Introduction to
PSYCHOLOGY

TENTH EDITION

Introduction to
PSYCHOLOGY

TENTH EDITION

Rita L. Atkinson
University of California, San Diego

Richard C. Atkinson
University of California, San Diego

Edward E. Smith
University of Michigan

Daryl J. Bem
Cornell University

HBJ

HARCOURT BRACE JOVANOVICH, PUBLISHERS

San Diego   New York   Chicago   Austin   Washington, D.C.
London   Sydney   Tokyo   Toronto

Preface

This is the tenth edition of *Introduction to Psychology*. The first edition was published in 1953 under the authorship of Ernest R. Hilgard of Stanford University. In the intervening years this textbook has become one of the most widely used books in the history of college publishing, and has been translated into many languages, including Russian, Spanish, French, Chinese, and German. In fact, since its publication more introductory psychology students have used this book than any other. Many young students studying the text today will have parents who used an earlier edition.

What accounts for the book's success? We believe that it is a combination of two factors: one is our excitement and enthusiasm for the field of psychology; the other is our commitment to present ideas and research in a scholarly manner. Psychology is in a period of great progress, with major advances being made on almost every front. We consider it important for an introductory book not only to describe that progress, but also to convey the excitement and enthusiasm associated with it. In doing so, however, we have not resorted to pop psychology or tried to enlist the reader's interest by over-simplifying the facts or by glossing over difficult concepts. There is enough excitement in psychology today that one can present the information in a scholarly and balanced way without losing the reader's interest.

Accordingly, we have attempted to write for the student, but in a manner that will satisfy the critical psychologist as well. To accomplish this goal we have relied on feedback from three sources: students, instructors, and specialists. To make certain our subject matter was comprehensible to students and pertinent to the issues with which they are concerned, we asked a number of students to comment on each section of the manuscript in terms of interest and clarity. Their responses were extremely helpful. Several college instructors who specialize in teaching the introductory course read the manuscript as it evolved, commenting on its suitability for their students and on problems they foresaw in teaching the material. We also benefited from comments and suggestions received from instructors who used the previous edition. Finally, to keep abreast of research developments, we asked experts to review the material. Several specialists commented on each chapter, both in the early stages of revision and in its final form. By such consultation, we sought to ensure that the coverage was attuned to current research. (The reviewers are listed following the preface.)

This edition represents a major revision. As a simple measure of the amount of change, approximately one-fourth of the references have been published since the last edition went to press. Those familiar with the book will realize that the three chapters in Part III, "Consciousness and Perception," have been reordered and changed to reflect recent research and theoretical developments in perception. A major change also occurs in Part VI, "Personality and Individuality," with the addition of a new chapter entitled

"Personality through the Life Course." This chapter discusses the interplay of forces that shape an individual's personality throughout life, examines the evidence for continuity of personality, and provides some fascinating new data on the consequences in adulthood of certain childhood personality traits. This new chapter precedes the chapter on "Personality Theory and Assessment," which has been reorganized and rewritten.

Readers familiar with earlier editions should also take note of a new section in Chapter 6 entitled "Psi Phenomena." We have discussed parapsychology in previous editions but have been very critical of the research and skeptical of the claims made in the field. And although we still have strong reservations about most of the research in parapsychology, we do find the recent work on telepathy using the ganzfeld procedure worthy of careful consideration.

In the last edition we introduced an appendix called "How to Read a Textbook: The PQRST Method." We have received a great deal of positive feedback on this appendix and recommend that it be carefully studied by the student before beginning the text. Chapter 8, "Memory," includes an expanded discussion of the principles underlying the PQRST method.

We have tried to cover contemporary psychology in a textbook of reasonable length. However, each instructor must design his or her course according to course objectives and available time. Even if all chapters are not assigned, students will have them for reference. For a short course, we believe that it is better to treat fewer chapters fully than to cover the entire book. Two possible 14-chapter courses are proposed below, one for a course with an experimental–biological emphasis, the other for a course with a personal–social emphasis. These proposals only illustrate possible combinations, however. Each instructor must choose the order of topics he or she finds congenial; the book has been written so that a variety of arrangements is possible.

For example, some instructors feel that student interest can be better piqued by beginning the course with material on personality, abnormal psychology, and social psychology, leaving more experimental topics, such as memory, perception, and physiological psychology, until later. The authors have tried this approach but have found it unsatisfactory. Beginning with the more personally relevant topics may get the course off to a fast start, but it often gives students a distorted idea of what psychology is. In addition, many students are ill-prepared for the experimental material when it is introduced later. Our preferred approach is to cover the chapter on developmental psychology early in the course, thereby exposing students to a wide range of provocative topics in psychology. We then turn to the more technical areas, such as perception, memory, and motivation, and we end the course with personality, abnormal psychology, and social psychology.

The many decisions that must be made in teaching the introductory psychology course are discussed in the *Instructor's Manual*, which is useful for both beginning and experienced instructors, as well as for teaching assistants. As a further instructional aid, we have provided students with an entirely new *Study Guide and Unit Mastery Program*. This aid can be used by students in preparing for a traditional course or in preparing for a course taught by the unit mastery method.

As noted earlier, Ernest R. Hilgard was the original author of *Introduction to Psychology*. Over successive editions he was joined by Richard C. Atkinson, Rita L. Atkinson, and Edward E. Smith. Daryl J. Bem has contributed chapters to several earlier editions, and in this edition we are pleased to finally welcome him as a full-fledged co-author. Lynn L. Atkinson, M.D., a

CHAPTER	EXPERIMENTAL–BIOLOGICAL EMPHASIS	PERSONAL–SOCIAL EMPHASIS
1 Nature of Psychology	1	1
2 Biological Basis of Psychology	2	—
3 Psychological Development	3	3
4 Sensory Processes	4	—
5 Perception	5	5
6 Consciousness and Its Altered States	6	6
7 Learning and Conditioning	7	7
8 Memory	8	8
9 Thought and Language	9	—
10 Basic Motives	10	—
11 Emotion	—	—
12 Mental Abilities and Their Measurement	12	12
13 Personality through the Life Course	13	13
14 Personality Theory and Assessment	—	14
15 Stress and Coping	15	15
16 Abnormal Psychology	—	16
17 Methods of Therapy	—	17
18 Social Information Processing	18	18
19 Social Influence	—	19

neurosurgeon at the Medical College of Virginia, has provided an up-to-date treatment of the neurosciences in Chapter 2.

Ernest R. Hilgard, after all these years, has finally chosen not to continue as an author. The many individuals who have used earlier editions of this book will understand our feelings of regret. Despite the absence of his name on the cover, his guiding force is still with us and his enthusiasm for psychology remains the hallmark of this book.

We would like to give special thanks to our colleagues whose suggestions were particularly helpful: Avshalom Caspi, University of Wisconsin; and John Jonides, University of Michigan.

Finally, in addition to those listed below, we would like to thank the staff at Harcourt Brace Jovanovich who contributed their skills in helping us put the new edition together—Marcus Boggs, acquisitions editor; Debbie Hardin, manuscript editor; Christopher Nelson, production editor; Ann Smith, designer; Rebecca Lytle, art editor; and Lesley Lenox, production manager.

RITA L. ATKINSON
RICHARD C. ATKINSON
EDWARD E. SMITH
DARYL J. BEM

ACKNOWLEDGMENTS

Michael Atkinson
University of Western Ontario

Elaine Baker
Marshall University

Guido Barrientos
University of Texas at El Paso

Hall Beck
Appalachian State University

Paul Bedell
*State University of New York,
College of Technology at Farmingdale*

Thomas Berndt
University of California, Los Angeles

Robert Bjork
University of California, Los Angeles

Randolph Blake
Vanderbilt University

Anne Bogart
Michigan State University

Glen Bradley
Pensacola Junior College

Eileen Brady
College of Mount Saint Vincent

L. Brandt
Pacific Lutheran University

Marc Breedlove
University of California, Berkeley

Raeford Brown
Florida A & M University

Mark Byrd
University of Kansas

Thomas Carr
Michigan State University

Daniel Cervone
University of Illinois

Garvin Chastain
Boise State University

John Childers
East Carolina University

A. Clark
University of Saskatchewan

Margaret Cleek
*University of Wisconsin,
Washington County*

Caroline Coile
Florida State University

William Cooper
Tulane University

A. Derick Dalhouse
Moorhead State University

James Dannemiller
University of Wisconsin, Madison

Douglas Detterman
Case Western Reserve University

H. Mitz Doane
University of Minnesota, Duluth

James Doyle
Roane State Community College

J. D. Duke
Appalachian State University

Christine Dunkel-Schette
University of California, Los Angeles

R. S. Dytell
College of Mount Saint Vincent

Brian M. Earn
University of Guelph

Matthew Erdelyi
*City University of New York,
Brooklyn College*

S. Feist
*State University of New York,
College of Technology at Farmingdale*

Robyn Fivush
Emory University

Earl Folse
Nicholls State University

Roy Fontaine
*Williamsport Area Community
College*

Paul Fox
Appalachian State University

William Frederickson
Central State University

David Galinsky
*University of North Carolina at
Chapel Hill*

Charles Geist
University of Alaska, Fairbanks

G. David Gentry
College of Charleston

Betty H. Gibbons
Shelton State Junior College

Kenneth Good
Mankato State University

Donald R. Gorassini
*King's College,
University of Western Ontario*

P. C. Gram
Pensacola Junior College

David Griese
*State University of New York,
College of Technology at Farmingdale*

Richard Griggs
University of Florida

Philip Groves
University of California, San Diego

E. B. Gurman
University of Southern Mississippi

Catherine Hackett-Renner
University of Tennessee

Thomas Harbin
*University of North Carolina at
Greensboro*

Richard Harris
Kansas State University

John Hartman
Southwestern Michigan College

Albert Heldt
Grand Rapids Junior College

Joyce Hemphill
Elmhurst College

Sidney Hochman
Nassau Community College

Donald Hoffman
University of California, Irvine

S. Hotard
University of Southwestern Louisiana

Wayne Houchins
University of Southwestern Louisiana

Dalton Howard
Valencia Community College

Kenneth Howard
Northwestern University

I-Ning Huang
University of Wisconsin, Whitewater

William Iacono
University of Minnesota, Minneapolis

Gene Indenbaum
*State University of New York,
College of Technology at Farmingdale*

Sherri Jackson
University of Florida

Judith Jankowski
Grand Rapids Junior College

Randy Jarrell
Shelton State Community College

Robert Johnson
Arkansas State University

Cecil P. Jones
Daytona Beach Community College

Craig Jones
Arizona State University

Charles Kaiser
College of Charleston

James Kalat
North Carolina State University

Jane Kelly
Hinds Community College

Norbert Kerr
Michigan State University

Alrene Kestner
Southern University, Baton Rouge

Cheryl A. King
University of Michigan, Dearborn

Melvyn King
*State University of New York,
State University College at Cortland*

Sherry Kirksey
Shelton State Community College

Stephen C. Klein
Fort Hays State University

Ronald Kleinknecht
Western Washington University

Mike Knight
Central State University

Ralph Kolstoe
University of North Dakota

Stuart Korsharn
Saint Norbert College

Rosemary Kraweczyk
Mankato State University

Kevin Krull
Florida State University

Michael Lambert
Brigham Young University

Joan Lauer
IU-PU Indianapolis

Manuel Leon
Boise State University

Judith Levine
*State University of New York,
College of Technology at Farmingdale*

Harlan Linsley
University of Wisconsin, Oshkosh

John Lombardo
*State University of New York,
State University College at Cortland*

Lola Lopes
University of Wisconsin, Madison

G. William Lucker
University of Texas at El Paso

Wesley Lynch
Montana State University

Jane Maddy
University of Minnesota, Duluth

Ruth Maki
North Dakota State University

Tom Martoccia
East Carolina University

Robert Mauro
University of Oregon

Roy Maxwell
East Central University

James Mazur
Southern Connecticut State University

J. R. McCallum
Birmingham Southern College

David McDonald
University of Missouri, Columbia

Charles McMullen
*State University of New York,
Tompkins Cortland Community
College*

Mary J. Meadow
Mankato State University

Rick Medlin
Stetson University

Janet Metcalf
University of California, San Diego

Steven Mewaldt
Marshall University

David Miller
Daytona Beach Community College

Charles C. Mitchell
East Carolina University

Thomas Mitchell
*Southern Illinois University at
Carbondale*

Charles Moore
East Carolina University

William T. Moss
Appalachian State University

Lawrence A. Mosse
Michigan State University

Gregory Murphy
Brown University

Thomas Natsoulas
University of California, Davis

Donald Novin
University of California, Los Angeles

Gayle Olson
University of New Orleans

David Olton
Johns Hopkins University

Howard B. Orenstein
Western Maryland College

Nicky Ozbek
University of Tennessee, Chattanooga

Philip Peake
Smith College

Robert Plomin
Pennsylvania State University

Mark Plonsky
University of Wisconsin, Stevens Point

Bobby Poe
Belleville Area College

Samuel B. Pond III
North Carolina State University

Benjamin Popper
Broward Community College

Lillian Rank
University of Southern Mississippi

Michael Raulin
State University of New York, Buffalo

William Revelle
Northwestern University

Dean Richards
University of California, Los Angeles

Paul Rokke
North Dakota State University

Paul Ronco
Salem State College

Frank Rosekrans
Eastern Washington University

Edna Ross
University of Louisville

Gail Ross
Pittsburgh State University

Gary Ross-Reynolds
Nicholls State University

Peter Salovey
Yale University

Daniel Schacter
University of Arizona

Ann-Marie Scheerbaum
Michigan State University

David Schlundt
Vanderbilt University

David Schroeder
University of Arkansas

Jerry Schulenbarger
Tacoma Community College

Dale Sengelaub
Indiana University

Ronald Senzig
Okaloosa-Walton Junior College

Joe Shelton
Southwest Baptist University

Cheryl Sisk
Michigan State University

Art Skibbe
Appalachian State University

M. Dale Smalley
Memphis State University

Timothy Smith
University of Utah

Timothy Smock
University of Colorado, Boulder

John W. Staas
Monroe County Community College

Mary Stegall
Okaloosa-Walton Junior College

Faye Steuer
College of Charleston

Vince Sullivan
Pensacola Junior College

William Swann
University of Texas at Austin

Charles Thompson
Kansas State University

Francine Tougas
University of Ottawa

Robin Vallacher
Florida Atlantic University

Eric Vernberg
University of Miami

Charles R. Vior
Dyersburg State Community College

Rick Wagner
Florida State University

Paul Watson
University of Tennessee, Chattanooga

Sheldon Weinstock
Community College of Baltimore

David H. Westendorf
University of Arkansas

Paul Whitney
Washington State University

Maxine Wintre
York University

M. W. Wolff
Florida State University

P. Jeffrey Wright
Middle Tennessee State University

Karl Wuensch
East Carolina University

Fred Yaffe
Washburn University

James Zacks
Michigan State University

Rose Zacks
Michigan State University

Mark Zanna
University of Waterloo

Contents

PART III   Consciousness and Perception

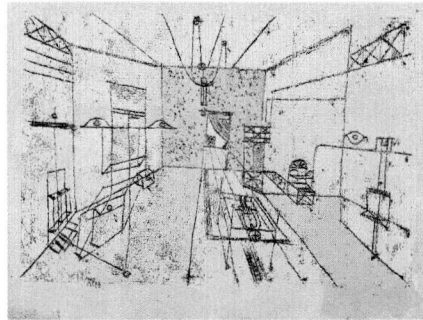

PART IV
Learning, Remembering, and Thinking

PART V   Motivation and Emotion

PART VI Personality and Individuality

PART VII

Stress, Psychopathology, and Therapy

PART VIII Social Behavior

Appendixes

Introduction to
PSYCHOLOGY

TENTH EDITION

Paul Klee. Nearly Hit, 1928.
Oil on board, 20″ x 15½″, San Francisco Museum of Modern Art, Albert N.
Bender Collection, Albert M. Bender Bequest Fund Purchase, 44: 2640. E3 (143)

Chapter 1

Detail, Nearly Hit.

Nature of Psychology

NOTE TO THE STUDENT

A method for effectively reading a textbook is described in Appendix I; you may wish to read the appendix before starting this chapter.

No one today can afford *not* to know psychology; it touches virtually every aspect of your life. For example: How does the way your parents raised you affect the way you raise your own children? What is the best way to break a drug habit? Can a man care for an infant as ably as a woman? To what extent are political surveys self-fulfilling prophecies? Can you recall childhood experiences in more detail under hypnosis? How should instruments in a nuclear power plant be designed to minimize human error? What effect does prolonged stress have on your immune system? How effective is psychotherapy in treating depression? Can learning be improved by the use of drugs that facilitate neural transmission? Psychologists are working on these and many other questions.

Psychology also affects our life through its influence on laws and public policy. Psychological theories and research have influenced laws concerning discrimination, capital punishment, pornography, sexual behavior, and the conditions under which individuals may be held legally responsible for their actions. For example, laws pertaining to sexual deviancy have changed markedly in the past 40 years as research has shown that many sexual acts previously classed as perversions are "normal" in the sense that most people engage in them. Consider also the effect of television violence on children. Only since psychological studies provided evidence of the harmful effects of such programs has it been possible to modify television programming policies. Programs designed for children now contain less violence, and an effort is made to restrict particularly brutal television to late-evening viewing hours.

Because psychology affects so many aspects of our life, it is essential that even those who do not intend to specialize in the field know something about its basic facts and research methods. An introductory course in psychology should give you a better understanding of why people think and act as they do, and provide insights into your own attitudes and reactions. It should also help you evaluate the many claims made in the name of psychology. Everyone has seen newspaper headlines like these:

- New drug discovered to improve memory
- Anxiety controlled by self-regulation of brain waves
- Proof of mental telepathy found
- Hypnosis effective in the control of pain
- Emotional stability and family size closely related
- Homosexuality linked to parental attitudes
- Transcendental meditation facilitates problem solving
- Multiple personality linked to childhood abuse

You can judge the validity of such claims in part by knowing what psychological facts have been firmly established; you can then assess whether the new claim is compatible with these established facts. You can also judge the validity in part by knowing the kind of evidence necessary to give credence to a new "discovery," so that you can determine whether the arguments in support of the new claim meet the usual standards of evidence. This book reviews the current state of knowledge in psychology and examines the nature of research—that is, how a psychologist formulates a hypothesis and designs a research program to provide evidence for or against it.

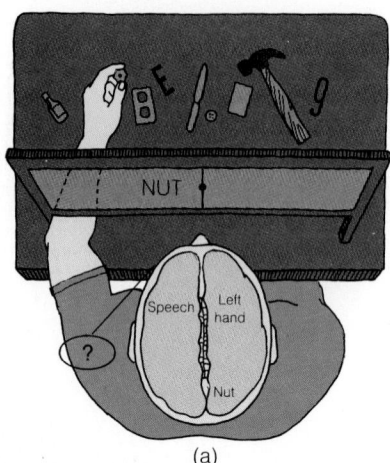

FIGURE 1-1
Testing the Abilities of the Two Hemispheres *The split-brain subject correctly retrieves an object by touch with the left hand when its name is flashed to the right hemisphere, but he cannot name the object or describe what he has done.*

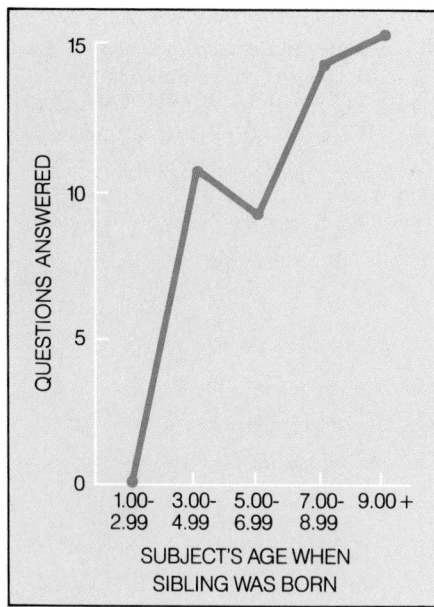

FIGURE 1-2
Recall of an Early Memory *In an experiment on childhood amnesia, college-age subjects were asked 20 questions about the events surrounding the birth of a younger sibling. The average number of questions answered is plotted as a function of the subject's age when the sibling was born. If the birth occurred before the fourth year of life, no subject could recall a thing about it; if the birth occurred after that, recall increased with age at the time of the event. (After Sheingold & Tenney, 1982)*

SCOPE OF PSYCHOLOGY

Psychology can be defined as the *scientific study of behavior and mental processes.* An astonishing variety of topics is covered by this definition. To get a better grasp on this variety, we briefly describe five representative problems psychologists examine. (All of these problems will be discussed in more detail at various points in the text.)

LIVING WITH A DIVIDED BRAIN The human brain is divided into a left and a right hemisphere. Normally, the two hemispheres are connected by a band of neural fibers, but some people who suffer from severe epilepsy have had these fibers surgically disconnected and are living with a divided brain (this separation prevents a seizure that originates in one hemisphere from spreading to the other). Casual interaction with such people would not indicate anything unusual. But psychological experiments show that a split-brain person can have unusual perceptual and conscious experiences.

In a standard experiment, a split-brain person is seated in front of a screen that hides his hands from view (see Figure 1-1). The word "nut" is flashed very briefly on the screen in such a way that its image goes only to the right hemisphere of the person's brain. Because the right hemisphere controls the left side of the body, the subject can use his left hand to pick out a nut from a pile of tools hidden from view. But the subject cannot tell the experimenter what word flashed on the screen, because speech is controlled by the left hemisphere and the image of "nut" was not transmitted to that hemisphere. When asked what his left hand is doing, the split-brain person cannot answer! The normal unity of experience has been disrupted.

CONDITIONED FEAR Suppose a rat is placed in an enclosed compartment and periodically subjected to mild electric shock through the floor. Just before the shock occurs a tone sounds. After the tone and shock have been presented in succession a number of times, the tone alone will produce reactions that are indicative of fear, including crouching and defecating. The animal is said to have been *conditioned* to fear what was once an innocuous stimulus.

Many human fears may be learned this way, particularly in early childhood. Suppose a young child is subjected to repeated physical or emotional abuse by a particular relative. After a number of painful experiences, the mere sound of the relative's voice may elicit a fear reaction in the child. Such a fear, learned with little thought or conscious awareness, is hard to combat by verbal assurances ("There's nothing to be afraid of now"). But the fear may be reduced by a form of therapy that is based on the principles of conditioning, discussed in Chapters 7 and 17.

CHILDHOOD AMNESIA Most adults, even elderly ones, can recall events from their early years. But only up to a certain point. Virtually no one can recall events from the first 3 years of life. Consider a significant event like the birth of a sibling. If the birth occurred after you were 3 years old you may have some memory of it, the amount you remember being greater the older you were at the time of the birth. But if the birth occurred before age 3, most people have trouble remembering a single incident about the event (see Figure 1-2).

This phenomenon, discovered by Sigmund Freud, is called *childhood amnesia.* It is particularly striking because our first three years are so rich in experience. So much is new in a way that it never will be again; we develop from helpless newborns to crawling, babbling infants to walking, talking kids. But these remarkable transitions leave little trace on our memory.

OBESITY   Roughly 35 million Americans are obese, which technically means they are 20 percent or more above the appropriate weight for their body structure and height. Obesity is dangerous—it contributes to a higher incidence of diabetes, high blood pressure, and heart disease. At the other end of the spectrum, some people (especially young women) suffer from an-orexia nervosa, a disorder in which people severely restrict their eating, sometimes to the point of self-imposed starvation. Anorexia can even result in death.

Psychologists are interested in what factors lead people to eat too much or too little. One factor seems to be a history of deprivation. If rats are first deprived of food, then allowed to feed back to normal weights, and finally allowed to eat as much as they want, they eat more than other rats who have no history of deprivation. In this instance prior deprivation leads to subse-quent overeating. This may explain why many cases of anorexia paradox-ically record binge eating as well: the deprivation required to stay thin even-tually leads to overeating.

EXPRESSION OF AGGRESSION   Many people believe that they can lessen their aggressive feelings by expressing them either directly or vicari-ously. Psychological research indicates the opposite is more often the case. To study vicarious expression of aggression, researchers have looked at chil-dren's viewing of television. In one experiment, one group of children watched violent cartoons, while another group watched nonviolent cartoons for the same amount of time. The children who watched violent cartoons became more aggressive in their interactions with peers, whereas the chil-dren who viewed nonviolent cartoons showed no change in aggression. Moreover, these effects of television violence can be lasting: the more vio-lent programs a boy watches at age 9, the more aggressive he is likely to be at age 19 (see Figure 1-3).

These five problems—divided brains, conditioned fear, childhood am-nesia, weight control, and expression of aggression—will surface again in our discussion of perspectives in psychology.

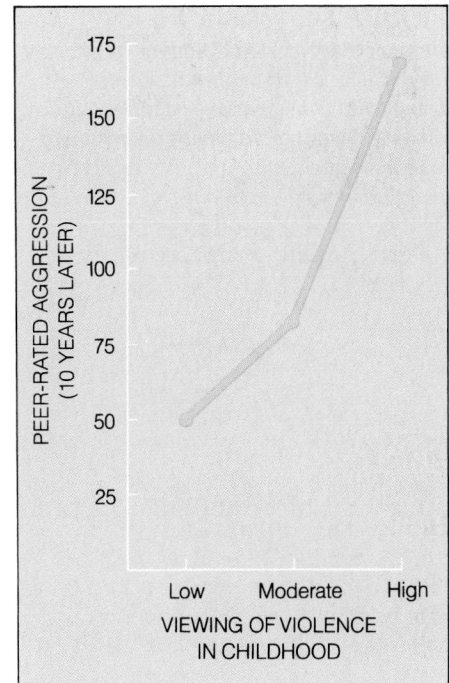

FIGURE 1-3
Relationship between Childhood Viewing of Violent Television and Adult Aggression *Preference for viewing violent TV programs by boys at age 9 is related to aggressive behavior as rated by peers at age 19.* (After Eron, Huesmann, Lefkowitz, & Walder, 1972)

PERSPECTIVES IN PSYCHOLOGY

Any topic in psychology can be approached from a variety of perspectives. Indeed, this is true of any action a person takes. Suppose you walk across the street. From a *biological* perspective, this act can be described as the firing of the nerves that activate the muscles that move the legs that transport you across the street. From a *behavioral* perspective, the act can be described without reference to anything within your body: rather, the green light is interpreted as a stimulus to which you respond by crossing the street. One may also take a *cognitive* perspective of crossing the street, focusing on the *mental processes* involved in producing the behavior. From a cognitive per-spective, your action might be explained in terms of your goals and plans: your goal is to visit a friend, and crossing the street is part of your plan for achieving that goal.

FIGURE 1-4
Perspectives in Psychology *The analysis of psychological phenomena can be approached from several perspectives. Each offers a somewhat different explanation of why individuals act as they do, and each can make a contribution to our conception of the total person. The Greek letter psi, ψ, is sometimes used as an abbreviation for psychology.*

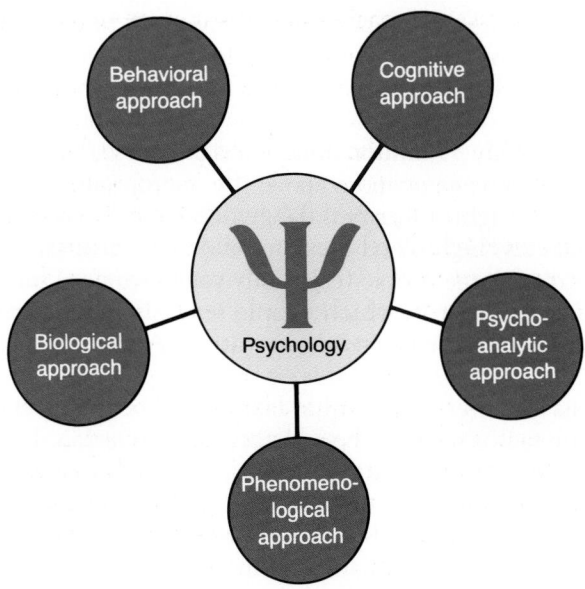

While there are many possible ways to describe any psychological act, the following five perspectives represent the major approaches to the modern study of psychology. These five include the three mentioned above—biological, behavioral, and cognitive—plus two others: psychoanalytic and phenomenological (see Figure 1-4). Because some of these perspectives arose in reaction to other views, we first consider the origin of psychological perspectives, and then describe the five contemporary perspectives.

Origins of Psychological Perspectives*

The roots of modern psychology can be traced to the fourth and fifth centuries B.C. The great Greek philosophers Socrates, Plato, and Aristotle posed fundamental questions about mental life. For example: Do people perceive reality correctly? What is consciousness? Are people inherently rational or irrational? Are people capable of free choice? These questions, as important now as they were two thousand years ago, deal with the nature of *mind* and mental processes, rather than with the nature of *body* or *behavior*, and are precursors to a cognitive perspective.

The biological perspective has an equally long history. Hippocrates, usually credited as the "father of medicine," lived at roughly the same time as Socrates, and was much interested in physiology (the branch of biology that studies the normal functions of the living organism and its parts). He made many important observations about how the brain controlled various organs of the body, which set the stage for the modern approach to physiology and the biological perspective in psychology.

Two millennia later, in the latter part of the nineteenth century, scientific psychology was born. The fundamental idea behind its inception was that mind and behavior—like the planets or chemicals or human organs—could be the subject of scientific analysis. The beginning of psychology involved some mixing of the questions of philosophy and the methods of

---

*A fuller history of psychology is presented in Appendix II.

physiology, but these two approaches were distinct enough to emerge as the cognitive and biological perspectives to psychology.

The nineteenth-century version of the biological perspective differed markedly from the current version because relatively little was then known about the nervous system. Still, the development of this perspective has been relatively continuous compared to that of the cognitive perspective. The nineteenth-century cognitive perspective focused mainly on mental experiences, and its data were largely self-observations in the form of *introspections*. Introspection refers to an individual's observation and recording of the nature of his or her own perceptions, thoughts, and feelings; for example, one's self-reflections on one's immediate sensory impressions of a stimulus, such as the flash of a light. This extreme reliance on introspection, particularly for very rapid mental events, proved unworkable. Even after receiving extensive training in introspecting, different people produced very different introspections about simple sensory experiences, and little could be made of these differences. Introspectionism is not a critical part of the current cognitive perspective. As we will see, reactions by some psychologists to introspection played a role in the development of other modern perspectives.

Modern Perspectives

Because the five perspectives of interest are discussed throughout the book, we provide here only a brief description of some main points. Also keep in mind that these approaches need not be mutually exclusive; rather, they may focus on different aspects of the same complex phenomenon.

BIOLOGICAL PERSPECTIVE   The human brain contains well over 10 billion nerve cells and an almost infinite number of interconnections. It may well be the most complex structure in the universe. In principle, all psychological events correspond in some manner to the activity of the brain and nervous system. The biological approach to the study of human beings and other species attempts to relate overt behavior to electrical and chemical events taking place inside the body, particularly within the brain and nervous system. This approach seeks to specify the *neurobiological* processes that underlie behavior and mental processes.

We can use the problems described earlier to illustrate the biological perspective. The study of split-brain patients demonstrates that normal conscious experience is mediated by neural fibers connecting the two hemispheres of the brain; it also tells us where certain abilities are localized within the brain. Recall that if a word is presented only to the right hemisphere of a split-brain subject, the person can correctly select by touch the named object from a pile hidden from view. This indicates that the right hemisphere can make discriminations based on touch, and also that it can understand some language, since it can interpret single words. Recall further that the split-brain subject cannot name the word presented: this indicates that only the left hemisphere has the power of speech.

The biological perspective has also made progress in the study of learning and memory. Neurobiologists have proposed cell-by-cell accounts of learning by conditioning, as in the example of a rat being conditioned to fear a tone. The gist of these accounts is that conditioning involves changes in connections between *neurons*, or nerve cells, where these neural changes are themselves mediated by alterations in the amount of certain chemicals produced in the brain. The biological approach to memory has emphasized the

By studying the brain activity of animals, researchers gain insight into the human brain. In this single-cell recording experiment a microelectrode, which monitors the electrical activity of a single neuron, is implanted in the visual system of an anesthetized monkey.

importance of certain brain structures, including the *hippocampus*, which is involved in consolidating memories. Therefore, childhood amnesia may be partly due to an immature hippocampus, since this brain structure is not fully developed until a year or two after birth.

The biological perspective has had similar successes in the study of motivation and emotion, particularly with other species. We know from work with rats, cats, and monkeys that there are certain regions in the brain that when electrically stimulated produce excessive overeating and obesity, and other nearby regions that when stimulated produce aggressive behavior. While human obesity and aggression involve far more than stimulation of these particular regions, these studies with animals provide some idea of the contribution that biology alone makes to human motives and emotions.

Because of the complexity of the brain, tremendous gaps exist in our knowledge of neural functioning. For this reason, a psychological conception of ourselves based solely on biology would be inadequate.

BEHAVIORAL PERSPECTIVE   A person eats breakfast, rides a bike, talks, blushes, laughs, and cries. These are forms of behavior—the activities of an organism that can be observed. With the behavioral approach, a psychologist studies individuals by looking at their behavior rather than at their brain and nervous system.

The view that behavior should be the sole subject matter of psychology was first advanced by the American psychologist John B. Watson in the early 1900s. Before that, the dominant nonbiological approach was the nineteenth-century cognitive perspective, with its emphasis on introspectionism. Watson noted that introspections have a private quality that distinguishes them from observations in other fields of science. Any qualified scientist can replicate an observation in the natural sciences, whereas the introspective observation can be reported by only one observer—the person engaging in the introspection. Watson felt that introspection was a futile approach. He argued that if psychology were to be considered a science, its data must be observable by any qualified scientist. Only you can introspect about your perceptions and feelings, but others can observe your behavior, including verbal behavior about your perceptions and feelings. Watson maintained that only by studying what people do—their behavior—is an objective science of psychology possible.

Behaviorism, as Watson's position came to be called, helped shape the course of psychology during the first half of this century. The offspring of behaviorism, *stimulus-response psychology*, is still influential. Stimulus-response psychology (S-R psychology) studies the relevant stimuli in the environment, the responses that are elicited by these stimuli, and the rewards or punishments that follow these responses.

Again we can use our sample problems to illustrate the approach. In conditioned fear, the critical stimuli are the tone and the electric shock (recall that the tone consistently precedes the shock), and the relevant responses include withdrawal, defecation, and other specific behaviors associated with fear. Conditioning involves coming to respond to the tone in a fashion similar to how the organism naturally responds to the shock, where this change is a consequence of the tone reliably preceding the shock.

Similar analyses have proven useful in the areas of obesity and aggression. Some people may overeat (a specific response) only in the presence of specific stimuli, and learning to avoid these stimuli is now part of many weight-control programs. With regard to aggression, children are more likely to express aggressive responses, such as hitting another child, when such responses are rewarded—another child withdraws—than when their responses are punished—the other child counterattacks.

A strict behavioral approach does not consider the individual's mental processes. Psychologists other than behaviorists will often record what a person says about his or her conscious experiences (a verbal report), and from this objective data draw inferences about the person's mental activity. But, by and large, behavioral psychologists have chosen not to conjecture about the mental processes that intervene between the stimulus and the response (Skinner, 1981).*

Today, few psychologists would regard themselves as strict behaviorists. Nevertheless, many modern developments in psychology have evolved from the work of behaviorists.

COGNITIVE PERSPECTIVE   The modern cognitive perspective is in part a reaction to behaviorism and in part a return to the cognitive roots of psychology. Like the nineteenth-century version, the modern study of cognition is concerned with mental processes, such as perceiving, remembering, reasoning, deciding, and problem solving. Unlike the nineteenth-century version, however, modern cognitivism is not based on introspection. Thus, the modern study of cognition is premised on the assumptions that: a) only by studying mental processes can we fully understand what organisms do; and b) we can study mental processes in an objective fashion by focusing on

---

*Throughout this book the reader will find references, cited by author and date, that document or expand the statements made here. Detailed publishing information on these studies appears in the reference list at the end of the book. The reference list also serves as an index to the pages on which the citation appears.

Language is a uniquely human activity.

specific behaviors, just as the behaviorists do, but interpret them in terms of underlying mental processes.

The cognitive perspective (that from here on refers to the modern version) developed partly in reaction to the narrowness of the S-R view. To conceive of human actions solely in terms of stimulus and response may be adequate for the study of simple forms of behavior, but this approach neglects too many important areas of human functioning. People can reason, plan, make decisions on the basis of remembered information, and, perhaps most striking of all, use language to communicate with one another. But these more complex phenomena are somewhat neglected by the behavioral perspective. In many ways, the behavioral approach is like an old-fashioned telephone switchboard: the stimulus goes in, and after a series of cross connections and circuits through the brain, the response comes out. In contrast, an analogy for cognitive psychology is a modern computer, or what in its most general sense is called an information-processing system. Incoming information is processed in various ways: it is selected, compared and combined with other information already in memory, transformed, rearranged, and so on. The response output depends on these internal processes and their state at that moment.

We can use our sample problems once again to illustrate the cognitive approach. The rat learning to fear a tone may actually be developing a hypothesis, or rule, that "If you hear a tone, a painful shock is coming." And it is this rule that is responsible for the animal's reactions. The phenomenon of childhood amnesia also lends itself to a cognitive analysis. Perhaps we cannot remember events from the first few years of life because we change the way we organize our experience in memory. Such changes may be particularly pronounced around age 3 because at that point there is a great increase in our language abilities, and language offers us a new way of organizing our experience.

Cognitive analyses can also be used in the study of obesity and aggression. Some obese people fit the following pattern: they diet successfully for a while, then break down and overeat so excessively that they eventually consume more calories than they would have had they not dieted at all. The critical factor here seems to be a breakdown of a plan, and the feelings of lack of control that ensue from this loss of cognitive control. With regard to aggression, the importance of cognition or knowledge is straightforward. If someone insults you, you are far more likely to return the verbal aggression if the person is an acquaintance than if he or she is a mental patient you do not know. In both cases, acquaintance and mental patient, the stimulus situation is roughly the same; what differs is what you know about the other person, and it is this *knowledge* that controls your behavior.

PSYCHOANALYTIC PERSPECTIVE   The psychoanalytic conception of human behavior was developed by Sigmund Freud in Europe about the same time behaviorism was evolving in the United States. Freud was a physician by training, but he knew about the cognitive developments then going on in Europe. In some respects his psychoanalysis was a blend of nineteenth-century versions of cognition and physiology. In particular, Freud combined then-current cognitive notions of consciousness, perception, and memory, with ideas about biologically-based instincts to forge a bold new theory of human behavior.

The basic assumption of Freud's theory is that much of our behavior stems from processes that are unconscious. By *unconscious process* Freud meant beliefs, fears, and desires a person is unaware of but that nevertheless influence behavior. He believed that many of the impulses that are forbidden or punished by parents and society during childhood are derived from innate instincts. Because each of us is born with these impulses, they exert a pervasive influence that must be dealt with in some manner. Forbidding them merely forces them out of awareness into the unconscious, where they remain to affect dreams, slips of speech, or mannerisms, and to manifest themselves as emotional problems, symptoms of mental illness, or, on the other hand, socially approved behavior such as artistic and literary activity.

Freud believed that all of our actions have a cause but that the cause is often some unconscious motive rather than the rational reason we may give. Freud's view of human nature was essentially negative: he believed that we are driven by the same basic instincts as animals (primarily sex and aggression) and that we are continually struggling against a society that stresses the control of these impulses. While most psychologists do not completely accept Freud's view of the unconscious, they would probably agree that individuals are not fully aware of some important aspects of their personality.

The psychoanalytic perspective suggests new ways of looking at some of our sample problems. According to Freud (1905), childhood amnesia arises because some emotional experiences in the first few years of life are so traumatic that allowing them to enter consciousness years later (that is, remembering them) would cause the individual to be overwhelmed by anxiety. With regard to obesity, it is known that some people overeat when anxious; the psychoanalytic perspective suggests that these people may be responding to an anxiety-producing situation by doing the one thing that has brought them comfort all their lives—namely, eating. And of course, psychoanalysis has much to say about the expression of aggression. Freud claimed that aggression is an instinct, which means that people aggress to express an inborn desire. While this proposal is not widely accepted in human psychology, it is in agreement with the views of some biologists and psychologists who study aggression in animals.

PHENOMENOLOGICAL PERSPECTIVE   Unlike the other approaches we have considered, the phenomenological perspective focuses almost entirely on *subjective experience*. It is concerned with the individual's personal view of events—the individual's *phenomenology*. This approach developed partly as a reaction to what phenomenologists perceived as the overly mechanistic quality of the other perspectives to psychology. Thus, phenomenological psychologists tend to reject the notion that behavior is controlled by external stimuli (behaviorism), or by just the processing of information in perception and memory (cognitive psychology), or by unconscious impulses (psychoanalytic theories). Also, phenomenological psychologists have different goals than psychologists operating from the other perspectives: they are concerned more with describing the inner life and experiences of individuals than with developing theories or predicting behavior.

Phenomenological psychologists believe that we are not *acted on* by forces beyond our control, but instead we are *actors* capable of controlling our own destiny. We are the builders of our own lives because each of us is a free agent—free to make choices and set goals and therefore accountable for our life choices. This is the issue of free will versus determinism. Some phenomenological theories are also called *humanistic* because they emphasize those qualities that distinguish people from animals: for example, the drive toward self-actualization. According to humanistic theories, an individual's principal motivational force is a tendency toward growth and self-actualization. All of us have a basic need to develop our potential to the fullest, to progress

Sigmund Freud.

An encounter group.

beyond where we are now; although we may be blocked by environmental and social obstacles, our natural tendency is toward actualizing our potential.

With its emphasis on developing one's potential, phenomenological or humanistic psychology has been closely associated with encounter groups and various types of "consciousness-expanding" and mystical experiences. It is more aligned with literature and the humanities than with science. For this reason, it is difficult to give detailed descriptions of what the phenomenological perspective would say about our sample problems, such as conditioned fear and childhood amnesia, because these are not the kinds of problems that phenomenologists study.

In fact, some humanists reject scientific psychology altogether, claiming that its methods can contribute nothing to an understanding of human nature. This position, which is incompatible with our definition of psychology, seems far too extreme. The humanistic view makes a valuable point as a warning that psychology needs to focus its attention on solving problems relevant to human welfare rather than studying isolated bits of behavior that happen to lend themselves to an easy scientific analysis. But to assume that problems of mind and behavior can be solved by discarding all that we have learned about scientific methods of investigation seems fallacious. To quote one psychologist concerned with this issue, "We can no more afford a psychology that is humanistic at the expense of being scientific than we can afford one that is 'scientific' at the expense of human relevance" (M. B. Smith, 1973).

Relations among Perspectives

The biological perspective is at a different level than the other perspectives. The biological perspective uses concepts and principles that are drawn from physiology and other branches of biology, whereas the other perspectives rely on concepts and principles that are purely psychological (concepts such as perception, memory, the unconscious, and self-actualization).

There is a way, though, in which the biological perspective makes direct contact with the more psychological perspectives. Biologically-oriented researchers attempt to explain psychological concepts and principles in terms of their biological counterparts. For example, researchers might attempt to explain the conditioning of fear solely in terms of changes in neural connections in a certain region of the brain. Because this attempt involves reducing psychological notions to biological ones, this kind of explanation is called *reductionism*. Throughout this book we will present examples in which reductionism has been successful; that is, situations in which what was once understood at only the psychological level is now understood at the biological level.

If reductionism can be successful, why bother with psychological explanations at all? To put it another way, is psychology just something to do until the biologists get around to figuring everything out? The answer to this question is a resounding *No*. First and foremost, there seem to be many principles that can be stated *only* at the psychological level.

To illustrate, consider a principle about human memory for facts, namely, that memory preserves the meaning of a message and not the actual symbols used to communicate the meaning. So, 2 minutes after being presented some lines of text, people have no memory for the exact words used, although they do remember the meaning of the message. This principle seems to hold regardless of whether the message is read or heard. But because some of the biological (brain) processes involved are different for reading and listening, any attempt to reduce our psychological principle to the biological level would end up with two separate subprinciples—one for reading and one for listening. The single overarching principle would therefore be lost. There are many examples of this sort, and they justify the need for a psychological level of explanation that is distinct from the biological level (Fodor, 1981).

A second reason for having a psychological level of explanation is that psychological concepts and principles can be used to direct biological psychologists in their work. Given that the brain contains billions of brain cells and countless interconnections, biological researchers cannot hope to find something of interest by arbitrarily selecting some brain cells to study. Rather, they must have a way of directing their search to relevant groups of brain cells. Psychological findings can supply this direction. For example, if psychological research indicates that conditioning is a slow process that is hard to undo, then biological psychologists can direct their attention to brain processes that are relatively slow but that permanently alter neural connections (Churchland & Sejnowski, 1988).

Perspectives at the psychological level—particularly behavioral, cognitive, and psychoanalytic—are sometimes mutually compatible; at other times they compete with one another. The perspectives tend to be compatible when they focus on different aspects of the same phenomenon. For example, with regard to obesity there may be different reasons why people overeat, some of which are biological (for example, a genetic predisposition to be obese), some of which are behavioral (for example, the stimuli of a holiday-meal situation trigger overeating), and some of which are psychoanalytic (for example, eating is a familiar means of reducing anxiety). The perspectives are competitive when they offer different explanations for the very same phenomenon. This kind of conflict will arise many times throughout this book. Such a conflict may indicate only that our knowledge of the relevant phenomenon is imperfect. As more is learned about the phenomenon, the views may become compatible with one another. An initial conflict among the views may thus be just another step in the ongoing process of scientific psychology.

METHODS OF PSYCHOLOGY

Now that we have some idea of the topics studied in psychology and the perspectives adopted in studying them, we can consider the research methods used to investigate them.

As mentioned earlier, psychology can be defined as the *scientific study of behavior and mental processes*. The term "scientific" means that the research methods used to collect data are: a) *unbiased*, in that they do not favor one hypothesis over another; and b) *objective*, in that they allow other qualified people to repeat the observations and obtain the same results. The various methods to be considered next have these two characteristics. While some of the methods are used more by certain perspectives than others, each method can be used with each perspective. The only exception is that some phenomenological psychologists reject scientific methods entirely.

Experimental Method

CONTROL OF VARIABLES   The prototypical scientific method is the *experimental method*. The investigator carefully controls conditions—typically, in a laboratory—and takes measurements in order to discover *relations among variables*, where a variable is something that can occur with different values. For example, in an experiment seeking to discover the relation between learning ability and age, both learning ability and age can have different values. To the extent that learning ability changes systematically with increasing age, we can find an orderly relation between these two variables.

The ability to exercise precise control over variables distinguishes the experimental method from other methods of scientific observation. If the experimenter seeks to discover whether learning ability depends on the amount of sleep a person has had, the amount of sleep can be controlled by arranging to have several groups of subjects spend the night in the laboratory. Two groups might be allowed to go to sleep at 11:00 P.M. and 1:00 A.M., respectively, and a third group might be kept awake until 4:00 A.M. By waking all the subjects at the same time and giving each the same learning task, the experimenter can determine whether the subjects with more sleep learn more than those with less sleep.

In this study, the amount of sleep is called the *independent variable* because it is independent of what the subject does (the subject does not determine how much sleep he or she gets, the experimenter does); the amount learned is called the *dependent variable* because its values ultimately depend on the values of the independent variable. The dependent variable is almost inevitably some measure of the subject's behavior. The phrase "is a function of" is used to express the dependency of one variable on another. Thus, for this experiment we could say that the subjects' ability to learn a new task *is a function of* the amount of sleep they had.

An experiment concerned with the effect of marijuana on memory may make clearer the distinction between independent and dependent variables.

A researcher in a sleep experiment monitors the brain activity of a sleeping woman.

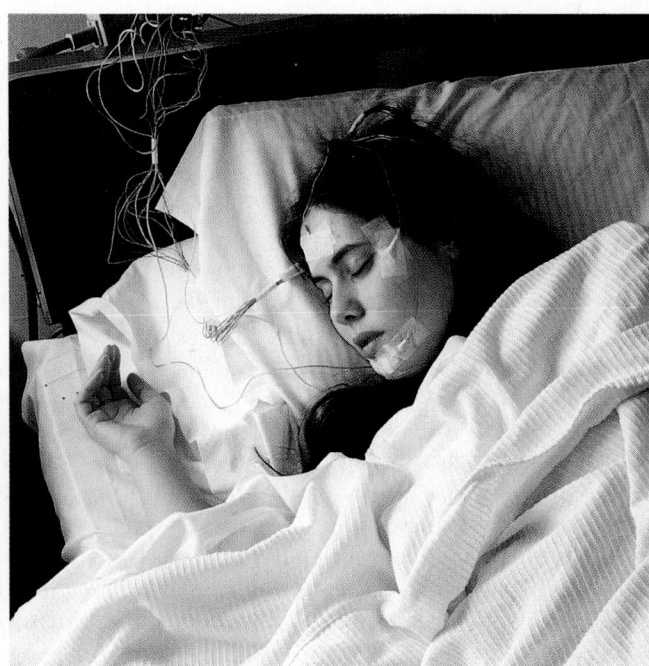

Subjects were randomly assigned to four groups. When subjects arrived at the laboratory, they were given an oral dose of marijuana in a cookie. All subjects were given the same type of cookie and the same instructions. But the dosage level of the marijuana was different for each group: 5, 10, 15, or 20 milligrams of THC, the active ingredient in marijuana.

After consuming the marijuana, the subjects were required to memorize several lists of unrelated words. One week later, the subjects were brought back to the laboratory and asked to recall as many words as possible. Figure 1-5 shows the percentage of words recalled for each of the four groups. Note that recall decreases as a function of the amount of marijuana taken at the time the subject studied the lists.

The experimenters had worked out a careful plan before bringing the subjects to the laboratory. Except for the dosage of marijuana, they held all conditions constant: the general setting for the experiment, the instructions to the subjects, the material to be memorized, the time allowed for memorization, and the conditions under which recall was tested. The only factor permitted to vary across the four groups was the dosage of marijuana—the independent variable. The dependent variable was the amount of material recalled one week later. The marijuana dosage was measured in milligrams of THC; memory was measured by the percentage of words recalled. The experimenters could plot the relation between the independent and dependent variables as shown in Figure 1-5. Finally, the experimenters used enough subjects (a sample of 20 per group) to justify expecting similar results if the experiment were repeated with a different sample of subjects. The letter N is generally used to denote the number of subjects in each group; in this study, N = 20.

The experimental method can be used outside the laboratory as well as inside. It is possible to investigate the effects of different psychotherapeutic methods by trying these methods on separate but similar groups of emotionally troubled individuals. The experimental method is a matter of logic, not of location.

Still, most experiments take place in special laboratories, chiefly because precision instruments are usually necessary to control the presentation of stimuli and to obtain exact measures of behavior. For example, the experimenter may need to produce colors of known wavelengths in vision studies, or to produce sounds of known frequency in audition studies, or to expose a visual display for a precisely timed fraction of a second in an experiment on attention. With precision instruments, time can be measured in thousandths of a second, and physiological activity can be studied by means of very slight currents amplified from the brain. Similarly, the psychological laboratory has other precision instruments, such as audiometers, photometers, oscilloscopes, electronic timers, electroencephalographs, and computers.

EXPERIMENTAL DESIGN   The expression *experimental design* refers to the procedure used in collecting data. The simplest experimental designs are those in which the investigator manipulates one independent variable and studies its effect on one dependent variable. Because everything is held constant except the independent variable, at the end of the experiment a statement like this can be made: "With everything else constant, when X is increased, Y also increases." Or, in other cases: "When X is increased, Y decreases." Almost any content can fit into this kind of statement, as is indicated by the following examples: a) "When the dosage of THC is increased, the recall of memorized material decreases"; b) "The more television aggression children are exposed to, the more aggressively they will act

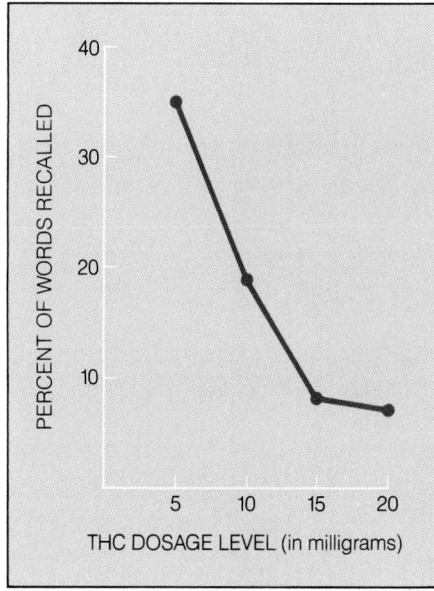

FIGURE 1-5
Marijuana and Memory *Subjects memorized word lists after taking varying dosages of THC (the active ingredient in marijuana). Recall tests administered a week later measured how much of the memorized material was retained. The figure shows the relationship between dosage level (independent variable) and recall score (dependent variable). (After Darley et al., 1973)*

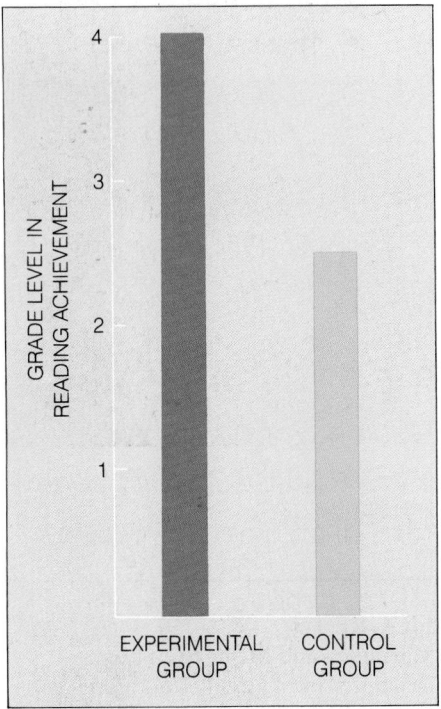

FIGURE 1-6
Experimental and Control Groups
Each day, grade-school children in the experimental group participated in a computer-assisted instruction (CAI) program in reading. The computer was programmed to present different types of materials and instructions to each student, depending on the difficulty a student was having at any point in the reading curriculum. CAI has the advantage of working with each student in a highly individualized way, concentrating on those areas in which the student is having the most difficulty. The control group had no supplementary CAI in reading. At the end of the third grade, all students in both groups were given a standardized reading test. It was administered by testers who had no knowledge of which students had received CAI and which had not. As the figure indicates, students in the experimental group scored higher on the test than students in the control group, suggesting that CAI had been beneficial. In this experiment, the independent variable is the presence or absence of CAI; the dependent variable is the student's score on the reading test. (After Atkinson, 1976)

with other children"; c) "When the physical frequency of a tone is increased, the perceived pitch increases"; or d) "The more prolonged stress one is under, the greater the likelihood of ulcers."

Sometimes an experiment focuses only on the influence of a single condition, which can be either present or absent (an independent variable with two values, presence and absence). The experimental design calls for an *experimental group* with the condition present and a *control group* with the condition absent. The results of such an experiment are presented in Figure 1-6. Inspecting the figure, we see that the experimental group, which received computer-assisted learning, scored higher on reading achievement tests than the control group, which did not receive such instruction.

Limiting an investigation to the effects of only one independent variable is too restrictive for some problems. It may be necessary to study how several independent variables interact to produce an effect on one or even several dependent variables. Studies involving the simultaneous manipulation of several variables are called *multivariate* experiments and are frequently used in psychological research.

MEASUREMENT   Psychologists using the experimental method often find it necessary to make statements about amounts or quantities. Sometimes the variables can be measured by physical means—for example, hours of sleep deprivation, dosage level of a drug, or time required to press a brake pedal when a light flashes. Other times variables have to be scaled in a manner that places them in some sort of order; in rating a patient's feelings of aggression, a psychotherapist might use a five-point scale ranging from "never" through "rarely," "sometimes," "often," and "always." Usually, for purposes of precise communication, numbers are assigned to variables. The term *measurement* is used when a procedure is specified for assigning numbers to different levels, amounts, or sizes of a variable.

Experiments usually involve making measurements on not just one subject, but on a sample of many subjects. Thus, the outcome of the research is data in the form of a set of numbers that must be summarized and interpreted. Basic to this task is *statistics*, the discipline that deals with sampling data from a population of individuals and then drawing inferences about the population from that sample. Statistics plays an important role not only in experimental research, but in other methods as well.* The most common statistic is the *mean*, which is simply the technical term for an arithmetic average. It is the sum of a set of scores divided by the number of scores. In studies involving an experimental and control group, there are two means to be compared: a mean for the scores of the subjects in the experimental group, and a mean for the scores of the subjects in the control group. The difference between these two means is, of course, what interests us.

If the difference between the means is large, we may accept it at face value. But what if the difference is small? What if our measures are subject to error? What if a few extreme cases are producing the difference? Statisticians have solved these problems by developing tests of the *significance of a difference*. A psychologist who says that the difference between the experimental group and the control group is "statistically significant" means that a statistical test has been applied to the data and that the observed difference is trustworthy. In other words, the statistical test indicates that the difference

---

*This discussion is designed to give the reader a brief introduction to the problems of measurement and statistics. A more thorough discussion is provided in Appendix III.

observed is extremely likely to occur again if the experiment is repeated. By using statistical tests, psychologists can judge the likelihood that the observed difference is, in fact, due to the effect of the independent variable rather than an unlucky accident of chance factors.

Correlational Method

NATURALLY OCCURRING DIFFERENCES   Not all problems are susceptible to the experimental method. There are many situations where the investigator has no control over which subjects go in which conditions. For example, if we want to test the hypothesis that obese people are more sensitive to changes in taste than normal-weight people, we cannot select a group of normal-weight subjects and require half of them to become obese! Rather, we select people who are already obese or already normal-weight and see if they also differ in taste sensitivity. More generally, we can use the *correlational method* to determine whether some difference that is not under our control is associated, or *correlated*, with another difference of interest.

COEFFICIENT OF CORRELATION   In the above example, there were only two values of the weight variable—obese and normal. It is more common to have many values of each variable, and to determine the degree to which values on one variable are correlated with values on another. This determination is made by using a statistic called the *coefficient of correlation*, usually symbolized by the lowercase letter r. The correlation coefficient is an estimate of the degree to which two variables are related and is expressed as a number between 0 and 1. No relation is indicated by 0; a perfect relation is indicated by 1. As r goes from 0 to 1, the strength of the relation increases.

The nature of a correlation coefficient can be made clearer by examining a graphic presentation of data from an actual study. In this study, subjects were tested for their susceptibility to hypnosis and were given a score: a low score indicated minimal susceptibility, whereas a high score indicated that they were easily hypnotized. Several weeks later, they were tested again to obtain a second measure of their susceptibility to hypnosis. The study was concerned with how effectively one can predict hypnotizability on one occasion from performance on a prior occasion. Each tally mark in Figure 1-7 represents the results for one subject on the two tests. For example, note that two subjects made scores of 1 on both test days (the two tallies in the box to the lower left), and two subjects made scores of 13 on both days (box to upper right). One subject (see lower right portion of diagram) made a score of 11 on the first test but only 5 on the second test, and so on.

If all subjects had exactly the same score on both tests, all of the tallies would have fallen in the diagonal squares (in yellow), and the coefficient of correlation would have been $r = 1$. Enough tallies fell to either side, however, so that in this study the correlation was $r = .86$. A correlation of .86 indicates that the first test of hypnotizability is a very good, but not perfect, predictor of hypnotizability on a later occasion. The numerical method for calculating a correlation coefficient is described in Appendix III. At this point, however, we will set forth some rules of thumb that will help you interpret correlation coefficients when you encounter them in later chapters.

A correlation can be either $+$ or $-$. The sign of the correlation indicates whether the two variables are positively or negatively correlated. For example, if the number of times a student is absent from class correlates $-.40$ with the final course grade, then the correlation between the number

Computer-assisted learning.

FIGURE 1-7
Scatter Diagram Illustrating
Correlation *Each tally indicates the scores of one subject on two separate tests of hypnotic susceptibility. Tallies in the yellow area indicate identical scores on both tests; those between the dark blue lines indicate a difference of no more than one point between the two scores. The correlation of r = +.86 means that the performances were fairly consistent on the 2 days. There were 49 subjects in this study; thus, N = 49. (After Hilgard, 1961)*

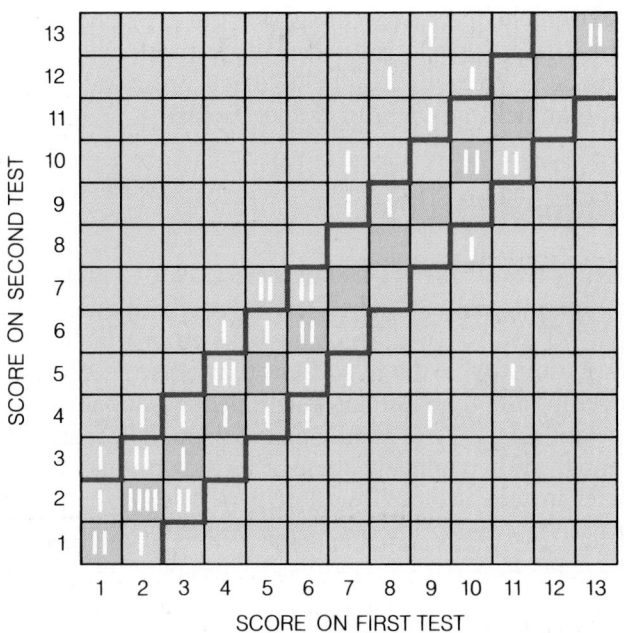

of classes attended and the course grade would be +.40. The strength of the relation is the same, but the sign indicates whether we are looking at classes missed or classes attended.

The strength of the relation between two variables is specified by the absolute value of r. As r goes from 0 to 1, the degree of the relation increases. Let us consider a few examples of correlation coefficients:

- A correlation coefficient of about .75 between grades received in the first year of college and grades received in the second year.
- A correlation of about .70 between scores on an intelligence test given at age 7 and a retest of intelligence at age 18.
- A correlation of about .50 between the height of a parent and the adult height of the child.
- A correlation of about .40 between scores on scholastic aptitude tests given in high school and grades in college.
- A correlation of about .25 between scores on paper-and-pencil personality inventories and judgments by psychological experts of individuals in a social setting.

In psychological research, a correlation coefficient of .60 or more is judged to be quite high. Correlations in the range from .20 to .60 are of practical and theoretical value and useful in making predictions. Correlations between 0 and .20 must be judged with caution and are only minimally useful in making predictions.

TESTS One familiar use of the correlation method involves tests that measure some aptitude, achievement, or other psychological trait. The test presents a uniform situation to a group of people who vary in some trait (such as mathematical ability, manual dexterity, or anxiety). The variation in scores on the test can then be correlated with variations on another variable. For example, people's scores on a mathematical ability test can be correlated with their subsequent grades in a college math course; if the correlation is high, then the test score may be used to determine which of a new group of students should be placed in advanced sections.

The test is an important research instrument in psychology. It enables the psychologist to obtain large quantities of data from people with minimal disturbance of their daily routines and without elaborate laboratory equipment. The construction of tests requires many steps in item preparation, scaling, and establishing norms. Later chapters will explore in some detail the problems of testing.

CAUSE-AND-EFFECT RELATIONS   There is an important distinction between experimental and correlational studies. In an experimental study, one variable (the independent variable) is systematically manipulated to determine its effect on some other variable (the dependent variable). Such cause-and-effect relations cannot be inferred from correlational studies. The fallacy of interpreting correlations as implying cause and effect can be illustrated with a couple of examples. The softness of the asphalt in the streets of a city may correlate with the number of sunstroke cases reported that day, but this does not mean that soft asphalt gives off some kind of poison that sends people to hospitals. We understand the cause in this example: a hot sun both softens the asphalt and produces sunstroke. Another common example is the high positive correlation obtained for the number of storks seen nesting in French villages and the number of childbirths recorded in the same villages. We shall leave it to the reader's ingenuity to figure out possible reasons for such a correlation without postulating a cause-and-effect relation between storks and babies. These examples provide sufficient warning against giving a cause-and-effect interpretation to a correlation. When two variables are correlated, variation in one may *possibly* be the cause of variation in the other, but in the absence of experimental evidence, no such conclusion is justified.

Observational Method

DIRECT OBSERVATION   In the early stages of research on a given topic, laboratory experiments and correlational studies may be premature and progress can best be made by observing the phenomenon of interest as it occurs naturally. Careful observation of animal and human behavior is the starting point for a great deal of research in psychology. For example, observation of primates in their native environment may tell us things about their social organization that will help in later laboratory investigations (see Figure 1-8). Study of preliterate tribes reveals the range of variation in human institutions, which would go unrecognized if we confined our study to people of our own culture. Motion pictures of newborn babies reveal the details of movement patterns shortly after birth and the types of stimuli to which babies are responsive.

In making observations of naturally occurring behavior, however, there is a risk that interpretive anecdotes may be substituted for objective descriptions. We may be tempted, for example, to say that an animal known to have been without food for a long time is "looking for food" when all we observe is heightened activity. Investigators must be trained to observe and record accurately to avoid projecting their own wishes or biases into what they report.

Observational methods can require the use of a laboratory if the problem being studied is partly a biological one. In their extensive study of the physiological aspects of human sexuality, Masters and Johnson (1966) developed

FIGURE 1-8
Baboons Observed in Their Natural Habitat *Field studies can often tell us more about social behavior than experimental studies. Professor Shirley Strum has observed the same troop of baboons in Kenya for more than 15 years, identifying individual animals and making daily recordings of their behaviors and social interactions. Her data have provided remarkable information about the mental abilities of baboons and the role of friendships in their social system.*

"How would you like me to answer that question? As a member of my ethnic group, income group, or religious category?"

Drawing by D. Fradon, © 1969 *The New Yorker Magazine,* Inc.

techniques that permitted direct observation of sexual responses in the laboratory. The intimate nature of the research required careful planning to devise procedures for making the subjects feel at ease in the laboratory and to develop appropriate methods for observing and recording their responses. The data included a) observations of behavior, b) recordings of physiological changes, and c) responses to questions asked about the subject's sensations before, during, and after sexual stimulation. While Masters and Johnson would be the first to agree that human sexuality has many dimensions in addition to the biological one, we still need to understand the biological dimension—the basic anatomical and physiological facts of sexual response—before we can fully understand the psychological aspects.

SURVEY METHOD   Some problems that are difficult to study by direct observation may be studied by indirect observation through the use of questionnaires or interviews. For example, prior to the Masters and Johnson research on sexual response, most of the information on how people behave sexually (as opposed to how laws, religion, or society said they should behave) came from extensive surveys conducted by Alfred Kinsey and his associates 20 years earlier. Information from thousands of individual interviews was analyzed to form the basis of *Sexual Behavior in the Human Male* (Kinsey, Pomeroy, & Martin, 1948) and *Sexual Behavior in the Human Female* (Kinsey, Pomeroy, Martin, & Gebhard, 1953).

Surveys have also been used to indirectly observe people's political opinions, product preferences, health care needs, and so on. The Gallup poll and the United States census are probably the most familiar surveys. An adequate survey requires a carefully pretested questionnaire, interviewers trained in its use, a sample of people selected to ensure they are representative of the population to be studied, and appropriate methods of data analysis to ensure that the results are properly interpreted.

CASE HISTORIES   Still another means of indirectly observing someone is to obtain a biography of him or her. Biographies for scientific use are known as *case histories,* and are important sources of data for psychologists studying individuals. There can also be case histories of institutions or groups of people.

Most case histories are prepared by *reconstructing the biography* of a person on the basis of remembered events and records. Reconstruction is necessary because the individual's history often does not become a matter of interest until that person develops some sort of problem; at such a time, knowledge of the past is important in understanding present behavior. The retrospective method may result in distortions of events or in oversights, compared to what natural observation would have uncovered, but it is often the only approach available.

PROFESSIONS IN PSYCHOLOGY

We have tried to gain some understanding of the nature of psychology by looking at its topics, perspectives, and methods. We can further our understanding of what psychology *is* by looking at what different kinds of psychologists *do*.

Fields of Psychology

About half the people who have advanced degrees in psychology work in colleges and universities. In addition to teaching, they may devote much of their time to research or counseling. Other psychologists work in the public schools, in hospitals or clinics, in research institutes, in government agencies, or in business and industry. Still others are in private practice and offer their services to the public for a fee. Table 1-1 gives an estimate of the proportion of psychologists engaged in different specialized fields; Table 1-2 gives proportions in terms of employment settings (where psychologists work).

We now turn to a description of some of the fields of specialization in psychology.

BIOLOGICAL PSYCHOLOGY   This is the specialization of those who adopt a biological perspective. As discussed earlier, *biological psychologists* (also referred to as *physiological psychologists*) seek to discover the relationship between biological processes and behavior. For example: How do sex hormones influence behavior? What area of the brain controls speech? How do drugs like marijuana and LSD affect personality and memory?

EXPERIMENTAL PSYCHOLOGY   The term "experimental" is really a misnomer because psychologists in other areas of specialization also carry out experiments. But *experimental psychology* usually consists of behaviorist and cognitive psychologists who use experimental methods to study how people react to sensory stimuli, perceive the world, learn and remember, reason, respond emotionally, and how they are motivated to action. Experimental psychologists also work with animals. Sometimes they attempt to relate animal and human behavior; sometimes they study animals in order to compare the behavior of different species (*comparative psychology*).

DEVELOPMENTAL, SOCIAL, AND PERSONALITY PSYCHOLOGY   The categories of developmental psychology, social psychology, and personality

TABLE 1-1
Field of Specialization *The percentage of individuals holding a doctorate degree in psychology and their primary fields of specialization.* (After Stapp & Fulcher, 1981)

FIELD	PERCENTAGE
Experimental and biological	6.9
Developmental, personality, and social	10.4
Clinical, counseling, and school	60.5
Engineering, industrial, and organizational	6.3
Educational	5.4
Other	10.5
	100.0

TABLE 1-2
Employment Setting *The percentage of individuals holding a doctorate degree in psychology and their principal employment settings.* (After Stapp & Fulcher, 1981)

SETTING	PERCENTAGE
Academic setting (university, medical school, college, other)	43.1
Schools and school systems	4.6
Clinics, hospitals, community mental health centers, and counseling centers	23.9
Private practice	14.7
Business, government, research organizations, industry	13.0
Other	.7
	100.0

psychology overlap. *Developmental psychologists* are concerned with human development and the factors that shape behavior from birth to old age. They might study a specific ability, such as how language develops in the growing child, or a particular period of life, such as infancy, the preschool years, or adolescence.

Because human development takes place in the context of other persons—parents, siblings, playmates, and school companions—a large part of development is social. *Social psychologists* are interested in the ways interactions with other people influence attitudes and behavior. They are concerned also with the behavior of groups, and are well known to the general public for their work in public opinion surveys and in market research. Social psychologists investigate topics such as persuasion, conformity, intergroup conflict, and the formation of attitudes.

To the extent that personality is a product of developmental and social factors, the province of personality psychology overlaps both of these categories. *Personality psychologists* focus on differences between individuals. They are interested in ways of classifying people for practical purposes, as well as in studying each individual's unique qualities.

CLINICAL AND COUNSELING PSYCHOLOGY The greatest number of psychologists are engaged in clinical psychology, which is the application of psychological principles to the diagnosis and treatment of emotional and behavioral problems—mental illness, juvenile delinquency, criminal behavior, drug addiction, mental retardation, marital and family conflict, and other less serious adjustment problems. Many clinical psychologists have a psychoanalytic perspective, though the behavioral, cognitive, and phenomenological perspectives are also well represented. *Clinical psychologists* may work in mental hospitals, juvenile courts or probation offices, mental health clinics, institutions for the mentally retarded, prisons, university medical schools, or in private practice.

Counseling psychologists serve many of the same functions as clinical psychologists, although they usually deal with less serious problems. They often work with high school or university students, providing help with problems of social adjustment and vocational and educational goals. Together, clinical and counseling psychologists account for about 55 percent of all psychologists in the United States.

SCHOOL AND EDUCATIONAL PSYCHOLOGY The elementary and secondary schools have a great need for psychologists. Because the beginnings of serious emotional problems often appear in the early grades, many elementary schools employ psychologists whose training combines courses in child development, education, and clinical psychology. These *school psychologists* work with individual children to evaluate learning and emotional problems. Administering and interpreting intelligence, achievement, and personality tests is also part of their job. In consultation with parents and teachers, they plan ways of helping the child both in the classroom and in the home.

Educational psychologists are specialists in learning and teaching. They may work in the schools, but more often they are employed by a university's school of education, where they do research on teaching methods and help train teachers and school psychologists.

INDUSTRIAL AND ENGINEERING PSYCHOLOGY *Industrial psychologists* (sometimes called *organizational psychologists*) typically work for a particular company. They are concerned with such problems as selecting people

Counseling psychologists often work with families to help them resolve problems.

most suitable for particular jobs, developing job training programs, and participating in management decisions that involve the motivation of employees. They also conduct research on consumer behavior, including how advertising and consumer preferences influence the purchase of a particular product.

Engineering psychologists (sometimes called *human factors engineers*) seek to improve the relationship between people and machines; they help design machines to minimize human error. For example, engineering psychologists were involved in developing space capsules in which astronauts could live and function efficiently. Designing air traffic control systems and underwater habitats for oceanographic research are other examples of their work. In computer systems, the design of the *person-machine interface*, the point at which the person interacts with the machine, is especially important.

Along with social psychologists and engineering psychologists, there is a group of *environmental psychologists* concerned with the problems of noise, air, and water pollution, as well as the optimal design of working and living areas.

OTHER SPECIALITIES In addition to the areas mentioned, there are other career possibilities in psychology. *Forensic psychologists* work within the legal, judicial, and correctional systems in a variety of ways. For example, they may consult with police departments and probation offices to increase the understanding of the human problems with which these institutions must deal. Also, they may work with prison inmates and their families, participate in decisions about whether an accused person is mentally competent to stand trial, or prepare psychological reports to help judges decide on the most appropriate course of action for a convicted criminal.

Because of their expertise in procedures for gathering and analyzing data, psychologists also work in the area of *evaluation research*. Many of the public and private programs designed to solve social problems involve large expenditures of money and extensive personnel. Consequently, it is essential to determine whether such programs—aimed, for example, at preventing drug

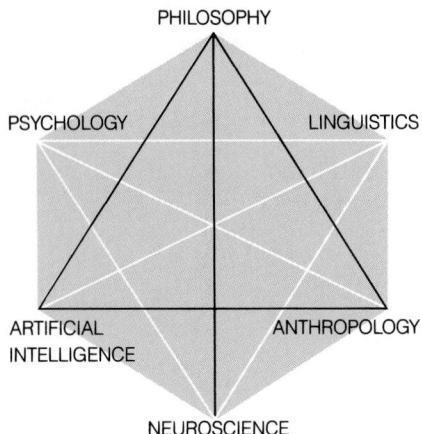

FIGURE 1-9
Cognitive Sciences *The figure shows the fields involved in cognitive science and their interrelationships. Artificial intelligence refers to a branch of computer science concerned with a) using computers to simulate human thought processes; and b) devising computer programs that act "intelligently" and can adapt to changing circumstances. This figure was included in an unpublished report commissioned by the Sloan Foundation (New York City) in 1978; the report was prepared by leading researchers in the cognitive sciences.*

abuse among high-school students, or providing job training for unemployed youths—are effective. Psychologists are involved in the evaluation of such programs.

Cognitive Science

Cognitive science describes those areas of psychological research that a) are concerned with cognitive processes like perceiving, remembering, reasoning, deciding, and problem solving; and b) overlap with other disciplines interested in these processes, such as philosophy and computer science. The term was introduced in the 1970s to focus attention on how people and machines carry out certain intelligent processes. A number of scientists from diverse disciplines believed that sufficient progress had been made on various fronts to form a "new" science dedicated to understanding cognitive processes. The new field's major objectives were to discover how information was represented in the mind (mental representations); what types of computations could be carried out on these representations to bring about perceiving, remembering, reasoning, and so on; and how these computations were realized biologically in the brain.

In addition to psychology, the disciplines that are particularly relevant to cognitive science are neuroscience, anthropology, linguistics, philosophy, and artificial intelligence. (The latter is a branch of computer science concerned with developing computers that act intelligently and computer programs that can simulate human thought processes.) The diagram in Figure 1-9 lists the contributing disciplines.

Gardner argues that cognitive science is based on at least two beliefs:

> First of all, there is the belief that, in talking about human cognitive activities, it is necessary to speak about mental representation and to posit a level of analysis wholly separate from the biological or neurological, on the one hand, and the sociological or cultural, on the other. Second, there is the faith that central to any understanding of the human mind is the electronic computer. Not only are computers indispensable for carrying out studies of various sorts, but, more crucially, the computer also serves as the most viable model of how the human mind functions. (1985, p. 6)

Cognitive science, whether viewed as a new discipline or as a label for a group of disciplines working on a common problem, represents an important milestone in the history of science. Recent developments in neuroscience, computers, linguistics, and psychology suggest that the necessary ingredients are in place to make headway on problems that have intrigued the human species throughout its history: problems concerning the nature of knowledge and how it is represented in the brain. Throughout this book, we will have numerous occasions to mention such interdisciplinary approaches to problems of knowledge.

OVERVIEW OF THE BOOK

Psychologists today are in the process of investigating thousands of different phenomena ranging from microelectrode studies of how individual brain cells change during learning to studies of the effects of population density and overcrowding on social behavior. Deciding how to classify these investigations topically and how to present the topics in the most meaningful order is difficult. Should we know how people perceive the world around them in order to understand how they learn new things? Or does learning determine how we perceive our environment? Should we discuss what motivates a person to action so that we can understand his or her personality? Or can motivation be better understood if we first look at the way personality develops over the course of a lifetime? Despite such unresolved questions, we have tried to arrange the topics in this book so that the understanding of the issues in each chapter will provide a background for the study of problems in the next.

To understand how people interact with their environment, we need to know something about their biological equipment. In Part II ("Biological and Developmental Processes"), the first chapter describes how the nervous and endocrine systems function to integrate and control behavior. Because behavior also depends on the interaction between inherited characteristics and environmental conditions, this chapter includes a discussion of genetic influences on behavior. The second chapter in Part II provides an overview of the individual's psychological development from infancy through adolescence and adulthood. By noting how abilities, attitudes, and personality develop, and the problems that must be faced at different stages of life, we can appreciate more fully the kinds of questions to which psychology seeks answers.

With this as background, we move on to Part III ("Perception and Consciousness"), where we will survey how humans and other species acquire information about the external world. Such information must first be registered by the sense organs, which mediate the sensations of light, sound, touch, and taste. We first discuss the nature of sensory information, and then consider how such information is organized into meaningful patterns and recognized as instances of familiar objects or events. Organization and recognition are parts of the *process* of perception. The *products* of perception often emerge in consciousness, and we will examine the characteristics of human consciousness under both normal and altered states.

In Part IV ("Learning, Remembering, and Thinking"), we will first consider how organisms learn about their environment, ranging from the learning of simple relations like "shock follows tone" to the complex knowledge taught in college courses. We will also consider how such information is remembered and used for purposes of reasoning and problem solving. In addition, we take up the critical problem of language—how we communicate what we know.

Part V ("Motivation and Emotion") deals with the forces that energize and direct behavior. Such forces include basic motives such as hunger, sex, and curiosity, as well as emotions such as joy, fear, and anger.

The ways in which individuals differ from one another is the substance of Part VI ("Personality and Individuality"). We will consider differences in both mental abilities and personality, paying close attention to how these differences are measured.

Dealing with stress and emotional problems are the major topics in Part VII ("Stress, Psychopathology, and Therapy"). We will consider the kinds of emotional problems that virtually everyone faces at some point, as well as more severe forms of mental disorders like schizophrenia. In addition, we discuss the various therapies that have been developed to deal with such problems and disorders.

Part VIII ("Social Behavior") is concerned with social interactions. We will discuss how we think, feel, and act in social situations, and how social situations in turn influence our thoughts, feelings, and actions. We will discuss how we perceive and interpret the behaviors of other people; how beliefs and attitudes are shaped; and how groups influence their members and vice versa.

CHAPTER SUMMARY

1. *Psychology* may be defined as the *scientific study of behavior and mental processes.* The variety of topics covered by this definition is illustrated by considering five specific problems: a) *split-brain perception*, where people with disconnected left and right hemispheres experience the world differently from people with connected hemispheres; b) *conditioned fear*, wherein an organism learns to fear what was once a neutral stimulus; c) *childhood amnesia*, the inability to remember events from the first few years of life; d) *causes of obesity*, including psychological and biological factors; and e) the *expression of aggression*, and whether such expression leads to more or less aggression.

2. The *roots of psychology* can be traced to the fourth and fifth centuries B.C. The Greek philosophers Socrates, Plato, and Aristotle posed fundamental questions about the mind, while Hippocrates, the "father of medicine," made many important observations about how the brain controlled other organs. *Scientific psychology* was born in the latter part of the nineteenth century, when the idea took hold that mind and behavior could be the subject of scientific analysis.

3. The study of psychology can be approached from several viewpoints. The *biological perspective* relates our actions to events taking place inside the body, particularly in the brain and nervous system. The *behavioral* perspective considers only those external activities of the organism that can be observed and measured. The *cognitive* perspective is concerned with mental processes such as perceiving, remembering, reasoning, deciding, and problem solving, and with relating these processes to behavior. The *psychoanalytic* perspective emphasizes unconscious motives stemming from sexual and aggressive impulses repressed in childhood. The *phenomenological* perspective focuses on the person's subjective experiences, freedom of choice, and motivation toward self-actualization. A particular area of psychological investigation often can be analyzed from a number of these viewpoints.

4. The *biological* perspective differs from the other viewpoints in that its principles are drawn from biology. Often biological researchers attempt to explain psychological principles in terms of biological ones. While such *reductionism* can be successful, there are some principles that can be stated only at psychological levels. Also, psychological research is often needed to direct the work of researchers taking the biological perspective.

5. When applicable, the *experimental method* is preferred for studying problems because it seeks to control all variables except the ones being studied. The *independent variable* is the one manipulated by the experimenter; the *dependent variable* (usually some measure of the subject's behavior) is the one being studied to determine if it is affected by changes in the independent variable. In the simplest *experimental design*, the experimenter manipulates one independent variable and observes its effect on one dependent variable.

6. In many experiments, the independent variable is something that is either present or absent. The simplest experimental design includes an *experimental group* (with the condition present for one group of subjects) and a *control group* (with the condition absent for another group of subjects). If the difference in *means* between the experimental and control groups is *statistically significant*, we know that the experimental condition had a reliable effect; that is, if the study were to be repeated, a similar difference in means would be observed.

7. If an investigator has no control over which subjects go in which conditions, a *correlational method* may be used. This method determines whether a naturally occurring difference is associated with another difference of interest. The degree of correlation between two variables is measured by the *correlation coefficient*, *r*. It is a number between 0 and 1. No relationship is indicated by 0; a perfect relationship is indicated by 1. As *r* goes from 0 to 1, the strength of the relationship increases. The correlation coefficient can be positive or negative, depending on whether one variable increases with another (+) or one variable decreases as the other increases (−).

8. Another approach to research is the *observational* method, in which one observes the phenomenon of interest. Researchers must be trained to observe and record accurately to avoid projecting their own wishes or biases into what they report. Phenomena that are difficult to observe directly may be observed indirectly by *surveys* (questionnaires and interviews) or by *reconstructing a case history*.

9. Psychology as a profession includes numerous areas of specialization: biological psychology; experimental psychology, developmental, social, and personality psychology; clinical and counseling psychology; school and educational psychology; and industrial and engineering psychology.

FURTHER READING

The topical interests and theories of any contemporary science can often be understood best according to their history. Several useful books are Hilgard, *Psychology in America: A Historical Survey* (1987); Murphy and Kovach, *Historical Introduction to Modern Psychology* (3rd ed., 1972); Wertheimer, *A Brief History of Psychology* (rev. ed., 1979); and Schultz, *A History of Modern Psychology* (4th ed., 1987). A brief history of psychology is presented in Appendix II.

The various conceptual approaches to psychology are discussed in Medcof and Roth (eds.), *Approaches to Psychology* (1988); Anderson, *Cognitive Psychology and Its Implications* (3rd ed., 1989); Peterson, *Personality* (1988); Royce and Mos (eds.), *Humanistic Psychology: Concepts and Criticism* (1981); Bower and Hilgard, *Theories of Learning* (5th ed., 1981); Lundin, *Theories and Systems of Psychology* (3rd ed., 1985); and Gardner, *The Mind's New Science: A History of the Cognitive Revolution* (1985).

The methods of psychological research are presented in Wood, *Fundamentals of Psychological Research* (3rd ed., 1986); Snodgrass, Levy-Berger, and Haydon, *Human Experimental Psychology* (1985); Ray and Ravizza, *Methods Toward a Science of Behavior and Experience* (2nd ed., 1984); and Elmes, Kantowitz, and Roediger, *Research Methods in Psychology* (3rd ed., 1989).

A simple but elegant introduction to basic concepts in statistics is Phillips, *How to Think About Statistics* (1988).

Appendix IV to this book lists some of the major psychology journals and gives a description of the types of articles they publish. These journals are available in most college and university libraries. Current issues of the journals generally can be found on racks in an open section of the library. An excellent overview of psychology can be gained by spending some time perusing recent issues of these journals.

To find out more about career opportunities in psychology and the training required to become a psychologist, write to the American Psychological Association (1200 Seventeenth Street N.W., Washington, D.C. 20036) for a copy of their booklet, *A Career in Psychology*.

Paul Klee. Child and Aunt, 1937.
Oil on plaster-coated burlap, 28⅝″ x 20¾″, Galerie Beyeler, Basel.

PART II

Biological and Developmental Processes

Chapter 2

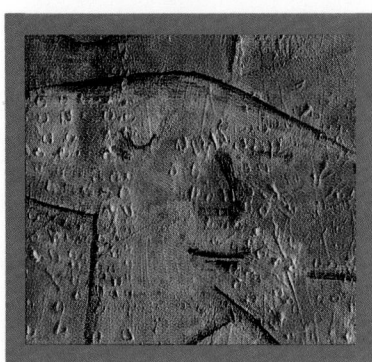

Detail, Child and Aunt.

Biological Basis of Psychology

Behavior, from blinking an eye to playing tennis to writing a computer program, depends on the integration of numerous processes within the body. This integration is provided by the nervous system, with help from the endocrine system. Consider, for example, all the processes that must coordinate effectively for you to stop your car at a red light. First you must see the light; this means that the light must register on one set of your sense organs, your eyes. Neural impulses from your eyes are relayed to your brain, where the stimulus is analyzed and compared with information about past events stored in your memory: you recognize that a red light in a certain context means "stop." The process of moving your foot to the brake pedal and pressing it is initiated by the motor areas of the brain that control the muscles of your leg and foot. In order to send the proper signals to these muscles, the brain must know where your foot is as well as where you want it to go. The brain maintains a register of the position of body parts relative to one another, which it uses to plan directed movements. You do not stop the car with one sudden movement of your leg, however. A specialized part of your brain receives continual *feedback* from leg and foot muscles so that you are aware of how much pressure is being exerted and you can alter your movements accordingly. At the same time, your eyes and some of your other body senses tell you how quickly the car is stopping. If the light turned red as you were speeding toward the intersection, some of your endocrine glands would also be activated, leading to increased heart rate, more rapid respiration, and other metabolic changes associated with fear; these processes speed your reactions in an emergency. Your stopping at a red light may seem quick and automatic, but it involves numerous complex messages and adjustments. The information for these activities is transmitted by large networks of nerve cells.

Many aspects of behavior and mental functioning can be better understood with some knowledge of the underlying biological processes. Our nervous system, sense organs, muscles, and glands enable us to be aware of and to adjust to our environment. Our perception of events depends on how our sense organs detect stimuli and how our brain interprets information coming from the senses. Much of our behavior is motivated by such needs as hunger, thirst, and the avoidance of fatigue or pain. Our ability to use language, to think, and to solve problems depends on a brain that is incredibly complex. Indeed, the specific patterns of electrical and chemical events in the brain are the very basis of our most intricate thought processes.

Some of the research relating psychological events to biological processes will be discussed in later chapters when we talk, for example, about perception, memory, or motivation. This chapter attempts only to provide an overview of the nervous system.

COMPONENTS OF THE NERVOUS SYSTEM

The basic unit of the nervous system is a specialized cell called the *neuron*. It is important to understand neurons because they undoubtedly hold the secrets of how the brain works. We know their role in the transmission of nerve impulses, and we know how some neural circuits work; but we are just beginning to unravel their more complex functioning in memory, emotion, and thought.

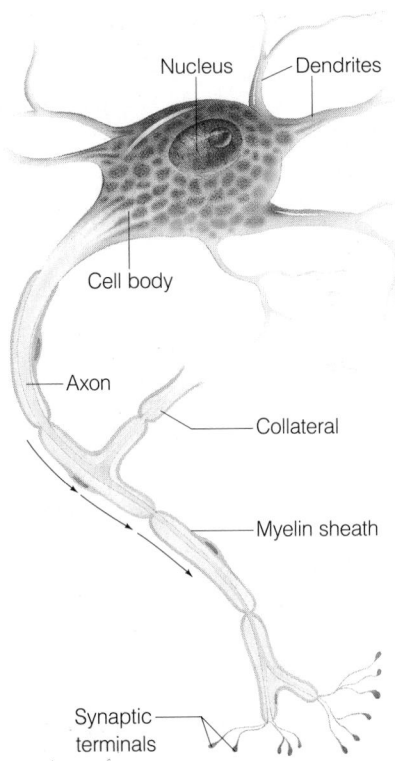

FIGURE 2-1
**Schematic Diagram of a
Neuron** *Arrows indicate the direction
of the nerve impulse. Some axons are
branched; the branches are called
collaterals. The axons of many neurons are
covered with a myelin sheath that helps to
increase the speed of the nerve impulse.*

Neurons and Nerves

Although neurons differ markedly in size and appearance, they have certain common characteristics (see Figure 2-1). Projecting from the *cell body* are a number of short branches called *dendrites* (from the Greek word *dendron*, meaning "tree"). The dendrites and cell body receive neural impulses from adjacent neurons. These messages are transmitted to other neurons (or to muscles and glands) by a slender tubelike extension of the cell called an *axon*. At its end the axon branches into a number of fine collaterals that end in small swellings called *synaptic terminals*.

The synaptic terminal does not actually touch the neuron that it will stimulate. Rather, there is a slight gap between the synaptic terminal and the cell body or dendrites of the receiving neuron. This junction is called a *synapse* and the gap itself is called the *synaptic gap*. When a neural impulse travels down the axon and arrives at the synaptic terminals, it triggers the secretion of a chemical called a *neurotransmitter*. The neurotransmitter travels across the synaptic gap and stimulates the next neuron, thereby carrying the impulse from one neuron to the next. The axons from a great many neurons (perhaps as many as 1,000) may synapse on the dendrites and cell body of a single neuron (see Figure 2-2).

Although all neurons have these general features, they vary greatly in size and shape (see Figure 2-3). A neuron in the spinal cord may have an axon three to four feet long, running from the tip of the spine to the big toe; a neuron in the brain may cover only a few thousandths of an inch.

There are three types of neurons. *Sensory neurons* transmit impulses received by *receptors* to the central nervous system. The receptors are specialized cells in the sense organs, muscles, skin, and joints that detect physical or chemical changes and translate these events into impulses that travel along the sensory neurons. *Motor neurons* carry outgoing signals from the brain or spinal cord to the effector organs, namely the muscles and glands.

FIGURE 2-2
**Synapses at the Cell Body of a
Neuron** *Many different axons, each of
which branches repeatedly, synapse on the
dendrites and cell body of a single neuron.
Each branch of an axon ends in a swelling
called a synaptic terminal, which contains
chemicals that are released and transmit the
nerve impulse across the synapse to the
dendrites or cell body of the receiving cell.*

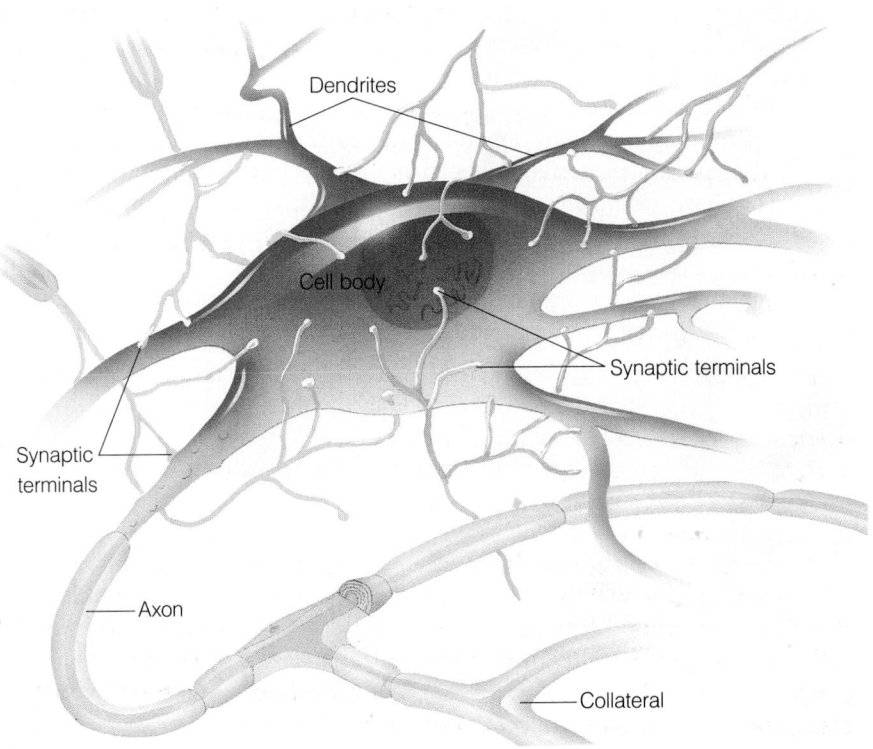

Interneurons receive the signals from the sensory neurons and send impulses to other interneurons or to motor neurons. Interneurons are found only in the brain, eyes, and spinal cord.

A *nerve* is a bundle of elongated axons belonging to hundreds or thousands of neurons. A single nerve may contain axons from both sensory and motor neurons.

In addition to neurons, the nervous system consists of a large number of nonneural cells, called *glial cells*. The name is derived from the Greek word *glia* (meaning glue), because one of their principal functions is to hold the neurons in place. Glial cells have neither axons nor dendrites and are not specialized to receive or transmit signals. Rather, they provide structural support and serve in other ways to ensure that neurons can perform their functions. Estimates of the number of neurons and glial cells in the human nervous system vary widely, depending on the method used to make the determination; as yet, there is no agreement among scientists on the best estimate. In the human brain alone, the estimates range from 10 billion to 1 trillion neurons; whatever the estimate for neurons, the number of glial cells is probably 10 times that number (Groves & Rebec, 1988). These are astronomical figures, but this number of cells is undoubtedly necessary to support the complexities of human behavior.

Axonal Conduction

The movement of a nerve impulse along an axon is quite different from the flow of electric current through a wire. Electricity travels at the speed of light (186,300 miles per second), whereas a nerve impulse in the human body may travel from 2 to 200 miles per hour, depending on the diameter of the axon and other factors. The analogy of a firework fuse has sometimes been used: when a fuse is lighted, one part of the fuse ignites the next part, the impulse being regenerated along the way. However, the details of neural transmission are more complex. The process is *electrochemical*. The thin membrane that holds together the protoplasm of the cell is not equally permeable to the many different types of *ions* (electrically charged atoms and molecules) that float in the protoplasm of the cell and in the liquid surrounding the cell. In its resting state, the cell membrane tends to keep out positively charged sodium ions (Na^+) and tends to keep within the cell various negatively charged ions. As a result, there is a small electrical potential, or voltage difference, across the membrane; the inside of a nerve cell is more negative than the outside.

When the axon is stimulated, the electrical potential across the membrane is reduced at the point of stimulation. If the reduction in potential is large enough, the permeability of the cell membrane suddenly changes, allowing Na^+ ions to enter the cell. This process is called *depolarization*; now the inside of the cell membrane becomes less negative than it was before. This change affects the adjacent portion of the axon, causing its membrane to depolarize. The process (repeating itself down the length of the axon) is the *nerve impulse*. Because the nerve impulse is generated anew at each stage along the axon, it does not diminish in strength during transmission.

Depolarization occurs because the cell membrane acts as a highly selective filter, ensuring different concentrations of ions inside and outside the cell. Ions can pass into and out of the cell only by way of *ion channels* and *ion pumps* embedded in the cell membrane. Ion channels are protein structures that form a pore across the cell membrane. The protein structure regulates

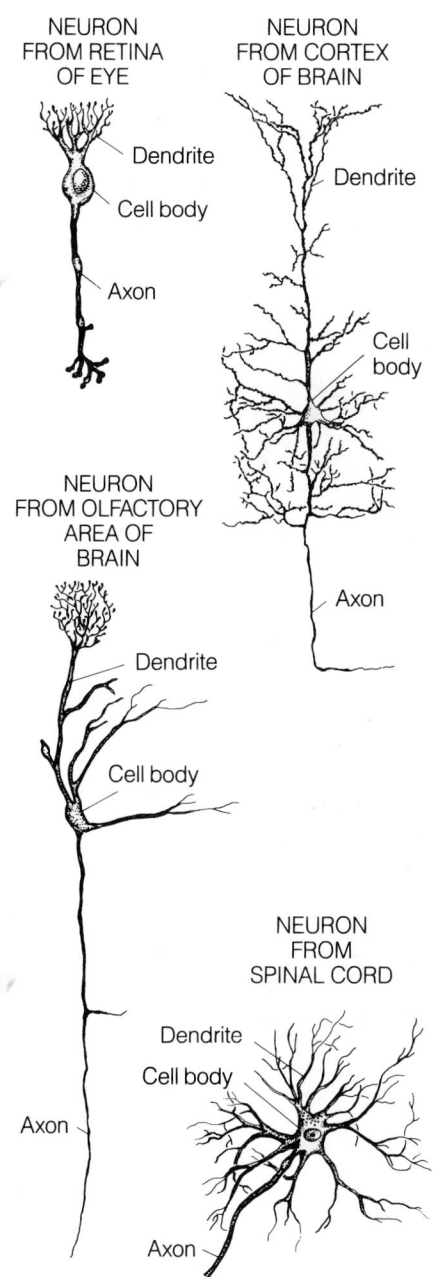

FIGURE 2-3
Shapes and Relative Sizes of Neurons *The axon of a spinal cord neuron (not shown in its entirety in the figure) may be several feet long.*

the flow of ions by opening and closing the pore. When the gates of the channels are open, ions rush through the pores and tend to equalize the differences in ion concentrations that exist between the interior and exterior of the cell. The ion channels may open or close in response to neuro-transmitters binding to them or in response to a change in the voltage across the membrane. In contrast to ion channels, ion pumps use metabolic energy to pump Na^+ ions (and other ions) back out of the cell to restore the resting potential of the membrane (Alberts et al., 1983).

The axons of most neurons are covered by a thin fatty sheath, the *myelin sheath*, which serves to insulate them. The sheath consists of a series of short segments separated by small gaps (refer back to Figure 2-1). The insulating function of the myelin sheath allows the nerve impulse to jump from gap to gap, thus greatly improving the speed of conduction. The myelin sheath is characteristic of the nervous systems of higher animals. *Multiple sclerosis*, a disease characterized by severe sensory and motor nerve dysfunction, is due to degeneration of areas of the myelin sheath.

Synaptic Transmission

The synaptic junction between neurons is of tremendous importance because it is there that nerve cells transfer signals. A single neuron dis-charges, or fires, when the stimulation reaching it via multiple synapses ex-ceeds a certain threshold level. The neuron fires in a single, brief pulse and is then inactive for a few thousandths of a second. The strength of the neural impulse is constant and cannot be triggered by a stimulus unless it reaches threshold level; this is referred to as the *all-or-none principle* of action. The nerve impulse, once started, travels down the axon to its many axon terminals.

As we have said, neurons do not connect directly at a synapse; there is a slight gap across which the signal must be transmitted (see Figure 2-4). Al-though in a few areas of the nervous system the electrical activity in one neuron can stimulate another neuron directly, neurotransmitters are respon-sible for transmitting the signal in the vast majority of cases. When a nerve impulse moves down the axon of a neuron and arrives at a synaptic terminal, it stimulates *synaptic vesicles* in the terminal. These vesicles are small spheri-cal or irregularly shaped structures that contain neurotransmitters; when stimulated they discharge the neurotransmitters. The neurotransmitter mol-ecules diffuse across the synaptic gap and bind to *receptor molecules* in the cell membrane of the receiving neuron. The neurotransmitter molecules and

FIGURE 2-4
Release of Neurotransmitters into a Synaptic Gap *The neurotransmitter is carried to the presynaptic membrane in synaptic vesicles, which fuse with the membrane and release their contents into the synaptic gap. The neurotransmitters diffuse across the gap and combine with receptor molecules in the postsynaptic membrane.*

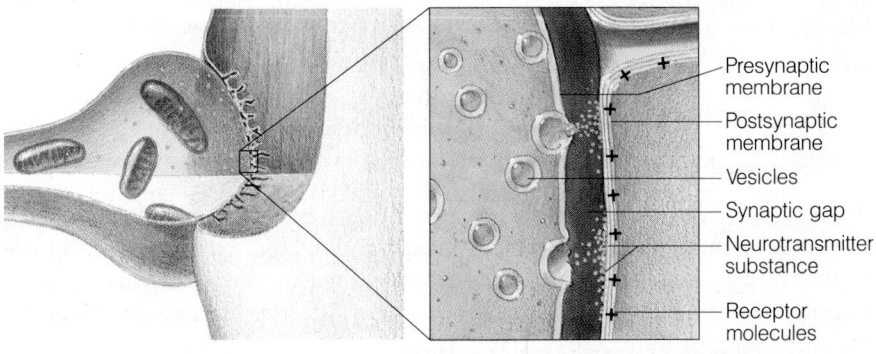

Presynaptic membrane

Postsynaptic membrane

Vesicles

Synaptic gap

Neurotransmitter substance

Receptor molecules

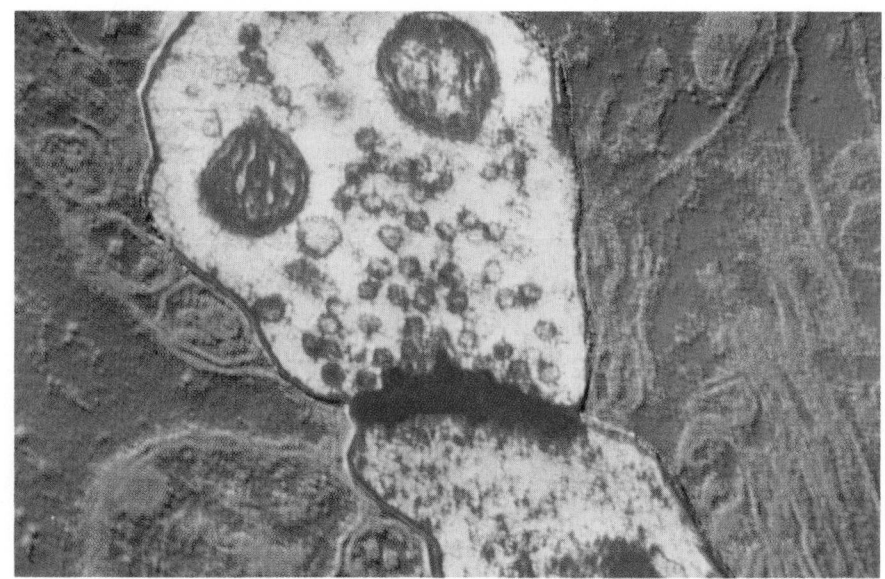

A micrograph of a synapse between two neurons in the cerebral cortex. The synaptic gap appears deep red. Vesicles containing neurotransmitters are seen as small red/ yellow spheres. The two larger circles are the sites of energy production in the nerve cell. (Magnification: x 17,600)

receptor molecules fit together in the same way that one piece of a jigsaw puzzle fits another, or the way a key fits a lock. This *lock-and-key* action of the two molecules causes a change in the permeability of the receiving neuron. When locked to their receptors some neurotransmitters have an excitatory effect and increase permeability in the direction of depolarization; others are inhibitory and decrease the permeability.

A given neuron may receive many thousands of synapses from a network of other neurons. Some of these synapses release neurotransmitters that are *excitatory*, while others release neurotransmitters that are *inhibitory*. Depending on their pattern of firing, different axons will release their neurotransmitter substances at different times. If, at any moment, the excitatory effects on a given neuron become large relative to the inhibitory effects, then depolarization occurs and the neuron fires an all-or-none impulse.

Once a neurotransmitter substance is released and diffuses across the synaptic gap, its action must be very brief. Otherwise, it will exert its effects for too long, and precise control will be lost. The brevity of the action is achieved in one of two ways. For some neurotransmitters, the synapse is almost immediately cleared of the chemical by *reuptake*, the process in which the neurotransmitter is reabsorbed by the synaptic terminals from which it was released. Reuptake cuts off the action of the neurotransmitter and spares the axon terminals from having to manufacture more of the substance. The effect of other neurotransmitters is terminated by *degradation*, the process in which enzymes in the membrane of the receiving neuron react with the neurotransmitter to break it up chemically and make it inactive.

Neurotransmitters and Receptor Molecules

Over 50 different neurotransmitters have been identified, and others surely will be discovered in the future. Moreover, some neurotransmitters can bind to more than one type of receptor molecule, causing different effects. For example, there are neurotransmitters that are excitatory at some sites in the nervous system and inhibitory at other sites because two different types of receptor molecules are involved.

CRITICAL DISCUSSION

Molecular Psychology

When the neural impulse reaches the end of an axon, neurotransmitter molecules are released that cross the synaptic gap and combine with receptor molecules in the membrane of the target neuron. The lock-and-key action of the two molecules changes the electrical properties of the target cell, either causing it to fire or preventing it from firing.

To serve its function, every key requires a lock and every neurotransmitter requires a receptor. Many commonly used drugs—from tranquilizers such as Valium to street drugs such as heroin and crack—interact with receptor molecules in very much the

same way as neurotransmitters. Molecules of these drugs are shaped enough like those of the neurotransmitters to work as if they were keys to the lock of receptor molecules.

A good example of look-alike molecules are *opiates*, a class of drugs that includes heroin and morphine. In molecular shape, opiates resemble a group of neurotransmitters in the brain called *endorphins*, which have the effect of blocking pain. The discovery that opiates mimic naturally occurring substances in the brain has prompted considerable research on the chemical control system in the body that copes with stress and pain. Individuals who appear indifferent to pain may have an unusual ability to increase the production of these natural painkillers when they are needed. Research with one of the endorphins, called *enkephalin*, has helped explain why a painkiller like morphine can be addictive. Under normal conditions, enkephalin occupies a

certain number of opiate receptors. Morphine relieves pain by binding to the receptors that are left unfilled. Too much morphine can cause a drop in enkephalin production, leaving opiate receptors unfilled. The body then requires more morphine to fill the unoccupied receptors and to reduce pain. When morphine is discontinued, the opiate receptors are left unfilled, causing painful withdrawal symptoms. The fact that the brain synthesizes substances that resemble opiates has been invoked to explain all sorts of effects. Joggers tout the theory that physical exertion increases enkephalin production to induce a "runner's high." Acupuncturists say their needles actuate enkephalins that act as natural anesthetics. There is, however, no definitive evidence to support these claims.

Drugs that influence mental functioning and mood, such as opiates, are called *psychoactive drugs*. By and large, they produce their effects by altering

Acetylcholine (ACh) is a neurotransmitter found at many synapses throughout the body. In general, it is an excitatory transmitter, but it can be inhibitory depending on the type of receptor molecule in the membrane of the receiving neuron. ACh is particularly prevalent in an area of the brain called the hippocampus, which plays a key role in the formation of new memories (Squire, 1987). Alzheimer's disease, a devastating disorder that affects many older people, involves impairment of memory and other cognitive functions. It has been demonstrated that brain cells producing ACh tend to degenerate in Alzheimer patients, and consequently the brain's production of ACh is reduced; the less ACh the brain produces, the more serious the memory loss.

ACh is also released at every synapse at which a nerve terminates at a skeletal muscle fiber. The ACh is directed onto small structures called *end plates*, located on the muscle cells. The end plates are covered with receptor molecules that, when activated by ACh, trigger a molecular linkage inside the muscle cells that results in their contraction. Certain drugs that affect ACh can produce muscle paralysis. For example, botulinum toxin, which forms from bacteria in improperly canned foods, blocks receptors for ACh at nerve-muscle synapses and can cause death when the muscles for breathing become paralyzed. Some nerve gases developed for warfare and many pesticides cause paralysis by destroying the enzyme that degrades ACh once the neuron has been fired; when the degradation process fails there is an uncontrolled buildup of ACh in the nervous system so that normal synaptic transmission becomes impossible.

one of the various neurotransmitter-receptor systems. Different drugs can have different actions at the same synapse. One drug might mimic the effect of a specific neurotransmitter, another might occupy the receptor site so that the normal neurotransmitter is blocked out, and still others might affect the reuptake or degradation processes. The drug action will either increase or decrease the effectiveness of neural transmission.

Two drugs, *chlorpromazine* and *reserpine*, have proved effective in treating schizophrenia (a mental illness to be discussed in Chapter 16). Both drugs act on norepinephrine and dopamine systems, but their antipsychotic action is primarily due to their effect on the neurotransmitter dopamine. It appears that chlorpromazine blocks dopamine receptors, whereas reserpine reduces dopamine levels by destroying storage vesicles in the synaptic terminals. The effectiveness of these drugs in treating schizophrenia has led to the *dopamine hypothesis*, which postulates that schizophrenia is due to an excess of dopamine activity in critical cell groups within the brain. The key evidence for the hypothesis is that antipsychotic drugs seem to be clinically effective to the extent that they block the transmission of impulses by dopamine molecules. The dopamine hypothesis has wide support, but as yet, efforts to demonstrate an actual increase in dopamine concentrations in schizophrenics, as compared with nonschizophrenics, have not been successful.

Research on neurotransmitter-receptor systems has increased our understanding of how drugs work. In an earlier period, psychoactive drugs were discovered almost entirely by accident and their development took years of research. Now, as we gain more knowledge about neurotransmitters and receptors, new drugs can be designed and developed in a systematic way.

During the last 10 years, a great deal has been learned about the molecular basis of interneural communication. The emerging picture is that thousands of different types of molecules are involved—not just transmitter and receptor molecules but also the enzymes that manufacture and degrade them and various other molecules that modulate their action (Groves & Rebec, 1988). Of course, each time a new molecule is identified, we have discovered the potential for at least two diseases or forms of mental illness; some people will surely have too much of that molecule and others too little. Research on these problems has proved so productive that the field has been given the name *molecular psychology* (Franklin, 1987). The basic idea behind this new discipline is that mental processes and their aberrations can be analyzed in terms of the molecular interplay that takes place between neurons.

Norepinephrine (NE) is a neurotransmitter that is produced mainly by neurons in the brain stem. Two well-known drugs, *cocaine* and *amphetamines*, prolong the action of NE by slowing down its reuptake process. Because of the delay in the reuptake, the receiving neurons are activated for a longer period of time, thus causing the stimulating psychological effects of these drugs. In contrast, *lithium* is a drug that speeds up the reuptake of NE, causing a person's mood level to be depressed. Any drug that causes NE to increase or decrease in the brain is correlated with an increase or decrease in the individual's mood level.

Another prominent neurotransmitter is *gamma-aminobutyric acid* (GABA). This substance acts as an inhibitory transmitter. For example, the drug *picrotoxin* blocks GABA receptors and produces convulsions because without GABA's inhibiting influence there is a lack of control in muscle movement. The tranquilizing properties of certain drugs used to treat patients suffering from anxiety are related to a facilitation of GABA activity.

Some mood-altering drugs, such as *chlorpromazine* and *LSD*, create their effects by causing an excess or deficiency of specific neurotransmitters. Chlorpromazine, a drug used to treat schizophrenia, blocks the receptors for the neurotransmitter *dopamine* and allows fewer messages to get through. Too much dopamine at the synapse may cause schizophrenia; too little dopamine results in Parkinson's disease. LSD is similar in chemical structure to the neurotransmitter *serotonin*, which affects emotion. Evidence shows that LSD accumulates in certain brain cells, where it mimics the action of serotonin and overstimulates the cells.

A receptor molecule that has attracted special attention in the last several years is called the NMDA receptor (after the chemical, *N-methyl D-aspartate*, that is used to detect it). Neurons in the hippocampus (an area near the center of the brain) are particularly rich in NMDA receptors, and it is known that the hippocampus plays a critical role in the formation of new memories. The NMDA receptor is different from other receptors in that two successive signals are required to activate it. The first signal makes the receptor more responsive to future chemical signals—a phenomenon known as *long-term potentiation*, or LTP. Then when a second signal occurs (the neurotransmitter *glutanate*) the receptor is activated. The first signal cocks the trigger and the second fires the gun, so to speak. It is this two-stage action that has made NMDA a likely candidate for explaining how memories are stored by linking neurons to form new neural circuits (Cotman & Iversen, 1987; Brown et al., 1988).

ORGANIZATION OF THE NERVOUS SYSTEM

All parts of the nervous system are interrelated. But for purposes of discussion, the nervous system can be separated into the following divisions and subdivisions:

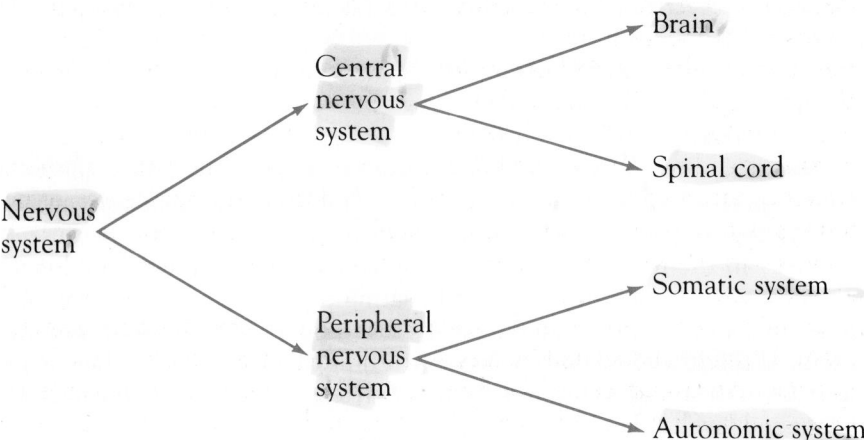

The *central nervous system* includes all the neurons in the brain and spinal cord. The *peripheral nervous system* consists of the nerves connecting the brain and spinal cord to the other parts of the body. The peripheral nervous system is further divided into the *somatic system* and the *autonomic system*.

The sensory nerves of the somatic system transmit information about external stimulation from the skin, muscles, and joints to the central nervous system; they make us aware of pain, pressure, and temperature variations. The motor nerves of the somatic system carry impulses from the central nervous system to the muscles of the body, where they initiate action. All the muscles we use in making voluntary movements, as well as involuntary adjustments in posture and balance, are controlled by these nerves.

The nerves of the autonomic system run to and from the internal organs, regulating such processes as respiration, heart rate, and digestion. The autonomic system, which plays a major role in emotion, is discussed later in this chapter.

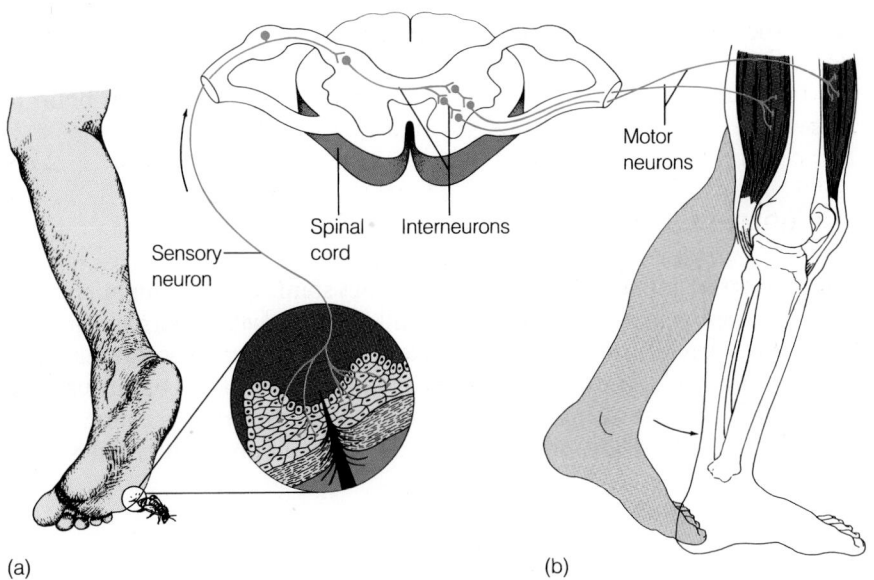

FIGURE 2-5
Four-Neuron Reflex Arc *This diagram illustrates how nerve impulses from a sense organ (a) in the skin reach a skeletal muscle (b) by a four-neuron arc in the spinal cord. Awareness of this automatic reflex occurs because impulses also reach the cerebral hemisphere by way of an ascending tract.*

Most of the nerve fibers connecting various parts of the body to the brain are gathered together in the *spinal cord*, where they are protected by the bony spinal vertebrae. The spinal cord is remarkably compact—barely the diameter of your little finger. Some of the simplest stimulus-response reflexes are carried out at the level of the spinal cord. One example is the knee jerk, the extension of the leg in response to a tap on the tendon that runs in front of the kneecap. Frequently a doctor uses this test to determine the efficiency of the spinal reflexes. The natural function of this reflex is to ensure that the leg will extend when the knee is bent by the force of gravity, so the organism remains standing. When the knee tendon is tapped, the attached muscle stretches, and a signal from sensory cells embedded in the muscle is transmitted through sensory neurons to the spinal cord. There the sensory neurons synapse directly with motor neurons, which transmit impulses back to the same muscle, causing it to contract and the leg to extend. Although this response can occur solely in the spinal cord without any assistance from the brain, it can be modulated by messages from higher nervous centers. If you grip your hands just before the knee is tapped, the extension movement is exaggerated. Or if you consciously want to inhibit the reflex just before the doctor taps the tendon, you can do so. The basic mechanism is built into the spinal cord, but it can be modified by higher brain centers.

The simplest reflex involves only sensory and motor neurons. Most reflexes, however, also involve one or more interneurons in the spinal cord, which mediate between sensory and motor neurons. Figure 2-5 shows a basic four-neuron reflex arc.

STRUCTURE OF THE BRAIN

Some brain structures are clearly demarcated. Others gradually merge into each other; this leads to debate about their exact boundaries and the functions they control. For descriptive purposes, it will be useful to think of the human brain as composed of three concentric layers: a) a *central core*; b) the *limbic system*; and c) the *cerebral hemispheres* (together known as the *cerebrum*). Figure 2-6 shows how these layers fit together; it can be compared with the more detailed labeling of the cross section of the human brain in Figure 2-7.

Central Core

The central core includes most of the brain stem. The first slight enlargement of the spinal cord as it enters the skull is the *medulla*, a narrow structure that controls breathing and some reflexes that help the organism maintain an upright posture. Also, at this point the major nerve tracts coming up from the spinal cord cross over so that the right side of the brain is connected to the left side of the body, and the left side of the brain to the right side of the body.

CEREBELLUM   Attached to the rear of the brain stem, slightly above the medulla, is a convoluted structure, the *cerebellum*. The cerebellum is concerned primarily with the coordination of movement. Specific movements may be initiated at higher levels, but their smooth coordination depends on the cerebellum. Damage to the cerebellum results in jerky, uncoordinated movements.

THALAMUS AND HYPOTHALAMUS   Located just above the brain stem inside the cerebral hemispheres are two egg-shaped groups of nerve cell nuclei that make up the *thalamus*. One region of the thalamus acts as a relay station and directs incoming information to the cerebrum from the sense receptors for vision, hearing, touch, and taste. Another region of the thalamus plays an important role in the control of sleep and wakefulness.

The *hypothalamus* is a much smaller structure, located just below the thalamus. Centers in the hypothalamus govern eating, drinking, and sexual behavior. The hypothalamus regulates endocrine activity and maintains *homeostasis*. Homeostasis refers to the normal level of functioning characteristic of the healthy organism, such as normal body temperature, heart rate, and blood pressure. Under stress homeostasis is disturbed and processes are set into motion to correct the disequilibrium. For example, if we are too warm, we perspire; and if we are too cool, we shiver. Both of these processes tend to restore normal temperature and are controlled by the hypothalamus.

The hypothalamus also plays an important role in emotion and in our response to stress-producing situations. Mild electrical stimulation of certain areas in the hypothalamus produces feelings of pleasure, while stimulation of adjacent regions produces sensations that are unpleasant or painful. By its influence on the pituitary gland, which lies just below it (see Figure 2-7), the hypothalamus controls the endocrine system and in turn the production of hormones. This control is particularly important when the body must mobilize a complex set of physiological processes (the "fight-or-flight" response) to deal with emergencies. The hypothalamus has been called the "stress center" in recognition of its special role in mobilizing the body for action.

RETICULAR SYSTEM   A network of neural circuits that extends from the lower brain stem up to the thalamus, traversing through some of the other central core structures, is the *reticular system*. This system plays an important role in controlling our state of arousal. When an electric current of a certain voltage is sent through electrodes implanted in the reticular

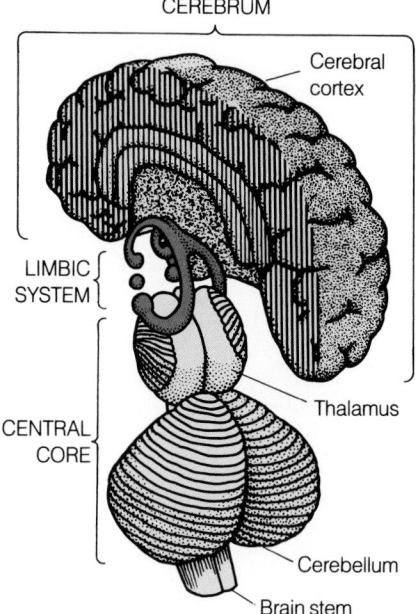

CEREBRUM

Cerebral cortex

LIMBIC SYSTEM

Thalamus

CENTRAL CORE

Cerebellum

Brain stem

FIGURE 2-6
Three Concentric Layers of the Human Brain *The central core and the limbic system are shown in their entirety, but the left cerebral hemisphere has been removed. The cerebellum of the central core controls balance and muscular coordination; the thalamus serves as a switchboard for messages coming from the sense organs; the hypothalamus (not shown but located below the thalamus) regulates endocrine activity and such life-maintaining processes as metabolism and temperature control. The limbic system is concerned with actions that satisfy basic needs and with emotion. The cerebral cortex (an outer layer of cells covering the cerebrum) is the center of higher mental processes, where sensations are registered, voluntary actions initiated, decisions made, and plans formulated.*

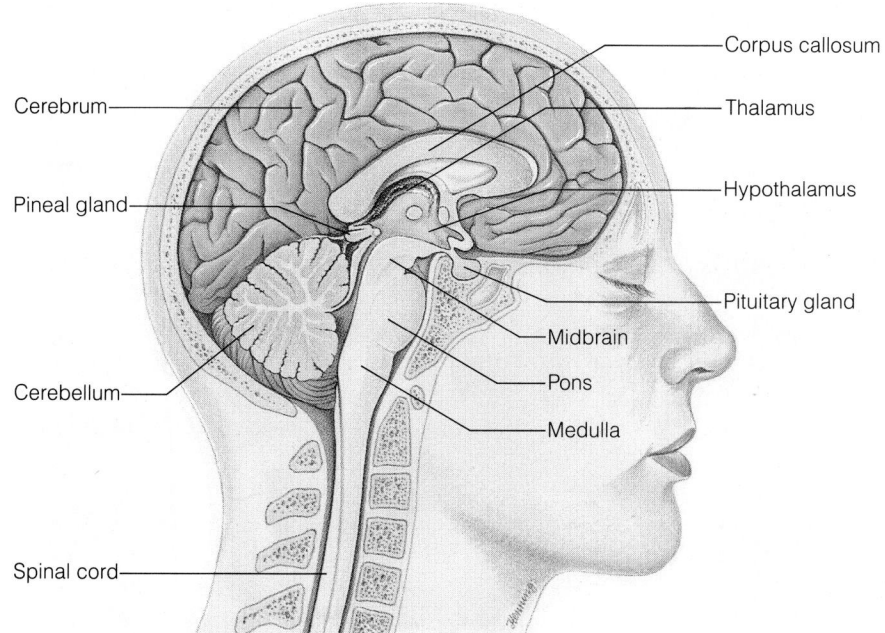

Cerebrum

Pineal gland

Cerebellum

Spinal cord

Corpus callosum

Thalamus

Hypothalamus

Pituitary gland

Midbrain

Pons

Medulla

FIGURE 2-7
Human Brain *This schematic drawing shows the main structures of the central nervous system. (Only the upper portion of the spinal cord is shown.)*

system of a cat or dog, the animal goes to sleep; stimulation by a current with a more rapidly changing waveform awakens the sleeping animal.

The reticular system also plays a role in our ability to focus attention on particular stimuli. All of the sense receptors have nerve fibers that feed into the reticular system. The system appears to act as a filter, allowing some of the sensory messages to pass to the cerebral cortex (to conscious awareness) while blocking others. Thus, our state of consciousness at any moment appears to be influenced by a filtering process in the reticular system.

Limbic System

Around the central core of the brain are a number of structures that together are called the *limbic system* (refer back to Figure 2-6). This system is closely interconnected with the hypothalamus and appears to impose additional controls over some of the instinctive behaviors regulated by the hypothalamus and brain stem. Animals that have only rudimentary limbic systems (for example, fish and reptiles) carry out activities such as feeding, attacking, fleeing from danger, and mating by means of stereotyped behaviors. In mammals, the limbic system seems to inhibit some of the instinctive patterns, allowing the organism to be more flexible and adaptive to changes in the environment.

One part of the limbic system, the *hippocampus*, plays a special role in memory. Surgical removal of the hippocampus or accidental damage to the structure demonstrates that it is critical for the storage of new events as lasting memories, but it is not necessary for the retrieval of older memories. Upon recovery from such an operation, the patient will have no difficulty recognizing old friends or recalling earlier experiences; he will be able to read and perform skills learned earlier in life. However, he will have little, if any, recall of events that occurred in the year or so just prior to the operation. He will not remember events and people he meets after the operation at all. For

CRITICAL DISCUSSION

Computer-Generated Pictures of the Living Brain

A number of new techniques have been developed to obtain detailed pictures of the living human brain without causing the patient distress or damage. Before these techniques were perfected, the precise location and identification of most types of brain injury could be determined only by exploratory neurosurgery, by a complicated neurological diagnosis, or by autopsy after the patient's death. The new techniques depend on sophisticated computer methods that have become feasible only recently.

One such technique is *computerized axial tomography* (abbreviated CAT or simply CT). This procedure involves sending a narrow X-ray beam through the patient's head and measuring the amount of radiation that gets through. The revolutionary aspect of the technique is that measurements are made at hundreds of thousands of different orientations (or axes) through the head. These measurements are then fed into a computer and, by making appropriate calculations, a cross-sectional picture of the brain is reconstructed that can be photographed or displayed on a television monitor. The cross-sectional slice can be at any level and angle desired. The term "computerized axial tomography" refers to the critical role of the computer, the many axes at which measurements are made, and the resulting image that is a cross-sectional slice through the brain (*tomo* is from the Greek word meaning "slice" or "cut").

A newer and even more powerful technique involves *magnetic resonance imaging* (abbreviated MRI). Scanners of this sort use strong magnetic fields, radio-frequency pulses, and computers

A technician administers a CT scan, which generates a computer picture of a "slice" of the patient's brain.

to compose the image. In this procedure the patient lies in a doughnut-shaped tunnel surrounded by a large magnet that generates a powerful magnetic field. When the anatomic part to be studied is placed in a strong magnetic field and exposed to a certain radio-frequency pulse, the tissues emit a signal that can be measured. As with the CT scanner, hundreds of thousands of such measurements are made and then manipulated by a computer into a two-dimensional image of the anatomic part. Among scientists, the

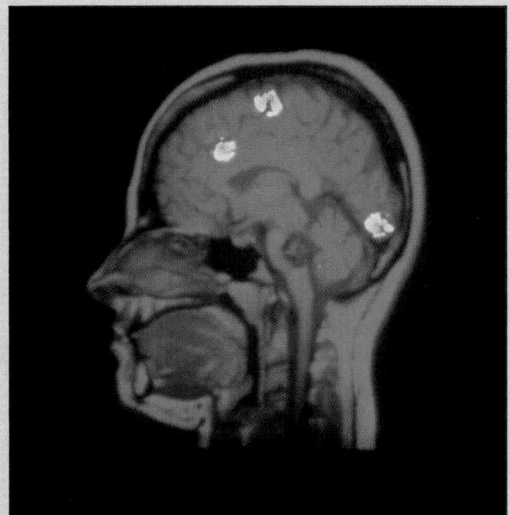

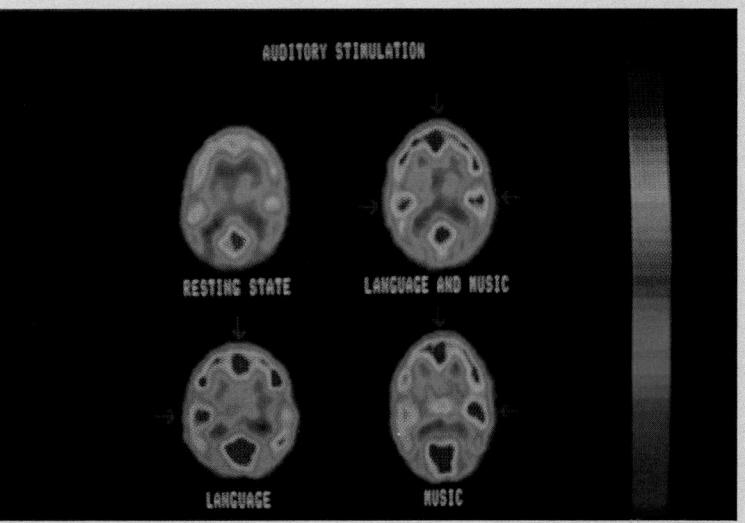

PET image shows three areas in the left brain active during a language task.

Red areas indicate maximum brain activity; blue areas show minimum activity.

technique is usually called nuclear magnetic resonance because what is being measured are variations in the energy level of hydrogen atom nuclei in the body caused by the radio-frequency pulses. However, many physicians prefer to drop the term "nuclear" and simply call it magnetic resonance imaging, since they fear the public may confuse the reference to the nucleus of an atom with nuclear radiation.

MRI offers greater precision than the CT scanner in the diagnosis of diseases of the brain and spinal cord. For example, an MRI cross section of the brain shows features characteristic of multiple sclerosis that are not detected by a CT scanner; previously, diagnosis of this disease required hospitalization and a test in which dye is injected into the canal around the spinal cord. MRI is also useful in the detection of abnormalities in the spinal cord and at the base of the brain, such as herniated disks, tumors, and birth malformations.

While CT and MRI provide a picture of the anatomical detail of the brain, it is often desirable to assess the level of neural activity at different spots in the brain. A computer-based scanning procedure called *positron*

emission tomography (abbreviated PET) provides this additional information. This technique depends on the fact that every cell in the body requires energy to conduct its various metabolic processes. In the brain, neurons utilize glucose (obtained from the bloodstream) as their principal source of energy. A small amount of a radioactive tracer compound can be mixed with glucose so that each molecule of glucose has a tiny speck of radioactivity (that is, a label) attached to it. If this harmless mixture is injected into the bloodstream, after a few minutes the brain cells begin to use the radio-labeled glucose in the same way they use regular glucose. The PET scan is essentially a highly sensitive detector of radioactivity (it is not like an X-ray machine, which *emits* X rays, but rather like a Geiger counter, which *measures* radioactivity). Neurons of the brain that are most active require the most glucose and, therefore, will be the most radioactive. The PET scan measures the amount of radioactivity and sends the information to a computer that draws a color cross-sectional picture of the brain, with different colors representing different levels of

neural activity. The measurement of radioactivity is based on the emission of positively charged particles called *positrons*—hence the term "positron emission tomography."

Comparing PET scans of normal individuals with those of persons who have neurological disorders indicates that a variety of brain problems (epilepsy, blood clots, brain tumors, and so on) can be identified using this technique. For psychological research, the PET scan has been used to compare the brains of schizophrenics with those of nonschizophrenics and has revealed differences in the metabolic levels of certain cortical areas (Andreasen, 1988). It has also been used to investigate the brain areas activated during such higher mental functions as listening to music, doing mathematics, or speaking, the goal being to identify the brain structures involved (Posner, Petersen, Fox, & Raichle, 1988).

The CT, MRI, and PET scanners are proving to be invaluable tools for studying the relationship between the brain and behavior. These instruments are an example of how progress in one field of science forges ahead because of technical developments in another.

The limbic system plays an important role in regulating certain instinctive behaviors, such as aggression.

example, the patient will fail to recognize a new person with whom he may have spent many hours earlier in the day. He will do the same jigsaw puzzle week after week, never remembering having done it before, and will read the same newspaper over and over without remembering the contents (Squire, 1987).

The limbic system is also involved in emotional behavior. Monkeys with lesions in some regions of the limbic system react with rage at the slightest provocation, suggesting that the destroyed area was exerting an inhibiting influence. Monkeys with lesions in other areas of the limbic system no longer express aggressive behavior and show no hostility, even when attacked. They simply ignore the attacker and act as if nothing had happened.

Describing the brain in terms of three concentric structures—the central core, the limbic system, and the cerebrum (to be discussed in the next section)—must not lead us to think of these structures as independent of one another. We might use the analogy of an array of interrelated computers. Each has specialized functions, but they must work together to produce the most effective result. Similarly, the analysis of information coming from the senses requires one kind of computation and decision process (for which the cerebrum is well adapted), differing from that which controls a reflexive sequence of activities (the limbic system). The finer adjustments of the muscles (as in writing or playing a musical instrument) require another kind of control system, in this case mediated by the cerebellum. All these activities are organized into an integrated system that maintains the integrity of the organism.

CEREBRAL HEMISPHERES

The cerebrum is more highly developed in human beings than in any other organism. Its outer layer is called the *cerebral cortex*; in Latin, *cortex* means "bark." The cerebral cortex (often simply called the cortex) of a preserved brain appears gray because it consists largely of nerve cell bodies and un-myelinated fibers—hence the term "gray matter." The inside of the cerebrum, beneath the cortex, is composed mostly of myelinated axons and appears white.

Structure of the Cerebrum

The cortex of a lower mammal, such as the rat, is small and relatively smooth. As we ascend the phylogenetic scale to the higher mammals, the amount of cortex relative to the amount of total brain tissue increases, and the cortex becomes progressively more wrinkled and convoluted, so that its actual surface area is far greater than it would be if it were a smooth covering of the cerebrum.

All of the sensory systems (for example, vision, audition, and touch) project information to specific areas of the cortex. The movements of body parts (motor responses) are controlled by another area of the cortex. The rest of the cortex, which is neither sensory nor motor, consists of association areas. These areas are concerned with other aspects of behavior—memory, thought, and language—and occupy the largest area of the human cortex.

Before discussing some of these locations, we need to introduce a few landmarks in describing areas of the *cerebral hemispheres*. The two hemispheres are basically symmetrical, with a deep division between them running from front to rear. So, our first classification is the division into *right* and *left hemispheres*. Each hemisphere is divided into four *lobes*: the *frontal, parietal, occipital,* and *temporal.* The divisions between these lobes are shown in Figure 2-8. The frontal lobe is separated from the parietal lobe by the *central fissure*, running from near the top of the head sideways to the ears. The division between the parietal lobe and the occipital lobe is less clear-cut; for our purpose, it suffices to say that the parietal lobe is at the top of the brain behind the central fissure and that the occipital lobe is at the rear of the brain. The temporal lobe is demarcated by a deep fissure at the side of the brain, the *lateral fissure*.

Cortical Areas and Their Functions

MOTOR AREA   The *motor area* controls the voluntary movements of the body; it lies just in front of the central fissure (see Figure 2-9). Electrical stimulation at certain spots on the motor cortex produces movement of specific body parts; when these same spots on the motor cortex are injured, movement is impaired. The body is represented on the motor cortex in approximately upside-down form. For example, movements of the toes are mediated near the top of the head, whereas tongue and mouth movements are mediated near the bottom of the motor area. Movements on the right side of the body are governed by the motor cortex of the left hemisphere; movements on the left side, by the right hemisphere.

SOMATOSENSORY AREA   In the parietal lobe, separated from the motor area by the central fissure, lies an area that if stimulated electrically produces a sensory experience somewhere on the opposite side of the body. It is as though a part of the body were being touched or moved. This is called the *somatosensory area* (body-sense area). Heat, cold, touch, pain, and the sense of body movement are all represented here.

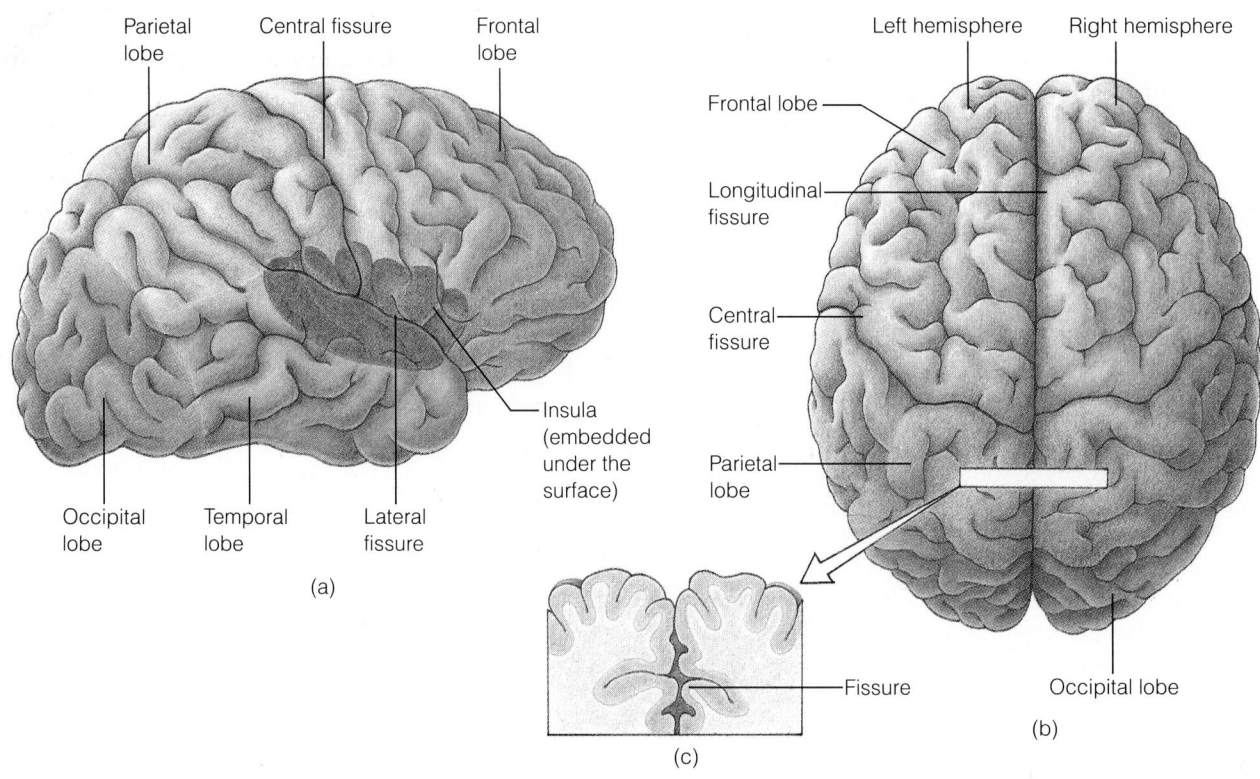

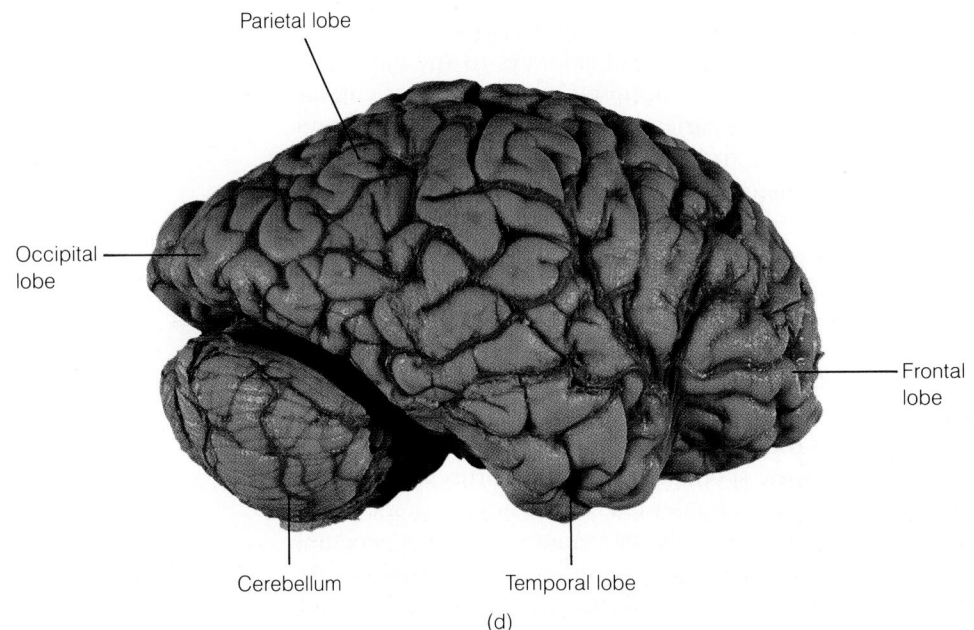

FIGURE 2-8
Cerebral Hemispheres *Each hemisphere has several large lobes separated by fissures. In addition to these externally visible lobes, a large internal fold of cortex, called the insula, lies deep in the lateral fissure. (a) Lateral view. (b) Superior view. (c) Transverse section through cerebral cortex. Note the distinction between the more superficial gray matter (shown in dark pink) and the deeper white matter. (d) Photograph of human brain.*

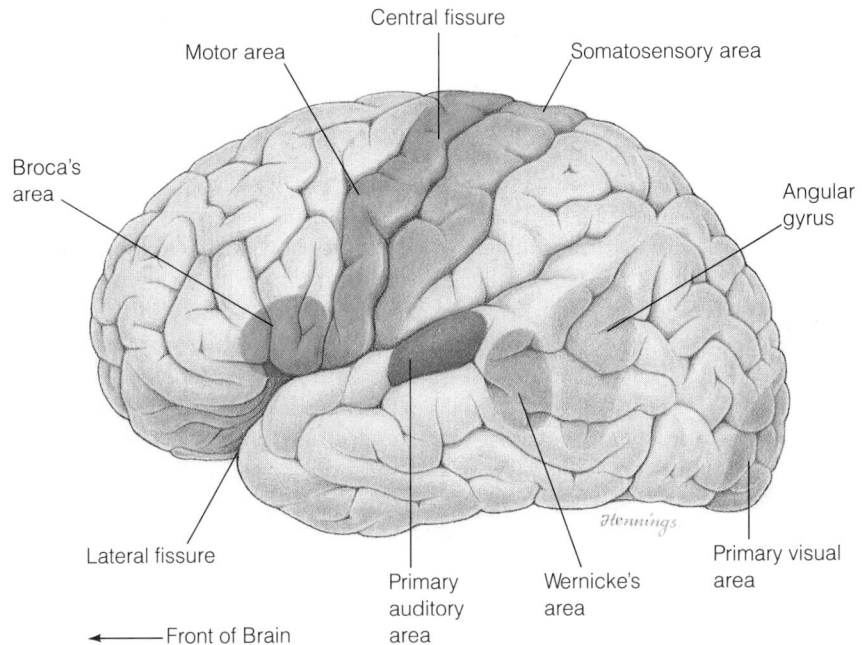

Central fissure

Motor area

Somatosensory area

Broca's area

Angular gyrus

Lateral fissure

Primary auditory area

Wernicke's area

Primary visual area

Hennings

← Front of Brain

FIGURE 2-9
Localization of Function in the Left Cortex *A major part of the cortex is involved in generating movements and in analyzing sensory inputs. These areas (which include motor, somatosensory, visual, auditory, and olfactory areas) are present on both sides of the brain. Other functions are found on only one side of the brain. For example, Broca's area and Wernicke's area are involved in the production and understanding of language, and the angular gyrus is involved in matching the visual form of a word with its auditory form; these functions exist only on the left side of the human brain.*

Most of the nerve fibers in the pathways that radiate to and from the somatosensory and motor areas cross to the opposite side of the body. Thus, the sensory impulses from the right side of the body go to the left somatosensory cortex, and the muscles of the right foot and hand are controlled by the left motor cortex.

It seems to be a general rule that the amount of somatosensory or motor area associated with a particular part of the body is directly related to its sensitivity and use. For example, among four-footed mammals the dog has only a small amount of cortical tissue representing the forepaws, whereas the raccoon—which makes extensive use of its forepaws in exploring and manipulating its environment—has a much larger representative cortical area, including regions for the separate fingers of the forepaw. The rat, which learns a great deal about its environment by means of its sensitive whiskers, has a separate cortical area for each whisker.

VISUAL AREA   At the back of each occipital lobe is an area of the cortex known as the *visual area*. Figure 2-10 shows the optic nerve fibers and neural pathways leading from each eye to the visual cortex. Notice that some of the optic fibers from the right eye go to the right cerebral hemisphere, whereas others cross over at a junction called the *optic chiasma* and go to the opposite hemisphere; the same arrangement holds true for the left eye. Fibers from the right sides of *both* eyes go to the right hemisphere of the brain, and fibers from the left sides of both eyes go to the left hemisphere. Consequently, damage to the visual area of one hemisphere (say, the left) will result in blind fields in the left sides of both eyes, causing a loss of vision to the right side of the environment. This fact is sometimes helpful in pinpointing the location of a brain tumor or other abnormalities.

AUDITORY AREA   The *auditory area* (found on the surface of the temporal lobe at the side of each hemisphere) is involved in the analysis of

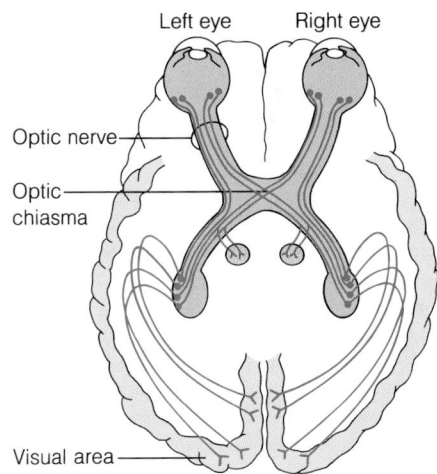

Left eye   Right eye

Optic nerve

Optic chiasma

Visual area

FIGURE 2-10
Visual Pathways *Nerve fibers from the inner, or nasal, half of the retina cross over at the optic chiasma and go to opposite sides of the brain. Thus, stimuli falling on the right side of each retina are transmitted to the right hemisphere, and stimuli impinging on the left side of each retina are transmitted to the left hemisphere.*

complex auditory signals. It is particularly concerned with the temporal patterning of sound, as in human speech. Both ears are represented in the auditory areas on both sides of the cortex; however, connections to the contralateral side are stronger.

ASSOCIATION AREAS   The many large areas of the cerebral cortex that are not directly concerned with sensory or motor processes are called *association areas*. The *frontal association areas* (the parts of the frontal lobes in front of the motor area) appear to play an important role in thought processes required for problem solving. In monkeys, for example, lesions in the frontal lobes destroy the ability to solve a delayed-response problem. In this kind of problem, food is placed in one of two cups while the monkey watches, and the cups are covered with identical objects. An opaque screen is then placed between the monkey and the cups; after a specified period of time the screen is removed, and the monkey is allowed to choose one of the cups. Normal monkeys can remember the correct cup after delays of several minutes, but monkeys with frontal lobe lesions cannot solve the problem if the delay is more than a few seconds. This delayed-response deficit following brain lesions is unique to the frontal cortex; it does not occur if lesions are made in other cortical regions (French & Harlow, 1962).

Human beings who have suffered damage to the frontal association areas can perform many intellectual tasks normally, including delayed-response problems. Their ability to use language probably enables them to remember the correct response. They do have difficulty, however, when it is necessary to shift frequently from one strategy to another while working on a problem (Milner, 1964).

The *posterior association areas* are located near the various primary sensory areas and appear to consist of subareas, each serving a particular sense. For example, the lower portion of the temporal lobe is related to visual perception. Lesions in this area produce deficits in the ability to recognize and discriminate different forms. A lesion here does not cause loss of visual acuity, as would a lesion in the primary visual area of the occipital lobe; the individual "sees" the forms (and can trace the outline) but cannot identify the shape or distinguish it from a different form (Goodglass & Butters, 1988).

ASYMMETRIES IN THE BRAIN

On casual examination, the two halves of the human brain look like mirror images of each other. But closer examination reveals asymmetries. When brains are measured during autopsies, the left hemisphere is almost always larger than the right hemisphere. Also, the right hemisphere contains many long neural fibers that connect widely separate areas of the brain, whereas the left hemisphere contains many shorter fibers that provide rich interconnections within a limited area (Geschwind & Galaburda, 1987).

As early as 1861, the French physician Paul Broca examined the brain of a patient who had suffered speech loss, and he found damage in an area of the left hemisphere just above the lateral fissure in the frontal lobe. This region, known as *Broca's area* and shown in Figure 2-9, is involved in the production of speech. Destruction of the equivalent region in the right hemisphere usually does not result in speech impairment. The areas involved in understand-

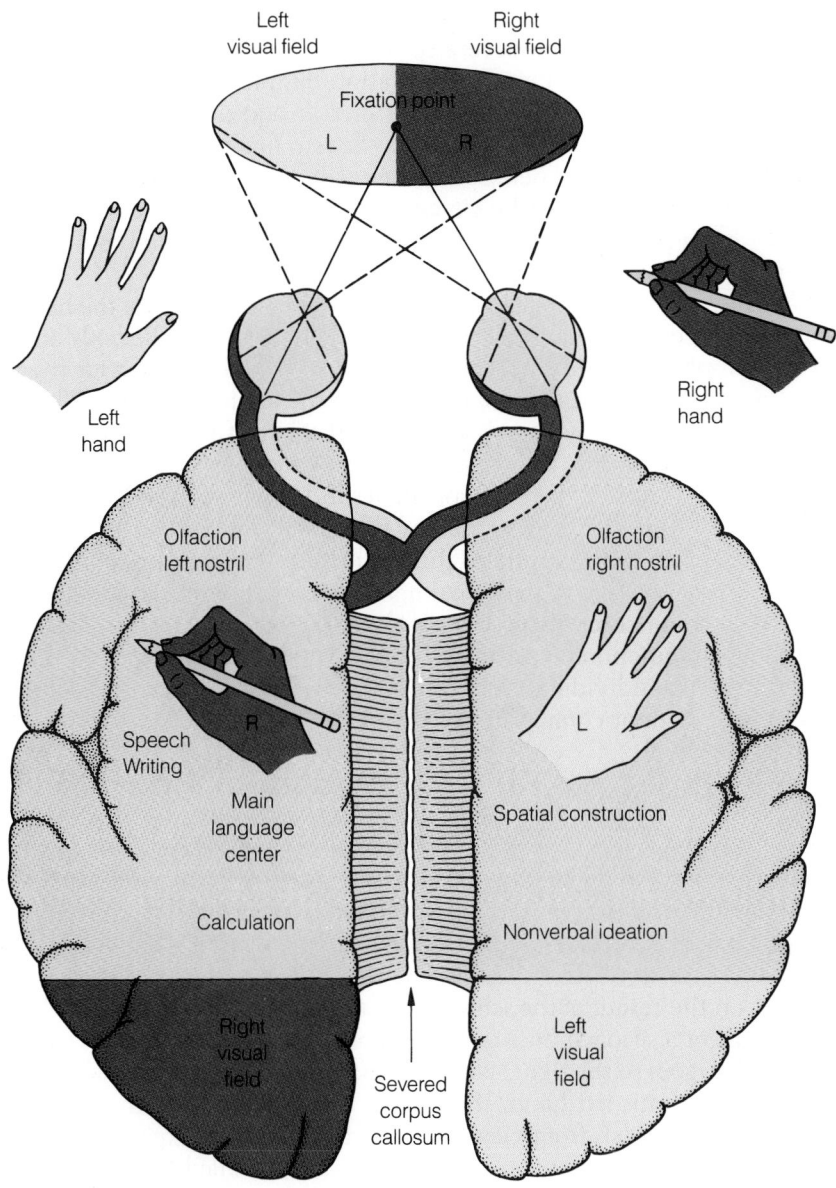

Left
visual field

Right
visual field

Fixation point

L R

Left
hand

Right
hand

Olfaction
left nostril

Olfaction
right nostril

R

L

Speech
Writing

Main
language
center

Spatial construction

Calculation

Nonverbal ideation

Right
visual
field

Severed
corpus
callosum

Left
visual
field

FIGURE 2-11
**Sensory Inputs to the Two
Hemispheres** *With the eyes fixated straight
ahead, stimuli to the left of the fixation point
go to the right cerebral hemisphere, and
stimuli to the right go to the left hemisphere.
The left hemisphere controls movements of
the right hand, and the right hemisphere
controls the left hand. Hearing is largely
crossed in its input, but some sound
representation goes to the hemisphere on the
same side as the ear that registered it. The
left hemisphere controls written and spoken
language and mathematical calculations.
The right hemisphere can understand only
simple language; its main ability seems to
involve spatial construction and pattern
sense.*

ing speech and in the ability to write and understand written words are also
usually located in the left hemisphere. Thus, a person who suffers a stroke
that damages the left hemisphere is more likely to show language impairment
than one whose damage is confined to the right hemisphere. A few left-
handed people have speech centers located in the right hemisphere, but the
great majority have language functions in the left hemisphere (the same as
right-handed individuals).

Although the left hemisphere's role in language has been known for some
time, only recently has it been possible to investigate what each hemisphere
can do on its own. In the normal individual, the brain functions as an integrated whole; information in one hemisphere is immediately transferred to
the other by way of a broad band of connecting nerve fibers called the *corpus
callosum.* This connecting bridge can cause a problem in some forms of epilepsy, because a seizure starting in one hemisphere may cross over and trigger

a massive discharge of neurons in the other. In an effort to prevent such generalized seizures in some severe epileptics, neurosurgeons have surgically severed the corpus callosum. The operation has proved successful for some individuals, resulting in a decrease in seizures. In addition, there appear to be no undesirable aftereffects; the patients seem to function in everyday life as well as individuals whose hemispheres are still connected. It took some very special tests to demonstrate how mental functions are affected by separating the two hemispheres. A little more background information is needed to understand the experiments we are about to describe.

We have seen that the motor nerves cross over as they leave the brain, so that the left cerebral hemisphere controls the right side of the body and the right hemisphere controls the left. We noted also that the area for the production of speech (Broca's area) is located in the left hemisphere. When the eyes are fixated directly ahead, images to the left of the fixation point go through both eyes to the right side of the brain and images to the right of the fixation point go to the left side of the brain (see Figure 2-11). Thus, each hemisphere has a view of that half of the visual field in which "its" hand normally functions; for example, the left hemisphere sees the right hand in the right visual field. In the normal brain, stimuli entering one hemisphere are rapidly communicated, by way of the corpus callosum, to the other, so that the brain functions as a unit. We will see what happens when the corpus callosum in an individual is severed—leaving a *split brain*—and the two hemispheres cannot communicate.

Split-Brain Subjects

Roger Sperry pioneered work in this field and was awarded the Nobel prize in 1981 for his research in neuroscience. In one of Sperry's test situations, a subject (who has undergone a split-brain operation) is seated in front of a screen that hides his hands from view (see Figure 2-12a). His gaze is fixed at a spot on the center of the screen and the word "nut" is flashed very briefly (one-tenth of a second) on the left side of the screen. Remember that this visual image goes to the right side of the brain, which controls the left side of the body. With his left hand, the subject can easily pick up the nut from a pile of objects hidden from view. But he cannot tell the experimenter what word flashed on the screen because speech is controlled by the left hemisphere and the visual image of "nut" was not transmitted to that hemisphere. When questioned, the split-brain subject seems unaware of what his left hand is doing. Since the sensory input from the left hand goes to the right hemisphere, the left hemisphere receives no information about what the left hand is feeling or doing. All information is fed back to the right hemisphere, which received the original visual input of the word "nut."

It is important that the word be flashed on the screen for no more than one-tenth of a second. If it remains longer, the subject can move his eyes so that the word is also projected to the left hemisphere. If the split-brain subject can move his eyes freely, information goes to both cerebral hemispheres; this is one reason why the deficiencies caused by severing the corpus callosum are not readily apparent in a person's daily activities.

Further experiments demonstrate that the split-brain subject can communicate through speech only what is going on in the left hemisphere. Figure 2-12b shows another test situation. The word "hatband" is flashed on the screen so that "hat" goes to the right hemisphere and "band" to the left. When asked what word he saw, the subject replies, "band." When asked

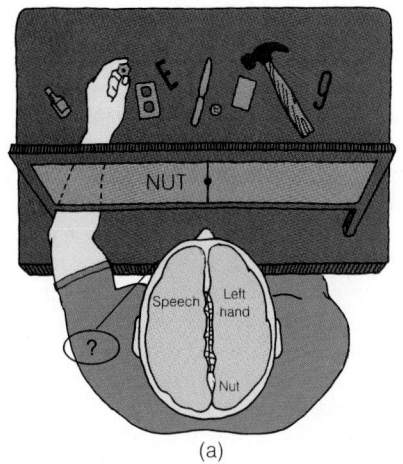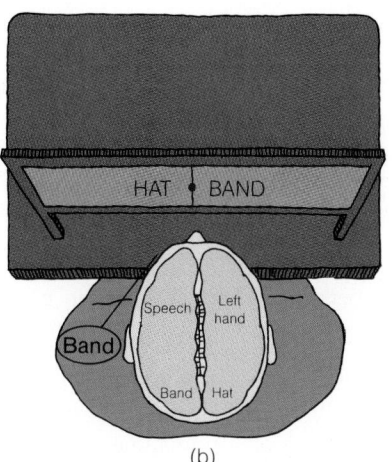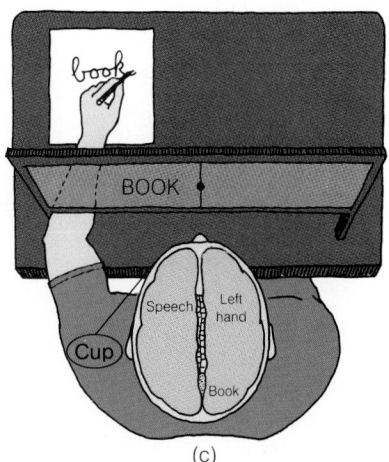

(a) (b) (c)

what kind of band, he makes all sorts of guesses—"rubber band," "rock band," "band of robbers," and so forth—and only hits on "hatband" by chance. Tests with other word combinations (such as "keycase" and "suitcase") show similar results. What is perceived by the right hemisphere does not transfer to the conscious awareness of the left hemisphere. With the corpus callosum severed, each hemisphere seems oblivious to the experiences of the other.

If the split-brain subject is blindfolded and a familiar object (such as a comb, toothbrush, or keycase) is placed in his left hand, he appears to know what it is; for example, he can demonstrate its use by appropriate gestures. But he cannot express his knowledge in speech. If asked what is going on while he is manipulating the object, he has no idea. This is true as long as any sensory input from the object to the left (talking) hemisphere is blocked. But if the subject's right hand inadvertently touches the object or if it makes a characteristic sound (like the jingling of a keycase), the speaking hemisphere immediately gives the correct answer.

Although the right hemisphere cannot speak, it does have some linguistic capabilities. It recognized the meaning of the word "nut," as we saw in our first example, and it can write a little. In the experiment illustrated in Figure 2-12c, a split-brain subject is first shown a list of common objects such as cup, knife, book, and glass. This list is displayed long enough for the words to be projected to both hemispheres. Next, the list is removed, and one of the words (for example, "book") is flashed briefly on the left side of the screen so that it goes to the right hemisphere. If the subject is asked to write what he saw, his left hand will begin writing the word "book." If asked what his left hand has written, he has no idea and will guess at any of the words on the original list. The subject knows he has written something because he feels the writing movements through his body. But because there is no communication between the right hemisphere that saw and wrote the word and the left hemisphere that controls speech, the subject cannot tell you what he wrote.

Hemispheric Specialization

Studies with split-brain subjects indicate that the two hemispheres function differently. The left hemisphere governs our ability to express ourselves in language. It can perform many complicated logical and analytic activities

FIGURE 2-12
Testing the Abilities of the Two Hemispheres *(a) The split-brain subject correctly retrieves an object by touch with the left hand when its name is flashed to the right hemisphere, but he cannot name the object or describe what he has done. (b) The word "hatband" is flashed so that "hat" goes to the right cerebral hemisphere and "band" goes to the left hemisphere. The subject reports that he sees the word "band" but has no idea what kind of band. (c) A list of common objects (including "book" and "cup") is initially shown to both hemispheres. One word from the list ("book") is then projected to the right hemisphere. When given the command to do so, the left hand begins writing the word "book," but when questioned the subject does not know what his left hand has written and guesses "cup." (After Sperry, 1970; Nebes & Sperry, 1971)*

CRITICAL DISCUSSION

Language and the Brain

A great deal of our information about brain mechanisms for language comes from observations of patients suffering from brain damage. The damage may be due to tumors, penetrating head wounds, or the rupture of blood vessels. The term *aphasia* is used to describe language deficits caused by brain damage.

As already noted, Broca observed in the 1860s that damage to a specific area on the side of the left frontal lobe was linked to a speech disorder called *expressive aphasia*. Individuals with damage in Broca's area have difficulty enunciating words correctly and speak in a slow, labored way. Their speech often makes sense, but it includes only key words. Nouns are generally expressed in the singular, and adjectives, adverbs, articles, and conjunctions are apt to be omitted. However, these individuals have no difficulty understanding either spoken or written language.

In 1874, Carl Wernicke, a German investigator, reported that damage to another site in the cortex (also in the left hemisphere, but located in the temporal lobe) was linked to a language disorder called *receptive aphasia*. People with damage in this location, *Wernicke's area*, are not able to comprehend words; they can hear words, but they do not know their meaning. They can produce strings of words without difficulty and with proper articulation, but there are errors in word usage and their speech tends to be meaningless.

Based on an analysis of these defects, Wernicke developed a model for language production and understanding. Although the model is 100 years old, its general features still appear to be correct. Norman Geschwind has built on them and developed the theory known as the *Wernicke-Geschwind model* (Geschwind, 1979). According to the model, Broca's area is assumed to store *articulatory codes* that specify the sequence of muscle actions required to pronounce a word. When these codes are transferred to the motor area, they activate the muscles of the lips, tongue, and larynx in the proper sequence and produce a spoken word (see figure).

Wernicke's area, on the other hand, is where auditory codes and the meanings of words are stored. If a word is to be spoken, its auditory code must be activated in Wernicke's area and transmitted by a bundle of nerves to Broca's area, where it activates the corresponding articulatory code. In turn, the articulatory code is transmitted to the motor area for the production of the spoken word.

If a word spoken by someone else is to be understood, it must be transmitted from the auditory area to Wernicke's area, where the spoken form of the word is matched to its auditory code, which in turn activates the word's meaning. When a written word is presented, it is first registered in the visual area and then relayed to the *angular gyrus*, which associates the visual form of the word with its auditory code in Wernicke's area; once the word's auditory code has been found, so has its meaning. Thus, the meanings of words are stored along with their acoustical codes in Wernicke's area. Broca's area stores articulatory codes, and the angular gyrus matches the written form of a word to its auditory code; neither of these two areas, however, stores information about word meaning. The meaning of a word is retrieved only when its acoustical code is activated in Wernicke's area.

The model explains many of the language deficits shown by aphasics. Damage restricted to Broca's area disrupts speech production but has less effect on the comprehension of spoken or written language. Damage to Wernicke's area disrupts all aspects of language comprehension, but the individual can still articulate words properly (since Broca's area is intact) even though the output is meaningless. The model also predicts that individuals with damage in the angular gyrus will not be able to read but will have no problem in comprehending speech or

and is skilled in mathematical computations. The right hemisphere can comprehend very simple language. It can respond to simple nouns by selecting objects such as a nut or comb, and it can even respond to associations of these objects. For example, if the right hemisphere is asked to retrieve from a group of objects the one used "for lighting fires," it will instruct the left hand to select a match. But the right hemisphere cannot comprehend more abstract linguistic forms; if it is presented with such simple commands as "wink," "nod," "shake head," or "smile," it seldom responds.

The right hemisphere can add simple two-digit numbers but can do little beyond this in the way of calculation. However, the right hemisphere appears to have a highly developed spatial and pattern sense. It is superior to

in speaking. Finally, if damage is restricted to the auditory area, a person will be able to read and to speak normally; but he or she will not be able to comprehend spoken speech.

There are some research findings that the Wernicke-Geschwind model does not adequately explain. For example, when the language areas of the brain are electrically stimulated in the course of a neurosurgical operation, both receptive and expressive functions may be disrupted at a single site. This suggests that some brain areas may share common mechanisms for producing and understanding speech.

We are still a long way from a comprehensive model of language function, but there can be no doubt that some aspects of language function are highly localized in the brain (Geschwind & Galaburda, 1987).

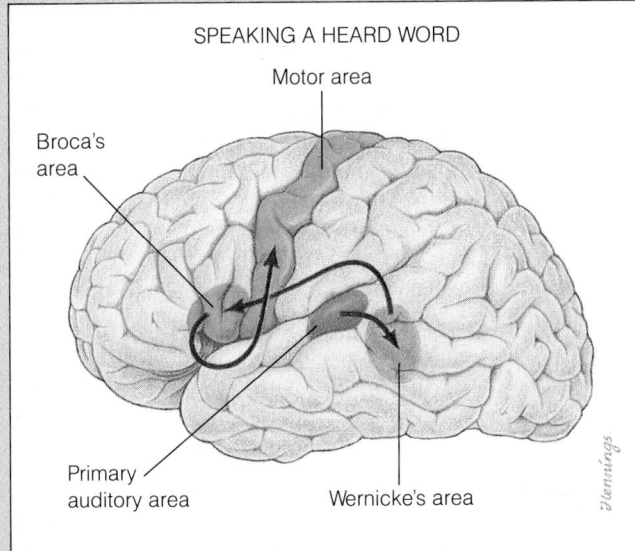 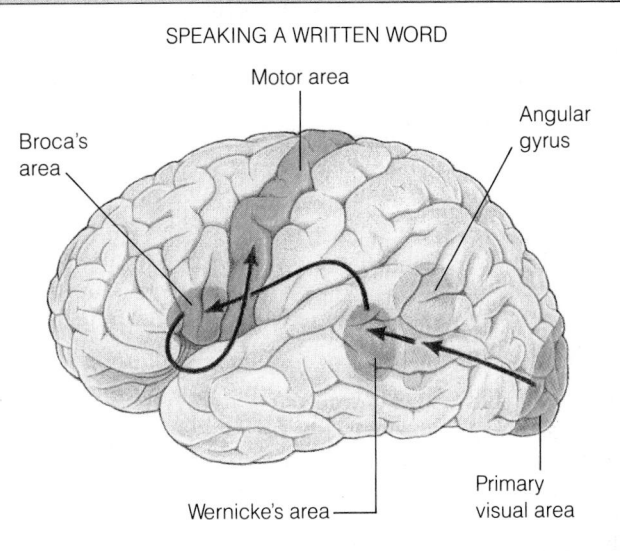

Wernicke-Geschwind Model *The left panel illustrates the sequence of events when a spoken word is presented and the individual repeats the word in spoken form. Neural impulses from the ear are sent to the primary auditory area, but the word cannot be understood until the signal is next transmitted to Wernicke's area. In Wernicke's area, the word's acoustical code is retrieved and transmitted via a bundle of nerve fibers to Broca's area. In Broca's area, an articulatory code for the word is activated, which in turn directs the motor area. The motor area drives the lips, tongue, and larynx to produce the spoken word. In the right panel, a written word is presented and the individual is to speak the word. The visual input to the eye is first transmitted to the primary visual cortex and then relayed to the angular gyrus. The angular gyrus associates the visual form of the word with the related acoustical code in Wernicke's area. Once the acoustical code is retrieved and the meaning of the word is established, speaking the word is accomplished through the same sequence of events as before.*

the left hemisphere in constructing geometric and perspective drawings. It can assemble colored blocks to match a complex design much more effectively than the left hemisphere. When split-brain subjects are asked to use their right hand to assemble the blocks according to a picture design, they make numerous mistakes. Sometimes they have trouble keeping their left hand from automatically correcting the mistakes being made by the right hand.

Studies with normal individuals tend to confirm the different specializations of the two hemispheres. For example, verbal information (such as words or nonsense syllables) can be identified faster and more accurately when flashed briefly to the left hemisphere (that is, in the right visual field) than to the right hemisphere. In contrast, the identification of faces, facial expressions of emotion, line slopes, or dot locations occurs more quickly when flashed to the right hemisphere. And *electroencephalogram* (EEG) studies indicate that electrical activity from the left hemisphere increases during a verbal task, whereas during a spatial task, EEG activity increases in the right hemisphere (Springer & Deutsch, 1985; Kosslyn, 1988).

One should not infer from this discussion that the two hemispheres work independently of each other. Just the opposite is true. The hemispheres differ in their specializations, but they integrate their activities at all times. It is this interaction that gives rise to mental processes greater than and different from each hemisphere's special contribution. As noted by Levy,

> These differences are seen in the contrasting contributions each hemisphere makes to all cognitive activities. When a person reads a story, the right hemisphere may play a special role in decoding visual information, maintaining an integrated story structure, appreciating humor and emotional content, deriving meaning from past associations and understanding metaphor. At the same time, the left hemisphere plays a special role in understanding syntax, translating written words into their phonetic representations and deriving meaning from complex relations among word concepts and syntax. But there is no activity in which only one hemisphere is involved or to which only one hemisphere makes a contribution. (1985, p. 44)

AUTONOMIC NERVOUS SYSTEM

We noted earlier that the peripheral nervous system consists of two divisions. The somatic system controls the skeletal muscles and receives information from the skin, muscles, and various sensory receptors. The autonomic system controls the glands and the smooth muscles, which include the heart, the blood vessels, and the lining of the stomach and intestines. These muscles are called "smooth" because that is how they look when examined under a microscope. (Skeletal muscles, in contrast, have a striped appearance.) The autonomic nervous system derives its name from the fact that many of the activities it controls are autonomous, or self-regulating—such as digestion and circulation—and continue even when a person is asleep or unconscious.

The autonomic nervous system has two divisions, the *sympathetic* and the *parasympathetic*, which are often antagonistic in their actions. Figure 2-13 shows the contrasting effects of the two systems on various organs. For example, the parasympathetic system constricts the pupil of the eye, stimulates the flow of saliva, and slows the heart rate; the sympathetic system has the opposite effect in each case. The normal state of the body (somewhere between extreme excitement and vegetative placidity) is maintained by the balance between these two systems.

The sympathetic division tends to act as a unit. During emotional excitement, it simultaneously speeds up the heart, dilates the arteries of the skeletal muscles and heart, constricts the arteries of the skin and digestive organs, and causes perspiration. It also activates certain endocrine glands to secrete hormones that further increase arousal.

Unlike the sympathetic system, the parasympathetic division tends to affect one organ at a time. If the sympathetic system is thought of as dominant during violent and excited activity, the parasympathetic system may be

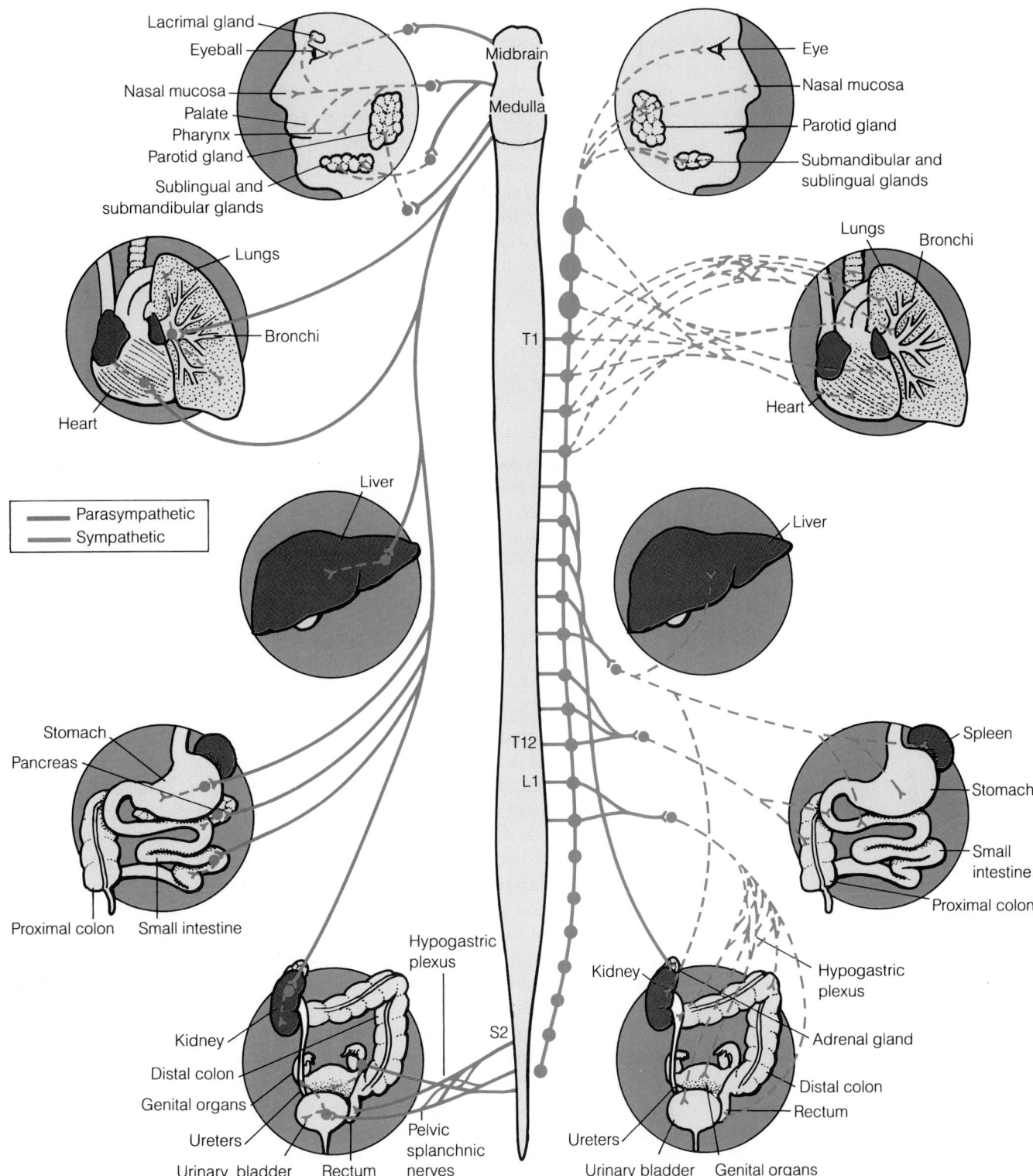

FIGURE 2-13

Motor Fibers of the Autonomic Nervous System *In this diagram the sympathetic division is indicated in blue and the parasympathetic is in red. Solid lines indicate preganglionic fibers and dashed lines indicate postganglionic fibers. Neurons of the sympathetic division originate in the thoracic and lumbar regions of the spinal cord; they form synaptic junctions with ganglia lying just outside the cord. Neurons of the parasympathetic division exit from the medulla region of the brain stem and from the lower (sacral) end of the spinal cord; they connect with ganglia near the organs stimulated. Most internal organs are innervated by both divisions, which function in opposition to each other.*

thought of as dominant during quiescence. It participates in digestion and, in general, maintains the functions that conserve and protect bodily resources.

While the sympathetic and parasympathetic systems are usually antagonistic to one another, there are some exceptions to this principle. For example, the sympathetic system is dominant during fear and excitement; however, a not-uncommon parasympathetic symptom during extreme fear is the involuntary discharge of the bladder or bowels. Another example is the complete sex act in the male, which requires erection (parasympathetic) followed by ejaculation (sympathetic). Thus, although the two systems are often antagonistic, they interact in complex ways.

ENDOCRINE SYSTEM

We can think of the nervous system as controlling the fast-changing activities of the body by its ability to directly activate muscles and glands. The *endocrine system* is slower acting and indirectly controls the activities of cell groups throughout the body by means of chemicals called *hormones*. These hormones are secreted by the various endocrine glands into the bloodstream (see Figure 2-14). The hormones then travel through the body, acting in various ways on cells of different types. Each target cell is equipped with receptors that recognize only the hormone molecules meant to act on that cell; the receptors pull the appropriate hormone molecules out of the bloodstream and into the cell. Some endocrine glands are activated by the nervous system, while others are activated by changes in the internal chemical state of the body.

One of the major endocrine glands, the *pituitary*, is partly an outgrowth of the brain and lies just below the hypothalamus (refer back to Figure 2-7). The pituitary gland has been called the "master gland" because it produces the largest number of different hormones and controls the secretion of other endocrine glands. One of the pituitary hormones has the crucial job of controlling body growth. Too little of this hormone can create a dwarf, while oversecretion can produce a giant. Other hormones released by the pituitary trigger the action of other endocrine glands, such as the thyroid, the sex glands, and the outer layer of the adrenal gland. Courtship, mating, and reproductive behavior in many animals are based on a complex interaction between the activity of the nervous system and the influence of the pituitary on the sex glands.

The relationship between the pituitary gland and the hypothalamus illustrates the complex interactions that take place between the endocrine system and the nervous system. In response to stress (fear, anxiety, pain, emotional events, and so forth) certain neurons in the hypothalamus secrete a substance called *corticotropin-release factor* (CRF). The pituitary is just below the hypothalamus and CRF is carried to it through a channel-like structure. The CRF stimulates the pituitary to release *adrenocorticotrophic hormone* (ACTH), which is the body's major stress hormone. ACTH, in turn, is carried by the bloodstream to the adrenal glands and to various other organs of the body, causing the release of some 30 hormones, each of which plays a role in the body's adjustment to emergency situations. This sequence of events indicates that the endocrine system is under the control of the hypothalamus and thereby under the control of other brain centers via the hypothalamus.

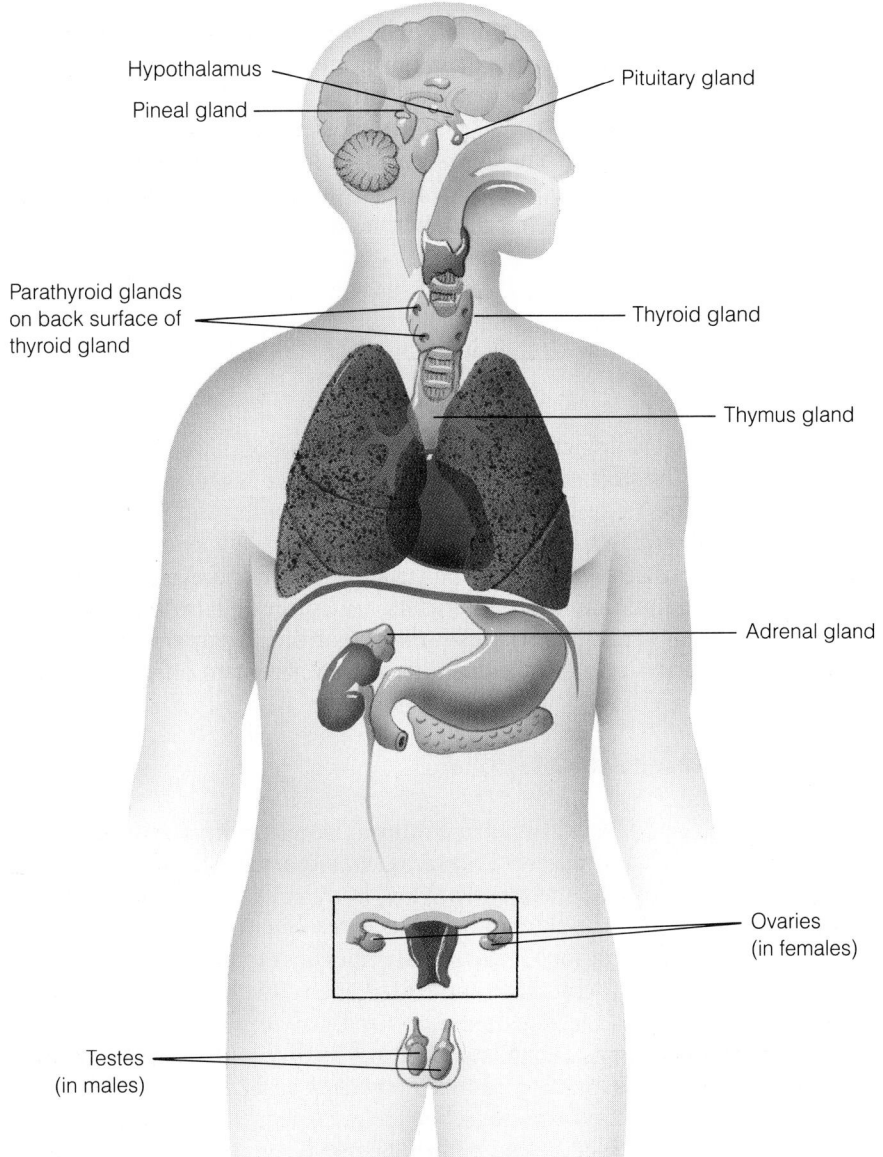

Hypothalamus

Pineal gland

Parathyroid glands
on back surface of
thyroid gland

Pituitary gland

Thyroid gland

Thymus gland

Adrenal gland

Ovaries
(in females)

Testes
(in males)

FIGURE 2-14
Some of the Endocrine
Glands *Hormones secreted by the
endocrine glands are as essential as the
nervous system to the integration of
the organism's activity. The endocrine
system and the nervous system, however,
differ in the speed with which they can act.
A nerve impulse can travel through the
organism in a few hundredths of a second.
Seconds, or even minutes, may be required
for an endocrine gland to produce an effect;
the hormone, once released, must travel to
its target site via the bloodstream—a much
slower process.*

The *adrenal glands* play an important role in determining an individual's
mood, level of energy, and ability to cope with stress. The inner core of the
adrenal gland secretes *epinephrine* and *norepinephrine* (also known as *adrenaline* and *noradrenaline*). Epinephrine acts in a number of ways to prepare
the organism for an emergency, often in conjunction with the sympathetic
division of the autonomic nervous system. Epinephrine, for example, affects
the smooth muscles and the sweat glands in a way similar to that of the
sympathetic system. It causes constriction of the blood vessels in the stomach and intestines and makes the heart beat faster (as anyone who has ever
had a shot of adrenaline knows).

Norepinephrine also prepares the organism for emergency action. When
it reaches the pituitary in its travels through the bloodstream, it stimulates
the gland to release a hormone that acts on the outer layer of the adrenal
glands; in turn, this second hormone stimulates the liver to increase the
blood-sugar level so the body has energy for quick action.

The hormones of the endocrine system and the neurotransmitters of
neurons have similar functions; they both carry *messages* between cells of the

body. A neurotransmitter carries messages between adjacent neurons, and its effect is highly localized. In contrast, a hormone may travel a long distance through the body and act in various ways on many different types of cells. The basic similarity between these chemical messengers (despite their differences) is shown by the fact that some serve both functions. Epinephrine and norepinephrine, for example, act as neurotransmitters when released by neurons, and as hormones when released by the adrenal gland.

GENETIC INFLUENCES ON BEHAVIOR

To understand the biological foundations of psychology, we need to know something about hereditary influences. The field of *behavior genetics* (also called *psychogenetics*) combines the methods of genetics and psychology to study the inheritance of behavioral characteristics. We know that many physical characteristics—height, bone structure, hair and eye color, and so on—are inherited. Behavioral geneticists are interested in the degree to which psychological characteristics—mental ability, temperament, emotional stability, and so on—are transmitted from parent to offspring.

Chromosomes and Genes

The hereditary units we receive from our parents and transmit to our offspring are carried by structures known as *chromosomes*, which are found in the nucleus of each cell in the body. Most body cells contain 46 chromosomes. At conception, the human being receives 23 chromosomes from the father's sperm and 23 chromosomes from the mother's ovum. These 46 chromosomes form 23 pairs, which are duplicated each time the cells divide (see Figure 2-15).

Each chromosome is composed of many individual hereditary units called *genes*. A gene is a segment of *deoxyribonucleic acid* (DNA), which is the actual carrier of genetic information. The DNA molecule looks like a twisted ladder or a double-stranded helix (spiral), as shown in Figure 2-16. All DNA has the same chemical composition, consisting of a simple sugar (deoxyribose), phosphate, and four bases—adenine, guanine, thymine, and cytosine (A, G, T, C). The two strands of the DNA molecule are composed of phosphate and sugar, and the strands are held apart by pairs of bases. Due to the structural properties of these bases, A always pairs with T and G always pairs with C. The bases can occur in any sequence along a strand, and these sequences constitute the genetic code. The fact that many different arrangements of bases are possible is what gives DNA the ability to express many different genetic messages. The same four bases specify the characteristics of every living organism and, depending on their arrangement, determine whether a creature turns out to be a bird, a lion, a fish, or Michelangelo.

A segment of the DNA molecule, the gene, will give coded instructions to the cell, directing it to perform a specific function (usually to manufacture a particular protein). Although all cells in the body carry the same genes, the specialized nature of each cell is due to the fact that only 5 to 10 percent of the genes are active in any given cell. In the process of developing from a fertilized egg, each cell switches on some genes and switches off all others. When "nerve genes" are active, for example, a cell develops as a neuron

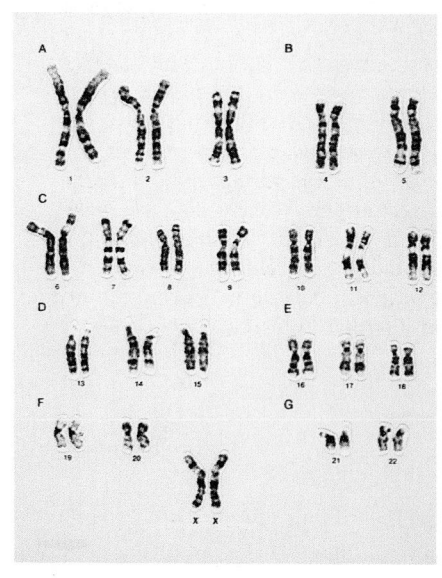

FIGURE 2-15
Chromosomes *This photo (greatly enlarged) shows the 46 chromosomes of a normal human female. A human male would have the same pairs 1 through 22, but pair 23 would be XY rather than XX.*

because the genes are directing the cell to make the products that allow it to perform neural functions (which would not be possible if the genes irrelevant to a neuron, such as "muscle genes," were not switched off).

Genes, like chromosomes, exist in pairs. One gene of each pair comes from the sperm chromosomes and one gene comes from the ovum chromosomes. Thus, a child receives only half of each parent's total genes. The total number of genes in each human chromosome is around 1,000—perhaps higher. Because the number of genes is so high, it is extremely unlikely that two human beings would have the same heredity, even if they were siblings. The only exception is *identical twins*, who, because they developed from the same fertilized egg, have exactly the same genes.

DOMINANT AND RECESSIVE GENES An important attribute of some genes is *dominance* or *recessiveness*. When both members of a gene pair are dominant, the individual manifests the form of the trait specified by these dominant genes. When one gene is dominant and the other recessive, the dominant gene again determines the form of the trait. Only if the genes contributed by both parents are recessive is the recessive form of the trait expressed. The genes determining eye color, for example, act in a pattern of dominance and recessiveness; blue is recessive and brown is dominant. Thus, a blue-eyed child may have two blue-eyed parents, or one blue-eyed parent and one brown-eyed parent (who carries a recessive gene for blue eyes), or two brown-eyed parents (each of whom carries a recessive gene for blue eyes). A brown-eyed child, in contrast, never has two blue-eyed parents.

Some of the characteristics that are carried by recessive genes are baldness, albinism, hemophilia, and a susceptibility to poison ivy. Not all gene pairs follow the dominant-recessive pattern, and as we shall see, most human characteristics are determined by many genes acting together, rather than by a single gene pair.

Even though most human characteristics are not determined by the actions of a single gene pair, there are some striking exceptions. Of special interest from a psychological viewpoint are diseases like *phenylketonuria* (PKU) and *Huntington's disease* (HD), both of which involve deterioration of the nervous system and correlated behavioral and cognitive problems. Geneticists have identified the gene responsible for PKU and they have been able to establish the approximate location of the gene responsible for HD.

PKU results from the action of a recessive gene that is inherited from each parent. The infant cannot digest an essential amino acid (phenylalanine), which then builds up in the body, poisoning the nervous system and causing irreversible brain damage. PKU children are severely retarded and usually die before the age of 30. If the PKU disorder is discovered at birth and the infants are placed on a diet that controls the level of phenylalanine, their chances of surviving with good health and intelligence are fairly high. Until the PKU gene was located, the disorder could not be diagnosed until an infant was at least 3 weeks old. Now it is possible to determine prenatally whether the fetus has the PKU gene so that the proper diet can begin at birth.

HD is caused by a single dominant gene. The long-term course of the disease involves a degeneration of certain areas in the brain and the ultimate outcome is death. Victims gradually lose their ability to talk and to control their movements, and they show a marked deterioration in memory and mental ability. The disease usually strikes when a person is 30 to 40 years of age. Before then there are no symptoms or other evidence of the disease. In fact, until recently, a person with a parent with HD had no way of knowing

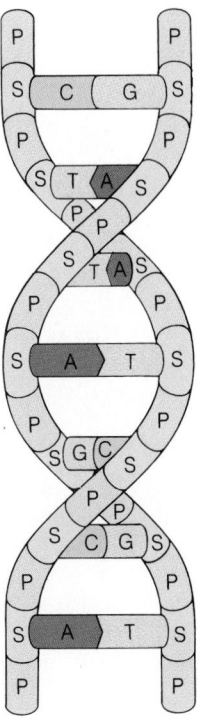

FIGURE 2-16
Structures of the DNA Molecule *Each strand of the molecule is made up of an alternating sequence of sugar (S) and phosphate (P); the rungs of the twisted ladder are made up of four bases (A, G, T, C). The double nature of the helix and the restriction on base pairings make possible the self-replication of DNA. In the process of cell division, the two strands of the DNA molecule come apart with the base pairs separating; one member of each base pair remains attached to each strand. Each strand then forms a new complementary strand using excess bases available in the cell; an A attached to a strand will attract a T, and so forth. By this process, two identical molecules of DNA come to exist where previously there was one.*

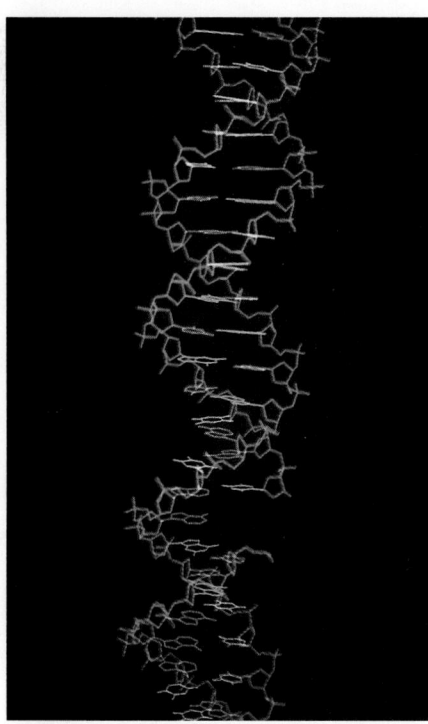

A computer-generated graphic of DNA.

whether or not he carried the Huntington gene; he only knew that he had a fifty-fifty chance of developing the disease sometime during his life. Once HD strikes, victims will typically live for 10 to 15 years with progressive deterioration and the agonizing experience of knowing what is happening to them.

Although the Huntington gene has not yet been isolated, geneticists have established that it is located on a specifiable part of a particular chromosome. As a consequence of this work, it is now possible to test individuals at risk and tell them with 99 percent accuracy whether or not they carry the gene. Hopefully, the gene will soon be isolated and its DNA structure established. Once this has been done, the protein produced by the gene can be determined. It is this protein that must in some way be responsible for HD and will provide a key for treating the disease.

SEX-LINKED GENES   Male and female chromosomes appear the same under a microscope, except for pair 23, which determines the sex of the individual and carries genes for certain traits that are sex-linked. A normal female has two similar-looking chromosomes in pair 23, called X chromosomes. A normal male has one X chromosome in pair 23 and one that looks slightly different, called a Y chromosome (refer back to Figure 2-15). Thus, the normal female chromosome pair 23 is represented by the symbol XX and the normal male pair by XY.

When most body cells reproduce, the resulting cells have the same number of chromosomes (46) as the parent cell. However, when sperm and egg cells reproduce, the chromosome pairs separate, and half go to each new cell. Thus, egg and sperm cells have only 23 chromosomes. Each egg cell has an X chromosome, and each sperm cell has either an X or a Y chromosome. If an X-type sperm is the first to enter an egg cell, the fertilized ovum will have an XX chromosome pair and the child will be a female. If a Y-type sperm fertilizes the egg, the 23rd chromosome pair will be XY and the child will be a male. The female inherits one X chromosome from the mother and one from the father; the male inherits his X chromosome from the mother and his Y chromosome from the father. Thus, it is the father's chromosome contribution that determines a child's sex (see Figure 2-17).

The X chromosome may carry either dominant or recessive genes; the Y chromosome carries a few genes dominant for male sexual characteristics but otherwise seems to carry only recessive genes. Thus, most recessive characteristics carried by a man's X chromosome (received from his mother) are expressed since they are not blocked by dominant genes. For example, color blindness is a recessive sex-linked characteristic. A man will be color-blind if he inherits a color-blind gene on the X chromosome he receives from his mother. Females are less often color-blind, because a color-blind female has to have both a color-blind father and a mother who is either color-blind or who carries a recessive gene for color blindness. A number of genetically determined disorders are linked to abnormalities of the 23rd chromosome pair, or by recessive genes carried by this pair. These are called sex-linked disorders.

CHROMOSOMAL ABNORMALITIES   On rare occasions, a female may be born with only one X chromosome instead of the usual XX. Females with this condition, which is known as *Turner's syndrome,* fail to develop sexually at puberty. Although usually of normal intelligence, they show some specific cognitive defects: they do poorly in arithmetic and on tests of visual form perception and spatial organization.

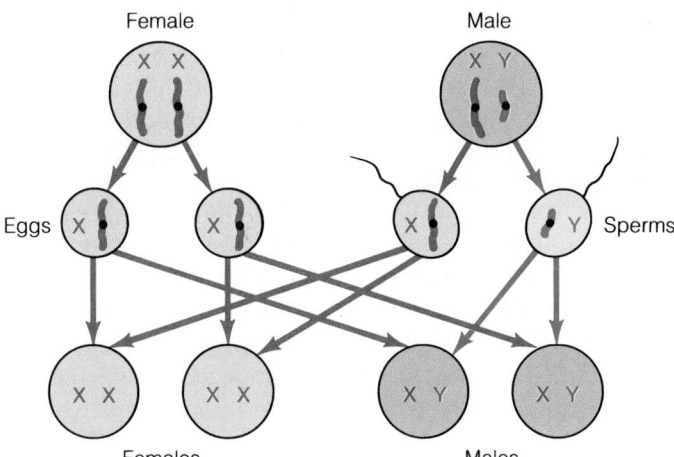

Female   Male

Eggs

Sperms

Females   Males

FIGURE 2-17
Sex of Offspring *Females have XX cells and all of their eggs contain a single X chromosome. Males have XY cells; half of their sperm are X-bearing and half are Y-bearing. The sex of the offspring is determined by the sex chromosome contained in the sperm that fertilizes the egg.*

Sometimes when the 23rd chromosome fails to divide properly, the developing organism ends up with an extra X or Y chromosome. An individual with an XXY chromosome is physically a male, with penis and testicles, but with marked feminine characteristics. His breasts are enlarged and his testes are small and do not produce sperm. This condition, known as *Klinefelter's syndrome*, is surprisingly common—about 1 in every 400 births.

Another sex chromosome abnormality in males has received considerable publicity. Men with an extra Y chromosome (type XYY) are taller than average and are reported to be unusually aggressive. Early studies suggested that the incidence of XYY males among prison inmates—particularly those convicted of violent crimes—was much higher than in the population at large. Newspaper accounts exaggerated these findings, however, portraying the XYY male as an individual genetically predisposed toward aggression and violence.

More recent studies, however, question whether there is a link between the presence of an extra Y chromosome and aggression. They find that XYY males in the general population are no more aggressive than normal males (Owen, 1972; Hook, 1973). Nevertheless, survey data indicate that males with this genetic makeup are more likely than normal males to be convicts. We do not know why this is so; however, XYY males do test lower on intelligence tests. Their higher incarceration rate may be related to low intelligence, which would increase the likelihood of being apprehended when committing a crime (Witkin et al., 1976).

Genetic Studies of Behavior

A few disorders result from chromosomal abnormalities, and some traits are determined by single genes. But most human characteristics are determined by many genes: they are *polygenic*. Traits such as intelligence, height, and emotionality do not fall into distinct categories, but show continuous variation. Most people are neither dull nor bright; intelligence is distributed over a broad range, with most individuals located near the middle. Sometimes a specific genetic defect can result in mental retardation, but in most instances, a person's intellectual potential is determined by a large number of genes that influence the factors underlying different abilities. Of course, what happens to this genetic potential depends on environmental conditions.

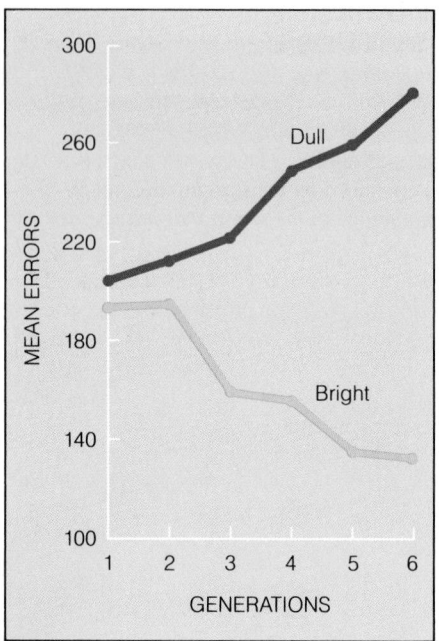

FIGURE 2-18
Inheritance of Maze Learning in Rats *Mean error scores of "bright" and "dull" rats selectively bred for maze-running ability.* (After Thompson, 1954)

SELECTIVE BREEDING One method of studying the heritability of traits in animals is by selective breeding. Animals that are high or low in a certain trait are mated with each other. For example, to study the inheritance of learning ability in rats, the females that do poorly in learning to run a maze are mated with males that do poorly; the females that do well are mated with the males that do well. The offspring of these matings are tested on the same maze. On the basis of performance, the brightest are mated with the brightest and the dullest with the dullest. (To ensure that environmental conditions are kept constant, the offspring of "dull" mothers are sometimes given to "bright" mothers to raise so that genetic endowment rather than adequacy of maternal care is being tested.) After a few rodent generations, a "bright" and a "dull" strain of rats can be produced (see Figure 2-18).

Selective breeding has been used to show the inheritance of a number of behavioral characteristics. For example, dogs have been bred to be excitable or lethargic; chickens, to be aggressive and sexually active; fruit flies, to be more drawn or less drawn to light; and mice, to be more attracted or less attracted to alcohol. If a trait is influenced by heredity, it should be possible to change it by selective breeding. If selective breeding does not alter a trait, we assume that the trait is primarily dependent on environmental factors (Plomin, 1986).

TWIN STUDIES Since, ethically, breeding experiments cannot be carried out with human beings, we must look instead at similarities in behavior among individuals who are related. Certain traits often run in families. But families are not only linked genetically, they also share the same environment. If musical talent runs in the family, we do not know whether inherited ability or parental emphasis on music is more important to this development. Sons of alcoholic fathers are more likely than sons of nonalcoholic fathers to develop alcoholism. Do genetic tendencies or environmental conditions play the major role? In an effort to answer questions of this sort, psychologists have turned to studies on twins.

Identical twins develop from a single fertilized egg and thus share the same heredity; they are also called *monozygotic* since they come from a single zygote, or fertilized egg. Fraternal twins develop from different egg cells and

Identical twins.

IDENTICAL TWINS

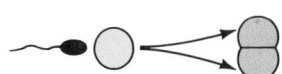 

1. Accounting for about 1 in 250 births, identical twins are created when a single egg is fertilized by one sperm.

2. The egg splits into halves. Each develops into a fetus with the same genetic composition.

FRATERNAL TWINS

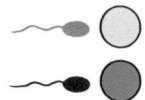 

1. Twice as common as identicals, fraternals arise when two eggs are released at once.

2. If both are fertilized by separate sperm, two fetuses form. Genetically they are just ordinary siblings.

HALF-IDENTICAL TWINS

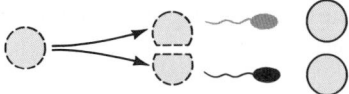 

1. A rare type, half-identicals form when a precursor to an egg splits evenly and is fertilized by two sperm.

2. The fetuses have about half of their genes in common—those from the mother.

TWINS OF DIFFERENT FATHERS

  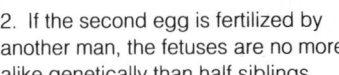

1. In extremely rare cases, an egg is released even though the previous month's egg was fertilized.

2. If the second egg is fertilized by another man, the fetuses are no more alike genetically than half siblings.

FIGURE 2-19
Types of Twins *Besides identical and fraternal twins, there may be "half-identical" twins. Half-identicals arise when a precursor to a true ovum divides into identical halves and is fertilized by two sperm. Thus they are more alike than fraternals, but less alike than identicals. Twins can also have different fathers. If an ovum is released after the previous month's ovum has begun developing into an embryo, it can be fertilized by the next act of sexual intercourse. They are, in essence, step-siblings, for they have the same mother but different fathers.*

are no more alike genetically than are ordinary siblings; they are also called *dizygotic*, or two-egged. Fraternal twins are about twice as common as identical twins. As Figure 2-19 indicates, there are other types of twins, but they are extremely rare.

Studies comparing identical and fraternal twins help to sort out the influence of environment and heredity. Identical twins are found to be more similar in intelligence than fraternal twins, even when they are separated at birth and reared in different homes (see Chapter 12). Identical twins are also more similar than fraternal twins in some personality characteristics and in susceptibility to the mental disorder of schizophrenia (see Chapter 16). Twin studies have proved to be a useful method of investigating genetic influences on human behavior.

Environmental Influences on Gene Action

The inherited potential with which an individual enters the world is very much influenced by the environment that he or she encounters. This interaction will be made clear in later chapters, but two examples will suffice to illustrate the point here. The tendency to develop diabetes is hereditary, although the exact method of transmission is unknown. Diabetes is a disease in which the pancreas does not produce enough insulin to burn carbohydrates as an energy source for the body. Scientists assume that genes determine the production of insulin. But people who carry the genetic potential for diabetes do not always develop the disease; for example, if one identical twin has diabetes, the other twin will develop the disorder in only about half the cases. Not all of the environmental factors that contribute to diabetes are known, but one variable that seems fairly certain is obesity. A fat person requires more insulin to metabolize carbohydrates than a thin person. Consequently, an individual who carries the genes for diabetes is more likely to develop the disorder if he or she is overweight.

A similar situation is found in the mental illness called *schizophrenia*. As we shall see in Chapter 16, substantial evidence indicates a hereditary component to the disorder. If one identical twin is schizophrenic, chances are high that the other twin will exhibit some signs of mental disturbance. But whether or not the other twin develops the full-blown disorder will depend on a number of environmental factors. The genes may predispose, but the environment shapes the outcome.

✖ CHAPTER SUMMARY

1. The nervous system is composed of cells called *neurons*, which receive stimulation by way of their *dendrites* and *cell bodies* and transmit impulses via their *axons*. *Sensory neurons* carry messages from the sense *receptors* to the brain and spinal cord; *motor neurons* transmit signals from the brain and spinal cord to the muscles and glands. Axon fibers group together to form *nerves*.

2. Two aspects of the transmission of the nerve impulse are important: conduction along axon fibers and transmission across the synaptic junction between neurons. Axonal conduction involves an electrochemical process called *depolarization*; the *nerve impulse*, once started, travels down the axon to its many *synaptic terminals*. Chemical intermediaries called *neurotransmitters* pass the impulse from one neuron to the next across a *synapse*. Neurotransmitters are released from synaptic terminals and act on the dendrites and cell body of the receiving neuron to change its membrane permeability; some neurotransmitters are excitatory and others are inhibitory.

3. The nervous system is divided into the *central nervous system* (the brain and spinal cord) and the *peripheral nervous system* (the nerves connecting the brain and spinal cord to other parts of the body). Subdivisions of the peripheral nervous system are the *somatic system* (which carries messages to and from the sense receptors, muscles, and the body surface) and the *autonomic system* (which connects with the internal organs and glands).

4. The human brain is composed of three concentric layers: a *central core*, the *limbic system*, and the *cerebrum*.

   a. The central core includes the *medulla*, responsible for respiration and postural reflexes; the *cerebellum* is concerned with motor coordination; the *thalamus* is a relay station for incoming sensory information; and the *hypothalamus* is important in emotion and in maintaining homeostasis. The *reticular system*, which crosses through several of the above structures, controls the organism's state of wakefulness and arousal.

   b. The *limbic system* controls some of the instinctive activities (feeding, attacking, fleeing from danger, mating) regulated by the hypothalamus; it also plays an important role in emotion and memory.

   c. The *cerebrum* is divided into two *cerebral hemispheres*. The convoluted surface of these hemispheres, the *cerebral cortex*, plays a critical role in discrimination, decision making, learning, and thinking—the higher mental processes. Certain areas of the cerebral cortex represent centers for specific sensory inputs or for control of specific movements. The remainder of the cerebral cortex consists of *association areas*.

5. When the *corpus callosum* (the band of nerve fibers connecting the two cerebral hemispheres) is severed, significant differences in the functioning of the two hemispheres can be observed. The left hemisphere is skilled in language and mathematical abilities. The right hemisphere can understand some language but cannot communicate through speech; it has a highly developed spatial and pattern sense.

6. The *autonomic nervous system* is made up of the *sympathetic* and the *parasympathetic* divisions. Because its fibers mediate the action of the smooth muscles and of the glands, the autonomic system is particularly important in emotional reactions. The sympathetic division is active during excitement and the parasympathetic during quiescence.

7. The *endocrine glands* secrete hormones into the bloodstream that are important for emotional and motivational behavior. They complement the nervous system in integrating behavior, and their action is closely tied to the activity of the hypothalamus and the autonomic nervous system.

8. An individual's hereditary potential, transmitted by the *chromosomes* and *genes*, influences psychological and physical characteristics. Genes are segments of DNA *molecules*, which store genetic information. Some genes are *dominant*, some *recessive*, and some *sex-linked*. Most human characteristics are *polygenic*— that is, determined by many genes acting together, rather than by a single gene pair.

9. *Selective breeding* (mating animals that are high or low in a certain trait) is one method of studying the influence of heredity. Another method for sorting out the effects of environment and heredity is *twin studies*, in which the characteristics of *identical twins* (who share the same heredity) are compared with those of *fraternal twins* (who are no more alike genetically than ordinary siblings).

10. Behavior depends on the *interaction* between heredity and environment; the genes set the limits of the individual's potential, but what happens to this potential depends on the environment.

FURTHER READING

Introductions to physiological psychology are Carlson, *Foundations of Physiological Psychology* (1988); Groves and Rebec, *Introduction to Biological Psychology* (3rd ed., 1988); Kolb and Whishaw, *Fundamentals of Human Neuropsychology* (2nd ed., 1985); Schneider and Tarshis, *An Introduction to Physiological Psychology* (3rd ed., 1986); and Rosenzweig and Leiman, *Physiological Psychology* (2nd ed., 1989).

For a review of the molecular basis of neural processes see Alberts et al., *Molecular Biology of the Cell* (1983). Also see Squire, *Memory and Brain* (1987) for a discussion of the neural basis of memory and cognition.

A survey of genetic influences on behavior is provided by Plomin, DeFries, and McClearn, *Behavioral Genetics: A Primer* (2nd ed., 1989). For a review of psychoactive drugs and their effects on the body, brain, and behavior, see Julien, *A Primer of Drug Action* (5th ed., 1988) and Julien, *Drugs and the Body* (1988).

For a survey of research on the function of the two cerebral hemispheres, see Springer and Deutsch, *Left Brain, Right Brain* (3rd ed., 1989) and Beaton, *Left Side/Right Side: A Review of Laterality Research* (1986).

Chapter 3

Detail, Child and Aunt.

Psychological Development

Of all mammals, human beings are the most immature at birth and require the longest period of development before they are self-sufficient. In general, the higher on the phylogenetic scale an organism is, the more complex its nervous system is and the longer the time required to reach maturity. For example, the lemur, a primitive primate, can move about on its own shortly after birth and is soon able to fend for itself; the newborn monkey is dependent on its mother for several months, the infant baboon for several years. The human offspring, in contrast, is dependent for many years and requires a long period of learning and interaction with others before becoming self-sufficient.

We tend to think that development is complete once a person reaches physical maturity. But the circumstances of our lives and the way we deal with these circumstances continually shape us, so that development is actually a lifelong process. Developmental psychologists are concerned with describing and analyzing the regularities of human development throughout the life span. They study *physical development*, such as changes in height and weight, and the acquisition of motor skills; *perceptual development*, such as changes in hearing and seeing; *cognitive development*, such as changes in thought processes, language abilities, and memory; and *personality and social development*, such as changes in gender identity or moral behavior.

Developmental psychologists often study the average, or "typical," rate of development. At what age, for instance, does the average child begin to speak? How rapidly does a typical child's vocabulary increase with age? Such normative data are important for planning educational programs and for evaluating an individual child's development. Psychologists are concerned also with how certain behaviors develop and why they appear when they do. Why do most children not walk or utter their first word until they are about a year old? What physiological developments and behaviors must precede these accomplishments?

Environmental influences on behavior are another concern. Psychologists may study the effect of a child's viewing television violence on his or her behavior or study different approaches to instruction on reading skills. Psychologists have also looked at the effects of day care, divorce, and parental unemployment on the emotional development of children.

In this chapter, we discuss several general principles of development, as well as some behavior and attitude changes that occur as the individual matures from infancy through adulthood. Our purpose is to provide an overview of psychological development. The development of certain specific abilities, such as language and perception, will be considered in later chapters devoted to these topics.

BASIC QUESTIONS ABOUT DEVELOPMENT

Two basic questions underlie theories about the course of human development: a) Is development guided primarily by heredity—that is, by genetic programs locked into the body's cells—or is it subject to fundamental changes determined by events in the environment? and b) Is development a continuous process of change, or is it best understood as a series of distinct stages? The assumptions that theorists make about the sources of change and about continuity shape their interpretations of what they observe and their proposals for guiding development.

Nature versus Nurture

The question of whether heredity ("nature") or environment ("nurture") is more important in determining the course of human development has been debated through the centuries. The seventeenth-century British philosopher John Locke, for example, rejected the prevailing notion of his day that babies were miniature adults who arrived in the world fully equipped with abilities and knowledge and who simply had to grow in order for these inherited characteristics to appear. On the contrary, Locke believed that the mind of a newborn infant is a "blank slate" (*tabula rasa*). What gets written on this slate is what the baby experiences—what he or she sees, hears, tastes, smells, and feels. According to Locke, all knowledge comes to us through our senses. It is provided by experience; no knowledge or ideas are built in.

The advent of Charles Darwin's theory of evolution (1859), which emphasizes the biological basis of human development, led to a return to the hereditarian viewpoint. With the rise of behaviorism in the twentieth century, however, the environmentalist position gained dominance. Behaviorists such as John B. Watson and B. F. Skinner argued that human nature is completely malleable: early training can turn a child into any kind of adult, regardless of his or her heredity. Watson believed that the environment has tremendous power to shape a child's development. "Give me a dozen healthy infants, well-formed, and my own specified world to bring them up in," he wrote, "and I'll guarantee to take any one at random and train him to be any type of specialist I might—doctor, lawyer, artist, merchant, chief, and, yes, even beggar man and thief!" (Watson, 1950, p. 104).

Today most psychologists agree that both nature and nurture play an important role in development. Human development is determined by continuous interaction between heredity and environment. At the moment of conception, a remarkable number of personal characteristics are already determined by the genetic structure of the fertilized ovum. Our genes program our growing cells so that we develop into a person rather than a fish, a bird, or a monkey. They decide the color of our skin and hair, general body size, sex, and (to some extent) our intellectual abilities and emotional temperament. The genetically specified characteristics present at birth interact with the experiences encountered in the course of growing up to determine individual development. Our experiences depend on the specific culture, social group, and family in which we are reared.

The development of speech provides an example of the interaction between genetically determined characteristics and the experiences provided by the environment. Almost all human infants are born with the ability to learn a spoken language; other species are not. In the normal course of development, human beings learn to speak. But they are not able to talk before they have attained a certain level of neurological development—no infant less than a year old speaks in sentences. Children reared in an environment in which people talk to them and reward them for making speechlike sounds will talk earlier than children who do not receive such attention. For example, children reared in middle-class American homes begin to speak at about 1 year of age. Children reared in San Marcos, a remote village in Guatemala, have little verbal interaction with adults and do not utter their first words until they are over 2 years old (Kagan, 1979). The language children speak, of course, will be that of their own culture. Thus, the development of speech has both genetic and environmental components. Most other aspects of human development likewise depend on the interaction between inherited characteristics and environmental experiences.

MATURATION   Genetic determinants are expressed through the process of *maturation*. Maturation refers to innately determined sequences of growth or bodily changes that are relatively independent of environmental events. We say "relatively" because such changes occur over a wide range of environmental conditions; however, an environment decidedly atypical or inadequate in some way *will* affect maturational processes. Although maturation is most apparent during childhood, it continues well into adult life. Some of the changes that occur at adolescence, as well as some of the changes that occur with aging (the appearance of gray hair, for instance), are regulated by a genetically determined time schedule.

Maturation is demonstrated clearly by fetal development. The human fetus develops within the mother's body according to a fairly fixed time schedule, and fetal behavior (such as turning and kicking) also follows an orderly sequence that depends on the stage of growth. Premature infants who are kept alive in an incubator develop at much the same rate as infants who remain in the uterus to the full term. The regularity of development before birth illustrates what we mean by maturation. However, if the uterine environment is seriously abnormal in some way, maturational processes can be disrupted. For example, if the mother contracts German measles during the first 3 months of pregnancy (when the fetus's basic organ systems are developing according to the genetically programmed schedule), the infant may be born deaf, blind, or brain-damaged (the type of defect depends on which organ system was in a critical stage of development at the time of infection). Maternal malnutrition, smoking, and consumption of alcohol and drugs are among the other environmental factors that can affect the normal maturation of the fetus.

Motor development after birth—using the hands and fingers, standing, and walking—also follows a regular sequence. For example, such activities as rolling over, crawling, and pulling up to a standing position occur in the same *order* in most children. Unless we believe that all parents subject their offspring to the same training regimen (an unlikely possibility), we must assume that growth processes determine the order of behavior. As Figure 3-1 shows, not all children go through the sequence at the same rate; some infants are 4 or 5 months ahead of others in standing alone or walking. But the order in which they go from one stage to the next is generally the same in all infants.

Because the child's mastery of the movements necessary for sitting, standing, walking, and using hands and fingers follows such an orderly sequence, and because children in all cultures accomplish these skills at *roughly* the same age, motor development appears to be primarily a maturational process, little influenced by the environment in which the child is reared.

Stages and Critical Periods

Many behaviors follow a natural sequence of development. Infants reach for an object before they are able to pick it up. Toddlers walk before they can

Despite warnings of abnormal fetal development, some pregnant women continue to put their babies at risk by drinking and smoking.

FIGURE 3-1
Babies Develop at Different
Rates *Although development is orderly,*
some infants reach each stage ahead of other
infants. The left end of the bar indicates the
age by which 25 percent of infants have
achieved the stated performance, whereas
the right end gives the age by which 90
percent have accomplished the behavior. The
vertical mark on each bar gives the age by
which 50 percent have achieved it. (After
Frankenburg & Dodds, 1967)

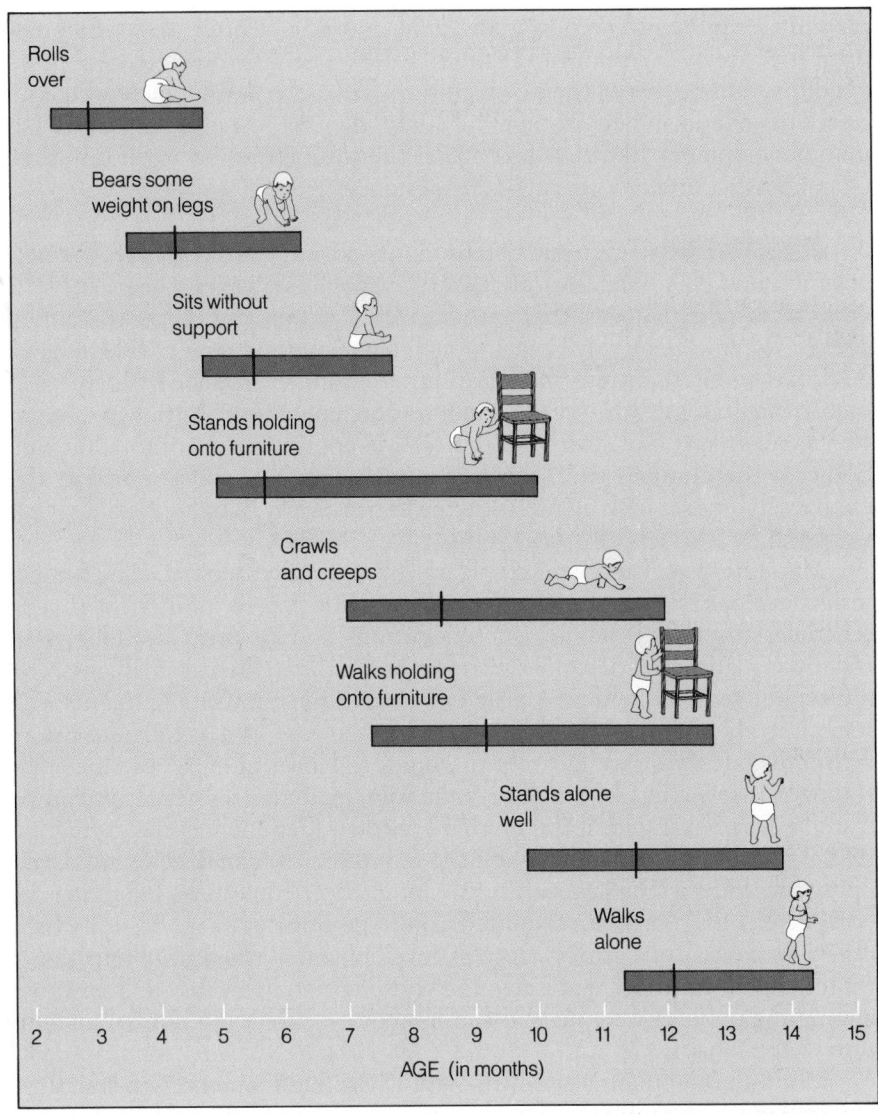

run; they speak words before they can combine them into sentences. Children learn to count by rote before they understand the concept of numbers. Sequences in development usually proceed from simple behaviors to those that are more differentiated and complex. For example, newborn infants can clasp and unclasp their fingers and wave their arms about, occasionally managing to connect the thumb with the mouth. As infants mature, these simple actions become differentiated into increasingly more complex behaviors: patting an object, grasping it, picking it up, moving it toward the mouth, or throwing it.

Psychologists generally agree that there are orderly sequences in development that depend on the maturation of the organism as it interacts with its environment. In explaining developmental sequences, some psychologists prefer to interpret them as a *continuous process*, in which biological factors interplay with learning to produce a smooth and continuous change in behavior. Other psychologists agree on the sequential character of development but are less impressed by the continuity of the process; they see development more as a series of steps. For this reason, Piaget and other stage theorists such as Kohlberg, Erikson, and Freud have introduced the concept of *stages*.

We identify broad stages when we divide the life span into successive periods of infancy, childhood, adolescence, and adulthood. Parents use the term "stage" when they refer to a "negative stage" their 2-year-old is going through (saying no to every request) or a "rebellious stage" their adolescent is in (challenging parental authority). When psychologists refer to developmental stages, they have a more precise concept in mind: the concept of stages implies that a) behaviors at a given stage are organized around a *dominant theme*; b) behaviors at one stage are *qualitatively different* from behaviors that appear at earlier or later stages; and c) all children go through the same stages *in the same order*. Environmental factors may speed up or slow down development, but the order of stages is invariant; a child cannot achieve a later stage without going through an earlier one first.

Later in this chapter we will look at several stage theories: one focuses on stages of cognitive development; another, on stages of moral development; and the third, on stages of social development. Although some psychologists believe that stage theories are a useful way of describing development, others believe that development is better interpreted as a continuous process of acquiring new behaviors through experience. They do not accept the qualitative shifts in behavior that stage theories imply. We will examine the evidence for both the continuous process and the stage theory viewpoints as we go along.

Closely related to the concept of stages is the idea that there may be *critical periods* in human development—that is, crucial time periods in a person's life during which specific events must occur for development to proceed normally. Critical periods have been firmly established for some aspects of the physical development of the human fetus. For example, the period 6 to 7 weeks after conception is critical for the normal development of the fetus's sex organs. Whether the primitive sex organ develops into a male or female sexual structure depends on the presence of male hormones, regardless of the XX or XY arrangement of chromosomes. The absence of male hormones means that female sexual organs will develop in either case. If male hormones are injected later in development, they cannot reverse the changes that have already taken place.

During postnatal development, there is a critical period for the development of vision. If children who are born with cataracts have them removed before the age of 7, their vision will develop fairly normally. But if a child goes through the first seven years without vision, extensive permanent disability will result (Kuman, Fedrov, & Novikova, 1983).

The existence of critical periods in the *psychological* development of the child has not been established. It is probably more accurate to say that there are *sensitive periods*—periods that are optimal for a particular kind of development. If a certain behavior is not well established during this sensitive period, it may not develop to its full potential. For example, the first year of life may be sensitive for the formation of close attachment to the parents. The preschool years may be especially significant for intellectual development and the acquisition of language. Children who for some reason have not had sufficient exposure to language prior to the age of 6 or 7 years may fail to acquire it altogether (Goldin-Meadow, 1982). The experiences of the child during such sensitive periods may shape his or her future course of development in a manner that will be difficult to change later.

Motor development in infants *Sitting alone, crawling, and standing alone are major developments in an infant's mobility.*

EARLY YEARS

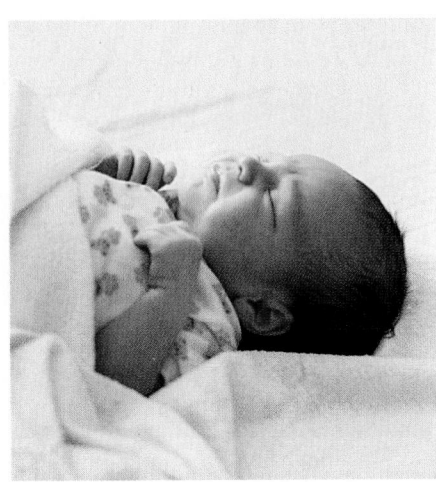

The human infant is helpless at birth.

Infancy (from the Latin word meaning "without language") is difficult to study because babies cannot explain what they are doing or tell us what they are thinking. Until recently, newborn infants were assumed to be helpless, unsensing, and unresponsive creatures who had little awareness of what was going on around them. Psychologist William James' notion that the newborn child experiences the world as a "buzzing, blooming confusion" was still prevalent as late as the 1960s. Parents were often told that their infants were essentially blind at birth and could not taste, smell, or feel pain.

Newborn infants are indeed physically weak and helpless; most cannot hold up their heads. But research of recent decades has demonstrated that normal, full-term infants enter the world with all sensory systems functioning and prepared to learn about events in their environment.

Capacities of the Newborn

The basic method used to study infant sensory capacities is to introduce some change in the baby's environment and observe its effects on the baby. For example, an investigator might present a tone or a flashing light and watch for indicators in the newborn that it has been sensed, such as a turn of the head, a change in heart rate or brain waves, or a change in the rate at which the baby sucks on a nipple. In some instances, the researcher will present two stimuli at the same time to determine if infants look longer at one than the other. If they do, it presumably shows that they can tell the stimuli apart, and may also indicate that they prefer one to the other (Cole & Cole, 1989).

Another method frequently used depends on the processes of *habituation* and *dishabituation*. A stimulus to which the newborn attends is presented repeatedly until the infant stops paying attention to it. This response pattern is called habituation—a reduction in the strength of a response to a repeated stimulus. Then some aspect of the stimulus is changed. If the infant continues to ignore the stimulus, despite the change, it can be concluded that the change is not psychologically significant to the baby. But if the infant's attention is renewed (that is, the baby dishabituates) the investigator can conclude that the baby did notice the change in the stimulus.

For example, while monitoring the infant's heart rate, an investigator presents a tone of a given pitch for a series of trials. When a baby—or anyone, for that matter—is presented with a new stimulus, the heart rate slows down. This reduction in heart rate is a sign that the infant is attending to the stimulus. After the tone is presented a number of times, the heart rate no longer decelerates at the onset of the sound; the heart rate response has habituated. We assume that the sound has become familiar and the infant ceases to attend to it. The experimenter then presents a new tone of higher pitch. If the infant's heart rate decelerates (that is, dishabituates), the investigator infers that the infant is attending to the new sound and therefore able to detect the difference between the two tones. Studies using this habituation-dishabituation technique have shown that newborn infants can detect the difference between very similar sounds, such as two tones that are only one note apart on the musical scale (Bridger, 1961).

HEARING Newborn infants will startle at the sound of a loud noise. They will also turn their heads toward the source of a sound. Interestingly

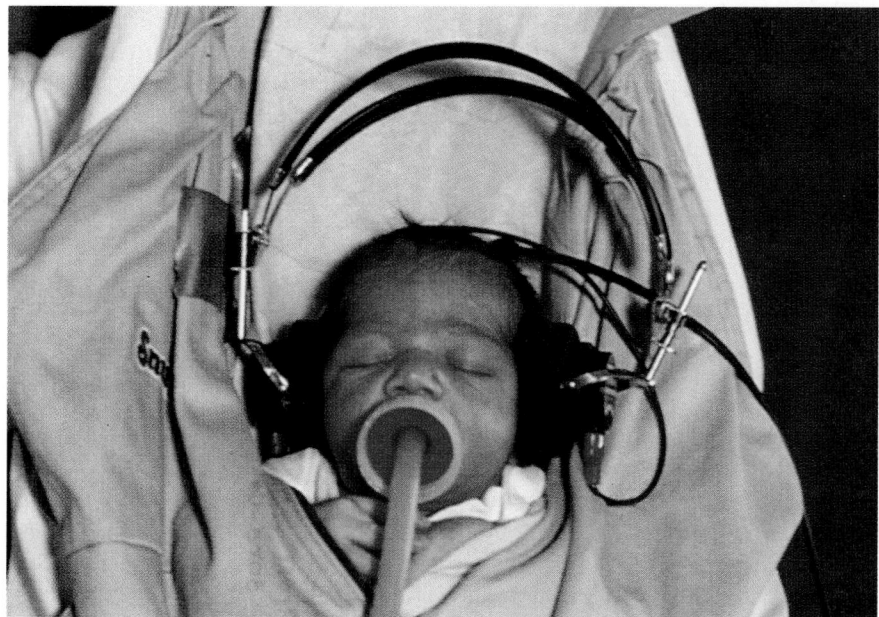

FIGURE 3-2
Preference for Mother's Voice *A newborn increases the vigor of his sucking on a non-nutritive nipple when he hears the sound of his mother's voice through the earphones.*

enough, the head-turning response disappears at about 6 weeks and does not reemerge until 3 or 4 months of age, at which time the infants will also search with their eyes for the source of the sound. The reasons for the temporary disappearance of the head-turning response are unclear; it probably represents a maturational transition from a reflexive response (controlled by subcortical areas of the brain) to a voluntary attempt to locate the sound source. By 6 months infants show a marked increase in their responsiveness to sounds that are accompanied by interesting sights (Field, 1987).

Newborn infants are able to distinguish the sound of the human voice from other kinds of sounds, and they seem to prefer it. Infants tested within a few days of birth will learn to suck on an artificial nipple in order to turn on recorded speech or vocal music, but they will not suck as readily in order to hear non-speech sounds or instrumental music (Butterfield & Siperstein, 1972). They also prefer listening to their own mother's voice over that of an unfamiliar woman (DeCasper & Fifer, 1980) (see Figure 3-2). It is believed that infants become accustomed to mother's voice before birth; we know that low-frequency sounds, such as those of human speech, can penetrate the uterus, and that the fetus is responsive to sounds in the external environment.

One of the most startling discoveries about the hearing of young infants is that they can perceive a number of critical characteristics of human speech (Eimas, 1975). For example, 1-month-old infants can tell the difference between the sounds of *p* and *b*. The investigators used sucking as a response and a decrease in sucking rate as a measure of habituation. They discovered that the infants would suck strongly on a pacifier connected to a recording mechanism in order to hear the sound "bah." Gradually they became habituated to that sound and sucked less. When the sound changed to "pah," they sucked harder again, indicating that they were hearing something new. Using this method, researchers have found that infants are able to discriminate most of the sound contrasts that occur in any language. Thus, human infants appear to be born with perceptual mechanisms already tuned to the properties of human speech that will help them in their mastery of language.

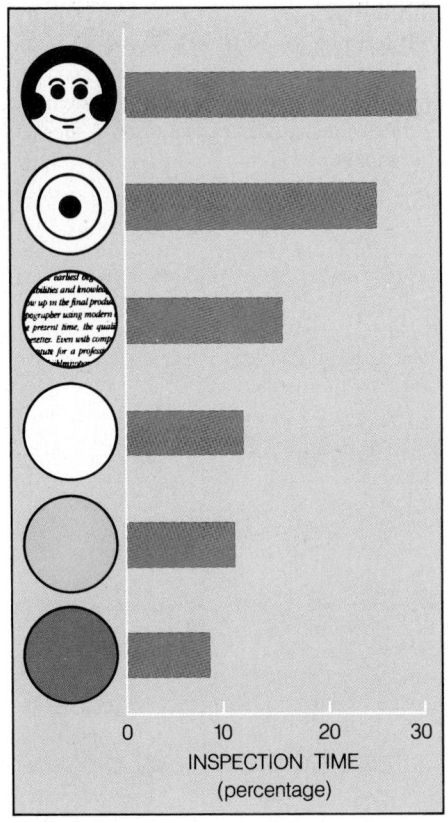

FIGURE 3-3
Visual Preferences *Newborns as young as 10 hours to 5 days old were shown disks that differed in particular ways—a facelike circle, a bull's-eye, an array of fine print, and disks colored white, yellow, or red. Infants could tell the difference between them and preferred one pattern over another.* (After Fantz, 1961)

VISION The visual system is not well-developed at birth. Newborns have poor visual acuity and their ability to change focus is limited, so that objects appear fuzzy. They are very near-sighted, so they see things better at close distances. The infant's visual capacities improve rapidly over the first few months and by the time they are able to crawl on their own—at 7 or 8 months—they can see almost as well as an adult (Cornell & McDonnell, 1986).

Despite their visual immaturity, newborns spend a lot of time actively looking about. They scan the world in an organized way and pause when their eyes encounter an object or some change in the visual field. They are particularly attracted to areas of high visual contrast, such as the edges of an object. Instead of scanning the entire object, as an adult would, they keep looking at areas that have the most edges. Crib ornaments and toys are now being designed with patterns of high contrast, using black and white or bright primary colors rather than the traditional baby pastels.

Newborn infants prefer to look at certain patterns over others. Using a specially constructed "looking chamber" (see Chapter 5), the investigator presents infants with pairs of stimuli that differ in a particular way—a yellow circle paired with a red circle, for example, or a gray square paired with a gray triangle. If the infants consistently look longer at one stimulus than the other (regardless of its position), the investigator can draw two conclusions: the infants can tell the difference between the stimuli, and they prefer one over the other. Using this method, investigators discovered that newborns prefer complex patterns to plain ones, prefer patterns with curved lines to patterns with straight lines, can discriminate fine print from gray surfaces, and are especially interested in faces (see Figure 3-3).

The suggestion that newborns might have an unlearned preference for human faces aroused great interest. However, later research showed that infants are attracted to faces not because they are human, but because they have the kinds of stimulus characteristics that babies like: curved lines, high contrast, interesting "edges," movement, and complexity (Banks & Salapatek, 1983; Aslin, 1987).

Newborns look mostly at the outside contour of a face (the hairline), but by 2 months they focus their attention on the inside of the face—the eyes, nose, and mouth (Haith, Bergman, & Moore, 1977). At this point a parent may notice, with delight, that the baby has begun to make eye contact.

TASTE AND SMELL Infants can discriminate differences in taste shortly after birth. They much prefer sweet-tasting liquids to those that are salty, bitter, sour, or bland. The characteristic response of the newborn to a sweet liquid is a relaxed expression resembling a slight smile, sometimes accompanied by lip-licking. A sour solution produces pursed lips and a wrinkled nose. In response to a bitter-tasting solution, the baby will open its mouth with the corners turned down and stick out its tongue in what appears to be an expression of disgust.

Newborns can also discriminate among odors. They will turn their heads toward a sweet smell, and their heart rate and respiration will slow down, indicating attention. Noxious odors, such as ammonia or rotten eggs, cause them to turn their heads away; heart rate and respiration accelerate, indicating distress. Infants are even able to discriminate subtle differences in smells. After nursing for only a few days, an infant will consistently turn its head toward a pad saturated with its mother's milk in preference to one saturated with another mother's milk (Russell, 1976). The innate ability to distinguish among smells has a clear adaptive value: it helps infants avoid noxious substances, thereby increasing their likelihood of survival.

EARLY SIGNS OF LEARNING AND MEMORY Because the brain is not well-developed at birth, it was once thought that infants could neither learn nor remember. A large body of research has demonstrated that this is not the case. Habituation itself is an indication of very elementary memory processes. By paying less attention to a repeated stimulus, a baby indicates that he or she has seen or heard it before and is now becoming bored with it. Habituation provides an indication of how well the infant's brain and nervous system are functioning. Infants who have brain damage or have suffered birth traumas, such as lack of oxygen, do not habituate well.

Learning to discriminate between stimuli has also been demonstrated with newborns. In one study, infants only a few hours old learned to turn their heads right or left, depending on whether they heard a buzzer or a tone. In order to taste a sweet liquid, the baby had to turn to the right when a tone sounded; to get the sweet drink when a buzzer sounded, the baby had to turn to the left. In only a few trials, the babies were performing without error—turning to the right when the tone sounded and to the left when they heard the buzzer. The experimenter then reversed the situation so that the infant had to turn the opposite way when either the buzzer or the tone sounded. The babies mastered this new task very quickly (Siqueland & Lipsitt, 1966).

By the time they are 3 months old, infants show that they have surprisingly good memories. When a mobile over an infant's crib was attached by a ribbon to one of the baby's limbs, 3-month-old infants quickly discovered which arm or leg would move the mobile. Eight days later, the same infants were placed in the same situation, and they remembered which arm or leg to move—even though they were no longer attached to the mobile (Rovee-Collier & Hayne, 1987).

All in all, the research we have described challenges the view of the newborn as a "blank slate." It suggests that the infant enters the world prepared to perceive and recognize reality and to learn quickly the relations between events that are important for human development.

INDIVIDUAL DIFFERENCES IN TEMPERAMENT In discussing the capacities of the infant, we have emphasized ways in which infants are alike. Barring some sort of physical damage, all babies have similar sensory abilities at birth and can experience the same kinds of events around them. But babies differ markedly in their *temperament*. By temperament we mean a person's characteristic mood, sensitivity to stimulation, and energy level.

As early as the first weeks of life, infants show individual differences in activity level, responsiveness to change in their environment, and irritability. One infant cries a lot; another cries very little. One endures diapering or bathing without much fuss; another kicks and thrashes. One is responsive to every sound; another is oblivious to all but the loudest noises. Infants even differ in "cuddliness." Some seem to enjoy being cuddled and mold their bodies to the person holding them; others stiffen and squirm and do less body adjusting (Korner, 1973).

The traditional view has been that parents shape their children's behavior. Parents of a fussy baby, for example, tend to blame themselves for their infant's difficulties. But research with newborns makes it increasingly clear that some temperamental differences are innate, and that the relationship between parent and infant is reciprocal—in other words, the infant's

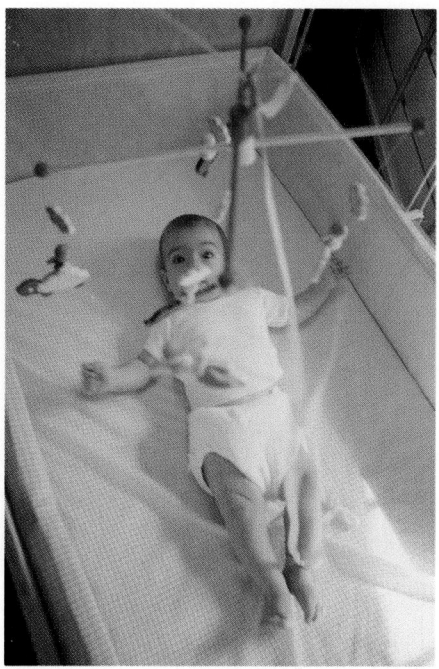

Early Learning *If a mobile is attached to an infant so that the infant's movements activate the mobile, the infant soon discovers this relationship and seems to delight in activating the mobile with the appropriate kick. Two-month-old babies can learn to do this, but soon forget. Three-month-old babies can remember the correct action over several days.*

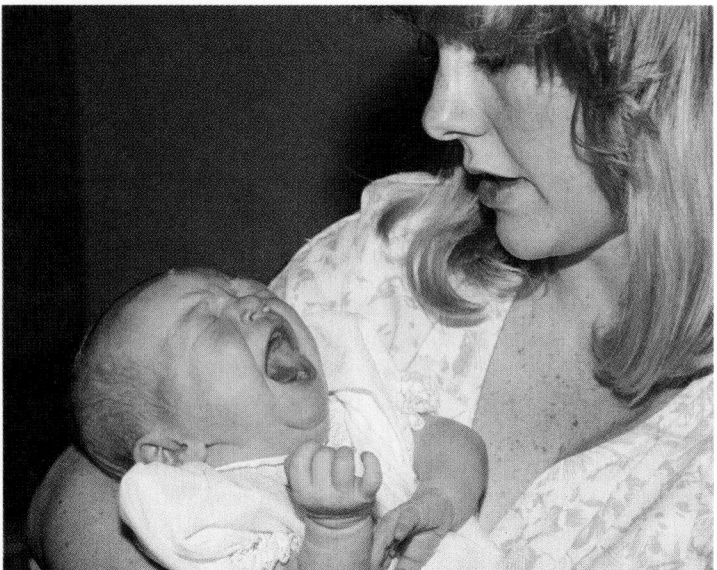

behavior also shapes the parent's response. An infant who is easily soothed, who snuggles and stops crying when picked up, increases the mother's feelings of competency and attachment. The infant who stiffens and continues to cry, despite efforts to comfort it, makes the mother feel inadequate and rejected. The more responsive a baby is to the stimulation provided by the parent (snuggling and quieting when held, attending alertly when talked to or played with), the easier it is for the parent and child to establish a loving bond.

Researchers do not assume that a child's temperament is unchangeable or immune to environmental influences. Temperamental differences observed in infants often persist to some degree throughout childhood; thus, babies with "difficult" temperaments are more likely than "easy" babies to have school problems later on (Riese, 1987; Thomas & Chess, 1977). But temperamental traits can also change with development: an easygoing infant may become a tantrum-throwing toddler. Inborn temperament predisposes an infant to react in certain ways, but temperament and life experiences interact to form personality. Still, an infant's temperament affects how parents and infant interact with one another, no matter how long that temperament persists.

Early Experience and Child Development

A child's development from an alert but fairly helpless newborn to a walking and talking 2-year-old progresses at an astonishing rate. As we noted earlier, the achievement of such physical skills as sitting, reaching for objects, crawling, and walking depends on the maturation of the muscles and the nervous system. All babies achieve these skills without being taught. But psychologists have long been interested in whether environmental conditions can accelerate or retard maturational processes.

Although no training is required for a child to walk at the appropriate time, a certain amount of environmental stimulation appears to be necessary. Children who are reared in institutions in which they are handled infrequently and are given little opportunity to move about will sit, stand, and walk much later than normal. One study of an orphanage in Iran found that only 42 percent of the children were able to sit without support at 2 years, and only 15 percent could walk unaided at age 4 (Dennis, 1960). Go back and contrast these percentages with the norms given for home-reared children in Figure 3-1. It should be emphasized that this particular orphanage provided a more impoverished environment than most. The care-givers had little education; they provided for the physical needs of the children but made no effort to play with or talk to them. Infants remained in their cribs all day except when being fed or changed. Older children were placed in a playpen for part of the day, but there were few toys to play with.

To determine whether increased stimulation and the opportunity to move about improve the development of motor skills, two psychologists tested 30 of the Iranian orphans on a scale measuring various aspects of infant development and then divided them into two groups. One group remained in their cribs as before. The other babies were taken to a playroom for an hour each day, propped into a sitting position, and allowed to play with a variety of toys. When the two groups were tested again a month later, the infants in the experimental group showed a marked gain in development compared with those who had remained in their cribs. So, although motor development is largely dependent on maturation, the experiences of being able to move about freely and to reach for interesting objects are also necessary.

These studies demonstrate that when opportunities for exercise and movement are greatly restricted, there is some retardation in motor development, but in most cases the retardation can be remedied by appropriate stimulation. A related question is whether special training can accelerate the development of basic motor skills. Some classic studies with identical twins in the 1920s and 1930s focused on this question (Gesell & Thompson, 1929; McGraw, 1935). Typically, one twin was given a lot of early practice on a particular skill (such as stair climbing). Later, the other twin was given a brief period of practice, and then the two twins were tested. In general, if the untrained twin had received even the briefest period of practice, the two performed almost equally well on the task. For the elementary motor skills, a small amount of practice later (when the muscles and nervous system are more mature) is as good as a lot of practice earlier.

More recent studies indicate that practice or extra stimulation can accelerate the appearance of motor behaviors to some extent. For example, newborn infants have a *stepping reflex*—if they are held in an upright position with their feet touching a solid surface, their legs will make stepping movements that are very similar to walking. A group of infants who were given stepping practice for a few minutes several times a day during the first two months of life began walking five to seven weeks earlier than babies who had not had this practice (Zelazo, Zelazo, & Kolb, 1972).

Long-Term Effects of Early Experience

How permanent are the effects of early stimulation or deprivation? As far as motor skills are concerned, early experiences probably do not have a lasting effect. Children from the Iranian orphanage who were adopted before the age of 2 quickly attained, and thereafter maintained, normal development (Dennis, 1973). Infants in an isolated Indian village in Guatemala are kept inside the family's windowless hut for the first year of life in the belief that sunshine and air will cause sickness. They have little opportunity to crawl about, and their parents seldom play with them. When these children are allowed to leave the hut, they are behind American children in physical skills. But they catch up, and by the age of 3 they are as well coordinated as other children (Kagan & Klein, 1973).

In other areas of development—language ability, intellectual skills, and emotional development—the effects of early deprivation appear to be more lasting. Children whose learning opportunities are restricted during the first 2 or 3 years of life—who are not talked to, read to, or encouraged to explore their environment—will be seriously behind in language and intellectual skills by the time they enter school and may never catch up.

The importance of a stimulating environment in the early years for intellectual development is illustrated by a classic study by Skeels and Dye (1939). A group of orphaned children whose development at about 2 years of age was so retarded that they were not considered adoptable was transferred to an institution for the mentally retarded. In this institution, in contrast to the overcrowded orphanage, each child was placed in the care of a mildly retarded older girl or young woman who served as a surrogate mother and spent great amounts of time playing with and talking to the child. In addition, the living quarters were spacious and well-equipped with toys. As soon as the children could walk, they began to attend a nursery school in which additional play materials and stimulation were provided. After a period of four years, this experimental group showed an average gain in intelligence of 32 IQ points; a group matched in age and intelligence that remained in the orphanage showed a *loss* of 21 points. A follow-up study over 20 years later found the experimental group still superior to the control group (Skeels, 1966). Most of the experimental group had completed high school (one-third had gone to college), were self-supporting, married, and had children of normal intelligence. Most of the control group, on the other hand, had not progressed beyond the third grade and either remained institutionalized or did not earn enough to be self-supporting.

Although the number of subjects in this study was small and the possibility of some innate differences between the experimental group and control group cannot be completely ruled out, the results are sufficiently impressive to indicate the importance of a stimulating early environment for later intellectual development. As we will see in the discussion of Head Start programs in Chapter 12, early intellectual stimulation can have a significant impact on school achievement and on performance in adult life.

COGNITIVE DEVELOPMENT

Although most parents are aware of the intellectual changes that accompany their children's physical growth, they would have difficulty describing the nature of these changes. The Swiss psychologist Jean Piaget studied children's cognitive development intensively. After many years of careful observation, he developed a theory of how children's abilities to think and to reason progress through a series of distinct stages as they mature (see Table 3-1).

Sensorimotor Stage

Noting the close interplay between motor activity and perception in infants, Piaget designated the first 2 years of life as the *sensorimotor stage*.

TABLE 3-1
**Piaget's Stages of Cognitive
Development** *The ages given are averages.
They may vary considerably depending on
intelligence, cultural background, and
socioeconomic factors, but the order of
progression is assumed to be the same for all
children. Piaget has described more detailed
phases within each stage; only a very
general characterization of each stage is
given here.*

STAGE	CHARACTERIZATION
1. Sensorimotor (birth–2 years)	Differentiates self from objects Recognizes self as agent of action and begins to act intentionally: for example, pulls a string to set a mobile in motion or shakes a rattle to make a noise Achieves object permanence: realizes that things continue to exist even when no longer present to the senses
2. Preoperational (2–7 years)	Learns to use language and to represent objects by images and words Thinking is still egocentric: has difficulty taking the viewpoint of others Classifies objects by a single feature: for example, groups together all the red blocks regardless of shape or all the square blocks regardless of color
3. Concrete operational (7–12 years)	Can think logically about objects and events Achieves conservation of number (age 6), mass (age 7), and weight (age 9) Classifies objects according to several features and can order them in series along a single dimension, such as size
4. Formal operational (12 years and up)	Can think logically about abstract propositions and test hypotheses systematically Becomes concerned with the hypothetical, the future, and ideological problems

During this period, infants are busy discovering the relationships between their actions and the consequences of these actions. They discover, for example, how far they have to reach to grasp an object, what happens when they push their food dish over the edge of a table, and that their hand is part of their body and the crib rail is not. Through countless "experiments," infants begin to develop a concept of themselves as separate from the external world.

An important discovery during this stage is the concept of *object permanence*: an awareness that an object continues to exist even when it is not present to the senses. If a cloth is placed over a toy that an 8-month-old is reaching for, the infant immediately stops and appears to lose interest. The baby seems neither surprised nor upset, makes no attempt to search for the toy, and acts as if the toy has ceased to exist (see Figure 3-4). In contrast, a 10-month-old will actively search for an object that has been hidden under a cloth or behind a screen. The older baby seems to realize that the object exists even though it is out of sight. He or she has attained the concept of object permanence, indicating that the baby possesses a *mental representation* of the missing object. But even at this age, search is limited. If the infant has had repeated success in retrieving a toy hidden in one place, he or she will continue to look for it in that spot even after watching an adult conceal it in a new location. The baby repeats the action that produced the toy earlier rather than looking for it where it was last seen. Not until about 1 year of age will a child consistently look for an object where it was last seen to disappear, regardless of what happened on previous trials.

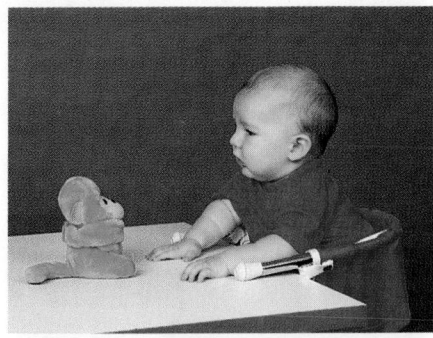

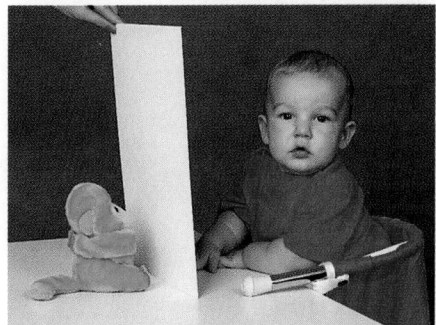

FIGURE 3-4
Object Permanence *When the toy is hidden by a screen, the infant acts as if it no longer exists. The infant does not yet have the concept of object permanence.*

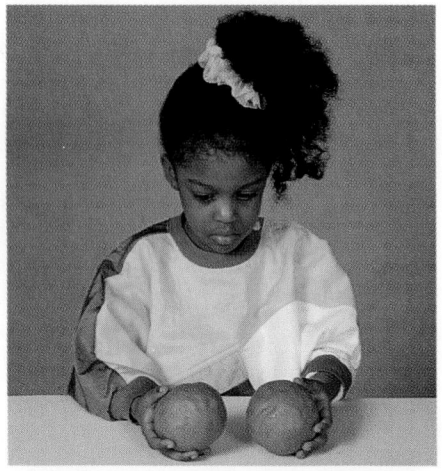

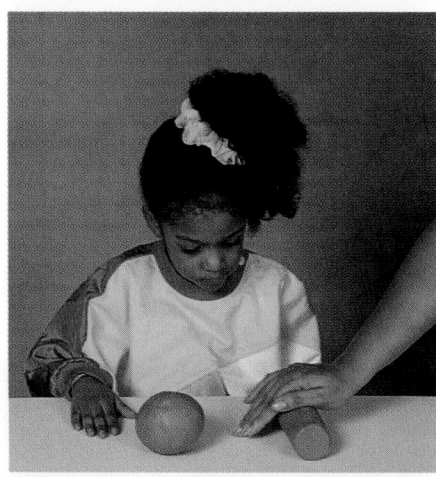

FIGURE 3-5
Concept of Conservation *A 4-year-old acknowledges that the two balls of clay are the same size. But when one ball is rolled into a long thin shape, she says that it has more clay. Not until she is several years older will she state that the two different shapes contain the same amount of clay.*

Preoperational Stage

By about 1½ to 2 years of age, children have begun to use language. Words, as symbols, can represent things or groups of things, and one object can represent (symbolize) another. Thus, in play a 3-year-old may treat a stick as if it were a horse and ride it around the room; a block of wood can become a car; one doll can become a mother and another, a baby.

Although 3- and 4-year-olds can think in symbolic terms, their words and images are not yet organized in a logical manner. Piaget calls the 2- to 7-years stage of cognitive development *preoperational,* because the child does not yet comprehend certain rules or *operations.* An operation is a mental routine for transposing information, and it is reversible, meaning that every operation has its logical opposite. Cutting a circle into four equal pie-shaped wedges is an operation because we can reverse the procedure and put the pieces back to form a whole. The rule that we square the number 3 to get 9 is an operation because we can reverse the operation and take the square root of 9 to get 3. In the preoperational stage of cognitive development, a child's understanding of such rules is absent or weak. Piaget illustrates this deficit by some experiments on the development of what he calls *conservation.*

As adults, we take conservation principles for granted: the amount (mass) of a substance remains the same when its shape is changed or when it is divided into parts; the total weight of a set of objects will remain the same no matter how they are packaged together; likewise, liquids do not change in amount when they are poured from a container of one shape to a container of another shape. For children, however, attainment of these concepts is an aspect of intellectual growth that requires several years.

In a study of the conservation of mass, a child is given some clay to make into a ball that is equal to another ball of the same material; after doing this, the child declares them to be "the same." Then, leaving one ball for reference, the experimenter rolls the other into a long sausage shape while the child watches. The child can plainly see that no clay has been added or subtracted. In this situation, children about 4 years old believe that the two objects no longer contain the same amount of clay: "The longer one contains more," they say (see Figure 3-5). Not until the age of 7 do the majority of children perceive that the clay in the longer object is equal in amount to that in the reference ball.

The same kind of experiment can be used to study the conservation of weight. For example, children who know that equal things will balance on a scale (they can test this with the two balls) are asked whether the sausage-shaped form will keep the scale arm balanced, as did the original ball. Conservation of weight is a more difficult concept than conservation of mass, and it comes a year or so later in development.

One reason why children younger than 7 have difficulty with conservation concepts is because their thinking is still dominated by visual impressions. A change in the appearance of the clay mass means more to them than less obvious qualities, such as weight. The young child's reliance on visual impressions is made clear by an experiment on the conservation of number. If two rows of checkers are matched one for one against each other, the 5- or 6-year-old will say the rows have the same number of checkers (see Figure 3-6). If the checkers in one row are brought closer together to form a cluster, the 5-year-old says there are now more checkers in the vertical row—even though no checkers have been removed. The visual impression of a long row of checkers overrides the numerical equality that was obvious when the checkers appeared in matching rows. In contrast, 7-year-olds assume that if

FIGURE 3-6
Conservation of Number *When the two rows of seven checkers are evenly spaced, most children report that they contain the same amount. When one row is then clustered into a smaller space, children under 6 or 7 will say the original row contains more.*

the number of objects was equal before, it must remain equal. At this age, numerical equality has become more significant than visual impression.

Operational Stage

Between the ages of 7 and 12, children master the various conservation concepts and begin to perform still other logical manipulations. They can order objects on the basis of a dimension, such as height or weight. They can also form a mental representation of a series of actions. Five-year-olds can find their way to a friend's house but cannot direct you there or trace the route with paper and pencil. They can find the way because they know they have to turn at certain places, but they have no overall picture of the route. In contrast, 8-year-olds can readily draw a map of the route.

Piaget calls this period the *concrete operational stage*: although children are using abstract terms, they are doing so only in relation to concrete objects—that is, objects to which they have direct sensory access. Not until the final stage of cognitive development, the *formal operational stage* that begins around age 11 or 12, are youngsters able to reason in purely symbolic terms.

In one test for formal operational thinking, the subject tries to discover what determines the amount of time that a pendulum will swing back and forth (its period of oscillation). The subject is presented with a length of string suspended from a hook and several weights that can be attached to the lower end. He or she can vary the length of the string, change the attached weight, and alter the height from which the bob is released.

Children still in the concrete operational stage will experiment by changing some of the variables, but not in a systematic way. Adolescents of even average ability will set up a series of hypotheses and proceed to test them systematically. They reason that if a particular variable (weight) affects the period of oscillation, the effect will appear only if they change one variable and hold all others constant. If this variable seems to have no effect on the time of swing, they rule it out and try another. Considering all the possibilities—working out the consequences for each hypothesis and confirming or denying these consequences—is the essence of what Piaget called formal operational thought. This ability to conceive of possibilities beyond what is present in reality—in other words, to think of alternatives to the way things are—permeates adolescent thinking and is related to the adolescent tendency to be concerned with philosophical and ideological problems and to question the way in which adults run the world.

Evaluation of Piaget's Stages

Piaget's theory provides a broad overview of cognitive development. It is the most comprehensive theory to date and has influenced much of the research on the way children think and solve problems. Most studies support Piaget's observations on the sequences in cognitive development, although the ages at which children reach the different levels vary considerably, depending on such factors as intelligence and experiences.

Newer, more sophisticated methods of testing the intellectual functioning of infants and preschool children indicate that Piaget underestimated their abilities. As we saw earlier, very young infants possess some intellectual abilities that they are unable to demonstrate under normal circumstances. And preschoolers are capable of handling concepts more complex than those of Piaget's preoperational stage, given appropriate testing conditions.

For example, if test conditions are carefully arranged in conservation experiments so that the children's responses do not depend on their language ability (their understanding of what the experimenter means by "more" or "longer"), then even 3- and 4-year-olds show some awareness of number conservation; they can distinguish between the number of items in a set and the way in which the items are spatially arranged (Gelman & Gallistel, 1978).

This and similar studies suggest that the quality of a child's thinking does not change dramatically from one stage to the next. Transition between stages of intellectual growth is gradual, involving a consolidation of earlier skills so they become automatic. Consider conservation of liquid. If the task is simplified in various ways (for example, by drawing the child's attention to both the height and the width of the containers), preschoolers are able to conserve. A 7- or 8-year-old, in contrast, hardly needs to glance at the containers. He or she *knows* that the quantity of liquid remains the same regardless of the shape of the container into which it is poured.

Recent research raises other questions about some of Piaget's ideas. For example, Piaget believed that early cognitive development depends on sensorimotor activities. He did not conceive of the possibility that infants' minds may be ahead of their motor abilities. He believed that infants do not recognize contingencies—that their own actions are making something happen—until at least 4 or 5 months, when they begin to have some control of arm movements. At this age, for example, they discover that hitting a rattle suspended above the crib makes an interesting noise, and they delight in repeating the movement. Recent studies show that infants as young as 2 months, who cannot manipulate objects with their hands, can still recognize when something they have done has had an effect on the environment. For example, if a mobile that can be operated by a pressure-sensitive pillow is attached to the crib, 2-month-old infants quickly learn to move their heads in a way that makes the mobile rotate. Moreover, after a few days of playing with the mobile, they begin to smile and coo at it (in advance of the normal time for this kind of emotional expression), suggesting that they are delighted by their ability to make something happen (Watson, 1983; Bahrick &

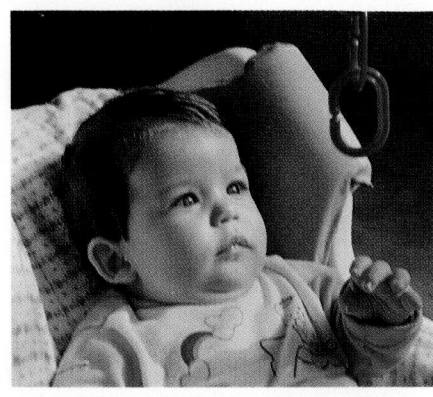

Watson, 1985). This study indicates that sensorimotor activities (moving about and handling objects) may not be essential for early cognitive development, although they undoubtedly play a major role.

Information-Processing Approaches

Instead of focusing on stages, some psychologists view cognitive development as a gradual increase in knowledge and in the ability to process information. The term "information-processing" refers to a variety of approaches to the study of memory and thinking that are concerned with the way the human mind attends to, represents, organizes, stores, and retrieves information. From a developmental perspective, the focus is on how the strategies children use for remembering and organizing information change with age.

Many of the differences in performance between an older and younger child may be due to differences in their ability to remember. The younger child may be unable to acquire certain concepts (such as conservation) because to do so would require holding more items of information in mind simultaneously than the child's current memory capacity permits.

Preschool children perform poorly on tests of memory, such as recalling a series of words they have heard or objects they have been shown. With increasing age, their performance improves. For example, if children hear a list of 15 simple words and are then asked to recall them, a 6-year-old will recall about 4 words; a 9-year-old, 5 words; and an 11-year-old, 7 words (Yussen & Berman, 1981). The poorer performance of the younger children may be due to a limited memory capacity, which increases as their brains mature. But preschool children, even as young as 2 or 3 years, can remember events, names of friends, and the location of familiar toys with surprising accuracy. It is the more deliberate kind of memory, a purposeful attempt to remember a series of things, that gives them trouble. Thus, it seems likely that what changes with age is the ability to organize knowledge and to use various strategies to improve memory.

For example, a common strategy for remembering is rehearsal; when you look up a telephone number you repeat it under your breath or in your mind until you dial. Children age 5 years or younger seldom use rehearsal spontaneously, while 8- to 10-year-olds usually do. Five-year-olds can be *taught* to rehearse, and when they use this strategy, they remember better. But if given a new problem and not reminded to rehearse, they will forget and go back to their original memory strategy (Flavell, 1970).

Organization is another aid to memory. If you have a list of things to remember, it helps to organize them into categories. A grocery list, for example, could be organized mentally into fruits, vegetables, canned goods, dairy products, meat, and so forth. This kind of "chunking" is helpful because it reduces the number of pieces of information you have to remember (see Chapter 8). Children as young as 2 show some indication of organizing things to be remembered, but they get steadily better at this strategy as they grow older (Goldberg, Perlmutter, & Myers, 1974). Again, if young children are taught a way of grouping things into sets, their memories improve, but they do not generalize the strategy very well to other situations (Brown et al., 1983).

So, a major aspect of cognitive development is acquiring more efficient strategies for remembering and extending these strategies to a wider range of situations. In addition, as children learn more about the world and about their native language, their increased knowledge provides them with richer associations between concepts, which in itself makes it easier to learn and remember (Ornstein & Naus, 1985).

As they mature, children also develop a greater understanding of how their minds work—what psychologists call *metacognition*. Metacognition is knowledge and control of one's own mental processes. It involves knowing how to use good strategies for learning and remembering, such as rehearsal and organization. It also involves knowing when you don't fully comprehend something. The ability to monitor one's own comprehension—to recognize whether or not one has understood something—is important for success in school. The difference between good students and poor students lies partly in their awareness of what they do and do not know.

PERSONALITY AND SOCIAL DEVELOPMENT

Our first social contacts are with the person who cares for us in early infancy, usually our mother. The manner in which the caregiver responds to the infant's needs—patiently, with warmth and concern, or brusquely, with little sensitivity—will influence the child's attitudes toward other people. Some psychologists believe that a person's basic feelings of trust in others are determined by experiences during the first years of life (Erikson, 1963; Bowlby, 1973). In the discussions that follow, we will use the word "mother" to refer to the primary caregiver, recognizing, nevertheless, that fathers and other family members sometimes assume this role.

Early Social Behavior

By 2 months of age, the average child will smile at the sight of its mother's face. Delighted with this response, mothers will go to great lengths to encourage repetition. Indeed, the infant's ability to smile at such an early age may play an important role in strengthening the mother-child bond. The first smiles tell the mother that the infant recognizes (loves) her—which is actually not true in any personal sense at such a young age—and encourages her to be even more affectionate and stimulating in response. The infant smiles and coos at the mother; she pats, smiles, and vocalizes in return, thereby stimulating an even more enthusiastic response from her infant. Each reinforces social responses in the other.

Infants all over the world begin to smile at about the same age, whether raised in a remote African village or a middle-class American home. This suggests that maturation is more important in determining the onset of smiling than are the conditions of rearing. The fact that blind babies smile at about the same age as sighted infants (in response to their parents' voices or touch rather than faces) indicates that smiling is an innate response (Eibl-Eibesfeldt, 1970).

By their third or fourth month, infants show that they recognize and prefer familiar members of the household—by smiling or cooing more when seeing these familiar faces or hearing their voices—but infants are still fairly receptive to strangers. At about 7 or 8 months, however, this indiscriminate acceptance changes. The infant begins to show wariness or actual distress at

The delight of an infant's smile.

the approach of a stranger (even while being held by the mother) and, at the same time, to protest strongly when left by the parent in an unfamiliar setting or with an unfamiliar person. Parents are often disconcerted to find that their formerly gregarious infant, who had always happily welcomed the attentions of a baby-sitter, now cries inconsolably when they prepare to leave—and continues to cry for some time after they have left.

"Stranger anxiety" increases dramatically from about 8 months of age until the end of the first year. Distress over separation from the parent—a distinct but related phenomenon—reaches a peak between 14 to 18 months and then gradually declines. By the time they are 3 years old, most children are secure enough in their parents' absence to be able to interact comfortably with other children and adults.

The waxing and waning of these two fears appears to be only slightly influenced by conditions of child rearing. The same general pattern has been found among American children reared entirely at home and those attending a day-care center, as well as in Israeli infants reared in a kibbutz, Indian children living in a Guatemalan village, and Bushmen children living in the Kalahari Desert (Kagan, 1979).

How do we explain these fears? Two factors seem to be important in both their onset and their decline. One is the growth of memory capacity. During the second half of the first year infants gain in their ability to remember past events and to compare past and present. This makes it possible for the baby to detect, and sometimes to fear, unusual or unpredictable events. The emergence of "stranger anxiety" coincides with the emergence of fears to a variety of stimuli that are unusual or unexpected; a weird-looking mask or a Jack-in-the-box that brings smiles to a 4-month-old often causes an 8-month-old to look apprehensive and distressed. As children learn that strangers and unusual objects are not generally harmful, such fears gradually diminish.

We noted in our discussion of cognitive development that object permanence, the awareness that an object exists even when it is not present, begins to develop at about 10 months. This ability to remember absent objects is weak at first; a 10-month-old infant will not search for a hidden object if there is a delay of 10 seconds. But by 12 to 14 months the infant will respond correctly with delays of a minute or more. It seems reasonable to assume that memory development is involved in "separation anxiety." The infant cannot "miss" the mother unless he or she can recall her presence a minute earlier and compare this with her absence. When mother leaves the room, the infant is aware that something is amiss. This awareness leads to anxiety and distress. As the child's memory improves for past instances of separation and return, the child becomes better able to anticipate the return of the absent parent, and anxiety declines.

The second factor is the growth of autonomy. One-year-olds are still highly dependent on care from adults, but children of 2 or 3 can head for the snack plate or toy shelf on their own. Also, they can use language to communicate their wants and feelings. Thus, dependency on caregivers in general, and on familiar caregivers in particular, decreases, and the issue of the parent's presence becomes less critical for the child.

Attachment

The infant's tendency to seek closeness to particular people and to feel more secure in their presence is called *attachment*. The young of other species show attachment to their mothers in different ways. An infant monkey clings to its mother's chest as she moves about; puppies climb over each other in their attempts to reach the warm belly of their mother; ducklings and baby chicks follow their mother about, making sounds to which she responds and going to her when they are frightened. These early, unlearned responses to the mother have a clear adaptive value: they prevent the organism from wandering away from the source of care and getting lost.

Psychologists at first theorized that attachment to the mother developed because she, as a source of food, satisfied one of the infant's most basic needs. But some facts did not fit. For example, ducklings and baby chicks feed themselves from birth, yet they still follow their mothers about and spend a great deal of time with them. The comfort they derive from the mother's presence cannot come from her role in feeding. A series of well-known experiments with monkeys showed that there is more to mother-infant attachment than nutritional needs (Harlow & Suomi, 1970).

ATTACHMENT IN MONKEYS Infant monkeys were separated from their mothers shortly after birth and placed with two artificial "mothers" constructed of wire mesh with wooden heads: the torso of one mother was bare wire; the other was covered with foam rubber and terry cloth, making it more cuddly and easy to cling to (see Figure 3-7). Either mother could be equipped to provide milk by means of a bottle attached to its chest.

The experiment sought to determine whether the "mother" that was always the source of food would be the one to which the young monkey would cling. The results were clear-cut; no matter which mother provided food, the infant monkey spent its time clinging to the terry-cloth, cuddly mother. This purely passive, but soft-contact mother was a source of security. For example, the obvious fear of the infant monkey placed in a strange environment was allayed if the infant could make contact with the cloth mother. While holding on to the cloth mother with one hand or foot, the monkey was willing to explore objects that were otherwise too terrifying to approach. Similar responses can be observed in 1- to 2-year-old children who are willing to explore strange territory as long as their mothers are close by.

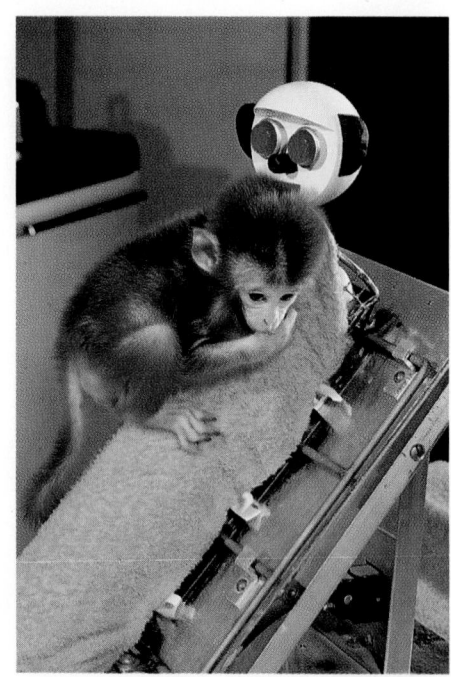

FIGURE 3-7
A Monkey's Response to an Artificial Mother *Although fed via a wire mother, the infant spends more time with the terry-cloth mother. The terry-cloth mother provides security and a safe base from which to explore strange objects.*

Further studies revealed additional features that infant monkeys seek in their mothers. They prefer an artificial mother that rocks to an immobile one, and they prefer a warm mother to a cold one. Given a choice of a cloth mother or a wire mother of the same temperature, the infant monkeys always preferred the cloth mother. But if the wire mother was heated, the newborns chose it over a cool cloth mother for the first 2 weeks of life. After that, the infant monkeys spent more and more time with the cloth mother.

The infant monkey's attachment to its mother is thus an innate response to certain stimuli provided by her. Warmth, rocking, and food are important, but *contact comfort*—the opportunity to cling to and rub against something soft—seems to be the most important attribute for monkeys.

Although contact with a cuddly, artificial mother provides an important aspect of "mothering," it is not enough for satisfactory development. Infant monkeys raised with artificial mothers and isolated from other monkeys during the first 6 months of life showed various types of bizarre behavior in adulthood. They rarely engaged in normal interaction with other monkeys later on (either cowering in fear or showing abnormally aggressive behavior), and their sexual responses were inappropriate. When female monkeys that had been deprived of early social contact were successfully mated (after considerable effort), they made poor mothers, tending to neglect or abuse their infants. For monkeys, interaction with other members of their species during the first 6 months of life appears to be crucial for normal social development.

ATTACHMENT IN HUMAN INFANTS   Although we should be careful in generalizing from research on monkeys to human development, there is evidence that the human infant's attachment to the mother serves the same functions: it provides the security necessary for the child to explore his or her environment, and it forms the basis for interpersonal relationships in later years. It has been hypothesized that the failure to form a secure attachment to one or a few primary persons in the early years is related to an inability to develop close personal relationships in adulthood (Bowlby, 1973).

A series of studies designed to investigate attachment in young children has revealed some interesting differences in the quality of the mother-child relationship (Ainsworth, Blehar, Walters, & Wall, 1978). The laboratory setup, called the *Strange Situation*, involves the following episodes:

1. The mother brings the child into the experimental room, places the child on a small chair surrounded by toys, and then goes to sit at the opposite end of the room.
2. After a few minutes, a female stranger enters the room, sits quietly for a while, and then attempts to engage the child in play with a toy.
3. The mother leaves the room, leaving her handbag on her chair as a sign that she will return.
4. The mother returns and engages the child in play while the stranger slips out.
5. The mother leaves again, and the child is left alone for three minutes.
6. The stranger returns.
7. The mother returns.

The child is observed through a one-way mirror during the entire sequence, and any number of different measures can be recorded: child's activity level and play involvement, crying and other distress signs, proximity to and attempts to gain attention of the mother, proximity to and willingness to interact with the stranger, and so on. From studying the reactions of 1- to

1½-year-olds in the Strange Situation, especially their behavior when reunited with their mothers, the investigators categorized children into three groups.

- *Securely Attached*   As long as the mother is present, these babies play comfortably with toys and are friendly to the stranger. They are clearly upset when the mother leaves; signs of distress range from fussing and visually searching for her to loud crying. When she returns, they go to her immediately, calm down after being held or hugged, and resume playing with the toys. About 65 percent of the children studied were classified in this category.
- *Insecurely Attached: Avoidant*   These babies pay little attention to the mother when she is in the room and do not seem distressed when she leaves. If distressed, they are as easily comforted by the stranger as the mother. They ignore the mother when she returns, or they may approach her tentatively, turning or looking away. About 25 percent of the sample fit into this pattern.
- *Insecurely Attached: Resistant*   These babies have trouble with the Strange Situation from the start. They stay close to their mothers and appear anxious when she is not at hand. They become very upset during the mother's absence and seem ambivalent toward her when she returns. They simultaneously seek and resist physical contact. For example, they may cry to be picked up and then squirm angrily to get down. They do not resume playing; instead they keep a wary eye on the mother. About 10 percent of the babies fit this category.

The first group of children, those who sought contact with their mothers on reunion, were labeled securely attached on the basis of observations in the home. They seemed generally more secure (cried less often, were more responsive to their mothers' verbal commands, and were less upset by their mothers' coming and going) than children who were either avoidant or resistant on reunion in the Strange Situation. The latter two groups showed signs of conflict in their relationship with their mothers. The avoidant babies seemed to dislike physical contact with her, while the resistant babies were clingy and seemed to demand more from their mothers than the mothers were willing to give (Ainsworth, 1979).

The investigators concluded, on the basis of these and other data, that all babies become attached to their mothers by the time they are 1 year old, but the quality of the attachment differs depending on each mother's responsiveness to her baby. Most babies show *secure attachment*, but some show *insecure attachment*. Insecure attachment is associated with insensitive or unresponsive mothering during the first year of life. The mothers of babies who show insecure attachment tend to respond more on the basis of their own wishes or moods than to signals from the baby. For example, they will respond to the baby's cries for attention when they feel like cuddling the baby but will ignore such cries at other times (Stayton, 1973). Mothers of infants who are securely attached are more responsive to their infants' needs, provide more social stimulation (talking to and playing with the infant), and express more affection (Clarke-Stewart, 1973). Looking at the two classifications of insecure attachment, resistant behavior appears to be related to maternal unresponsiveness and general lack of emotional involvement with the baby, while avoidant behavior is related to maternal hostility and rejection (Lyons-Ruth et al., 1987; Belsky, Rovine, & Taylor, 1984).

ATTACHMENT AND LATER DEVELOPMENT   An infant's attachment classification has been found to remain quite stable when retested in the Strange Situation several years later, unless the family experiences major changes in life circumstances (Thompson, Lamb, & Estes, 1982; Main & Cassidy, 1988). Stressful life changes are likely to affect maternal responsiveness to the infant that, in turn, would affect the baby's feelings of security.

There appears to be a relationship between the pattern of early attachment and the way that an infant copes with new experiences during the next few years. For example, in one study, 2-year-olds were given a series of problems requiring the use of tools. Some of the problems were within the child's capacity; others were quite difficult. The toddlers who had been rated as securely attached (at 12 months of age) approached the problems with enthusiasm and persistence. When they encountered difficulties, they seldom cried or became angry; rather, they sought help from the adults who were present. Those who had been rated earlier as insecurely attached behaved quite differently. They became easily frustrated and angry, seldom asked for help, tended to ignore or reject directions from the adults, and quickly gave up trying to solve the problems (Matas, Arend, & Sroufe, 1978).

Another study looked at the social behavior of nursery school children (age 3½ years) whose attachment relationships had been assessed at 15 months of age. The children rated as securely attached earlier tended to be the social leaders: they were active in initiating and participating in activities and were sought out by the other children. Their teachers rated them as self-directed and eager to learn. The insecurely attached children tended to be socially withdrawn and hesitant about participating in activities. Their teachers rated them as less curious about new things and less forceful in pursuing their goals. These differences were not related to intelligence (Waters, Wippman, & Sroufe, 1979).

These studies suggest that children who are securely attached by the time they enter their second year of life are better equipped to cope with new experiences and relationships. However, we cannot be certain that the quality of children's early attachments is directly responsible for their later competence in problem solving and social skills. Mothers who are responsive to their children's needs in infancy probably continue to provide effective mothering during early childhood—encouraging autonomy and efforts to cope with new experiences, yet ready with help when needed. Thus, the child's competency and social skills at age 3½ may reflect the current state of the parent-child relationship rather than the relationship that existed two years earlier.

Moreover, some critics believe that the child's behavior in the Strange Situation and his or her competency as a preschooler reflect characteristics of the child more than the quality of the mother-child relationship (Chess & Thomas, 1982; Lamb et al., 1984). As we noted earlier, some children appear to be more cautious and easily upset than others, almost from birth. Such children may find it hard to cope with new tasks and to form relationships, despite receiving quite adequate parenting.

Child-rearing practices may also affect the child's behavior in the Strange Situation. For example, Japanese child-rearing customs encourage a great deal of physical closeness between mother and child, little exposure to strange adults, and little experience in the sort of free play environment characteristic of the Strange Situation. As a result, Japanese babies tend to be anxious and wary throughout all episodes of the Strange Situation and are particularly upset when left alone—they become so distressed, in fact, that the experimenter usually curtails the episode when the child is alone (Takahashi, 1986).

Thus, at least some of the observed differences in infant attachment behavior that have been attributed to the mother's responsiveness may arise

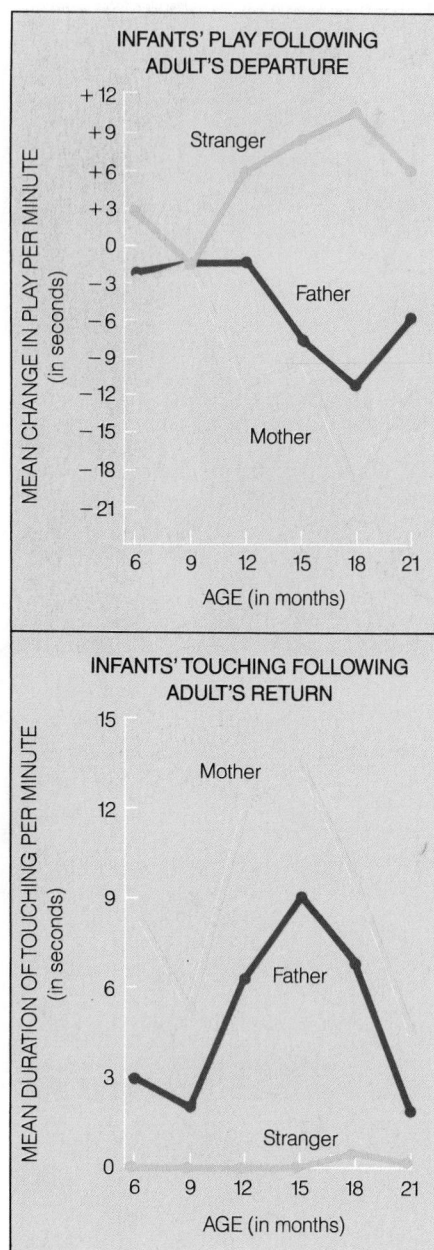

FIGURE 3-8
Age Changes in Infants'
Responses *Children (6 to 21 months)*
were observed in the Strange Situation with
either their mothers, fathers, or a stranger.
When the mother or father left briefly, the
child's play was disrupted, although such
responses to father's departure appeared at a
later age. When the stranger left, the child
played more actively, apparently feeling
more comfortable alone than with a
stranger. The return of either parent was
followed by a period of touching or clinging.

from temperamental predispositions of the child and cultural expectations that influence both mother and child. Nevertheless, it seems likely that early patterns of mother-child attachment have an important influence on later development.

ATTACHMENT TO FATHERS   Although an infant's primary attachment is to the person who provides most of the early care, other familiar persons are a source of security, too. Studies of the Strange Situation using the father indicate that infants react to his presence or absence in ways similar to those described for the mother, although attachment to the father seems to develop more slowly (Kotelchuck, 1976). For example, a 1-year-old usually cries and stops playing when the mother leaves him or her alone; such responses to the father's departure do not appear (on the average) until the child is 15 months old. In addition, the 1-year-old infant usually protests the mother's departure more vigorously than the father's and clings to her somewhat longer on reunion. These differences lessen with age (see Figure 3-8).

Fathers differ greatly in the amount of time they devote to child care. Children whose fathers are actively involved in their day-to-day care tend to be less disturbed when left alone with a stranger than children from families in which the mother provides most of the care (Kotelchuck, 1976). Yet babies also become attached to fathers who spend little time with them. Most of the brief interactions between fathers and their babies are play episodes. Fathers provide fun and excitement; they tend to engage in more physical, rough-and-tumble play than mothers. If given a choice of whom to play with, 18-month-old babies will choose their fathers more often than they will their mothers. But in times of stress, mothers are generally preferred (Clarke-Stewart, 1978).

INTERACTION WITH PEERS   Although a close relationship with a warm and responsive adult is important for a child's emotional development, interaction with other children plays a role, too. As we have seen, infant monkeys that are raised only with their mothers and that have no opportunity to play with other young monkeys do not develop normal patterns of behavior. When introduced to other monkeys later on, they may be abnormally fearful of contact or overly aggressive. They also show inappropriate sexual responses (Suomi, 1977).

In the normal course of development, an infant monkey spends the first 8 weeks of life exclusively with its mother. From then on, the young monkey spends more and more time swinging, chasing, and wrestling with its age-mates. From these early play activities, the young monkey learns to enjoy physical contact, to control aggression, and to develop the grasping and mounting responses that will lead to adult sexual behavior. Human children also learn many of their social skills by interacting with each other. They learn to give and take, to share in cooperative ventures, and to understand how another person feels. Peers become models to imitate as well as dispensers of rewards and punishments. By watching the actions of peers, children may learn a new skill (how to build a bridge with blocks) or the consequences of certain behaviors (aggressive children get into trouble).

A number of experiments have shown the influence of peer models on children's behavior. For example, 4- and 5-year-olds who watched one of their classmates being very generous in sharing some prizes were much more generous when their turn came to share than were children who had not watched the generous model (Hartup & Coates, 1967). As we will see in

Chapter 11, if a child watches a model being rewarded for certain behaviors, the child is more likely to imitate those behaviors than if he or she sees the model being punished.

The way in which other children respond to a child's behavior is also an important modifying influence. For example, selfishness that is accepted by doting parents may not be tolerated by the child's peers. Children reinforce certain actions in their playmates by approval and attention and punish others.

Acquiring Sex Roles

All cultures define ways in which men and women are expected to behave. Certain personality characteristics, work tasks, and activities are considered appropriate for males, and others are appropriate for females. The definitions of sex-appropriate behavior vary from culture to culture and may change over time within a culture. Certainly, our view of appropriate masculine and feminine behavior today is radically different from what it was 50 years ago. Women are no longer expected to be dependent, submissive, and noncompetitive; men are not criticized for enjoying such domestic activities as cooking and child care or for expressing artistic and tender feelings. Standards of dress and appearance have also become much more unisex—indeed, from a distance it is often difficult to determine whether the individual in jeans with medium-length hair is male or female. In all areas, earlier sex-role differentiations have been breaking down. Nevertheless, within any culture the roles of men and women and the behavior expected of them still differ.

SEX TYPING   *Sex typing* refers to the acquisition of characteristics and behaviors that a culture considers appropriate for females and males. Sex typing must be distinguished from *gender identity*, which is the degree to which one regards oneself as female or male. A girl may have a firm acceptance of herself as female and still not adopt all of the behaviors that her culture considers feminine or avoid all behaviors labeled masculine. A boy may identify with an artistic and sensitive father whose behavior does not fit the cultural masculine stereotype; even though the boy may be secure in his masculine identity, his behavior will not be strongly sex-typed.

Despite the current trend toward equality of the sexes, sex-role stereotypes are still prevalent in our culture. By *sex-role stereotypes*, we mean the belief that an individual should behave in certain ways or should show certain characteristics because that person is male or female. For example, it is difficult to distinguish newborn boys from girls when their diapers are on. Yet adults, viewing newborn infants through the window of a hospital nursery, believe that they can detect differences. Infants thought to be boys are described as robust, strong, and large-featured; girls are seen as delicate, fine-featured, and "soft" (Luria & Rubin, 1974). To cite another example, college students viewed a videotape of a 9-month-old infant's responses to a variety of situations. Some students were led to believe that the infant was a boy, and others that the infant was a girl. When the infant showed a strong reaction to a Jack-in-the-box, the reaction was more often labeled "anger" if the child was thought to be a boy and "fear" when the infant was thought to be a girl (Condry & Condry, 1976). In general, male infants are perceived by both parents as hardier and less in need of nurturance than female infants (Block, 1982).

Sex-typed behavior begins early in life.

CRITICAL DISCUSSION

Day Care: Effects on Children's Development

More and more women today are working outside of the home. Over half the mothers in the United States with children age 1 and under are employed, and the number is increasing. In view of the research on infant attachment and on the benefits of a stimulating environment during the early years, it is important to consider how this trend will affect future generations.

Working parents provide a variety of arrangements for their children's care. The majority leave their preschoolers at home to be cared for by a sitter or a relative while they work. The rest leave their young ones at someone else's home (to be cared for alone or with other children) or at day-care centers. Clearly, the effects of maternal employment on the child's development depend, to a large extent, on the quality of the substitute care.

Most of the research on day-care has been conducted at university-affiliated centers of high quality. Such centers are run by trained personnel in charge of small groups of children. They have good equipment, educationally stimulating activities, and they attempt to provide each child with emotional support. The experience of children in these centers is probably not representative of the experiences of day-care children in the United States as a whole. This limitation must be kept in mind when considering the reported findings.

In terms of intellectual development, children from middle-class families appear to do as well at a good day-care center as they do with parental care at home (Kagan, Kearsley, & Zelazo, 1978; Clarke-Stewart, 1982). Children from homes with poorly educated parents who have low incomes benefit intellectually from their day-care experience. The enrichment programs provided seem to prevent the decline in intellectual performance that often occurs after the age of 2 if such children remain at home (Ramey, 1981). Middle-class mothers are better educated than lower-class mothers; they are more effective teachers and provide greater intellectual stimulation for their children (Goldberg, 1978).

How does day-care affect the emotional ties between parents and their children? Critics of day-care have voiced concern that the repeated separations of mother and child that are a part of day-care could seriously interfere with the security of young children's attachment to their mothers. Most of the studies on this issue have compared the responses of home-reared children and day-care-reared children under the age of 2 in the Strange Situation. Some of these studies found no significant difference in attachment behavior between the two groups of children; day-care infants were as likely to become distressed as home-reared children when confronting a stranger or being separated from their mothers, and they clearly preferred their mothers to the day-care teachers as a source of comfort (McCartney & Phillips, 1988). Other studies reported that day-care toddlers did not stay as close to their mothers when playing in the Strange Situation or seek as much physical contact on reunion as did the home-reared children (Hock, 1980; Goossens, 1987). The latter finding has been interpreted by some to indicate that day-care children become more independent as part of their adaptation to daily separation (Clarke-Stewart, 1989). Others, however, believe that this behavior reflects an underlying doubt about the availability of the mother to meet the baby's needs and, thus, an insecure attachment (Belsky & Rovine, 1988). They suggest that an insecure avoidant pattern of attachment (in which the baby refuses to look at or approach the mother when reunited in the Strange Situation) is seen more often in infants who start day-care during the first year

By the time they are 2 years old, children identify themselves as male or female, and they evidence some awareness of sex-role stereotypes (see Table 3-2). They also begin to show sex-typed behavior in their choice of toys and play activities. In a day-care setting with a wide selection of toys available, male toddlers will spend more time playing with "masculine" toys (trucks, trains, tools) than with "feminine" toys (dolls, tea sets) or with neutral toys (chimes, blocks). Likewise, female toddlers will spend more time with "feminine" toys (O'Brien & Huston, 1985). As they grow older, boys make increasingly more sex-typed choices. But beginning about age 7, girls often decline in their preference for feminine activities and become increasingly interested in masculine ones (Huston-Stein & Higgins-Trenk, 1978). Boys are more sex-typed than girls: they show a preference for same-sex activities

of life and/or who experience frequent changes in caretakers (Schwartz, 1983).

The most clear-cut influence of day-care appears to be in the area of social development. Compared to home-reared children, those who attend day-care centers have been described as more self-sufficient, more cooperative with peers, and more comfortable in new situations. They are also less polite, less compliant with adults, and more aggressive (Clarke-Stewart & Fein, 1983). Some of these results may depend on the child-rearing attitudes of the parents and the teachers. Children attending day-care centers in the Soviet Union, Israel, and Sweden also show greater self-sufficiency and ease in social situations, but they do not act as aggressively or rudely as day-care children in the United States. Such behavior is strongly disapproved of by parents and teachers in those countries (Cole & Cole, 1989).

It should be emphasized again that all of these generally positive findings pertain to quality day-care centers. They undoubtedly do not hold for the many day-care facilities that provide for the child's physical needs but little more. Since experiences during the preschool years form the basis for later development, children who spend most of their waking hours under conditions that are not very stimulating lose a great deal. In view of the fact that the number of mothers of young children who are employed is steadily increasing, the provision of quality, affordable child care is a vital social issue.

The age of the child is important when deciding between individual care and group care for children of working mothers. Most experts recommend individual care in a home for the younger children (up to age 2 or 3) and group care for older preschool children (Scarr, 1984). Infants and toddlers need the consistent care of one person (turnover of personnel is frequent in most day-care centers). Older children can benefit from the intellectual stimulation and peer interaction provided by a good day-care center. In fact, 3- and 4-year-olds attending day-care centers show better social and intellectual development than do their age-mates cared for at home by sitters (Clarke-Stewart, 1982).

Day-care centers are one solution for working parents.

earlier than girls, and they continue to show such preference more strongly than girls at every age (Huston, 1983).

How do we account for this difference? For one thing, there is an unfortunate tendency for both sexes to view "masculine" activities as superior to "feminine" ones. In addition, the taboos in our culture against feminine behavior for boys are stronger than those against masculine behavior for girls. Conforming to the masculine stereotype seems to be largely a matter of avoiding any behavior regarded as "sissyish." Four- and five-year-old boys are more likely to experiment with feminine toys and activities (such as dolls, a lipstick and mirror, hair ribbons) when no one is watching than when an adult or another boy is present. For girls, the presence of an observer makes little difference in their choice of play activities (Hartup & Moore, 1963;

TABLE 3-2
Gender-Role Stereotypes in Young Children *Two- and three-year-olds were introduced to male and female paper dolls, Michael and Lisa, and then played a game in which they were asked to identify the doll that said or did certain things. The children's choices for a number of statements were tabulated. Many items were not sex-typed. On other items, boys and girls disagreed. The items listed in the table are the gender-role stereotypes on which both boys and girls agreed.* (After Kuhn, Nash, & Brucken, 1978)

Both boys and girls believe that girls
  like to play with dolls
  like to help mother
  talk a lot
  never hit
  say "I need some help"
  will grow up to be a nurse or a teacher

Both boys and girls believe that boys
  like to play with cars
  like to help father
  like to build things
  say "I can hit you"
  will grow up to be boss

Kobasigawa, Arakaki, & Awiguni, 1966). These findings suggest that young boys are interested in feminine activities but have learned to expect negative reactions for showing interest in them.

CAUSES OF SEX-TYPED BEHAVIOR   Parents clearly play a major role in sex typing. They serve as the child's first models of feminine and masculine behavior. Their attitudes toward their own gender roles and the way they interact with each other will influence the child's views. In addition, parents shape sex-typed behavior in numerous ways: by the toys they provide, the activities they encourage, and their responses to behaviors considered appropriate or inappropriate for the child's sex. From infancy on, most parents dress boys and girls differently and provide them with different toys. When they are old enough to be given household chores, girls are usually assigned such tasks as caring for younger children and helping with cleaning and food preparation. Boys are usually asked to do things outside the house, such as raking leaves or shoveling snow. Parents tend to emphasize independence, competition, and achievement in raising boys; girls are expected to be trustworthy, sensitive, and concerned with the welfare of others (Block, 1980).

Fathers appear to be more concerned with sex-typed behavior than mothers, particularly with their sons. They tend to react negatively (interfering with the child's play or expressing disapproval) when their sons play with "feminine" toys, whereas mothers do not. Fathers are less concerned when their daughters engage in "masculine" play, but they still show more disapproval than mothers do (Langlois & Downs, 1980).

Once children enter nursery school or kindergarten, their peers serve as models for imitation and also exert pressure toward sex-typed behavior. Parents who consciously seek to raise their children without the traditional sex-role stereotypes (by encouraging the child to engage in a wide range of activities without labeling any activity as masculine or feminine) are often dismayed to find their efforts undermined by peer pressure. Again, boys tend to experience more pressure than girls. Girls seem not to object to other girls playing with "boys'" toys or engaging in masculine activities. Boys, on the other hand, criticize other boys when they see them engaged in "girls'" activities. They are quick to call another boy a sissy if he plays with dolls, cries when he is hurt, or shows tender concern toward another child in distress (Langlois & Downs, 1980).

In addition to parental and peer influences, children's books and television programs play an important part in promoting sex-role stereotypes. Until recently, most children's books portrayed boys in active, problem-solving roles. They were the characters who displayed courage and heroism, persevered in the face of difficulty, constructed things, and achieved goals. Girls were usually much more passive. Female storybook characters were apt to display fear and avoidance of dangerous situations; they would give up easily, ask for help, and watch while someone else achieved a goal. Similar differences have been noted in the sex roles portrayed in children's television programs (Sternglanz & Serbin, 1974).

Attempts to modify children's sex-role stereotypes by exposing them to television programs in which the stereotypes are reversed (for example, the girls win in athletic events or a girl is elected president) have shown some success (Davidson, Yasuna, & Tower, 1979). But exposure to television cannot counteract real-life experiences. When 5- and 6-year-olds were shown films in which the usual sex-typed occupations were reversed (the doctors were women and the nurses were men), the children tended to relabel the occupations of the characters; when questioned about the films afterward and shown pictures of the actors, they were apt to identify the female actor as the nurse and the male actor as the doctor. Having a mother who worked outside the home or being exposed to female physicians and male nurses in real life increased the likelihood that the child would accept the less conventional roles (Cordua, McGraw, & Drabman, 1979).

Moral Reasoning

Understanding the values of society and regulating behavior accordingly are important aspects of development. Children's concepts of right and wrong change in interesting ways as they grow older. Most 5-year-olds say that it is wrong to lie, to steal, or to injure another person. But their comprehension of these statements changes with age. Only gradually do they begin to understand what kinds of statements are lies, how borrowing differs from stealing, and that injuring someone intentionally evokes greater blame than accidental injury.

Children's ability to make judgments about moral issues is related to their cognitive development. Older children are more capable of handling abstract concepts and making inferences about social relationships than are younger children. Although maturing cognitive abilities play a role in the development of a child's sense of right and wrong, other factors (the models provided by parents and peers, for example) are equally important. And children's moral behavior (their ability to inhibit actions that are disapproved of by society and to be concerned about the welfare of others) depends on much more than an understanding of moral problems.

Piaget was the first to investigate the development of moral reasoning (Piaget, 1932). He told stories to children of various ages and asked the children to make moral judgments about the fictional characters in the stories. For example, one story was about a boy who broke a teacup while trying to steal some jam when his mother was not home. Another boy broke a whole trayful of teacups, but it was just an accident; he was not doing anything wrong. Piaget asked his subjects, "Which boy is naughtier?" He presented a number of such stories varying the amount of damage done, as well as the character's intentions. Piaget found that preschool children tend to attribute blame according to the amount of damage done, regardless of intention. Older children take motives or intentions into account. A person with good intentions is not considered morally blameworthy, even if he or she does a great deal of damage.

The American psychologist Laurence Kohlberg extended Piaget's work on moral reasoning to include adolescence and adulthood (Kohlberg, 1969; Colby & Kohlberg, 1987). By presenting moral dilemmas in story form, he sought to determine if there are universal stages in the development of moral judgments. For example:

> In Europe, a woman was near death from a special kind of cancer. There was one drug that the doctors thought might save her. It was a form of radium that a druggist in the same town had recently discovered. The drug was expensive to make, but the druggist was charging 10 times what the drug cost him to make. He paid $400 for the radium and charged $4000 for a small dose of the drug. The sick woman's husband, Heinz, went to everyone he knew to borrow the money, but he could only get together about $2000, which is half of what it cost. He told the druggist that his wife was dying and asked him to sell it cheaper or let him pay later. But the druggist said, "No, I discovered the drug and I'm going to make money from it." So Heinz gets desperate and considers breaking into the man's store to steal the drug for his wife. (After Kohlberg, 1963, pp. 18–19)

Concern for others is one aspect of moral development.

TABLE 3-3
Stages of Moral Reasoning *Kohlberg believed that moral judgment develops with age according to the following stages.* (After Kohlberg, 1969)

LEVELS AND STAGES		ILLUSTRATIVE BEHAVIOR
LEVEL I	Preconventional morality	
Stage 1	Punishment orientation	Obeys rules to avoid punishment
Stage 2	Reward orientation	Conforms to obtain rewards, to have favors returned
LEVEL II	Conventional morality	
Stage 3	Good-boy/good-girl orientation	Conforms to avoid disapproval of others
Stage 4	Authority orientation	Upholds laws and social rules to avoid censure of authorities and feelings of guilt about not "doing one's duty"
LEVEL III	Postconventional morality	
Stage 5	Social-contract orientation	Actions guided by principles commonly agreed on as essential to the public welfare; principles upheld to retain respect of peers and, thus, self-respect
Stage 6	Ethical principle orientation	Actions guided by self-chosen ethical principles (that usually value justice, dignity, and equality); principles upheld to avoid self-condemnation

The subject is asked, "Should Heinz steal the drug? Why or why not? Would it be wrong or right? Why?" By analyzing the answers to a series of stories of this type, each portraying a moral dilemma, Kohlberg arrived at six developmental stages of moral judgment grouped into three levels (see Table 3-3). The answers are scored as appropriate to a certain stage, not on the basis of whether the action is judged right or wrong, but on the reasons given for the decision. For example, agreeing that Heinz should have stolen the drug because "If you let your wife die, you'll get in trouble" or condemning him for his actions because "If you steal the drug, you'll be caught and sent to jail" are both scored at Stage 1 of Level I. In both instances, the man's actions are evaluated as right or wrong on the basis of anticipated punishment.

Kohlberg believed that all children start at Level I, *preconventional morality*: they evaluate actions in terms of whether or not the actions avoid punishment or lead to rewards. His studies indicate that below age 10, preconventional responses are dominant. Some people never progress beyond this level. From age 10 on, responses at Level II, *conventional morality*, increase: youngsters begin to evaluate actions in terms of maintaining a good image in the eyes of other people. By age 13, a majority of moral dilemmas are resolved at Level II. In the first stage of this level (Stage 3), one seeks approval by being "nice." This orientation expands in the next stage (Stage 4) to include "doing one's duty," showing respect for authority, and conforming to the social order in which one is raised.

According to Kohlberg, many individuals never progress beyond Level II. He sees the stages of moral development as closely tied to Piaget's stages of cognitive development, and only those people who have achieved the later stages of formal operational thought are capable of the kind of abstract thinking necessary for *postconventional morality* at Level III. The highest stage of moral development (Level III, Stage 6) requires formulating abstract ethical principles and upholding them to avoid self-condemnation. Kohlberg reports that fewer than 10 percent of his adult subjects show the kind of "clear-principled" Stage-6 thinking exemplified by the following response of a 16-year-old to Heinz's dilemma: "By the law of society [Heinz] was wrong but by the law of nature or of God the druggist was wrong and the husband was justified. Human life is above financial gain. Regardless of who was dying, if it was a total stranger, man has a duty to save him from dying" (Kohlberg, 1969, p. 244).

A longitudinal study of moral reasoning that followed one group of 58 American boys over a 20-year period (from the time they were between 10 and 16 to age 30 and 36) found the developmental progression up through Stage 4 to be as Kohlberg predicted (Colby et al., 1983). And a shorter longitudinal study of boys in Turkey obtained similar results (Nisan & Kohlberg, 1982). In these studies no subject skipped a stage, and only 5 to 10 percent showed regression (that is, moved down a stage) in any of their responses. However, less than 10 percent of the subjects attained consistent Stage-5 reasoning, and none reached Stage 6. Consequently, postconventional morality (Level III) cannot be considered part of the normal or expected course of development. It represents a philosophical ideal rather than a developmental sequence through which most people pass. Progress beyond the conventional level of moral reasoning may depend on formal schooling or a particular cultural viewpoint (namely, one that emphasizes democracy and individual judgment).

Kohlberg viewed children as "moral philosophers" who develop moral standards of their own. These standards do not necessarily come from parents or peers; rather, they emerge from the cognitive interaction of children with their social environment. Movement from one stage to the next involves an internal cognitive reorganization rather than a simple acquisition of the moral concepts prevalent in their culture (Kohlberg, 1973).

Other psychologists disagree, pointing out that the development of a conscience, a sense of right and wrong, is not simply a function of maturing cognitive abilities. Children's imitation of their parents and the way in which they are rewarded or punished in specific situations will influence their moral views, as will the moral standards espoused by the children's peers and by characters on television and in books. Studies have shown that moral judgments can be modified by exposure to models: when children see adults reinforced for expressing a moral viewpoint based on principles different from their own, they may change their judgments up or down a level (Bandura & McDonald, 1963).

Thus, although there are obviously *age trends* in the way children think about moral issues, these may be partly a function of what parents teach and reinforce in children at different ages. Very young children may need the threat of punishment to keep them from doing something wrong ("If you hit your little sister, I will put you to bed *right now*"). As children mature, social sanctions become more effective ("If you hit your little sister, I will be very angry; good children don't hurt other people").

MORAL BEHAVIOR How well does *moral reasoning*—as measured by responses to moral dilemmas—correlate with *moral behavior*? Are youngsters who show advanced moral judgment more likely to resist temptation or behave unselfishly than those less advanced? There is clearly some relationship between moral thought and moral action. For example, juvenile delinquents show lower levels of moral judgment than law-abiding youngsters of the same age and intelligence. And people who attain higher moral levels on Kohlberg's dilemmas are more likely than low scorers to offer help to a person in distress (Blasi, 1980). But, in general, research relating Kohlberg's levels to behavior in specific situations—for example, whether a child will cheat on a test or behave unselfishly—has found low correlations (Mischel & Mischel, 1976; Rest, 1983).

Often we know how we *should* act; however, we may not do so when our own self-interest is involved. For example, children's judgment of "fairness" tended to be more mature and just in a hypothetical situation (how should candy bars be distributed among workers in a group?) than their reasoning was when the situation became real. Those who had suggested giving the most candy to the person who produced the most when the situation was hypothetical were apt to say that everyone should share equally when it came to dividing the candy among their own work group—particularly if they had been among the less productive workers. Some of those who had earlier advocated an equal division demanded the largest share in the real situation (Damon, 1977).

Moral conduct depends on a number of factors, in addition to the ability to reason about moral dilemmas. Two important factors are the ability to consider the long-range consequences of one's actions (rather than the immediate gain) and to control one's behavior. Equally important is the ability to empathize with other people—that is, to be able to put oneself in someone else's place. Understanding what another person is feeling motivates us to help.

ADOLESCENCE

Adolescence refers to the period of transition from childhood to adulthood. Its age limits are not clearly specified, but it extends roughly from age 12 to the late teens, when physical growth is nearly complete. During this period, the young person develops to sexual maturity, establishes an identity as an individual apart from the family, and faces the task of deciding how to earn a living.

A few generations ago, adolescence as we know it today was nonexistent. Many teenagers worked 14 hours a day and moved from childhood into the responsibilities of adulthood with little time for transition. With a decrease in the need for unskilled workers and an increase in the length of apprenticeship required to enter a profession, the interval between physical maturity and adult status has lengthened. Symbols of maturity, such as financial independence from parents and completion of school, are accomplished at later ages. Young people are not given many adult privileges until late in their teens; in most states, adolescents cannot work full-time, sign legal documents, drink alcoholic beverages, marry without parental consent, or vote.

A gradual transition to adult status has some advantages. It gives the young person a longer period in which to develop skills and to prepare for the future, but it tends to produce a period of conflict and vacillation between dependence and independence. It is difficult to feel completely self-sufficient while living at home or receiving financial support from one's parents.

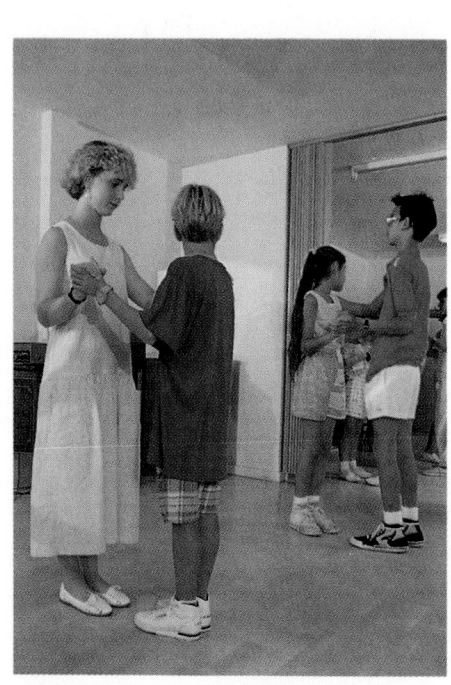

Adolescent variations in physical development are evident in junior high school.

Sexual Development

Puberty, the period of sexual maturation that transforms a child into a biologically mature adult capable of sexual reproduction, takes place over a period of about 3 or 4 years. It starts with a period of very rapid physical growth (the *adolescent growth spurt*) accompanied by the gradual development of the reproductive organs and *secondary sex characteristics* (breast development in girls, beard growth in boys, and the appearance of pubic hair in both sexes).

Menarche, the first menstrual period, occurs relatively late in puberty—about 18 months after a girl's growth spurt has reached its peak velocity. The first menstrual periods tend to be irregular, and ovulation (the release of a mature egg) does not usually begin until a year or so after menarche. A boy's first ejaculation typically occurs about 2 years after the growth spurt begins. The first seminal fluid does not contain sperm; the number of sperm and their fertility gradually increase.

There is wide variation in the age at which puberty begins and the rate at which it progresses. Some girls attain menarche as early as 11, others as late as 17; the average age is 12 years, 9 months. Boys, on the average, experience their growth spurt and mature 2 years later than girls (see Figure 3-9). They begin to ejaculate semen with live sperm sometime between age 12 and 16; the average age is 14½ years. The wide variation in the timing of puberty is strikingly apparent in seventh- and eighth-grade classrooms. Some of the girls may look like mature women with fully developed breasts and rounded hips, while others may still have the size and shape of little girls. Some of the boys may look like gangly adolescents, while others may look much as they did at the age of 9 or 10.

PSYCHOLOGICAL EFFECTS OF PUBERTY   How do the biological changes of puberty affect adolescents' behavior, attitudes, and emotions? An earlier view, and one still popularly held, considers adolescence as a period of "storm and stress," characterized by moodiness, inner turmoil, and rebellion. But current research indicates that puberty does not have the overwhelming psychological impact that clinicians and researchers once assumed it did. A recent study followed more than 300 young adolescents as they progressed from the sixth through the eighth grades, assessing them and their parents twice a year through interviews and psychological tests. The young people and their parents were assessed again during the adolescents' last year of high school (Petersen, 1988a). The timing of puberty was estimated by determining when each youngster's adolescent growth spurt peaked. The data indicate that puberty does have significant effects on body image, self-esteem, moods, and relationships with parents and members of the opposite sex. However, most of the adolescents made it through this period without major turmoil.

Being an early or late maturer (one year earlier or later than average) affected the adolescents' satisfaction with their appearance and their body image. Girls who were physically mature were generally less satisfied with their weight and appearance than their less mature classmates. The early maturing girls tended to be embarrassed by the fact that their bodies were more womanly in shape than those of their female classmates—particularly since the current standards for female attractiveness, as promoted by the media, emphasize the lean look.

The reverse pattern was found among boys. Those who were physically more mature tended to be more satisfied with their weight and their overall appearance than those who were less mature. In view of the importance of

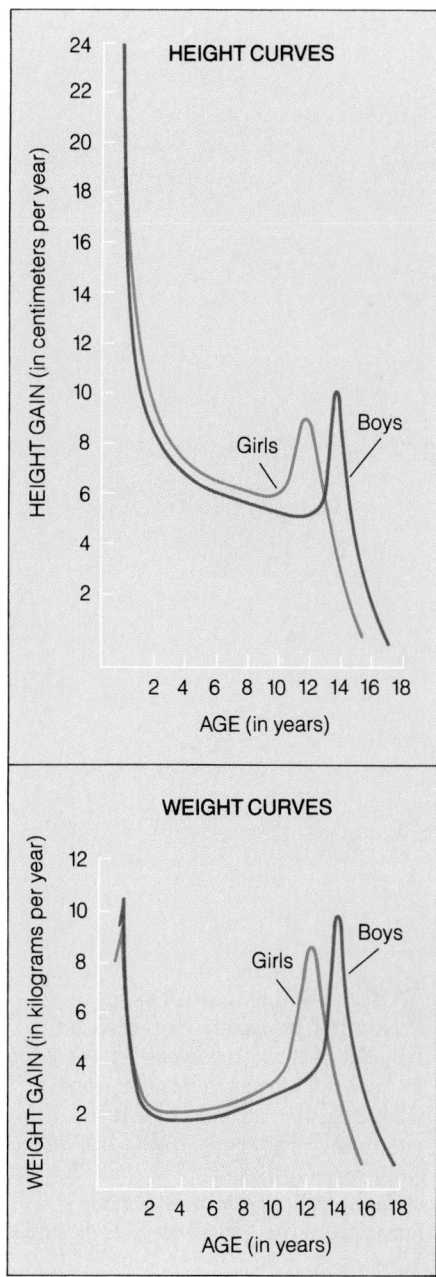

FIGURE 3-9
Annual Gains in Height and Weight *The period of most rapid growth comes earlier for girls than for boys. (After Tanner, 1970)*

strength and physical prowess in their peer activities, early maturing boys have an advantage over their less mature classmates.

Seventh- and eighth-grade boys who had reached puberty reported positive moods more often than their prepubertal male classmates did. While pubertal status was less clearly related to mood among girls in this study, other studies indicate that early maturing girls experience more depression and anxiety (Brooks-Gunn & Ruble, 1983) and have lower self-esteem (Simmons & Blyth, 1988) than their less mature classmates.

Puberty also affected the girls' relationship with their parents; girls who were developmentally advanced talked less with their parents and had less positive feelings about family relationships than did less developed girls. Although puberty brings some gains in rights and privileges for both sexes, it also brings increased limitations and restrictions for girls related to their emerging womanhood. Girls perceive more control by their families after menarche than before (Hill, 1988). In general, pubertal change appears to be a positive experience for boys but a negative one for girls.

Overall, the researchers found that early adolescence was relatively trouble-free for more than half of those studied. About 30 percent of the group had only intermittent problems. Fifteen percent were caught in a "downward spiral of trouble and turmoil"; emotional and academic problems that were evident in the eighth grade continued or worsened into twelfth grade. The authors of this study conclude that for youngsters whose lives are already troubled, the changes that come with early adolescence add further burdens so that their problems are likely to persist.

Sexual Standards and Behavior

The last 30 years have witnessed a revolutionary change in attitudes toward sexual activity in most Western societies. Views regarding premarital sex, homosexuality, extramarital sex, and specific sexual acts are probably more open and permissive today than they have been at any time in recent history. Young people are exposed to sexual stimuli in magazines, on television, and by the movies to a greater extent than ever before. Satisfactory birth control methods and the availability of abortions have lessened fear of pregnancy. All of these changes give the newly matured individual more freedom today. These changes produce more conflict, too, since guidelines for "appropriate behavior" are less clear-cut than they were in the past. In some families, the divergence between adolescent and parental standards of sexual morality may be great.

Have more permissive attitudes toward sex been accompanied by changes in actual behavior? At first, some experts maintained that young people were simply being more open about activities that their predecessors carried on in secret. But the data indicate definite changes in adolescent sexual behavior. A nationwide survey of 13- to 19-year-olds in 1973 found that 59 percent of the boys and 45 percent of the girls had engaged in sexual intercourse, most of them before age 16 (Sorensen, 1973). A 1976 survey found that 55 percent of the 19-year-old females interviewed had experienced sex (Zelnik & Kanter, 1977). Recent estimates remain about the same as those for 1976: more than half of all young men and women have experienced sexual intercourse by the age of 19 (Brooks-Gunn & Furstenberg, 1989).

Although strictly comparable data from earlier periods are not available, the studies conducted by Alfred Kinsey in the late 1930s and the 1940s found

TABLE 3-4
Premarital Intercourse of Teenage Females *The table gives the percentage of 19-year-old, unmarried females who reported having experienced sexual intercourse. The period of data collection is given below each study. This and other evidence indicate a marked increase in premarital sexual experience over the past 50 years.*

STUDY AND YEAR	PERCENTAGE REPORTING SEXUAL INTERCOURSE
Kinsey et al. (1938–1949)	18
Sorensen (1973)	45
Zelnik & Kantner (1976)	55

The AIDS epidemic has prompted schools to initiate programs that promote safe sex practices.

that fewer than 20 percent of the females and about 40 percent of the males reported experiencing sexual intercourse by the time they were 20 years old. Today's adolescents are engaging in sexual activity at an earlier age than their parents did. The change is most dramatic for girls, who are now as likely as boys to have intercourse while still in their teens (see Table 3-4).

Recently, with the advent of AIDS (Acquired Immune Deficiency Syndrome) and the spread of venereal disease and genital infections (such as herpes), there is some indication that the trends toward initiating sexual activity earlier in life and toward having many sexual partners may be slowing. A recent survey found that one in five Americans between the ages of 18 and 24 reported that AIDS had exerted a "large impact" on their lives (Steinbrook, 1987). Of those, 37 percent said that having sex with only one partner was the most practical precaution against AIDS, and 7 percent favored refraining from sexual activity altogether.

Adolescent–Family Conflict

The traditional view is that adolescents and their parents suffer from a "generation gap" and that adolescent–parent relationships are inevitably stormy. Indeed, so strong is this belief that parents often anticipate their youngsters' approaching puberty with great trepidation, and some parents with well-behaved teenagers worry that their offspring aren't developing properly.

Research indicates that there is no real evidence of a generation gap. Parents and their offspring have more similar values and attitudes than do adolescents and their friends (Lerner et al., 1975), and they agree about most important issues (Youniss & Smollar, 1985). Adolescents seek their parents' advice on important matters; they consult their peers about areas of "adolescent culture"—such as how to dress, what music to listen to, and so forth.

CRITICAL DISCUSSION

Teenage Pregnancy

The most troubling aspect of the increase in adolescent sexual activity is teenage pregnancy. The pregnancy rate for unmarried mothers under age 18 has been increasing rapidly in the United States since 1960. Close to one million American teenage girls become pregnant each year and many of them are under age 15 (Hayes, 1987).

An adolescent girl who became pregnant 25 years ago usually married or gave up her baby for adoption. Abortion was not a legal option until 1973, when the Supreme Court ruled that the procedure could not be outlawed. Today, if a girl chooses not to abort her pregnancy (and some 45 percent of teenagers decide to follow this course), chances are she will keep the baby and raise it as a single parent. A decade ago, more than 90 percent of babies born out of wedlock were given up for adoption; today, almost 90 percent are kept by the mother.

Children raising children has enormous social consequences. Teenage mothers often do not complete high school, and many live below the poverty level, dependent on welfare. Their infants have high rates of illness and mortality and often experience emotional and educational problems later in life. Many are victims of child abuse

The one on the left will finish high school before the one on the right.

Adolescent pregnancy isn't just a problem in America, it's a crisis. To learn more about a social issue that concerns all of us, write: Children's Defense Fund, 122 C Street, N.W., Washington, D.C. 20001.
The Children's Defense Fund.

A poster prepared by the Children's Defense Fund for its campaign aimed at reducing teenage pregnancies.

at the hands of parents too immature to understand why their baby is crying or how their doll-like plaything has suddenly developed a will of its own.

A 17-year follow-up study of some 300 adolescents born to teenage mothers indicates that teenage pregnancy can perpetuate a cycle of failure and early childbearing. Compared to the offspring of later childbearers, the adolescent children of teenage mothers had a much higher incidence of school failure, behavior problems, and delinquency. They were also more likely to engage in intercourse at an early age and to become pregnant or father a child (Furstenberg, Brooks-Gunn, & Morgan, 1987).

With effective methods of contraception more widely available than ever before, why do so many girls have unplanned pregnancies? Part of the explanation is ignorance about the process of reproduction. Surveys find that fewer than half of the teenagers questioned know when in the menstrual cycle a woman is most likely to become pregnant (Morrison, 1985). Since low pregnancy risk due to "time of month" is a common reason adolescents give for not using contraception, this lack of information has important consequences. Other frequently reported bits of misinformation include the

However, family conflict, in the form of nagging, squabbling, and bickering, *is* more common during adolescence than during any other period of development. The arguments usually involve mundane aspects of daily life, such as chores, schoolwork, messy rooms, blaring stereos, and curfews. More potentially explosive issues, such as sex, tend not to be discussed.

Parent–adolescent conflict is more intense during early and middle adolescence (roughly ages 11 to 15), and puberty appears to play a central role in triggering this conflict. If physical maturity comes early, so does the arguing and bickering; if it is late, the period of heightened tension is delayed (Steinberg, 1987). Adolescents of both sexes have significantly more conflicts with their mothers than with their fathers, probably because mothers are more involved in regulating the everyday details of family life (Smetana, 1988).

In order for an adolescent to become a competent and self-sufficient adult, the adolescent–parent relationship has to change. Young people need to have more autonomy and responsibility within the family as they proceed through adolescence, and the onset of puberty is an appropriate signal for the

belief that you cannot become pregnant from your first intercourse, or if you have sex infrequently, or if you do it standing up.

Fewer than one-third of sexually active adolescents regularly use a method of contraception. About 25 percent never use contraception; the rest do sometimes (Morrison, 1985). Among the reasons given for not using contraceptive methods (in addition to erroneous beliefs about the likelihood of getting pregnant) is the unplanned nature of intercourse and a generally negative attitude toward contraception. Many adolescents say that contraceptives are "embarrassing," "messy," or "unnatural" and interfere with the enjoyment of sex. A theme underlying these complaints is the feeling that being prepared robs sex of its spontaneity and is also somewhat immoral. Adolescent girls who are uncomfortable admitting their sexuality to themselves prefer to be swept away romantically rather than to prepare for sex: if you are swept away by passion, then you did not do anything wrong, but if you go on a date with a diaphragm or if you take the pill, then you are "looking for sex" and can be labeled promiscuous.

Teenage pregnancy rates in the United States are more than double that of any other industrialized country

(see figure). American adolescents are not more sexually active than their foreign peers. Nor is the difference due to higher abortion rates abroad; indeed, abortion rates are much higher here (Brozan, 1985). Most experts attribute the high rates of teenage pregnancy in

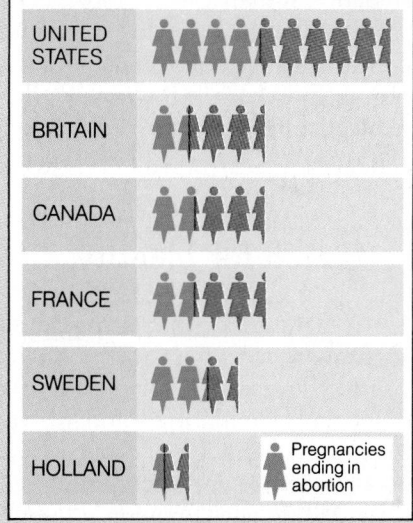

Teenage Pregnancy Rates *Each figure represents 10 pregnancies out of every 1,000 female teenagers. The teenage pregnancy rate in the United States (9.5 percent) is more than double that of any of the other countries.*

this country to a cultural ambivalence about teenage sex. The popular media—television, rock music, movies—encourage early experimentation with sex. They convey the message that to be sophisticated one must be sexually hip. Yet at the same time we are reluctant to acknowledge adolescent sexuality and to help teenagers prevent pregnancy. The television networks are unwilling to show programs dealing with contraception; many teenagers report that their parents are reluctant to discuss birth control; sex education in the schools is still a controversial topic; and high-school clinics that give birth control counseling and dispense contraceptives are even more controversial. Hopefully, the current concern about preventing the spread of AIDS will lead Americans to a more realistic approach to teenage sexuality.

In contrast are countries like Sweden where schoolchildren, starting at age 7, receive instruction in reproductive biology and by age 10 or 12 have been introduced to the various types of contraceptives. The aim is to demystify sex so that familiarity will make the child less likely to fall prey to unwanted pregnancy and venereal disease. These efforts appear to be successful; Sweden has one of the lowest rates of teenage pregnancy.

timing of this change. Although conflicts between adolescents and their parents often center on seemingly unimportant matters of taste ("This skirt is *not* too short to wear to school"; "All the kids wear their hair this way") and timing ("Why do I have to be home by 10:00?"; "Why can't I clean my room later?"), they represent an adolescent's attempts to exert more control over his or her life.

A study of parents' and adolescents' interpretations of issues that were sources of conflict showed that many were in areas that the adolescent thought should be under his or her personal jurisdiction, such as bedtime and curfew hours, appearance, and hygiene. The parents viewed the same issues in conventional or pragmatic terms, that is, according to social customs or as necessary for the efficient running of the family (Smetana, 1988). Parents are often torn between the necessity of maintaining the family system and allowing their child increasing jurisdiction over his or her own behavior. Adolescents are caught between two worlds, one of dependence, the other of responsibility. They would like the power to decide for themselves, but are not certain they want the increased responsibility that accompanies adult-hood. Their parents, who pay the bills and pick up the clothing tossed on the floor, demand that independence be matched by responsibility.

Most parents and teenagers manage to negotiate a new form of interde-pendence that grants the adolescent more autonomy, a more equal role in family decisions, *and* more responsibilities. If a youngster fails to negotiate a working relationship with his or her parents in early adolescence (if the parents are authoritative and unwilling to grant more autonomy), then con-flict may escalate into major difficulties by late adolescence (Petersen, 1988b). This may be why we commonly think of adolescent–parent conflict as typi-cal of the last years of high school with the already mature and fully grown student. Actually, as we have seen, conflict peaks much earlier, at puberty.

Parents who provide explanations for their decisions, who relax parental control during adolescence, and who employ a democratic structure of deci-sion making within the family give their offspring a sense of autonomy that reduces conflict and eases the transition to adulthood (Maccoby & Martin, 1983).

Search for Identity

A major task confronting the adolescent is to develop a sense of individ-ual *identity*, to find answers to the questions "Who am I?" and "Where am I going?" The search for personal identity involves deciding what is worth doing and formulating standards of conduct for evaluating one's own behav-ior and the behavior of others. It also involves feelings about self-worth and competence, as well as defining oneself with regard to sexuality and gender roles. While development of a self-image and gender identity starts in early childhood and continues throughout the life span, adolescence is a partic-ularly critical period. Compared to younger children, early adolescents (be-ginning about age 12) are highly self-conscious and have uncertain images of themselves.

An adolescent's sense of identity develops gradually out of the various identifications of childhood. Young children's values and moral standards are largely those of their parents; their feelings of self-esteem stem primarily from their parents' view of them. As youngsters move into the wider world of junior high school, the values of the peer group become increasingly impor-tant, as do the appraisals of teachers and other adults. Adolescents try to synthesize these values and appraisals into a consistent picture. If parents, teachers, and peers project consistent values, the search for identity is easier.

When parental views and values differ markedly from those of peers and other important figures, the possibility for conflict is great and the adolescent may experience what has been called *role confusion*: the adolescent tries one role after another and has difficulty synthesizing the different roles into a single identity. As one teenage girl put it,

> I'm fairly prim and proper at home because my parents have firm views about how a young girl should behave. At school, I toe the line too, although I don't hesitate to express my opinions. When I'm with my girl friends, I relax and act fairly silly; I'm usually the first to suggest smoking pot or doing something crazy. On a date, I tend to act helpless and docile. Who am I really?

In a simple society in which identification models are few and social roles are limited, the task of forming an identity is relatively easy. In a society as

In order to feel accepted, teenagers tend to conform to a group standard—listening to the same music, engaging in the same activities, and wearing the same clothing styles.

complex as ours, it is a difficult task for many adolescents. They are faced with an almost infinite array of possibilities of how to behave and what to do in life.

One way of approaching the identity problem is to experiment with various roles and ways of behaving. Many experts believe that adolescence should be a period of "role experimentation," in which the youngster can explore different ideologies and interests. They are concerned that today's academic competition and career pressures are depriving many adolescents of the opportunity to explore. As a result, some are "dropping out" temporarily to have time to think about what they want to do in life and to experiment with various identities. Youth movements, both political and religious, often provide temporary commitments to an alternative life-style; they give the young person a group to identify with and time to formulate a more permanent set of beliefs.

The search for identity can be resolved in a number of ways. Some young people, after a period of experimentation and soul-searching, commit themselves to a life goal and proceed toward it. For some, the *identity crisis* may not occur at all; these are adolescents who accept their parents' values without question and adopt adult roles that are consistent with their parents' views. In a sense, their identity crystallized early in life.

Still other young people adopt a *deviant identity*, one that is at odds with the values of their family and/or society. For example, a young man who has been pressured all his life to go to law school and join the family firm rebels and decides to become a ski bum. Some ghetto adolescents, rather than risk failure in attempting to rise above their social conditions, adopt a deviant identity and take pride in being "nothing."

Other adolescents go through a prolonged period of *identity confusion* and have great difficulty "finding themselves." In some cases, a defined identity may ultimately be worked out after much trial and error. In others, the person never has a strong sense of personal identity even as an adult. This is the individual who never develops commitments or loyalties.

An individual's personal identity, once formed, is not necessarily static. People can acquire new interests, ideas, and skills during their adult years

TABLE 3-5
Stages of Psychosocial
Development *Problems in relating to other people change with age. Erikson defines eight major life stages in terms of the psychosocial problems, or crises, that must be resolved. (After Erikson, 1963)*

STAGES	PSYCHOSOCIAL CRISES	FAVORABLE OUTCOME
1. First year of life	Trust versus mistrust	Trust and optimism
2. Second year	Autonomy versus doubt	Sense of self-control and adequacy
3. Third through fifth years	Initiative versus guilt	Purpose and direction; ability to initiate one's own activities
4. Sixth year to puberty	Industry versus inferiority	Competence in intellectual, social, and physical skills
5. Adolescence	Identity versus confusion	An integrated image of oneself as a unique person
6. Early adulthood	Intimacy versus isolation	Ability to form close and lasting relationships; to make career commitments
7. Middle adulthood	Generativity versus self-absorption	Concern for family, society, and future generations
8. The aging years	Integrity versus despair	A sense of fulfillment and satisfaction with one's life; willingness to face death

that may change their sense of who they are. Women who have been "house-wives" all of their adult lives, for example, often find a new sense of identity as their child-rearing duties diminish and they have time to develop new interests or pursue a career.

DEVELOPMENT AS A LIFELONG PROCESS

Development does not end with the attainment of physical maturity. It is a continuous process extending from birth through adulthood to old age. Bodily changes occur throughout life, affecting the individual's attitudes, cognitive processes, and behavior. The kinds of problems people must cope with change throughout the life span, too.

Erik Erikson has proposed a series of eight stages to characterize develop-ment from the cradle to the grave. He calls them *psychosocial stages* because he believes that the psychological development of individuals depends on the social relations established at various points in life. At each stage, there are special problems or crises to be confronted. Although these stages, shown in Table 3-5, are not based on scientific evidence, they call attention to the kinds of problems people encounter during life.

We touched on some of these problems earlier in the chapter, noting that an infant's feelings of trust in other people depend to a large extent on the way early needs are handled by the mother. During the second year of life (when children begin to move about on their own), they want to explore, to investigate, and to do things for themselves. To the extent that parents en-courage such activities, children begin to develop a sense of autonomy. They learn to control some of their impulses and to feel pride in their accomplishments. Overprotection—restricting what the child is permitted to do—or ridiculing unsuccessful attempts may cause the child to doubt his or her abilities.

During the preschool years (ages 3 through 5), children progress from simple self-control to an ability to initiate activities and carry them out. Again, parental attitudes—encouraging or discouraging—can make children feel inadequate (or guilty, if the child initiates an activity that the adult views as shameful).

During the elementary-school years, children learn the skills valued by society. These include not only reading, writing, and physical skills, but also the ability to share responsibility and to get along with other people. To the extent that efforts in these areas are successful, children develop feelings of competence; unsuccessful efforts result in feelings of inferiority.

Finding one's personal identity, as we noted in the last section, is the major psychosocial crisis of adolescence.

Early Adulthood

During the early adult years, people commit themselves to an occupation, and many will marry or form other types of intimate relationships. Intimacy means an ability to care about others and to share experiences with them. People who cannot commit themselves to a loving relationship—because they fear being hurt or are unable to share—risk being isolated. Studies indicate that an intimate relationship with a supportive partner contributes significantly to a person's emotional and physical health. People who have someone to share their ideas, feelings, and problems with are happier and healthier than those who do not (Traupmann & Hatfield, 1981).

The percentage of young adults who marry today is lower than it was a generation ago. More people are living alone or cohabitating without legalities. Nevertheless, most people do marry, and most of them do so during the early adult years. Individuals tend to look for marriage partners whose ethnic, social, and religious backgrounds match their own. Contrary to popular opinion, women appear to be less romantic in their approach to mate selection than men. Men tend to fall in love more quickly than women and to be satisfied with the qualities of their prospective mate. Women, on the other hand, are more practical and cautious in deciding whom to marry (Rubin, 1973).

This finding is not surprising when we consider that marriage traditionally requires a greater change in life-style for women than for men. A married man usually continues in his career, whereas a woman may be required to give up the relative independence of single life for the responsibilities of wife and mother. Egalitarian marriages, in which responsibilities are shared and the careers of both partners are given equal consideration, are increasing in number. Nevertheless, young working wives usually experience greater pressure as they struggle to meet the conflicting demands of home and work responsibilities than do their spouses. This difference is reflected in the fact that married women report more unhappiness with their lives than married men, although they are still happier than single women—both nevermarrieds and divorced women (Greeley, 1988).

The arrival of children brings added responsibilities and adjustments. The high divorce rate indicates that such adjustments are not easy in a society as complex as ours. More than 38 percent of all *first* marriages in the

United States end in divorce. Taking into account remarriages and divorces, about 40 percent of *all* marriages end in divorce.

A survey of 300 couples who had been happily married for 15 years or more provides some clues for a successful marriage. The most frequently named reason for an enduring and happy marriage was having a generally positive attitude toward one's spouse: viewing one's partner as one's best friend and liking him or her as a person. Among the characteristics that the partners liked in each other were qualities of caring, giving, integrity, and a sense of humor. In essence, they said, "I am married to someone who cares about me, who is concerned for my well-being, who gives as much or more than he or she gets, who is open and trustworthy and not mired down in a somber, bleak outlook on life" (Lauer & Lauer, 1985, p. 24). They also liked the fact that their spouses had changed and grown more interesting over the years.

Other elements important to a lasting marriage were a belief in marriage as a long-term commitment, agreement on common goals, and the ability to communicate with each other and to resolve problems calmly without venting anger. Surprisingly, sexual fulfillment was far down the list of reasons for a happy marriage. While most were generally satisfied with their sex lives, few listed it as a major reason for their happiness; those who were dissatisfied felt that sex was less important than understanding, friendship, and respect (Lauer & Lauer, 1985).

Middle Adulthood

For many people, the middle years of adulthood (roughly ages 40 to 65) are the most productive period. Men in their forties are usually at the peak of their careers. Women who are mothers have less responsibility at home because the children are growing up, and can devote more time to career or civic activities. This is the age-group that essentially runs society, in terms of both power and responsibility.

Erikson uses the term *generativity* to refer to a concern with guiding and providing for the next generation. Feelings of satisfaction in middle adulthood come from helping teenage children become adults, providing for others who need help, and seeing your contributions to society as valuable. Feelings of despair may come from the realization that you have not achieved the goals you set for yourself as a young adult. The may also come from the belief that what you are doing is not important.

Much has been written in the popular literature about the so-called "midlife crisis." Several longitudinal studies have reported that men in their early forties experience a period of emotional turmoil centered around conflicts about sexual relationships, family roles, and work values (Vaillant, 1977; Levinson, 1978). And a similar midlife crisis has been proposed for women (Sheehy, 1976). The transition to middle adulthood, according to this view, is a time of upheaval not unlike a second adolescence, during which life goals are reevaluated and questions such as "Who am I?" and "Where am I going?" become important again.

Many researchers question the concept of midlife crisis as a developmental stage that most people experience. They find little evidence that people in their forties report more symptoms of emotional distress than younger or older people (Costa & McCrae, 1980; Schaie & Willis, 1986a). And studies of how middle-aged women react to events such as menopause and children leaving home report that few perceive these changes as traumatic (Neugarten, 1968).

Middle age is often a time of transition. As people approach the midpoint in life, their view of the life span tends to change. Instead of looking at life in terms of time since birth, as younger people do, they begin to think in terms of years left to live. Having faced the aging or death of their parents, they begin to realize the inevitability of their own death. At this point, many people restructure their lives in terms of priorities, deciding what is important to do in the years remaining. A man who has spent his years building a successful business may leave it to return to school. A woman who has raised her family may develop a new career or become active in politics. A couple may leave their jobs in the city to purchase a small farm. While some people find this kind of reevaluation and change stressful enough to constitute a midlife crisis, most perceive it as a challenge rather than a threat.

The Later Years

Until recently, the years after 65 were called "old age." But our idea of what it means to be old, in terms of chronological age, is changing. This is true partly because the population of older people in the United States has increased dramatically, and partly because many people 65 and beyond do not act "old." It has been said that the attitudes and activities of a 70-year-old today are equivalent to those of a 50-year-old two decades ago. In essence, our society is getting older, but the old are getting younger.

People older than 65 now compose approximately 12 percent of the population, a percentage that is expected to approach 20 percent by the year 2020 (see Figure 3-10). Because of better medical care, improved diet, and increasing interest in physical fitness, more people are reaching the ages of 65, 75, and older in excellent health. Research has shown that aging does not mean inevitable physical and mental debility. Normal aging is a gradual process that brings some changes: slower reflexes, dimmer eyesight and hearing, decreased stamina. But the more extreme debilities that we associate with old age are the result of disease (such as Alzheimer's, which destroys mental and physical functioning); abuse of the body by improper diet or use of alcohol and cigarettes; and failure to keep physically and mentally active.

The belief that mental abilities decline with age has also been challenged by research findings. Elderly adults do not process information as quickly as younger people (Cerella, 1985), and they perform worse on some problem-solving tasks (Denny, 1980). But there is no evidence that the general ability to learn decreases with age (Schaie & Willis, 1986b). Even brief training can improve the problem-solving skills of older people (Willis, 1985). The number of individuals in their 60s and 70s who work under demanding schedules and make important decisions (such as judges, corporate heads, and political leaders) attests to the fact that cognitive abilities need not diminish with age.

This is the bright side of the picture; for some older people the later years are not so happy. Those who are in poor health find that declining physical strength limits their activities and debilitating illnesses make them feel helpless. Mandatory retirement, which brings idle hours to be filled, may lessen feelings of worth and self-esteem, especially in a society in which one's contributions are usually evaluated in economic terms. The death of a spouse, siblings, and friends can make life unbearably lonely.

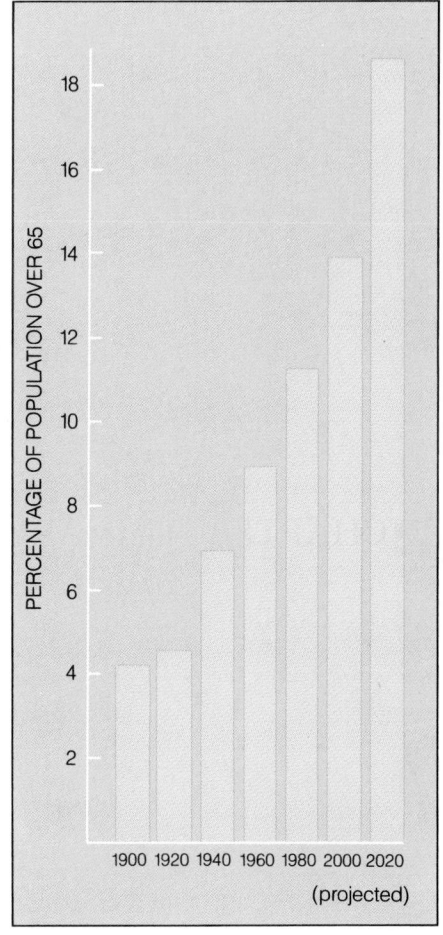

FIGURE 3-10

Aging America *The percentage of the population in the United States over age 65 is increasing at a steady rate and is projected to continue to increase. For babies born in the United States today, life expectancy is an unprecedented 71.1 years for a boy and 78.3 years for a girl. For those who survive through middle age, the expected length of life is dramatically longer. A man who reaches 65 today can expect to live until 79.5 and a woman, to 83.7.* (U.S. Bureau of the Census, 1989)

The increasing proportion of older people in the population has spurred the growth of research centers on aging, retirement villages, continuing education programs for senior citizens, and volunteer programs that involve older people in community life—as teacher aides, library assistants, and guards at school crossings, for example. Active involvement has proven to be a major factor in helping to maintain the physical and emotional health of the elderly.

Erikson's last psychosocial crisis—integrity versus despair—is concerned with the way a person faces the end of life. Old age is a time of reflection, of looking back on the events of a lifetime. To the extent that an individual has successfully coped with the problems posed at each of the earlier stages of life, he or she has a sense of wholeness and integrity, of a life well-lived. If the elderly person looks back on life with regret, seeing it as a series of missed opportunities and failures, the final years will be ones of despair.

⚡ CHAPTER SUMMARY

1. Human development is determined by a continuous interaction between *heredity or nature* (characteristics specified by the individual's genes) and *environment or nurture* (the experiences encountered while growing up in a particular family and culture). Genetic determinants express themselves through the process of *maturation*: innately determined sequences of growth or bodily changes that are relatively independent of the environment. Motor development, for example, is largely a maturational process because all children master skills such as crawling, standing, and walking in the same sequence and at roughly the same age.

2. Development proceeds in *orderly sequence* from simple behaviors to those that are more differentiated and complex. Two unresolved questions concern a) whether development should be viewed as a *continuous process* or a series of successive *stages* that are qualitatively different from each other, and b) the existence of *critical periods* during which specific experiences must occur for psychological development to proceed normally.

3. Infants are born with all sensory systems functioning; they are preprogrammed to learn about the world, and they show individual differences in *temperament*. Although the development of physical skills depends largely on maturation, restricted environments can delay motor development, and increased stimulation can accelerate it. Early deprivation or stimulation do not appear to have a lasting effect on motor skills, but development in other areas—language, intelligence, personality—may be permanently affected by early experiences.

4. Piaget's theory describes stages in *cognitive development*; proceeding from the *sensorimotor stage* (in which an important discovery is *object permanence*), through the *preoperational stage* (symbols begin to be used), and the *concrete operational stage* (*conservation* concepts develop), to the *formal operational stage* (hypotheses are tested systematically in problem solving).

5. Information-processing approaches view cognitive development as a gradual increase in knowledge, strategies for remembering (such as rehearsal and organization) and *metacognition* (knowledge and control of one's own mental processes).

6. Early social attachments form the basis for close interpersonal relations in adulthood. Insensitive mothering may undermine the child's trust and produce *insecure attachment*. Children who are *securely attached* are better able to cope with new experiences and to relate to others. Interactions with siblings and peers are also important for normal development.

7. *Sex typing*, the acquisition of those characteristics and behaviors society considers appropriate for one's gender, develops through parental, peer, and cultural influences. It is distinct from *gender identity*, which is the degree to which one regards oneself as male or female.

8. Children's concepts of right and wrong change as they mature. Younger children tend to evaluate moral actions in terms of anticipated *rewards* and *punishments*; with increasing age, *avoiding disapproval* and *conforming to social norms* become important. In the highest stage of moral reasoning, actions are evaluated in terms of one's own ethical principles. *Moral behavior* depends on a number of factors, in addition to the ability to reason about moral issues.

9. Although the age at which sexual maturation (*puberty*) begins varies widely, on the average girls mature two years earlier than boys. Compared to their pre-pubertal classmates, early maturing boys report greater satisfaction with their appearance and more frequent positive moods; early maturing girls, in contrast, report more depression, anxiety, family conflict, and dissatisfaction with their appearance than do their less mature classmates. Survey data indicate that adolescents today are engaging in sexual intercourse at an earlier age than did their parents.

10. In their search for personal *identity*, adolescents try to synthesize the values and views of people important to them (parents, teachers, and peers) into a cohesive self-portrait. When these values are not consistent, adolescents may experience *role confusion*, trying out one social role after another before finding a sense of individual identity.

11. Development is a lifelong process: individuals change both physically and psychologically, and they encounter new adjustment problems throughout life. Erikson's *psychosocial stages* describe problems, or crises, in social relations that must be confronted at various points in life. These range from "trust versus mistrust" during the first year of life, through "intimacy versus isolation" in early adulthood, to "integrity versus despair" as individuals face death.

▤ FURTHER READING

Comprehensive textbooks on development include Skolnick, *The Psychology of Human Development* (1986); Cole and Cole, *The Development of Children* (1989); Mussen, Conger, Kagan, and Huston, *Child Development and Personality* (6th ed., 1984); and Bee, *The Developing Child* (4th ed., 1985). For a discussion of the major approaches to the study of development see Miller, *Theories of Developmental Psychology* (2nd ed., 1989).

Books focusing on infancy include Osofsky (ed.), *Handbook of Infant Development* (2nd ed., 1987); Lamb and Bornstein, *Development in Infancy: An Introduction* (2nd ed., 1987); and Rosenblith and Sims-Knight, *In the Beginning: Development in the First Two Years* (1985). A four-volume overview of the major theories and research in child development may be found in Mussen (ed.), *Handbook of Child Psychology* (4th ed., 1983).

Cognitive Development (2nd ed., 1985) by Flavell presents a thorough introduction to this topic. *The Development of Memory in Children* (3rd ed., 1989) by Kail provides a very readable summary of research on children's memory. *Children's Thinking* (1986) by Siegler is written from the perspective of information-processing theories. For a brief introduction to Piaget, see Phillips, *Piaget's Theory: A Primer* (1981).

Kohlberg, *The Psychology of Moral Development: The Nature and Validity of Moral Stages* (1984) brings together many of Kohlberg's papers on moral development. For examples of children's thinking about important moral issues see Coles, *The Moral Life of Children* (1986).

The problems of adolescence are dealt with in Santrock, *Adolescence: An Introduction* (3rd ed., 1987); Kimmel and Wiener, *Adolescence: A Developmental Transition* (1985); and Youniss and Smollar, *Adolescent Relations with Mother, Father, and Friends* (1985).

For the later years, see Woodruff and Birren, *Aging: Scientific Perspectives and Social Issues* (2nd ed., 1983); and Perlmutter and Hall, *Adult Development and Aging* (1985).

Paul Klee. Phantom Perspective, 1920.
Watercolor and transferred printing ink on laid paper mounted on light cardboard.
9½" x 12". The Metropolitan Museum of Art, The Berggruen Klee Collection,
1984. (1984.315.22) 174

PART III

Consciousness and Perception

Chapter 4

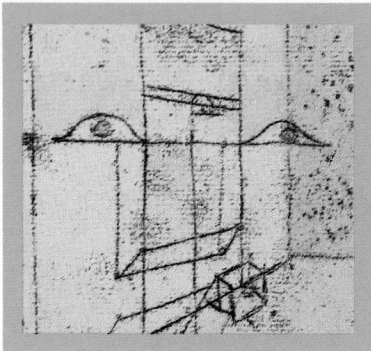

Detail, Phantom Perspective.

Sensory Processes

To survive, an organism must know the world around it, and much of this knowledge comes through the senses. Scholars have long wondered about the nature of our senses. How, for example, does the brain differentiate between seeing a light and hearing a sound? Democritus, a Greek philosopher in the fifth century B.C., proposed that we sense the external world by means of small, faint copies of objects that are transmitted from the objects to us (Jung, 1984). According to this theory, copies enter the body through the sense organs and are carried by spirits along hollow tubes to the sensory part of the brain, where they somehow evoke perceptual experiences. Because copies of lights and sounds are carried by different tubes, they evoke different sensations. Implausible as this theory sounds now, the notion of a copy dominated the study of sensation until the early eighteenth century. In 1825 Johannes Müller proposed a different kind of idea. He theorized that the stimuli reaching our sense organs produce responses in sensory nerves and that different nerves evoke different types of sensations. Thus the brain can differentiate light and sound (and other senses as well) because the different energies stimulate different nerves. This idea remains the cornerstone of the biological approach to sensation.

Cognitive and phenomenological approaches to sensation also have a long history. When Wilhelm Wundt founded the science of psychology in the late 1800s, his goal was to model the new field after the science of chemistry. He wanted to break down conscious experience into its basic elements and analyze how they relate. His method was *introspection*, which involved trained observers describing their own experience of some object or event. Introspection turned out to be too subjective (see Chapter 1), and the principal goal of sensory research increasingly shifted from the description of experience to the broader cognitive question of how stimuli are processed by the perceiver so as to guide behavior. Methods changed as well. Today, most experiments measure performance on a task for which the subject can be scored as right or wrong, rather than simply recording his or her introspections. The study of the cognitive aspects of sensory processes has proceeded in close association with the search for the biological basis of sensations. Thus the dominant approaches to the study of sensory processes are cognitive and biological, with phenomenological observation playing a secondary role (see Chapter 1).

Wundt made a sharp distinction between sensation and perception. A sensation was thought to be an indivisible unit of experience characterized by a quality and an intensity, such as "loud and high-pitched" or "bright red," while a perception was thought to be a combination of several sensations, such as the percept of a fire engine (Boring, 1942). Today, the same kind of distinction is often made, but it is not as sharp. Sensations are thought to be experiences elicited by simple stimuli (color patches, for example), while perceptions are thought to be occasioned by complex and often meaningful stimuli (fire engines, for example). Thus perception is still assumed to involve an *integration* of sensations, though the latter are no longer considered indivisible atoms of experience.

Another way to roughly distinguish between sensation and perception is to start with the notion that we have a system of processes for directly knowing the world around us. *Sensory processes* are those associated with the sense organs and peripheral levels of the nervous system, whereas *perceptual processes* are those associated with the higher levels of the nervous system.

This chapter deals with sensory processes. Chapter 5 deals with perceptual processes. The bulk of the present chapter is organized around the different senses: vision, hearing, smell, taste, touch (including pressure, temperature, and pain), and what are called the "body senses." Before beginning our analysis of individual senses, or *sensory modalities*, we will discuss some properties that are common to all senses.

COMMON PROPERTIES OF SENSORY MODALITIES

In this section we consider two properties common to all sensory modalities. The first one describes sensory modalities at a psychological level, while the second focuses on the biological level. (The Critical Discussion on decision processes in detection describes a third common property.)

Sensitivity

One of the most striking aspects about our sensory modalities is that they are extremely sensitive at detecting changes in the environment. To appreciate this fact, first we need a measure of sensitivity.

ABSOLUTE THRESHOLDS   In sensory psychology, the *stimulus* refers to one of the forms of physical energy to which we are sensitive (light for vision, pressure changes for hearing, and so on). A common way to assess the sensitivity of a sensory modality is to determine the minimum magnitude of a stimulus that can be reliably discriminated from no stimulus at all—for example, the weakest light that can be reliably discriminated from darkness. This minimum magnitude is referred to as the *absolute threshold*.

The procedures used to determine such thresholds are called *psychophysical methods*. In the commonly used *method of constant stimuli*, the experimenter first selects a set of stimuli with magnitudes varying around the threshold (for example, a set of dim lights varying in intensity). The stimuli are presented to a subject one at a time in random order, and the subject is instructed to say "yes" if the stimulus is detected and "no" if it is not. Each stimulus is presented many times, and the percentage of "yes" responses is determined for each stimulus magnitude.

Figure 4-1 is a graph of the percentage of "yes" responses as a function of stimulus magnitude (light intensity, for example). This graph is called a *psychometric function*. The data are typical of those obtained in this kind of experiment; the percentage of "yes" responses rises gradually as intensity is increased. The subject detects some stimuli with intensities as low as three units, yet occasionally fails to detect some with intensities of eight units. When performance is characterized by a psychometric function, the definition of a threshold must be somewhat arbitrary. Psychologists have agreed to define the absolute threshold as the value of the stimulus at which it is detected 50 percent of the time. Thus, for the data displayed in Figure 4-1, the absolute threshold is six units. (The absolute threshold may vary considerably from one individual to the next, and vary within an individual from time to time, depending on the person's physical and motivational state.)

As we mentioned earlier, our sensory modalities are extremely sensitive. See Table 4-1 for some estimates of absolute thresholds for human senses.

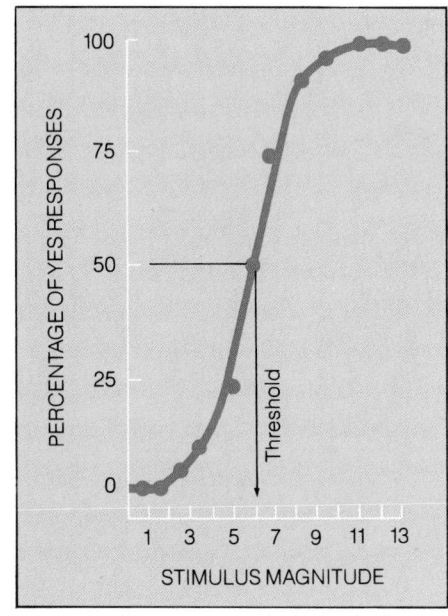

FIGURE 4-1
Psychometric Function *Plotted on the ordinate is the percentage of times the subject responds, "Yes, I detect the stimulus"; on the abscissa is the measure of the magnitude of the physical stimulus. Psychometric functions may be obtained for any stimulus dimension.*

SENSE	THRESHOLD
Vision	A candle flame seen at 30 miles on a dark, clear night
Hearing	The tick of a watch at 20 feet under quiet conditions
Taste	One teaspoon of sugar in 2 gallons of water
Smell	One drop of perfume diffused into the entire volume of six rooms
Touch	The wing of a fly falling on your cheek from a distance of 1 centimeter

TABLE 4-1
Absolute Thresholds *Approximate values of absolute thresholds for various sense modalities.* (After Galanter, 1962)

What is most noticeable about these thresholds is how low they are—that is, how sensitive the corresponding modality is. This is particularly true for vision. A classic experiment by Hecht, Shlaer, and Pirenne (1942) demonstrated that human vision is virtually as sensitive as is physically possible. The smallest unit of light energy is a *quantum*; Hecht and his colleagues showed that a person can detect a flash of light that contains only 100 quanta. Furthermore, they showed that only 7 of these 100 quanta actually contact the critical chemicals (molecules) in the eye that are responsible for translating light into vision, and that each of these 7 quanta affects a different molecule. The critical receptive unit of the eye is therefore sensitive to the minimal possible unit of light energy.

DETECTING CHANGES IN INTENSITY   Psychologists have also studied our ability to detect *changes* in intensity. As we will see, how much change is needed in order for us to detect a difference depends on the original intensity of the stimulus.

Just as there must be a certain minimum stimulus before we can perceive anything, so there must be a certain difference between two stimulus magnitudes before we can reliably distinguish one from the other. For instance, two tones must differ in intensity by a certain amount before one is heard as louder than the other; they must also differ in frequency by a certain amount before one is heard as different in pitch than the other. The minimum difference in stimulus magnitude necessary to tell two stimuli apart is called the *difference threshold* or the *just noticeable difference*. Like the absolute threshold, the just noticeable difference is defined statistically. In the method of constant stimuli, it is the amount of change necessary for a subject to detect a difference between two stimuli on 50 percent of the trials.

An experiment to determine a just noticeable difference, or *jnd* for short, proceeds as follows. A spot of light (standard) is flashed, and above it another smaller spot of light (increment) is flashed for a shorter duration. The standard spot is the same on every trial but the increment spot varies in intensity from trial to trial. The subject responds "yes" or "no" to indicate whether or not the increment spot seems more intense than the standard. If the subject can discriminate an intensity of 51 watts in the increment spot of light from a standard of 50 watts on 50 percent of the trials, then the jnd is 1 watt under these conditions.

The size of the jnd critically depends on the intensity of the standard. In an experiment in which the intensities of both the standard and the increment flash varies, the more intense the standard, the larger the jnd. The results of such an experiment are shown by the curved function in Figure 4-2.

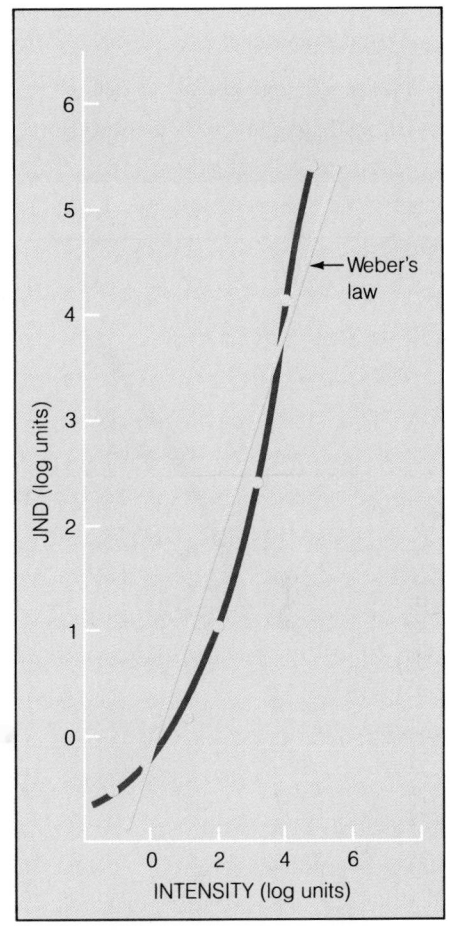

FIGURE 4-2
Jnd for Light *Here the subject's task was to detect the difference between a flash of intensity I and this same flash plus light of intensity ΔI. The jnd (measured in logarithmic units) was determined at several different intensities (also measured in logarithmic units). The graph shows that the size of the jnd increases with intensity in a way that corresponds only roughly to Weber's law. In other cases, Weber's law holds more accurately.* (After Geisler, 1978)

TABLE 4-2
Weber's Constant *Approximate values of Weber's constant for various stimulus dimensions.*

STIMULUS DIMENSION	WEBER'S CONSTANT
Sound frequency	.003
Sound intensity	.15
Light intensity	.01
Odor concentration	.07
Taste concentration	.20
Pressure intensity	.14

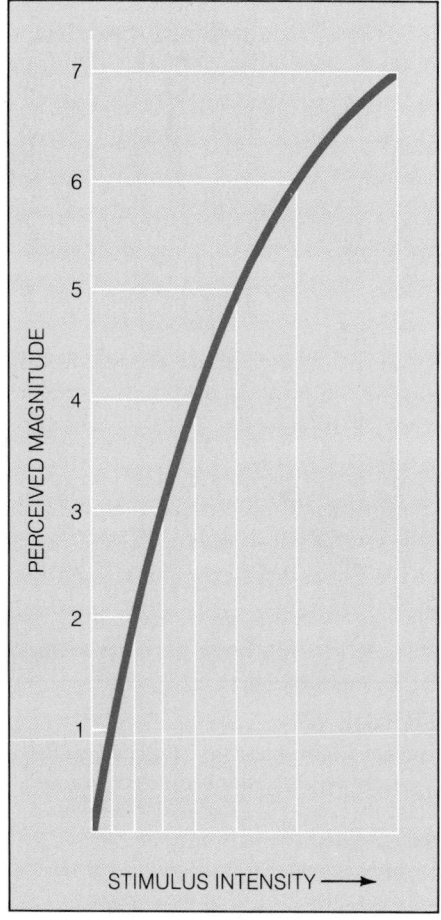

FIGURE 4-3
Fechner's Law *As the physical intensity of a stimulus increases, our perception of it increases rapidly at first, and then more slowly.*

In 1834 Ernst Weber, a German physiologist, first determined that the more intense the stimulus is to begin with, the larger the change must be for the subject to notice it. He measured jnds for intensity for several senses, including vision and hearing. He noted that a jnd increased with the intensity of the standard, and proposed that the jnd is a constant fraction of stimulus intensity (*Weber's law*). For example, if a jnd is 1 at an intensity of 50, it will be 2 at 100, 4 at 200, and so forth (the jnd always being 0.02 of the intensity of the standard in this example). This relation between the intensity of a standard and a jnd may be written as

$$\frac{\Delta I}{I} = k$$

where I is the intensity of the standard, ΔI is the increase in the intensity for a jnd, and k is *Weber's constant* (0.02 in our example). Weber's law does not give a precise account of the data in Figure 4-2 (see the straight line in the figure), but does provide a very good approximation. This is true in general. Values of Weber's constant for different modalities are given in Table 4-2. The smaller the constant, the more sensitive we are to a change in intensity in that modality.

Soon after Weber proposed his law, it was generalized by Gustav Fechner (1860), a German physicist. Fechner assumed not only that a jnd is a constant fraction of stimulus intensity, but also that one jnd is perceptually equal to any other jnd. (The latter assumption means that the perceived magnitude of a stimulus is simply the number of jnds it is above the absolute threshold.) From these two assumptions, Fechner derived the relation that the perceived magnitude of a stimulus, P, is proportional to the logarithm of its physical intensity; that is,

$$P = c \log I.$$

This relation is known as *Fechner's law*. To see what it tells us, suppose $c = 1$. Then, doubling I, say from 10 to 20 units, increases P only from 1 to approximately 1.3 units. Hence, doubling a light's intensity does not double its perceived brightness (a 100-watt bulb does not look twice as bright as a 50-watt bulb), doubling a sound's intensity does not double its perceived loudness, and so on for smell, taste, touch, and the other senses. More generally, as the physical intensity of a stimulus increases, its perceived magnitude increases rapidly at first, and then more and more slowly (see Figure 4-3). Like Weber's law, Fechner's law is only an approximation; modern researchers have proposed many variations on it to fit a wide variety of experimental results (Stevens, 1957). Nevertheless, the logarithmic relation has been useful in many practical applications of sensory psychology.

Sensory Coding

FROM RECEPTORS TO THE BRAIN   The brain has a formidable problem in sensing the world. Each sense responds to a certain kind of stimulus—light energy for vision, mechanical energy for audition and touch, chemical energy for smell and taste. But the brain understands none of this. It speaks only the language of electrical signals associated with neural discharges. Somehow, each sensory modality must first translate its physical energy into electrical signals, so that these signals can eventually make their way to the brain. This translation process is called *transduction*, and it is accomplished by specialized cells in the sense organs, called *receptors*. The receptors for vision, for instance, are located in a thin layer on the inside of the eye; each visual receptor contains a chemical that reacts to light, and this reaction triggers a series of steps that results in a neural impulse. The receptors for audition are fine hair cells located deep in the ear; the vibrations in the air that are the stimulus for sound succeed in bending these hair cells, which results in a neural impulse. Similar descriptions apply to the other sensory modalities.

A receptor is a specialized kind of nerve cell or *neuron* (see Chapter 2), and once activated, it passes its electrical signal to connecting neurons. The signal travels up the spinal cord until it reaches its receiving area in the cortex, with different receiving areas for different sensory modalities. Somewhere in the brain—perhaps in the cortical receiving area, perhaps elsewhere—the electrical signal results in a sensory experience. Thus when we experience a touch, the experience is "occurring" in our brain, not in our skin. However, the electrical impulses in our brain that directly mediate the experience of touch are themselves caused by electrical impulses in touch receptors that are located in the skin. In this way, our sensory systems relate external events to subjective experience.

CODING INTENSITY AND QUALITY   In every sensory modality, we experience both the *intensity* of the stimulus and the *quality* (or nature) of the stimulus. For example, when we see a saturated red, we experience the quality of redness at an intense level; when we hear a faint, high-pitched tone, we experience the quality of the pitch at an un-intense level. The receptors and their neural pathways to the brain must therefore code both intensity and quality.

Researchers who study these coding processes need a way of determining which specific neurons are activated by which specific stimuli. The usual means is to record from single cells in the receptors and neural pathways to the brain while the subject is presented various stimuli. A typical *single-cell recording* experiment is illustrated in Figure 4-4. This is a vision experiment, but the procedure is similar for experiments that test other senses. An animal (in this case a monkey) is placed in a device that holds its head in a fixed position. The animal is anesthetized so it does not feel pain, and its eyes are prevented from moving. Facing the animal is a screen on which various stimuli can be projected. A thin wire (microelectrode), insulated except at its tip, is inserted into a selected area of the visual cortex through a small hole drilled in the animal's skull. The electrode is positioned so that it will pick up the electrical responses of a single neuron while the animal's eyes are being stimulated. These tiny electrical signals are amplified and displayed on an oscilloscope, which converts the electrical signals into a graph of the changing electrical voltage. Most neurons emit a series of nerve impulses that appear on the oscilloscope as vertical spikes. Even in the absence of a stimulus, many cells will respond at a slow rate (*spontaneous activity*). If a stimulus is presented to which the neuron is sensitive, a fast train of spikes will be seen. The electrode can be moved to test different neurons.

With the aid of single-cell recordings, researchers have learned a good deal about how sensory systems code intensity and quality. The primary means for coding the intensity of a stimulus is in terms of the rate of neural

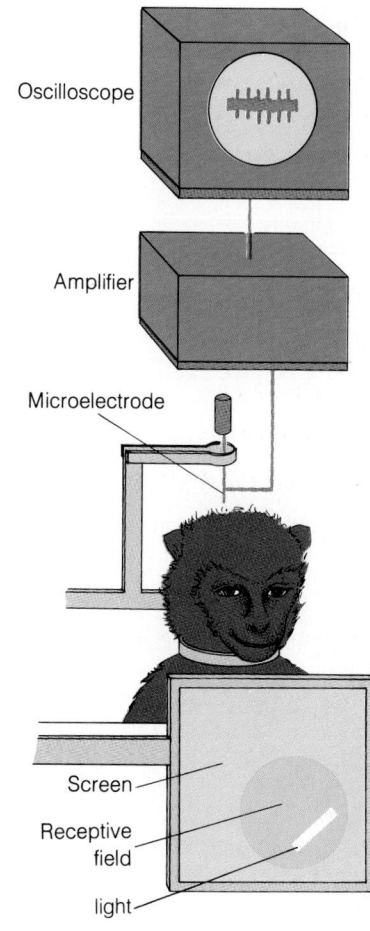

FIGURE 4-4
Single-Cell Recording *An anesthetized monkey is placed in a device that holds its head in a fixed position. A stimulus, often a flashing or moving bar of light, is projected onto the screen. A microelectrode implanted in the visual system of the monkey monitors activity from a single neuron, and this activity is amplified and displayed on an oscilloscope.*

CRITICAL DISCUSSION

Decision Processes in Detection

The notion of an absolute threshold dates back to the early 1800s. The key idea is that an absolute threshold is a fixed, sensory barrier; above the threshold people can detect a stimulus; below it they cannot. (This seemingly all-or-none property suggests that a threshold *should* be defined as the value of the stimulus that can be detected 100 percent of the time. The reason why the threshold is *in fact* defined by 50 percent detection is that on any trial of an experiment, numerous factors can be less than optimal: the sense organ may not function perfectly, the subject's attention may wander, and so on.) The idea of a threshold as a fixed barrier implies that what subjects do in experiments is report whether or not the stimulus passed the threshold. Detailed research on this issue, however, indicates that rather than observers simply reporting whether or not a stimulus crossed a fixed barrier, they are instead making a relatively complex decision about whether their sensory experience is due to a stimulus or to random perturbations in their sensory system.

PROBLEMS WITH THRESHOLDS
Researchers have long been aware of certain difficulties in establishing thresholds. To illustrate the problem, suppose we want to determine the likelihood that a subject will detect a weak auditory signal. On each trial of an experiment, the auditory signal is presented and the subject indicates whether or not she heard it. Suppose that on 100 such trials the subject reported hearing the signal 89 times. How should this result be interpreted? Because the subject knows that the same signal will be presented on each trial, and because she will often be uncertain whether to respond "yes" or "no" on a given trial, she may unconsciously tend toward "yes" answers to impress the experimenter with her ability. To deal with this problem, experimenters introduce *catch trials* (on which there are no signals) to see how the subject will respond.

The following results are typical of a subject's performance in an experiment involving several hundred trials, 10 percent of which were catch trials.

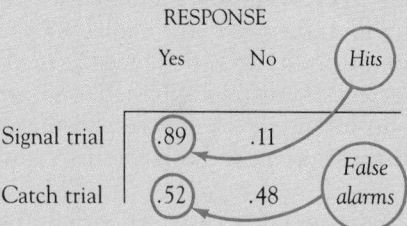

These results represent the proportion of times the subjects answered "yes" or "no" when the signal was or was not presented. For example, on 89 percent of the trials on which a signal was presented, the subject said "yes." We refer to this as the probability of a *hit*. The probability of a hit is a kind of measure of an absolute threshold: if it is around .5 (50 percent), the stimulus is at threshold, whereas if the probability is greater than .5 the stimulus is above threshold, whereas if the probability is "yes" on a trial in which no signal was presented, the response is called a *false alarm*. In the example, the probability of a false alarm is .52. This result suggests that even a zero stimulus can cross the threshold, which seems at odds with the idea of an absolute threshold.

The notion of a threshold runs into more problems when we do an experiment that varies the percentage of catch trials. Suppose that the subject is tested for several days with the same signal but with the percentage of catch trials varied from day to day. Results of an experiment in which the percentage of catch trials ranged from 10 to 90 percent are given in the table to the right. These data show that hits and false alarms both decrease as the proportion of catch trials increases. Presumably, with more catch trials, subjects come to *expect* trials with no signals, and accordingly are biased to say "no." Given that expectancy affected the probability of a hit, it follows that expectancy can affect the absolute threshold. But again, this is at odds with the idea that a threshold is fixed and with the idea that it is a purely sensory barrier. Results like these have led to an alternative theory of how people detect sensory stimuli.

THEORY OF SIGNAL DETECTION
The alternative theory is referred to as the *theory of signal detection*. It assumes that there is always some random activity or *noise* in sensory systems; hence, *there is no such thing as a zero stimulus*. A person in a detection task is always in the position of deciding whether the sensory activity experienced is more likely to be due to a presented signal than to random noise in his or her sensory system. Thus, the task of detecting weak stimuli requires a decision process, rather than simply reporting whether or not a sensory barrier has been passed.

Two factors affect the decision that must be made. One factor is the subject's *sensitivity* to the stimulus—

Hits and False Alarms *The table presents data on the relationship between hits and false alarms as the percentage of catch trials is increased.*

PERCENT CATCH TRIALS	HITS	FALSE ALARMS
10	.89	.52
30	.83	.41
50	.76	.32
70	.62	.19
90	.28	.04

how well he can hear a faint tone or see a dim light. The other factor is the subject's *criterion*—how willing he is to say "yes." The subject's sensitivity is assumed to be influenced by the intensity of the stimulus, while his criterion is influenced by expectancies. In particular, a subject's criterion will be lower when a stimulus is expected than when it is not (Green & Swets, 1966).

According to the theory of signal detection, one can get separate measures of a subject's sensitivity and criterion by plotting on the same graph the hit and false-alarm probabilities obtained in an experiment. We have plotted the probability of hits and false alarms from the table in the upper graph of the figure. Note, for example, that the point on the graph farthest to the right is for data obtained when 10 percent of the trials were catch trials; referring to the table, we see the hit probability plotted on the ordinate is .89 and the false-alarm probability on the abscissa is .52. When all five points are plotted, an orderly picture emerges. The points fall on a symmetric, bow-shaped curve. While every point on this curve reflects a different perfor-

mance (different hit and false-alarm probabilities), these differences reflect only the criterion and not the subject's sensitivity. Thus, if we performed other experiments with the same signal but different percentages of catch trials, the hit and false-alarm probabilities would differ from those in the table but would fall somewhere on this curve. This curve is called the *receiver-operating-characteristic curve* (or ROC curve for short) because it measures the operating characteristics of a person receiving signals.

Points along the same ROC curve indicate changes in criteria, while different ROC curves indicate changes in sensitivity. The points that are plotted in the upper graph in the figure are for a particular signal intensity. When the signal is more intense, sensitivity is greater and the ROC curve arches higher; when the signal is weaker, sensitivity is less and the ROC curve is closer to the diagonal line. The curvature of the ROC curve is therefore determined by the subject's sensitivity, and the measure used for the curvature is called d'. The lower graph in the figure gives ROC curves for values of d' ranging from 0 to 2. Thus, hit and false-alarm probabilities can be converted into a d' value that measures the subject's sensitivity to a particular signal. Manipulating the percentage of catch trials may affect hits and false alarms for a fixed signal, but the various probabilities will fall on an ROC curve corresponding to a particular d' value (Egan, 1975).

Given this view of detecting signals, we need to reinterpret the threshold measurements obtained in other experiments. From the perspective of the theory of signal detection, a threshold is defined as the stimulus intensity at which d' has a particular value, such as 1. Nevertheless, the older methods for determining thresholds remain convenient indicators of sensitivity.

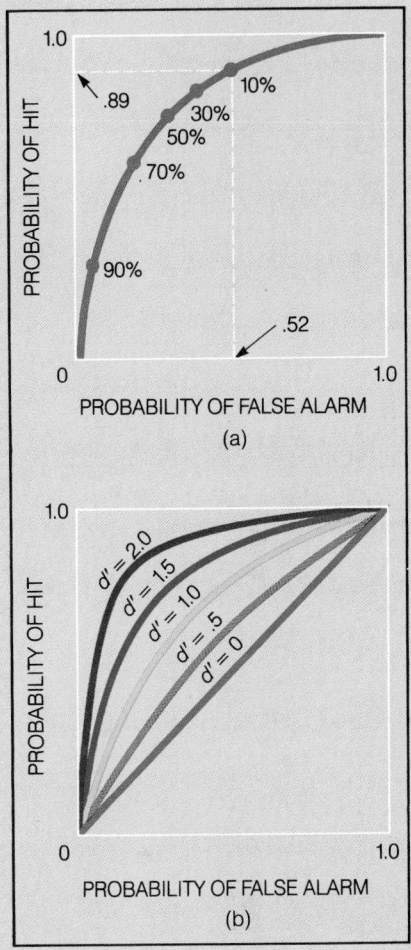

Plotting ROC Curves from Data (*a*) *A plot of the same data from the table in the form of an ROC curve. The percentages on this curve indicate the percentages of catch trials.* (*b*) *ROC curves for several different values of* d'. *The more intense the signal, the higher the value of* d'; *the* d' *value for the data in the table is 1.18.*

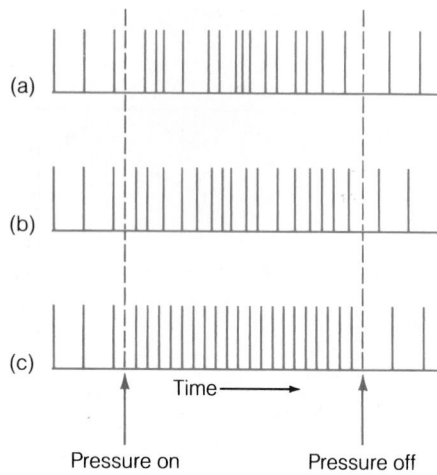

FIGURE 4-5
Coding Intensity *Response of a nerve fiber from the skin to (a) soft, (b) medium, and (c) strong pressure applied to the fiber's receptor. Increasing the stimulus strength increases both the rate and regularity of nerve firing in this fiber. (After Goldstein, 1984)*

impulses. We can illustrate with touch. If a light pressure is applied to the skin, a series of electrical impulses will be generated in a nerve fiber. If the pressure is increased, the impulses stay the same in size but increase in number (see Figure 4-5). The same story holds for other modalities. In general, the greater the intensity of the stimulus, the higher the rate of neural firing and the greater the perceived magnitude of the stimulus.

However, the intensity of a stimulus can also be coded by the *temporal pattern* of the electrical impulses. At low intensities, nerve impulses are relatively spaced in time and the exact time between successive impulses is variable. At high intensities, though, the time between impulses may be quite constant (see Figure 4-5). Thus the regularity of neural firing may also serve as a code for intensity.

Coding the quality of a stimulus is a more complex matter, and one that will continually crop up in our discussion. We mentioned earlier Müller's 1842 proposal that the brain can tell different sensory modalities apart because they involve different sensory nerves (some nerves lead to visual experiences, others to auditory experiences, and so on). Müller's idea, which came to be called the *doctrine of specific nerve energies*, received support from subsequent research demonstrating that neural pathways originating in different receptors terminate in different areas of the cortex. One thing seems clear—the brain codes the qualitative differences between sensory modalities by the specific neural pathways involved.

But what about distinguishing qualities *within* a sense? It is likely that again the coding is based on the specific neurons involved. To illustrate, there is evidence that we distinguish sweet from sour tastes by virtue of the fact that each kind of taste has its own nerve fibers. Thus, *sweet fibers* respond primarily to sweet tastes, *sour fibers* primarily to sour tastes, and ditto for *salty fibers* and *bitter fibers*.

But *specificity* is not the only plausible coding principle. A sensory system may also use the *pattern* of neural firing to code the quality of a sensation. While a particular nerve fiber may respond maximally to a sweet taste, it may respond to other tastes as well, but to varying degrees. One fiber may respond best to sweet tastes, less to bitter tastes, and even less to salty tastes; a sweet-tasting stimulus would thus lead to activity in a large number of fibers, with some firing more than others, and this particular pattern of neural activity would be the system's code for sweet. As we will see when we discuss the senses in detail, both specificity and patterning are used in coding quality.

VISUAL SENSE

Humans are generally credited with the following senses: a) vision; b) audition; c) smell; d) taste; e) touch (or the *skin senses*); and f) the *body senses* (which are responsible for sensing the position of the head relative to the trunk, for example). Only the first three of these senses are capable of obtaining information that is at a distance from us, and of this group vision is the most finely tuned in the human species. In discussing vision, first we consider the nature of the stimulus to which vision is sensitive; next we describe the visual system with particular emphasis on how its receptors carry out the transduction process; and then we consider how the visual modality processes information about intensity and quality.

Visual Stimulus

Each sense responds to a particular form of physical energy, and for vision the stimulus is light. Light is *electromagnetic radiation* (energy produced by oscillation of electrically charged matter) and belongs to the same continuum as cosmic rays, X rays, ultraviolet and infrared rays, and radio and television waves. Think of electromagnetic energy as traveling in waves, with wavelengths (the distance from one crest of a wave to the next) varying tremendously from the shortest cosmic rays (4 trillionths of a centimeter) to the longest radio waves (several miles). Our eyes are sensitive to only a small range of this continuum—wavelengths of approximately 400 to 700 nanometers. Since a nanometer is one-billionth of a meter, visible energy makes up only a very small part of electromagnetic energy. Radiation within the visible range is called *light*; we are blind to all other wavelengths. A light may be specified by the wavelengths it contains and the physical intensity (energy per unit time per unit area) at each wavelength; this is called the *energy spectrum* of the light.

Visual System

The human visual system consists of the eyes, several parts of the brain, and the pathways connecting them. (Go back to Figure 2-10 for a simplified illustration of the visual system.) Our primary concern will be with the inner workings of the eyes. The eye contains two systems, one for forming the image and the other for transducing the image into electrical impulses. The critical parts of these systems are illustrated in Figure 4-6.

The image-forming system consists of the cornea, the pupil, and the lens. Without them, we could see light but not pattern. The *cornea* is the transparent front surface of the eye: light enters here, and rays are bent inward by it to begin image formation. The *lens* completes the process of focusing the light on the retina (see Figure 4-7). To focus objects at different distances, the lens changes shape. It becomes more spherical for near objects and flatter for far ones. In some eyes, the lens does not become flat enough to bring far objects in focus, although it focuses near objects well; people with such eyes are said to be *myopic* (nearsighted). In other eyes, the lens does not become spherical enough to focus on near objects, although it focuses well on far objects; people with such eyes are said to be *hyperoptic* (farsighted). Such optical defects are common and can easily be corrected with eyeglasses

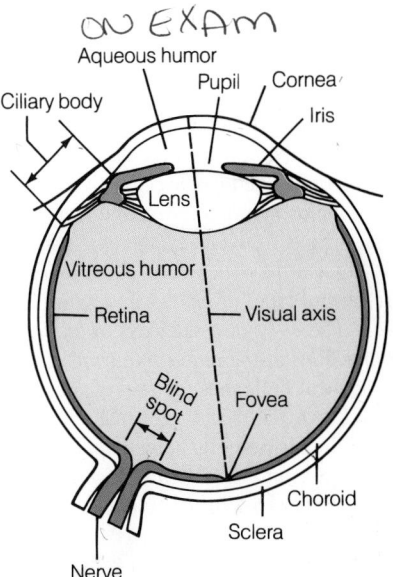

ON EXAM

FIGURE 4-6
Top View of Right Eye *Light entering the eye on its way to the retina passes through the following:* cornea; aqueous humor; lens; *and vitreous humor. The amount of light entering the eye is regulated by the size of the* pupil, *a small hole toward the front of the eye formed by the iris. The iris consists of a ring of muscles that can contract or expand, thereby controlling pupil size. The iris gives the eyes their characteristic color (blue, brown, and so forth).*

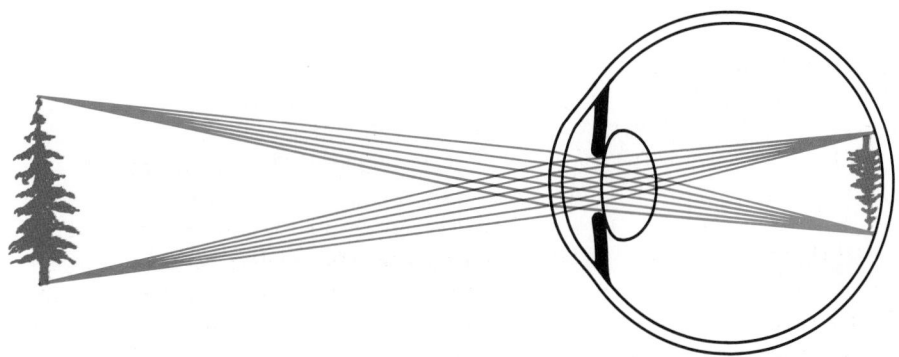

FIGURE 4-7
Image Formation in the Eye *Each point on an object sends out light rays in all directions, but only some of these rays actually enter the eye. Light rays from the same point on an object pass through different places on the lens. If a sharp image is to be formed, these different rays have to come back together (converge) at a single point on the retina. For each point on the object, there will be a matching point in the retinal image. Note that the retinal image is inverted and is generally much smaller than the actual object. Note also that most of the bending of light rays is at the cornea.*

FIGURE 4-8

Schematic Picture of the Retina *This is a schematic drawing of the retina based on an examination with an electron microscope. The bipolar cells receive signals from one or more receptors and transmit those signals to the ganglion cells, whose axons form the optic nerve. Note that there are several types of bipolar and ganglion cells. There are also sideways or lateral connections in the retina. Neurons called* horizontal cells *make lateral connections at a level near the receptors; while neurons called* amacrine cells *make lateral connections at a level near the ganglion cells. (After Dowling & Boycott, 1966)*

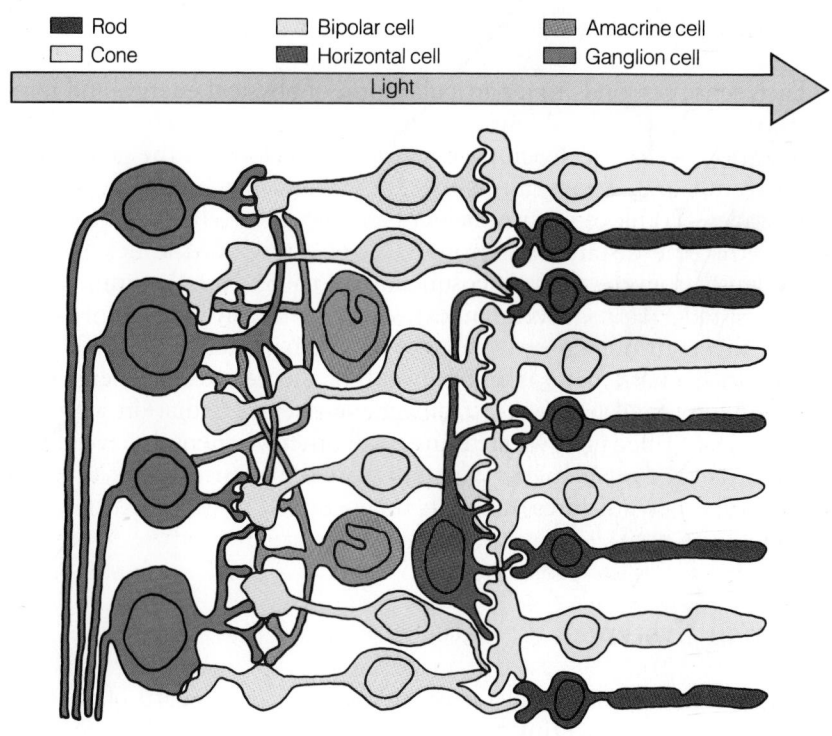

or contact lenses. The *pupil*, the third component of the image-forming system, is a circular opening in the iris (the colored part of the eye). The pupil varies in diameter in response to the light level, being largest in dim light and smallest in bright light. This variation in pupil size helps to maintain image quality at different light levels.

The system for transduction is contained in the *retina*, a thin layer that covers the inside of the back of the eyeball. The retina contains the receptor cells and a network of neurons (see Figure 4-8), plus support cells and blood vessels. There are two types of receptor cells, *rods* and *cones*, so called because of their distinctive shapes. The two kinds of receptors are specialized for different purposes. Rods are designed for seeing at night, because they operate at low intensities and lead to colorless sensations; cones are best for

FIGURE 4-9

Locating Your Blind Spot *(a) With your right eye closed, stare at the cross in the upper right-hand corner. Put the book about a foot from your eye and move it forward and back. When the black circle on the left disappears, it is projected onto the blind spot. (b) Without moving the book and with your right eye still closed, stare at the cross in the lower right-hand corner. When the white space falls in the blind spot, the black line appears to be continuous. This phenomenon helps us to understand why we are not ordinarily aware of the blind spot. In effect, the visual system fills in the parts of the visual field that we are not sensitive to; thus, they appear like the surrounding field.*

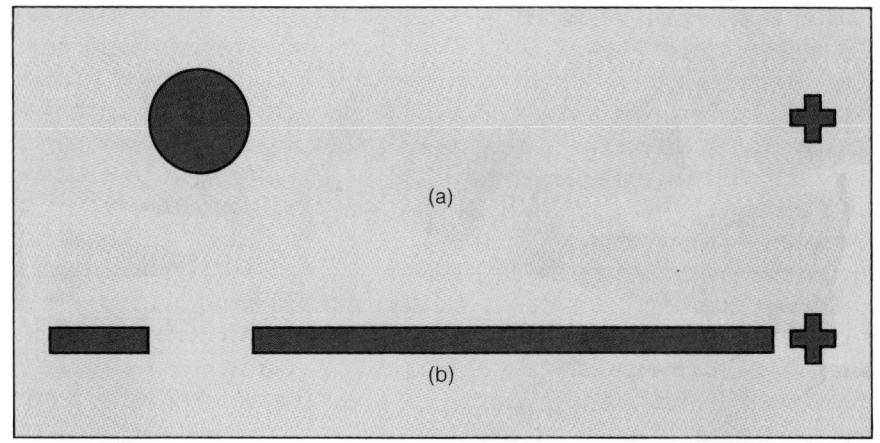

seeing during the day, because they respond to high intensities and result in sensations of color. Curiously, the rods and cones are located in the layer of the retina farthest from the cornea (note the direction-of-light arrow in Figure 4-8).

The receptors are not distributed evenly across the retina. In the center of the retina there is a region called the *fovea*, and here the receptors are plentiful and closely packed; outside of the fovea, in the *periphery*, there are fewer receptors. Not surprisingly, the fovea is the region of the eye that is best at seeing details. To ensure good acuity, we are constantly moving our eyes so that the object under view falls on the fovea (try reading this book while looking off the side of the page). These rapid eye movements are accomplished by six muscles that are attached to the outside of the eyeball.

The rods and cones contain chemicals, called *photoreceptors*, that absorb light. The absorption of light by the photoreceptors starts a process that results in a neural impulse; this is the critical transduction step. Once this transduction step is completed, the electrical impulses must make their way to the brain via connecting neurons. The responses of the rods and cones are first transmitted to *bipolar cells*, and from bipolar cells to other neurons called *ganglion cells* (refer to Figure 4-8). The long axons of the ganglion cells extend out of the eye to form the *optic nerve* to the brain. At the place where the optic nerve leaves the eye, there are no receptors; we are blind to a stimulus in this region (see Figure 4-9).

Seeing Light

SENSITIVITY Our sensitivity to a light's intensity is determined by the rods and cones. There are two critical differences between rods and cones that explain a number of phenomena involving perceived intensity, or *brightness*. One difference is that, on the average, more rods connect to a single ganglion cell than do cones; rod-based ganglion cells therefore get more inputs than cone-based ones, and consequently vision is more sensitive when based on rods than on cones. Secondly, rods and cones differ in where they are located. The fovea of the retina contains many cones but no rods, whereas the periphery (the rest of the retina) is rich in rods and relatively sparse in cones.

One consequence of these differences is that we are better able to detect a dim light in the rod-rich periphery than in the fovea. So while acuity— that is, seeing exactly *what* happened—is greater in the fovea than in the periphery, sensitivity—that is, seeing that *something* happened—is greater in the periphery. Greater sensitivity in the periphery may be established by measuring a subject's absolute threshold for light flashes presented in a dark room. The threshold is lower (which means sensitivity is greater) when the subject looks off to the side so that the light falls on the periphery, than when the subject looks directly at the flash so that the light falls on the fovea.

Brightness sensitivity also depends on the wavelength of the light. Although we see electromagnetic radiation within the 400-to-700 nanometer range, we are not equally sensitive to all these wavelengths. If we measure a subject's absolute threshold for light flashes of different wavelengths, the results differ when the stimulus is presented to the cone-rich fovea or the rod-rich periphery. This is shown in Figure 4-10. Not only are thresholds lower in the periphery (rods) than in the fovea (cones), but the minimum thresholds

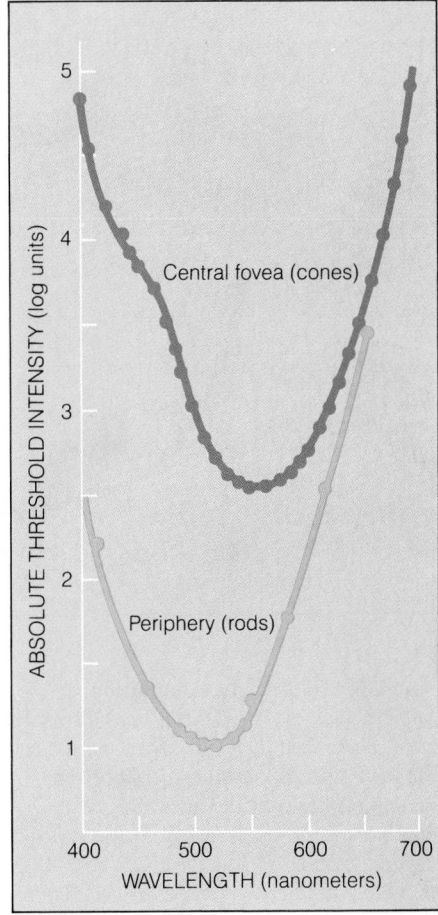

FIGURE 4-10
Absolute Threshold for Light Intensity at Different Wavelengths *The graph plots the absolute threshold as a function of wavelength (in nanometers). The curve is different depending on whether the subject looks directly at the flash, so the image falls on the central fovea, or off to the side, so that it falls on the periphery. The upper curve is attributed to the cones and the lower curve to the rods. Thus, the rods are more sensitive than the cones. The precise form of the curves and the value of the thresholds will depend on the duration of exposure, the area of the stimulus, and its exact retinal position. The thresholds are in log units; such units are often used for intensity. (After Hecht & Hsia, 1945)*

ROYGBU
400-750 nm

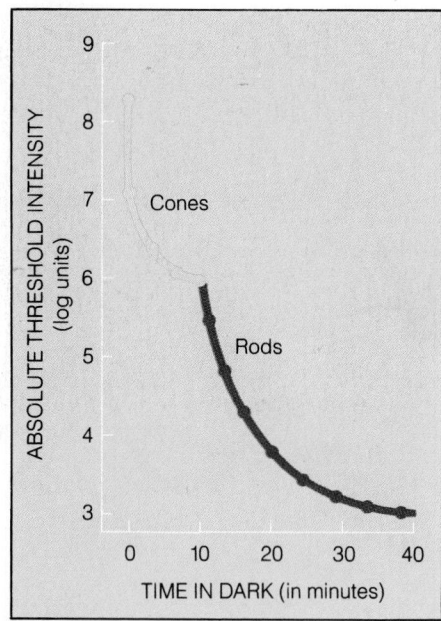

FIGURE 4-11
The Course of Light Adaptation
Subjects look at a bright light until the retina has become light adapted. When the subjects are then placed in darkness, they become increasingly sensitive to light, and their absolute thresholds decrease. This is called light adaptation. The graph shows the threshold at different times after the adapting light has been turned off. The pink data points correspond to threshold flashes whose color could be seen; the brown data points correspond to flashes that appeared white regardless of their wavelength. Note the sharp break in the curve at about 10 minutes; this is called the rod-cone break. A variety of tests show that the first part of the curve is due to cone vision and the second part to rod vision. (Data are approximate, from various determinations.)

for the areas also occur at different wavelengths; about 500 nanometers in the periphery, as compared to 550 nanometers in the fovea. These differences arise because the chemicals in the rods and cones differ in their ability to absorb light at various wavelengths. This difference in the sensitivity of rods and cones to various wavelengths explains why, as night falls, we become relatively more sensitive to short-wave light (light near the blue end of the spectrum). As night falls our vision shifts from cones to rods, since rods operate at low intensities, and the rods are more sensitive than the cones to short-wave or blue light.

LIGHT ADAPTATION   Thus far we have emphasized our sensitivity to flashes of lights presented in dark rooms; however, there are other aspects of brightness perception. Suppose a subject looks at an illuminated surface for a few minutes. The person's visual system will change, adjusting to the prevailing level of illumination. This adjustment is called *light adaptation*.

Adaptation allows us to see well over a wide range of intensities, but with our effective range at any given moment depending on the prevailing level of illumination. Adaptation to a higher intensity is very rapid (Adelson, 1982), while adaptation to darkness or to a very low intensity may take half an hour or more. When you enter a dark movie theater from a bright street, you get a good demonstration of adaptation to a low-intensity light level. At first you can see hardly anything in the dim light reflected from the screen. However, in a few minutes you are able to see well enough to find a seat. Eventually you are able to recognize faces in the dim light. When you re-enter the bright street, almost everything will seem painfully bright at first and it will be impossible to discriminate among these bright lights. Everything will look normal in less than a minute, though, because adaptation to this higher light level is rapid.

Figure 4-11 shows how the absolute threshold decreases with time in the dark. The curve has two limbs. The upper limb is mediated by the cones and the lower limb by the rods. The rod system takes much longer to adapt, but it is sensitive to much dimmer lights. Adaptation to light appears to be due largely to processes in the retina rather than in the brain, because adaptation of one eye has little effect on the threshold in the other (Battersby & Wagman, 1962).

As we adapt to a light, it appears to become dimmer. A dramatic illustration of this occurs when the image on the retina is kept from moving across the receptors. Usually even when we are trying to look steadily at a single point our eyes are moving slightly, which means that the image is always moving over the retina. When this movement is eliminated, the visual world disappears within a few seconds. It takes delicate equipment to stabilize a retinal image completely (see Figure 4-13), but approximate stabilization will cause the image to fade and almost disappear. This phenomenon appears to be a consequence of adaptation. The fact that the visual system ceases to respond to an unchanging stimulus indicates that it is designed to detect change, a hallmark of all sensory systems.

Seeing Color

All light is alike except for wavelength. Our visual system does something wonderful with wavelength—it turns it into color, with different wavelengths resulting in different colors. For example, *short-wavelength* lights, those 450–500 nanometers, appear blue; *medium-wavelength* lights, those

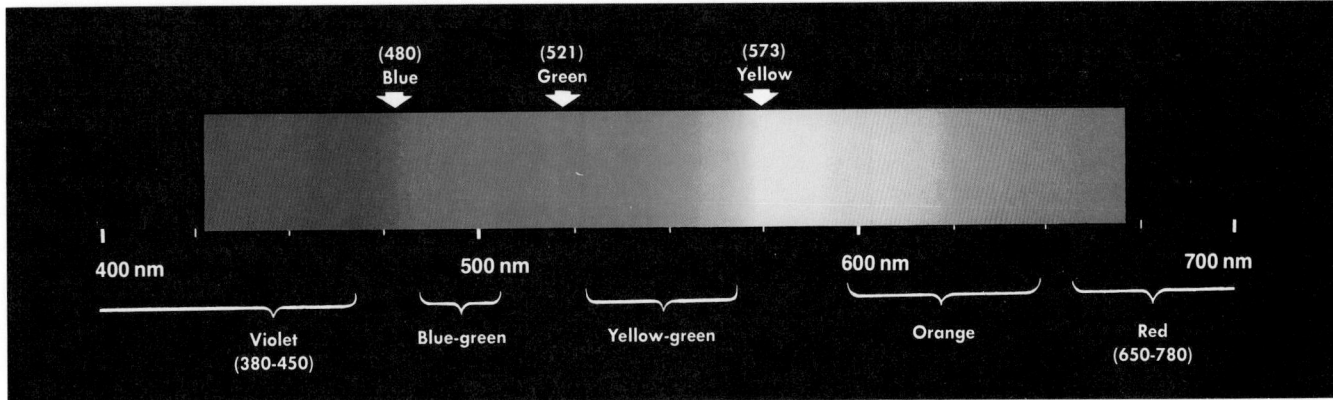

FIGURE 4-12
Solar Spectrum *The numbers given are the wavelengths of the various colors in nanometers (nm).*

roughly 500–570 nanometers, appear green; and *long-wavelength* lights, those about 620–700 nanometers, appear red (see Figure 4-12).

COLOR APPEARANCE   Seeing color seems like a very subjective experience, but to study color scientifically we have to be able to describe it. Consider a spot of light seen against a dark background. Physically, it can be described by its energy spectrum (intensities at different wavelengths), whereas phenomenologically it is described by three dimensions: brightness, hue, and saturation. *Brightness*, as we've seen, refers to the perceived intensity of the light. The other two dimensions say something about the color itself. *Hue* refers to the quality described by the color name, such as red or greenish-yellow. *Saturation* means the colorfulness or purity of the light: unsaturated colors appear pale or whitish (for example, pink); saturated colors appear to contain no white. In a complex way, both hue and saturation depend on the energy spectrum. Albert Munsell, an artist, proposed a scheme for specifying colored surfaces by assigning them one of 10 hue names and two numbers, one indicating saturation and the other brightness.* The colors in the Munsell system are represented by the color solid (see Figure 4-14).

Given a means for describing colors, we can ask how many different colors we are capable of seeing. Within the 400–700 nanometer range to which we are sensitive, we can discriminate about 150 different wavelengths. This means that, on the average, we can discriminate two wavelengths that are only 2 nanometers apart; that is, the jnd for wavelength is 2 nanometers (see Figure 4-15). Given that each of the 150 discriminable colors can have many different values of brightness and many different values of saturation, the estimated number of colors that we can discriminate is over seven million! Furthermore, according to estimates of the National Bureau of Standards, we have names for about 7,500 of these colors (Judd & Kelly, 1965); it is hard to think of any other domain of experience that is so extensively coded in our language. These numbers give some indication of the importance of color to our lives (Goldstein, 1984).

It would be very difficult for researchers to study seven million or even 7,500 different colors. Fortunately, all the hues we can discriminate can be generated by mixing together just a few basic colors.

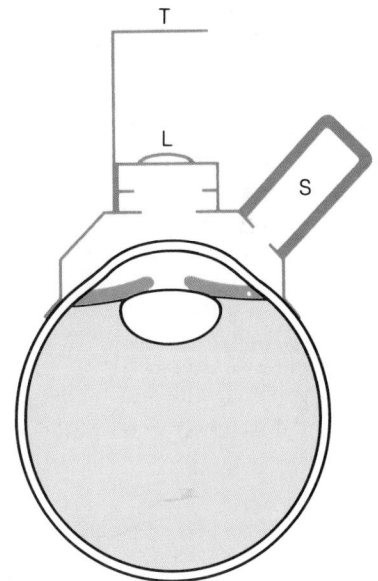

FIGURE 4-13
Stabilized Image *A device for stabilizing a retinal image using a contact lens. The target (T) is viewed through a powerful lens (L) mounted on a contact lens that is firmly attached to the cornea via a sucker (S). With each movement of the eyeball, the lens and target also move so that the projected image always falls on the same area of the retina. After a few seconds, the image of the target will fade and disappear.*

---

*The term "lightness," rather than "brightness," is used when referring to a surface; it refers to the shade—light or dark—of a surface, which depends on the percentage of light reflected by the surface.

FIGURE 4-14
Color Solid *The three dimensions of color can be represented on a double cone. Hue is represented by points around the circumference, saturation by points along the radius, and lightness by points on the vertical axis. A vertical slice taken from the color solid will show differences in saturation and lightness of a single hue.*

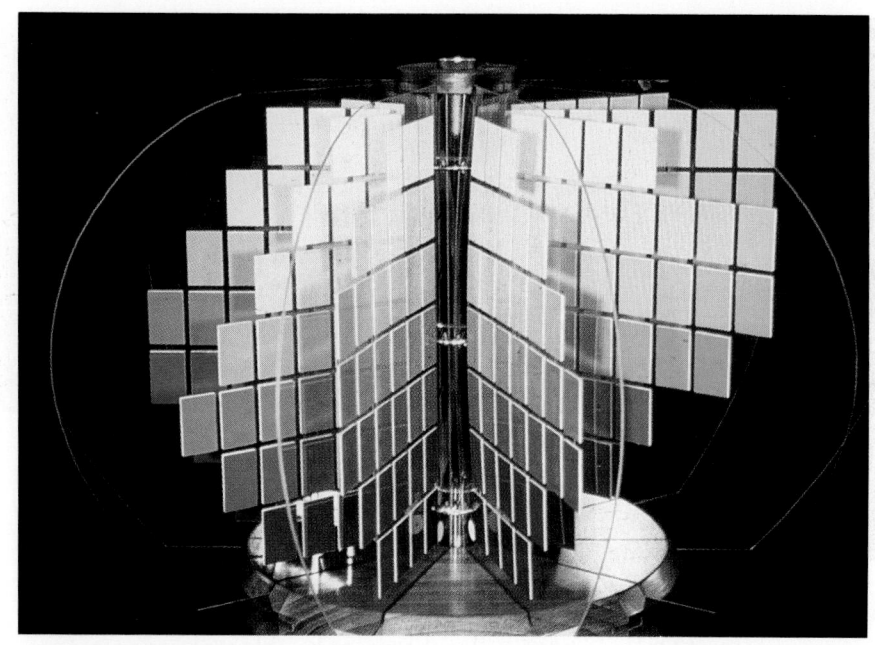

COLOR MIXTURE Suppose that we superimpose different colored lights on a projection screen—that is, project different wavelengths to the same region of the retina. The result of this light mixture will be a new color. For example, a mixture of 650-nanometer light (red) and 500-nanometer light (green) in the proper proportion will look yellow; in appearance the mixture will perfectly match a light of 580 nanometers. Mixtures of lights other than this particular one can also result in a light that perfectly matches a yellow light of 580 nanometers. Thus, light mixtures whose physical components are grossly different can appear to be identical.

A cautionary note is in order. Here and throughout this section we are referring to mixing lights, called an *additive mixture*; we are *not* referring to mixing paints or pigments, a *subtractive mixture* (see Figure 4-16). The rules of color mixture are different for mixing colors (paints) and mixing lights. This is to be expected. In mixing paints, the physical stimulus is itself altered, the mixture takes place outside the eye, and hence is a topic of study for physics. In contrast, in mixing lights, the mixture occurs in the eye itself, and thus is a topic for psychology.

With regard to mixing lights, in general, *three widely spaced wavelengths can be combined to match almost any color of light.* To illustrate, a subject in an

FIGURE 4-15
Wavelength Discrimination *This graph shows the difference threshold for wavelength at various wavelengths. In this experiment, lights of the two wavelengths were presented side by side, and the subjects had to judge whether they were the same or different. Over most of the range we can discriminate a change of 1 to 3 nanometers.* (After Wright, 1946)

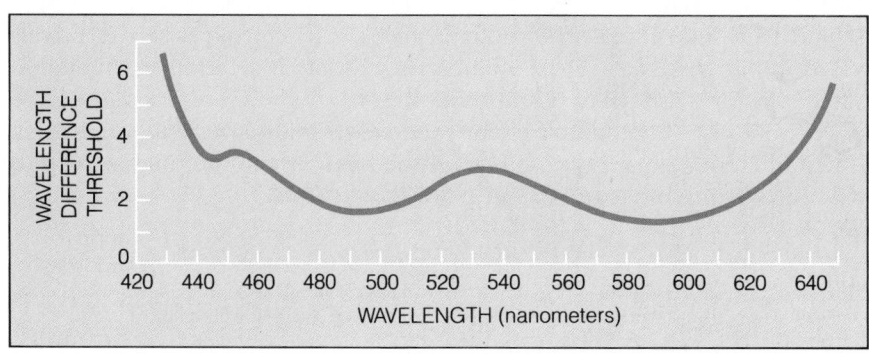

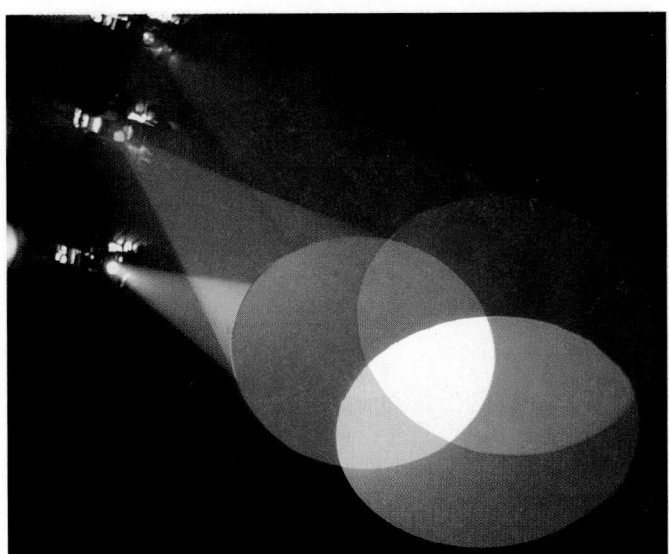 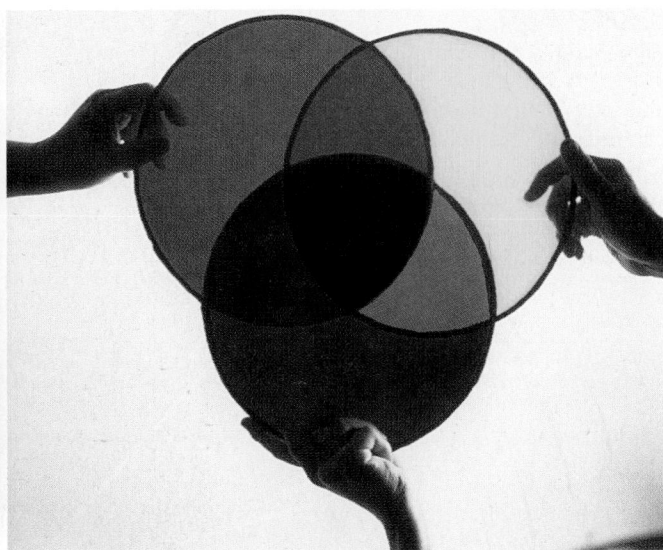

FIGURE 4-16
Additive and Subtractive Color Mixtures *Additive color mixture (illustrated by the figure at the left) combines lights. Red and green lights are mixed to appear yellow; green and purple appear blue; and so on. In the center, where the three colors overlap, the mixture appears white.*

Subtractive color mixture (illustrated in the figure at the right) takes place when pigments are mixed or when light is transmitted through colored filters placed one over another. Usually blue-green and yellow will mix to give green, and complementary colors will combine to appear black. Unlike additive mixture, one cannot always tell from the color of the components what color will result. For example, blue and green commonly yield blue-green by subtractive mixture, but with some filters they may appear red. This depends on the exact nature of the filters.

experiment on color matching might be asked to match the color of a test light by mixing together three other colored lights. As long as the three mixture lights are widely spaced in wavelength—for example, 450 (blue), 560 (green), and 640 nanometers (red)—the subject will always be able to match the test light. The subject will not, however, be able to match any test light if he or she is provided only two mixture lights—for example, the 450- and 640-nanometer lights. The number three, therefore, is significant.

Because some lights that are grossly different physically look identical to humans, we have to conclude that we are blind to the differences. Without this blindness, color reproduction would be impossible. Realistic color reproduction in television or photography relies on the fact that a wide range of colors can be produced by mixing just a few colors. For example, examination of a television screen with a magnifying glass will reveal that it is composed of tiny dots of only three colors (blue, green, and red). Additive color mixture occurs because the dots are so close together that their retinal images overlap. (See Figure 4-17 for a way of representing color mixtures.)

COLOR DEFICIENCY   Most people match a wide range of colors with a mixture of three appropriately selected lights—such as blue, green, and red—and different people make very similar matches. Such people are called *color normal.* Some people match colors with three lights but make matches different from those considered normal; they also tend to be poor at discriminating one wavelength from another. They are called *color anomalous.* Still other people can match a wide range of colors by using mixtures of only two lights (*dichromats*) or, in rare cases, simply by adjusting the intensity of a single light (*monochromats*). Dichromats have a major weakness in discriminating wavelengths; monochromats are unable to discriminate wavelength at all. Both groups are called *color-blind.* Screening for color deficiency is done with tests like that shown in Figure 4-18, a simpler procedure than conducting color mixture experiments.

Most color deficiencies are genetic in origin. They occur much more frequently in males than in females because the critical genes are recessive genes on the X chromosome (see Chapter 2); these genes have been isolated and analyzed (Nathans, Thomas, & Hogness, 1986). About 6 percent of

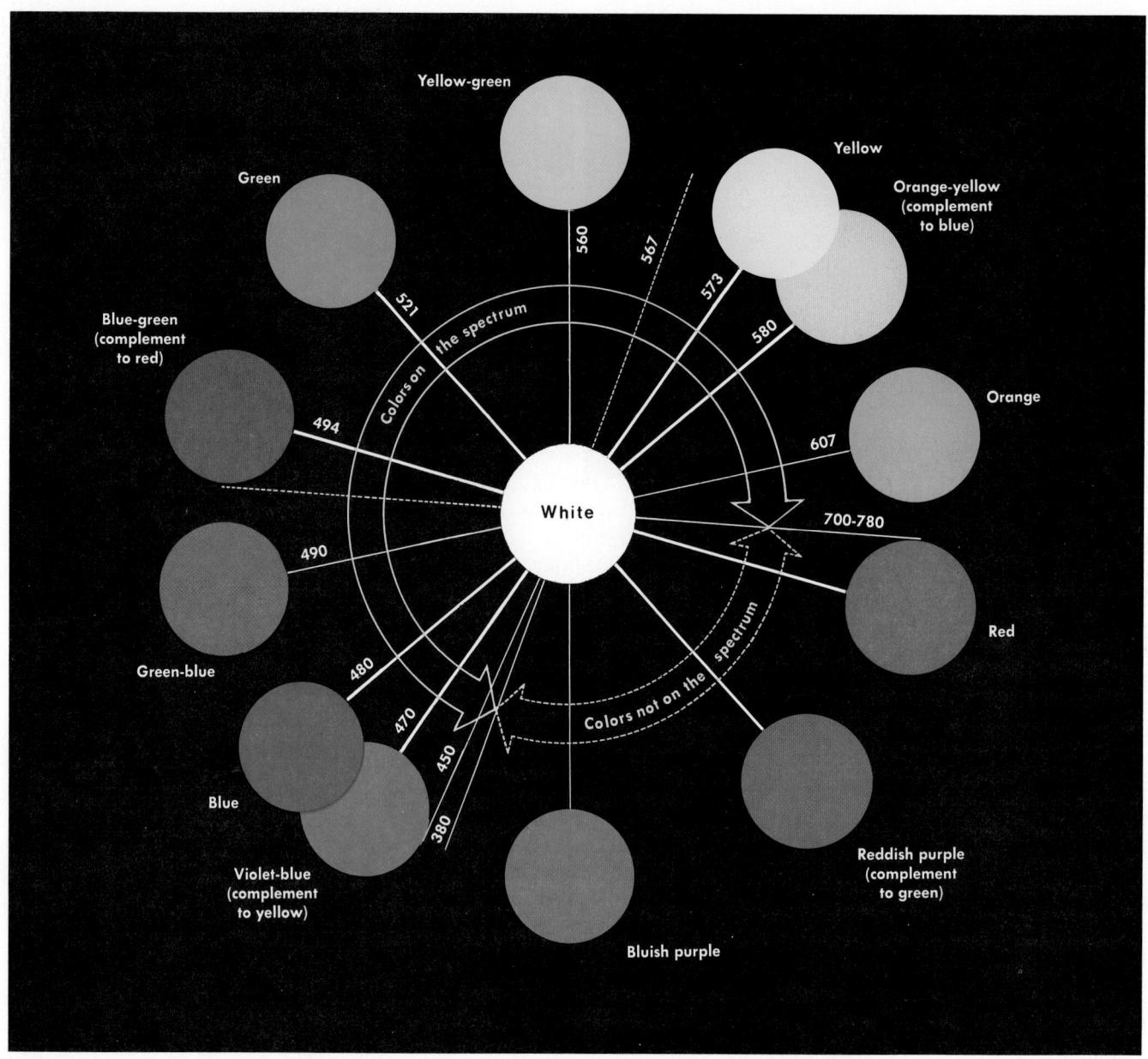

FIGURE 4-17
Color Circle *A simple way to represent color mixture is by means of the color circle. The spectral colors (colors corresponding to wavelengths in our region of sensitivity) are represented by points around the circumference of the circle. The two ends of the spectrum do not meet; the space between them corresponds to the nonspectral reds and purples, which can be produced by mixtures of long and short wavelengths. The inside of the circle represents mixtures of lights. Lights toward the center of the circle are less saturated (or whiter); white is at the very center. Mixtures of any two lights lie along the straight line joining the two points. When this line goes through the center of the circle, the lights, when mixed in proper proportions, will look white; such pairs of colors are called complementary colors.*

males are color anomalous and 2 percent are color-blind. For females, the percentages are 0.4 percent and 0.03 percent, respectively. Some color-deficient persons make such skillful use of their remaining color vision, combining it with learned associations of the relative intensities and color names of familiar objects, that they are unaware of their own deficiency!

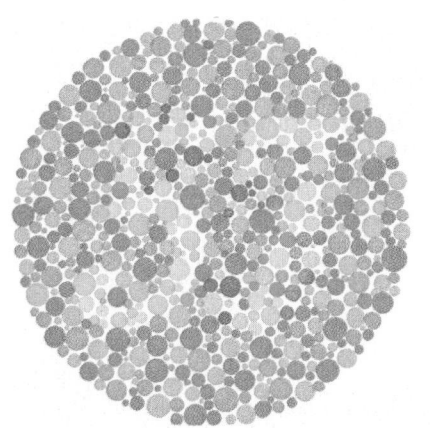 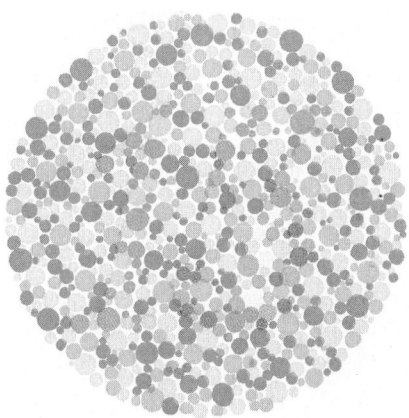

FIGURE 4-18
Color Blindness *Two plates used in color blindness tests. In the left plate, individuals with certain kinds of red-green blindness will see only the number 5; others see only the 7; still others, no number at all. Those with normal vision see 57. Similarly, in the right plate, people with normal vision see the number 15, whereas those with red-green blindness see no number at all.*

OBJECT COLOR   So far we have been concerned primarily with the color of lights that are generated by sources like sunlight and light bulbs. But most of the light we see is reflected from objects; in these cases, we experience the color of an object rather than the color of a light.

So what determines the color of an object? One major determinant is the wavelengths that the object reflects. A blue object is one that reflects predominantly short wavelengths, a green object reflects mainly medium wavelengths, and a red object reflects mainly long wavelengths. Another determinant of an object's color is the color of the objects that surround it. For example, an object looks greyer when it is surrounded by lighter-colored objects than darker-colored ones. For a familiar object, there is still another determinant of color, namely the characteristic color of the object. Thus, knowing that an object is a banana makes the object appear yellower (Delk & Fillenbaum, 1965).

The above discussion indicates that color perception is affected by factors in addition to the wavelengths falling on our eye. Wavelength, however, is still a critical factor, and it has been the main concern of theories of color perception.

THEORIES OF COLOR VISION   Over the years, two major theories of color vision have arisen. The first of these was initially proposed by Thomas Young in 1807. Fifty years later, Hermann von Helmholtz further developed Young's theory and put it on a quantitative basis.

According to the *Young-Helmholtz* or *trichromatic theory*, there are only three types of receptors (cones) for color. Each receptor is sensitive to a wide range of wavelengths, but is most responsive in a narrow region. As shown in Figure 4-19, the *short receptor* is maximally sensitive to short wavelengths (blues), the *medium receptor* is most sensitive to medium wavelengths (greens and yellows), and the *long receptor* is maximally sensitive to long wavelengths (reds). The joint action of these three receptors determines the sensation of color. That is, a light of a particular wavelength stimulates the three receptors to different degrees, and the specific ratios of activity in the three receptors leads to the sensation of a specific color. Hence, with regard to our earlier discussion of coding quality, the trichromatic theory holds that the *quality* of color is coded by the *pattern* of activity of three receptors rather than by specific receptors for each color.

The trichromatic theory explains the facts about color vision that we mentioned previously. We can discriminate different wavelengths because

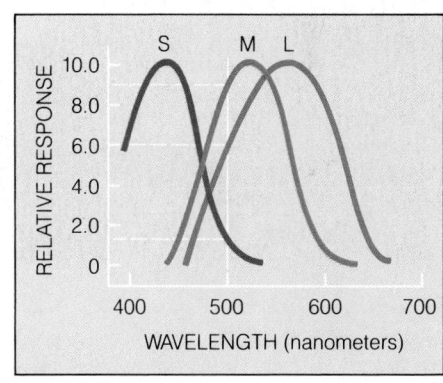

FIGURE 4-19
Trichromatic Theory *Response curves for the short-, medium-, and long-wave receptors proposed by trichromatic theory. These curves enable us to determine the relative response of each receptor to light of any wavelength. In the example shown here, the response of each receptor to a 500-nanometer light is determined by drawing a line up from 500 nanometers and noting where this line intersects each curve. (After Wald & Brown, 1965)*

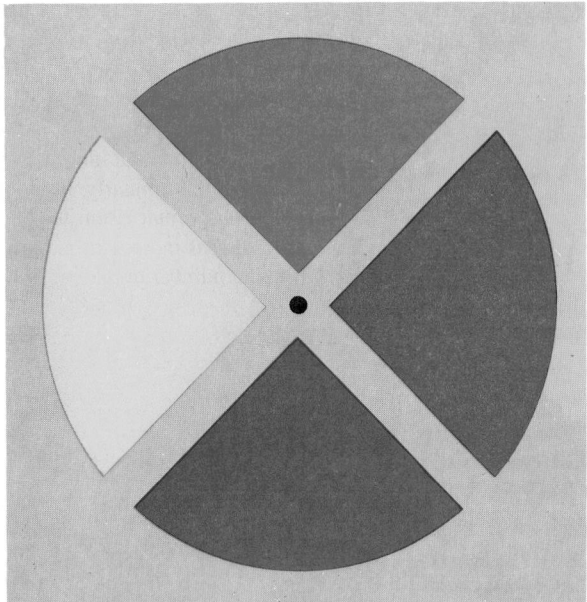 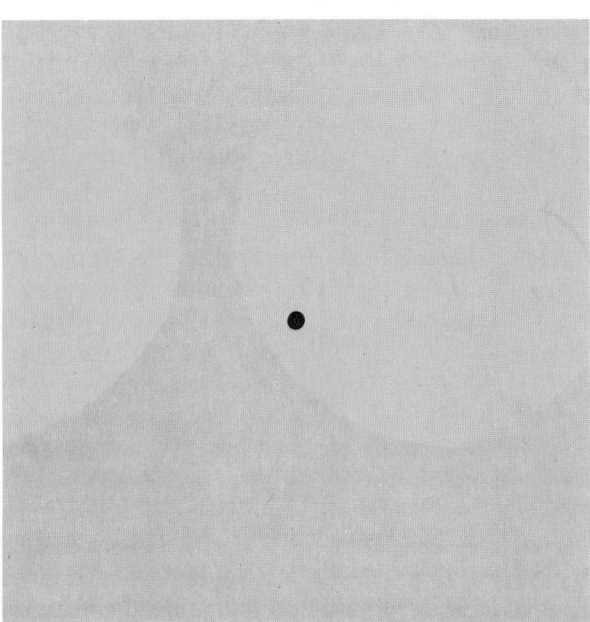

FIGURE 4-20

Complementary Afterimages *Look steadily for about a minute at the dot in the center of the colors, then transfer your gaze to the dot in the gray field at the right. You should see a blurry image with colors that are complementary to the original: the blue, red, green, and yellow are replaced by yellow, green, red, and blue.*

they lead to different responses in the three receptors. We can match a mixture of three widely spaced wavelengths to any color, because the three widely spaced wavelengths will activate the three different receptors, and activity in these receptors is what lies behind perception of the test color. (Now we see the significance of the number three.) Trichromatic theory explains the various kinds of color blindness by positing that one or more of the three types of receptors is missing: dichromats are born missing one type of receptor, whereas monochromats are born missing two of the three types of receptors.

Despite its successes, the trichromatic theory cannot explain some well-established findings about the phenomenology of color. In 1878 Ewald Hering observed that all colors may be described phenomenologically as consisting of one or two of the following sensations: red, green, yellow, and blue. Hering also noted that nothing is perceived to be reddish-green or yellowish-blue; rather, a mixture of red and green may look yellow, and a mixture of yellow and blue may look white. These observations suggested that red and green form an *opponent pair*, as do yellow and blue, and that the colors in an opponent pair cannot be perceived simultaneously. Further support for the notion of opponent-pairs comes from studies in which a subject first stares at a colored light and then looks at a neutral surface. The subject reports seeing a color on the neutral surface that is the complement of the original one (see Figure 4-20).

These phenomenological observations led Hering to propose an alternative theory of color vision called *opponent-color theory*. Hering believed that the visual system contains two types of color-sensitive units. One type of unit responds to red or green, the other to blue or yellow. Each unit responds in opposite ways to its two opponent colors: the red-green unit, for example, increases its response rate when a red is presented and decreases it when a green is presented. Because a unit cannot respond in two ways at once, reddish-greens and yellowish-blues cannot occur; white is perceived when both types of opponent units are in balance (see Figure 4-21). Opponent-color theory is thereby able to explain Hering's phenomenological observations about color.

The theory also accounts for why we see the hues that we do. We perceive a single hue—red, green, yellow, or blue—whenever only one type of opponent unit is out of balance, and we perceive combinations of hues when both types of units are out of balance. Opponent-color theory received a great impetus from the discovery of *color opponent cells* in the retina (Svaetichin, 1956) and in the lateral geniculate nucleus of the thalamus (DeValois & Jacobs, 1984). The cells in the thalamus are spontaneously active, increasing their activity rate in response to one range of wavelengths and decreasing it in response to another. Thus, some cells at a higher level in the visual system fire more rapidly if the retina is stimulated by a blue light, and less rapidly when the retina is exposed to a yellow light; such cells seem to be the biological basis of the blue-yellow opponent pair.

The opponent-color theory and trichromatic theory competed for more than half a century; each could explain some facts but not others. Some researchers proposed that the theories might be reconciled in a two-stage theory in which the three types of receptors in the trichromatic theory feed into color-opponent units at a higher level in the visual system. The most completely developed theory of this kind is by Jameson and Hurvich (Hurvich, 1981). Figure 4-22 illustrates the basics of a two-stage color theory. The figure shows how the short, medium, and long receptors of trichromatic theory might connect with color-opponent cells to produce sensations of color. The blue-yellow opponent cells receive excitatory input from the short receptor and inhibitory input from the long receptor. If only short-wavelength light is presented, the sensation will be that of blue; if long- as well as short-wavelength lights are presented the sensation will be different—namely, purple. A similar analysis applies to the red-green opponent cell. This theory accounts for much of what is known about color vision. However, theories of this kind do not account for color constancy (see Chapter 5), nor do they account for all known facts about the detection and appearance of isolated spots of light (Hood & Finkelstein, 1983). Nevertheless, the analysis of color vision is one of the major theoretical accomplishments of psychology, and serves as a prototype for the analysis of other sensory systems.

AUDITORY SENSE

Our discussion of audition will follow the same plan as our discussion of vision. We will first consider the nature of the stimulus that audition is sensitive to, then describe the auditory system with particular emphasis on how the receptors execute the transduction process, and finally consider how the auditory system codes the intensity of sound and its quality.

Auditory Stimulus

Sound originates from the motion or vibration of an object, as when the wind rushes through the branches of a tree. When something moves, the molecules of air in front of it are pushed together. These molecules push other molecules and then return to their original position. In this way, a

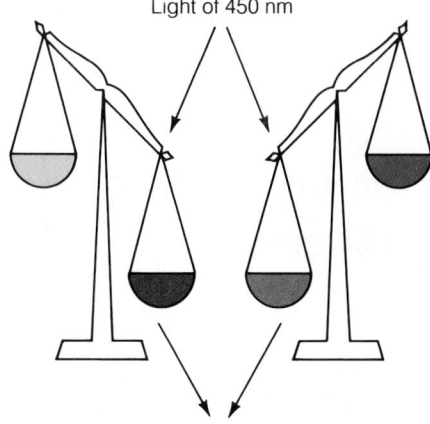

FIGURE 4-21
Opponent-Process Theory *The diagram shows how an opponent process responds to light of a particular wavelength. The light is in the short-wave region of the visible spectrum, 450 nanometers. This will affect both the blue-yellow and the red-green systems. It will tip the blue-yellow balance toward blue, and the red-green balance toward red. The resulting hue will be a mixture of red and blue (that is, violet).* (After Hurvich & Jameson, 1957)

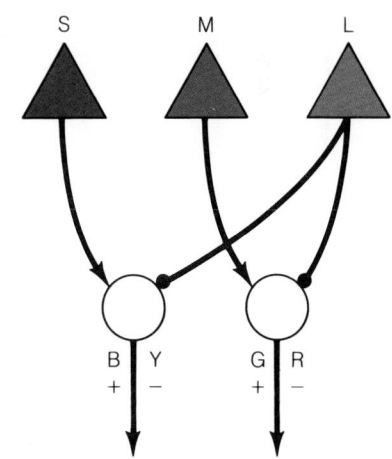

FIGURE 4-22
Two-Stage Color Theory *A simplified diagram showing how the short, medium, and long receptors might connect with color-opponent cells to produce sensations of color. An arrowhead indicates an excitatory connection, while a filled circle indicates an inhibitory connection.* (After Goldstein, 1984)

CRITICAL DISCUSSION

Seeing Spatial Patterns

A factor that enables you to distinguish an object from its background is the sudden change in intensity that defines the object's borders. Such an abrupt change, or *contrast*, is critical for our ability to see spatial patterns, an ability referred to as *spatial resolution*. Normally, spatial resolution is measured in the way that it is done by an optometrist. The person looks at a chart of letters that become progressively smaller and is asked to read the smallest line of letters that she can identify. This kind of test allows the eye specialist to determine a threshold for the minimum size of detail that the tested person can detect; the result is expressed as a measure called *visual acuity*.

Recently, researchers have developed a new way to study the perception of spatial patterns. The stimuli used in this research are patterns of alternating dark and light bars, called *gratings*, and spatial resolution is measured by our ability to distinguish the dark and light bars under various conditions. Two sample gratings are shown in Figure 1. There are three critical properties of a grating that affect how easy it is to distinguish the black from the white bars. One property is obviously the intensity difference between the black and white bars. A second property is the *waveform*, which tells us how the intensity of the grading changes from one spatial location to the next. In the left-hand grating of the figure, the intensity changes abruptly from high (a light bar) to low (a dark bar). This grating is therefore said to have a *square waveform*, or to be a *square-wave* grating. The intensity for the right-hand grating changes more gradually; because this grating's distribution of intensity over locations follows a mathematical function called a *sine wave*, the grating is called a *sine-wave* grating. As is evident from Figure 1, the apparent contrast between successive bars is greater in the square-wave grating than the sine-wave grating; consequently, the bars are easier to resolve (distinguish) in the square-wave grating.

A third critical property of a grating is its *spatial frequency*. Spatial frequency is a measure of how long it takes a basic pattern (a dark and a light bar) to repeat; a rough indication of a grating's spatial frequency is the distance between successive dark bars. Figure 2 displays a pair of square-wave gratings that differ only in spatial frequency. The *low-frequency* grating (wide bars) has a higher contrast than the *high-frequency* grating (narrow bars), and consequently the low-frequency grating is easier to resolve.

Do contrast and resolution always

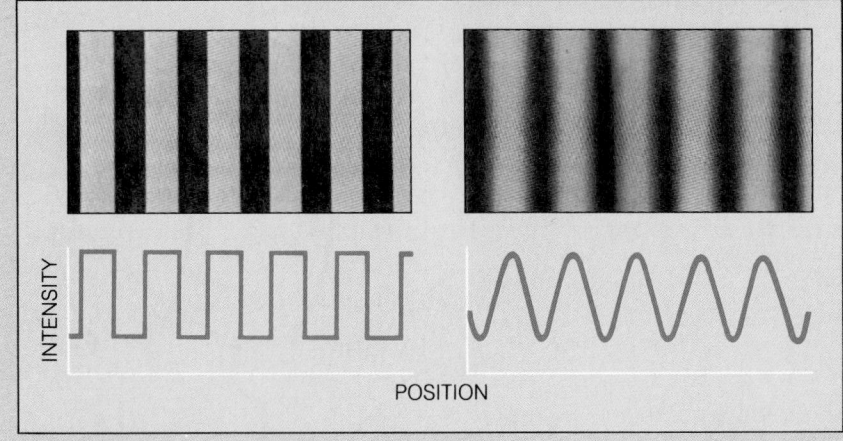

FIGURE 1

Gratings *The stripe pattern on the left is a square-wave grating; plotted below it is a curve giving intensity as a function of location. The pattern on the right is called a sine-wave grating because its intensity is a sinusoidal function of location. Different gratings also can be constructed by varying frequency (number of cycles/cm), or contrast (maximum difference between dark and light regions).*

wave of pressure changes (a *sound wave*) is transmitted through the air, even though the individual air molecules do not travel far. This wave is analogous to the ripples set up by throwing a stone into a pond.

A sound wave may be described by a graph of air pressure as a function of time. A pressure-versus-time graph of one type of sound is shown in Figure 4-23. The graph corresponds to a mathematical function called a *sine wave*. Sounds that correspond to sine waves are called *pure tones*, which play an important role in the analysis of sound. Pure tones vary with respect to their

 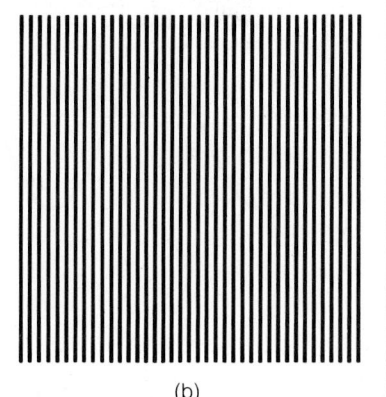

(a)   (b)

FIGURE 2
Spatial Frequency *The effect of spatial frequency on the apparent brightness and contrast of patterns. Notice that the higher frequency pattern on the right has less apparent contrast.* (After Coren, Porac, & Ward, 1984)

decrease as spatial frequency increases? To answer this question, an experimenter starts with a set of gratings that vary in spatial frequency, and determines for each grating the minimum difference in intensity between the dark and light bars that allows a subject to tell the bars apart. The inverse of this difference (that is, 1/difference) is used as a measure of sensitivity. The results of such an experiment (done with sine-wave gratings) are given in Figure 3. For low spatial frequencies (wide bars), sensitivity is at a moderate level; as spatial frequency increases, sensitivity increases; but for very high spatial frequencies (narrow bars), sensitivity decreases drastically. The visual system therefore appears to be most sensitive to intermediate spatial frequencies. This has led to the idea that there are neurons in the cortex that are sensitive to spatial frequencies, particularly at intermediate frequencies.

In addition to offering new insights about how the visual system analyzes patterns, an analysis in terms of spatial frequencies offers a more thorough test of spatial resolution than does the standard visual-acuity test used to prescribe eyeglasses. In an experiment to demonstrate this, a group of 18-year-olds and a group of 73-year-olds were tested. The two groups did not differ when the experimenters measured their visual acuity by the standard visual-acuity test. However, the groups differed when the experimenters measured their spatial resolutions for gratings of varying spatial frequency. The older subjects required a much larger contrast difference to resolve the low-frequency (wide bars) gratings (Sekular, Hutman, & Owsley, 1980). The older subjects' problems with low frequencies may be responsible for their occasional difficulties in recognizing faces: the distribution of features across a face creates a kind of grating with a low spatial frequency.

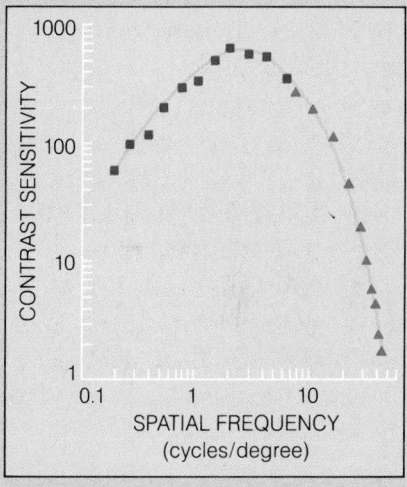

FIGURE 3
Contrast Sensitivity *A contrast sensitivity function for a sine-wave grating.* (After Campbell & Robson, 1968)

frequency (the number of cycles per second, called *hertz*), their intensity (the pressure difference between peak and trough), and the time at which they start (called *phase*). These physical aspects determine how we experience the tone, because frequency underlies our sensation of pitch and intensity our sensation of loudness.

Young adult humans can hear frequencies between 20 and 20,000 hertz; dogs, bats, and porpoises can hear much higher frequencies. Sound intensity is usually specified in *decibels*; a change of 10 decibels corresponds to a change

FIGURE 4-23
Pure Tone *As the tuning fork vibrates, it produces successive waves of compression and expansion of the air, which correspond to a sine wave. Such a sound is called a pure tone. It can be described by giving its frequency and intensity. If the tuning fork makes 100 vibrations per second, it produces a sound wave with 100 compressions per second and a frequency of 100 hertz. The intensity (or amplitude) of a pure tone is the pressure difference between the peaks and the troughs. The waveform of any sound can be decomposed into a series of sine waves of different frequencies with various amplitudes and phases. When these sine waves are added together, the result is the original waveform.*

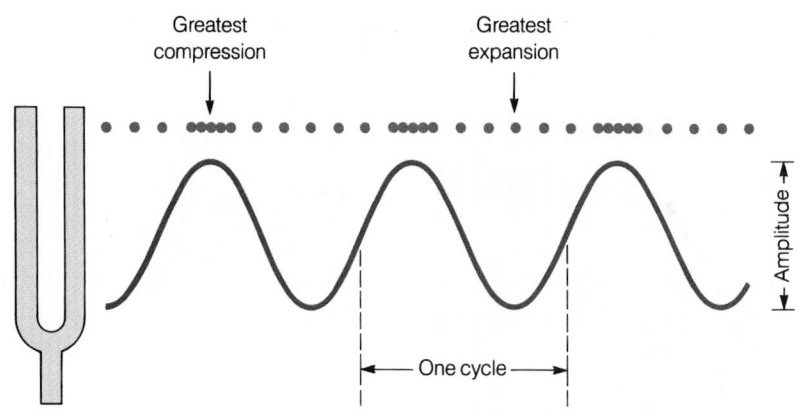

in sound power of 10 times; 20 decibels, a change of 100 times; 30 decibels, a change of 1,000 times; and so forth. Table 4-3 shows the intensities of some familiar sounds, and indicates which of them are so intense as to endanger our hearing.

Most sounds are not pure tones; nevertheless, such complex sounds can be decomposed into a number of different sine waves. The typical musical

TABLE 4-3
Decibel Ratings and Hazardous Time Exposures of Common Sounds *This table gives the intensities of common sounds in decibels. An increase of 3 decibels corresponds to a doubling of sound power. The sound levels given correspond approximately to the intensities that occur at typical working distances. The right-hand column gives the exposure times at which one risks permanent hearing loss.*

DECIBEL LEVEL	EXAMPLE	DANGEROUS TIME EXPOSURE
0	Lowest sound audible to human ear	
30	Quiet library, soft whisper	
40	Quiet office, living room, bedroom away from traffic	
50	Light traffic at a distance, refrigerator, gentle breeze	
60	Air conditioner at 20 feet, conversation, sewing machine	
70	Busy traffic, office tabulator, noisy restaurant (constant exposure)	Critical level begins
80	Subway, heavy city traffic, alarm clock at 2 feet, factory noise	More than 8 hours
90	Truck traffic, noisy home appliances, shop tools, lawnmower	Less than 8 hours
100	Chain saw, boiler shop, pneumatic drill	2 hours
120	Rock concert in front of speakers, sandblasting, thunderclap	Immediate danger
140	Gunshot blast, jet plane	Any exposure is dangerous
180	Rocket launching pad	Hearing loss inevitable

note, for example, will contain frequencies that are multiple (*harmonies*) of the frequency being played (the *fundamental*).

Auditory System

The auditory system consists of the ears, parts of the brain, and the various connecting neural pathways. Our primary concern will be with the ears; this includes not just the appendages on the sides of the head, but the entire hearing organ, most of which lies within the skull (see Figure 4-24).

The ear includes three main parts: the *outer ear*, which consists of the external ear (or *pinna*) and the *auditory canal*; the *middle ear*, which consists of the *eardrum* and a chain of three bones; and the *inner ear*, or *cochlea*, which contains the receptors for sound. The major functions of the outer and middle ears are to amplify and transmit sound waves to the receptors in the inner ear.

Let us take a more detailed look at the middle and inner ear (see Figure 4-25). At the outermost part of the middle ear is a taut membrane called the eardrum, which is set into vibration by sound waves funneled to it through the outer ear. The middle ear's job is to transmit these vibrations of the eardrum across an air-filled cavity to another membrane, the *oval window*, which is the gateway to the inner ear and the receptors. The middle ear accomplishes this transmission by means of a mechanical bridge built of three bones, called *malleus, incus,* and *stapes*. The vibrations of the eardrum move the first bone, which then moves the second, which in turn moves the third, which results in vibrations of the oval window. This mechanical arrangement not only transmits the sound wave, but amplifies it as well.

The inner ear, or cochlea, is a coiled tube of bone. It is divided into sections of fluid by membranes, one of which, the *basilar membrane*, supports

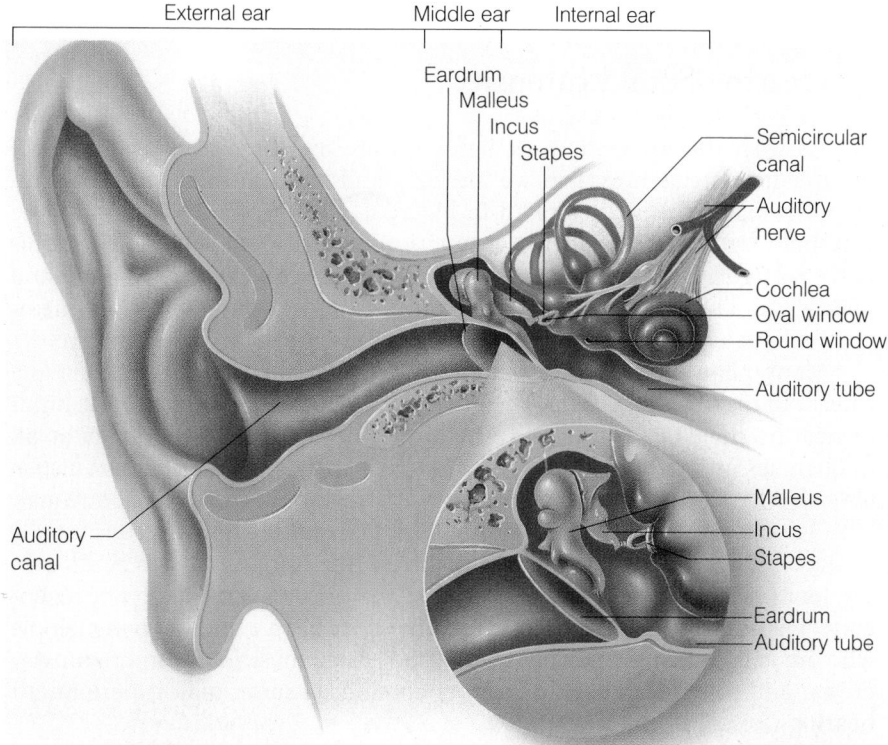

External ear   Middle ear   Internal ear

Eardrum
Malleus
Incus
Stapes

Semicircular canal
Auditory nerve
Cochlea
Oval window
Round window
Auditory tube

Malleus
Incus
Stapes
Eardrum
Auditory tube

Auditory canal

FIGURE 4-24
A Cross Section of the Ear *This drawing shows the overall structure of the ear. The inner ear includes the cochlea, which contains the auditory receptors, and the vestibular apparatus (semicircular canals and vestibular sacs), which is the sense organ for our sense of balance and body motion.*

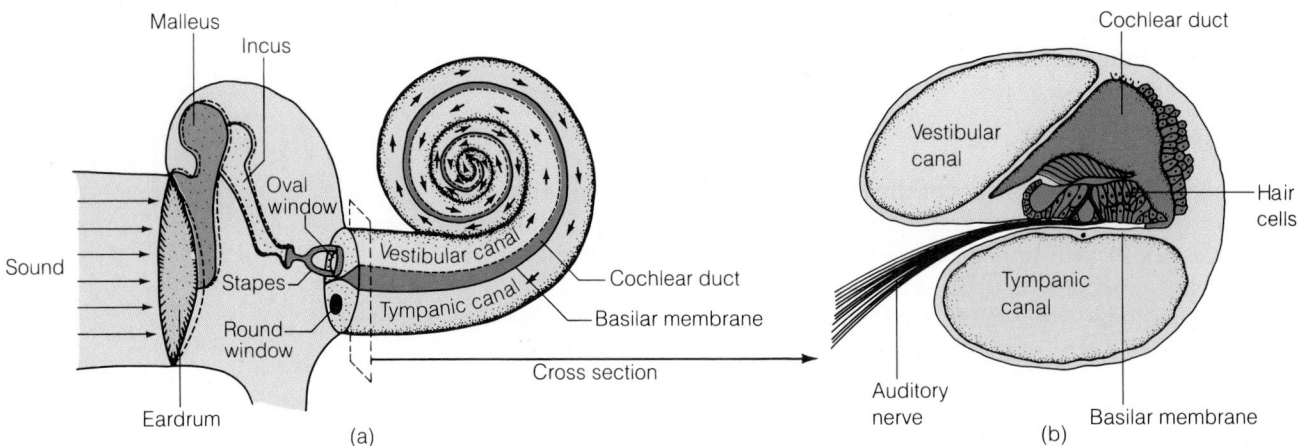

(a)

Cross section

(b)

FIGURE 4-25
Schematic Diagram of the Middle and Inner Ear *(a) Movement of the fluid within the cochlea deforms the basilar membrane and stimulates the hair cells that serve as the auditory receptors. (b) Cross section of the cochlea showing the basilar membrane and the hair cell receptors.*

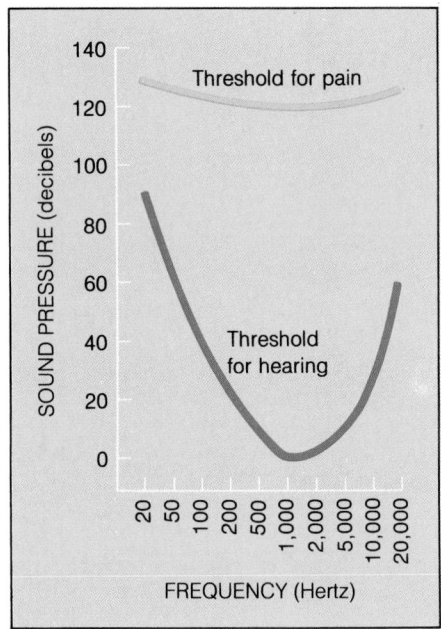

FIGURE 4-26
Absolute Threshold for Hearing *The lower curve shows the absolute intensity threshold at different frequencies. Sensitivity is greatest in the vicinity of 1,000 hertz. The upper curve describes the threshold for pain. (Data are approximate, from various determinations.)*

the auditory receptors (Figure 4-25). The receptors are called *hair cells* because they have hairlike structures that extend into the fluid. Pressure at the oval window (which connects the middle and inner ear) leads to pressure changes in the cochlear fluid, which in turn causes the basilar membrane to vibrate, resulting in a bending of the hair cells and an electrical impulse. By this complex process, a sound wave is transduced into an electrical impulse. The neurons that synapse with the hair cells have long axons that form part of the acoustic nerve. Most of these auditory neurons are connected to a single hair cell. There are about 31,000 auditory neurons in the acoustic nerve, many fewer than the one million neurons in the optic nerve (Yost & Nielson, 1985).

The central auditory pathways are relatively complex. The pathway from each ear goes to both sides of the brain and has synapses in several nuclei before reaching the auditory cortex. Additional pathways descend from the cortex to the cochlea and modulate the activity in ascending pathways.

Hearing Sound Intensity

As with the wavelength of light, we are more sensitive to sounds of intermediate frequency than we are to sounds near either end of our frequency range. This is illustrated in Figure 4-26, which shows the absolute threshold for sound intensity as a function of frequency. The shape of this curve is largely a consequence of the transmission of sound by the outer and middle ear. The complex acoustics of these structures amplify the intermediate frequencies more than those at the extremes of the frequency range.

Many people have some deficit in hearing and consequently have a threshold higher than those shown in Figure 4-26. There are two basic kinds of hearing deficits. In one, thresholds are elevated roughly equally at all frequencies as the result of poor conduction in the middle ear (*conduction loss*). In the other kind of hearing loss, the threshold elevation is unequal, with large elevations occurring at higher frequencies. This pattern is usually a consequence of inner-ear damage, often involving some destruction of the hair cells (*sensory-neural loss*). Hair cells, once destroyed, do not regenerate. Sensory-neural loss occurs in many older people and in young people who are exposed to excessively loud sound. Rock musicians, airport-runway crews, and pneumatic drill operators commonly suffer major, permanent hearing loss.

Hearing Pitch

PITCH AND FREQUENCY   When hearing a pure tone, we experience not only its loudness but also its *pitch*. Just as color is the prime quality of light, so pitch is the prime quality of sound, ordered on a scale from low to high. And just as color is determined by the frequency of light, pitch is determined by the frequency of sound. As frequency increases, pitch increases. (When frequency doubles—that is, increases by one octave—pitch increases by an approximately constant amount; this phenomenon is the basis of musical scales.) As with the wavelength of light, we are very good at discriminating the frequency of a sound. The jnd is less than 1 hertz at 100 hertz and increases to 100 hertz at 10,000 hertz.

However, there is nothing analogous to color mixture in audition. When two or more frequencies are sounded simultaneously, we can hear the pitch associated with each frequency, provided that they are sufficiently separated. When the frequencies are close together, the sensation is more complex but still does not sound like a single, pure tone. In color vision, the fact that a mixture of three lights results in the sensation of a single color led to the idea of three types of cones. The absence of a comparable phenomenon in audition suggests that, if there are receptors specialized for different frequencies, then many different types of such receptors exist.

To determine whether there are cells in the auditory system that respond to different frequencies, researchers have used the phenomenon of *masking*. If the threshold for a tone is increased by the simultaneous presentation of a second tone, the second tone is said to mask the first. This happens only when the tones are close in frequency. Assuming that masking occurs when the two tones activate the same cell, the lack of masking between widely separated frequencies implies that there are different cells for widely different frequencies. Masking experiments also provide a way to determine what frequencies each cell responds to and how well (see Figure 4-27).

THEORIES OF PITCH PERCEPTION   As was the case with color vision, two different kinds of theories have been proposed to account for how the ear codes frequency into pitch.

The first kind of theory originated with Lord Rutherford, a British physicist, in 1886. He proposed that: a) a sound wave causes the entire basilar membrane to vibrate, and the rate of vibration matches the frequency of the sound; and b) the rate at which the membrane vibrates determines the rate of impulses of nerve fibers in the auditory nerve. Thus a 1,000-hertz tone causes the basilar membrane to vibrate 1,000 times per second, which causes nerve fibers in the auditory nerve to fire at 1,000 impulses per second, and the brain interprets this as a particular pitch. Because this theory proposes that pitch depends on how the sound varies with time, it is called a *temporal theory*.

Rutherford's hypothesis soon ran into a major problem. Nerve fibers were shown to have a maximum firing rate of about 1,000 impulses per second, which left the temporal theory with no way to explain how we perceive the pitch of tones whose frequency exceeds 1,000 hertz. Wever (1949) proposed a way to salvage temporal theories. He argued that frequencies over 1,000 hertz could be coded by different groups of nerve fibers, each group firing at a slightly different pace. If one group of neurons is firing at 1,000 impulses per second, for example, and then 1 millisecond later a second group of neurons begins firing at 1,000 impulses per second, the combined rate of impulses per second for the two groups will be 2,000 impulses per second. This version of

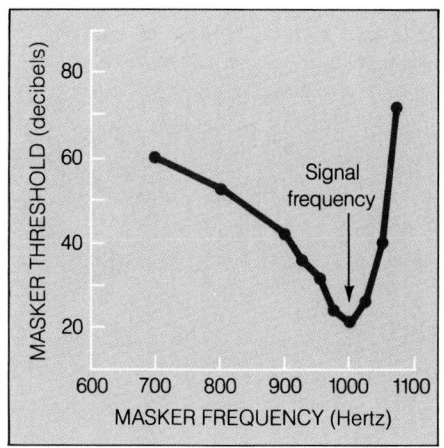

FIGURE 4-27
Auditory Masking *The subject's task was to detect a 1,000-hertz tone of constant intensity (signal). The graph shows the intensity of a second tone (masker) that just masks the signal. As the masker frequency moves away from the signal frequency, the masker becomes less and less effective; its threshold increases. This curve closely resembles a threshold curve for a single neuron in the auditory nerve. It is thought to correspond to one of the frequency-sensitive cells in the human auditory system. (After Moore, 1978)*

Sitting in front of the speakers at a rock concert can cause permanent hearing loss.

temporal theory received support from the discovery that the pattern of nerve impulses in the auditory nerve follows the waveform of the stimulus tone even though individual cells do not respond on every cycle of the wave (Rose, Brugge, Anderson, & Hind, 1967).

However, the ability of nerve fibres to follow the waveform breaks down at about 4,000 hertz; nevertheless, we can hear pitch at much higher frequencies. This suggests that there must be another means of coding the quality of pitch, at least for high frequencies.

The second kind of theory of pitch perception dates back to 1683 when Joseph Guichard Duverney, a French anatomist, proposed that frequency was coded into pitch mechanically by resonance (Green & Wier, 1984). He theorized that the ear contained a structure like a stringed instrument. Different parts of this structure are tuned to different frequencies, so that when a frequency is presented to the ear, the corresponding part of the structure vibrates—just as when a tuning fork is struck near a piano, the piano string that is tuned to the frequency of the fork will begin to vibrate. This idea proved to be essentially correct; the structure turned out to be the basilar membrane, which, unlike a set of strings, is continuous.

In the 1800s, Hermann von Helmholtz developed the resonance hypothesis into the *place theory* of pitch perception. It holds that each specific place along the basilar membrane will, when it responds, lead to a particular pitch sensation. This does not mean that we hear with our basilar membrane; rather, the places on the membrane that vibrate most determine what neural fibers are activated, and that determines the pitch that we hear. This is an example of a sensory modality coding quality by the specific nerves involved.

How the basilar membrane actually moves was not established until the 1940s when Georg von Békésy measured its movement through small holes drilled in the cochlea. Working with the cochleas of guinea pigs and human cadavers, he showed that high frequencies cause vibration at the far end of the basilar membrane; as frequency increases, the vibration pattern moves toward the oval window (Békésy, 1960). For this and other research on audition, von Békésy received a Nobel prize in 1961.

Like temporal theories, place theories explain many phenomena of pitch perception, but not all. A major difficulty for place theory arises with low-frequency tones. With frequencies below 50 hertz, all parts of the basilar membrane vibrate roughly the same amount. This means that all receptors are equally activated, which implies that we have no way of discriminating between frequencies below 50 hertz. In fact, though, we can discriminate frequencies as low as 20 hertz.

Hence, place theories have problems explaining our perception of low-frequency tones, while temporal theories have problems dealing with high-frequency tones. This led to the idea that pitch depends on both place and temporal pattern (*duplicity theory*). Unlike the two-stage color theory, the duplicity theory of pitch has yet to be developed into a complete theory.

Localizing Sounds

In addition to sensing the intensity and pitch of a sound, we can also determine the direction of its source. This ability to *localize sound* depends on us having two ears that receive somewhat different inputs.

A sound may arrive at the two ears at slightly different times. When the source of a sound is located to the right of the head, for example, the sound has to travel less distance to reach the right ear than the left ear, and consequently it arrives at the right ear a split second before it reaches the left one. At low frequencies, we employ this *interaural time difference* as a cue for localizing sounds, being able to use arrival time differences as brief as 10 microseconds (Durlach & Colburn, 1978). At high frequencies, we favor another cue: the difference in intensity of the sounds reaching the two ears. This *interaural intensity* difference occurs because the head causes a "sound shadow," which *decreases* the intensity of the sound reaching the far ear (see Figure 4-28).

An analysis of the physics of the two cues supports the idea that at high frequencies we localize sound by intensity differences while at low frequencies we localize by arrival time. Intensity differences are greater at high frequencies than at low frequencies, because the head blocks high frequencies more than low frequencies. In contrast, arrival-time differences are easier to detect at low frequencies, because the peaks of the waves are not close together. A number of phenomena are compatible with the two-cue theory, particularly the fact that we tend to confuse sounds coming from in front of us with sounds coming from behind. Both intensity and time cues are almost the same for sound sources directly in front of and behind the observer.

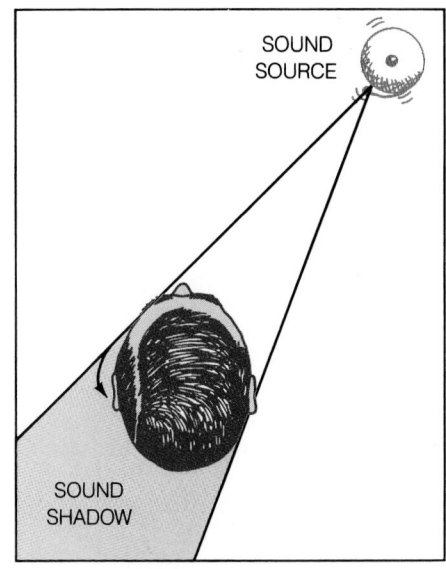

FIGURE 4-28
Cues to Sound Source Location *If a sound source is to the right of the head, the distance from the source to the right ear is shorter than the distance to the left ear. Consequently, the sound will arrive at the right ear first. This cue is effective at low sound frequencies. Because of the partial sound shadow cast by the head, intensity will be less at the left ear. This cue is effective at high frequencies.*

OTHER SENSES

Senses other than vision and audition lack the richness of patterning and organization that have led sight and hearing to be called the "higher senses." Our symbolic experiences are expressed largely in visual and auditory terms: spoken language is to be heard, written language to be seen. Still, these other senses are vitally important.

In discussing each of these other senses, as with vision and audition we will consider: the nature of the stimulus to which the sensory modality is sensitive, how the receptors carry out the transduction process, and how the sensory modality codes intensity and quality.

CRITICAL DISCUSSION

Artificial Ears and Eyes

The science fiction fantasy of replacing defective sense organs with artificial, functioning ones is becoming a reality. Researchers have been working for several years on artificial replacements (called *prostheses*) for damaged eyes and ears. In the mid-1980s the United States Food and Drug Administration approved a device that directly stimulates the auditory nerve. This work has important implications for both the reduction of sensory handicaps and for our understanding of auditory processes.

Research on auditory prostheses has concentrated on devices that apply electrical stimulation to the auditory nerve. They are designed to aid people whose hair cells (the receptors) have been destroyed, and consequently suffer a total sensory-neural hearing loss, but whose auditory nerve is intact and functional. Most of these devices use an electrode, which is inserted through the round window into the cochlea, to stimulate the neurons along the basilar membrane (a *cochlea implant*). Because the electrode goes directly into the cochlea, the functional part of the ear is bypassed (including the receptors); the cochlea is simply a convenient place to stimulate auditory neurons where they are accessible and laid out in an orderly array.

In addition to the stimulating electrode, a cochlea implant has three other components that operate in sequence: a) a microphone located near the external ear that picks up sound; b) a small battery-operated electronic processor worn on the outside of the body that converts the sound into electrical signals; and c) a transmission system that transmits the electrical signal through the skull and to the electrode implanted in the cochlea. The last step in this process is accomplished by radio transmission to avoid a wire through the skull.

A relatively simple device of this kind was developed in the early 1970s by William House (see the figure). The House implant extends only 6 millimeters into the cochlea and has only one electrode. The signal applied to this electrode is an electrical wave having essentially the same form as the sound wave. When sound is presented to a deaf patient using this device, he or she hears a complex noise that varies in loudness. These devices have been implanted in hundreds of profoundly deaf people. Most of the recipients believe that the device provides a marked improvement over their previously deaf state. With it, they at least hear sounds and have some ability to discriminate intensity.

More recent developments include a number of devices with multiple electrodes. These extend further into the cochlea and are designed to independently stimulate several sets of neurons along the basilar membrane. Because the cochlea is only the size of a pea, with a solid bony shell and very delicate interior structures, there are difficult technical problems involved in designing and implanting the electrodes. Accompanying most of these multichannel implants is a more elaborate electronic processor that filters the sound into separate frequencies, one for each electrode. The sound wave in each frequency band is converted into an electrical signal and applied to one of the electrodes. Although preliminary results vary greatly, some patients show good performance, including word recognition scores of more than 70 percent (Loeb, 1985).

The multiple-electrode devices are based on the place theory of pitch perception. In the normal ear, mechanical means are used to get different frequencies to vibrate specific parts of the basilar membrane, which lead to the activation of specific nerve fibers; in the multiple-electrode device, electronic filtering is used to accomplish this task. The electronically filtered signal is sent to the same place that it would be applied in the normal ear. To some extent the success of the device supports the theory.

However, use of the multiple-electrode devices has turned up some findings that don't fit well with place theory. According to the latter, when electrical stimulation is applied to a single small region on the basilar membrane, a sound with a pitch is heard and this pitch varies with place. However, the sound that is heard with a multiple-electrode device is not at all like a pure tone; it is more like the "quacking of ducks" or the "banging of garbage cans," even though it does have a crude pitch. Nor do results with multiple-electrode devices provide

Smell

EVOLUTIONARY SIGNIFICANCE   Before turning to our usual considerations about a sensory modality, it is useful to view the sense of smell from an evolutionary perspective. Smell is one of the most primitive and most important of the senses. The sense organ for smell has a position of prominence in the head appropriate to a sense intended to guide the organism. Smell has a more direct route to the brain than any other sense: the receptors, which

much support for temporal theories of pitch. Temporal theorists might expect that the sensation would change when the frequency of electrical stimulation changes. In fact, this produces only slight changes. The results suggest that another factor, apart from place and temporal pattern, is involved in pitch perception. This may be a complex spatiotemporal pattern of stimulation along the basilar membrane that cannot be mimicked by a few electrodes (Loeb, 1985).

The development of artificial eyes for the blind has not progressed as far as the development of artificial ears. The problem is not one of picking up the optical image; a video camera can do this well. Rather, the problem is putting the image's information into the visual system in a form that the brain can use. Research has focused on the direct electrical stimulation of the visual cortex in volunteer subjects who are either blind or undergoing brain surgery. If we know what a person sees when different places in the cortex are electrically stimulated, then by controlling the electrical stimulation it should be possible to evoke different experiences. The next step would be to use a video camera to form an image of the scene in front of a blind person and then evoke an experience of that scene.

Results obtained thus far suggest we are a long way from developing an artificial eye. When a small region of the visual cortex is stimulated with a weak electrical signal, the person experiences rudimentary, visual sensations. These sensations have been described as small spots of light that are seen in front of the person in different direc-

tions. They range in size from that of a "grain of rice" to a "coin." Most are white, but some are colored. If several places in the visual cortex are stimulated simultaneously, the corresponding spots will usually be experienced together. Although multiple stimulation of the visual cortex provides the

basis for a crude pattern vision (Dobelle, Meadejovsky, & Girvin, 1974), it is questionable whether this approach will lead to a successful prosthesis for damaged eyes. The neural input to the visual cortex is so complicated that it is unlikely to be adequately duplicated.

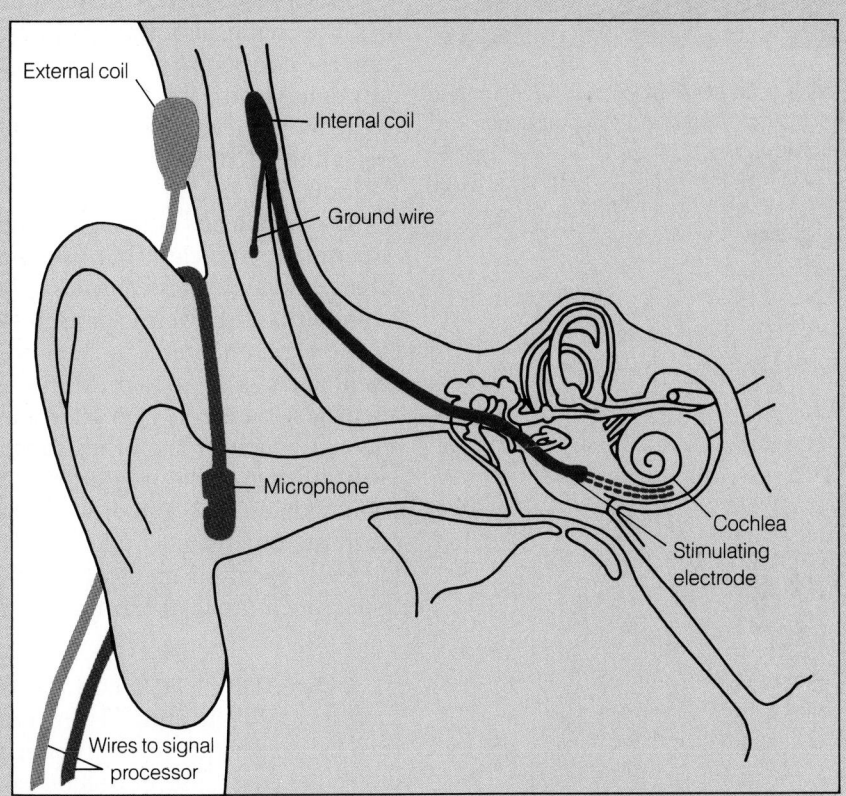

Cochlear Implant *This diagram illustrates the auditory prosthesis developed by William House and his associates. Sound is picked up by a microphone and filtered by a signal processor (not shown) worn outside the body. The electrical waveform produced by the processor is then transmitted by radio waves through the skull to the electrode inside the cochlea.*

are in the nasal cavity, are connected without synapse to the brain.

While smell (or *olfaction*) is not essential for our species, it is essential for the survival of many other animals. Not surprisingly, then, a larger area of the cortex is devoted to smell in other species than in our own. In fish, the olfactory cortex makes up almost all of the cerebral hemispheres; in dogs, about one-third; in humans, only about one-twentieth. These differences are related to differences in sensitivity among the species. Taking advantage of the superior smell capability of dogs, both the United States Postal

A dog's acute sense of smell is helpful in law enforcement, as this drug-sniffing canine demonstrates.

Service and the Bureau of Customs have trained them to check unopened packages for heroin. And specially trained police dogs can sniff out hidden explosives.

Because smell is so well developed in other species, it is often used as a major means of communication. Insects and some higher animals secrete chemicals, known as *pheromones*, that float through the air to be sniffed by other members of the species. For example, a female moth can release a pheromone so powerful that males are drawn to her from a distance of several miles. It is clear that the male moth responds only to the pheromone and not to the sight of the female; the male will be attracted to a female in a wire container even though she is blocked from view, but not to a female who is clearly visible in a glass container from which the scent cannot escape.

Insects use smell to communicate death as well as "love." After an ant dies, the chemicals formed from its decomposing body stimulate other ants to carry the corpse to a refuse heap outside the nest. If a living ant is experimentally doused with the decomposition chemicals, it is carried off by other ants to the refuse heap. When it returns to the nest, it is carried out again. Such premature attempts at burial continue until the "smell of death" has worn off (Wilson, 1963).

Do we humans have a remnant of this primitive communication system? Experiments indicate that we can use smell at least to tell ourselves from others, and males from females. In one study, subjects wore undershirts for 24 hours without showering or using deodorant. The undershirts were collected by the experimenter. He then presented each subject with three shirts to smell: one was the subject's own shirt, another was a male's, and the third was a female's. Based only on odor, most subjects could identify their own shirt and tell which of the other shirts was worn by males or females (Russell, 1976). Other studies suggest that we may communicate subtler matters by odor. Women who live or work together seem to communicate where they are in their menstrual cycle by means of smell, and over time this results in a tendency for their menstrual cycles to synchronize and begin at the same time (McClintock, 1971; Russell, Switz, & Thompson, 1980).

OLFACTORY STIMULUS AND SYSTEM   The molecules given off by a substance are the stimulus for smell. The molecules leave the substance, travel through the air, and enter the nasal passage (see Figure 4-29). The molecules must also be soluble in fat, because the receptors for smell are covered with a fatlike substance. Researchers have been hampered in their study of smell because the stimuli are hard to control. It is difficult to know exactly when the molecules reach the olfactory receptors, and difficult to determine the exact concentration of the stimulus that reaches the receptors.

The olfactory system consists of the receptors in the nasal passage, regions of the brain, and interconnecting neural pathways. The receptors for smell are located high in the nasal cavity. When the *cilia* (hairlike structures) of these receptors are contacted by molecules of odorant, an electrical impulse results; this is the transduction process. This impulse travels along nerve fibers to the *olfactory bulb*, a region of the brain that lies just below the frontal lobes. The olfactory bulb in turn is connected to the olfactory cortex on the inside of the temporal lobes.

SENSING INTENSITY AND QUALITY   Human sensitivity to the intensity of a smell depends dramatically on the substance involved. Absolute thresholds can be as low as 1 part per 50 billion parts of air. Still, as noted

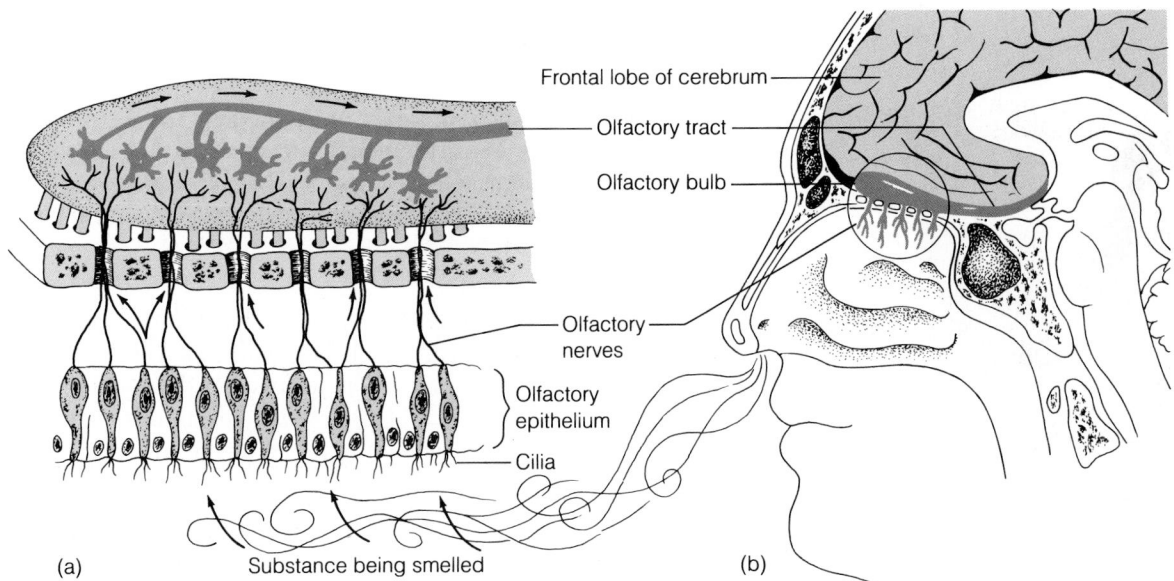

Frontal lobe of cerebrum

Olfactory tract

Olfactory bulb

Olfactory nerves

Olfactory epithelium

Cilia

(a) Substance being smelled (b)

FIGURE 4-29
Olfactory Receptors *(a) Detail of receptors interspersed among numerous supporting cells. (b) The placement of the olfactory receptors in the nasal cavity.*

earlier, we are far less sensitive to smell than other species. Dogs, for example, can detect substances in concentrations 100 times lower than concentrations humans can detect (Moulton, 1977). Our relative lack of sensitivity is not due to our having less sensitive olfactory receptors. Rather, we just have fewer of them: roughly 10 million receptors for people versus 1 billion for dogs.

Some researchers have proposed that there are six basic odor qualities—spicy, fragrant, putrid, etheral, resinous, and burned—and that all odors can be analyzed phenomenologically into one more of these six qualities (Woodworth, 1938). Other researchers (Amoore, 1970) have proposed seven or more different basic odors. At this point in time, no clear consensus exists on how to describe phenomenologically the qualities of different odors.

Still, progress has been made on how the olfactory system codes the quality of odor. Unlike the coding of color in vision or pitch in audition, each olfactory receptor responds to many different odorants rather than to just one type of odorant or to one class of similarly smelling odorants (Matthews, 1972). Such diffuse coding is also the rule higher in the olfactory system, at the olfactory bulb. Qualitatively different odors activate roughly the same set of neurons, though the precise pattern differs from odor to odor. The difference in smell between lemon and turpentine, for example, is due more to the pattern of activation in the receptors, than to the specific cells activated.

Taste

Taste gets credit for a lot of experiences that it does not provide. We say that a meal "tastes" good, but when smell is eliminated by a bad cold our dinner becomes an impoverished experience. Still, taste (or *gustation*) is a sense in its own right. Even with a bad cold, we can tell salted from unsalted food.

In what follows, we will talk about the taste of particular substances, but note that the substance being tasted is not the only factor that determines its taste. Our genetic makeup and past experience also affect taste. For example,

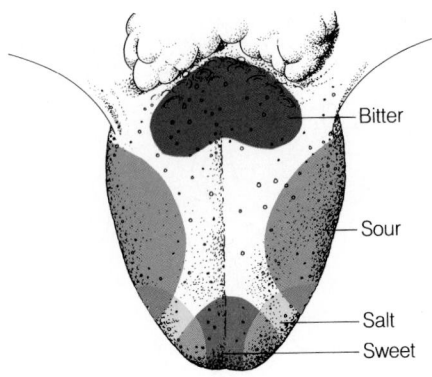

FIGURE 4-30
Taste Areas *Different areas of the tongue are sensitive to different tastes. The center of the tongue is relatively insensitive.*

some people detect a bitter taste in caffeine and saccharine, whereas many do not, and this difference among people appears to be genetically determined (Bartoshuk, 1979). As another case in point, Indians living in the Karnataka province of India eat many sour foods, and experience citric acid and quinine as pleasant tasting: most of us experience the opposite. This particular difference between people seems to be a matter of past experience, for Indians who have been raised in a western country find citric acid and quinine unpleasant (Moskowitz et al., 1975).

GUSTATORY STIMULUS AND SYSTEM   The stimulus for taste is a substance that is soluble in saliva, which is a fluid much like salt water. The gustatory system includes the receptors located on the tongue, parts of the brain, and interconnecting neural pathways. The taste receptors occur in clusters, called *taste buds*, on the bumps of the tongue and around the mouth. At the ends of the taste buds are short, hairlike structures that extend out and make contact with the solutions in the mouth. This contact results in an electrical impulse; this is the transduction process. The electrical impulse then travels to the brain.

SENSING INTENSITY AND QUALITY   Sensitivity to different taste stimuli varies from place to place on the tongue, with sensitivity to salty and sweet substances best near the front of the tongue, sour along the sides, and bitter on the soft palate (see Figure 4-30). In the center of the tongue is a region insensitive to taste (the place to put an unpleasant pill). While absolute thresholds for taste are generally very low, jnds for intensity are relatively high (Weber's constant is about 0.2). This means that if you are increasing the amount of spice in a dish you must add more than 20 percent or you will not taste the difference.

With regard to sensing quality, taste shows many of the phenomena with which we are already familiar. Thus, exposure to one substance will temporarily change the taste of other substances, and one taste can even mask

Taste discrimination by an expert.

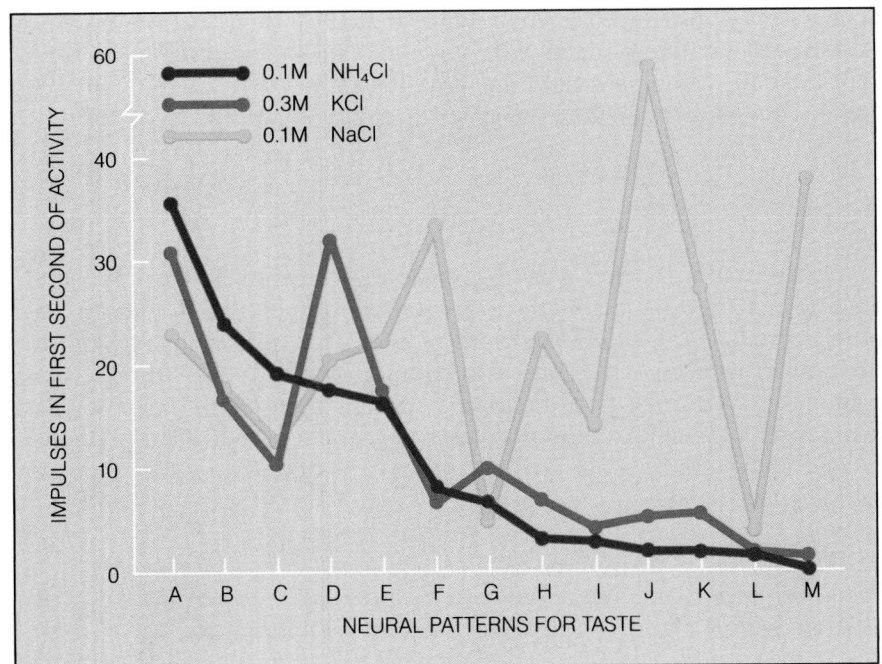

FIGURE 4-31
Pattern of Neural Impulses *Each letter on the horizontal axis indicates a different neural fiber. For each fiber the responses to three stimuli are plotted.* (After Erickson, 1963)

another. As examples: sugar masks the bitterness of coffee, toothpaste reduces the sweetness of sugar and makes citrus juice extra sour (another reason for brushing your teeth *after* breakfast), and a berry called miracle fruit makes anything eaten after it taste sweet. Although new tastes sometimes appear in mixtures (Schiffman & Erickson, 1980), we do not know if substances can be mixed to match the tastes of other substances in any general way, as is the case in color vision.

Any taste can be described as one or a combination of the four basic taste qualities: sweet, sour, salty, and bitter (McBurney, 1978). These four tastes are best revealed in sucrose (sweet), hydrochloric acid (sour), sodium chloride (salty), and quinine (bitter). When subjects are asked to describe the tastes of various substances in terms of just the four basic tastes, they have no trouble doing this; even if given the option of using additional qualities of their own choice, they tend to stay with the four basic tastes (Goldstein, 1984).

The gustatory system codes taste in terms of both the specific nerve fibers activated and the pattern of activation across nerve fibers. There appear to be four different types of nerve fibers, corresponding to the four basic tastes. While each fiber responds somewhat to all four basic tastes, it responds best to just one of them. Hence, it makes sense to talk of "salty fibers," whose activity signals saltiness to the brain.

To appreciate how the gustatory system uses the pattern of activation to code taste, look at the graph in Figure 4-31. These data are from a study in which the experimenter presented various substances to a rat to taste, and simultaneously recorded electrical activity in nerve fibers leaving the tongue. The letters along the horizontal axis of the graph correspond to 13 different nerve fibers, and the vertical axis shows the number of impulses in each of these fibers. The blue curve presents the results for one substance, the red curve the results for a second substance, and the yellow curve the results for a third substance. To the extent the curves for two substances differ, their pattern of impulses across the 13 fibers differ. Clearly, the pattern of impulses for the third substance differs markedly from that of the other two substances, and independent evidence shows that the third substance is perceived as tasting different from the other two (which taste alike). The brain is using the pattern to "tell" the taste (Erickson, 1963).

Skin Senses

Traditionally, touch was thought to be a single sense. Today, it is considered to include three distinct skin senses, one responding to pressure, another to temperature, and the third to pain. The reason for making this division is that each of the three skin senses: a) responds to a distinct class of stimuli; b) has the ability to discriminate among these stimuli; c) possesses a distinct set of receptors; and d) leads to experiences that differ phenomenologically when the sense is stimulated. These are the standard criteria for telling senses apart.

PRESSURE   The stimulus for sensed pressure is physical pressure on the skin. Although we are not aware of steady pressure on the entire body (such as air pressure), we are sensitive to variations in pressure over the body surface. Some parts of the body are more effective than others at coding the intensity of pressure; the lips, nose, and cheek are the most sensitive to pressure, while the big toe is least sensitive. These differences are closely related to the number of receptors that respond to the stimulus at each of these body loci. In sensitive regions, we can detect a force as small as 5 milligrams applied to a small area.

Our sensitivity to pressure depends on factors other than just location on the body. If the stimulus vibrates up and down on the skin, we are most sensitive to vibration frequencies of about 250 hertz and less sensitive to higher and lower frequencies. Recordings from single cells at higher levels in the pressure system suggest that some cells are specialized for certain vibration frequencies (Loomis & Lederman, 1986). The pressure system shows profound adaptation effects. If you hold your friend's hand for several minutes without moving, you will become insensitive to it and cease to feel the hand.

In addition to single points of pressure, we are also sensitive to patterns of pressure, which can be thought of as *qualities* of pressure. Most studies of pattern sensation have measured the *two-point threshold*, the minimum distance by which two very thin rods touching the skin must be separated before they are felt as two points rather than one. Like the pressure threshold, the two-point threshold varies greatly over the body surface, but the correlation between the two is not perfect. The two-point threshold is lowest in the fingers and highest on the calves (see Figure 4-32).

In the above discussion, we focused on what happens when we experience pressure in a passive way, that is, when we are being touched. But what about when we are actively exploring the environment, that is, when we are doing the touching. Such *active touching* results in a different experience than its passive counterpart, and involves the activity of the motor senses (see below), as well as the pressure sense. By active touch alone, we can readily identify familiar objects, even though we are rarely required to identify objects in this manner (Klatzky, Lederman, & Metzger, 1985).

TEMPERATURE   The stimulus for temperature is the temperature of our skin. The receptors are neurons with free nerve endings just under the skin.

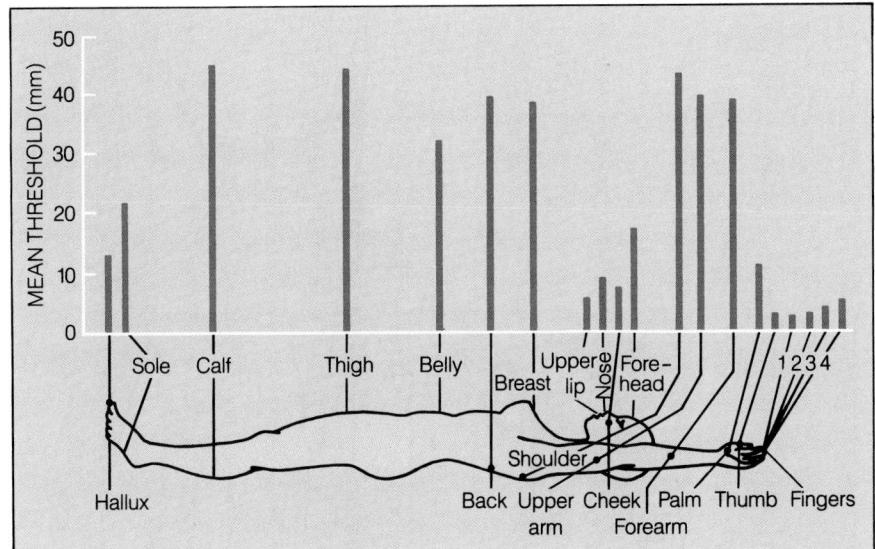

FIGURE 4-32
Two-Point Threshold *This graph shows the two-point threshold in millimeters at different places on the body surface. The threshold is determined by touching the skin with two thin rods separated by a small distance. The subject indicates whether one or two rods are sensed. The rod separation is adjusted to find the minimum separation at which two rods are sensed. The data given are for females, but male thresholds are very similar. (After Weinstein, 1968)*

In the transduction stage, *cold receptors* generate a neural impulse when there is a decrease in skin temperature, while *warm receptors* generate an impulse when there is an increase in skin temperature (Hensel, 1973; Duclauz & Kenshalo, 1980). Hence, different qualities of temperature can be coded primarily by the specific receptors activated. However, this specificity of neural reaction has its limits. Cold receptors respond not only to low temperatures but also to very high temperatures (above 45 degrees centigrade). Consequently a very hot stimulus will activate both warm and cold receptors, which in turn evoke a hot sensation.

Because maintaining body temperature is crucial to our survival, it is important that we can sense small changes in our skin temperature. When the skin is at its normal temperature, we can detect a warming of only 0.4 degrees centigrade and a cooling of just 0.15 degrees centigrade (Kenshalo, Nafe, & Brooks, 1961). Our temperature sense adapts completely to moderate changes in temperatures, so that after a few minutes the stimulus feels neither cool nor warm. This adaptation explains the strong differences of opinion about the temperature of a swimming pool between those who have been in it for a while and those first dangling a foot in.

PAIN Any stimulus that is intense enough to cause tissue damage is a stimulus for pain. It may be pressure, temperature, electric shock, or irritant chemicals. The effect of such a stimulus is to cause the release of chemical substances in the skin, which in turn stimulate distinct high-threshold receptors (the transduction stage). These receptors are neurons with specialized free nerve endings, and researchers have distinguished at least four types (Brown & Deffenbacher, 1979).

More than any other sensation, the intensity and quality of pain is influenced by factors other than the precipitating stimulus. These factors include the person's culture, attitudes, and previous experience. The striking influence of culture is illustrated by the fact that some non-western societies engage in rituals that would be unbearably painful to westerners. A case in point is the hook-swinging ceremony practiced in some parts of India:

FIGURE 4-33
Culture and Pain *Right: two steel hooks in the back of the "celebrant" in the Indian hook-swinging ceremony. Left: the celebrant hangs onto the ropes as a cart takes him from village to village. As he blesses the village children and crops, he swings freely, suspended by the hooks in his back. (After Kosambi, 1967)*

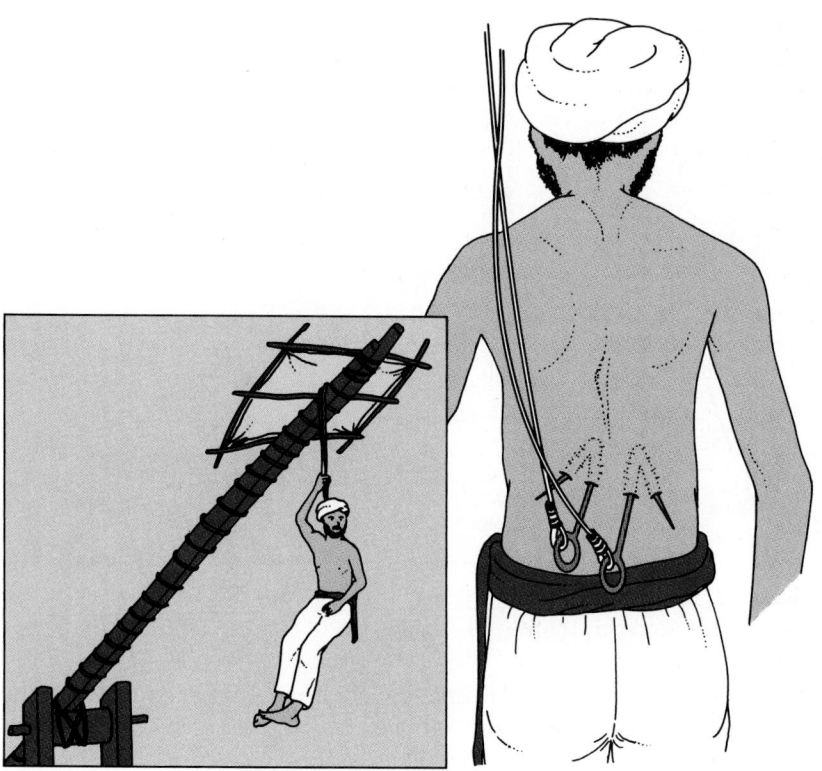

The ceremony derives from an ancient practice in which a member of a social group is chosen to represent the power of the gods. The role of the chosen man (or "celebrant") is to bless the children and crops in a series of neighboring villages during a particular period of the year. What is remarkable about the ritual is that steel hooks, which are attached by strong ropes to the top of a special cart, are shoved under his skin and muscles on both sides of his back [see Figure 4-33]. The cart is then moved from village to village. Usually the man hangs on to the ropes as the cart is moved about. But at the climax of the ceremony in each village, he swings free, hanging only from the hooks embedded in his back, to bless the children and crops. Astonishingly, there is no evidence that the man is in pain during the ritual; rather, he appears to be in a "state of exaltation." When the hooks are later removed, wounds heal rapidly without any medical treatment other than the application of wood ash. Two weeks later the marks on his back are scarcely visible (Melzak, 1973).

Clearly, pain is as much a matter of mind as of sensory receptors.

Phenomena like the above have led to the *gate control theory* of pain (Melzak, 1973). According to the theory, the sensation of pain requires not only that pain receptors on the skin be active, but also that a neural gate in the spinal cord allow these signals to pass to the brain (the gate is "closed" when critical fibers in the spinal cord are activated). Because the neural gate can be influenced by signals sent down from the brain, the perceived intensity of pain can be influenced by mental state, as in the hook-swinging ceremony.

Many phenomena fit with gate control theory. For one, pressure stimulation tends to close the neural gate (activate the critical fibers), which is why rubbing a hurt area may relieve pain. A more extreme version of this phenomenon is *stimulation-produced analgesia*, in which stimulation of a region in the midbrain acts like an anesthetic. One can perform abdominal surgery on a rat with no anesthetic other than electrical stimulation of the midbrain, yet the rat shows no sign of experiencing pain (Reynolds, 1969). A related phenomenon is the reduction in pain resulting from *acupuncture*. Acupuncture is a healing procedure developed in China, in which needles are inserted into the skin at critical points; twirling these needles has been reported to eliminate pain entirely, making it possible to perform major surgery in a conscious patient (see Figure 4-34). Presumably, the needles stimulate nerve fibers that lead to a closing of the pain gate.

Body Senses

In addition to skin senses, we also have a set of *body senses*, each of which informs us about our movements and orientation in space.

KINESTHESIS   *Kinesthesis* is a sense of the position and movement of the head and limbs relative to the trunk. If you doubt whether you have such a sense, next time you wake in the middle of the night ask yourself where your arms are. Kinesthesis will enable you to answer correctly without looking. The receptors that are responsible for transduction are located in the muscles, tendons, joints, and skin. Often, kinesthesis does not work alone. When we actively control our limbs, kinesthesis is aided by signals from the motor center of the brain to the perceptual system. And when we actively touch something, kinesthesis can be involved along with the pressure sense.

ORIENTATION AND BODY MOVEMENT   We sense the orientation of our body with respect to gravity as well as the movement of our body through space (both linear and angular movement). These capacities are often grouped together because the receptors involved are all in the *vestibular apparatus* adjoining the inner ear.

The receptors for orientation and *linear movement* (movement in a straight line) are located in fluid-filled chambers. These chambers, called the *vestibular sacs*, consist of hair cells; when the cilia of these hair cells are bent by body tilt or linear acceleration, a neural impulse results (the transduction stage). Typically, our senses of orientation and linear movement do not lead to conscious sensations, as their main function is the largely unconscious regulation of motor activity.

The receptors for angular movements (movement of our body or parts of it rotating through space) are located in the *semicircular canals* (see Figure 4-24 again). Movement of the fluid in these canals bends the cilia of the hair cells embedded in the canals and causes them to respond (transduction), producing a sensation of acceleration. The hair cells do not respond to motion at constant velocity, but extreme stimulation of this sense produces dizziness and nausea.

In many cases, then, the body senses do not give rise to conscious sensations of intensity and quality. In this respect, they are most unlike the other senses. Among the skin senses, pain in particular is notorious for filling one's consciousness. To a lesser extent, smells and tastes can also command our attention. And vision and hearing, our higher senses, are responsible for a good deal of the richness of conscious experience.

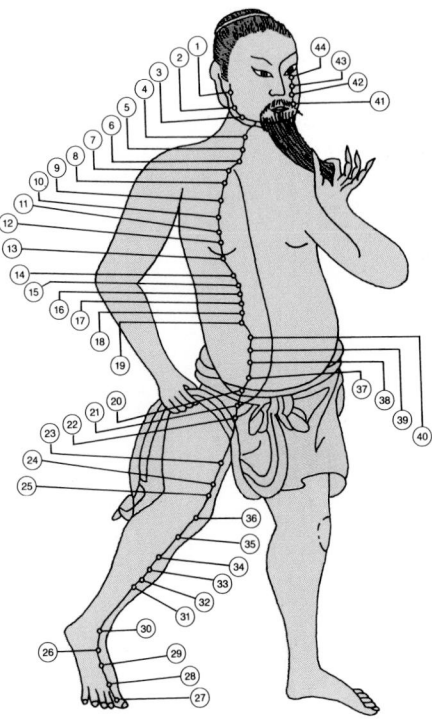

FIGURE 4-34
Typical Acupuncture Chart *The numbers indicate sites at which needles can be inserted, and then either twisted, electrified, or heated. An impressive analgesia results in many cases.*

⚡ CHAPTER SUMMARY

1. Sensations result from processes associated with organs like the eye and ear, and presumably are elicited by simple stimuli (a color pattern, for example). The senses include vision, hearing (*audition*), smell (*olfaction*), taste (*gustation*), the *skin senses* (including pressure, temperature, and pain), and the *body senses* (including our senses of orientation and body movement).

2. One property common to all senses is a sensitivity for detecting change. Sensitivity to intensity is measured by the *absolute threshold*, the minimum amount of a stimulus that can be reliably detected. Sensitivity to a change in intensity is measured by the *difference threshold* or *jnd*, the minimum difference between two stimuli that can be reliably detected. The amount of change needed for detection to occur increases with the initial intensity of the stimulus, and is approximately proportional to it (*Weber's law*).

3. Every sense modality must recode its physical energy into neural impulses. This *transduction* process is accomplished by the *receptors*. The receptors and connecting neural pathways code the *intensity* of a stimulus by the rate of neural impulses and their patterns; they code the *quality* of a stimulus by the specific nerve fibers involved and their pattern of activity.

4. The stimulus for vision is electromagnetic radiation from 400 to 700 nanometers, and the sense organs are the eyes. Each eye contains a system for forming the image (including the *cornea, pupil*, and *lens*), and a system for transducing the image into electrical impulses. The transduction system is in the *retina*, which contains the visual receptors, the *rods* and *cones*. Cones operate at high intensities, lead to sensations of color, and are found only in the center (or *fovea*) of the retina; rods operate at low intensities, lead to colorless sensations, and predominate in the *periphery* of the retina.

5. Our sensitivity to a light's intensity is mediated by properties of the rods and cones. Sensitivity is greater in the rod-rich periphery than in the fovea. Sensitivity also depends on the *wavelength* of the light: in the periphery (rod vision), sensitivity is greatest for a light of about 500 nanometers; in the fovea (cone vision), sensitivity peaks at about 550 nanometers. These differences arise because the chemicals in the rods and cones, the *photoreceptors*, differ in their ability to absorb light at various wavelengths.

6. Different wavelengths of light lead to sensations of different colors. Any color can be described phenomenologically by three dimensions: *brightness, hue*, and *saturation*. A mixture of three lights widely separated in wavelength can be made to match almost any color of light. There are four *basic color sensations*: red, yellow, green, and blue. Mixtures of these make up our experiences of color, except that we do not see reddish-greens and yellowish-blues. These facts can be explained by a *two-stage theory*. It postulates three types of cones (each of which is maximally sensitive to wavelengths in a different region) followed at a higher level in the visual system by red-green and yellow-blue *opponent processes* (each of which responds in opposite ways to its two opponent colors).

7. The stimulus for audition is a wave of pressure changes (a *sound wave*), and the sense organs are the ears. The ear includes: the *outer ear* (the external ear and the *auditory canal*); the *middle ear* (the *eardrum* and a chain of bones); and the *inner ear*. The inner ear, or *cochlea*, is a coiled tube that contains the *basilar membrane*, which supports the *hair cells* that serve as the receptors for sound. Sound waves transmitted by the outer and middle ear cause the basilar membrane to vibrate, which results in a bending of the hair cells, and eventuates in a neural impulse.

8. *Pitch*, the most striking quality of sound, increases with the frequency of the sound wave. The fact that *masking* occurs only for tones close in frequency indicates that there are many cells in the auditory system that respond to different frequencies. *Temporal theories* of pitch perception postulate that the pitch heard depends on the temporal pattern of neural responses in the auditory system, which itself is determined by the temporal pattern of the sound wave. *Place*

theories postulate that each frequency stimulates one place along the basilar membrane, and each place, when stimulated, results in one pitch heard. There is evidence for and against both theories.

9. Smell is more important to nonhuman species than to humans. Many species use specialized odors (*pheromones*) for communication, and humans seem to have a remnant of this system. The stimuli for smell are the molecules given off by a substance. The molecules travel by air and activate the olfactory receptors located high in the *nasal cavity*. Each receptor responds to many different odors rather than just one; consequently, coding of odor depends on the pattern of neurons activated.

10. Taste is affected not only by the substance being tasted, but also by genetic makeup and past experience. The stimulus for taste is a substance that is soluble in saliva. The receptors occur in clusters on the tongue (*taste buds*). Sensitivity varies from place to place on the tongue. Any taste can be described as one or a combination of the four basic taste qualities: *sweet, sour, salty,* and *bitter*. Different qualities of taste are coded partly in terms of the specific nerve fibers activated—different fibers respond best to one of the four taste sensations—and partly in terms of the pattern of fibers activated.

11. Three *skin senses* are distinguished: *pressure, temperature,* and *pain*. Our sensitivity to pressure is greatest at the lips, nose, and cheeks, and least at the big toe. We are very sensitive to temperature, being able to detect a change of less than one degree centigrade. We code different kinds of temperatures primarily by whether *hot* or *cold receptors* are activated. Our sensitivity to pain is greatly influenced by factors other than the noxious stimulus, including culture, attitudes, and previous experience. These factors may have their influence by opening or closing a *neural gate* in the spinal cord; pain is experienced only when pain receptors are activated and the gate is open.

12. The *body senses* include *kinesthesis,* and the senses of *orientation* and *body motion*. Kinesthesis is a sense of the position and movement of the limbs and head relative to the trunk; its receptors are located in the muscles, tendons, joints, and skin. We also sense our orientation with respect to gravity, as well as our movement through space (both *linear* and *angular movement*). These capacities are often grouped together because the receptors involved are all in the *vestibular apparatus* adjoining the inner ear.

FURTHER READING

There are several good general texts on sensory processes and perception. A particularly clear one is Goldstein, *Sensation and Perception* (3rd ed., 1989). Other useful texts include: Barlow and Mollon, *The Senses* (1982); Coren and Ward, *Sensation and Perception* (3rd ed., 1989); Schiffman, *Sensation and Perception* (1982); and Sekuler and Blake, *Perception* (1985).

For treatments of color vision, see Boynton, *Human Color Vision* (1979); and Hurvich, *Color Vision* (1981). Introductory books on audition include Moore, *An Introduction to the Psychology of Hearing* (2nd ed., 1982); and Yost and Nielson, *Fundamentals of Hearing* (2nd ed., 1985). For smell, see Engen, *The Perception of Odors* (1982); for touch, *Tactual Perception,* edited by Schiff and Foulke (1982); and for pain, *The Psychology of Pain,* edited by Sternbach (2nd ed., 1986).

For reference there are four multivolume handbooks, each of which has several chapters on sensory systems. They are the *Handbook of Perception* (1974–1978), edited by Carterette and Friedman; the *Handbook of Physiology: The Nervous System*: Section 1, Volume 3, *Sensory Processes* (1984), edited by Darian-Smith; the *Handbook of Perception and Human Performance*: Volume 1, *Sensory Processes and Perception* (1986), edited by Boff, Kaufman, and Thomas; and *Stevens' Handbook of Experimental Psychology: Volume 1* (1988), edited by Atkinson, Herrnstein, Lindzey, and Luce.

Chapter 5

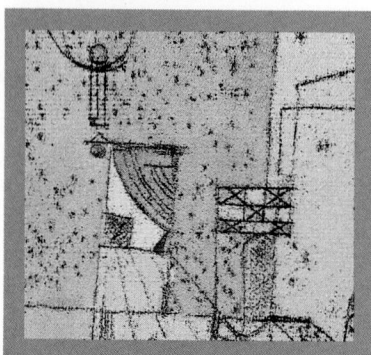

Detail, Phantom Perspective.

Perception

*I*nformation may enter our senses in bits and pieces, but that is not how we *perceive* the world. We perceive a world of objects and people, a world that bombards us with integrated wholes, not piecemeal sensations. Only under unusual circumstances do we notice the individual features and parts of stimuli; most of the time we see three-dimensional objects and hear words and music.

FUNCTIONS OF PERCEPTION

The study of perception is the study of how we integrate sensations into percepts of the objects in our world (a *percept* is an outcome of a perceptual process). The study of perception is also concerned with how we use these percepts in getting around in the world. Researchers are increasingly approaching the study of perception with the following question: What problems does our perceptual system solve? David Marr (1982) argued that our visual system must construct a description of the stimulus objects that allows us to determine a) *what* the objects are (apples, tables, cats, and so on); and b) *where* the objects are (arm's length on my left, hundreds of yards straight ahead, and so on). The same two problems are involved in auditory perception (*what* was that sound, a phone or a siren? *Where* was it coming from, the front or the back?).

In vision, determining what the objects are is referred to as the process of *pattern recognition*, or *recognition* for short. It is crucial for survival because often we have to know what an object is before we can infer some of its critical properties. So, once we know an object is an apple, we know it is edible; once we know an object is a wolf, we know not to perturb it. Determining where visual objects are is referred to as *spatial localization*, or *localization*. It is also necessary for survival. Localization is the means we use to navigate through our environment. Without such an ability, we would constantly be bumping into objects, failing to grasp things we are reaching for, and moving into the path of dangerous objects and predators.

Although visual recognition and localization are not completely independent (both tasks require some information about shape, for example), the idea that they are qualitatively different tasks is supported by the finding that they are carried out by different regions of the brain. Recognition of objects depends on a branch of the visual system that includes the cortical receiving area for vision (discussed in the previous chapter) and a region near the bottom of the brain. In contrast, localization of objects depends on a branch of the visual system that projects to a region of the cortex near the top of the brain. If the recognition branch of an animal's visual system is impaired, it can still perceive spatial relations between objects (one in front of the other, for example), but it cannot discriminate the actual objects—for example, it cannot tell a cube from a cylinder; if the location branch is impaired, it can distinguish a cube from a cylinder, but it does not know where they are in relation to each other (Mishkin & Appenzeller, 1987). In view of these arguments and others (Livingstone & Hubel, 1988), we will treat localization and recognition separately.

There is, however, more to perception than the functions it accomplishes. There is also the phenomenological question of why our world *looks* the way it does, and in particular, why the appearance of things remains relatively constant. Such *perceptual constancy* will be another concern to us.

FIGURE 5-1
Reversible Figure and Ground *The reversible goblet illustrates figure-ground reversal. Note that you can perceive either the light portion (the goblet) or the dark portion (two profiles) as a figure against a background, but only one at a time.*

Finally, we will consider what is known about the development of the various aspects of perception. Throughout the chapter, we will be concerned primarily with visual perception, since this is the area that has been most investigated.

LOCALIZATION

To know where the objects in our environment are, we first have to *segregate* the objects from one another and from the background. Then the perceptual system can determine the position of the objects in a three-dimensional world, including their *distance* from us and their *movement* patterns. The idea that these three perceptual abilities—segregation, determining distance, and determining movement—belong together is supported by physiological findings indicating that all three abilities are mediated by the same branch of the visual system (Livingstone & Hubel, 1988). We will discuss each of these perceptual abilities in turn.

Segregation of Objects

The image projected on our retina is a mosaic of varying brightnesses and colors. Somehow our perceptual system organizes the mosaic into a set of discrete objects projected against a background. This kind of organization was of great concern to *Gestalt psychology*, an approach to psychology that began in Germany early in this century. The Gestalt psychologists emphasized the importance of perceiving whole objects or forms, and proposed a number of principles of how we organize objects.

FIGURE AND GROUND If a stimulus contains two or more distinct regions, we usually see part of it as a *figure* and the rest as *ground*. The regions seen as a figure contain the objects of interest—they appear more solid than the ground and appear in front of the ground. This is the most elementary form of perceptual organization. Figure 5-1 illustrates that figure-ground organization can be reversible. The fact that either region can be recognized as a figure indicates that figure-ground organization is not part of the physical

FIGURE 5-2
The Slave Market with Disappearing Bust of Voltaire *A reversible figure is in the center of this painting by Salvador Dali (1940). Two nuns standing in an archway reverse to form a bust of Voltaire.*

stimulus, but rather is an accomplishment of our perceptual system. Figure 5-2 illustrates a more complex reversible figure-ground effect. Interestingly, a stimulus need not contain identifiable objects in order for a person to organize it into figure and ground. (Note that we can perceive figure-ground relations in senses other than vision. For example, we may hear the song of a bird against a background of outdoor noises, or the melody played by the violin against the harmonies of the rest of the orchestra.)

GROUPING OF OBJECTS   We see not only objects against a ground, but a particular grouping of the objects as well. Even simple patterns of lines or dots fall into groups when we look at them. In the top part of Figure 5-3, we tend to see three pairs of lines, with an extra line at the right. But notice that the stimulus can be described equally well as three pairs beginning at the right with an extra line at the left. The slight modification of the lines shown in the lower part of the figure causes us to perceive the second grouping.

The Gestalt psychologists proposed a number of determinants of grouping. One is *proximity*: elements that are near to one another will tend to be grouped together. This principle explains the preferred grouping of the lines in the top part of Figure 5-3. *Closure*, or our tendency to group elements to complete figures with gaps, explains the grouping preferred in the bottom part of the figure. In the bottom part of the figure closure is a stronger factor than proximity.

Many determinants of grouping were first noted by Max Wertheimer (1923), the founder of Gestalt psychology. Wertheimer's research strategy was to construct demonstrations such as the one in Figure 5-3, and leave it to the reader's intuition to verify the grouping. In modern times, researchers have used experiments to show that different ways of grouping objects have marked effects on perceptual performance. In one set of experiments, on each of the trials subjects were presented with a display (see Figure 5-4). The subject's task was to decide as quickly as possible whether or not the display contained a target letter, either a T or an F. On those trials where the display contained a target, subjects responded faster when the target was relatively far from the nontargets, as in the display on the top, than when the target was relatively close to the nontargets, as in the display on the bottom. Apparently, when the target was close to the nontargets the principle of proximity led the target and nontargets to be grouped together, which resulted in extra time being needed to extract the target.

The same task can be used to study another determinant of grouping, namely *good continuation*, our tendency to group together objects that form an unbroken contour. Look at the displays in Figure 5-5. The target F forms part of a contour with the nontargets in the display on the bottom but not in the display on the top. Because it requires extra time to extract the target from its grouping with the nontargets, subjects took longer to respond to the display on the bottom than to the one on the top. Still another determinant of grouping that deserves mention is *similarity*, our tendency to group together similar objects. If we replaced the F in the bottom display of Figure 5-5 with an O, subjects would be less likely to group it with the nontargets because an O is very dissimilar to the nontargets.

In addition to segmenting and grouping objects, our perceptual system also groups features like shape and color into a single object. In such cases, there are other determinants of grouping. For example, we can group features on the basis of common *distance* (two contours are likely to be features of the same object only if they are at the same distance from the observer), or on the basis of their *motion* (two contours moving in the same direction are

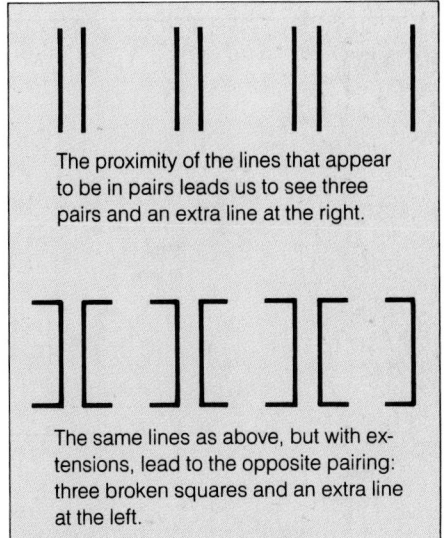

The proximity of the lines that appear to be in pairs leads us to see three pairs and an extra line at the right.

The same lines as above, but with extensions, lead to the opposite pairing: three broken squares and an extra line at the left.

FIGURE 5-3
Perceptual Grouping

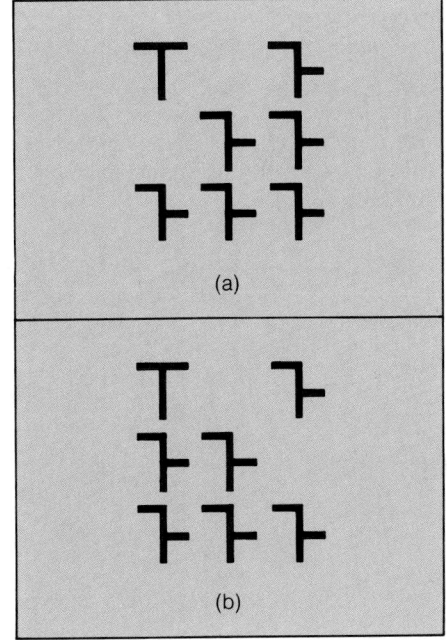

FIGURE 5-4
Grouping by Proximity *Subjects found the target T faster when it was relatively far from the nontargets (a) than when it was relatively close to the nontarget (b). (After Banks & Prinzmetal, 1976)*

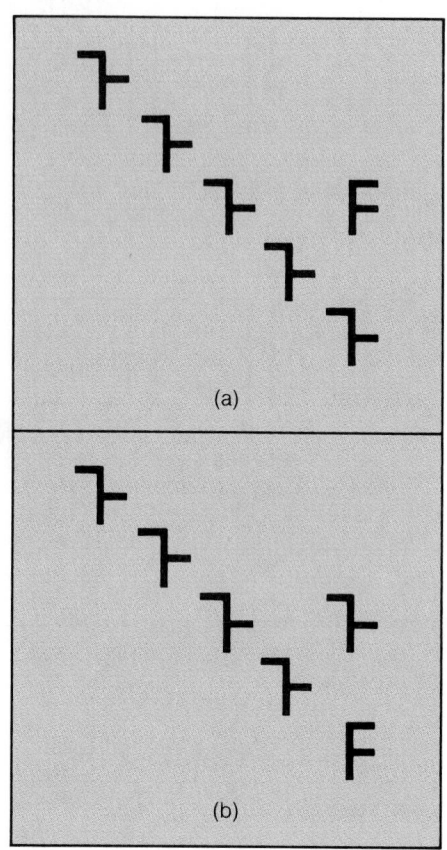

FIGURE 5-5
Grouping and Good Continuation
Subjects found the target F faster when it did not form a part of the contour with the nontargets (a) than when it did form a part of the contour (b). (After Prinzmetal & Banks, 1977)

likely to be features of the same object). These examples highlight the close connection between our ability to segment objects and features on the one hand, and our abilities to determine distance and movement on the other.

Although perceptual grouping has been studied mainly in visual perception, the same determinants of grouping appear in audition. Proximity clearly operates in audition (though it is proximity in time rather than in space): four drumbeats with a pause between the second and third will be heard as two pairs. Similarity and good continuation are also known to play important roles in hearing tones and more complex stimuli (Bregman & Reidnicky, 1975).

Perceiving Distance

To know where an object is, we must know its *depth*. Although perceiving an object's depth seems effortless, it is a remarkable achievement given the physical structure of our eyes.

DEPTH CUES   The retina, the starting point of vision, is a two-dimensional surface. This means the retinal image is flat and has no depth at all. This fact has led many students of perception (artists as well as scientists) to the idea of *distance cues*, two-dimensional aspects that a perceiver uses to infer distance in a three-dimensional world. There are a number of distance cues that combine in complex ways to determine perceived distance. The cues can be classified as *monocular* or *binocular*, depending on whether they involve one or both eyes.

People using only one eye can perceive depth remarkably well by picking up monocular depth cues. Figure 5-6 illustrates three of these cues. The first is *relative size*. If an image contains an array of similar objects that differ in size, people interpret the smaller objects as being further away (see Figure 5-6a). A second monocular cue is *superposition*. If one object is positioned so that it obstructs the view of the other, people perceive the overlapping object as being nearer (see Figure 5-6b). A third cue is *relative height*. Among similar objects, those that are higher in an image are perceived as being further away (see Figure 5-6c). These three cues have been known to artists for centuries—they are called *pictorial cues* for this reason—and a single painting will often use more than one of the cues.

Seeing with both eyes rather than one has advantages for depth perception. Because the eyes are separated in the head, each eye perceives a three-dimensional object from a slightly different angle. Consequently each eye has a slightly different view of the object. Fusing these different views gives rise to an impression of depth. This can be demonstrated by a device called a

FIGURE 5-6
Monocular Distance Cues *The figure illustrates three monocular distance cues. These are used by artists to portray depth on a two-dimensional surface and are also present in photographs.*

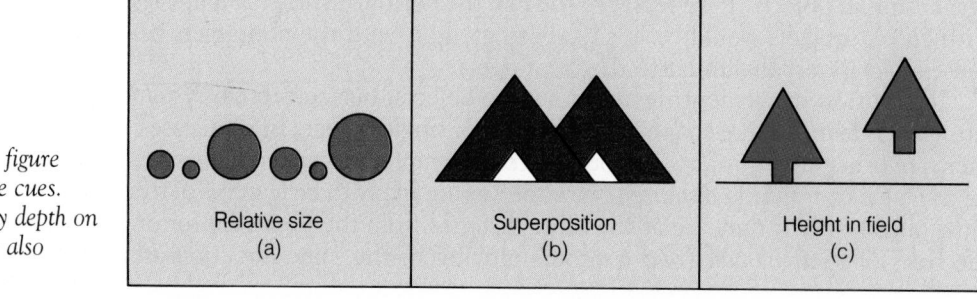

Relative size
(a)   Superposition
(b)   Height in field
(c)

stereoscope (see Figure 5-7). The stereoscope displays a different photograph or drawing to each eye. If the two pictures are taken from slightly separated camera positions or drawn from slightly different perspectives, the viewer will experience vivid depth.

Binocular parallax is one cue that is responsible for this perception of depth. Any visible point will differ slightly in its direction to the two eyes. A related cue is *binocular disparity*, referring to the difference between the retinal images on the two eyes when we look at an object in depth. Both binocular parallax and binocular disparity are consequences of the fact that our eyes are separated. You can easily demonstrate these cues to yourself. Hold a pencil about a foot in front of you and, with only one eye open, line it up with a vertical edge of the wall opposite you. Then close that eye and open the other. The pencil will now appear in a different direction; the difference between these directions is binocular parallax. Also, the two edges that were lined up in the first eye will appear separated when you open the second eye, and indeed the images in the eye are separated; the difference between the retinal images in the two eyes is binocular disparity.

Binocular disparity is a particularly powerful cue. It leads to a vivid impression of depth even with completely meaningless stimuli, such as a random pattern of dots that contain no other depth cues (Julesz, 1971). Furthermore, binocular disparity seems to be coded directly by the visual system. Researchers have found single neurons in the visual cortex of cats that respond best to particular disparities. Thus, some of these cells respond most to one particular degree of disparity, while other cells are most responsive to another degree of disparity (Barlow, Blakemore, & Pettigrew, 1967). Binocular disparity, then, is treated by the nervous system in the same manner as the wavelength of light or the frequency of sounds.

DIRECT PERCEPTION   The idea behind distance cues is that the observer notes a critical cue—for instance, that one object appears larger than another—and then unconsciously infers distance information from the cue. This notion of *unconscious inference* was introduced by Helmholtz in 1909.

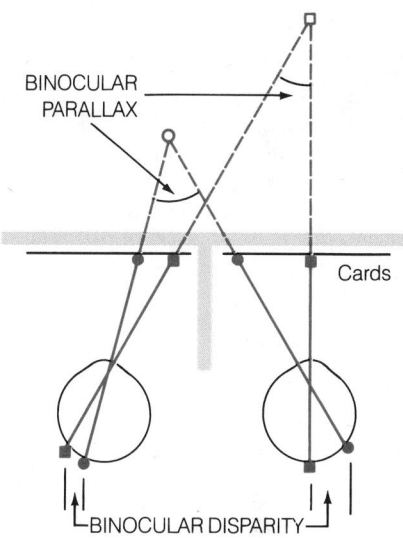

FIGURE 5-7

A Stereoscope and Binocular Distance Cues *A stereoscope is a device that presents different images to the two eyes. This very simple model holds a different card in front of each eye; a barrier between the eyes allows each eye to see only one card. If each card contains the same two symbols (here a circle and a square) separated by a different amount of space, the stimulus is the same as that produced by a circle and a square at different distances behind the cards. The dashed lines show how the images on the cards simulate two objects at different distances in space. When presented with stereo images such as these, people will experience vivid depth. Binocular parallax refers to the angle between the two lines of sight; binocular disparity refers to the difference between the separations of the retinal images of the symbols in the two eyes.*

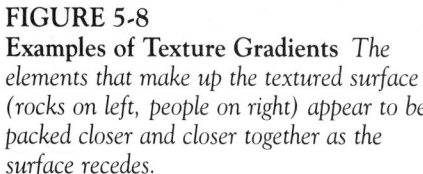

FIGURE 5-8
Examples of Texture Gradients *The elements that make up the textured surface (rocks on left, people on right) appear to be packed closer and closer together as the surface recedes.*

While it continues to be a key idea in the study of perception (Rock, 1983), some psychologists, most notably Gibson, have argued for another approach to depth perception.

Gibson (1950; 1966; 1979) claims that we do not infer depth, but rather perceive it directly. To appreciate Gibson's ideas, it is useful to consider *where* people routinely look for information about depth. Gibson argues that instead of looking for cues that characterize objects protruding in the air—such as relative size, superposition, and relative height—people look at information on the ground itself. The best example of such information is a *texture gradient* (see Figure 5-8). A texture gradient arises when we view a surface in perspective. The elements that make up the textured surface appear to be packed closer and closer together as the surface recedes. This gradient gives rise to a powerful impression of depth.

Unlike the standard distance cues, the gradient extends over a large visual area, and were you to move forward you could determine your distance to any other point on the gradient. The gradient information on the retina, therefore, remains constant or, to use Gibson's term, *invariant*. Depth perception, according to Gibson, is a matter of directly perceiving such invariants. Thus, when we perceive depth in a scene, we need not process the information provided by scattered depth cues, but instead we can directly perceive the depth information provided by the texture gradient (Goldstein, 1984).

Although Gibson's ideas about direct perception are controversial (Fodor & Pylyshyn, 1981), they have influenced many areas of perception. They will surface again in our discussion of localization.

Perceiving Motion

If we are to move around our environment effectively, we need to know not only the locations of static objects, but also the trajectories of moving ones. This brings us to the issue of how we perceive motion.

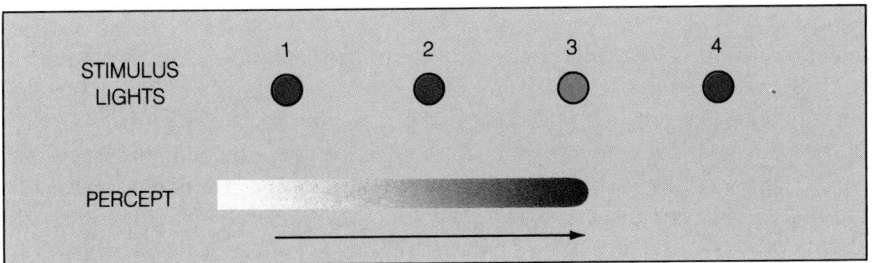

FIGURE 5-9
Stroboscopic Motion *The four circles in the top row correspond to four lights. If these are flashed one after the other with a short dark interval in between, they will appear to be a single light in continuous motion, such as that suggested in the second row. This is stroboscopic motion; motion in movies and on television is of this kind.*

STROBOSCOPIC MOTION   What causes us to perceive motion? One might suspect that we perceive an object in motion whenever its image moves across our retina. This answer turns out to be too simple, though, for we can see motion even when *nothing* moves on our retina. This phenomenon was demonstrated in 1912 by Wertheimer in his studies of *stroboscopic motion* (see Figure 5-9). Stroboscopic motion is produced most simply by flashing a light in darkness and then, a few milliseconds later, flashing another light near the location of the first light. The light will seem to move from one place to the other in a way that is indistinguishable from real motion. Stroboscopic motion, though, has its limits. When the time interval between the flashes is too short, the lights appear to be simultaneous; when the interval is too long, the lights appear as two isolated flashes without motion.

The motion that we see in movies is stroboscopic. The film is simply a series of still photographs (frames), each slightly different than the preceding. The frames are projected on the screen in rapid sequence, with dark intervals in between. The rate at which the frames are presented is critical. In the early days of motion pictures, the frame rate was 16 per second. This was too slow, and as a consequence movement in these early films appears jerky and disjointed. Today, the rate is usually 24 frames per second. Even at this rate the picture would appear to flicker because of the fine temporal resolution of our visual system if each frame were not flashed on and off three times.

INDUCED MOTION   Another case in which we perceive motion in the absence of movement across our retina is the phenomenon of *induced motion*. When a large object surrounding a smaller one moves, the smaller object may appear to be the one that is moving even if it is static. This phenomenon was first studied by the Gestalt psychologist, Duncker, in 1929. Duncker had subjects sit in a darkened room and observe a small luminous circle inside a larger luminous rectangular frame. When the rectangle was moved to the right, subjects reported that the circle appeared to move to the left. This same phenomenon may be at play on a windy night when the moon seems to be racing through the clouds.

REAL MOTION   Of course, our visual system is also sensitive to *real motion* (that is, motion induced by movement across the retina). Under optimal conditions, our threshold for seeing motion is strikingly low: an object need move only about one-fifth the diameter of a single cone in the retina in order for us to detect movement (Nakayama & Tyler, 1981).

We are much better at detecting motion when we can see an object against a structured background (*relative motion*) than when the background is dark or neutral and only the moving object can be seen (*absolute motion*). According to Gibson (1966; 1979), relative motion is easier to perceive because it provides a pattern of information about motion; specifically, as the object moves, it covers and uncovers parts of the background. Gibson argues that we can use this pattern to directly perceive motion, just as we can directly perceive depth.

Some aspects of real movement are coded by specific cells in the visual cortex. These cells respond to some motions and not to others, and each cell responds best to one direction and speed of motion. Some evidence for these claims comes from experiments on *selective adaptation*. Selective adaptation is a loss in sensitivity to motion that occurs when we view motion; the adaptation is selective in that we lose sensitivity to the motion viewed and to similar motions, but not to motion that differs significantly in direction or speed. If we look at upward-moving stripes, for example, we lose sensitivity to upward motion but our ability to see downward motion is not affected (Sekuler & Ganz, 1963). Presumably, this selectivity occurs because the cortical cells specialized for upward motion have become fatigued, whereas those specialized for downward motion are functioning as usual.

As with other types of adaptation, we do not usually notice the sensitivity loss but we do notice the aftereffect produced by adaptation. If we view a waterfall for a few minutes and then look at the cliff beside it, the cliff will appear to move upward. Most motions will produce such a *motion aftereffect* in the opposite direction.

Other evidence for the existence of movement cells in the visual system comes from studies of animals. The evidence is obtained by recording from single cells in the visual cortex while presenting stimuli with different patterns of motion (refer back to Figure 4-4). Such single-cell recording studies have found cortical cells tuned to a particular direction of movement. Most of these cells are tuned to other features as well, but some are highly specialized for motion (Nakayama, 1985). There are even cells specifically tuned to detect an object moving toward the head (Regan, Beverley, & Cynader, 1979), clearly useful for survival.

However, there is more to the perception of real motion than the activation of specific cells. We can see motion when we track a luminous object moving in darkness (such as an airplane at night). Because our eyes follow the object, the image makes only a small, irregular motion on the retina (due to imperfect tracking), yet we perceive a smooth, continuous motion. Why? The answer seems to be that information about how our eyes are moving is sent to our visual system and influences the motion that we see. In essence, the visual system is being informed by the motor system that the latter is responsible for the lack of regular motion on the retina, and the visual system then corrects for this lack. In more normal viewing situations, there are both eye movements and large retinal-image movements. The visual system must combine these two sources of information to determine the perceived motion.

MOTION AND CAUSALITY   The motion of objects tells us not only about where the objects are, but also about what they are doing. In particular, when two objects are in motion, we may perceive one as having *caused* the motion of the other. In a demonstration of this, Michotte (1963) used squares like those in Figure 5-10 as stimuli. When square A moves to square B, and then B immediately begins to move in the direction A was moving, subjects report that A caused B's movement; more specifically, A seems to launch B. (This perception of causality, however, obtains only when the interval between when A reaches B and when B starts to move is very brief, roughly, less than one-fifth of a second.) Furthermore, the perception of causality appears to be direct in the same way that Gibson has argued the

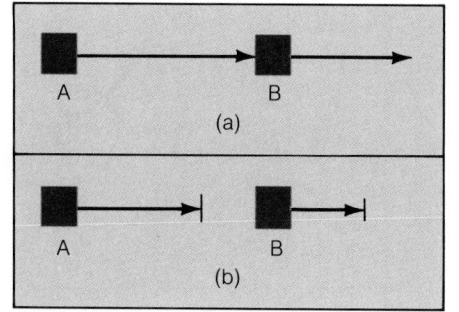

FIGURE 5-10
Motion and the Perception of Causality *When square A moves to square B, and B then immediately begins to move, subjects report that A "launches" B (a). The perception of causality is somewhat different when A stops before it reaches B (b).*

perception of depth or motion is direct. The subject does not reason to herself that "A hit B and B moved, so A must have caused B to move." Rather, causality appears to be perceived without any intervening reasoning (Goldstein, 1984).

While we have emphasized what motion perception tells us about the location of objects, the findings on causality make it clear that motion perception tells us other things as well. Indeed, in addition to providing information about causality, the motion of objects can be used to: a) segregate objects from their background (a moving object is likely to be seen as figure); b) control eye movements (motion in the periphery may trigger an eye movement to that region); and c) sense the movements of our own body (Nakayama, 1985). With regard to the latter, when we move in a normal, illuminated environment, we produce complex patterns of retinal image motion; these patterns of motion are potentially rich sources of information about both the scene and our own motion (Gibson, 1979; Ullman, 1979).

RECOGNITION

We turn now to the second major function of perception: recognizing what an object is. Recognizing an object amounts to assigning it to a category—that's a shirt, that's a cat, that's a daisy, and so on. Of course, we can also recognize people, which amounts to assigning the visual input to a particular individual—that's Ben Murphy, or this is Irene Paull. In either case, objects or people, recognition allows us to infer many hidden properties of the object—if it's a shirt then it's made of cloth and I can wear it; if it's a cat then it may scratch me if I pull its tail; if it's Ben Murphy he'll want to tell me one of those silly jokes, and so on. Recognition is what allows us to go beyond the information given, which is a hallmark of mental activity.

What attributes of an object do we use to recognize it? Shape, size, color, texture, orientation, and so on? While all of these attributes may make some contribution, shape appears to play the critical role in recognition. We can recognize a cup, for example, regardless of whether it is large or small (a variation in size), or brown or white (a variation in color), or smooth or bumpy (a texture variation), or presented upright or tilted slightly (an orientation variation). In contrast, our ability to recognize a cup is strikingly affected by variations in shape; if part of the cup's shape is occluded, we may not recognize it at all. One of the strongest pieces of evidence for the importance of shape to recognition is that we can recognize many objects about as well from simple line drawings, which preserve only the shapes of the objects, as from detailed color photographs, which preserve many attributes of the objects (Biederman & Ju, 1988).

The critical question then becomes: How do we use the shape of an object to assign it to its appropriate category? In dealing with this question, first we focus on simple objects like letters, and later consider natural objects like animals and furniture.

Early Stages of Recognition

Following Marr (1982), we may distinguish between *early* and *late* stages in recognizing an object. In early stages, the perceptual system uses information on the retina, particularly variations in intensity, to describe the object in terms of primitive components like lines, edges, and angles. The system uses these primitive components to construct a description of the object itself. In later stages, the system compares the object's description to shape descriptions of various categories of objects stored in memory and selects the best match. To recognize a particular object as the letter B, for example, is to say that the object's shape matches that of B's better than it matches that of other letters. For now, our concern is with the early stages, which construct the shape descriptions of the object.

FEATURE DETECTORS IN THE CORTEX   Much of what is known about the primitive features of object perception comes from studies of other species (cats, monkeys) that use single-cell recordings in the visual cortex (refer back to Figure 4-4). These studies examine the sensitivity of specific cortical neurons when different stimuli are presented to the regions of the retina associated with these neurons; such a retinal region is called a *receptive field* of a cortical neuron. These single-cell studies were pioneered by Hubel and Wiesel (1968), who shared a Nobel prize in 1981 for their research.

Hubel and Wiesel identified three types of cells in the visual cortex that can be distinguished by the features to which they respond. *Simple cells* respond when the eye is exposed to a line stimulus (such as a thin bar or straight edge between a dark and a light region) at a particular orientation and position within their receptive field. Figure 5-11 illustrates how a simple cell will respond to a vertical bar and to bars tilted away from the vertical. The response decreases as the orientation varies from the optimal one. Other simple cells are tuned to other orientations and positions. A *complex cell* also responds to a bar or edge in a particular orientation, but it does not require that the stimulus be at a particular place within its receptive field. A complex cell responds to the stimulus anywhere within its receptive field, and it responds continuously as the stimulus is moved across its receptive field. *Hypercomplex cells* require not only that the stimulus be in a particular orientation, but also that it be of a particular length. If a stimulus is extended beyond the optimal length, the response will decrease and may cease entirely.

Since Hubel and Wiesel's initial reports, investigators have found cells that respond to shape features other than single bars and edges. Thus, there are hypercomplex cells that respond to corners or angles of a specific length.

FIGURE 5-11
Response of a Simple Cell *This figure illustrates the response of a simple cortical cell to a bar of light. The stimulus is on the top, the response on the bottom; each vertical spike on the bottom corresponds to one nerve impulse. When there is no stimulus, only an occasional impulse is recorded. When the stimulus is turned on, the cell may or may not respond, depending on the position and orientation of the light bar. For this cell a horizontal bar produces no change in response, a bar at 45 degrees produces a small change, and a vertical bar produces a very large change.*

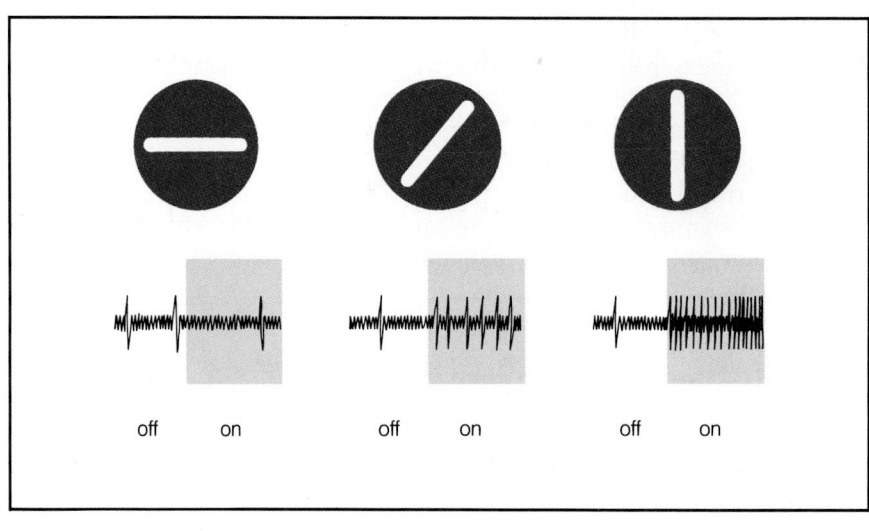

And there are cells that are more sensitive to a grating consisting of several bars than to a single bar (DeValois & DeValois, 1980; Shapley & Lennie, 1985).

All of the cells described above are referred to as *feature detectors*. Because the edges, bars, corners, and angles to which these detectors respond can be used to approximate many shapes, the feature detectors might be thought of as the building blocks of shape perception. As we will see later, though, this proposal seems more true of simple shapes like letters than of complex shapes like those of tables and tigers.

BEHAVIORAL INDICATORS OF FEATURES   In addition to single-cell recordings, researchers have developed behavioral indicators of primitive features of objects. One of the best-known techniques is due to Treisman (Treisman & Gormican, 1988). On each trial of the task subjects are presented an array of items and have to decide as quickly as possible whether the array contains a target. For example, the target might be a curve and the nontargets straight lines, as illustrated in Figure 5-12. What varies from trial to trial is the number of nontargets—which can be between 3 and 30—and the question of interest is how this number affects the time to detect the target. If the target is defined by a primitive feature, a viewer should be able to search an array for it *in parallel*, rather than examining each nontarget in series. Consequently, the number of nontargets should have no effect on the time to detect a primitive feature. This is exactly what happens with arrays like that in Figure 5-12, which suggests that curvature is a primitive feature of objects. Phenomenologically, the curve seems to "pop out" of the array; for this reason, a demonstration of parallel search in this task is referred to as the *pop-out* effect.

Treisman has found pop-out effects for a number of other features. Two such features are the length of a line (a long line pops out from an array of short ones) and the amount of brightness contrast between neighboring dots (a high contrast pair pops out). These two features, like curvature, could well play a role in determining shape. Other features that pass the pop-out test, though, seem to have little to do with shape. Examples include color and orientation. These results indicate that the primitive features of objects are simple properties that characterize points and lines, with only some of these properties being related to shape.

RELATIONS BETWEEN FEATURES   There is more to a description of a shape than just its features: relations between features must also be specified. The importance of such relations is illustrated in Figure 5-13. The features of a printed T include a vertical line and a horizontal line, but unless these lines are combined in the right way, the resulting pattern is not a T. The description of a T must include mention of the fact that the horizontal line is attached to the top of the vertical line at its center. It is this kind of relation between features that the Gestalt psychologists had in mind when they cautioned psychologists years ago that "the whole is greater than the sum of its parts."

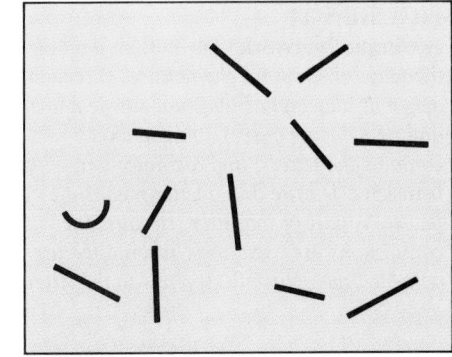

FIGURE 5-12
Searching for a Curve *The time it takes to find the curve does not depend on the number of straight lines surrounding it.* (After Treisman & Gormican, 1988)

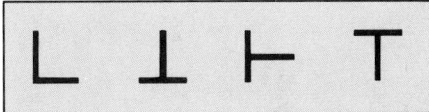

FIGURE 5-13
Relations between Features *All forms include the features of a vertical line and a horizontal line, but only the right-most form has the relation between features characteristic of the letter T.*

The Matching Stage and Connectionist Models

Now that we have some idea of how an object's shape is described, we can consider how that description is matched to stored shape descriptions to find the best match.

FIGURE 5-14
A Simple Network *The bottom level of the network contains the features (ascending diagonal, descending diagonal, vertical line, and right-facing curve), the top level contains the letters, and a connection between a feature and a letter means the feature is part of the letter. Because the connections are excitatory, when a feature is activated the activation spreads to the letter.*

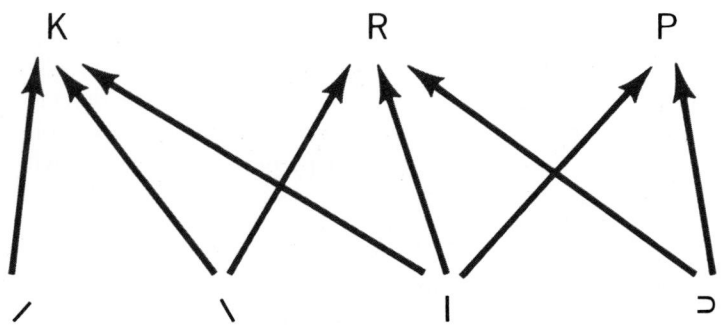

SIMPLE NETWORKS Much of the research on the matching stage has used simple patterns, specifically handwritten or printed letters or words. Figure 5-14 illustrates a proposal about how we store shape descriptions of letters. The basic idea is that letters are described in terms of certain features, and that knowledge about what features go with what letter is contained in a network of connections (hence the term, *connectionist* models). What is appealing about connectionist models is that it is easy to conceive how these networks could be realized in an actual nervous system with its array of interconnected neurons and receptors. Thus *connectionism* offers a bridge between a hypothetical model of how the mind might work and a neural network that resembles the human brain.

The bottom level of the network in Figure 5-14 contains the features—ascending diagonal, descending diagonal, vertical line, and right-facing curve, for example—and the top level contains the letters themselves, and a connection between a feature and a letter means that the feature is part of the letter. The fact that the connections have arrowheads at their ends means they are *excitatory* connections; if the feature is activated, the activation spreads to the letter (in a manner analogous to how electrical impulses spread in a network of neurons).

The network in Figure 5-14 tells us that the category of K is described by an ascending diagonal, a descending diagonal, and a vertical line; Rs are described by a descending diagonal, a vertical line, and a right-facing curve, and Ps are described by a vertical line and a right-facing curve. (To keep the discussion simple, we will ignore relations between features.) To see how this network can be used to recognize (or match) a letter, consider what happens when the letter K is presented. It will activate the features of descending diagonal, ascending diagonal, and vertical line. All three of these features will activate the category K; two of them—the descending diagonal and vertical line—will activate the category R; and one of them—the vertical line—will activate P. Only the category K has all of its features activated, and consequently it will be selected as the best match.

The above model is too simple to account for many aspects of recognition. To see what the model lacks, consider what happens when the letter R is presented. It activates the features of descending diagonal, vertical line, and right-facing curve. Now both the categories R and P will have all their features activated, and the perceptual system has no way of deciding which of the two categories provides a better match. What the system needs to know to choose between these categories is that the presence of a descending diagonal means the input *cannot* be a P. This kind of negative knowledge is included in the augmented network in Figure 5-15. This network has everything the preceding one had, plus *inhibitory connections* (symbolized by solid circles at their ends) between features and letters that do not contain these

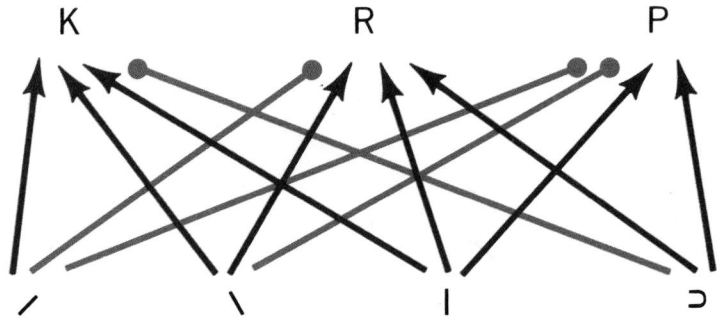

FIGURE 5-15
An Augmented Network *The network contains inhibitory connections between features and letters that do not contain these features, as well as excitatory connections.*

features. When a feature is connected to a letter by an inhibitory connection, activating the feature *decreases* activation of the letter. When R is presented to the network in Figure 5-15, the descending diagonal sends inhibition to the category P, thereby decreasing its overall level of activation; now the category R will receive the most activation and consequently will be selected as the best match.

The preceding discussion illustrates some critical properties of connectionist networks, which many have claimed offer a revolutionary new way of understanding cognitive processes (Rumelhart & McClelland, 1986; McClelland & Rumelhart, 1986). The networks in Figures 5-14 and 5-15 are composed of only two kinds of entities: a) *nodes* designating features or patterns (such as the node for an upright line, or that for the letter R); and b) connections between nodes that are either excitatory or inhibitory. All connectionist networks are restricted to just nodes and connections.* Furthermore, the networks in Figures 5-14 and 5-15 allow an object to be compared to all stored categories *simultaneously* (the feature information is passed to all letter nodes at once); this is in contrast to comparing the object to the stored categories one at a time or *sequentially*. Simultaneous processing (also called *parallel processing*) is characteristic of connectionist models.

NETWORKS WITH TOP-DOWN ACTIVATION The basic idea behind the model we just considered—that a letter must be described by the features it lacks as well as the features it contains—was originally proposed by researchers in artificial intelligence who were trying to write computer programs to simulate human letter perception (Selfridge & Neisser, 1960). Although the ideas were relatively successful for a time, ultimately they proved inadequate to explain findings about how context affects our ability to perceive letters. In particular, they could not explain why a letter is easier to perceive when presented as part of a word than when presented alone. Thus, if subjects are briefly presented a display containing either the single letter K or the word WORK, and are then asked whether the last letter was a K or a D, they are more accurate when the display contained a word than when it contained only a letter (see Figure 5-16).

To account for this result, our network of feature-letter connections has to be altered in a few ways. First, we have to add a level of words to our network, and along with it excitatory and inhibitory connections that go from letters to words (see Figure 5-17). In addition, we also have to add excitatory connections that go from words down to letters; these *top-down*

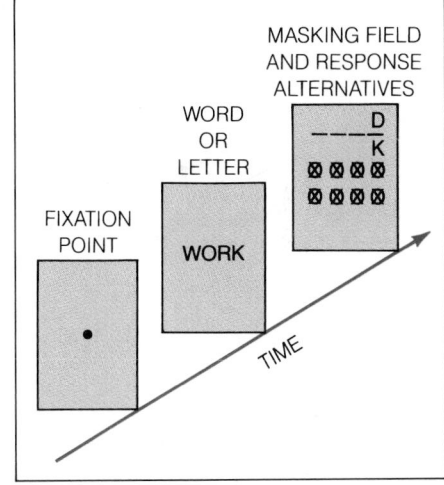

FIGURE 5-16
Perception of Letters and Words *This figure illustrates the sequence of events in an experiment that compares the perceptibility of a letter presented alone or in the context of a word. First, subjects saw a fixation point, followed by a word or a single letter, which was present for only a few milliseconds. Then the experimenter presented a stimulus that contained a visual mask in the positions where the letters had been, plus two response alternatives. The subjects' task was to decide which of the two alternatives occurred in the word or letter presented earlier. (After Reicher, 1969)*

---

*Each connection is usually accompanied by a number, or *weight*, indicating the strength of the connection.

FIGURE 5-17
Network with Top-Down
Activation *The network contains*
excitatory and inhibitory connections
between letters and words (as well as
between features and letters), and some of
the excitatory connections go from words to
letters.

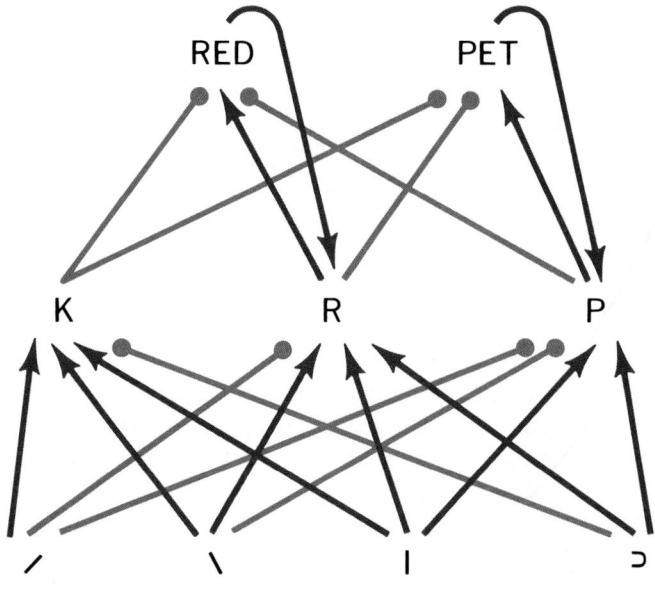

connections explain why a letter is more perceptible when presented briefly in the context of a word than when presented briefly alone. When R is presented alone, for example, the features of vertical line, descending diagonal, and right-facing curve are activated, and this activation spreads to the node for R. Because the letter was presented very briefly, not all the features may have been fully activated, and the activation culminating at the R node may not be sufficient for recognition to occur. In contrast, when R is presented in RED, there is activation not only from the features of R to the R node, but also from the features of E and D to their nodes; all of these partially activated letters then partially activate the RED node, which in turn sends activation back to its letters via its top-down connections.

The upshot is that there is an additional source of activation for R when it is presented in a word, and this is why it is easier to recognize a letter in a word than when it is presented alone. Many other findings about letter and word patterns have been shown to be consistent with this connectionist model (McClelland & Rumelhart, 1981).

Recognizing Natural Objects

We know quite a bit about the recognition of letters and words, but what about more natural objects—animals, plants, people, furniture, and clothing?

FEATURES OF NATURAL OBJECTS   The shape features of natural objects are more complex than lines and curves, and more like simple geometric forms. The features must be such that they can combine to form the shape of any recognizable object (just as lines and curves can combine to form any letter). The features of objects must also be such that they can either be determined solely by information on the retina (just as lines and curves are), or be constructed from primitive features of objects. These criteria have guided the search for a possible set of object features.

One proposal assumes that cylinders of various kinds are the features of objects. Figure 5-18 illustrates how cylinders of different sizes can be

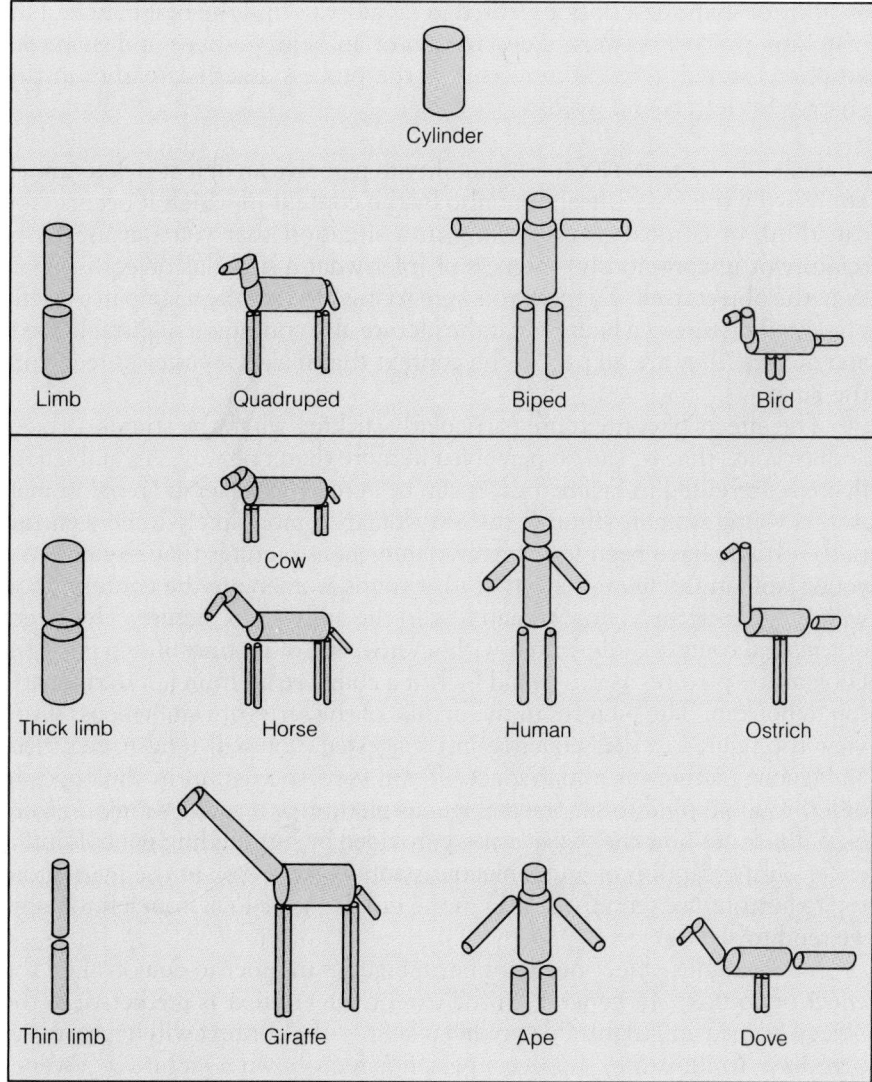

FIGURE 5-18
Cylinder as Features of Natural Objects *The figure illustrates how cylinders of various sizes can be combined to represent the shapes of various objects and parts of objects. (After Marr & Nishihara, 1978)*

combined to form the shapes of various objects or parts of objects. Another proposed set of features includes a number of geometric forms, such as cylinders, cones, blocks, and wedges, as illustrated in Figure 5-19. Biederman (1987) has argued that about 35 features like those in Figure 5-19 are sufficient to describe the shapes of all objects that people can possibly recognize. Evidence suggesting the proponents of these features are on the right track comes from experiments in which subjects try to recognize forms that are presented briefly. Fewer errors are committed on a complex object like an airplane, which is composed of many features like those in Figure 5-19, than on a simple object like a lamp, which is composed of only a few such features. The more features there are in an object, the more likely a few of them will be extracted, even when the object is briefly presented, and even a few features can suffice to recognize a complex object.

As usual, the description of an object includes not just its features but also the relations between them. This is illustrated in Figure 5-20 with the features of an arc and a cylinder. When the arc is connected to the side of the cylinder, it forms a cup; when connected to the top of the cylinder, it forms a pail. Once a description of an object's shape is constructed, it is matched to

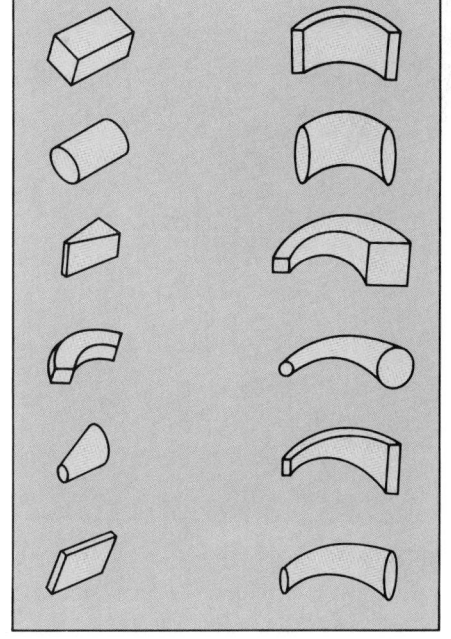

FIGURE 5-19
Another Possible Set of Features for Natural Objects *Cylinders, cones, blocks, and wedges may all be features of complex objects. (After Biederman, 1987)*

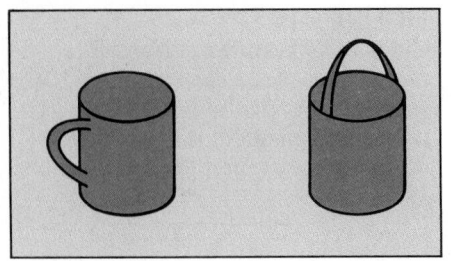

FIGURE 5-20
Relations between Features:

Objects *Both objects contain the same features, an arc and a cylinder. When the arc is connected to the side of the cylinder, it forms a cup; when connected to the top of the cylinder, it forms a pail.* (After Biederman, 1987)

FIGURE 5-21
Ambiguous Stimulus *An ambiguous drawing that can be seen either as a young woman or as an old woman. Most people see the old woman first. The young woman is turning away, and we see the left side of her face. Her chin is the old woman's nose, and her necklace is the old woman's mouth.* (After Boring, 1930)

an array of shape descriptions stored in memory to find the best match. This matching process between a description of an object's shape and shape descriptions stored in memory resembles the process described earlier in this chapter for letters and words.

EFFECTS OF CONTEXT   Our ability to perceive an object is determined not only by the object itself, but also by the context in which it occurs. You can think of context as everything in a situation that you can use (consciously or unconsciously) to guess or infer what a stimulus object is, apart from the object itself. Suppose you were trying to recognize a lamp in a briefly presented picture of a bedroom; if the picture also contains a nighttable, bed, and dresser, they are all part of the context that makes it easier to recognize the lamp.

The effects of context are particularly striking when the stimulus object is *ambiguous*, that is, can be perceived in more than one way. An ambiguous figure is presented in Figure 5-21; it can be perceived either as an old woman or as a young woman (though the old woman is more likely to be seen initially). If you have been looking at unambiguous pictures that resemble the young woman in Figure 5-21 (that is, if young women are the context), you will tend to see the young woman first in the ambiguous picture. This effect of *temporal context* is illustrated with another set of pictures in Figure 5-22. Look at the pictures as you would look at a comic strip, from left to right and top to bottom. The pictures in the middle of the series are ambiguous. If you view the figures in the sequence just suggested, you will tend to see these ambiguous pictures as a man's face. If you view the figures in the opposite order, you will tend to see the ambiguous pictures as a young woman. Figure 5-23 illustrates how the *spatial context* provided by surrounding symbols influences our perception of an ambiguous symbol. If we look at the figure from top to bottom, we tend to see a 13 in the middle; if we look from left to right, we tend to see a B.

The stimulus object need not be ambiguous in order to demonstrate the effect of context. In general, to the extent the context is predictive of the object—a bed and nighttable predict a lamp—the context will improve recognition. To illustrate, suppose a person is first shown a picture of a scene, and is then briefly presented a picture of an unambiguous object to identify; identification will be more accurate if the object is appropriate to the scene. For example, after looking at a kitchen scene, a subject will correctly identify a briefly presented loaf of bread more often than he or she will a briefly presented mailbox (Palmer, 1975). Likewise, when a scene is flashed very rapidly before a subject, who must then identify an unambiguous object at some position in the scene, the subject will identify the object more accurately if it is in a normal location in the scene than if it is in an unusual location. For example, we have difficulty seeing fire hydrants on top of mailboxes (Biederman, 1981). We identify words, too, more rapidly in the context of appropriate sentences. Consider the sentence "Babe Ruth swung his bat and hit the _____." The last word is recognized as "ball" almost before the eye fixates it.

Sometimes context produces conscious expectations. When you are at an airport waiting for a friend to get off a plane, you have a conscious expectation. If that friend comes along, you are not likely to miss him or her, and recognition will be very rapid. Context, however, produces its effects even in the absence of conscious expectation; you do not even have to be aware of the context for it to affect you. If researchers flash a word on a screen for a few milliseconds and immediately follow it by a pattern of random lines, the

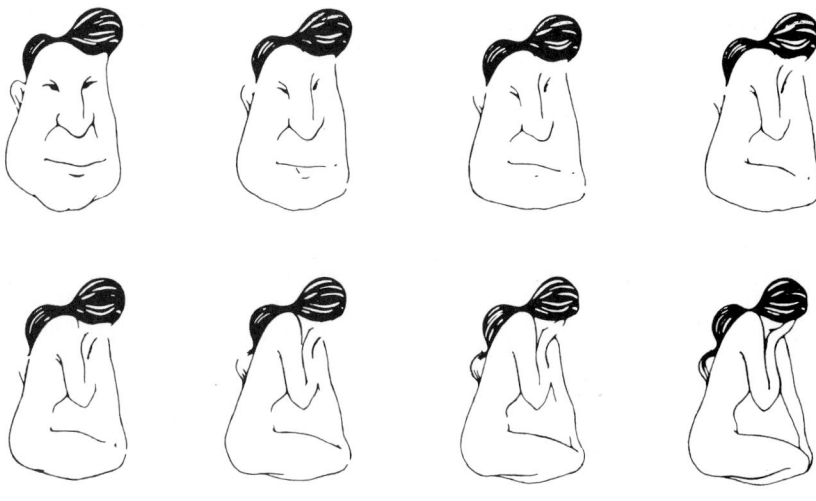

FIGURE 5-22
Effect of Temporal Context *What you see here depends on the order in which you look at the pictures. The pictures in the middle of the series are ambiguous. If you have been looking at pictures of a man's face, they will appear to be distorted faces. If you have been looking at pictures of a young woman, they will look like a young woman. (After Fisher, 1967)*

subject cannot report the word (this phenomenon is called *masking*). The unseen word, nevertheless, may have an effect on the perception of a word that follows. For example, if the word "Bread" is flashed and masked, then the word "Butter" is flashed, subjects will recognize "Butter" faster than they would if "Bread" had not been presented (Schvaneveldt & Meyer, 1973; Marcel, 1983).

Role of Attention

Most of the time we are bombarded with so many stimuli that we are unable to recognize all of them. Although a few objects intrude into our consciousness no matter what we do, within limits we select what we perceive. As you sit reading, stop for a moment, close your eyes, and attend to the various stimuli that are reaching you. Notice, for example, the tightness of your left shoe. What sounds do you hear? Is there an odor in the air? You probably were not aware of these stimuli before, because you had not selected them for recognition. The process by which we select is called *selective attention*.

SELECTIVE LOOKING   How exactly do we direct our attention to objects of interest? The simplest means is by physically reorienting our sensory receptors so as to favor those objects. For vision, this means moving our eyes until the object of interest falls on the most sensitive region of the retina.

Studies of visual attention often involve observing a subject looking at a picture or scene. If we watch the subject's eyes it is evident that they are not stationary; rather, they are scanning. Scanning is not a smooth continuous motion, however. The eyes are still for a brief period, then jump to another position, are still for another brief period, then jump again, and so on. The periods during which the eyes are still are called *fixations*, and the quick, almost instantaneous, movements between fixations are called *saccades* ("saccade" is French for "jump"). There are a number of techniques for recording these eye movements. The simplest method is to monitor the eyes with a television camera in such a way that what the eye is gazing at is reflected on the cornea of the eye so it appears on television superimposed on the image of the eye. From this superimposed image, the experimenter can determine the point in the scene where the eye is fixated. The procedure

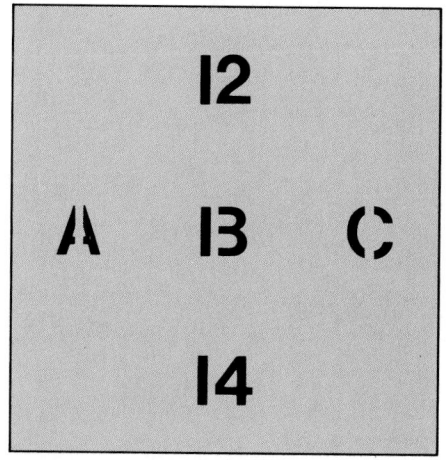

FIGURE 5-23
Effect of Spatial Context *The figure in the center is ambiguous, and the way we see it depends on whether we are attending to the row or the column.*

CRITICAL DISCUSSION

Unconscious Perception and Emotion

The studies discussed in the text suggest that stimuli that are not consciously recognized can still affect behavior. Such *unconscious perception* has been assumed by many theorists to play a role in our emotional lives. In particular, Sigmund Freud and others suggested that an individual's unconscious perceptual system can rapidly detect an anxiety-producing situation, and then somehow prevent the individual's conscious perceptual system from recognizing the situation. This kind of *perceptual defense* serves the function of protecting the individual from painful anxiety.

Early studies provided support for perceptual defense. In a famous experiment, McGinnies (1949) briefly presented his subjects with words that were considered either *neutral*, such as "house" and "apple," or *sexual*, such as "vagina" and "penis." The subjects had more difficulty recognizing the sexual words than the neutral ones. This result, according to McGinnies, indicated that subjects were defending against the sexual words (and their attendant anxiety), that is, their unconscious perceptual systems recognized the sexual words quickly and then blocked their conscious systems from identifying them. As further support for this interpretation, McGinnies measured the subjects' galvanic skin response (GSR), which is an indicator of emotionality, while they were trying to recognize the words. He found that subjects' GSRs were higher for the sexual words than the neutral ones, which presumably reflected the workings of the unconscious perceptual system.

McGinnies' study, and many others like it, engendered a great deal of controversy. Two major criticisms of the work emerged. First, the poorer recognition of the sexual words may have been due to subjects' reluctance to report the words, either because they considered such words unlikely in the context of an "academic-type" experiment, or because they were somewhat embarrassed to report the words given the meager evidence of a quick glance. According to this criticism, then, poor recognition of emotional material may reflect a *report bias* rather than a defensive action of an unconscious system. The second criticism of the McGinnies study is that the

provides an unobtrusive method for monitoring eye movements, and researchers using the procedure can replay the television tape to measure the duration of each fixation.

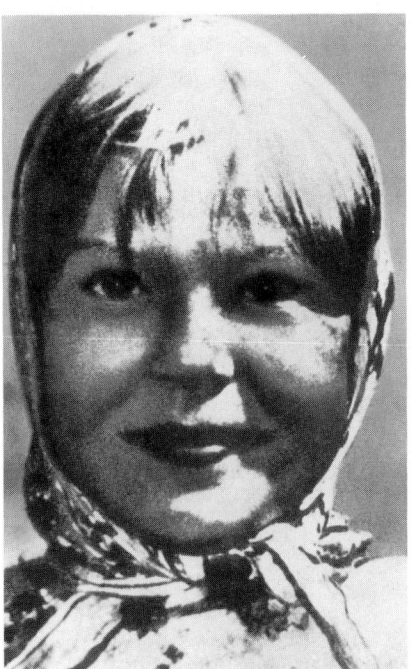 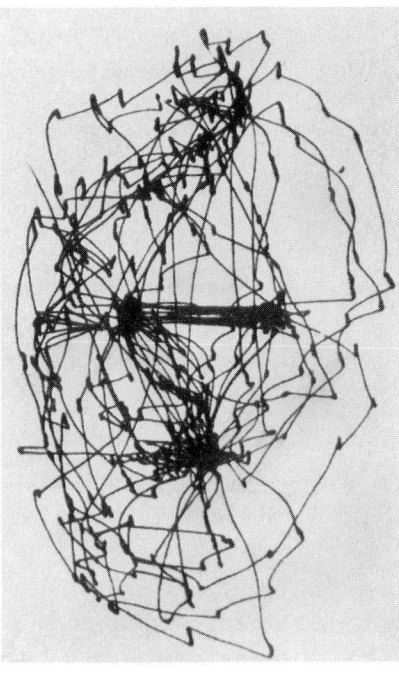

FIGURE 5-24
Eye Movements in Viewing a Picture *Next to the picture of the young girl is a record of the eye movements made by a subject inspecting the picture. (After Yarbus, 1967)*

heightened GSRs to the sexual words may have been due to any number of things other than the words' activity in an unconscious system, for example, their embarrassment potential, their lack of familiarity in print, and so on. According to this criticism, measures of emotionality may reflect many different processes, not just unconscious ones. These two criticisms applied to many studies of perceptual defense, not just McGinnies', and they continue to be widely accepted today (Erdelyi, 1985).

More recent studies have been designed to avoid these criticisms. One such experiment took as its starting point the well-known finding that the more often one is exposed to a particular stimulus, the more one likes it (see Chapter 18). Subjects in the experiment of interest were repeatedly presented geometric figures, but at levels of exposure too brief to permit recognition. Then, on each of a series of test trials, subjects were presented a pair of geometric forms, one of which had previously been presented and one of which was brand new. For each pair, subjects had to answer two questions: a) Which of the two had previously been presented? (a *recognition test*); and b) Which of the two was more attractive? (a *feeling test*). Subjects showed no discrimination on the recognition test—they were completely unable to tell old forms from new ones; but subjects could discriminate on the feeling test, as they consistently favored old forms over new ones. Thus, information that is unavailable for conscious recognition seems to be available to an unconscious system that is linked to affect and emotion (Kunst-Wilson & Zajonc, 1980).

The above study shows us a link between unconscious perception and affect. But it does not speak to the original claim behind perceptual defense, namely that stimuli capable of eliciting unpleasant emotions are harder to perceive. Studies on perceptual defense continue to be done and continue to remain controversial. In addition, other experiments suggest new mechanisms by which strong emotions can disrupt perception. In one study, for example, the subjects were religious Jews and their task was to recognize a briefly presented neutral object. The object was presented either alone or contiguously with a swastika or Star of David. For religious Jews, a swastika was expected to elicit negative emotions, a Star of David positive ones. Perception of the neutral object was hurt as much by the positive Star of David as by the negative swastika. Apparently, positive emotions as well as negative ones can disrupt perception, a notion quite different from perceptual defense (Erdelyi & Applebaum, 1973).

The eye movements used in scanning a picture ensure that different parts of the picture will fall on the fovea so that all of its details can be seen. (As noted in the previous chapter, the fovea has the best resolution; visual acuity diminishes rapidly toward the periphery of the retina.) The points on which the eyes fixate are not evenly distributed, nor are they random. They tend to be places that are most informative about the picture, places where important features are located. Perceiving the picture requires the perceptual system to combine these various glimpses into a single representation of the scene, a process akin to assembling a picture from a series of snapshots of its parts (see Figure 5-24).

There are objects in which the various glimpses cannot be combined into a single representation: such *impossible figures* are illustrated in Figure 5-25. In either of these figures, recognition seems normal as we attend to each part, but the different glances will not fuse into a single, coherent picture. Consider the bottom object in Figure 5-25. When we attend to the right part, we see something like a perspective drawing of three rectangular beams joined together; when we attend to the left part, we see three round rods; when we try to put the products of our eye movements together, they will not gel. The problem is clearly one of integrating separate snapshots, for if the figure is made small enough that its image fits in the fovea, it tends to lose both its depth and its impossible quality, and it appears simply as lines on a flat surface (Hochberg, 1978).

SELECTIVE LISTENING   In audition, the closest thing to eye movements is moving our head so that our ears are directed at the source of interest. This

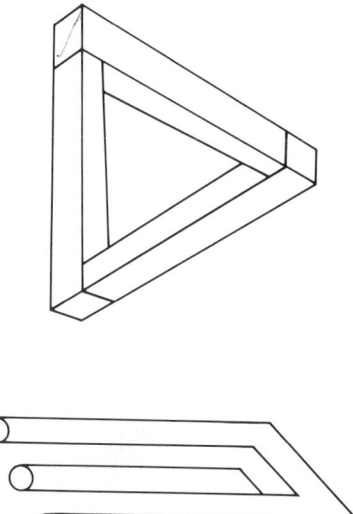

FIGURE 5-25
Impossible Figures *If one looks at any one part of either of these two figures, it makes perceptual sense, but the whole figure does not.*

mechanism of attention is of limited use in many situations, though. Consider, for example, a crowded cocktail party. The sounds of many voices bombard our ears, and their sources are not far enough apart that adjusting our ears would allow us to selectively follow one conversation. We are able, however, to use purely mental means (as opposed to the physical adjustments of our ears) to selectively attend to the desired message. Some of the cues that help us to do this are the direction of the sound, the lip movements of the speaker, and the particular voice characteristics of the speaker (pitch, speed, and intonation). Even in the absence of any of these cues, we can, with difficulty, select one of two messages to follow on the basis of its meaning.

Research on what is called the *cocktail party* phenomenon indicates that we remember very little of messages that we do not attend to. A common procedure in this research is to put earphones on a subject and play one message through one ear and another message through the other ear. The subject is asked to repeat (or *shadow*) one of the messages as it is heard. After proceeding in this way for a few minutes, the messages are turned off and the listener is asked about the unshadowed message. The person can report very little about it. The listener's remarks are usually limited to the physical characteristics of the sound in the unshadowed ear—whether the voice was high or low, male or female, and so forth; he or she can say almost nothing about the content of the message (Moray, 1969).

⤳ The fact that we can report so little about unattended messages initially led researchers to the idea that nonattended stimuli are filtered out completely at a low level in the perceptual system (Broadbent, 1958). However, there is now considerable evidence that our perceptual system retains nonattended stimuli for a brief period and processes them to some extent, even though they never reach consciousness. One piece of evidence for partial processing of nonattended stimuli is that we are very likely to hear the sound of our own name even when spoken softly in a nonattended conversation. This could not happen if the entire nonattended message (such as another person's conversation across the room) were lost at lower levels of the perceptual system. Hence, a lack of attention does not block messages entirely, but rather *attenuates* them, much like a volume control that is turned down but not off (Treisman, 1969).

CONJOINING FEATURES   Thus far we have discussed the role of attention in selecting one object or message from another, or selecting one part of an object from another part. But attention does more than select. It also conjoins, or "glues," the features of an object together. This idea can best be understood in reference to the case of looking *very briefly* at an array of objects, such as pieces of furniture in a living room. Even without paying attention, you may quickly register that there is a couch in the room, and that there is something gold in the room, but it takes a bit of attention to determine that it is the couch that is gold. That is, it takes attention to allocate color and other properties to shapes.

Support for this claim comes from the following experiment. On each trial of the task, subjects had to determine as quickly as possible whether or not an array of letters contained a target letter; the number of nontarget letters varied from trial to trial. In one condition, the target was defined as "either a T or a blue letter," and the nontarget letters in the array were all brown S's (see the top panel of Figure 5-26). In this condition, there is no need to conjoin the features of a nontarget—just checking its color is sufficient to eliminate it—hence there is no need to attend to each nontarget

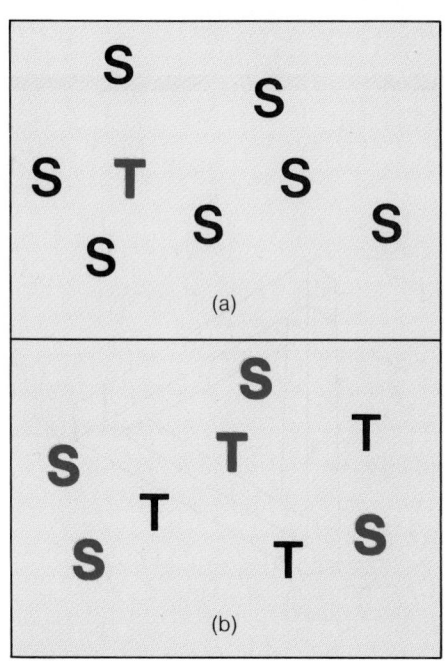

FIGURE 5-26
Attention and Conjoining Features In (a), subjects had to search for either a T or a blue letter; the time to find the target was unaffected by the number of nontarget letters. In (b), subjects had to search for a blue T; in this case the time to find the target increased with the number of nontarget letters. (After Treisman & Gelade, 1980)

separately. Rather, all the nontargets could be analyzed in parallel. In line with this reasoning, subjects in this condition responded very quickly, and took no longer to detect a target when there were 30 nontarget letters than when there were 3 (this is the "pop-out" effect discussed earlier). In another condition, the target was defined as "a blue T," and the nontargets were blue S's and brown T's (see the bottom panel of Figure 5-26). Now, there is a need to conjoin features for every nontarget in the array, which means that attention has to be paid to every letter. In line with this, subjects responded much more slowly, with their times increasing with the number of nontarget letters in the array. Thus, conjoining the features of an object requires attending to that object, which results in processing one object at a time.

There is other evidence that attention is required to conjoin features. An experimenter briefly flashes an array of colored letters, including green S's, brown T's, and pink R's. The subjects' task is simply to report what they see. Because subjects do not always have enough time to attend to every letter in the array, sometimes they will be left with unconjoined features— "there was an S and some pink"—and consequently report an erroneous conjunction—"a pink S." Such *illusory conjunctions* provide striking support for the notion that extra processing is needed to conjoin features (Treisman & Schmidt, 1982).

PERCEPTUAL CONSTANCIES

There is more to perception than the functions it accomplishes. There is the way the world looks to us, and the question of why it looks the way it does.

A striking aspect about how the world appears is that we usually perceive an object as remaining relatively constant regardless of changes in lighting, the position from which we view it, or its distance from us. Your car does not appear to get larger as you walk toward it, distort in shape as you walk around it, or change in color when you view it in artificial light, even though the image on your retina does undergo these changes. This tendency toward constancy is referred to as *perceptual constancy*. Although constancy is not perfect, it is a salient aspect of visual experience.

Lightness and Color Constancy

When an object is illuminated it reflects a certain amount of the light into your eye. The amount reflected is related to the apparent *lightness* of the object. The phenomenon of *lightness constancy* refers to the fact that the perceived lightness of a particular object may barely change even when the amount of reflected light changes dramatically. Thus, black velvet looks nearly as black to us in sunlight as in shadow, even though it reflects thousands of times more light toward our eyes when it is directly illuminated by the sun.

Although the above effect holds under normal circumstances, a change in the surroundings can destroy it. Attach the black velvet to a white board and shine a bright light on both, and the velvet still looks black. But now place an opaque black screen with a small opening in it between you and the velvet so that you can see only a small patch of the velvet. This screen reduces what you see through the opening to the actual light reflected from

CRITICAL DISCUSSION

Reading as a Perceptual Skill

Reading is a remarkable skill and an important means of learning about the world. In our society, most adults are proficient at this skill, and read about 100–400 words per minute, with college students averaging 300 words per minute for nontechnical material. Because reading is in part a perceptual skill, with an emphasis on the recognition of words, it should manifest some of the same phenomena as other topics in recognition. But reading is also a comprehension skill, so it should reveal some new aspects as well.

EYE MOVEMENTS   As was the case with viewing a picture, when we read our eyes do not move continuously across the page; rather, they move in a series of saccades interspersed with fixations. Contrary to many people's impressions, when reading our eyes move only a short distance in each saccade, usually from one word to the next, ignoring certain function words like "a," "of," "the," and so on. The duration of

fixations average about 250 milliseconds, but varies greatly from one fixation to the next. As the text becomes more readable saccades go further (for example, two words rather than one) and fixations become shorter (Rayner, 1978). Occasionally, a reader will move his or her eyes backward to a word already passed, but skilled readers do this less often than beginners.

The display below presents some eye movement data from an experiment by Just and Carpenter (1980). Their subjects read a series of passages that contained scientific material; the figure presents the fixation times of one subject reading two sentences from such a passage. The researchers combined consecutive fixations on the same word into units called *gazes* and numbered the gazes in sequence for each sentence. The duration of each gaze, recorded in milliseconds, is also indicated.

Note, first of all, that almost every word is fixated. The words that are not fixated tend to be short function words like "of," "a," and "the." This is the typical pattern when a reader encounters new text materials that are fairly difficult to comprehend. Note also the word-to-word variation in the duration of gazes. For example, the word "flywheel" is fixated for over a second on each of its two occurrences; no other word was inspected for so long. Longer

gazes occur for words that are unfamiliar to the reader in part because such words take longer to recognize. Longer gazes also occur for words that have special thematic importance. Fixations at the end of a sentence also tend to be long, suggesting that the reader is taking time to integrate information from the whole sentence.

CONTEXT EFFECTS   Various kinds of context effects facilitate normal reading. Our knowledge of words and how they are spelled speeds the identification of letters within the context of words. For example, when we fixate on "C_T," we expect a vowel in the second position. This kind of context effect fits with the connectionist model described earlier: the C and T both activate the word CAT, which in turn activates the missing A. In addition, our knowledge of grammatical rules helps us to identify words in sentences, and our general knowledge of the topic further augments the recognition of words. The possible words that can occur at any position in a text are limited by both grammar and meaning.

When fixating on a word, how much of the material in the periphery is providing useful context? One way to test this is to allow a reader to see only a small region around the fixation point and then determine how the size of this

1	2	3	4	5	6	7	8	9	1	2
1566	267	400	83	267	617	767	450	450	400	616

Flywheels are one of the oldest mechanical devices known to man. Every internal-

3	5	4	6	7	8	9	10	11	12	13
517	684	250	317	617	1116	367	467	483	450	383

combustion engine contains a small flywheel that converts the jerky motion of the pistons into the

14	15	16	17	18	19	20	21
284	383	317	283	533	50	366	566

smooth flow of energy that powers the drive shaft.

Eye Fixations in Reading *Eye fixations of a college student reading a scientific passage. A gaze is the total time a person fixates on a word or group of words. Gazes within each sentence are numbered sequentially above the fixated words, with the durations in milliseconds indicated below the sequence number. Note that there is only one regress— from fixation 4 to 5 in the second sentence. (After Just & Carpenter, 1980)*

the velvet, independent of its surroundings. Now the velvet looks white because the light that reaches your eye through the hole is more intense than that from the screen itself. This demonstration provides a clue as to why the lightness of an object remains constant. When we perceive objects in natural settings, several other objects are usually visible. Lightness constancy

region affects reading performance. Using a computer-driven display controlled by the reader's eye movements, researchers masked all of the text except a small region around the fixation point. When the readers saw only one or two letters around the fixation point, their reading performance slowed and they made errors. As the amount of text seen by the readers increased, their performance improved, but they did not achieve normal reading speed until the window exposed about four words at a time (Rayner et al., 1981). This does not mean that we read four words in one fixation. The words in the periphery are too blurry to read, but apparently these blurs help somewhat, if only to guide the next fixation.

SPEED READING Many speed-reading courses claim to increase both reading speed and comprehension. The critical idea behind these courses is that the bottleneck in reading is the number of eye movements that are usually made. Hence the objective is to train readers to make fewer eye movements and take in several words or a whole phrase in each fixation. Some proponents of speed reading even argue that one can register a whole line of printed text in a single fixation and thus read straight from the top to the bottom of the page rather than from left to right on each line. Students are told to imagine a line down the center of the page and to move their eyes down that imaginary line, registering a whole line of print with each fixation. The instructor may suggest that they move the tip of a finger slowly down the center of the page at the same time, as a guide.

Many claims have been made about the benefits of speed-reading courses,

such as improvements in *both* reading speed and comprehension, but the claims tend not to hold up when evaluated under controlled conditions (Carver, 1981). For example, some early studies reported that readers could greatly increase their speed while showing only a minimal decrease in their score on a comprehension test. However, the comprehension tests used in these studies turned out to be so insensitive that it was possible to obtain reasonable scores on them by not even reading the text and just guessing.

Nevertheless, often people who have taken speed-reading courses are convinced that they have substantially improved their reading skills, and there is a sense in which they are right. What they have learned is the skill of *skimming*. This enables them to pick out key words and main ideas and thereby obtain a great deal of informa-

tion about the passage. Some reading material contains so little new information that skimming is all that is required. Even with difficult material, skimming can be helpful. For example, before reading a chapter in a textbook it is helpful to skim the material to identify key topics and gain a general impression of the chapter (see Appendix I). However, difficult material cannot be fully comprehended by speed reading. Under these conditions the reader must fixate on almost every word to comprehend the material.

These findings do not mean that there is no way to improve reading skills. On the contrary, we know that the more reading a person does, the more his or her reading skills improve. This is particularly true for younger children. Attempts to force yourself to read at a faster rate, however, do not lead to improved reading skills.

depends on the relations among the intensities of light reflected from the different objects. Thus, we continue to see snow as light even in shadow because the snow continues to reflect a greater percentage of its light than does its surroundings. It is the relative percentage of light reflected that determines its brightness.

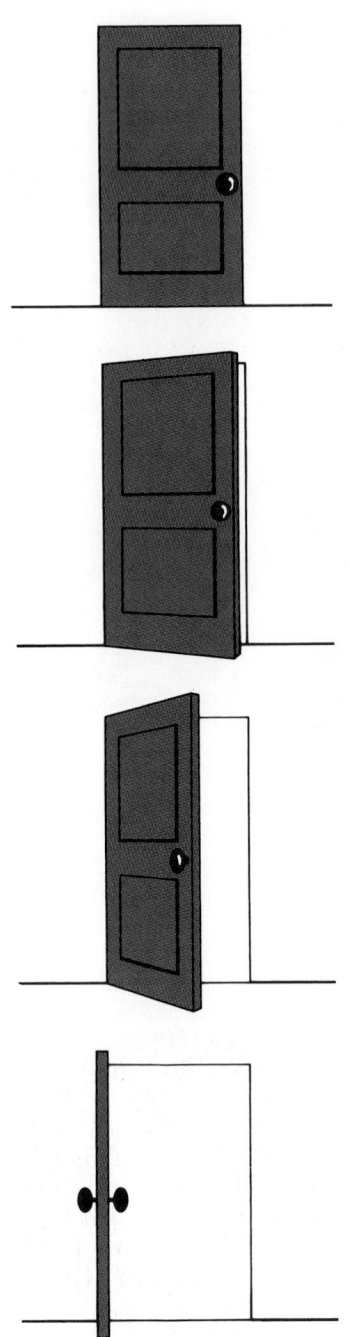

FIGURE 5-27
Shape Constancy *The various retinal images produced by an opening door are quite different, and yet we perceive a door of constant rectangular shape.*

This also holds with regard to color. Recall that the color of an object is partly determined by the wavelengths it reflects. A blue object is one that reflects predominantly short wavelengths, a red object is one that reflects mainly long wavelengths, and so on. However, there is a complication in this—the wavelengths reflected by an object depend not only on the object, but on the light source as well. The cover of this book, for example, reflects somewhat different wavelengths when seen in sunlight than when illuminated by a tungsten light bulb. Remarkably, though, the apparent colors of the cover remain roughly the same with different light sources. This is called *color constancy*.

As was the case with lightness constancy, color constancy can be eliminated by removing the object from its background. For example, if you look at a ripe tomato through a tube that obscures the surroundings and the nature of the object, the tomato may appear any color—blue, green, or pink—depending on the wavelengths reflecting from it. Hence color constancy, like lightness constancy, depends on a heterogeneous background (Land, 1977). Indeed it has been shown mathematically that a sufficiently heterogeneous background is necessary for a visual system to maintain color constancy, be the system a human eye, a camera, or a robot eye (Maloney & Wandell, 1986).

Shape and Location Constancy

When a door swings toward us, the shape of its retinal image goes through a series of changes (see Figure 5-27). The door's rectangular shape produces a trapezoidal image, with the edge toward us wider than the hinged edge; then the trapezoid grows thinner, until finally all that is projected on the retina is a vertical bar the thickness of the door. Nevertheless, we perceive an unchanging door swinging open. The fact that the perceived shape is constant while the retinal image changes is an example of *shape constancy*.

Still another constancy involves the locations of objects. Despite the fact that a series of changing images strike the retina as we move, the positions of fixed objects appear to remain constant. We tend to take this *location constancy* for granted, but it requires that the perceptual system take account of both our movements and the changing retinal images. Consider the case in which we move our eyes over a static scene. The image moves across the receptors in the same way it would if the objects in the scene moved, yet we do not perceive movement in the scene. The visual system must receive information that the eyes are moving, and it must take this information into account in interpreting image motion. Some of this accounting is wired into the brain. Using single-cell recordings, researchers have found cells in the brain that respond only when an external object moves, not when the eye moves over a static object (Robinson & Wurtz, 1976).

Although the preceding paragraphs focus on the way objects look to us, shape constancy and location constancy also have implications for our earlier discussion of localization and recognition. In general, the constancies make the tasks of localization and recognition easier. If an object appeared to change its location every time we moved our eyes, determining its depth (an important part of localization) might be exceedingly difficult. If the shape of an object changed every time it or we moved, then the description of the object that we construct in the early stages of recognition would also change, and recognition might be an impossible task.

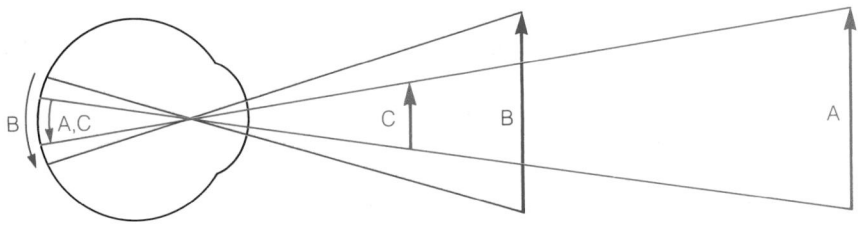

FIGURE 5-28
Retinal Image Size *This figure illustrates the geometric relationship between the physical size of an object and the size of its image on the retina. Arrows A and B represent objects of the same size, but one is twice as far from the eye as the other. As a result, the retinal image of A is about half the size of the retinal image of B. The object represented by arrow C is smaller than that of A, but its location closer to the eye causes it to produce a retinal image of the same size as A.*

Size Constancy

The most studied of all the constancies is *size constancy*, the fact that an object's size remains relatively constant no matter what its distance. As an object moves farther away from us, we generally do not see it as decreasing in size. Hold a quarter a foot in front of you and then move it out to arm's length. Does it appear to get smaller? Not noticeably so. Yet the retinal image of the quarter when it is 24 inches away is half the size of the retinal image when it is 12 inches away (see Figure 5-28). We certainly do not perceive the quarter as becoming half its size as we move it an arm's length. Like other constancies, however, size constancy is not perfect; *very* distant objects appear to be smaller than the same objects close up, as anyone knows who has looked down from a tall building or from an airplane in flight.

DEPENDENCE ON DEPTH CUES The moving quarter example indicates that when we perceive the size of an object, we consider something in addition to the size of the retinal image. That additional something is the *perceived distance* of the object. As long ago as 1881, Emmert was able to show that size judgments depend on distance. Emmert used an ingenious method that involved judging the size of afterimages.

Emmert first had subjects fixate on (stare at) the center of an image for about 1 minute (see Figure 5-29 for an example of such an image). Then subjects looked at a white screen and saw an afterimage. Their task was to judge the size of the afterimage; the independent variable was how far away the screen was. Because the retinal size of the afterimage was the same regardless of the distance of the screen, any variations in the judged size of the afterimage had to be due to its perceived distance. When the screen was far away, the afterimage looked large; when the screen was near, the afterimage looked small. Emmert's experiment is so easy to do that you can perform it on yourself.

Based on such experiments, Emmert proposed that the perceived size of an object increases with both: a) the retinal size of the object; and b) the perceived distance of the object. More specifically, perceived size is equal to the product of retinal size multiplied by perceived distance. This is known as the *size-distance invariance* principle. The principle explains size constancy in the following way. When the distance to an object increases, the object's retinal size decreases; but if distance cues are present, perceived distance will increase. Hence, the product of retinal size and perceived distance will remain approximately constant, which means that perceived size will remain approximately constant. To illustrate: When a person walks away from you, the size of her image on your retina gets smaller, but her perceived distance gets larger; these two changes cancel each other out, and the net result is that your perception of the person's size remains relatively constant.

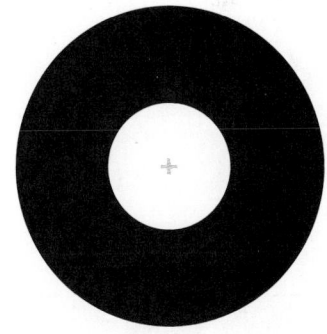

FIGURE 5-29
Emmert's Experiment *Hold the book at normal reading distance under good light. Fixate on the cross in the center of the figure for about 1 minute, then look at a distant wall. You will see an afterimage of the two circles that appears larger than the stimulus. Then look at a piece of paper held close to your eyes; the afterimage will appear smaller than the stimulus. If the afterimage fades, blinking can sometimes restore it.*

The size-distance invariance principle tells us that retinal size and perceived distance can compensate for one another, but it does not tell us *how* the perceiver combines the two sources of information. The best proposal about how we combine the two sources involves Helmholtz's (1909) notion of unconscious inference (encountered earlier in our discussion of depth perception). According to Helmholtz, from experience the perceiver has learned the following rule: "the farther away an object is, the smaller the sensation derived from its retinal image." The perceiver uses this rule to combine the sources of information he has available—size of retinal image and perceived distance—adjusting the perceived size up if the object is seen as far away, and adjusting it down if the object is perceived as close. The perceiver has used the rule to *infer* the size of the object, and this inference has been drawn unconsciously.

ILLUSIONS   The size-distance principle seems to be fundamental to understanding a number of size illusions. (An *illusion* is a percept that is false or distorted; it differs from the state of affairs described by physical science with the aid of measuring instruments.) A good example of a size illusion is the *moon illusion*. When the moon is near the horizon, it looks as much as 50 percent larger than when it is at its zenith, even though in both locations the moon produces the same size retinal image. One explanation of this illusion is that the perceived distance to the horizon is judged to be greater than that to the zenith; hence, it is the greater perceived distance that leads to the greater perceived size (Holway & Boring, 1941).

Another size illusion is the *Ames room* (named after its inventor, Adelbert Ames). Figure 5-30 shows a view of how the Ames room looks to an observer seeing it through a peephole. When the boy is in the left-hand corner of the room (photograph on the left) he appears much smaller than when he is in the right-hand corner (photograph on the right). Yet it is the same boy in both pictures. Here we have a case in which size constancy has broken down. Why? The reason lies in the construction of the room.

FIGURE 5-30

The Ames Room *A view of how the Ames room looks to an observer viewing it through the peephole. The size of the boy and dog depends on which one is in the left-hand corner of the room and which one is in the right-hand corner. The room is designed to wreak havoc with our perceptions. Because of the perceived shape of the room, the relative sizes of the boy and the dog seem impossibly different. Yet it is the same boy and dog in both photographs.*

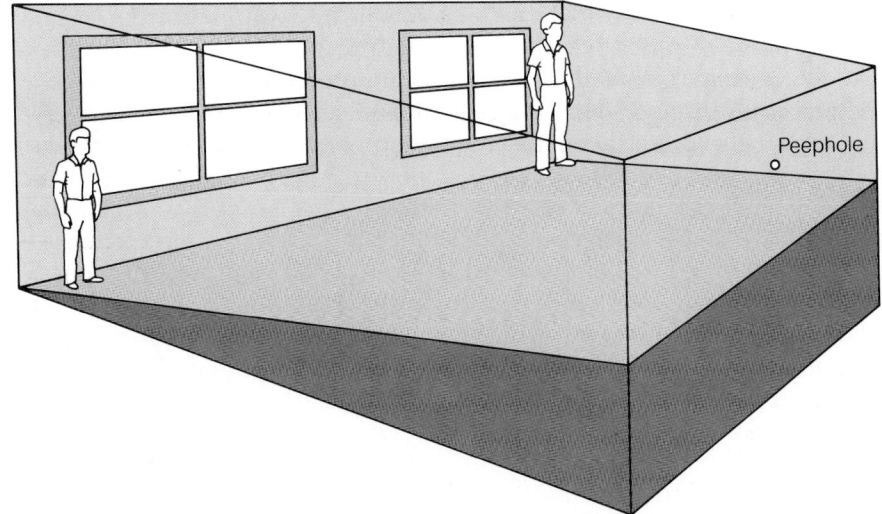

FIGURE 5-31
True Shape of the Ames Room *This figure shows the true shape of the Ames room. The boy on the left is actually almost twice as far away as the boy on the right; however, this difference in distance is not detected when the room is viewed through the peephole. (After Goldstein, 1984)*

Although the room looks like a normal rectangular room to an observer seeing it through the peephole, it is in fact shaped so that its left corner is almost twice as far from us as its right corner (see the diagram in Figure 5-31). Hence, the boy on the left is in fact much farther away than the one on the right, and consequently projects a smaller retinal image. We do not correct for this difference in distance, though, because we believe we are looking at a normal room and thus assume that both boys are at the same distance. In essence, our assumption that the room is normal blocks our usual application of the size-distance invariance principle, and consequently size constancy breaks down.

The Ames room is a particularly dramatic demonstration of a general phenomenon: size constancy becomes imperfect as distance cues are eliminated. To return to our earlier example of a moving quarter, the quarter will change size more as its distance from us varies if it is viewed with one eye rather than two. Using only one eye eliminates the distance cues of binocular parallax and disparity, which reduces size constancy.

Although all of the examples of constancy we have described are visual, and visual constancies are the most studied, constancies do occur in the other senses as well. For example, a person will hear the same tune if the frequencies of all its notes double. All constancies depend on relations between features of the stimulus—between retinal size and distance in the case of size constancy, between the intensity of two adjacent regions in the case of lightness constancy, and so forth. Somehow the perceptual system integrates these features to respond in a constant way, even though the individual features are changing.

PERCEPTUAL DEVELOPMENT

An age-old question about perception is whether our abilities to perceive are learned or innate—the familiar nature vs. nurture problem. Its investigation goes back to the philosophers of the seventeenth and eighteenth centuries. One group, the *nativists* (including Descartes and Kant), argued that we are born with the ability to perceive the way we do. In contrast, the *empiricists* (including Berkeley and Locke), maintained that we learn our ways of perceiving through experience with objects in the world about us. A good example of the empiricist viewpoint is Helmholtz's claim, mentioned earlier, that size constancy depends on the application of a rule (about retinal size and perceived distance) that is *learned from experience*. Contemporary psychologists believe that a fruitful integration of the empiricist and nativist viewpoints is possible. No one today doubts that both genetics and experience influence perception. The question is to what *extent* is perceptual capacity inborn and to what *extent* is it acquired as a function of experience.

For the modern researcher, the question "Must we learn to perceive?" has given way to more specific questions: a) What discriminatory capacity do infants have (that tells us something about inborn capacities), and how does this capacity change with age under normal rearing conditions? b) If animals are reared under conditions of controlled stimulation (that restricts what they can learn), what effects does this have on their later discriminatory capacity? c) What effects does rearing under controlled conditions have on perceptual-motor coordination?

Discrimination by Infants

Perhaps the most direct way to find out what perceptual capacities are inborn is to see what capacities an infant has. At first, you might think that the research should consider only newborns, because if a capacity is inborn it should be present from the first day of life. This idea turns out to be too simple, though. Some inborn capacities, such as form perception, can appear only after other more basic capacities, such as seeing details, have developed. Thus the study of inborn capacities traces perceptual development from the first minute of life through the early years of childhood.

METHODS OF STUDYING INFANTS   It is hard for us to know what an infant perceives because it cannot talk or follow instructions, and has a fairly limited set of behaviors. To study infant perception, a researcher needs to

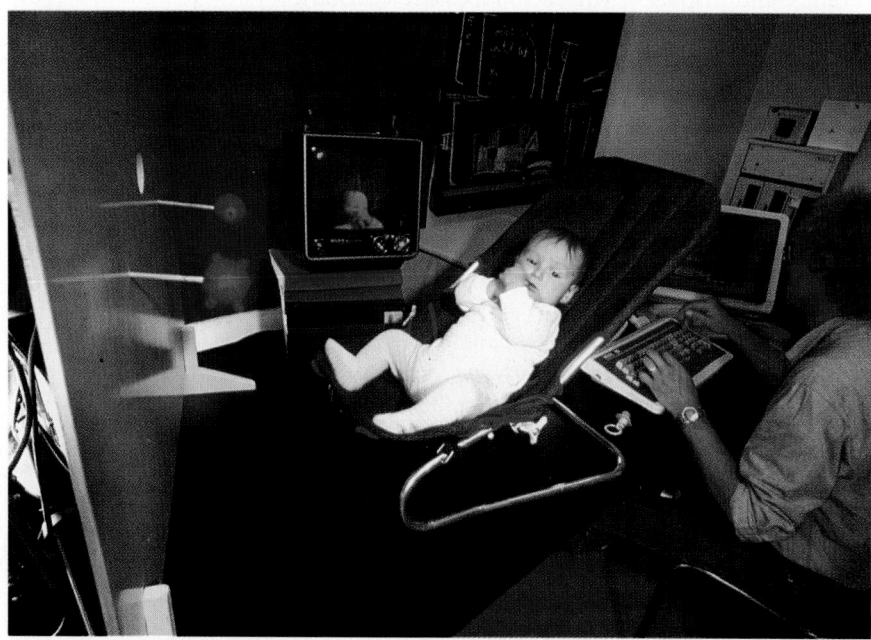

Testing the visual preferences of an infant.

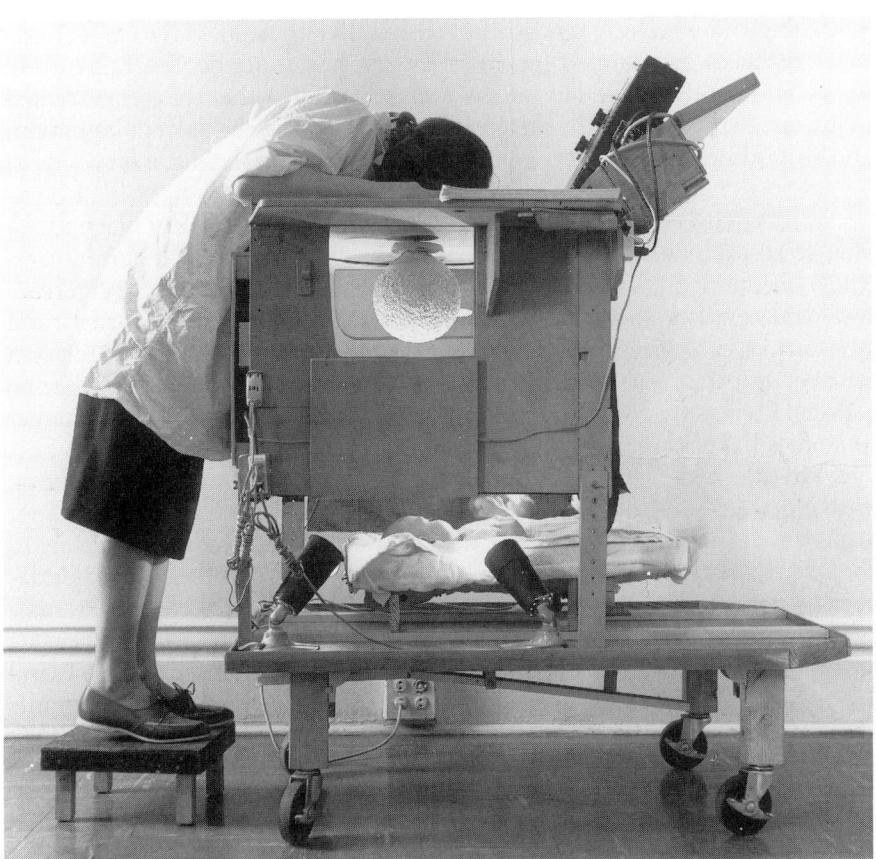

FIGURE 5-32
Preferential Looking Apparatus *This
"looking chamber" has been used to study
preferential looking in infants. An infant lies
in a crib and looks up at pictures and objects
on the ceiling. The experimenter, watching
through a peephole, records the infant's
looking behavior.* (After Fantz, 1961)

find a form of behavior through which an infant indicates what it can discriminate. The behavior often used for this purpose is an infant's tendency to look at some objects more than others, and psychologists study this by using the *preferential looking method.*

The method, which was discussed in Chapter 3, is illustrated in Figure 5-32. Two stimuli are presented to the infant side by side. The experimenter, who is hidden from the infant's view, looks through a partition behind the stimuli and, by watching the infant's eyes, measures the amount of time that the infant looks at each stimulus. (Usually the experimenter will use a television camera to record the infant's viewing pattern to ensure accuracy.) From time to time, the stimulus positions are switched randomly. If an infant consistently looks at one stimulus more than the other, the experimenter concludes that the infant can tell them apart (discriminate between them). The method would not work unless infants looked at some things more than others; hence, it shows that infants have definite looking preferences. For example, given a choice, infants will look at a pattern rather than a blank field (Fantz, Ordy, & Udelf, 1962).

Psychologists have also used *visual evoked potentials* to study infant perception. To record evoked potentials, an experimenter places electrodes on the back of the baby's head over the visual cortex. The electrodes are not annoying, and the infant quickly adapts to them. If a pattern consisting of broad stripes is presented to the infant, the electrodes will pick up an electrical response (the evoked potential); when the stripes are made very narrow, the response disappears. The response is thought to be closely related to how well the infant can see the stripes.

Using these techniques, psychologists have studied a variety of perceptual capacities in infants. Some of these capacities are needed to perceive forms, and hence are used in the task of recognition; other capacities studied in infants, particularly depth perception, are involved in the task of localization; and still other capacities are involved in the perceptual constancies.

PERCEIVING FORMS To be able to perceive an object, first one must be able to discriminate one part of it from another, an ability referred to as *acuity*. Related to acuity is *contrast sensitivity*, roughly the ability to discriminate between dark and light stripes under various conditions. (The dark and light stripes can correspond to different parts of a pattern, hence the relation between contrast sensitivity and acuity; for a review of these ideas, see the Critical Discussion on Seeing Spatial Patterns in Chapter 4.) A large number of studies have focused on acuity and contrast sensitivity in infants.

The method typically used in studying acuity is preferential looking, with a pattern of stripes as one stimulus and a uniform gray field as the other stimulus. Initially, the stripes are relatively wide, and the infant prefers to look at the pattern rather than the uniform field. Then the researcher decreases stripe width until the infant no longer shows a preference. Presumably at this point the infant can no longer discriminate a stripe from its surrounding so that the pattern of stripes no longer has perceptible parts and looks like a uniform field. When first studied at about 1 month of age, infants can see some patterns, but their acuity is very low. Acuity increases rapidly over the first 6 months of life; then it increases more slowly, reaching adult levels between 1 and 5 years of age (Teller, Morse, Borton, & Regal, 1974; Pirchio, Spinelli, Fiorentini, & Maffei, 1978).

Researchers have used the same method to study contrast sensitivity. Now both stimuli are patterns of alternating dark and light stripes, and what varies is the *spatial frequency* of the stripes, where the higher the spatial frequency of a pattern the smaller the distance between successive dark stripes. Infant contrast sensitivity is better at low spatial frequencies (big distances between stripes) than at other frequencies, but is less than adult sensitivity at all frequencies. Like acuity, contrast sensitivity increased rapidly over the first 6 months of life (Banks, 1982). Visual evoked-potentials studies give comparable results. The basis of this development in pattern vision is not completely understood, but we do know that the optics of the eye, the retina, and the cortex continue to develop over this period.

What do these studies tell us about the infant's perceptual world? At 1 month, infants can distinguish no fine details; their vision can discriminate only relatively large objects. Such vision is sufficient, though, to perceive some gross characteristics of an object, including some of the features of a face (which create something like a pattern of dark and light stripes). Figure 5-33 uses the results of acuity and contrast-sensitivity experiments to simulate what a 1-, 2-, and 3-month-old infant sees when viewing a woman's face from a distance of 6 inches. At 1 month, acuity is so poor that it is difficult to perceive facial expressions (and indeed newborns look mostly at the outside contours of a face). By 3 months, acuity has improved to the point where an infant can decipher facial expressions (Goldstein, 1984). No wonder that infants seem so much more socially responsive at 3 months than 1 month.

Being able to discriminate dark from light edges is critical for seeing forms, but what about other aspects of object recognition? Our sensitivity to some of the shape features of objects is manifested early. When presented with a triangle, even a 3-day-old infant will direct its eye movements toward

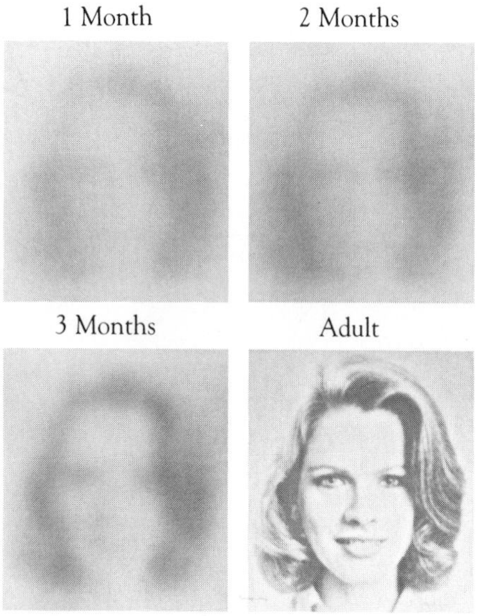

1 Month   2 Months

3 Months   Adult

FIGURE 5-33
Visual Acuity and Contrast-Sensitivity *Simulations of what 1-, 2-, and 3-month-old infants see when they look at a woman's face from a distance of about six inches; the bottom right photograph is what an adult sees. The simulations of infant perception were obtained by first determining an infant's contrast sensitivity, and then applying this contrast-sensitivity function to the photograph on the bottom right. (After Ginsburg, 1983)*

the edges and vertices, rather than look randomly over the form (Salapatek, 1975). Also, infants find some shapes more interesting than others. Infants tend to look more at forms that resemble human faces, which appears to be based on a preference for some of the features that comprise a face, like a preference for curved rather than straight contours (Fantz, 1961; 1970). By age 3 months, an infant can recognize something about the mother's face, even in a photograph, as revealed by an infant's preference to look at a photograph of the mother rather than one of an unfamiliar woman (Barrera & Maurer, 1981).

PERCEIVING DEPTH   Depth perception begins to appear at about 3 months of age but is not fully established until about 6 months. Evidence for this conclusion comes from studies like the following one on binocular disparity. An infant views a random pattern of dots that look like a moving object *only* if the observer is sensitive to binocular-disparity information. Thus, if an infant moves his eyes to follow the object, he is probably sensitive to disparity. In fact, infants younger than 3 months will not follow the moving object, whereas infants between 3 and 6 months do follow it (Fox, Aslin, Shea, & Dumais, 1980).

The use of monocular cues shows a similar developmental course. At 5½ months, but not before, infants will reach for the nearer of two objects, where nearness is signaled by the monocular cue of relative size. Further evidence about the development of monocular depth perception comes from studies of the *visual cliff*. The visual cliff (illustrated in Figure 5-34) consists of a center board placed across a sheet of glass, with a surface of patterned material located directly under the glass on the *shallow side*, and at a distance of a few feet below the glass on the *deep side*. An infant old enough to crawl (about 6 months) is placed on the center board; one of her eyes is patched to eliminate binocular depth cues. The infant will consistently crawl across the

FIGURE 5-34
Visual Cliff *The "visual cliff" is an apparatus used to show that infants and young animals are able to see depth by the time they are able to move about. The visual cliff consists of two surfaces, both displaying the same checkerboard pattern and covered by a sheet of thick glass. One surface is directly under the glass; the other is several feet below it. When placed on the center board between the deep and the shallow sides, the kitten refuses to cross to the deep side but will readily move off the board onto the shallow side. (After Gibson & Walk, 1960)*

shallow side to get to her mother, but will not cross the "cliff" or deep side. Thus when old enough to crawl, an infant's depth perception is relatively well developed.

PERCEPTUAL CONSTANCIES   Compared to the perception of form and depth, the perceptual constancies take much longer to develop. For example, although there is some degree of size constancy in infancy, 8-year-old children still show less constancy than adults (Zeigler & Leibowitz, 1957). Constancies are about the way the world looks to us, and of course there is no way for us to be sure what an infant is experiencing. But a number of investigators have been impressed by the fact that infants' natural responses to stimuli often resemble those of adults. They turn toward sounds, defend themselves when an object flies toward them, and do not fall off raised platforms. The similarity of infant and adult responses to the same stimuli suggests that infants and adults may experience these stimuli in a similar way (Bower, 1982).

Rearing with Controlled Stimulation

We turn now to the question of how experience affects perceptual capacities. To answer this question, researchers have systematically varied the kinds of perceptual experiences a young organism has, and then looked at the effects of this experience on subsequent perceptual performance.

ABSENCE OF STIMULATION   The earliest experiments on controlled stimulation sought to determine the effects of rearing an animal in the total absence of visual stimulation. The experimenters kept animals in the dark for several months after birth until they were mature enough for visual testing. The idea behind these experiments was that if animals have to *learn* to perceive, they would be unable to perceive when first exposed to the light. The results turned out as expected: chimpanzees reared in darkness for their first 16 months could detect light but could not discriminate patterns (Riesen, 1947). However, subsequent studies showed that prolonged rearing in the dark does more than prevent learning; it causes neuronal deterioration in various parts of the visual system. It turns out that a certain amount of light stimulation is necessary to maintain the visual system. Without any light stimulation, nerve cells in the retina and visual cortex begin to atrophy. Though this fact does not tell us much about the role of learning in perceptual development, it is important in itself.

Single-cell recording studies provided a more thorough account of the devastating effects of no stimulation. Recordings from the visual cortex in newborn cats and monkeys show that they have simple, complex, and hypercomplex cells very similar to those in adult animals (see p. 166) (Hubel & Wiesel, 1963; Wiesel & Hubel, 1974). These cells, however, respond more slowly and are less sharply tuned than adult cells. In kittens, for instance, the cells become adultlike in 4 to 6 weeks if the kittens receive some visual stimulation. If they are reared in darkness, many of their cortical cells do not respond when they are introduced to an illuminated room. Similarly, animals that are raised with one eye patched have few cortical cells that respond to stimulation of that eye, and are essentially blind in that eye.

In general, when an animal is deprived of visual stimulation from birth, the longer the time of deprivation, the greater the deficit. Adult cats, on the other hand, can have one eye patched for a long period without losing vision in that eye. These observations led to the idea that a *critical period* exists for visual development early in life; lack of stimulation during this period permanently impairs the visual system.

LIMITED STIMULATION Because a prolonged, total lack of stimulation can destroy inborn capacities, researchers have shifted strategy. Researchers no longer deprive animals of stimulation for a long period of time; instead they study the effects of rearing animals with stimulation in both eyes, but only of a certain kind. Researchers have raised kittens in an environment in which they see only vertical stripes, or only horizontal stripes (see Figure 5-35). The kittens become blind to stripes in the orientation—vertical or horizontal—that they do not experience. And single-cell recording studies show that many cells in the visual cortex of a "horizontally-reared" cat respond to horizontal stimuli and none respond to vertical stimuli, whereas the opposite pattern of results obtains for a "vertically-reared" cat (Blakemore & Cooper, 1970; Hirsch & Spinelli, 1970). What happens to the cortical cells that are not stimulated? Do they degenerate or do they become "rewired" to respond to the available stimuli? If degeneration occurs, there should be areas of the visual cortex that are unresponsive. The evidence on this issue is mixed, but it seems to favor the degeneration hypothesis (Movshon & Van Sluyters, 1981).

Of course researchers do not deprive humans of normal visual stimulation, but sometimes this happens naturally or as a consequence of medical treatment. For example, after eye surgery the operated eye is usually patched. If this happens to a child in the first year of life, the acuity of the patched eye is reduced (Awaya et al., 1973). Similarly, if a person's eyes do not point in the same direction early in life (a condition called *strabismus*), he or she will not have binocular depth perception in later life, even if the strabismus is corrected by surgery. Likewise, if *astigmatism* (an optical defect that prevents horizontal and vertical contours from being in focus at the same moment) is not corrected early in life, the individual will later have low acuity for one orientation (Mitchell & Wilkinson, 1974). These facts suggest that there is a critical period early in the development of the human visual system similar to that in animals; if stimulation is restricted during this period, the system will not develop normally. The critical period is much longer in humans than in animals. It may last as long as eight years, but the greatest vulnerability occurs during the first two years of life (Aslin & Banks, 1978).

None of these facts indicate that we have to learn to perceive. Rather, the facts show that certain kinds of stimulation are essential for the *maintenance* and *development* of perceptual capacities that are present at birth. If there is any learning going on in the situations described above, it is of a very special kind in that it occurs only during an early critical period and involves a partial rewiring of the cortex.

For clearer cases of learning affecting perception, we need only consider our ability to recognize common objects, and how this ability is influenced by context and expectation. The fact that we can more readily recognize a familiar object than an unfamiliar one—a dog versus an aardvark, for example—must certainly be due to learning (because had we been reared in an environment rich in aardvarks and sparse in dogs, we could have recognized the aardvark more readily than the dog). Likewise, the fact that certain contexts can facilitate the recognition of particular objects—for example, a farm scene facilitates recognition of a cow—is also almost certainly a consequence of learning.

FIGURE 5-35
Controlled Visual Environment *In one experiment, kittens were kept in the dark from birth to 2 weeks of age. They were then placed in this tube for five hours a day and spent the rest of the time in the dark. The kitten is on a clear Plexiglass platform, and the striped tube extends above and below it. It is wearing a neck ruff that blocks its view of its own body and prevents head turning. The kittens did not appear to be distressed in this situation. After five months of this exposure, the kittens could see vertical stripes very well but were essentially blind to horizontal stripes. Further, single-cell recording found few cells in their cortices that responded to horizontal stripes. (After Blakemore & Cooper, 1970)*

FIGURE 5-36
Learning Perceptual-Motor Coordination *(a) Kitten wearing a collar that prevented it from seeing its limbs and torso. The collar was lightweight and had little effect on locomotion. Kittens were permitted to move freely 6 hours daily in a lighted and patterned environment while wearing the collar. The rest of the time, they were kept without collars in a dark room. (b) Apparatus for testing visually guided paw placement. The prongs were 2.5 cm. wide and 7.5 cm. apart. During the test trials, the torso, hindlimbs, and one forelimb were supported as shown. The kitten was carried downward toward the pronged edge. The kitten was scored on the basis of whether or not its paw landed on a prong. (After Hein & Held, 1967)*

(a) (b)

PERCEPTUAL-MOTOR COORDINATION When it comes to coordinating perceptions with motor responses, learning plays a major role. The evidence for this comes from studies in which subjects receive normal stimulation but are prevented from making normal responses to that stimulation. Under such conditions, perceptual-motor coordination does not develop.

For example, kittens were reared in the dark until they were 4 weeks old and then for 6 hours a day placed in a lighted and patterned environment in which they were allowed to move about freely. While they were in this situation, they wore lightweight collars that prevented them from seeing their bodies or paws (see Figure 5-36a). Except for this 6-hour exposure period each day, they stayed in a dark room. After 12 days of this regimen, they were tested for visual-motor coordination. The test consisted of lowering the kitten (with one front paw held and the other free to move) toward a table that had horizontal prongs (see Figure 5-36b). The researcher was interested in determining if the kitten would extend a paw and guide it to a prong. This is a response that a normally reared kitten will make very reliably. All the experimental kittens extended their free paw as they approached the table, indicating that they could see that the table was within reach. But on 50 percent of the trials, the kittens missed the prongs, indicating that they had not learned to guide their limbs to a visual target. After a few hours without the collar in a normally illuminated room, the kittens learned the paw-placing response (Hein & Held, 1967).

Not only is learning required for perceptual motor coordination, but the learning must involve self-produced movements in response to the stimulation. In one experiment, two dark-reared kittens had their first visual experience in the "kitten carousel" illustrated in Figure 5-37. As the active kitten walked, it moved the passive kitten riding in the carousel. Although both kittens received roughly the same visual stimulation, only the active kitten had this stimulation produced by its movement. And only the active kitten successfully learned sensory-motor coordination; for example, only the active kitten learned to put out its paws to ward off a collision.

Very similar results have been obtained with humans. In some experiments people have worn prism goggles that distort the directions of objects. Immediately after putting on these goggles, a person temporarily has trouble reaching for objects and often bumps into things. If a person moves about

FIGURE 5-37
Importance of Self-Produced Movements *Both kittens received roughly the same visual stimulation, but only the active kitten had this stimulation produced by its own movement.* (After Held & Hein, 1963)

and attempts to perform motor tasks while wearing the goggles, he or she learns to behave adaptively. On the other hand, if the person is pushed in a wheelchair, he or she does not adapt to the goggles. Apparently, self-produced movement is essential to prism adaptation (Held, 1965).

Is perception innate or learned? The answer to this question is clearly some of each. The evidence indicates that we are born with considerable perceptual capacity, which is then shaped and developed by learning.

CHAPTER SUMMARY

1. The study of perception deals with two major tasks: *localization*, or determining where objects are, and *recognition*, or determining what objects are. Localization and recognition are carried out by different regions of the cortex. The study of perception also deals with phenomenological issues about why the world looks the way it does, and with developmental issues about the growth of perceptual capacities.

2. To localize objects, first we have to *segregate* objects from one another and then *organize* them into groups. These processes were first studied by *Gestalt* psychologists, who proposed principles of organization. One such principle is that we organize a stimulus into regions corresponding to *figure* and *ground*. Other principles concerned the bases that we use to group objects together, including: *proximity, closure, good continuation,* and *similarity*.

3. Localizing an object requires that we know its depth. *Depth perception* is usually thought to be based on *depth cues*. Monocular depth cues include *relative size, superposition,* and *relative height*. Binocular depth cues include *parallax* and *disparity*, with disparity due to the fact that any object provides slightly different images to the two eyes. An alternative to inferring distance on the basis of depth cues is Gibson's notion of *direct perception*, wherein a source of information like a *texture gradient* provides direct information about the depth of an object.

4. Localizing an object requires knowing the motion of moving objects. *Motion perception* can be produced in the absence of an object moving across our retina; one case of this is *stroboscopic motion* in which a series of rapid, still images

induces apparent movement; another case of motion perception without a moving object is *induced motion* in which movement of a large object induces apparent movement of a smaller stationary object. *Real motion* (induced by an object moving across the retina) is partly coded by specific cells in the visual system, as indicated by experiments on *selective adaptation* and by single-cell recordings.

5. Recognizing an object amounts to assigning it to a category and is based mainly on the shape of the object. In *early stages* of recognition, the visual system uses retinal information to describe the object in terms of *features* like lines and angles; cells that detect such features (*feature detectors*) have been found in the visual cortex. In the *later stages* of recognition, the system matches the description of the object to shape descriptions stored in memory to find the best match.

6. Much of the research on the *matching stage* of recognition has used letter patterns. Matching can be explained by a *connectionist model* or network. The bottom level of the network contains features and the next level contains letters; a *facilitatory connection* between a feature and a letter means that the feature is part of a letter, while an *inhibitory connection* means the feature is not part of the letter. When a letter is presented, it activates some features in the network, which pass their activation or inhibition up to letters; the letter that receives the most activation is the best match to the input. The network can be expanded to include a level of words and to explain why a letter is easier to recognize when presented in a word than when presented alone.

7. The shape features of natural objects are more complex than lines, being more like simple geometric forms such as cylinders, cones, blocks, and wedges. We can perceive an object more readily if it fits the *context* in which it occurs; this is particularly true of *ambiguous figures*, which are figures that are perceived in more than one way. Context works by setting up expectations that can be either conscious or unconscious.

8. *Selective attention* is the process by which we select some stimuli for further processing while ignoring others. In vision, the primary means for directing our attention are *eye movements*. Usually, our eyes are still for a brief period (a *fixation*), then jump to a new location (a *saccade*), with most of the fixations being on the more informative parts of a scene. Selective attention also occurs in audition. Usually, we are able to *selectively listen* by using cues like the direction of the sound and the voice characteristics of the speaker. In addition to its selective function, attention is also needed to conjoin the features of an object.

9. *Perceptual constancy* is a tendency for objects to appear the same in spite of large changes in the stimuli received by our sense organs. *Lightness constancy* refers to the fact that an object appears equally light regardless of how much light it reflects, whereas *color constancy* means an object looks roughly the same color regardless of the exact wavelengths it reflects when illuminated. In both cases, constancy depends on relations between object and background elements. Two other well known constancies are *shape* and *location constancy*.

10. The most studied of all constancies is *size constancy*, the fact that any object's size remains relatively constant no matter what its distance from us. The perceived size of an object increases with both the *retinal size* of the object and the *perceived distance* of the object, in accordance with the *size-distance invariance* principle. Thus, as an object moves away from the perceiver, the retinal size decreases but the perceived distance increases, and the two changes cancel each other out, resulting in constancy. This principle can explain certain *illusions*.

11. Research on *perceptual development* is concerned with the extent to which perceptual capacity is inborn and the extent to which it is acquired by experience. To determine inborn capacities, researchers study the discrimination capacities of infants using the methods of *preferential looking* and *visual evoked potentials*. *Acuity* increases rapidly over the first 6 months of life, then increases more

slowly until it reaches adult levels between 1 and 5 years of age. *Depth perception* begins to appear at about 3 months of age, but is not fully established until about 6 months.

12. Animals raised in darkness suffer permanent visual impairment, and animals raised with a patch over one eye become blind in that eye. Adult animals do not lose vision even when deprived of stimulation for long periods. These results suggest a *critical period* early in life, during which lack of normal stimulation produces an abnormal perceptual system. If stimulation is controlled early in life, so that certain kinds of stimuli are absent, both animals and people become insensitive to the stimuli of which they have been deprived.

13. *Perceptual-motor* coordination must be learned. Animals that cannot see their own limbs do not develop normal coordination. Both animals and people require *self-produced movement* to develop normal coordination.

FURTHER READING

Many of the textbooks listed under Further Reading in Chapter 4 also pertain to the topics considered in this chapter. Several additional sources are appropriate as well.

General treatments of perception are available in Coren and Ward, *Sensation and Perception* (3rd ed., 1989), and Rock, *The Logic of Perception* (1983). Gibson's distinctive approach to issues like depth and motion perception in particular, and to perception in general, is presented in *The Ecological Approach to Visual Perception* (1979). Marr's equally distinctive, cognitive-science approach to perception is given in his book *Vision* (1982). A more elementary introduction to some of Marr's work is presented in the early chapters of Johnson-Laird, *The Computer and the Mind* (1988).

Problems of recognition and attention are discussed in Spoehr and Lehmkuhle, *Visual Information Processing* (1982), and Posner and Marin, (ed.), *Mechanisms of Attention* (1985). The connectionist approach to problems of recognition and localization are contained in an advanced, two-volume set by Rumelhart and McClelland, *Parallel Distributed Processing* (1986).

Chapter 6

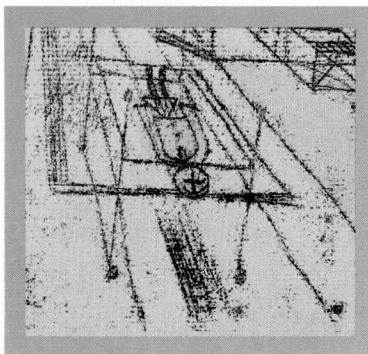

Detail, Phantom Perspective.

Consciousness and Its Altered States

As you read these words, are you awake or dreaming? Hardly anyone is confused by this question. We all know the difference between an ordinary state of wakefulness and the experience of dreaming. We also recognize other *states of consciousness*, including those induced by drugs such as alcohol and marijuana.

A person's conscious awareness is readily subject to change. At this moment, your attention may be focused on this book; in a few minutes, you may be deep in reverie. To most psychologists, an *altered state of consciousness* exists whenever there is a change from an ordinary pattern of mental functioning to a state that *seems* different to the person experiencing the change. Although this is not a very precise definition, it reflects the fact that states of consciousness are personal and therefore subjective. Altered states of consciousness can vary from the distraction of a vivid daydream to the confusion and perceptual distortion of drug intoxication. In this chapter we will look at some altered states of consciousness that are experienced by everyone (sleep and dreams, for instance), as well as some that result from special circumstances (meditation, hypnosis, and the use of drugs).

ASPECTS OF CONSCIOUSNESS

Many topics discussed in other chapters have a direct bearing on the study of consciousness. When psychologists ask how we interpret sensory information (Chapters 4 and 5), how we store and retrieve memories (Chapters 7 and 8), and how we think and solve problems (Chapter 9), they are essentially raising questions about consciousness.

But what is consciousness? The early psychologists equated "consciousness" with "mind." They defined psychology as "the study of mind and consciousness" and used the introspective method to study consciousness. As noted in Chapter 1, both introspection as a method for investigation and consciousness as a topic for investigation fell from favor with the rise of *behaviorism* in the early 1900s. John Watson, the founder of behaviorism, and his followers believed that if psychology were to become a science, its data must be objective and measurable. Behavior could be publicly observed and various responses could be objectively measured. In contrast, an individual's private experiences revealed through introspection could not be observed by others or objectively measured. In other words, if psychology dealt with actual behavior, it would be dealing with *public events*, instead of *private events*, which are observable only to the experiencing person.

Behaviorism did not require as radical a change as its pronouncements seemed to imply. The behaviorists themselves dealt with private events when their research required them to. They accepted *verbal responses* as a substitute for introspection when the subject's own experiences were studied. What subjects said was objective, regardless of the uncertainties about the underlying subjective condition. Still, many psychologists continued to believe, regardless of the behaviorists, that when people said they experienced a series of colored afterimages after staring at a bright light, they probably did see colors in succession. That is, their words were not the whole story: the words referred to something of additional psychological interest. While behaviorists could deal with many phenomena in terms of verbal responses,

Reflection is one aspect of consciousness.

their preoccupation with observable behavior caused them to neglect interesting psychological problems, such as dreaming, meditation, and hypnosis, because the subjective aspects made the topics distasteful to them.

By the 1950s, psychologists began to recognize that the facts of consciousness are too pervasive and important to be neglected. This does not mean that psychology must again be defined exclusively as the study of consciousness; it means only that a complete psychology cannot afford to neglect consciousness. A strict behaviorist's insistence on confining psychology to the study of observable behavior is too limiting. If one can theorize about the nature of consciousness, and that theory leads to testable predictions about behavior, then such theorizing represents a valuable contribution to understanding how the mind works.

Within a period of 50 years, the focus of psychology has come full circle. After rejecting consciousness as ill-suited to scientific investigation and turning to the study of behavior, psychologists are once again theorizing about the nature of conscious experience, but this time with new and more powerful research tools. The gain from behaviorism has been an emphasis on objectivity and reproducibility of research findings.

Consciousness

Despite the reemergence of consciousness in psychology, there is still no common agreement on a definition of the term. Many textbooks simply define consciousness as the individual's current awareness of external and internal stimuli—that is, of events in the environment and of bodily sensations, memories, and thoughts. This definition identifies only one aspect of consciousness and ignores the fact that we are conscious also when we try to solve a problem or deliberately select one course of action over others in response to environmental circumstances and personal goals. Thus we are conscious when we monitor the environment (internal and external), but also when we seek to control ourselves and our environment. In short, consciousness involves a) *monitoring* ourselves and our environment so that percepts, memories, and thoughts are accurately represented in awareness; and b) *controlling* ourselves and our environment so that we are able to initiate and terminate behavioral and cognitive activities (Kihlstrom, 1984).

MONITORING   Processing information from the environment is the main function of the body's sensory systems, leading to awareness of what is going on in our surroundings as well as within our own bodies. But we could not possibly attend to all of the stimuli that impinge on our senses; there would be an information overload. Our consciousness focuses on some stimuli and ignores others. Often the information selected has to do with changes in our external or internal world. While concentrating on this paragraph, you are probably unaware of numerous background stimuli. But should there be a change—the lights dim, the air begins to smell smoky, or the noise of the air conditioning system ceases—you would suddenly be aware of such stimuli.

Our attention is selective; some events take precedence over others in gaining access to consciousness and in initiating action. Events that are important to survival usually have top priority. If we are hungry, it is difficult for us to concentrate on studying; if we experience a sudden pain, we push all other thoughts out of consciousness until we do something to make it go away.

CONTROLLING   Another function of consciousness is to plan, initiate, and guide our actions. Whether the plan is simple and readily completed (such as meeting a friend for lunch) or complex and long-range (such as preparing for a lifetime career), our actions must be guided and arranged to coordinate with events around us.

In planning, events that have not yet occurred can be represented in consciousness as future possibilities; we may envision alternative "scenarios," make choices, and initiate appropriate activities.

Subconscious Processes and Preconscious Memories

From all that is going on around us now and from our store of knowledge and memories of past events, we can focus attention on only a few stimuli at a given moment. We ignore, select, and reject all the time, so that consciousness is continually changing. But objects or events that are not the focus of attention can still have some influences on consciousness. For example, you may not be aware of hearing a clock strike the hour. After a few strokes, you become alert; then you can go back and count the strokes that you did not know you heard. Another example of peripheral attention is the *cocktail party phenomenon*: you are talking to someone in a crowded room, ignoring the other voices and general noise, when the sound of your own name in another conversation catches your attention. Clearly, you would not have detected your name in the other conversation if you had not, in some sense, been monitoring that conversation; you were not consciously aware of the other conversation until a special signal drew your attention to it. A considerable body of research indicates that we register and evaluate stimuli that we do not consciously perceive (Kihlstrom, 1987). These stimuli are said to influence us *subconsciously*, or to operate at a subconscious level of awareness.

Many memories and thoughts that are not part of your consciousness at this moment can be brought to consciousness when needed. At this moment you may not be conscious of your vacation last summer, but the memories are accessible if you wish to retrieve them; then they become a vivid part of your consciousness. Memories that are accessible to consciousness are called *preconscious memories*. They include specific memories of personal events, as well as the information accumulated over a lifetime, such as one's knowledge of the meaning of words, the layout of the streets of a city, or the location of a particular country. They also include knowledge about learned skills like the procedures involved in driving a car or the sequence of steps in tying one's shoelace. These procedures, once mastered, generally operate outside conscious awareness, but when our attention is called to them we are capable of describing the steps involved. The collection of such memories and processes is called the *preconscious*.

The Unconscious

According to the psychoanalytic theories of Sigmund Freud and his followers, some memories, impulses, and desires are not accessible to consciousness. Psychoanalytic theory assigns these to the *unconscious*. Freud believed that some emotionally painful memories and wishes are *repressed*—that is, diverted to the unconscious, where they may continue to influence our actions even though we are not aware of them. Thoughts and impulses repressed to the unconscious cannot enter our consciousness, but they can

"Good morning, beheaded—uh, I mean beloved"

Drawing by Dana Fradon; © 1979 *The New Yorker Magazine,* Inc.

affect us in indirect or disguised ways—through dreams, irrational behaviors, mannerisms, and slips of the tongue. The term "Freudian slip" is commonly used to refer to unintentional remarks that are assumed to reveal hidden impulses. Saying "I'm sad you're better," when intending to say "I'm glad you're better," would be an example.

Freud believed that unconscious desires and impulses are the cause of most mental illnesses. He developed the method of psychoanalysis, the goal of which is to draw the repressed material to consciousness and, in so doing, cure the individual (see Chapter 17).

Most psychologists accept the idea that there are memories and mental processes that are inaccessible to introspection and accordingly may be described as unconscious. However, many would argue that Freud placed undue emphasis on the emotionally laden aspects of the unconscious and not enough on other aspects. They would include in the unconscious a large array of mental processes that we depend on constantly in our everyday lives but to which we have no conscious access (Kihlstrom, 1987). For example, during perception, the viewer may be aware of two objects in the environment but have no awareness of the mental calculations she performed almost instantaneously to determine that one is closer or larger than the other (see Chapter 5). Although we have conscious access to the outcome of these mental processes—in that we are aware of the size and distance of the object—we have no conscious access to their operations.

Fodor (1983) has proposed that these types of unconscious mental processes are innately specified and operate as independent modules. His *modularity thesis* asserts that the mind consists of a number of innate mental structures (modules) controlling such activities as language and visual perception, hardwired in the nervous system (in the sense of being associated with specific, localized neural structures) and operating outside of conscious awareness and voluntary control.

In this section we have introduced four concepts—consciousness, subconscious processes, preconscious memories, and the unconscious—and assigned them definitions. Not all psychologists will agree with these definitions. Nevertheless, versions of these concepts are so pervasive in psychology that one needs to be familiar with them, even though different theorists define them somewhat differently.

DIVIDED CONSCIOUSNESS

An important function of consciousness is the control of our actions. But some activities are practiced so often that they become habitual, or automatic. Learning to drive a car requires intense concentration at first. We have to concentrate on coordinating the different actions (shifting gears, releasing the clutch, accelerating, steering, and so forth) and can scarcely think about anything else. However, as we mentioned earlier, once the movements become automatic, we can carry on a conversation or admire the scenery without being conscious of driving—unless a potential danger appears that quickly draws our attention to the operation of the car.

Skills, like driving a car or riding a bike, once well-learned no longer require our attention. They become automatic, thereby permitting a

Extreme familiarity with a skill makes actions automatic, so that we can perform two tasks simultaneously.

relatively uncluttered consciousness to focus on other matters. Such *automatic processes* may have negative consequences on occasion, for example, when a driver cannot remember landmarks he passed along the way.

Dissociation

The more automatic an action becomes, the less it requires conscious control. Another example is the skilled pianist who carries on a conversation with a bystander while performing a familiar piece. The pianist is exercising control over two activities—playing and talking—but does not think about the music unless a wrong key is hit, alerting her attention to it and temporarily disrupting the conversation. You can undoubtedly think of other examples of well-learned, automatic activities that require little conscious control. One way of interpreting this is to say that the control is still there (we can focus on automatic processes if we want to), but it has been *dissociated* from consciousness. (To "dissociate" means to sever the association of one thing from another.)

The French psychiatrist Pierre Janet (1889) originated the concept of *dissociation*. He proposed that under certain conditions some thoughts and actions become split off, or dissociated, from the rest of consciousness and function outside of awareness. Dissociation differs from Freud's concept of repression because the dissociated memories and thoughts are readily accessible to consciousness. Repressed memories, in contrast, cannot be brought to consciousness; they have to be inferred from signs or symptoms (such as slips of the tongue). Dissociated memories, therefore, are part of the preconscious.

When faced with a stressful situation, we may temporarily put it out of our minds in order to be able to function effectively; when bored, we may lapse into reverie or daydreams. These are mild examples of dissociation; they involve dissociating one part of consciousness from another. More extreme examples of dissociation are demonstrated by cases of *multiple personality*.

Multiple Personality

Multiple personality is the existence of two or more integrated and well-developed personalities within the same individual. In most cases, each personality has its own name and age and a specific set of memories and characteristic behaviors; frequently, the different personalities will differ in handwriting, artistic talent, or even in knowledge of foreign languages. Typically, the attitudes and behavior of the alternating personalities are markedly different. For example, if personality A is shy, inhibited, and rigidly moral, personality B may be extraverted, unrestrained, and prone to excessive drinking and sexual promiscuity. In most cases, some of the personalities have no awareness of the experiences of the others. Periods of unexplained amnesia—the loss of memory for hours or days each week—are a clue to the presence of multiple personality.

One of the most famous cases of multiple personality is that of Chris Sizemore, whose alternative personalities—Eve White, Eve Black, and Jane—were portrayed in the movie *The Three Faces of Eve* (Thigpen & Cleckley, 1957) and later elaborated more fully in her autobiography *I'm Eve* (Sizemore & Pittillo, 1977). Another well-studied case of multiple personality is that of Jonah, a 27-year-old man who was admitted to a hospital complaining of severe headaches that were often followed by memory loss. Hospital attendants noticed striking changes in his personality on different days, and the psychiatrist in charge detected three distinct secondary personalities. The relatively stable personality structures that emerged are diagrammed in Figure 6-1 and can be characterized as follows:

- *Jonah.* The primary personality. Shy, retiring, polite, and highly conventional, he is designated "the square." Sometimes frightened and confused during interviews, Jonah is unaware of the other personalities.
- *Sammy.* He has the most intact memories. Sammy can coexist with Jonah or set Jonah aside and take over. He claims to be ready when Jonah needs legal advice or is in trouble; he is designated "the mediator." Sammy remembers emerging at age 6, when Jonah's mother stabbed his stepfather and Sammy persuaded the parents never to fight again in front of the children.
- *King Young.* He emerged when Jonah was 6 or 7 years old to straighten out Jonah's sexual identity after his mother occasionally dressed him in girls' clothing at home and Jonah became confused about boys' and girls' names at school. King Young has looked after Jonah's sexual interests ever since; hence he is designated "the lover." He is only dimly aware of the other personalities.
- *Usoffa Abdulla.* A cold, belligerent, and angry person. Usoffa is capable of ignoring pain. It is his sworn duty to watch over and protect Jonah; thus he is designated "the warrior." He emerged at age 9 or 10, when a gang of white boys beat up Jonah without provocation. Jonah was helpless, but Usoffa emerged and fought viciously against the attackers. He too is only dimly aware of the other personalities.

The four personalities tested very differently on all measures having to do with emotionally laden topics but scored essentially alike on tests relatively free of emotion or personal conflict, such as intelligence or vocabulary tests.

In cases of multiple personality, consciousness is divided so sharply that several different personalities seem to be living in the same body. Observers note that the switch from one personality to another is often accompanied by subtle changes in body posture and tone of voice. The new personality talks, walks, and gestures differently. There may even be changes in such physiological processes as blood pressure and brain activity (Putnam, 1984).

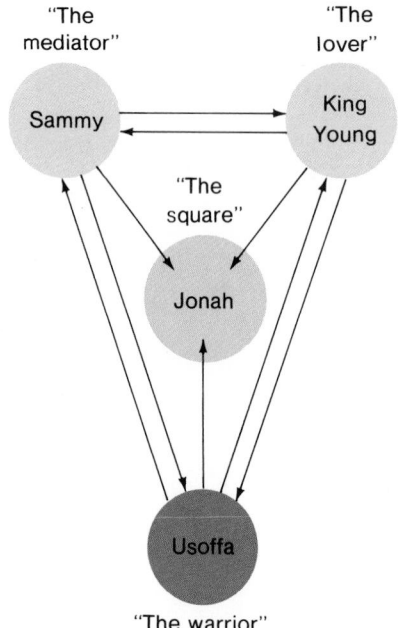

FIGURE 6-1
Jonah's Four Component Personalities *The three personalities on the periphery have superficial knowledge of each other but are intimately familiar with Jonah, who in turn is totally unaware of them.* (After Ludwig et al., 1972)

Although individuals with multiple personalities are relatively rare, enough cases have been studied to uncover some common features that provide us with clues as to how multiple personalities develop in an individual. The initial dissociation seems to occur in response to a traumatic event in childhood (usually between ages 4 and 6). The child copes with a painful problem by creating another personality to bear the brunt of the difficulty (Frischholz, 1985). In Jonah's case, Sammy (the mediator) emerged when Jonah had to deal with his mother's attack on his stepfather. This hypothesis is supported by the fact that most people with multiple personalities were physically or sexually abused as young children.

The gist of the idea is that the child learns to defend himself from the pain of abuse by dissociating the memory from consciousness. In extreme cases in which the child is severely and repeatedly abused, this method of defense over time leads to multiple personalities in which only one or two subpersonalities are conscious of the abuse, while the others have no memory of the pain. It is adaptive for the child to keep the personalities separate, so that he can keep awareness of the abuse from his other selves. That way the feeling and memories of abuse do not continuously flood the child when he cannot handle it, for instance while he is at school or playing with friends (Braun, 1986).

Another factor in the development of multiple personality appears to be an enhanced susceptibility to self-hypnosis, a process by which one is able to put oneself at will into the kind of trance state characteristic of hypnosis (discussed later in this chapter). There is evidence that multiple-personality patients make excellent hypnotic subjects, and when hypnotized for the first time, some report that the trance experience is identical to experiences they have had dating back to their childhood. One of the personalities of a patient said, "She creates personalities by blocking everything from her head, mentally relaxes, concentrates very hard, and wishes" (Bliss, 1980, p. 1392). This description sounds very much like self-hypnosis.

Once individuals discover that creating another personality by self-hypnosis relieves them of emotional pain, they are apt to create other personalities in the future when confronted by emotional problems. Thus, when Jonah was beaten by a gang of white boys at age 9 or 10, he created a third personality, Usoffa Abdulla, to handle the problem. Some multiple-personality patients become so accustomed to defending against problems by means of alternate personalities that they continue the process throughout adulthood, creating new personalities in response to new problems; thus they may end up with a dozen or more different personalities (Spanos, Weekes & Bertrand, 1985).

SLEEP AND DREAMS

Sleep seems the opposite of wakefulness, yet the two states have much in common. We think when we sleep, as dreams show, although the type of thinking in dreams departs in various ways from the type we do while awake. We form memories while sleeping, as we know from the fact that we remember dreams. Sleep is not entirely quiescent: some people walk in their sleep. People who are asleep are not entirely insensitive to the environment: parents are awakened immediately by their baby's cry. Nor is sleep entirely planless: some people can decide to wake at a given time and do so.

Many aspects of sleep have interested investigators. Researchers have looked at normal rhythms of waking and sleeping, the depth of sleep at different periods of the night, and individual and environmental factors that affect sleep.

Sleep Schedules

Newborn babies tend to alternate frequently between sleeping and waking. Much to the relief of parents, a rhythm of two naps a day and longer sleep at night is eventually established. An infant's total sleeping time drops from about 17 hours per day to about 13 hours per day within the first six months of life. Most adults average about 8 hours of sleep per night. However, some people manage on as little as 4 or 5 hours of sleep per night, and there are occasional reports of people who get by on less. Sleep patterns also vary from person to person. We all know "larks" who go to bed early and rise early and "owls" who go to bed late and rise late (Webb, 1975).

Many of our body functions (such as temperature, metabolism, blood and urine composition) have their own inherent tidelike ebb and flow, peaking sometime during the day and slowing down at night in approximate 24-hour cycles. These cyclical patterns form a kind of "internal clock" known as the *circadian rhythm* (whose name comes from the Latin phrase meaning "about a day"). In conditions in which a person has no way to mark the passing of day and night, the cycle tends to have a natural period of approximately 25 hours. The cause of this departure from a 24-hour cycle is a matter of speculation. In any case, cues from the environment (most importantly the daily cycle of light and dark) are needed to keep our internal clock synchronized with the world around us. In short, we need daily clock resettings, and anything that prevents this or otherwise disturbs our circadian rhythm can disturb our sleep (Kripke, 1985).

In one carefully studied case, a young man, blind since birth, had a circadian rhythm of 24.9 hours. As a consequence, he was completely out of phase with the night-day cycle about every two weeks. The only way he could stay in phase and meet the requirements of his professional life was to take stimulants and sedatives to counteract the rhythmical changes during the different phases of his cycle. Careful efforts to modify his sleep cycle by monitoring and controlling his sleep in a sleep laboratory did not prove successful (Miles, Raynal, & Wilson, 1977).

The jet lag that bothers many people when they travel to a different time zone is caused by disruption of the normal circadian rhythm. Their internal clocks that regulate sleep and metabolism are out of sync with the new light-dark cycle, and it may take several days before they adjust to the new schedule. The fatigue and lack of alertness characteristic of jet lag are not simply the result of the rigors of travel: travel in a north-south direction (with no changes in time zones) does not produce the same symptoms.

Depth of Sleep

Some people are readily aroused from sleep; others are hard to awaken. Research begun in the 1930s (Loomis, Harvey, & Hobart, 1937) has produced sensitive techniques for measuring the depth of sleep, as well as for determining when dreams are occurring (Dement & Kleitman, 1957). This research uses devices that measure electrical changes on the scalp associated

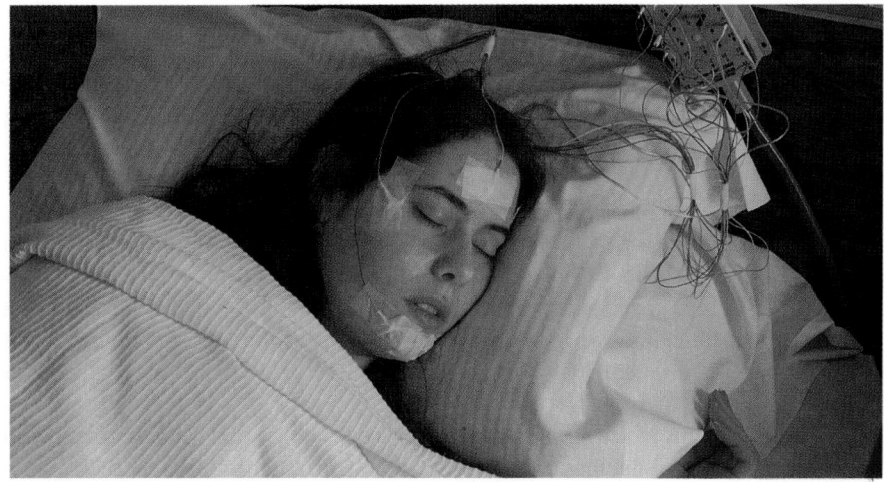

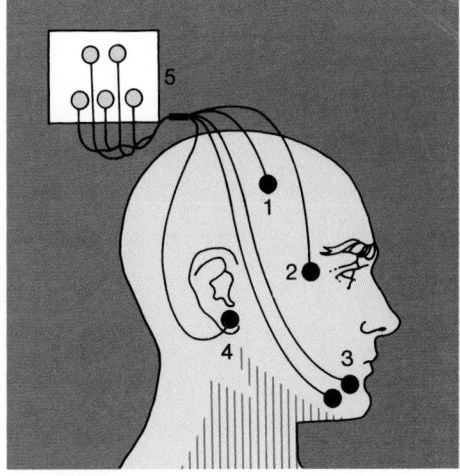

FIGURE 6-2
Arrangement of Electrodes for Recording the Electrophysiology of Sleep *The diagram shows the way in which electrodes are attached to the subject's head and face in a typical sleep experiment. Electrodes on the scalp (1) record the patterns of brain waves. Electrodes near the subject's eyes (2) record eye movements. Electrodes on the chin (3) record tension and electrical activity in the muscles. A neutral electrode on the ear (4) completes the circuit through amplifiers (5) that produce graphical records of the various patterns.*

with spontaneous brain activity during sleep, as well as eye movements that occur during dreaming. The graphic recording of the electrical changes, or brain waves, is called an *electroencephalogram*, or EEG (see Figures 6-2 and 6-3).

   FIVE STAGES OF SLEEP   Analysis of the patterns of brain waves suggests that sleep involves five stages: four depths of sleep and a fifth stage, known as *rapid eye movement* (or REM) sleep. When a person closes her eyes and relaxes, the brain waves characteristically show a regular pattern of 8 to 12 hertz (cycles per second); these are known as *alpha waves*. As the individual drifts into *Stage 1* sleep, the brain waves become less regular and are reduced in amplitude. *Stage 2* is characterized by the appearance of *spindles*—short runs of rhythmical responses of 12 to 16 hertz—and an occasional sharp rise

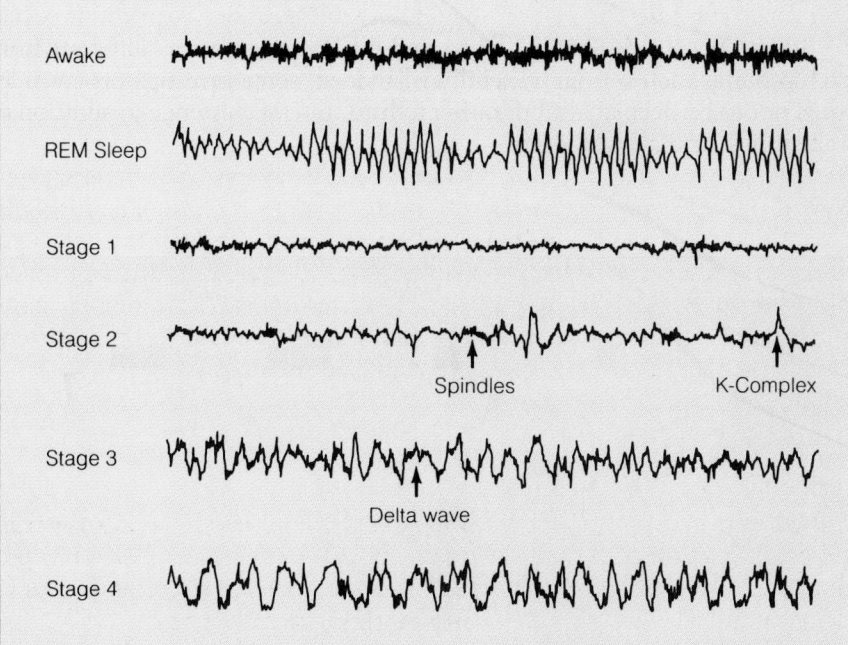

FIGURE 6-3
Electrophysiological Activity During Sleep *The figure presents EEG recordings during wakefulness and during the various stages of sleep. The Awake Stage is characterized by alpha waves (8–12 hertz). Stage 1 is basically a transition from wakefulness to the deeper stages of sleep. Stage 2 is defined by the presence of sleep spindles (brief bursts of 12–16 hertz waves) and K-complexes (a sharp rise and fall in the brain-wave pattern). Stages 3 and 4 are marked by the presence of delta waves (1–2 hertz) and the only difference between these two stages is the amount of delta wave found. Stage 3 is scored when 20 to 50 percent of the record contains delta waves, and Stage 4 for 50 percent or more.*

and fall in the amplitude of the whole EEG. The still deeper *Stages 3 and 4* are characterized by slow waves (1 to 2 hertz), which are known as *delta waves*. Generally the sleeper is hard to awaken during Stages 3 and 4, although she can be aroused by something personal, such as a familiar name or a child crying. A more impersonal disturbance, such as a loud sound, may be ignored.

After an adult has been asleep for an hour or so, another change occurs. The EEG becomes very active (even more so than when the subject is awake), but the subject does not wake. The electrodes placed near the subject's eyes detect rapid eye movements; these eye movements are so pronounced that one can even watch the sleeper's eyes move around beneath the closed eyelids. This stage is known as REM sleep; the other four stages are known as non-REM sleep (or NREM).

These various stages of sleep alternate throughout the night. Sleep begins with the NREM stages and consists of several sleep cycles, each containing some REM and some NREM sleep. Figure 6-4 illustrates a typical night's sleep for a young adult. As you can see, the person goes from wakefulness into a deep sleep (Stage 4) very rapidly. After about 70 minutes, Stage 2 reoccurs, immediately followed by the first REM period of the night. Notice that the deeper stages (3 and 4) occurred during the first part of the night, whereas most REM sleep occurred in the last part. This is the typical pattern: the deeper stages tend to disappear in the second half of the night as REM becomes more prominent. There are usually four or five distinct REM periods over the course of an 8-hour night, with an occasional brief awakening as morning arrives.

The exact pattern of the sleep cycles varies from person to person and with age. Newborn infants, for instance, spend about half their sleeping time in REM sleep. This proportion drops to 20 to 25 percent of total sleep time by the age of 5 and remains fairly constant until old age, when it drops to 18 percent or less. Older people tend to experience less Stage 3 and 4 sleep (sometimes these stages disappear completely) and more frequent and longer nighttime awakenings. A natural kind of insomnia seems to occur with age (Gillin, 1985).

REM AND NREM SLEEP   REM and NREM sleep are as different from each other as each is from wakefulness. Indeed, some investigators consider REM not to be sleep at all, but rather a third state of existence in addition to wakefulness and NREM sleep.

FIGURE 6-4
Succession of Sleep Stages *The graph provides an example of the sequence and duration of sleep stages during a typical night. The subject went successively through Stages 1 to 4 during the first hour of sleep. He then moved back through Stages 3 and 2 to REM sleep. Thereafter the subject cycled between NREM and REM periods, with two brief awakenings at about 3½ and 6 hours of sleep.*

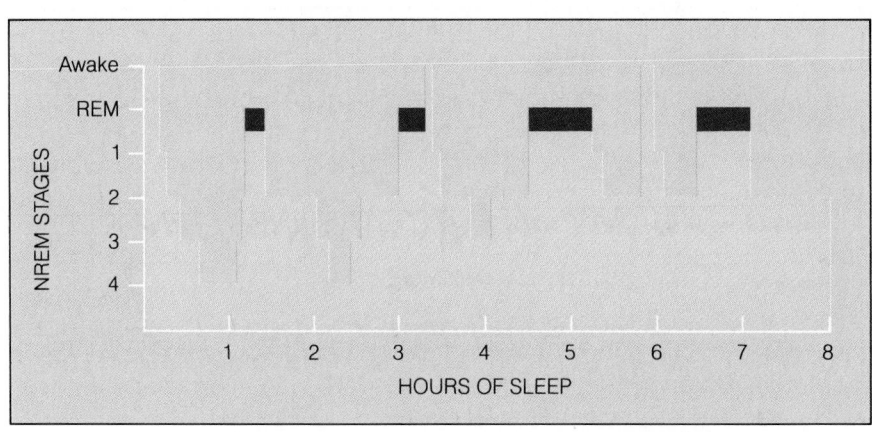

During NREM sleep, eye movements are virtually absent, heart and breathing rates decrease markedly, there is increased muscle relaxation, and there is diminished brain activity. In contrast, during REM sleep eye movements occur about 40 to 60 times per minute, heart rate increases to its daytime level, and the brain appears (from viewing the EEG) to be more active than it is when we are awake. Further, during REM sleep we are almost completely paralyzed—only the heart, diaphragm, eye muscles, and smooth muscles (such as the muscles of the intestines and blood vessels) are spared. To summarize, NREM sleep is characterized by an idle brain in a very relaxed body, whereas REM sleep is characterized by a brain that appears to be wide awake in a virtually paralyzed body.

Physiological evidence indicates that in REM sleep the brain is isolated to a large extent from its sensory and motor channels; stimuli from other parts of the body are blocked from entering the brain, and there are no motor outputs. Nevertheless, the brain is still very active in REM sleep, being spontaneously driven by the discharge of giant neurons that originate in the brain stem. These neurons extend into parts of the brain that control eye movements and motor activities. Thus, during REM sleep the brain registers the fact that the neurons normally involved in walking and seeing are activated, even though the body itself is doing neither (Hobson, 1989).

Sleepers awakened during REM sleep almost always report having a dream, but when awakened during NREM sleep they will report a dream only about 25 percent of the time. The dreams reported when aroused from REM sleep tend to be visually vivid and have a bizarre, illogical character—they represent the type of experience we typically associate with the word "dream." In contrast, NREM dreams are more like normal thinking, neither as visual nor as emotionally charged as REM dreams, and more related to what is happening in waking life. Thus, mental activity is different in REM and NREM periods, as indicated by the type of dream we report (bizarre and illogical versus thoughtlike) and the frequency of reporting a dream (almost always versus occasionally).

It is important to realize that we become conscious of a dream only if we awaken while dreaming. If we then pay attention and make an effort to remember the dream, some of it will be recalled at a later time. Otherwise, our dream is transient and fades quickly; we may know that we have had a dream but will be unable to remember its contents.

If you are interested in remembering your dreams, keep a notebook and pencil beside your bed. Tell yourself you want to wake up when you have a dream. When you do, immediately write down the dream. As your dream recall improves, look for patterns. Underline anything that strikes you as odd and tell yourself that the next time something similar happens, you are going to recognize it as a sign you are dreaming. The problem, of course, is that you will lose some sleep if you follow this regime.

Theorists have proposed that sleep fulfills two separate functions: one being physical restoration and the other, psychological restoration. The physical restoration presumably takes place during the slow-wave, deep-sleep stages, whereas the psychological restoration occurs during REM sleep. There is some evidence to support this view. For example, strenuous physical exercise increases the time spent in slow-wave sleep (particularly Stage 4 sleep) without affecting REM time (Horne, 1988). In contrast, a higher percentage of REM sleep has been found to occur in hospital patients who have serious psychological problems. Further, women tend to have longer REM periods during their premenstrual phase, a time characterized by irritability, depression, and anxiety (Hartmann, 1984).

Sleep Disorders

About 90 percent of adults sleep 6 to 9 hours per night, with the largest number sleeping 8 to 9 hours. While some people sleep only 6 to 7 hours, most of these people have measurable signs of sleepiness during the daytime, even if they do not realize it. It appears that 8 to 9 hours of sleep are required by most people to be free from daytime sleepiness (Kripke & Gillin, 1985). A *sleep disorder* exists whenever the inability to sleep well produces impaired daytime functioning or excessive sleepiness.

INSOMNIA   The term *insomnia* is used in reference to complaints about a symptom, namely, dissatisfaction with the amount or quality of one's sleep. Whether or not a person has insomnia is almost always a subjective decision. Many people who complain of insomnia are found to have perfectly normal sleep when studied in a sleep laboratory, whereas others who do not complain of insomnia have detectable sleep disturbances (Trinder, 1988).

A perplexing feature of insomnia is that people seem to overestimate their sleep loss. One study that monitored the sleep of people who identified themselves as insomniacs found that only about half of them were actually awake as much as 30 minutes during the night (Carskadon, Mitler, & Dement, 1974). The problem may be that light or restless sleep sometimes feels like wakefulness or that some people remember only time spent awake and think they have not slept because they have no memory of doing so. Table 6-1 provides some helpful information on how to ensure that you have a restful sleep.

NARCOLEPSY AND APNEA   Two relatively rare but severe sleep disorders are narcolepsy and apnea. A person with *narcolepsy* may fall asleep while writing a letter, driving a car, or carrying on a conversation. If a student falls asleep while a professor is lecturing, that is perfectly normal; but if a professor falls asleep while lecturing, that may indicate narcolepsy. Individuals with this dysfunction have recurring, irresistible attacks of drowsiness, and simply fall asleep at totally inappropriate times. These episodes can occur several times a day in severe cases, and last from a few seconds to 15–30 minutes. Narcoleptics have difficulty keeping jobs because of their daytime sleepiness and are potentially dangerous if they are driving a car or operating machinery when an attack occurs. Approximately one in a thousand individuals suffers from debilitating narcolepsy, and the incidents of milder, unrecognized cases may be much higher.

Essentially, narcolepsy is the intrusion of REM episodes into daytime hours. During attacks victims go quickly into a REM state, so rapidly in fact that they may lose muscle control and collapse before they can lie down. Moreover, many will report experiencing hallucinations during an attack as reality is replaced by vivid REM dreams. Narcolepsy runs in families, and there is evidence that a specific gene or combination of genes confers susceptibility to the disorder (Hobson, 1988).

In *sleep apnea*, the individual stops breathing while asleep. There are two reasons for apnea attacks. One reason is that the brain fails to send a "breathe" signal to the diaphragm and other breathing muscles, thus causing breathing to stop. The other reason is that muscles at the top of the throat become too relaxed, allowing the windpipe to partially close, thereby forcing the breathing muscles to pull harder on incoming air, which causes the airway to completely collapse. During an apnea, the oxygen level of the blood

TABLE 6-1
Advice for a Good Night's Sleep *There is considerable agreement among researchers and clinicians on how to avoid sleep problems. These recommendations are summarized in the table; some are based on actual research, and others are simply the best judgments of experts in the field.*

REGULAR SLEEP SCHEDULE

Establish a regular schedule of going to bed and getting up. Set your alarm for a specific time every morning, and get up at that time no matter how little you may have slept. Be consistent about naps. Take a nap every afternoon or not at all; when you take a nap only occasionally, you probably will not sleep well that night. Waking up late on weekends can also disrupt your sleep cycle.

ALCOHOL AND CAFFEINE

Having a stiff drink of alcohol before going to bed may help put you to sleep, but it disturbs the sleep cycle and can cause you to wake up early the next day. In addition, stay away from caffeinated drinks like coffee or cola for several hours before bedtime. Caffeine works as a stimulant even on those people who claim they are not affected by it, and the body needs 4 to 5 hours to halve the amount of caffeine in the bloodstream at any one time. If you must drink something before bedtime, try milk; there is evidence to support the folklore that a glass of warm milk at bedtime induces sleep.

EATING BEFORE BEDTIME

Don't eat heavily before going to bed, since your digestive system will have to do several hours of work. If you must eat something before bedtime, have a light snack.

EXERCISE

Regular exercise will help you sleep better, but don't engage in a strenuous workout just before going to bed.

SLEEPING PILLS

Be careful about using sleeping pills. All of the various kinds tend to disrupt the sleep cycle, and long-term use inevitably leads to insomnia. Even on nights before exams, avoid using a sleeping pill. One bad night of sleep tends not to affect performance the next day, whereas a hangover from a sleeping pill may.

RELAX

Avoid stressful thoughts before bedtime and engage in soothing activities that help you relax. Try to follow the same routine every night before going to bed; it might involve taking a warm bath or listening to soft music for a few minutes. Find a room temperature at which you are comfortable and maintain it throughout the night.

WHEN ALL FAILS

If you are in bed and have trouble falling asleep, don't get up. Stay in bed and try to relax. But if that fails and you become tense, then get up for a brief time and do something restful that reduces anxiety. Doing push-ups or some other form of exercise to wear yourself out is not a good idea.

drops dramatically, leading to the secretion of emergency hormones. This reaction causes the sleeper to awaken in order to begin breathing again.

Most people have a few apneas a night, but people with severe sleep problems may have several hundred apneas per night. With each apnea they wake up in order to resume breathing, but these arousals are so brief they are generally unaware of doing so. The result is that those who suffer from apnea can spend 12 or more hours in bed each night and still be so sleepy the next day that they cannot function and will fall asleep even in the middle of a conversation (Ancoli-Israel, Kripke, & Mason, 1987).

Sleep apnea is common among older men. Sleeping pills, which make arousal more difficult, lengthen periods of apnea (during which the brain is deprived of oxygen) and may prove fatal. Not waking up is probably one of the main reasons people die in their sleep.

SLEEP DEPRIVATION   The need for sleep seems so important that we might expect being deprived of sleep for several nights to have serious consequences. Numerous studies have shown, however, that the only consistent effects of sleep deprivation are drowsiness, a desire to sleep, and a tendency to fall asleep easily. Subjects kept awake for 50 hours or more show nothing more noticeable than "transient inattentions, confusions, or misperceptions" (Webb, 1975). Even sleepless periods exceeding four days produce little in the way of severely disturbed behavior. In one study in which a subject was kept awake for 11 days and nights, there were no unusually deviant responses (Gulevich, Dement, & Johnson, 1966). Intellectual activities such as answering short test questions seem unaffected by several nights of sleep deprivation.

If sleep deprivation has no serious consequences, what about dream deprivation? This question has been investigated by depriving subjects of REM sleep. Dement (1960) woke his subjects at the onset of every REM period. He found that after five nights there was a *rebound effect*, with an abnormal amount of time spent in REM sleep during the recovery night. Control tests were run by awakening subjects an equal number of times during NREM sleep; no rebound of REM was found. Dement's findings have been confirmed by many others. Researchers had hoped that REM deprivation would provide clues to the function of REM sleep, but answers have not been forthcoming even though the search has continued. Some effects of REM deprivation on memory have been reported, but memory disturbances have also been found to occur after deprivation of NREM sleep (McGaugh, Jensen, & Martinez, 1979; Horne, 1988).

Dreams

Dreaming is an altered state of consciousness in which remembered images and fantasies are temporarily confused with external reality. Investigators do not yet understand why people dream at all, much less why they dream what they do. However, modern methods of study have answered a great many questions about dreaming.

DOES EVERYONE DREAM?   Although many people do not recall their dreams in the morning, REM-sleep evidence suggests that nonrecallers do as much dreaming as recallers. If you take people who have sworn that they never dreamed in their life, put them in a dream research laboratory and wake them from REM sleep, you will get dream recall at rates comparable to other people. If someone says "I never dream," what they mean is "I can't recall my dreams."

Researchers have proposed several hypotheses to account for differences in dream recall. One possibility is that nonrecallers simply have more difficulty than recallers in remembering their dreams. Another hypothesis suggests that some people awaken relatively easily in the midst of REM sleep and thus recall more dreams than those who sleep more soundly. The most generally accepted model for dream recall supports the idea that what happens on awakening is the crucial factor. According to this hypothesis, unless a distraction-free waking period occurs shortly after dreaming, the memory of the dream is not consolidated (Koulack & Goodenough, 1976; Hobson, 1988).

HOW LONG DO DREAMS LAST? Some dreams seem almost instantaneous. The alarm clock rings and we awaken to complex memories of a fire breaking out and fire engines arriving with their sirens blasting. Because the alarm is still ringing, we assume that the sound must have produced the dream. Research suggests, however, that a ringing alarm clock or other sound merely reinstates a complete scene from earlier memories or dreams. This experience has its parallel during wakefulness when a single cue may tap a rich memory that takes some time to tell. The length of a typical dream can be inferred from a REM study in which subjects were awakened and asked to act out what they had been dreaming (Dement & Wolpert, 1958). The time it took them to pantomime the dream was almost the same as the length of the REM sleep period, suggesting that the incidents in dreams commonly last about as long as they would in real life.

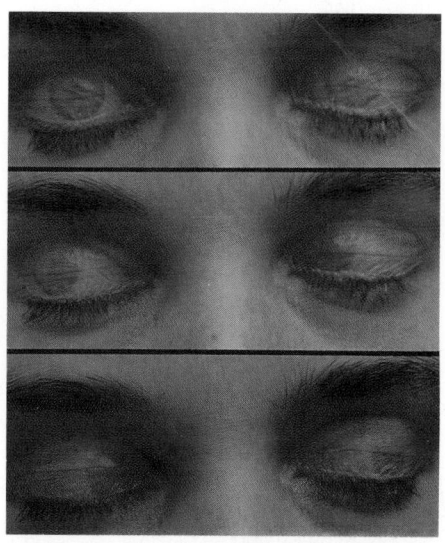

This multiple-exposure photograph shows the rapid eye movements associated with dreaming.

DO PEOPLE KNOW WHEN THEY ARE DREAMING? The answer to this question is "sometimes yes." People can be taught to recognize that they are dreaming, and their awareness does not interfere with the dream's spontaneous flow. For example, subjects have been trained to press a switch when they notice that they are dreaming (Salamy, 1970).

Some people have *lucid dreams* in which events seem so normal (lacking the bizarre and illogical character of most dreams) that they feel they are awake and conscious. Only on awakening do they realize it was a dream. Lucid dreamers report doing various "experiments" within their dreams to determine whether they are awake or dreaming. A Dutch physician, van Eeden (1913), was one of the first to give an accurate account of initiating actions within a lucid dream to prove that events were not occurring normally. In a later report, Brown (1936) described a standard experiment in which he jumped and suspended himself in the air. If he did this successfully, he knew he was dreaming. Both Brown and van Eeden report an occasional "false awakening" within a dream. For example, in one of Brown's dreams, he discovered that he was dreaming and decided to call a taxicab as an indication of his control over events. When he reached into his pocket to see if he had some change to pay the driver, he thought that he woke up. He then found the coins scattered about the bed. At this point, he really awoke and found himself lying in a different position and, of course, without any coins.

CAN PEOPLE CONTROL THE CONTENT OF THEIR DREAMS? Psychologists have demonstrated that some control of dream content is possible by making suggestions to subjects in the presleep period and then analyzing the content of the dreams that followed. In a carefully designed study of an *implicit predream suggestion*, researchers tested the effect of wearing red goggles prior to sleep. Although the researchers made no actual suggestion, and the subjects did not understand the purpose of the experiment, many subjects reported that their visual dream worlds were tinted red (Roffwarg, Herman, Bowe-Anders, & Tauber, 1978). In a study of the effect of an *overt predream suggestion*, subjects were asked to try to dream about a personality characteristic that they wished they had. Most of the subjects had at least one dream in which the intended trait could be recognized (Cartwright, 1974).

CRITICAL DISCUSSION

Theories of Dream Sleep

A great deal of research on sleep and dreams has been conducted in recent years, and a number of theories have been proposed. Here we summarize two theories of dream sleep, one proposed by Evans (1984) that takes a cognitive approach and the other by Crick and Mitchison (1983; 1986) that takes a neurobiological approach.

Evans' theory views sleep as a period when the brain disengages from the external world and uses this off-line time to sort through and reorganize the vast array of information that was input during the day. According to the theory, the brain is like a computer with large data banks and an assortment of control programs. Some of these programs are inherited and relate to what we call instincts; others are acquired and continually modified by experience. Sleep, particularly REM sleep, is when the brain comes off-line, isolating itself from the sensory and motor neural pathways. In this off-line period the various data banks and program files are opened and become available for modification and reorganization based on the experiences of the day. According to Evans, the reorganization of memory that occurs during REM sleep involves updating the memory files and programs rather than erasing or deleting information.

In Evans' theory, we are not consciously aware of the full array of off-line processing that occurs during REM sleep. During dreaming, however, the brain comes back on-line for a brief time and the conscious mind observes a small sample of the programs being run. The brain attempts to interpret this information the same way it would interpret stimuli in the outside world, giving rise to the kind of pseudo-event that characterizes dreams. Thus, according to Evans, dreams are nothing more than a small subset of the vast amount of information that is being scanned and sorted during REM sleep, a momentary glimpse by the conscious mind that we remember if we wake. Evans believes that dreams can be useful in inferring the full array of processing that occurs during REM sleep, but they are an extremely small sample on which to base inferences.

Crick and Mitchison base their theory on the fact that the cortex—unlike other parts of the brain—is made up of richly interconnected *neuronal networks* in which each cell has the capacity to excite its neighbors. They believe that memories are encoded in these networks, with neurons and their many synapses representing different features of a memory. These networks are like spiderwebs, and

A *posthypnotic predream suggestion* is another way of influencing dream content. In one extensive study using this method, detailed dream narratives were suggested to highly responsive hypnotic subjects. After the suggestion, the subject slept until roused from REM sleep. Some of the resulting dreams reflected the thematic aspects of the suggestion without including many of the specific elements, whereas other dreams reflected specific elements of the suggestion (Tart & Dick, 1970).

SLEEPWALKING?   Virtually all research on sleepwalking indicates that it occurs only in NREM periods. Typically, people will sleepwalk during the first third of the night; sometimes they just sit up in bed, but at other times they may leave the room or even the house. Though the sleepwalker's eyes may be open, they are glassy and unseeing, so the person could have a serious accident. Sleepwalkers usually forget about what they have done, and the dreams they report bear no resemblance to what they do while walking about (Jacobson & Kales, 1967). About 15 percent of children have one or more episodes of sleepwalking, but these usually stop before age 15 with no aftereffects.

Dream Content

Freud's theory that dreams are mental products that can be understood and interpreted was one of the earliest and most comprehensive attempts to

when one point in the web is excited, perhaps by hearing a few notes of a song, a pulse travels throughout the network, prompting recall of the rest of the song. The problem with such network systems is that they malfunction when there is an overload of incoming information. Too many memories in one network may produce either bizarre associations to a stimulus (fantasies) or the same response whatever the stimulus (obsessions), or associations may be triggered without any stimulus (hallucinations).

To deal with information overload, the brain needs a mechanism to debug and tune the network. Such a debugging mechanism would work best when the system was isolated from external inputs and it would have to have a way of randomly activating the network in order to eliminate spurious connections. The mechanism Crick and Mitchison propose is REM sleep: the hallucinatory quality of dreams is nothing more than the random neural

firing needed for the daily cleanup of the network.

As noted earlier, the brain is very active during REM sleep, barraged with neural signals traveling from the brain stem to the cortex. According to the theory, these signals somehow erase the spurious memory associations formed during the previous day; we awake with the network cleaned up, and the brain ready for new input. Crick and Mitchison also suggest that trying to remember one's dreams—a key aspect of psychoanalysis—may not be a good idea. They believe that such remembering could help to retain patterns of thought that are better forgotten, the very patterns the system is attempting to tune out.

The two theories have some common features, but there are clear differences. Evans views REM sleep as a time when the brain reorganizes memory by a process of updating, rather than deleting, information. Crick and Mitchison, on the other hand, see REM sleep

as a time when spurious or useless information is purged from memory. Evans regards conscious dreams as a surface indicator of the rich reorganizational process taking place during REM sleep, whereas Crick and Mitchison suggest that dreams are little more than random noise with no real content. But both theories assume that REM sleep plays a role in the storage of memories and in preparing the brain from one day to the next to deal with new information inputs. Neither theory assigns to dreams the rich symbolism and concealed meaning that typifies a psychoanalytic approach to the analysis of dream content.

We still have no direct test to prove one theory clearly superior to the other; the same comment applies to psychoanalytic theories of dreams. Thus these theories are speculative, awaiting the outcome of further research. Nevertheless, each theory provides intriguing possibilities about the nature of dreams.

explain the content of dreams without reference to the supernatural. In his book, *Interpretation of Dreams* (1900), Freud proposed that dreams provide the "royal road to a knowledge of the unconscious activities of the mind." He believed that dreams are a disguised attempt at *wish fulfillment*. By this he meant that the dream touches on wishes, needs, or ideas that the individual finds unacceptable and have been repressed to the unconscious. These wishes and ideas then appear in symbolic form as the *latent content* of the dream. Freud used the metaphor of a censor to explain the conversion of latent dream content to *manifest content* (the characters and events that make up the actual narrative of the dream). In effect, Freud said, the censor protects the sleeper, enabling him to express repressed impulses while avoiding the frightening intensity of the unconscious wish that is being expressed.

The transformation of latent content into manifest content is done by the "dream work," as Freud called it, the function of which is to code and disguise material in the unconscious in such a way that it can reach consciousness. However, sometimes the dream work fails, and anxiety awakens the dreamer. The dream essentially expresses the fulfillment of wishes or needs that are too painful or guilt-inducing to acknowledge consciously (Freud, 1933).

The cognitive side of dreaming—its role in problem solving and thinking—has been increasingly recognized (see the Critical Discussion, "Theories of Dream Sleep"). Although cognitive psychologists reject many of Freud's ideas, they also note that his theory has cognitive aspects. In fact,

Freud's emphasis on thought transformations through free association goes far beyond the oversimplified popular notion that all the transformations in dreams can be explained as wish fulfillment.

PSYCHOACTIVE DRUGS

Since ancient times, people have used drugs to alter their state of consciousness—to stimulate or relax, to bring on sleep or prevent it, to enhance ordinary perceptions, or to produce hallucinations. Drugs that affect behavior, consciousness, and mood are called *psychoactive*. They include not only street drugs such as heroin and marijuana but also tranquilizers, stimulants, and such familiar drugs as alcohol, tobacco, and coffee. Table 6-2 lists and classifies the psychoactive drugs that are commonly used and abused.

It may be difficult for students today to appreciate the major changes in patterns of drug-taking behavior that have occurred over the past 40 years. In the 1950s, very few young people used drugs (other than cigarettes and alcohol). Since the 1950s, however, we have moved from a relatively drug-free society to a drug-using society. A number of factors have contributed to this change. For instance, the widespread use of tranquilizers for the treatment of mental illness and emotional problems, which began in the 1950s, and the appearance of oral contraceptives in 1960 did much to change people's attitudes toward drugs. Drugs became an option available to solve problems—problems other than physical illness. In the 1960s and 1970s, Americans also explored new life-styles, following the opportunities provided by easier transportation and expanding job markets. With increased leisure time people looked for new outlets, and the recreational use of drugs became such an outlet.

For these and other reasons, drug use, particularly among young people, increased steadily through the 1960s and 1970s. In the 1980s, however, drug use began a gradual downward trend that we hope will continue (see Figure 6-5). The factors contributing to the decline are many, but certainly one has been a significant increase in the number of young people who believe that using drugs, even experimentally, is dangerous. Another factor appears to be an increased concern for health and physical fitness. Even with this modest downturn in recent years, the United States still has the highest rates of drug usage among the world's industrialized nations (Johnston, O'Malley, & Bachman, 1989).

All of the drugs listed in Table 6-2 are assumed to affect behavior and consciousness because they act in specific biochemical ways on the brain. With repeated use, an individual can become physically or psychologically dependent on any of these drugs. *Physical dependence*, also called addiction, is characterized by *tolerance* (that is, with continued use, the individual must take more and more of the drug to achieve the same effect) and *withdrawal* (if use is discontinued, the person experiences unpleasant physical symptoms). *Psychological dependence* refers to a need that develops through learning. People who habitually use a drug to relieve anxiety may become dependent on it, even though no physical need develops. For example, marijuana smokers do not appear to build up tolerance for the drug, and they experience minimal withdrawal symptoms. Nevertheless, a person who learns to use marijuana

TABLE 6-2
Psychoactive Drugs That Are Commonly Abused *Only a few examples of each class of drug are given. The generic name (for example, psilocybin) or the brand name (Miltown for meprobamate; Seconal for secobarbital) is used, depending on which is more familiar.*

DEPRESSANTS (SEDATIVES)

Alcohol (ethanol)
Barbiturates
   Nembutal
   Seconal
Minor tranquilizers
   Miltown
   Valium

OPIATES (NARCOTICS)

Opium and its derivatives
   Codeine
   Heroin
   Morphine
Methadone

STIMULANTS

Amphetamines
   Benzedrine
   Dexedrine
   Methedrine
Cocaine
Nicotine
Caffeine

HALLUCINOGENS

LSD
Mescaline
Psilocybin
PCP (Phencyclidine)

CANNABIS

Marijuana
Hashish

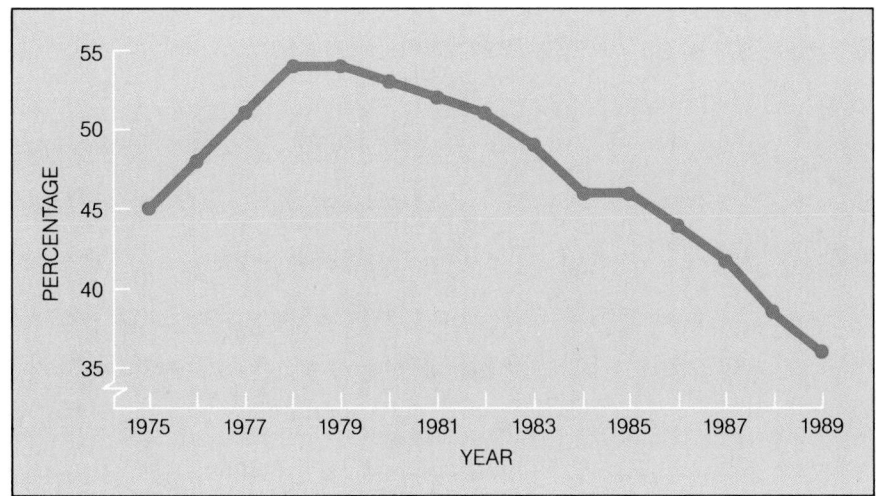

FIGURE 6-5
Illicit Drug Use *Percentage of American high-school seniors who reported using an illicit drug in the 12-month period prior to graduation. Drugs include marijuana, hallucinogens, cocaine, and heroin, and any nonprescribed use of opiates, stimulants, sedatives, and tranquilizers.* (After Johnston, O'Malley, & Bachman, 1989)

when faced with stressful situations will find the habit difficult to break. With some drugs, such as alcohol, psychological dependence progresses to physical dependence as more and more of the substance is consumed.

Depressants

Drugs that depress the central nervous system include the minor tranquilizers, barbiturates (sleeping pills), and ethyl alcohol. Of these, the one most frequently used and abused is alcohol. Almost every society, primitive or industrialized, consumes alcohol. It can be produced by fermenting a wide variety of materials: grains, such as rye, wheat, and corn; fruits, such as grapes, apples, and plums; and vegetables, such as potatoes. Through the process of distillation, the alcoholic content of a fermented beverage can be increased to obtain "hard liquors" such as whiskey or rum.

EFFECTS OF ALCOHOL   In small quantities, alcohol appears to increase people's energy and make them feel lively and sociable. In reality, it is a central nervous system depressant, not a stimulant. The initial stimulating effect of alcohol is believed to occur because the inhibitory synapses in the brain are depressed slightly earlier than the excitatory synapses. Since the brain's neurons maintain a close balance between excitation and inhibition, the depression of inhibitory synapses results in a feeling of excitation, or stimulation. However, the excitatory synapses soon become depressed, too; the stimulating effects are overridden, causing drowsiness and slowed sensory and motor functions.

Measuring the amount of alcohol in the air we exhale (as in a breath analyzer) gives a reliable index of alcohol in the blood. Consequently, it is easy to determine the relationship between *blood alcohol concentration* (BAC) and behavior. At concentrations of .03 to .05 percent in the blood (that is, 30 to 50 milligrams of alcohol per 100 milliliters of blood), alcohol produces light-headedness, relaxation, and release of inhibitions. People say things they might not ordinarily say; they tend to become more sociable and expansive. Self-confidence may increase, whereas motor reactions will begin to slow (a pair of effects that makes it dangerous to drive after drinking).

FIGURE 6-6

BAC and Alcohol Intake *Approximate values of BAC as a function of alcohol consumption in a 2-hour period. For example, if you weigh 180 pounds and had four beers in two hours, your BAC would be between .05 and .09 percent and your driving ability would be seriously impaired. Six beers in the same 2-hour period would give you a BAC of over .10 percent—the level accepted as proof of intoxication.* (After National Highway Traffic Safety Administration)

WEIGHT	DRINKS IN A TWO-HOUR PERIOD (1.2 ozs. 80-Proof Liquor or 12 ozs. Beer)											
100	1	2	3	4	5	6	7	8	9	10	11	12
120	1	2	3	4	5	6	7	8	9	10	11	12
140	1	2	3	4	5	6	7	8	9	10	11	12
160	1	2	3	4	5	6	7	8	9	10	11	12
180	1	2	3	4	5	6	7	8	9	10	11	12
200	1	2	3	4	5	6	7	8	9	10	11	12
220	1	2	3	4	5	6	7	8	9	10	11	12
240	1	2	3	4	5	6	7	8	9	10	11	12

BE CAREFUL DRIVING
BAC TO .05%

DRIVING IMPAIRED
.05–.09%

DO NOT DRIVE
.10% & UP

At a BAC of .10 percent, sensory and motor functions become noticeably impaired. Speech becomes slurred, and people have difficulty coordinating their movements. Some people tend to become angry and aggressive; others grow silent and morose. The drinker is seriously incapacitated at a level of .20 percent, and a level above .40 percent may cause death. The legal definition of intoxication in most states is a BAC of .10 percent (that is, one-tenth of 1 percent).

How much can a person drink without becoming legally intoxicated? The relationship between BAC and alcohol intake is not simple. It depends on a person's sex, body weight, and speed of consumption. Age, individual metabolism, and experience with drinking are also factors. Although the effects of alcohol intake on BAC vary a great deal, the average effects are shown in Figure 6-6. Moreover, it is not true that beer or wine is less likely to make someone drunk than so called hard drinks. A 4-ounce glass of wine, a 12-ounce can of beer, and 1.2 ounces of 80-proof whiskey have about the same alcohol content and will have about the same effect.

Drinking is viewed as an integral part of social life for many college students. It promotes conviviality, eases tensions, releases inhibitions, and generally adds to the fun. Nevertheless, social drinking can create problems in terms of lost study time, poor performance on an exam because of feeling hung over, and arguments or accidents while intoxicated. Clearly the most serious problem is accidents: alcohol-related automobile accidents are the leading cause of death among 15- to 24-year-olds. When the legal drinking age was lowered from 21 to 18 years of age in a number of states, traffic fatalities of 18- and 19-year-olds increased 20 to 50 percent. Most states have since raised their minimum drinking age, and a significant decrease in traffic accidents has followed.

About two-thirds of American adults report that they drink alcohol. At least 10 percent of them have social, psychological, or medical problems resulting from alcohol use. Probably half of that 10 percent are physically dependent on alcohol. Heavy or prolonged drinking can lead to serious health problems. High blood pressure, stroke, ulcers, cancers of the mouth, throat, and stomach, cirrhosis of the liver, and depression are some of the conditions associated with the regular use of substantial amounts of alcohol.

Nearly all high-school seniors have had experience with alcohol and two-thirds are current users (that is, have used it in the past 30 days). About 5 percent are daily drinkers and about 40 percent report at least one occasion of heavy drinking in the past two weeks (that is, consuming five or more drinks in a row). None of these figures has shown much change over the last several years (Johnston, O'Malley, & Bachman, 1989).

Alcohol can also produce risks for a developing fetus. Mothers who drink heavily are twice as likely to suffer repeated miscarriages and to produce low birth-weight babies. A condition called *fetal alcohol syndrome*, characterized by mental retardation and multiple deformities of the face and mouth, is caused by maternal drinking. The amount of alcohol needed to produce this syndrome is unclear, but it is thought that as little as a few ounces of alcohol a week can be detrimental (Streissguth, Clarren, & Jones, 1985).

ALCOHOLISM   The stereotype of an alcoholic—the skid-row drunk—constitutes only a small proportion of the individuals who have drinking problems. The depressed housewife who takes a few drinks to gear up for a social evening, the businessman who needs a three-martini lunch to make it through the afternoon, the overworked physician who keeps a bottle in her desk drawer, and the high-school student who drinks more and more to gain acceptance from peers—all are on their way to becoming alcoholics. There are various definitions of alcoholism, but almost all of them include the *inability to abstain* (the feeling that you cannot get through the day without a drink) or a *lack of control* (an inability to stop after one or two drinks). Table 6-3 lists some questions to help people determine whether or not they have a drinking problem.

The peak drinking years for most people are between ages 16 and 25. In the late 20s to early 30s, the average drinker decreases his or her alcohol consumption. The alcoholic, in contrast, maintains or increases his or her

Ages 16 through 25 are peak drinking years for most people.

TABLE 6-3
Signs of Alcoholism *Questions developed by the National Institute on Alcohol Abuse and Alcoholism to help people determine whether or not they have a drinking problem.*

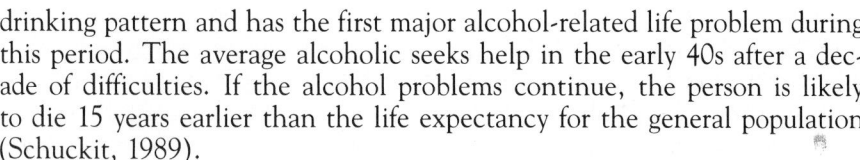

The sooner you recognize a drinking problem in yourself, the easier it is to get out from under it. Below are some questions that will help you learn how dependent you are on drinking. This is a time to be absolutely honest with yourself—only you can know how seriously you are being hurt by the role alcohol plays in your life.

1. Has someone close to you sometimes expressed concern about your drinking?
2. When faced with a problem, do you often turn to alcohol for relief?
3. Are you sometimes unable to meet home or work responsibilities because of drinking?
4. Have you ever required medical attention as a result of drinking?
5. Have you ever experienced a blackout—a total loss of memory while still awake—when drinking?
6. Have you ever come in conflict with the law in connection with your drinking?
7. Have you often failed to keep the promises you have made to yourself about controlling or cutting out your drinking?

If you have answered yes to any of the above questions, your drinking is probably affecting your life in some major ways and you should do something about it—before it gets worse.

drinking pattern and has the first major alcohol-related life problem during this period. The average alcoholic seeks help in the early 40s after a decade of difficulties. If the alcohol problems continue, the person is likely to die 15 years earlier than the life expectancy for the general population (Schuckit, 1989).

While this scenario describes the *average* alcoholic, heavy drinking can progress to alcoholism at any age. People who become psychologically dependent on alcohol—who habitually use alcohol to handle stress and anxiety—stand a good chance of becoming alcoholics. They are apt to become trapped in a vicious cycle. By resorting to alcohol when confronted with problems, they handle these problems ineffectively. As a consequence, they feel even more anxious and inadequate and consume more alcohol in an attempt to bolster their self-esteem. Prolonged heavy drinking leads to physical dependency: a person's tolerance rises so that more and more alcohol must be consumed to achieve the same effect, and the individual begins to experience withdrawal symptoms when he or she abstains from drinking. Withdrawal symptoms may range from feelings of irritability and general malaise to tremors and intense anxiety. In some instances, they include confusion, hallucinations, and convulsions. This syndrome, called *delirium tremens* (DTs), usually occurs only in chronic alcoholics who stop drinking after a sustained period of heavy consumption.

Although our definition of alcoholism includes the inability to abstain from drinking or the lack of control after starting to drink, very few alcoholics stay drunk until they die. They usually alternate periods of abstinence (or light drinking) with periods of serious abuse. Thus, the ability to go for weeks, or even months, without drinking does not mean that an individual is not an alcoholic. Perhaps the most useful criterion for diagnosing alcoholism is whether alcohol is causing problems with health, job performance, or family relationships.

Opiates

Opium and its derivatives, collectively known as *opiates*, are drugs that diminish physical sensation and the capacity to respond to stimuli by depressing the central nervous system. (These drugs are commonly called "narcotics," but opiates is the more accurate term; the term "narcotics" is not well defined and covers a variety of illegal drugs.) Opiates are medically useful for their painkilling properties, but their ability to alter mood and reduce anxiety has led to widespread illegal consumption. Opium, which is the air-dried juice of the opium poppy, contains a number of chemical substances, including morphine and codeine. Codeine, a common ingredient in prescription painkillers and cough suppressants, is relatively mild in its effects (at least at low doses). Morphine and its derivative, heroin, are much more potent. Most illegal drug use involves heroin because, being more concentrated, it can be concealed and smuggled more easily than morphine.

Heroin can be injected, smoked, or inhaled. At first, the drug produces a sense of well-being. Experienced users report a special thrill, or rush, within a minute or two after an intravenous injection. Some describe this sensation as intensely pleasurable, similar to an orgasm. Young people who sniff heroin report that they forget everything that troubles them. Following this, the user feels fixed, or gratified, with no awareness of hunger, pain, or sexual urges. The person may "go on the nod," alternately waking and drowsing while comfortably watching television or reading a book. Unlike the alcoholic, the heroin user can readily produce skilled responses to agility and intellectual tests and seldom becomes aggressive or assaultive.

The changes in consciousness produced by heroin are not very striking; there are no exciting visual experiences or feelings of being transported elsewhere. Apparently, it is the change in mood—the feeling of euphoria and reduced anxiety—that prompts people to *start* using this drug. However, heroin is very addictive; even a brief period of usage can create physical dependency. After a person has been smoking or "sniffing" (inhaling) heroin for a while, tolerance builds up, and this method no longer produces the desired effect. In an attempt to recreate the original high, the individual may progress to "skin popping" (injecting under the skin) and then to "mainlining" (injecting into a vein). Once the user starts mainlining, stronger and stronger doses are required to produce the high, and the physical discomforts of withdrawal from the drug become intense (chills, sweating, stomach cramps, vomiting, headaches). Thus, the motivation to continue using the drug stems from the need to avoid pain and discomfort.

Most heroin users who restrict themselves to smoking or sniffing are able to give up the habit. Only about 7 percent of American soldiers who sniffed heroin regularly in Vietnam (where the drug was easily available) continued to use the drug after they returned to the United States (Robins, 1974). However, once larger amounts are absorbed into the body through injection, the majority of users become addicted.

The hazards of heroin use are many. Death from an overdose is always a possibility because the concentration of street heroin fluctuates widely. Thus, the user can never be sure of the potency of the powder in a newly purchased supply. Death is caused by suffocation resulting from depression of the brain's respiratory center. Heroin use is generally associated with a serious deterioration of personal and social life. Because maintaining the habit is costly, the user often becomes involved in illegal activities.

Additional dangers of heroin use include AIDS (Acquired Immune Deficiency Syndrome), hepatitis, and other infections associated with unsterile

PET scans show the effects of opiates on the neural activity of different brain areas.

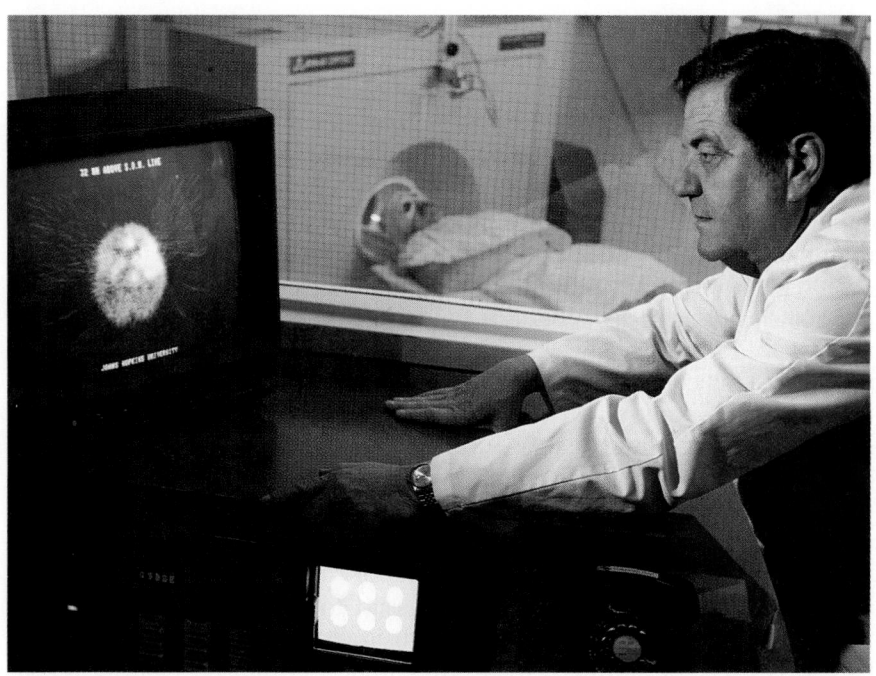

injections. Sharing drug needles, even once, is an extremely easy way to be infected with the AIDS virus. Blood from an infected person can be trapped in the needle or syringe, and then injected directly into the bloodstream of the next person who uses the needle. The sharing of needles and syringes by those who shoot drugs is the most rapidly increasing way that the AIDS virus is being spread.

In the 1970s, researchers made a major breakthrough in understanding opiate addiction with the discovery that opiates act on very specific receptor sites in the brain (see Chapter 2). In molecular shape, the opiates resemble a group of neurotransmitters called *endorphins*. One of these endorphins, *enkephalin*, occupies a certain number of opiate receptors. Morphine and heroin relieve pain by binding to receptors that are unfilled. Repeated heroin use causes a drop in enkephalin production; the body then requires more heroin to fill the unoccupied receptors and to reduce pain. The person experiences painful withdrawal symptoms when heroin is discontinued because many opiate receptors are left unfilled (since the normal enkephalin production has decreased). In essence, the heroin has replaced the body's own natural opiates (Koob & Bloom, 1988).

The research findings on opiate receptors have led to two important treatment methods. First, there are drugs called opiate antagonists that can block the action of an opiate—such as heroin or morphine—because they have a greater affinity for the receptor site than do the opiates themselves. Thus, an opiate antagonist, such as *naloxone*, is often used in hospital emergency rooms to reverse the effects of a drug overdose. Interestingly, this drug is very specific: it will reverse the potentially fatal depression of the respiratory center caused by an opiate overdose, but it will not reverse depression resulting from other classes of drugs such as alcohol or barbiturates.

Second, a synthetic opiate called *methadone*, which prevents withdrawal symptoms by occupying the opiate receptor sites, is sometimes used to treat heroin-dependent individuals. Methadone is addictive, but it produces less psychological impairment than heroin and its effects last much longer.

When taken orally in low doses, it suppresses the craving for heroin without producing feelings of euphoria.

Stimulants

AMPHETAMINES   In contrast to depressants and opiates, stimulants are drugs that increase arousal. Amphetamines are powerful stimulants, sold under such trade names as Methedrine, Dexedrine, and Benzedrine and known colloquially as "speed," "uppers," or "Bennies." The immediate effects of consuming such drugs are an increase in alertness and a decrease in feelings of fatigue and boredom. Strenuous activities that require endurance seem easier when amphetamines are taken. As with other drugs, the ability of amphetamines to alter mood and increase self-confidence is the principal reason for their use. People also use them to stay awake, to increase endurance and strength during athletic competition, and to lose weight. Most prescription weight-control medications contain amphetamines.

Low doses that are taken for limited periods to overcome fatigue (as during nighttime driving) seem to be relatively safe. However, as the stimulating effects of amphetamines wear off, there is often a period of compensatory letdown during which the user feels depressed, irritable, and fatigued. He or she may be tempted to take more of the drug. Tolerance develops quickly, and the user needs increasingly larger doses to produce the desired effect. Since high doses can have dangerous side effects—agitation, confusion, heart palpitations, and elevated blood pressure—medications containing amphetamines should be used with caution.

When tolerance develops to the point at which oral doses are no longer effective, many users inject amphetamines into a vein. Large intravenous doses produce an immediate pleasant experience (a flash or rush); this sensation is followed by irritability and discomfort, which can be overcome only by an additional injection. If this sequence is repeated every few hours over a period of days, it will end in a "crash," a deep sleep followed by a period of lethargy and depression. The amphetamine abuser may seek relief from this discomfort by turning to alcohol or heroin.

Long-term amphetamine use is accompanied by drastic deterioration of physical and mental health. The user, or "speed freak," may develop symptoms that are indistinguishable from those of acute schizophrenia (see Chapter 16). These symptoms include paranoid delusions (the false belief that people are persecuting you or out to get you) and visual or auditory hallucinations. The paranoid delusions may lead to unprovoked violence. For example, in the midst of an amphetamine epidemic in Japan (during the early 1950s when amphetamines were sole without prescription and advertised for "elimination of drowsiness and repletion of the spirit"), 50 percent of the murder cases in a 2-month period were related to amphetamine abuse (Hemmi, 1969).

COCAINE   Like other stimulants, cocaine, or "coke," a substance obtained from the dried leaves of the coca plant, increases energy and self-confidence; it makes the user feel witty and hyperalert. In the early part of this century, cocaine was widely used and easy to obtain; in fact, it was an ingredient in the early recipe of Coca-Cola. Its use then declined, but recently its popularity has been increasing, even though it is now illegal. Indeed, cocaine is the drug of choice for many conventional and upwardly mobile young adults who consider it safer than heroin or amphetamines.

Cocaine can be inhaled or it can be made into a solution and injected directly into a vein. It can also be converted into a flammable compound known as *crack* and smoked.

One of the earliest studies of the effects of cocaine is reported by Freud (1885). In an account of his own use of cocaine, he was at first highly favorable to the drug and encouraged its use. He noted

> . . . the exhilaration and lasting euphoria, which in no way differs from the normal euphoria of the healthy person. . . . You perceive an increase of self-control and possess more vitality and capacity for work. . . . In other words, you are simply normal, and it is so hard to believe that you are under the influence of any drug. . . . Long intensive mental or physical work is performed without any fatigue. . . . This result is enjoyed without any of the unpleasant after-effects that follow exhilaration brought about by alcohol. (1885/1974, p. 9).

Freud soon withdrew this unreserved support, however, after he treated a friend with cocaine and the results were disastrous. The friend developed a severe addiction, demanded larger dosages of the drug, and was debilitated until his death.

Despite earlier reports to the contrary, and as Freud soon discovered, cocaine is highly addictive. In fact, it has become more addictive and dangerous in recent years with the emergence of crack. Tolerance develops with repeated use, and withdrawal effects, while not as dramatic as with the opiates, do occur. The restless irritability that follows the euphoric high becomes, with repeated use, a feeling of depressed anguish. The down is as bad as the up was good and can be alleviated only by more cocaine (see Figure 6-7).

Heavy cocaine users can experience the same abnormal symptoms as high-level amphetamine users, including hallucinations and paranoid delusions. A common visual hallucination is flashes of light ("snow lights") or moving lights. Less common but more disturbing is the feeling that bugs are crawling under the skin—"cocaine bugs." The hallucination may be so strong that the individual will use a knife to cut out the bugs. These experiences (sensory stimulation in the absence of sensory input) occur because cocaine is causing the sensory neurons to fire spontaneously.

Studies of babies exposed to cocaine before birth suggest that the drug is causing an epidemic of damaged infants, some of whom will be impaired for life because the mother used cocaine even briefly during pregnancy. The damaging effects include retarded growth in the womb, neurological abnormalities, malformed genital and urinary organs, and brain-damaging strokes. The research indicates that even a single exposure to cocaine during pregnancy can cause lasting damage. Cocaine readily crosses the placenta and the fetus converts a significant portion into norcocaine—an even more potent drug. Norcocaine does not leave the womb; the fetus excretes it into the amniotic fluid and then swallows it, re-exposing itself repeatedly to the drug. While a single dose of cocaine and its metabolites clear out of an adult body in about 2 days, a fetus is exposed for 5 or 6 days. As a consequence, almost no cocaine-exposed baby escapes its damaging effects.

Just as there is a heroin–AIDS connection, injecting cocaine can lead to AIDS and other diseases if drug needles are shared among several people. In some ways AIDS may be more of a problem for cocaine users than for heroin users. One reason is "binge use," with cocaine users sharing a needle for injection many times in a short period, unlike heroin addicts, who fall asleep after injection.

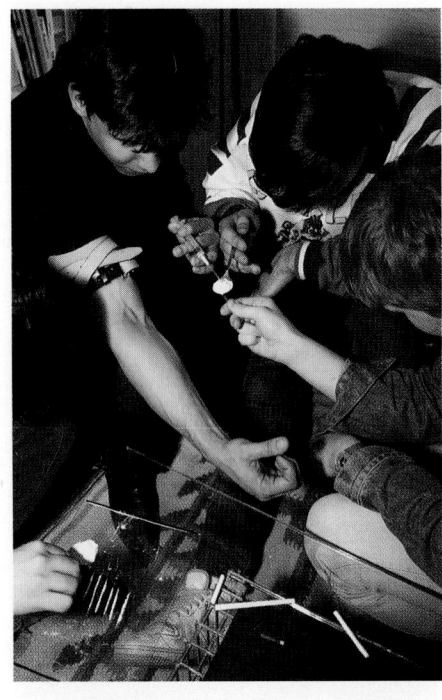

Drug users who share needles increase their risk of contracting AIDS.

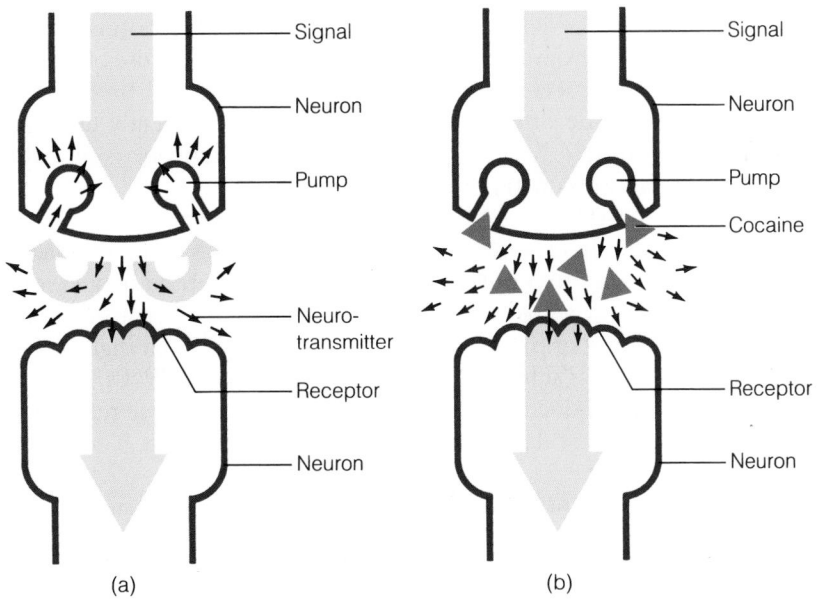

(a) (b)

FIGURE 6-7
Molecular Effects of Cocaine *(a) A nerve impulse causes the release of neurotransmitters that carry the signal across the synapse to a receiving neuron. Some of the neurotransmitters are then reabsorbed into the originating neuron* (reuptake process), *while the rest are broken up chemically and made inactive* (degradation process). *These processes are discussed in Chapter 2. (b) Several lines of research indicate that cocaine blocks the reuptake process for three neurotransmitters* (dopamine, serotonin, and norepinephrine) *that are involved in the regulation of mood. With reuptake hampered by cocaine, the normal effects of these neurotransmitters are amplified; in particular, an excess of dopamine is associated with feelings of euphoria. However, prolonged cocaine use produces a shortage of these neurotransmitters since their reuptake for later use is blocked; that is, the body degrades them at a faster rate than it can manufacture them anew. With the normal supply depleted by repeated cocaine use, euphoria is replaced by anxiety and depression.*

In recent years cocaine ranked second only to marijuana among illicit drugs in active use. A great many young people have been putting themselves at risk by trying cocaine—39 percent of those who reached their late twenties in the past few years have tried cocaine and 7 percent have tried crack specifically. Fortunately, there is evidence of some downturn in cocaine use (Johnston, O'Malley, & Bachman, 1989). Undoubtedly, the tragic deaths from cocaine use of sports stars and other media luminaries attracted the attention of young Americans and conveyed the message that no one is invincible.

Hallucinogens

Drugs whose main effect is to change perceptual experience are called *hallucinogens*, or *psychedelics*. Hallucinogens typically change the user's perception of both his or her internal and external worlds. Usual environmental stimuli are experienced as novel events—for example, sounds and colors seem dramatically different. Time perception is so altered that minutes may seem like hours. The user may experience auditory, visual, and tactile hallucinations and will have a decreased ability to differentiate between himself and his surroundings.

Some hallucinogenic drugs are derived from plants—such as mescaline from cactus and psilocybin from mushrooms. Others are synthesized in the laboratory, such as LSD (lysergic acid diethylamide) and PCP (phencyclidine).

LSD The drug LSD, or "acid," is a colorless, odorless, tasteless substance (solution or powder) that is often sold dissolved on sugar cubes or pieces of paper. It is a very potent drug that produces hallucinations at low doses. Some users have vivid hallucinations of colors and sounds, whereas others have mystical or semireligious experiences. Anyone can have an unpleasant, frightening reaction (or "bad trip"), even those who have had many pleasant LSD experiences. Another adverse LSD reaction is the flashback, which may occur days, weeks, or months after the last use of the drug. The individual experiences illusions or hallucinations similar to those experienced when using the drug. Since LSD is almost completely eliminated from the body within 24 hours after it is taken, the flashback is probably a restoration of memories of the prior experience.

More threatening to the LSD user is the loss of reality orientation that can occur during mystical states associated with the drug. This alteration in consciousness can lead to a highly irrational and disoriented behavior and, occasionally, to a panic state in which the victim feels that he cannot control what the body is doing or thinking. People have jumped from high places to their death when in this state. LSD was popular during the 1960s, but its use has declined, probably due to widespread reports of severe drug reactions, as well as reports of genetic damage to users and their offspring.

PCP   Next to alcohol, PCP is now the most widely misused drug in Western cultures. Although it is sold as a hallucinogen (under such street names as "Angel Dust," "Shermans," and "Superacid"), PCP is technically classified as a dissociative anesthetic. It may cause hallucinations, but it also makes the user feel dissociated or apart from the environment.

PCP was first synthesized in 1956 for use as a general anesthetic. It had the advantage of eliminating pain without producing a deep coma. However, its legal manufacture was discontinued when doctors found that the drug produced agitation, hallucinations, and a psychotic-like state resembling schizophrenia among many patients. Because the ingredients are cheap and the drug is relatively easy to manufacture in a kitchen laboratory, PCP is widely used as an adulterant of other, more expensive street drugs. Much of what is sold as THC (the active ingredient of marijuana) is really PCP.

PCP can be taken in liquid or pill form, but more often it is smoked or snorted. In low doses it produces an insensitivity to pain and an experience similar to a moderately drunken state—one of confusion, loss of inhibition, and poor psychomotor coordination. Higher doses produce a disoriented, comalike condition. Unlike the person who experiences LSD, the PCP user is unable to observe his or her drug-induced state and frequently has no memory of it.

The effects of PCP are not clearly understood. While the drug reduces a person's sensitivity to pain, the user also seems to experience heightened sensory input; the person feels bombarded by an overload of stimuli. This may explain why trying to talk down or physically handle a person on PCP usually makes things worse.

Contrary to the popular image, PCP users are seldom violent. When the police or someone else try to help the person because he or she looks drunk or sick, the increased stimulation of being picked up or grabbed increases the PCP user's arousal. In flailing around to get away, the user may injure others and himself, especially since the user is insensitive to pain.

Cannabis

The *cannabis* plant has been harvested since ancient times for its psychoactive effects. The dried leaves and flowers, or *marijuana*, is the form in which it is most often used in this country, while the solidified resin of the plant, called *hashish* ("hash"), is commonly used in the Middle East. The active ingredient in both substances is THC (tetrahydrocannabinol). Taken orally in small doses (5 to 10 milligrams), THC produces a mild high; larger doses (30 to 70 milligrams) produce severe and longer-lasting reactions that resemble those of hallucinogenic drugs. As with that of alcohol, the reaction often has two stages: a period of stimulation and euphoria followed by a period of tranquillity and, with higher doses, sleep.

Regular users of marijuana report a number of sensory and perceptual changes: a general euphoria and sense of well-being, some distortions of space and time, changes in social perception, and a number of out-of-body experiences (Tart, 1971). Not all marijuana experiences are pleasant. Sixteen percent of regular users report anxiety, fearfulness, and confusion as a "usual occurrence," and about one-third report that they occasionally experience such symptoms as acute panic, hallucinations, and unpleasant distortions in body image (Halikas, Goodwin, & Guze, 1971; Negrete & Kwan, 1972).

Drug use among young people, including marijuana, has declined since the late 1970s.

Marijuana interferes with performance on complex tasks. Motor coordination and signal detection (the ability to detect a brief flash of light) are significantly impaired by low to moderate doses; and tracking (the ability to follow a moving stimulus) is especially sensitive to the effects of marijuana (Institute of Medicine, 1982). These findings make it clear that driving while under the drug's influence is dangerous. The number of automobile accidents related to marijuana use is difficult to determine because, unlike alcohol, THC declines rapidly in the blood, quickly going to the fatty tissues and organs of the body. A blood analysis two hours after a heavy dose of marijuana may show no signs of THC, even though an observer would judge the person to be clearly impaired. Nevertheless, it is estimated that one-fourth of all drivers involved in accidents are under the influence of marijuana alone or marijuana in combination with alcohol (Jones & Lovinger, 1985).

The effects of marijuana may persist long after the subjective feelings of euphoria or sleepiness have passed. A study of aircraft pilots using a simulated flight-landing task found that performance was significantly impaired as much as 24 hours after smoking one marijuana cigarette containing 19 milligrams of THC—despite the fact that the pilots reported no awareness of any aftereffects on their alertness or performance (Yesavage, Leier, Denari, & Hollister, 1985). These findings have led to concern about marijuana use by those whose jobs involve the public safety.

Most studies of the effects of long-term marijuana use have been confounded by the subjects' use of other drugs. One study in which this factor was carefully controlled found few measurable effects of prolonged use (Schaeffer, Andrysiak, & Ungerleider, 1981). The subjects, all Caucasians born and raised in the United States, were members of a religious sect that uses marijuana, in the form of ganja (a potent preparation used especially for smoking), as part of its religious sacrament. Members of the sect abstain from alcohol and other psychoactive drugs. The subjects had used between 2 and 4 ounces of ganja-tobacco mixture each day for over seven years, and their urine specimens indicated the presence of large amounts of THC. Nevertheless, their intelligence levels were unimpaired, they performed adequately on other cognitive measures, and they showed no signs of poor health. However, the long-range effect that smoking may have on these subjects' lungs remains to be determined. Indications are that marijuana smoke is at least as harmful to the lungs as tobacco smoke (Tashkin et al., 1985).

CRITICAL DISCUSSION

Drug Dependence

All of the drugs we have discussed—with the possible exception of marijuana—have profound effects on the central nervous system, and an individual can become psychologically or physically dependent on any of them. The fact that students as young as 11 and 12 years are experimenting with drugs is of concern not only because of possible damage to the still-developing nervous system but because early involvement with drugs predicts a more extensive use of drugs later on.

A longitudinal study of high-school students in New York State indicates the following stages in the sequence of drug usage:

beer and wine → hard liquor → marijuana → other illegal drugs

This does not mean that the use of a particular drug invariably leads to the use of others in the sequence. Only about one-fourth of the students who drank hard liquor progressed to marijuana, and only one-fourth of the marijuana users went on to try such drugs as LSD, amphetamines, or heroin. The students stopped at different stages of usage, but none of them progressed directly from beer or wine to illegal drugs without drinking liquor first, and very few students progressed from liquor to hard drugs without trying marijuana first (Kandel, 1975; Kandel et al., 1986). Positive experiences with one drug may encourage experimentation with another.

This stepping-stone theory of drug usage has been criticized because the majority of young people who smoke marijuana do not go on to use other drugs. Nevertheless, heavy use of marijuana does appear to increase the likelihood of using other illegal drugs. A nationwide survey of men 20 to 30 years of age showed that, of those who had smoked marijuana 1,000 times or more (roughly equivalent to daily usage for three years), 73 percent later tried cocaine and 35 percent tried heroin. In contrast, less than 1 percent of the people surveyed who did not smoke marijuana used these harder drugs. Of those who had used marijuana fewer than 100 times, only 7 percent later tried cocaine and 4 percent tried heroin (O'Donnell & Clayton, 1982). So, studies indicate that heavy marijuana smoking does increase the likelihood of becoming involved with more dangerous drugs.

Many studies have been conducted to determine what personality characteristics and social factors prompt people to use psychoactive drugs. Because some of these studies involved individuals who were already taking drugs, the results must be viewed with caution. For example, heroin addicts have been described as antisocial personalities who have difficulty relating to other people and who seek to escape responsibility through drugs. But we cannot be certain that these characteristics did not *result from* addiction rather than precede it. Nevertheless, the following factors seem important in determining whether a person will try illegal drugs.

PARENTAL INFLUENCES   One finding is that young people who come

MEDITATION

In *meditation*, a person achieves an altered state of consciousness by performing certain rituals and exercises. These exercises include controlling and regulating breathing, sharply restricting one's field of attention, eliminating external stimuli, assuming yogic body positions, and forming mental images of an event or symbol. The result is a somewhat mystical state in which the individual is extremely relaxed and feels divorced from the outside world; the person loses self-awareness and gains a sense of being involved in a wider consciousness, however defined. That such meditative techniques may cause a change in consciousness goes back to ancient times and is represented in every major world religion. Buddhists, Hindus, Sufis, Jews, and Christians all have literature describing rituals that induce meditative states (West, 1987).

Traditional Forms of Meditation

Traditional forms of meditation follow the practices of *yoga*, a system of thought based on the Hindu religion, or *Zen*, which is derived from Chinese and Japanese Buddhism. Two common techniques of meditation are an

from unhappy homes, those in which parents show little interest in their children or inflict harsh physical punishment, are more apt to use drugs than young people who come from happier home environments (Baer & Corrado, 1974). Parental values also play an important role in drug usage. Youths from conservative homes, in which traditional social and religious values are emphasized, are less apt to become involved with drugs than youths from more permissive and liberal homes, where "doing your own thing" is encouraged (Blum et al., 1972). Perhaps the most powerful influence is the degree to which parents model drug use. The children of parents who freely use alcohol, tranquilizers, and other legal drugs are likely to sample drugs themselves (Smart & Fejer, 1972; Newcomb & Bentler, 1988).

PEER INFLUENCES Numerous studies have revealed a correlation between the variety of drugs a young person tries, and the likelihood that his or her friends are users. This finding is subject to several interpretations: drug-using friends may encourage the youth to experiment with drugs, or the youth may start using drugs and then select friends who are drug users. Both explanations may be true to some degree (Marlatt, Baer, Donovan, & Kivlahan, 1988).

PERSONALITY FACTORS No single personality type is associated with drug use. People try drugs for a variety of reasons, such as curiosity or the desire to experience a new state of consciousness, escape from physical or mental pain, or as a relief from boredom. However, one personality trait that is predictive of drug usage is social conformity. People who score high on various tests of social conformity (who see themselves as conforming to the traditional values of American society) are less apt to use drugs than those who score low on such tests. The nonconformist may be either a loner who feels no involvement with other people or a member of a subculture that encourages drug use. A study of teenagers identified several additional personality traits, related to social conformity, that are predictive of drug use. Eighth- and ninth-graders who were rated by their classmates as impulsive, inconsiderate, not trustworthy, lacking in ambition, and having poor work habits were more likely to smoke, drink alcohol, and take other drugs. They were also more likely to start using these drugs early and to be heavy users 12 years later as young adults (Smith, 1986).

These factors may influence initial drug use, but once an individual becomes physically dependent, the motivation changes radically. The person has acquired a new need that may be so powerful he or she ignores all other concerns and lives only for the next fix.

Newcomb and Bentler (1988) have conducted a major study of the effects of drug use on young people. They conclude that a life-style that involves regular use of drugs also includes nonconformity to traditional values, involvement with other deviant or illegal behaviors and involvement with individuals engaged in such behaviors, poor family relations, few educational interests, experiences of emotional turmoil, and feelings of alienation and rebellion.

---

opening-up meditation, in which the subject clears his or her mind for receiving new experiences, and a *concentrative meditation*, in which the benefits are obtained through actively attending to some object, word, or idea. The following is a representative statement of opening-up meditation:

> This approach begins with the resolve to do nothing, to think nothing, to make no effort of one's own, to relax completely and let go of one's mind and body . . . stepping out of the stream of ever-changing ideas and feelings which your mind is in, watch the onrush of the stream. Refuse to be submerged in the current. Changing the metaphor . . . watch your ideas, feelings, and wishes fly across the firmament like a flock of birds. Let them fly freely. Just keep a watch. Don't let the birds carry you off into the clouds. (Chauduri, 1965, pp. 30–31)

Here is a corresponding statement used in an experimental study of concentrative meditation:

> The purpose of these sessions is to learn about concentration. Your aim is to concentrate on the blue vase. By concentration I do not mean analyzing the different parts of the vase, but rather, trying to see the vase as it exists in itself, without any connections to other things. Exclude all other thoughts or feelings or sounds or body sensations. (Deikman, 1963, p. 330)

Traditional forms of meditation have been practiced for hundreds of years as part of some eastern religions.

After a few sessions of concentrative meditation, subjects typically report a number of effects: an altered, more intense perception of the vase; some time shortening, particularly in retrospect; conflicting perceptions, as if the vase fills the visual field and does not fill it; decreasing effectiveness of external stimuli (less distraction and eventually less conscious registration); and an impression of the meditative state as pleasant and rewarding.

Experimental studies of meditation, which necessarily are of short duration, provide only limited insight into the alterations of consciousness that a person can achieve when meditative practice and training extend over many years. In his study of the *Matramudra*, a centuries-old Tibetan Buddhist text, Brown (1977) has described the complex training required to master the technique. He has also shown that cognitive changes can be expected at different meditative levels. (In this type of meditation, people proceed through five levels until they reach a thoughtless, perceptionless, selfless state known as concentrative samdhi.)

Meditation for Relaxation

A somewhat commercialized and secularized form of meditation has been widely promoted in the United States and elsewhere under the name of *Transcendental Meditation* or TM (Forem, 1973). The technique is easily learned from a qualified teacher who gives the novice meditator a *mantra* (a special sound) and instructions on how to repeat it over and over to produce the deep rest and awareness characteristic of TM.

A similar state of relaxation can be produced without the mystical associations of TM. Developed by Benson and his colleagues, the technique includes the following steps:

1. Sit quietly in a comfortable position and close your eyes.
2. Deeply relax all your muscles, beginning at your feet and progressing to your face. Keep them deeply relaxed.

Secular forms of TM have become a popular and lucrative business.

3. Breathe through your nose. Become aware of your breathing. As you breathe out, say the word "one" silently to yourself. For example, breathe in . . . out, "one"; in . . . out, "one"; and so on. Continue for 20 minutes. You may open your eyes to check the time, but do not use an alarm. When you finish, sit quietly for several minutes at first with closed eyes and later with opened eyes.

4. Do not worry about whether you are successful in achieving a deep level of relaxation. Maintain a passive attitude and permit relaxation to occur at its own pace. Expect other thoughts. When these distracting thoughts occur, ignore them by thinking "oh well" and continue repeating "one." With practice, the response should come with little effort.

5. Practice the technique once or twice daily but not within two hours after a meal, since the digestive processes seem to interfere with the subjective changes. (Benson, Kotch, Crassweller, & Greenwood, 1977, p. 442)

During this kind of meditation, a person develops a reduced state of physiological arousal. Subjects report feelings quite similar to those generated by other meditative practices: peace of mind, a feeling of being at peace with the world, and a sense of well-being.

Effects of Meditation

Meditation is an effective technique for inducing relaxation and reducing physiological arousal. Almost all studies of the phenomenon report a significant lowering of the respiratory rate, a decrease in oxygen consumption, and less elimination of carbon dioxide. The heart rate is lowered, blood flow stabilizes, and the concentration of lactate in the blood is decreased (Benson & Friedman, 1985; Shapiro, 1985). Early research findings suggested that meditation could be discriminated as a unique physiological state, but more recent experiments indicate that the physiological state is no different from that induced by other relaxation techniques such as hypnosis, biofeedback, or deep muscle relaxation. Holmes (1984; 1987) goes even

further and argues that there is no reliable evidence to indicate that meditating is more effective in reducing physiological arousal than simply resting.

A number of people involved in *sports psychology* believe that meditation can be useful in getting maximum performance from an athlete (Syer & Connolly, 1984). Engaging in meditation helps reduce stress before an event, and with experience the athlete can learn to relax different muscle groups and appreciate subtle differences in muscle tension. The meditation may also involve forming mental images of the details of an upcoming event, such as a downhill ski race, until the athlete is in total synchrony with the flow of actions. The skier visualizes the release from the starting platform, speeding down the hill, and moving between the gates, and goes through every action in her mind. By creating visual sensations of a successful performance, the athlete is attempting to program the muscles and body for peak efficiency. Golfing great Jack Nicklaus developed this technique on his own years ago. In describing how he images his performance, Nicklaus wrote:

> I never hit a shot, even in practice, without having a sharp, in-focus picture of it in my head. It's like a color movie. First, I "see" the ball where I want it to finish, nice and white and sitting up high on the bright green grass. Then the scene quickly changes, and I "see" the ball going there: its path, trajectory, and shape, even its behavior on landing. Then there's a sort of fade-out, and the next scene shows me making the kind of swing that will turn the previous images into reality. Only at the end of this short, private, Hollywood spectacular do I select a club and step up to the ball. (1974, p. 79)

The research literature on meditation is of mixed quality and some claims, particularly by those who have a commercial interest in the outcome, are suspect. Nevertheless, on balance, the evidence suggests that meditation may reduce arousal (especially in easily stressed individuals) and may be valuable for those suffering from anxiety and tension. To summarize, we quote from Harré and Lamb:

> The value of meditating for an individual depends on attitude and context. In the spiritual market place many contemporary cults of meditation, with their emphasis on gurus and membership of self-defining elitist institutions, may perhaps be seen as an expression of the disintegration of the family system in the modern West and attendant uncertainty regarding parental and sexual roles and mores. Young people, often desperate for guidance, find parental substitutes in strange places and are liable to become brainwashed practitioners of powerful psychosomatic exercises, access to which is made dependent on cult membership and financial contribution. Only where meditation is used as a means to personal development, insight and above all autonomy can its true potential be realized. (1983, p. 377)

HYPNOSIS

Of all altered states of consciousness, none raises more questions than the *hypnotic condition*. Once associated with the bizarre and the occult, hypnosis has now become the subject of rigorous scientific investigation. As in all fields of psychological investigation, uncertainties remain, but by now many facts have been established. A definition of hypnosis proposed by Kihlstrom serves as an introduction to the topic:

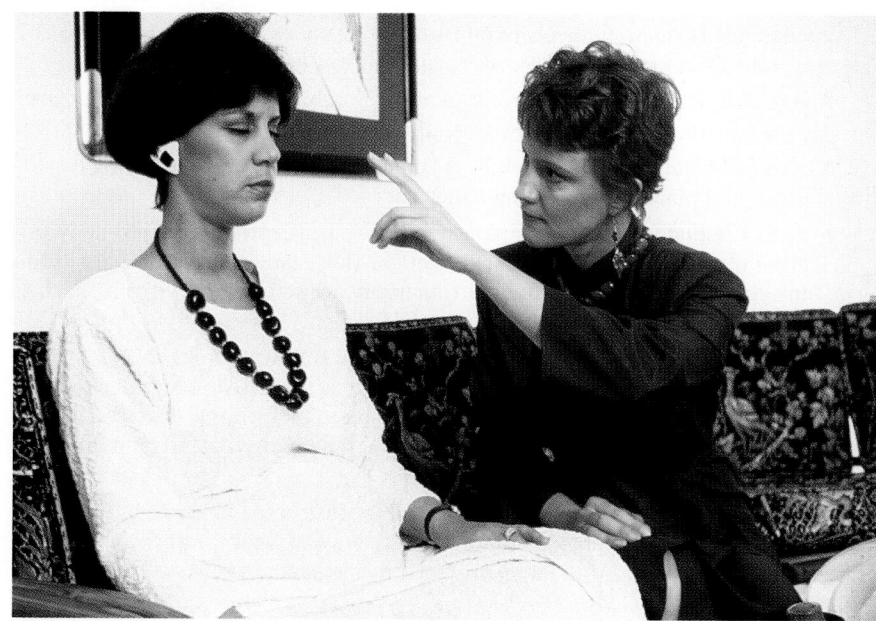

Hypnosis may be defined as a social interaction in which one person (designated the subject) responds to suggestions offered by another person (designated the hypnotist) for experiences involving alterations in perception, memory, and voluntary action. In the classic case, these experiences and their accompanying behaviors are associated with subjective conviction bordering on delusion, and involuntariness bordering on compulsion. (1985, pp. 385–86)

Induction of Hypnosis

In hypnosis, a willing and cooperative subject (the only kind that can be hypnotized under most circumstances) relinquishes some control over his behavior to the hypnotist and accepts some reality distortion. The hypnotist uses a variety of methods to induce this condition. For example, the subject may be asked to concentrate all thoughts on a small target (such as a thumbtack on the wall) while gradually becoming relaxed. A suggestion of sleepiness may be made because, like sleep, hypnosis is a relaxed state in which a person is out of touch with ordinary environmental demands. But sleep is only a metaphor. The subject is told that he will not really go to sleep but will continue to listen to the hypnotist.

The same state can be induced by methods other than relaxation. A hyperalert hypnotic trance is characterized by increased tension and alertness, and the trance-induction procedure is an active one. For example, in one study, subjects riding a stationary laboratory bicycle while receiving suggestions of strength and alertness were as responsive to hypnotic suggestions as were conventionally relaxed subjects (Banyai & Hilgard, 1976). This result denies the common equation of hypnosis with relaxation, but it is consistent with the trance-induction methods of sects like the whirling dervishes.

Modern hypnotists do not use authoritarian commands. Indeed, with a little training, subjects can hypnotize themselves (Ruch, 1975). The subject enters the hypnotic state when the conditions are right; the hypnotist merely helps set the conditions. The following changes are characteristic of the hypnotized state.

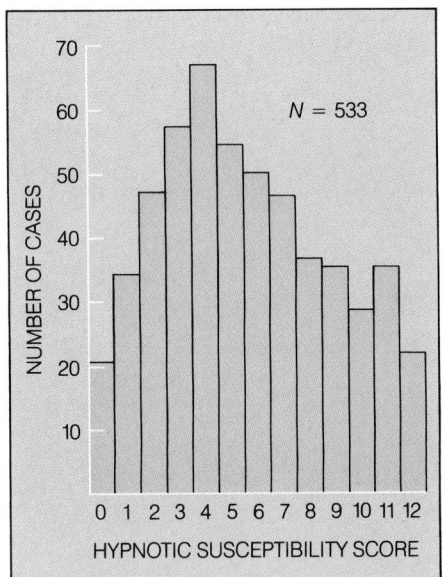

FIGURE 6-8
Individual Differences in Hypnotizability *After using a standard procedure designed to induce hypnosis, researchers administered 12 test suggestions from the Stanford Hypnotic Susceptibility Scale to 533 subjects. The object of the experiment was to test the appearance of hypnotic responses such as those described in the text (for example, being unable to bend one's arm or separate interlocked fingers when the hypnotist suggests these possibilities). The response was scored as present or absent, and the present responses were totaled for each subject to yield a score ranging from 0 (totally unresponsive) to 12 (most responsive). Most subjects fell in the middle ranges with a few very high and a few very low. (After Hilgard, 1965)*

- *Planfulness ceases.* A deeply hypnotized subject does not like to initiate activity and would rather wait for the hypnotist to suggest something to do.
- *Attention becomes more selective than usual.* A subject who is told to listen only to the hypnotist's voice will ignore any other voices in the room.
- *Enriched fantasy is readily evoked.* A subject may find herself enjoying experiences at a place distant in time and space.
- *Reality testing is reduced and reality distortion is accepted.* A subject may uncritically accept hallucinated experiences (for example, conversing with an imagined person believed to be sitting in a nearby chair) and will not check to determine whether that person is real.
- *Suggestibility is increased.* A subject must accept suggestions in order to be hypnotized at all, but whether suggestibility is increased under hypnosis is a matter of some dispute. Careful studies have found some increase in suggestibility following hypnotic induction, although less than is commonly supposed (Ruch, Morgan, & Hilgard, 1973).
- *Posthypnotic amnesia is often present.* When instructed to do so, a highly responsive hypnotic subject will forget all or most of what transpired during the hypnotic session. When a prearranged release signal is given, the memories are restored.

Responsiveness to suggestions is typical of relatively superficial levels of hypnosis. When highly responsive subjects are encouraged to go deeper into hypnosis, they eventually reach a state in which they are unresponsive to the hypnotist's suggestions (except when a prearranged signal returns them to a level at which they can communicate). People who have been deeply hypnotized describe a sense of mind-body separation, a feeling of oneness with the universe, an impression of gaining knowledge of a kind that cannot be communicated (Tart, 1979). This state seems similar to the kind of mystical experience reported by those who have had extensive training in meditation, suggesting that meditation may be a kind of self-hypnosis.

Not all individuals are equally responsive to hypnosis, as Figure 6-8 indicates. Roughly 5 to 10 percent of the population cannot be hypnotized even by a skilled hypnotist, and the remainder show varying degrees of susceptibility. However, if a person is hypnotized on one occasion, he probably will be equally susceptible on another (Hilgard, 1961).

One might suspect that individuals who are highly responsive to hypnosis would also be highly suggestible or compliant in other social situations. However, research findings indicate that this is not true; personality tests designed to measure for compliance do not correlate significantly with hypnotic susceptibility. What does appear to be a good predictor of responsiveness to hypnosis is whether or not the individual has a rich imagination, enjoys daydreaming, and has the ability to generate vivid mental images (Hilgard, 1979).

Hypnotic Suggestions

Suggestions given to a hypnotized subject can result in a variety of behaviors and experiences. The person's motor control may be affected, new memories may be lost or old ones reexperienced, and current perceptions may be radically altered.

CONTROL OF MOVEMENT Many hypnotic subjects respond to direct suggestion with involuntary movement. For example, if a person stands with arms outstretched and hands facing each other and the hypnotist suggests that the subject's hands are attracted to one another, the hands will soon begin to move together, and the subject will feel that they are propelled by some force that she is not generating. Direct suggestion can also inhibit movement. If a suggestible subject is told that an arm is stiff (like a bar of iron or an arm in a splint) and then is asked to bend the arm, it will not bend, or more effort than usual will be needed to make it bend. This response is less common than suggested movement.

Subjects who have been roused from hypnosis may respond with movement to a prearranged signal from the hypnotist. This is called a *posthypnotic response*. Even if the suggestion has been forgotten, subjects will feel a compulsion to carry out the behavior. They may try to justify such behavior as rational, even though the urge to perform it is impulsive. For example, a young man searching for a rational explanation of why he opened a window when the hypnotist took off his glasses (the prearranged signal) remarked that the room felt a little stuffy.

POSTHYPNOTIC AMNESIA   At the suggestion of the hypnotist, events occurring during hypnosis may be "forgotten" until a signal from the hypnotist enables the subject to recall them. This is called *posthypnotic amnesia*. Subjects differ widely in their susceptibility to posthypnotic amnesia, as Figure 6-9 shows. The items to be recalled in this study were 10 actions the subjects performed while hypnotized. A few subjects forgot none or only one or two items; most subjects forgot four or five items. However, a sizable number of subjects forgot all 10 items. This type of bimodal distribution, showing two distinct groups of subjects, has been found in many studies of posthypnotic amnesia. The group of subjects with the higher recall is larger and presumably represents the average hypnotic responders; the smaller group, the subjects who forgot all 10 items, has been described as hypnotic virtuosos. Differences in recall between the two groups following posthypnotic suggestion do not appear to be related to differences in memory capacity: once the amnesia is cancelled at a prearranged signal from the hypnotist, highly amnesic subjects remember as many items as those who are less amnesic. Some researchers have suggested that hypnosis temporarily interferes with the person's ability to search for a particular item in memory but does not affect actual memory storage (Kihlstrom, 1987).

AGE REGRESSION   In response to hypnotic suggestion, some individuals are able to relive episodes from earlier periods of life, such as a birthday at age 10. To some subjects, the episode seems to be pictured as if it were on a television screen; the subjects are conscious of being present and viewing the event but do not feel as if they are producing it. In another type of regression, subjects feel as if they are reexperiencing the events. They may describe the clothing they are wearing, run a hand through their hair and describe its length, or recognize their elementary-school classmates. Occasionally, a childhood language, long forgotten, emerges during regression. For example, an American-born boy whose parents were Japanese and who had spoken Japanese at an early age but had forgotten it began speaking the language fluently again while under hypnosis (Fromm, 1970).

POSITIVE AND NEGATIVE HALLUCINATIONS   Some hypnotic experiences require a higher level of hypnotic talent than others. The vivid and convincing perceptual distortions of hallucinations, for instance, are relatively rare. Two types of suggested hallucinations have been documented:

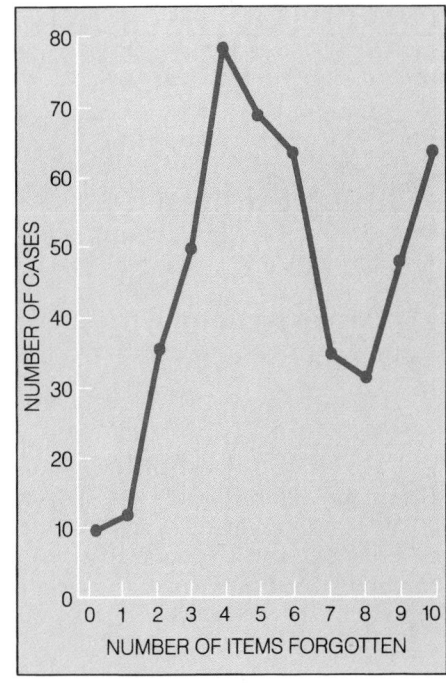

FIGURE 6-9
Distribution of Posthypnotic Amnesia *Subjects performed 10 actions while hypnotized and were then given posthypnotic amnesia instructions. When asked what occurred during hypnosis, subjects varied in the number of actions they failed to recall: the level of forgetting for a given subject ranged from 0 to 10 items. The experiment involved 491 subjects, and the graph plots the number of subjects at each level of forgetting. The plot shows a bimodal distribution for posthypnotic amnesia with peaks at 4 and 10 items forgotten. (After Cooper, 1979)*

CRITICAL DISCUSSION

The "Hidden Observer" in Hypnosis

The neodissociation theory of hypnosis originated with Hilgard's (1977) observation that in many hypnotized subjects, a part of the mind that is not within awareness seems to be watching the subject's experience as a whole. His finding has been described as follows:

The circumstances of Hilgard's discovery of a doubled train of thought in hypnosis were suitably dramatic. He was giving a classroom demonstration of hypnosis using an experienced subject who, as it happened, was blind. Hilgard induced deafness, telling him that he would be able to hear when a hand was put on his shoulder. Cut off from what was going on around him, he became bored and began to think of other things. Hilgard showed the class how unresponsive he was to noise or speech, but then the question arose as to whether he was as unresponsive as he seemed. In a quiet voice, Hilgard asked the subject whether, though he was hypnotically deaf, there might be "some part of him" that could hear; if so, would he raise a forefinger? To the surprise of everyone—including the hypnotized subject—the finger rose.

At this, the subject wanted to know what was going on. Hilgard put a hand on his shoulder so he could hear, promised to explain later, but in the meantime asked the subject what he remembered. What he remembered was that everything had become still, that he was bored and had begun thinking about a problem in statistics. Then he felt his forefinger rise, and he wanted to know why.

Hilgard then asked for a report from "that part of you that listened to me before and made your finger rise," while instructing the hypnotized subject that he would not be able to hear what he himself said. It turned out that this second part of the subject's awareness had heard all that went on and was able to report it. Hilgard found a suitable metaphor to describe this detached witness—the *hidden observer* (Hebb, 1982, p. 53).

Thus, the hidden-observer metaphor refers to a mental structure that monitors everything that happens, including events that the hypnotized subject is not consciously aware of perceiving.

The presence of the hidden observer has been demonstrated in many experiments (Kihlstrom, 1985; Zamansky & Bartis, 1985). In studies on pain relief, subjects are able to describe how the pain feels, using automatic writing or speaking, at the same time that their conscious system accepts and responds to the hypnotist's suggestion of pain relief. In other studies using automatic writing, hypnotized subjects have written messages of which they were unaware while their attention was directed to another task, such as reading aloud or naming the colors on a display chart (Knox,

---

positive hallucinations, in which the subject sees an object or hears a voice that is not actually present; and *negative hallucinations*, in which the subject does not perceive something that normally would be perceived. Many hallucinations have both positive and negative components. In order not to see a person sitting in a chair (a negative hallucination), a subject must see the parts of the chair that would ordinarily be blocked from view (a positive hallucination).

Hallucinations can also occur as the result of posthypnotic suggestion. For example, subjects may be told that on arousal from the hypnotic state they will find themselves holding a rabbit that wants to be petted and that the rabbit will ask, "What time is it?" Seeing and petting the rabbit will seem natural to most of the subjects. But when they find themselves giving the correct time of day, they are surprised and try to provide an explanation for the behavior: "Did I hear someone ask the time? It's funny, it seemed to be the rabbit asking, but rabbits can't talk!" is a typical response.

Negative hallucinations can be used effectively to control pain. In many cases, hypnosis completely eliminates pain, even though the source of the pain—a severe burn or a bone fracture, for example—continues. The failure to perceive something (pain) that would normally be perceived qualifies this response as a negative hallucination. The pain reduction need not be complete in order for hypnosis to be useful in giving relief. Reducing the pain by

Crutchfield, & Hilgard, 1975). Hilgard and his colleagues have compared these phenomena to everyday experiences in which an individual divides attention between two tasks, such as driving a car and conversing at the same time or making a speech and simultaneously evaluating her performance as an orator.

Hidden-observer experiments, although replicated in many laboratories and clinics, have been criticized on methodological grounds. Skeptics argue that implied demands for compliance may have produced the results (see, for example, Spanos & Hewitt, 1980). In a careful experiment designed to determine the role of compliance, researchers have shown that it is possible to distinguish the responses of the truly hypnotized from those of the merely compliant. They asked subjects of proven low hypnotizability to simulate hypnosis while highly responsive subjects behaved naturally. The experimenter did not know to which group each subject belonged. The simulators did conform to the implied demands in the way they were expected to, but

their reports of the subjective experiences differed significantly from those individuals who were actually hypnotized (Hilgard et al., 1978; Zamansky & Bartis, 1985).

An unresolved problem is why some highly responsive hypnotized subjects do not have access to a hidden observer. One difference between the two groups has been reported. Subjects without a hidden observer are more "compliant" to suggestions of age regression—that is, they report feeling like children again—whereas those with a hidden observer invariably report a persistent duality of awareness. During age regression, they see themselves simultaneously as adult observers and as children. This division between an active participant and an observer is spontaneous and not suggested by the hypnotist (Laurence, 1980).

These are complex matters, not to be simply explained or lightly dismissed. They have implications not only for theories of hypnosis but for our view of consciousness in general. For a further discussion of this topic, see Hilgard (1977).

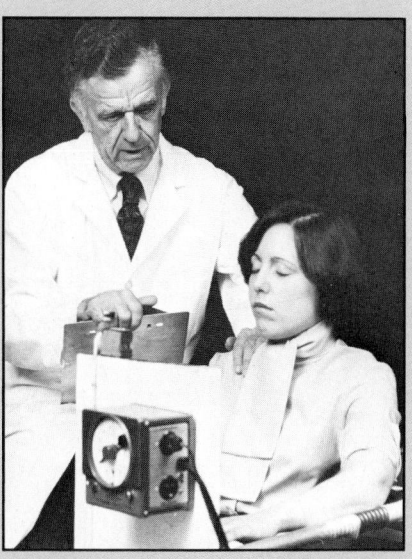

Pain under Hypnosis *Previously, when her hand was in the ice water, the subject felt no pain following suggestions of hypnotic anesthesia. By placing a hand on her shoulder, however, Dr. Hilgard can tap a "hidden observer" that reports the pain that the subject had felt at some level.*

as little as 20 percent can make the patient's life more tolerable. Experimental studies have shown that the amount of pain reduction is closely related to the degree of measured hypnotizability (Hilgard & Hilgard, 1975). Pain reduction through hypnosis is useful in dentistry, obstetrics, and surgery, especially when chemical anesthetics are ill-advised because of the patient's condition (see Figure 6-10) (Wadden & Anderton, 1982).

Theories of Hypnosis

Experts have been arguing about what hypnosis is and how it works since the late 1700s, when Franz Mesmer claimed that it was caused by "animal magnetism." A hundred years later, the French neurologist Charcot suggested that hypnosis is a sign of hysteria and classified it as a neurological disturbance. His views were opposed by Bernheim, a physician who argued that hypnosis is the result of suggestion and insisted that normal people can be hypnotized. Although Bernheim won the argument, hypnosis remained a source of controversy.

Pavlov, famed for his work on conditioned reflexes (see Chapter 7), believed that hypnosis is a form of sleep, from which, in fact, its name derives. His theory has been largely discredited by physiological studies that show a difference between sleep and hypnosis in the EEG and by demonstrations of alert hypnosis.

A psychoanalytic theory suggests that hypnosis is a state of *partial regression* in which the subject lacks the controls present in normal waking consciousness and therefore acts impulsively and engages in fantasy production. The idea is that hypnosis causes a regression in the thought processes to a more infantile stage; fantasies and hallucinations during hypnosis are indicators of a primitive mode of thought uncensored by higher levels of control (Gill, 1972).

A theory based on the dramatic nature of many hypnotic behaviors emphasizes a kind of involuntary *role enactment* as a response to social demands. This theory does *not* imply that the subject is playacting in a deliberate attempt to fool the hypnotist; it assumes that the subject becomes so deeply involved in a role that actions take place without conscious intent (Coe & Sarbin, 1977).

Yet another approach emphasizes the dissociative aspects of hypnosis. Dissociation involves a split of consciousness into several streams of thought, each somewhat independent of the others. Hypnosis theoretically induces a dissociative state in the subject so that he is not aware of all that is occurring in consciousness. The hypnotist, however, can tap into the various streams of thought. A special version of this theory, called *neodissociation theory*, has proved to be useful in analyzing hypnotic phenomena (see the following Critical Discussion).

Competing theories of hypnosis were argued more vehemently in the 1960s and 1970s than they are today. With the facts and relationships now better understood, differences between explanations fade in importance. Each theory calls attention to some significant features of hypnosis, and as new data become available, differences are being resolved (Kihlstrom, 1987).

PSI PHENOMENA

A discussion of consciousness would not be complete without considering some esoteric and mystical claims about the mind that have attracted widespread public attention. Of particular interest are questions about whether or not human beings can a) acquire information about the world or other people in ways that do not involve stimulation of the known sense organs, or b) influence physical events by purely mental means. These questions are the source of controversy over the existence of *psi*, processes of information and/or energy exchange not currently explicable in terms of known science (in other words, known physical mechanisms). The phenomena of psi are the subject matter of *parapsychology* ("beside psychology") and include the following:

1. *Extrasensory perception* (ESP). Response to external stimuli without any known sensory contact.
   a. *Telepathy*. Thought transference from one person to another without the mediation of any known channel of sensory communication (for example, identifying a playing card merely being thought of by another person)
   b. *Clairvoyance*. Perception of objects or events that do not provide a stimulus to the known senses (for example, identifying a concealed playing card whose identity is unknown to anyone)

     c. *Precognition.* Perception of a future event that could not be anticipated through any known inferential process (for example, predicting that a particular number will come up on the next throw of dice)

2. *Psychokinesis* (PK). Mental influence over physical events without the intervention of any known physical force (for example, willing that a particular number will come up on the throw of dice).

Experimental Evidence

Most parapsychologists consider themselves to be scientists applying the usual rules of scientific inquiry to admittedly unusual phenomena. Yet the phenomena of psi are so extraordinary and so similar to what are widely regarded as superstitions that some scientists declare psi to be an impossibility and reject the legitimacy of parapsychological inquiry. Such a priori judgments are out of place in science; the real question is whether the empirical evidence is acceptable by scientific standards. Many psychologists who are not yet convinced that psi has been demonstrated are nevertheless open to the possibility that new evidence might emerge that would be more compelling. For their part, many parapsychologists believe that several recent experimental procedures either provide that evidence already or hold the potential for doing so. We shall examine one of the most promising of these, the *ganzfeld procedure*.

The ganzfeld procedure tests for telepathic communication between a subject acting as the "receiver" and another subject who serves as the "sender." The receiver is sequestered in an acoustically isolated room and placed in a mild form of perceptual isolation: translucent ping-pong ball halves are taped over the eyes and headphones are placed over the ears; diffuse red light illuminates the room, and white noise is played through the headphones. (White noise is a random mixture of sound frequencies similar to the hiss made by a radio tuned between stations.) This homogeneous visual and auditory environment is called the *ganzfeld*, a German word meaning "total field."

The sender is sequestered in a separate acoustically isolated room, and a visual stimulus (picture, slide, or brief videotape sequence) is randomly selected from a large pool of similar stimuli to serve as the "target" for the session. While the sender concentrates on the target, the receiver attempts to describe it by providing a continuous verbal report of his or her ongoing imagery and free associations. Upon completion of the session, the receiver is presented with four stimuli—one of which is the target—and asked to rate the degree to which each matches the imagery and associations experienced during the ganzfeld session. A "direct hit" is scored if the receiver assigns the highest rating to the target stimulus.

More than 50 experiments have been conducted since the procedure was first introduced in 1974; the typical experiment involves about 30 ganzfeld sessions in which a receiver attempts to identify the target transmitted by the sender. An overall analysis of 28 studies (comprising a total of 835 ganzfeld sessions conducted by investigators in 10 different laboratories) reveals that subjects were able to select the correct target stimulus 38 percent of the time. Because a subject must select the target from four alternatives, we would expect a success rate of 25 percent if only chance were operating. Statistically this result is highly significant; the probability that it could have arisen by chance is less than one in a billion (Honorton, 1985).

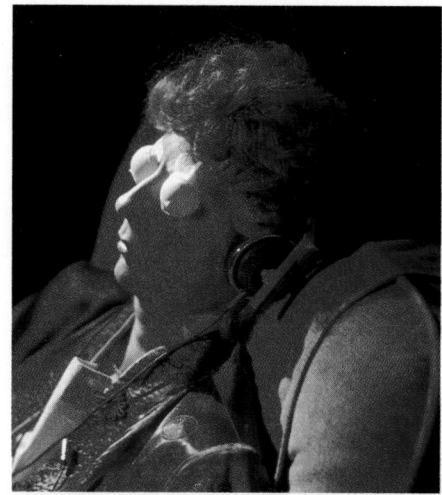

The receiver (top photograph) and the sender (bottom photograph) in a Ganzfeld experiment.

© Bill Yates; reprinted with special permission of King Features Syndicate, Inc., 1971.

Debate over the Evidence

In 1985 and 1986, the *Journal of Parapsychology* published an extended examination of the ganzfeld studies, focusing on a debate between Ray Hyman, a cognitive psychologist and critic of parapsychology, and Charles Honorton, a parapsychologist and major contributor to the ganzfeld database. They agree on the basic quantitative results but disagree on points of interpretation (Hyman, 1985; Hyman & Honorton, 1986; Honorton, 1985). We shall use their debate as a vehicle for examining the issues involved in evaluating claims of psi.

REPLICATION PROBLEM   In science generally, a phenomenon is not considered established until it has been observed repeatedly by several researchers. Accordingly, the most serious criticism of parapsychology is that it has failed to produce a single reliable demonstration of psi that can be replicated by other investigators. Even the same investigator testing the same individuals over time may obtain statistically significant results on one occasion but not on another. The ganzfeld procedure is no exception; fewer than half (43 percent) of the 28 studies analyzed in the debate yielded statistically significant results.

The parapsychologists' most effective response to this criticism actually comes from within psychology itself. Many statisticians and psychologists are dissatisfied with psychology's focus on the *statistical significance level* as the sole measure of a study's success. As an alternative, they are increasingly adopting the technique of *meta-analysis*, a statistical technique that treats the accumulated studies of a particular phenomenon as a single grand experiment and each study as a single observation. Thus any study that obtains results in the positive direction—even though it may not be statistically significant itself—contributes to the overall strength and reliability of the phenomenon rather than simply being dismissed as a failure to replicate (Glass, McGaw, & Smith, 1981; Rosenthal, 1984).

From this perspective, the ganzfeld studies provide impressive replicability: 23 of the 28 studies obtain positive results (more direct hits than chance would predict), a result whose probability of occurring by chance is less than one in a thousand.

The conventional criterion of replication further requires that any competent investigator be able to reproduce the claimed phenomenon, not just one or two gifted experimenters. This is often a difficult criterion to achieve in new areas of investigation because a number of unsuspected variables might affect the outcome. In psychological experiments, the experimenter is often an important social stimulus for the subject and hence a poorly controlled source of variability. Even in such an established area as classical conditioning, investigators at one university were obtaining positive results 94 percent of the time while other investigators could do so only 62 percent of the time (Rosenthal, 1966; Spence, 1964). Nor is the field of psychology alone here. Similar replication difficulties have been reported in medical studies of placebo efficacy (Moerman, 1981) and in such physical science areas as laser technology (Collins, 1974).

This problem may be even more acute in parapsychology because psi effects may legitimately depend on the motivational atmosphere established by the experimenter. Some parapsychologists further believe that the experimenter's own psi abilities and attitudes can have an effect.

Despite these potential difficulties, the replicability of the ganzfeld effect does not appear to rest on the success of one or two investigators. Six of the 10 investigators contributing to the 28 examined studies obtained statistically significant results; and, even if all the studies of the two most successful investigators are discarded from the analysis (half of the studies), the results remain significant (Palmer, Honorton, & Utts, 1988).

The power of a particular experiment to replicate an effect also depends on how strong the effect is and how many observations are made. If an effect is weak, an experiment with too few subjects or observations will fail to detect it at a statistically significant level—even though the effect actually exists.

This is strikingly illustrated by a recent medical experiment designed to determine whether aspirin can prevent heart attacks. The study was discontinued in 1987 because it was already clear the answer was yes. After six years, the aspirin group had already suffered 45 percent fewer heart attacks than a control group that received only placebo medication, a result that would occur by chance less than one time out of a million (The Steering Committee of the Physicians' Health Study Research Group, 1988). With such impressive results, it was considered unethical to keep the control group on placebo medication. This study was widely publicized as a major medical breakthrough.

The pertinent point here is that the study included over 22,000 subjects. If it were to be repeated with 3,000 subjects, a significant aspirin effect would be unlikely to emerge; the experiment would fail to replicate. Despite its undisputed reality and its practical importance, the aspirin effect is actually quite weak.

Now reconsider the ganzfeld effect. If the effect actually exists and has a true direct-hit rate of 38 percent, then statistically we should expect studies with 30 ganzfeld sessions (the average for the 28 studies) to obtain a statistically significant psi effect only about one-third of the time (Utts, 1986). The ganzfeld effect is about four times stronger than the aspirin effect.

In short, it is unrealistic to demand that any real effect be replicable at any time by any competent investigator. The replication issue is more complex than that, and meta-analysis is proving to be a valuable tool for dealing with some of those complexities.

INADEQUATE CONTROLS   The second major criticism of parapsychology is that many, if not most, of the experiments have inadequate controls and safeguards. Flawed procedures that would permit a subject to obtain the communicated information in normal sensory fashion either inadvertently, or through deliberate cheating, are particularly fatal. This is called the problem of *sensory leakage*. Inadequate procedures for randomizing (randomly selecting) target stimuli are another common problem.

Methodological inadequacies plague all the sciences, but the history of parapsychology is embarrassingly full of promising results that collapsed when the procedures were critically examined (Akers, 1984). One common charge against parapsychology is that preliminary, poorly controlled studies often obtain positive results but that as soon as better controls and safeguards are introduced, the results disappear.

Once a flaw is discovered in a completed experiment, there is no persuasive way of arguing that the flaw did not contribute illegitimately to a positive outcome; the only remedy is to redo the experiment correctly. In a database of several studies, however, meta-analysis can evaluate the criticism empirically by checking to see if, in fact, the more poorly controlled studies obtained more positive results than did the better controlled studies. If there is a correlation between a procedural flaw and positive results across the studies, then there is a problem. In the case of the ganzfeld database, both critic Hyman and parapsychologist Honorton agree that flaws of inadequate security and possible sensory leakage do not correlate with positive results. Hyman claimed to find a correlation between flaws of randomization and positive results, but both Honorton's analysis and two additional analyses by nonparapsychologists dispute his conclusion (Harris & Rosenthal, 1988; Saunders, 1985). Moreover, a series of 10 new studies designed to control for flaws identified in the original database yielded results consistent with the original set of 28 studies (Harris & Rosenthal, 1988).

FILE-DRAWER PROBLEM   Suppose that each of 20 investigators independently decides to conduct a ganzfeld study. Even if there were no genuine ganzfeld effect, there is a reasonable probability that at least one of these investigators would obtain a statistically significant result by pure chance. That lucky investigator would then publish a report of the experiment, but the other 19 investigators—all of whom obtained *null* results—are likely to become discouraged, put their data into a file drawer, and move onto something more promising. As a result, the scientific community would learn about the one successful study but have no knowledge of the 19 null studies buried away in the file drawers. The database of known studies would thus be seriously biased toward positive studies, and any meta-analysis of that database would arrive at similarly biased conclusions. This is called the *file-drawer problem*.

The problem is particularly tricky because it is impossible, by definition, to know how many unknown studies are languishing in file drawers somewhere. Nevertheless, parapsychologists offer two lines of defense against the charge that the file-drawer problem seriously compromises their database.

First, they point out that the *Journal of Parapsychology* actively solicits and publishes studies that report negative findings. Moreover, the community of parapsychologists is relatively small, and most investigators are cognizant of ongoing work in the various laboratories around the world. When conducting meta-analysis, parapsychologists actively attempt to scout out unpublished negative studies at conventions and through their personal networks.

But their major defense is statistical, and again meta-analysis provides an empirical approach to the problem. By knowing the overall statistical significance of the known database, it is possible to compute the number of studies with null results that would have to exist in file drawers to cancel out that significance. In the case of the ganzfeld database, there would have to be over 400 unreported studies with null results—the equivalent of 12,000 ganzfeld sessions—to cancel out the statistical significance of the 28 studies analyzed in the debate (Honorton, 1985). Not surprisingly, there is consensus that the overall significance of the ganzfeld studies cannot reasonably be explained by the file-drawer effect (Hyman & Honorton, 1986).

Rather than continuing their debate, Hyman and Honorton issued a joint communiqué in which they set forth their areas of agreement and disagreement and made a series of suggestions for the conduct of future ganzfeld studies (Hyman & Honorton, 1986). Their debate and the subsequent discussion provide a valuable model for evaluating disputed domains of scientific inquiry.

Anecdotal Evidence

In the public's mind, the evidence for psi consists primarily of personal experiences and anecdotes. Such evidence is unpersuasive in science because it suffers fatally from the same problems that jeopardize the experimental evidence—nonreplicability, inadequate controls, and the file-drawer problem.

The replication problem is acute because most such evidence consists of one-time occurrences. A woman announces a premonition that she will win the lottery that day—and she does. You dream about an unlikely event that actually occurs a few days later. A "psychic" correctly predicts the assassination of a public figure. Such incidents may be subjectively compelling, but there is no way to evaluate them because they are not repeatable.

The problem of inadequate controls and safeguards is decisive because such incidents occur under unexpected and ambiguously specified conditions. There is thus no way of ruling out such alternative interpretations as coincidence (chance), faulty memories, and deliberate deception.

A psychic at work in New Orleans.

And finally, the file-drawer problem is also fatal. The lottery winner who announced ahead of time that she would win is prominently featured in the news. But the thousands of others with similar premonitions who did *not* win are never heard from; they remain in the file drawers. It is true that the probability of this woman's winning the lottery was very low. But the critical criterion in evaluating this case is not the probability that *she* would win but the probability that any *one* of the thousands who thought they would win would do so. That probability is much higher. Moreover, this woman has a personal file drawer that contains all those past instances in which she had similar premonitions and then lost.

The same reasoning applies to *precognitive dreams* (in other words, dreams that anticipate an unlikely event that then occurs a few days later). We tend to forget our dreams unless and until an event happens to remind us of them. We thus have no way of evaluating how often we might have dreamed of similar unlikely events that did *not* occur. We fill our database with positive instances and unknowingly exclude the negative instances.

Perhaps the fullest file drawers belong to the so-called psychics who make annual predictions in the tabloid newspapers. Nobody remembers the predictions that fail, but everybody remembers the occasional direct hits. In fact, these psychics are almost always wrong (Frazier, 1987; Tyler, 1977).

Skepticism about Psi

If some of the experimental evidence for psi is as impressive as it seems, why hasn't it become part of established science? Why do we continue to be skeptical?

EXTRAORDINARY CLAIMS Most scientists believe that extraordinary claims require extraordinary proof. A study reporting that students who study harder get higher grades will be believed even if the study was seriously flawed because the data accord well with our understanding of how the world works. But the claim that two people in a ganzfeld study communicate telepathically is more extraordinary; it violates our a priori beliefs about reality. We thus rightly demand a higher measure of proof from parapsychologists because their claims, if true, would require us to radically revise our model of the world—something we should not undertake lightly. In this way, science is justifiably conservative. Many open-minded nonparapsychologists are genuinely impressed by the ganzfeld studies, for example, but reasonably they can and do ask to see more evidence before committing themselves to the reality of psi.

Extraordinariness is a matter of degree. Telepathy seems less extraordinary to most of us than precognition because we are already familiar with the invisible transmission of information through space. We may not all understand how television pictures get to our living rooms, but we know that they do so. Why should telepathy seem that much more mysterious? Precognition, on the other hand, seems more extraordinary because we have no familiar phenomena in which information flows backward in time.

Extraordinariness also depends on our current model of reality. As our understanding of the world changes, a phenomenon that seemed extraordinary at an earlier time may no longer seem so—even if the quality of the evidence has not changed. Any child who has visited a museum of natural history has seen fragments of a meteorite. But before the nineteenth century, the scientific community did not believe in meteorites. Those who reported seeing them were ridiculed—Stones falling out of the sky? Does God hurl them at us from heaven?—and alternative, natural explanations were advanced to explain away the evidence (Nininger, 1933).

In the twentieth century, quantum mechanics is challenging our everyday model of reality far more radically than most people realize (Herbert, 1987). Some parapsychologists believe that modern physics will provide a model of reality within which psi phenomena will fit comfortably and unremarkably (Stokes, 1987), and many studies of psychokinesis are conducted by physical scientists who explicitly base their theories of psi on quantum mechanics (Jahn & Dunne, 1987). If they are right, the scientific community may come to accept psi not because the data became more convincing but because psi became less extraordinary.

SKEPTICISM OF PSYCHOLOGISTS   Psychologists are a particularly skeptical group. National polls find that about one-half of all adult Americans believe in ESP, a figure that rises to two-thirds among Americans with college backgrounds. A survey of over 1,000 college professors found that about 66 percent believe that ESP is either an established fact or a likely possibility. Moreover, these favorable views were expressed by a majority of professors in the natural sciences (55 percent), the social sciences excluding psychology (66 percent), and the arts, humanities, and education (77 percent). The comparable figure for psychologists was 34 percent (Wagner & Monnet, 1979).

Psychologists may be more skeptical than others for several reasons. First, claims of psi might seem more extraordinary to psychologists than to others because it is their conceptual world that would require the most radical revisions if psi were shown to exist. Second, they are the most familiar with past instances of extraordinary claims within psychology that turned out to be based on flawed experimental procedures, faulty inference, or even on fraud and deception.

Third, psychologists know that popular accounts of psychological findings are frequently exaggerated. For example, the genuinely remarkable findings from research on asymmetries in the human brain (see p. 50) have spawned a host of pop-psychology books and media reports containing unsubstantiated claims about left-brained and right-brained persons. Irresponsible reports about states of consciousness—including hypnosis and psi—appear daily in the media. It is thus pertinent to note that when the college professors in the survey cited above were asked to name the sources for their beliefs about ESP, they most frequently cited reports in newspapers and magazines.

And finally, research in cognitive and social psychology has sensitized psychologists to the biases and shortcomings in our abilities to draw valid inferences from our everyday experiences (see Chapter 18). This makes them particularly skeptical of anecdotal reports of psi where, as we saw above, our judgments are subject to many kinds of errors.

For these several reasons, then, much of the skepticism of psychologists toward psi is well-founded. But some of it is not. As we noted earlier, some scientists declare psi to be an impossibility and reject the legitimacy of parapsychological inquiry—a priori judgments that we believe to be out of place in science. Only 4 percent of the college professors in the survey declared psi to be an impossibility—but 34 percent of the psychologists did so. Two hundred years ago, these same skeptics would have been equally certain that God does not hurl stones at us from heaven.

⚡ CHAPTER SUMMARY

1. A person's perceptions, thoughts, and feelings at any moment in time constitute that person's *consciousness*. An *altered state of consciousness* is said to exist when mental functioning seems changed or out of the ordinary to the person experiencing the state. Some altered states of consciousness, such as sleep and dreams, are experienced by everyone; others result from special circumstances, such as meditation, hypnosis, or the use of drugs.

2. The functions of consciousness are a) *monitoring* ourselves and our environment so that we are aware of what is happening within our bodies and in our surroundings; and b) *controlling* our actions so that they coordinate with events in the outside world. Not all events that influence consciousness are at the center of our awareness at a given moment. Memories of personal events and of the knowledge accumulated during a lifetime that are accessible but are not currently part of one's consciousness are called *preconscious memories*. Events that affect behavior even though we are not aware of perceiving them influence us *subconsciously*.

3. According to psychoanalytic theory, some emotionally painful memories and impulses are *not* available to consciousness because they have been repressed—that is, diverted to the *unconscious*. Unconscious thoughts and impulses influence our behavior even though they reach consciousness only in indirect ways through dreams, irrational behavior, and slips of the tongue.

4. The notion of a divided consciousness assumes that thoughts and memories may sometimes be *dissociated*, or split off, from consciousness, rather than repressed to the unconscious. Extreme examples are cases of *multiple personality*, in which two or more well-developed personalities alternate within the same individual.

5. *Sleep*, an altered state of consciousness, is of interest because of the rhythms evident in sleep schedules and in the depth of sleep. These rhythms are studied with the aid of the *electroencephalogram* (EEG). Patterns of brain waves show four stages (depths) of sleep, plus a fifth stage characterized by *rapid eye movements* (REMs). These stages alternate throughout the night. Dreams occur more often during REM sleep than during the other stages (non-REM sleep).

6. In 1900, Sigmund Freud proposed the most influential theory of dreams. It attributes psychological causes to dreams, distinguishing between the *manifest* and *latent* content of dreams and stating that dreams are wishes in disguise.

7. *Psychoactive drugs* have long been used to alter consciousness and mood. They include *depressants*, such as alcohol and tranquilizers; *opiates*, such as heroin and morphine; *stimulants*, such as amphetamines and cocaine; *hallucinogens*, such as LSD and PCP; and *cannabis*, such as marijuana and hashish.

8. All of these drugs can produce *psychological dependence* (compulsive use to reduce anxiety), and most result in *physical dependence* (increased tolerance and withdrawal symptoms) if used habitually.

9. Alcohol is an integral part of social life for many college students, but it can create serious social, psychological, and medical problems. Prolonged heavy drinking can lead to *alcoholism*, which is marked by an *inability to abstain* from or a *lack of control* over drinking.

10. *Meditation* represents an effort to alter consciousness by following planned rituals or exercises such as those of yoga or Zen. The result is a somewhat mystical state in which the individual is extremely relaxed and feels divorced from the outside world. Simple exercises combining concentration and relaxation can help novices experience meditative states.

11. *Hypnosis* is a responsive state in which subjects focus their attention on the hypnotist and the hypnotist's suggestions. Some people are more readily hypnotized than others, though most people show some susceptibility. Self-hypnosis can be learned by those who are responsive to hypnosis induced by others.

12. Characteristic hypnotic responses include enhanced or diminished *control over movements*, the distortion of memory through *posthypnotic amnesia*, *age*

regression, and positive and negative *hallucinations*. The reduction of pain, as a variety of negative hallucination, is one of the beneficial uses of hypnosis in the treatment of burns and in obstetrics, dentistry, and surgery.

13. Theories of hypnosis have long been a source of controversy, with each explaining some aspect of hypnotic behavior but none explaining all. With better agreement on the empirical facts, the theories are gradually becoming complementary rather than antagonistic.

14. There is considerable controversy over *psi*, the idea that human beings can acquire information about the world in ways that do not involve stimulation of known sense organs or can influence physical events by purely mental means. The phenomena of psi includes *extrasensory perception* (ESP) in its various forms (telepathy, clairvoyance, precognition) and *psychokinesis*, movement of objects by the mind.

15. A number of carefully controlled studies (called *ganzfeld experiments*) have been conducted to evaluate ESP via telepathy. These experiments are subject to criticism (replicability, inadequate controls, file-drawer problems). However, a careful analysis of the results does not preclude the possibility of a real ESP effect. Nevertheless, most psychologists remain skeptical about ESP and psi in general, in part because so many past instances of extraordinary claims turned out to be based on flawed experimental procedures, faulty inferences, or even on fraud and deception.

FURTHER READING

Several books deal in general with the problems of consciousness and its alterations, such as Baars, *Cognitive Theory of Consciousness* (1988); Pope and Singer (eds.), *The Stream of Consciousness* (1978); and Bowers and Meichenbaum (eds.), *The Unconscious Reconsidered* (1984). For philosophical/psychological discussions of consciousness see Lycan, *Consciousness* (1987); Jackendoff, *Consciousness and the Computational Mind* (1987); and Churchland, *Matter and Consciousness* (1988).

Problems of divided consciousness are treated in Hilgard, *Divided Consciousness* (1977); Kluft (ed.), *Childhood Antecedents of Multiple Personality* (1985); and Braun (ed.), *Treatment of Multiple Personality Disorder* (1986).

Useful books on sleep and dreams include Hobson, *Sleep* (1989); Horne, *Why We Sleep* (1988); Hobson, *The Dreaming Brain* (1988); and Hauri, *The Sleep Disorders* (1982).

General textbooks on drugs include Julien, *A Primer of Drug Action* (5th ed., 1988); Julien, *Drugs and the Body* (1988); and Ray, *Drugs, Society, and Human Behavior* (3rd ed., 1983). *Drug and Alcohol Abuse* (3rd ed., 1989) by Schuckit provides a guide to diagnosis and treatment. For a thoughtful discussion of the legal and social problems of heroin, as well as an evaluation of possible solutions, see Kaplan, *The Hardest Drug; Heroin and Public Policy* (1983).

On meditative practices, see West (ed.), *The Psychology of Meditation* (1987); Goleman, *The Varieties of Meditative Experience* (1977); or Naranjo and Ornstein, *On the Psychology of Meditation* (1977). On meditation for relaxing, see Benson, *The Relaxation Response* (1975). For a discussion of relaxation and mental images in athletics see Syer and Connolly, *Sporting Body Sporting Mind; An Athlete's Guide to Mental Training* (1984) and Butt, *The Psychology of Sport* (2nd ed., 1987).

There are a number of books on hypnosis. Presentations that include methods, theories, and experimental results are E. R. Hilgard, *The Experience of Hypnosis* (1968); Fromm and Shor (eds.), *Hypnosis; Developments in Research and New Perspectives* (2nd ed., 1979); and J. R. Hilgard, *Personality and Hypnosis* (2nd ed., 1979).

For a review of parapsychology, see Wolman, Dale, Schmeidler, and Ullman (eds.), *Handbook of Parapsychology* (1985); Frazier (ed.), *Science Confronts the Paranormal* (1986); Kurtz (ed.), *A Skeptic's Handbook of Parapsychology* (1985); Marks and Kammann, *The Psychology of the Psychic* (1980); and Gardner, *Science: Good, Bad, and Bogus* (1981).

Paul Klee. Open Book, 1930.
Gouache over white lacquer on canvas, 17⅝″ x 16⅜″, Solomon R. Guggenheim
Museum, New York. E6 (206)

PART IV

Learning, Remembering, and Thinking

Chapter 7

Detail, Open Book.

Learning and Conditioning

*L*earning pervades our lives. It is involved not only in mastering a new skill or academic subject but also in emotional development, social interaction, and even personality development. We learn what to fear, what to love, how to be polite, how to be intimate, and so on. Given the pervasiveness of learning in our lives, it is not surprising that we have already discussed many instances of it—how, for example, children learn to perceive the world around them, to identify with their own sex, and to control their behavior according to adult standards. Now, however, we turn to a more systematic analysis of learning.

In this chapter we focus on *associative* learning, or learning that certain events go together. This is among the most basic forms of learning. Traditionally, two kinds of associative learning have been of particular interest: *classical conditioning* and *operant conditioning*. In classical conditioning, an organism learns that one event follows another—for example, a baby learns that the sight of a breast will be followed by the taste of milk. In operant conditioning, an organism learns that a response it makes will be followed by a particular consequence; for example, a young child learns that striking a sibling will be followed by disapproval from his or her parents.

PERSPECTIVES ON CONDITIONING

Recall from Chapter 1 that there are various perspectives on psychology, with three of the most important ones being the behavioristic, cognitive, and biological perspectives. As much as any area in psychology, the study of learning has recently undergone a shift in perspectives. Until about 20 years ago, psychologists who studied conditioning usually took a behavioristic perspective, focusing mainly on external stimuli and responses. More recently, many researchers have moved toward either a cognitive perspective, which emphasizes internal process, or a variant of the biological perspective, called *ethology*, which studies animal behavior from an evolutionary-biological point of view. Currently, all three perspectives are reflected in research on conditioning.

In view of the pivotal role that the behavioristic perspective has played in the study of learning, it is important to understand the assumptions that comprise this approach to conditioning, particularly those assumptions that have been challenged by the other perspectives. Three such assumptions follow:

1. Simple associations of the classical or operant kind are the building blocks of all learning, no matter how complex. Thus, even something as complex as learning a language presumably is a matter of learning many simple associations (Staats, 1968).
2. The laws of learning are roughly the same for all species and can be revealed in experiments even with lower organisms in relatively barren environments. Thus, the laws that govern how a rat learns to run a maze presumably govern how a child learns long division (Skinner, 1938).
3. Learning can be better understood in terms of external or environmental causes than internal or intentional ones. That is, the ultimate causes of behavior presumably lie not inside the organism—not, for example, in a

person's beliefs and desires—but rather in environmental events, particularly those that are rewarding or punishing. Thus, we may *not* be able to advance our understanding of how a child learns language by inquiring about his or her mental activities (Skinner, 1971).

These three assumptions led behaviorists to focus on how the behaviors of lower organisms, particularly rats and pigeons, are influenced by rewards and punishments in simple laboratory situations. This work uncovered a wealth of findings about simple associative learning, and some of these findings will be presented in the next three sections of this chapter. The three assumptions also led to challenges from the ethological and cognitive perspectives. The ethological approach disputed the claim made by behaviorists that the laws of learning are the same for all organisms and all situations, while the cognitive approach disputed the behaviorists' assumptions that associations are the only building blocks of learning and that learning can be understood by considering only environmental factors. We will discuss the ethological and cognitive approaches in the final section of this chapter.

CLASSICAL CONDITIONING

The study of classical conditioning began in the early years of this century when Ivan Pavlov, a Russian physiologist who had already won the Nobel prize for research on digestion, turned his attention to learning. While studying digestion, Pavlov noticed that a dog began to salivate at the mere sight of a food dish. While any dog will salivate when food is placed in its mouth, this dog had learned to associate the sight of the dish with the taste of food. Pavlov decided to see whether a dog could be taught to associate food with other things, such as a light or a tone.

Ivan Pavlov with his assistants.

Pavlov's Experiments

In Pavlov's basic experiment, a researcher first attaches a capsule to the dog's salivary gland to measure salivary flow. Then the dog is placed in front of a pan, in which meat powder can be delivered automatically. A researcher turns a light on in a window in front of the dog. After a few seconds, some meat powder is delivered to the pan, and the light is turned off. The dog is hungry, and the recording device registers copious salivation. This salivation is an *unconditioned response*, or UCR, for no learning is involved; by the same token, the meat powder is an *unconditioned stimulus*, or UCS. The procedure is repeated a number of times. Then, to test if the dog has learned to associate the light with food, the experimenter turns on the light but does not deliver any meat powder. If the dog salivates, it has learned the association. This salivation is a *conditioned response*, or CR, while the light is a *conditioned stimulus*, or CS. The dog has been taught, or conditioned, to associate the light with food and to respond to it by salivating. Pavlov's experiment is diagramed in Figure 7-1.

EXPERIMENTAL VARIATIONS   Psychologists over the years have devised many variations of Pavlov's experiments, and we will be discussing some of these in what follows. To appreciate these variations, we need to note some critical aspects of the conditioning experiment. Each paired presentation of the conditioned stimulus (CS) and the unconditioned stimulus (UCS) is called a *trial*. The trials during which the subject is learning the association between the two stimuli is the *acquisition* stage of conditioning. During this stage, repeated pairings of the CS (light) and UCS (meat) are said to strengthen, or *reinforce*, the association between the two, as illustrated in the left-hand curve of Figure 7-2. If the CR is not reinforced (the UCS is omitted repeatedly), the response will gradually diminish; this is called *extinction* and is illustrated by the right-hand curve in Figure 7-2. Acquisition and extinction make intuitive sense if we think of classical conditioning as learning to predict what will happen next. When the prediction is successful (reinforced), the animal learns to keep making that prediction

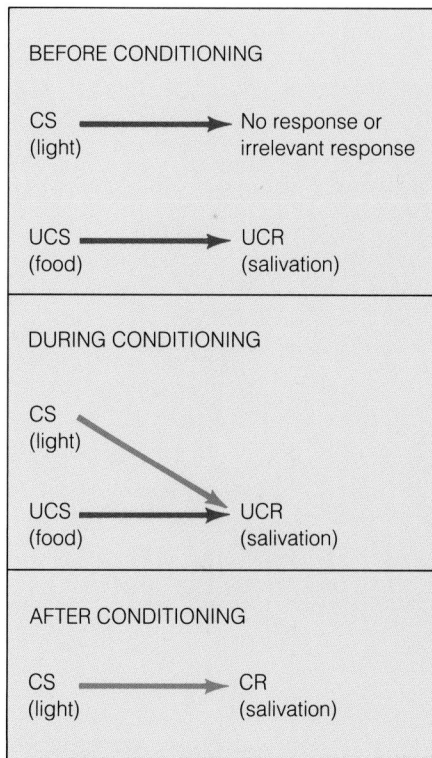

FIGURE 7-1
Diagram of Classical Conditioning *The association between the unconditioned stimulus and the unconditioned response exists at the start of the experiment and does not have to be learned. The association between the conditioned stimulus and the conditioned response is learned. It arises through the pairing of the conditioned and unconditioned stimuli.*

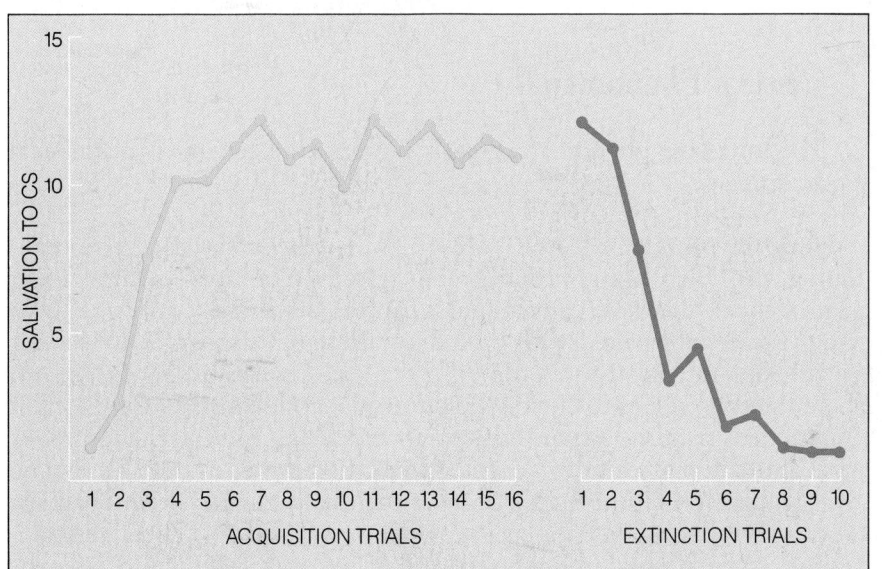

FIGURE 7-2
Acquisition and Extinction of a Conditioned Response *The curve in the panel on the left depicts the acquisition phase of an experiment. Drops of salivation in response to the conditioned stimulus (prior to the onset of the UCS) are plotted on the vertical axis; the number of trials, on the horizontal axis. After 16 acquisition trials, the experimenter switched to extinction; the results are presented in the panel at the right. (After Pavlov, 1927)*

(acquisition); when things change in the world so that the prediction is outdated (not reinforced), the animal unlearns that prediction (extinction).

Conditioning in Different Species

Classical conditioning is pervasive in the animal kingdom and can occur with organisms as primitive as the flatworm. Flatworms contract their bodies when subjected to mild electric shock, and if they experience sufficient pairings of shock (the UCS) and light (the CS), eventually they will contract to the light alone (Jacobson, Fried, & Horowitz, 1967). At the other end of the spectrum, numerous human responses can be classically conditioned. Many of these are involuntary responses, such as *vasoconstriction*, which is a constriction of small blood vessels near the body surface that occurs automatically when our body is exposed to cold. If a buzzer (the CS) routinely sounds just before a person's left hand is immersed in ice water (the UCS), eventually vasoconstriction will occur in response to the buzzer alone (Menzies, 1937).

Classical conditioning also plays a role in emotional reactions such as fear. Suppose a rat is placed in an enclosed compartment in which it is periodically subjected to electric shock (by electrifying the floor). Just before the shock occurs a tone sounds. After repeated pairings of the tone (the CS) and shock (the UCS), the tone alone will produce reactions that are indicators of fear, including stopping in its tracks and crouching; in addition, its blood pressure increases. The rat has been conditioned to be fearful when exposed to what was once a neutral stimulus.

Many human fears may be acquired in this way, particularly in early childhood (Jacobs & Nadel, 1985). Perhaps the best evidence that they can be classically conditioned is that some of these fears, especially irrational ones, can be eliminated by therapeutic techniques based on classical-conditioning principles. A person with an intense fear of cats, for example, may overcome the fear by gradually and repeatedly being exposed to cats. Presumably, a cat was a CS for some noxious UCS a long time ago, and when the person now repeatedly experiences the CS without the UCS, the conditioned fear extinguishes. (See Chapter 16 for a discussion of conditioning and phobias and Chapter 17 for conditioning therapies.)

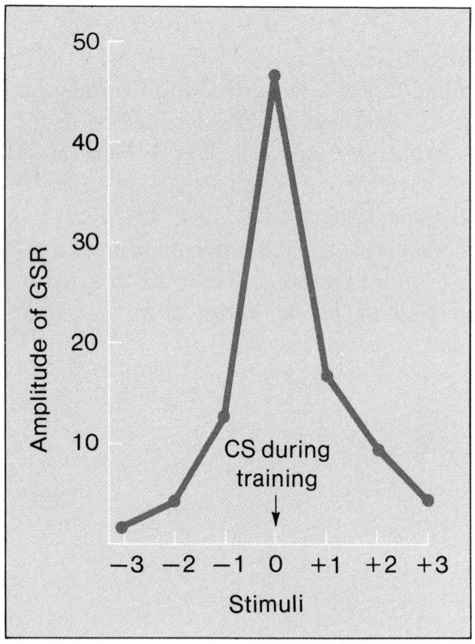

Critical Phenomena

The following phenomena greatly increase the generality of classical conditioning.

SECOND-ORDER CONDITIONING   Thus far in our discussion of conditioning, the UCS has always been biologically significant, such as food, cold, or shock. However, any stimulus can acquire the power of a UCS by being consistently paired with a biologically significant UCS. Recall the example of a rat exposed to a tone (CS) followed by electric shock (UCS), where the tone comes to elicit a conditioned fear response. Once the rat is conditioned, the tone acquires the power of a UCS. Thus, if the rat is now put in a situation in which it is exposed to a light followed by the tone (but no shock) on each trial, the light alone will eventually elicit a conditioned fear response even though it has never been paired with shock. (There must also be other trials in which the tone is again paired with shock; otherwise, the

FIGURE 7-3
Gradient of Generalization *Stimulus 0 denotes the tone to which the galvanic skin response (GSR) was originally conditioned. Stimuli +1, +2, and +3 represent test tones of increasingly higher pitch; stimuli −1, −2, and −3 represent tones of lower pitch. Note that the amount of generalization decreases as the difference between the test tone and the training tone increases.*

originally conditioned relation between tone and shock will extinguish.) The existence of such *second-order* conditioning greatly increases the scope of classical conditioning, especially for humans where biologically significant UCSs occur relatively rarely.

GENERALIZATION AND DISCRIMINATION   When a conditioned response has been associated with a particular stimulus, other similar stimuli will evoke the same response. Suppose that a person is conditioned to have a mild emotional reaction to the sound of a tuning fork producing a tone of middle C. (The emotional reaction is measured by the *galvanic skin response*, or GSR, which is a change in the electrical activity of the skin that occurs during emotional stress.) The person will also show a GSR to higher or lower tones without further conditioning (see Figure 7-3). The more similar the new stimuli are to the original CS, the more likely they are to evoke the conditioned response. This principle, called *generalization*, accounts in part for an individual's ability to react to novel stimuli that are similar to familiar ones.

A process complementary to generalization is *discrimination*. Whereas generalization is a reaction to similarities, discrimination is a reaction to differences. Conditioned discrimination is brought about through selective reinforcement and extinction, as shown in Figure 7-4. Instead of just one tone, for instance, now there are two. The low-pitched tone, CS_1, is always followed by a shock, and the high-pitched tone, CS_2, is not. Initially, subjects will show a GSR to both tones. During the course of conditioning, however, the amplitude of the conditioned response to CS_1 gradually increases while the amplitude of the response to CS_2 decreases. Thus, by the process of *differential reinforcement*, the subjects are conditioned to discriminate between the two tones.

Generalization and discrimination occur in everyday life. The young child who has been frightened by a snapping dog may initially respond with fear to all dogs (generalization). Eventually, through differential reinforcement, the child's range of fearful stimuli narrows to include only dogs that behave in a threatening way (discrimination).

Importance of Predictability

CONTIGUITY VERSUS PREDICTABILITY   Since Pavlov, researchers have tried to determine the critical factor needed for classical conditioning to occur. Pavlov thought the critical factor was *temporal contiguity* of the CS and UCS—that is, the two stimuli must occur within a limited time frame (close together) for an association to develop. Some evidence supporting this idea comes from experiments that have varied the time interval between the presentation of the CS and the UCS. Typically, conditioning is most effective when the CS precedes the UCS by approximately one-half second, and becomes progressively less effective as the time between CS and UCS increases. There is, however, an alternative to temporal contiguity as the critical factor in classical conditioning, namely that the CS be a *reliable predictor* of the UCS. In other words, for conditioning to occur, perhaps there must be a higher probability that the UCS will occur when the CS has been presented than when it has not.

Rescorla (1967), in an important experiment, contrasted contiguity and predictability. On certain trials of the experiment, Rescorla exposed dogs to

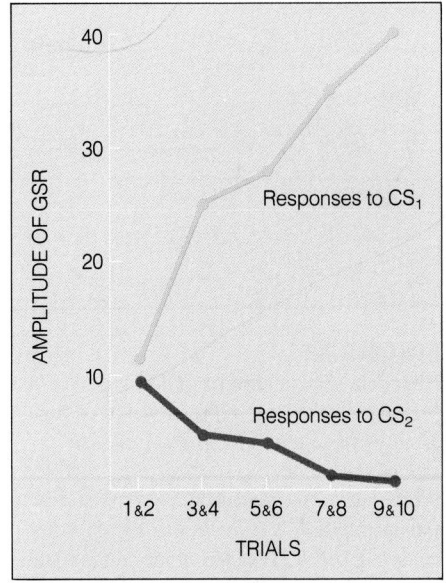

FIGURE 7-4
Conditioned Discrimination *The discriminative stimuli were two tones of clearly different pitch (CS_1 = 700 hertz and CS_2 = 3,500 hertz). The unconditioned stimulus, an electric shock applied to the left forefinger, occurred only on trials when CS_1 was presented. The strength of the conditioned response, in this case the GSR, gradually increased following CS_1 and extinguished following CS_2. (After Baer & Fuhrer, 1968)*

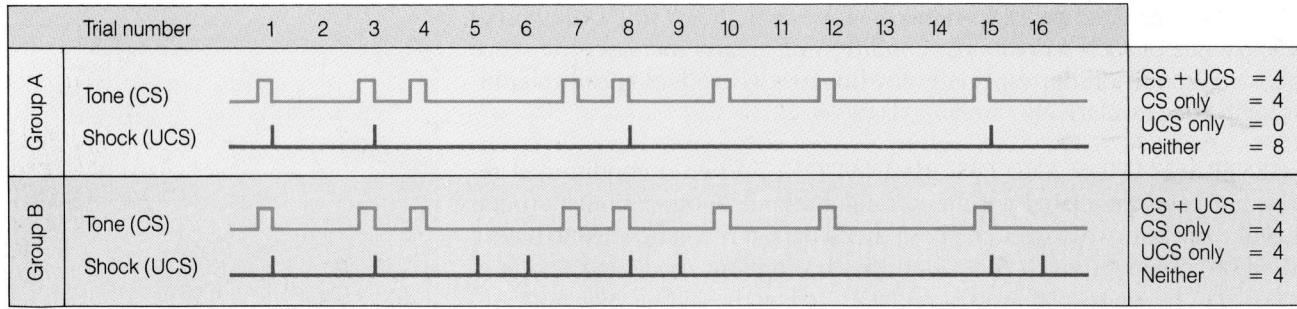

Trial number	1	2	3	4	5	6	7	8	9	10	11	12	13	14	15	16	

Group A

Tone (CS) / Shock (UCS)

CS + UCS = 4
CS only = 4
UCS only = 0
neither = 8

Group B

Tone (CS) / Shock (UCS)

CS + UCS = 4
CS only = 4
UCS only = 4
Neither = 4

FIGURE 7-5

Rescorla's Experiment *The figure presents a schematic representation of two groups from Rescorla's study. For each group, the events for 16 trials are presented. Note that on some trials CS occurs and is followed by UCS (CS + UCS); on other trials CS or UCS occurs alone; and on still other trials, neither CS nor UCS occurs. The boxes to the far right give a count of these trial outcomes for the two groups. The number of CS + UCS trials is identical for both groups, as is the number of trials on which only the CS occurs. But the two groups differ in the number of trials on which UCS occurred alone (never in Group A and as frequently as any other type of trial in Group B). Thus, for Group A, the experimenter established a situation in which the tone was a useful (but not perfect) predictor that shock would follow shortly, whereas for Group B the tone was of no value in predicting subsequent shock. A conditioned response to CS developed readily for Group A but did not develop at all for Group B.*

shock (the UCS), and on some of these trials he preceded the shock by a tone (the CS). The procedures for two of the groups from the experiment are illustrated in Figure 7-5. The number of temporally contiguous pairings of tone and shock was the same in both groups. The independent variable was that tones preceded all shocks in Group A, whereas in Group B shocks were as likely to be preceded by no tones as tones, so the tone had no real predictive power for Group B. This predictive power of the tone proved critical: Group A became rapidly conditioned, whereas Group B did not (as determined by whether or not the dog responded to the tone in such a way as to avoid the shock). In other groups in the experiment (not shown in Figure 7-5), the strength of the conditioning was directly related to the predictive value of the CS in signaling the occurrence of the UCS. Subsequent experiments support the conclusion that the predictive relation between the CS and UCS is more important than either temporal contiguity or the frequency with which the CS and UCS are paired (Rescorla, 1972).

The importance of predictability is also shown by the phenomenon of *blocking*, discovered by Kamin (1969). In the first phase of Kamin's experiment, an experimental group of animals was repeatedly presented a light, the CS, followed by a shock, the UCS. The animals easily learned the light-shock association. In the second phase of the study, the experimental animals were repeatedly presented the same light plus a tone, a compound CS, followed by a shock, the UCS. Now, the animals learned little about the tone-shock relation, compared to control animals who had not received any earlier training with just the light and shock. For the experimental animals, the previously learned light-shock association *blocked* the learning of the new tone-shock association. Why? Presumably because the earlier learning made the shock predictable, and once a UCS is predictable there is little need for further conditioning.

MODELS OF CLASSICAL CONDITIONING   The above findings about predictability have led to a number of models of classical conditioning, the best known of which is due to Rescorla and Wagner (1972). According to this model, the amount of conditioning between a CS and a UCS on any trial depends on the predictability of the UCS: the *less* predictable the UCS, the *greater* the amount of conditioning. Furthermore, the predictability of the UCS on any trial is determined by all the CSs present on that trial. For example, if there are two CSs present on a trial, the amount of conditioning possible for one CS is less the more conditioning that has already occurred to the other CS. This explains the blocking phenomenon described above. Essentially, CSs that occur together compete with one another for associative strength, where the amount to be won in the competition is the amount of unpredictability left in the UCS.

Other models of classical conditioning also focus on predictability, and give even greater emphasis to cognitive factors. According to Wagner (1981), just as humans have a short-term memory in which they can rehearse information (see Chapter 8), so do lower animals. Furthermore, an animal's short-term memory plays a critical role in conditioning. Early in the course of conditioning, a UCS is novel and unpredictable. Consequently, the organism actively rehearses the CS–UCS connection in short-term memory; this rehearsal process is presumably what mediates the acquisition of a classically conditioned response. Once the UCS is no longer surprising, rehearsal decreases and no further learning occurs. This explains the blocking phenomenon: once the UCS is completely predictable, there will be no rehearsal of any new association involving that UCS.

Another cognitive model views classical conditioning as the *generation* and *testing* of rules about what events are likely to follow other events (Holyoak, Koh, & Nisbett, 1989). According to this model, an animal is likely to generate a rule whenever two unexpected events occur in close proximity, or whenever an old rule fails. For a rat in a classical conditioning experiment, an unexpected light followed closely by an unexpected shock would lead to the generation of the rule, "If light, then shock." Once a rule is formed, it is strengthened every time it leads to a correct prediction and weakened every time it leads to an incorrect prediction. The "If light, then shock" rule, for example, would be strengthened whenever the light is in fact followed by the shock, and weakened whenever it is not. The rule model clearly predicts that predictability is necessary for conditioning to occur, because only correct predictions can strengthen a rule. The model also accounts for the blocking phenomenon: as long as a UCS is predicted by a known rule, no new rule involving that UCS will be generated.

PREDICTABILITY AND EMOTION   Predictability is equally important for emotional reactions: if a particular CS reliably predicts that pain is coming, then the absence of that CS predicts that pain is not coming and the organism can relax. The CS is therefore a "danger" signal, and its absence represents a "safety" signal. When such signals are erratic, the emotional toll on the organism can be devastating. When rats have a reliable predictor that shock is coming, they respond with fear only when the danger signal is present; if they have no reliable predictor, they appear to be continually anxious and may even develop ulcers (Seligman, 1975).

There are clear parallels to human emotionality. If a doctor gives a child a danger signal by telling her that a procedure will hurt, the child will be fearful until the procedure is over. In contrast, if the doctor always tells a child "it won't hurt" when in fact it sometimes does, the child has no danger or safety signals and may become terribly anxious whenever in the doctor's office. As adults, many of us have experienced the anxiety of being in a situation where something disagreeable is likely to happen but no warnings exist for us to predict it. Unpleasant events are, by definition, unpleasant, but unpredictable unpleasant events are downright intolerable.

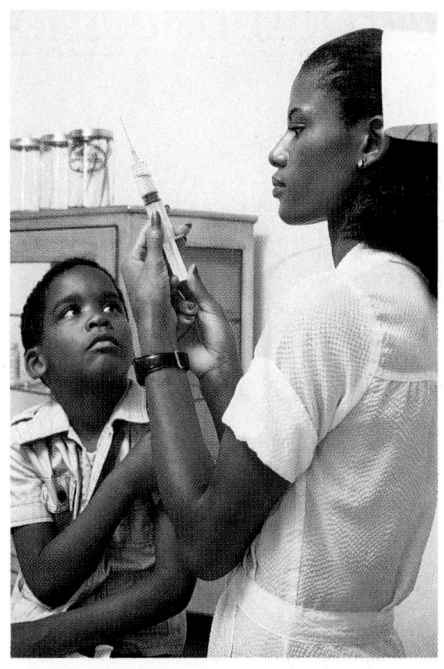

Knowing when to expect pain lessens anxiety.

OPERANT CONDITIONING

In classical conditioning, the conditioned response typically resembles the normal response to the unconditioned stimulus: salivation, for example, is a dog's normal response to food. But when you want to teach an organism

CRITICAL DISCUSSION

Neural Basis of Elementary Learning

Classical and operant conditioning may be the simplest forms of *associative* learning, but there are more elementary forms of learning, namely those that are considered *nonassociative*. One example is *habituation*, by which an organism learns to ignore a weak stimulus that has no serious consequences—such as tuning out the sound of a loud clock. Another kind of nonassociative learning is *sensitization*, whereby an organism learns to strengthen its reaction to a weak stimulus if a threatening or painful stimulus follows. For instance, we learn to respond more intensely to the sound of a piece of equipment if it is frequently followed by a crash. Researchers have made remarkable progress in determining the biological bases of these two forms of learning.

Consider some of the research of Eric Kandel and his associates, who use snails in their work. The neurons of a snail are similar in structure and function to those of a human, yet its ner-

vous system is simple enough to allow researchers to study individual cells. Indeed, the total number of cells in a snail is only in the thousands (compared to billions in a human). Moreover, the cells of a snail are collected into discrete groups (or *ganglia*) of 500 to 1,500 neurons, and a single ganglion can control an instance of habituation or sensitization. This makes it possible to give a "cell-by-cell" account of elementary learning.

The *Aplysia*, a large marine animal, is the snail of choice for researchers, and the behavior of particular interest is a withdrawal response. As shown in Figure 1, the *Aplysia's* gill is housed in a cavity that is covered by a protective sheet called the mantle shelf; the sheet ends in a fleshy spout called a siphon. When the siphon is stimulated by touch, both the siphon and gill contract into the cavity. The withdrawal is controlled by a single ganglion and is subject to habituation and sensitization.

In studies of habituation, the researchers lightly touch the snail's siphon on each trial of the experiment. In the initial trials, the gill-withdrawal reflex is strong, but it gradually weakens after 10 or 15 trials. What cellular events mediate this habituation behavior? The stimulus to the siphon activates 24 sensory neurons, each of which activates the 6 motor neurons in the gill that innervate the contracting

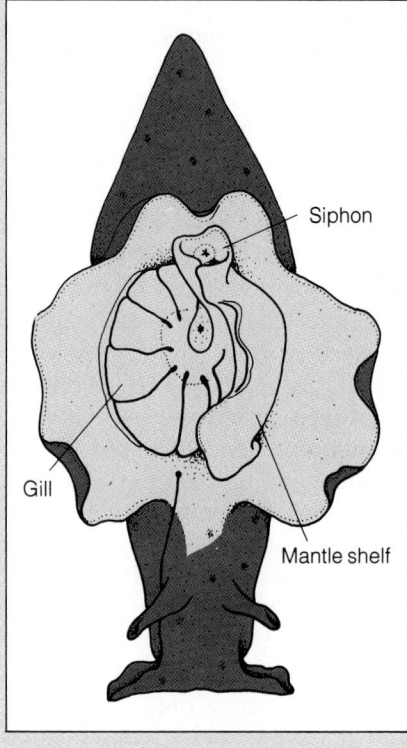

FIGURE 1
Gill Withdrawal in the *Aplysia*
When the siphon is stimulated, the animal retracts its gill into the protective sheet of the mantle cavity; this sheet is called the mantle shelf. (After Kandel, 1979)

something novel—such as teaching a dog a new trick—you cannot use classical conditioning. What unconditioned stimulus would make a dog sit up or roll over? To train the dog, you must first persuade it to do the trick and *afterward* reward it with either approval or food. If you keep doing this, eventually the dog will learn the trick.

Much of real-life behavior is like this: responses are learned because they *operate* on, or affect, the environment. Referred to as *operant conditioning*, this kind of learning occurs in our own species, as well as in lower species. Alone in a crib, a baby may kick and twist and coo spontaneously. When left by itself in a room, a dog may pad back and forth; sniff; or perhaps pick up a ball, drop it, and play with it. Neither organism is responding to the onset or offset of a specific external stimulus. Rather, they are operating on their environment. Once the organism performs a certain behavior, however, the

muscle. The structure of the system can be understood by looking at the neural connections for a single sensory neuron and a single motor neuron (see the top of Figure 2). The small triangles in the figure depict *synaptic* connections between neurons, where a synapse involves a space that must be bridged by a chemical *neurotransmitter.* In the *Aplysia,* a neurotransmitter released by the sensory neuron onto the motor neuron causes initial gill withdrawal, and a decrease in the amount of the neurotransmitter mediates the habituation of gill withdrawal. Thus, this form of elementary learning is due to chemically induced changes in synaptic connections between cells (Kandel, 1979).

Sensitization functions in a similar, though more complex, manner. To sensitize gill withdrawal, again the researchers apply a weak tactile stimulus to the siphon, but this time they also apply simultaneously a strong stimulus to the tail. After a number of such trials, gill withdrawal becomes more pronounced. Some of the mediating neural connections are illustrated in the bottom half of Figure 2. Some neural connections from the tail are now added to the circuit from the siphon. The new connections include a synapse between a tail sensory neuron and a *facilitator interneuron* (a neuron that connects other neurons) and a synapse that connects the facilitator inter-

neuron with the circuit that supports gill withdrawal. In essence, the neural activity from the strong stimulus to the tail modifies the neural connection that underlies gill withdrawal. Once more, learning is mediated by changes in the neurotransmitter that bridges the synapse between the siphon's sensory neuron and the gill's motor neuron. But in this case, the change consists of an increase in the amount of the neurotransmitter released by the sensory neuron (Castelluci & Kandel, 1976).

Our discussion of sensitization suggests that a cell-by-cell analysis may be possible for classical conditioning. Gill withdrawal in the *Aplysia* can be classically conditioned; and such conditioning, like sensitization, involves modifying the gill withdrawal by a second stimulus. Indeed, researchers have proposed a cellular account of classical conditioning that is remarkably similar to that for sensitization (Hawkins & Kandel, 1984). This proposal has generated some controversy (Gluck & Thompson, 1987), but should the basic ideas of the proposal prove defensible, it would indicate that some forms of associative learning are built on more primitive forms of nonassociative learning. It would also indicate that the biological basis of simple learning is not distributed diffusely through the brain; rather, it can be localized to the activity of specific neurons.

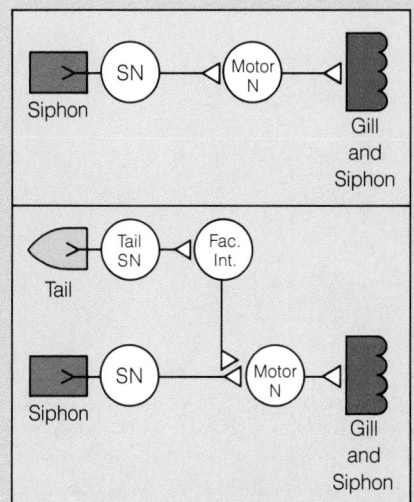

FIGURE 2
Neural Circuits for Habituation and Sensitization *The top panel illustrates the connection between a single sensory neuron (SN) and a single motor neuron (Motor N) for the gill-withdrawal reflex. Stimulation of the siphon excites the sensory neuron, which in turn excites the motor neuron to innervate the gill. Habituation of gill withdrawal is mediated by a change at the synaptic connection between the sensory and motor neurons. The bottom panel illustrates the connections involved in sensitization of gill withdrawal. Now, stimulation of the tail excites a facilitator interneuron (Fac. int.), which facilitates the impulse being sent from the siphon's sensory neuron.*

likelihood that the action will be repeated depends on the nature of its consequences. The baby will coo more often if each such occurrence is followed by parental attention, and the dog will pick up the ball more often if this action is followed by petting or a food reward. If we think of the baby as having a goal of parental attention, and the dog as having a goal of food, then operant conditioning amounts to learning that a particular behavior leads to attaining a particular goal (Rescorla, 1987).

Law of Effect

The study of operant conditioning began at the turn of the century with a series of experiments by E. L. Thorndike (1898). A typical experiment proceeded as follows. A hungry cat is placed in a cage whose door is held fast by a simple latch, and a piece of fish is placed just outside the cage. Initially, the cat tries to reach the food by extending its paws through the bars. When this fails, the cat moves about the cage, engaging in a variety of different behaviors. At some point it inadvertently hits the latch, frees itself, and eats the fish. The researchers then place the cat back in its cage and put a new piece of fish outside. The cat goes through roughly the same set of behaviors until once more it happens to hit the latch. The procedure is repeated again and again. Over trials, the cat eliminates many of its irrelevant behaviors, eventually efficiently opening the latch and freeing itself as soon as it is placed in the cage. The cat has learned to open the latch in order to obtain food.

It may sound as if the cat is acting intelligently, but Thorndike argued that there is little "intelligence" operative here. There is no moment in time at which the cat seems to have an insight about the solution to its problem. Instead, the cat's performance improves gradually over trials. Even if at one point the experimenter places the cat's paw on the latch and pushes it down, thereby demonstrating the solution, the cat's progress continues to be slow. Rather than insight, the cat appears to be engaging in *trial-and-error* behavior, and when a reward immediately follows one of these behaviors, the learning of the action is strengthened. Thorndike referred to this strengthening as the *law of effect*. He argued that in operant learning, the law of effect selects from a set of random responses just the responses that are followed by positive consequences. The process is similar to evolution, in which the law of *survival of the fittest* selects from a set of random species variations just the changes that promote survival of the species. The law of effect, then, promotes the survival of the *fittest responses* (Schwartz, 1984).

Skinner's Experiments

B. F. Skinner has been responsible for a number of changes in how researchers conceptualize and study operant conditioning. His method of studying operant conditioning is simpler than Thorndike's and has been widely accepted.

In a Skinnerian experiment, a hungry animal—usually a rat or a pigeon—is placed in a box like the one shown in Figure 7-6, which is popularly called a "Skinner box." The inside of the box is bare except for a protruding bar with a food dish beneath it. A small light above the bar can be turned on at the experimenter's discretion. Left alone in the box, the rat moves about, exploring. Occasionally it inspects the bar and presses it. The rate at which the rat first presses the bar is the baseline level of bar pressing. After establishing the baseline level, the experimenter activates a food magazine located outside the box. Now, every time the rat presses the bar, a small food pellet is released into the dish. The rat eats the food pellet and soon presses the bar again; the food *reinforces* bar pressing, and the rate of pressing increases dramatically. If the food magazine is disconnected so that pressing the bar no longer delivers food, the rate of bar pressing will diminish. Hence, an operantly conditioned response (or, simply, an *operant*) undergoes *extinction* with nonreinforcement just as a classically conditioned response does. The experimenter can set up a *discrimination* test by presenting food only if the rat presses the bar while the light is on, hence conditioning the rat through selective reinforcement. In this example, the light serves as a *discriminative stimulus* that controls the response.

FIGURE 7-6
Apparatus for Operant Conditioning *The photograph shows a Skinner box with a magazine for delivering food pellets. The computer is used to control the experiment and record the rat's responses.*

Thus, operant conditioning increases the likelihood of a response by following the behavior with a reinforcer (often something that can satisfy a basic drive). Experimenters can measure the strength of an operantly conditioned response (or, simply, *response strength*) in different ways. Because the bar is always present in the Skinner box, the rat can respond to it as frequently or infrequently as it chooses; the organism's *rate of response* is therefore a useful measure of response strength (that is, the more frequently the response occurs during a given time interval, the greater its strength). Another possible measure of response strength is the *total number of responses during extinction*: the more times the rat presses the bar, even though the experimenter is withholding reward, the greater the strength of the response (Skinner, 1938).

As is the case in classical conditioning, the temporal relations between the events in a trial are important. In particular, immediate reinforcement is more effective than delayed; the more time between an operant and a reinforcer, the less the response strength. Many developmental psychologists have noted that the delay of reinforcement is an important factor in dealing with young children. If a child acts kindly to a pet, the act can best be strengthened by praising (rewarding) the child immediately, rather than waiting until later. Similarly, if a child hits someone without provocation, this aggressive behavior will more likely be eliminated if the child is reprimanded immediately, rather than waiting until later.

B. F. Skinner.

Conditioning in Different Species

Although rats and pigeons have been the favored experimental subjects, operant conditioning applies to many species, including our own. A particularly illuminating instance of operant conditioning in human behavior is illustrated by the following case. A young boy had temper tantrums if he did not get enough attention from his parents, especially at bedtime. Since the parents eventually responded, their attention probably reinforced the tantrums. To eliminate the tantrums, the parents were advised to go through the normal bedtime rituals and then to ignore the child's protests, painful though that might be. By withholding the reinforcer (the attention), the tantrums should extinguish—which is just what happened. The time the child spent crying at bedtime decreased from 45 minutes to not at all over a period of only 7 days (Williams, 1959).

Operant conditioning applies to many responses. For years, psychologists believed that operant conditioning occurred only with voluntary behavior (responses of skeletal muscles mediated by the somatic nervous system) and not with involuntary responses (responses of glands and viscera mediated by the autonomic nervous system). Responses mediated by the autonomic nervous system were thought to be susceptible to classical conditioning but not operant conditioning. Researchers successfully challenged this belief by ingeniously demonstrating that heart rate and other visceral responses can be operantly conditioned.

It might seem that life already provides such demonstrations, since some people—yogis in India and other Eastern countries, for example—are reputed to be able to control their heart rates. Yogis can indeed control their heart rate, but they do it *indirectly* by manipulating their skeletal muscles, specifically those in their chest and abdomen (see Kimble & Perlmuter, 1970). We are interested in the possibility of *directly* controlling heart rate.

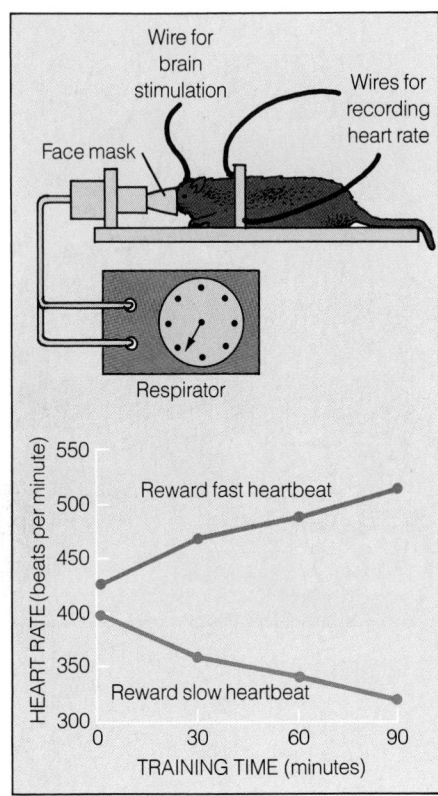

FIGURE 7-7
Operant Conditioning of Heart Rate *The top panel gives a schematic view of an apparatus used to study operant conditioning of heart rate. The rat, paralyzed by* curare, *is kept alive by a respirator. Reinforcement is administered through wires for brain stimulation; other wires record the rat's heart rate. The bottom panel shows the results of the experiment: heart rate increases when rats are reinforced for an increase and decreases when they are reinforced for a decrease. (After DiCara, 1970)*

Think of the difficulties in demonstrating such direct control. The organism's skeletal muscles must be paralyzed (to prevent indirect control); but then how is the organism to breathe since skeletal muscles are needed in breathing? And if the organism is paralyzed, what kind of reinforcer can it enjoy? Some remarkable experiments by Miller and his colleagues overcame these difficulties (for example, Miller, 1969) (see Figure 7-7). They injected rats with *curare*, a drug that paralyzes skeletal muscle but does not affect visceral reactions. An artificial respirator maintained the animals' breathing, and electrical stimulation of regions of the brain known to be associated with a feeling of reward served as reinforcement. Some animals were reinforced when their heart rate decreased; others were reinforced when their heart rate increased. The procedure worked: heart rate changed in accordance with reinforcement (see Figure 7-7). Experimenters have conditioned other autonomic responses using similar procedures. For example, curarized rats have learned to relax or contract their lower intestines.

These results have great practical implications. Human subjects have been trained by operant methods to control such autonomic responses as heart rate, blood pressure, and the secretion of stomach acids that may produce ulcers. To control blood pressure, for example, the individual watches a machine that provides continuous visual feedback about blood pressure. Whenever the blood pressure falls below a specified level, a light flashes. The subject then analyzes whatever he or she was thinking or doing when the blood pressure dropped and tries to repeat that thought or emotion to keep the blood pressure low. This procedure is called *biofeedback* training: the subject is given information (feedback) about some aspect of his or her biological state and is reinforced for altering that state.

The medical applications of such research are obvious. People with high blood pressure are better off learning to control it themselves than depending on medications that are only partially successful and that may have undesirable side effects. In addition to their use with high blood pressure, biofeedback techniques have been successfully used with a host of other disorders, such as cardiovascular disorders, migraine headaches, and visceral problems that range from the treatment of stomach ulcers in adults to toilet training children who have difficulty controlling their bowels (Miller, 1985). What is particularly noteworthy about these applications is that they were spawned by intricate experiments that used rats as subjects and were designed to demonstrate a scholarly point. The practical benefits of pure research are often difficult to foresee.

Critical Phenomena

The following phenomena increase the generality of operant conditioning.

CONDITIONER REINFORCERS Most of the reinforcers we have discussed are called *primary* because, like food, they satisfy basic drives. If operant conditioning occurred only with primary reinforcers, it would not be that common in our lives because primary reinforcers are not that common. However, virtually any stimulus can become a *secondary* or *conditioned* reinforcer by being consistently paired with a primary reinforcer; conditioned reinforcers greatly increase the range of operant conditioning (just as second-order conditioning greatly increases the range of classical conditioning).

A minor variation in the typical operant-conditioning experiment illustrates how conditioned reinforcement works. When a rat in a Skinner box presses a lever, a tone sounds momentarily, followed shortly by a delivery of food (the food is a primary reinforcer; the tone will become a conditioned reinforcer). After the animal has been conditioned in this way, the experimenter begins extinction, so that when the rat presses the lever neither the tone nor the food occurs. In time, the animal virtually ceases to press the lever. Then the tone is reconnected but not the food. When the animal discovers that pressing the lever turns on the tone, its rate of pressing markedly increases, overcoming the extinction even though no food follows. The tone has acquired a reinforcing quality of its own through classical conditioning; because the tone was reliably paired with food, it came to signal food.

Our lives abound with conditioned reinforcers. Two of the most prevalent are money and praise. Presumably, money is a powerful reinforcer because it has been paired so frequently with so many primary reinforcers—we can buy food, drink, and comfort, to mention just a few of the obvious things. And mere praise, without even the promise of a primary reinforcer, can sustain many an activity.

GENERALIZATION AND DISCRIMINATION   What was true for classical conditioning holds for operant conditioning as well: organisms generalize what they have learned, although generalization can be curbed by discrimination training. If a young child is reinforced by her parents for petting the family dog, she will soon generalize this petting response to other dogs. Since this can be dangerous (say, the neighbors have a vicious watchdog), the child's parents may provide some discrimination training, so that she is reinforced when she pets the family dog but not the neighbor's.

SHAPING   Suppose you want to use operant conditioning to teach your dog a trick—for instance, to press a buzzer with its nose. You cannot wait until the dog does this naturally (and then reinforce it), because you may wait forever. When the desired behavior is truly novel, you have to condition it by taking advantage of natural variations in the animal's actions. To train a dog to press a buzzer with its nose, you can give the animal a food reinforcer each time it approaches the area of the buzzer, requiring it to move closer and closer to the desired spot for each reinforcer until finally the dog's nose is touching the buzzer. This technique of reinforcing only the responses that meet the experimenter's specifications and extinguishing all others is called *shaping* the animal's behavior.

Animals can be taught elaborate tricks and routines by means of shaping. Two psychologists and their staff have trained thousands of animals of many species for television shows, commercials, and county fairs (Breland & Breland, 1966). One popular show featured "Priscilla, the Fastidious Pig." Priscilla turned on the TV set, ate breakfast at a table, picked up dirty clothes and put them in a hamper, vacuumed the floor, picked out her favorite food (from among foods competing with that of her sponsor!), and took part in a quiz program, answering questions from the audience by flashing lights that indicated yes or no. She was not an unusually bright pig; in fact, because pigs grow so fast, a new "Priscilla" was trained every 3 to 5 months. The ingenuity was not the pig's but the experimenters', who used operant conditioning and shaped the behavior to produce the desired result. Pigeons have been trained by the shaping of operant responses to locate persons lost at sea (see Figure 7-8), and porpoises have been trained to retrieve underwater equipment.

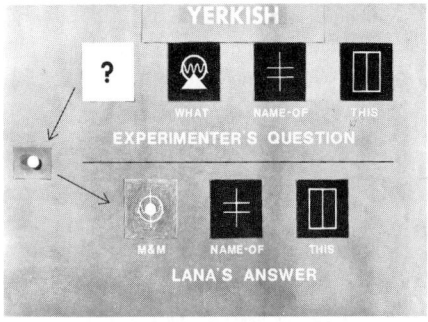

Animals have been taught very complex responses by means of shaping techniques. At the Yerkes Primate Research Center in Atlanta, a chimpanzee named Lana has learned to answer questions and to make requests by pressing symbols on a computer console. At bottom is an example of how the experiment works. A researcher outside the room asked Lana a question by pressing the symbols on the console for the words "What name of this" and also holding up candy. The chimpanzee answered by pressing the symbols for "M & M name of this."

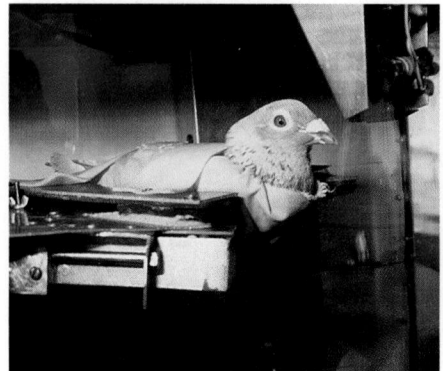

Pigeon sitting

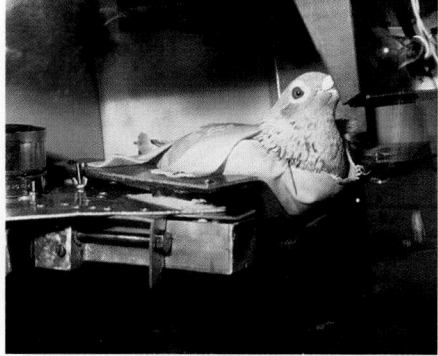

Pigeon pecking key

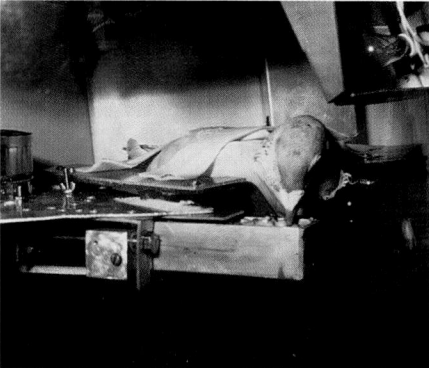

Pigeon rewarded

FIGURE 7-8
Search and Rescue by Pigeons *The Coast Guard has used pigeons to search for people lost at sea. The pigeons are trained, using shaping methods, to spot the color orange—the international color of life jackets. Three pigeons are strapped into a plexiglass chamber attached to the underside of a helicopter. The chamber is divided into thirds so that each bird faces a different direction. When a pigeon spots an orange object, or any other object, it pecks a key that buzzes the pilot. The pilot then heads in the direction indicated by the bird that responded. Pigeons are better suited than people for the task of spotting distant objects at sea. They can stare over the water for a long time without suffering eye fatigue, have excellent color vision, and can focus on a 60- to 80-degree area, whereas a person can only focus on a 2- to 3-degree area. (After Simmons, 1981)*

AUTOSHAPING   Thus far, the phenomena of operant conditioning have been distinct from those of classical conditioning. But there are cases of behavior that appear to be determined by principles of both operant and classical conditioning. One is *autoshaping*. A hungry pigeon, never before an experimental subject, is placed in a chamber. A key in the chamber is lit once every minute for 6 seconds. When the light is turned off (by the automated apparatus), a bit of food is provided. The key then remains unlit for 54 seconds, turns on again, and so on. Note that food is delivered independent of the pigeon's behavior toward the key; that is, food appears whenever the light goes off whether or not the pigeon pecks the key. Nonetheless, after a few trials the pigeon begins to peck the key as soon as it is lit. The procedure is called *autoshaping* because it does not require an experimenter as shaping does (Brown & Jenkins, 1968).

Classical conditioning is involved in autoshaping: by virtue of repeated pairings of light and food, the light becomes a conditioned stimulus (CS) for the response to food (pecking, the UCR). Once the pigeon pecks the lit key, it is given food almost immediately, as in an operant-conditioning experiment. Hence, it is likely that operant conditioning serves to maintain an autoshaped response.

It seems that by pairing the lit key with food, the light comes to substitute for food and the pigeon responds to the light in a manner similar to the way it responds to food. Photographs of a pigeon's autoshaped pecks support this notion (see Figure 7-9). When the beak hits the key, it is positioned as if seizing food when food is the reinforcer but *not* when water is the reinforcer. Thus, stimuli paired with food come to elicit the same response as the food itself, as in classical conditioning (Schwartz & Gamzu, 1977).

PARTIAL REINFORCEMENT   In real life, every instance of a behavior is rarely reinforced—sometimes hard work is followed by praise, but often it goes unacknowledged. If operant conditioning occurred only with continuous reinforcement, it might play a limited role in our lives. It turns out, however, that a behavior can be conditioned and maintained when it is reinforced only a fraction of the time. This phenomenon is known as *partial reinforcement*, and it can be illustrated in the laboratory by a pigeon who learns to peck at a key for food. Once this operant is established, the pigeon continues to peck at a high rate, even if it receives only occasional reinforcement. In some cases, pigeons who were rewarded with food on the average of once every 5 minutes (12 times an hour) pecked at the key as often as 6,000 times per hour!

Extinction following the acquisition of a response on partial reinforcement is much slower than extinction following the acquisition of a response on continuous reinforcement. This phenomenon is known as the *partial-reinforcement effect*. It makes intuitive sense because there is less difference between extinction and acquisition when reinforcement during acquisition is only partial. Human examples are plentiful. If a slot machine is broken, gamblers may still insert hundreds of coins into it, for they are accustomed to infrequent payoffs. When a food machine fails to operate, however, rarely will people insert more than one extra coin because vending machines operate on a continuous-reinforcement basis.

Other examples of partial reinforcement can be seen in child rearing. A parent who *occasionally* reinforces a child's temper tantrums by giving in to the child is ensuring more potent and more persistent tantrums than the parent who *always* gives in. The child with a history of partial reinforcement of tantrums will "throw" them with remarkable persistence even when the parent attempts to extinguish the tantrums by ignoring them.

Importance of Control

As was the case in classical conditioning, we want to know what factor is critical for operant conditioning to occur. Again, one of the options is temporal contiguity: an operant is conditioned whenever reinforcement immediately follows the behavior (Skinner, 1948). Another option, closely related to predictability, is that of *control*: an operant is conditioned only when the organism interprets the reinforcement as being dependent on its response. Some important experiments by Maier and Seligman (1976) provide more support for the control view than for the temporal contiguity view.

Their basic experiment includes two stages. In the first stage, some dogs learn that whether they receive a shock or not depends on (is controlled by) their behavior, while other dogs learn that they have no control over the shock. Think of the dogs as being tested in pairs. Both members of a pair are in a harness that restricts their movements, and occasionally they receive an electric shock. One member of the pair, the "control" dog, can turn off the

FIGURE 7-9
Water and Food Autoshaped Responses *The two photographs show the autoshaped responses of a pigeon at the moment of contact with the key. The top response is to a key paired with food, whereas the bottom response is to a key paired with water. The pigeon's beak movements are clearly different in the two situations. The top photo resembles a pigeon eating, whereas the bottom photo resembles a pigeon drinking. The pigeon appears to "eat" the key when working for food and "drink" the key when working for water. (After Jenkins & Moore, 1973)*

shock by pushing a nearby panel with its nose; the other member of the pair, the "yoked" dog, cannot exercise any control over the shock. Whenever the control dog is shocked, so is the yoked dog; and whenever the control dog turns off the shock, the yoked dog's shock is also terminated. The control and yoked dogs therefore receive exactly the same number of shocks.

In the second stage of the study, experimenters place both dogs in a new apparatus—a box divided into two compartments by a barrier. On each trial a tone is first sounded, indicating that the compartment that the dog currently occupies is about to be subject to electric shock. To avoid shock, the dogs must learn to jump the barrier into the other compartment when they hear the warning tone. Control dogs learn this response rapidly, but the yoked dogs are another story: initially they make no movement across the barrier, and as trials progress their behavior becomes increasingly passive, lapsing finally into utter helplessness. Why? Because during the first stage the yoked dogs learned that shocks were not under their control, and this belief in noncontrol made conditioning in the second stage impossible. If a belief in noncontrol makes operant conditioning impossible, then a belief in control must be what makes it possible. Many other experiments support the notion that operant conditioning occurs only when the organism perceives reinforcement as being under its control (Seligman, 1975).

NATURE OF REINFORCEMENT

We have talked about reinforcement as if it is an all-or-none property of an event—food has the property of reinforcement but a light does not. We have also talked as if a reinforcer is always positive (again, food is a good example). In addition, we have focused on reinforcers at the behavioral level rather than at the physiological level. This description of reinforcement is somewhat misleading:

1. Whether or not an event is reinforcing can be determined only *relative* to the activity it reinforces.
2. Negative or *aversive* events, such as shock or painful noise, also have dramatic effects on behavior.
3. Electrical stimulation of the brain can be as reinforcing as food or other behavioral reinforcers.

These three aspects of reinforcement are considered in the following discussion.

Relativity of Reinforcement

It is natural to think of reinforcement as an all-or-none property of stimuli or events. But it is more useful to think of reinforcers as *activities*; it is not the food pellet that reinforces lever pressing, but the eating of the pellet. What must be the relation between the two activities such that one reinforces the other?

PREMACK'S PRINCIPLE According to David Premack (1959), any activity that an organism performs can reinforce any other activity that the organism engages in less frequently. For example, Premack offered children

the choice of operating a pinball machine or eating candy. Children who preferred eating candy would increase their rate of playing the pinball machine if playing the machine led to eating candy; thus, eating candy reinforced playing pinball. For children who preferred playing pinball, however, the reverse was true: they increased their intake of candy only if this increased their chance to play pinball.

From this experiment, Premack developed a two-tiered conception of reinforcement: a) for any organism, a reinforcement hierarchy exists in which reinforcers at the top of the hierarchy are those activities engaged in with greatest likelihood, given the opportunity; and b) any activity in the hierarchy may be reinforced (made more likely) by any activity above it— and may itself reinforce any activity below it. This second statement is *Premack's principle*. It expresses a technique that has long been applied by parents who require a child to do homework before going out to play rather than letting the child play first provided he or she agrees to do the homework later.

Teachers have also used Premack's principle in classrooms to give them control over children's activities. Allowing students to play after successfully completing a writing assignment, for example, has enhanced their writing abilities. Even 3-year-old nursery school children have responded well to use of the principle. For these students, activities high on their reinforcement hierarchies included screaming and running around the room. These reinforcing activities were permitted if the children first displayed the desired behavior. For example, the behavior of sitting quietly while attending to the blackboard was followed occasionally by the sounding of a bell and the instruction "run and scream" (which was duly followed). After a few days, the teachers achieved virtually perfect control of classroom behavior (Homme et al., 1963).

IMPORTANCE OF DEPRIVATION   Is the reinforcement hierarchy stable or does it change according to the organism's motivational state? Although eating candy did not reinforce pinball playing in the children who preferred pinball over candy, Premack found that when the children became sufficiently hungry, the reinforcement relation reversed: eating candy came to reinforce pinball playing. Premack (1962) also found similar results in more

The threat of punishment is an effective motivator.

extensive studies with rats: a thirsty rat will run in order to drink, whereas a long-idle rat will drink for the opportunity to run in a running wheel. Other studies give an even greater role to deprivation in determining the reinforcement potency of an activity. Whenever an organism is deprived of its usual amount of a naturally occurring activity, such as running for rats, that activity becomes a more potent reinforcer (Timberlake & Allison, 1974).

Punishment

We have focused primarily on cases in which a behavior leads to a positive event or *reward* and have only briefly mentioned cases in which a behavior leads to an aversive event or *punisher*. But punishers have dramatic effects on behavior and therefore deserve our attention.

Suppose a young child is learning to draw with crayons; if he is slapped on the hand whenever he draws on the walls, he will learn not to do so. Similarly, if a rat learning to run a maze is shocked whenever it chooses a wrong path, it will soon learn to avoid past mistakes. In both cases, punishment is used to decrease the likelihood of an undesirable behavior. *

Although punishment can suppress an unwanted response, it has several significant disadvantages. First, its effects are not as predictable as the results of reward. Reward essentially says, "Repeat what you have done"; punishment says, "Stop it!" but fails to give an alternative. As a result, the organism may substitute an even less desirable response for the punished one. Second, the by-products of punishment may be unfortunate. Punishment often leads to dislike or fear of the punishing person (parent, teacher, or employer) and of the situation (home, school, or office) in which the punishment occurred. Finally, an extreme or painful punishment may elicit aggressive behavior that is more serious than the original undesirable behavior.

These cautions do not mean that punishment should never be employed. It can effectively eliminate an undesirable response if the available alternative responses are rewarded. Rats that have learned to take the shorter of two paths in a maze to reach food will quickly switch to the longer one if they are shocked in the shorter path. The temporary suppression produced by punishment provides the opportunity for the rat to learn to take the longer path. In this case, punishment is an effective means of redirecting behavior because it is informative, and this seems to be the key to the humane and effective use of punishment. A child who gets a shock from an electrical appliance may learn which connections are safe and which are hazardous; a teacher's corrections of a student's paper can be regarded as punishing, but they are also informative and can provide an occasion for learning.

Brain Stimulation as Reinforcement

Thus far the reinforcers we have considered tend to be defined at the behavioral level, things like food (or eating) and shock (or avoiding shock). But reinforcers can also be defined at the physiological level.

---

* It is worth noting the relation between the terms *reward* and *punisher* on the one hand, and *positive* and *negative reinforcers* on the other. *Reward* is sometimes used synonymously with *positive reinforcer*— an event whose occurrence following a response increases the probability of that response. But a *punisher* is not the same as a *negative reinforcer*. Negative reinforcement means termination of an aversive event following a response; this increases the probability of that response. Punishment has the opposite effect: it decreases the probability of a response.

REWARDING AND PUNISHING STIMULATION   In the 1950s, James Olds and Peter Milner made the startling discovery that electrical stimulation of certain regions of the brain can be reinforcing. Olds and Milner were investigating the rat's brain with microelectrodes. These tiny electrodes can be implanted permanently in specific brain areas without interfering with the rat's health or normal activity. When connected with an electrical source, they can supply stimulation of varying intensities to a very localized site in the brain. The researchers accidentally implanted an electrode in an area near the hypothalamus and delivered a very mild current through the electrodes. The animal repeatedly returned to the place in the cage where it had been when stimulated. Further stimulations at the same cage location caused the animal to spend most of its time there. Later, Olds and Milner found that other animals with electrodes implanted in the same region of the brain learned to press a bar in a Skinner box to produce their own electrical stimulation (see Figure 7-10). These animals pressed the bar at a phenomenal rate: a not unusual record would show an average of over 2,000 responses an hour for 15 or 20 hours, until the animal finally collapsed from exhaustion.

Since the initial discovery, experiments with microelectrodes implanted in many different areas of the brain and brain stem have been carried out using rats, cats, and monkeys in a wide variety of tasks. The reinforcing effects of stimulation in certain areas (primarily the hypothalamus) are powerful. In some situations, if given a choice between food and electric brain stimulation in a *T-maze* (a maze that has a straight runway ending in two armlike corridors that the animal must choose between—see Figure 7-11), even hungry rats may choose the arm that offers brain stimulation. On the other hand, stimulation of certain areas of the brain stem serves as a *punisher*. When the electrodes were moved to these different brain areas, rats that had previously pressed the bar at a rapid rate to receive stimulation suddenly stopped responding and avoided the bar entirely. Apparently the new stimulation was unpleasant. And other animals have learned various responses to terminate stimulation in these areas—for example, pressing a lever to turn *off* the current. Considerable progress has been made in mapping the neutral, punishing, and reinforcing areas of the brain (Carr & Coons, 1982).

Part of the significance of brain stimulation studies lies in their potential to reveal the anatomical and neurological bases of reinforcement in general. It would be convenient for us to think that these studies map the anatomical location of reinforcement; that when we stimulate one brain area in a rat, the sensations are similar to those experienced when the animal is reinforced with food, and that the sensations in another area are similar to reinforcement with water. Unfortunately, the rat cannot describe its sensations. What data we have on human subjects are sparse and come from patients with abnormal conditions (such as epilepsy or the intractable pain of terminal cancer), so the results cannot be readily generalized to normal individuals. These patients report feeling relief from pain and anxiety and feeling "wonderful," "happy," and "drunk" following stimulation of certain areas of the limbic system (Campbell, 1973).

REWARD AND THE MOTOR SYSTEM   There are, however, some difficulties in interpreting studies of brain stimulation. In some experiments, brain stimulation may affect the nearby motor system, as well as the reward system. Consequently, in these studies the high rates of responding obtained with stimulation may reflect heightened motor activity (Stellar & Stellar, 1985). Evidence for this comes from experiments in which two different levels of stimulation were used. The stimulation level that rats responded to

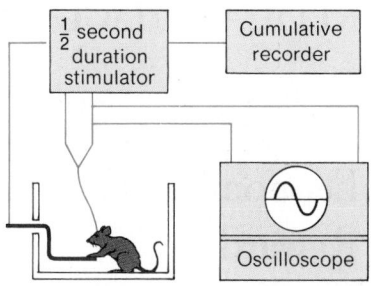

FIGURE 7-10
Brain Stimulation *The animal's bar-press delivers a 60-cycle current for half a second, after which the animal must release the bar and press again for more current. The animal's response rate is recorded on the cumulative recorder, and the delivery of the current is monitored by means of the oscilloscope. Rats respond with rates up to 100 bar presses per minute when they have electrodes in the medial-forebrain region of the hypothalamus.*

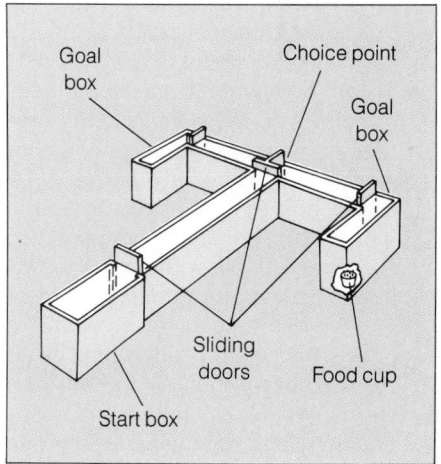

FIGURE 7-11
T-Maze *A maze used in the study of simple choice learning. The sliding doors (which usually are operated by a system of strings and pulleys from above) prevent the animal from retracing its path once it has made a choice. Note that the goal boxes are arranged so that the rat cannot see what is in them from the choice point.*

CRITICAL DISCUSSION

Economics of Reward

The simple operant experiments that we have discussed fail to capture an important aspect of human behavior: many responses that we make represent a *choice* among alternatives. To study choice, operant researchers use experiments in which the animal has at least two responses. The choices that the animal has may differ in their reinforcer or in their schedule of reinforcement, or both. To illustrate, a pigeon may have a choice between two keys, where pecks on one key produce food and pecks on the other, water; alternatively, both keys may lead to food but may have different *schedules*, so that one key may require five pecks for a reinforcement while the other may require ten.

In analyzing behavior in choice experiments, researchers have found that some concepts and principles of economics are useful (Rachlin, 1980). To see the relation between economic principles and pigeons pecking keys, note that a pigeon in a choice experiment can be thought of as having to choose how to distribute its limited responses—its resources—and that economic theory deals with questions about how to allocate one's limited resources.

We will illustrate the economic approach to operant conditioning by discussing three examples. In each case, we first provide the relevant economic principles and then consider their application to operant experiments.

DEMAND CURVES An important concept in economics is that of *demand* for a commodity; this is the amount of the commodity—say, bread or chocolate—that will be purchased at a given price. If we change the price, we generate a *demand curve* like those presented in Figure 1. Note that the curve for chocolate decreases sharply as price is increased; the more it costs, the

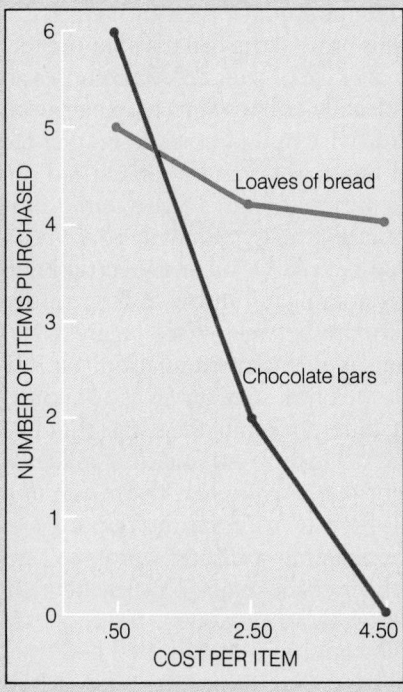

FIGURE 1

Hypothetical Demand Curves for Bread and Chocolate *As the price of a loaf of bread increases from $.50 to $4.50, the amount of bread purchased decreases hardly at all; the demand for bread is inelastic. In contrast, as the price of a chocolate bar increases from $.50 to $4.50, the amount purchased decreases sharply; the demand for chocolate is elastic.*

less chocolate we will buy. The demand for chocolate is therefore said to be *elastic*. In contrast, the curve for bread is barely affected by price; we will purchase roughly the same amount of bread regardless of its cost. Thus, the demand for bread is *inelastic*. All of this conforms to the belief that bread is a necessity and chocolate a luxury.

Consider now the relevance of this to operant conditioning. For rats and pigeons, the equivalent of price is the number of responses that must be made to obtain a reinforcer (which is the *schedule of reinforcement*). This equivalence is illustrated in Figure 2, which includes a rat's demand curve for food. The curve tells us how much food (reinforcement) a rat will "purchase" (work to obtain) at different "prices" (schedules of reinforcement). Rats purchase the same amount of food reinforcements regardless of whether they are rewarded after every two or every eight responses: the demand curve for food is inelastic. The other demand curve in Figure 2 is for brain stimulation. The demand for brain stimulation is clearly elastic, because the amount purchased decreases sharply with price (the number of responses required for a reinforcement).

The curves in Figure 2 have implications for questions about the nature of reinforcement. It is natural to ask whether one kind of reinforcement is more or less potent than another, say, food versus brain stimulation. In the past, researchers interested in this question had devised an experiment in which one response leads to food reinforcement, another leads to brain stimulation, and both are on the same schedule of reinforcement. As Figure 2 makes clear, the results from such an experiment will depend entirely on the choice of the schedule. Specifically

more was not always the one they preferred if offered a choice. The level that led to the higher response rate may have done so because it activated the motor system, while the other level may have actually been the more rewarding level. Brain stimulation has also been shown to produce an aftereffect consisting of a general motor arousal, which makes subsequent

when a reinforcement requires two responses, brain stimulation is the overwhelming choice, but at higher prices (eight responses) food is slightly preferred. The question of which reinforcer is more potent only has a straightforward answer when the demand for both reinforcers is inelastic, or when the demand for both are elastic and their demand curves are the same (Hirsh & Natelson, 1981).

SUBSTITUTABILITY OF COMMODITIES

An economic analysis of choice considers the interactions between the choices. Suppose we are interested in a choice between gasoline and public transportation. Because the demand curves for both commodities are elastic, we expect that when gas prices increase, people more often choose public transportation. This of course is what happens, but it does so because gas and public transportation can *substitute* for one another. In contrast, consider the choice between gas and inexpensive downtown parking, where the two commodities *complement* one another (the more you have of one commodity, the more you want of the other). Now, increases in gas prices will no longer lead to increases in the preference for the other commodity.

Similarly, operant studies of choice must consider whether the two reinforcers substitute for or complement one another. Suppose a pigeon can peck at either of two keys, and both are associated with food reinforcement. The reinforcers, therefore, are substitutes. Consequently, if we give one key a lower price (it requires only five responses per reinforcement, for instance, while the other key requires 10), the pigeon will increase its pecks to the lower price key and de-

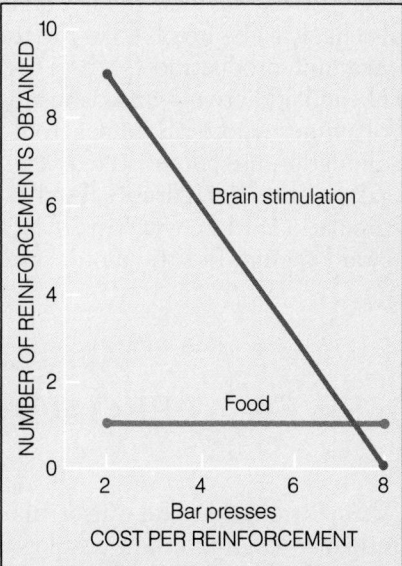

FIGURE 2
Demand Curves for Food and Brain-Stimulation Reinforcers *As the "price" of a food pellet increased from two to eight bar presses, the amount of food reinforcement the rats obtained was essentially unchanged; the demand for food is inelastic. In contrast, as the price of brain stimulation increased from two to eight presses, the amount of reinforcement obtained decreased substantially; the demand for brain stimulation is elastic. (After Hirsh & Natelson, 1981)*

crease its pecks to the more expensive one. In contrast, if the reinforcers are food and water, which are complements, and we lower the price on the key leading to food, the pigeon will peck at both keys more often (the more it eats, the more it wants to drink). The influence of price differences on choice, therefore, depends on the relation between the commodities (Schwartz, 1982).

OPEN VERSUS CLOSED SYSTEM

The economic principles that we have discussed so far hold only in a *closed system*—that is, in a situation in which there are no alternative sources of the commodities. We can illustrate this concept with a commodity like soda, which has an elastic demand. A decrease in the price of soda should lead you to purchase more, but this is true only if you have no way of obtaining soda other than buying it at market prices. Should you have a benefactor who will supply you for free, there is no reason why your purchases should follow price changes; in this case we are in an *open system*, and the concept of demand does not apply.

There is a parallel to this in operant research. An operant experiment that uses, say, food reinforcement can be performed in two different ways, which correspond to open and closed systems. In the open-system version, if an animal does not obtain enough food reinforcement during an experimental session, it is given a supplement before the next session; the animal has an alternative way of obtaining the desired commodity. In the closed-system version of the experiment, there are no between-session supplements. If the reinforcement schedule is made increasingly demanding (100 rather than 50 responses are required for reinforcement), the resulting behaviors seem to differ for the two versions of the study. In the open-system version, the amount of reinforcement purchased decreases with very demanding schedules; this does not fit with the idea that the demand for food is inelastic. In the closed-system version, the amount of reinforcement purchased often is the same regardless of the schedule, which is exactly what should happen if the demand for food is inelastic (Schwartz, 1982).

responding to receive electrical stimulation more likely and more vigorous (Gallistel, 1973).

The evidence that brain stimulation affects both the reward and motor systems fits nicely with the hypothesis that the effects of brain stimulation are mediated by the neurotransmitter *dopamine* (Wise, 1984). Dopamine is known to be involved in motor functioning. Dopamine loss is a major cause of *Parkinson's disease*, which is a syndrome that includes such motoric disfunctions as muscular rigidity and resting tremors. Dopamine production is also likely to be involved in the reward system, because drugs that stimulate dopamine production (such as cocaine and amphetamines) can be pleasurable and addictive—and dangerous. Perhaps the strongest evidence for the dopamine hypothesis comes from studies in which animals receiving brain stimulation are administered *neuroleptics*, drugs that disrupt the production of dopamine. Such drugs substantially reduce the rate of responding for brain stimulation. Moreover, this reduction in response is due to changes in the reward system, not the motor system (Stellar & Stellar, 1985).

NEWER APPROACHES

We mentioned at the outset that in recent years many researchers have turned to cognitive and ethological approaches to conditioning. To some extent, both of these newer approaches developed as reactions to the behaviorist approach. The ethologists (biologists and psychologists who study animal behavior in the natural environment) claim that the laws of learning are not the same for all species; indeed, they differ even within a species for different situations. The cognitive psychologists believe that behavior, even for animals, can be understood only by considering internal factors, such as goals and mental representations, as well as external factors. We will consider these challenges in turn.

Ethological Approach

Although both ethologists and behaviorists are concerned with the behavior of animals, the two approaches differ in a number of respects. For one, ethologists usually study behavior by observing it in the natural environment, rather than by analyzing it in the laboratory, as is generally the case for behaviorists. Another difference is that ethologists place greater emphasis on evolution and genetics than on learning, while behaviorists do the reverse. In some cases, this difference in emphasis leads to a difference in what is studied—ethologists focusing on unlearned, innate behaviors, and behaviorists on learned ones. In other cases, this difference in emphasis leads to a clash of views: when ethologists turn their attention to learning, they argue that it is rigidly constrained by an animal's genetic endowment; behaviorists, on the other hand, assume that the laws of learning are the same for different species. As ethologists put it, when an animal learns, it must conform to a genetically determined "behavioral blueprint"; just as an architectural blueprint imposes constraints on the kinds of functions that a building may serve, so a behavioral blueprint imposes genetic constraints on the kinds of associations that an organism may learn. That is, animals are pre-programmed to learn particular things in particular ways.

Some early support for the ethological view came from psychologists who were using operant techniques to teach animals tricks. These trainers reported that instead of learning the desired trick, occasionally the animal learned something else that was closer to one of its instinctive behaviors. In one case, the trainers tried to get a chicken to stand still on a platform, but the chicken insisted on scratching the ground instead. Scratching the ground is related to the chicken's instinctual food-gathering behavior, which successfully competed with the behavior that the trainers were trying to instill. Thus, an instinct sets limits on what could be acquired. In other cases, an animal would succeed initially in learning the desired response only to drift later to a response that was an instinctual food-gathering behavior of its particular species (Breland & Breland, 1961).

CONSTRAINTS IN CLASSICAL CONDITIONING   Some of the best evidence for constraints in conditioning comes from studies of *taste aversion*. In a typical study, a rat is permitted to drink a flavored solution—say, vanilla. After drinking it, the rat is mildly poisoned and made ill. When the rat recovers, it is again presented the vanilla solution. Now the rat scrupulously avoids the solution because it has learned to associate the vanilla taste with poison. There is good evidence that such avoidance is an instance of classical conditioning: the initial taste of the solution is the CS, the feeling of being sick is the UCS, and after conditioning, the taste signals that sickness is on its way.

According to the behaviorist perspective, a light or a sound might be expected to play the same signaling role as taste. An association between a light and feeling sick should be no more difficult to establish than one between a taste and feeling sick. But the facts turn out to be otherwise, as revealed by the following experiment. Rats are allowed to lick at a tube that contains a flavored solution; each time the rat licks the tube, a click and a light are presented. Thus the rat experiences three stimuli simultaneously—the taste of the solution, as well as the light and the click. Subsequently, the rat is mildly poisoned. The question is, What stimuli—the taste or the light-plus-click—will become associated with feeling sick? To answer this, in the final phase of the study, the rat is again presented the same tube; sometimes the solution in the tube has the same flavor as before but there is no light or click, while other times the solution has no flavor but the light and click are presented. The animal avoids the solution when it experiences the taste, but not when the light-plus-click is presented; hence, the rat has associated only taste with feeling sick. These results cannot be attributed to taste being a more potent CS than light-plus-click, because in another condition of the experiment, instead of being mildly poisoned the rat is shocked. Now, in the final phase of the study, the animal avoids the solution only when the light-plus-click is presented, not when it experiences the taste alone (Garcia & Koelling, 1966).

Thus, taste is a better signal for sickness than for shock, while light-plus-sound is a better signal for shock than for sickness. Why does this selectivity of association exist? It does not fit with the behaviorist perspective: since taste and light-plus-click can both be effective CSs, and since being sick and being shocked are both effective UCSs, then either CS should have been associatable with either UCS. In contrast, this *selectivity of association* fits perfectly with the ethological perspective and its emphasis on an animal's evolutionary adaptation to its environment. In their natural habitat, rats (like other mammals) rely on taste to select their food. Consequently, there may be a genetically determined, or "built-in," relation between taste and intestinal reactions, which constrains what associations the rat may learn. In particular, the built-in relation fosters an association between taste and sickness but not between light and sickness. Furthermore, in a rat's natural environment, pain resulting from external factors like cold or injury is invariably

Water squirting (a preprogrammed behavior for walruses) can be easily conditioned to occur on command.

Since pecking is part of a pigeon's natural eating behavior, it is a response that is easily conditioned when food is the reward.

due to external stimuli. Consequently, there may be a built-in relation between external stimuli and "external pain," which fosters an association between light and shock, but not one between taste and shock.

If rats learn to associate taste with sickness because it fits with their natural means of selecting food, then another species with a different means of selecting food might have trouble learning to associate taste with sickness. This is exactly what happens. Birds naturally select their food on the basis of looks rather than taste, and they readily learn to associate a light with sickness, but not a taste with sickness. In short, if we want to know what may be conditioned to what, we cannot consider the CS and UCS in isolation; rather, we must focus on the two in combination and consider how well that combination reflects built-in relations. This conclusion differs considerably from the behaviorist assumption that the laws of learning are the same for all species and situations.

CONSTRAINTS IN OPERANT CONDITIONING   Constraints on learning also occur in operant conditioning, though now the constraints involve response-reinforcer relations. We can illustrate this point with pigeons in two different situations; *reward learning*, where the animal acquires a response that is reinforced by food; and *escape learning*, where the animal acquires a response that is reinforced by the termination of shock. In the case of reward, pigeons learn much faster if the response is pecking a key rather than flapping their wings. In the case of escape, the opposite is true; pigeons learn faster if the response is wing flapping rather than pecking (Bolles, 1970).

Again, the results seem inconsistent with the assumption that the same laws of learning apply to all situations, but they make sense from an ethological perspective. The reward case with the pigeons involved eating, and pecking (but not wing flapping) is part of the bird's natural eating activities. Hence, a genetically determined connection between pecking and eating is reasonable. Similarly, the escape case involved a danger situation, and the pigeon's natural reactions to danger include flapping its wings (but not pecking). Birds are known to have a small repertoire of defensive reactions, and they will quickly learn to escape only if the relevant response is one of these natural defensive reactions. In sum, rather than being a means for learning arbitrary associations, operant conditioning also honors the behavioral blueprint.

DIFFERENT KINDS OF LEARNING   Constraints on associations are not the only problem that ethologists have raised for behaviorists. Ethologists have also studied some important forms of animal learning that differ from associative learning. Two striking instances of such learning are imprinting and song learning in birds.

Imprinting refers to the type of learning that forms the basis for a young bird's attachment to its parents. A newly hatched duckling reared without its mother will follow a human being, a wooden decoy, or almost any other moving object that it first sees after birth (see the Critical Discussion, "Instincts and Maternal-Infant Behavior," in Chapter 10). Imprinting is different from standard associative learning because it occurs *only* during a *critical period*, which begins right after birth and typically ends when a suitable parent model is learned. No form of associative learning seems to have the feature that it occurs *only* very early in life.

Bird songs offer another challenge to associative learning. Learning the song that is characteristic of their species is an important task for birds, because the song allows them to be recognized by other members of their species. In part, birds learn their songs from other birds. For example, if a male white-crowned sparrow is raised in isolation, as an adult it will not vocalize normally; instead, it will sing a crude version of its species song. Imitation, therefore, seems to be involved. But imitation is not the whole story, for if the white-crowned sparrow is exposed only to the songs of other species, the songs will have no effect on the sparrow's learning. These results suggest that the sparrow has a kind of inborn *template* or model of what its adult song is like, and its learning is influenced only by songs that fit the template. The idea of "fitting an inborn template" is far removed from associative learning (Marler, 1970; Gould & Marler, 1987).

BEHAVIORIST COUNTERARGUMENTS   The above challenges to behaviorism—different kinds of learning, and constraints on classical and operant conditioning—have not gone unanswered. Thus, some behaviorists have argued that the constraints on classical conditioning do not necessarily show that different laws of learning apply to different situations, but rather that the situations need to be analyzed in more detail. To illustrate, consider again the finding that taste is a better signal for sickness than is light-plus-sound, but light-plus-sound is a better signal for shock than is taste. Some researchers have argued that what is critical here is not that rats are evolutionarily prepared to associate taste with sickness, and light-plus-sound with shock; but rather that taste is *similar* to sickness, while light-plus-sound is *similar* to shock, and the more similar the CS and UCS the more rapid the conditioning. Thus, sensations of taste and sickness both start slowly, persist for a relatively long period, and then end slowly. These similarities make it easy to associate taste and sickness (Garcia & Koelling, 1966; Testa, 1975). The general point, then, is that the behaviorist account of conditioning may be partially salvaged by positing new laws relating aspects of situations to conditioning, such as similar stimuli lead to rapid conditioning.

At this point in time, it is unclear how persuasive or general these behaviorist counterarguments will prove to be. A careful analysis of the issues suggests that, even when factors like the similarity of the CS and the UCS are taken into account, some of the constraints on conditioning result from evolutionary adaptation (Domjan, 1983). Our best guess, then, is that the ethological approach will continue to change our conception of conditioning and associative learning in animals. Instead of assuming there is always a sharp distinction between instincts and learning, increasingly researchers think that learning is often guided by instincts. More and more, there is a call for a synthesis of ethology and behaviorism: a synthesis in which much of animal learning is still assumed to be based on conditioning, but where the learning is specialized for the learning of tasks that the animal is likely to encounter in its natural environment (Gould & Marler, 1987).

Cognitive Approach

In a sense, the cognitive challenge to behaviorism is the opposite of the ethological one. Whereas the ethologist tells us that animals are not as flexible as the behaviorists thought, the cognitivist argues that animals, particularly higher species, are more intelligent than the behaviorists thought. According to the cognitivist, the crux of intelligence lies in an organism's ability to mentally represent aspects of the world and then to *operate* on these *mental representations* rather than on the world itself. In some cases, the costly trial and error of actual behavior can be replaced by a mental trial and

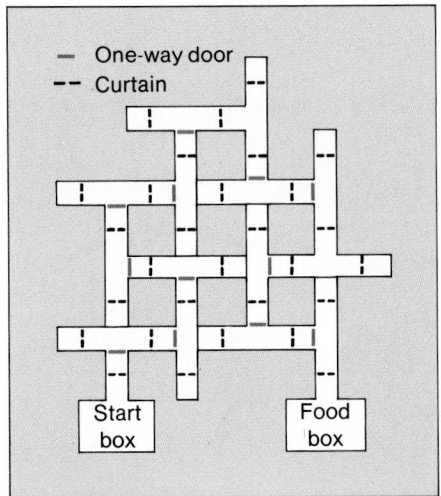

FIGURE 7-12
Diagram of One of Tolman's Mazes *A diagram of a maze used by Tolman in his learning experiments with rats. The complexity of the maze (with right and left turns, one-way doors, and curtains limiting the view of the route) tested the rat's ability to form a cognitive map.*

error, in which the organism tries out different possibilities in its mind. In other cases, the operations on mental representations are less like trial and error and more like a multistep strategy; that is, the organism takes some mental steps only because they enable subsequent ones. Such notions contradict the behaviorist assumption that an organism's behavior can be explained without considering its internal processes. Furthermore, the idea of a strategy seems at odds with the behaviorist assumption that complex learning is built out of simple associations.

The cognitive view of learning has gained support rapidly. No doubt, this is partly due to the advent of computers. Computers are capable of complex learning (for example, learning to play chess), yet no one thinks that the way to understand a computer is by considering just its external behavior—its inputs and outputs. Rather, the standard way to understand the behavior of a computer is in terms of its internal representations (its data, for example) and its procedures for operating on them. Animal and human learning may require the same kind of explanation. The analogy of a computer, however, is not the only reason for adopting a cognitive view of learning. There are numerous phenomena in learning that directly point to the need to consider mental representations. Some of these phenomena involve animals, whereas others involve humans performing tasks that are similar to conditioning.

COGNITIVE PHENOMENA IN ANIMALS   An early advocate of the cognitive approach to learning was Edward Tolman, whose research dealt with the problem of rats learning their way through complex mazes (Tolman, 1932). In his view, a rat running through a complex maze was not learning a sequence of right- and left-turning responses but rather was developing a *cognitive map*—a mental representation of the layout of the maze. In a typical experiment of Tolman's, rats in an experimental group were first allowed to explore a maze, like the one in Figure 7-12, in the absence of any reinforcer such as food. A control group had no opportunity to explore the maze. Then food was introduced as a reinforcer, and both experimental and control animals had to find their way through the maze. The experimental group learned to run the maze more quickly than the controls, presumably because they had learned the layout of the maze during their unreinforced exploration, and this cognitive map facilitated their learning of a specific route when the food was introduced.

More recent research provides additional evidence for cognitive maps in rats. To illustrate, consider the maze diagramed in Figure 7-13. The maze consists of a center platform with eight identical arms radiating out. On each trial, the researcher places food at the end of each arm; the rat needs to learn to visit each arm (and obtain the food there) without returning to those it has already visited. Rats learn this remarkably well; after 20 trials, they will virtually never return to an arm they have already visited. (Rats will do this even when the maze has been doused with after-shave lotion to eliminate the odor cues about which arms still have food.) Most important, a rat rarely employs the strategy that would occur to humans—such as always going through the arms in an obvious order, say clockwise. Instead, the rat visits the arms randomly, indicating that it has not learned a rigid sequence of responses. What, then, has it learned? Probably, the rat has developed a representation of the maze, which specifies the spatial relations between arms, and on each trial it makes a mental note of each arm that it has visited (Olton, 1978; 1979).

While many researchers have tried to make the case for the cognitive view with lower species, other researchers assumed that the best evidence for a cognitive approach would come from higher species, especially primates. Among these researchers, Wolfgang Köhler's work with chimpanzees, carried out in the 1920s, remains particularly important. The problems that Köhler set for his chimpanzees left some room for insight, because no parts of the problem were hidden from view (in contrast, the workings of a food dispenser in a Skinner box are hidden from the animal's view). Typically, Köhler placed a chimpanzee in an enclosed area with a desirable piece of fruit, often a banana, out of reach. To obtain the fruit, the animal had to use a nearby object as a tool. Usually the chimpanzee solved the problem, and did it in a way that suggested he had some insight. The following description from Köhler is typical:

> Sultan [Köhler's most intelligent chimpanzee] is squatting at the bars but cannot reach the fruit which lies outside by means of his only available short stick. A longer stick is deposited outside the bars, about two meters on one side of the object and parallel with the grating. It cannot be grasped with the hand, but it can be pulled within reach by means of the small stick. [See Figure 7-14 for an illustration of a similar multiple-stick problem.] Sultan tries to reach the fruit with the smaller of the two sticks. Not succeeding, he tears at a piece of wire that projects from the netting of his cage, but that too is in vain. Then he gazes about him (there are always in the course of these tests some long pauses, during which the animals scrutinize the whole visible area). He suddenly picks up the little stick once more, goes up to the bars directly opposite to the long stick, scratches it towards him with the "auxiliary," seizes it, and goes with it to the point opposite the objective (the fruit), which he secures. From the moment that his eyes fall upon the long stick, his procedure forms one consecutive whole, without hiatus, and although the angling of the bigger stick by means of the smaller is an action that could be complete and distinct in itself, yet observation shows that it follows, quite suddenly, on an interval of hesitation and doubt—staring about—which undoubtedly has a relation to the final objective, and is immediately merged in the final action of the attainment of the end goal. (Köhler, 1925, pp. 174–75)

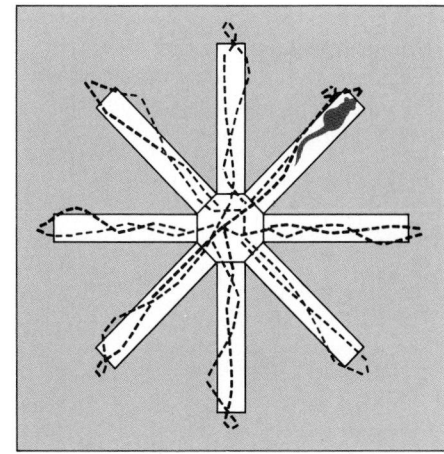

FIGURE 7-13
Maze for Studying Cognitive Maps *With food placed at the end of every arm, the rat's problem is to find all the food without retracing its steps. The pattern shown here reflects perfect learning: this rat visited each arm of the maze only once, eating whatever it found there; it did not go back to an empty arm even one time.*

FIGURE 7-14
Multiple-Stick Problem *Using the shorter sticks, the chimpanzee pulls in a stick long enough to reach the piece of fruit. It has learned to solve this problem by understanding the relationship between the sticks and the piece of fruit.*

FIGURE 7-15
Chimpanzee Constructing a Platform *To reach the bananas hanging from the ceiling, the chimpanzee stacks boxes to form a platform.*

Several aspects of the performance of these chimpanzees are unlike those of Thorndike's cats or Skinner's rats and pigeons. For one thing, the solution was sudden, rather than being the result of a gradual trial-and-error process. Another point is that once a chimpanzee solved a problem, thereafter it would solve the problem with few irrelevant moves. This is most unlike a rat, which continues to make irrelevant responses in the Skinner box for many trials. Also, Köhler's chimpanzees could readily transfer what they had learned to a novel situation. For example, in one problem, Sultan was not encaged, but some bananas were placed too high for him to reach, as shown in Figure 7-15. To solve the problem, Sultan stacked some boxes strewn around him, climbed the "platform," and grabbed the bananas. In subsequent problems, if the fruit was again too high to reach, Sultan found other objects to construct a platform; in some cases, Sultan used a table and a small ladder, and in one case Sultan pulled Köhler himself over and used the experimenter as a platform.

There are, therefore, three critical aspects of the chimpanzee's solution: its suddenness, its availability once discovered, and its transferability. These aspects are at odds with the behaviorist notion of trial-and-error behaviors of the type observed by Thorndike, Skinner, and their students. Instead, the chimpanzee's solutions may reflect a mental trial and error. That is, the animal forms a mental representation of the problem, manipulates components of the representation until it hits on a solution, and then enacts the solution in the real world. The solution, therefore, appears sudden because the researchers do not have access to the chimpanzee's mental process. The solution is available thereafter because a mental representation persists over time, and the solution is transferable because the representation is either abstract enough to cover more than the original situation or malleable enough to be extended to a novel situation.

More recent studies of primates provide even stronger evidence for cognition in animal learning. Particularly striking are studies showing that chimpanzees can acquire abstract concepts that were once believed to be the sole province of humans. In the typical study, chimpanzees learn to use plastic tokens of different shapes, sizes, and colors as words. For example, they might learn that one token refers to "apples" and another to "paper," where there is no physical resemblance between the token and the object. The fact that chimpanzees can learn these references means they understand concrete concepts like "apple" and "paper." More impressively, they also have abstract concepts like "same," "different," and "cause." Thus, chimpanzees can learn to use their "same" token when presented either two "apple" tokens or two "orange" ones and their "different" token when presented one "apple" and one "orange" token. Likewise, chimpanzees seem to understand causal relations: they will apply the token for "cause" when shown some cut paper and scissors, but not when shown some intact paper and scissors (Premack, 1985a; Premack & Premack, 1983).

Finally, we note that in previous sections of this chapter we described some phenomena in classical and operant conditioning that require a cognitive interpretation, particularly the importance of predictability and control

Using the technique developed by Premack, an experimenter tests a chimpanzee's ability to use language by manipulating plastic chips that represent specific words.

in conditioning. Recall that in classical conditioning a rat will learn an association between a tone and a shock to the extent the tone predicts the shock; in operant conditioning dogs will not learn to jump a hurdle to avoid shock if they have previously learned that shocks are not under their control. The notions of *predictability* and *control* are cognitive; *predictability*, for example, refers to a belief that something will happen, and *beliefs* are part of the mental world, not the physical one.

LEARNING LESS THAN PERFECT RELATIONS   Research on animal learning has emphasized the learning of *perfectly predictable* relations. For example, in most studies of classical conditioning, the CS is followed by the UCS 100 percent of the time. But in real life, relations between stimuli or events are usually less than perfectly predictable. The study of associative learning with less than perfect relations has been conducted mainly with humans; and in these studies, learning clearly seems to be mediated by cognitive processes.

In the studies of interest, a different pair of stimuli is presented on each trial—say, a picture and a description of a person—and the subject's task is to learn the relation between the members of the pairs—say, that pictures of tall men tend to be associated with brief descriptions. Some striking evidence for cognitive processes comes from cases in which, objectively, there is *no* relation between the stimuli, yet subjects "learn" such a relation. In one experiment, subjects were concerned with the possible relation between the drawings that mental patients made and the symptoms that the patients manifested. On each trial of the experiment, subjects were presented a patient's drawing of a person and one of six symptoms, including, for example, the symptoms "suspiciousness of other people" and "concerned with being taken care of." The subject's task was to determine whether any of the signs in the drawing—some aspect of the eyes or mouth, for instance—were associated with any of the symptoms. In fact, the six symptoms had been randomly paired with the drawings so that there was no association between sign (drawing) and symptom. Yet subjects consistently reported there were such relations, where the relations they reported were ones they probably believed *before* participating in the experiment: for example, that large eyes are associated with suspiciousness, or that a large mouth is associated with a desire to be taken care of by others. These nonexistent but plausible relations are referred to as *spurious associations*.

The same spurious associations have been made by some clinical psychologists who tried to use the so-called *Draw-a-Person* test to diagnose psychological problems. Objective assessments of this test have shown it has virtually no correlation with emotional problems. But, in the past, some clinical psychologists insisted that the test had diagnostic value, and in particular that exaggerated eyes in a drawing were associated with suspiciousness of others, and that an exaggerated mouth was associated with a desire to be taken care of (Chapman & Chapman, 1967).

For both the clinical psychologists and the subjects in the experiment described above, prior beliefs about what things generally go together—such as our belief that big eyes go with suspiciousness—influenced the learning of what in fact goes together in the situation at hand. Thus, prior beliefs about the stimuli constrain the process of associative learning, which attests to the cognitive nature of such learning.

The above research shows the power of prior beliefs on associative learning, but it does not say anything about how learning proceeds when there is in fact an objective association to be learned. Nor does the above work say anything about associative learning when the learner has no relevant prior beliefs. Both of these issues were analyzed in the following study.

On each of a set of trials, subjects were presented a picture of a man with a walking stick, and the heights of both the men and the walking sticks varied from trial to trial. The subjects' task was to estimate the strength of the relation between the two heights by choosing a number between 0 (which indicated no relation) and 100 (a perfect relation). Because the task was novel, subjects presumably had no prior beliefs about the relation of interest; consequently, their learning should be driven by only the input or data (for this reason, it is referred to as *data-driven learning*). Data-driven learning turns out to be conservative, tending to underestimate the objective relations involved. When the objective relation between the two heights was low (as measured by the correlation coefficient between the two heights), often subjects failed to detect any relation; when the objective relation was moderate, subjects generally succeeded in learning there was a relation, but underestimated its strength; only when the objective relation was high and close to perfectly predictive did subjects learn that there was a relation, and estimate it to have a high strength (Jennings, Amabile, & Ross, 1980).

The obvious question is, What would happen to subjects' estimates of low, moderate, and high predictive relations if subjects *did* have prior beliefs about the relations? Given the previous work on spurious associations that shows that people learn even nonexistent relations if they are consistent with their beliefs, we would expect that *belief-driven learning* would tend to overestimate the objective relations involved. This is exactly what researchers have found. When the task involves estimating the relation between things that people believe ought to be related—for example, on each trial, two different measures of a person's honesty taken from two completely different situations are presented—subjects never fail to detect a relation that exists, and consistently overestimate its predictive strength (Jennings et al., 1980).

These studies further demonstrate the importance of prior beliefs in human associative learning, thereby strengthening the case for a cognitive approach to associative learning. In a way, however, the above studies also have a connection to the ethological approach to associative learning. Just as rats and pigeons may be constrained to learn only those associations that evolution has prepared them for, so we humans seem to be constrained to learn those associations that our prior beliefs have prepared us for. Without prior constraints of some sort, perhaps there would simply be too many potential associations to consider, and associative learning would be chaotic.

CHAPTER SUMMARY

1. Two forms of *associative learning* are *classical conditioning* and *operant conditioning*. In classical conditioning, an organism learns that one event follows another. In operant conditioning, an organism learns that a response leads to a particular consequence.

2. The behavioristic approach to conditioning assumes that a) simple associations are the building blocks of all learning; b) the laws of association are the same for all species and situations; and c) learning is better understood in terms of external causes than internal ones.

3. In Pavlov's experiments, if a *conditioned stimulus* (CS) consistently precedes an *unconditioned stimulus* (UCS), the CS comes to serve as a signal for the UCS and will elicit a *conditioned response* (CR) that often resembles the *unconditioned response* (UCR). Stimuli that are similar to the CS also elicit the CR to some extent, though such *generalization* can be curbed by *discrimination training*. These phenomena occur in organisms as diverse as flatworms and humans.

4. For classical conditioning to occur, the CS must be a reliable predictor of the UCS; that is, there must be a higher probability that the UCS will occur when the CS has been presented than when it has not. The importance of *predictability* is also evident in the phenomenon of *blocking*: if one CS reliably predicts a UCS, and another CS is added, the relation between the added CS and the UCS will not be learned.

5. Operant conditioning deals with situations in which the response operates on the environment rather than being elicited by an unconditioned stimulus. The earliest systematic studies were performed by Thorndike, who showed that animals engage in *trial-and-error* behavior, and that any behavior followed by reinforcement is strengthened (the *law of effect*).

6. In Skinner's experiments, typically a rat or pigeon learns to make a simple response, such as pressing a lever, to obtain reinforcement. The rate of response is a useful measure of *response strength*. Even responses mediated by the autonomic nervous system, like blood pressure, can be modified through operant conditioning.

7. There are a number of phenomena that increase the generality of operant conditioning. One is *conditioned reinforcement*, wherein a stimulus associated with a reinforcer acquires its own reinforcing properties. Another phenomenon is *generalization*, wherein organisms generalize operant responses to similar situations. Another relevant phenomenon is *partial reinforcement*: responses learned under partial reinforcement are more difficult to extinguish. Finally, there is *shaping*, a training procedure used when the desired response is novel, where the organism is reinforced for any behavior that brings it closer to the desired response.

8. It is useful to think of reinforcers as activities rather than stimuli. According to *Premack's Principle*, activities that are engaged in more frequently reinforce activities that are engaged in less frequently. Reinforcers can also be *punishers*, which are events that suppress or eliminate responses. Punishment is beneficial to learning to the extent that it is informative. Direct stimulation of the brain can also serve as a reinforcer. Stimulation of certain areas of the brain serves as a reward, while stimulation of other regions serves as a punisher.

9. The *ethological* approach challenges the behaviorist assumption that the laws of learning are the same for all species or for all situations that a given species encounters. According to ethologists, what an animal learns is constrained by its genetically determined "behavioral blueprint." Evidence for such constraints on learning comes from studies of *taste aversion*. While rats readily learn to associate the feeling of being sick with the taste of a solution, they cannot learn to associate sickness with a light. Conversely, birds can learn to associate light and sickness, but not taste and sickness. These distinctions are the result of innate differences between rats and birds in their food-gathering activities.

10. The *cognitive* approach challenges the behaviorist assumption that behavior can be understood by considering only external or environmental factors. According to cognitivists, intelligence is an organism's ability to represent aspects of the world mentally and then to operate on those *mental representations* rather than on the world itself. In some cases, the operations are like mental trial and error. Studies of cognitive phenomena in animals indicate that rats develop a mental representation, or *cognitive map*, of a maze. Other studies demonstrate that chimpanzees can solve problems by mental trial and error, and can acquire abstract concepts such as *same*, *different*, and *cause*.

11. When learning relations between stimuli that are not perfectly predictive, people often invoke prior beliefs about the relations. This can lead to people detecting relations that are not objectively present (*spurious associations*). When the relation is objectively present, having a prior belief about it can lead to overestimating the relation's predictive strength (*belief-driven learning*), while lacking a prior belief about it can lead to underestimating the relation's predictive strength (*data-driven learning*).

Pavlov's *Conditioned Reflexes* (1927) is the definitive work on classical conditioning. Skinner's *The Behavior of Organisms* (1938) is the corresponding statement on operant conditioning. The major points of view about conditioning and learning, presented in their historical settings, are summarized in Bower and Hilgard, *Theories of Learning* (5th ed., 1981).

For a general introduction to learning, a number of textbooks are recommended. Schwartz's *Psychology of Learning and Behavior* (3rd ed., 1989) is a particularly well-balanced review of conditioning, including discussion of ethology and cognition. Another useful textbook is Domjan and Burkhard's *The Principles of Learning and Behavior* (1986). Staddon's *Adaptive Behavior and Learning* (1983) tries to synthesize traditional work on conditioning with the ethological findings, while Mackintosh's *Conditioning and Associative Learning* (1983) takes a cognitive approach to classical conditioning. At the advanced level, the six-volume Estes (ed.), *Handbook of Learning and Cognitive Processes* (1975–1979), covers most aspects of learning and conditioning; and Honig and Staddon (eds.), *Handbook of Operant Behavior* (1977), provides a comprehensive treatment of operant conditioning.

The early cognitive approach is well described in two classics: Tolman's *Purposive Behavior in Animals and Men* (1932; reprint ed. 1967) and Köhler's *The Mentality of Apes* (1925; reprint ed. 1976). For a recent statement of the cognitive approach to animal learning, see Roitblat's *Introduction to Comparative Cognition* (1987) and Premack's unusually titled *Gavagai: The Future of the Animal Language Controversy* (1985).

FURTHER READING

Chapter 8

Detail, Open Book.

Memory

All learning implies memory. If we remembered nothing from our experiences, we could learn nothing. Life would consist of momentary episodes that had little relation to one another. We could not even carry on a simple conversation. To communicate, we have to remember the thoughts we want to express as well as what has just been said to us. Without memory we could not even reflect on ourselves, for the very notion of a *self* depends on a sense of continuity that only memory can bring. In short, when we think of what it means to be human, we must acknowledge the centrality of memory.

DISTINCTIONS ABOUT MEMORY

Psychologists find it useful to make a few basic distinctions about memory. One distinction concerns three stages of memory: *encoding, storage*, and *retrieval*. Other distinctions deal with different types of memory. Different memories may be used to store information for short and long periods and to store different kinds of information (for example, one memory for facts and another for skills).

Three Stages of Memory

Suppose one morning you are introduced to a student and told her name is Barbara Cohn. That afternoon you see her again and say something like, "You're Barbara Cohn. We met this morning." Clearly, you have remembered her name. But how exactly did you remember it?

Your minor memory feat can be broken into three stages (see Figure 8-1). First, when you were introduced, you somehow "deposited" Barbara Cohn's name into memory; this is the *encoding stage*. You transformed a physical input (sound waves) that corresponds to her spoken name into the kind of code or representation that memory accepts, and you placed that representation in memory. Second, you retained—or stored—the name during the time between the two meetings; this is the *storage stage*. And, third, you recovered the name from storage at the time of your second meeting; this is the *retrieval stage*.

Memory can fail at any of these three stages. Had you been unable to recall Barbara's name at the second meeting, this could have reflected a failure in encoding, storage, or retrieval. Much of current research on memory attempts to specify the mental operations that occur at each of the three stages of memory and to explain how these operations can go awry and result in memory failure.

FIGURE 8-1
Three Stages of Memory *Theories of memory attribute forgetting to a failure at one or more of these stages.*

Different Types of Memory

SHORT-TERM VERSUS LONG-TERM MEMORY   The three stages of memory do not operate the same way in all situations. Memory seems to differ between those situations that require us to store material for a matter of seconds and those that require us to store material for longer intervals—from minutes to years. The former situations are said to tap *short-term memory*, whereas the latter reflect *long-term memory*.

We can illustrate this distinction by amending our story about meeting Barbara Cohn. Suppose that during the first meeting, as soon as you had heard her name, a friend came up and you said, "Doug, have you met Barbara Cohn?" In this case, remembering Barbara's name would be an example of short-term memory: you retrieved the name after only a second or two. Remembering her name at the time of your second meeting would be an example of long-term memory, because then retrieval would take place hours after the name was encoded.

When we recall a name immediately after encountering it, retrieval seems effortless, as if the name were still active, still in our consciousness. But when we try to recall the same name hours later, retrieval is often difficult because the name is no longer in our consciousness. This contrast between short- and long-term memory is similar to the contrast between conscious knowledge and preconscious knowledge—the knowledge we have but are not currently thinking about. We can think of memory as a vast body of knowledge, only a small part of which is active at any moment. The rest is passive. Short-term memory corresponds to the active part, long-term memory to the passive part.

The need to distinguish between short- and long-term memory is further supported by studies of people with *amnesia*, or severe memory loss. Amnesia takes several forms. In one form, people have profound difficulty remembering material for long time intervals but rarely have any trouble remembering material for a few seconds. Thus, a patient with this form of amnesia may be unable to recognize his doctor when she enters the room—even though the patient has seen this doctor every day for years—yet will have no trouble repeating back the physician's full name when she is reintroduced (Milner, Corkin, & Teuber, 1968). In contrast, in another form of amnesia, people have trouble only when they have to remember material for a short time interval (Warrington & Shallice, 1972).

DIFFERENT MEMORIES FOR DIFFERENT KINDS OF INFORMATION
Until recently, psychologists assumed that the same memory system was used for all contents that had to be stored. For example, the same long-term memory was presumably used to store both one's recollection of a grandmother's funeral and the skill one needs to ride a bike. Recent evidence suggests that this assumption is wrong. In particular, we seem to use a different long-term memory for storing *facts* (such as who the current president is) than we do for retaining *skills* (such as how to ride a bicycle). We may also use different long-term memories for storing *general facts* about the world (for example, "12 squared is 144") versus *personal facts* about our experiences ("I couldn't stand the teacher who taught me squares").

Ideally, we should first specify the different memory systems corresponding to different contents and for each one describe the nature of encoding, storage, and retrieval stages in its short-term and long-term memory. This goal is too ambitious given present knowledge. Most of what we know concerns memory for facts, particularly personal ones, and aside from a few subsections, such memory will be the focus of this chapter. The next two sections consider primarily the nature of encoding, storage, and retrieval in short-term and long-term fact memory. Then we will examine how long-term memory can be improved. In the last section, we will focus on memory for more complex factual material, with an emphasis on how we embellish what we put into memory.

SHORT-TERM MEMORY

Even in those situations in which we must remember information for only a few seconds, memory involves the three stages of encoding, storage, and retrieval.

Encoding

To encode information into short-term memory, we must attend to it. Since we are selective about what we attend to (see Chapter 5), our short-term memory will contain only what has been selected. This means that much of what we are exposed to never even enters short-term memory and, of course, will not be available for later retrieval. Indeed, many difficulties labeled "memory problems" are really lapses in attention. For example, if you bought some groceries and someone asked you later for the color of the checkout clerk's eyes, you might well be unable to answer because you had not paid attention to them in the first place.

ACOUSTIC CODING   When information is encoded into memory, it is deposited in a certain code or representation. For example, when you look up a phone number and retain it until you have dialed it, in what form do you represent the digits? Is the representation visual—a mental picture of the digits? Is it acoustic—the sounds of the names of the digits? Or is it semantic (based on meaning)—some meaningful association that the digits have? Research indicates that we can use any of these possibilities to encode information into short-term memory, although we seem to favor an acoustic code when we are trying to keep the information active by *rehearsing* it—that is, by repeating it over and over in our minds. Rehearsal is a particularly popular strategy when the information consists of verbal items such as digits, letters, or words. So in trying to remember a phone number, we are most likely to encode the number as the sounds of the digit names and to rehearse these sounds to ourselves until we have dialed the number.

In one experiment that provided evidence for an acoustic code, researchers briefly showed subjects a list of six consonants (for example, RLBKSJ); when the letters were removed, the subject had to write all six letters in order. Although the entire procedure took only a second or two, subjects occasionally made errors. When they did, the incorrect letter tended to be similar in sound to the correct one. For the list mentioned, a subject might have written RLTKSJ, replacing the B with the similar-sounding T (Conrad, 1964). This finding supports the idea that the subjects encoded each letter acoustically (for example, "bee" for B), sometimes lost part of this code (only the "ee" part of the sound remained), and then responded with a letter ("tee") that was consistent with the remaining part of the code.

Short-term recall of digits.

FIGURE 8-2
Testing for Eidetic Images *This test picture was shown for 30 seconds to elementary school children. After removal of the picture, one boy saw in his eidetic image "about 14" stripes in the cat's tail. The painting, by Marjorie Torrey, appears in Lewis Carroll's* Alice in Wonderland, *abridged by Josette Frank.*

Experiments such as this one have produced another result that points to an acoustic code: it is more difficult to recall the items in order when they are acoustically similar (for example, TBCGVE) than when they are acoustically distinct (RLTKSJ). A striking example of this occurs with Chinese readers. Written Chinese consists of syllable-like units called characters. Usually, there are two characters per word, and each character typically shares its name with several others. When Chinese subjects are briefly shown a sequence of characters that they then have to write down in order, they get about six correct if all the characters have different names but only three correct if all have the same name (and hence cannot be coded acoustically). Eliminating the use of an acoustic code thus cuts recall in half (Zhang & Simon, 1985).

VISUAL CODING   The fact that the Chinese readers in the previous study were able to remember the correct order of three characters with the same name suggests that they also maintained these items in a visual representation. Other experiments indicate that although we can use a visual code for verbal material, the code often fades quickly. To illustrate, after looking at the address 7915 THIRD AVENUE, you may have a visual code of it for a second or two. This representation would preserve visual details, such as the fact that the address is written in all capital letters. After a couple of seconds, however, all that would remain would be the sound of the address (the acoustic code), and this code would not preserve information about the form of the letters (Posner & Keele, 1967).

This dominance of the acoustic code may apply mainly to verbal materials. When a person must store nonverbal items (such as pictures that are difficult to describe and therefore difficult to rehearse acoustically), the visual code may become more important. A few people, most of them children, are able to hold in their short-term memory images of visual material that are almost photographic in clarity. They can look briefly at a picture and, when it is removed, still see its image before their eyes. They can maintain the image for as long as several minutes, scan it, and when questioned, provide a wealth of detail, such as the number of stripes on a cat's tail (see Figure 8-2). Such children seem to be reading the details directly from an *eidetic* image (Haber, 1969). Eidetic imagery is quite rare, though. Studies with children indicate that only about 5 percent report visual images that are long-lasting and possess sharp detail. The existing evidence suggests that even fewer individuals have eidetic images after adolescence.

Storage

LIMITED CAPACITY   Perhaps the most striking fact about short-term memory is that it has a very limited capacity. On the average, the limit is seven items, give or take two (7 ± 2). Some people store as few as five items; others can retain as many as nine. It may seem strange to give such an exact number to cover all people when it is clear that individuals differ greatly in their memory abilities. These differences, however, are primarily due to long-term memory. For short-term memory, most normal adults have a capacity of 7 ± 2. This constancy has been known since the earliest days of experimental psychology. Hermann Ebbinghaus, who began the experimental study of memory in 1885, reported results showing that his own limit was seven items. Some 70 years later, George Miller (1956) was so struck by the

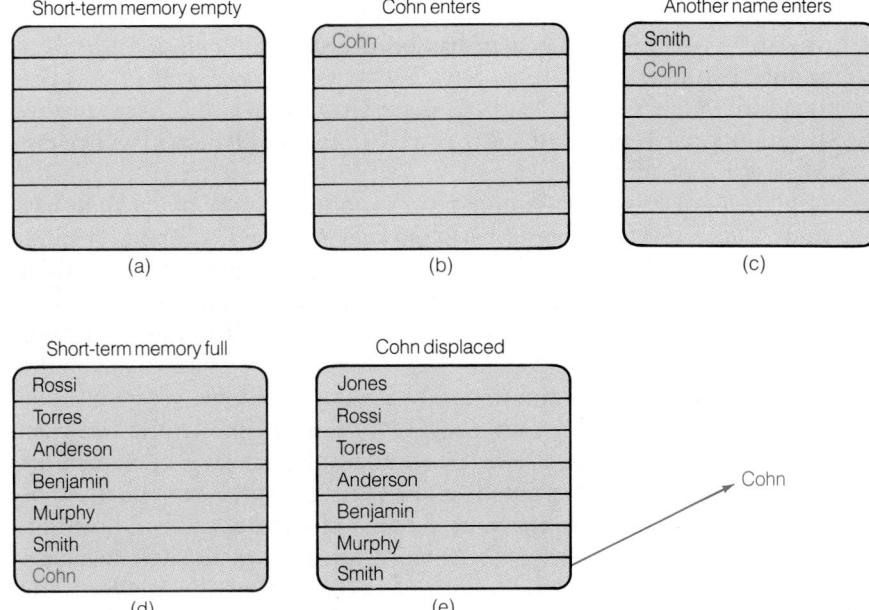

Short-term memory empty
(a)

Cohn enters
Cohn
(b)

Another name enters
Smith
Cohn
(c)

Short-term memory full
Rossi
Torres
Anderson
Benjamin
Murphy
Smith
Cohn
(d)

Cohn displaced
Jones
Rossi
Torres
Anderson
Benjamin
Murphy
Smith
(e)

Cohn

FIGURE 8-3
Forgetting Due to Displacement *Due to the limited capacity of short-term memory, 7 ± 2 "slots," the addition of a new item can result in the displacement or loss of an old one.*

constancy that he referred to it as the "magic number seven." And the limit has been shown to hold in non-Western cultures (Yu et al., 1985).

Psychologists determined this number by showing subjects various sequences of unrelated items (digits, letters, or words) and asking them to recall the items in order. The items are presented rapidly, and the subject does not have time to relate them to information stored in long-term memory; hence, the number of items recalled reflects only the storage capacity for short-term memory. On the initial trials, subjects have to recall just a few items, say, three or four digits, which they can easily do. Then the number of digits increases over trials until the experimenter determines the maximum number a subject can recall in perfect order. The maximum (almost always between five and nine) is the subject's *memory span*. This task is so simple that you can easily try it yourself. The next time you come across a list of names (a directory in a business or university building, for example), read through the list once and then look away and see how many names you can recall in order. It will probably be between five and nine.

FORGETTING   We may be able to hold on to seven items briefly, but in most cases they will soon be forgotten. Forgetting occurs either because the items are *displaced* by newer ones or because the items *decay* with time.

The notion of displacement fits with short-term memory having a fixed capacity. The fixed capacity suggests that we might think of short-term memory as a sort of mental box with roughly seven slots. Each item entering short-term memory goes into its own slot. As long as the number of items does not exceed the number of slots, we can recall the items perfectly, but when all the slots are filled and a new item enters, one of the old ones must go. The new item displaces an old one. To illustrate, suppose your short-term memory is empty (see Figure 8-3). An item enters. Let us say you have been introduced to Barbara Cohn, and the name Cohn enters your short-term memory. Others are introduced soon after, and the list of names in short-term memory grows. Finally, the limit of your memory span is reached. Then

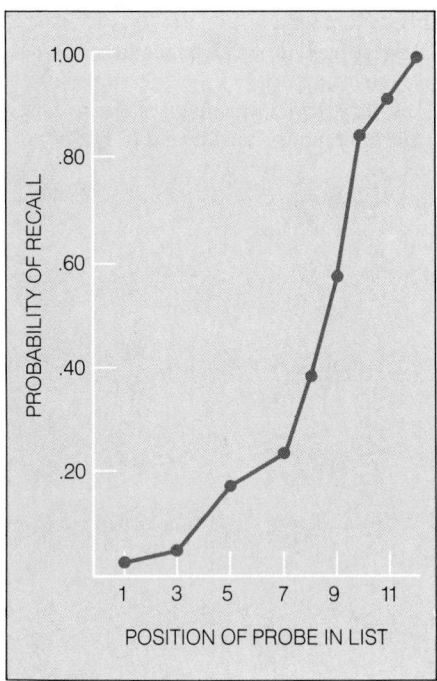

FIGURE 8-4
Recall as a Function of Probe Position *When probes are drawn from the end of the list, few items have followed the one to be recalled, and the probability of recall is high. When probes are drawn from the beginning of the list, many items have followed the one to be recalled, and the probability of recall is low. (After Waugh & Norman, 1965)*

each new item that enters short-term memory has a chance to displace Cohn. After one new item, there has been only one chance to displace Cohn; after two new items, there have been two chances; and so on. The likelihood that Cohn will be lost from short-term memory increases steadily with the number of items that have followed it. Eventually, Cohn will be lost from short-term memory.

Displacement has been demonstrated experimentally many times. In one study, subjects were given a list of 13 digits, presented one at a time. After the last digit in the list was presented, a *probe* digit was given (it is called a probe because subjects must use it to probe their memory). The probe was always the same as one of the digits in the list, and the subject was required to recall the item that came after the probe. For example, given the list 3 9 1 6 9 7 5 3 8 2 5 6 4 and the probe 2, subjects should report 5. (The probe always occurred just once in the list.) When the probe is drawn from the end of the list, the item following it should still be in short-term memory (because it has just been presented) and hence should be very likely to be recalled. When the probe is drawn from the beginning of the list, however, many items have followed the one to be recalled. Most likely it has been displaced and will not be recalled. For probes drawn from the middle of the list, the chance of displacement is moderate, as is the chance of recall. Figure 8-4 shows that the data from this experiment support the principle of displacement. The more items that intervene between the occurrence of a particular digit and the attempt to recall it, the less the chance of recall.

There is another way to think about the fixed capacity of short-term memory and the tendency of new items to displace old ones. As noted earlier, being in short-term memory may correspond to being in a state of activation. The more items we try to keep active, the less activation there is for any one of them. Perhaps only about seven items can be simultaneously maintained at a level of activation that permits recall of all of them. Once seven items are active, if a new item is attended to, the activation that it receives will be usurped from items presented earlier; consequently these earlier items may fall below the critical level of activation needed for recall (Anderson, 1983).

The other major cause of forgetting in short-term memory is that information simply decays in time. We may think of the representation of an item as a trace that fades within a matter of seconds. One piece of evidence for this view is that an item may be lost from memory within seconds even if no new information follows it (Reitman, 1974). Another source of evidence for decay is that our short-term memory span holds fewer words when the words take longer to say; for example, the span is less for long words such as "harpoon" and "cyclone" than for shorter words such as "bishop" and "pewter" (try saying the words to yourself to see the difference in duration). Presumably this effect arises because as the words are presented we say them to ourselves, and the longer it takes to do this, the more likely it is that some of the words' traces will have faded before they can be recalled (Baddeley, Thompson, & Buchanan, 1975).

It appears, then, that information at the forefront of our memory must soon give way. The one major exception to this involves rehearsal: items that we rehearse are not readily subject to displacement or decay. (In experiments that demonstrate displacement or decay, subjects are typically discouraged from rehearsing.) Rehearsing information may protect it from displacement because we cannot encode new items at the same time we are rehearsing old ones. Rehearsal may offset decay more directly: rehearsing an item that has partly faded may bring it to full strength again.

Retrieval

Let us think of the contents of short-term memory as being active in consciousness. Intuition suggests that access to this information is immediate. You do not have to dig for it; it is right there. Retrieval, then, should not depend on the number of items in consciousness. But in this case intuition is wrong.

Evidence shows that the more items there are in short-term memory, the slower retrieval becomes, suggesting that retrieval requires a search of short-term memory in which the items are examined one at a time (just as you might examine a set of dishes one at a time to find the one with a chip). This *serial* search of short-term memory takes place at a very fast rate—so fast, in fact, that we are not aware of it. Most of the evidence for such a search comes from a type of experiment introduced by Sternberg (1966). On each trial of the experiment, a subject is shown a set of digits, called the *memory list*, that he or she must temporarily hold in short-term memory. It is easy for the subject to maintain the information in short-term memory because each memory list contains between one and six digits. The memory list is then removed from view, and a probe digit is presented. The subject must decide whether the probe was on the memory list. For example, if the memory list is 3 6 1 and the probe is 6, the subject should respond "yes"; given the same memory list and a probe of 2, the subject should respond "no." Subjects rarely make an error on this task; what is of interest, however, is the speed at which the subject makes the decision. The *decision time* is the elapsed time between the onset of the probe and the subject's press of a "yes" or a "no" button to indicate whether the probe was or was not on the memory list. The decision times are extremely fast and must be measured with equipment that permits accuracy in milliseconds (thousandths of a second).

Figure 8-5 presents data from such an experiment, indicating that decision time increases directly with the length of the memory list. What is remarkable about these decision times is that they fall along a straight line. This means that each additional item in short-term memory adds a fixed amount of time to the search process—approximately 40 milliseconds. The subject, of course, is not aware of such brief time intervals, but the data indicate that decision time increases with the amount of information that must be searched through in short-term memory. The same results are found when the items are letters, words, auditory tones, or pictures of people's faces: the addition of an extra item usually adds about 40 milliseconds to retrieval time (Sternberg, 1975). Psychologists have obtained similar results with groups as varied as schizophrenic patients, college students under the influence of marijuana, and people from preliterate societies. *

Short-Term Memory and Thought

Short-term memory plays an important role in conscious thought. When consciously trying to solve a problem, we often use short-term memory as a mental work space: we use it to store parts of the problem as well as

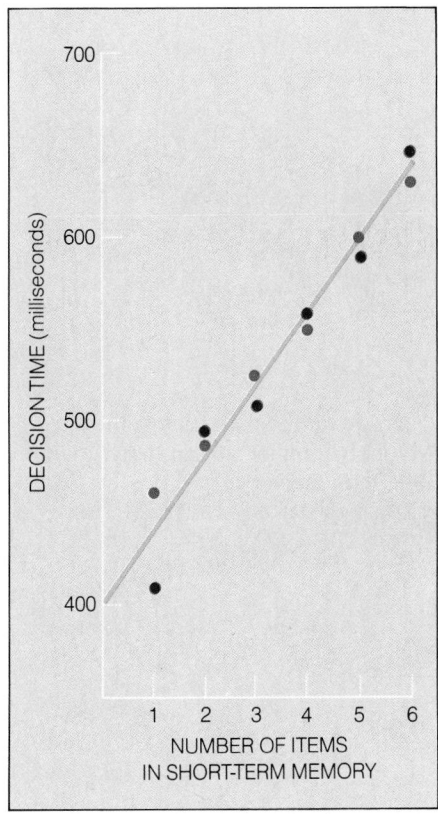

FIGURE 8-5
Retrieval as a Search Process *Decision times increase in direct proportion to the number of items in short-term memory. Blue circles represent "yes" responses; red circles, "no" responses. The times for both types of decision fall along a straight line.* (After Sternberg, 1966)

---

* While the data in Figure 8-5 are consistent with a serial (one at a time) search of short-term memory, other interpretations are possible. Some researchers have taken the view that short-term memory corresponds to a state of activation, and have argued that retrieval is based on activation reaching a critical level. One decides a probe is in short-term memory if its representation is above a critical level of activation, and the more items in short-term memory, the less the activation for any one of them (Monsell, 1979).

"Can we hurry up and get to the test? My short-term memory is better than my long-term memory."

© 1985, reprinted courtesy of Bill Hoest and *Parade* Magazine.

information accessed from long-term memory that is relevant to the problem. To illustrate, consider what it takes to multiply 35 by 8 in your head. You need short-term memory to store the given numbers (35 and 8), the nature of the operation required (multiplication), and arithmetic facts such as $8 \times 5 = 40$ and $3 \times 8 = 24$. Not surprisingly, performance on mental arithmetic declines substantially if you have to remember simultaneously some words or digits; try doing the above mental multiplication while remembering the phone number 745–1739 (Baddeley & Hitch, 1974). Other research indicates that short-term memory is used not only in numerical problems but also in the whole gamut of complex problems that we routinely confront. For this reason, researchers increasingly refer to short-term memory as "working memory," and conceptualize it as a kind of blackboard in which the mind performs its computations and posts the partial results for later use (Baddeley, 1986; Just & Carpenter, 1987).

The role that short-term memory plays in understanding language is more complicated. The short-term memory system we have described appears not to be involved in understanding relatively simple sentences. The best evidence for this comes from studies of brain-damaged patients with memory disorders. When presented with a list of unrelated words, some patients can correctly repeat only a single word (their memory span is 1), yet when presented with a whole sentence they can repeat and understand the entire thing. In contrast, other brain-damaged patients have a normal memory span, yet are unable to repeat or understand a simple sentence. These findings suggest that we have a special memory system for processing language. A patient who has a defective memory span but normal language understanding has an impaired short-term memory but an intact language memory. On the other hand, a patient who has a normal memory span but defective language understanding has the opposite memory problem (McCarthy & Warrington, 1987a).

The special memory for language seems limited to relatively simple sentences. Once sentences become complex—for example, "The salesman that the doctor met departed"—short-term memory is brought in for help (you can sense yourself using short-term memory to understand the preceding example). Hence short-term memory serves as a back up in sentence understanding (McCarthy & Warrington, 1987b).

When it comes to higher-level language processes like following a conversation or reading a text, short-term memory appears to play a crucial role. When reading for understanding, often we must consciously relate new sentences to some prior material in the text. This relating of new to old seems to occur in short-term memory because people who have more short-term capacity score higher than others on reading comprehension tests (Daneman & Carpenter, 1980). Other work shows that the readability of text depends partly on the likelihood that relevant connecting material is still in short-term memory (Malt, 1985).

Chunking

In the preceding discussion, we considered only short-term memory, but in real life, both short-term and long-term memory often play a role in the same situation. One particularly important interaction between short-term and long-term memory is the phenomenon of *chunking*, which can occur in memory-span tasks.

Recall that in a memory-span task, subjects can repeat a sequence of verbal items in perfect order as long as the number of items is 7 ± 2. As a result, you would probably be unable to repeat the letter sequence SRUOYYLERECNIS since it contains 14 letters. Should you notice, however, that these letters spell the phrase SINCERELY YOURS in reverse order, your task would become easier. By using this knowledge, you have decreased the number of items that must be held in short-term memory from 14 to 2. But where did this spelling knowledge come from? From long-term memory, of course, where knowledge about words is stored. Thus, you can use long-term memory to recode new material into larger meaningful units and then store those units in short-term memory. Such units are called *chunks*, and the capacity of short-term memory is best expressed as 7 ± 2 chunks (Miller, 1956).

Sometimes we can chunk letters without forming words when the letters stand for some meaningful (but nonword) unit. The letter string IB-MFB-ITVU-SA is hard to recall. But suppose the spacing is changed so that the string reads IBM-FBI-TV-USA. Each component is now a familiar unit. The result is four chunks and a string that is easy to remember (Bower & Springston, 1970). Chunking can occur with numbers as well. The string 149-2177-619-90 is beyond our capacity, but 1492-1776-1990 is well within it. The general principle is that we can boost our short-term memory by regrouping sequences of letters and digits into units that can be found in long-term memory.

Transfer from Short-Term to Long-Term Memory

DUAL-MEMORY THEORY   If information in short-term memory is to persist, it must be transferred to long-term memory. A number of theories about this transfer have been advanced. One such proposal, called *dual-memory theory*, illustrates the ideas involved (Atkinson & Shiffrin, 1971; 1977). This theory assumes that information we have attended to enters short-term memory, wherein it can be either maintained by rehearsal or lost by displacement or decay (see Figure 8-6). In addition, the information can be transferred into long-term memory. While there are a number of different ways to implement the transfer, one of the most commonly investigated is rehearsal. As the diagram in Figure 8-6 suggests, rehearsing an item not only maintains it in short-term memory but also causes it to be transferred to long-term memory.

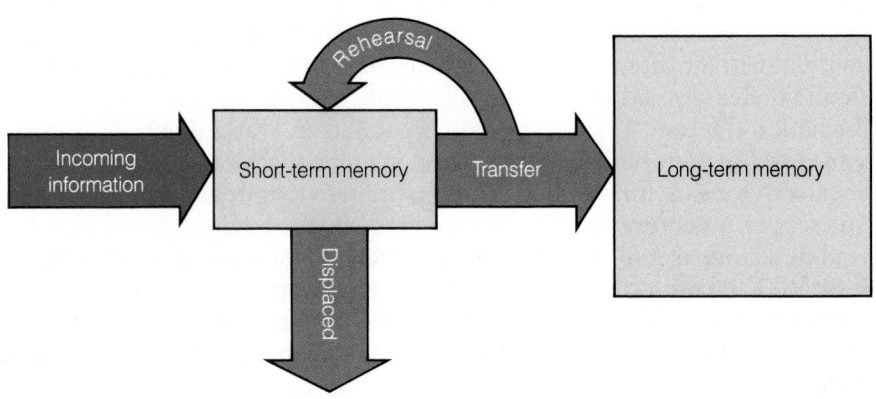

FIGURE 8-6
Dual-Memory Theory *Incoming items enter the memory system through short-term memory. Once in short-term memory, an item can be maintained there by rehearsal. As an item is rehearsed, information about it is transferred to long-term memory. Once rehearsal of an item is terminated, the item soon will be displaced by a new incoming item and thus be lost from short-term memory.*

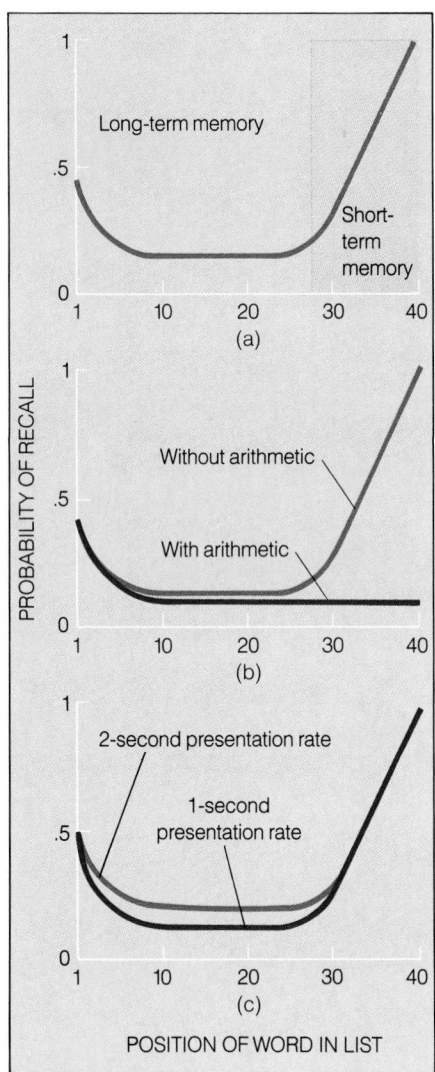

FIGURE 8-7
Curves of Free-Recall
Experiments *Probability of recall varies with an item's position in a list, with the probability being highest for the last five or so positions, next highest for the first few positions, and lowest for the intermediate positions. (a) Recall of the last few items is based on short-term memory, whereas recall of the remaining items is based on long-term memory. (b) If an arithmetic task occurs between the list presentation and free recall, only recall from short-term memory is reduced. (c) Slower presentation of items results in better recall from long-term memory. (After Murdock, 1962; Glanzer, 1972)*

Some of the best support for the dual-memory theory comes from experiments on *free recall*. In a free-recall experiment, subjects first see a list of, for example, 40 unrelated words which are presented one at a time. After all the words have been presented, subjects must immediately recall them in any order (hence the designation "free"). The results from such an experiment are shown in Figure 8-7a. The chance of correctly recalling a word is graphed as a function of the word's position in the list. The part of the curve to the left in the graph is for the first few words presented, whereas the part to the right is for the last few words presented.

The dual-memory theory assumes that at the time of recall the last few words presented are still likely to be in short-term memory, whereas the remaining words are in long-term memory. Hence, we would expect recall of the last few words to be high, because items in short-term memory can easily be retrieved. Figure 8-7a shows this is the case. But recall for the first words presented is also quite good. Why is this? Dual-memory theory has an answer. When the first words were presented, they were entered into short-term memory and rehearsed. Since there was little else in short-term memory, they were rehearsed often and were therefore likely to be transferred to long-term memory. As more items were presented, short-term memory quickly filled up, and the opportunity to rehearse and transfer any given item to long-term memory decreased to a low level. So, only the first few items presented enjoyed the extra opportunity of transfer, which is why they were later recalled so well from long-term memory.

Varying the procedure of the free-recall experiment produces results that support the preceding analysis. Suppose that after the list is presented but before subjects try to recall it they do arithmetic problems for 30 seconds. Doing arithmetic requires short-term memory capacity and should therefore displace many of the list words that are in short-term memory (the last words presented). Figure 8-7b shows that, as expected, the last few words were displaced. The rate at which the words are presented should also affect recall. A slower rate of presentation—for instance, a word every 2 seconds instead of every second—will allow more time for rehearsal and, hence, for transfer to long-term memory. The slower rate should therefore boost recall for the words that have to be retrieved from long-term memory—that is, all words but the last few. The results of this variation, shown in Figure 8-7c, again conform to predictions. The slower rate improved recall for all but the last few words.

PROBLEMS FOR THE THEORY   Although the dual-memory theory has successfully accounted for a wide range of phenomena, it does not answer some questions (Craik & Lockhart, 1972). One major dispute concerns rehearsal. The dual-memory theory assumes that simply repeating words to yourself, with no attempt to organize them or relate them to other memories, should increase your long-term recall. While some experiments support this prediction (Nelson, 1977), others do not (Craik & Watkins, 1973). Indeed, some psychologists have suspected for a long time that simple rehearsal is not an effective means for transferring information to long-term memory. Three-quarters of a century ago, the psychologist E. C. Sanford noted that his reading a group of five morning prayers aloud almost every day for 25 years (at least 5,000 repetitions) did not succeed in implanting the prayers in permanent memory. When Sanford tested his memory by cueing himself with a word from a prayer to see how much of the litany he could recall, he found that for some of the prayers he could not even recall three words per cue.

That is not much memory for two and a half decades of rehearsal (Sanford, 1917; cited in Neisser, 1982).

Another challenge for dual-memory theory involves the free-recall evidence for the theory. When presenting this evidence, we noted that recall was particularly good for the most recently presented items and assumed that this *recency effect* was due to the words still being in short-term memory. However, a recency effect does not necessarily implicate short-term memory, because such an effect can arise even when recall is from long-term memory. For example, when soccer players were asked at the end of a season to free-recall all their rivals, recall was best for the last few competitors. This recency effect cannot possibly reflect short-term memory because the recall occurred weeks after the games. Rather, this effect probably results from searching long-term memory chronologically (Baddeley & Hitch, 1977). Perhaps the same is true of the recency effect in the free-recall studies described earlier. Thus, the existence of a long-term memory recency effect dilutes the evidence for the dual-memory model. These challenges to dual-memory theory have led to the development of alternative theories of the relation between short- and long-term memory (Baddeley, 1986).

LONG-TERM MEMORY

Long-term memory involves information that has been retained for intervals as brief as a few minutes (such as a point made earlier in a conversation) or as long as a lifetime (such as an adult's childhood memories). In experiments on long-term memory, psychologists generally have studied forgetting over intervals of minutes, hours, or weeks, but a few studies have involved years or even decades.

Our discussion of long-term memory will again distinguish between the three stages of memory—encoding, storage, and retrieval—but this time there are two complications. First, unlike the situation in short-term memory, important interactions between encoding and retrieval occur in long-term memory. In view of these interactions, we will consider some aspects of retrieval in our discussion of encoding and will present a separate discussion of encoding-retrieval interactions. The other complication is that it is often difficult to know whether forgetting from long-term memory is due to a loss from storage or a failure in retrieval. To deal with this problem, we will delay our discussion of storage until after we have considered retrieval, so that we will have a clearer idea of what constitutes good evidence for a storage loss.

Encoding

ENCODING MEANING   For verbal materials, the dominant long-term memory representation is neither acoustic nor visual; instead, it is based on the meanings of the items. If you memorize a long list of unrelated words and try to recall them an hour later, you will undoubtedly make errors. Many of the erroneous words, however, will be similar in meaning to the correct ones. For example, if "quick" is on the original list, you may mistakenly recall "fast" instead (Kintsch & Buschke, 1969). Encoding items according to their meanings is more striking when the items are sentences. Several minutes

"Honus Wagner had a lifetime batting average of .329 and wrote 'Lohengrin.' Ask me another."

Drawing by Handelsman. © 1988. Reprinted by permission of *The New Yorker Magazine*, Inc.

after hearing a sentence, most of what you can recall or recognize is the sentence's meaning. Suppose you heard the sentence, "The author sent the committee a long letter." Two minutes later you could not tell whether you had heard that sentence or one that has the same meaning: "A long letter was sent to the committee by the author" (Sachs, 1967).

Encoding meaning is pervasive in real life. When people report on complex social or political situations, they may misremember many of the specifics (who said what to whom, when something was said, who else was there) yet can accurately describe the basic situation that took place. Thus, in the famous Watergate scandal of the early 1970s, the chief government witness (John Dean) was subsequently shown to have made many mistakes about what was said in particular situations, yet his overall testimony accurately described the events that had taken place (Neisser, 1981).

Although meaning may be the dominant way of representing verbal material in long-term memory, we sometimes code other aspects as well. We can, for example, memorize poems and recite them word for word. In such cases, we have coded not only the meaning of the poem but the words themselves. We can also use an acoustic code in long-term memory. When you get a phone call and the other party says "hello," often you recognize the voice. To do this, you must have coded the sound of that person's voice in long-term memory. Visual impressions, tastes, and smells are also coded in long-term memory. Thus, like short-term memory, long-term memory has a preferred code for verbal material (namely, meaning for long-term memory and acoustic for short-term memory), but other codes can be used as well.

ADDING MEANINGFUL CONNECTIONS   Often the items we have to remember are meaningful but the connections between them are not. In such cases, memory can be improved by creating real or artificial links between the items. For example, people learning to read music must remember that the five lines in printed music are referred to as EGBDF; although the symbols themselves are meaningful (they refer to notes on a keyboard), their order seems arbitrary. What many learners do is convert the symbols into the sentence "Every Good Boy Does Fine"; the first letter of each word names each symbol, and the relations between the words in the sentence supply meaningful connections between the symbols. These connections aid memory because they provide retrieval paths between the words: once the word "Good" has been retrieved, for example, there is a path or connection to "Boy," the next word that has to be recalled.

One of the best ways to add connections is to elaborate on the meaning of the material while encoding it. The more deeply or elaborately one encodes the meaning, the better memory will be. If you have to remember a point made in a textbook, you will recall it better if you concentrate on its meaning rather than on the exact words. And the more deeply and thoroughly you expand on its meaning, the better you will recall it.

An experiment by Bradshaw and Anderson (1982) illustrates some of these points. Subjects read facts about famous people that they would later have to recall, such as "At a critical point in his life, Mozart made a journey from Munich to Paris." Some facts were elaborated by either their causes or consequences, as in "Mozart wanted to leave Munich to avoid a romantic entanglement." Other facts were presented alone. When subjects were later tested for memory, they recalled more facts that were given elaborations than those presented alone. Presumably, in adding the cause (or consequence) to their memory representation, subjects set up a retrieval path from the cause to the target fact in the following manner:

Mozart journeyed from Munich to Paris

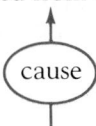

Mozart wanted to avoid a romantic entanglement in Munich

At the time of recall, subjects could retrieve the target fact directly, or indirectly, by following the path from its cause. Even if they forgot the target fact entirely, they could infer it if they retrieved the cause.

Material as complex as a textbook chapter also benefits from elaboration. This has been demonstrated in an experiment in which subjects had to read part of a text and later answer questions about the material. Prior to reading the text, one group of subjects was given a set of advance questions (which were different from the test questions they would later be asked). These subjects were to find answers to the advance questions while reading the text. Trying to find these answers should have led the subjects to elaborate on parts of the text as it was being read. A control group of subjects studied the text without any advance questions. When both groups were later given the test questions, the first group answered more correctly than the control group. Again, an experimental technique that fostered elaboration enhanced memory (Frase, 1975; Anderson, 1989).

Retrieval

Many cases of forgetting from long-term memory result from a loss of access to the information rather than from a loss of the information itself. That is, poor memory often reflects a retrieval failure rather than a storage

TABLE 8-1
**Examples from a Study of Retrieval
Failures** *Subjects not given the retrieval
cues recall fewer words from the memorized
list than other subjects who did have the
cues. This finding shows that problems at
the retrieval stage of long-term memory are
responsible for some memory failures.*
(After Tulving & Pearlstone, 1966)

LIST TO BE MEMORIZED		
dog	cotton	oil
cat	wool	gas
horse	silk	coal
cow	rayon	wood
apple	blue	doctor
orange	red	laywer
pear	green	teacher
banana	yellow	dentist
chair	knife	football
table	spoon	baseball
bed	fork	basketball
sofa	pan	tennis
knife	hammer	shirt
gun	saw	socks
rifle	nails	pants
bomb	screwdriver	shoes

RETRIEVAL CUES		
animals	cloth	fuels
fruit	color	professions
furniture	utensils	sports
weapons	tools	clothing

failure. (Note that this is unlike short-term memory, where forgetting is a
result of exceeding the storage capacity, while retrieval is thought to be error-
free.) Trying to retrieve an item from long-term memory is analogous to
trying to find a book in a large library. Failure to find the book does not
necessarily mean it is not there; you may be looking in the wrong place, or it
may simply be misfiled and therefore inaccessible.

EVIDENCE FOR RETRIEVAL FAILURES   Common experience provides
much evidence for retrieval failures. Everyone at some point has been unable
to recall a fact or an experience, only to have it come to mind later. How
many times have you taken an exam and not been able to recall a specific
name or date, only to remember it after the exam? Another example is the
"tip-of-the-tongue" experience in which a particular word or name lies tanta-
lizingly outside our ability to recall it (Brown & McNeill, 1966). We may feel
quite tormented until a search of memory (dredging up and then discarding
words that are close but not quite right) finally retrieves the correct word.

A more striking example of retrieval failure is the occasional recovery by
a person under hypnosis of a childhood memory that had previously been
forgotten. Similar experiences may occur in psychotherapy. Although we
lack firm evidence for some of these observations, they at least suggest that
some seemingly forgotten memories are not lost. They are just difficult to get
at and require the right kind of *retrieval cue* (anything that can help us retrieve a memory).

For stronger evidence that retrieval failures can cause forgetting, consider the following experiment. Subjects were asked to memorize a long list
of words. Some of the words were names of animals, such as dog, cat, horse;
some named specific fruits, such as apple, pear, orange; some named items of
furniture, and so on (see Table 8-1). At the time of recall, the subjects were
divided into two groups. One group was supplied with retrieval cues such as
"animal," "fruit," and so on; the other group, the control group, was not. The
group given the retrieval cues recalled more words than the control group. In
a subsequent test, when both groups were given the retrieval cues, they recalled the same number of words. Hence, the initial difference in recall
between the two groups must have been due to retrieval failures.

Thus, the better the retrieval cues, the better our memory. This principle explains why we usually do better on a recognition test of memory than
on a recall test. In a recognition test, we are asked if we have seen a particular
item before (for example, "Was Bessie Smith one of the people you met at the
party?"). The test item itself is an excellent retrieval cue for our memory of
that item. In contrast, in a recall test we have to produce the memorized
items with minimal retrieval cues (for example, "Recall the names of everyone you met at the party"). Since the retrieval cues in a recognition test are
generally more useful than those in a recall test, recognition tests usually
show better memory performance than recall tests (Tulving, 1974).

INTERFERENCE   Among the factors that can impair retrieval, the most
important is *interference*. If we associate different items with the same cue,
when we try to use that cue to retrieve one of the items (the target item), the
other items may become active and interfere with our recovery of the target.
For example, if your friend, Dan, moves and you finally learn his new phone
number, you will find it difficult to retrieve the old number. Why? You are
using the cue "Dan's phone number" to retrieve the old number, but instead
this cue activates the new number, which interferes with recovery of the old
one. Or suppose that your reserved space in a parking garage, which you have

used for a year, is changed. You may initially find it difficult to retrieve from memory your new parking location. Why? You are trying to learn to associate your new location with the cue "my parking place," but this cue retrieves the old location, which interferes with the learning of the new one. In both examples, the power of retrieval cues ("Dan's phone number" or "my parking place") to activate particular target items decreases with the number of other items associated with those cues. The more items associated with a cue, the more overloaded it becomes and the less effectively it can retrieve.

Interference can operate at various levels, including that of whole facts. In one experiment, subjects first learned to associate various facts with the names of professions. For example, they learned that:

1. The banker was asked to address the crowd.
2. The banker broke the bottle.
3. The banker did not delay the trip.
4. The lawyer realized the seam was split.
5. The lawyer painted an old barn.

The occupational names "banker" and "lawyer" were the retrieval cues here. Since "banker" was associated with three facts, whereas "lawyer" was associated with just two, "banker" should have been less useful in retrieving any one of its associated facts than "lawyer" was ("banker" was the more overloaded retrieval cue). When subjects were later given a recognition test, they did take longer to recognize the facts learned about the banker than those learned about the lawyer. In this study, then, interference slowed the speed of retrieval. Many other experiments show that interference can lead to a complete retrieval failure if the target items are very weak or the interference is very strong (Anderson, 1983).

These interference effects suggest that retrieval from long-term memory may be thought of as a search process. To illustrate, consider how a sentence from the preceding study, "The banker broke the bottle," might be recognized (see Figure 8-8). The term "banker" accesses its representation in

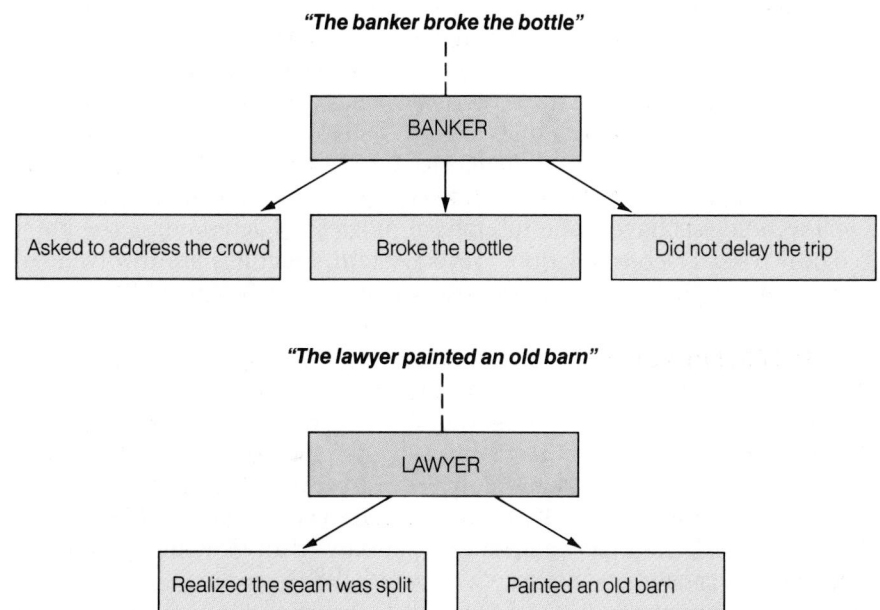

FIGURE 8-8
Illustration of Retrieval as a Search Process *When presented the sentence, "The banker broke the bottle," the term "banker" accesses the banker representation in long-term memory; once at this representation, there are three paths to be searched. When presented "The lawyer painted an old barn," "lawyer" accesses the lawyer representation, from which there are two paths to be searched. Alternatively, the term "banker" may activate the banker representation, where this activation then spreads simultaneously along the three paths (and similarly for the "lawyer" example).*

memory, which localizes the search to the relevant part of long-term memory. Once there, three paths need to be searched to find the fact "broke the bottle." In contrast, if the test sentence was "The lawyer painted an old barn," there are only two paths to be searched (see Figure 8-8). Since the duration of a search increases with the number of paths to be considered, retrieval will be slower for the "banker" sentence than the "lawyer" one. Retrieval generally is more difficult when more facts are associated with a retrieval cue, because each fact adds a path to be searched.

An alternative way to think about the retrieval process is in terms of activation. When trying to recognize "The banker broke the bottle," for example, the subject activates the representation for "banker," which then spreads simultaneously along the three paths emanating from "banker" (see Figure 8-8). When sufficient activation reaches "broke the bottle," the sentence can be recognized. Interference arises because the activation from the banker representation must be subdivided among the paths emanating from it. Hence, the more facts associated with "banker," the thinner the activation on each path, and the longer it will take for sufficient activation to reach any particular fact. So, thinking of retrieval in terms of spreading activation can also account for why interference slows retrieval (Anderson, 1983).

Storage

Retrieval failures are unlikely to be the only cause of forgetting. The fact that *some* forgetting is due to retrieval failures does not imply that *all* forgetting is. It seems most unlikely that everything we ever learned is still there in memory waiting for the right retrieval cue. Some information is almost certainly lost from storage (Loftus & Loftus, 1980).

Direct evidence of storage loss comes from people who receive *electroconvulsive shock* (a mild electric current applied to the brain produces a brief epileptic-like seizure and momentary unconsciousness; see Chapter 16) to alleviate severe depression. In such cases, the patient loses some memory for events that occurred in the months prior to the shock, but not for earlier events (Squire & Fox, 1980). Memory loss due to electroconvulsive shock has been demonstrated with animal subjects in the laboratory [though with rats, the memory loss covers a period of minutes rather than months (McGaugh & Herz, 1972)]. These memory losses are unlikely to be due to retrieval failures, because if the shock disrupted retrieval, then all memories should be affected, not just the recent ones. More likely, the shock disrupts storage processes that *consolidate* new memories over a period of months or longer, and information that is not consolidated is lost from storage.

Psychologists have made substantial progress in determining the physiological bases of consolidation. Several brain structures are involved, including the *hippocampus* and *amygdala*, which are located below the cerebral cortex. The hippocampus' role in consolidation seems to be that of a cross-referencing system, linking together aspects of a particular memory that are stored in separate parts of the brain (Squire, Cohen, & Nadel, 1984). Damage to the hippocampus alone can result in severe memory disturbance. This fact was recently demonstrated by a study that started with an analysis of a particular patient's memory problems (due to complications from coronary bypass surgery), and ended with a detailed autopsy of his brain following the patient's death; the hippocampus was the only brain structure found to be damaged (Zola-Morgan, Squire, & Amaral, 1989).

More frequently, damage to just the hippocampus does not result in severe memory loss; the amygdala seems to be able to pick up the slack. If both
the hippocampus and amygdala are damaged, then a global memory loss
ensues. In addition, severe memory loss can arise when there is damage to
another brain site, the *diencephalon*, a cluster of nuclei below the cortex. This
structure is often damaged when the memory loss arises from tumors, strokes,
and severe alcoholism (Mishkin & Appenzeller, 1987).

The brain structures described above—hippocampus, amygdala, and diencephalon—are all part of the lower brain. They are not believed to be the
places in which memories are ultimately stored. Rather, the anatomical
locus of long-term storage is almost certainly the cortex, particularly those
regions in which sensory information is interpreted.

Encoding-Retrieval Interactions

In describing the encoding stage, we noted that operations carried out
during encoding (for instance, elaboration) later make retrieval easier. Two
other encoding factors also increase the chances of successful retrieval: a)
organizing the information at the time of encoding, and b) ensuring that the
context in which information is encoded is similar to that in which it will be
retrieved.

ORGANIZATION   The more we organize the material we encode, the
easier it is to retrieve. Suppose you were at a conference at which you met
various professionals—doctors, lawyers, and journalists. When later you try
to recall their names, you will do better if initially you organize the information by profession. Then you can ask yourself, Who were the doctors I met?
Who were the lawyers? And so forth. A list of names or words is far easier to
recall when we encode the information into categories and then retrieve it
on a category-by-category basis.

The following experiment illustrates the use of categories in organizing
encoding. The subjects were asked to memorize lists of words. For some
subjects, the words in a list were arranged in the form of a hierarchical tree,
much like the example shown in Figure 8-9. For the other subjects, the words
were arranged randomly. When tested later, the subjects presented with
the hierarchical organization recalled 65 percent of the words, whereas the

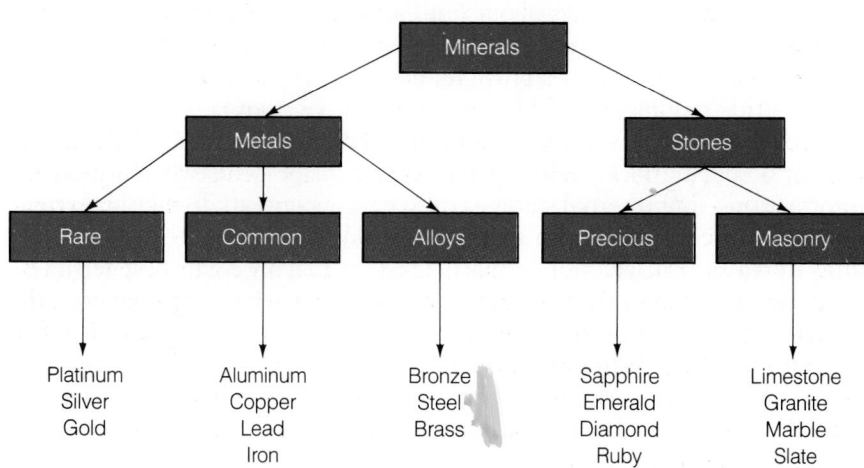

FIGURE 8-9
**Hierarchical Organization to Improve
Retrieval** *Trees like this are constructed
according to the following rule: all items
below a node are included in the class
labeled by that node. For example, the items
"bronze," "steel," and "brass" are included
in the class labeled "alloys."* (After Bower,
Clark, Winzenz, & Lesgold, 1969)

subjects presented with random arrangements recalled only 19 percent of the same words. Studies like this leave little doubt that memory is best when the material is highly organized.

Why does hierarchical organization improve memory? Probably because it makes the process underlying retrieval—search or activation—more efficient. To illustrate, suppose that subjects in the preceding experiment used a serial search. Subjects who had seen the words hierarchically organized, as in Figure 8-9, might have proceeded as follows: first they found a high-level cluster, such as "metals"; from that high-level cluster, they then searched for a low-level cluster, such as "common metals"; and then they searched that low-level cluster for specific words ("aluminum," "copper," "lead," "iron"); and so on. By operating in this way, at no point would subjects have to search a large set. There are only two high-level clusters, never more than three low-level clusters connected to a high-level one, and never more than four specific words in a low-level cluster. Hierarchical organization thus allows us to divide a big search into a sequence of little ones. And with a little search, there is less chance we will bog down by turning up the same words again and again, which is exactly what seems to happen when we search material that is not organized (Raaijmakers & Shiffrin, 1981; Gillund & Shiffrin, 1984).

Organization can also offset the detrimental effects of interference. In the experiment in which subjects memorized such facts as "The banker was asked to address the crowd," "The banker broke the bottle," and "The banker did not delay the trip," subjects took longer to recognize one of these three facts than they did to recognize one of two facts learned about some other occupation term. This interference effect can be eliminated by organizing the facts. Thus, if the first sentence is replaced by "The banker was asked to christen the ship," the "banker" facts will be integrated around the theme of christening a ship. Now, subjects take no longer to recognize one of the three facts about the banker than one of the two learned about some other occupation; organization has offset interference (Smith, Adams, & Schorr, 1978).

CONTEXT   It is easier to retrieve a particular fact or episode if you are in the same context in which you encoded it (Estes, 1972). For example, it is a good bet that your ability to retrieve the names of your classmates in the first and second grades would improve were you to walk through the corridors of your elementary school. Similarly, your ability to retrieve an emotional moment with your parents would be greater if you were back in the place where the incident occurred. This may explain why we are sometimes overcome with a torrent of memories about our earlier life when we visit a place we once lived. The context in which an event was encoded is itself one of the most powerful retrieval cues possible, and a mass of experimental evidence supports this (see Figure 8-10 for a representative study).

Context is not always external to the memorizer, such as a physical location or a specific face. What is happening inside of us when we encode information—our internal state—is also part of context. To take an extreme example, if we experience an event while under the influence of a particular drug (for instance, alcohol or marijuana), perhaps we can best retrieve it when we are again in that drug-induced state. In such cases, memory would be partly dependent on the internal state during learning; we call this *state-dependent learning*. While the evidence on state-dependent learning is controversial, it suggests that memory does indeed improve when our internal state during retrieval matches that during encoding (Eich, Weingartner, Stillman, & Gillian, 1975).

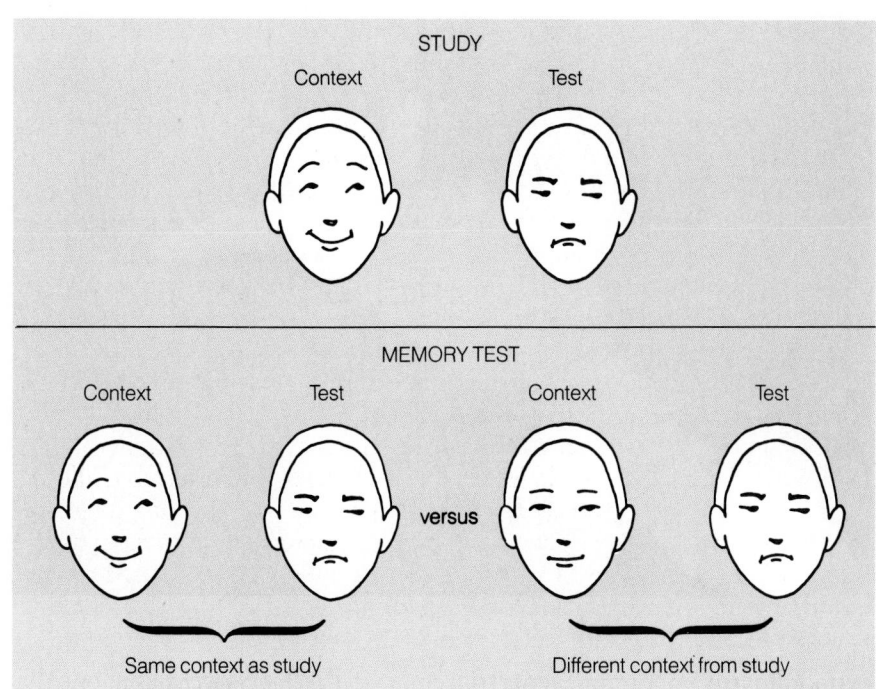

STUDY
Context   Test

MEMORY TEST
Context   Test   Context   Test

versus

Same context as study   Different context from study

FIGURE 8-10
Effects of Context on Retrieval *In an experiment to demonstrate how context affects retrieval, subjects first studied pairs of faces like the one at the top. (Since only the right-hand face was ever tested, it was the test face, whereas the left-hand one was the context face.) Later, in a memory test, subjects were again shown pairs of faces and asked whether the test face (the one on the right) was one they had previously studied. In some cases, the context face was the same one that had appeared in the original pair; in other cases, it was not. Subjects made more accurate decisions when the context face was the same. (After Watkins, Ho, & Tulving, 1976)*

Emotional Factors in Forgetting

So far, we have treated memory as if it were divorced from the emotional part of our lives. But don't we sometimes remember material because of its emotional content? Or for that matter, forget material because of its emotional content? There has been a great deal of research on these questions. The results suggest that emotion can influence long-term memory in at least five distinct ways.

The simplest idea is that we tend to think about emotionally charged situations, negative as well as positive, more than we think about neutral ones. We rehearse and organize exciting memories more than we do their blander counterparts. For example, you may forget where you saw this or that movie, but if a fire breaks out while you are in a theater, you will describe the setting over and over to friends, as well as think about the setting over and over to yourself, thereby rehearsing and organizing it. Since we know that rehearsal and organization can improve retrieval from long-term memory, it is not surprising that many researchers have found better memory for emotional than for unemotional situations (Rapaport, 1942; Neisser, 1982).

The second way that emotion can affect memory is via *flashbulb memories*. A flashbulb memory is a vivid and permanent record of the circumstances in which you learned of an emotionally charged, significant event, such as the explosion of the space shuttle *Challenger* in 1986. Many people remember exactly where they were when they learned of the *Challenger* disaster, and exactly who told them about it, even though these are the kinds of details that we usually forget quickly. Americans 30 years of age or older may have flashbulb memories of the assassination attempt on Ronald Reagan in 1981, while those 40 or older may have such memories of the assassinations of John F. Kennedy and Martin Luther King in the 1960s. What is responsible for such memories? According to Brown and Kulik (1977),

For many people, the explosion of the space shuttle Challenger *is a "flashbulb memory."*

extraordinarily important events trigger a *special memory mechanism*, one that makes a permanent record of everything the person is experiencing at the moment. It is as if we took a picture of the moment, which is why the recollection is dubbed a "flashbulb memory."

While few doubt that our memories of emotionally charged, national events can be detailed and long-lasting, some researchers have disputed the idea that a special memory mechanism is involved. In particular, flashbulb memories become less retrievable with time, in the same way that normal long-term memories do. In one study, a few days after the *Challenger* explosion, people were asked where they were and what they were doing when they heard of the disaster; nine months later, the same people were asked the same questions. Although the people had unusually detailed memories of the event 9 months after it occurred, there was some forgetting during the interval (McCloskey, Wible, & Cohen, 1988). Similarly, people's memories of the assassination attempt on President Reagan show some decrease in recall as the event recedes in time (Pillimer, 1984). Results like these suggest that memory for national tragedies could be an instance of normal memory. The reason we remember the events so vividly is that we keep on hearing and talking about them, the way we do other emotionally charged situations (McCloskey, Wible, and Cohen, 1988).

In some cases, however, negative emotions hinder retrieval, which brings us to the third way that emotion can affect memory. An experience that many students have at one time or another illustrates this:

> You are taking an exam about which you are not very confident. You can barely understand the initial question, let alone answer it. Signs of panic appear. Although the second question really isn't hard, the anxiety triggered by the previous question spreads to this one. By the time you look at the third question, it wouldn't matter if it just asked for your name. There's no way you can answer it. You're in a complete panic.

What is happening to memory here? Failure to deal with the first question produced anxiety. Anxiety is often accompanied by extraneous thoughts, such as "I'm going to flunk out" or "Everybody will think I am stupid." These thoughts then interfere with any attempt to retrieve the information relevant to the question, and that may be why memory utterly fails. According to this view, anxiety does not directly cause memory failure; rather, it causes, or is associated with, extraneous thoughts, and these thoughts cause memory failure by interfering with retrieval (Holmes, 1974).

Emotion may also affect memory by *context effects*. As we have noted, memory is best when the context at retrieval matches that at encoding. Since our emotional state during learning is part of the context, if we feel sad when we learn some material, then we can best retrieve that material when we feel sad again. Experimenters have demonstrated such an emotional-context effect in the laboratory. Subjects agreed to keep diaries for a week, recording daily every emotional incident that occurred and noting whether it was pleasant or unpleasant. One week after they handed in their diaries, the subjects returned to the laboratory and were hypnotized (they had been preselected to be highly hypnotizable). Half the subjects were put in a pleasant mood, and the other half were put in an unpleasant mood. All were asked to recall the incidents recorded in their diaries. For subjects in a pleasant mood, most of the incidents they recalled had been rated as pleasant when experienced; for subjects in an unpleasant mood at retrieval, most of the incidents recalled had been rated as unpleasant when experienced. As expected, recall was best when the dominant emotion during retrieval matched that during encoding (Bower, 1981).

Thus far, aside from the possibility of a special purpose mechanism for flashbulb memories, all of the means by which emotions can influence memory rely on principles already discussed—namely, rehearsal, interference, and context effects. The fifth view of emotion and memory, Freud's theory of the unconscious, brings up new principles. Freud proposed that some emotional experiences in childhood are so traumatic that allowing them to enter consciousness many years later would cause the individual to be totally overwhelmed by anxiety. (This is different from the example of the exam, where the anxiety was tolerable to consciousness.) Such traumatic experiences, as well as later ones associated with them, are said to be stored in the unconscious, or *repressed*; and they can be retrieved only when some of the emotion associated with them is defused, usually by therapeutic means. Repression, therefore, represents the ultimate retrieval failure: access to the target memories is actively blocked. This notion of active blocking makes the *repression hypothesis* qualitatively different from the ideas about forgetting we considered earlier. (For a fuller discussion of Freud's theory, see Chapter 14.)

Repression is such a striking phenomenon that we would of course like to study it in the laboratory, but this has proved difficult to do. To induce true repression in the laboratory, the experimenter must have the subject experience something extremely traumatic; ethical considerations prohibit this. The studies that have been done have exposed subjects to only mildly upsetting experiences. The bulk of the evidence from these studies lends some support to the repression hypothesis (Erdelyi, 1985).

Amnesia: Breakdown of Memory

We have learned a great deal about memory from people who have suffered *amnesia*. Amnesia refers to a partial or total loss of memory. It may result from very different causes, including accidental injuries to the brain,

"And then I say to myself, 'If I really wanted to talk to her, why do I keep forgetting to dial 1 first?'"
Drawing by Modell; © 1981 *The New Yorker Magazine*, Inc.

strokes, encephalitis, alcoholism, electroconvulsive shock, and surgical procedures (for example, removal of the hippocampus to reduce epilepsy). Whatever its cause, the primary symptom of amnesia is a profound inability to acquire new factual information or to remember day-to-day events; this is referred to as *anterograde amnesia*, and it can be very extensive. There are cases of amnesiacs who have spent years in the same hospital but have never learned their way to the bathroom. There is an intensively studied patient, identified as NA, who is unable to participate in a normal conversation because he loses his train of thought with the least distraction. Another patient identified as HM—the most intensively studied of all amnesiacs—reads the same magazines over and over and continually needs to be reintroduced to doctors who have been treating him for more than two decades.

A secondary symptom of amnesia is an inability to remember events that occurred *prior* to the injury or disease. The extent of such *retrograde amnesia* varies from patient to patient. Aside from retrograde and anterograde memory losses, the typical amnesiac appears normal: he or she has a normal vocabulary, the usual knowledge about the world, and in general shows no loss of intelligence.

EFFECTS ON DIFFERENT STAGES   Do the memory losses in amnesia reflect a breakdown in a particular stage of memory or in all of them? The evidence indicates that each stage can be affected. Some patients show an encoding deficit. If they are allowed more time than normal subjects to encode the material in a recall task, their subsequent recall can equal that of normals. Other patients may exhibit retrieval and storage deficits. For some amnesiacs, memory loss for events prior to the injury or disease (retrograde amnesia) extends over the majority of their lives. This loss must be due to retrieval failure, because events that occurred many years prior to the injury must have been normally encoded and consolidated. In contrast, in other patients retrograde amnesia extends only over a period of months. Such a restricted memory loss suggests a disruption of the storage stage, because consolidation processes presumably require only a period of months (Hirst, 1982; Squire & Cohen, 1984).

It is possible that there are two distinct kinds of amnesia, each corresponding to a distinct site of brain damage and affecting different stages of memory. Thus, patients who have damage in their hippocampal regions may suffer primarily from a storage deficit; these are the patients whose retrograde amnesia is limited to relatively recent events. In contrast, a person with an intact hippocampus but a damaged thalamus (part of the diencephalon) may suffer from encoding and retrieval deficits; these are the patients whose retrograde amnesia is unlimited in time and whose recall of new information is relatively normal only if given extra encoding time. While the hypothesis that different kinds of amnesia are related to damage in different regions of the brain makes sense of the varied findings, it is quite controversial (Squire & Cohen, 1984; Corkin et al., 1985).

FACT VERSUS SKILL MEMORY   A striking aspect of amnesia is that not all kinds of memory are disrupted. Thus, while amnesiacs are generally unable to remember old facts about their lives or to learn new ones, they have no difficulty remembering and learning perceptual and motor skills. This suggests that there is a different memory for facts than for skills.

The skills preserved in amnesia include *motor skills*, such as tieing one's shoelaces or riding a bike; *perceptual skills*, such as normal reading or reading words that are projected into a mirror (and hence reversed); and *cognitive skills*, such as defining a word or generating a word given only a fragment of its letters. Consider the ability of reading mirror-reversed words. To do this well takes a bit of practice (try holding this book in front of a mirror). Amnesiacs improve with practice at the very same rate as normal subjects, though they have no memory of having participated in prior practice sessions (Cohen & Squire, 1980). They show normal memory for the skill but virtually no memory for the learning episodes that developed it (the latter being *facts*).

A similar story emerges for cognitive skills, like that involved in word completion (for example, what word is *MOT _ _*?). In one experiment, both amnesiac and normal subjects were first presented a list of words to study. Then fragments of words on the list and fragments of words not on the list were presented, and subjects tried to complete them. The normal subjects performed as expected, completing more words when the fragmented words were drawn from the list than when they were not, but interestingly, amnesiacs were also able to complete more words for fragments drawn from the list. In fact, the extent to which amnesiacs did better with fragments from the list than with fragments not on the list was the same as normal subjects. Hence, when memory is manifested in skill, amnesiacs perform normally. However, in another condition of the experiment, the original words were presented again along with some novel words, and subjects had to recognize which words had appeared on the list. Now, amnesiacs remembered far fewer words than normals. Thus, when memory is manifested in "facts" ("This was one of the words that I saw on this list"), amnesiacs perform far below normals (Warrington & Weiskrantz, 1978).

The notion of different memories for skills and facts is not surprising once we reflect on how different these two kinds of knowledge are. Skill knowledge is "knowing how"; fact knowledge is "knowing that" (Ryle, 1949), and often the twain never meet. We know how to tie our shoelaces, for example, but we would have trouble describing it as a set of facts. The knowledge in a skill seems to be represented by the procedures needed to perform the skill, and such knowledge can be retrieved only by executing the procedures (Anderson, 1987).

There are different memories for motor skills and for facts.

PERSONAL-FACT VERSUS GENERAL-FACT MEMORY   Even within the domain of facts, there is an important distinction to be drawn. Some facts refer to personal episodes, while others are general truths. To illustrate, your memory of high-school graduation is a *personal fact*, and so is your memory for what you had for dinner last night. Even your memory for a memory experiment you read about in which amnesiacs had to read mirror-reversed words is a personal fact. In each of these cases, the episode is encoded with respect to you the individual (your graduation, your dinner, and so on), and often the episode is coded with respect to a specific time and place as well. All of this is in contrast to *general facts*, examples of which include your memory, or knowledge, that the word "bachelor" means an unmarried man, that September has 30 days, and that Abraham Lincoln was president of the United States. In these cases, the knowledge is encoded in relation to other knowledge rather than in relation to yourself, and there is no coding of time and place. For example, you probably cannot remember much about the context in which you learned that February has 29 days every fourth year (Tulving, 1985).

Are personal facts and general facts stored in different memories? The very existence of amnesia suggests that they are. Aside from their severe memory loss, most amnesiacs seem to have normal intelligence. This implies they have a normal vocabulary and normal knowledge about the world,

CRITICAL DISCUSSION

Childhood Amnesia

One of the most striking aspects of human memory is that everyone suffers from a particular kind of amnesia: virtually no person can recall events from the first years of life, though this is the time when experience is at its richest. This curious phenomenon was first discussed by Freud (1905), who called it *childhood amnesia*.

Freud discovered the phenomenon by observing that his patients were generally unable to recall events from their first 3 to 5 years of life. At first you might think there is nothing unusual about this, because memory for events declines with time, and for adults there has been a lot of intervening time since early childhood. But childhood amnesia cannot be reduced to a case of normal forgetting. Most 30-year-olds can recall a good deal about their high school years, but it is a rare 18-year-old that can tell you anything about his third year of life; yet the time interval is roughly the same in the two cases (about 15 years). More rigorous evidence along these lines comes from a study in which 18-year-old subjects tried to recall personal memories from all periods of their lives. Memory for an event, of course, declined with the number of years that had passed since that event, but the *rate* of decline was much steeper for events in the first 6 years of life than for events thereafter (Wetzler & Sweeney, cited in Rubin, 1986).

In other studies, people have been asked to recall and date their childhood memories. For most subjects, their first memories are of something that occurred when they were age 3 or older; a few subjects, however, will report memories prior to the age of 1. A problem with these reports, however, is that we can never be sure that the "remembered" event actually occurred (the person may have reconstructed what he or she thought happened). This problem was overcome in an experiment in which subjects were asked a total of 20 questions about a childhood event that was known to have occurred—the birth of a younger sibling—the details of which could be verified by another person. The questions asked of each subject dealt with events that transpired during the mother's leaving for the hospital (for example, "What time of day did she leave?"),

This little girl will not remember the events surrounding the birth of her baby brother.

which in turn imply they are relatively normal with respect to general facts. In most forms of amnesia, then, memory for general facts is spared while memory for personal episodes is disrupted, suggesting that the two types of facts are indeed stored in different memories. In addition, specific experiments have shown that amnesiacs perform normally on tasks requiring the retrieval of general facts (Weingartner et al., 1983).

Implicit versus Explicit Memory

As was the case with amnesiacs, findings with normal subjects suggest that perceptual or cognitive skills, like identifying a word or completing a word fragment, seem to be stored separately from personal facts.

when the mother was in the hospital ("Did you visit her?"), and when the mother and infant returned home ("What time of day did they come home?"). The subjects were college students, and their ages at the birth of their siblings varied from 1 to 17 years. The results are shown in the figure. The number of questions answered is plotted as a function of the subject's age when the sibling was born. If the sibling was born before the subject was 3 years old, the person could not recall a thing about it. If the birth occurred after that, recall increased with age at the time of the event. These results suggest an almost total amnesia for the first 3 years of life.

What causes childhood amnesia? Freud (1905) thought that it was due to the repression of sexual and aggressive feelings that a young child experiences toward his parents. But this account predicts amnesia only for events related to sexual and aggressive thoughts, when in fact childhood amnesia extends to all kinds of events. A more accepted explanation is that childhood amnesia is due to a massive difference between how young children encode experience and how adults organize their memories. Adults structure their memories in terms of categories and schemata ("She's that kind of person," "It's that kind of situation"), while young children encode their experiences without embellishing them or connecting them to related events. Once a child begins to form associations between events and to categorize those events, early experiences become lost (Schachtel, 1947).

What causes the shift from early-childhood to adult forms of memory? One factor is biological development. The hippocampus, a brain structure involved in consolidating memories, is not mature until roughly a year or two after birth. Therefore, events that take place in the first 2 years of life cannot be sufficiently consolidated and consequently cannot be recalled later. Other causes of the shift to adult memory involve more cognitive factors, particularly the development of language and the beginning of schooling. Both language and the kind of thinking emphasized in school provide new ways of organizing experiences, ways that may be incompatible with how the young child encodes experiences. Interestingly, language development reaches an early peak at age 3, while schooling generally begins at age 5; and the age span from 3 to 5 is when childhood amnesia seems to end.

Organizational changes may not be the whole story of childhood amnesia. The difference between memory for skills and memory for facts may also play a role. Much of what we learn in infancy are skills, and they will not be represented in fact memory, which develops later. There is evidence for this hypothesis in studies with monkeys. Three-month-old monkeys can learn a "skill" task as readily as adult monkeys, but they cannot master a fact task that adults find easy (Mishkin, Malamut, & Bachevalier, 1984).

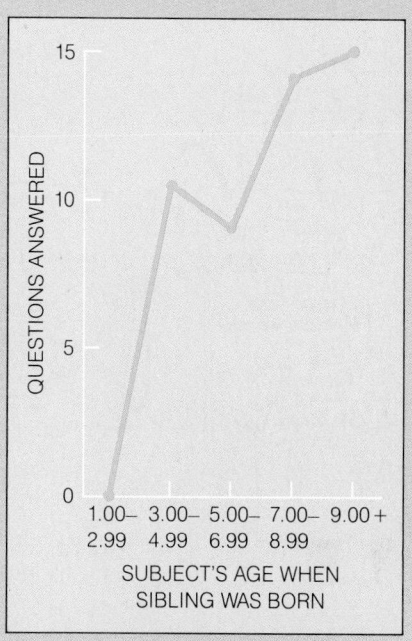

Recall of an Early Memory *In an experiment on childhood amnesia, college-age subjects were asked 20 questions about the events surrounding the birth of a younger sibling. The average number of questions answered is plotted as a function of the subject's age when the sibling was born. If the birth occurred before the fourth year of life, no subject could recall a thing about it; if the birth occurred after that, recall increased with age at the time of the event. (After Sheingold & Tenney, 1982)*

One major difference between the two kinds of memory is how they are typically expressed. The memory behind perceptual and cognitive skills is often expressed *implicitly*, as an improvement on some perceptual or cognitive task without conscious recollection of the experiences that led to this improvement. For example, with practice we can steadily improve our ability to recognize words in a foreign language, but at the moment we are recognizing a word, and thereby demonstrating our skill, we need not have any conscious recollection of the lessons that led to our improvement. In contrast, our memory of a personal fact is often expressed *explicitly*, as a conscious recollection of something in the past (Schacter, 1987).

Other differences between *fact memory* and *skill memory* in normal individuals have been documented by experiments. These studies generally show

that an independent variable that affects fact memory has no effect on skill memory, or vice versa, thereby strengthening the case for two different kinds of memory.

In one such experiment, subjects were first presented a list of 20 words to study. Subjects had to process each word in a way that could either elaborate its meaning—"Rate each word for how concrete it is"—or not elaborate its meaning—"Count the number of vertical lines in the letters of a word." After all the words had been processed, subjects were presented their initial stems, for example DE _ _ _. Sometimes subjects were instructed to treat these stems as cues for recall of the original words (a fact memory test); in such cases, recall was better for words whose meaning had been elaborated during study than for words whose meanings had not been elaborated. This much is to be expected given our earlier discussion of encoding in long-term memory. In other cases, subjects were instructed to respond to the same word-stems by completing them with the first word that came to mind (a skill-memory task); now subjects were no more likely to produce an original word whose meaning had been elaborated than an original word whose meaning had not been elaborated. In short, elaborating meaning boosts memory for facts but not for skill (Graf & Mandler, 1984).

There are also variables that affect skill memory but not fact memory. In one experiment, a group of subjects was presented a list of words visually, whereas a second group was presented them auditorially. Both groups studied the words and were then given two memory tests. One was a recognition test—which taps fact memory—where the original words and some new ones were presented visually; the subjects' task was to identify the old words. Subjects who were initially presented the words visually did no better at recognizing the old words than those who were initially presented the words auditorially. Changing the modality from study to test thus had no effect on recognition. The second memory test required subjects to identify words that are presented very briefly—this task taps skill memory. Again, some of the words presented were old and some were new, and now the measure of memory was the extent to which old words were easier to identify than new ones. Subjects who were initially presented the words visually showed more skill memory than subjects who were initially presented the words auditorially. In short, changing the modality from study to test hurts skill memory but has no effect on fact memory (Jacoby & Dallas, 1981).

These studies suggest that we all have a bit of a split personality, or at least a split memory system. As the philosopher Bergson pointed out years ago (1911), the past survives in us in two distinct forms: first in the physical and mental operations needed to carry out various tasks (skills), and second in independent conscious recollections (facts). Rarely are we aware of this striking dissociation.

IMPROVING MEMORY

Having considered the basics of short-term and long-term memory, we are ready to tackle the question of improving memory. We will consider here only memory for facts. First, we will consider how to increase the short-term memory span. Then we will turn to a variety of methods for improving long-term memory; these methods work by increasing the efficiency of encoding and retrieval.

Chunking and Memory Span

For most of us, the capacity of short-term memory cannot be increased beyond 7 ± 2 chunks. However, we can enlarge the size of a chunk and thereby increase the number of items in our memory span. We demonstrated this point earlier: given the string 149-2177-619-90, we can recall all 12 digits if we recode the string into 1492-1776-1990 and then store just these three chunks in short-term memory. Although recoding digits into familiar dates works nicely in this example, it will not work with most digit strings because we have not memorized enough significant dates. But if a recoding system could be developed that worked with virtually *any* string, then short-term memory span could be dramatically improved.

There is a study of a particular subject who discovered such a general-purpose recoding system and used it to increase his memory span from seven to almost 80 random digits (see Figure 8-11). The subject, referred to as SF, had average memory abilities and average intelligence for a college student. For a year and a half, he engaged in a memory-span task for about 3 to 5 hours per week. During this extensive practice, SF, a good long-distance runner, devised the strategy of recoding sets of four digits into running times. For example, SF would recode 3492 as "3:49.2—world class time for the mile," which for him was a single chunk. Since SF was familiar with many running times (that is, had them stored in long-term memory), he could readily chunk most sets of four digits. In those cases in which he could not (1771 cannot be a running time because the second digit is too large), SF tried to recode the four digits into either a familiar date or the age of some person or object.

Use of the above recoding systems enabled SF to increase his memory span from seven to 28 digits (because each of SF's seven chunks contains four digits). SF then built to nearly 80 digits by hierarchically organizing the running times. Thus, one chunk in SF's short-term memory might have pointed to three running times; at the time of recall, SF would go from this chunk to the first running time and produce its four digits, then move to the second running time in the chunk and produce its digits, and so on. One chunk was therefore worth 12 digits. Now we can see how SF could achieve his remarkable span of nearly 80 digits. It was due to increasing the *size* of a chunk (by relating the items to information in long-term memory), not to increasing the *number* of chunks that short-term memory can hold. For when SF switched from digits to letters, his memory span went back to seven—that is, seven letters (Ericsson, Chase, & Faloon, 1980).

Lest you think that SF is somehow unique, researchers have recently used the same procedure—constant practice on a memory-span task—to produce another short-term memory whiz. This subject, referred to as DD, is also a runner and used a similar method of recoding to running times, and he was able to increase his memory span to 106 digits (Waldrop, 1987).

This research is among the first major projects to deal with improvement in a short-term memory task. In contrast, there has long been interest in how to improve long-term memory, which is the focus of the rest of this section. We will look first at how material can be encoded to make it easier to retrieve and then consider how the act of retrieval itself can be improved.

Imagery and Encoding

We mentioned earlier that we can improve the recall of unrelated items by adding meaningful connections between them at the time of encoding, for these connections will later facilitate retrieval. Mental images turn out to

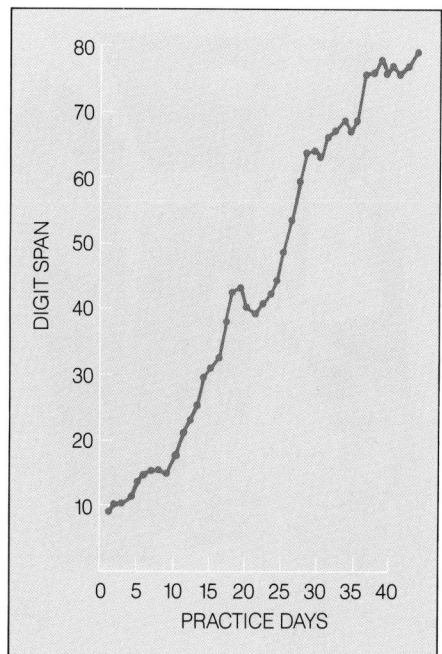

FIGURE 8-11
Number of Digits Recalled by SF *This subject greatly increased his memory span for digits by devising a recoding system using chunking and hierarchical organization. Total practice time was about 215 hours.* (After Ericsson, Chase, & Faloon, 1980)

FIGURE 8-12
A Mnemonic System *The method of loci aids memory by associating items (here, entries on a shopping list) with an ordered sequence of places.*

Key-word Method *Examples of key words used to link Spanish words to their English translation. For example, when the Spanish word muleta is pronounced, part of it sounds like the English word "mule." Thus, "mule" could be used as the key word and linked to the English translation by forming an image of a mule standing erect on a crutch.*

SPANISH	KEY WORD	ENGLISH
caballo	(eye)	horse
charco	(charcoal)	puddle
muleta	(mule)	crutch
clavo	(claw)	nail
lagartija	(log)	lizard
payaso	(pie)	clown
hiio	(eel)	thread
tenaza	(tennis)	pliers
jabon	(bone)	soap
carpa	(carp)	tent
pato	(pot)	duck

be particularly useful for connecting pairs of unrelated items, and for this reason imagery is the major ingredient in many *mnemonic* (memory-*aiding*) systems.

One famous mnemonic system is called the *method of loci* (*loci* is Latin for "places"). The method works especially well with an ordered sequence of arbitrary items, like unrelated words. The first step is to commit to memory an ordered sequence of places, say the locations you would come upon in a slow walk through your house. You enter through the front door into a hallway, move next to the bookcase in the living room, then to the television in the living room, then to the curtains at the window, and so on. Once you can easily take this mental walk, you are ready to memorize as many unrelated words as there are locations on your walk. You form an image that relates the first word to the first location, another image that relates the second word to the second location, and so on. If the words are items on a shopping list—for example, "bread," "eggs," "beer," "milk," and "bacon"—you might imagine a slice of bread nailed to your front door, an egg hanging from the light cord in the hallway, a can of beer in the bookcase, a milk commercial playing on your television, and curtains made from giant strips of bacon (see Figure 8-12). Once you have memorized the items this way, you can easily recall them in order by simply taking your mental walk again. Each location will retrieve an image, and each image will retrieve a word. The method clearly works and is a favorite among those who perform memory feats professionally.

Imagery is also used in the *key-word method* of learning a foreign vocabulary. Suppose you had to learn that the Spanish word *caballo* means "horse." The key-word method has two steps. The first is to find a part of the foreign word that sounds like an English word. Since *caballo* is pronounced "cob-eye-yo," "eye" could serve as the key word. The next step is to form an image that connects the key word and the English equivalent—for example, a horse kicking a giant eye (see Figure 8-13). This should establish a meaningful connection between the Spanish and English words. To recall the meaning of *caballo*, you would first retrieve the key word "eye" and then the stored image that links it to "horse." Note that the key-word method can also be used to get from English words to Spanish words. If you want to recall the Spanish word for "horse," you would first retrieve the image involving a horse, thereby obtaining the key word "eye" that serves as a retrieval cue for *caballo*. The key-word method may sound complicated, but studies have shown that it greatly facilitates learning the vocabulary of a foreign language (Atkinson, 1975; Pressley, Levin, & Delaney, 1982).

Elaboration and Encoding

We have seen that the more we elaborate items, the more we can subsequently recall or recognize them. This phenomenon arises because the more connections we establish between items, the larger the number of retrieval possibilities. The practical implications of these findings are straightforward: if you want to remember some fact, expand on its meaning. To illustrate, suppose you read a newspaper article about an epidemic in Detroit that health officials are trying to contain. To expand on this, you could ask yourself questions about the causes and consequences of the epidemic: Was the disease carried by a person or an animal? Was the disease transmitted through the water supply? To contain the epidemic, will officials go so far as to stop outsiders from visiting the city? How long is the epidemic likely to last?

Questions about the causes and consequences of an event are particularly effective elaborations because each question sets up a meaningful connection, or retrieval path, to the event.

Context and Retrieval

Since context is a powerful retrieval cue, we can improve our memory by restoring the context in which the learning took place. If your psychology lecture always meets in one room, your memory for the lecture material will be best when you are in that room, because the context of the room is a retrieval cue for the lecture material. This has direct educational implications. Students will do better on exams when they are tested in their habitual classroom and when the proctor is their instructor than they will when these factors are changed (Abernathy, 1940).

Most often, though, when we have to remember something, we cannot physically return to the context in which we learned it. If you are having difficulty remembering the name of a particular high-school classmate, you are not about to go back to your high school just to recall it. In these situations, however, you can try to recreate the context mentally. To retrieve the long-forgotten name, you might think of different classes, clubs, and other activities that you were in during high school to see if any of these bring to mind the name you are seeking. When subjects used these techniques in an actual experiment, they were often able to recall the names of high-school classmates that they were sure had been forgotten (Williams & Hollan, 1981).

Another illustration of mentally recreating context is as follows (adapted from Norman, 1976). Suppose someone asks you, "What were you doing at 1:00 P.M. on the third Monday of October two years ago?" "Ridiculous," you might say. "No one can remember things like that." But recreating the context can lead to surprising results:

> Well, two years ago, I was a senior in high school; let me see, October—that's fall semester. Now what courses did I take that semester? Oh yes, chemistry. That's it—I had a chemistry lab every afternoon; that's where I was at 1:00 P.M. on the third Monday of October two years ago.

In this example, restoring the context seems to have done the trick. However, we cannot be sure that you actually remembered being in chemistry lab. Perhaps you inferred that you must have been there. Either way, though, you may come up with the right answer.

Organization

We know that organization during encoding improves subsequent retrieval. This principle can be put to great practical use: we are capable of storing and retrieving a massive amount of information if only we organize it.

Some experiments have investigated organizational devices that can be used to learn many unrelated items. In one study, subjects memorized lists of unrelated words by organizing the words in each list into a story, as illustrated in Figure 8-14. Later, when tested for 12 such lists (a total of 120 words), subjects recalled more than 90 percent of the words. This appears to be a truly remarkable memory feat, but anyone can do it easily.

Caballo → eye → Horse

Pato → pot → Duck

FIGURE 8-13
Foreign Language Learning *Mental images can be used to associate spoken Spanish words with corresponding English words. Here, possible images for learning the Spanish words for "horse" and "duck" are illustrated.*

FIGURE 8-14
Organizing Words into a Story *Three examples of turning a list of 10 unrelated words into a story. The capitalized items are the words on the list. (After Bower & Clark, 1969)*

A LUMBERJACK DARTed out of a forest, SKATEd around a HEDGE past a COLONY of DUCKs. He tripped on some FURNITURE, tearing his STOCKING while hastening toward the PILLOW where his MISTRESS lay.

A VEGETABLE can be a useful INSTRUMENT for a COLLEGE student. A carrot can be a NAIL for your FENCE or BASIN. But a MERCHANT of the QUEEN would SCALE that fence and feed the carrot to a GOAT.

One night at DINNER I had the NERVE to bring my TEACHER. There had been a FLOOD that day, and the rain BARREL was sure to RATTLE. There was, however, a VESSEL in the HARBOR carrying this ARTIST to my CASTLE.

At this point, you might concede that psychologists have devised some ingenious techniques for organizing lists of unrelated items. But, you argue, what you have to remember are not lists of unrelated items but stories you were told, lectures you have heard, and readings like the present chapter. Isn't this kind of material already organized, and doesn't this mean that the previously mentioned techniques are of limited value? Yes and no. Yes, this chapter is more than a list of unrelated words, but—and this is the critical point—there is always a problem of organization with any lengthy material, including this chapter. Later you may be able to recall that elaborating meaning aids learning, but this may not bring to mind anything about, say, acoustic coding in short-term memory. The two topics do not seem to be intimately related, but there is a relation between them: both deal with encoding phenomena. The best way to see that relationship is to note the headings and subheadings in the chapter, because these show how the material in the chapter is organized. A most effective way to study is to keep this organization in mind. You might, for example, try to capture part of this chapter's organization by sketching a hierarchical tree like the one shown below. Then you can use such a hierarchy to guide your memory search whenever you have to retrieve information about this chapter. It may be even more helpful, though, to make your own hierarchical outline of the chapter. Memory seems to benefit most when the organization is done by the rememberers themselves.

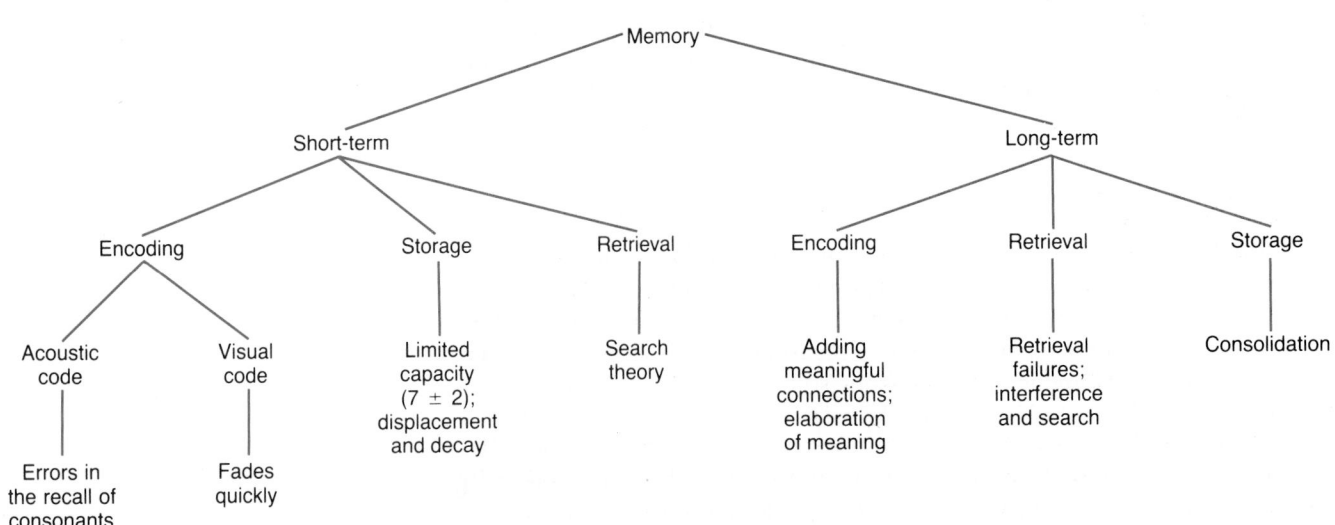

Practicing Retrieval

Another way to improve retrieval is to practice it—that is, to ask yourself questions about what you are trying to learn. Suppose you have 2 hours in which to study an assignment that can be read in approximately 30 minutes. Reading and rereading the assignment four times is generally much less effective than reading it once and asking yourself questions about it. You can then reread selected parts to clear up points that were difficult to retrieve the first time around, perhaps elaborating these points so they become particularly well connected to each other and to the rest of the assignment. Attempting retrieval is an efficient use of study time. This was demonstrated long ago by experiments using unrelated items, as well as material like that actually learned in courses (see Figure 8-15).

PQRST Method

Thus far in this section, we have considered particular principles of memory (for example, the principle that organization aids memory search) and then shown their implications for improving memory. In establishing the practical application of memory principles, we can also go in the opposite direction. We can start with a well-known technique for improving memory and show how it is based on principles of memory.

One of the best-known techniques for improving memory, called the *PQRST method*, is intended to improve a student's ability to study and remember material presented in a textbook (Thomas & Robinson, 1982). The method takes its name from the first letters of its five stages: *Preview, Question, Read, Self-Recitation,* and *Test.* We can illustrate the method by showing how it would apply to studying a chapter in this textbook. In the first stage, students preview the material in a chapter to get an idea of its major topics and sections. Previewing involves reading the chapter outline at the beginning of the chapter, skimming the chapter while paying special attention to the headings of main sections and subsections, and carefully reading the summary at the end of the chapter. This kind of preview induces students to organize the chapter, perhaps even leading to the rudiments of a hierarchical organization like that shown above. As we have repeatedly noted, organizing material aids one's ability to retrieve it.

The second, third, and fourth stages (Question, Read, and Self-Recitation) apply to each major section of the chapter as it is encountered. In this book, for example, a chapter typically has five to eight major sections, and students would apply the Question, Read, and Self-Recitation stages to each section before going on to the next one. In the Question stage, students carefully read the section and subsection headings and turn these into questions. In the Read stage, students read the section with an eye toward answering these questions. And in the Self-Recitation stage, the reader tries to recall the main ideas in the section and recites the information (either subvocally or, preferably, aloud). For example, if you were applying these stages to the present section of this chapter, you might look at the headings and make up such questions as "How much can the short-term memory span be increased?" or "What exactly is the PQRST method?" Next you would read this section and try to determine answers to your questions (for example, "One person was able to increase his short-term memory span to nearly 80 digits"). Then you would try to recall the main ideas (for example, "You can

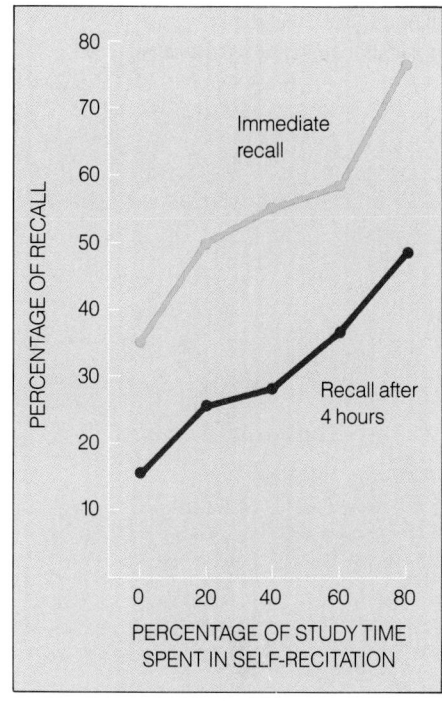

FIGURE 8-15
Practicing Retrieval *Recall can be improved by spending a large proportion of study time attempting retrieval rather than silently studying. Results are shown for tests given immediately and 4 hours after completing study.* (After Gates, 1917)

The PQRST method increases understanding and retention.

increase the size of a chunk but not the number of chunks"). The Question and Read stages almost certainly induce students to elaborate the material while encoding it; the Self-Recitation stage induces the student to practice retrieval.

The fifth, or Test, stage occurs after finishing an entire chapter. Students try to recall the main facts from what they have read and to understand how the various facts relate to one another. This stage prompts elaboration and offers further practice at retrieval. In summary, the PQRST method relies on three basic principles for improving memory: organizing the material, elaborating the material, and practicing retrieval. (For a more in-depth description of the method, see Appendix I.)

CONSTRUCTIVE MEMORY

Throughout this chapter, we have considered research using simple verbal materials (lists of unrelated words, for instance) and more complex material (sentences, textbook chapters). We did this because many principles apply to both simple and complex materials. However, some principles seem to apply only to memory for complex, meaningful materials; the most important of these principles is that memory can be *constructive*.

When we hear a sentence or story, we often take it as an incomplete description of a real event, and we use our general knowledge about how the world works to construct a more complete description of the event. How do we do this? By adding to the sentences and stories statements that are likely to follow from them. For example, on hearing "Mike broke the bottle in a barroom brawl," we are likely to infer that it was a beer or whiskey bottle, not a milk or soda bottle. We add this inference to our memory of the sentence itself. Our total memory therefore goes beyond the original information given. We fill in the original information by using our general knowledge about what goes with what (for example, that beer bottles go with bars). We do this because we are trying to explain to ourselves the events we are hearing about. Constructive memory, then, is a by-product of our need to understand the world.

Simple Inferences

Often when we read a sentence we draw inferences from it and store the inferences along with the sentence. This tendency is particularly strong when reading real text, because inferences are often needed to connect different lines. To illustrate, consider the following story, which was presented to subjects in an experiment.

1. Provo is a picturesque kingdom in France.
2. Corman was heir to the throne of Provo.
3. He was so tired of waiting.
4. He thought arsenic would work well.

When reading this story, subjects draw inferences at certain points. At line 3, they infer that Corman wanted to be king, which permits them to connect line 3 to the preceding line. But this is not a necessary inference (Corman could have been waiting for the king to receive him). At line 4, subjects infer that Corman had decided to poison the king, so they can connect this line to what preceded it. Again, the inference is not a necessary one (there are people other than the king to poison, and there are other uses of arsenic). When subjects' memories were later tested for exactly which lines had been presented, they had trouble distinguishing the story lines from the inferences we just described. It is hard to keep separate what was actually presented from what we added to it (Seifert, Robertson, & Black, 1985).

Inferences can also affect memory for visual scenes. This is illustrated by the following study. Subjects were shown a film of a traffic accident and then were asked questions about their memory of the accident. One question about the speed of the vehicles was asked in two different ways. Some subjects were asked, "How fast were the cars going when they smashed into each other?" whereas others were asked, "How fast were the cars going when they hit each other?" Subjects asked the "smashed" question might infer that the accident was a very destructive one, perhaps more destructive than they had actually remembered. These subjects were likely to use this inference somehow to alter their memory of the accident to make it more destructive (see Figure 8-16). Subjects asked the "hit" question, however, should be less likely to do this, since "hit" implies a less severe accident than does "smashed."

This line of reasoning was supported by the results of a memory test given 1 week later. In this test, subjects were asked, "Did you see any broken glass?" There was no broken glass in the film of the accident, but subjects who had been asked the "smashed" question were more likely to say mistakenly that there had been glass than were subjects who had been asked the "hit" question. The "smashed" question may have led to reconstruction of the memory for the accident, and the reconstructed memory contained details, such as broken glass, that were never actually part of the accident (Loftus, Schooler, & Wagenaar, 1985). Alternatively, subjects may not have integrated inferences about "smashed" with their memory of the accident; rather, they may have consulted such inferences at the time of the memory test (McCloskey &

FIGURE 8-16
Reconstructing a Memory of an Accident *The picture at the top represents the subject's original memory for the accident. Then comes the "smashed" question, which leads the subject to draw inferences about the destructiveness of the accident. These inferences may be used to reconstruct the original memory so that it looks more like the picture on the bottom.* (After Loftus & Loftus, 1975)

The stereotype of a Scandinavian: blond hair and blue eyes.

Zaragoza, 1985). Either interpretation of the results has important implications for eyewitness identification: a question phrased in a particular way ("smashed" rather than "hit") can alter a witness's memory structures that an attorney is trying to probe.

Stereotypes

Another means by which we fill in, or construct, memories is through the use of social *stereotypes*. A stereotype is a packet of inferences about the personality traits or physical attributes of a whole class of people. We may, for example, have a stereotype of the typical German (intelligent, meticulous, serious) or of the typical Italian (artistic, carefree, fun loving). These descriptions rarely apply to many people in the class and can often be misleading guides for social interaction. Our concern here, however, is not with the effects of stereotypes on social interaction (see Chapter 18 for a discussion of this) but with the effects of stereotypes on memory.

When presented with information about a person, we sometimes stereotype that person (for example, "He's your typical Italian") and then combine the information presented with that in our stereotype. Our memory of the person is thus partly constructed from the stereotype. To the extent that our stereotype does not fit the person, our recall can be terribly distorted. Hunter, a British psychologist, provides a firsthand account of such a distortion:

> In the week beginning 23 October, I encountered in the university, a male student of very conspicuously Scandinavian appearance. I recall being very forcibly impressed by the man's nordic, Viking-like appearance—his fair hair, his blue eyes, and long bones. On several occasions, I recalled his appearance in connection with a Scandinavian correspondence I was then conducting and thought of him as the "perfect Viking," visualizing him at the helm of a longship crossing the North Sea in quest of adventure. When I again saw the man on 23 November, I did not recognize him, and he had to introduce himself. It was not that I had forgotten what he looked like but that his appearance, as I recalled it, had become grossly distorted. He was very different from my recollection of him. His hair was darker, his eyes less blue, his build less muscular, and he was wearing spectacles (as he always does). (Hunter, 1974, pp. 265–66)

Clearly, Hunter's memory of the student was severely distorted. His stereotype of Scandinavians seems to have so overwhelmed any information he actually encoded about the student's appearance that the result was a highly constructed memory. It bore so little resemblance to the student that it could not even serve as a basis for recognition.

Stereotypes may also work retroactively on memory. We may first hear a relatively neutral description of a person, later find out this person belongs to a particular category, and then use our stereotype of that category to augment our memory of the original description. In a study demonstrating this phenomenon, subjects first read a narrative about events in the life of a woman named Betty K. The narrative followed Betty K's life from birth to early adulthood and contained facts about her social life, such as, "Although she never had a steady boyfriend in high school, she did go out on dates." After reading the story, subjects were given additional facts about Betty K that would lead to stereotyping her. One group of subjects was told that Betty later adopted a lesbian life-style. A second group was told that she later married. Apparently, the first group fit Betty to their stereotype of lesbians, whereas the second group fit her to their stereotype of married women. Such stereotyping affected subsequent recognition of the original narrative. Subjects told about Betty's later lesbian activities were more likely to remember that "she never had a steady boyfriend" than that "she did go out on dates." Subjects told about Betty's later marriage did the reverse. Both groups may have reconstructed their memory of the original narrative to make it fit their stereotypes, or they may have used their stereotypes to answer questions when they could not remember the original narrative (Snyder & Uranowitz, 1978; Bellezza & Bower, 1981). Thus, memory for people seems to be particularly susceptible to construction; our memory is a compromise between what is and what we think should be.

Schemata

Psychologists use the term *schema* (*schemata* for plural) to refer to a mental representation of a class of people, objects, events, or situations. Stereotypes, as described above, are thus a kind of schema because they represent classes of people (for example, Italians, women, homosexuals). Similarly, common categories such as *dog* and *table* are another kind of schema because they represent classes of objects. Schemata can be used to describe not only our knowledge about particular objects and events but also our knowledge about how to act in certain situations. For example, most adults have a schema for how to drive a car (sit behind the wheel, insert the key into the ignition, turn the key while pressing the gas pedal, and so on) and a schema for how to eat in a restaurant (enter the restaurant, find a table, get a menu from the waiter, order food, and so on). Everyone but very young children would have schemata for how to find his or her way home from various locations.

Perceiving and thinking in terms of schemata permits us to filter, organize, and process large amounts of information swiftly and economically. Instead of having to perceive and remember all the details of each new person, object, or event we encounter, we can simply note that it is like a schema already in memory and encode and remember only its most distinctive features. The price we pay for such "cognitive economy," however, is that an object or event can be distorted if the schema used to encode it does not quite fit.

Bartlett (1932) was perhaps the first psychologist to study systematically the effect of schemata on memory. He suggested that memory distortions, much like those that occur when we fit people into stereotypes, can occur when we attempt to fit stories into schemata. Research has confirmed Bartlett's suggestion. For example, after reading a brief story about a character going to a restaurant, subjects are likely to recall statements about the character eating and paying for a meal, even when those actions were never mentioned in the story (Bower, Black, & Turner, 1979).

On the other hand, schemata are often a great aid to memory. For example, some stories we read may be difficult to comprehend and remember unless we can fit them into their appropriate schemata. To illustrate this, read the following paragraph and try to recall it.

The procedure is actually quite simple. First you arrange things into different groups. Of course, one pile may be sufficient, depending on how much there is to do. If you have to go somewhere else due to lack of facilities, that is the next step; otherwise you are pretty well set. It is important not to overdo things. That

The schemata of eating in a restaurant includes knowing that one normally orders a salad, an entree, and a dessert, rather than three bowls of soup.

is, it is better to do too few things at once than too many. In the short run this may not seem important but complications can easily arise. A mistake can be expensive as well. At first the whole procedure will seem complicated. Soon, however, it will become just another facet of life. It is difficult to foresee any end to the necessity for this task in the immediate future, but then one never can tell. After the procedure is completed, one arranges the materials into different groups again. Then they can be put into their appropriate places. Eventually, they will be used once more and the whole cycle will then have to be repeated. However, that is part of life. (After Bransford & Johnson, 1973)

In reading the paragraph, you no doubt had some difficulty in trying to understand exactly what it was about. Consequently, your recall of it is probably relatively poor. But given the hint that the paragraph describes "washing clothes," you can now use your schema for washing clothes to interpret all the cryptic parts of the passage. The "procedure" referred to in the first sentence is that of "washing clothes," the "things" referred to in the second sentence are "clothes," the "different groups" are "groups of clothing of different colors," and so on. Your memory for the paragraph, if you reread it, should now be quite good. Schemata, then, can help or hurt memory.

Schemata seem to affect both the encoding and retrieval stages of long-term memory. If a particular schema is active when we read a story, we tend to encode mainly the facts that are related to the schema. We can illustrate with the following simple story:

1. Steven and Edgar went to a movie.
2. Steven and Edgar talked about business while waiting in line.
3. Steven liked the film, but Edgar thought it was too sentimental.

Assuming that Sentence No. 1 activates our movie schema, we are more likely to encode Sentence No. 3 than No. 2 because Sentence No. 3 is more related to the schema. In later recalling this story, if we could remember that it had to do with going to a movie, we could use our movie schema to search our memory: for example, was there anything in the story about a reaction to the film? Thus, schemata can affect retrieval by guiding search processes (Brewer & Nakamura, 1984).

In the case of a difficult memory task, retrieval may be almost totally guided by schemata. As one example, if asked to remember where you met a particular person, you might check one schema after another to see if any of them have been used as the encoding context for the target person ("Was it a party, a class, a restaurant, a movie?"). The relevant schemata—parties, classes, and so on—have become the critical retrieval cues, and memory is almost entirely constructive (Kolodner, 1983).

As another example of schema-guided retrieval, suppose that in September you were asked what you did on your summer vacation. To answer this, you might retrieve various situation schemata, such as going to movies and playing tennis, and then report the basics of these schemata ("I played a lot of tennis, mainly with my brother, saw a few good movies. . . .") (Barsalou, 1987).

Situations in which memory is schema-driven and heavily constructive seem a far cry from the simpler situations we covered earlier. Consider, for example, memory for a list of unrelated words: here, memory processes appear more to *preserve* the input than to *construct* something new. However, there is a constructive aspect even to this simple situation, for techniques such as using imagery give meaning to the input. Similarly, when we read a paragraph such as the one about washing clothes, we must still preserve some of its specifics if we are to recall it correctly in detail. Thus, the two aspects of memory—to preserve and to construct—may always be present, although their relative emphasis may depend on the exact situation.

CHAPTER SUMMARY

1. There are three stages of memory: *encoding, storage,* and *retrieval.* Encoding refers to the transformation of information into the kind of code or representation that memory can accept; storage is the retention of the encoded information; and retrieval refers to the process by which information is recovered from memory. The three stages may operate differently in situations that require us to store material for a matter of seconds (*short-term memory*) and in situations that require us to store material for longer intervals (*long-term memory*).

2. Information in short-term memory tends to be encoded *acoustically,* although we can also use a *visual code.* The dominance of the acoustic code may apply mainly to verbal materials. The most striking fact about short-term memory is that its storage capacity is limited to 7 ± 2 items, or *chunks.* When this limit is reached, a form of forgetting occurs: a new item can enter short-term memory only by *displacing* an old one. The other major cause of forgetting in short-term memory is that information *decays* with time. Both displacement and decay can be offset by *rehearsal.*

3. Retrieval slows down as the number of items in short-term memory increases, suggesting that retrieval may involve a *search process.* Short-term memory seems to serve as a mental "work space" in solving certain kinds of problems, such as mental arithmetic and answering questions about text. However, short-term memory does not seem to be involved in the understanding of relatively simple sentences.

4. There are interactions between short-term and long-term memory. In *chunking,* information in long-term memory is used to recode incoming material into large, meaningful units (chunks), which are then stored in short-term memory.

Information may also be transferred from short-term to long-term memory, sometimes by the process of *rehearsal*. A theory of this transfer process (*dual-memory theory*) accounts for the results of experiments on *free recall*: items at the end of a list are remembered well because they are still in short-term memory, whereas items at the beginning of a list are remembered well because they are rehearsed more often.

5. Information in long-term memory is usually encoded according to its *meaning*. If the items to be remembered are meaningful but the connections between them are not, memory can be improved by adding meaningful connections that provide retrieval paths. The more one *elaborates* the meaning, the better memory will be.

6. Many cases of forgetting in long-term memory are due to *retrieval failures* (the information is there but cannot be found). Retrieval failures are more likely to occur when there is *interference* from items associated with the same retrieval cue. Such interference effects indicate that retrieval from long-term memory is accomplished by either a *sequential search* process or a *spreading activation* process.

7. Some forgetting from long-term memory is due to a loss from storage, particularly when there is a disruption of the processes that *consolidate* new memories. The biological locus of consolidation includes the *hippocampus*, *amygdala*, and *diencephalon*, brain structures located below the cerebral cortex.

8. Retrieval failures in long-term memory are less likely to happen when the items are *organized* during encoding and when the *context* at retrieval is similar to that at encoding. Retrieval processes can also be disrupted by *emotional factors*. In some cases, anxious thoughts interfere with retrieval of the target memory; in others, the target memory (*repression hypothesis*) may be actively blocked. In still other cases, emotion can enhance memory, as in *flashbulb memories*.

9. The symptoms common to all forms of amnesia are an inability to acquire new information (*anterograde amnesia*) and an inability to remember events that occurred prior to the injury or disease (*retrograde amnesia*). In some cases of amnesia, the breakdown of memory seems to happen at the storage stage, while in other cases the breakdown seems to occur at the encoding and retrieval stages. In most forms of amnesia, the lost memories are for personal episodes or facts. Memory for skills and for general facts are usually spared, suggesting that there may be separate memories for *personal facts*, *general facts*, and *skills*.

10. Research with normal subjects also supports the idea that there are separate memories for facts and skills. Skill memory is often expressed *implicitly*, as an improvement on some task, whereas fact memory is usually expressed *explicitly*, as a conscious recollection of the past. Experiments reveal that an independent variable that affects fact memory (amount of elaboration during encoding) has no effect on skill memory; conversely, a variable that affects skill memory (changing the modality from study to test) has no effect on fact memory.

11. Although we cannot increase the capacity of short-term memory, we can use *recoding* schemes to enlarge the size of a chunk and thereby increase the memory span. Long-term memory for facts can be improved at the encoding and retrieval stages. One way to improve encoding and retrieval is to use imagery, which is the basic principle underlying mnemonic systems such as the *method of loci* and the *key-word method*.

12. Other ways to improve encoding (and subsequent retrieval) are to elaborate the meaning of the items and to organize the material during encoding (hierarchical organization seems best). The best ways to improve retrieval are to attempt to restore the encoding context at the time of retrieval and to practice retrieving information while learning it. Most of these principles for improving encoding and retrieval are incorporated into the *PQRST method* of studying a textbook, whose five stages are *Preview, Question, Read, Self-Recitation,* and *Test*.

13. Memory for complex materials, such as stories, is often *constructive*. We tend to use our general knowledge of the world to construct a more complete memory of a story or an event. Construction can involve adding simple *inferences* to the material presented; it can also involve fitting the material into *stereotypes* and other kinds of *schemata* (mental representations of classes of people, objects, events, or situations).

☰ FURTHER READING

There are several introductory books on memory that are readable and up-to-date: Anderson, *Cognitive Psychology and Its Implications* (3rd ed., 1989); Glass and Holyoak, *Cognition* (2nd ed., 1986); Klatzky, *Human Memory: Structures and Processes* (2nd ed., 1980); Reed, *Cognition: Theory and Applications* (1981); Baddeley, *Your Memory: A User's Guide* (1982); and Gregg, *Introduction to Human Memory* (1986). In addition to these textbooks, Neisser (ed.), *Memory Observed* (1982), provides a survey of remembering in natural contexts.

For an advanced treatment of theoretical issues in memory, see Anderson, *The Architecture of Cognition* (1983); Tulving, *Elements of Episodic Memory* (1983); the second volume of Atkinson, Herrnstein, Lindzey, and Luce (eds.), *Steven's Handbook of Experimental Psychology* (1988); and Baddeley, *Working Memory* (1986).

For a review of research on the biological bases of memory and learning, see Squire and Butters (eds.), *The Neuropsychology of Memory* (1984); and Squire, *Memory and Brain* (1987).

Chapter 9

Detail, Open Book.

Thought and Language

The greatest accomplishments of our species stem from our ability to entertain complex thoughts and to communicate them. Thinking includes a wide range of mental activities. We think when we try to solve a problem that has been presented to us in class; we think when we daydream while waiting for that class to begin. We think when we decide what groceries to buy, plan a vacation, write a letter, or worry about a troubled relationship.

In all cases, thought can be conceived of as a "language of the mind." Introspection suggests that there is more than one language. One *mode of thought* corresponds to the stream of sentences that we seem to "hear in our mind"; this is referred to as *propositional thought* (because it expresses a proposition or claim). Another mode corresponds to images, particularly visual ones, that we can "see" in our mind; this is *imaginal thought*. Finally, there may be a third mode, *motoric thought*, which corresponds to sequences of "mental movements" (Bruner, Olver, Greenfield et al., 1966). While studies of cognitive development have paid some attention to motoric thought in children, research on thinking in adults has emphasized the other two modes, particularly the propositional one; this emphasis is reflected in the current chapter.

The next four sections discuss major topics in propositional thinking, including: the components of a proposition, or the study of *concepts*; the organization of propositional thought, or the study of *reasoning*; the communication of propositional thought, or the study of *language*; and the development of such communication, or the study of *language acquisition*. We then turn to the imaginal mode of thought. In the final section, we will discuss thought in action—the study of *problem solving*—and consider the uses of both propositional and imaginal thought.

CONCEPTS

We can think of a proposition as a statement that expresses a factual claim. "Irene is a mother" is one proposition, and "Cats are animals" is another. It is easy to see that such a thought consists of concepts—such as "Irene" and "mother" or "cat" and "animal"—combined in a particular way. To understand propositional thought, we first need to understand the concepts that compose it.

Concepts are our means of dividing the world into manageable units. The world is full of so many different objects that if we treated each one as distinct, we would soon be overwhelmed. For example, if we had to refer to every single object we encountered by a different name, our vocabulary would have to be gigantic—so immense that communication might be impossible. (Think of what it would be like if we had a separate name for each of the seven million colors we can discriminate!) Fortunately, we do not treat each object as unique; rather, we see it as an instance of a concept or class. Thus, many different objects are seen as instances of the concept "apple," many others as instances of the concept "chair," and so on. By treating different objects as members of the same concept, we reduce the complexity of the world that we have to represent mentally.

Treating different objects as members of the same concept means that we treat them as if they were roughly the same with respect to those properties

The concept of "apple" includes roundness and distinctness of flavor.

that characterize the concept. For example, our concept of "apple" is characterized by the properties of having seeds, growing on trees, being edible, being round, having distinctive colors, and so on, and when we categorize an object as an "apple" we assume that the object has these characteristic properties. Categorization has an enormous impact on how we deal with the objects around us. Having perceived some visible properties of an object (something round and red on a tree), we assign it to the concept of "apple." This allows us to infer properties that are not visible—for instance, that it has seeds inside of it and is edible. Concepts, then, enable us to go beyond the information immediately available.

We also have concepts of activities, such as "eating"; of states, such as "being old"; and of abstractions, such as "truth," "justice," or even the number "two." In each case we know something about the properties common to members of the concept. Widely used concepts like these generally are associated with a one-word name. This allows us to communicate quickly about experiences that occur frequently.

Prototypes

Every concept has a *prototype* that contains the properties that describe the best examples of the concept. In the concept "bachelor," for example, your prototype might include such properties as a man who is in his 30s, lives alone, and has an active social life. These properties may be true of the typical examples of a bachelor, but they are clearly not true of all instances (think of an uncle in his 60s who boards with his sister and rarely goes out). This means that a concept must contain something in addition to a prototype; this additional something is a *core* that comprises the properties that are most important for being a member of the concept. Your core of the concept "bachelor" would probably include the properties of being adult, male, and unmarried; these properties are essential for being a member of the concept (Armstrong, Gleitman, & Gleitman, 1983).

As another example, consider the concept "bird." Your prototype likely includes the properties of flying and chirping—which works for the best examples of "bird," such as robins and blue jays, but not for other examples, such as ostriches and penguins. Your core would likely specify something about the biological basis of birdhood—the fact that it involves having certain genes or, at least having parents that are birds. Note that in this example and the previous one, the prototype properties are salient but not perfect indicators of concept membership, whereas the core properties are diagnostic of concept membership.

The prototype and core play different roles in concepts like "bachelor" than they do in concepts like "bird." In "bachelor," because the core properties (being adult, for example) are as salient as the prototype properties (being in one's 30s), we primarily use the core to determine whether or not something is an instance of the concept. In "bird," the core properties (genes) are hidden from view, and consequently we primarily use the prototype in determining membership in the concept. Thus, happening on a small animal, we can hardly inspect its genes or inquire about its parentage. All we can do is check whether it does certain things such as fly and chirp, and use this information to decide whether it is a bird. Concepts like "bachelor" are called *classical* concepts, while concepts like "bird" are called *fuzzy*—because we cannot always be sure about our decisions (Smith & Medin, 1981).

Some instances of fuzzy concepts will have more prototype properties than other instances. Among birds, for example, a robin will have the property of flying, whereas an ostrich will not. And the more prototype properties an instance has, the more typical people will consider that instance to be of the concept. Thus, of "bird," most people rate a robin as more typical than an ostrich; of "apple," they rate red apples as more typical than green ones (since red seems to be a property of the concept "apple"); and so on.

Further, the *typicality* of an instance affects many mental processes. One is *categorization*. When people are asked whether or not a pictured animal is a "bird," a robin produces an immediate "yes," whereas a chicken requires a longer decision time. When young children are asked the same question, a robin will almost inevitably be correctly classified, whereas often a chicken will be declared a nonbird. Another process affected by typicality is *memory*. When asked to retrieve the names of all the pieces of "clothing" they can think of, people produce such typical items as "suit" before the less typical ones such as "vest." Typicality also affects inferences. Suppose people are told that one member of a fraternity voted for a particular candidate; the more typical that member of the concept "fraternity man," the more people will infer that other members of the fraternity also voted for that candidate. Thus, we are more likely to make inferences from an individual to a group, the more typical the individual is of the group. Finally, typicality affects what we think of when we think of a particular concept. Imagine that you have just witnessed a minor crime and think about finding a police officer. The object of your thought will likely be the American prototype of *police officer*, and it will fit burly, male, police officers better than others. Why? Because most police officers you have seen, either directly or through the media, have been burly males, and these have become properties of your prototype. Should you find an officer Murphy and the person turns out to be a slim female, you will probably be surprised (Rosch, 1978; Rothbart & Lewis, 1988).

Hierarchies of Concepts

In addition to knowing the properties of concepts, we also know how they relate to one another. For example, "apples" are members (or a subset) of a larger concept, "fruit"; "robins" are a subset of "birds," which in turn are a subset of "animals." These two types of knowledge (properties of a concept and relationships between concepts) are represented in Figure 9-1 as a hierarchy. Such a hierarchy allows us to infer that a concept has a particular property even when it is not associated directly with that concept. Suppose you do not have the property of being sweet associated directly with "McIntosh apple." If you were asked, "Is a McIntosh apple sweet?" presumably you would enter your mental hierarchy at "McIntosh apple" (see Figure 9-1), trace a path from "McIntosh apple" to "fruit," find the property of being sweet stored at "fruit," and respond "yes." This idea implies that the time needed to establish a relation between a concept and a property should increase with the distance between them in the hierarchy. This prediction has been confirmed in experiments in which subjects were asked questions such as, "Is an apple sweet?" and "Is a McIntosh apple sweet?" Subjects took longer to answer the McIntosh apple question than the apple question, because the distance in the hierarchy between "McIntosh apple" and "sweet" is greater than that between "apple" and "sweet" (Collins & Loftus, 1975).

As the hierarchy in Figure 9-1 makes clear, an object can be identified at different levels. The same object is at once a "McIntosh apple," an "apple," and a "fruit." However, in any hierarchy, one level is the "basic" or preferred one for classification; this is the level at which we first categorize an object. For the hierarchy in Figure 9-1, the level that contains "apple" and "pear" would be the basic one. Evidence for this claim comes from studies in which people are asked to name pictured objects with the first names that come to mind. People are more likely to call a pictured McIntosh apple an "apple" than either a "McIntosh apple" or a "fruit." It seems then that we first divide the world into basic-level concepts; membership in more abstract concepts is then inferred ("If an object is an 'apple,' it must also be a 'fruit'"), whereas membership in more concrete concepts is decided by observation of additional properties ("If an object is an 'apple,' and it's red and green, it is probably a 'McIntosh apple'") (Mervis & Rosch, 1981).

What determines which level is basic? The answer seems to be that the basic level is the one that has the most *distinctive properties*. In Figure 9-1,

FIGURE 9-1

Hierarchy of Concepts *Words in capital letters represent concepts; lowercase words depict properties of these concepts. The blue lines show relationships between concepts, and the red lines connect properties and concepts.*

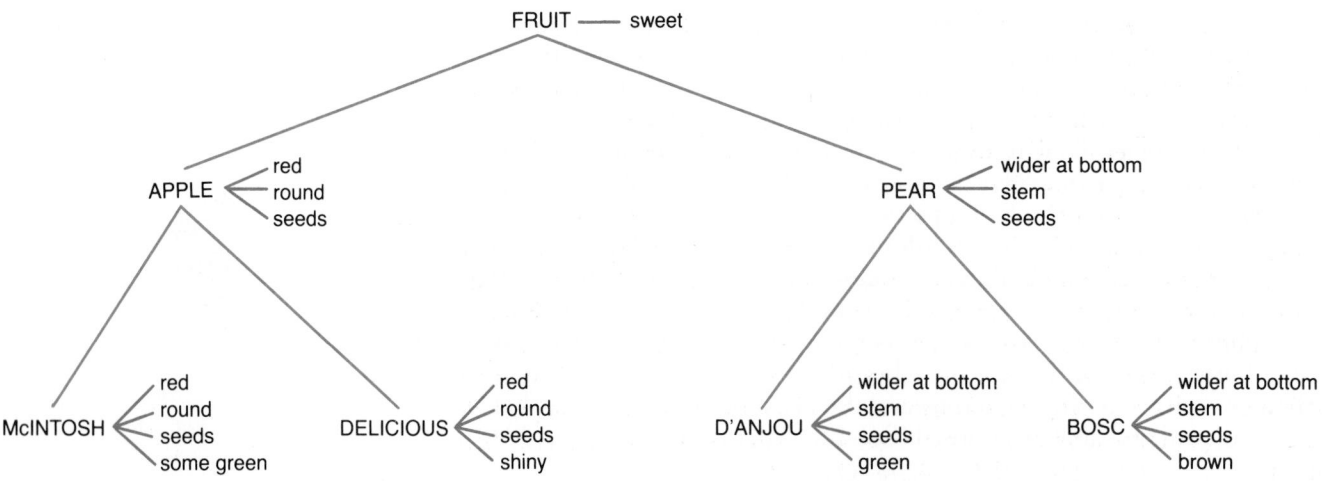

"apple" has several properties that are distinctive—they are not shared by other kinds of fruit (for example, red and round are not properties of "pear"). In contrast, "McIntosh apple" has few distinct properties; most of its properties are shared by "Delicious apple," for example (see Figure 9-1). And "fruit," which is at the highest level of Figure 9-1, has few properties of any kind. Thus, we categorize the world first at what turns out to be the most informative level.

Acquiring Concepts

How do we acquire the multitude of concepts that we have? Some concepts may be inborn, such as the concepts of "time" and "space." Other concepts have to be learned. We can learn about a concept in two different ways: either we are explicitly taught something about the concept, or we learn it through experience. Which way we learn depends on *what* we are learning. Explicit teaching is likely to be the means by which we learn cores of concepts, while experience seems to be the standard means by which we acquire prototypes. Thus, someone explicitly tells a child a "robber" is someone who takes another person's possessions with no intention of returning them (the core), while the child's experiences lead him or her to expect robbers to be shiftless, disheveled, and dangerous (the prototype).

Children must also learn that the core is a better indicator of concept membership than the prototype is. It takes a while for them to learn this. In one study, children aged 5 to 10 were presented with descriptions of items and had to decide whether or not they belonged to particular concepts. We can illustrate the study with the concept of "robber." One description given for "robber" depicted a person who matched its prototype but not its core:

> A smelly, mean old man with a gun in his pocket who came to your house and takes your TV set because your parents didn't want it anymore and told him he could have it.

Another description used for "robber" was of a person who matched its core but not its prototype:

> A very friendly and cheerful woman who gave you a hug, but then disconnected your toilet bowl and took it away without permission and no intention to return it. (Keil & Batterman, 1984, p. 226)

The younger children often thought the prototypical description was more likely than the core description to be an instance of the concept. Not until age 10 did children show a clear shift from the prototype to the core as the final arbitrator of concept decisions (Keil & Batterman, 1984).

Perhaps the reason why young children put so much stock in the prototype of a concept is that they learn it before they do the core. Even an 18-month-old child seems to have acquired the prototypes of "person," "baby," "dog," "cup," "food," and so on. Children can learn prototypes very early because they can use a simple strategy that requires them only to note similarities, not to make abstractions. In this *exemplar strategy*, when children encounter a known instance (or *exemplar*) of a concept, they store a representation of it. Later, when they have to decide whether or not a new item is an instance of that concept, they determine its similarity to stored examplars of the concept. If the similarity is great enough, they decide that the new item is an instance of the concept (Kemler Nelson, 1984).

CRITICAL DISCUSSION

Linguistic Relativity Hypothesis

In our discussion of concepts, we assume that words reflect existing concepts. We assume that language is designed to express propositional thought and, therefore, that the structure of language reflects the structure of thought. However, some have suggested that the relationship between language and thought is the other way around. Rather than thought determining language, it may be that language determines thought. This is the *linguistic relativity hypothesis* proposed by Benjamin Whorf (1956). Whorf argued that the kinds of concepts and perceptions we can have are affected by the particular language we speak. Therefore, people who speak different languages perceive the world in different ways. This provocative idea has caused considerable debate over the years.

Much of the evidence cited in favor of the hypothesis is based on vocab-

ulary differences. For example, English has only one word for snow, whereas Eskimo has four. Consequently, speakers of Eskimo may perceive differences in snow that speakers of English do not. Do such observations constitute strong evidence for the linguistic relativity hypothesis? Critics of the hypothesis argue that they do not (for example, Slobin, 1979; Brown, 1986). According to the critics, language may embody distinctions that are important to a culture, but it does not create those distinctions, nor does it limit its speakers' perceptions to them. English speakers may have the same capacity for perceiving variations in snow as Eskimo speakers, but since such variations are more important in Eskimo cultures than in Anglo cultures one language assigns different words to the variations whereas the other does not. The best evidence for this view is the development of jargons. For example, American skiers talk of "powder" and "corn," not jut "snow." This growth in vocabulary may be accompanied by changes in perception: Eskimos and skiers are more likely to notice variations in snow than are Hawaiians. But the critical point is that such changes do not depend on the language spoken. If anything, the language seems to depend on changes in perception.

The linguistic relativity hypothesis has fared no better when it comes to explaining cultural variations in terms describing colors. At one time, many linguists believed that languages differed widely in how they divided the color spectrum and that this led to differences in the perception of colors. Subsequent research showed just the opposite. Berlin and Kay (1969), two anthropologists, studied the *basic color terms* of many languages. Basic color terms are simple, nonmetaphoric words that are used to describe the colors of many different objects. Berlin and Kay found striking commonalities in such terms across languages. For instance, every language takes its basic color terms from a restricted set of 11 names. In English these are "black," "white," "red," "yellow," "green," "blue," "brown," "purple," "pink," "gray," and "orange." No matter what color terms a particular language has, they inevitably correspond to some subset of the colors listed here. In addition, if a language uses fewer than 11 terms, the basic terms chosen are not arbitrary. If a language has only two terms (none has fewer), they correspond to "black" and "white"; if it has three, they correspond to "black," "white," and "red"; if it has six, they correspond to these three plus "yellow," "green," and "blue."

The exemplar strategy works better with typical instances than atypical ones. Because the first exemplars a child learns tend to be typical ones, new instances are more likely to be correctly classified to the extent they are similar to typical instances. Thus, a young child's concept of "furniture" might consist of just the most typical instances (say, table and chair). The child could use the exemplar strategy to classify many other instances of the concept, such as desk and sofa, because they are so similar to the learned exemplars. But the child may not correctly classify instances of the concept that look different from the learned exemplars, such as "lamp" and "bookshelf." When learning is based on exemplars, typical instances will fare well, but atypical ones may not even be included in the concept (Mervis & Pani, 1981).

Although the exemplar strategy remains part of our repertory for acquiring concepts, as we grow older we start to use another strategy, *hypothesis testing*. We hypothesize what properties are critical for determining whether an item belongs to a concept, analyze any potential instance for these critical

Thus, the ordering of basic color terms seems to be universal, rather than varying from language to language as the linguistic relativity hypothesis might suggest.

In addition, people whose languages use corresponding basic color terms agree on what particular color is most typical of a color term. Suppose two different languages have terms corresponding to "red." When speakers of these languages are asked to pick the best example of red from an array of hues, they make the same choice. Even though the range of hues for what they would call red may differ, their idea of a typical red is the same. Their perceptions are identical, even though their vocabularies are different. Further work by Rosch (1974) suggests that the Dani (a New Guinea people), whose language has only two basic color terms, perceive color variations in exactly the same way as people whose language has all 11. So, the perception of color gives little support to the linguistic relativity hypothesis.

We should not dismiss the hypothesis too quickly, however. Few language domains have been investigated in the same detail as color terms, and perhaps support for the hypothesis will be found in other domains (for example, whether a language codes a particular thing or event by a noun or a verb). Also, the linguistic relativity hypothesis calls attention to an important point. In learning to make fine discriminations in a particular field, it is helpful to have a vocabulary that expresses these discriminations. As we gain expertise in a field (whether skiing, psychology, or something else), we enlarge our vocabulary for distinctions in that field. Jargons help us to think about and communicate these distinctions. Although a distinction must exist in someone's mind before a term can be created to embody it, the importance of that embodiment should not be underestimated.

Eskimos may perceive differences in snow that we do not.

properties, and then maintain our hypothesis if it leads to correct decisions. This strategy is clearly appropriate for classical concepts like "bachelor," because the core properties may be taken as the critical ones.

Combining Concepts

We need to understand not only the nature of individual concepts but also how we combine them to form propositional thoughts. One general rule of combination is that we join concepts to produce a proposition that contains a *subject* and a *predicate* (a description). In the proposition "Lorri has beautiful eyes," "Lorri" is the subject, and "has beautiful eyes" is the predicate. In the proposition "The tailor is asleep," "the tailor" is the subject, and "is asleep" is the predicate. And in "Teachers work too hard," "teachers" is the subject, and "work too hard" is the predicate. Note that in some cases the predicate is an attribute ("has beautiful eyes"); in other cases, it is a state ("is asleep"); and in still other cases, it is an activity ("work too hard").

Combining concepts into propositions is the first step toward complex thoughts. The rest of the way is accomplished by combining the propositions themselves. Again, there appear to be only certain ways we can do this. The easiest way to combine propositions into thoughts is by simply joining them—for example, "Anne likes vegetables, but Ed prefers pizza." A more complex way of combining propositions is to attach one proposition to part of another. In "Ben likes the blue blanket," we have two propositions: "Ben likes the blanket" and "the blanket is blue." The second proposition is attached to part of the predicate of the first. Perhaps the most complex way to combine propositions or thoughts is to insert one into another. For example, "Anne's liking the restaurant was a surprise to everyone" contains two propositions. The first is "Anne liked the restaurant." This proposition then serves as the subject of the second proposition, in which "was a surprise to everyone" is the predicate. Thus, the first proposition has been *embedded* into the second, and such embedding enables us to form very complex thoughts (Clark & Clark, 1977).

REASONING

When we think propositionally our sequence of thoughts is organized. Sometimes our thoughts are organized by the structure of long-term memory. A thought about calling your father, for example, leads to one about a recent conversation you had with him in your house, which in turn leads to a thought about fixing the house's attic. This sequence arises because different incidents about your father are interconnected in your memory, as are different facts about your house, and these connections supply the links between your thoughts. But memory associations are not the only means we have of organizing propositional thought. The kind of organization of interest to us here manifests itself when we try to *reason*. In such cases, our sequence of thoughts often takes the form of an argument, in which one proposition corresponds to a claim, or *conclusion*, that we are trying to draw. The remaining propositions are reasons for the claim, or *premises* for the conclusion.

Deductive Reasoning

LOGICAL RULES   According to logicians, the strongest arguments are *deductively valid*, which means that it is impossible for the conclusion of the argument to be false if its premises are true (Skyrms, 1986). An example of such an argument is the following:

1. If it's raining, I'll take an umbrella.
2. It's raining.
3. Therefore, I'll take an umbrella.

When asked to decide whether or not an argument is deductively valid, people are reasonably accurate in their assessments of simple arguments. How do we make such judgments? Some theories of deductive reasoning assume that we operate like intuitive logicians and use logical rules in trying to prove that the conclusion of an argument follows from the premises. To illustrate, consider the following rule:

If you have a proposition of the form *If p then q*, and another proposition *p*, then you can infer the proposition *q*.

Presumably, adults know this rule (perhaps unconsciously) and use it to decide that the previous argument is valid. Specifically, they identify the first premise ("If it's raining, I'll take an umbrella") with the *If p then q* part of the rule. They identify the second premise ("It's raining") with the *p* part of the rule, and then they infer the *q* part ("I'll take an umbrella").

Rule-following becomes more conscious if we complicate the argument. Presumably, we apply our sample rule twice when evaluating the following argument:

1. If it's raining, I'll take an umbrella.
2. If I take an umbrella, I'll lose it.
3. It's raining.
4. Therefore, I'll lose my umbrella.

Applying our rule to Propositions No. 1 and No. 3 allows us to infer "I'll take an umbrella"; and applying our rule again to Proposition No. 2 and the inferred proposition allows us to infer "I'll lose my umbrella," which is the conclusion. The best evidence that people are using rules like this is that the number of rules an argument requires is a good predictor of the argument's difficulty. The more rules that are needed, the more likely it is that people will make an error, and the longer it will take them when they do make a correct decision (Osherson, 1976; Rips, 1983).

OTHER RULES AND HEURISTICS   Logical rules do not capture all aspects of deductive reasoning. Such rules are triggered only by the logical *form* of propositions, yet our ability to evaluate a deductive argument often depends on the *content* of the propositions, as well. We can illustrate this point by the following experimental problems. Subjects are presented four cards. In one version of the problem, each card has a letter on one side and a digit on the other (see the top half of Figure 9-2). The subject must decide which cards to turn over to determine whether the following claim is correct: "If a card has a vowel on one side, then it has an even number on the other side." While most subjects correctly choose the "E" card, fewer than 10 percent of them also choose the "7" card, which is the other correct choice. (To see that the "7" card is critical, note that if it has a vowel on its other side, the claim is disconfirmed.)

Performance improves drastically, however, in another version of the above problem (see the bottom half of Figure 9-2). Now the claim that subjects must evaluate is "If a person is drinking beer, he or she must be over 19." Each card has a person's age on one side, and what he or she is drinking on the other. This version of the problem is logically equivalent to the preceding version (in particular, "Beer" corresponds to "E," and "16" to "7"); but now most subjects make the correct choices (they turn over the "Beer" and "16" cards). Thus, the content of the propositions affects our reasoning.

Results such as the above imply that we do not always use logical rules when faced with deduction problems. Rather, sometimes we use rules that are less abstract and more relevant to everyday problems, what are called

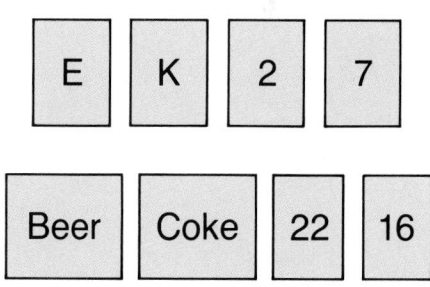

FIGURE 9-2
Content Effects in Deductive Reasoning *The top row illustrates a version of the problem in which subjects had to decide which two cards should be turned over to test the hypothesis, "If a card has a vowel on one side, it has an even number on the other side." The bottom row illustrates a version of the problem where subjects had to decide which cards to turn over to test the hypothesis, "If a person is drinking beer, he or she must be over 19." (After Wason & Johnson-Laird, 1972; Griggs & Cox, 1982)*

pragmatic rules. An example is the *permission rule*, which states that "If a particular action is to be taken, often a precondition must be satisfied." Though less abstract than a logical rule, the permission rule can be applied to many different domains of life (voting, driving, and so on). Most people know this rule, and activate it when presented the drinking problem in the bottom half of Figure 9-2; that is, they would think about the problem in terms of permission. Once activated, the rule would lead people to look for failures to meet the relevant precondition (being under 19), which in turn would lead them to choose the "16" card. In contrast, the permission rule would not be triggered by the letter-number problem in the top half of Figure 9-2, so there is no reason for people to choose the "7" card. Thus, the content of a problem affects whether or not a pragmatic rule is activated, which in turn affects the correctness of reasoning (Cheng, Holyoak, Nisbett, & Oliver, 1986).

In addition to rules, we sometimes use *heuristics* in deductive reasoning. Heuristics are shortcut procedures that are relatively easy to apply and that often yield the correct answers, but not inevitably so. Subjects may solve the drinking version of the aforementioned problem by retrieving from long-term memory a relevant fact about drinking (that only young drinkers must be checked to see if the law is being violated) and then applying this fact to the present problem (Rips, 1988). Alternatively, subjects may solve the drinking problem by setting up a concrete representation of the situation. They may, for example, imagine two people, each with a number on his back and a drink in his hand. They may then inspect this representation and see what happens, for example, if the drinker with "16" on his back has a beer in his hand. According to this idea, we reason in terms of concrete examples suggested by the content of the problem (Johnson-Laird, 1983).

All of the procedures just described—applying pragmatic rules, retrieving specific facts, and constructing concrete examples—have one thing in common. They are determined by the content of the problem. This is in contrast to the application of logical rules, which should not be affected by problem content. Hence, our sensitivity to content often prevents us from operating as intuitive logicians.

Inductive Reasoning

LOGICAL RULES Logicians have noted that an argument can be good even if it is not deductively valid. Such arguments are *inductively strong*, which means that it is *improbable* that the conclusion is false if the premises are true (Skyrms, 1986). An example of an inductively strong argument is as follows:

1. Mitch majored in accounting in college.
2. Mitch now works for an accounting firm.
3. Therefore, Mitch is an accountant.

This argument is not deductively valid (Mitch may have tired of accounting courses and taken a night-watchman's job in the only place he had contacts). Inductive strength, then, is a matter of probabilities, not certainties, and inductive logic is based on the theory of probability.

We make and evaluate inductive arguments all the time. In doing this, do we rely on the rules of probability theory as a logician or mathematician would? One probability rule that is relevant is the *base-rate rule*, which states that the probability of something being a member of a class (such as Mitch being a member of the class of accountants) is greater the more class members there are (that is, the higher the base rate of the class). Thus, our sample argument about Mitch being an accountant can be strengthened by adding the premise that Mitch joined a club in which 90 percent of the members are accountants. Another relevant probability rule is the *conjunction rule*: the probability of a proposition cannot be less than the probability of that proposition conjoined with another proposition. For example, the probability that "Mitch is an accountant" cannot be less than the probability that "Mitch is an accountant and makes more than $30,000 a year." The base-rate and conjunction rules are rational guides to inductive reasoning, and most people will defer to them when the rules are made explicit. However, in the rough-and-tumble of everyday reasoning, people frequently violate these rules, as we are about to see.

HEURISTICS   In a series of ingenious experiments, Tversky and Kahneman have shown that people violate basic rules of probability theory when making inductive judgments. Violations of the base-rate rule are particularly common. In one experiment, one group of subjects was told that a panel of psychologists had interviewed 100 people—30 engineers and 70 lawyers—and had written personality descriptions of them. These subjects were then given five descriptions and for each one were asked to indicate the probability that the person described was an engineer. Some descriptions were prototypical of an engineer (for example, "Jack shows no interest in political issues and spends his free time on home carpentry"); other descriptions were neutral (for example, "Dick is a man of high ability and promises to be quite successful"). Not surprisingly, these subjects rated the prototypical description as more likely to be an engineer than the neutral description. Another group of subjects was given the identical instructions and five descriptions, except they were told that the 100 descriptions were of 70 engineers and 30 lawyers (the reverse of the first group). The base rate of engineers therefore differed greatly between the two groups. This difference had virtually no effect: subjects in the second group gave essentially the same ratings as those in the first group. Thus, subjects in both groups rated the neutral description as having a 50–50 chance of being an engineer (whereas the rational move would have been to rate the neutral description as more likely to be in the profession with the higher base rate). Subjects completely ignored the information about base rates (Tversky & Kahneman, 1973).

People pay no more heed to the conjunction rule. In one study, subjects were presented the following description:

Linda is 31 years old, single, outspoken, and very bright. In college, she majored in philosophy . . . and was deeply concerned with issues of discrimination.

Subjects then estimated the probabilities of the following statements:

1. Linda is a bank teller.
2. Linda is a bank teller and is active in the feminist movement.

Is this bank teller a feminist?

Statement No. 2 is the conjunction of Statement No. 1 and the proposition "Linda is active in the feminist movement." In flagrant violation of the conjunction rule, most subjects rated No. 2 more probable than No. 1. Note that this is a fallacy because every feminist bank teller is a bank teller, but some female bank tellers are not feminists, and Linda could be one of them (Tversky & Kahneman, 1983).

Subjects in this study based their judgments on the fact that Linda seems more similar to a feminist bank teller than to a bank teller. Though they were asked to estimate *probability*, subjects instead estimated the *similarity* of Linda to the prototype of the concepts "bank teller" and "feminist bank teller." Thus, estimating similarity is used as a heuristic for estimating probability, because similarity often relates to probability yet is easier to calculate. Use of the *similarity heuristic* also explains why people ignore base rates. In the engineer-lawyer study described earlier, subjects may have considered only the similarity of the description to their prototypes of "engineer" and "lawyer." Hence, given a description that matched the prototypes of "engineer" and "lawyer" equally well, subjects judged that that engineer and lawyer were equally probable.

Another heuristic that we employ to estimate probabilities is the *causality heuristic*: people estimate the probability of a situation by the strength of the causal connections between the events in the situation. For example, people judge Statement No. 4 to be more probable than Statement No. 3:

3. Sometime during 1994, there will be a massive flood in North America, in which more than 1,000 people will drown.
4. Sometime during 1994, there will be an earthquake in California, causing a massive flood, in which more than 1,000 people will drown.

Judging No. 4 to be more probable than No. 3 is another violation of the conjunction rule. This time, the violation arises because in Statement No. 4 the flood has a strong causal connection to another event, the earthquake; whereas in Statement No. 3, the flood alone is mentioned and hence has no causal connections.

So, there are rational rules for inductive reasoning, including the base-rate and conjunction rule, which are established by experts. Although we generally accept these rules as ideals, and defer to them when they are explicitly mentioned, our everyday reasoning differs from their prescriptions. In particular, often we use judgments of similarity and causality rather than the rational rules, perhaps because judgments of similarity and causality are more natural ways for us to think. Although the rules of probability theory may not always seem natural to us, explicit training in them can increase the extent to which we use the rules in everyday situations (Nisbett, Fong, Lehman, & Cheng, 1987).

LANGUAGE AND COMMUNICATION

Language is the primary means for communicating propositional thought. Moreover, it is a universal means: every human society has a language, and every human being of normal intelligence acquires his or her native language and uses it effortlessly. The naturalness of language sometimes lulls us into thinking that language use requires no special explanation. Nothing could be further from the truth. Some people can read, and others cannot; some can do arithmetic, and others cannot; some can play chess, and others cannot. But virtually everyone can master and use an enormously complex linguistic system. This is among the fundamental puzzles of human psychology.

Levels of Language

Language use has two aspects: *production* and *comprehension*. In producing language, we start with a propositional thought, somehow translate it into a sentence, and end up with sounds that express the sentence. In comprehending language, we start by hearing sounds, attach meanings to the sounds in the form of words, combine the words to create a sentence, and then somehow extract a proposition from it. Language use thus seems to involve moving through various levels, and Figure 9-3 makes these levels explicit. At the highest level are sentence units, including sentences and phrases. The next level is that of words and parts of words that carry meaning (the prefix "non" or the suffix "er," for example). The lowest level contains speech sounds. The adjacent levels are closely related to one another: the phrases of a sentence are built from words and prefixes and suffixes, which in turn are constructed from speech sounds. Language is therefore a multilevel system for relating thoughts to speech by word and sentence units (Chomsky, 1965).

There are striking differences in the number of units at each level. All languages have only a limited number of speech sounds; English has about 40 of them. But rules for combining these speech sounds make it possible to produce and understand thousands of words (a vocabulary of 40,000 words is not unusual for an adult). Similarly, rules for combining words make it possible to produce and understand millions of sentences (if not an infinite number of them). Thus, two of the basic properties of language are that it is *structured* at multiple levels and that it is *productive*: rules allow us to combine units at one level into a vastly greater number of units at the next level. Every human language has these two properties.

Language Units and Processes

With the above as background, let us now consider the units and processes involved at each level of language.

SPEECH SOUNDS In speaking, we use the lips, tongue, mouth, and vocal cords to produce a variety of physical sounds. Not all of these sounds are perceived as distinct, however. In English, we discriminate about 40 *phonemes*, or categories of speech sounds. The sound corresponding to the first letter in "boy" is a phoneme symbolized as /b/. We are good at discriminating different sounds that correspond to different phonemes in our language. But we are poor at discriminating different sounds that correspond to the same phoneme—for example, the sound of the first letter in "pin" and the sound of the second letter in "spin" (Liberman, Cooper, Shankweiler, & Studdert-Kennedy, 1967). They are the same phoneme, /p/, and they sound the same to us even though they have different physical characteristics. The /p/ in "pin" is accompanied by a small puff of air, but the /p/ in "spin" is not (try holding your hand a short distance from your mouth as you say the two words). Thus, we are "equipped" with phonemic categories that act as filters (they convert a stream of speech into the phonemes of our language).

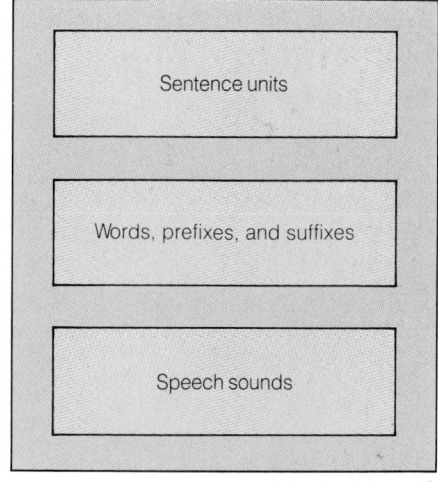

FIGURE 9-3
Levels of Language *At the highest level are sentence units, including phrases and sentences. The next level is that of words and parts of words that carry meaning. The lowest level contains speech sounds.*

Every language has a different set of phonemes, which is one reason why we often have difficulty learning to pronounce foreign words. Another language may use speech sounds that never appear in ours. It may take us a while even to hear the new phonemes, let alone produce them. For example, in the Hindi language, the two different /p/ sounds illustrated above correspond to two different phonemes. Or another language may not make a distinction between two sounds that our language treats as two phonemes. For example, in Japanese the English sounds corresponding to "r" and "l" (/r/ and /l/) are treated as the same phoneme.

When phonemes are combined in the right way, they form words. Each language has its own rules about which phonemes can follow others. In English, for example, /b/ cannot follow /p/ at the beginning of a word (try pronouncing "pbet"). Such rules show their influence when we speak and listen. For example, we have no difficulty pronouncing the plurals of nonsense words we have never heard before. Consider "zuk" and "zug." In accordance with a simple rule, the plural of "zuk" is formed by adding the phoneme /s/, as in "hiss." In English, however, /s/ cannot follow "g" at the end of a word, so to form the plural of "zug" we must use another rule—one that adds the phoneme /z/, as in "fuzz." We may not be aware of these differences in forming plurals, but we have no difficulty producing them. It is as if we "know" the rules for combining phonemes even though we are not consciously aware of the rules: we conform to rules we cannot verbalize.

WORD UNITS   A *morpheme* is the smallest linguistic unit that carries meaning. Most morphemes are themselves words, such as "time." Others are suffixes, such as "ly," or prefixes, such as "un," which are added onto words to form more complex ones, such as "timely" or "untimely." Most words denote some specific content, such as "house" or "run." A few words, however, primarily serve to make sentences grammatical; such grammatical words, or *grammatical morphemes*, include what are commonly labeled articles and prepositions, such as "a," "the," "in," "of," "on," and "at." Some prefixes and suffixes also play primarily a grammatical role. These grammatical morphemes include the suffixes "ing," "ed," and "s" (added to nouns to form the plural—"boys"—and added to verbs in the present tense for the third person singular—"The boy kicks"). As we shall see later, grammatical morphemes are acquired in a different manner than are content words.

Every language has rules about how prefixes or suffixes are combined with words. In English, for example, the suffix "er" is regularly added to many verbs to form nouns that refer to people who habitually perform the action described by the verb, as in "speak–speaker" and "paint–painter." Do we actually use these rules, or something like them, in production and comprehension? Our slips of the tongue suggest we do. For example, a speaker who intended to say "Smith favors busting pushers" uttered instead "Smith favors pushing busters" (Garrett, 1975). The morphemes "bust" and "push" were interchanged, whereas the morphemes "ing" and "er + s" stayed in their correct positions. This implies that morphemes like "push" and "er + s" are treated as separate units (which are usually combined by application of a rule).

The most important aspect of a word is, of course, its meaning. A word can be viewed as the name of a concept; hence, its meaning is the concept it names. Some words are *ambiguous* because they name more than one concept. "Club," for example, names both a social organization and an object used for striking. Sometimes we may be aware of a word's ambiguity, as when hearing the sentence "He was interested in the club." In most cases, however, the sentence context makes the meaning of the word sufficiently clear

Club as a social organization.

so we do not consciously experience any ambiguity—for example, "He wanted to join the club." Even in the latter cases, though, there is evidence that we *unconsciously* consider both meanings of the ambiguous word for a brief moment. In one experiment, a subject was presented a sentence like, "He wanted to join the club," followed immediately by a test word that the subject had to read aloud as quickly as possible. Subjects read the test word faster if it was related to *either* meaning of "club" (for example, "group" or "struck") than if it was unrelated to either meaning (for example, "apple"). This suggests that both meanings of "club" were activated during comprehension of the sentence, and that either meaning could prime related words (Tanenhaus, Leiman, & Seidenberg, 1979; Swinney, 1979).

SENTENCE UNITS   Sentence units include sentences and phrases. An important property of these units is that they can correspond to parts of a proposition. Such correspondences allow speakers to "put" propositions into sentences and listeners to "extract" propositions from sentences.

Recall that any proposition can be broken into a subject and predicate. A sentence can be broken into phrases in such a way that each phrase corresponds either to the subject or the predicate of a proposition or to an entire proposition. For example, intuitively we can divide the simple sentence "Maria sells insurance" into two phrases, "Maria" and "sells insurance." The first phrase, which is called a *noun phrase* because it centers on a noun, specifies the subject of an underlying proposition. The second phrase, a *verb phrase*, gives the predicate of the proposition. For a more complex example, consider the sentence "Serious scholars read books." This sentence divides into two phrases, the noun phrase "serious scholars" and the verb phrase "read books." The noun phrase expresses an entire proposition, "scholars are serious"; the verb phrase expresses part (the predicate) of another proposition, "scholars read books" (see Figure 9-4). Again, sentence units correspond closely to proposition units.

Thus, when reading or listening to a sentence, people seem to first divide it into noun phrases, verb phrases, and the like, and then extract propositions from these phrases. Evidence that we in fact divide sentences into phrases comes from memory experiments. In one study, subjects listened to sentences such as "The poor girl stole a warm coat." Immediately after each sentence was presented, they were given a probe word from the sentence and asked to say the word that came after it. People responded faster when the probe and the response words came from the same phrase ("poor" and "girl") than when they came from different phrases ("girl" and "stole"). Thus, people break the sentence into phrases, and each phrase becomes a unit in memory. When the probe and response are from the same phrase, only one unit needs to be retrieved (Wilkes & Kennedy, 1969).

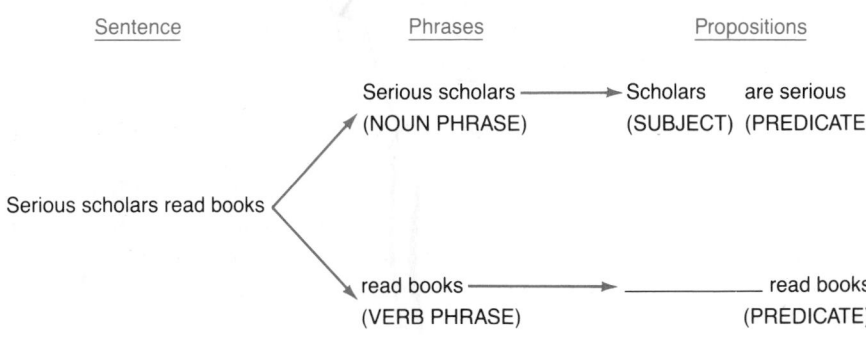

FIGURE 9-4
Phrases and Propositions *The first step in extracting the propositions from a complex sentence is to break the sentence into phrases.*

Analyzing a sentence into noun and verb phrases, and then dividing these phrases into smaller units like nouns, adjectives, and verbs, is called a *syntactic analysis* (*syntax* deals with the relations between words in phrases and sentences). Usually, in the course of understanding a sentence we perform such an analysis effortlessly and unconsciously. Sometimes, however, our syntactic analysis goes awry and we become aware of the process. Consider the sentence, "The horse raced past the barn fell." Many people experience difficulty understanding this sentence. Why? Because on first reading, we assume that "The horse" is the noun phrase and "raced past the barn" the verb phrase, which leaves us with no place for the word "fell." To correctly understand the sentence, we have to repartition it so that the entire phrase "The horse raced past the barn" is the noun phrase, and "fell" is the verb phrase (that is, the sentence is just a shortened version of "The horse who was raced past the barn fell"). In this example people initially run into trouble because they unconsciously commit themselves to one particular syntactic analysis when another one is possible. Other work, however, suggests that in certain cases we are capable of simultaneously considering more than one analysis of a sentence (Gorrell, 1987).

Effects of Context on Comprehension and Production

By way of summary, Figure 9-5 presents an amended version of our levels description of language. The figure suggests that understanding a sentence is the inverse of producing a sentence. To produce a sentence, we start with a propositional thought, translate it into the phrases and morphemes of a sentence, and finally translate these morphemes into phonemes. We work from the top level down to the bottom level ("top-down processing"). To understand a sentence, however, we move in the opposite direction—from the bottom level to the top. We hear phonemes, use them to construct the morphemes and phrases of a sentence, and finally extract the proposition from the sentence unit ("bottom-up processing").

Although this analysis describes some of what occurs in sentence production and understanding, it is oversimplified because it does not consider the *context* in which language processing occurs. Consider, for example, a case of language understanding in which the context makes what is about to be said predictable. After comprehending just a few words, we jump to conclusions about what we think the entire sentence means (the propositions behind it), and then use our guess about the propositions to help understand the rest of the sentence. In such cases, understanding proceeds from the top level down as well as from the bottom level up. To illustrate, suppose that in a conversation about eating in a restaurant, your friend says, "The food was so bad that I complained to the manager." Immediately after hearing the word "bad," you might hypothesize that the rest of the sentence will express a thought about complaining to someone on the staff. In this case, you could use your stored knowledge about eating in restaurants (what we called the restaurant schema in Chapter 8) to guide sentence understanding. Such schema guidance is very common in understanding conversations and stories (Adams & Collins, 1979; Schank, 1982).

Perhaps the most salient part of the context, though, is the other person (or persons) we are communicating with. In understanding a sentence, it is not enough to understand its phonemes, morphemes, and phrases; we must also understand the *speaker's intention* in uttering that particular sentence. For example, when someone at dinner asks you, "Can you pass the potatoes,"

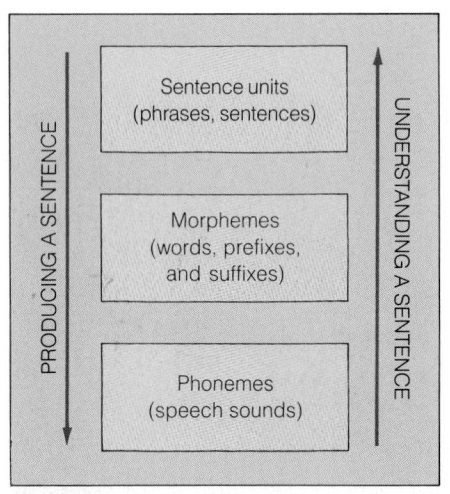

FIGURE 9-5
Levels of Understanding and Producing Sentences *In producing a sentence, we translate a propositional thought into the phrases and morphemes of a sentence and translate these morphemes into phonemes. In understanding a sentence, we go in the opposite direction—we use phonemes to construct the morphemes and phrases of a sentence and from these units extract the underlying propositions.*

usually you assume that their intention was not to find out if you are physically capable of lifting the potatoes, but rather to induce you to actually pass the potatoes. However, had your arm been in a sling, then given the identical question you might assume that the speaker's intention *was* to determine your physical capability. In both cases, the sentence (and proposition) is the same; what changes is the speaker's goal for uttering that sentence (Grice, 1975). And there is abundant evidence that people extract the speaker's intention as part of the process of comprehension (Clark, 1984).

There are similar effects in the production of language. If someone asks you, "Where is the Empire State Building?" you will say very different things depending on the physical context and the assumptions that you make about the questioner. If the question is asked of you in Cincinnati, for example, you might answer "In New York"; if the question is asked in Brooklyn, you might say "Near Midtown Manhattan"; and if the question is asked in Manhattan, you might say "On 34th Street." Therefore, in speaking, as in understanding, one must determine how the utterance fits the context.

DEVELOPMENT OF LANGUAGE

Our discussion of language should indicate the enormity of the task confronting children. They must master all levels of language—not only the proper speech sounds but also how these sounds are combined into thousands of words and how these words can be combined into sentences to express thoughts. It is a wonder that virtually all children in all cultures accomplish so much of this in a mere 4 to 5 years. What is perhaps even more amazing is that all children, regardless of their culture, seem to go through the same sequence of development. At age 1, the child speaks a few isolated words; at about age 2, the child speaks two- and three-word sentences; at age 3, sentences become more grammatical; and at age 4, the child speaks much like an adult (Gleitman, 1984).

We will first discuss what is acquired at each level of language and then consider how it is acquired and what roles learning and innate factors play. Our discussion of innate factors will consider a number of critical issues, including the possibility of another species learning human language and the localization of language abilities in the human brain.

What Is Acquired?

Development occurs at all three levels of language. It starts at the level of phonemes, proceeds to the level of words and other morphemes, and then moves on to the level of sentence units, or syntax.

PHONEMES AND THEIR COMBINATION Recall that adults are good at discriminating different sounds that correspond to different phonemes in their language, but poor at discriminating different sounds that correspond to the same phoneme in their language. Remarkably, children come into the world able to discriminate different sounds that correspond to different phonemes in *any* language. What changes over the first year of life is that infants learn which phonemes are relevant to their language, and lose their ability to discriminate between sounds that correspond to the same phoneme in their language. These remarkable facts were determined by experiments in which

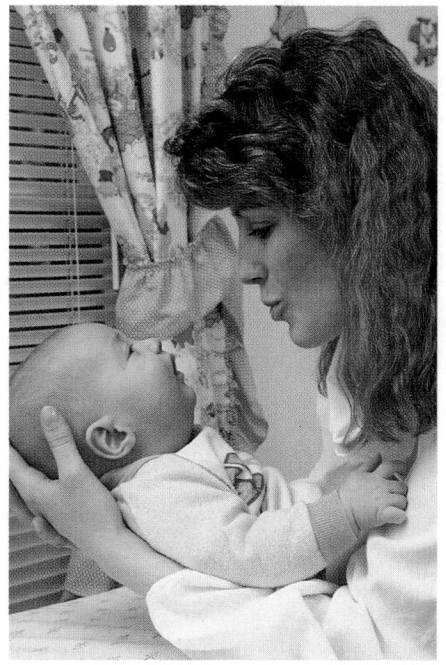

Infant vocalization is an initial stage of language acquisition.

A child learns to recognize objects as his mother reads to him.

infants were presented pairs of sounds in succession while they were sucking on pacifiers. Since infants suck more to a novel stimulus than to a familiar one, their rate of sucking can be used to tell whether they perceive two successive sounds as the same or different. Six-month-old infants increase their rate of sucking when the successive sounds correspond to different phonemes in *any* language, whereas 1-year-olds increase their rate of sucking only when the successive sounds correspond to different phonemes in their own language. Thus, a 6-month-old Japanese child can distinguish /l/ from /r/ but loses this ability by the end of the first year of life (Eimas, 1985).

While children learn which phonemes are relevant in their first year of life, it takes several years for children to learn how phonemes can be combined to form words. When children first begin to talk, they occasionally produce "impossible" words, like "dlumber" for "lumber." They do not yet know that in English /l/ cannot follow /d/ at the beginning of a word. By age 4, children have learned most of what they need to know about phoneme combinations. In one study, children of about 4 years of age were asked to say which of two made-up sequences of speech sounds would make a better name for a toy. One sequence was consistent with rules for combining phonemes (for example, "klek"), whereas the other was not (for example, "lkel"). Most of the children chose the name that conformed to the rules (Messer, 1967).

WORDS AND CONCEPTS   At about 1 year of age, children begin to speak. One-year-olds already have concepts for many things (including family members, household pets, food, toys, and body parts), and when they begin to speak, they are mapping these concepts onto words that adults use. To learn which word goes with which concept, children look at what is happening around them when a word is used and take the important aspects of the situation as the meaning of the word. For example, a child might think, "Mommy said 'Fang' when she pointed to my pet, so 'Fang' means my pet."

The beginning vocabulary is roughly the same for all children. Children 1 to 2 years old talk mainly about people ("Dada," "Mama," "baby"), animals ("dog," "cat," "duck"), vehicles ("car," "truck," "boat"), toys ("ball," "block," "book"), food ("juice," "milk," "cookie"), body parts ("eye," "nose," "mouth"), and household implements ("hat," "sock," "spoon"). While these words name some of the young child's concepts, by no means do they name them all. Consequently, young children often have a gap between the concepts they want to communicate and the words they have at their disposal. To bridge this gap, children aged 1 to 2½ years old *overextend* their words to neighboring concepts. For example, a 2-year-old child might use the word "doggie" for cats and cows, as well as dogs (the child is not unsure of the word's meaning—if presented pictures of various animals and asked to pick the "doggie," the child makes the correct choice). At about the age of 2½ years, overextensions begin to disappear, presumably because the child's vocabulary begins to increase markedly, thereby eliminating many of the gaps (Rescorla, 1980; Clark, 1983).

Thereafter, vocabulary development virtually explodes. At 1½ years, a child might have a vocabulary of 25 words; at 6 years, the child's vocabulary is around 15,000 words. To achieve this incredible growth, children have to learn new words at the rate of almost 10 per day (Templin, 1957; Miller & Gildea, 1987). Children seem to be tuned to learning new words. When they hear a word they do not know, they may assume it maps onto one of their concepts that is as yet unlabeled, and they use the context in which the word was spoken to find that concept (Clark, 1983; Markman, 1987).

TABLE 9-1
Intentions of Two-Word Sentences in Children's speech *Children's earliest*
sentences in many languages serve the same basic intentions. (After Slobin, 1971)

INTENTION OF UTTERANCE	LANGUAGE			
	English	German	Russian	Samoan
Locate, name	there book that car see doggie	buch da (book there) gukuk wauwau (see doggie)	Tosya tam (Tosya there)	Keith lea (Keith there)
Demand, desire	more milk give candy want gum	mehr milch (more milk) bitte apfel (please apple)	yeschē moloko (more milk) day chasy (give watch)	mai pepe (give doll) fia moe (want sleep)
Negate	no wet no wash no hungry allgone milk	nicht blasen (not blow) kaffee nein (coffee no)	vody net (water no) gus' tyu-tyu (goose gone)	le 'ai (not eat) uma mea (allgone thing)
Describe event, action, or situation	Bambi go mail come hit ball block fall baby highchair	puppe kommt (doll comes) tiktak hängt (clock hangs) sofa sitzen (sofa sit)	mama prua (mama walk) papa bay-bay (papa sleep) korka upala (crust fell)	pa'u pepe (fall doll) tapale 'oe (hit you) tu'u lalo (put down)
Indicate possession	my shoe mama dress	mein ball (my ball) mama hat (mama's hat)	mami chaska (mama's cup) pup moya (navel my)	lole a'u (candy my) polo 'oe (ball your)
Modify, qualify	pretty dress big boat	milch heiss (milk hot) armer wauwau (poor dog)	mama khoroshaya (mama good) papa bol'shoy (papa big)	fa'ali'i pepe (headstrong baby)
Question	where ball	wo ball (where ball)	gde papa (where papa)	fea Punafu (where Punafu)

FROM PRIMITIVE TO COMPLEX SENTENCES   At about 1½ to 2½ years, the acquisition of phrase and sentence units, or syntax, begins. Children start to combine single words into two-word utterances, such as "There cow" (where the underlying proposition is "There's the cow"), "Jimmy bike" (the proposition is "That's Jimmy's bike"), or "Towel bed" (the proposition is "The towel's on the bed"). There is a *telegraphic* quality about two-word speech. The child leaves out the grammatical words (such as "a," "an," "the," and "is"), as well as other grammatical morphemes (such as the suffixes "ing," "ed," and "s") and puts in only the words that carry the most important content. Despite their brevity, these utterances express most of the basic intentions of speakers, such as locating objects and describing events and actions (see Table 9-1).

Children progress rapidly from two-word utterances to more complex sentences that express propositions more precisely. Thus, "Daddy hat" may become "Daddy wear hat" and finally "Daddy is wearing a hat." Such expansions of the verb phrase appear to be the first complex, syntactic constructions that occur in children's speech. The next step is the use of conjunctions like "and" and "so" to form compound sentences ("You play with the doll *and* I play with the block") and the use of grammatical morphemes like the past tense "ed." The sequence of language development is remarkably similar for all children.

Learning Processes

Now that we have an idea about what children acquire in the language process, we can ask how they acquire it. Learning undoubtedly plays a role; that is why children who are brought up in an English-speaking household learn English and why children raised in a French-speaking household learn French. And innate factors undoubtedly play a role; that is why all children in a household learn language but none of the pets do (Gleitman, 1984). We discuss learning in this section and consider innate factors in the next section. In both discussions, we emphasize sentence units and syntax, for it is at this level of language that the important issues about language acquisition are most clearly illustrated.

IMITATION AND CONDITIONING   One possibility is that children learn language by *imitating* adults. While imitation may play some role in learning words (a parent points to a telephone, says "phone," and the child tries to repeat it), it cannot be the principal means by which children learn to produce and understand sentences. Young children constantly utter sentences they have never heard an adult say, such as "All gone milk." Even when children at the two-word stage try to imitate longer adult sentences (for example, "Mr. Miller will try"), they produce their usual telegraphic utterances ("Miller try"). In addition, the mistakes children make (for instance, "Daddy taked me") show that they are trying to apply rules, not simply trying to copy what they have heard adults say (Ervin-Tripp, 1964).

Some linguists and psychologists have argued that it is *impossible in principle* for a child to learn a language by imitation. Thus, the number of 20-word sentences that we can understand has been estimated to be 10^{20}. To learn sentences by imitation, a person first must listen to them; but if 10^{20} sentences were spoken at a normal rate, the amount of time needed to listen to them would exceed the estimated age of the earth (Miller, 1965)!

A second possibility is that children acquire language through *conditioning*. Adults may reward children when they produce a grammatical sentence and reprimand them when they make mistakes. For this to work, parents would have to respond to every detail in a child's speech. However, Brown, Cazden, and Bellugi (1969) found that parents do not pay attention to how the child says something as long as the statement is comprehensible. Rare attempts to correct a child (and hence to apply conditioning) are often futile.

CHILD: Nobody don't like me.
MOTHER: No, say, "nobody likes me."
CHILD: Nobody don't like me.
MOTHER: No, now listen carefully; say "nobody likes me."
CHILD: Oh! Nobody don't LIKES me.   (McNeill, 1966, p. 49)

HYPOTHESIS TESTING   The problem with imitation and conditioning is that they focus on specific utterances (one can only imitate or reinforce something specific). However, children often learn something general, such as a rule; they seem to form a hypothesis about a rule of language, test it, and retain it if it works.

Consider the morpheme "ed." As a general rule in English, "ed" is added to the present tense of verbs to form the past tense (as in "cook–cooked"). Many common verbs, however, are irregular and do not follow this rule (like "go–went" and "take–took"). Many of these irregular verbs express concepts that children use from the beginning. So at an early point, children use the past tense of some irregular verbs correctly (presumably because they learned them by imitation). They learn the past tense for some regular verbs and discover the hypothesis "add 'ed' to the present tense to form the past tense." This hypothesis leads them to add the "ed" ending to all verbs, including the irregular ones. They say things such as "Annie goed home" and "Jackie taked the book," which they have never heard before. Eventually, they learn that some verbs are irregular and stop overgeneralizing their use of "ed."

How do children generate these hypotheses? There are a few *operating principles* that all children use as a guide to forming hypotheses. One is to pay attention to the ends of words. Another is to look for prefixes and suffixes that indicate a change in meaning. A child armed with these two principles is likely to hit the hypothesis that "ed" at the end of verbs signals the past tense, since "ed" is a word ending associated with a change in meaning. A third operating principle is to avoid exceptions, which explains why children initially generalize their "ed"-equals-past-tense hypothesis to irregular verbs. Some of these principles appear in Table 9-2 and they seem to hold for the 40 languages studied by Slobin (1971; 1985).

Recently, there has been a challenge to the idea that learning a language amounts to learning rules by hypothesis testing. Some researchers have argued that what looks like an instance of learning a single rule may in fact be a case of learning numerous associations or *connections* (like the connections we considered in our discussion of perceptual recognition in Chapter 5). Consider again a child learning to form the past tense of verbs in English. Instead of learning a rule about adding "ed" to the present tense of a verb, perhaps children are learning associations between the past tense ending "ed" and various *phonetic properties* of verbs that can go with "ed." The phonetic properties of a verb include properties of the sounds that make up the verb, such as whether the vocal chords are vibrating when producing the sound, as well as properties of the whole verb, such as whether it contains an "alk" sound at the end. Thus, a child may learn (unconsciously) that verbs containing an "alk" sound at the end—such as "talk," "walk," and "stalk"— are likely to take "ed" as a past tense ending. This proposal has in fact been shown to account for some aspects of learning verb endings, including the finding that at some point in development children add the "ed" ending even to irregular verbs (Rumelhart & McClelland, 1987). However, there appear to be other aspects of learning verb endings that can be explained only by assuming the child is learning rules. So the link between language learning and rules may still stand (Pinker & Prince, 1988).

Innate Factors

As noted earlier, some of our knowledge about language is inborn, or innate. There are, however, controversial questions about the extent and

TABLE 9-2
Operating Principles Used by Young Children *Children from many countries seem to follow these principles in learning to talk and to understand speech.* (After Slobin, 1971)

1. Look for systematic changes in the form of words.

2. Look for grammatical markers that clearly indicate changes in meaning.

3. Avoid exceptions.

4. Pay attention to the ends of words.

5. Pay attention to the order of words, prefixes, and suffixes.

6. Avoid interruption or rearrangement of constituents (that is, sentence units).

nature of this innate knowledge. One question concerns its *richness*. If our innate knowledge is very rich, or specific, then all human languages should bear strong similarities to one another (because they are all based on the same innate knowledge), and the process of language acquisition should be similar for different languages. A second question about innate factors involves *critical periods*. As noted in Chapters 5 and 7, a common feature of innate behavior is that it will be acquired more readily if the organism is exposed to the right cues during a critical time period. Are there such critical periods in language acquisition? A third question about the innate contribution to language concerns its possible *uniqueness*: Is the ability to learn a language system unique to the human species? We will consider these three questions in turn.

SIMILARITIES IN LANGUAGE AND LANGUAGE ACQUISITION   The study of different languages has revealed a number of specific features that may be common to *all* languages. We will illustrate with an example from Chomsky (1980a). In English, simple declarative sentences can be transformed into yes–no questions, as in:

> The man is here. Is the man here?
> The man will leave. Will the man leave?

What rule describes how to transform the declarative into the question form? One possibility is that the rule involves only word units, not syntactic units.

> Word Rule: Go through the declarative form from left to right until reaching the first occurrence of "is," "will," and so on; transpose this occurrence to the beginning of the sentence to get the question form.

Another possibility is that the rule involves a syntactic unit, namely that of a noun phrase:

> Syntactic Rule: Go through the declarative form from left to right until reaching the first occurrence of "is," "will," and so on, *following the first noun phrase*; transpose this occurrence to the beginning of the sentence to get the question form.

The syntactic rule is clearly the correct one for English. In the declarative "The man who is here is tall," we wait until the second occurrence of "is"—the one after the noun phrase ("the man who is here")—before transposing. The same principle—that the rule for transforming declaratives into questions depends on syntactic units, not just words—holds for every human language that has ever been studied. This universality is remarkable, given that there are thousands of natural languages. One might have thought that one or two languages would have evolved so that a simpler word rule could handle the transformation. The fact that there are *no* exceptions suggests that all languages must conform to specific innate constraints.

The sequence of language acquisition offers another source of evidence that our innate knowledge about language is very rich. The sequence (from single words to two-word telegraphs to complex sentences) is remarkably similar for all children, despite large variations in the language of the adults around them. Indeed, children go through the normal course of language acquisition even when there are no language users around them to serve as models. A group of researchers studied six deaf children of parents who could hear and who had decided not to have the children learn sign language. Before the children received any instruction in lip reading and vocalization—indeed, before they had acquired any knowledge of English—they began to use a system of gestures called *home sign*. Initially, their home sign was a kind of simple pantomime, but eventually it took on the properties of a language. For example, it was organized at both morphemic and syntactic levels, including individual signs and combinations of signs. In addition, these deaf children (who essentially created their own language) went through the same stages of development as normal hearing children. Thus, the deaf children initially gestured one sign at a time, then later put their pantomimes together into two- and three-concept "sentences." These striking results support the idea that our innate knowledge about language is indeed very specific (Feldman, Goldin-Meadow, & Gleitman, 1978).

Deaf children go through the same stages of language development as children who can hear.

CRITICAL PERIODS   Like other innate behaviors, language learning has some critical periods. This is particularly evident when it comes to acquiring the sound system of a new language—that is, learning new phonemes and their rules of combination. We have already noted that infants less than 1 year old can discriminate phonemes of any language, but lose this ability by the end of their first year. Hence, the first months of life are a critical period for honing in on the phonemes of one's native language. There is also evidence for a critical period in acquiring the sound system of a second language. After a few years of learning a second language, young children are more likely than adults to speak it without an accent, and better able to understand the language when it is spoken in noisy conditions (Lenneberg, 1967; Snow, 1987).

The case is not as strong for a critical period in learning syntax. Some of the most important evidence concerns a few children whose dire circumstances prohibited them from learning any language until they were in their teens. The best-documented case is that of "Genie," who suffered as horrible a childhood as one can imagine. She was 14 when she was discovered. Apparently, Genie had lived tied to a chair without ever being spoken to since the age of 20 months. She had had virtually no social contact. Her blind mother would feed her hurriedly, and she was punished if she uttered a sound. Not surprisingly, Genie had developed no language. After her discovery, she was taught language by psychologists and linguists, but she never became proficient at syntax. Although Genie learned to use many words and to combine them into simple phrases, she could not combine phrases to form elaborate sentences. In this case, the crucial factor behind the lack of language development seems to be the relatively late age at which she learned language. This is consistent with the idea of a critical period for learning syntax; it is also compatible with the idea that Genie's lack of language during her early years led to some atrophy of the left hemisphere of her brain (Curtiss, 1977).

Can Another Species Learn Human Language?

Some experts believe that our innate capacity to learn language is unique to our species (Chomsky, 1972). They acknowledge that other species have communication systems but argue that these are qualitatively different from ours. Consider the communication system of the chimpanzee. This species' vocalizations and gestures are limited in number, and the *productivity* of its communication system is very low in comparison to human language, which

CRITICAL DISCUSSION

Brain Localization

Given that innate factors play a large role in language acquisition, it is not surprising that regions of the human brain are specialized for language. In a Critical Discussion in Chapter 2 ("Language and the Brain"), we discussed how damage to certain regions of the left hemisphere results in *aphasia*, or language deficits. There we emphasized the relationship between the site of the brain damage and whether the resulting deficit was primarily one of production or comprehension. In the current discussion, we focus on the relation between the site of the damage and whether the deficit involves syntactic or conceptual knowledge.

Recall from Chapter 2 that there are two regions of the left hemisphere of the cortex that are critical for language: *Broca's area*, which lies in the frontal lobes, and *Wernicke's area*, which lies in the temporal-occipital region (see Figure 2-9). Damage to either of these areas leads to specific kinds of aphasia.

The disrupted language of a patient with *Broca's aphasia* is illustrated by the following interview in which "E" designates the interviewer and "P," the patient:

E: Were you in the Coast Guard?
P: No, er, yes, yes . . . ship . . . Massachu . . . chusetts . . . Coast Guard . . . years. [Raises hands twice with fingers indicating "19"]
E: Oh, you were in the Coast Guard for 19 years.
P: Oh . . . boy . . . right . . . right.
E: Why are you in the hospital?
P: [Points to paralyzed arm] Arm no good. [Points to mouth] Speech . . . can't say . . . talk, you see.
E: What happened to make you lose your speech?
P: Head, fall, Jesus Christ, me no good, str, str . . . oh Jesus . . . stroke.
E: Could you tell me what you've been doing in the hospital?
P: Yes sure. Me go, er, uh, P. T. nine o'cot, speech . . . two times . . . read . . . wr . . . ripe, er, rike, er, write . . . practice . . . get-ting better.

(Gardner, 1975, p. 61)

The speech is very disfluent. Even in simple sentences, pauses and hesitations are plentiful. This is in contrast to the fluent speech of a patient with *Wernicke's aphasia*:

Boy, I'm sweating, I'm awful nervous, you know, once in a while I get caught up. I can't mention the tarripoi, a month ago, quite a little, I've done a lot well, I impose a lot, while, on the other hand, you know what I mean, I have to run around, look it over, trebbin and all that sort of stuff. (Gardner, 1975, p. 68)

In addition to fluency, there are other marked differences between Broca's and Wernicke's aphasias. The speech of a Broca's aphasic consists mainly of content words. It contains few grammatical morphemes and complex sentences and, in general, has a telegraphic quality that is reminiscent of the two-word stage of language acquisition. In contrast, the language of a Wernicke's aphasic preserves syntax but is remarkably devoid of content. There are clear problems in finding the right noun, and occasionally words are invented for the occasion (as in the use of "tarripoi" and "trebbin"). These observations suggest that Broca's aphasia involves a disruption at the syntactic stage, while Wernicke's aphasia involves a disruption at the level of words and concepts.

---

permits the combination of a relatively small number of phonemes into thousands of words and the combination of these words into an unlimited number of sentences. Another difference is that human language is structured at several levels, whereas chimpanzee communications are not. In particular, in human language, a clear distinction exists between the level of morphemes—at which the elements have meaning—and the level of sounds—at which the elements do not. There is no hint of such a *duality of structure* in chimpanzee communication, because every symbol carries meaning. Still another difference is that chimpanzees do not vary the *order* of their symbols to vary the meaning of their messages, while we do. For instance, "Jonah ate the whale" means something quite different from "The whale ate Jonah."

The fact that chimpanzee communication is impoverished compared to our own does not prove that chimpanzees lack the capacity for a more productive system. Their system may be adequate for their needs. To determine if chimpanzees have the same innate capacity we do, we must see if they can learn our language.

Until about 1970, attempts to teach chimpanzees to *speak* had failed. The failures, however, may have been due to limitations in the chimpanzees'

These characterizations of the two aphasias are supported by experiments. In a study that tested for a syntactic deficit, subjects had to listen to a sentence on each trial and show that they understood it by selecting a picture (from a set) that the sentence described. Some sentences could be understood without using much syntactic knowledge. For example, given "The bicycle the boy is holding is broken," one can figure out that it is the bicycle that is broken and not the boy, solely from one's knowledge of the concepts involved. Understanding other sentences requires extensive syntactic analysis. In "The lion that the tiger is chasing is fat," one must rely on syntax (word order) to determine that it is the lion who is fat and not the tiger. On those sentences that did not require much syntactic analysis, Broca's aphasics did almost as well as nonaphasics, scoring close to 90 percent correct. But with sentences that required extensive analysis, Broca's aphasics fell to the level of guessing (for example, given the sentence about the lion and tiger, they were as likely to select the picture with a fat tiger as the one with the fat lion). In contrast, the performance of Wernicke's aphasics did not depend on the syntactic demands of the sentence. Thus, Broca's aphasia, but not Wernicke's, seems to be partly a disruption of syntax (Caramazza & Zurif, 1976). The disruption is not total, though, in that Broca's aphasics are capable of handling certain kinds of syntactic analysis (Grodzinski, 1984).

Other experiments have tested for a conceptual deficit. In one study, subjects were presented three words at a time and were asked to select the two that were most similar in meaning. The words included animal terms, such as "dog" and "crocodile," as well as human terms, such as "mother" and "knight." Normal subjects used the distinction between humans and animals as the major basis for their selections; given "dog," "crocodile," and "knight," for example, they selected the first two. Wernicke's patients, however, ignored this basic distinction. Although Broca's aphasics showed some differences from normals, their selections at least respected the human–animal distinction. A conceptual deficit is thus more pronounced in Wernicke's aphasics than in Broca's aphasics (Zurif, Caramazza, Myerson, & Galvin, 1974).

While Broca's and Wernicke's are the most common forms of aphasia, other kinds exist as well, each associated with a specific area of brain damage. A particularly interesting case is *conduction aphasia*. A patient with this problem manifests relatively good syntax and conceptual knowledge but cannot repeat a sentence, or sometimes even a word, that he or she has just heard.

Thus, one patient, after being prompted again and again to repeat just the word "no," exclaimed, "No, no, I told you I can't say no," and still could not repeat the word in isolation (Gardner, 1975). This peculiar symptom makes sense, given that the part of the brain damaged in conduction aphasia is the region connecting Broca's and Wernicke's areas. In order to repeat a spoken sentence, the sentence must first be registered by Wernicke's area and then passed to Broca's area, where it is given the syntactic frame needed for production. Since the passageway is damaged in conduction aphasia, repetition is disrupted, though comprehension and production remain intact. This line of reasoning indicates that the exact nature of a patient's language deficit can be used to diagnose the specific brain region that has been damaged (Geschwind, 1972).

vocal abilities, not their linguistic abilities. Subsequent studies attempted to teach chimpanzees to communicate with their hands. In one of the best known studies, Gardner and Gardner (1972) taught a female chimpanzee, named Washoe, signs adapted from American Sign Language. Training began when Washoe was about a year old and continued until she was 5. During this time, Washoe's caretakers communicated with her only by means of sign language. They first taught her signs by shaping procedures, waiting for her to make a gesture that resembled a sign, and then reinforcing her. Later they found that Washoe could learn signs if they put her hands into the proper position and guided her through the desired movement. Ultimately, Washoe learned signs simply by observing and imitating.

By age 4, Washoe could produce 130 different signs and understand even more. She could also generalize a sign from one situation to another. For example, she first learned the sign for *more* in connection with *more tickling* and then generalized it to indicate *more milk*. Washoe is not unique. Other chimpanzees have acquired comparable vocabularies. Some of these studies have used methods of manual communication other than sign language. Premack (1971; 1983) taught a chimpanzee named Sarah to use plastic symbols

Signing "toothbrush" (left) and "baby" (right).

as words and to communicate by manipulating these symbols. And Lana, a chimpanzee studied by Rumbaugh (1977), communicates by means of a keyboard console. The console has about a hundred keys, each representing a different word, and Lana types her messages on the keyboard. In a series of similar studies, Patterson (1978) taught sign language to a gorilla named Koko, starting when Koko was 1 year old. By age 10, Koko had a vocabulary of more than 400 signs (Patterson & Linden, 1981).

Do these studies prove that another species—the apes—can learn human language? There seems to be little doubt that the apes' signs are equivalent to our words and that the concepts behind some of these signs are equivalent to ours. But there are grave doubts that apes can learn to combine these signs in the manner that humans combine words into a sentence. Thus, not only can people combine the words "snake," "Eve," "killed," and "the" into the sentence "The snake killed Eve," but we can also combine the same words in a different order to produce a sentence with a different meaning, "Eve killed the snake." Although we have some evidence that apes can combine signs into a sequence resembling a sentence, little evidence exists to show that they can alter the order of the signs to produce a different sentence (Slobin, 1979; Brown, 1986).

Even the evidence that apes can combine signs into a sentence has come under attack. In early work, researchers reported cases in which an ape produced what seemed to be a meaningful sequence of signs, such as "Gimme flower" and "Washoe sorry" (Gardner & Gardner, 1972). As data have accumulated, it has become apparent that, unlike human sentences, the utterances of an ape are often highly repetitive. Thus, "You me banana me banana you" is typical of the signing chimps but would be odd for a human child. These utterances are so repetitive that some researchers have claimed they are qualitatively different from human sentences (Seidenberg & Petitto, 1979). In the cases in which an ape utterance is more like a sentence, the ape may simply be imitating the sequence of signs made by its human teacher. Thus, some of Washoe's most sentence-like utterances occurred when she was answering a question; for example, the teacher signed "Washoe eat?" and then Washoe signed "Washoe eat time." Here, Washoe's combination of signs may have been a partial imitation of her teacher's combination, which is not how human children learn to combine words (Terrace et al., 1979; but see VanCantfort & Rimpau, 1982, for counterarguments).

No doubt, research and debate will continue on whether apes can learn our language. Perhaps novel training methods will enable apes to learn to string signs into sentences as we do. Alternatively, future research may support the conclusion that, although apes can develop a human-like vocabulary, they cannot learn to combine their signs in the systematic way we do. If this turns out to be the case, we will at last have evidence to support the age-old belief that language separates us from other species.

IMAGINAL THOUGHT

We mentioned at the beginning of the chapter that, in addition to propositional thought, we can also think in an imaginal mode, particularly in terms of visual images. Such visual thinking is the concern of the present section.

Imagery and Perception

Many of us feel that we do some of our thinking visually. Often it seems that we retrieve past perceptions, or parts of them, and then operate on them in the way we would a real percept. For example, when asked, "What shape are a German shepherd's ears?" most people report that they form a visual image of a German shepherd's head and "look" at the ears to determine their shape. If asked, "What new letter is formed when an upper case N is rotated 90 degrees?" people report first forming an image of a capital N, then mentally "rotating" it 90 degrees and "looking" at it to determine its identity. And if asked, "How many windows are there in your parents' living room?" people report imagining the room and then "scanning" the image while counting the windows (Shepard & Cooper, 1982; Kosslyn, 1983).

The above examples rest on subjective impressions, but they and other evidence suggest that imagery involves the same representations and processes that are used in perception (Finke, 1985). Our images of objects and places have visual detail: we see the German shepherd, the N, or our parents' living room in our "mind's eye." Moreover, the mental operations that we perform on these images seem to be analogous to the operations that we carry out on real visual objects: we scan the image of our parents' room in much the same way we would scan a real room, and we rotate our image of the N the way we would rotate the real object.

Imagery may be like perception because it is mediated by the same parts of the brain. Some support for this idea comes from studies of people who have suffered brain damage in a certain region of the right hemisphere. Such patients may develop *visual neglect* of the left side; though not blind, they ignore everything on the left side of their visual field. A male patient, for example, may forget to shave the left side of his face. This visual neglect extends to imagery. When patients are asked to construct a mental image of a familiar location (say, a shopping area) and report all of its contents, they may report only those things on the right side of their image (Bisiach & Luzzatti, 1978). The brain damage has led to the identical problem in perception and imagery.

More recent studies provide further evidence that the parts of the brain involved in perception are also involved in imagery. In one experiment, subjects performed both a mental arithmetic task ("Start at 50, and count

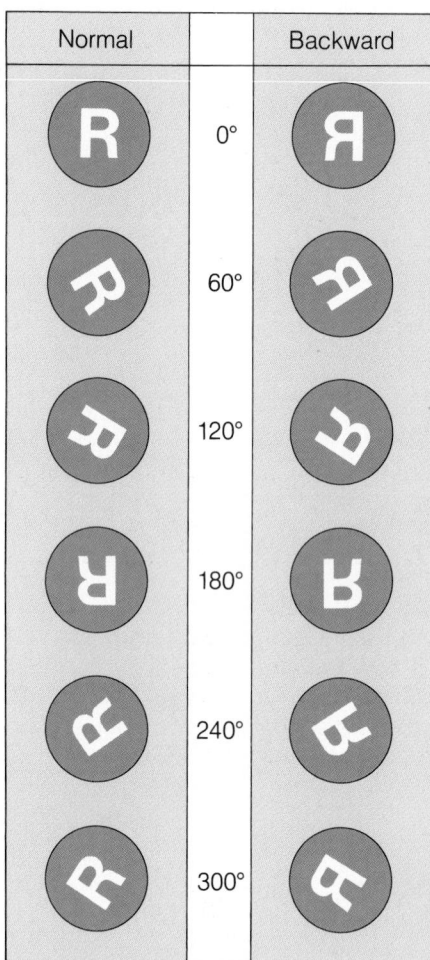

Normal		Backward
R	0°	Я
R	60°	Я
R	120°	Я
R	180°	Я
R	240°	Я
R	300°	Я

FIGURE 9-6
Study of Mental Rotation *Shown are examples of the letters presented to subjects in studies of mental rotation. On each presentation, subjects had to decide whether the letter was normal or backward. Numbers indicate deviation from the vertical in degrees.* (After Cooper & Shepard, 1973)

down, subtracting by 3s") and a visual imagery task ("Visualize a walk through your neighborhood, making alternating right and left turns starting at your door"). While a subject was doing each task, the amount of blood flow in various areas of his or her cortex was measured. There was more blood flow in the visual cortex when subjects engaged in the imagery task than the mental arithmetic one. Moreover, the pattern of blood flow found during the imagery task was like that normally found in perceptual tasks (Roland & Friberg, 1985). Similar results have been obtained in studies that use other measures of cortical activity, such as EEG techniques that measure brain waves in various regions of the brain (Farah, 1988).

Imaginal Operations

We have noted that the mental operations performed on images seem to be analogous to those we carry out on real visual objects. Numerous experiments provide objective evidence for these subjective impressions.

One operation that has been studied intensively is mental rotation. In one experiment, subjects saw the capital letter R on each trial. The letter was presented either normally (R) or backward (Я) and in its usual vertical orientation or rotated various degees (see Figure 9-6). The subjects had to decide if the letter was normal or backward. The more the letter had been rotated from its vertical orientation, the longer it took the subjects to make the decision (see Figure 9-7). This finding suggests that subjects made their decisions by mentally rotating the image of the letter until it was vertical and then checking whether it was normal or backward.

Another operation that is similar in imagery and perception is that of scanning an object or array. In an experiment on scanning an image, subjects first studied the map of a fictional island, which contained seven critical locations. The map was removed, and subjects were asked to form an image of it and fixate on a particular location (for example, the tree in the southern part of the island—see Figure 9-8). Then the experimenter named another location (for example, the tree at the northern tip of the island). Starting at the fixated location, the subjects were to scan their images until they found the named location and were to push a button on "arrival" there. The greater the distance between the fixated location and the named one, the longer the subjects took to respond. Thus, responses were longer when the fixated and named locations were on different sides of the island than when they were on the same side. This suggests subjects were scanning their images in much the same way they scan real objects.

Another commonality between imaginal and perceptual processing is that both are limited by *grain size*. On a television screen, for instance, the grain of the picture tube determines how small the details of a picture can be and still remain perceptible. While there is no actual screen in the brain, we can think of our images as occurring in a mental medium, the grain of which limits the amount of detail we can detect in an image. If this grain size is fixed, then smaller images should be more difficult to inspect than larger ones. There is a good deal of support for this claim. In one experiment, subjects first formed an image of a familiar animal—say, a cat. Then they were asked to decide whether or not the imaged object had a particular property. Subjects made decisions faster for larger properties, such as the head, than for smaller ones, such as the claws. In another study, subjects were asked to image an animal at different relative sizes—small, medium, or large. Subjects were then asked to decide whether their images had a particular property. Their decisions were faster for larger images than smaller ones. Thus, in imagery as in perception, the larger the image, the more readily we can see the details of an object (Kosslyn, 1980).

Visual Creativity

There are innumerable stories about scientists and artists producing their most creative work through visual thinking (Shepard & Cooper, 1982). Although not hard evidence, these stories are among the best indicators that we have of the power of visual thinking. It is surprising that visual thinking appears to be quite effective in highly abstract areas like mathematics and physics. Albert Einstein, for example, said he rarely thought in words; rather, he worked out his ideas in terms of "more or less clear images which can be 'voluntarily' reproduced and combined." Perhaps the most celebrated example is in chemistry. Friedrich Kekule von Stradonitz was trying to determine the molecular structure of benzene. One night he dreamed that a writhing, snakelike figure suddenly twisted into a closed loop, biting its own tail. The structure of the snake proved to be the structure of benzene. A dream image had provided the solution to a major scientific problem. Visual images can also be a creative force for writers. Samuel Coleridge's famous poem "Kubla Khan" supposedly came to him in its entirety as a prolonged visual image.

THOUGHT IN ACTION: PROBLEM SOLVING

For many people, solving a problem epitomizes thinking itself. In problem solving, we are striving for a goal but have no ready means of obtaining it. We must break the goal into subgoals and perhaps divide these subgoals further into smaller subgoals, until we reach a level that we have the means to obtain (Anderson, 1985).

We can illustrate these points with a simple problem. Suppose you need to figure out the combination of an unfamiliar lock. You know only that the combination has four numbers and that whenever you come across a correct number, you will hear a click. Your overall goal is to find the combination. Rather than trying four numbers at random, most people decompose the overall goal into four subgoals, each corresponding to finding one of the four numbers in the combination. Your first subgoal is to find the first number, and you have a procedure for accomplishing this—namely, turning the lock slowly while listening for a click. Your second subgoal is to find the second number, and you can use the same procedure, and so on for the remaining subgoals.

The strategies that people use to decompose goals into subgoals is thus a major issue in the study of problem solving. Another issue is how people mentally represent a problem, because this also affects how readily we can solve the problem. The following discussion considers both of these issues.

FIGURE 9-7
Decision Times in Mental Rotation Study *The time taken to decide whether a letter had normal or reversed orientation was greatest when the rotation was 180° so that the letter was upside down.*

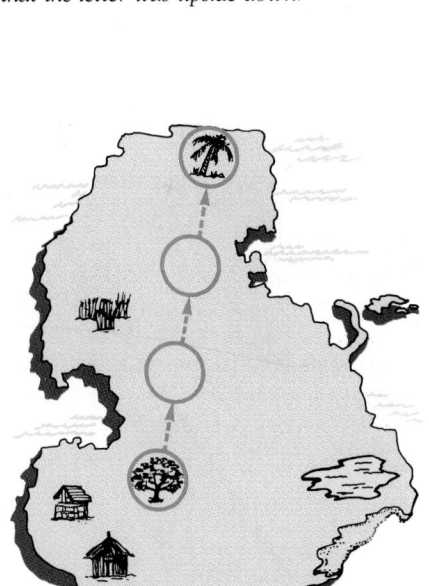

FIGURE 9-8
Scanning Mental Images *The subject scans the image of the island from south to north, looking for the named location. It appears as though the subject's mental image is like a real map and that it takes longer to scan across the mental image if the distance to be scanned is greater. (After Kosslyn, Ball, & Reiser, 1978)*

Problem-Solving Strategies

Much of what we know about strategies for decomposing goals derives from the research of Newell and Simon (see, for example, Newell & Simon, 1972). Typically, the researchers have subjects think aloud while trying to solve a difficult problem, and they analyze the subjects' verbal responses for clues to the underlying strategy. A number of general-purpose strategies have been identified.

One strategy is to reduce the difference between our *current state* in a problem situation and our *goal state*, wherein a solution is obtained. Consider again the combination lock problem. Initially, our current state includes no knowledge of any of the numbers, while our goal state includes knowledge of all four numbers. We therefore set up the subgoal of reducing the difference between these two states; determining the first number accomplishes this subgoal. Our current state now includes knowledge of the first number. There is still a difference between our current state and our goal state, and we can reduce it by determining the second number, and so on. Thus, the critical idea behind *difference reduction* is that we set up subgoals that, when obtained, put us in a state that is closer to our goal.

A similar but more sophisticated strategy is *means-ends analysis*. Here, we compare our current state to the goal state in order to find the most important difference between them; eliminating this difference becomes our main subgoal. We then search for a means or a procedure to achieve this subgoal. If we find such a procedure but discover that something in our current state prevents us from applying it, we introduce a new subgoal of eliminating this obstacle. Many commonsense problem-solving situations involve this strategy. Here is an example:

> I want to take my son to nursery school. What's the most important difference between what I have and what I want? One of distance. What [procedure] changes distance? My car. My car won't work. What is needed to make it work? A new battery. What has new batteries? My auto repair shop. (After Newell & Simon, 1972, as cited in Anderson, 1985, p. 211)

Means-ends analysis is more sophisticated than difference reduction because it allows us to take action even if it results in a temporary decrease in similarity between our current state and the goal state. In the example, the auto repair shop may be in the opposite direction from the nursery school. Going to the shop thus temporarily increases the distance from the goal, yet this step is essential for solving the problem.

Another strategy is to work backward from the goal. This is particularly useful in solving mathematical problems, such as that illustrated in Figure 9-9. The problem is this: given that ABDC is a rectangle, prove that AD and BC are the same length. In *working backward*, one might proceed as follows:

> What could prove that AD and BC are the same length? I could prove this if I could prove that the triangles ACD and BDC are congruent. I can prove that ACD and BDC are congruent if I could prove that two sides and an included angle are equal. (After Anderson, 1985, p. 216)

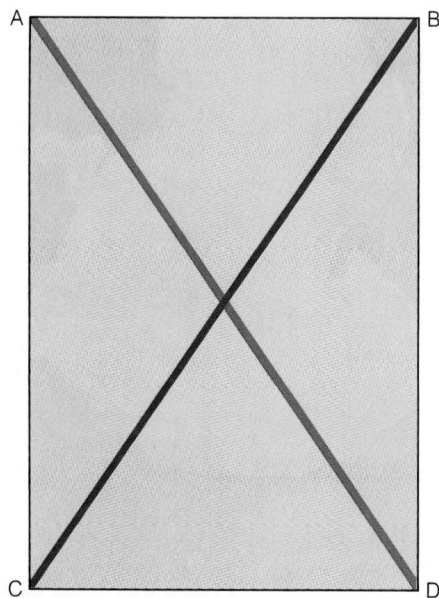

FIGURE 9-9
An Illustrative Geometry Problem
Given that ABDC is a rectangle, prove that the line segments AD and BC are the same length.

We reason from the goal to a subgoal (proving the triangles congruent), from that subgoal to another subgoal (proving the sides and angle equal), and so on, until we reach a subgoal that we have a ready means of obtaining.

Representing the Problem

Being able to solve a problem depends not only on our strategy for decomposing it but also on how we represent it. Sometimes a propositional mode, or representation, works best; at other times, a visual image is more effective. To illustrate, consider the following problem:

> One morning, exactly at sunrise, a monk began to climb a mountain. A narrow path, a foot or two wide, spiraled around the mountain to a temple at the summit. The monk ascended at varying rates, stopping many times along the way to rest. He reached the temple shortly before sunset. After several days at the temple, he began his journey back along the same path, starting at sunrise and again walking at variable speeds with many pauses along the way. His average speed descending was, of course, greater than his average climbing speed. Prove that there exists a particular spot along the path that the monk will occupy on both trips at precisely the same time of day. (Adams, 1974, p. 4)

Learning aids help visualize a math problem.

In trying to solve this problem, many people start with a propositional representation. They may even try to write out a set of equations and soon confuse themselves. The problem is far easier to solve when it is represented visually. All you need do is visualize the upward journey of the monk superimposed on the downward journey. Imagine one monk starting at the bottom and the other, at the top. No matter what their speed, at some time and at some point along the path the two monks will meet. Thus, there must be a spot along the path the monk occupied on both trips at precisely the same time of day. (Note that the problem did not ask you where the spot was.)

Some problems can be readily solved by manipulating either propositions or images. We can illustrate with the following problem: "Ed runs faster than David but slower than Dan; who's the slowest of the three men?" To solve this problem in terms of propositions, note that we can represent the first part of the problem as a proposition that has "David" as subject and "is slower than Ed" as predicate. We can represent the second part as a proposition with "Ed" as subject and "is slower than Dan" as predicate. We can then deduce that David is slower than Dan, which makes David the slowest. To solve the problem by imagery, we might, for example, imagine the three men's speeds as points on a line, like this:

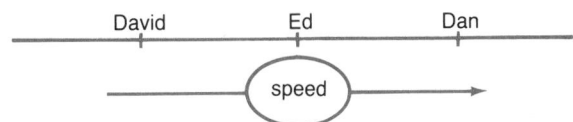

Then we can simply "read" the answer to the question directly from the image. Apparently, some people prefer to represent such problems as propositions, while others tend to represent them visually (Johnson-Laird, 1985).

In addition to the issue of propositions versus images, there are questions about *what* gets represented. Often, we have difficulty with a problem because we fail to include something critical in our representation or because we include something in our representation that is *not* an important part of the problem. We can illustrate with an experiment. One group of subjects was posed the problem of supporting a candle on a door, given only the materials depicted in Figure 9-10. The solution was to tack the box to the door and use the box as a platform for the candle. Most subjects had difficulty

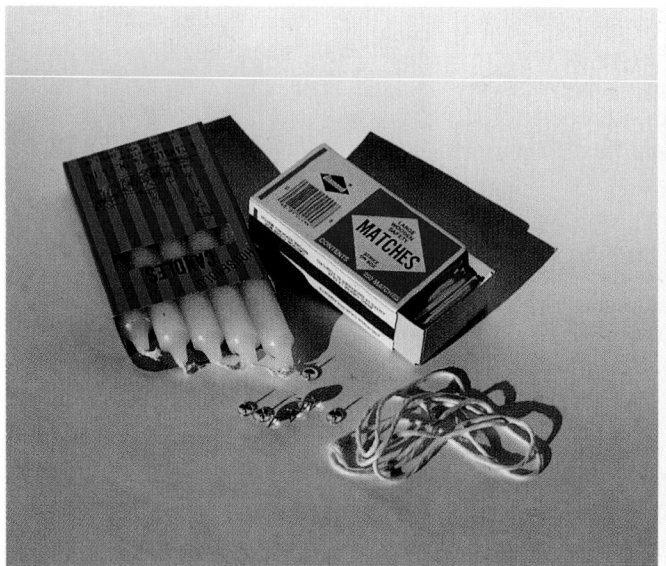 

FIGURE 9-10
Materials for Candle Problem
Given the materials depicted (left), how can you support a candle on a door? The solution is shown in the right-hand photo.

with the problem, presumably because they represented the box as a container, not as a platform. Another group of subjects was given the identical problem, except that the contents of the box were removed. These subjects had more success in solving the problem, presumably because they were less likely to include the box's container property in their representation and more likely to include its supporter property.

Experts versus Novices

In a given content area (physics, geography, or chess, for instance), experts solve problems qualitatively differently than novices. These differences are due to the representations and strategies that experts use and those that novices use. Experts have many more specific representations stored in memory that they can bring to bear on a problem. A master chess player, for example, can look for 5 seconds at a complex board configuration of over 20 pieces and reproduce it perfectly; a novice in this situation can reproduce only the usual 7 ± 2 items (see Chapter 8). Experts can accomplish this memory feat because, through years of practice, they have developed representations of many possible board configurations; these representations permit them to encode a complex configuration in just a chunk or two. Further, these representations are presumably what underlies their superior chess game. A master may have stored as many as 50,000 configurations and has learned what to do when each arises. Thus, master chess players can essentially "see" possible moves; they do not have to think them out the way novices do (Chase & Simon, 1973; Simon & Gilmartin, 1973).

Even when confronted with a novel problem, experts represent it differently than novices. This point is nicely illustrated in studies of problem solving in physics. An expert (say, a physics professor) represents a problem in terms of the physical principle that is needed for solution: for example, "this is one of those every-action-has-an-equal-and-opposite-reaction problems." In contrast, a novice (say, a student taking a first course in physics) tends to represent the same problem in terms of its surface features: for example, "this is one of those inclined-plane problems" (Chi, Glaser, & Rees, 1982).

A novice player solves chess problems differently from an expert.

Experts and novices also differ in the strategies they employ. In studies of physics problem solving, experts generally try to formulate a plan for attacking the problem before generating equations, whereas novices typically start writing equations with no general plan in mind (Larkin, McDermott, Simon, & Simon, 1980). Another difference is that experts tend to reason from the givens of a problem toward a solution, while novices tend to work in the reverse direction (the working-backward strategy). This difference in the direction of reasoning has also been obtained in studies of how physicians solve problems. More expert physicians tend to reason in a forward direction—from symptom to possible disease—while the less expert tend to reason in a backward direction—from possible disease to symptom (Patel & Groen, 1986).

Computer Simulation

To study how people solve problems, researchers often use the method of *computer simulation*. After having people think aloud while solving a complex problem, researchers use their verbal reports as a guide in programming a computer to solve the problem. Then the output of the computer can be compared to aspects of people's performance on the problem—say, the sequence of moves—to see if they match. If they match, the computer program offers a theory of some aspects of problem solving.

Why use computers to learn about people? Perhaps the most interesting answer is Simon's claim: "The reason human beings can think is because they are able to carry out with neurons the simple kinds of processes that computers do with tubes or chips" (1985, p. 3). These simple processes include reading, outputting, storing, and comparing symbols; we do one thing if the symbols match and another if they differ. To the extent that we can closely simulate human problem solving on a digital computer, which uses just these simple processes, we have support for Simon's claim.

A computer simulation of mental processes.

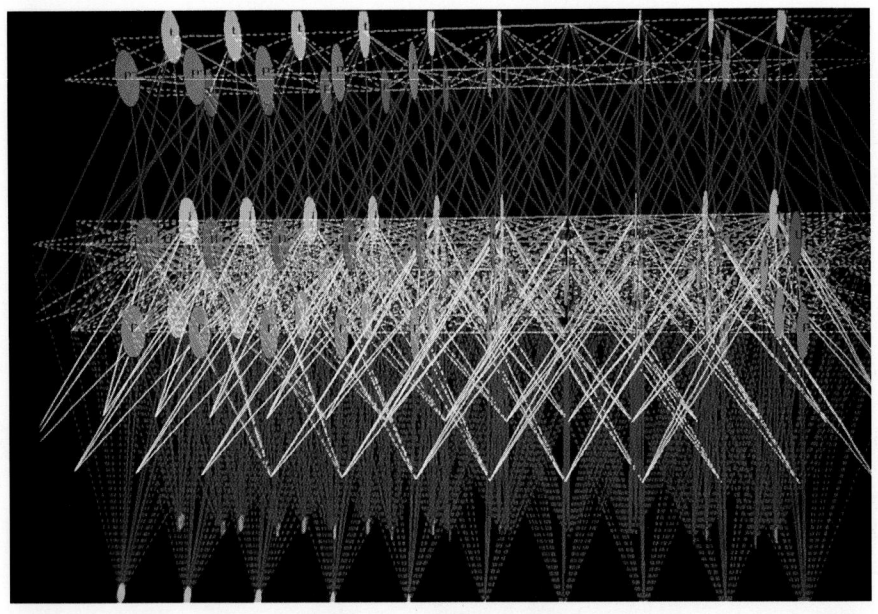

Consider what is involved in trying to write a computer program that simulates the way many of us solve simple algebraic equations. When confronted with the equation $3X + 4 = X + 10$, you might have learned to reason as follows:

> The solution of the equation looks like an X followed by an = sign followed by a number—not any number, it has to be one that will fit the equation if I substitute it back in. If I start out with something that has a number on the left side where I don't want it, then I better get rid of it since I'm trying to get something with an X and an = and a number. So given $3X + 4 = X + 10$, I subtract the 4 (I know I have to subtract it from both sides). Then I have a new equation $3X = X + 6$. But I don't want an X on the right side of the equation. So I subtract it and now have $2X = 6$. Now I don't want a 2X, but instead just a plain X on the left side of the equation, so I divide by 2. Then I have $X = 3$. (After Simon, 1985, p. 6)

The above reasoning can be captured by four rules:

1. If there is a number on the left side of the equation, then subtract it from both sides.
2. If there is an X or a multiple of X on the right side of the equation, then subtract it from both sides.
3. If there is a number in front of the X on the left side of the equation, then divide both sides of the equation by it.
4. If you arrive at an equation that looks like "X = Number," quit and check your answer.

Though probably you do not articulate these rules, presumably they underlie your ability to solve algebraic equations. These rules can readily be translated into a computer program. A program is simply a detailed set of instructions (written in a language designed for a computer) that specifies every step the machine must take. Our rules can be treated as such instructions. Thus, simulation requires that we first be precise about the knowledge involved and then translate it into the language of a computer.

Computer simulation is not without its critics. Some argue that we do not yet know enough about human mental processes to evaluate the computer programs. How, for example, can we be sure that the computer memory resembles human memory? Other critics have challenged the basic analogy between computers and people: computers, they say, can only do what they have been programmed to do. However, it is quite possible that humans can also do only what heredity and experience have "programmed" them to do. Another criticism is that the physical basis of human thought, the brain, is very different from the electrical circuitry of computers. Clearly, a brain and a computer differ physically, but they may be similar in how they are organized and how they function. How far one can trust the computer as a guide to human mental life remains an open question.

At points in this chapter on human thought and language, we have raised questions about these abilities in nonhumans. We have discussed apes that talk or almost talk, and computers that appear to think. These discussions and comparisons suggest that we can improve our understanding of human intelligence by comparing it to nonhuman intelligence, be it natural or of our own making.

⚡ CHAPTER SUMMARY

1. Thought occurs in different modes, including *propositional, imaginal,* and *motoric*. The basic component of a proposition is a *concept*, the set of properties that we associate with a class. A concept includes both a *prototype* (properties that describe the best examples) and a *core* (properties that are most essential for being a member of the concept). Core properties play a major role in *classical* concepts, such as "bachelor"; prototype properties dominate in *fuzzy* concepts such as "bird." Concepts are sometimes organized into hierarchies; in such cases, one level of the hierarchy is the *basic* or preferred level for categorization.

2. Children often learn the prototype of a concept by an *exemplar strategy*. With this technique, a novel item is classified as an instance of a concept if it is sufficiently similar to a known exemplar of the concept. As children grow older, they use *hypothesis testing* as another strategy for learning concepts. Concepts can be combined to form *propositions*, with each proposition containing a *subject* (for example, "the tailor") and a *predicate* (for example, "is asleep").

3. In reasoning, we organize our propositions into an argument. Some arguments are *deductively valid*: it is impossible that the conclusion of the argument is false if its premises are true. When evaluating a deductive argument, we sometimes try to prove that the conclusion follows from the premises by using logical rules. Other times, however, we use *heuristics*—rules of thumb—that operate on the content of propositions rather than on their logical form.

4. Some arguments are *inductively strong*: it is improbable that the conclusion is false if the premises are true. In generating and evaluating such arguments, we often ignore the principles of probability theory and rely instead on heuristics that focus on similarity or causality. For example, we may estimate the probability that a person belongs to a category by determining the person's similarity to the category's prototype.

5. Language, the means for communicating propositions, is structured at three levels. At the highest level are sentence units, including phrases that can be related to units of propositions. The next level is that of words and parts of words that carry meaning. The lowest level contains speech sounds. The phrases of a sentence are built from words (and other parts of words), whereas the words themselves are constructed from speech sounds.

6. A *phoneme* is a category of speech sounds. Every language has its own set of phonemes and rules for combining them into words. A *morpheme* is the smallest unit that carries meaning. Most morphemes are words; others are prefixes and

suffixes that are added onto words. A language also has *syntactic* rules for combining words into phrases and phrases into sentences. Understanding a sentence requires not only analyzing phonemes, morphemes, and phrases, but also understanding the *speaker's intention.*

7. Language development occurs at all three levels. Infants come into the world preset to learn phonemes, but they need several years to learn the rules for combining them. When children begin to speak, they learn words that name familiar concepts. If they want to communicate a concept that is as yet unnamed, they may *overextend* the name of a neighboring concept (for example, they use "doggie" to name cats and cows). In learning to produce sentences, children begin with one-word utterances, progress to two-word *telegraphic speech*, and then elaborate their noun and verb phrases.

8. Children learn language mainly by testing hypotheses. Children's hypotheses appear to be guided by a small set of *operating principles*, which call the children's attention to critical characteristics of utterances, such as word endings. Innate factors also play a role in language acquisition. Our innate knowledge of language seems to be very rich, as suggested by the facts that all languages share some specific features and that all children seem to go through the same stages in acquiring a language. Like other innate behaviors, some language abilities are learned only during a *critical period*. It is a matter of controversy whether or not our innate capacity to learn language is unique to our species. Recent studies suggest that chimpanzees and gorillas can learn signs that are equivalent to our words, but they have difficulty learning to combine these signs in the systematic manner that humans do.

9. Not all thoughts are expressed in propositions; some are manifested as visual images. Such images contain the kind of visual detail found in perceptions. Moreover, brain damage that results in certain perceptual problems, *visual neglect*, also results in the comparable problem in imagery. In addition, the mental operations performed on images (such as scanning and rotation) are like the operations carried out on perceptions.

10. Problem solving requires decomposing a goal into subgoals that are easier to obtain. Strategies for such decomposition include *reducing differences* between the *current state* and the *goal state*; *means-ends analysis* (eliminating the most important differences between the current and goal states); and *working backward*. Some problems are easier to solve by using a propositional representation; for other problems, a visual representation works best.

11. Expert problem solvers differ from novices in three basic ways: they have more representations to bring to bear on the problem; they represent novel problems in terms of solution principles rather than surface features; and they tend to reason forward rather than working backward. A useful method for studying problem solving is *computer simulation*, in which one tries to write a computer program that solves problems the same way people do.

■ FURTHER READING

There are two recent introductions to the psychology of thinking: Sternberg and Smith, *The Psychology of Thinking* (1988), and Baron, *Thinking and Deciding* (1988). The study of concepts is reviewed in Smith and Medin, *Categories and Concepts* (1981). Research on reasoning is reviewed by Kahneman, Slovic, and Tversky (eds.), *Judgment Under Uncertainty: Heuristics and Biases* (1982); for a more advanced treatment of reasoning, see Holland, Holyoak, Nisbett, and Thagard, *Induction: Processes of Inference, Learning, and Discovery* (1986). For an introduction to the study of imagery, see Kosslyn, *Ghosts in the Mind's Machine* (1983). For more advanced treatments of imagery, see Kosslyn, *Image and Mind* (1980), and Shepard and Cooper, *Mental Images and their Transformations* (1982). For an introduction to problem solving, see Mayer, *Thinking, Problem Solving, and Cognition* (1983); for an advanced treatment, see the classic by Newell and Simon, *Human Problem Solving* (1972).

Numerous books deal with the psychology of language. Standard introductions include Clark and Clark, *Psychology and Language: An Introduction to Psycholinguistics* (1977); Foss and Hakes, *Psycholinguistics: An Introduction to the Psychology of Language* (1978); Tartter, *Language Processes* (1986); and Carroll, *Psychology of Language* (1985). For a more advanced treatment, particularly of issues related to Chomsky's theory of language and thought, see Chomsky, *Rules and Representations* (1980); and Fodor, Bever, and Garrett, *The Psychology of Language* (1974). For an account of early language development, see Brown, *A First Language: The Early Stages* (1973); and Pinker, *Language Learnability and Language Development* (1984).

Paul Klee. Love Song by the New Moon, *1939.*
Watercolor on lined burlap, 39⅜″ x 27⅝″, Klee Foundation, Bern. Y2 (342)

PART

V Motivation and Emotion

Chapter 10

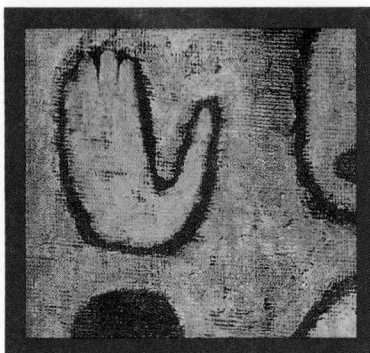

Detail, Love Song by the New Moon.

Basic Motives

H aving discussed what people can *do*—for instance, learn, remember, think—we will now consider what they *want*. The study of wants and needs goes under the heading of *motivation* and is concerned with factors that give behavior *direction* and *energize* it. A hungry organism will direct its behavior toward food and a thirsty organism toward drink. Both will engage in activity more vigorously than an unmotivated organism.

But hunger and thirst are just two among many motives. In this chapter, we deal with *basic* motives—unlearned motives that humans share with other animals. Such basic motives appear to be of several types: one corresponds to *survival* needs of the organism, such as hunger and thirst; a second deals with biologically based *social* needs, such as sex and maternal behavior; and a third involves *curiosity* motives, which are not directly related to the welfare of the organism. A fundamental question concerns what the motives within a type have in common. Do the motives corresponding to, say, survival needs all operate by the same principles? If so, do any of these principles apply to the other types of basic motives? We will consider these questions throughout our discussion.

SURVIVAL MOTIVES AND HOMEOSTASIS

Nature of Homeostasis

Many survival motives operate according to the principle of *homeostasis*, which is the body's tendency to maintain a constant internal environment in the face of a changing external environment. The healthy individual maintains a body temperature that varies only a degree or two, even though the temperature of the environment can vary by more than 100 degrees. Similarly, the healthy person maintains a relatively constant amount of water in his or her body, though the availability of water in the environment may vary drastically. Such internal constancies are essential for survival, since a body temperature that remains substantially above or below normal for hours can result in death, as can a lack of water for 4 to 5 days.

A thermostat is an example of a mechanical homeostatic system. Its purpose is to keep the temperature in your house (the internal environment) relatively constant while the temperature outside your house (the external environment) varies. The operation of a thermostat can tell us a good deal about the principles of homeostasis, as illustrated in the top half of Figure 10-1. The temperature of the room acts as input to the thermostat. The thermostat contains a *sensor* to measure the room temperature, an *ideal value* to represent the desired temperature, and a *comparator* to compare the sensed temperature to the ideal value. If the sensed temperature is less than the ideal value, the mechanism turns the furnace on; this action raises the room temperature until it matches the ideal value, at which point the thermostat turns the furnace off.

We can generalize this description to all homeostatic systems, as shown in the bottom half of Figure 10-1. The core of the system is a particular variable that is being regulated (such as room temperature in the thermostat example). To regulate the variable, the system contains an ideal value of the variable, sensors that measure the variable, a comparator (or central

FIGURE 10-1

Homeostatic Systems *The top half of the figure illustrates the workings of a thermostat. The temperature of the room is input to the thermostat; there, a sensor detects the input temperature and compares it to an ideal value. If the sensed temperature is less than the ideal value, the furnace is turned on. The bottom half of the figure illustrates a homeostatic system in general. The system consists of a regulated variable, sensors that detect the variable, and a comparator that gauges the sensed variable against an ideal value. If the sensed variable is less than the ideal value, adjustments are made.*

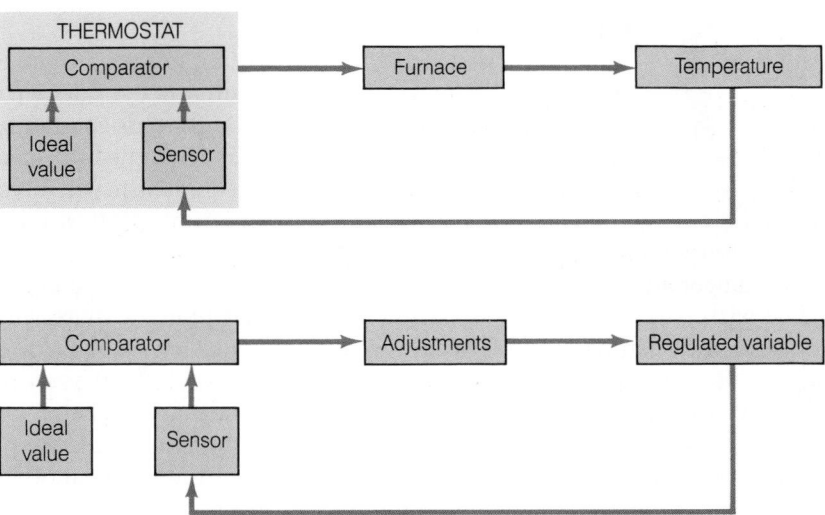

control), and programmed adjustments that the system makes when the variable is at a value above or below the ideal (such as turning the furnace on or off). This framework enables us to understand a number of human motives. In the case of body temperature control, the variable regulated is body temperature; for thirst, the amounts of water in the cells and in the blood are the variables that are being regulated; and for hunger, several regulated variables correspond to various sources of energy (blood sugar, fat, and so on). In each case, sensors in the body detect changes from ideal values and activate adjustments that correct the imbalance. In studying these homeostatic systems, researchers seek to determine where the sensors are located, what adjustments are possible, and what region of the brain plays the role of a comparator.

We can use the homeostatic framework to distinguish between the concepts of *need* and *drive*. A need is any substantial physiological departure from the ideal value; its psychological counterpart is a drive, an aroused state or urge that results from the need. Using hunger as an example, a need arises when the level of blood sugar drops substantially below an ideal value. This physiological imbalance may be corrected automatically by the pancreas signaling the liver to release sugar into the bloodstream. But when these automatic mechanisms cannot maintain a balanced state, a drive is activated and the aroused organism takes action to restore the balance (it seeks foods with a high sugar content).

Temperature Regulation as a Homeostatic System

Of all human motives, the ability to keep ourselves at a comfortable temperature offers the most straightforward case of a homeostatic system. While temperature regulation may not be our prototype of a motive, it is critical for survival. Our cells cannot function outside certain limits of temperature: above 45 degrees Centigrade (113 degrees Fahrenheit), most proteins in cells become inactive and cannot carry out their functions; below 0 degrees Centigrade (32 degrees Fahrenheit), the water inside the cells begins to form ice crystals that destroy the cells.

The regulated variable is blood temperature, which is usually an accurate reflection of body temperature. There are sensors of blood temperature in the mouth (we can taste hot and cold foods), the skin (we can feel hot or cold), the spinal cord, and the brain. The chief region of the brain involved is the *hypothalamus*, a small collection of cell nuclei at the base of the brain that is directly linked with the pituitary gland and with other parts of the brain (see Figure 2-7). In addition to sensors, the anterior (front) region of the hypo-thalamus appears to contain the comparator and the ideal temperature value (really, an ideal temperature *zone*). The anterior hypothalamus therefore functions like a thermostat. If this region is destroyed in a rat, the animal can no longer regulate its temperature. And if the anterior hypothalamus is heated directly (through a wire implanted there), the rat's body temperature drops, even though the body itself is not hot (Barbour, 1912); by heating the hypothalamus, the rat has been "fooled" about the temperature of the rest of its body. (This is analogous to applying a hot burst of air directly to a thermo-stat: even though room temperature is cool, the thermostat is fooled into dropping the temperature.)

Once the hypothalamic thermostat has determined that the body's tem-perature is outside of an ideal zone, it can make a variety of adjustments. Some adjustments are automatic, physiological responses. If body tempera-ture is too high, the skin's capillaries may dilate, which increases the amount of warm blood just under the surface of the skin. The additional heat then radiates off the skin, which subsequently lowers the temperature of the blood. Sweating is another physiological means of heat loss for species that have sweat glands all over their bodies (such as humans, horses, and cattle). Species that have sweat glands in their tongues (dogs, cats, and rats) will pant to release heat. If body temperature dips too low, the first physiological adjustment is a constriction of the skin's capillaries; this pulls blood away from the cold periphery, which conserves the remaining heat for the vital organs. The body will also generate heat by shivering.

In addition to physiological reactions, we also make behavioral adjust-ments. When we feel cool or chilly, we put on extra clothing or seek a warmer place; when we feel too warm, we take off clothing or seek a cooler spot. These behavioral adjustments differ from the physiological ones in sev-eral respects. The behavioral adjustments are voluntary acts that we attribute to our "self," while the physiological adjustments are involuntary reactions that we attribute more to our body parts (for example, our sweat glands). Our bodies make a physiological adjustment in response to a physical need (a biological imbalance), and we make a behavioral adjustment in response to a drive. Physiological adjustments directly affect our internal environment, whereas behavioral adjustments affect our external environment (putting on a sweater protects us from the cool air), which in turn influences our internal environment. These two types of adjustments appear to be localized in differ-ent regions of the hypothalamus: the preoptic area regulates our physiologi-cal changes, whereas the lateral area regulates our behavior (Satinoff & Rut-stein, 1970; Satinoff & Shan, 1971).

Thirst as a Homeostatic System

The regulation of water intake is another critical ingredient of our sur-vival. Water is a major element of our bodies. It makes up about two thirds of our weight; it is the main component of most tissues and blood; and it is used to carry nutrients and oxygen to our tissues, as well as to carry away wastes. But we are constantly losing water—either by evaporation from the surface of the lungs, or by sweating and urination. We therefore have to constantly replace our water losses.

The homeostatic system for thirst is more complex than that for temperature because our bodies must regulate two variables: the amount of water inside the body's cells (*intracellular fluid*); and the amount outside the cells, including the blood (*extracellular fluid*). We will examine these two regulated variables in turn.

The typical cause of intracellular fluid loss is a greater concentration of sodium in the water outside the cells than in the water inside the cells. Since sodium cannot permeate the cells' membranes, water leaves the cells by osmosis (a pressure to balance the concentrations of sodium on both sides of the membrane). While all cells may dehydrate, only certain ones play the role of sensors. These are *osmoreceptors* (so named because of their connection to osmosis), which are located in the hypothalamus and in the *preoptic area* that lies in front of the hypothalamus, and which respond to dehydration by becoming slightly deformed or shriveled. Thus, though the variable being regulated is water, the sensors are detecting changes in cell shape and size. In addition to the sensors, the anterior region of the hypothalamus may also contain the comparator and ideal values relevant to intracellular fluid loss (Blass & Epstein, 1971; Peck & Novin, 1971).

Once the hypothalamus detects these changes, it sets homeostatic adjustments in motion. The physiological adjustment involves recovering water from the kidneys before it is excreted as urine. Specifically, axons from osmoreceptors project into the pituitary gland (which is located just below the hypothalamus) and release the *antidiuretic hormone* (ADH). ADH regulates the kidneys so they release water back into the bloodstream and form only very concentrated urine. (After a night's sleep, you may notice that your urine is a darker color and has a stronger odor than it does at other times of the day; your body has recovered water from your kidneys to compensate for your not having consumed fluids while asleep.) This physiological mechanism can maintain the body's water balance only to a certain point, however. When the water deficit is too great, behavioral adjustments are required; you feel thirsty and seek water. All of this makes it clear why a hamburger and fries makes us thirsty. Eating salty food increases the concentration of salt outside the cells and causes water to leave the cells; the shrunken cells then activate sensors that mediate the thirst drive.

There is more to thirst, though, than a deficit of intracellular fluid. Loss of blood volume, which is part of extracellular fluid, produces thirst even when the cells are not dehydrated. An injured person who has lost a considerable amount of blood feels extremely thirsty, even though the chemical concentration of the remaining blood is unchanged. Likewise, people engaged in vigorous exercise lose salt through perspiration but still have the urge to drink a lot of water, which will only further dilute the salt concentration of their blood. These observations indicate that there is another variable being regulated, namely the total volume of fluid in blood, regardless of its concentration.

The sensors for this variable are located in the kidneys, and what they actually detect is a change in blood pressure. The kidneys then secrete a substance called *renin* into the bloodstream. Renin plays a role in two different kinds of homeostatic adjustments to decreased blood volume. It causes the blood vessels to constrict, thereby preventing further blood loss; this reaction is a physiological adjustment. Renin also reacts with a substance circulating in the blood to produce another hormone called *angiotensin*, which induces the feeling of thirst as well as an appetite for salt (Fitzsimons, 1969; Stricker & Verbalis, 1988).

A homeostatic analysis suggests that a thirsty organism should drink until its intracellular and extracellular elements become rehydrated. But this is not the case. Subjects deprived of water and then allowed to drink will stop before their intracellular and extracellular levels are replenished. Thus, there must be a special mechanism to stop drinking—namely, satiety sensors that determine when there is sufficient water in the system to replenish the parched cells and the blood. Some of these sensors (osmoreceptors again) are located in the mouth, while others are located in the intestines. In experiments with monkeys, infusion of a small amount of water into the small intestine stops drinking, even if the animal has not had anywhere near enough water to make up its deficit. Thus, our system for regulating water intake is quite complex; it involves a satiety mechanism as well as the regulation of intracellular and extracellular fluid.

HUNGER

Hunger is a powerful motivator. When food becomes sparse, all of our energies and thoughts are directed to obtaining it. What exactly triggers eating? To say that people eat because it is mealtime is not sufficient. The number of meals people eat each day differs widely among cultures (as many as five in some European cultures and as few as one in some African cultures). Yet as long as food is available, people in different cultures weigh about the same. Similarly, it is not enough to say that we eat when we feel "hunger pangs" in our stomach, because people who have had their stomachs removed (due to cancer or large ulcers) still regulate their food intake. Nor do we eat simply because food tastes good, or smells good, or looks good; while food cues can stimulate hunger, people continue to regulate their food intake even when all such cues are eliminated.

Social customs influence eating.

External influences can arouse hunger.

What, then, triggers eating? Current research suggests that we automatically monitor the quantities of various nutrients stored in our body (for example, glucose and fats) and are motivated to eat whenever these energy stores fall below critical levels. Again, the system is basically homeostatic; indeed, it is a common observation among researchers that most animals have stable body weights and that if they are given all they want to eat, they somehow eat just enough to maintain their weight. But hunger is too complex for us to give a simple homeostatic analysis. For one thing, several variables have to be regulated. For another, eating is terminated not by the food stores returning to their ideal values but, instead, by satiety sensors detecting that sufficient food has entered the system. Also, clearly not every person is able to maintain homeostasis: just walking down a street, we can see examples of extreme overeating (*obesity*) and extreme undereating (*anorexia*). In trying to understand hunger, we will first consider the variables that are regulated (along with the sensors that gauge them and trigger eating), then we will discuss the satiety detectors that tell us when we have eaten enough, the brain mechanisms that integrate the feeding and satiety cues, and finally the breakdown of homeostasis found in obesity.

Variables of Hunger

The study of hunger is closely tied to the study of metabolism and digestion. In order for our body cells to function, they require certain nutrients. These needed nutrients are the end products of digestion and include glucose (blood sugar), fats, and amino acids. All three appear to be regulated variables in hunger.

Glucose's role is the best documented. Typically, the brain uses only glucose for its energy supply (the rest of the body is more flexible), and it contains sensors for the nutrient. The sensors, located in the hypothalamus, reflect the extent to which glucose has been absorbed by the cells. Roughly, they measure the difference in the amount of glucose in the arteries versus that in the veins. Researchers have implanted microelectrodes in the hypothalami of dogs and cats to record neural activity before and after injections of glucose and insulin (which lowers glucose level). They found that after glucose injections cells in the lateral region of the hypothalamus decrease in activity (signaling that glucose levels are sufficient) and after insulin injections they increase their activity (signaling that glucose levels are insufficient). When the sensors indicate too low a glucose level, physiological and behavioral adjustments ensue: either the liver releases stored glucose into the bloodstream or the hungry organism searches for food. There are also glucose sensors outside the brain, specifically in the liver. These detectors are particularly well situated since the liver is among the first organs to receive the products of digestion (Stricker, Rowland, Saller, & Friedman, 1977).

We also regulate the amount of amino acids and fat stored in special fat cells. We would expect amino acids to be regulated, for they are essential in building protein, but it is surprising that a decline in stored fat can trigger feeding. This makes sense, however, when one realizes that between meals stored fat is converted into free fatty acids, which are a major source of energy for the body. A lack of fat deposits can therefore lead to a lack of energy. The hypothalamus appears to be able to detect decreases in the size of fat cells. The substance *glycerol*, which is produced during the conversion of fat into free fatty acids, also seems to be a regulated variable. Hunger, then, involves multiple homeostatic systems.

Satiety Detectors

If we did not stop eating until our stores of nutrients reached their ideal levels, we would routinely eat for the roughly four hours that it takes to digest a meal. Nature has spared us by providing *satiety sensors*, detectors located in the early parts of the digestive system that signal the brain that the needed nutrients are on their way and that feeding can stop. The termination of feeding is thus handled by a different system—one located earlier in the digestive system—than that responsible for the initiation of feeding.

Where are the satiety sensors located? One obvious place to look is the mouth and throat. To establish definitively whether the mouth and throat contain satiety sensors, researchers have severed the esophagus of an animal and brought the cut ends out externally through incisions in the skin. When such an animal eats, the food it swallows cannot make its way to the stomach (hence satiety sensors in the stomach and beyond can have no effect). Such an animal will swallow a somewhat larger than normal meal, then stop eating, which implies that satiety sensors must exist in the mouth and throat. However, the animal soon begins to eat again, which implies that these satiety sensors have only a short-term effect (Janowitz & Grossman, 1949). There must be other satiety sensors farther down the digestive tract.

The next places to look are the stomach and *duodenum* (the part of the small intestine connected directly to the stomach). Both organs also contain satiety sensors. If nutrients are injected directly into the stomach of a hungry animal before it is given access to food, it will eat less than usual. Thus, although the stomach may play little role in "feeling hungry," it has a substantial role in "feeling full." Nutrients injected directly into the duodenum also lead to a decrease in eating. Here, the satiety sensor may be the hormone *cholecystokinin* (CCK). When food enters the duodenum, the upper intestinal mucosa produces CCK, which limits the rate at which food passes from the stomach to the duodenum. Blood levels of CCK may be monitored by the brain as a satiety signal. Consistent with this hypothesis, many studies have found that injections of CCK inhibit eating (Gibbs, Young, & Smith, 1973).

Another major depository of satiety sensors is the liver. It is the first organ to receive water-soluble nutrients from the digestive system, and hence its receptors have an accurate gauge of the nutrients being digested. If glucose is injected directly into the liver of a hungry animal, the animal will feed less. Sensors in the liver appear to monitor the level of nutrients that are in the intestines and then to pass this information on to the brain (Russek, 1971). In short, we can think of satiety sensors throughout the body as constituting a homeostatic system in which the variable being regulated is the total amount of nutrients in the system.

Brain Mechanisms

The system for satiety must be integrated with that for feeding. The likely locus of this is the brain, specifically the hypothalamus, which has already been shown to figure centrally in temperature control and fluid regulation and in aspects of feeding. The hypothalamus is particularly well suited for housing a control center for hunger, since it contains more blood vessels than any other area of the brain and consequently is readily influenced by the chemical state of the blood. Two regions of the hypothalamus are particularly important: the *lateral hypothalamus* and *ventromedial hypothalamus*.

FIGURE 10-2
Hypothalamic Overeating *Lesions in the ventromedial hypothalamus caused this rat to overeat and gain more than three times its normal weight. Its weight is 1,080 grams, not 80 grams.*

One way to study the function of a brain area is to destroy cells and nerve fibers in the region and observe the animal's behavior when the area no longer exerts control. This technique has led to the discovery of two important syndromes. The first, *LH syndrome*, occurs when tissue in the lateral hypothalamus is destroyed. Initially, the animal—typically a rat—refuses to eat or drink and will die unless it is fed intravenously. After several weeks of being intravenously nourished, most of the rats begin to recover: first they eat only palatable wet food but will not drink; eventually they will eat dry food and begin to drink (Teitelbaum & Epstein, 1962). The second syndrome, *VMH syndrome*, occurs when tissue in the ventromedial hypothalamus is destroyed. It has two distinct phases. In the initial or *dynamic phase*, which lasts between 4 and 12 weeks, the animal overeats voraciously, sometimes tripling its body weight within a matter of weeks (see Figure 10-2). In the second or *static phase*, the animal no longer overeats. Rather, it reduces its food intake to slightly more than normal level and maintains its new obese weight. The VMH syndrome has been observed in all animal species studied—from rat to chicken and monkey. For humans, researchers have noted that people with tumors or injuries in the ventromedial hypothalamus may overeat and become extremely obese.

Initially, psychologists interpreted the VMH and LH syndromes as implying the existence of dual hunger centers—a *feeding center* in the lateral hypothalamus and a *satiety center* in the ventromedial hypothalamus. They believed that destruction of the lateral tissue disrupts the feeding center, thereby making it difficult for the animal to eat, while destruction of ventromedial tissue disrupts the satiety center, thereby making it difficult for the animal not to eat. But why, then, do rats nursed through the first few weeks after their lateral-hypothalamic lesions eventually come to regulate their food intake with precision, albeit at a lower weight? Similarly, if destruction of the ventromedial hypothalamus impairs a satiety center, why do the animals actually reduce their food intake during the static phase? These puzzles, and the findings to be presented below, have largely overthrown the dual-center interpretation.

One new account holds that the lateral and ventromedial areas are concerned with the regulation of overall body weight. Consider again a fat rat with a ventromedial lesion. We have already noted that eventually it will reach a static phase where it maintains its new obese weight. But if the animal's diet is now restricted, body weight will decrease until it reaches the original, normal weight; if the rat is allowed to eat freely again, it will overeat

FIGURE 10-3
Effects of Forced Feeding and Starvation on Rats with VMH Lesions *Following lesioning of the ventromedial hypothalamus, the rat overeats and gains weight until it stabilizes at a new, obese level. Forced feeding or starvation alters the weight level only temporarily; the rat returns to its stabilized level. (After Hoebel & Teitelbaum, 1966)*

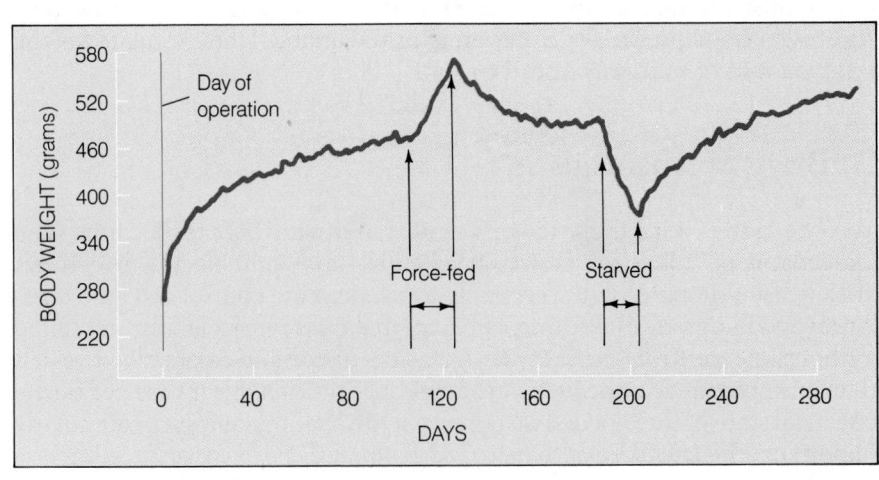

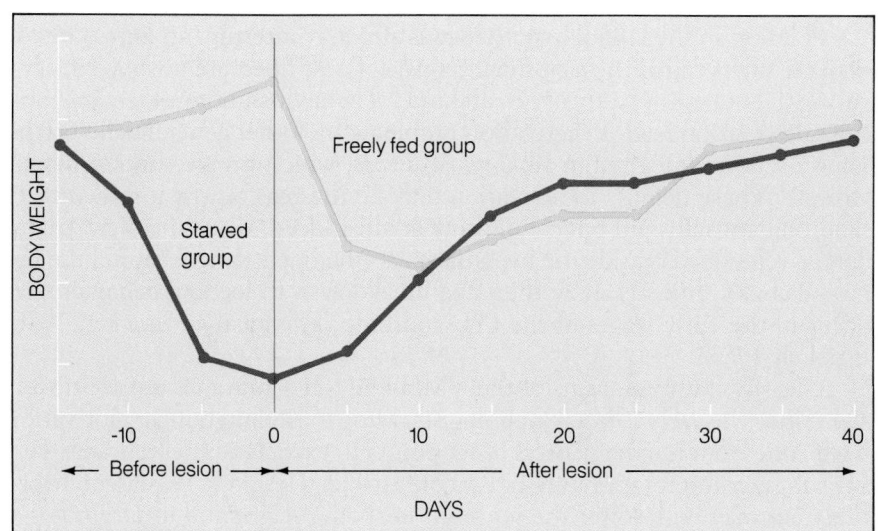

FIGURE 10-4
Body Weight and the Lateral Hypothalamus *Prior to lesioning the lateral hypothalamus, one group of rats was starved while another group was allowed to feed freely. Following surgery, the starved animals increased their food intake and gained weight while the freely fed group lost weight. Both groups stabilized at the same weight level. (After Powley & Keesey, 1970)*

until it returns to its obese state. Damage to the ventromedial area apparently disturbs the animal's long-term weight control system, so it regulates its weight at a higher level. Further, if these obese rats are force-fed until they become extremely obese, they will reduce their food intake until their weight returns to its "normal obese" level (see Figure 10-3).

Similarly, damage to the lateral hypothalamus apparently disturbs weight control so that the animal regulates its weight at a lower level. Recall that after initially refusing all food and water, rats with the LH syndrome resume eating and drinking on their own. But they stabilize at a lower weight level, just as rats with the VMH syndrome stabilize at an obese level (Mitchel & Keesey, 1974). Again, this behavior indicates impairment of a long-term weight control system. Rats that are starved prior to lesioning of the lateral hypothalamus do not refuse to eat after the operation. In fact, many of them overeat, but only until their weight reaches a new level that is lower than their normal weight but higher than their starved, preoperational weight (see Figure 10-4).

These findings indicate that the lateral and ventromedial hypothalamus have reciprocal effects on the *set point* for body weight, or the weight at which an individual body functions best. Damage to the ventromedial areas raises the set point; damage to the lateral area lowers it. If *both* areas in a rat are lesioned carefully so that an equivalent amount of tissue is destroyed in each area, the animal does not overeat or undereat; rather, it maintains its presurgery weight level (Keesey & Powley, 1975).

Another explanation of the VMH and LH syndromes proposes that the effects are due not to the destruction of hypothalamic nuclei but to interference with some of the 50 different nerve tracts that pass through these hypothalamic locations. Consider again a fat rat with a lesion in its ventromedial hypothalamus. While the researchers may have been interested in the effects of the lesion on just the hypothalamus per se, such a lesion also affects certain branches of the parasympathetic nervous system that pass through this region. These latter effects alter metabolism so that too many nutrients are converted into fat (for storage) and too few are left as fuel for metabolic processes. As a result, the animal is constantly in need of nutrients, so it constantly overeats. Thus the VMH-lesioned rat may overeat because, in a sense, it is starving.

A lesion in the lateral hypothalamus also may interrupt an important set of nerve fibers called the *nigrostriatal bundle*. These fibers are involved in activating the organism to engage in all kinds of behaviors, not just feeding, and their destruction leads to activation problems and other general deficits (the same fibers are impaired in *Parkinson's disease*, which involves motor inactivation). These deficits in activation may be the reason why a rat with LH syndrome initially will not eat or drink at all. Indeed, when the nigrostriatal bundle is lesioned outside the hypothalamus (the tracts extend beyond the hypothalamus), animals show the same breakdowns in feeding behavior that occur in the early stages of the LH syndrome (Friedman & Stricker, 1976; Stricker, 1983).

Clearly, interpretations of the VMH and LH syndromes are controversial. Since the early 1960s, psychologists trying to explain hunger motivation have gone from hunger centers to set points to extraneous nerve tracts. Perhaps these interpretations are not incompatible: a lesion in the lateral hypothalamus may both lower the set point for body weight and interrupt nerve tracts that activate the organism. The brain is an enormously complex organ, and we cannot expect simple correspondences between its regions and psychological functions.

OBESITY

We have emphasized homeostatic processes in hunger, but our eating behavior shows several departures from homeostasis. Some people's body weights are not as constant as the homeostatic viewpoint suggests. And while the sight, taste, and smell of food may not be the basic factors in regulating feeding, they do have some influence. For example, after a full meal you may still want to eat dessert; here your cue for hunger is not internal, because there is no physiological need.

The most frequent deviation from homeostatic regulation of eating—at least for humans—is obesity. It is very common in our culture. Roughly 25 percent of Americans are obese, a condition usually defined as being 30 percent or more in excess of one's appropriate body weight. Obesity is also dangerous: a 1985 National Institute of Health panel concluded that obesity is a major health hazard, contributing to a higher incidence of diabetes, high blood pressure, and heart disease. It is not surprising that each year millions of people spend billions of dollars on special diets and drugs to lose weight. Unfortunately, most dieters are not successful, and those who succeed in shedding pounds often regain them. Part of the difficulty in losing weight is that being fat is self-perpetuating: both gaining additional weight and dieting can change your metabolism and energy expenditure in such a way as to keep you fat.

Most researchers agree that obesity is a complex problem and can involve genetic, metabolic, nutritional, psychological, sociological, and environmental factors. Obesity probably is not a single disorder but a host of disorders that all have fatness as their major symptom (Rodin, 1981). The question of how one becomes obese is like that of how one gets to Pittsburgh—there are many ways to do it, and which one you "choose" depends on where you are coming from (Offir, 1982).

We will be concerned with three major causes of weight gain: *calorie intake, calorie expenditure,* and *genetics.* Roughly speaking, people become

Binge eating after an attempt to diet.

obese because they a) eat too much, b) expend too little effort, or c) are genetically predisposed to be fat. Keep in mind that no single factor needs to apply to all people (there are many ways to get to Pittsburgh).

Factors Increasing Calorie Intake

BREAKDOWN OF CONSCIOUS RESTRAINTS   Some people stay obese by binge eating after they diet. An obese man may break his two-day diet and then overeat so much that he eventually consumes more calories than he would have had he not dieted at all. Since the diet was a conscious restraint, the breakdown of control is a factor in increased calorie intake.

To have a more complete understanding of the role of conscious restraints, researchers have developed a questionnaire that asks about diet and weight history (for example, How often do you diet? and What is the maximum amount of weight that you have ever lost in a month?), as well as about the individual's concern with food and eating (for instance, Do you eat sensibly in front of others, yet overeat when alone? and Do you feel guilty after overeating?). The results show that almost everyone—whether thin, plump, or fat—can be classified into one of two categories: people who consciously restrain their eating and people who do not. In addition, regardless of their actual weight, the eating behavior of restrained eaters is closer to that of obese individuals than is that of unrestrained eaters (Herman & Polivy, 1980; Ruderman, 1986).

A laboratory study shows what happens when restraints are dropped. Restrained and unrestrained eaters (both of normal weight) were required to drink either two milk shakes, one milk shake, or none; they then sampled several flavors of ice cream and were encouraged to eat as much as they wanted. The more milk shakes the unrestrained eaters were required to drink, the less ice cream they consumed later. In contrast, the restrained eaters who had been preloaded with two milk shakes ate more ice cream than did those who drank one milk shake or none.

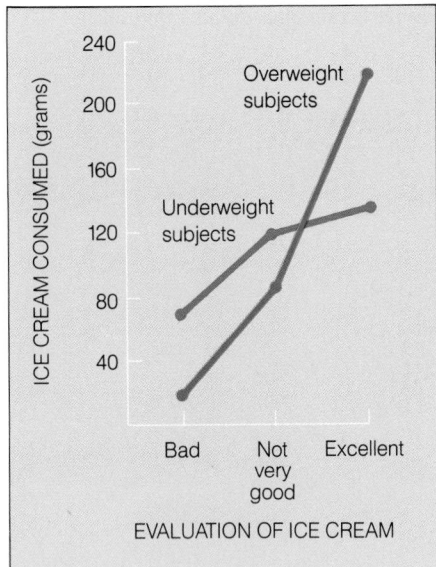

FIGURE 10-5
Taste and Obesity *The effects of food quality on the amount eaten by overweight and underweight subjects. The subjects rated the quality of ice cream and could eat as much as they desired.* (After Nisbett, 1968)

In the above experiment, the preloading of milk shakes makes the subjects lose control of their eating behavior. Once restrained eaters lose control, they eat much more than unrestrained eaters do. But loss of control may not be the only reason why restraint eventually leads to overeating. Deprivation per se can lead to binge eating, independent of the organism's feelings of control. In some experiments, rats were first deprived of food for 4 days, then allowed to feed back to their normal weights, and finally allowed to eat as much food as they wanted. These once-deprived rats ate more than did control rats that had no history of deprivation. Thus, prior deprivation leads to subsequent overeating, even after the weight lost from the deprivation has been regained (Coscina & Dixon, 1983).

Why should prior deprivation lead to future overeating? Evolutionary theory suggests an answer. Until very recently in historical time—and, indeed, still in underdeveloped countries—whenever human beings experienced deprivation, it was because of scarcity in the environment. An adaptive response to such scarcity is to overeat and store in our bodies as much food as possible whenever it is available. Hence, evolution may have selected for an ability to overeat following deprivation. In times of famine, this tendency has served our species well, but once famine is not a concern, the tendency keeps obese dieters overweight (Polivy & Herman, 1985).

EMOTIONAL AROUSAL   Overweight individuals often report that they tend to eat more when they are tense or anxious, and experiments support this. Obese subjects eat more in a high-anxiety situation than they do in a low-anxiety situation, while normal-weight subjects eat more in situations of low anxiety (McKenna, 1972). Other research indicates that any kind of emotional arousal seems to increase food intake in some obese people. In one study, overweight and normal-weight subjects saw a different film in each of four sessions. Three of the films aroused various emotions: one was distressing; one, amusing; and one, sexually arousing. The fourth film was a boring travelogue. After viewing each of the films, the subjects were asked to taste and evaluate different kinds of crackers. The obese subjects ate significantly more crackers after viewing any of the arousing films than they did after seeing the travelogue. Normal-weight individuals ate the same amount of crackers regardless of which film they had seen (White, 1977).

RESPONSIVENESS TO EXTERNAL CUES   Compared to normal-weight people, obese individuals may be more sensitive to external hunger cues (the sight, aroma, and taste of food) and less sensitive to internal hunger cues (such as satiety signals from the intestines). One study examined the effects of taste on the eating behavior of underweight and overweight subjects. The subjects were allowed to eat as much vanilla ice cream as they wanted and then were asked to rate its quality. Some subjects were given a creamy, expensive brand; the others, a cheap brand with quinine added. Figure 10-5 plots the subjects' ratings against the amount of ice cream they ate. Overweight subjects ate much more ice cream when they rated it "excellent" than when they rated it "bad," while the ice-cream consumption by underweight subjects was less affected by taste. Other experiments indicate that while people do indeed differ in their *externality* (sensitivity to external cues), by no means are all obese people "externals," nor are all externals obese. Rather, there are externals and internals in every weight category, and only a moderate correlation exists between degree of externality and degree of obesity (Rodin, 1981).

Factors Decreasing Energy Expenditure

METABOLIC RATE   Two-thirds of a normal person's energy expenditure is devoted to metabolic processes (basic bodily functions). Hence, our *metabolic rate* is a major determinant of weight control: low rates of metabolism expend fewer calories and result in more body weight. One recent study showed that the risk of gaining 15 pounds in a 2-year period was four times greater for a person with a low metabolic rate than for a person with a high rate (Ravusin et al., 1988). Also, metabolic rate is lower in fat tissue than in lean tissue, which means an individual's basal metabolic rate will decrease as lean tissue is replaced by fat. This explains why obese people may stay fat even when their caloric intake is normal.

Metabolic rate also decreases during periods of deprivation, such as when dieting. Consequently, the caloric reduction during dieting is partly offset by the lowered metabolic rate, making it difficult for dieters to meet their goal. The reduction in metabolic rate with dieting may also explain why many people find it harder and harder to lose weight with each successive diet: the body responds to each bout of dieting with a reduction in metabolic rate (Brownell, 1988). While it may seem that nature, in the guise of metabolism, is conspiring against the obese, an evolutionary account provides some perspective. Since deprivation has usually indicated a scarcity of food in the environment, it is adaptive for organisms to respond to deprivation by decreasing the rate at which they expend their limited amount of calories.

ACTIVITY AND EXERCISE   General activity and exercise account for the remaining third of a person's energy expenditure. Exercise, of course, burns off calories: the more that people exercise, the more calories they expend. But exercise also indirectly affects basal metabolism. If a person is sedentary, the metabolic mechanism fails to operate properly and so produces a lower metabolic rate (Garrow, 1978). Lack of exercise for an overweight person sets up a vicious cycle: obesity makes physical exercise more difficult and less enjoyable, and inactivity results in fewer calories being

Overweight people find exercise difficult, thereby perpetuating their obesity.

Exercise is critical in weight loss; it burns calories, but even more important, it helps regulate body metabolism.

burned—directly through a lack of exercise and indirectly through a reduced basal metabolic rate. Thus, exercise is critical in weight loss, not only because it burns calories but also because it helps to regulate normal metabolic functioning (Thompson, Jarvie, Lakey, & Cureton, 1982).

Weight Control

Our discussion of obesity has uncovered a number of factors that tend to maintain fatness: eating to assuage emotions; the tendency of dieting to lead to binge eating; and the slowed metabolic rate caused by fat tissue, dieting, and lack of exercise. Each of these factors can perpetuate a vicious cycle. But the cycle can be broken, as witnessed by the success of certain weight-reduction programs. To lose weight and keep it off, overweight individuals must recognize that anxiety and emotional situations tend to cause them to overeat, that dieting can seduce them into binges, and—perhaps most important—that exercise is a vital part of success.

To control weight, the individual must establish a new set of eating and exercise habits. A study comparing methods for treating obesity illustrates this conclusion. For 6 months, obese individuals followed one of three treatment regimens: a) behavior modification of eating and exercise habits, b) drug therapy using an appetite suppressant (fenfluramine), and c) a combination of behavior modification and drug therapy. Subjects in all three treatment groups were given information on exercise and extensive nutritional counseling, including a diet of no more than 1,200 calories per day. Subjects in the behavior modification groups were taught to become aware of situations that prompted them to overeat, to change the conditions associated with their overeating, to reward themselves for appropriate eating behavior, and to develop a suitable exercise regimen. In addition to the three treatment groups, there were two control groups: one consisted of subjects waiting to take part in the study, and the other comprised subjects who saw a physician for traditional office treatment of weight problems.

Table 10-1 presents the results of the study. The subjects in all three treatment groups lost more weight than the subjects in the two control groups, with the group combining behavior modification and drug therapy losing the most weight and the behavior-modification-only group losing the least. However, during the year after treatment, a striking reversal developed. The behavior-modification-only group regained far less weight than the other two treatment groups; these subjects maintained an average weight loss of 19.8 pounds by the end of the year, whereas the weight losses for the drug-therapy-only group and the combined-treatment group averaged only 13.8 and 10.1 pounds each.

What caused this reversal? An increased sense of self-efficacy may have been a factor. Subjects who received the behavior-modification-only treatment could attribute their weight loss to their own efforts, thereby strengthening their resolve to continue controlling their weight after the treatment ended. Subjects who received an appetite suppressant, on the other hand, probably attributed their weight loss to the medication and so did not develop a sense of self-control. Another possible factor is that the medication had decreased the subjects' feelings of hunger, and consequently subjects in the drug-therapy-only group and the combined-treatment group may not have been sufficiently prepared to cope with the increase in hunger that they felt when the medication was stopped.

	WEIGHT LOSS AFTER TREATMENT	WEIGHT LOSS ONE YEAR LATER
Treatment groups		
Behavior modification only	24.0	19.8
Drug therapy only	31.9	13.8
Combined treatment	33.7	10.1
Control groups		
Waiting list	2.9 (gain)	—
Physician office visits	13.2	—

TABLE 10-1
Weight Loss Following Different Treatments *Weight loss in pounds at the end of 6 months of treatment and on a follow-up 1 year later. Subjects in the two control groups were not available for the 1-year follow-up. (After Craighead, Stunkard, & O'Brien, 1981)*

Genetic Factors

Obesity runs in families: fat parents tend to have fat children. This observation does not necessarily imply a biological explanation (perhaps the child is simply imitating the parents), but there is evidence that some aspects of obesity are biologically based. For instance, twin studies indicate that genetics does play a role; identical twins share the same level of obesity twice as often as fraternal twins (Stunkard, Foch, & Hrubec, 1986).

FAT CELLS Research on the biological basis of obesity has focused on *fat cells*, where all body fat is stored. Organisms—people and animals—vary in how many fat cells they have; the variation, due partly to genetics, has consequences for obesity. In one sample, obese subjects were found to have three times as many fat cells as normal subjects (Knittle & Hirsch, 1968). In other studies, researchers have shown that rats that have double the usual number of fat cells tend to be twice as fat as the control rats. And when researchers cut some of the fat cells out of young rats, so they had only half as many fat cells as their littermates, the operated rats grew up to be only half as fat as their littermates (Hirsch & Batchelor, 1976; Faust, 1984).

The number of fat cells is not entirely fixed by genes. Overeating during the early months of life can increase the number of fat cells. Recent work suggests that even in adulthood overeating can increase an organism's fat-cell count, though to a lesser extent. Still, genetics sets important limits on the total number of fat cells. It determines the minimum number of fat cells, since—barring surgery for obesity—an organism can never lose fat cells. In addition, the extent to which overeating produces new fat cells may itself be determined genetically.

The number of fat cells is not the only critical factor; the size of fat cells also matters. Overeating increases the size of fat cells, while deprivation decreases their size. In most organisms, however, fat cells stay relatively constant in size.

SET POINTS We therefore have two biologically based factors—the number and the size of fat cells—that vary from person to person and are critically related to obesity. Researchers believe that the combination of these two factors may determine an individual's *set point*, which the hypothalamus tries to maintain. Thus, the set points for obese and nonobese individuals who have the same height and bone structure may be different if the two people differ in the number and size of their fat cells. If this is true,

CRITICAL DISCUSSION

Anorexia and Bulimia

While obesity is our most frequent eating disorder, the opposite kind of problem has also surfaced in the form of *anorexia nervosa* and *bulimia*. Both of these eating disorders are characterized by a pathological desire *not* to gain weight.

Anorexia is distinguished by an extreme, self-imposed weight loss. A person may lose 25 percent or more of their normal body weight, resulting in emaciation, susceptibility to infection, and other symptoms of undernourishment. Despite these striking symptoms, the typical anorexic denies there is any problem and refuses to gain weight. In fact, anorexics frequently think they look "too fat," which suggests there is a disturbance in their body image (Bruch, 1973). While anorexia is relatively rare (its incidence in the United States is only about 1 or 2 percent), it is a matter of great concern because anorexics can sometimes starve themselves to death.

Anorexia is 20 times more likely to occur in women than in men, particularly young women in their late high-school and early college years. Often the anorexic has been a model girl, with high grades in school and an upwardly mobile family that stresses achievement (Garfinke & Gardner, 1982). Some researchers have suggested that this kind of background contributes to the development of anorexia; in the context of stressful family demands and expectations, refusing to eat may seem (unconsciously) like a blow for autonomy. Others have argued that society's overemphasis on thinness in women is partly responsible for the disorder. Still other researchers have focused on a biological component of anorexia; once the self-starvation begins, it may lead to the production of *endorphins* in the brain, which function like

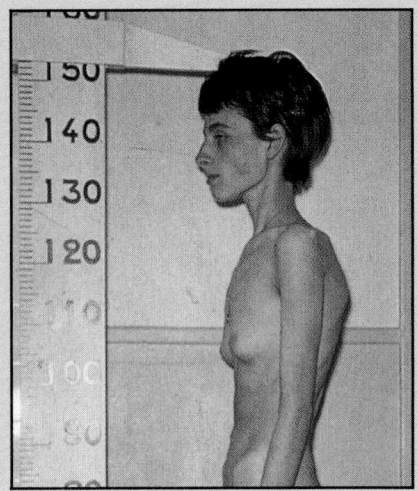

Anorexic female.

obesity for some individuals is their "normal" weight. Attempts at weight reduction by such individuals would hold them below their biologically determined set point, in a state of chronic deprivation; they would feel hungry all the time—just as a thin person would feel on a starvation diet (Nisbett, 1972).

In pursuing the *set-point hypothesis*, Stunkard (1982) has argued that appetite-suppressant drugs such as fenfluramine act primarily to lower the set point and only secondarily to suppress appetite. His account explains the findings on drug therapy for obesity discussed earlier—namely, the rapid regaining of body weight following the withdrawal of fenfluramine in contrast to the relative stability of weight loss achieved by behavior modification. The drug lowered the set point of patients, thereby facilitating weight loss; but discontinuation of the drug caused the set point to return to its pretreatment level. The resulting biological pressure for the individuals to gain weight until they reached their original set points produced a greater weight gain in the drug-therapy subjects than in those who lost weight without the aid of drugs. These interpretations cast doubt on the effectiveness of appetite-suppressant medication in the treatment of obesity.

The set-point hypothesis has generated considerable research, but there are too many contrary findings for it to serve as a general theory of obesity. However, as noted earlier, no such general theory may be possible. The set-point hypothesis may account for certain types of problems, particularly the individual who was moderately overweight as a child and remains moderately overweight throughout life. A higher than normal set point may be one reason for overconsumption, but undoubtedly others exist.

painkillers (see Chapters 2 and 6), and which may reinforce the starvation. It is conceivable that all three factors—personality, societal norms, and brain physiology—play a role.

Like anorexia, bulimia primarily afflicts young women. It is characterized by episodes of binge eating, followed by attempts to purge the excess eating by means of vomiting and laxatives. Because of these purges, a bulimic's weight may stay roughly normal. Consequently, a bulimic woman can often keep her eating disorder hidden. Bulimia is more frequent than anorexia, with 5 to 20 percent of American young women affected to some degree. Rather than being restricted to just the upwardly mobile, bulimia is found in all racial, ethnic, and socio-economic groups in our society.

Again researchers have considered personality, societal factors, and physiological factors as possible causes of the disorder. Therapists who work with bulimic patients often see them as lacking a sense of identity and self-esteem; such people may use food to try to fulfill their feelings of longing and emptiness. Others view bulimic women as people who have been forced by societal pressure to decrease their weight below their natural set point; their binge eating may result from the pressure to return to the set point. Still other researchers favor a totally biological approach, and suggest that bulimia results from a deficit of the neurotransmitter *serotonin*, which leads to both a depressed mood and a craving for carbohydrates (Bruch, 1973).

While the origins of anorexia and bulimia remain somewhat obscure, treatments for these disorders have been developed. The treatment involves some form of therapy. Traditional psychotherapies are useful in dealing with the personality problems involved; behavior modification programs, like that described in the text,

seem particularly useful for helping such people bring their eating habits under control.

Some women with eating disorders become compulsive exercisers to control their weight.

ADULT SEXUALITY

Sexual and maternal drives are other powerful motivators. Sexual desire sometimes can be so strong that it becomes almost an obsession, and a mother's (or father's) desire to protect its young can be so intense as to make her insensitive to pain. Like the survival motives we have considered, sex (and to some extent maternal behavior) is an unlearned motive that human beings share with other species, and whose biological basis psychologists are beginning to understand. There are, however, important differences between sex and maternal behavior, on the one hand, and temperature, thirst, and hunger on the other. Sex and maternal behavior are *social* motives—their satisfaction typically involves another organism—whereas the survival motives concern only the biological self. In addition, motives such as hunger and thirst stem from tissue needs, while sex and maternal behavior do not involve an internal deficit that needs to be regulated and remedied for the organism to survive. Consequently, social motives do not lend themselves to a homeostatic analysis.

With regard to sex, two critical distinctions should be kept in mind. The first stems from the fact that, although we begin to mature sexually at puberty, the basis for our sexual identity is established in the womb. We therefore distinguish between adult sexuality (that is, beginning with changes at puberty) and early sexual development. The second distinction is between the biological and environmental determinants of sexual behaviors and feelings. For many aspects of sexual development and adult sexuality, a

fundamental question is the extent to which the behavior or feeling in question is a product of biology (particularly hormones), of environment (early experiences and cultural norms), or of an interaction between the two.

Hormonal Control

At puberty—roughly ages 11 to 14—hormone changes produce the bodily changes that serve to distinguish males from females. The hormonal system involved is illustrated in Figure 10-6. The general idea is that endocrine glands manufacture hormones (chemical messengers), which travel through the bloodstream to target organs. The process begins in the hypothalamus when it secretes *gonadotropin-releasing factors*; these chemical messengers direct the pituitary gland to produce *gonadotropins*, which are hormones whose targets are the *gonads*—the ovaries and testes. There are two kinds of gonadotropins. One is called *follicle-stimulating hormone* (FSH). In women, FSH stimulates the growth of *follicles*, clusters of cells in the ovaries that support developing eggs and secrete the female hormone *estrogen*. In men, FSH stimulates sperm production in the testes. The other gonadotropin produced by the pituitary is called *luteinizing hormone* (LH) in women and *interstitial-cell stimulating hormone* (ICSH) in men. The secretion of LH brings on ovulation—the release of a mature egg from the follicle—and then causes the ruptured follicle to secrete *progesterone*, another female hormone. ICSH, the male equivalent, stimulates the production of the male hormone *androgen*. Although a number of technical terms have been mentioned here, the basic scheme is simple: by way of hormones, the hypothalamus directs the pituitary, which in turn directs the gonads.

The hormones produced by the gonads—estrogen, progesterone, and androgen—are called the *sex hormones* (a bit of a misnomer because all three hormones are produced by males and females, albeit in different amounts). These hormones are responsible for the body changes at puberty. In girls, estrogen causes the development of breasts, the changes in the distribution of body fat that result in a more feminine form, and the maturation of the female genitals. In boys, *testosterone* (a kind of androgen) is responsible for the sudden growth of facial, underarm, and pubic hair; it also causes a deepening of the voice, the development of muscles that lead to a more masculine form, and the growth of the external genitals.

What role do these hormones play in adult sexual desire and arousal? In other species, sexual arousal is closely tied to variations in hormonal levels; in humans, however, hormones play less of a role. One way to assess the contribution of hormones to sexual arousal is to study the effects of castration. In males, castration usually involves removal of the testes, which essentially eliminates production of the sex hormones. In experiments with lower species (such as rats and guinea pigs), castration results in the rapid decline and eventual disappearance of sexual activity. For humans, of course, there are no controlled experiments; psychologists rely instead on observations of males with serious illnesses (for example, cancer of the testes) who have undergone *chemical castration* (synthetic hormones administered to suppress or block the use of androgen). These studies typically show that some men lose their interest in sex, while others continue to lead a normal sex life (Money, Wiedeking, Walker, & Gain, 1976; Walker, 1978). Apparently, androgen contributes to sexual desire only in some cases.

Another way to measure the contribution of hormones to sexual desire and arousal in men is to look for a relation between hormonal fluctuation

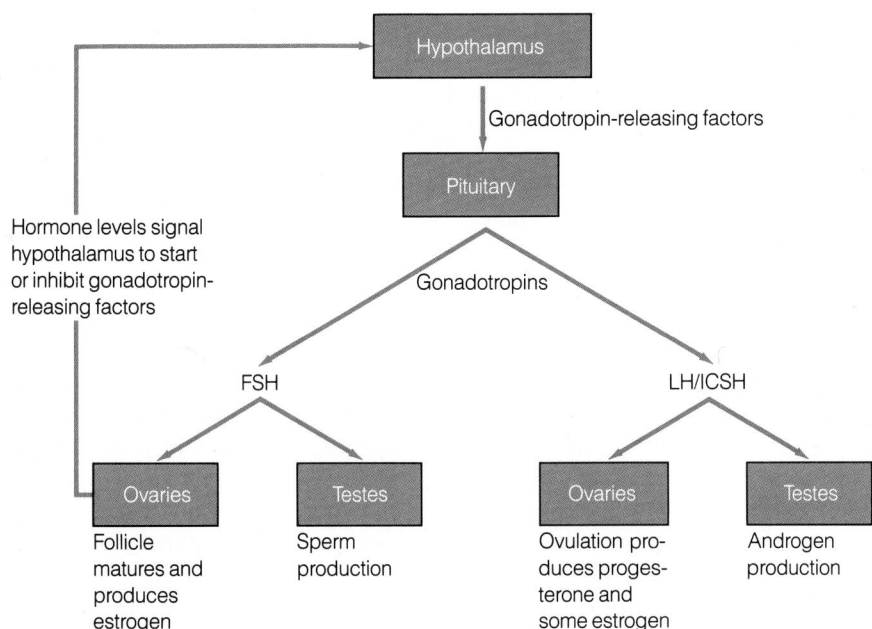

and sexual interest. For example, is a man more likely to feel aroused when
his testosterone level is high? For years, researchers had failed to find strong
evidence for a relation between hormone levels and arousal. However, some
recent work (Davidson, 1988) suggests that while testosterone level may
have no effect on *arousal*—as indicated by the ability to have an erection—it
does increase *desire*—as indicated by sexual fantasies. [The major determinants of sexual desire in men, however, seem to be emotional factors; thus,
for males as well as females, the most common cause of low desire in couples
seeking sex therapy is marital conflict (Goleman, 1988).]

The lack of hormonal effects on arousal is even more striking in women,
particularly in contrast to other species. In all animals, from reptiles to monkeys, castration in a female (removal of the ovaries) results in cessation of
sexual activity. The castrated female ceases to be receptive to the male and
usually resists sexual advances. The major exception is the human female;
following menopause (when the ovaries have ceased to function), sexual
desire in most women does not diminish. In fact, some women show an
increased interest in sex after menopause, possibly because they are no longer
concerned about becoming pregnant.

Studies looking at the relation between hormonal fluctuation and sexual
arousal in premenopausal females present a similar conclusion: hormones
have substantial control of arousal in lower species but not in humans. In
female mammals, hormones fluctuate cyclically with accompanying changes
in fertility. During the first part of the mammalian cycle (while the egg is
being prepared for fertilization), the ovaries secrete estrogen, which prepares
the uterus for implantation and also tends to arouse sexual interest. After
ovulation occurs, both progesterone and estrogen are secreted. This *fertility*
or *estrous cycle* is accompanied by a consequent variation in sexual motivation in most mammalian species. Most female animals are receptive to sexual
advances by a male only during the period of ovulation, when the estrogen
level is at its highest in the cycle (when they are "in heat"). Among primates, however, sexual activity is less influenced by the fertility cycle; monkey, ape, and chimpanzee females copulate during all phases of the cycle,

although ovulation is still the period of most intense sexual activity. In the human female, sexual desire and arousal seems to be barely influenced by the fertility cycle, being affected much more by social and emotional factors.

In sum, the degree of hormonal control over adult sexual behavior decreases from the lower to the higher vertebrates. Still, even for humans there may be some hormonal control, as witnessed by the relation between testosterone and sexual desire in men.

Neural Control

The nervous system also is responsible for aspects of sexual arousal and behavior, the mechanisms of which are complex and vary from one species to the next. In humans, some of the neural mechanisms involved are at the level of the spinal cord. In males, an erection following direct stimulation of the penis is controlled by a spinal reflex, as are pelvic movements and ejaculations. All of these actions are still possible in men whose spinal cords have been severed by injury. Similarly, clinical studies of women with spinal cord injuries suggest that lubrication of the vagina may be controlled by a spinal reflex (Offir, 1982).

But the organ most responsible for the regulation of sexual arousal and behavior is the brain (sex therapists call it "the most erogenous zone"). The spinal reflexes are regulated by the brain, and erections can be directly controlled by the brain through thoughts and images. Some of our more precise knowledge about the role of the brain in sex comes from experiments with animals. In male rats, electrical stimulation of the posterior hypothalamus produces not only copulation but the entire repertoire of sexual behavior. A male rat stimulated in that area does not mount indiscriminately; instead, he courts the female by nibbling her ears and nipping the back of her neck until she responds. Intromission and ejaculation follow unless the electrical stimulation is terminated. Even a sexually satiated male rat will respond to electrical stimulation by pressing a bar to open a door leading to the female and will court and mate with her (Caggiula & Hoebel, 1966).

Early Experiences

The environment also has great influence on adult sexuality, one class of determinants being early experience. Experience has little influence on the mating behavior of lower mammals—inexperienced rats will copulate as efficiently as experienced ones—but it is a major determinant of the sexual behavior of higher mammals.

Experience can affect specific sexual responses. For instance, young monkeys exhibit in their play many of the postures required later for copulation. In wrestling with their peers, infant male monkeys display hindquarter grasping and thrusting responses that are components of adult sexual behavior. Infant female monkeys retreat when threatened by an aggressive male infant and stand steadfastly in a posture similar to the stance required to support the weight of the male during copulation. These presexual responses appear as early as 60 days of age and become more frequent and refined as the monkey matures (see Figure 10-7). Their early appearance suggests that they are innate responses to specific stimuli, and the modification and refinement of these responses through experience indicates that learning plays a role in the development of the adult sexual pattern.

Sexual play among snow monkeys.

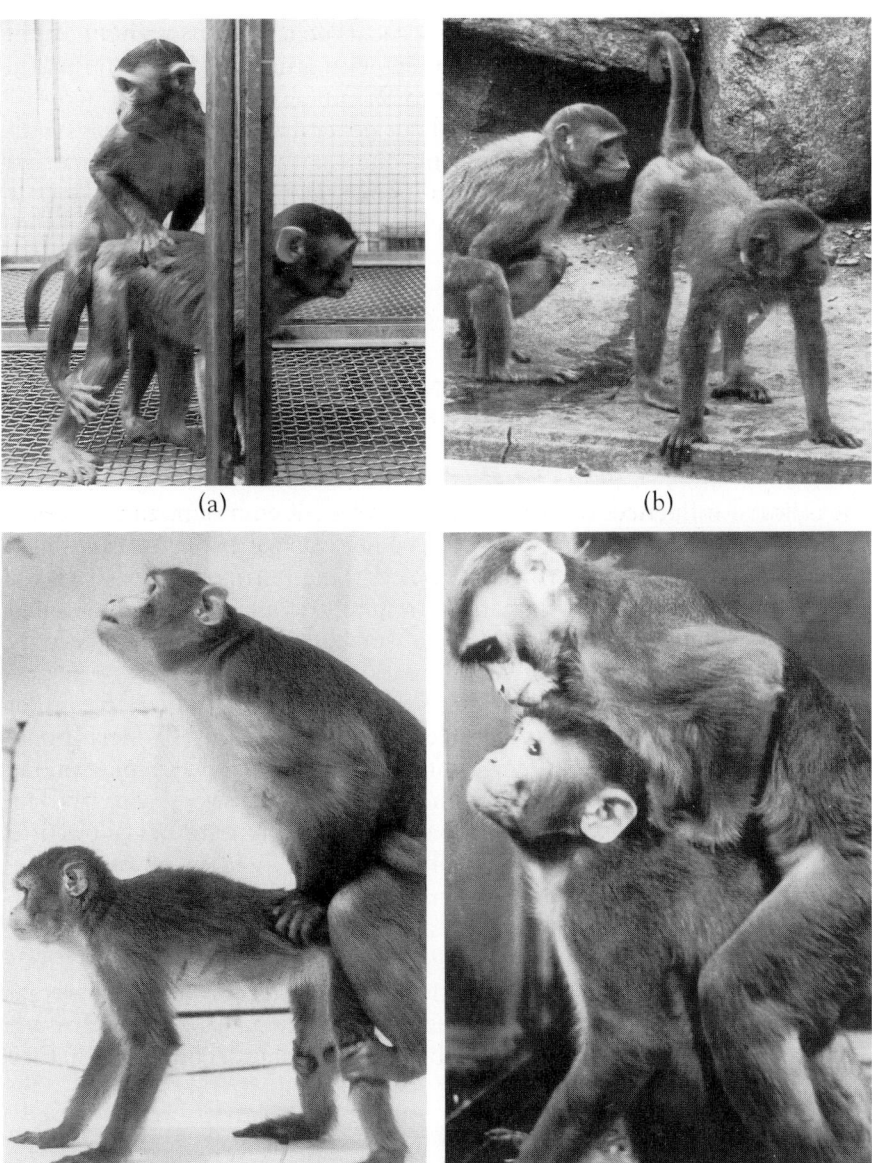

FIGURE 10-7
Infant Play and Adult Sexual Behavior *(a) The first presexual step. (b) Inappropriate sexual response: female correct, male incorrect. (c) Basic sexual posture. (d) Inappropriate sexual response: male correct, female incorrect.*

(a)

(b)

(c)

(d)

Experience also affects the interpersonal aspect of sex. Monkeys raised in partial isolation (in separate wire cages, where they can see other monkeys but cannot have contact with them) are usually unable to copulate at maturity. The male monkeys are able to perform the mechanics of sex: they masturbate to ejaculation at about the same frequency as normal monkeys. But when confronted with a sexually receptive female, they do not seem to know how to assume the correct posture for copulation. They are aroused but aimlessly grope the female or their own bodies. Their problem is not just a deficiency of specific responses. These once-isolated monkeys have social or affectional problems: even in nonsexual situations, they are unable to relate to other monkeys, exhibiting either fear and flight or extreme aggression. Apparently, normal heterosexual behavior in primates depends not only on hormones and the development of specific sexual responses, but also on an affectional bond between two members of the opposite sex. This bond is an outgrowth of earlier interactions with the mother and peers, through which the young monkey learns to trust, to expose its delicate parts without fear of harm, to accept and enjoy physical contact with others, and to be motivated to seek the company of others (Harlow, 1971).

Although we must be cautious about generalizing these findings with monkeys to human sexual development, clinical observations of human infants suggest certain parallels. Human infants develop their first feelings of trust and affection through a warm and loving relationship with the mother or primary caretaker (see Chapter 3). This basic trust is a prerequisite for sastisfactory interactions with peers. And affectionate relationships with other youngsters of both sexes lay the groundwork for the intimacy required for sexual relationships among adults.

Cultural Influences

Cultural influences constitute another class of environmental determinants. Unlike that of other primates, human sexual behavior is strongly determined by culture. Every society places some restrictions on sexual behavior. Incest (sexual relations within the family), for example, is prohibited by almost all cultures. Other aspects of sexual behavior—sexual activity among children, homosexuality, masturbation, and premarital sex—are permitted in varying degrees by different societies. Among preliterate cultures studied by anthropologists, acceptable sexual activity varies widely. Some very permissive societies encourage autoerotic activities and sex play among children of both sexes and allow them to observe adult sexual activity. The Chewa of Africa, for example, believe that if children are not allowed to exercise themselves sexually, they will be unable to produce offspring later. The Sambia of New Guinea have institutionalized bisexuality: from prepuberty until marriage, a boy lives with other males and engages in homosexual practices (Herdt, 1984).

In contrast, very restrictive societies try to control preadolescent sexual behavior and to keep children from learning about sex. The Cuna of South America believe that children should be totally ignorant about sex until they

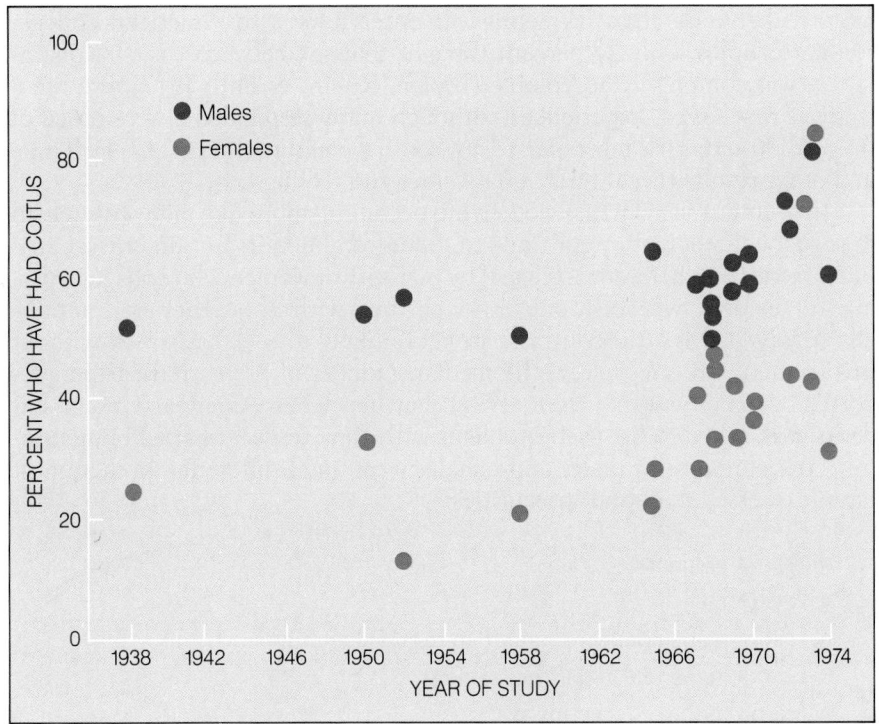

FIGURE 10-8
Reported Incidence of Premarital Coitus *Each data point represents findings from a study of the incidence of premarital sex among college men and women. Note the marked upward trend starting in the 1960s. (After Hopkins, 1977)*

are married; they do not even permit their children to watch animals give birth. And among the Ashanti of Africa, intercourse with a girl who has not undergone the puberty rites is punishable by death for both participants. Similar extreme attitudes are found toward other aspects of sexual behavior: homosexuality, for example, is viewed by some nonliterate societies as an essential part of growing up and by others as an offense punishable by death.

In the 1940s and 1950s, the United States and most other western countries would have been classified as sexually restrictive. Traditionally, the existence of prepubertal sexuality had been ignored or denied. Marital sex was considered the only legitimate sexual outlet, and other forms of sexual expression (homosexual activities, premarital and extramarital sex) were generally condemned and often prohibited by law. Of course, many members of these societies engaged in such activities, but often with feelings of shame.

Over the years, sexual activities became less restricted. Premarital intercourse, for example, became more acceptable and more frequent. Among American college-educated individuals interviewed in the 1940s, 27 percent of the women and 49 percent of the men had engaged in premarital sex by the age of 21 (Kinsey, Pomeroy, & Martin, 1948; Kinsey, Pomeroy, Martin, & Gebhard, 1953). In contrast, several surveys of American college students in the 1970s reported percentages ranging from 40 to over 80 for both males and females (Hunt, 1974; Tavris & Sadd, 1977). Figure 10-8 gives the reported incidence of premarital intercourse in studies conducted over a 35-year span. Note that the change in sexual behavior was greater among women than men and that the biggest changes occurred in the late 1960s. These changes led many observers of the social scene in the 1970s to conclude that there had been a sexual revolution.

Today, it seems that the sexual revolution has been stymied by the fear of sexually transmitted diseases, particularly the Acquired Immunodeficiency Syndrome, or *AIDS*. Furthermore, the revolution may always have pertained more to behavior than to feelings. In interviews with American college-student couples, only 20 percent thought that sex between casual acquaintances was completely acceptable (Peplau, Rubin, & Hill, 1977). And in a study of first sexual experiences, although many respondents were proud of losing their virginity, few reported any sensual pleasures (Hunt, 1974). These and other results reveal traditional values and feelings.

In a similar vein, while women are becoming more like men with regard to sexual behavior, they continue to differ from men in certain critical attitudes toward sex before marriage. The majority of women who engage in premarital sex do so with only one or two partners with whom they are emotionally involved. Men, in contrast, are more likely to seek casual sex without involvement; in one survey, the median number of premarital partners reported by males was six (Hunt, 1974). Further, when American college students were asked to list their problems with "any respect of sexual functioning," the concerns of males and females were quite different. Women most often expressed fears and insecurities:

- Fear of pregnancy
- Fear of rape
- Fear of being conquered and then regarded as of no further use
- Fear of being rejected if they said no
- Masturbation—accepting it
- Fear that their partners would be physically repulsed by them
- Fear of losing self-respect
- Fear of becoming too attached when the feeling was not mutual
- Guilt feelings about premarital sex
- Pressure to have sex even when they did not want to
- Fear of not satisfying their partners
- Embarrassment or concern over not being orgasmic

Men were more apt to list complaints about women rather than to express their own conflicts or worries:

- Finding partners who were open to varying sexual experiences
- Always having to be on the hunt
- Not being able to have sexual relations when they wanted to
- Women who "tease," without wanting to engage in sexual activity
- Women's refusal to take responsibility for their own sexuality
- Women who used their sexual attractiveness in a manipulatory fashion
- The excessive modesty of women (they wanted the lights off)
- Passive women
- Aggressive women
- Necessity to say you loved the woman even if it was not true
- Being expected to know all about sex
- Inability to communicate feelings or needs during sex

(Tavris & Offir, 1977, p. 68)

These response differences reflect different attitudes—at least among males and females who are young and unmarried—about the relation between sex and love.

Homosexuality

The term "homosexual" can be applied to either a man or a woman, but female homosexuals are usually called "lesbians." Someone is considered homosexual if they are sexually attracted primarily to members of the same sex. Most experts agree with Kinsey's view that homosexuality is not an either–or matter; sexual behavior falls on a continuum, with exclusively heterosexual and exclusively homosexual individuals at either end and various mixtures of sexual behavior in between. Most young boys engage in erotic play with other boys at some time during their childhood, and many men have one or more homosexual encounters. According to some estimates, only about 4 percent of men become exclusively homosexual. Women are less apt than men to have sexual interactions with each other during childhood or a homosexual episode in later life; and only 1–2 percent of women are exclusively homosexual. Some individuals are *bisexual*, having sexual relations with members of both sexes. And some married individuals may have extramarital homosexual encounters.

Until the advent of the sexual revolution in the late 1960s, homosexuality was considered a mental illness or an abnormal perversion. Although many people still view homosexuality as unnatural, most psychologists and psychiatrists consider it to be a variant rather than a perversion of sexual expression and not, in itself, an indication or cause of mental illness. In some studies of mental health homosexuals seemed as well adjusted as heterosexuals in certain areas of life (Bell & Weinberg, 1978). Their job stability and job satisfaction was equal to that of heterosexuals. In other areas of life, homosexuals fared less well. They reported themselves as being more tense and depressed than did a comparable group of heterosexuals. However, this difference between homosexuals and heterosexuals all but disappears if one considers only those homosexuals that are "close-coupled," that is, living in a quasi-marriage. Also, the greater unhappiness of other homosexuals may stem less from their sexual preference than from their treatment as a disapproved-of minority: being attracted to people of the same sex may or may not make you depressed, but being scorned and ostracized because of your sexual preference almost certainly will (Brown, 1986). In any event, these data on homosexuality and mental health were obtained before AIDS had reached epidemic proportions in the homosexual community. No doubt, living (and dying) with AIDS is bad for one's mental health, but this is true of any group at high risk for a deadly disease.

ENVIRONMENTAL AND BIOLOGICAL DETERMINANTS   Despite considerable research, little of certainty is known about the causes of homosexuality. With regard to environmental causes, common wisdom has it that male homosexuality can result from a young boy identifying with his mother. The most relevant evidence for this "mothering" hypothesis comes from a large study involving extensive interviews with hundreds of homosexuals and heterosexuals about their early development (Bell, Weinberg, & Hammersmith, 1981; Bell & Weinberg, 1978). This study found no difference between homosexual and heterosexual males in the frequency with which they reported that when growing up they wanted to be like their mothers. Thus, there is no evidence for the mothering hypothesis. On the other hand, the two groups of males did differ with regard to identifying with their fathers; many fewer homosexuals reported that while growing up they wanted to be like their fathers. But there is no simple link between a poor relation with a father and male homosexuality, because poor relations with a father were

Homosexual couples.

TABLE 10-2
Variables Influencing Sexual Preference *Results are based on interviews conducted in 1969–70 with approximately 1,500 homosexual men and women living in the San Francisco Bay area. The investigators analyzed the respondents' relationships with their parents and siblings while growing up, the degree to which the respondents conformed during childhood to the stereotypical concepts of what it means to be male or female, the respondents' relationships with peers and others outside the home, and the nature of their childhood and sexual experiences. Statistical analyses traced the relationship between such variables and adult sexual preference.* (After Bell, Weinberg, & Hammersmith, 1981)

1. The respondents' identification with their opposite-sex parents while growing up appeared to have had no significant impact on whether they turned out to be homosexual or heterosexual.

2. For both the men and the women in the study, poor relationships with fathers seemed to play a more important role in predisposing them to homosexuality than the quality of their relationships with their mothers.

3. For both men and women, homosexuals were no more likely than heterosexuals to report a first sexual encounter with a member of the same sex.

4. By the time both the boys and the girls reached adolescence, their sexual preference was likely to be determined, even though they might not yet have become very active sexually.

5. Among the respondents, homosexuality was indicated or reinforced by sexual feelings that typically occurred 3 years or so before their first "advanced" homosexual activity. These feelings, more than homosexual activities, appeared to play a crucial role in the development of adult homosexuality.

6. The homosexual men and women in the study were not particularly lacking in heterosexual experiences during their childhood and adolescent years. They were distinguishable from their heterosexual counterparts, however, in that they found such experiences ungratifying.

7. Among both the men and the women in the study, there was a powerful link between gender nonconformity as a child and the development of homosexuality.

8. Insofar as differences can be identified between male and female psychosexual development, gender nonconformity appeared to be somewhat more important for males and family relationships appeared to be more important for females in the development of sexual preference.

also more prevalent among lesbians than their heterosexual counterparts. (These findings, along with other results from the Bell, Weinberg, and Hammersmith study, are summarized in Table 10-2.)

A more promising approach may be to consider the interaction between environment and biology. Storms (1981) has proposed that sexual preference results in part from an interaction between sex-drive development and social development during early adolescence. Specifically, the onset of the sex drive during adolescence (due to the surge of hormones) initiates the development of a sexual orientation, and the various people in an individual's social environment at that time determine the direction of the sexual orientation. An unusually early onset of the sex drive may contribute to homosexuality, because the individual's social environment at that time is composed primarily of youngsters of the same sex (boys and girls tend to form separate, same-sexed groups from early childhood through preadolescence). Thus, sexual preference in adulthood may depend on the social environment that is present when the individual's sex drive comes into full force during adolescence. This hypothesis suggests that if the environment is primarily of the same sex, the adult's sexual preference will tend to be homosexual; if heterosocial, the adult's sexual preference will tend to be heterosexual.

This "first encounter" theory is at least compatible with the earlier mentioned findings about identification with parents. But it is not compatible with another finding from the Bell, Weinberg, and Hammersmith study, namely that, for both males and females, homosexuals were no more likely than heterosexuals to report having a first sexual encounter with a member of the same sex. This result should be interpreted with caution in view of the difficulty people have recalling a specific episode from memory; still, it at least suggests that first encounter theory is unlikely to be the major cause of homosexuality (Brown, 1986).

Some proposals about biological causes of homosexuality seem equally tenuous. Thus, there are no reliable differences in body characteristics between homosexuals and heterosexuals. Although some male homosexuals may look quite feminine—and some female homosexuals, quite masculine—this is often not the case. A more plausible locus of biological differences is hormones. With regard to hormone levels in adulthood, the evidence is at best inconsistent. Some studies have found that male homosexuals have lower levels of testosterone than do heterosexual males, while other studies show no difference in overall levels of hormones. Moreover, when male homosexuals are given additional male hormones, their sex drive may increase but their sexual preferences do not change.

A more promising hypothesis is that homosexuals and heterosexuals may differ with respect to the hormones they were exposed to while still in the womb. Specifically, during prenatal life male fetuses secrete testosterone (as will be discussed in the section on early sexual development), and this testosterone may masculinize the brain. It is possible that males who get too little testosterone at some critical point in prenatal life are predisposed toward homosexuality in adult life. Similarly, female fetuses exposed to too much testosterone may be predisposed toward lesbianism in adult life. Though the hypothesis may seem far-fetched, there are some data that indirectly support it. Girls who are known to have been exposed to too much prenatal testosterone are extremely likely to be "tomboys" in childhood, and more likely than normal girls to have lesbian fantasies during early adulthood (Money, 1980; Money, Schwartz, & Lewis, 1984). Also, the prenatal hypothesis seems compatible with the findings listed in Table 10-2, in particular the early emergence of homosexual feelings (Brown, 1986). Still, at this

Lesbian partners at a gay wedding.

point in time, the hypothesis remains speculative, and is intended only for those people classified as exclusively homosexual. Even proponents of the hypothesis think that for some people, homosexuality is entirely learned, and if desired, potentially changeable by therapy.

SEX DIFFERENCES   In our earlier discussion of heterosexuality, we noted that young men and women differ in their attitudes about sex, with women being more likely than men to view sex as a part of a loving relationship. This same kind of difference appears between male and female homosexuals. Lesbians are more likely than male homosexuals to have long-term relations with their lovers. Lesbians also have many fewer sexual partners. In the study by Bell and Weinberg (1978), the majority of gay females reported having a total of fewer than 10 sexual partners, while the average gay male reported hundreds of sexual partners. (However, male homosexuals have become far less promiscuous in the last few years in a determined effort to reduce the transmission of AIDS.) Also, lesbians place more emphasis on the romantic aspects of their relations than do gay men. The way that people conduct their sexual-romantic lives, therefore, may have less to do with being homosexual or heterosexual than with being male or female.

EARLY SEXUAL DEVELOPMENT

For social and sexual experiences to be gratifying in adult life, one needs to develop an appropriate *gender identity*—that is, males need to think of themselves as males, and females as females. This development is quite complex and begins in the womb.

Prenatal Hormones

For the first couple of months after conception, only the chromosomes of a human embryo indicate whether it will develop into a boy or girl. Up to this stage, both sexes are identical in appearance and have tissues that will eventually develop into testes or ovaries, as well as a genital tubercle that will become either a penis or a clitoris. But between 2 and 3 months, a primitive sex gland, or gonad, develops into testes if the embryo is genetically male (that is, has XY chromosomes—see Chapter 2) or into ovaries if the embryo is genetically female (XX chromosomes). Once testes or ovaries develop, they produce the sex hormones, which then control the development of the internal reproduction structures and the external genitals. The sex hormones are more important for prenatal development than they are for expressions of adult sexuality.

The critical hormone in genital development is androgen. If the embryonic sex glands produce enough androgen, the newborn will have male genitals; if there is insufficient androgen, the newborn will have female genitals, *even* if it is genetically male (XY). The anatomical development of the female embryo does not require female hormones, only the absence of male hormones. In short, nature will produce a female unless androgen intervenes.

The influence of androgen, called *androgenization*, extends far beyond anatomy. After it has molded the genitals, androgen begins to operate on the brain cells. Studies with rats provide direct evidence that prenatal androgen

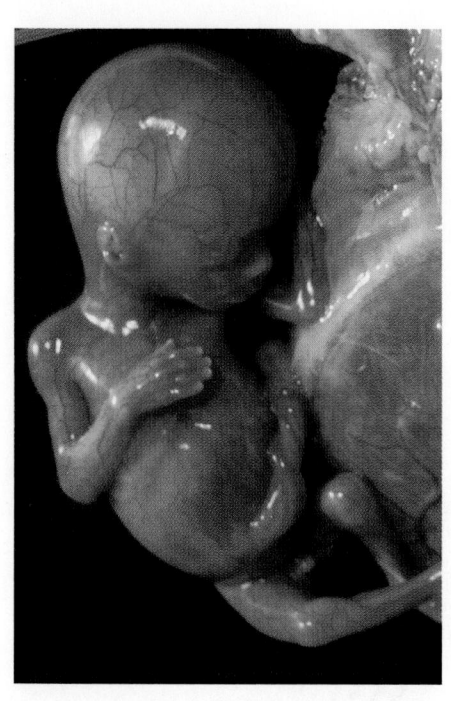

Prenatal development: 4 months.

painkillers (see Chapters 2 and 6), and which may reinforce the starvation. It is conceivable that all three factors—personality, societal norms, and brain physiology—play a role.

Like anorexia, bulimia primarily afflicts young women. It is characterized by episodes of binge eating, followed by attempts to purge the excess eating by means of vomiting and laxatives. Because of these purges, a bulimic's weight may stay roughly normal. Consequently, a bulimic woman can often keep her eating disorder hidden. Bulimia is more frequent than anorexia, with 5 to 20 percent of American young women affected to some degree. Rather than being restricted to just the upwardly mobile, bulimia is found in all racial, ethnic, and socioeconomic groups in our society.

Again researchers have considered personality, societal factors, and physiological factors as possible causes of the disorder. Therapists who work with bulimic patients often see them as lacking a sense of identity and self-esteem; such people may use food to try to fulfill their feelings of longing and emptiness. Others view bulimic women as people who have been forced by societal pressure to decrease their weight below their natural set point; their binge eating may result from the pressure to return to the set point. Still other researchers favor a totally biological approach, and suggest that bulimia results from a deficit of the neurotransmitter *serotonin*, which leads to both a depressed mood and a craving for carbohydrates (Bruch, 1973).

While the origins of anorexia and bulimia remain somewhat obscure, treatments for these disorders have been developed. The treatment involves some form of therapy. Traditional psychotherapies are useful in dealing with the personality problems involved; behavior modification programs, like that described in the text, seem particularly useful for helping such people bring their eating habits under control.

Some women with eating disorders become compulsive exercisers to control their weight.

ADULT SEXUALITY

Sexual and maternal drives are other powerful motivators. Sexual desire sometimes can be so strong that it becomes almost an obsession, and a mother's (or father's) desire to protect its young can be so intense as to make her insensitive to pain. Like the survival motives we have considered, sex (and to some extent maternal behavior) is an unlearned motive that human beings share with other species, and whose biological basis psychologists are beginning to understand. There are, however, important differences between sex and maternal behavior, on the one hand, and temperature, thirst, and hunger on the other. Sex and maternal behavior are *social* motives—their satisfaction typically involves another organism—whereas the survival motives concern only the biological self. In addition, motives such as hunger and thirst stem from tissue needs, while sex and maternal behavior do not involve an internal deficit that needs to be regulated and remedied for the organism to survive. Consequently, social motives do not lend themselves to a homeostatic analysis.

With regard to sex, two critical distinctions should be kept in mind. The first stems from the fact that, although we begin to mature sexually at puberty, the basis for our sexual identity is established in the womb. We therefore distinguish between adult sexuality (that is, beginning with changes at puberty) and early sexual development. The second distinction is between the biological and environmental determinants of sexual behaviors and feelings. For many aspects of sexual development and adult sexuality, a

painkillers (see Chapters 2 and 6), and which may reinforce the starvation. It is conceivable that all three factors—personality, societal norms, and brain physiology—play a role.

Like anorexia, bulimia primarily afflicts young women. It is characterized by episodes of binge eating, followed by attempts to purge the excess eating by means of vomiting and laxatives. Because of these purges, a bulimic's weight may stay roughly normal. Consequently, a bulimic woman can often keep her eating disorder hidden. Bulimia is more frequent than anorexia, with 5 to 20 percent of American young women affected to some degree. Rather than being restricted to just the upwardly mobile, bulimia is found in all racial, ethnic, and socioeconomic groups in our society.

Again researchers have considered personality, societal factors, and physiological factors as possible causes of the disorder. Therapists who work with bulimic patients often see them as lacking a sense of identity and self-esteem; such people may use food to try to fulfill their feelings of longing and emptiness. Others view bulimic women as people who have been forced by societal pressure to decrease their weight below their natural set point; their binge eating may result from the pressure to return to the set point. Still other researchers favor a totally biological approach, and suggest that bulimia results from a deficit of the neurotransmitter *serotonin*, which leads to both a depressed mood and a craving for carbohydrates (Bruch, 1973).

While the origins of anorexia and bulimia remain somewhat obscure, treatments for these disorders have been developed. The treatment involves some form of therapy. Traditional psychotherapies are useful in dealing with the personality problems involved; behavior modification programs, like that described in the text, seem particularly useful for helping such people bring their eating habits under control.

Some women with eating disorders become compulsive exercisers to control their weight.

ADULT SEXUALITY

Sexual and maternal drives are other powerful motivators. Sexual desire sometimes can be so strong that it becomes almost an obsession, and a mother's (or father's) desire to protect its young can be so intense as to make her insensitive to pain. Like the survival motives we have considered, sex (and to some extent maternal behavior) is an unlearned motive that human beings share with other species, and whose biological basis psychologists are beginning to understand. There are, however, important differences between sex and maternal behavior, on the one hand, and temperature, thirst, and hunger on the other. Sex and maternal behavior are *social* motives—their satisfaction typically involves another organism—whereas the survival motives concern only the biological self. In addition, motives such as hunger and thirst stem from tissue needs, while sex and maternal behavior do not involve an internal deficit that needs to be regulated and remedied for the organism to survive. Consequently, social motives do not lend themselves to a homeostatic analysis.

With regard to sex, two critical distinctions should be kept in mind. The first stems from the fact that, although we begin to mature sexually at puberty, the basis for our sexual identity is established in the womb. We therefore distinguish between adult sexuality (that is, beginning with changes at puberty) and early sexual development. The second distinction is between the biological and environmental determinants of sexual behaviors and feelings. For many aspects of sexual development and adult sexuality, a

fundamental question is the extent to which the behavior or feeling in question is a product of biology (particularly hormones), of environment (early experiences and cultural norms), or of an interaction between the two.

Hormonal Control

At puberty—roughly ages 11 to 14—hormone changes produce the bodily changes that serve to distinguish males from females. The hormonal system involved is illustrated in Figure 10-6. The general idea is that endocrine glands manufacture hormones (chemical messengers), which travel through the bloodstream to target organs. The process begins in the hypothalamus when it secretes *gonadotropin-releasing factors*; these chemical messengers direct the pituitary gland to produce *gonadotropins*, which are hormones whose targets are the *gonads*—the ovaries and testes. There are two kinds of gonadotropins. One is called *follicle-stimulating hormone* (FSH). In women, FSH stimulates the growth of *follicles*, clusters of cells in the ovaries that support developing eggs and secrete the female hormone *estrogen*. In men, FSH stimulates sperm production in the testes. The other gonadotropin produced by the pituitary is called *luteinizing hormone* (LH) in women and *interstitial-cell stimulating hormone* (ICSH) in men. The secretion of LH brings on ovulation—the release of a mature egg from the follicle—and then causes the ruptured follicle to secrete *progesterone*, another female hormone. ICSH, the male equivalent, stimulates the production of the male hormone *androgen*. Although a number of technical terms have been mentioned here, the basic scheme is simple: by way of hormones, the hypothalamus directs the pituitary, which in turn directs the gonads.

The hormones produced by the gonads—estrogen, progesterone, and androgen—are called the *sex hormones* (a bit of a misnomer because all three hormones are produced by males and females, albeit in different amounts). These hormones are responsible for the body changes at puberty. In girls, estrogen causes the development of breasts, the changes in the distribution of body fat that result in a more feminine form, and the maturation of the female genitals. In boys, *testosterone* (a kind of androgen) is responsible for the sudden growth of facial, underarm, and pubic hair; it also causes a deepening of the voice, the development of muscles that lead to a more masculine form, and the growth of the external genitals.

What role do these hormones play in adult sexual desire and arousal? In other species, sexual arousal is closely tied to variations in hormonal levels; in humans, however, hormones play less of a role. One way to assess the contribution of hormones to sexual arousal is to study the effects of castration. In males, castration usually involves removal of the testes, which essentially eliminates production of the sex hormones. In experiments with lower species (such as rats and guinea pigs), castration results in the rapid decline and eventual disappearance of sexual activity. For humans, of course, there are no controlled experiments; psychologists rely instead on observations of males with serious illnesses (for example, cancer of the testes) who have undergone *chemical castration* (synthetic hormones administered to suppress or block the use of androgen). These studies typically show that some men lose their interest in sex, while others continue to lead a normal sex life (Money, Wiedeking, Walker, & Gain, 1976; Walker, 1978). Apparently, androgen contributes to sexual desire only in some cases.

Another way to measure the contribution of hormones to sexual desire and arousal in men is to look for a relation between hormonal fluctuation

changes the volume and detailed structure of cells in the fetus' hypothalamus, an organ that regulates motivation in humans as well as rats (Money, 1988). These effects of androgen essentially masculinize the brain, and may be responsible for masculine traits and behaviors that appear months or years later.

In a series of experiments, pregnant monkeys were injected with testosterone (a kind of androgen), and their female offspring were observed in detail. These female offspring showed some anatomical changes (penises instead of clitorises) and also acted differently than normal females. They were more aggressive in play, more masculine in sexual play, and less intimidated by approaching peers (Goy, 1968; Phoenix, Goy, & Resko, 1968). These findings indicate that some gender-appropriate behaviors (such as greater aggression for males) may be hormonally determined in monkeys. If the same is true in humans, then some typical aspects of our gender identity are controlled by hormones rather than by the social environment. We noted in our discussion of homosexuality that there is suggestive evidence that androgen levels in the womb may influence sexual preference in adult life. Some researchers have even suggested that such unusual traits as mathematical genius and *dyslexia* (a reading disability), which are more common in men than women, are partly the products of excessive androgenization (Geschwind, 1984). The question of hormonal control in humans remains controversial, however.

Hormones versus Environment

In humans, much of what is known about the effects of prenatal hormones and early environment has been uncovered by studies of *hermaphrodites*. Hermaphrodites are individuals who are born with both male and female tissue; they may have genitals that appear to be ambiguous (an external organ that could be described as a very large clitoris or a very small penis) or external genitals that conflict with internal sex organs (a penis and ovaries). These conditions arise because of prenatal hormonal imbalances, in which a genetically female fetus has too much androgen or a genetically male fetus has too little of it. What, then, will be the eventual gender identity of a hermaphroditic infant who is assigned the wrong sex label at birth— say, an infant with ambiguous external genitalia who is called a boy at birth but is later determined to be genetically female (XX) and to have ovaries?

In most cases such as this, the assigned label and the sex role in which the individual is raised have a much greater influence on gender identity than do the individual's genes and hormones. For example, two genetically female infants had ambiguous external genitals because their fetal sex glands had produced too much androgen (their internal organs were clearly female, though). Both infants had surgery to correct their enlarged clitorises. One infant's genitals were "feminized," and she was raised as a girl; the other infant's genitals were modified to resemble a penis, and he was raised as a boy. Reports indicate that both children grew up secure in their respective sex roles. The girl was somewhat "tomboyish," but feminine in appearance. The boy was accepted as a male by his peers and expressed a romantic interest in girls. Cases such as this suggest that an individual's gender identification is influenced more by the way a person is labeled and raised than by his or her hormones (Money, 1980).

But there are also cases that point to the opposite conclusion. The most famous occurred several years ago in remote villages of the Dominican Republic. It involved 18 genetic males who, owing to the fact that their cells were insensitive to the androgen their bodies generated prenatally, were born with internal organs that were clearly male but external genitals that were closer to females, including a clitoris-like sex organ. All 18 were raised as girls, which was at odds with both their genes and their prenatal hormonal environment. When they reached puberty, the surge of male hormones produced the usual bodily changes and turned their clitoris-like sex organs into penis-like organs. The vast majority of these males-reared-as-females rapidly turned into males. They seemed to have little difficulty adjusting to a male gender identity; they went off to work as miners and woodsmen and some found female sexual partners. In this case, biology triumphed over environment (Imperato-McGinley, Peterson, Gautier, & Sturla, 1979). There is controversy, however, about these Dominican hermaphrodites. They do not seem to have been raised as ordinary girls (not surprising since they had ambiguous genitals). Rather, they seemed to have been treated as half-girl, half-boy, which could have made their subsequent transition to males easier (Money, 1987).

Proponents of environmental determination can point to their own incredible case. Identical twin boys had a completely normal prenatal environment. But at the age of 7 months, in a tragic mistake, one of the boys had his penis completely severed in what was supposed to be a routine circumcision. Ten months later, the agonized parents authorized surgery to turn their child into a little girl—the testes were removed and a vagina was given preliminary shape. The child was then given female sex hormones and raised as a girl. Within a few years, the child seemed to have assumed a female gender identity: she preferred more feminine clothes, toys, and activities than her twin brother. What is striking about this case is a) that environment won out over both genes and a *normal* prenatal environment (in all other cases considered, the prenatal environment has not been entirely normal), and b) that a comparison can be made between individuals who have identical genes and prenatal hormones but different upbringings. Still, advocates of biological determination are skeptical about basing too much on a single case.

What can we conclude about gender identity? Clearly, prenatal hormones and environment are both major determinants of gender identity that typically work in harmony. When they clash, as they do in certain hermaphrodites, most experts believe that environment will dominate. But this is a controversial area, and expert opinion may change as additional data are gathered.

Transsexualism

Some people feel that their body is compatible with one sex—say, their internal and external organs are all male—but their gender identity is that of the other sex—they think of themselves as females. Such *transsexuals* (usually males) feel that they were born into the wrong body. They are not homosexuals in the usual sense. Most homosexuals are satisfied with their anatomy and identify themselves as appropriately male or female; they have an appropriate gender identity but are sexually attracted to members of their own sex. Transsexuals, in contrast, think of themselves as members of the *opposite* sex (often from early childhood) and may be so desperately unhappy with their physical appearance that they request hormonal and surgical treatment to change their genitals and secondary sex characteristics.

Doctors have performed several thousand sex-change operations in the United States. For males, hormone treatments can enlarge their breasts, reduce beard growth, and make their bodies more rounded; surgical procedures involve removing the testes and part of the penis and shaping the remaining tissue into a vagina and labia. For women, hormone treatments can increase beard growth, firm their muscles, and deepen their voices; surgical procedures involve removing the ovaries and the uterus, reducing breast tissue, and in some instances constructing a penislike organ. Although a sex-change operation does not make reproduction possible, it can produce a remarkable change in physical appearance. Because the surgery is so drastic, though, it is undertaken only after careful consideration. The individual is usually given counseling and hormone treatments and is required to live as a member of the opposite sex for a year or more prior to the operation. Expert opinion remains divided on whether sex-change surgery genuinely helps transsexual individuals to feel better adjusted to their environment (Hunt & Hampson, 1980).

MATERNAL BEHAVIOR

In many species, care of the offspring is a more powerful determinant of behavior than is sex, or even hunger and thirst. A mother rat, for example, will more frequently overcome barriers and suffer pain to reach its young than it will to obtain food when hungry or water when thirsty. While humans are not always as dutiful parents as rats are, caring for the young is one of the basic motives in our species, too.

Biological Determinants

As is the case with sex, hormones play more of a role in the maternal behavior of lower species than in primates. Virgin rats presented with rat pups for several days will begin to build a nest, lick the pups, retrieve them, and finally hover in a nursing posture. If blood plasma from a mother rat that has just given birth is injected into a virgin rat, it will begin to exhibit maternal behavior in less than a day (Terkel & Rosenblatt, 1972). Maternal behavior patterns appear to be innately programmed in the rat's brain, and hormones serve to increase the excitability of these neural mechanisms. The hormonal effects depend on the balance between the female hormones (estrogen and progesterone) and prolactin from the anterior pituitary gland, which stimulates the production of milk.

For humans, hormones have much less influence. If human maternal behavior were chiefly guided by hormones, one would not expect parents to abuse their children as often as they do. Some women abandon their newborn infants or even kill them, and battered children are more commonplace than people realize. In the United States, according to a conservative estimate, approximately 350,000 children each year are physically, sexually, or emotionally abused by their caretakers; a less conservative estimate holds that between 1.4 and 1.9 million children each year are at risk of a serious injury from a family member (Wolfe, 1985). The parents involved in these cases generally received little or no love as children and frequently were beaten by their own parents, indicating the importance of early experience on parental behavior. In primates and humans, experience far overrides whatever influence maternal hormones may have.

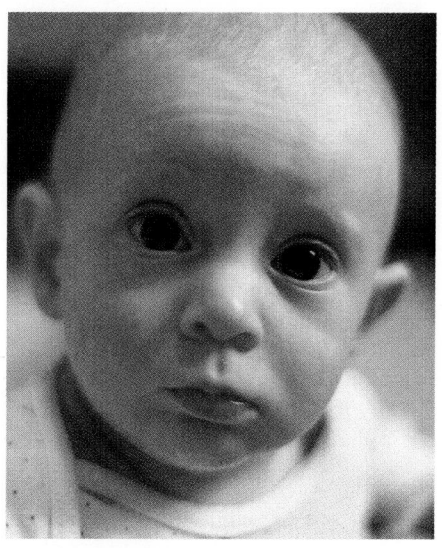

Cuteness acts as an innate releaser of parental feelings.

CRITICAL DISCUSSION

Instincts and Maternal-Infant Behavior

The concept of an "instinct" has a long history in the study of behavior. Around the turn of the century, psychologists relied heavily on the concept, attempting to explain all human behavior in terms of instincts (McDougall, 1908). During the 1920s, the concept fell into disrepute, partly because many acts were being cavalierly labeled "instinctive" and partly because the concept did not fit with the emerging theory of behaviorism (Stellar & Stellar, 1985). But later, starting in the 1950s, a group of European ethologists brought the study of instinct under scientific scrutiny and revived interest in the concept. For a behavior to be labeled instinctive, it has to be innately determined and it must be specific to a certain species and appear in the same form in all members of the species. Thus, *innateness, species specificity,* and *fixed-action patterns* are the hallmarks of the ethological approach to instinctive behavior.

One area where the ethological approach has succeeded is in the analysis of maternal behavior. The response patterns that animals display in the care of their young provide a clear example of instinctive behavior. Building nests, removing the amniotic sac so the newborn can breathe, feeding the young, and retrieving them when they stray from the nest are all complex behavior patterns that animals exhibit without having had the opportunity to learn them; hence, they must be innate. A squirrel performs maternal duties in the same manner as all other mothers of its species; therefore, the behavior is species-specific and fixed in its action pattern.

Among the more startling discoveries of ethologists is the phenomenon of *imprinting.* As you may recall from Chapter 7, imprinting refers to a type of early learning that forms the basis for the young animal's attachment to its parents. A newly hatched duckling that has been incubated artificially will follow a human being, a wooden decoy, or almost any other moving object that it first sees after birth. Following a wooden decoy for as little as 10 minutes is enough to imprint the duckling on the decoy; the duckling will then remain attached to this object, follow it even under adverse circumstances, and prefer it to a live duck. Imprinting occurs most readily 14 hours after hatching, but can happen any time during the first 2 days of life. After this interval, imprinting is difficult, probably because the duckling has acquired a fear of strange objects.

Ethologists have found imprinting in a number of species—including dogs, sheep, and guinea pigs—but it is most clearly developed in birds that are able to walk or swim immediately after birth. An innate mechanism ensures that the young will follow and will remain close to their mothers (normally

Imprinting in Ducklings *The newly hatched duckling follows the model duck around a circular track. The duckling soon becomes imprinted on the model and will follow it in preference to a live duck of its own species. The more effort the duckling has to exert to follow the model (such as climbing a hurdle), the stronger the imprinting. (After Hess, 1958)*

But we cannot dismiss biology entirely. A number of possible biological determinants of human parental behavior have been suggested by *ethologists* (scientists who study animal behavior in the natural environment). One such possibility is that the distinctive, cute features of a baby (large protruding forehead, large eyes, upturned nose, chubby cheeks, and so forth) serve as *innate releasers* of parental feelings and behavior. That is, our species—and most others—may have evolved so that the characteristic cute features of babies elicit feelings of parenting in adults. Babies that have fewer of these cute features are somewhat more likely to be abused by their parents (see Mook, 1987). In a similar vein, a baby's smile, which appears to be innately

the first moving object they see), rather than wander off into a perilous world.

Studies of mallard ducks have identified the stimuli that are important for imprinting in birds and indicate that the phenomenon begins even before birth. Ducklings begin to make sounds in their eggs a week before they break through the shells. Mallard mothers respond to these sounds with clucking signals, which increase in frequency about the time the ducklings hatch. Auditory stimuli before and after hatching, together with tactile stimulation in the nest after birth, thoroughly imprint the ducklings on the female mallard in the nest. An unhatched duckling that hears a recording of a human voice saying "Come, come, come" instead of its mother's clucking will imprint on a decoy that utters "Come, come, come" as easily as it will imprint on a decoy that utters normal mallard clucks. Ducklings that have been exposed to a mallard female's call prior to hatching are more likely to imprint on decoys that utter mallard clucks (Hess, 1972).

In addition to the concepts of species specificity and fixed-action patterns, ethologists have developed the concept of a *releaser*, a particular environmental stimulus that sets off a species-specific behavior. In some young sea gulls, a red or yellow spot on the mother's beak releases a pecking response by the hatchling, which causes the mother to regurgitate the food that the infant will eat. By varying the color and shape of the spot on cardboard models and by observing whether the young gull pecks at the beak, researchers can determine the characteristics of the releaser to which the bird responds. (Releasers also play a major role in the sexual behavior of lower animals.)

The higher an animal is on the evolutionary scale, the fewer instinctive behaviors it exhibits and the more that learning determines its actions. But even humans have some instinctual behavior patterns, including the *rooting reflex* of the human infant. Touching a nipple (or a finger) to the cheek of a newborn elicits head turning and simultaneous mouth opening. If the mouth contacts the nipple, it closes on the nipple and begins to suck. This behavior pattern is automatic and can occur even when the infant is sleeping. At about 6 months, the rooting reflex is superseded by voluntary behavior; the typical 6-month-old sees the nipple, reaches for it, and tries to bring it to his or her mouth.

Austrian ethologist Konrad Lorenz demonstrates how young ducklings follow him instead of their mother because he was the first moving object they saw after they were hatched.

determined, seems to be a preprogrammed elicitor of parental behavior. (See the Critical Discussion, "Instincts and Maternal-Infant Behavior," for greater detail.)

Environmental Determinants

Among primates, maternal behavior is largely influenced by experience and learning. If female monkeys are raised in isolation, they exhibit none of the normal maternal behaviors when they later become mothers (see Chapter 3). They appear to develop little love for their offspring and generally ignore them. When they do pay attention to their young, they sometimes abuse them savagely. A mother might try to crush her infant's head or, in extreme cases, even bite the infant to death (Suomi, Harlow, & McKinney, 1972). There is a parallel here between the dreadful parenting of these monkey mothers originally reared in isolation and the child abuse by people who were raised by inadequate parents. Those who are themselves subjected to poor parenting seem destined to pass it on to their offspring.

CURIOSITY MOTIVES

Thus far, all of the motives discussed have been related to the survival of either the individual or the species. An earlier generation of psychologists believed that once an organism has satisfied its motives, it prefers a quiescent state, but this belief has turned out to be wrong. Both people and animals are motivated to *seek* stimulation—to explore actively their environment, even when the activity satisfies no bodily need. Thus, there appears to be a third general class of motives, *curiosity*, which we will briefly survey.

Exploration and Manipulation

We seem to have inborn drives to manipulate and investigate objects. We give babies rattles, crib gymnasiums, and other toys because we know they like to hold, shake, and pull them. Monkeys enjoy the same sort of activities; in fact, the word "monkey," used as a verb, describes casual manipulation for whatever satisfaction it brings. A number of experiments have shown that monkeys do indeed like to "monkey." If various mechanical devices are placed in a monkey's cage, it will begin to take them apart, becoming more skilled with practice, without receiving any evident reward other than the satisfaction of manipulating them. If the monkey is fed each time it takes a puzzle apart, its behavior changes; it loses interest in manipula-

Young monkeys "monkeying."

tion and views the puzzle as a means of acquiring food (Harlow, Harlow, & Meyer, 1950).

While manipulation sometimes is done for its own sake, other times it is for purposes of *investigation*. The monkey—or person—picks up the object, looks at it, tears it apart, and examines the parts, apparently attempting to discover more about it. Piaget made a number of observations bearing on such responses in the early life of the human infant. Within the first few months of life, infants learn to pull a string to activate a hanging rattle—a form of manipulation that might be considered merely entertaining. Between 5 and 7 months, they will remove a cloth from their faces in anticipation of the peekaboo game. At 8 to 10 months, infants look for objects behind or beneath other objects; by 11 months, they begin to experiment with objects, varying the toys' placement or positions (Piaget, 1952). This kind of inquisitive or investigative behavior is typical of the growing child, and it seems to develop as a motive apart from any physiological need of the organism.

Sensory Stimulation

REDUCED STIMULATION STUDIES   Both exploration and manipulation provide the organism with new and changing sensory input. This change in input may be one reason why humans and animals manipulate and investigate objects: perhaps we have a need for sensory stimulation. Studies in which sensory stimulation is markedly reduced provide some support for this hypothesis. In the initial studies of this type, subjects were paid to spend their time lying on a cot, cut off from most forms of sensory stimulation. Reduced stimulation (or sensory deprivation, as it was originally called) proved very detrimental: subjects became disoriented in time and space, began to experience visual hallucinations, and were unable to think clearly.

Subsequent work, however, showed that many of these extreme reactions were due not to subjects being deprived of environmental stimulation, but rather to their feeling disoriented and anxious about the experimental situation (Suedfeld, 1975). In more recent experiments, care is taken to alleviate the subjects' anxiety and disorientation, in part by familiarizing them with the experimental situation before a session begins. In a typical session, the subject lies on a comfortable bed in a dark, sound-reduced room for 24 hours. Water and food are available through plastic tubes fastened near the pillow, and a chemical toilet is at the foot of the bed (see Figure 10-9). These experiments show no evidence of the extreme reactions that characterized the earlier studies, but they do show decrements in perception. Reduced-stimulation subjects experience some distortions in color and in spatial orientation, and are slower in reacting to visual stimuli than control subjects (Zubek, 1969). Stimulus reduction also produces decrements in problem-solving tasks such as thinking of as many uses as possible for a common object. Thus, people apparently require sensory stimulation for normal perceptual and intellectual functioning.

Interestingly, though, the absence of stimulation can be helpful in getting someone to make a major change in their behavior. For example, reduced stimulation has been used in programs to help people stop smoking. Subjects who are first presented anti-smoking messages and then given 24 hours of reduced stimulation are more likely to stay off cigarettes for a year than subjects provided only the anti-smoking messages (Suedfeld &

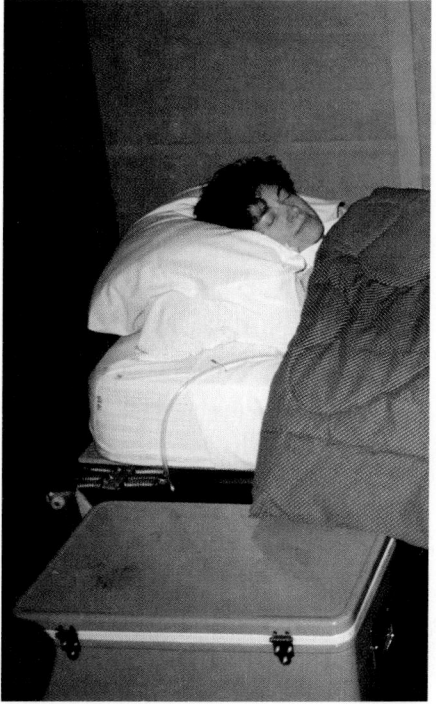

FIGURE 10-9
Reduced Stimulation Experiment
The room is dark and sound-deadened. Food and water stored in the blue box are delivered via the plastic tube. An intercom behind the subject's head permits communication when necessary.

TABLE 10-3
Sensation Seeking Scale *A sample of items from the SSS and a scoring procedure. Each item contains two choices. Choose the one that best describes your likes or feelings. If you do not like either choice, mark the choice you dislike the least. Do not leave any items blank.* (Test items courtesy of Marvin Zuckerman)

1. A. I have no patience with dull or boring persons.
   B. I find something interesting in almost every person I talk to.

2. A. A good painting should shock or jolt the senses.
   B. A good painting should provide a feeling of peace and security.

3. A. People who ride motorcycles must have some kind of unconscious need to hurt themselves.
   B. I would like to drive or ride a motorcycle.

4. A. I would prefer living in an ideal society in which everyone is safe, secure, and happy.
   B. I would have preferred living in the unsettled days of history.

5. A. I sometimes like to do things that are a little frightening.
   B. A sensible person avoids dangerous activities.

6. A. I would not like to be hypnotized.
   B. I would like to be hypnotized.

7. A. The most important goal of life is to live to the fullest and experience as much as possible.
   B. The most important goal in life is to find peace and happiness.

8. A. I would like to try parachute jumping.
   B. I would never want to try jumping from a plane, with or without a parachute.

9. A. I enter cold water gradually, giving myself time to get used to it.
   B. I like to dive or jump right into the ocean or a cold pool.

10. A. When I go on a vacation, I prefer the comfort of a good room and bed.
    B. When I go on a vacation, I prefer the change of camping out.

11. A. I prefer people who are emotionally expressive even if they are a bit unstable.
    B. I prefer people who are calm and even-tempered.

12. A. I would prefer a job in one location.
    B. I would like a job that requires traveling.

13. A. I can't wait to get indoors on a cold day.
    B. I am invigorated by a brisk, cold day.

14. A. I get bored seeing the same faces.
    B. I like the comfortable familiarity of everyday friends.

Scoring:

Count one point for each of the following items that you have circled: 1A, 2A, 3B, 4B, 5A, 6B, 7A, 8A, 9B, 10B, 11A, 12B, 13B, 14A. Add your total for sensation seeking and compare it with the norms below:

0–3	Very low	6–9	Average	12–14	Very high
4–5	Low	10–11	High		

Baker-Brown, 1986). Reduced stimulation is also being explored in the treatment of other health-related problems, such as tension headaches, high blood pressure, and insomnia (Suedfeld & Coren, 1989). Thus, while sensory stimulation may generally be needed for normal functioning, there seem to be times when a decrease in stimulation is useful, perhaps to allow us to attend more to our own feelings and thoughts.

INDIVIDUAL DIFFERENCES IN STIMULATION SEEKING While persons differ in the extent to which they manifest some of the other motives discussed in this chapter, individual differences in curiosity motives seem particularly salient. To try to measure these differences, Zuckerman (1979a) has developed a test called the *Sensation Seeking Scale*, abbreviated SSS. The scale includes a range of items designed to assess an individual's desire to engage in adventurous activities, to seek new kinds of sensory experiences, to enjoy the excitement of social stimulation, and to avoid boredom. Table 10-3 presents a sample of items on the scale; you may want to answer them before reading further.

Research using the SSS has revealed large differences in stimulation seeking (Carrol, Zuckerman, & Vogel, 1982). Moreover, sensation seeking appears to be a trait that is consistent across a variety of situations; individuals who report enjoying new experiences in one area of life tend to describe themselves as adventurous in other areas. Psychologists have related high scores on the SSS to a number of behavioral characteristics: engaging in risky sports, occupations, or hobbies (parachuting, motorcycle riding, fire fighting, scuba diving); seeking variety in sexual and drug experiences; behaving fearlessly in common phobic situations (heights, darkness, snakes); taking risks when gambling; and preferring exotic foods. Even when asked to describe their normal driving habits, high-sensation seekers report driving at faster speeds than low-sensation seekers (see Figure 10-10).

COMMON PRINCIPLES FOR DIFFERENT MOTIVES

Motives generally can be categorized according to survival needs, social needs, and the need to satisfy curiosity. While the differences between these types are real, we have not addressed some similarities among them.

In the 1940s and 1950s, many psychologists believed that all basic motives operated according to the principle of *drive reduction*: supposedly motives are directed at the reduction of a psychological state that a person experiences as tension, and the person experiences pleasure from this reduction in tension or drive. Drive reduction seems applicable to the survival motives. When deprived of food, we do indeed feel a tension that is reduced by eating, and we experience that reduction as pleasurable. But for such motives as sex, drive reduction sounds less plausible; according to both everyday observation and laboratory experiments, sexual stimulation is rewarding in its own right. Similarly, drive-reduction theory has never been able to come to grips with the curiosity motive. Drive-reduction theory suggests that everyone would avoid extreme tension-producing situations; but some people (perhaps mainly those who are high on the SSS) seek out such situations, like riding roller coasters and sky diving (Geen, Beatty, & Arkin, 1984).

Psychologists today generally reject drive reduction in favor of the principle of *arousal level*, according to which people seek an optimal level of drive or arousal. The optimal level varies from person to person—as demonstrated by individual differences in stimulation seeking. Physiological deprivation, as in hunger and thirst, increases arousal level above the optimum and leads to behavior that brings the level down. In contrast, too little stimulation can sometimes motivate an organism to increase its arousal level. We seek

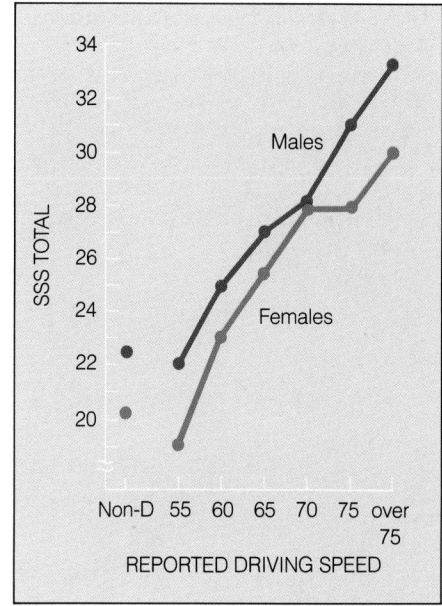

FIGURE 10-10
SSS Scores and Driving Speed *Subjects were asked at what speed they would usually drive on a highway if conditions were good and the posted speed limit was 55 MPH. Results revealed a significant relationship between reported driving speed and SSS score. Nondrivers (Non-D) and those who drove at or below the speed limit had the lowest SSS scores; scores increased with each increment in driving speed. The sex difference observed in this study is generally the case; males typically score higher on SSS than females. (After Zuckerman & Neeb, 1980)*

Sensation-seeking individuals are attracted to dangerous sports.

stimulation (including sexual stimulation), novelty, and complexity in our environments, but only up to a point. Though the notion of arousal level is not without its critics, it seems more likely than drive reduction to emerge as a unifying principle of the basic drives.

✦ CHAPTER SUMMARY

1. Motives, which give behavior *direction* and *energize* it, are of different types, including *survival, social,* and *curiosity.* Survival motives, such as hunger and thirst, operate according to *homeostasis:* they maintain a constant internal environment. Homeostasis involves a *regulated variable, sensors* that measure the variable, an *ideal value* of the variable, a *comparator,* and *adjustments* that the system makes when the variable is at a value above or below the ideal value.

2. Our regulation of temperature is an example of homeostasis. The regulated variable is the temperature of the blood, and sensors for this are located in various regions of the body, including the *hypothalamus.* The ideal value and comparator are also located in the hypothalamus. Adjustments are either automatic physiological responses (for example, shivering) or voluntary behavioral ones (such as putting on a sweater).

3. Thirst is another homeostatic motive. There are two regulated variables, *intracellular fluid* and *extracellular fluid.* The loss of intracellular fluid is detected by *osmoreceptors,* cells in the hypothalamus that respond to dehydration; this in turn leads to the release of the *antidiuretic hormone* (ADH), which regulates the kidneys, allowing water to be reabsorbed into the bloodstream. Extracellular fluid is detected by *blood-pressure sensors* in the kidneys.

4. Hunger is a complex, homeostatic motive with numerous regulated variables, including *glucose, fats,* and *amino acids.* Glucose sensors have been found in the hypothalamus and liver. In addition to sensors that trigger feeding, there are also *satiety detectors,* which are found in the digestive system (particularly the stomach, duodenum, and liver) and signal the brain that the needed nutrients are on their way.

5. Two regions of the brain are critical for hunger: the *lateral hypothalamus* and the *ventromedial hypothalamus.* Destruction of the lateral hypothalamus leads to undereating; destruction of the ventromedial hypothalamus to overeating. One interpretation of these effects is that the ventromedial and lateral regions have reciprocal effects on the *set point* for body weight: damage to the ventromedial region raises the set point, whereas damage to the lateral region lowers it. Another interpretation proposes that the effects are due to interference with nerve tracts that pass through the hypothalamic locations.

6. People become obese when they (a) take in too many calories, (b) expend too few calories, or (c) are genetically predisposed to be fat. With regard to why they

take in too many calories, obese people tend to overeat when they break a diet, eat more when emotionally aroused, and are more responsive than normal-weight individuals to external hunger cues. With regard to why they expend too few calories, obese people often have a relatively low metabolic rate (due to dieting or to a high proportion of fat tissue) and usually do not exercise enough. In treating obesity, it appears that keeping weight off permanently depends on establishing self-control over eating habits, which can be done by behavior modification, and exercising regularly.

7. The female hormones (*estrogen* and *progesterone*) and male hormones (*androgens*) are responsible for the body changes at puberty but play only a limited role in human sexual arousal. In contrast, there is substantial hormonal control over sex in lower species. Early social experiences with parents and peers have a large influence on adult sexuality in primates and humans. Monkeys raised in isolation have sexual problems as adults. For humans, other environmental determinants of adult sexuality are cultural norms and attitudes. Although western society is becoming increasingly permissive about premarital sex, men and women still differ in their attitudes toward sex.

8. Sexual interactions with members of the same sex are not uncommon during childhood, but only a small percentage of people become exclusively *homosexual* as adults. Extensive interviews with homosexuals suggest that they do not differ from heterosexuals with regard to their identifications with parents of the opposite sex, or with regard to the nature of their first sexual encounter. For exclusive homosexuals, there may be a biological predisposition.

9. Prenatal hormones are important for sexual development. If the embryonic sex glands produce enough androgen, the newborn will have male genitals; if there is insufficient androgen, the newborn will have female genitals, even if it is genetically male. In cases in which hormonal imbalances result in *hermaphrodites* (individuals born with both male and female tissue), the assigned label and the sex role in which the individual is raised seem to have greater influence on gender identity than do the individual's genes and hormones.

10. In lower animals, maternal behavior appears to be innately programmed and triggered by hormones. In primates and humans, however, maternal behavior is largely influenced by experience. Monkeys reared in isolation do not exhibit the usual maternal behaviors when they later become mothers.

11. People and animals appear to have inborn curiosity motives to explore and manipulate objects. Manipulation of objects provides the organism with changing sensory input, and studies of *reduced sensory stimulation* show that the absence of changing input can disrupt normal perceptual and intellectual functioning.

12. Psychologists used to believe that all basic motives operate by *drive reduction*, the principle that all motives are directed toward the reduction of tension. But drive reduction does not offer a satisfactory account of sex or the curiosity motives. A more promising principle is that organisms seek an *optimal level of arousal*.

FURTHER READING

The biological approach to temperature regulation, thirst, hunger, and sex is surveyed in Carlson, *Physiology of Behavior* (3rd ed., 1985); and Rosenzweig and Leiman, *Physiological Psychology* (2nd ed., 1989). An introduction to human sexuality is provided by Offir, *Human Sexuality* (1982). An explanation of normal and abnormal patterns of eating and drinking is given in Logue, *The Psychology of Eating and Drinking* (1986); also see Stunkard (ed.), *Obesity* (1980).

For reviews of motivation in general, see Mook, *Motivation: The Organization of Action* (1987); Geen, Beatty, and Arkin, *Human Motivation: Physiological, Behavioral, and Social Approaches* (1984); and Stellar and Stellar, *The Neurobiology of Motivation and Reward* (1985). A review of ethology is presented in Lorenz, *The Foundations of Ethology* (1981); and in McFarland, *Animal Behaviour: Psychobiology, Ethology and Evolution* (1985).

Chapter 11

Detail, Love Song by the New Moon.

Emotion

The most basic feelings that we experience include not only motives such as hunger and sex but also emotions such as joy and anger. Emotions and motives are closely related. Emotions can activate and direct behavior in the same way that basic motives do. Emotions may also accompany motivated behavior: sex, for example, is not only a powerful motive but a potential source of joy, as well.

Despite their similarities, motives and emotions need to be distinguished. One common distinction is that emotions are triggered from the outside, while motives are activated from within. That is, emotions are usually aroused by external events, and emotional reactions are directed toward these events; motives, in contrast, are often aroused by internal events (a homeostatic imbalance, for example) and are naturally directed toward particular objects in the environment (such as food, water, or a mate). Another distinction between motives and emotions is that a motive is usually elicited by a specific need, whereas an emotion can be elicited by a wide variety of stimuli. These distinctions are not absolute. An external source can sometimes trigger a motive, as when the sight of food triggers hunger. And the discomfort caused by a homeostatic imbalance—severe hunger, for example—can arouse emotions. Nevertheless, emotions and motives are sufficiently different in their sources of activation, subjective experience, and effects on behavior that they merit separate treatment.

COMPONENTS OF AN EMOTION

An intense emotion includes several components. One component is bodily reaction. When angered, for example, you may sometimes tremble or raise your voice, even though you don't want to. Another component is the collection of thoughts and beliefs that accompany the emotion. Experiencing joy, for example, often involves thinking about the reasons for the joy ("I did it—I'm accepted into college!"). A third component of an emotional experience is facial expression. When you experience disgust, for example, you probably frown, often with your mouth open wide and your eyelids partially closed. Finally, a fourth component concerns your reactions to the experience. These include specific reactions—anger may lead you to aggression, for instance—and more global ones—a negative emotion may darken your outlook on the world.

Thus, our final list of the components of an emotion includes:

1. Internal bodily responses, particularly those involving the autonomic nervous system
2. Belief or cognitive appraisal that a particular positive or negative state of affairs is occurring
3. Facial expression
4. Reactions to the emotion

The critical questions in the study of emotion concern the relations between these components and the subjective experience of an emotion.

Facial expression is a component of emotion.

One set of questions concerns how autonomic responses, beliefs and cognitions, and facial expressions contribute to the intensity of an experienced emotion. Do you feel angrier, for example, when you experience more autonomic arousal? Indeed, could you even feel angry if you had no autonomic arousal? Similarly, does the intensity of your anger depend on your having a certain kind of thought, or a certain kind of facial expression? In contrast to these questions about the intensity of an emotion, there are also questions about which components of an emotion are responsible for making the different emotions *feel* different. Which components *differentiate* the emotions? To appreciate the difference between questions about intensity and questions about differentiation, note that it is possible that autonomic arousal greatly increases the intensity of our emotions, but that the pattern of arousal is roughly the same for several emotions; if this were the case, autonomic arousal could not differentiate between emotions.

These questions will guide us as we consider in turn autonomic arousal, cognitive appraisal, and facial expression. We will then turn our attention to general reactions of an emotional experience. In the final part of the chapter, we will focus on a specific reaction to an emotion, and consider in detail the topic of aggression. We will be concerned throughout primarily with the more intense affective states, although the ideas and principles that will emerge in our discussion are relevant to a variety of feelings.

AROUSAL AND EMOTION

Physiological Basis

When we experience an intense emotion, such as fear or anger, we may be aware of a number of bodily changes—including rapid heartbeat and breathing, dryness of the throat and mouth, increased muscle tension, perspiration, trembling of the extremities, and a sinking feeling in the stomach (see Table 11-1). Most of the physiological changes that take place during emotional arousal result from activation of the *sympathetic division* of the autonomic nervous system as it prepares the body for emergency action (see Chapter 2). The sympathetic system is responsible for the following changes (all of which need not occur at once):

1. Blood pressure and heart rate increase.
2. Respiration becomes more rapid.
3. The pupils dilate.
4. Perspiration increases while secretion of saliva and mucous decreases.
5. Blood-sugar level increases to provide more energy.
6. The blood clots more quickly in case of wounds.
7. Motility of the gastrointestinal tract decreases; blood is diverted from the stomach and intestines to the brain and skeletal muscles.
8. The hairs on the skin become erect, causing goose pimples.

The sympathetic system gears the organism for energy output. As the emotion subsides, the *parasympathetic system*—the energy-conserving system—takes over and returns the organism to its normal state.

TABLE 11-1
Symptoms of Fear in Combat Flying
Based on reports of combat pilots during World War II. (After Shaffer, 1947)

DURING COMBAT MISSIONS DID YOU FEEL...?	OFTEN	SOMETIMES	TOTAL
A pounding heart and rapid pulse	30%	56%	86%
That your muscles were very tense	30	53	83
Easily irritated or angry	22	58	80
Dryness of the throat or mouth	30	50	80
Nervous perspiration or cold sweat	26	53	79
Butterflies in the stomach	23	53	76
A sense of unreality—that this could not be happening to you	20	49	69
A need to urinate very frequently	25	40	65
Trembling	11	53	64
Confused or rattled	3	50	53
Weak or faint	4	37	41
That right after a mission you were unable to remember the details of what had happened	5	34	39
Sick to the stomach	5	33	38
Unable to concentrate	3	32	35
That you had wet or soiled your pants	1	4	5

These activities of the autonomic nervous system are themselves triggered by activity in certain critical regions of the brain, including the *hypothalamus* (which, as we saw in the last chapter, plays a major role in many biological motives) and parts of the *limbic system*. Impulses from these areas are transmitted to nuclei in the brain stem that control the functioning of the autonomic nervous system. The autonomic nervous system then acts directly on the muscles and internal organs to initiate some of the bodily changes previously described and acts indirectly by stimulating the adrenal hormones to produce other bodily changes. Additional hormones that play a crucial role in an individual's reaction to stress are secreted by the pituitary gland on direct signal from the hypothalamus.

Note that the kind of heightened physiological arousal we have described is characteristic of emotional states such as anger and fear, during which the organism must prepare for action—for example, to fight or flee. (The role of this fight-or-flight response in threatening or stressful situations is elaborated in Chapter 15.) Some of the same responses may also occur during joyful excitement or sexual arousal. During emotions such as sorrow or grief, however, some bodily processes may be depressed, or slowed down.

Intensity of Emotions

What is the relation between heightened physiological arousal and the subjective experience of an emotion? To answer this question, researchers

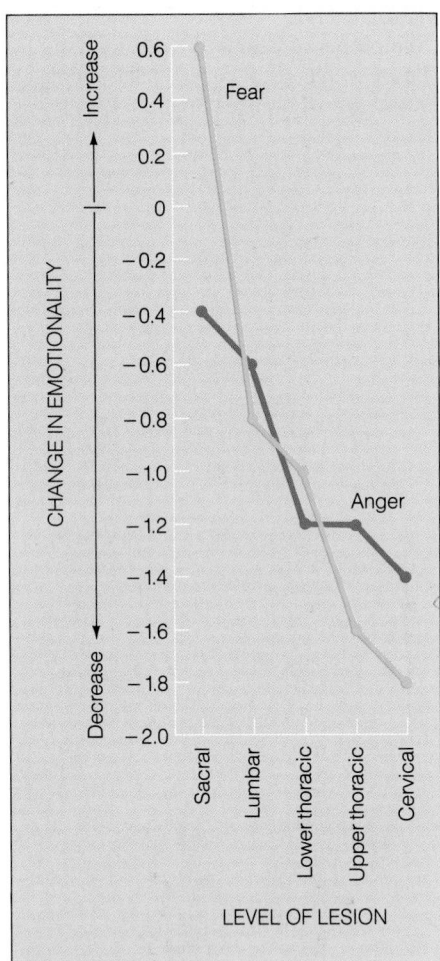

FIGURE 11-1
Relationship Between Spinal Cord Lesions and Emotionality *Subjects with spinal cord lesions compared the intensity of their emotional experiences before and after injury. Their reports were coded according to the degree of change: 0 indicates no change; a mild change ("I feel it less, I guess") is scored −1 for a decrease or +1 for an increase; and a strong change ("I feel it a helluva lot less") is scored −2 or +2. Note that the higher the lesion, the greater the decrease in emotionality following injury.* (After Schachter, 1964; Hohmann, 1962)

have studied the emotional life of individuals with spinal cord injuries. When the spinal cord is severed or lesioned, sensations below the point of injury cannot reach the brain. Since some of these sensations arise from the sympathetic nervous system, the injuries reduce the contributions of autonomic arousal to felt emotion. In one study, army veterans with spinal cord injuries were divided into five groups, according to the location on the spinal cord at which the lesion occurred. In one group, the lesions were near the neck (at the cervical level), with no innervation of the sympathetic system. In another group, the lesions were near the base of the spine (at the sacral level), with at least partial innervation of the sympathetic nerves. The other three groups fell between these two extremes. The five groups represented a continuum of bodily sensation: the higher the lesion on the spinal cord, the less the feedback of the autonomic nervous system to the brain.

The subjects were interviewed to determine their feelings in situations of fear, anger, grief, and sexual excitement. Each person was asked to recall an emotion-arousing incident prior to the injury and a comparable incident following the injury, and to compare the intensity of emotional experience in each case. The data for states of fear and anger are shown in Figure 11-1. The higher the person's lesion was on the spinal cord (that is, the less the feedback from the autonomic nervous system), the more his emotionality decreased following injury. The same relation was true for states of sexual excitement and grief. A reduction in autonomic arousal resulted in a reduction in the intensity of experienced emotion.

Comments by patients with the highest spinal cord lesions suggested that they could *react* emotionally to arousing situations, but that they did not really *feel* emotional. For example, "It's sort of a cold anger. Sometimes I act angry when I see some injustice. I yell and cuss and raise hell, because if you don't do it sometimes, I've learned people will take advantage of you; but it doesn't have the heat to it that it used to. It's a mental kind of anger." Or, "I say I am afraid, like when I'm going into a real stiff exam at school, but I don't really feel afraid, not all tense and shaky with the hollow feeling in my stomach, like I used to."

The preceding study is important, but it is not entirely objective—the emotional situations varied from person to person, and subjects rated their own experiences. A follow-up study provides a more objective situation: all subjects were exposed to the same situations, and their emotional experiences were rated by independent judges. Male subjects with spinal cord injuries were presented with pictures of clothed and nude females and were told to imagine that they were alone with each woman. Subjects reported their "thoughts and feelings," which then were rated by judges for expressed emotion. Patients who had higher lesions reported less sexual excitement than those whose lesions were lower on their spines (Jasmos & Hakmiller, 1975).

Differentiation of Emotions

Clearly, autonomic arousal contributes to the intensity of emotional experience. But does it differentiate the emotions? Is there one pattern of physiological activity for joy, another for anger, still another for fear, and so on? This question dates back to a seminal paper that William James wrote over a century ago (James, 1884), in which he proposed that the perception of bodily changes *is* the subjective experience of an emotion: "We are afraid because we run"; "we are angry because we strike." The Danish physiologist

Carl Lange arrived at a similar position at about the same time, but for him the bodily changes included autonomic arousal. Their combined position is referred to as the *James-Lange theory*, and it argues as follows: because the perception of autonomic arousal (and perhaps of other bodily changes) constitutes the experience of an emotion, and because different emotions feel different, there must be a distinct pattern of autonomic activity for each emotion. The James-Lange theory therefore holds that autonomic arousal differentiates the emotions.

The theory came under severe attack in the 1920s by the physiologist Walter Cannon (1927), who offered three major criticisms:

1. Since the internal organs are relatively insensitive structures and not well supplied with nerves, internal changes occur too slowly to be a source of emotional feeling.

2. Artificially inducing the bodily changes associated with an emotion—for example, injecting a drug such as epinephrine—does not produce the experience of a true emotion.

3. The pattern of autonomic arousal does not seem to differ much from one emotional state to another; for example, while anger makes our heart beat faster, so does the sight of a loved one.

The third argument, then, explicitly denies that autonomic arousal can differentiate the emotions.

Psychologists have pursued Cannon's third point while developing increasingly more accurate measures of the components of autonomic arousal. Although a few experiments in the 1950s reported distinct physiological patterns for different emotions (Ax, 1953; Funkenstein, 1955), until recently most studies on this topic had found little evidence for different patterns of arousal being associated with different emotions. A study by Ekman and his collaborators (1983), however, provides strong evidence that there are autonomic patterns distinct to different emotions. Subjects produced emotional expressions for each of six emotions—surprise, disgust, sadness, anger, fear, and happiness—by following instructions about which particular facial muscles to contract (most of the subjects were actors, and they were aided in their task by a mirror and coaching). While they held an emotional expression for 10 seconds, the researchers measured their heart rate, skin temperature, and other indicators of autonomic arousal. A number of these measures revealed differences between the emotions (see Figure 11-2). Heart rate was faster for the negative emotions of anger, fear, and sadness than it was for happiness, surprise, and disgust; and the former three emotions themselves could be partially distinguished by the fact that skin temperature was higher in anger than in fear or sadness. Thus, even though both anger and the sight of a loved one make our heart beat faster, only anger makes it beat *much* faster; and though anger and fear have much in common, anger is hot and fear cold (no wonder people describe their anger as their "blood boiling," and their fear as "bone-chilling" or as "getting cold feet").

These results are important, but by no means do they provide unequivocal evidence for the James-Lange theory or the claim that autonomic arousal is the *only* component that differentiates the emotions. All the Ekman study demonstrated was that there are some physiological differences between emotions, not that these differences are perceived and experienced as *the* qualitative differences between the emotions. Even if autonomic arousal does help differentiate some emotions, it is unlikely that it differentiates *all* emotions; the difference between contentment and pride, for example, is

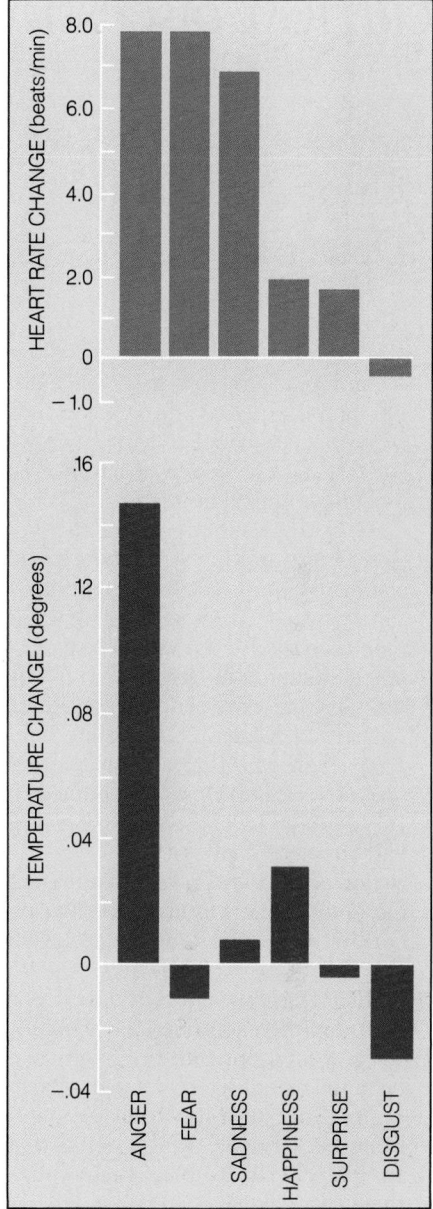

FIGURE 11-2
Arousal Differences for Different Emotions *Changes in heart rate (upper graph) and right finger temperature (lower graph). For heart rate, the changes associated with anger, fear, and sadness were all significantly greater than those for happiness, surprise, and disgust. For finger temperature, the change associated with anger was significantly different from that for all other emotions. (After Ekman, Levenson, & Frieson, 1983)*

CRITICAL DISCUSSION

Using Arousal to Detect Lies

If autonomic arousal is part of an emotion and if experiencing an emotion is a likely consequence of lying, then we can use the presence of autonomic arousal to infer that a person is lying. This is the theory behind the *lie-detector* test, in which a machine called a *polygraph* (meaning "many writings") simultaneously measures several physiological responses known to be part of autonomic arousal (see Figure 1). The measures most frequently recorded are changes in heart rate, blood pressure, respiration, and the galvanic skin response or GSR (a change in the electrical conductivity of the skin that occurs with emotional arousal).

In operating a polygraph, the standard procedure is to make the first recording while the subject is relaxed; this recording serves as a *baseline* for evaluating subsequent responses. The examiner then asks a series of carefully worded questions that the subject has been instructed to answer with a "yes" or "no" response. Some of the questions are "critical," which means that the guilty are likely to lie in response to them (for example, "Did you rob Bert's Cleaners on December 11?"). Other questions are "controls"; even innocent people are somewhat likely to lie in response to these questions (for example, "Have you ever taken something that didn't belong to you?"). Yet other questions are "neutral" (for example, "Do you live in San Diego?"). Critical questions are interspersed among control and neutral ones; sufficient time is allowed between questions for the polygraph measures to return to normal. Presumably, only the guilty should show greater physiological responses to the critical questions than to the others.

However, the use of the polygraph in detecting lies is far from foolproof. A response to a question may show that a subject is aroused but not *why* he or she is aroused. An innocent subject may be very tense or may react emotionally to certain words in the questions and therefore appear to be lying when telling the truth. On the other hand, a practiced liar may show little arousal when lying. And a knowledgeable subject may be able to "beat" the machine by thinking about something exciting or by tensing muscles during neutral questions, thereby creating a baseline comparable to reactions to the critical questions. The recording in Figure 1 shows the responses to an actual lie and a simulated lie. In this experiment, the subject picked a number and then tried to conceal its identity from the examiner. The number was 27, and a marked change in heart rate and GSR can be seen when the subject denies number 27. The subject simulates lying to number 22 by tensing his toes, producing noticeable reactions in heart rate and GSR.

Because of these and other problems, most state and federal courts will not admit polygraph tests; the courts that do generally require that both sides agree to its introduction. Such tests are frequently used, however, in preliminary criminal investigations and by employers interviewing prospective personnel for trusted positions.

Representatives of the American Polygraph Association have claimed an accuracy rate of 90 percent or better for polygraph tests conducted by a skilled operator. Critics, however, consider the accuracy rate to be much lower. For example, Lykken (1984) claims that in studies involving real-life situations, the lie-detector test is correct only about 65 percent of the time, and an innocent person has a 50-50 chance of failing the test. He argues that the polygraph detects not only the arousal that accompanies

FIGURE 1
Polygraph *The arm cuff measures blood pressure and heart rate, the pneumograph around the rib cage measures rate of breathing, and the finger electrodes measure GSR. The recording on the right shows the physiological responses of a subject as he lies and as he simulates lying. The respiratory trace (top line) shows that he held his breath as he prepared for the first simulation. He was able to produce sizable changes in heart rate and GSR at the second simulation.* (After Kubis, 1962)

lying but also the stress that an honest person experiences when strapped to the equipment. Also, guilty people who are less socialized may be less aroused while lying, and consequently harder to detect (Saxe, Dougherty, & Cross, 1985). Nevertheless, many businesses believe that the benefits of these tests outweigh the risks, and the use of polygraph tests is increasing in private industry. Their use in law enforcement is also increasing. The FBI, for example, administers several thousand polygraph tests per year, mostly to follow up leads and to verify specific facts—areas in which, experts agree,

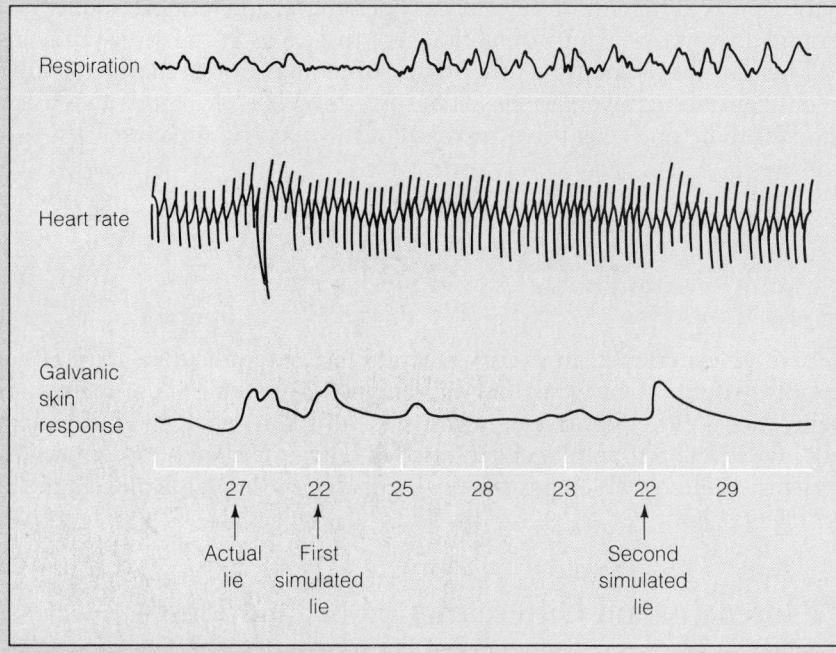

Respiration

Heart rate

Galvanic
skin
response

27   22   25   28   23   22   29

↑   ↑   ↑
Actual First   Second
lie   simulated   simulated
      lie   lie

a speaker is under stress, the tremors are suppressed (see the right-hand graph in Figure 2).

The voice-stress analyzer is used in lie detection in essentially the same way as a polygraph; neutral questions are interspersed with critical questions, and recordings of the subject's responses to both are compared. If answers to the critical questions produce the relaxed wave form, the person is probably telling the truth (as far as we know, vocal cord tremors cannot be controlled voluntarily). A stressed wave form, on the other hand, indicates only that the individual is tense or anxious, not necessarily that he or she is lying.

There are, however, two serious problems with the use of the voice-stress analyzer in detecting lies. First, since the analyzer can work over the telephone, from radio or television messages, or from tape recordings, there is potential for the unethical use of this instrument. The second concern is the accuracy of the voice-stress analyzer. Some investigators claim that it is as accurate as the polygraph in distinguishing between the guilty and the innocent; others claim that it is no more accurate than chance. Much more research is required to determine the relationship between voice changes and other physiological measures of emotion (Rice, 1978; Lykken, 1980).

the polygraph is more useful. In criminal and private cases, anyone has the legal right to refuse a polygraph test. However, this is hardly a safeguard for someone whose refusal, for whatever reason, may endanger a career or job opportunity.

Another type of lie detector measures changes in a person's voice that are undetectable to the human ear. All muscles, including those controlling the vocal cords, vibrate slightly when

in use. This tremor, which is transmitted to the vocal cords, is suppressed by activity of the autonomic nervous system when a speaker is under stress. When a tape recording of a person's voice is played through a device called a *voice-stress analyzer*, a visual representation of the voice can be produced on a strip of graph paper. The tremors of the vocal cords in the voice of a relaxed speaker resemble a series of waves (see the left-hand graph in Figure 2). When

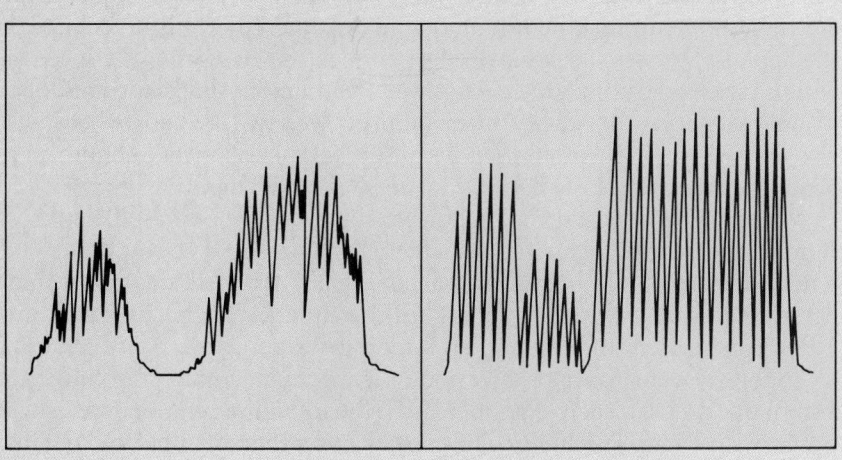

FIGURE 2
Effects of Stress on Voice Patterns
A voice-stress analyzer produces graphic records of speech. The voice printout for a relaxed speaker resembles a series of waves, such as those shown on the left. The waves are produced by tiny tremors of the vocal cords. Under stress, the tremors are suppressed, producing a printout similar to that shown on the right. (After Holden, 1975)

unlikely to be found in visceral reactions. Also, the first two points that Cannon raised against the James-Lange theory still stand: autonomic arousal is too slow to differentiate emotional experiences, and artificial induction of arousal does not yield a true emotion. For these reasons, many psychologists still believe that something other than autonomic arousal must be involved in differentiating the emotions. That something else (or part of it) is usually thought to be one's cognitive appraisal of the eliciting situation.

COGNITION AND EMOTION

When we experience an event or action, we interpret the situation with respect to our personal goals and well-being; the outcome of the appraisal is a belief that is either positive or negative ("I won the match and I feel happy" or "I failed the test and I feel depressed"). This interpretation is known as a *cognitive appraisal*, which has two distinct parts: the appraisal process and the resulting belief.

Intensity and Differentiation of Emotions

Clearly, our appraisal of a situation can contribute to our emotional experience. If we are in a car that starts to roll down a steep incline, we experience fear, if not terror; but if we know the car is part of a roller coaster, the fear is usually much less. If we are told by someone that he or she cannot stand the sight of us, we may feel very angry or hurt if that person is a friend, but feel barely perturbed if the person is a mental patient whom we have never met before. If we watch a film of African tribesmen making an incision in a young boy's body, we may feel outrage if we believe the men are torturing the boy but feel relatively detached if we believe the men are performing a rites-of-passage ritual. In these cases, and countless others, our cognitive appraisal of the situation determines the intensity of our emotional experience (Lazarus, Kanner, & Folkman, 1980).

Cognitive appraisal may also be heavily responsible for differentiating the emotions. Unlike autonomic arousal, the beliefs resulting from appraisal are rich enough to distinguish among many different kinds of feelings, and the appraisal process itself may be fast enough to account for the speed with which some emotions arise. Also, we often emphasize emotional beliefs when we describe the quality of an emotion. We say, "I felt angry because she was unfair" or "I felt frightened because I was abandoned"; unfairness and abandonment are clearly beliefs that result from a cognitive process.

Observations suggest that cognitive appraisals are often sufficient to determine the quality of experience. That is, if people could be induced to be in a neutral state of autonomic arousal, the quality of their emotion would be determined solely by their appraisal of the situation. Schachter and Singer (1962) first tested this claim in an important experiment.

Subjects were given an injection of epinephrine, which typically causes autonomic arousal, such as an increase in heart and respiration rates, muscle tremors, and a jittery feeling. The experimenter then manipulated the information that the subjects were given regarding the effects of epinephrine. Some subjects were correctly informed about the arousal consequences of the drug (heart-rate acceleration, muscle tremors, and so on); other subjects

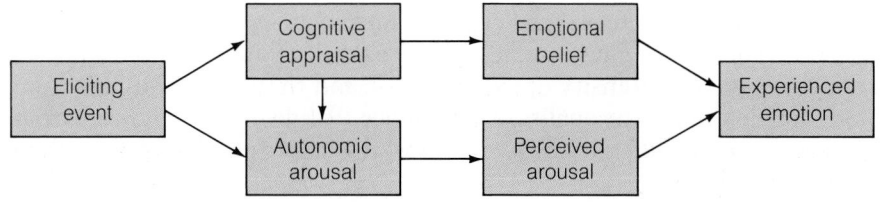

FIGURE 11-3
Components of an Emotional
Experience: 1 *The beliefs resulting from*
a cognitive appraisal and the perception
of autonomic arousal both contribute to
the experience of an emotion. (After
Reisenzein, 1983)

were misinformed about the drug and told it would produce feelings of numbness. The *informed* subjects had an explanation of their arousal; the *misinformed* subjects did not. How the misinformed subjects interpreted their symptoms depended on the situation they were placed in. Subjects were left in a waiting room with another person, ostensibly another subject but actually a confederate of the experimenter, who created either a happy situation (by making paper airplanes, playing basketball with wads of paper, and so on), or an angry situation (by complaining about the experiment, tearing up a questionnaire, and so on). Misinformed subjects who were placed in a happy situation rated their feelings as relatively happy, whereas misinformed subjects placed in an angry situation rated their feelings as relatively angry. Although the autonomic arousal was the same in the two situations (they all experienced rapid heart rate, muscle tremors, and so on), the emotions experienced by misinformed subjects were not; their emotions were determined by their appraisals of the situation. In contrast, the informed subjects' feelings were unaffected by whether they were placed in a happy or angry situation; they already had an explanation of their arousal, and they did not need to rely on an appraisal of the situation.

However, while the autonomic arousal may have been the same in the happy and angry situations, apparently it was not neutral. Follow-up experiments to the Schachter and Singer study have found that subjects rate their experiences more negatively (less happy, or more angry) than the situation warrants, suggesting that the physiological arousal produced by epinephrine is experienced as somewhat unpleasant. Also, these follow-up experiments have sometimes had difficulty reproducing the Schachter and Singer results (Maslach, 1979; Marshall & Zimbardo, 1979). Hence, we still need a demonstration that completely neutral arousal may be misattributed. A subsequent study supplied this demonstration. Subjects first engaged in strenuous physical exercise and then participated in a task where they were provoked by a confederate of the experimenter. The exercise induced physiological arousal that was neutral and that persisted until the subject was provoked; this arousal should have combined with any that was elicited by the provocation, thereby resulting in a more intense experience of anger. In fact, subjects who exercised responded more aggressively to the provocation than subjects who did not (Zillman & Bryant, 1974).

The conclusions that emerge from this line of research are depicted in Figure 11-3. In an emotional situation, an eliciting event typically results in both autonomic arousal and cognitive appraisal; the arousal and appraisal lead, respectively, to *perceived* arousal and an emotional belief, which then determine the experienced emotion. (The perceived arousal and emotional belief are not experienced as independent; rather, the arousal is *attributed* to the belief—"My heart is racing *because* I'm so angry.") Usually, the same eliciting event is responsible for both the arousal and the appraisal. In the studies just reviewed, however, the experimenters arranged the situation so that arousal and appraisal had different sources (for example, injection versus

TABLE 11-2
Primary Emotions and Their Causes
Eight primary emotions and their associated situations. (After Plutchik, 1980)

EMOTION	SITUATION
Grief (Sorrow)	Loss of loved one
Fear	Threat
Anger	Obstacle
Joy	Potential mate
Trust	Group member
Disgust	Gruesome object
Anticipation	New territory
Surprise	Sudden novel object

TABLE 11-3
Primary Situation Aspects and Their Consequences *Combinations of two situational aspects and their associated emotions.* (After Roseman, 1979; 1984)

SITUATION	EMOTION
Desirable and occurs	Joy
Desirable and doesn't occur	Sorrow
Undesirable and occurs	Distress
Undesirable and doesn't occur	Relief

situation), thereby allowing the experimenter to analyze separately the role of each component. These studies indicate that both arousal and appraisal contribute to the intensity of experience—and that sometimes appraisal alone can determine the quality of experience. While research indicates that arousal may aid in differentiating emotions, it seems to play less of a role than does appraisal.

Contents of Cognitive Appraisal

We have emphasized that people's appraisal of a situation can determine their emotions, but thus far have had little to say about which aspects or dimensions of a situation determine which emotions occur.

Psychologists have taken two different approaches to this problem. One approach assumes that there is a relatively small set of "primary" emotions and associates each emotion with a fundamental life situation. Table 11-2 lists several emotions (such as fear) and their respective triggering situations (threat). These primary emotions can be found in every human culture and throughout the animal kingdom. Their universality provides a reason for singling out these emotions as primary and for describing the situations in terms that are appropriate even for lower species.

The other approach to specifying the situational aspects of emotion emphasizes cognitive processes and, consequently, may be more appropriate for humans than for lower species. Instead of starting with a primary set of emotions, this approach begins with a primary set of situational aspects or dimensions that a person attends to. The theory then associates various combinations of these dimensions with specific emotions. An example is given in Table 11-3. One dimension of a situation is the desirability of an anticipated event, and another is whether or not the event occurs. When we combine these two dimensions, we get four possible situations (the left-hand side of Table 11-3), each of which seems to produce a distinct emotion. (We are using only four emotions in our example just to keep the explanation simple.) When a desired event occurs, we experience *joy*; when a desired event does not occur, we experience *sorrow*; when an undesired event occurs, we experience *distress*; and when an undesired event does not occur, we experience *relief*. To illustrate, if a young woman marries an attractive young man who is known to have a drinking problem, she may feel mainly joy, her rival sorrow, her parents distress, and his parents relief.

The preceding example invokes only two dimensions, but most theories of cognitive appraisal assume that multiple dimensions are involved. For example, Smith and Ellsworth (1985; 1987) found that at least six dimensions were needed to describe 15 different emotions (including, for example, anger, guilt, and sadness). These dimensions included: a) the desirability of the situation (pleasant or unpleasant); b) the effort that one anticipates spending on the situation; c) the certainty of the situation; d) the attention that one wants to devote to the situation; e) the control that one feels over the situation; and f) the control that one attributes to nonhuman forces in the situation. To illustrate how the last two dimensions operate, anger is associated with an unpleasant situation caused by another person, guilt is associated with an unpleasant situation brought about by one's self, and sadness is associated with an unpleasant situation controlled by circumstances. The virtue of this kind of approach is that it specifies the appraisal process in detail and accounts for a wide range of emotional experiences.

The sensation of joy may be the same whether we are 3 or 30 years of age.

Some Clinical Implications

The fact that cognitive appraisals can differentiate emotions helps make sense of a puzzling clinical observation. Clinicians report that sometimes a patient appears to be experiencing an emotion but is not conscious of it. That is, the patient has no subjective experience of the emotion, yet reacts in a manner consistent with the emotion—for example, though the patient may not feel angry, he acts in a hostile manner. Also, at a later point he may experience the emotion and agree that in some sense he must have been having it earlier. Freud (1915) thought that this phenomenon involved the repression of painful ideas, and modern work on appraisal and emotion is compatible with his hypothesis. Because the belief about a situation usually gives the emotion its quality, preventing that belief from entering consciousness (repression) prevents one from experiencing the quality of the emotion.

Another point of contact between clinical analysis and experimental research concerns emotional development. Clinical work suggests that a person's sensations of pleasure and distress change very little as he or she develops from child to adult; what does develop, however, are the ideas associated with the sensations (Brenner, 1980). Thus, the sensation of joy may be the same when we are 3 or 30, but what makes us joyous is very different. This developmental pattern fits perfectly with the facts that we have reviewed about emotion. Sensations of pleasure and distress are probably due to feedback from autonomic arousal, and the nature of this arousal may not change over the life span. In contrast, ideas associated with the sensations are simply emotional beliefs, and they should show the same kind of development as other aspects of cognition.

Finally, the work on appraisal fits with a phenomenon that is familiar not just to clinicians but to all of us: the extent to which a situation elicits an emotion depends on our past experience. When confronted with an overly critical employer, some people will be annoyed while others will be enraged. Why the difference? Presumably because of differences in past experience: perhaps those who are enraged suffered a hypercritical authority figure in the past, while those who are only annoyed had no such experience. A possible link between past experience and current emotion is the appraisal process; that is, our past experience affects our beliefs about the current situation, and these beliefs then influence the emotion we experience. (Another possible link between past experience and current emotion is classical conditioning, which we will consider next.)

Emotion without Cognition

Although cognitive appraisal is clearly important for experiencing an emotion, it is worth noting that there are cases of emotion in which no cognitive appraisal seems to be involved. When a rat receives an electric shock for the first time, for example, presumably it has little to think about, and its emotional reaction is devoid of cognitive activity. Similarly, if you are suddenly punched in the nose, you may experience an emotion before you interpret the event. In addition to such one-shot experiences, there are recurrent situations in which emotional experience may bypass the cognitive system. In particular, some fear experiences that were acquired in childhood by classical conditioning may not involve any cognitive appraisal. For example, if painful sessions with a doctor were reliably preceded by being in a waiting room, the person may experience substantial fear when in a waiting room even as an adult; in this case, the adult experience is not the result of an interpretation of a situation with respect to present goals (Zajonc, 1980; 1984).

There is also some experimental evidence that directly shows emotion can be independent of cognition. The experiment of interest (which was mentioned in Chapter 5) took as its starting point the well-known finding that the more often one is exposed to a particular stimulus, the more one likes it. In the first part of the experiment, subjects were presented 10 geometric forms one at a time. The forms were presented many times, but the presentation of each was so brief (1 millisecond) that subjects reported they were unable to see the forms. In the second part of the experiment, on each trial subjects were presented a pair of geometric forms, an old one from the first part and a new one. For each pair, subjects had to answer two questions: a) which of the two had previously been presented? (a cognitive decision) and b) which of the two they liked better? (an emotional decision). Subjects' cognitive decisions were at chance: they were completely unable to tell the old forms from the new ones. Subjects' emotional decisions, however, consistently favored the forms that had been presented earlier. Apparently, the brief presentations of the forms in the first part had not left enough residue to influence cognitive processes, but had left enough to alter emotional processes. This is striking evidence that emotional reactions can be independent of cognitive processes (Kunst-Wilson & Zajonc, 1980; Seamon, Brody, & Kauff, 1983).

How can we reconcile the above results with the earlier evidence that cognitive appraisal influences the intensity and quality of an emotion? One resolution is that we can have emotional experiences without cognitive appraisal, but such experiences are restricted to undifferentiated positive or negative feelings. In more complex emotional experiences, such as pride, disappointment, jealousy, or contempt, cognitive appraisal must play a role. Thus, not all emotional experiences are characterized by the same principles. For many subjective feelings, cognitive appraisal is a necessary ingredient, but for others it is not (Zajonc, Murphy, & Inglehart, 1989).

EXPRESSION AND EMOTION

The facial expression that accompanies an emotion clearly serves to communicate that emotion. Since the publication of Charles Darwin's 1872 classic, *The Expression of Emotion in Man and Animals*, psychologists have regarded the communication of emotion as an important function, one with survival value for the species. Thus, looking frightened may warn others that danger is present, and perceiving that someone is angry tells us that he or she may be about to act aggressively. More recent work goes beyond the Darwinian tradition, suggesting that, in addition to their communicative function, emotional expressions contribute to the subjective experience of emotion, just as arousal and appraisal do.

Emotional expression in the mandrill monkey.

Communication of Emotional Expressions

Certain facial expressions seem to have a universal meaning, regardless of the culture in which an individual is raised. The universal expression of anger, for example, involves a flushed face, brows lowered and drawn together, flared nostrils, a clenched jaw, and bared teeth. When people from five different countries (the United States, Brazil, Chile, Argentina, and Japan) viewed photographs showing facial expressions of happiness, anger, sadness, disgust, fear, and surprise, they had little difficulty in identifying the emotion that each expression conveyed. Even members of remote, preliterate tribes that had had virtually no contact with Western cultures (the Fore and Dani tribes in New Guinea) were able to identify the facial expressions correctly. Likewise, American college students who viewed videotapes of emotions expressed by Fore natives identified the emotions accurately, although they sometimes confused fear and surprise (Ekman, 1982).

The universality of certain emotional expressions supports Darwin's claim that they are innate responses with an evolutionary history. According to Darwin, many of the ways in which we express emotion are inherited patterns that originally had some survival value. For example, the expression of disgust or rejection is based on the organism's attempt to rid itself of something unpleasant that it has ingested. To quote Darwin (1872),

> The term "disgust," in its simplest sense, means something offensive to the taste. But as disgust also causes annoyance, it is generally accompanied by a frown, and often by gestures as if to push away or to guard oneself against the offensive object. Extreme disgust is expressed by movements around the mouth identical with those preparatory to the act of vomiting. The mouth is opened widely, with the upper lip strongly retracted. The partial closure of the eyelids, or the turning away of the eyes or of the whole body, are likewise highly expressive of disdain. These actions seem to declare that the despised person is not worth looking at, or is disagreeable to behold. Spitting seems an almost universal sign of contempt or disgust; and spitting obviously represents the rejection of anything offensive from the mouth.

While some facial expressions and gestures seem to be innately associated with particular emotions, others are learned from culture. One psychologist reviewed Chinese novels to determine how Chinese writers portray various human emotions. Many of the bodily changes in emotion (flushing, paling, cold perspiration, trembling, goose pimples) represent the same symptoms of emotion in Chinese fiction as they do in western writing.

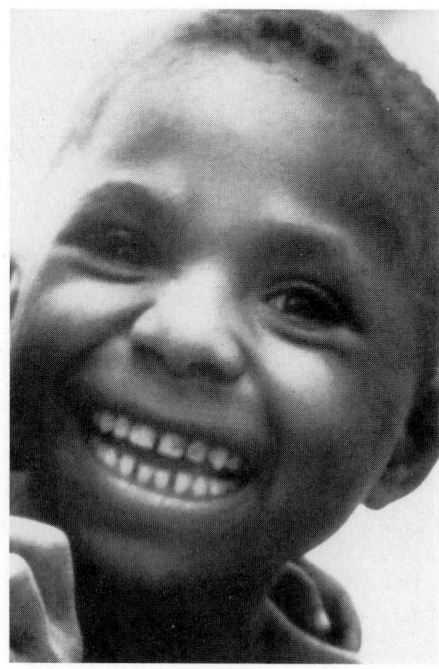

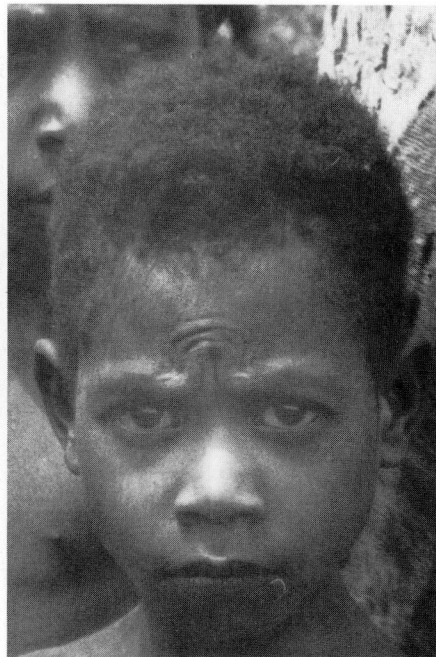

Facial expressions are universal in the emotions they convey. Photographs of people from New Guinea and from the United States demonstrate that emotions are conveyed by the same facial expressions. From left to right are happiness, sadness, and disgust.

However, the Chinese have other, quite different ways of expressing emotion. The following quotations from Chinese novels would surely be misinterpreted by an American reader unfamiliar with the culture (Klineberg, 1938).

"They stretched out their tongues."
(They showed signs of surprise.)

"He clapped his hands."
(He was worried or disappointed.)

"He scratched his ears and cheeks."
(He was happy.)

"Her eyes grew round and opened wide."
(She became angry.)

Thus, superimposed on the basic expressions of emotion, which appear to be universal, are conventional forms of expressions—a kind of language of emotion recognized by others within a culture. Skilled actors are able to convey to their audiences an intended emotion by using facial expressions, tones of voice, and gestures in patterns that the audience will recognize. In simulating emotion, those of us who are less skilled actors can convey our intent by exaggerating the conventional expressions: gritting our teeth and clenching our fists to indicate anger, raising our eyebrows to express doubt or disapproval, and so on.

Brain Localization

The emotional expressions that are universal (for example, those associated with joy, anger, and disgust) are also highly specific: particular muscles

  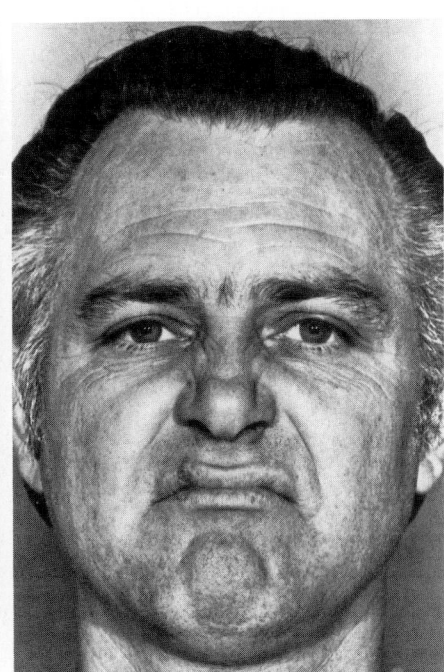

are used to express particular emotions. This combination of universality and specificity suggests that a specialized neurological system may have evolved in humans to interpret the primitive emotional expressions, and recent evidence indicates that this system is localized in the right cerebral hemisphere.

One source of evidence comes from studies in which pictures of emotional expressions are presented to either the left side or the right side of the subject's visual field. (Recall from Chapter 2 that a stimulus presented to the left visual field projects to the right hemisphere, and a stimulus presented to the right visual field projects to the left hemisphere.) When subjects have to decide which of two emotions the picture manifests, they are faster and more accurate when the picture is presented to their left visual field—that is, when it is projected to their right hemisphere. In addition, when the two halves of the face convey different emotions (one half may be smiling while the other half is frowning), the expression presented to the left visual field has the most impact on the subject's decision. Another source of evidence about the localization of emotional expressions comes from studies of patients who have suffered brain damage from strokes or accidents. Patients who have only right-hemisphere damage have more difficulty recognizing facial expressions of emotion than do patients who have only left-hemisphere damage (Etcoff, 1985).

Our system for recognizing emotional expressions seems to be highly specialized. In particular, it is distinct from our ability to recognize faces. Consider a *prosopagnosic*, a person who has such extreme difficulty recognizing familiar faces that he (or she) sometimes fails to recognize his own face! He can, however, recognize emotional expressions: he can tell you that a particular person is happy even when he does not know that the person is his wife (Bruyer et al., 1983). The abilities to recognize faces and to recognize emotions also are differentially affected by electrical stimulation of various regions of the right hemisphere: face recognition is disrupted by stimulation in the parieto-occipital region, whereas emotion recognition is disrupted by stimulation of the middle temporal gyrus (Fried et al., 1982).

Emotions, in addition to being communicated by facial expressions, are also expressed by variations in voice patterns (particularly variations in pitch, timing, and stress). Some of these variations appear to be universal and specific: a sharp increase in pitch indicates fear, for example. The specialized neurological system for perceiving these emotional clues is located in the right cerebral hemisphere, and the evidence for this is similar to that for facial expressions. If an emotional voice is presented to either the left or right ear (which project to the right and left hemispheres, respectively), subjects are more accurate in identifying the emotion when the sound is presented to the left ear. And patients who have solely right-hemisphere damage have more trouble identifying emotions from voice clues than do patients who have solely left-hemisphere damage (Ley & Bryden, 1982).

Intensity and Differentiation of Emotions

The idea that facial expressions, in addition to their communicative function, also contribute to our experience of emotions is sometimes called the *facial feedback hypothesis* (Tomkins, 1962). According to the hypothesis, just as we receive feedback about (or perceive) our autonomic arousal, so we receive feedback about our facial expression, and this feedback combines with the other components of an emotion to produce a more intense experience. This implies that if you make yourself smile and hold the smile for several seconds, you will begin to feel happier; if you scowl, you will feel tense and angry. (Try it.) In support of the hypothesis, subjects who exaggerate their facial reactions to emotional stimuli report more emotional response than subjects who do not (Laird, 1974), though this may be true mainly for cases in which the emotional stimuli are relatively weak (Tourangeau & Ellsworth, 1979). Other studies indicate that facial expressions may have an

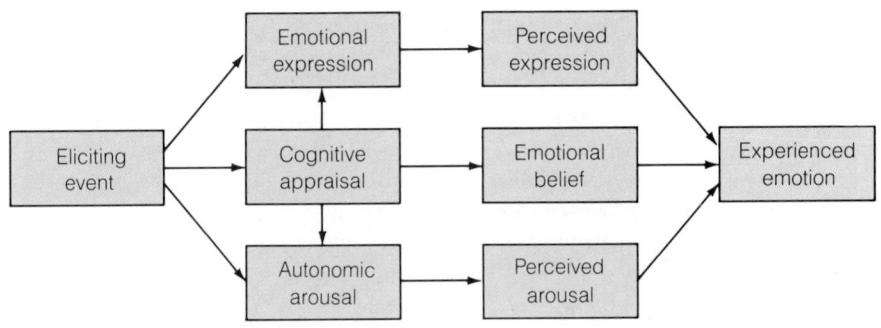

FIGURE 11-4
**Components of an Emotional
Experience: 2** *Emotional expression,
emotional belief, and perceived arousal all
contribute to the experience of an emotion.*
(After Reisenzein, 1983)

indirect effect on emotion by increasing autonomic arousal. Such an indirect influence was demonstrated in an experiment we discussed earlier, where producing particular emotional expressions led to changes in heartbeat and skin temperature. We therefore need to add emotional expression to our list of contributors to emotional experience (see Figure 11-4).

Some researchers also believe that facial expressions can determine the *quality* of emotions. Since the expressions for the primary emotions are distinct and occur rapidly, they are at least plausible candidates for contributing to the differentiation of emotions. Tomkins (1980) has proposed that the feedback from a facial expression is inherently positive or negative, thereby suggesting a means by which facial expressions can distinguish the positive from the negative emotions. Should this suggestion prove true, we are back (in part) to the James-Lange theory mentioned earlier, which holds that emotion is the perception of certain bodily changes; facial expressions are bodily changes—we *are* happy *because* we laugh.

But exactly which aspects of a facial expression makes it inherently positive or negative? A possible answer may be found in the fact that the contraction of certain facial muscles can affect the blood flow in neighboring blood vessels. This, in turn, affects cerebral blood flow, which can determine brain temperature, which in turn can facilitate and inhibit the release of various neurotransmitters—and the latter may well be part of the cortical activity that underlies emotion. For example, when smiling, the configuration of facial muscles may lead to a lowering of the temperature in a region of the brain in which the neurotransmitter serotonin is released; this temperature change may block the release of the neurotransmitter, resulting in a positive feeling. The critical path, then, moves from facial expression to brain temperature to emotional experience (Zajonc, Murphy, & Inglehart, 1989).

This path from expression to emotion is supported by recent experiments. One study takes advantage of the fact that pronunciation of the German vowel "ü" (as in Für) requires extending a facial muscle that is contracted when smiling. This suggests that the facial expression associated with pronouncing ü can lead to a negative feeling. To test this hypothesis, German subjects read aloud stories that contained either many words with ü or no words with ü; the stories were equated for their content and emotional tone. When asked how much they liked the stories, subjects rated those with ü words as less favorable than those with no ü words. Also, while subjects read the stories, the temperature of their foreheads was measured to provide an estimate of brain temperature. Temperatures rose during stories with ü words but not during stories without such words. Thus, the facial expression needed to produce ü led to both increased brain temperature and negative feeling, which supports the proposed path from facial expression to brain temperature to emotion experience (Zajonc, Murphy, & Inglehart, 1989).

CRITICAL DISCUSSION

Opponent Processes in Emotion

Given that intense emotions can be disruptive, why do some people repeatedly engage in highly arousing activities such as skydiving? According to an old joke, they do it because "it feels good when they stop." Surprisingly, there appears to be some truth to this punch line, which is captured by the *opponent-process theory* of emotion (Solomon & Corbit, 1974; Solomon, 1980).

The theory assumes that the brain is organized to oppose or suppress emotional states, whether the states are positive or negative. Each emotional state has an opposite that can cancel it; when one member of a pair is elicited (call it A), it soon triggers its opposite (call it B), which in time returns the system to its baseline:

Baseline → A → B → Baseline

This type of process is illustrated by reports on the emotional reactions typically experienced by parachutists in training (Epstein, 1967). During their first free-fall (before the parachute opens), the response is one of fear (this is State A). After landing, a trainee usually walks about with a stunned expression for a few minutes and then begins to smile and become very sociable. A feeling of euphoria follows (this is State B), which eventually fades to a baseline of normal behavior. (See Figure 1.)

The temporal course of this emotional process can be understood by looking first at the middle curve on the left-hand side of Figure 2. When the emotional event occurs, it elicits an *a*-process; this gives rise to State A. Sometime after the *a*-process is activated, the *b*-process is aroused and functions to oppose and suppress the affective state generated by the *a*-process. At any moment, the difference between the magnitude of the *a*-process and the magnitude of the *b*-process determines the emotional response; this difference is plotted in the top left-hand curve of Figure 2.

The top left-hand curve also gives us the time course of an emotional experience. When an emotion-producing stimulus is first presented, an emotion occurs that rises to a peak in a few seconds. Then, as the event continues, the emotion recedes slightly from its peak and remains steady. This sequence occurs because initially the *a*-process is unopposed, giving rise to a peak level for State A; but as the *b*-process gradually becomes activated, it subtracts from the *a*-process, thereby reducing the peak level for State A. Once the emotion-producing stimulus is removed, the opposite emotion is experienced. This happens because the *a*-process disappears almost immediately but the *b*-process recedes more slowly; thus, State B is experienced until the *b*-process has run its course.

Let us return to skydiving and interpret it in terms of these underlying processes. The free-fall is clearly an emotion-producing event. At its onset, the *a*-process will be activated immediately, leading to an emotional peak for State A—namely, intense fear. Shortly afterward (still during free-fall), the *b*-process will be aroused gradually and will reduce the intensity of State A, but the jumper will still feel considerable fear. When the parachute opens, fear will be lessened further. When the jumper lands, removing the fear-producing event, the *a*-process will disappear quickly but the *b*-process

will persist, giving rise to State B—a feeling of relief. This pattern of emotional response can be observed in our everyday experiences, but it is often complicated by cultural factors and our efforts to control our emotions. In well-controlled laboratory situations, the temporal course of an emotional state presented in Figure 2 can be demonstrated.

Thus far, we have considered only the first time an emotion-producing event is encountered. But skydivers repeat the activity of parachuting many times, and opponent-process theory considers this repetition of the event. According to the theory, the first time an arousing stimulus is experienced, the *b*-process is fairly weak and slow

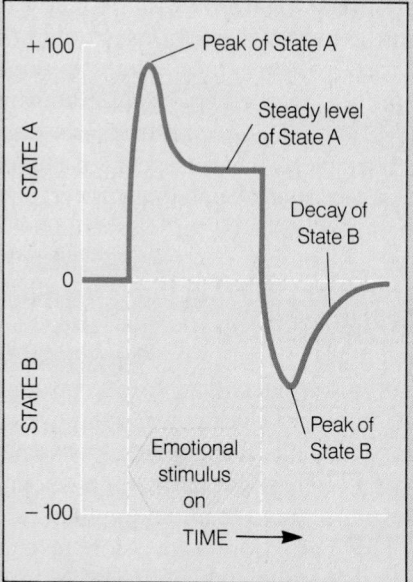

FIGURE 1
Temporal Dynamics of an Affective Response *The standard pattern of an affective response produced by an emotion-arousing stimulus on its initial presentation. This curve is the same as the one at the top of the left-hand panel in Figure 2.*

to occur. Repeated exposures to the stimulus strengthen the *b*-process until it becomes activated much more quickly and with much greater intensity; this is indicated in the middle curve of the right-hand panel of Figure 2. As a result, the manifest level for State A is reduced, and when the stimulus is removed, the intensity of State B is greatly amplified (see the top curve on the right-hand side of Figure 2). This pattern of reactions also has been verified by experimentation. Thus, the initial encounter with an arousing event will lead to a strong State A experience followed by a mild State B experience; but after repeated exposures, the intensity of State A will be diminished, whereas the intensity of State B will be greatly amplified. Hence, we can see why some people continue to engage in highly arousing activities such as skydiving and roller-coaster riding: the negative A state is more than compensated for by the positive B state.

This analysis of the effects of repeated exposures to arousing events can also illuminate drug addictions. The first few doses of an opiate produce a potent experience of pleasure, called a rush, which has been described as an intense type of sexual pleasure felt throughout the body. The rush is followed by a less intense state of euphoria. After the drug has worn off, the user lapses into an aversive state of craving called withdrawal, which fades in time. This pattern conforms to the curve in the top left-hand panel of Figure 2. The opiate produces a peak level for State A (the rush), followed by a slight decline in intensity (euphoria); when the drug dose loses its effect, State B (withdrawal) emerges and then gradually disappears. If the user repeats the drug doses frequently, the course of the emotional experience changes as predicted by the opponent-process theory (see the right-hand panel of Figure 2). The rush is no longer experienced,

and the feeling of euphoria is minimal or absent. The withdrawal syndrome becomes much more intense, and its duration lengthens dramatically. Experienced drug users have mild highs followed by intense and extended lows.

Initially, addictive drugs are taken because they produce pleasant effects. After repeated use, however, they are taken to counteract the unpleasant opponent process that persists from prior drug use. A vicious circle is formed: the more often a drug is used, the more intense and longer-lasting the opponent process becomes. To get rid of this

unpleasant aftereffect, the drug user takes the drug again, further strengthening the opponent process. An experienced drug user continues to take a drug to reduce the low that occurs after the previous dose rather than to produce the high originally associated with the drug. This cycle is not easily broken, as indicated by the high failure rates of most drug-treatment programs. The opponent-process theory does not offer a prescription for the treatment of drug addiction, but it provides a framework within which to evaluate such programs (Solomon, 1980).

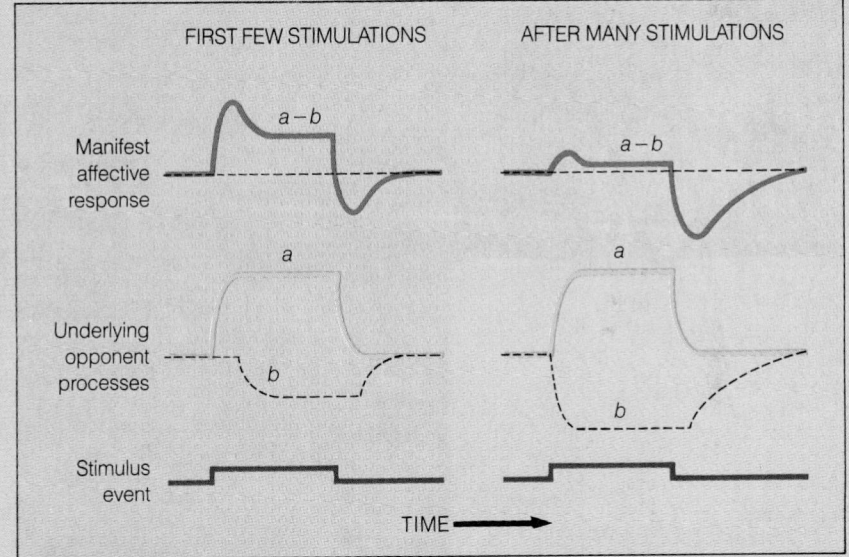

FIGURE 2

Opponent Processes in Emotion *The left-hand panel illustrates the affective response to the first few presentations of a stimulus; the right-hand panel shows the response after repeated presentations of the stimulus. The top curve in each panel is the manifest response produced by the interplay of the opponent processes; it is obtained by taking the difference between the underlying opponent processes a and b shown in the middle row of the figure (that is, subtracting the b-curve from the a-curve). The bottom row in the figure indicates the onset and offset of the emotion-arousing stimulus. Note that the b-process has a shorter latency, an increased intensity, and a slower decay as the stimulus is presented repeatedly and becomes familiar. These changes in the b-process explain why there is a change in the manifest emotional response as a stimulus is repeatedly experienced. (After Solomon, 1980)*

GENERAL CONSEQUENCES OF EMOTION

Although some consequences of being in an emotional state are specific to the emotion experienced—smiling when happy or withdrawing when frightened, for example—other consequences seem to apply to emotions in general. In particular, being in an emotional state: a) can energize or disrupt us; b) determine what we attend to and learn; and c) determine what kinds of judgments we make about the world.

Energy and Disruption

Being in an emotional state sometimes energizes people, but other times disrupts them—depending on the intensity of the experience, the individual who is experiencing it, and the duration of the experience. With regard to intensity, a mild level of emotional arousal tends to produce alertness and interest in the current situation. When emotions become intense, however, whether pleasant or unpleasant, they usually result in some disruption of thought or behavior. The curve in Figure 11-5 represents the relation between a person's level of emotional arousal and his or her effectiveness on a task. At very low levels of emotional arousal (for example, at the point of waking up), sensory information may not be well attended to, and performance will be relatively poor. Performance is optimal at moderate levels of arousal. At high levels of emotional arousal, performance begins to decline, probably because the person cannot devote enough cognitive resources to the task. The optimum level of arousal and the shape of the curve differ for different tasks. A simple, well-learned routine would be much less susceptible to disruption by emotional arousal than a more complex activity that depends on the integration of several thought processes. During a moment of intense fear, you would probably still be able to spell your name but not be able to play chess well.

Exactly what constitutes an excessive level of emotional arousal depends on the individual, as shown by studies of behavior during crises such as fires or sudden floods. About 15 percent of people show organized, effective behavior, suggesting that their optimum level of emotional arousal has not been exceeded. The majority of people, about 70 percent, show various degrees of disorganization but are still able to function with some effectiveness. The remaining 15 percent are so disorganized that they are unable to function at all; they may panic or exhibit aimless and completely inappropriate behavior, suggesting they are far above their optimal level of emotional arousal (Tyhurst, 1951).

Sometimes intense emotions are not quickly discharged but continue to remain unresolved. Perhaps the situation that makes a person angry (for example, prolonged conflict with an employer) or fearful (such as worry over the illness of a loved one) continues for a long time period. While the physiological changes that accompany anger and fear can have adaptive value (they mobilize us to fight or flee), when maintained too long they can exhaust our resources and even cause tissue damage. A chronic state of heightened arousal can thus take its toll on the individual's health. We will have more to say about the relationship between stress and the body's vulnerability to illness in Chapter 15.

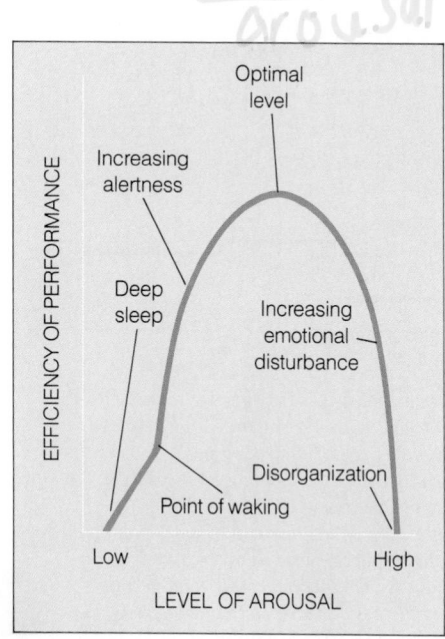

FIGURE 11-5
Emotional Arousal and Performance
The curve shows the hypothetical relationship between level of emotional arousal and efficiency of performance. The precise shape of the curve differs for various tasks. (After Hebb, 1972)

Attention and Learning

When experiencing an emotion, we tend to pay more attention to events that fit our mood than to events that do not. As a consequence, we learn more about the events that are congruent with our mood.

One experiment that demonstrates these phenomena involved three stages. In the first stage, subjects were hypnotized and induced to be in either a happy or sad mood (the subjects had been preselected for being hypnotizeable). In the second stage, the hypnotized subjects read a brief story about an encounter between two men—a happy character and a sad one. The story vividly described the events of the two men's lives and their emotional reactions. After reading the story, subjects were asked who they thought the central character was, and with whom they identified. Subjects who had been induced to be happy identified more with the happy character and thought the story contained more statements about him; subjects who had been induced to be sad identified more with the sad character and estimated that more story statements were about him. These results indicate that subjects paid more attention to the character and events that were congruent with their moods than to those that were not.

Evidence that subjects also *learned* more about mood-congruent events than mood-incongruent ones comes from the third part of the experiment. One day after reading the story, subjects returned to the laboratory, now in a neutral mood. They were asked to recall the story. Subjects recalled more about the character they had identified with: for the previously happy subjects, 55 percent of the facts they recalled were about the happy character; for the previously sad subjects, 80 percent of their recalled facts were about the sad character.

Exactly how does the congruence between one's mood and some new material affect the learning of that material? We know that we can learn new material better if we can relate it to information already in memory. One's mood during learning may increase the availability of memories that fit that mood, and such memories will be easier to relate to new material that also fits that mood. Suppose you hear a story about a person losing a job. If you are in a bad mood when hearing the story, some of your memories about failure experiences may be easily accessible, and the similarity of these memories to the new fact of someone losing her job will make it easy to relate them. In contrast, if you are in a good mood when hearing the story, your most accessible memories may be too dissimilar to a job loss to foster a relation between the old memories and the new fact. So, our mood determines what memories are more accessible, and those memories determine what is easy for us to learn at the moment (Bower, 1981; Isen, 1985).

Evaluation and Estimation

Our emotional mood can affect our evaluation of other people. Everyday experiences provide numerous examples of this. For example, when we are in a good mood, a friend's habit of constantly checking his appearance in a mirror may seem just an idiosyncrasy; when we are in a bad mood, we may judge our friend's behavior more harshly. Our mood affects our evaluation of inanimate objects as well. In one experiment, subjects were asked to evaluate their major possessions. Subjects who had just been put in a good mood by receiving a small gift rated their televisions and cars more positively than did control subjects who were in a neutral mood (Isen et al., 1978).

Our mood also affects our judgments about the frequency of various risks in the world. Bad moods lead us to see these risks as more likely; good moods lead us to see the risks as less likely. In an experiment dealing with estimating risks, subjects in the experimental group first read a newspaper story that recounted a tragic death, putting the subjects in a negative mood. Control subjects read a bland newspaper story, putting them in a neutral mood. Then all subjects were asked to estimate the frequencies of various fatalities, including diseases like leukemia and heart disease, and accidents like fires and floods. Subjects who were in a negative mood estimated the frequencies of these fatalities to be almost twice as great as did subjects in a neutral mood. Further, all that mattered for estimating frequencies was the subject's mood, not the content of the story that had put them in that mood. The tragic story that some experimental subjects read involved a case of leukemia, whereas the story that other experimental subjects read involved a death due to fire; both kinds of subjects overestimated the frequencies of leukemia and fire to the same degree. The similarity between the story and the risk had no effect on the estimate of frequency. It is as if the affect was separated from the content of a story, and only the affect guided subsequent estimates. Comparable results were obtained for the effects of being in a good mood. Reading a story about someone's good fortune led subjects to make relatively low estimates about the frequencies of various fatalities, and the extent to which subjects did this did not depend on the similarity between the story and the risk being evaluated (Johnson & Tversky, 1983).

Being in a bad mood, then, makes the world seem a more dangerous place. Such a perception can reinforce the bad mood. Also, as noted earlier, being in a bad mood leads us to selectively attend and learn negative-toned facts; this too can reinforce a bad mood. A similar analysis applies to a good mood. It makes the world seem less risky, and leads us to attend and learn positively-toned material. Thus, the general consequences of a mood serve to perpetuate that mood.

AGGRESSION AS AN EMOTIONAL REACTION

Emotions cause not only general reactions, but specific ones as well. We may laugh when happy, withdraw when frightened, get aggressive when angry, and so forth. Among these typical emotional reactions, psychologists have singled out one in particular for extensive study: aggression.

This special attention is partly due to the social significance of aggression. At the societal level, in an age when nuclear weapons are widely available, a single aggressive act can spell disaster. At the individual level, many people experience aggressive thoughts and impulses frequently, and how they handle these thoughts will have major effects on their health and interpersonal relations. Another reason why psychologists have focused their research on aggression is because two major theories of social behavior make quite different assumptions about the nature of aggression. Freud's *psychoanalytic theory* views aggression as a drive, and *social-learning theory* views it as a learned response. Research on aggression helps us to evaluate these competing theories.

In the following discussion, we first describe these different views along with related research, and then consider how the views differ with respect to the effects of viewing aggression in the mass media. Keep in mind that what we mean by "aggression" is behavior that is *intended* to injure another person (physically or verbally) or to destroy property. The key concept in this definition is intent. If a person accidentally steps on your foot in a crowded elevator and immediately apologizes, you would not interpret the behavior as aggressive; but if someone walks up to you as you sit at your desk and stomps on your foot, you would not hesitate to label the act as aggressive.

Aggression as a Drive

We will present only those aspects of psychoanalytic theory and social-learning theory that are relevant to aggression. Both theories will be presented in more detail in Chapter 14, where we focus on personality, and Chapters 16 and 17, where we discuss abnormal behavior and its treatment.

According to Freud's early psychoanalytic theory, many of our actions are determined by instincts, particularly the sexual instinct. When expression of these instincts is frustrated, an aggressive drive is induced. Later theorists in the psychoanalytic tradition broadened this *frustration-aggression hypothesis* to the following claim: whenever a person's effort to reach *any* goal is blocked, an aggressive drive is induced that motivates behavior to injure the obstacle (person or object) causing the frustration (Dollard et al., 1939). There are two critical aspects of this proposal: one is that the usual cause of aggression is frustration; the other is that aggression has the properties of a basic drive—being a form of *energy* that *persists* until its goal is satisfied, as well as being an *inborn* reaction (hunger, sex, and other basic drives have these properties). As we will see, it is the drive aspect of the frustration-aggression hypothesis that has proved to be particularly controversial.

Is aggression a drive or a learned response?

SUDDEN VIOLENCE   The idea of an aggressive drive fits with the popular notion that there are people who have always been docile and then suddenly commit a violent act: it is as if aggressive energy builds up until it has to find an outlet. Newspaper and television accounts of crimes tend to encourage this view. Usually, however, the offender's background is anything but innocent. Most people who commit violent acts have a history of aggressive behavior (with the exception of the rare psychotic individual who is driven to a violent act by delusional beliefs). Today's most aggressive 30-year-olds were yesterday's most aggressive 10-year-olds. Aggressiveness seems to be established during childhood and remains relatively stable thereafter (Huesmann, Eron, Lefkowitz, & Walder, 1984; Eron, 1987).

BIOLOGICAL BASIS OF AGGRESSION   Findings on the biological basis of aggression in animals provide better evidence for an aggressive drive. Some studies show that mild electrical stimulation of a specific region of the hypothalamus produces aggressive, even deadly, behavior in animals. When a cat's hypothalamus is stimulated via implanted electrodes, the animal hisses, its hair bristles, its pupils dilate, and it will strike at a rat or other objects placed in its cage. Stimulation of a different area of the hypothalamus produces quite different behavior: instead of exhibiting any of these rage responses, the cat coldly stalks and kills a rat.

Similar techniques have produced aggressive behavior in rats. A laboratory-bred rat that has never killed a mouse, nor seen a wild rat kill one, may live quite peacefully in the same cage with a mouse. But if the rat's hypothalamus is stimulated, the animal will pounce on its mouse cage mate and kill it with exactly the same response that is exhibited by a wild rat (a hard bite to the neck that severs the spinal cord). The stimulation seems to trigger an innate killing response that had previously been dormant. Conversely, if a neurochemical blocker is injected into the same brain site in rats that spontaneously kill mice on sight, the rats become temporarily peaceful (Smith, King, & Hoebel, 1970). In these cases, then, aggression has some properties of a drive, as it involves inborn reactions.

In higher mammals, such instinctive patterns of aggression are controlled by the cortex and therefore are influenced more by experience. Monkeys living in groups establish a dominance hierarchy: one or two males become leaders, and the others assume various levels of subordination.

FIGURE 11-6
Brain Stimulation and Aggression
A mild electrical current is delivered to electrodes implanted in the monkey's hypothalamus via remote radio control. The animal's response (attack or flight) depends on its position in the dominance hierarchy of the colony. (Courtesy Dr. José Delgado)

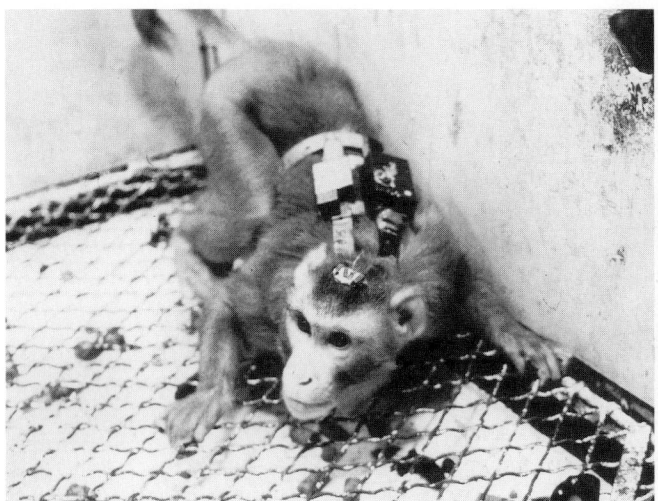

When the hypothalamus of a dominant monkey is electrically stimulated, the monkey attacks subordinate males but not females. When a low-ranking monkey is stimulated in the same way, it cowers and behaves submissively (see Figure 11-6). Thus, aggressive behavior in a monkey is not automatically elicited by stimulation of the hypothalamus; rather, in making its response a monkey considers the environment and its past experiences. Humans are similar. Although we are equipped with neurological mechanisms that are tied to aggression, the activation of these mechanisms is usually under cortical control (except in some cases of brain damage). Indeed, in most individuals, the frequency with which aggressive behavior is expressed, the forms it takes, and the situations in which it is displayed are determined largely by experience and social influences. (For further comparisons between aggression in humans and that in other animals, see the Critical Discussion, "On Aggressive Instincts and Their Inhibition.")

Aggression as a Learned Response

Social-learning theory is concerned with human social interaction, but it has its origins in behavioristic studies of animal learning (such as those discussed in Chapter 7). It focuses on the behavior patterns that people develop in response to environmental contingencies. Some social behaviors may be rewarded while others may produce unfavorable results; through the process of differential reinforcement, people eventually select the more successful behavior patterns. Social-learning theory differs from strict behaviorism, however, in that it stresses the importance of cognitive processes. Because people can represent situations symbolically, they are able to foresee the probable consequences of their actions and to alter their behavior accordingly.

Social-learning theory further differs from strict behaviorism in that it stresses the importance of *vicarious learning*, or learning by observation. Many behavior patterns are learned by watching the behavior of others and observing what consequences it produces for them. A child who observes the pained expressions of an older sibling in the dentist's chair will probably be fearful when the time comes for his or her first dental appointment. Social-learning theory emphasizes the role of *models* in transmitting both specific behaviors and emotional responses, and it focuses on such questions as what types of models are most effective and what factors determine whether the modeled behavior that is learned will actually be performed (Bandura, 1973; 1986).

With this emphasis on learning, it is no surprise that social-learning theory rejects the concept of aggression as an instinct or as a frustration-produced drive; the theory proposes instead that aggression is similar to any other learned response. Aggression can be learned through observation or imitation, and the more often it is reinforced, the more likely it is to occur. A person who is frustrated by a blocked goal or disturbed by some stressful event experiences an unpleasant emotion. The response that this emotion elicits will differ, depending on the kinds of responses the individual has learned to use in coping with stressful situations. The frustrated individual may seek help from others, aggress, withdraw, try even harder to surmount the obstacle, or anesthetize himself or herself with drugs or alcohol. The chosen response will be the one that has relieved frustration most successfully in the past. According to this view, frustration provokes aggression mainly in people who have learned to respond to adverse situations with aggressive behavior (Bandura, 1977).

CRITICAL DISCUSSION

On Aggressive Instincts and Their Inhibition

In the early phase of his work, Freud proposed that aggression is a frustration-induced drive. In later years, he adopted the more extreme position that aggression is based on a *death instinct* that can be directed either inward in the form of self-destructive behavior or outward in the form of aggression. The claim that aggression is an instinct means that people aggress to express an inborn desire: the ultimate goal of aggression is not removal of a frustrating agent but aggression itself.

Freud came to this pessimistic stance in an attempt to account for the senseless carnage of World War I. He expressed his views in a letter written to Albert Einstein in 1932. Einstein, concerned with the efforts of the League of Nations to promote world peace, asked Freud for his opinions on why people engage in war. Is it possible, Einstein inquired, that human beings have a "lust for hatred and destruction"? Freud replied:

You express astonishment at the fact that it is so easy to make men enthusiastic about a war and add your suspicion that there is something at work in them—an instinct for hatred and destruction—which goes halfway to meet the efforts of warmongers. I can only express my entire agreement. We believe in an instinct of that kind and have been occupied during the last few years in studying its manifestations. The death instinct turns into the destructive instinct. It is directed outwards, onto objects. The living creature preserves its own life, so to say, by destroying an extraneous one. (1963, p. 41)

Though Freud's instinct view of aggression is not widely accepted by clinicians, it is in agreement with some theories of aggression proposed by ethologists. The view of some ethologists is that both animals and humans have an aggressive instinct that must find some outlet (for example, Eibl-Eibesfeldt, 1970; Lorenz, 1981). Earlier work in ethology assumed that a major difference exists between humans and lower species—namely, that animals have evolved mechanisms to control their aggressive instincts, whereas humans have not (for example, Ardrey, 1966; Lorenz, 1966). More recent work, however, suggests that animals are no better at controlling their instincts than we are.

In the 1960s, Lorenz and other ethologists made a number of observations about animal aggression. They noted that, among their own species, animals usually fight to protect their young and to compete for food, mates, and nesting sites. Such aggression ensures that the strongest males will procreate—since they will be the winners in the competition for females—and also makes it likely that animals will be spaced over the inhabited area so that each group establishes a specific territory. According to Lorenz, animals can safely enjoy these benefits of aggression because, through the process of evolution, they have developed inhibitions that prevent them from destroying their own species. Many species exhibit ritualistic fighting behavior that appears to be largely innate. They ward off combat by threatening displays. They fight according to a stylized

(a) (b)

(c) (d)

Ritualistic Patterns of Fighting Behavior *The wildebeest bull defends its territory against a rival in a stylized challenge duel. These skirmishes, which may occur many times a day, seldom result in bloodshed. (a) The two antagonists stand grazing head to head, taking each other's measure. (b) Suddenly, they drop to their knees in the eye-to-eye combat attitude. (c) Pretending to sense danger, they raise their heads in mock alarm, apparently a means of easing tension. (d) At this point, the challenge may be called off or may progress to a brief, horn-locked battle.*

pattern that seldom results in serious injury, because the loser can display signals of submission that inhibit further aggression on the part of the victor (for example, a wolf lies down and exposes its throat). All of this, according to Lorenz, is in contrast to humans, who have developed powerful weapons that can cause instant death at great distances and who have no inhibitions to offset these destructive instincts.

More recent observations by ethologists challenge the earlier belief that animals know how to inhibit their aggression. It is now known that many animals do not employ innate signals to stop attacks, and that the stereotyped signals that they do employ have varying effects on the responses of their foes. The incidence of murder, rape, and infanticide among animals is much greater than was thought in the 1960s. One kind of murder involves border wars between chimpanzees (Goodall, 1978). In one well-documented case in the Gombe Stream National Park in Tanzania, a gang of five male chimpanzees defended their territory against any strange male that wandered into it. If the gang encountered a group of two or more strangers, their response would be raucous, but not deadly; but if there was only one intruder, then one member of the gang might hold his arm, another a leg, while a third member pounded the intruder to death. Or a couple of members of the gang would drag the intruder over the rocks until he died. In another chimpanzee border war observed during the 1970s, a tribe of about 15 chimpanzees destroyed a smaller neighboring group by killing the members off one male at a time. Furthermore, at least for primates, females engage in as many aggressive acts as males, though their encounters are less deadly because their teeth are shorter and less sharp (Smuts, 1986).

Observations such as this have led to a drastic revision in beliefs about the extent of animal aggression. Indeed, the well-known sociobiologist E. O.

Mutual grooming is a social response that inhibits aggression.

Wilson has gone so far as to claim that: "If you calculate the number of murders per individual animal per hour of observation, you realize that the murder rate is higher than for human beings, even taking into account our wars" (1983, p. 79).

Some experts believe that, in addition to comparable incidences of aggression, animals and humans have comparable inhibitions on aggression. Animal behaviors that appear to inhibit aggression include maintaining distance from a potential foe (strong odors and loud vocalizations that permit animals to detect and withdraw from one another at a distance serve this purpose) and evoking a social response that is incompatible with aggression. One such response is mutual grooming—touching or fingering the fur or feathers of another animal. Perhaps the most important factor in

reducing aggression is familiarity. Many of the social rituals in which animals engage (such as sniffing and inspecting body parts and stereotyped greeting behaviors) familiarize them with each other's smell and appearance, which helps them to distinguish group members from strangers.

Maintaining distance, engaging in social responses incompatible with aggression, and gaining familiarity are also activities that people use to ward off aggression. These parallels (and others mentioned in this discussion) between humans and other animals are of considerable interest, but they are only weak evidence for an aggressive instinct or drive in humans. At this point, the preponderance of evidence favors the idea that aggression in humans is a learned behavior (see the section "Aggression as a Learned Response").

FIGURE 11-7
Two Views of Aggression *The diagram schematically represents the determinants of aggression according to psychoanalytic theory (the frustration-aggression hypothesis) and social-learning theory. From the viewpoint of social-learning theory, the emotional arousal caused by unpleasant experiences can lead to any number of different behaviors, depending on the behavior that has been reinforced in the past.*

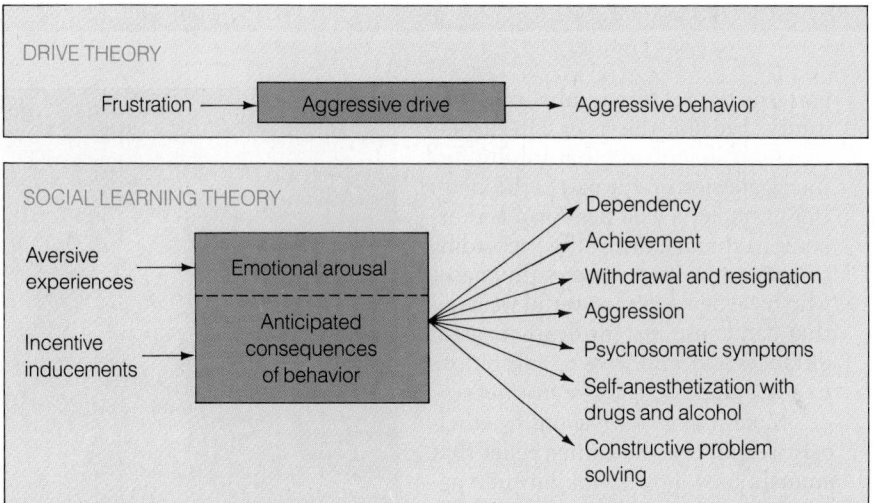

Figure 11-7 shows how social-learning theory differs from psychoanalytic theory (the frustration-aggression hypothesis) in conceptualizing aggression. Social-learning theory assumes that a) aggression is just one of several reactions to the aversive experience of frustration, and b) aggression is a response with no drivelike properties, and consequently is influenced by anticipated consequences of behavior.

IMITATION OF AGGRESSION   One source of evidence for social-learning theory is studies showing that aggression, like any other response, can be learned through imitation. Nursery-school children who observed an adult expressing various forms of aggression toward a large, inflated doll

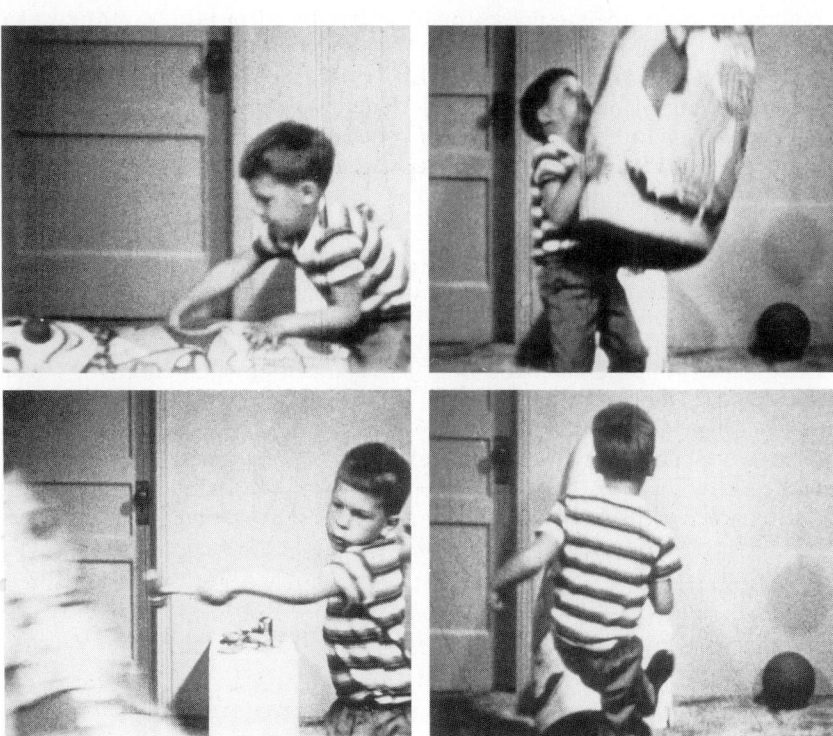

FIGURE 11-8
Children's Imitation of Adult Aggression *Nursery-school children observed an adult express various forms of aggressive behavior toward an inflated doll. After watching the adult, both boys and girls behaved aggressively toward the doll, performing many of the detailed acts of aggression the adult had displayed, including lifting and throwing the doll, striking it with a hammer, and kicking it.*

subsequently imitated many of the adult's actions, including unusual ones (see Figure 11-8). The experiment was expanded to include two filmed versions of aggressive modeling (one showing an adult behaving aggressively toward the doll, the other showing a cartoon character displaying the same aggressive behavior). The results were equally striking. Children who watched either of the two films behaved as aggressively toward the doll as children who had observed a live model displaying aggression. Figure 11-9 measures aggressive behavior for each of the groups and for two control groups who observed either no model or a nonaggressive model. The conclusion of such studies is that observation of either live or filmed models of aggression increases the likelihood of aggression in the viewer. This may be part of the reason why children whose parents punish them severely are likely to be more aggressive than average; the parents provide the model (Eron, 1987).

REINFORCEMENT OF AGGRESSION   Another source of evidence for social-learning theory is that aggression is sensitive to reinforcement contingencies in the same manner that other responses are. A number of studies show that children are more likely to express the aggressive responses they learned by watching aggressive models when they are reinforced for such actions or when they observe aggressive models being reinforced. In one study, investigators observed children for 10 weeks, recording instances of interpersonal aggression and the events that immediately followed aggression, such as positive reinforcers of the aggression (victim winced or cried), punishment of the aggression (victim counterattacked), or neutral reactions (victim ignored the aggressor). For the children who showed the highest overall level of aggression, the most common reaction to their aggressive act was positive reinforcement. For the children who showed the least aggression, punishment was a common reaction. Children who were initially unaggressive, but occasionally succeeded in stopping attacks by counteraggression gradually began to initiate attacks of their own (their aggression was being positively reinforced). Clearly, the consequences of aggression play an important role in shaping behavior (Patterson, Littman, & Bricker, 1967).

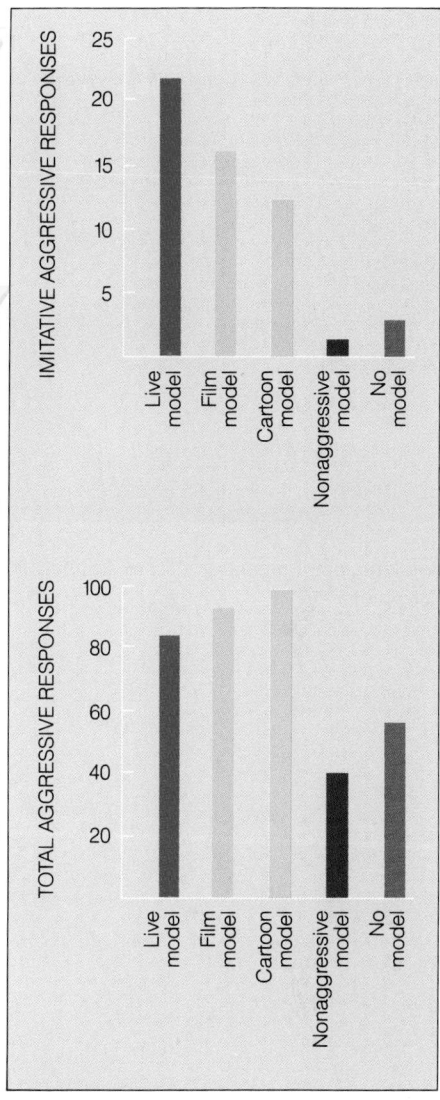

FIGURE 11-9
Imitation of Aggression *Observing aggressive models (either live or on film) greatly increases the amount of aggressive behavior that children display, compared to observing a nonaggressive model or no model at all. Note that observation of the live model results in the imitation of more specific aggressive acts, whereas observation of filmed (either real-life or cartoon) models instigates more aggressive responses of all kinds. (After Bandura, 1973)*

Aggressive Expression and Catharsis

Studies that try to distinguish between aggression as a drive and aggression as a learned response often focus on *catharsis* (purging an emotion by experiencing it intensely). If aggression is persistent energy, then the expression of aggression should be cathartic, resulting in a reduction in the intensity of aggressive feelings and actions. On the other hand, if aggression is a learned response, the expression of aggression could result in an increase in such actions (if the aggression is reinforced). Currently, the evidence favors the learned-response view.

ACTING AGGRESSIVELY   Psychologists have conducted numerous laboratory studies to determine whether or not aggression decreases once it has been partially expressed. Studies of children indicate that participation in aggressive activities either increases aggressive behavior or maintains it at the same level. Experiments with adults produce similar results. When given repeated opportunities to shock another person (who cannot retaliate), college students become more and more punitive. Subjects who are angry become even more punitive on successive attacks than subjects who are not

Children often imitate what they see on television.

angry. If aggression were cathartic, the angry subjects should reduce their aggressive drive by acting aggressively and become less punitive the more they aggress (Berkowitz, 1965; Geen & Quanty, 1977).

Some evidence about catharsis is also taken from real-life situations. In one case, California aerospace workers who had been laid off were first interviewed about how they felt about their companies and supervisors and subsequently were asked to describe their feelings in writing. If aggression were cathartic, men who expressed a lot of anger in the interviews should have expressed relatively little in the written reports. The results, however, showed otherwise: the men who let out anger in conversation expressed even more in their reports. Fuming in conversation may have kindled the aggression. Another study looked at the relation between the hostility of a country (vis-à-vis its neighboring countries) and the kinds of games it plays. More belligerent cultures were found to play more combative games. Again, aggression seems to breed aggression rather than dissipate it (Ebbesen, Duncan, & Konečni, 1975).

These results argue against aggression being cathartic. However, there are circumstances in which the expression of aggression decreases its incidence. For example, behaving aggressively may arouse feelings of anxiety in the aggressors that inhibit further aggression, particularly if they observe the injurious consequences of their actions. But in these instances, the effect on aggressive behavior can be explained without concluding that an aggressive drive is being reduced. Also, although expressing hostile feelings in action does not usually reduce the aggression, it may make the person feel better. But this may happen because the person feels more powerful and more in control, rather than because the person has reduced an aggressive drive.

VIEWING VIOLENCE   Most of the studies we have discussed deal with the consequences of directly expressing aggression. What about the effects of indirectly or vicariously expressing aggression through watching violence on television or in the movies? Is viewing violence cathartic, providing fantasy outlets for an aggressive drive? Or does it elicit aggression by modeling violent behavior? We have already seen that children will imitate live or filmed aggressive behavior in an experimental setting, but how will they react in more natural settings? The amount of violence to which we are exposed through the media makes this an important question.

Several experimental studies have controlled children's viewing of television: one group watched violent cartoons for a specified amount of time each day; another group watched nonviolent cartoons for the same amount of time. The amount of aggression the children showed in their daily activities was carefully recorded. The children who watched violent cartoons became more aggressive in their interactions with their peers, whereas the children who viewed nonviolent cartoons showed no change in interpersonal aggression (Steuer, Applefield, & Smith, 1971).

The above study involves an experimental group and a control group. However, most studies that deal with children's viewing habits are correlational; they determine the relation between the amount of exposure to televised violence and the degree to which children use aggressive behavior to solve interpersonal conflicts. This correlation is clearly positive (Singer & Singer, 1981), even for children in Finland, which has a limited number of violent programs (Lagerspetz, Viemero, & Akademi, 1986). Correlations, however, do not imply causal relationships. It may be that children who are more aggressive prefer to watch violent television programs—that is, aggression causes one to view violence, rather than vice versa.

To evaluate this alternative hypothesis, a study traced television viewing habits over a 10-year period. More than 800 children were studied between the ages of 8 and 9 years. Investigators collected information about each child's viewing preferences and aggressiveness (as rated by schoolmates). Boys who preferred programs that contained a considerable amount of violence were found to be much more aggressive in their interpersonal relationships than boys who preferred programs that contained little violence. So far, the evidence is of the same nature as that in previous studies. But 10 years later, more than half of the original subjects were interviewed concerning their television preferences, given a test that measured delinquency tendencies, and rated by their peers for aggressiveness. Figure 11-10 shows that high exposure to violence on television at age 9 is positively related to aggressiveness in boys at age 19. Most important, the correlation remains significant even when statistical methods are used to control for the degree of childhood aggressiveness, thereby reducing the possibility that the initial level of aggression determines both childhood viewing preferences and adult aggressiveness.

It is interesting that the results showed no consistent relation between the television viewing habits of girls and their aggressive behavior at either age. This agrees with the results of other studies indicating that girls tend to imitate aggressive behavior much less than boys do unless specifically reinforced for doing so. In our society, girls are less likely to be reinforced for behaving aggressively. And since most of the aggressive roles on television are male, females are less likely to find aggressive models to imitate. For boys, however, the majority of studies point to the conclusion that viewing violence does increase interpersonal aggression, particularly in young children. This argues against aggression catharsis and the view that aggression is a drive.

Our survey of aggression has by no means considered all of its possible causes. Common causes of anger and aggression include a loss of self-esteem or a perception that another person has acted unfairly (Averill, 1983); neither of these factors has figured centrally in our discussion of aggression as a drive versus aggression as a learned response. Also, many societal factors are involved in the instigation of aggression; conditions of poverty, overcrowding, the actions of authorities such as the police, and the values of one's

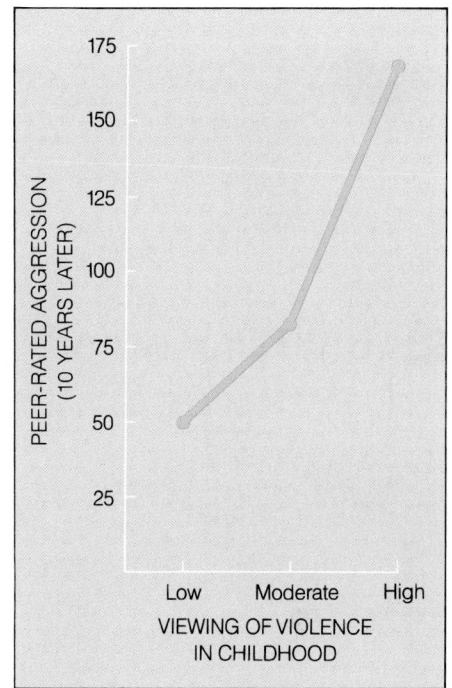

FIGURE 11-10
Relationship Between Childhood Viewing of Violent Television and Adult Aggression *Preference for viewing violent television programs by boys at age 9 is positively correlated with aggressive behavior at age 19.* (After Eron, Huesmann, Lefkowitz, & Walder, 1972)

cultural group are only a few. Some of these social influences will be considered in Chapter 19.

The study of aggression makes it clear that an emotional reaction is a complex event. Similarly, each component of an emotion that we considered—autonomic arousal, cognitive appraisal, and emotional expression—is itself a complex phenomenon involving multiple factors. It is no wonder that we still know so little about this side of our lives.

⚡ CHAPTER SUMMARY

1. The components of an emotion include *autonomic arousal, cognitive appraisal,* and *emotional expression.* One critical question is, How do arousal, appraisal, and expression contribute to the intensity of an emotional experience? Another question is, Which components *differentiate* the emotions?

2. Intense emotions usually involve physiological arousal caused by activation of the *sympathetic division* of the *autonomic nervous system.* People who have spinal cord injuries, which limit feedback from the autonomic nervous system, report experiencing less intense emotions. Autonomic arousal may also help differentiate the emotions, since the pattern of arousal (for example, heartbeat, skin temperature) differs for different emotions.

3. A *cognitive appraisal* is an analysis of a situation that results in an emotional belief. Such appraisals affect both the intensity and quality of an emotion. When people are induced into a state of undifferentiated arousal (say, by injection of epinephrine), the quality of their emotional experience is determined almost entirely by their appraisal of the situation. There are cases of emotion, however, in which no cognitive appraisal seems to be involved (for example, fear experiences that were acquired in childhood by classical conditioning).

4. The facial expressions that accompany primary emotions have a universal meaning: people from different cultures agree on what emotion a person in a particular photograph is expressing. The ability to recognize emotional expression is localized in the right cerebral hemisphere and is neurologically distinct from the ability to recognize faces. In addition to their communicative functions, emotional expressions may also contribute to the subjective experience of an emotion.

5. Being in an emotional state has some general consequences. One is that emotion can sometimes energize people, but at other times disrupt them. A mild emotion produces alertness whereas an intense emotion can be disruptive. Another general consequence of being in an emotional state is that we tend to pay more attention to and learn more about events that fit our mood than to events that do not. Another consequence is that our emotional mood affects our evaluation of people and objects, as well as our estimation of what will happen in the future. When in a bad mood, we estimate various risks in life to be relatively frequent; when in a good mood, we estimate these risks to be relatively infrequent.

6. *Aggression* is a typical reaction to anger (though it can occur for other reasons as well). According to early *psychoanalytic theory,* aggression is a *frustration-produced drive;* according to *social-learning theory,* aggression is a *learned response.*

7. In lower animals, aggression is controlled by neurological mechanisms in the *hypothalamus.* Stimulation of the hypothalamus of a rat or cat can lead to a rage or killing response. In humans and other higher mammals, aggressive behavior is under cortical control. In most people, the frequency with which aggressive behavior is expressed and the form it takes are determined largely by past experiences and social influences.

8. In keeping with the social-learning theory of aggression, aggressive responses can be learned through *imitation* and increased in frequency when positively reinforced. Children are more likely to express aggressive responses when they are reinforced for such actions (for example, their victims wince or cry) than when they are punished for the actions (their victims counterattack).

9. Evidence indicates that aggression either increases subsequent aggressive behavior or maintains it at the same level. The indirect or vicarious expression of aggression has similar effects: there is a positive relation between the amount of exposure children have to television violence and the extent to which they act aggressively.

FURTHER READING

For an introduction to various views on emotion, see Strongman, *The Psychology of Emotion* (2nd ed., 1978). Some chapters in Mook, *Motivation* (1987), also provide a useful introduction. For a more technical treatment of emotion, see Mandler, *Mind and Emotion* (1982); and Plutchik and Kellerman (eds.), *Emotion: Theory, Research, and Experience* (1980). The role of cognition in emotion is discussed in detail in Ortony, Clore, and Collins, *The Cognitive Structure of Emotions* (1988).

Interesting books on facial expressions and emotion include Ekman's *Emotion in the Human Face* (2nd ed., 1982) and his *Telling Lies: Clues to Deceit in the Marketplace, Politics and Marriage* (1985). For a review and critical analysis of lie detection procedures, see Lykken, *A Tremor in the Blood: Uses and Abuses of the Lie Detector* (1980).

The psychoanalytic theory of emotion is presented in two books by Freud: *Beyond the Pleasure Principle* (1920/1975) and *New Introductory Lectures on Psychoanalysis* (1933/1965). For the social-learning approach, see Bandura, *Social Learning Theory* (1977).

Books on aggression include Johnson, *Aggression in Man and Animals* (1972); Bandura, *Aggression: A Social Learning Analysis* (1973); Montagu (ed.), *Learning Non-aggression: The Experience of Non-Literate Societies* (1978); Tavris, *Anger: The Misunderstood Emotion* (1984); and Hamburg and Trudeau (eds.), *Biobehavioral Aspects of Aggression* (1981).

Paul Klee. Little Hope, *1938.*
Plaster and watercolor on burlap mounted on light cardboard, 15½″ x 17½″,
The Metropolitan Museum of Art, The Berggruen Klee Collection, 1984.
(1984.315.58) QU 14

PART VI Personality and Individuality

Chapter 12

Detail, Little Hope.

Mental Abilities and Their Measurement

People vary widely in personality characteristics and mental abilities. In this chapter, we will look at individual differences in ability and at tests designed to measure these differences. Methods of assessing personality differences will be discussed in Chapter 14. The features that make a test useful, however, are the same regardless of the test's purpose; the requirements for a good test apply equally to ability and personality tests.

The use of ability tests to assign schoolchildren to special classes, to admit students to college and professional schools, and to select individuals for jobs is a topic of public debate and controversy. When ability tests were first developed around the turn of the century, they were hailed as an objective and impartial method of identifying talent and ensuring individual opportunity. Testing permitted people to be selected for jobs or advanced schooling on the basis of merit rather than family background, wealth, social class, or political influence. America—a democratic society with a large, heterogeneous population—was particularly enthusiastic about the use of tests to classify students and select employees. To cite one example, the Civil Service Examinations that thousands of people now take annually when applying for government jobs were initiated during the 1880s in an attempt to ensure that such jobs would be given to qualified people instead of to those who had gained favor by supporting the newly elected politicians.

Many people still view ability tests as the best available means of determining what people can do and for advising them on jobs and professions. Others claim that such tests are narrow and restrictive: they do not measure the characteristics that are most important in determining how well a person will do in college or on the job—specifically, motivation, social skills, and qualities of leadership—and they discriminate against minorities. We will look at the evidence on both sides of this controversy.

TYPES OF ABILITY TESTS

By the time we finish high school, most of us have had some experience with ability tests. Driver's license examinations, grade-school tests of reading and math skills, the competency examinations required for graduation from many high schools, and tests that assess mastery of a particular course (typing, American history, chemistry, and so on) are all ability tests.

A test is essentially a sample of behavior taken at a given point in time. A distinction is often made between *achievement tests* (which are designed to measure accomplished skills and indicate what the person can do at present) and *aptitude tests* (which are designed to predict what a person can accomplish with training). But the distinction between these two types of tests is not clear-cut. All tests assess the individual's current status, whether the purpose of the test is to assess what has been learned or to predict future performance. Both kinds of tests often include similar types of questions and yield results that are highly correlated. Rather than considering aptitude and achievement tests as two distinct categories, it is more useful to think of them as falling along a continuum.

Aptitude versus Achievement

Tests at either end of the aptitude-achievement continuum are distinguished from each other primarily in terms of purpose. For example, a test of knowledge of mechanical principles might be given on completion of a course in mechanics to measure the student's mastery of the course material—to provide a measure of *achievement*. Similar questions might be included in a battery of tests administered to select applicants for pilot training, since knowledge of mechanical principles has been found to be a good predictor of success in flying. The latter test would be considered a measure of *aptitude*, since its results are used to predict a candidate's performance as a student pilot. Thus, whether the test is labeled an aptitude or an achievement test depends more on its purpose than on its content.

Tests at the two ends of the aptitude-achievement continuum can also be distinguished in terms of the *specificity of relevant prior experience*. At one end of the continuum are achievement tests designed to measure mastery of a fairly specific subject matter, such as music theory, European history, or the safe and legal operation of a motor vehicle. At the other extreme are aptitude tests that assume little more in terms of prior experience than the general experience of growing up in the United States. A musical aptitude test, for example, is intended to predict the degree to which a student will benefit from music lessons prior to any instruction. Thus, the Musical Aptitude Profile (Gordon, 1967) does not require any knowledge of musical techniques (see Figure 12-1). It tests a person's ability to identify tones and rhythms that sound similar and to discriminate musical selections that are tastefully performed. However, although no specific experience is required, a person's ability to understand instructions given in English and his or her prior experience listening to music (western versus eastern music, for example) would undoubtedly influence the test results.

We will see later that performance on "intelligence" tests (aptitude tests designed to measure a person's general capacity for learning) does depend to some extent on prior experience, even though every attempt is made to devise questions that do not reflect the results of special training.

FIGURE 12-1

Two Dimensions that Describe Ability Tests *Any given test falls somewhere along an aptitude-achievement continuum and also along a general-specific continuum. For example, a Spanish vocabulary test or a typing test would fall toward the achievement end of the aptitude-achievement continuum and toward the specific end of the general-specific continuum. The Musical Aptitude Profile, which requires no prior musical knowledge and is designed to predict an individual's capacity to profit from music lessons, also taps a fairly specific area of ability but falls toward the aptitude end of the aptitude-achievement dimension. Most intelligence tests (such as the Stanford-Binet and Wechsler Intelligence Scales) are fairly general in that they sample a range of abilities and are designed to measure aptitude more than achievement of skills. Scholastic achievement tests, such as the SAT and ACT, are fairly general; they measure achievement in verbal and mathematical reasoning but do not presume the mastery of specific courses.*

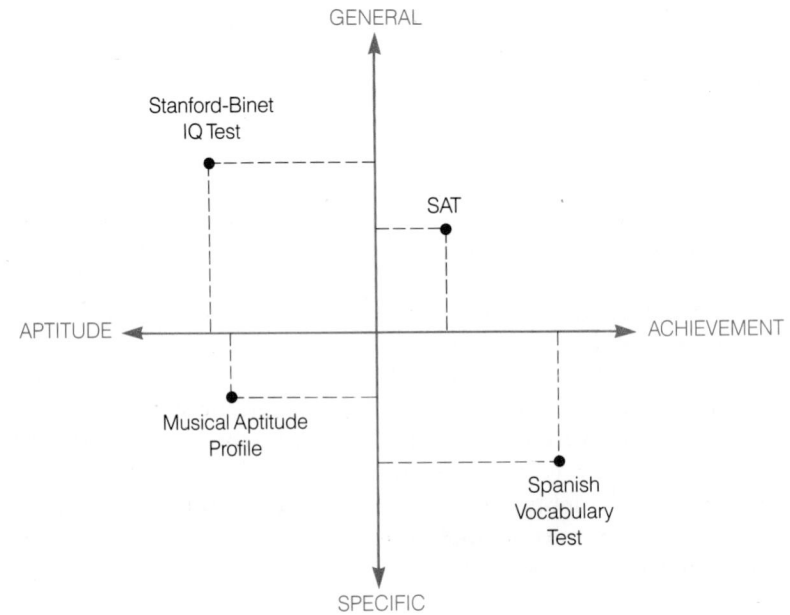

VERBAL ITEMS

Antonyms (tests extent of vocabulary)

1. Choose the word or phrase that is most nearly the *opposite* in meaning to the word in capital letters.

   PARTISAN: A   commoner   D   ascetic
   　　　　　　　 B   neutral   E   pacifist —
   　　　　　　　 C   unifier

Analogies (tests ability to see a relationship in a pair of words, to understand the ideas expressed in the relationship, and to recognize a similar or parallel relationship)

2. Select the lettered pair that *best* expresses a relationship similar to that expressed in the original pair.

   FLURRY: BLIZZARD: A   trickle: deluge   D   spray: foam
   　　　　　　　　　　　 B   rapids: rock   E   mountain: summit
   　　　　　　　　　　　 C   lightning: cloudburst

Sentence completion (tests ability to recognize the relationships among parts of a sentence)

3. Choose the word or set of words that *best* fits the meaning of the sentence as a whole.

   Prominent psychologists believe that people act violently because they have been _____ to do so, not because they were born _____:

   　　　A   forced–gregarious   D   taught–aggressive
   　　　B   forbidden–complacent   E   inclined–belligerent
   　　　C   expected–innocent

Reading passages (tests ability to comprehend a written passage)

Blocks of questions are presented following passages of roughly 400 to 500 words. Some questions ask about information that is directly stated in the passage; others require applications of the author's principles or opinions; still others ask for judgments (e.g., how well the author supports the claims).

TABLE 12-1
Scholastic Aptitude Test *A sample of items from the verbal section of the SAT. These items are of middle difficulty and are answered correctly by 50–60 percent of the test takers. The answers are 1: B, 2: A, 3: D.*

Somewhere between aptitude tests (which assume little in terms of relevant prior experience) and achievement tests (which measure the mastery of specific subject matter) are tests that measure both aptitude and achievement. An example is the Scholastic Aptitude Test (SAT), which is required for admission to many colleges. The SAT consists of a verbal section (see Table 12-1), which measures vocabulary skills and the ability to understand what is read, and a mathematical section (see Table 12-2), which tests the ability to solve problems requiring arithmetic reasoning, algebra, and geometry. Thus, although the test taps learned material (the verbal and quantitative skills that a person has acquired during 12 years of education), it attempts to avoid questions that depend on knowledge of specific topics and focuses instead on the ability to use acquired skills to solve newly posed problems.

TABLE 12-2
Scholastic Aptitude Test *A sample of items from the mathematical section of the SAT, also of middle difficulty. The answers are 1: C, 2: C, 3: B, 4: C.*

MATHEMATICAL ITEMS

1. If $x^3 = (2x)^2$ and $x \neq 0$, then $x =$

A 1	D 6
B 2	E 8
C 4	

$$l \frac{x°/y°}{P}$$

Note: Figure is not drawn to scale.

2. If P is a point on line l in the figure above and $x - y = 0$, then $y =$

A 0	D 135
B 45	E 180
C 90	

Each question consists of two quantities, one in Column A and one in Column B. You are to compare the two quantities and on the answer sheet blacken space:

A   if the quantity in Column A is greater;
B   if the quantity in Column B is greater; ✓
C   if the two quantities are equal;
D   if the relationship cannot be determined from the information given.

Note: In certain questions, information concerning one or both of the quantities to be compared is centered above the two columns.

	Column A	**Column B**
3.	Number of minutes in 1 week	Number of seconds in 7 hours

$$\frac{5}{x} = \frac{1}{3}$$

4.	$\dfrac{3}{x}$	$\dfrac{1}{5}$

Generality versus Specificity

Ability tests can also be distinguished along a general-specific continuum, because they vary in the broadness of their content. The Musical Aptitude Profile would be at the specific end of the continuum, as would a typing test, a driver's license examination, a test of mathematical ability, or a reading comprehension test. All of these tests measure fairly specific skills. At the general end of the continuum would be high-school competency exams and scholastic aptitude tests (like the SAT), which attempt to measure educational development in a number of areas, as well as most tests that are called *intelligence tests*. An intelligence test is an aptitude test designed to predict performance over a range of abilities. Such tests usually do not contain items that can be answered by simple recall or the application of practiced skills. Instead, they focus on items that require a mixture of the abilities to analyze, to understand abstract concepts, and to apply prior knowledge to the solution of new problems. Intelligence tests usually include verbal, figurative, and quantitative tasks. Although the attempt to measure general intellectual ability in order to predict what an individual can accomplish with education or training is certainly worthwhile, the label "intelligence test" is unfortunate. The wording implies that people possess an innate capacity, called intelligence, that is fixed in amount and is not influenced by education or experience. Later, we will see that many variables can influence a person's score on an intelligence test. In addition, although some individuals may be more able than others to accomplish a variety of tasks, abilities are not so consistent that a person who is above average at one task is above average at all tasks.

REQUIREMENTS FOR A GOOD TEST

In our society, much depends on test scores. In the elementary-school grades, children are often placed in instructional groups on the basis of their performances on tests of math and reading skills. Some high schools require students to pass minimum competency tests in order to graduate. Tests are part of the admissions procedure in many colleges and most professional and graduate schools. Most high-school students who are college-bound must take either the SAT or a similar admission test, the American College Testing Program (ACT). Scores on these tests, as well as high-school grades and other criteria, determine who is admitted to college. Applicants to law schools and medical schools must take special admission tests—the Law School Admissions Test (LSAT) and the Medical College Admissions Test (MCAT); many graduate-school departments require students to take the Graduate Record Exam (GRE). People applying to programs to be trained in most professions (dentistry, nursing, pharmacology, accounting, and business administration, to name a few) must also take special admission tests. And once the training program is completed, more tests must be passed to obtain a license to practice or a certificate of competency. Becoming certified or licensed in almost every trade or profession—as a plumber, beautician, physical therapist, doctor, clinical psychologist, or lawyer—requires the passage of a written examination. In addition, many industries and government agencies select job applicants and place or promote employees on the basis of test scores.

Since tests play such an important role in our lives, it is essential that they measure what they are intended to measure and that the scores accurately reflect the test taker's knowledge and skills. If a test is to be useful, its scores must be both *reliable* and *valid*.

Reliability

Test scores are *reliable* when they are reproducible and consistent. Tests may be unreliable for a number of reasons. Confusing or ambiguous test items may mean different things to a test taker at different times. Tests may be too short to sample the abilities being tested adequately, or scoring may be too subjective. If a test yields different results when it is administered on different occasions or scored by different people, it is unreliable. A simple analogy is a rubber yardstick. If we did not know how much it stretched each time we took a measurement, the results would be unreliable no matter how carefully we marked the measurement. Tests must be reliable if the results are to be used with confidence.

To evaluate reliability, two measures must be obtained for the same individual on the same test. This can be done by repeating the test, by giving the test in two different but equivalent forms, or by treating each half of the test separately. If each individual tested achieves roughly the same score on both measures, then the test is reliable. Of course, even for a reliable test, some differences are to be expected between the pair of scores due to chance and errors of measurement. Consequently, a statistical measure of the degree of relationship between the set of paired scores is needed. This degree of relationship is provided by the coefficient of correlation, r (discussed in Chapter 1). The coefficient of correlation between paired scores for a group of individuals on a given test is called a *reliability coefficient*. Well-constructed tests usually have a reliability coefficient of $r = .90$ or greater.

Validity

Tests are *valid* when they measure what they are intended to measure. A college examination in economics that is full of questions containing complex or tricky wording might be a test of a student's verbal ability rather than of the economics learned in the course. Such an examination might be *reliable* (a student would achieve about the same score on a retest), but it would not be a *valid* test of achievement for the course. A test of sense of humor might be made up of jokes that are hard to understand unless the test taker is very bright and well read. This test might be a reliable measure of something (perhaps intelligence or educational achievement), but it would not be a valid test of humor.

To measure validity, we must also obtain two scores for each person: the test score and some other measure of the ability in question. This measure is called a *criterion*. Suppose that a test is designed to predict success in learning to type. To determine whether the test is valid, it is given to a group of individuals before they study typing. After completing the course, the students are tested on the number of words per minute that they can type accurately. This is a measure of their success and serves as a criterion. A coefficient of correlation between the early test scores and the scores on the criterion can now be obtained. This correlation coefficient, known as the *validity coefficient*, tells something about the value of a given test for a given purpose. The higher the validity coefficient, the more accurate the prediction that can be made from the test results.

Many tests, however, are intended to predict abilities that are more wide-ranging and difficult to measure than typing skills. Scores on the Medical College Admissions Test (MCAT), for example, are used (along with other information) to select medical students. If the purpose of the test is to predict success in medical school, a person's grade point average could be used as a criterion; correlating MCAT scores with grade point averages would be one way of validating the test. But if the MCAT is intended to predict success as a physician, the problem of validation becomes much more difficult. What criterion should be chosen: annual income, research achievements, contributions to community welfare, evaluation by patients or colleagues, number of malpractice suits? Even if the test administrators could agree on one of these criteria, that criterion would probably be difficult to measure.

The validity of ability tests—how well they predict performance—will be discussed later. The important point to remember here is that the evaluation of a test's validity must take into account the intended uses of the test and the inferences to be made from its scores.

Uniform Procedures

To a large extent, the reliability and validity of a test depend on the uniformity of the procedures followed in administering and scoring the test. In measuring ability, as in obtaining any scientific measurement, we attempt to control conditions in order to minimize the influence of extraneous variables. Thus, well-accepted ability tests contain clearly specified instructions, time limits (or, in some cases, no time restrictions), and scoring methods. The explanations given by the examiner and the manner in which the examiner presents the test materials must be standard from one test administration to the next.

Of course, not all extraneous variables can be anticipated or controlled. The sex and race of the examiner, for example, will vary. These characteristics could influence a test taker's performance, as could the examiner's general demeanor (facial expression, tone of voice, and so on). Although such variables cannot be controlled, their influence should be taken into consideration in evaluating test results. Thus, if a black male child does poorly when tested by a white female examiner, the possibility that the child's motivation and anxiety levels would have been different with a black male examiner should be considered.

TESTS OF INTELLECTUAL ABILITY

Reliability, validity, and uniform testing procedures are essential requirements for any test—whether the test is designed to measure personality characteristics (to be discussed in Chapter 14), mastery of a specific subject matter, job skills, or the probability of succeeding in college or professional school. This chapter focuses primarily on tests that measure general intellectual ability. Such tests are often called "intelligence tests," but as we noted earlier, many psychologists consider that term inappropriate. There is no general agreement as to what constitutes intelligence, and intelligence cannot be considered apart from an individual's culture and experiences. During this discussion of intelligence tests, these qualifications should be kept in mind.

Historical Background

The first person to attempt to develop tests of intellectual ability was Sir Francis Galton a century ago. A naturalist and mathematician, Galton developed an interest in individual differences from the evolutionary theory of his cousin, Charles Darwin. Galton believed that certain families are biologically superior—stronger and smarter—than others. Intelligence, he reasoned, is a question of exceptional sensory and perceptual skills, which are

Alfred Binet with his daughters.

passed from one generation to the next. Since all information is acquired through the senses, the more sensitive and accurate an individual's perceptual apparatus, the more intelligent the person. In 1884, Galton administered a battery of tests (measuring such variables as head size, reaction time, visual acuity, auditory thresholds, and memory for visual forms) to over 9,000 visitors at the London Exhibition. To his disappointment, he discovered that eminent British scientists could not be distinguished from ordinary citizens on the basis of their head size and that measurements such as speed of reaction were not particularly related to other measures of intelligence. Although his tests did not prove very useful, Galton did invent the correlation coefficient, which plays an important role in psychology.

The first tests that approximated contemporary intelligence tests were devised by the French psychologist Alfred Binet. In 1881, the French government passed a law making school attendance compulsory for all children. Previously, slow learners had usually been kept at home; now teachers had to cope with a wide range of individual differences. The government asked Binet to create a test that would detect children who were too slow intellectually to benefit from a regular school curriculum.

Binet assumed that intelligence should be measured by tasks that required reasoning and problem-solving abilities rather than perceptual-motor skills. In collaboration with another French psychologist, Théophile Simon, Binet published a scale in 1905, which he revised in 1908 and again in 1911.

Binet's Method: A Mental-Age Scale

Binet reasoned that a slow or dull child was like a normal child retarded in mental growth. On tests, the slow child would perform like a normal child of younger age, whereas the mental abilities of a bright child were characteristic of older children. Binet devised a scale of test items of increasing difficulty that measured the kinds of changes in intelligence ordinarily associated with growing older. The higher a child could go on the scale in correctly answering the items, the higher his or her *mental age* (MA). The concept of mental age was critical in Binet's method; using this method, one could compare the MA of a child with his or her *chronological age* (CA) as determined by date of birth.

The scoring system for computing MA was structured so that the *average* MA for a large sample of children of a particular CA, in fact, equalled that CA. For example, the average MA for all 10-year-olds equalled 10 years, but for any particular 10-year-old, his or her MA could be below, equal to, or above 10 years. Thus a bright child's MA is above his or her CA; a slow child's MA is below his or her CA. This type of mental-age scale is easily interpreted by teachers and others who deal with children of differing mental abilities.

ITEM SELECTION Since intelligence tests are designed to measure brightness rather than the results of special training (that is, aptitude more than achievement), they should consist of items that do not assume any special training. There are two chief ways to select such items. One way is to choose *novel items*, which provide an uneducated child with just as much chance to succeed as a child who has been taught at home or in school. Figure 12-2 illustrates novel items; in this particular test, the child is asked to choose figures that are alike, on the assumption that the designs are unfamiliar to all children. The other way is to choose *familiar items*, on the assumption that all those for whom the test is designed have had the requisite prior experience to deal with the items. The following problem provides an example of a supposedly familiar item:

Mark F if the sentence is foolish; mark S if it is sensible.

S F Mrs. Smith has had no children, and I understand that the same was true of her mother.

Of course, this item is fair only for children who know the English language, who can read, and who understand all the words in the sentence. For such children, detection of the fallacy in the statement becomes a valid test of intellectual ability.

Many of the items on intelligence tests assume general knowledge and familiarity with the language of the test. But such assumptions can never be strictly met. The language spoken in one home is never exactly the same as that spoken in another; the available reading material and the stress on cognitive abilities also vary. Even the novel items test perceptual discriminations that may be acquired in one culture and not in another. Despite these difficulties, items can be chosen that work reasonably well. The items included in contemporary intelligence tests have survived in practice after many others have been tried and found defective. It should be remembered, however, that intelligence tests have been validated according to their success in predicting school performance within a particular culture.

STANFORD-BINET INTELLIGENCE SCALE   The test items originally developed by Binet were adapted for American schoolchildren by Lewis Terman at Stanford University. He standardized the administration of the test

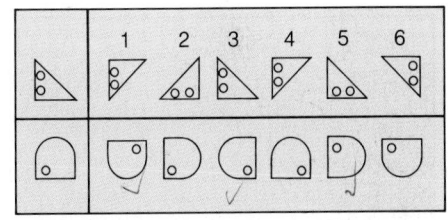

FIGURE 12-2
Novel Items Used in Intelligence Tests *The following instructions accompany the test: Mark every card to the right that matches the sample card on the left. You can rotate the sample card but not flip it over. (Cards 2, 3, and 6 are correct in the first line; cards 1, 3, and 5 are correct in the second line.)*

Test materials from the 1986 Stanford-Binet Intelligence Scale.

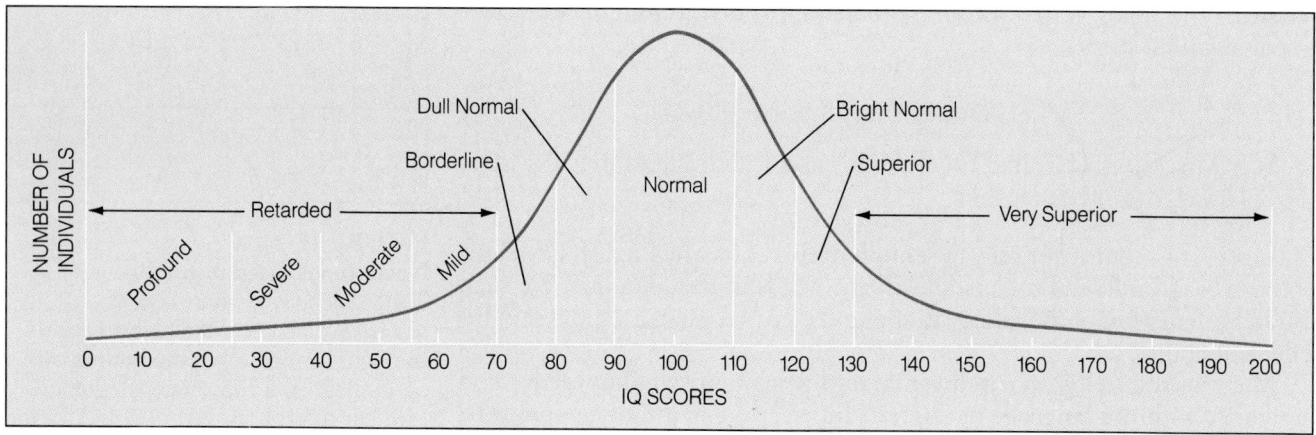

FIGURE 12-3

IQ Distribution *The distribution of IQ scores expected for a large sample of individuals and the adjectives used to describe various levels of IQ. An IQ between 90 and 110 is judged to be normal; above 130, very superior; and below 70, retarded.*

and developed age-level norms by giving the test to thousands of children. In 1916, he published the Stanford revision of the Binet tests, now referred to as the Stanford-Binet Intelligence Scale; it was revised in 1937, 1960, 1972, and most recently in 1986.

Terman retained Binet's concept of mental age. Each test item was age-graded at the level at which a substantial majority of the children passed it. A child's mental age could be obtained by summing the number of items passed at each age level. In addition, Terman adopted a convenient index of intelligence suggested by the German psychologist William Stern. This index is the *intelligence quotient*, commonly known as the IQ. It expresses intelligence as a ratio of mental age (MA) to chronological age (CA):

$$IQ = \frac{MA}{CA} \times 100$$

The 100 is used as a multiplier so that the IQ will have a value of 100 when MA is equal to CA. If MA is lower than CA, then the IQ will be less than 100; if MA is higher than CA, then the IQ will be more than 100.

How is the IQ to be interpreted? The distribution of IQs approximates the form of curve found for many differences among individuals, such as differences in height; this bell-shaped *normal distribution curve* is shown in Figure 12-3. Most cases cluster around a midvalue on the normal curve; from there, the number gradually decreases to just a few cases at both extremes. The adjectives commonly used to describe various IQ levels are also shown in the figure.*

Testing Specific Mental Abilities

The Stanford-Binet uses an assortment of different types of items to test intelligence. Until the 1986 revision, all items contributed equally to the total IQ score. A child might perform very well on a test of vocabulary but poorly on a test requiring drawing geometric forms. These strengths and weaknesses might be noted by the examiner but would not be reflected in the

---

*The most recent revision of the Stanford-Binet (Thorndike, Hagen, & Sattler, 1986) uses Standard Age Scores, instead of IQ scores. These can be interpreted in terms of percentiles which show the percent of subjects in the standardization group falling above or below a given score.

TABLE 12-3
Stanford-Binet Items *Typical examples of items from the 1986 Stanford-Binet Intelligence Scale for a 6- to 8-year-old.*

VERBAL REASONING

Vocabulary Defines words, such as "dollar" and "envelope."
Comprehension Answers questions, such as "Where do people buy food?" and "Why do people comb their hair?"
Absurdities Identifies the "funny" aspect of a picture, such as a girl riding a bicycle in a lake or a bald man combing his head.
Verbal Relations Tells how the first three items in a sequence are alike and how they differ from the fourth: scarf, tie, muffler, shirt.

QUANTITATIVE REASONING

Quantitative Performs simple arithmetic tasks, such as selecting a die with six spots because the number of spots equals the combination of a two-spot and a four-spot die.
Number Series Gives the next two numbers in a series, such as
20 16 12 8 __ __.
Equation Building Builds an equation from the following array:
2 3 5 + =. One correct response would be 2 + 3 = 5.

ABSTRACT/VISUAL REASONING

Pattern Analysis Copies a simple design with blocks.
Copying Copies a geometrical drawing demonstrated by the examiner, such as a rectangle intersected by two diagonals.

SHORT-TERM MEMORY

Bead Memory Shown a picture of different-shaped beads stacked on a stick. Reproduces the sequence from memory by placing real beads on a stick.
Memory for Sentences Repeats after the examiner sentences such as "It is time to go to sleep" and "Ken painted a picture for his mother's birthday."
Memory for Digits Repeats after the examiner a series of digits, such as 5-7-8-3, forward and backward.
Memory for Objects Shown pictures of individual objects, such as a clock and an elephant, one at a time. Identifies the objects in the correct order of their appearance in a picture that also includes extraneous objects; for example, a bus, a clown, an *elephant*, eggs, and a *clock*.

IQ score. In line with the current view of intelligence as a composite of different abilities, the 1986 revision groups its tests into four broad areas of intellectual abilities: *verbal reasoning, abstract/visual reasoning, quantitative reasoning,* and *short-term memory* (Sattler, 1988). A separate score is obtained for each area; Table 12-3 gives some examples of items, grouped by area.

WECHSLER INTELLIGENCE SCALES One of the first intelligence tests to measure separate abilities was developed by David Wechsler in 1939; it ranks with the Stanford-Binet as one of the best known intelligence tests. Wechsler originally developed his test because he felt the Stanford-Binet was not appropriate for adults, and also he felt it depended too heavily on language ability. The Wechsler Adult Intelligence Scale, or WAIS (1939, 1955, 1981), is divided into two parts—a *verbal* scale and a *performance* scale—

TABLE 12-4
Tests Composing the Wechsler Adult Intelligence Scale *The tests of the Wechsler Intelligence Scale for Children are similar with some modifications.*

TEST	DESCRIPTION
VERBAL SCALE	
Information	Questions tap a general range of information; for example, "How many nickels make a dime?"
Comprehension	Tests practical information and ability to evaluate past experience; for example, "What is the advantage of keeping money in a bank?"
Arithmetic	Verbal problems testing arithmetic reasoning.
Similarities	Asks in what way certain objects or concepts (for example, *egg* and *seed*) are similar; measures abstract thinking.
Digit span	A series of digits presented auditorily (for example, 7-5-6-3-8) is repeated in a forward or backward direction; tests attention and rote memory.
Vocabulary	Tests word knowledge.
PERFORMANCE SCALE	
Digit symbol	A timed coding task in which numbers must be associated with marks of various shapes; tests speed of learning and writing.
Picture completion	The missing part of an incompletely drawn picture must be discovered and named; tests visual alertness and visual memory.
Block design	Pictured designs must be copied with blocks; tests ability to perceive and analyze patterns.
Picture arrangement	A series of comic-strip pictures must be arranged in the right sequence to tell a story; tests understanding of social situations.
Object assembly	Puzzle pieces must be assembled to form a complete object; tests ability to deal with part–whole relationships.

which yield separate scores as well as a full-scale IQ. The test items are described in Table 12-4. A similar test for children, the Wechsler Intelligence Scale for Children (WISC), was developed later (1958, 1974).

Items on the performance scale require the manipulation or arrangement of blocks, pictures, or other materials. Both the stimulus displays and the responses are nonverbal. The Wechsler scales also provide scores for each of the subtests, so the examiner has a clearer picture of the individual's intellectual strengths and weaknesses. For example, separate scores can indicate how well the person performs under pressure (some subtests are timed; others are not) or how verbal skills compare with the ability to manipulate nonverbal material. Figure 12-4 shows a test profile and how scores are summed to yield IQs. The subject who obtained these particular scores tends to do better on performance (nonverbal) tasks. Looking at the profile of scores, this 16-year-old does not appear to be doing as well scholastically as he could be; he scores lowest on subtests that are more closely related to school learning

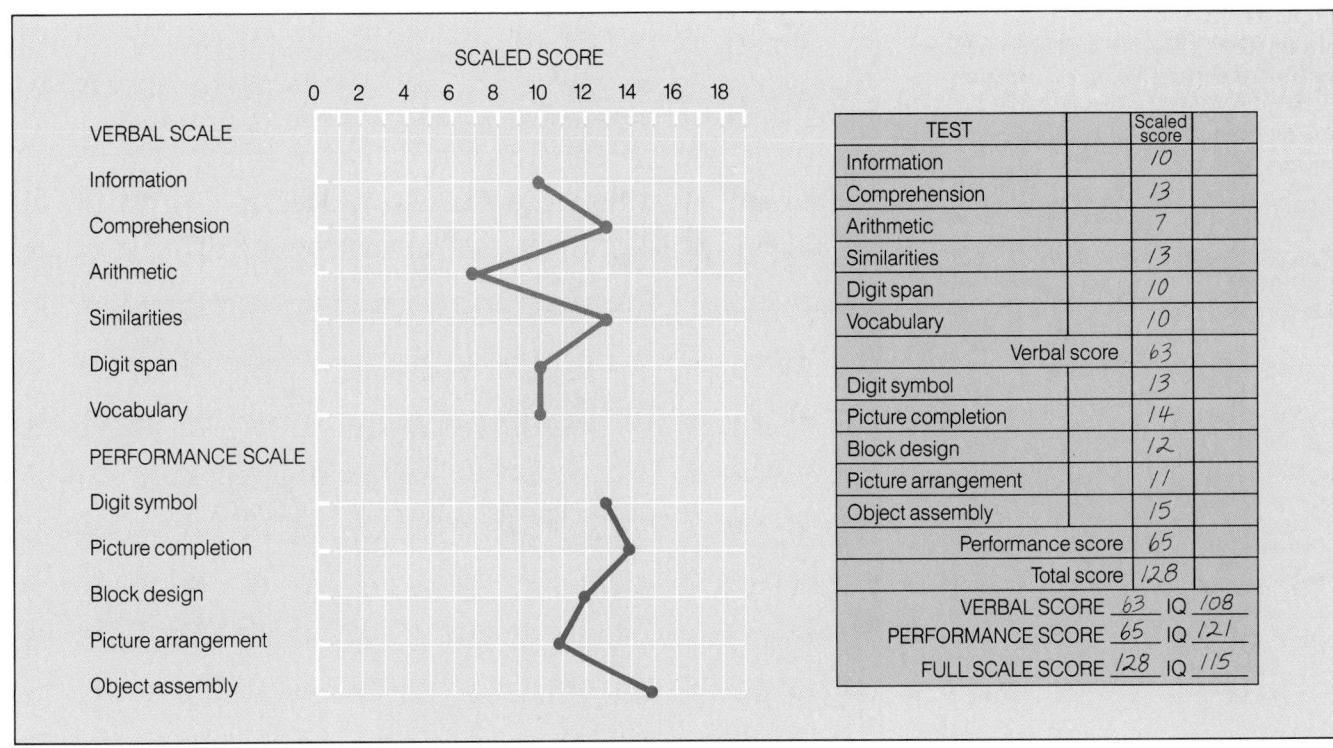

TEST	Scaled score	
Information	*10*	
Comprehension	*13*	
Arithmetic	*7*	
Similarities	*13*	
Digit span	*10*	
Vocabulary	*10*	
Verbal score	*63*	
Digit symbol	*13*	
Picture completion	*14*	
Block design	*12*	
Picture arrangement	*11*	
Object assembly	*15*	
Performance score	*65*	
Total score	*128*	
VERBAL SCORE *63* IQ *108*		
PERFORMANCE SCORE *65* IQ *121*		
FULL SCALE SCORE *128* IQ *115*		

(information, arithmetic, and vocabulary). A discrepancy between verbal and performance scores prompts the examiner to look for specific learning problems, such as reading disabilities or language handicaps.

Both the Stanford-Binet and the Wechsler scales meet the requirements for a good test; that is, they show good reliability and validity. The Stanford-Binet scale has a reliability coefficient of about .90 on retest; the WAIS has a retest reliability of .91. Both tests are fairly valid predictors of achievement in school; the correlation between IQ scores on these tests and school grades is approximately .40 to .60 (Sattler, 1988).

Group Tests

The Stanford-Binet and the Wechsler scales are *individual ability tests*; that is, they are administered to a single individual by a specially trained tester. *Group ability tests*, in contrast, can be administered to a large number of people by a single examiner and are usually in pencil-and-paper form (see Figure 12-5). The advantages of an individual test over a group test are many. The tester can be certain the subject understands the questions, can evaluate the person's motivation (is the subject really trying?), and can gain additional clues to intellectual strengths and weaknesses by carefully observing the subject's approaches to different tasks. Group ability tests are useful, however, when large numbers of people have to be evaluated. The armed services, for example, use a number of group tests that measure general intellectual ability and special skills to help select men and women for special jobs, including pilots, navigators, electronic technicians, and computer programmers. Similarly, the Professional and Administrative Career Examination (PACE) was developed by the U.S. Civil Service Commission for use in selecting employees for government jobs.

FIGURE 12-4
Profile for Wechsler Adult Intelligence Scale *The table on the right shows the test scores for a 16-year-old male combined to yield verbal, performance, and full-scale scores. The manual that accompanies the test provides tables (adjusted for age) for use in converting these scores into IQs. Note that the test taker's performance IQ is 13 points above his verbal IQ.*

FIGURE 12-5
Group Test *These are sample items from the Armed Services Vocational Aptitude Battery (ASVAB), the basic recruit selection and placement test used by all military services.*

Space Perception

Which of the four patterns would result when the box is unfolded?

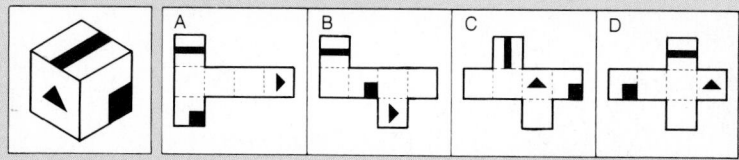

Mechanical Comprehension

Which bridge is the strongest?

Word Knowledge

Stench most nearly means

A. Puddle of slimy water.
B. Pile of debris.
C. Foul odor.
D. Dead animal.

Camaraderie most nearly means

A. Interest in photography.
B. Close friendship.
C. Petty jealousies.
D. Arts and crafts projects.

General Information

For which of the following taxes was it necessary to amend the U.S. Constitution?

A. Income.
B. Sales.
C. Liquor.
D. Tobacco.

Picasso was a famous

A. poet.
B. painter.
C. philosopher.
D. soldier.

Arithmetic Reasoning

It cost $0.50 per square yard to waterproof canvas. What will it cost to waterproof a canvas truck cover that is 15' x 24'?

A. $6.67
B. $18.00
C. $20.00
D. $180.00

The parcel post rate in the local zone is 18 cents for the first pound and 1½ cents for each additional pound. How many pounds can be sent in the local zone for $1.50?

A. 88
B. 89
C. 100
D. 225

Other examples of group tests used to measure general ability are the Scholastic Aptitude Test (SAT), developed by the Princeton-based Educational Testing Service, and the American College Test (ACT), developed by the Iowa-based American College Testing Program. Virtually all 4-year colleges require that applicants take either the ACT or SAT as a way of setting a common standard for students from high schools with different curricula and grading standards. The SAT is used mostly by colleges on the East and West coasts, whereas the ACT is dominant in the Midwest, Southeast, and Rocky Mountains.

The SAT has two sections of multiple-choice items, one testing verbal skills and the other mathematical skills (see Table 12-1). However, the developers of the SAT have begun a review of their test and plan to introduce a new essay section, open-ended (rather than multiple-choice) mathematics questions, and enough additional algebra items to provide two mathematics' subscores. The changes are seen as a way of a) providing students with more detailed feedback on their performance; b) increasing the usefulness of the test for educators and others who use it for student counseling and course placement; and c) comparing different high schools.

In past years, the ACT consisted of subtests in English, mathematics, social studies, and the natural sciences; students received scores in each of these four areas as well as a composite score. In 1989, the ACT test-developers revised the number of subtests to 12. These include an expanded mathematics section with more than one subscore, a new reading test, an English section that places more emphasis on writing skills, and separate science reasoning tests for biology, chemistry, physics, and the physical sciences. The tests require minimal knowledge of these subjects. Instead, they use graphs, tables, and summaries of research to measure how well students can deal with abstract concepts.

The changes in the ACT, and the proposed changes in the SAT, are in response to recent high-school curriculum trends that place a premium on more sophisticated reading, writing, and mathematics skills. Standards are being raised in the nation's high schools, and there is an increased emphasis on abstract thinking and reasoning skills.

CRITICAL DISCUSSION

Can Tests Be Culturally Fair?

A person's performance on an ability test clearly is dependent on the culture in which he or she is raised. Obviously, this is true of verbal tests that require familiarity with a particular language. We would not expect a child from a home in which English is spoken as a second language to score as well on verbal items as a child whose parents speak only English. But even among children from English-speaking families, the vocabulary in a middle-class home may differ significantly from the vocabulary in a lower-class home. In one study, for example, children were asked to consider the following item:

Pick ONE WORD that does not belong with the others.

cello   harp   drum   violin   guitar

Most children from upper- or middle-class homes chose "drum," the intended correct answer. Children from lower-class homes commonly answered "cello," an unfamiliar word that they thought did not belong (Eells et al., 1951). Children from upper-class homes are more likely to be acquainted with cellos, or at least to have heard the word, than are children from poorer homes.

Several tests have been developed that are based on black culture and language (see Williams, 1972; Boone & Adesso, 1974). The vocabulary and idioms used in these tests are more or less characteristic of Black English and include items similar to the following:

"Running a game" means:

A   writing a bad check
B   looking at something
C   directing a contest
D   getting what one wants

Those familiar with Black English will recognize that D is the correct answer.

These tests emphasize the extent to which cultural factors can influence test scores; blacks may score 20 IQ points higher than whites on such tests. But the test scores apparently bear little relationship to other measures of intelligence or achievement for members of either race (Matarazzo & Wiens, 1977).

Cultural experiences can also affect performance on nonverbal items. Numerical operations and mathematical concepts are taught primarily in school. And even items that presumably are unrelated to schooling (such as recognizing the missing element in a drawing of a common object or manipulating blocks to form a pattern) are not wholly independent of culture. For example, if children from poor families are shown a drawing of a comb with several teeth missing and asked to name the missing part (an item on the WISC), they may be puzzled; to them, a broken comb may be more common than a whole one (Hewitt & Massey, 1969).

In some nonliterate societies, drawings and pictures are rare. When Nigerian children were asked to manipulate colored blocks to form a design (a task included in several intelligence tests), they did quite well when the design to be copied was also made of blocks. But

PREDICTIVE VALIDITY OF TESTS

Tests of general ability, such as the Stanford-Binet and Wechsler Intelligence Scales, do predict achievement in school and do provide a measure of what most people think of as brightness. When elementary-school teachers are asked to rank children in their classrooms in terms of brightness, correlations between the teachers' rankings and scores on intelligence tests range from .60 to .80. These correlations would probably be higher except for some interesting biases in judgment. For example, teachers tend to overrate the youngest children in their classrooms and underrate the oldest; apparently, they base their judgments on mental age rather than on IQ, which expresses the relationship between mental age and chronological age. Teachers also tend to overrate girls and underrate boys. In general, children who are sociable, eager, and self-confident—who volunteer for activities and raise their hands to recite—are viewed by their teachers and peers as brighter than children who are withdrawn and quiet, even though their test scores may be the same. In such instances, ability test scores provide a more accurate estimate of ability than the teacher's judgments.

it was difficult for them to copy a design from a picture until the examiner demonstrated with the blocks (D'Andrade, 1967).

Psychologists have made a number of attempts to develop tests that are culturally fair (see the figure), but the results have not been promising. For one thing, the culture-fair tests do not predict scholastic performance (or, in some instances, performance on the job) as well as do more conventional ability tests. This finding is not surprising, since what is considered a good performance in school or on the job is also culture-dependent. For another thing, group differences on culture-fair tests are often as large as the differences on the tests they have been designed to replace.

In principle, it is probably impossible to design a completely culture-fair test; an individual's performance will always be affected by his or her cultural background. The abilities that a society considers important are the ones it will take the trouble to test. If writing and quantitative skills are valued in a society, these skills will be viewed as predictive of success. If social skills and the use of complex riddles in storytell-

ing are valued (as they are among the Kpelle people of Liberia), these skills will be considered the important ones to test (Cole, 1981).

In the absence of satisfactory culture-fair tests, the best we can do at present is to recognize the cultural

basis of our standard intelligence tests and interpret the scores with caution, keeping in mind the individual's background—the language spoken in the home and the kinds of learning experiences provided (Neisser, 1986; Miller-Jones, 1989).

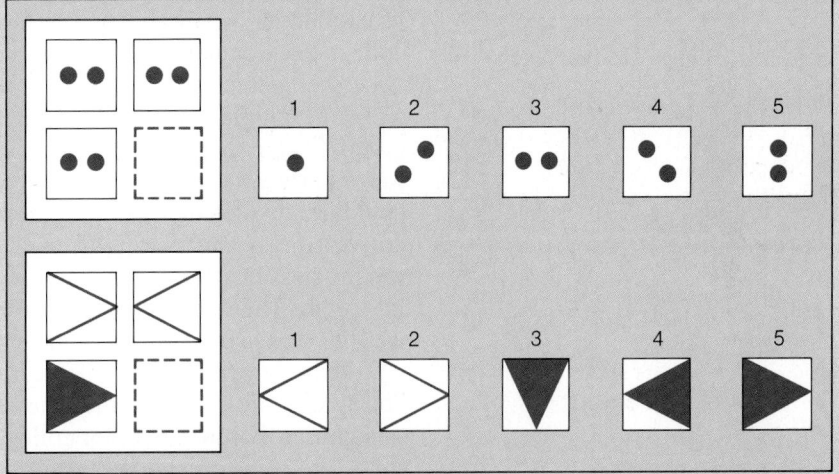

Culture-Fair Test *Sample items from a test designed to be relatively independent of the culture in which one is raised. The test taker is to select one of the five items on the right that best completes the pattern on the left.* (Taken from Culture Fair Intelligence Test, Scale 2, Form A test booklet. Copyright © 1949, 1960, Institute for Personality and Ability Testing, Inc. All rights reserved. Reproduced by permission.)

Test Scores and Academic Performance

Intelligence test scores correlate highly with measures of academic performance (for example, grades, continuation in school, likelihood of graduating), at least during the elementary- and high-school years. Youngsters who achieve higher scores on tests like the Stanford-Binet and Wechsler Intelligence Scales get better grades, enjoy school more, and stay in school longer. But as students move up the educational ladder—from elementary school to high school to college to graduate school—the correlations between intelligence test scores and measures of academic performance become progressively lower (see Table 12-5). A number of factors contribute to the progressive decrease in the size of validity coefficients as schooling increases. We will see shortly that one of the most important factors is *selection*.

Thus far, we have talked about the relationship between academic performance and tests designed to measure general aptitude for learning (so-called intelligence tests that yield an IQ score). What about scholastic aptitude tests, like the SAT, that measure developed abilities and are designed to predict performance in college? The SAT has been given to millions of college applicants over many years, and numerous studies have correlated SAT

TABLE 12-5
Correlation between IQ Scores and Academic Achievement *Table entries give the correlations typically observed between intelligence test scores and other measures of academic achievement (for example, grades or achievement test scores) at different levels of schooling.*

EDUCATIONAL LEVEL	TYPICAL CORRELATIONS
Elementary School	.60–.70
High School	.50–.60
College	.40–.50
Graduate School	.30–.40

scores with freshman grade point averages. The correlations vary from study to study, with a median correlation of about .38 for the verbal section of the SAT and .34 for the mathematics section (Linn, 1982).

These correlations underestimate to some extent the relationship between test scores and college grades, because the criterion data (grade point averages) are collected only for those individuals who actually attend college. If everyone who took the SAT attended college, and the test scores were correlated with his or her freshman grades, the correlations would be much higher. The size of a correlation coefficient is affected by the amount of variability in the measures being correlated; in general, the more select the group, the narrower the range of scores and the lower the correlation. College students are more capable than the population at large. If the entire college-age population were tested and attended college, the correlation between test scores and freshman grades would be higher still.

An example may help to explain why correlations are lower in a selected group. Before there were weight classifications in the sport of boxing, weight was a fairly good predictor of the outcome of a match. A 250-pound boxer could usually defeat a 150-pounder, regardless of differences in training; the correlation between weight and winning was quite high. However, once weight classifications were introduced and boxers fought only boxers of similar weight (heavyweights against heavyweights, lightweights against lightweights, and so on), weight became a poor predictor of outcome (Fricke, 1975).

Although the effects of selection on correlations between SAT scores and grades are less extreme than in the above example, they still can be substantial. For instance, for colleges with freshman classes that show a wide range of scores on the verbal section of the SAT, the correlation between SAT-Verbal scores and freshman grade point averages is .44. For colleges with less variability, the correlation is .31 (Schrader, 1971). The more select or homogeneous the group is, the lower the correlation.

If correlations between SAT scores and freshman grades are "corrected" statistically to take into account the selective nature of the population, the resulting correlations are around .50. What does a correlation of this size mean in terms of predictability? A correlation of .50 indicates that the chances are 44 out of 100 that a student in the top fifth of the distribution of SAT scores will also be in the top fifth of the distribution of freshman grade point averages, whereas the chances that a student in the bottom fifth of the SAT scores will earn such grades are only 4 out of 100. With no knowledge of the test scores, the chances would, of course, be 20 out of 100. Thus, SAT scores improve prediction considerably, but it is also clear that the freshman grades of students with the same SAT scores will vary widely.

Group Differences in Test Performance

Differences in average performance on ability tests are often found when certain subgroups of the population are studied. For example, children from middle- or upper-income families score higher, on the average, than children from poor families. Mean differences are found in performance on tests of general ability as well as on achievement tests, whether the group of children is defined in terms of parental occupation, education, or income (Speath, 1976). Members of some minority groups—blacks, Hispanic Americans, American Indians—also tend to score lower on ability tests than members of the white majority (Jones, 1984).

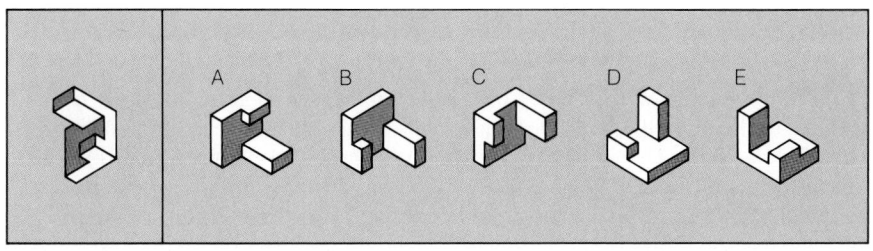

FIGURE 12-6
Visual-Spatial Skills *An example of the type of problem used to test for visual-spatial abilities. The testee is required to select from the five blocks on the right the one that is the same as the block on the left, except that it has been rotated and presented from a different perspective. The correct answer is B.*

Males and females score about the same on intelligence tests (such as the Stanford-Binet and the Wechsler Intelligence Scales). Most intelligence tests have been constructed to minimize sex differences either by deleting items showing large sex differences or by balancing items advantageous to females with those advantageous to males.

Until recently, however, tests of specific abilities have shown some differences between the sexes. Females, *on the average*, have scored higher than males on tests of verbal ability; males, *on the average*, have scored higher than females on tests of mathematical reasoning and visual-spatial skills. Visual-spatial skills are required in tasks such as conceptualizing how an object in space would look from a different perspective and reading maps or blueprints (see Figure 12-6).

These sex differences in cognitive abilities, which have been observed almost since the beginning of systematic testing, appear to be vanishing. An analysis of more than 3 decades (from 1947 to 1980) of scores on tests of specific abilities given to high-school students nationwide found that differences between boys and girls decreased progressively over that period (Feingold, 1988).

A recent analysis that looked at hundreds of studies of sex differences in ability conducted during the last 20 years reached similar conclusions: male verbal proficiency has been increasing over the years to match that of females, while female ability on tests of mathematical reasoning has been increasing to match that of males (Hyde & Linn, 1988; Linn & Hyde, 1989). The one test that continues to show differences in these abilities is the SAT; males and females score about the same on the verbal section, but males score significantly higher on the mathematical section.

The fact that sex differences in cognitive ability have decreased over the years suggests that earlier differences in test scores reflected differences in training and social expectations: until recently, girls were encouraged to develop interests in poetry and literature; boys were expected to be more concerned with science and mechanical things. Although society has become more egalitarian and parents and teachers are less stereotyped in the abilities they encourage, there are still differences in the way the sexes are treated that may make girls less confident in mathematics. Parents still believe science and mathematics to be less important for girls than for boys; they tend to exaggerate their sons' abilities in these areas and to underestimate the abilities of their daughters. And they are more likely to purchase computers and scientific toys for boys than for girls. Teachers of science and mathematics also tend to provide more encouragement and reinforcement for boys than for girls (Eccles & Jacobs, 1986).

Thus, differences on the SAT math test may reflect sex differences in self-confidence. It appears too that some of the math questions are biased toward males by subject content. For example, they involve situations taken from sports with which males may be more familiar.

CRITICAL DISCUSSION

Coaching and Test Sophistication

Courses that claim to improve an applicant's score on such admissions tests as the Scholastic Aptitude Test (SAT), the Law School Admissions Test (LSAT), the Medical College Admissions Test (MCAT), the Graduate Record Examination (GRE), and the Graduate Management Aptitude Test (GMAT) are offered daily in the newspapers. Coaching for such tests has become a profitable business. The degree to which coaching can improve test scores, however, is a controversial issue: if coaching does result in higher scores, applicants who can afford to pay for such courses have an advantage over those who cannot.

Being familiar with testing procedures is clearly helpful. An individual who has had prior experience in taking tests and who knows what to expect will be more confident than a person who has had limited test-taking experience. *Test sophistication* includes being familiar with separate answer sheets, considering *all* the answers in a multiple-choice item rather than picking the first one that seems right, knowing not to spend too much time on puzzling items, and spotting flaws in items that provide additional clues. It also helps to know when to guess. If there is no penalty for incorrect answers, it makes sense to guess when you do not know the correct answer. On tests such as the SAT, where a wrong answer on a four-choice item is scored $-\frac{1}{4}$ (compared to 1 point for a correct answer and 0 for no response), it pays to guess if the answer can be narrowed to two or three possible alternatives.

Instruction in test-taking strategies and practice with sample test questions are included in most courses that prepare applicants for admissions tests.

Commercially published practice booklets, available for the major admissions tests, can be used for a similar kind of self-coaching. Familiarity with the test format, knowledge of test-taking strategies, and practice on sample test items do result in higher test scores, but the gain is substantial only for naive test takers (for example, recent immigrants or students from schools that require little testing). Students who have graduated from American high schools, which provide substantial exposure to objective tests, probably would not benefit from spending more than a day on practice test items.

What about instruction in specific subjects? Admissions tests are designed to measure an individual's aptitude for a particular program of study, and test constructors try to avoid items on which performance can be raised by short-term drill or instruction in specialized topics. However, the verbal section of the SAT (and of the LSAT, MCAT, and GRE) relies heavily on vocabulary, and many of the problems in the quantitative section presume knowledge of

---

The one area of cognitive ability that continues to show a consistent sex difference is visual-spatial relations. Tests still show a superior performance for males in these skills, particularly when the tasks are timed and require mental rotation of objects (Burnett, 1986). Sex differences in spatial ability may partly account for sex differences in mathematical ability, since spatial visualization is one strategy for solving mathematical problems.

It will be interesting to see whether sex differences in spatial ability diminish in the years ahead as the environment for women changes. Some researchers think that this will be the case. Others believe that sex differences in visual-spatial abilities stem from the effect of sex hormones on the development of the brain during the fetal period. They propose that the ability to visualize objects mentally is related to the rate at which the two cerebral hemispheres develop; the male hormone, testosterone, presumably slows the development of the left hemisphere, resulting in a more highly specialized right hemisphere for males (Benbow, 1988). It remains to be seen whether the biological or the environmental explanation for sex differences in visual-spatial ability will prove to be correct.

Two points should be emphasized whenever group differences in performance are discussed. First, these are only *average* differences; the size of the differences between subgroups is usually small compared to the variability within groups. Thus, some girls will score higher than most boys on tests of spatial relations; conversely, some boys will score lower than most girls.

high-school algebra and geometry. For individuals who feel deficient in these subjects, a review would be worthwhile. Several studies have shown that coaching in mathematics raises scores on the quantitative section of the SAT for high-school students who are not currently studying math, but it is of little benefit for those enrolled in mathematics courses. Vocabulary flashcards and reading with the aid of a dictionary would be helpful in preparing for the verbal section.

Over the past 30 years, numerous studies have been conducted to determine the effects of coaching on SAT scores. The studies covered a variety of coaching methods and included commercial programs as well as programs offered to students in public and private high schools. The results vary markedly, depending on the length and type of program and the presence or absence of a control group. (Control groups are important because students who enroll in coaching courses are apt to differ from those who do not in a number of ways—especially in

level of motivation—and it is difficult to evaluate their test-score gains without referring to a comparable group of students.)

Messick and Jungeblut (1981) have published an analysis of research studies on SAT coaching that include control groups. They conclude that 30 hours of instruction in verbal skills, for instance, can result in average score gains of about 14 points on the verbal section of the SAT. An additional 30 hours of instruction in mathematics skills can result in average score gains of about 26 points on the mathematics section. These gains from 60 hours of instruction represent 40 points on the combined SAT scale. Since SAT scores range from a minimum of 400 to a maximum of 1600, gains of this size are not likely to affect college admission decisions. A subsequent study by Der Simonian and Laird (1983) comes to similar conclusions.

Several studies (without control groups) report much larger gains of 50–80 points on both sections of the SAT (Pallone, 1961; Marron, 1965).

However, the subjects in these studies were enrolled in fairly intensive, long-term coaching programs of up to 6 months. The issue here is the difference between *education* and *coaching*. The SAT is designed to assess *developed* abilities. One year of high-school courses in English and algebra does increase SAT scores; it is not surprising that a 6-month coaching course produces a similar effect (Jones, 1984).

What recommendations should be made regarding coaching for admissions tests? For purposes of equity, a brief course in test strategies plus practice on sample test items under examination conditions would help to equalize test sophistication among individuals who have different amounts of experience in taking objective tests. Reviews of vocabulary and of algebra and geometry skills would probably benefit individuals whose background in these areas is deficient. It is probably not worthwhile for people with a normal high-school education to spend a great deal of time or money on coaching courses.

Similarly, some children from poor families will score higher than most children from higher-income families, and some members of minority groups will score higher than most members of the white majority.

Second, as we have seen from the discussion of sex differences, group differences in average test scores cannot be viewed as evidence of innate differences in ability. They may reflect differences in home environment, social expectations, and opportunities to learn. However, to the extent that group differences in average test scores reflect differences in the probability of success in school or on the job, the distinctions need to be understood.

Later we will discuss some possible reasons for differences in test performance among racial, ethnic, and socioeconomic groups. But the existence of group differences does not mean that tests are not useful for predicting performance. Ability tests predict scholastic performance for minority students as well as they do for white students. For example, if black grade-school children are ranked according to scores on an intelligence test, the rankings predict school performance in mathematics and reading as well as they do for white children. And SAT scores predict college freshman grades for blacks and Mexican-Americans as well as they do for whites (Linn, 1982).

Saying that ability tests are not biased does not deny that society discriminates against minority groups. There is undoubtedly a bias in opportunity against minority groups that results in their lower scores on ability tests and on the criterion measure (grades, class standing, and so forth).

Using Tests to Predict Performance

Although ability tests are useful in predicting academic performance, they are only one measure and should always be used in combination with other information. For example, senior-year high-school grades correlate about as highly with freshman grade point averages as SAT scores do. This fact raises some questions about the usefulness of admissions tests. However, it can be argued that college admission test scores provide an adjustment for the variability in the quality of education among different high schools (grades from one high school may not be equivalent to grades from another). Indeed, a combination of SAT scores and high-school grades does predict college grades better than either of these variables alone.

Ability tests can provide a reasonably good indication of whether a person can read and comprehend certain material or solve quantitative problems. But tests cannot assess an individual's social concerns, willingness to work, or interpersonal skills. Tests provide some basis for predicting academic success, but they do not indicate which students will become creative writers, talented teachers, and outstanding physicians.

Scores on admissions tests provide one piece of information. They should be evaluated along with other measures (high-school grades, recommendations, special achievements) to predict an applicant's academic performance.

TABLE 12-6
Factor Analysis *An example of the data and computational methods involved in factor analysis.*

What are the data that enter into factor analysis, and what are the major steps in the analysis? The data are simply scores on a variety of tests designed to measure various psychological contents or processes. Each of a large number of individuals obtains a score for each of a number of tests. All these scores can then be intercorrelated; that is, we know how the scores of many individuals on Test 1 relate to their scores on Test 2, and so on. These intercorrelationships yield a table of correlations known as a *correlation matrix*. An example of such a correlation matrix, based on only nine tests, is given below.

TESTS	2	3	4	5	6	7	8	9
1	.38	.55	.06	−.04	.05	.07	.05	.09
2		.36	.40	.28	.40	.11	.15	.13
3			.10	.01	.18	.13	.12	.10
4				.32	.60	.04	.06	.13
5					.35	.08	.13	.11
6						.01	.06	.07
7							.45	.32
8								.32

The three color boxes of correlations indicate that these are groups of tests with something in common not shared by other tests (that is, they show high correlations). The inadequacy of making such a judgment from a table of correlations of this kind is shown by noting the additional high correlations of Test 2 with Tests 4, 5, and 6, not included in the outlined clusters. We can use factor analysis to tell us more precisely what underlies these correlations. If the correlation matrix contains a number of statistically significant correlations and a number of near-zero correlations, it is apparent that some tests measure similar abilities of one kind and that others measure abilities of other kinds. The purpose of factor analysis is to be more precise about these underlying abilities.

NATURE OF INTELLIGENCE

Some psychologists view intelligence as a general capacity for comprehension and reasoning that manifests itself in various ways. This was Binet's assumption. Although his test contained many different kinds of items (testing such abilities as memory span, arithmetic skills, and vocabulary knowledge), Binet noted that bright children tended to score higher than dull children on all of them. He assumed, therefore, that the different tasks sampled a basic ability or faculty.

> It seems to us that in intelligence there is a fundamental faculty, the alteration or the lack of which is of the utmost importance for practical life. This faculty is judgment, otherwise called good sense, practical sense, initiative, the faculty of adapting one's self to circumstances. To judge well, to comprehend well, to reason well, these are the essential activities of intelligence. (Binet & Simon, 1905)

Despite the diverse subscales that compose his tests, David Wechsler also believed that "intelligence is the aggregate or global capacity of the individual to act purposefully, to think rationally, and to deal effectively with his environment" (Wechsler, 1958).

Factor analysis then uses mathematical methods (assisted by high-speed computers) to compute the correlation of each of the tests with each of several possible underlying factors. Such correlations between test scores and factors are known as *factor loadings*; if a test correlates .05 on factor I, .10 on factor II, and .70 on factor III, it is most heavily "loaded" on factor III. For example, the nine tests with the above correlation matrix yield the *factor matrix* below.

TESTS	FACTORS		
	I	II	III
1	.75	−.01	.08
2	.44	.48	.16
3	.72	.07	.15
4	.08	.76	.08
5	−.01	.49	−.01
6	.16	.73	.02
7	−.03	.04	.64
8	.02	.05	.66
9	−.01	.10	.47

The color boxes in the factor matrix show which tests are most highly correlated with each of the underlying factors. The clusters are the same as the clusters in the correlation matrix but are now assigned greater precision. The problem of Test 2 remains because it is loaded almost equally on factor I and factor II; it is obviously not a "factor-pure" test. Having found the three factors that account for the intercorrelations of the nine tests, the factors can be interpreted by studying the content of the tests most highly weighted on each factor. The factor analysis itself is strictly a mathematical process, but the naming and interpretation of the factors depends on a psychological analysis.

Factorial Approach

Other psychologists question whether there is such a thing as "general intelligence." They believe that intelligence tests sample a number of mental abilities that are relatively *independent of one another*. One method of obtaining more precise information about the kinds of abilities that determine performance on intelligence tests is *factor analysis*. This mathematical technique is used to determine the minimum number of *factors*, or abilities, that are required to explain the observed pattern of correlations for an array of different tests. The basic idea is that two tests that correlate very highly with each other are probably measuring the same underlying ability. The factor analysis of data from an array of tests tells us how many distinguishable factors enter the set of correlations and the weight (or influence) of each factor. Factor analysis is too complicated to describe in detail, but Table 12-6 on pages 458–59 provides a brief account of the method.

The originator of factor analysis, Charles Spearman (1904), proposed that all individuals possess a general intelligence factor (called *g*) in varying amounts. A person could be described as generally bright or generally dull, depending on the amount of *g* he or she possessed. According to Spearman, the *g* factor is the major determinant of performance on intelligence test items. In addition, special factors, each called *s*, are specific to particular abilities or tests. For example, tests of arithmetic or spatial relationships would each tap a separate *s*. An individual's tested intelligence would reflect the amount of *g* plus the magnitude of the various *s* factors. Performance in mathematics would be a function of a person's general intelligence and mathematical aptitude.

A later investigator, Louis Thurstone (1938), objected to Spearman's emphasis on general intelligence. Thurstone felt that intelligence could be broken down into a number of primary abilities. To determine these abilities, he applied factor analysis to results from a large number of different tests. One set of test items was designed to measure verbal comprehension; another, to measure arithmetical computation; and so on. Thurstone hoped to find a more definitive way of grouping intelligence test items than the rather crude method of item sorting used in the Wechsler verbal and performance scales.

After intercorrelating the scores of all the tests (that is, correlating each test with every other test), Thurstone applied factor analysis to arrive at a set of basic factors. Test items that best represented each of the discovered factors were used to form new tests; these tests were then given to another group of subjects and the intercorrelations were reanalyzed. After several studies of this kind, Thurstone identified seven factors as the *primary mental abilities* revealed by intelligence tests: verbal comprehension, word fluency, number, space, memory, perceptual speed, and reasoning (see Table 12-7).

Thurstone devised a battery of tests, known as the *Test of Primary Mental Abilities*, to measure each of these abilities. Revised versions of this test are still widely used, but its predictive power is no greater than the predictability of general intelligence tests, such as the Wechsler scales. Thurstone's hope of discovering the basic elements of intelligence through factor analysis was not fully realized for several reasons. His primary abilities are not completely independent; the significant intercorrelations among them provide some support for Spearman's concept of a general intelligence factor. In addition, the number of basic abilities identified by factor analysis depends on the

ABILITY	DESCRIPTION
Verbal comprehension	The ability to understand the meaning of words; vocabulary tests represent this factor.
Word fluency	The ability to think of words rapidly, as in solving anagrams or thinking of words that rhyme.
Number	The ability to work with numbers and perform computations.
Space	The ability to visualize space-form relationships, as in recognizing the same figure presented in different orientations.
Memory	The ability to recall verbal stimuli, such as word pairs or sentences.
Perceptual speed	The ability to grasp details quickly and to see similarities and differences between pictured objects.
Reasoning	The ability to find a general rule on the basis of presented instances, as in determining how a number series is constructed after being presented with only a portion of that series.

TABLE 12-7
Thurstone's Primary Mental Abilities
Using factor analysis, Thurstone identified seven factors as the primary abilities revealed by intelligence tests. (After Thurstone & Thurstone, 1963)

nature of the test items. Other investigators, using different test items and alternative methods of factor analysis, have identified from 20 to 150 factors to represent the range of intellectual abilities (Ekstrom, French, Harman, & Derman, 1976; Ekstrom, French, & Harman, 1979; Guilford, 1982). This lack of consistency in the number and kinds of factors raises doubts about the validity of the *factorial approach.* Nevertheless, factor analysis continues to be a principal technique for studying intellectual performance (Carrol, 1988).

Information-Processing Approach

Until the 1960s, research on intelligence was dominated by the factorial approach. However, with the development of cognitive psychology and its emphasis on *information-processing models,* a new approach has emerged. This approach is defined somewhat differently by different investigators, but the basic idea is to try to understand intelligence in terms of the cognitive processes that operate when we engage in intellectual activities (Hunt, 1985). More specifically, the information-processing approach asks:

1. What mental processes are involved in the various tests of intelligence?
2. How rapidly and accurately are these processes carried out?
3. What types of mental representations of information do these processes act upon?

Rather than trying to explain intelligence in terms of factors, this approach attempts to identify the mental processes that underlie intelligent behavior.

TABLE 12-8
Components of Intelligence *Sternberg's scheme for classifying the many component processes operative in solving problems.* (After Sternberg, 1985)

COMPONENTS	PROCESSES
Metacomponents	Higher-order control processes used for executive planning and decision making in problem solving.
Performance components	Processes that execute the plans and implement the decisions selected by metacomponents.
Acquisition components	Processes involved in learning new information.
Retention components	Processes involved in retrieving information previously stored in memory.
Transfer components	Processes involved in carrying over retained information from one situation to another.

The information-processing approach assumes that individual differences on a given task depend on the specific processes that different individuals bring into play and the speed and accuracy of these processes. The goal is to use an information-processing model of a particular task to identify appropriate measures of the component processes. These measures may be as simple as the response to a multiple-choice item, or they may include the subject's speed of response, perhaps even eye movements and cortical evoked potentials associated with the response. The idea is to use whatever information is needed to estimate the efficiency of each component process.

The information-processing approach can be illustrated by the work of Sternberg (1985) and his *componential model* of intelligence. He assumes that the test taker possesses a set of mental processes, which he calls *components*, that operate in an organized way to produce the responses observed on an intelligence test. There are many components that fall into the five classes given in Table 12-8. Sternberg selects a specific task from an intelligence test and uses it in a series of experiments to try to identify the components involved in the task. For example, consider analogy tests of the following sort:

lawyer : client :: doctor : (medicine, patient)

A series of experiments with analogy problems led Sternberg to conclude that the critical components were the *encoding process* and the *comparison process*. The subject encodes each of the words in the analogy by forming a mental representation of the word—in this case, a list of attributes of the word that are retrieved from the subject's long-term memory. For example, a mental representation of the word "lawyer" might include the following attributes: college-educated, versed in legal procedures, represents clients in court, and so on. Once the subject has formed a mental representation for each word in the analogy, the comparison process scans the representations looking for matching attributes that solve the analogy.

Other processes are involved in analogy problems, but Sternberg has shown that individual differences on this task are principally determined by the efficiency of the encoding and comparison processes. The experimental evidence shows that individuals who score high on analogy problems (skilled performers) spend more time encoding and form more accurate mental representations than do individuals who score low on such problems (less-skilled performers). In contrast, during the comparison stage, the skilled performers are *faster* than the less-skilled performers in matching attributes, but both are *equally accurate* on matching attributes. Thus the better test scores for skilled performers are based on the increased accuracy of their encoding process, but the time they require to solve the problem is a complicated mix of slow encoding speeds and fast comparisons (Pellegrino, 1985; Galotti, 1989).

A factorial approach and an information-processing approach provide complementary interpretations of performance on intelligence tests. Factors such as Thurstone's primary mental abilities are useful in identifying broad areas of strengths and weaknesses. They may indicate that a person is strong in word fluency and verbal comprehension but weak in reasoning. If additional testing is conducted, an information-processing analysis could provide a diagnostic profile of the processes responsible for the observed deficiency. A process analysis may indicate a deficiency at the level of metacomponents (such as the choice of strategies used to attack the problem), or retention components (such as slow or inaccurate recall of relevant information), or transfer components (such as poor ability to transfer what has been learned in one situation to another).

Aspects of Intelligence

Sternberg (1985), in an attempt to generalize his approach, argues that a comprehensive theory of intelligence would involve a much larger set of component processes than have been identified to date by psychologists working in the restricted environment of a laboratory or a typical testing situation. He suggests that this larger set of components would relate not only to "academic intelligence" but also to "practical intelligence"; they would be organized and operate in clusters that might be labeled roughly as follows:

1. Ability to learn and profit from experience
2. Ability to think or reason abstractly
3. Ability to adapt to the vagaries of a changing and uncertain world
4. Ability to motivate oneself to accomplish expeditiously the tasks one needs to accomplish.

Other psychologists—whether working from the perspective of the factorial approach or the information-processing approach—would generally agree with this list. Most intelligence tests in use today are fairly effective in assessing the first two abilities, but they are of minimal value in assessing the last two. Undoubtedly, this is why conventional intelligence tests are very effective in predicting academic achievement but are far less predictive of personal achievement outside the academic world. Our ability to measure intelligence with the type of tests in use today probably has reached a ceiling (Sternberg & Wagner, 1986). New methods will have to be developed that more accurately assess motivation and practical problem-solving ability in order to improve the predictive power of intelligence tests. These new methods will probably require a more interactive testing situation than that provided by paper-and-pencil tests. Computer-controlled testing may provide the flexibility and richness of interaction required (Wenger, 1987).

CRITICAL DISCUSSION

Theory of Multiple Intelligences

Howard Gardner (1983) has proposed an approach to intelligence that is similar in many ways to the factorial and information-processing approaches. Nevertheless, his approach has so many unique features that it deserves special consideration.

According to Gardner, there is no such thing as a singular intelligence; rather, there are at least six distinct kinds of intelligence. These six intelligences are independent of one another, each operating as a separate system (or module) in the brain according to its own rules. The six intelligences are:

1. Linguistic
2. Logical-mathematical
3. Spatial
4. Musical
5. Bodily-kinesthetic
6. Personal

The first three are familiar components of intelligence, and Gardner's description of them is similar to what other theorists have proposed; they are what standard intelligence tests measure. The last three are surprising and may even seem frivolous in a discussion of intelligence, but Gardner believes that they deserve comparable status to the first three. He argues that musical intelligence, for example, has been more important than logical-mathematical intelligence throughout most of human history. The development of logical scientific thought occurred late in the evolution of the human species (as an invention of western culture in the aftermath of the Renaissance); in contrast, musical and artistic skills have been with us from the dawn of civilization.

Musical intelligence involves the ability to perceive pitch and rhythm and is the basis for the development of musical competence. Bodily-kinesthetic intelligence involves the control of one's own body motions and the ability to manipulate and handle objects skillfully: examples are dancers and gymnasts, who develop precise control over movements of their body; or artisans, tennis players, and neurosurgeons, who are able to manipulate objects with finesse.

Personal intelligence has two

GENETIC AND ENVIRONMENTAL INFLUENCES

People differ in intellectual ability. How much of this difference is due to the particular genes we inherit, and how much is due to the environment in which we are raised? The heredity-environment issue, which has been debated in regard to many aspects of human behavior, has focused primarily on the area of intelligence. Most experts agree that at least some aspects of intelligence are inherited, but opinions differ as to the relative contributions made by heredity and environment.

components that can be regarded as separate—namely, intrapersonal and interpersonal intelligence. *Intrapersonal* intelligence is the ability to monitor one's own feelings and emotions, to discriminate among them and use the information to guide one's actions. *Interpersonal* intelligence, on the other hand, is the ability to notice and understand the needs and intentions of other individuals and to monitor their moods and temperament as a way of predicting how they will behave in new situations.

Gardner analyzes each kind of intelligence from several viewpoints: the cognitive operations involved, the appearance of prodigies and other exceptional individuals, evidence from cases of brain damage, manifestations in different cultures, and the possible course of evolutionary development.

Because of heredity or training, some individuals will develop certain intelligences more than others, but every normal person should develop each to some extent. The intelligences interact with, and build on, one another but still operate as semi-autonomous systems. Each intelligence is an "encapsulated module" within the brain, operating according to its own rules and procedures; certain kinds of brain damage can impair one type of intelligence and have no effect on the others. Gardner is not the first to argue for the modularity of different mental functions, but most theorists of this persua-

sion still assume that a central control process (or executive routine) coordinates the activities of the various modules. Gardner, however, believes that one can explain behavior without postulating an executive control process.

In western society, the first three types of intelligence are highly regarded; they are what standard intelligence tests measure. But historical and anthropological evidence suggests that other intelligences have been more highly valued at earlier periods in human history and even today in some non-western cultures. Further, the activities a culture emphasizes will influence how a specific intelligence develops: for example, a boy endowed with unusual bodily-kinesthetic intelligence may become a baseball player in the United States or a ballet dancer in the Soviet Union.

Gardner's ideas about personal, musical, and bodily-kinesthetic intelligences are provocative and will undoubtedly lead to new efforts to measure these abilities and to use them as predictors of other variables. As noted earlier, conventional IQ tests are good predictors of college grades, but they are not particularly useful in predicting performance in later life on such indices as job success or career advancement. Measures of other abilities, such as personal intelligence, may help explain why some people with brilliant college records fail miserably in later life, while lesser students become char-

ismatic leaders. No matter how one judges Gardner's work, he makes a forceful case for the idea that intelligence encompasses more than verbal and quantitative skills, and that society would be better served by a broader conception of what we call intelligence (Walters & Gardner, 1986).

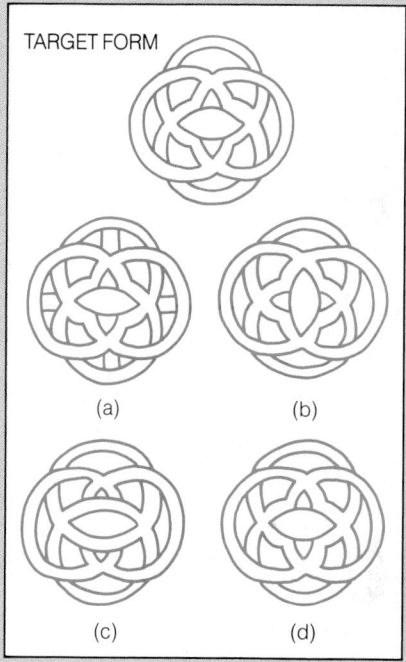

Spatial Ability *How quickly patterns can be matched is an indicator of spatial intelligence. From the array of four, choose the pattern that is identical to the target form. (After Gardner, 1983)*

Genetic Relationships and Intelligence

Most of the evidence bearing on the inheritance of intelligence is derived from studies correlating IQs between persons of various degrees of genetic relationship. Table 12-9 summarizes the results of over 100 studies of this type. In general, the closer the genetic relationship, the more similar the tested intelligence. The average correlation between the IQs of parents and their natural children is .40; between parents and their adopted children, the correlation is about .31. Identical twins, because they develop from a single egg, share precisely the same heredity; the correlation between their IQs is very high—about .86. The IQs of fraternal twins (who develop

TABLE 12-9
Familial Studies of Intelligence A *summary of 111 studies identified in a survey of the world literature on familial resemblances in measured intelligence. The data represent average correlation coefficients for IQ test scores between persons of various relationships. In general, the pattern of correlations indicates that the higher the proportion of genes two family members have in common, the higher the average correlation between their IQs.* (After Bouchard & McGue, 1981)

RELATIONSHIP	CORRELATION
Identical twins	
Reared together	.86
Reared apart	.72
Fraternal twins	
Reared together	.60
Siblings	
Reared together	.47
Reared apart	.24
Parent/child	.40
Foster parent/child	.31
Cousins	.15

from separate eggs and are no more alike genetically than ordinary siblings) have a correlation coefficient of about .60.

Although genetic determinants of intelligence are strong, the results shown in Table 12-9 indicate that environment is also important. Note that when siblings are reared together—in the same home environment—IQ similarity increases. Other studies have shown that the intellectual ability of adopted children is higher than would be predicted on the basis of their natural parents' ability (see Scarr & Weinberg, 1976). Environment does make a difference in intelligence.

It is possible to estimate what portion of the variability in test scores is due to environment and what portion is due to heredity from data similar to those given in Table 12-9. Several methods are used to make these estimates; the most common is to compare the variability of fraternal and identical twins on a given trait. To do this, two quantities are estimated: a) the total variability due to both environment and heredity (V_T) is estimated from the observed differences between pairs of fraternal twins, and b) the environmental variability alone (V_E) is estimated from the observed differences between pairs of identical twins. The difference between the two quantities (V_G) is the variability due to genetic factors (that is, $V_T = V_E + V_G$). The heritability ratio, or simply *heritability* (H), is the ratio between genetic variability and total variability:

$$H = \frac{V_G}{V_T}$$

In other words, heritability is the proportion of a trait's variation within a specified population that can be attributed to genetic differences. Heritability ranges between 0 and 1. When identical twins resemble each other much more than fraternal twins on a given trait, H approaches 1. When the resemblance between identical twins is about the same as the resemblance between fraternal twins on a given trait, H approaches 0.

There are a number of ways to estimate H other than comparing identical and fraternal twins. The theory that permits us to make such estimates is too lengthy to present here, but it is discussed in most genetics textbooks. For our purposes, it is sufficient to say that H measures the fraction of the observed variance in a population that is caused by differences in heredity. It is important to note that H refers to a *population* of individuals, not to a single individual. For example, height has an H of .90, which means that 90 percent of the variance in height observed in a population is due to genetic differences and 10 percent is due to environmental differences. (It does not mean that an individual who is 5 feet 10 inches tall grew to a height of 63 inches due to genetic factors and grew another 7 inches due to environmental factors.) In discussing intelligence, H is often misused to designate the fraction of an individual's intelligence that is due to heredity; the use of the term in this way is incorrect.

Heritability estimates for intelligence have ranged widely from one study to another. Some researchers have reported values as high as .87; others, values as low as .10. For the data presented in Table 12-9, the estimate of H is .46 (Chipuer, Rovine, & Plomin, 1989). The fact that heritability estimates vary so widely suggests that the research is plagued by a number of uncontrolled variables that influence the results in ways that cannot be specified. It must be kept in mind that heritability research is based on field studies and not on well-controlled laboratory experiments; individual cases are observed where they can be found. Field studies are always subject to the influence of uncontrolled variables and are particularly suspect when different investigators report quite different conclusions.

Complicating the situation further is the fact that assumptions made in assessing heritability may not always be correct. In research on twins, for example, it is assumed that twins who are reared together experience roughly the same environment, whether they are fraternal or identical twins. But this may not be true. Identical twins look more alike than fraternal twins, and this fact alone may cause parents and others to treat them more alike than fraternal twins (for example, identical twins are more likely to be dressed in identical outfits than fraternal twins).

In the absence of better-controlled studies, a reliable estimate of heritability is not possible. Heredity clearly has an effect on intelligence, but the degree of this effect is uncertain. It is probably less influential than some researchers have claimed (see Jensen, 1980) but not completely nonexistent, as others have claimed (Kamin, 1976). Most probably, intellectual ability is determined by a number of genes whose individual effects are small but cumulative. If as few as 5 to 10 pairs of genes are involved, the possible combinations would produce a normal distribution of IQ scores and would allow for a wide range of intellectual ability, even within a single family; it would not be uncommon for offspring of high IQ parents to have low IQs and vice versa (Bouchard, 1976).

Environmental Influences

The environmental conditions that determine how an individual's intellectual potential will develop include nutrition, health, quality of stimulation, emotional climate of the home, and type of feedback elicited by behavior. Given two children with the same genes, the child with the better prenatal and postnatal nutrition, the more intellectually stimulating and emotionally secure home, and the more appropriate rewards for academic accomplishments will attain the higher IQ score when tested in first grade. Studies have shown that IQ differences between children of low and high socioeconomic status become progressively greater between birth and entrance into school, suggesting that environmental conditions accentuate whatever differences in intelligence are present at birth (Bayley, 1970).

HEAD START PROGRAMS   Because children from underprivileged families tend to fall behind in cognitive development even before they enter school, efforts have been made to provide more intellectual stimulation for these children during their early years. In 1965, as part of President Johnson's War on Poverty, Congress authorized funds for a number of programs designed to provide learning experiences for 2- to 5-year-olds from poor homes. These programs, funded by Project Head Start, varied in approach. In some, special teachers visited the children at home several times a week to play with them. They engaged the children in such activities as building with blocks, looking at pictures, and naming colors, and they taught them such concepts as big–little and rough–smooth. In brief, the teachers provided the kind of intellectual stimulation that children in upper-class homes usually receive from their parents. The visiting teachers also taught the parents how to provide the same kinds of activities for their children. In other programs, the children attended special classes in which they interacted with teachers

Preschoolers in a Head Start program.

CRITICAL DISCUSSION

Race and Intelligence

The debate over genetic contributions to intelligence has focused on the possibility of inherited racial differences in intelligence—specifically, on the question of whether blacks are innately less intelligent than whites. In view of the heated controversy about this issue and its significance for social policy, it is important that we examine the available evidence.

On standard intelligence tests, black Americans as a group score 10–15 points lower than white Americans as a group. This fact is not debated; the controversy revolves around the interpretation of this difference. Some behavioral scientists and geneticists believe that the two groups differ in inherited ability (see Jensen, 1980; 1985). Others argue that black-white differences in average IQ can be attributed entirely to environmental differences between the two groups (see Kamin, 1976). Many believe that genetic and environmental differences are so confounded that the question is unanswerable at present (Loehlin, Lindzey, & Spuhler, 1975; Neisser, 1986).

The issues involved are exceedingly complex; the best we can do here is to summarize a few of the main points.

1. Although blacks and whites may differ in physical appearance, they do not represent two distinct biological groups. In fact, differences in gene structures (where known) in most cases are greater *within* the races than between them.

2. Heritability is a population statistic (like infant mortality or birthrate); it depends on the environmental and genetic variation among a given group of people at a given time. Thus, although heritability ratios estimated for white populations indicate that variations in IQ are partly a function of heredity, such estimates do not permit us to make inferences about heritability ratios among black populations. More importantly, heritability estimates do not tell us anything about differences *between* populations. The heritability of a characteristic could be the same for two groups, even though the differences between them are caused entirely by environmental factors. For example, suppose the heritability of height is the same for two populations, A and B. If individuals in Population A are raised on a starvation diet, they will be shorter, on the average,

than individuals in Population B. Variations in adult height within each group are still influenced by heredity (that is, undernourished individuals with tall parents will be taller than undernourished individuals with short parents), but the difference in average height between the two groups is clearly the result of environment. To summarize, heritability estimates do not permit us to draw conclusions about differences between populations (Mackenzie, 1984).

3. Among black populations, there is some tendency for lightness of skin color (presumably an indication of the degrees of intermixture with whites) to correlate positively with IQ. But such correlations are very low (typically .15) and can be explained on the basis of environmental differences—a lighter skin color is associated with less discrimination and greater opportunity.

4. A study of illegitimate children fathered by U.S. servicemen during the occupation of Germany after World War II found no overall difference in average IQ between children whose fathers were black and those whose fathers were white. Since these children were all raised by German mothers of similar social status and were matched with

in similar play-learning activities. Some of these programs involved the parents; others did not.

In general, the results of these early education programs have been promising. Children who have participated in such programs score higher on the Stanford-Binet or WISC on entering school and tend to be more self-confident and socially competent than children who have not received special attention.

Follow-up studies indicate that early education programs produce some lasting benefits. For example, several studies have followed progress through high school of disadvantaged children who participated in special preschool programs when they were 3 years old. By the age of 15, these students were more than a full grade ahead of a matched control group of students who had received no preschool experience. In addition, compared with the control group, the students with preschool experience a) scored higher on tests of

children of the same age in the classroom, the results provide strong support for viewing environment as the major determinant of racial IQ differences (Eyferth, Brandt, & Wolfgang, 1960).

5. When black or interracial children (those with one black parent) are adopted before they are 1 year old and raised by white families with above-average incomes and educations, they score more than 15 IQ points higher than underprivileged black children reared by their biological families. The performance of the adopted children on school achievement tests is slightly above the national norms (Scarr & Weinberg, 1976).

6. Ogbu (1986) has theorized that blacks in America are in a social position similar to other castelike minorities elsewhere in the world, such as the Harijans (untouchables) of India, the Maoris in New Zealand, and the Burakumi of Japan. The average IQ difference between blacks and whites is about the same as between the privileged and deprived groups in each of these other countries. A study of the Burakumi proves particularly interesting in this regard; in 1871 they were emancipated from their pariah status (due to their despised work as tanners) but continue to be treated as outcasts in Japan. Nevertheless, when Burakumi have emigrated to America, their children (treated as any other Japanese in the United States) do as well on IQ tests and in school as other Japanese-Americans. Being born into a castelike minority leads one to grow up with the conviction that life will be restricted to a limited set of opportunities. The lower IQ scores of these children become a self-fulfilling prophecy; teachers expect less and so tacitly treat them in ways that make those expectations come true. Fordham and Ogbu (1986) reported on a study of two groups of equally bright black high-school students, one group doing well and the other failing in school. Those who did poorly regarded being studious as betraying their racial identity ("acting white," in the students' words). They saw doing well in school and getting a high-status job as selling out to the white persons' values. Similar dynamics occur among Mexican-American children: they identify school achievement with betraying their roots.

7. Findings from the National Assessment of Educational Progress and from the College Entrance Examination Board demonstrate a consistent reduction over the last 20 years in the achievement differences between black and white students. These reductions occur for reading and mathematics achievement tests in grades 1 through 12 and for the SAT. The consistency of the trend suggests that further reductions in white-black differences will be seen in future years (Jones, 1984). The social changes affecting blacks have been enormous in the last 20 years; such changes might be expected to elevate aspirations of black youth and give them evidence that school achievement will enhance their prospects for career success. The improvement of black achievement levels in recent years is consistent with this supposition.

The authors of this text believe that it is not possible to draw valid conclusions about innate racial differences in intelligence from the available evidence. Cultural and environmental differences between blacks and whites influence the development of cognitive abilities in complex ways, and no study has succeeded in estimating or eliminating these effects. As long as systematic differences remain in the conditions under which blacks and whites are raised (and as long as the effects of these differences cannot be reliably estimated), no valid conclusions can be drawn concerning innate differences in intelligence.

reading, arithmetic, and language usage; b) were less apt to need special remedial classes; c) exhibited less antisocial behavior; and d) were more likely to hold after-school jobs (Hohmann, Banet, & Weikart, 1979; Palmer & Anderson, 1979; Lazar & Darlington, 1982; Zigler & Berman, 1983; Lee, Brooks-Gunn, & Schnur, 1988).

Head Start programs have shown that early intellectual stimulation can have a significant impact on later school performance. But the specific method used appears to be less important than parental involvement. Programs that actively involve the parents, that interest them in their children's development and show them how to provide a more stimulating home environment, tend to produce the greatest gains (Darlington, 1986).

KIBBUTZIM   Environmental effects on intellectual performance even more dramatic than Head Start are evidenced by studies of children living in

Children in an Israeli kibbutz.

Israeli kibbutzim. For some time, Israel has been faced with the problem of large differences in intellectual and educational background among Jews of different cultural ancestry. The average intellectual ability of Jews of European ancestry generally is considerably higher than that of Jews from Arabic countries. The average difference in IQ between the two groups is at least as large as the average difference in IQ between blacks and whites in the United States. The exceptions to this observation are Israeli children who are raised on certain types of kibbutzim, where they do not reside with their parents but live in a children's house under the care of women specially trained in child rearing. Under these special conditions, the children's IQ scores tend to be unrelated to the country of parental origin. Children whose parents came from Arabic countries score as well as children whose parents came from Europe. Although individual differences in IQ scores still exist, the differences are not related to ancestry (Smilansky, 1974; Rabin & Beit-Hallahmi, 1982). Thus, we have some indication of the contribution an enriched environment can make toward helping children reach their intellectual potential.

ABILITY TESTS IN PERSPECTIVE

Despite their limitations, ability tests are one of the most widely used tools that psychology has developed. If these tests are to continue to be useful, however, they must be viewed realistically. They should not be overvalued as providing a fixed, unchangeable measure of what a person can do. Nor should they be discarded because of their obvious shortcomings and replaced by other methods of evaluation that may be less valid.

One area of concern has been the use of ability tests to determine class placement for schoolchildren. Children who achieve low scores may be assigned to a slower "track" or placed in a special class for "slow learners";

"I'm sorry, but these records are somewhat mixed up. It turns out that 184 is your weight, not your I.Q."

children who earn high scores may be placed in accelerated or "enriched" programs. Unless schools provide periodic reassessment and unless slow-learner classes emphasize academic skills, a child's initial placement may well determine his or her academic future. Some youngsters who have the potential to succeed in college may be discouraged on the basis of early test scores from taking college preparatory courses. Both parents and teachers must realize that test scores—whether the test is called an intelligence test or an achievement test—can only measure current performance. Questions on an intelligence test are less dependent on schooling, but they do not measure innate capacity; thus, test scores can change with changes in the environment.

The use of tests to classify schoolchildren is a controversial social issue, because a disproportionately large number of minority and underprivileged children have been assigned to special classes for slow learners on the basis of their scores on group intelligence and achievement tests. Legal suits have prompted some states to prohibit the use of group intelligence tests for purposes of classification.

The issue is complicated. Ability tests (both intelligence and achievement) probably have been overused and misused in the schools. Teachers often do not know how to interpret test results and may draw sweeping conclusions about a child's ability on the basis of a single test score. More importantly, decisions about placement in special classes should be based on many factors—never on test scores alone. A child's medical and developmental history, social competency, and home environment are some of the variables that should be considered before the child is classified as a slow learner.

Ability tests can serve an important function when properly used. They help the teacher separate a large class of pupils of varying skills into homogeneous learning groups. (Children who are at roughly the same level in mastering reading or mathematical concepts can be taught together.) Ability tests can also be used diagnostically to improve the educational opportunities for disadvantaged and minority children. A child who scores low on a group intelligence test (and such tests should be used only as initial screening devices) should be given a more intensive evaluation. Individual testing can help to reveal a) whether the group test scores represent an accurate assessment of the child's current abilities, b) the child's particular intellectual strengths and weaknesses, and c) the best instructional program for improving his or her skills. Tests should be used to match instruction with individual needs, not to label a child.

A comparison of intelligence and achievement test scores often yields valuable information. For example, some children whose achievement test scores in math or reading are low may score quite high on an intelligence test. This discrepancy should alert the teacher to the possibility that the child's math and reading skills are not well developed and require special attention. This child may do quite well scholastically once his or her specific learning problems are remedied. Without the information from the intelligence test, such a child might be inappropriately placed in a slow-learner group.

Another point of concern is the type of talent measured by ability tests. As noted earlier, the SAT and other admissions tests have proved successful in predicting college grades. But when college admission officials place too much emphasis on test scores, they are apt to overlook students who may have an extraordinary talent in art, drama, or music. They may also overlook students who have aimed all of their energy and enthusiasm toward creative efforts in a specific area (for example, an award-winning science project or an

Elementary-school student taking a standardized test.

innovative community program). In any selection procedure, scores on intelligence and scholastic aptitude tests should be considered in conjunction with other information.

We must always question the validity of a test score for a particular individual or for a particular purpose, and we must continue to improve methods of assessment. But despite their limitations, ability tests are still the most effective aids we have for judging what job or class or type of training is most appropriate for a given individual (Hartigan & Wigdor, 1989). The alternatives are few. To rely entirely on subjective judgment would introduce the kinds of biases that such tests were designed to eliminate. To assign people at random to jobs or educational programs would benefit neither society nor the individual.

⚡CHAPTER SUMMARY

1. Ability tests include *aptitude tests* (which are designed to predict what a person can accomplish with training) and *achievement tests* (which measure accomplished skills and indicate what the individual can do at present). Both tests may contain similar types of items, but they differ in their purposes and in the amount of *prior experience* they assume. Some ability tests measure very specific abilities; others cover a range of skills.

2. To be useful, tests must meet certain specifications. Studies of *reliability* tell us whether test scores are consistent over time. Studies of *validity* tell us how well a test measures what it is intended to measure—how well it predicts according to an acceptable criterion. *Uniform testing procedures* are necessary for a test to be reliable and valid.

3. The first successful intelligence tests were developed by the French psychologist Alfred Binet, who proposed the concept of *mental age*. A bright child's mental age is above his or her chronological age; a slow child's mental age is below his or her chronological age. The revision of the Binet scales (the Stanford-Binet) adopts the *intelligence quotient* (IQ) as an index of mental development. The IQ expresses intelligence as a ratio of mental age (MA) to chronological age (CA).

4. Two widely used ability tests, the Wechsler Adult Intelligence Scale (WAIS) and the Wechsler Intelligence Scale for Children (WISC), have both verbal and performance scales so that separate information can be obtained about each type of ability. The Stanford-Binet and the Wechsler scales are *individual tests* that are administered to a single individual by a specially trained tester. *Group ability tests* can be administered to a large number of people at one time.

5. Scores on ability tests correlate quite highly with what we think of as "brightness" and with measures of academic performance. But they do not measure motivation, leadership, and other characteristics that are important for success.

6. Both Binet and Wechsler assumed that intelligence is a *general capacity* for reasoning. Spearman proposed a general factor (*g*) plus specific abilities (each called *s*), which could be identified by the method of *factor analysis*. Thurstone used factor analysis to arrive at seven *primary mental abilities* he considered to be the basic elements of intelligence; variants of his test are still widely used, but their predictive power is no greater than that of tests of general intelligence, such as the Wechsler scales. Factor analysis continues to be an important method for the analysis of test data; this perspective on intelligence is called the *factorial approach*.

7. An alternative perspective on intelligence is the *information-processing approach*. The basic idea of this approach is to try to understand intellectual behavior in terms of the underlying cognitive processes that are brought into play when we are confronted with a problem-solving task. The information-processing approach has yielded some detailed analyses of the mental processes involved in many tasks used to assess intelligence. A factorial approach and an information-processing approach provide complementary interpretations of performance on

intelligence tests. Both approaches have enhanced our understanding of academic intelligence, but their common shortcoming is that they have not proved particularly effective in assessing practical intelligence.

8. Studies correlating IQs between persons with varying degrees of genetic relationship show that heredity plays a role in intelligence. Estimates of *heritability* vary, however; such environmental factors as nutrition, intellectual stimulation, and the emotional climate of the home will influence where a person's IQ will fall within the *reaction range* determined by heredity.

9. Despite their limitations, ability tests are still the most objective method available for assessing individual capabilities. But test scores must be considered in conjunction with other information.

FURTHER READING

For an introduction to individual differences and psychological testing, see Kaplan and Sacuzzo, *Psychological Testing* (2nd ed., 1989); Cronbach, *Essentials of Psychological Testing* (4th ed., 1984); Kail and Pellegrino, *Human Intelligence: Perspectives and Prospects* (1985); Sattler, *Assessment of Children* (1988); Sternberg (ed.), *Human Abilities: An Information-Processing Approach* (1984); and Anastasi, *Psychological Testing* (6th ed., 1988). More advanced treatments of these topics are Sternberg (ed.), *Handbook of Human Intelligence* (1982); and Wigdor and Garner (eds.), *Ability Testing: Uses, Consequences, and Controversies* (1982).

For a more general overview of intellectual abilities, see Sternberg, *Intelligence Applied: Understanding and Increasing Your Intellectual Skills* (1986). For a historical perspective on intelligence tests and the controversies associated with them, see Fancher, *The Intelligence Men: Makers of the IQ Controversy* (1985).

The genetics of intelligence is discussed in Plomin, *Development, Genetics and Psychology* (1986) and in Plomin, DeFries, and McClearn, *Behavioral Genetics: A Primer* (2nd ed., 1989). For a discussion of racial and social class differences in intelligence, see Scarr, *Race, Social Class, and Individual Differences in IQ* (1981); and Lewontin, Rose, and Kamin, *Not in Our Genes: Biology, Ideology and Human Nature* (1984).

For a discussion of Head Start programs and day care for children, see Bond and Joffe (eds.), *Facilitating Infant and Early Childhood Development* (1982); and Zigler and Gordon (eds.), *Day Care: Scientific and Social Policy Issues* (1981).

Chapter 13

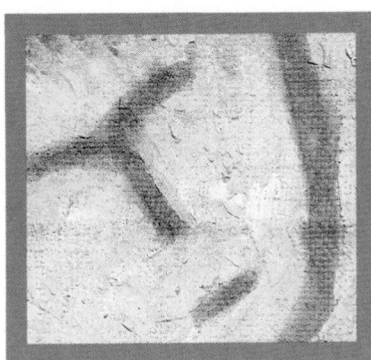

Detail, Little Hope.

Personality through the Life Course

The mental abilities that we examined in Chapter 12 are a subset of variables that constitute what we call *personality*—the characteristic patterns of thought, emotion, and behavior that define an individual's personal style and influence his or her interactions with the environment. In this chapter, we examine the interplay of forces that shape an individual's personality through the course of life; promote, disrupt, or transform the continuity of personality across time; and enable the individual's personality, in turn, to affect the life course itself. In Chapter 14 we will consider theories of personality and methods for assessing it.

SHAPING OF PERSONALITY

Genetic Influences

First-time parents are often surprised that their infant seems to possess a distinctive personality so early in life; when they have a second child, they are often surprised at how different the second is from the first. These parental observations are valid. Research shows that reliable differences can be observed among infants beginning at about 3 months of age in such characteristics as activity level, attention span, adaptability to changes in the environment, and general mood. One infant might be active, easily distracted, and not easily comforted when distressed; another might be predominantly quiet, persistent in concentrating on an activity, and easily comforted. Such mood-related personality characteristics, called *temperaments*, constitute early building blocks for the individual's later personality (Thomas & Chess, 1977).

The early appearance of such characteristics suggests that they are determined in part by genetic factors and are inherited from the parents—despite large differences among children from the same family. As we noted in Chapter 12, one way of investigating this possibility is to study pairs of twins. If identical twins (who share all their genes in common) are significantly more alike on a characteristic than fraternal twins (who, like ordinary siblings, share about half their genes in common) then the characteristic probably has a genetic or heritable component.

In several studies of this type, same-sex twins, whose average age was about 5 years, were rated by their parents on the temperaments of emotionality, activity, and sociability. Correlations between identical twins ranged from .5 to .6, whereas correlations between fraternal twins were not significantly different from zero, suggesting that genetic inheritance is an important determinant of these personality attributes (Buss & Plomin, 1984). One problem with these studies is that they rely on ratings by parents, who might exaggerate the similarities of identical twins or the differences between fraternal twins (Neale & Stevenson, 1989). Fortunately, other studies, using more objective methods, have confirmed that these characteristics have a substantial heritable component (Plomin et al., 1988).

Genetic effects on personality characteristics can also be detected in adulthood. A Swedish study examined the traits of extraversion (a combination of sociability and impulsiveness) and neuroticism (emotional instability) in a sample of over 12,000 pairs of adult twins. On both traits, there

Identical twins.

were correlations of .5 between members of identical-twin pairs and .2 between members of fraternal-twin pairs, again implying a genetic influence (Floderus-Myred, Petersen, & Rasmuson, 1980).

As we noted in Chapter 12, however, one difficulty in interpreting the results of twin studies is that identical twin pairs may be treated more alike than fraternal twin pairs, which may account for the greater personality similarities. Ideally one should study a sample of identical twins who had been separated at birth and raised in randomly selected environments. Fortunately there is an ongoing research project that comes close to fulfilling these conditions—the Minnesota Study of Twins Reared Apart (Bouchard, 1984). As of 1986, 44 pairs of identical twins had been brought to the laboratory for study. On average, these twin pairs had been separated at 10 weeks of age and had not seen each other again until 34 years later; some had not met until the study brought them together. The Minnesota researchers have now compared these twins with those in an earlier Minnesota study on twins reared together (Lykken, 1982; Tellegen et al., 1988).

These studies reveal that across a wide range of personality characteristics twins reared apart are just as similar to one another as twins reared together. The median correlations were .49 for identical twins reared apart and .52 for identical twins reared together; the corresponding correlations for fraternal twins were .21 and .23. These results permit us to conclude with greater confidence that identical twins are more similar to one another on personality characteristics than are fraternal twins because identical twins are more similar genetically.

The differences in correlations between identical and fraternal twins found in the Minnesota studies are themselves in accord with results from many other twin studies and imply that about 50 percent of the variability among individuals in many personality characteristics can be attributed to genetic differences among those individuals. This can be expressed by saying that these characteristics have heritabilities of about .5 in the populations studied.

The nature of an infant's early attachment to the parents is related to personal relationships in adulthood.

In general, the highest heritabilities are found in measures of abilities and intelligence. High heritabilities are also found in measures of sociability and emotional stability/instability. In the Minnesota study, the correlations on some ability and personality tests between pairs of identical twins reared apart were as high as if the same person took the test twice. (See the Critical Discussion for a further discussion of the Minnesota study.)

Environmental Influences

Even if genetic factors account for as much as 50 percent of the variability in many personality characteristics, this still leaves 50 percent of the variability to be accounted for by factors primarily related to the environment. It also leaves many other behavioral patterns that arise more from experience than from heredity. Because most psychological theories of development assume that forces acting early in life have more influence in shaping our personalities than do later forces, research has focused intensively on the home environment of early childhood.

CHILDREARING PRACTICES   We noted in Chapter 3 that infants differ from one another in the degree to which they form secure attachments to their primary caregivers in the first year of life. Those who form such attachments are observed in later childhood to approach difficult problems with enthusiasm and persistence, to be self-directed and eager to learn, and to be social leaders among their peers. In contrast, children who are less securely attached at the end of their first year are more easily frustrated, are more dependent on adults, and tend to be socially withdrawn (Matas, Arend, & Sroufe, 1978; Sroufe, Fox & Pancake, 1983; Waters, Wippman, & Sroufe, 1979). The failure to form secure attachments in the early years has been related to an inability to develop close personal relationships in adulthood (Bowlby, 1973; Rutter, 1979).

CRITICAL DISCUSSION

Minnesota Study of Twins Reared Apart

The participants in the Minnesota Study of Twins Reared Apart were assessed on a number of ability and personality measures. In addition, they participated in lengthy interviews,

during which they were asked questions about such topics as childhood experiences, fears, hobbies, musical tastes, social attitudes, and sexual interests. A number of startling similarities were found.

The twins with the most dramatically different backgrounds are Oskar Stohr and Jack Yufe. Born in Trinidad of a Jewish father and a German mother, they were separated shortly after birth. The mother took Oskar to Germany, where he was raised by his grandmother as a Catholic and a Nazi. Jack remained with his father, was raised as a Jew, and spent part of his youth on an Israeli kibbutz. The families never corresponded, and the two brothers now

lead quite different lives. They were in their late forties when they participated in the study and had met only once before about 20 years earlier. Remarkable similarities were evident when the pair showed up for the study. Both men were wearing blue double-breasted epauletted shirts, mustaches, and wire-rimmed glasses. Their mannerisms and temperaments were similar, and they shared certain idiosyncrasies; both liked spicy foods and sweet liqueurs, were absentminded, flushed the toilet before using it, liked to dip buttered toast in their coffee, and enjoyed surprising people by sneezing in elevators.

Another pair of twins with fairly

Do these differences in attachment among children stem from the childrearing practices of their parents? This possibility is suggested by the observation that mothers of infants who are securely attached are more responsive to their infants' needs, provide more social stimulation, and express more affection than do mothers of insecurely attached infants (Clarke-Stewart, 1973). But it may be that both a child's early attachment and his or her later behavioral style reflect common inborn temperamental factors, and the mother's responsiveness is a function of the child's behavior rather than the other way around. As we shall see below, this ambiguity of cause-and-effect arises whenever we seek to assess environmental influences on personality (Bell, 1968).

After the first year of a child's life, childrearing becomes more complex as parents take on the trickier tasks of discipline, control, and character building. Parents differ markedly from one another in how they approach these tasks. Some are warm, nurturant, and relaxed; others are cold, aloof, and tense. Some are highly controlling; others tend to let the children do their own thing. Some are child-centered, highly involved in their children's lives; others are parent-centered, more occupied with their own interests and activities. A basic task for psychology is to categorize and summarize these many differences and to determine if and how they help shape the child's personality.

One classification that has proven useful for this purpose is displayed in Figure 13-1. It divides parenting practices on two dimensions: the first distinguishes parents who are demanding and controlling from those who are undemanding of their children; the other distinguishes parents who are accepting, responsive, and child-centered from those who are rejecting, unresponsive, and parent-centered. The intersection of these two dimensions produces four kinds of parenting patterns which have been shown empirically to be associated with different outcomes for the children (Baumrind, 1967, 1971; Maccoby & Martin, 1983).

As shown in Figure 13-1, parents who combine control with acceptance and child-centered involvement are called authoritative. They exercise high

different backgrounds are now British housewives who were separated during World War II and were raised by families of different socioeconomic status. Both twins, who had never met before, arrived for their interviews wearing seven rings on their fingers.

There are not, of course, toast-dipping or ring-loving genes; such similarities reflect similarities in the heritable components of more basic personality characteristics. But as we shall see later, it is unlikely that genetics alone can account for these extraordinary similarities of twins reared apart. Moreover, we will look at a number of other puzzling findings that emerge from twin studies.

These twins, separated at birth, showed remarkable similarities in interests and habits when they first met at age 31.

levels of control and require their children to behave at intellectual and social levels consistent with their age and abilities. But authoritative parents combine their control and demands with warmth, nurturance, and two-way communication. They solicit their children's opinions and feelings when family decisions are made, and they offer explanations and reasons for punitive or restrictive measures whenever they feel these must be imposed. Research shows that children of such parents tend to be independent, self-assertive, friendly with peers, and cooperative with parents. They are also likely to be successful both intellectually and socially; they seem to enjoy life; and they have strong motivation to achieve.

Controlling and demanding parents who simply assert their power without warmth, nurturance, or two-way communication are labeled *authoritarian.* They attempt to control and evaluate the behavior and attitudes of their children in accordance with an absolute set of standards; they also value obedience, respect for authority, work, tradition, and preservation of order. Children of such parents tend to be moderately competent and responsible, but they also tend to be socially withdrawn and to lack spontaneity. The girls

	Accepting Responsive Child-centered	Rejecting Unresponsive Parent-centered
Demanding Controlling	Authoritative	Authoritarian
Undemanding Not controlling	Indulgent	Neglecting

FIGURE 13-1
Childrearing Patterns *The Demanding-Undemanding and the Accepting-Rejecting dimensions combine to produce four childrearing patterns. (After Maccoby & Martin, 1983)*

Children raised by parent-centered parents often engage in impulsive behavior, such as experimenting with smoking at an early age.

seem to be particularly dependent on their parents and lacking in achievement motivation; the boys tend to be more aggressive than other boys. Some studies also find a link between authoritarian parenting and low self-esteem in boys (Coopersmith, 1967).

Indulgent parents are accepting, responsive, child-centered parents who place few demands on their children. Such children are more positive in their moods and show more vitality than children of authoritarian families, but their behavior tends to be immature in that they lack impulse control, social responsibility, and self-reliance. There is also evidence that permissiveness for aggression is one factor contributing to children's aggressiveness. It is interesting that even though authoritarian and indulgent parents have almost opposite childrearing styles, both have children who tend to display little self-reliance and may have problems with aggression.

The fourth category contains *neglecting* parents. Most such parents are not neglecting in the extreme ways that would constitute child abuse. Rather, they are concerned with their own activities and uninvolved with those of their children—they are parent-centered rather than child-centered. Interviewers describe them as not knowing their children's whereabouts, activities, and associates when the children are away from home; they are uninterested in events at the children's schools; they have few daily conversations with their children; and they do not consider their children's opinions.

A large-scale longitudinal study conducted in Finland assessed the children of parent-centered parents at ages 8, 14, and 20 years. Compared with children of child-centered parents, children of parent-centered parents at age 14 were impulsive: they lacked concentration, were moody, spent money quickly rather than saving it, and had difficulty controlling aggressive outbursts. They were uninterested in school, likely to be truant, and spent time on the streets and at hangouts. They tended to start drinking, smoking, and dating at earlier ages. At age 20, they were hedonistic and lacked frustration tolerance and emotional control; they also lacked long-term goals, drank to excess, and often had a record of arrests (Pulkkinen, 1982).

More extreme cases of neglecting parents are those who are emotionally unavailable to their children. They are detached, emotionally uninvolved, often depressed, and uninterested in their children. Children of such parents show clear disturbances in their attachment relationships and increasing deficits in all aspects of psychological functioning by age 2; in fact, their deficits are greater than those of children whose parents actually physically abuse them (Egeland & Sroufe, 1981a, 1981b).

This four-fold classification of childrearing patterns helps to summarize the results of many studies conducted over the years, but it should not be interpreted to mean that a particular parent can be easily assigned to a single category. Many parents use different approaches at different times, under different circumstances, and with different children. Some parents may be noncontrolling when their children are young but controlling as they get older. They may be indulgent about toilet training but restrictive about displays of aggression. They may demand more obedience from a daughter than from a son or be more involved with a firstborn than with a laterborn child. And, of course, many two-parent homes contain a mother and father with very different childrearing styles.

The results of studies on childrearing practices and children's personalities are reasonably consistent but they are fairly weak. In fact, they are much weaker than many researchers had expected. Some psychologists are even coming to believe that, in general, differences between families have little to do with differences in children's personalities. We shall examine this startling conclusion later in the chapter.

Personality—Environment Influences

GENOTYPE–ENVIRONMENT CORRELATION   In shaping personality, genetic and environmental influences do not act independently of one another but are intertwined from the moment of birth. Parents give their biological offspring both their genes and a home environment, and both are functions of the parents' own genes. As a result, there is a built-in correlation between the child's own inherited characteristics (*genotype*) and his or her environment. For example, because general intelligence is partially heritable, parents with high intelligence are likely to have children with high intelligence. But parents with high intelligence are also likely to provide an intellectually stimulating environment for their children—both through their own interactions with them and through the books, piano lessons, trips to museums, and other intellectual experiences that are likely to be a part of their home. Because the child's genes and environment are positively correlated in this way, he or she will get a double-dose of intellectual advantage.

Some parents may deliberately construct an environment that is negatively correlated with the child's genotype. For example, introverted parents may encourage social activities in order to counteract the child's own likely introversion: "We make an effort to have people over because we don't want Chris to grow up to be as shy as we are." Parents of a very active child may try to provide more interesting quiet activities. But whether the correlation is positive or negative, the pertinent point is that the child's genotype and environment are joint contributors to his or her personality from the very beginning.

The child's genotype interacts with the environment in a number of other ways (Plomin, DeFries, & Loehlin, 1977; Scarr, 1988; Scarr & McCartney, 1983). In particular, we should like to propose that the environment becomes a function of the child's personality through three forms of dynamic interaction: *reactive*, *evocative*, and *proactive*.

REACTIVE INTERACTION   Different individuals exposed to the same environment experience it, interpret it, and react to it differently. An anxious, sensitive child will experience and react to authoritarian parents in very different ways from a calm, resilient child; the harsh tone that provokes the sensitive child to tears might pass unnoticed by his sister. An extraverted child will attend to people and events around her; her introverted brother will ignore them. A brighter child will get more out of being read to than a less bright child. Each child's personality thus extracts a subjective psychological environment from the objective surroundings, and it is that subjective environment that shapes subsequent personality development. Even if parents provided exactly the same environment for all their children— which they usually do not—it will not be psychologically equivalent for all of them.

EVOCATIVE INTERACTION   Every individual's personality evokes distinctive responses from others. An infant who squirms and fusses when picked up will evoke less nurturance from a parent than one who likes to be

A sociable child will choose environments that enhance her sociability.

cuddled. Docile children will evoke a less controlling style of childrearing from parents than will aggressive children. This is why we cannot simply conclude from the research reviewed earlier that parents' childrearing styles shape a child's personality (for example, that responsive mothers *create* securely attached infants, that authoritative parents *create* self-assertive children, and so forth). Rather, the child's personality shapes the parenting style which, in turn, further shapes the personality. Such evocative interaction occurs throughout the life course.

PROACTIVE INTERACTION   As children get older, they can move beyond the environments imposed by their parents and begin to select and construct environments of their own. These environments, in turn, further shape their personalities. A sociable child will choose to go to the movies with friends rather than stay home alone and watch television; her sociable personality thus selects her into an environment that further reinforces and sustains her sociability. And what she cannot select, she will construct: if nobody invites her to the movies, she will organize the event herself. As the name implies, proactive interaction is a process through which individuals become active agents in their own personality development.

The relative importance of these several kinds of personality–environment interaction shifts over the course of development (Scarr, 1988; Scarr & McCartney, 1983). The built-in correlation between a child's genotype and his or her environment is strongest when the child is young and confined almost exclusively to parent-imposed environments. As the child gets older and begins to select and construct environments of his or her own, this initial correlation decreases and the influence of proactive interaction increases. Reactive and evocative interactions remain important throughout life.

SOME UNSOLVED PUZZLES   Studies of twins have produced a number of puzzling patterns that are still not completely understood. One is the greater similarity of identical twins compared with fraternal twins. The problem is that the data are "too good." As we saw earlier, the striking similarities of identical twins do not seem to diminish across time or separate rearing environments. In contrast, the similarities of fraternal twins (and ordinary siblings) diminish from childhood through adolescence even when they are reared together; the longer they live together in the same home, the *less* similar they become (Scarr, 1988; Scarr & McCartney, 1983). And finally, the observed similarities of fraternal twins and ordinary siblings are often lower than they should be if the traits are as heritable as the identical twin correlations would imply.

Some of these patterns could emerge if the genes themselves interact with one another so that having all one's genes in common (as identical twins do) is more than twice as effective as having only half one's genes in common (as fraternal twins and ordinary siblings do). But personality–environment interactions may also be responsible.

Consider identical twins. Because they have identical genotypes, they also react to situations in similar ways (reactive interaction); they evoke similar responses from others (evocative interaction); and their similar, genetically-guided talents, interests, and motivations lead them to seek out and construct similar environments (proactive interaction). The important point is that these processes all occur whether the twins are reared together or apart.

For example, because each twin independently evokes similar responses from others, identical twins are treated more alike by others than are fraternal twins. But this is true not just of parents and others who interact with both twins but by people who only interact with one of them. Proactive interaction operates in similar ways. Each twin's personality influences him or her to select friends and environments that are similar to the friends and environments chosen independently by the other twin. But friends and environments that are similar will treat each twin in similar ways. And so it goes. Because the twins begin with identical genotypic personalities, all the processes of personality–environment interaction act together to promote and sustain their similarity across time—even if they are never together after birth.

In contrast, the environments of fraternal twins and ordinary siblings increasingly diverge as they get older, even within the same home. They are most alike in early childhood when parents impose a common environment. (Although even here, siblings will react somewhat differently from one another and evoke different responses from the parents.) But as soon as they begin to select and construct environments outside the home, their moderately different talents, interests, and motivations will take them down increasingly divergent paths, thereby producing increasingly divergent personalities.

A CONTROVERSIAL FINDING   Twin studies not only permit researchers to estimate how much of the variation among individuals is due to genetic variation but also to estimate how much of the remaining environmentally-related variation is due to differences between families as compared with differences within families. Surprisingly, differences between families seem to account for almost none of the environmental variation: after their genetic similarities are subtracted out, two children from the same family

Twins holding twins.

seem to be no more alike than two children chosen randomly from the population (Plomin & Daniels, 1987). This implies, for example, that except for their genetically-produced similarities, siblings raised by authoritative parents are likely to be as different from one another as they are from children raised by indulgent parents. More generally, this conclusion implies that the kinds of between-family variables that psychologists typically study (such as childrearing practices, quality of education, social class) are contributing virtually nothing to individual differences in personality. How can this be the case?

We suggest that one possible explanation might be that the reactive, evocative, and proactive processes act to diminish the differences between environments as long as those environments permit some flexibility of response. A bright child from a neglecting or impoverished home is more likely than a less bright sibling to absorb more information from a television program (reactive interaction), to attract the attention of a sympathetic teacher (evocative interaction), and to go to the library on his or her own (proactive interaction). This child's genotype acts to counteract the potentially debilitating effects of the imposed home environment, and therefore he or she develops differently from a less bright sibling. Only if the environment is severely restrictive will these personality-driven processes be thwarted (Scarr, 1988; Scarr & McCartney, 1983). This explanation is supported by the finding that the most dissimilar pairs of identical twins reared apart are those in which one was severely restricted in environmental opportunity.

Although this explanation seems plausible, there is no direct evidence that it is correct. In any case, if further research continues to show between-family effects to be negligible, then research will have to shift from the usual comparisons of children from different families to comparisons of children within the same families—with particular attention paid to the personality-environment interactions within those families.

Cultural Influences

One reason that differences between families in childrearing practices do not appear to produce systematic differences in children's personalities may be that the studies do not include a large enough range of family environments or children's personalities to detect such differences. For example, families in virtually all twin studies are drawn from a single culture—usually a western industrialized culture. Compared with differences between cultures, the families and children within a single culture may be relatively homogeneous.

Most western industrialized nations value and attempt to shape citizens who are independent, self-assertive, and motivated to achieve. As a member of such a culture, you can confirm this set of values by reviewing your own reactions to the personality types associated with the different parenting patterns summarized in Figure 13-1. In our culture, the authoritative parents and their confident, self-assertive children are clearly the preferred group.

In contrast, most non-western cultures place much less value on independence and self-assertiveness than our own society. This is especially true for girls and women. Such cultures stress the interdependence of persons with others in the community rather than the independence of persons from one another. Children are encouraged to be part of the functioning community rather than to compete and do better than others (Edwards & Whiting, 1980; Whiting & Edwards, 1988; Whiting & Whiting, 1975; Whiting & Child, 1953).

Parents in many non-western cultures also differ from parents in our culture in that they punish wrong behavior but do not explicitly praise or otherwise reward good behavior. Cross-cultural observations suggest that western children do not behave more appropriately overall than do non-western children, but they are more likely to do so when their parents are present and to seek attention from adults generally (LeVine, 1980). Western parents may sometimes find such attention-seeking annoying, but they willingly put up with it because it expresses the valued trait of self-assertiveness—a trait that is considered disruptive of community functioning in less achievement-oriented cultures.

It appears, then, that each culture manages to shape the kinds of personality characteristics that it values. It also appears that each culture values the kinds of personality characteristics it needs in order to survive and prosper. For example, in agricultural societies

Non-western families emphasize interdependence more than western families.

> carelessness in performance of routine duties leads to a threat of hunger, not for the day of carelessness itself but for many months to come. Individual initiative attempts to improve techniques may be feared because no one can tell immediately whether the changes will lead to a greater harvest or to a disastrous failure. Under those conditions, there might well be a premium on obedience to the older and wiser, and on responsibility in faithful performance to the routine laid down by custom for one's economic role.

> At the opposite extreme is subsistence through hunting or fishing with no means for extended storing of catch. Here individual initiative and development of high skill seem to be at a premium. Where each day's food comes from that day's catch, variations in the energy and skill exerted in food-getting lead to immediate reward or punishment. (Barry, Child, & Bacon, 1959, p. 52)

To test these speculations, Barry, Child, and Bacon (1959) looked at the relationship between childrearing practices and the degree of food

TABLE 13-1
Childrearing Practices and Food Accumulation *The table shows the relationship between traits emphasized in childrearing and the degree of food accumulation in six societies. Cultures high in food accumulation stress responsibility and obedience; cultures low in food accumulation stress achievement, self-reliance, and independence. (After Barry, Child, & Bacon, 1959)*

TRAIT STRESSED IN CHILDREARING	CORRELATION WITH FOOD ACCUMULATION	
	BOYS	GIRLS
Responsibility	+.74	+.62
Obedience	+.50	+.59
Nurturance	−.01	+.10
Achievement	−.60	−.62
Self-Reliance	−.21	−.46
Independence	−.41	−.11

accumulation in six societies. (Food accumulation is high in agricultural societies and low in hunting societies.) As the correlations in Table 13-1 show, high food-accumulation societies stress responsibility and obedience in their childrearing practices; low food-accumulation societies stress achievement, self-reliance, and independence.

To test whether these different kinds of societies do, in fact, tend to produce individuals with the valued attributes, one investigator assessed conformity in samples of individuals from high and low food-accumulating cultures. The participants were given a visual task in which they were required to identify which of several lines matched a standard line. Prior to making their own judgment, they were told on each trial which line had been selected most often by other members of their culture. In some cases, these responses were clearly incorrect. The investigator found that individuals from high food-accumulating cultures were significantly more likely than those from low food-accumulating cultures to conform to the alleged responses of others—even when those responses were clearly incorrect (Berry, 1967).

These results are consistent with the hypothesis that different lifestyles put a premium on different personalty traits and that cultures shape these traits in their members through different childrearing practices.

CONTINUITY OF PERSONALITY

When you look back over your life, you can probably discern personal patterns and styles that have always seemed a part of your personality. Perhaps you have always been shy or had a problem with procrastination. At the same time, you can probably identify ways in which you have changed; perhaps you are less impulsive than you used to be or better able to relate to others. Sometimes you might be able to identify specific experiences that have changed you. Going to college often affects attitudes, values, and personality in far-reaching ways. Understanding the interplay of continuity and change in personality across the life course is a basic task for both personality and developmental psychology.

Longitudinal studies follow the same individual over many years.

Evidence for Continuity

The only effective way to investigate continuity and change in personality over the life course is to conduct *longitudinal studies*, studies that observe or assess the same persons over time. But because these are very difficult to conduct (see the Critical Discussion, "Studying Personality the Long Way"), there are only a handful of longitudinal studies that cover extensive time periods.

Two of the most ambitious longitudinal studies ever conducted are housed at the Institute of Human Development (IHD) at the University of California in Berkeley. Investigators began the *Berkeley Guidance Study* in 1929 by contacting the parents of every third baby born in Berkeley over an 18-month period and asking them to enroll their newborns in the study; in all, 248 infants and their families were included. The *Oakland Growth Study* began in 1932 with 212 fifth-grade children from elementary schools in Oakland, California. The children from both samples were studied intensively up through adolescence and were interviewed again when the Berkeley subjects were about 30, 40, and 50 and the Oakland subjects were about 37, 47, and 57. Both studies are still in progress, and IHD has generously made its archive available to many investigators around the world.

As described in the Critical Discussion, independent clinical psychologists used a set of personality statements (Q items) to describe the IHD subjects when they were in junior high school (age 13), senior high school (age 16), and as adults (age 30 or 37). The three personality profiles for each subject were then correlated with one another to assess the continuity of the overall personality across these time intervals. Each profile was also correlated with a hypothetical profile of the optimally adjusted person, yielding a measure of overall adjustment that can range from -1 to $+1$.

The results show that in general there was strong continuity of personality from early to later adolescence; the mean correlations between the two sets of adolescent Q sorts were .77 and .75 for men and women, respectively. The correlations between the senior high-school and adult Q sorts were lower but still quite impressive: .56 for men and .54 for women.

TABLE 13-2
Continuity of Personality *The table lists some of the personality characteristics that showed the greatest continuity over the years from early adolescence to adulthood.* (After Block, 1971)

Q ITEMS	CORRELATIONS JUNIOR HIGH TO SENIOR HIGH SCHOOL	CORRELATIONS SENIOR HIGH SCHOOL TO ADULTHOOD
Males		
Is a genuinely dependable and responsible person	.58	.53
Tends toward undercontrol of needs and impulses; unable to delay gratification	.57	.59
Is self-defeating	.50	.42
Enjoys aesthetic impressions; is aesthetically reactive	.35	.58
Females		
Basically submissive	.50	.46
Emphasizes being with others; gregarious	.39	.43
Tends to be rebellious and nonconforming	.48	.49
Is concerned with philosophical problems (for example, religion, values, meaning of life)	.45	.42

The strongest continuities related to intelligence and intellectual interests. For example, the continuities from adolescence to adulthood for the item "Appears to have a high degree of intellectual capacity" were .60 and .61 for men and women, respectively. The corresponding correlations for the item "Genuinely values intellectual and cognitive matters" were .59 and .51. Table 13-2 lists correlations for other personality characteristics that showed substantial continuities.

In general, studies of individuals across the life course find that measures of intellectual performance show the strongest continuities; personality variables like extraversion, emotional stability, and impulse control are next; and political attitudes and measures of self-opinions (for example, self-esteem, life satisfaction) are last—showing correlations between .2 and .4 over 5–10-year intervals (Conley, 1984; 1985). Interestingly, these results are roughly parallel to those from heritability studies: variables with higher heritabilities appear to show stronger continuities. This suggests that genetic and genotype–environment processes may be helping to sustain the intellectual and personality characteristics across time.

Individual Differences

As we have just noted, different characteristics show different degrees of continuity. There are also differences among individuals. Subjects in the

IHD studies whose personalities remained stable from adolescence to adulthood (*nonchangers*) were quite different from those whose personalities changed (*changers*).

In general, nonchangers were better adjusted than changers during adolescence. Relative to male changers, male nonchangers in adolescence were described as having wide interests, valuing intellectual matters, being ambitious, insightful, productive, verbally fluent, dependable, and satisfied with self. They also scored higher on IQ tests. They retained these qualities in adulthood, when they were additionally described as socially perceptive, ethically consistent, warm, calm, and overcontrolled. The correlational measure of overall adjustment increased from $+.13$ to $+.23$ between their junior high-school years and senior high-school years and then remained constant at $+.23$ until adulthood ($+1$ is optimal adjustment).

In contrast, male changers were described in adolescence as psychologically brittle, uncomfortable with uncertainty, self-defensive, self-defeating, self-pitying, other-directed, and hostile toward adults. The changes they underwent from adolescence to adulthood did not appear to improve them much. Some of these same adjectives were used to describe them as adults, when they were additionally described as undercontrolled, self-indulgent, irritable, deceitful, and moody. Their psychological adjustment showed only a slight trend toward greater maturity, increasing from $-.07$ in adolescence to $+.06$ in adulthood.

A similar but not identical picture emerges for the women in the study. Relative to female changers, female nonchangers in adolescence were described as dependable, straightforward, consistent, productive, ambitious, sympathetic, arousing liking and nurturance in others, warm, intellectual, self-satisfied, conservative, and submissive. As adults, they retained their greater conservatism and ambition, but no longer differed from changers on

CRITICAL DISCUSSION

Studying Personality the Long Way

Only investigators with a strong ability to delay gratification or an unselfish devotion to science undertake longitudinal studies. For studies designed to span many years, the original investigators may not even be around to reap the final rewards; their studies may outlive them. Other practical reasons also deter most would-be investigators. Longitudinal studies are expensive, and funding cannot usually be guaranteed over the required time interval. Second, subjects who start out in the study move away, die, decide to discontinue their participation, or cannot otherwise be located for follow-up. In

general, the administrative tasks involved in conducting such a study take as much time and effort as collecting the data. For these reasons, many longitudinal studies are conducted under the auspices of research institutes rather than single investigators.

In addition to the practical problems, there is a more substantive problem that arises in many long-term longitudinal studies. As the interests of the field change over time, the kinds of data collected in a longitudinal study also change. A study that begins with a focus on academic achievement may fail to gather personality information that later investigators wish to have. Sometimes assessment instruments used early in the study become obsolete and are discarded for better instruments as the study progresses. All of these factors make it difficult to compare later observations with earlier ones.

This was the major problem with the two studies discussed in the text that were conducted at the Institute of

Human Development (IHD) in Berkeley. Not only were noncomparable measurements made at different points in time, the two studies were themselves not comparable to each other in many ways. These problems were elegantly solved by Jack Block, who used the Q-sort method of personality description to standardize the data (Block, 1961/1978; Block, 1971). (The "Q" in "Q-sort" was arbitrarily chosen and has no particular meaning.)

In the Q-sort technique, a rater or sorter describes an individual's personality by sorting a set of approximately 100 cards into piles. Each card contains a personality statement (for example, "Has a wide range of interests," "Is self-defeating"). The rater sorts the cards into nine piles, placing those cards that are least descriptive of the individual in pile 1 on the left and those cards that are most descriptive in pile 9 on the right. The other cards are distributed in the intermediate piles, with those that seem neither characteristic nor uncharacteristic of the individual

the other traits. In fact, as adults they were described as more moralistic, conventional, and self-defensive than the changers. Their overall level of adjustment remained virtually unchanged from adolescence to adulthood (.13 versus .16).

Female changers in adolescence were similar to the male changers, being described as psychologically brittle, self-defensive, undercontrolled, self-indulgent, hostile, deceitful, distrustful, self-dramatizing, and rebellious. In contrast to the male changers, however, these women grew out of it. By the time they became adults, most of these negative traits had vanished, and they were described as thinking unconventionally, being sensuous, initiating humor—and still rebellious. Their level of overall adjustment increased from −.08 to +.15 between senior high school and adulthood, thus achieving the same level of adjustment attained by the female nonchangers.

Environmental Influences

Although we have been able to describe differences between changers and nonchangers in the IHD study, it is still not clear why changers change and nonchangers do not. Part of the answer may be maturation. The changers do appear to be less mature as adolescents than the nonchangers, and the changes they undergo as they reach adulthood may simply reflect the further maturation of late bloomers. It also seems likely that the personalities

going into the middle pile (pile 5). Thus each Q item receives a score ranging from 1 to 9, with higher numbers indicating that the item is more characteristic of the person.

Two Q sorts can be compared with each other quantitatively by computing a correlation between them: the 100 scores from the first sort are correlated with the corresponding 100 scores of the other—just as if they were 100 observations of one variable being correlated with 100 observations of a second variable. Like the more standard correlation between variables, this index of similarity between two Q sorts can range from −1 to +1. Two identical Q sorts will thus have a similarity index of +1. If two Q sorts are descriptions of the same individual at two different times, then this index of similarity will assess the continuity of that individual's overall personality profile over time. The continuity of individual Q items can also be assessed by using the usual method of correlation between variables.

The method of correlating two Q sorts can also be used to derive a score from a Q sort for any personality variable the investigator wishes. This is accomplished by first preparing a hypothetical Q sort that describes the desired personality type. For example, Block had a set of clinical psychologists prepare a Q sort of a hypothetical person with an optimally adjusted personality. Individual Q sorts were then "scored" for psychological adjustment by correlating each of them with this ideal sort. Any Q sort that perfectly matches the clinicians' conception of optimal adjustment thus receives an adjustment score of +1.

Using this general method, Q sorts can be scored for personality variables that were not even conceived until long after the data were collected. For example, a researcher who is interested in investigating the motivation to achieve would not find any data specifically designed to assess that variable in the IHD archives. But he or she could prepare a Q sort of the hypothetical

person who—according to the researcher's theory—best exemplifies high-achievement motivation. Every Q sort in the IHD archives could then be scored for achievement motivation simply by correlating it with this criterion sort.

In the IHD studies, all the data on a single subject from the junior high-school years were placed into a single folder. Two to four clinical psychologists independently examined the folder and prepared Q-sort descriptions of the subject. A different set of sorters did the same thing for the data gathered during the senior high-school period. And finally, the interviewers and independent clinicians prepared Q-sort descriptions of the subjects when they were interviewed as adults in 1960, 1970, and 1980. This total procedure thus converted a bewildering variety of data to a set of independent but standardized personality descriptions on each subject at different ages that could be directly compared with one another.

of the adolescent changers were more aversive, causing other people to pressure them to change. These explanations can only be part of the story, however, because we also saw that male changers did not display more mature, pleasant, or adjusted personalities as adults than they had as adolescents.

SOCIAL NORMS   One environmental source of pressure to change is social norms. Individuals who violate social norms or expectations—who do not fit well into their social environments—are particularly likely to be subjected to such pressures. For example, the finding that the female nonchangers in the IHD study were more conservative, more submissive, and better adjusted in adolescence than the rebellious female changers suggests that the culture's sex-role norms were playing a part. The IHD subjects became adults between 1945 and 1960, a time of quite traditional sex roles in America. Conservative, submissive young women fit better into the prescribed roles than rebellious young women then and would thus not have been under as much pressure to change. (Those of us who are feminists can be encouraged that the female changers became well-adjusted adults, while remaining unconventional and rebellious.)

Further evidence for the influence of sex-role norms comes from an extensive longitudinal study conducted at the Fels Research Institute in Yellow Springs, Ohio from 1929 to 1954, and reported in the book *Birth to Maturity* (Kagan & Moss, 1962). The study began with 89 infants and was able to

Individuals who rebel against social norms are usually pressured to change—particularly if they are female.

follow 71 of them through early adulthood. They were assessed repeatedly on a number of variables, including passivity/dependency and aggression.

A number of continuities were found from childhood to adulthood, but they were related to the sex of the individual and the sex-role appropriateness of the behaviors being assessed. For example, girls who were strongly dependent on adults during childhood were passive and dependent on their families and males in adulthood. The male subjects did not show similar continuities in passivity/dependency. The opposite was observed for aggression: continuities were found for male subjects but not for female subjects.

These findings suggest again that individuals who do not conform to the culture's norms are likely to be pressured to change. Passivity is acceptable for females but not for males; aggression is acceptable for males but not for females. There was also some evidence that behavior inconsistent with sex-role expectations in childhood may not be entirely suppressed but may be expressed in adulthood in more socially acceptable ways. For example, boys who were passive during childhood became men who were noncompetitive in adulthood. We shall see a more compelling example of this pattern later in the chapter.

Personality–Environment Influences

We suggested above that the unpleasant personalities of the adolescent changers in the IHD study might have provoked others to pressure them to change. If this occurred, it would be another example of evocative interaction between the person and his or her social environment. In general, the same processes of personality–environment interaction that shape personality in the first place also influence its continuity.

Consider an adolescent boy who has temper tantrums. His ill temper may provoke school authorities to expel him (*evocative interaction*) or cause him to experience school so negatively (*reactive interaction*) that he chooses to quit as soon as he is legally permitted to do so (*proactive interaction*). In either case, leaving school might limit his future career opportunities, channeling him into frustrating life circumstances that further evoke a pattern of striking out explosively against the world. His personality thus creates future environments that themselves perpetuate his original personality.

His ill temper can promote its own continuity in other ways. For example, his tantrums might coerce his parents into giving in to his demands, thereby reinforcing his behavior (*evocative interaction*). This reinforcement not only short-circuits the learning of more controlled ways of behaving that might have greater adaptability in the long run, but it also increases the likelihood that he will react to future situations with similar behavior (*reactive interaction*). He has learned an interactional style that becomes self-perpetuating because it continues to work in later years. Later in this chapter, we shall see evidence in support of these scenarios.

PROACTIVE CHOICES   Although we might think of the ill-tempered boy as choosing future environments that promote the continuity of his personality, we generally think of "choosing" as the selection of alternatives that the individual prefers. Such positive choices can also have continuity-promoting consequences for personality. For example, in our earlier discussion of proactive interaction, we cited the sociable child who, in selectively choosing to enter and create social situations, places herself into environments that further reinforce and sustain her sociability. We do the same thing when we choose friends and spouses. Because we are likely to choose companions who are compatible with our personalities, they are likely to be people who, in turn, reinforce and sustain our personalities. Through positive proactive interaction, our personalities thus promote their own continuity.

Evidence for this process comes from a recent study of the IHD archives (Caspi & Herbener, 1989). When the subjects were interviewed in 1970 and 1980, so were their spouses, thereby providing Q sorts of subjects and spouses that could be directly correlated with each other. The researchers were interested in whether spouses who were more alike in personality would produce greater personality continuity in each other. To do this, they compared the similarity of each couple's Q sorts from 1970 with the personality continuity of each spouse from 1970 to 1980.

The results confirmed the hypothesis: when the researchers divided the 126 couples into three groups of equal size on the basis of the similarity between the spouses' 1970 Q sorts, they found that the least similar spouses showed individual continuities of .4 from 1970 to 1980; moderately similar spouses showed individual continuities of .5; and the most similar spouses showed continuities of .6. Further analyses demonstrated that these findings were not simply due to spouses' similarities in age, social class, or education.

The study also found that spouses who were more similar in personality were also more similar in their enjoyment of daily activities like visiting friends, going out for dinner, and participating in community activities and professional meetings. They also reported less marital conflict and greater closeness, friendliness, and marital satisfaction than less similar spouses. (This last finding exemplifies a well-known phenomenon. We discuss the similarity-produces-liking effect further in Chapter 18.)

The proactive selection process that promotes the continuity of personality has also been found in the domain of political attitudes. Politically conservative women who attended Bennington College in the 1930s became increasingly liberal during their 4 years there. A follow-up of these women 25 years later found that they had remained liberal, and that they had done so,

Couples who enjoy similar activities report greater marital satisfaction.

in part, because they had chosen politically liberal friends and husbands who reinforced and sustained their political attitudes (Newcomb, 1943; Newcomb, Koenig, Flacks, & Warwick, 1967). (This study is discussed in more detail in Chapter 19.)

CONSEQUENCES OF PERSONALITY

We have seen how the processes of reactive, evocative, and proactive interaction enable an individual's personality both to shape itself and to promote its own continuity through the life course. These same processes also enable an individual's personality to influence the life course itself. In particular, personality-environment interactions can produce two kinds of consequences in the life course: *cumulative consequences* and *contemporary consequences.*

Consider once again the boy whose temper tantrums lead him to quit school and thereby channel him into low-level jobs. His low occupational status might then lead to an erratic worklife characterized by frequent job changes and bouts of unemployment. This erratic worklife, in turn, might disrupt his marriage and lead to divorce. In this hypothetical scenario, these occupational and marital outcomes are *cumulative* consequences of his childhood personality. Once set in motion by childhood temper tantrums, the chain of events takes over and culminates in the adult outcomes—*even* if he is no longer ill-tempered as an adult.

On the other hand, if he *does* carry his ill temper into adulthood, then contemporary consequences are also likely to arise. He is likely to explode when frustrations arise on the job or when conflicts arise in his marriage. This can lead to an erratic worklife, low-level occupational status, and divorce. In this scenario, the same occupational and marital outcomes are contemporary consequences of his current personality rather than consequences of earlier events like quitting school.

Consequences of Childhood Ill-Temperedness

Evidence for both cumulative and contemporary consequences of childhood ill-temperedness was obtained by investigators who used the IHD archive from the Berkeley Guidance Study. Subjects in this study had been assessed annually on several rating scales when they were children. The investigators combined the ratings from two of these scales—severity and frequency of temper tantrums—into a single 5-point scale and averaged this scale across the annual assessments at ages 8, 9, and 10. Any subject who obtained a mean score greater than 3 on the 5-point scale was designated as having had a history of childhood ill-temperedness. The investigators then traced the continuities and consequences of this personality style across the subsequent 30 years of the subjects' lives (Caspi, Bem, & Elder, 1989; Caspi, Elder, & Bem, 1987).

MALE SUBJECTS   Beginning with male subjects, the investigators first asked the continuity question: Do ill-tempered boys become ill-tempered men? Apparently so. Correlations between the temper-tantrum scores in late

Do ill-tempered children become ill-tempered adults?

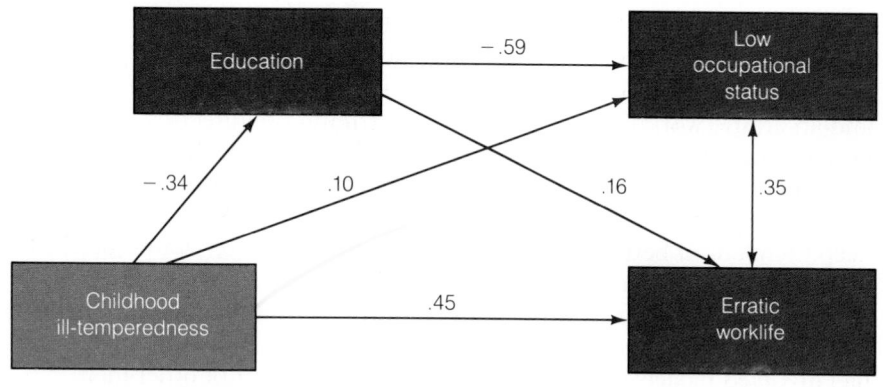

FIGURE 13-2
Path Analysis for Male Ill-
Temperedness *The figure traces the*
separate paths from childhood ill-
temperedness to low occupational status and
an erratic worklife at age 40 for middle-class
men. Childhood ill-temperedness leads to
lower occupational status because ill-
tempered children quit school sooner
(cumulative consequences). Childhood ill-
temperedness leads directly to an erratic
worklife because the subjects remain ill-
tempered as adults, and this handicaps them
in the world of work (contemporary
consequences). (After Caspi, Elder, &
Bem, 1987)

childhood and the Q-sort ratings 20 years later reveal that ill-tempered boys are later described as significantly more undercontrolled, irritable, and moody than their even-tempered peers.

The investigators then examined the subjects' work histories. The major finding was that ill-tempered boys who came from middle-class homes suffered a progressive deterioration of socioeconomic status as they moved through the life course. They were somewhat more likely than their even-tempered peers to terminate their formal education earlier; the occupational status of their first jobs was significantly lower, and by midlife (age 40), their occupational status was indistinguishable from that of men born into the working class. A majority of them held jobs of lower occupational status than those held by their fathers at a comparable age. They also had more erratic worklives, changing jobs more frequently and experiencing more unemployment between ages 18 and 40.

Having established an overall correlation between childhood ill-temperedness and occupational outcomes, the investigators then asked about the path between these two things. Did these subjects become occupationally disadvantaged because their earlier ill-temperedness started them down a particular path (cumulative consequences) or because their current ill-temperedness handicapped them in the world of work (contemporary consequences)? To answer this, the investigators used a correlational procedure called *path analysis*, which divides an overall correlation into separate components or paths. Figure 13-2 shows the results of this analysis.

As the figure shows, there is a significant path from childhood ill-temperedness through education to lower occupational status. In particular, childhood ill-temperedness is negatively correlated with education (ill-tempered children quit school sooner), and education, in turn, is correlated with occupational status (the less education, the lower the occupational status). At the same time, there is no significant *direct* correlation between ill-temperedness and occupational status (.10 is not significantly different from zero). This implies that occupational status is a cumulative consequence of earlier childhood ill-temperedness, not a contemporary consequence of adult ill-temperedness: The reason that ill-tempered children hold lower occupational status at age 40 is that they quit school sooner.

The path from childhood ill-temperedness to an erratic worklife shows just the opposite pattern. There is no significant path from education to an erratic worklife, but there is a significant direct path between childhood ill-temperedness and an erratic worklife. This implies that an erratic worklife is a contemporary consequence of adult ill-temperedness, not a cumulative consequence of truncated education. Apparently ill-tempered children have a more erratic worklife at age 40, in part, because they are still ill-tempered in ways that handicap them in the world of work.

Finally, there is a significant correlation between low occupational status and an erratic worklife, but we cannot determine the direction of causality because these two variables are both assessed at the same point in time. Ill-tempered men may become frustrated with low-status jobs and thus become erratic by quitting or being fired. Alternatively, their erratic worklife may keep them out of better jobs, thus forcing them into lower-status jobs. Both sequences could be in effect.

A history of childhood ill-temperedness also affects the domestic sphere. Almost half (46 percent) of men with histories of childhood ill-temperedness had divorced by age 40 compared with only 22 percent of other men.

FEMALE SUBJECTS   Like the men, women who had been ill-tempered as young girls also showed personality continuity. Compared with other women, these women were described by both their husbands and their children at the time of the 1970 interviews as less adequate, more ill-tempered mothers.

As noted earlier, the Berkeley subjects became adults when sex roles were quite traditional (1945–1960). Accordingly, few of the women had occupations outside the home, and the investigators were not able to analyze their occupational status as they had done for the men. But this was also a time when a woman's socioeconomic status was defined by her husband's occupation, and so the investigators looked at the occupational status of these women's husbands. They found that compared with other women, women with a history of childhood ill-temperedness married men who had lower occupational status both at the time of marriage and at midlife. When the jobs held by their fathers at a comparable age were compared with the jobs held by their husbands at the time of marriage, it was found that 40 percent of the ill-tempered women married down compared with only 24 percent of other women.

Ill-temperedness in childhood not only consigned these women to marriages "below their station," it also contributed to the deterioration of these relationships. Over a quarter (26 percent) of these women had divorced by age 40 compared with only 12 percent of other women. Husbands of those women who were married at the time of the 1970 interviews reported more marital conflict than husbands of other women.

Consequences of Childhood Dependency

The personality characteristic of dependency is a particularly interesting one to examine across the life course. On the one hand, dependency may well be even more self-perpetuating than ill-temperedness because dependent individuals are *positively* motivated to select and construct environments that would sustain their dependency (proactive interaction). On the other hand, sex-role norms discourage boys and men from being dependent. What might be the result of these two competing forces?

In order to find out, the investigators who had conducted the study of ill-temperedness conducted a parallel study of men and women who had histories of childhood dependency (Caspi, Elder, & Bem, 1989). Again they used two rating scales from the childhood records. The *dependency* scale ranged from 1, "easy attachments, not possessive," to 5, "intense attachments;

Men tend to be more nurturant if they have a history of childhood dependency.

parents' approval dominates the child's interests and values." The *attention-demanding* scale ranged from 1, "self-reliant," to 5, "constant demanding of attention; insecure and anxious without the attention of others." These scales were combined into a single 5-point scale and averaged across the annual assessments at ages 8, 9, and 10. Any subject who obtained a mean score greater than 3 on the 5-point scale was designated as having had a history of childhood dependency.

MALE SUBJECTS   Once again the investigators began with the continuity question: Do dependent boys become dependent men? The answer this time was both more complex and more interesting. Compared with other men, those who had histories of childhood dependency were characterized in adulthood as calm, warm, giving, sympathetic, insightful, undefensive, incisive, and socially poised. Although they sought reassurance from others—a possible echo of their earlier childhood dependency—others felt nurturant toward them and sought them out for advice. It appears that the negative childhood attribute of dependency had been transformed into a related but remarkably positive nurturant personality style in adulthood. These data are also consistent with the findings from the Fels longitudinal study, discussed earlier, which found that boys who were passive became men who were noncompetitive. Behavior patterns that are at odds with cultural norms may change their form to become more acceptable.

Not unexpectedly, the warm, nurturant adult style of men with a history of childhood dependency conferred its most obvious advantages in the domestic sphere. These men were significantly more likely to have an intact first marriage at midlife than other men (83 percent versus 62 percent); their wives expressed more satisfaction with their marriages than wives of other men; and, they and their wives agreed more with one another on such child-rearing practices as discipline, affection, and attention. Dependent adolescent boys who worry about being insufficiently assertive should take note—as should adolescent girls who will someday come to appreciate nurturant, lovable men and wonder where to find them.

Women who have a history of childhood dependency are more likely to have children at a younger age.

FEMALE SUBJECTS   Compared with the men, women with a history of childhood dependency are not nearly so agreeable. As adults, they are described as not valuing their own independence, having a low aspiration level, lacking personal meaning in life, having narrow interests, and being unassertive, moody, and self-pitying. A concern over the adequacy of their bodily functioning and a tendency to suffer psychosomatic symptoms adds to this already unflattering portrait.

It also appears that women who were dependent as children remained dependent throughout life, moving early into a circumscribed world in which they could create a life focused on their husbands and children. For example, these women were significantly more likely to marry earlier and to become mothers earlier than other women. Twenty percent of these women were married by age 18 compared with only 7 percent of other women; 38 percent had their first child by age 20 compared with only 13 percent of other women. And although these women did not bear more children, their childbearing period was spread out over more years. For example, 38 percent had a childbearing period longer than 10 years compared with only 17 percent of other women. This heavy investment in parenting also displaced higher education for these women. Whereas nearly three quarters (73 percent) of other women either went to college immediately after high school or resumed their formal education after marriage and childbearing, only half (54 percent) of these women did so.

In sum, childhood dependency produced sympathetic and nurturant men but constricted and self-pitying women, confirming again how dramatically a society's sex-role norms can influence both personality and the life course. It remains to be seen how the recent changes in America's views of appropriate behavior for males and females will affect the personalities and life courses of children coming of age today. The specific findings catalogued in this final section may become historical curiosities. But the general processes they illustrate will continue to remain valid: reactive, evocative, and proactive interactions between our genotypes and our environments will continue to shape our personalities; promote, disrupt, or transform their continuity across time; and enable our personalities, in turn, to shape the course of life itself.

CHAPTER SUMMARY

1. Mood-related personality differences that show up in infants as young as 3 months are called *temperaments* and constitute early building blocks for the individual's later personality. Comparisons of identical and fraternal twins indicate that genetic factors account for about 50 percent of the variability among individuals on many personality characteristics. This is particularly well documented for measures of sociability and emotional stability/instability.

2. Parental childrearing practices can be distinguished on two dimensions: the first distinguishes parents who are demanding and controlling of their children from those who are undemanding; the other distinguishes parents who are accepting, responsive, and child-centered from those who are rejecting, unresponsive, and parent-centered. The combination of these two dimensions produces four kinds of parenting patterns: *authoritative, authoritarian, indulgent,* and *neglecting*.

3. *Authoritative* parents combine high control with acceptance and have children who tend to be independent, self-assertive, motivated to achieve, and socially successful. *Authoritarian* parents exercise high control, but have a low level of acceptance. Their children tend to be responsible but socially withdrawn and lacking in spontaneity and achievement motivation. *Indulgent* parents are accepting but place few demands on their children. Their children show vitality but tend to be immature and lack impulse control, social responsibility, and self-reliance. Finally, *neglecting* parents are more concerned with their own activities and are uninvolved with their children. Their children tend to be impulsive, uninterested in school, and lack long-term goals. Extremely neglecting parents have children who show clear disturbances in their attachment relationships and psychological functioning by age 2. These childrearing practices may not cause the observed differences in children's behaviors so much as they reflect parents' reactions to the children's behavior. Also, the correlations are very low.

4. In shaping personality, genetic and environmental influences do not act independently of one another but are intertwined from the moment of birth. Because parents give a child both their genes and the environment, there is a built-in correlation between the child's *genotype* (inherited personality characteristics) and that environment.

5. Three dynamic processes of personality–environment interaction are a) *reactive interaction*—different individuals exposed to the same environment experience it, interpret it, and react to it differently; b) *evocative interaction*—an individual's personality evokes distinctive responses from others; and c) *proactive interaction*—individuals select or create environments of their own. As a child gets older, the influence of proactive interaction becomes increasingly important.

6. Studies of twins have produced a number of puzzling patterns: the differences between identical twin similarities and fraternal twin similarities are too great to be explained by simple genetic models; identical twins reared apart are as similar to one another as identical twins reared together; and fraternal twins and ordinary siblings become less similar over time, even when they are reared together. These patterns might be accounted for by the three processes of personality-environment interaction (reactive, evocative, and proactive).

7. After their genetic similarities are subtracted out, children from the same family seem to be no more alike than children chosen randomly from the population, a startling and controversial finding. If further research confirms it, then the kinds of between-family variables that psychologists typically study (such as childrearing practices, quality of education, social class) are contributing virtually nothing to individual differences in personality. Research will have to begin looking more closely at differences between children within the same family. This finding, too, might be partially accounted for by the three processes of personality–environment interaction.

8. Differences between families drawn from Western industrial societies may be too small for between-family effects to show up. Compared with these societies, most non-Western cultures place less value on independence and self-assertiveness and more on the interdependence of persons with others in the community. In general, agricultural societies stress responsibility and obedience in their childrearing practices; hunting and fishing societies stress achievement, self-reliance, and independence.

9. *Longitudinal studies* observe the same individuals over time and provide the only effective way to assess the continuity of personality through the life course. In general, measures of intellectual performance show the strongest continuities; personality variables like extraversion, emotional stability/instability, and impulse control are next; political attitudes and measures of self-opinions (for example, self-esteem, life satisfaction) are last. Genetic and genotype–environment factors may contribute to the continuity of the intellectual and personality characteristics across time.

10. Many factors affect the continuity of personality variables across time. In one study, those who were well adjusted in adolescence tended to show stronger continuities from adolescence to adulthood than those who were less well adjusted. Men who changed did not tend to become any better adjusted, but women who changed became as well adjusted as those who had not changed from adolescence.

11. Cultural norms are an important environmental influence on personality and its continuity. Individuals who do not conform to the culture's norms are likely to be pressured to change. Sex-role norms provide an example. Passivity and dependency show continuity for females but not for males; aggression shows continuity for males but not for females. Childhood behavior that is inconsistent with sex-role norms may be transformed into more acceptable forms in adulthood. For example, passive boys in one study became noncompetitive men.

12. The three processes of personality–environment interaction influence the continuity of personality. For example, continuity produced by proactive interaction occurs when we choose friends and spouses who are compatible with our personalities, and they, in turn, reinforce and sustain our personalities. One study showed that personalities of spouses who were more alike changed less over a decade than those of spouses who were less alike. More similar spouses also reported more similarities in the activities they enjoyed, less marital conflict, and greater marital satisfaction than less similar spouses.

13. The three processes of personality–environment interaction also enable an individual's personality to shape the life course itself. *Cumulative consequences* arise when an individual's early personality selects or channels him or her into particular life paths. *Contemporary consequences* arise when the early personality is itself carried forward into adulthood where it evokes distinctive responses from the environment. Both kinds of consequences were demonstrated in studies that followed ill-tempered or dependent children across the subsequent 30 years of their lives. The particular consequences of these personality styles depended strongly on the individual's sex, illustrating again how dramatically a society's sex-role norms can influence both personality and the life course.

A general text on personality development through the life course is Goldhaber, *Life-Span Human Development* (1986). Texts that focus on development up through adolescence include Scarr, Weinberg, and Levine, *Understanding Development* (1986); and Damon, *Social and Personality Development* (1983). Background information on genetics is provided in Plomin, *Development, Genetics, and Psychology* (1986); and Plomin, DeFries, and McClearn, *Behavioral Genetics: A Primer* (2nd ed., 1989).

Cross-cultural studies are reviewed in Munroe, Munroe, and Whiting (eds.), *Handbook of Cross-Cultural Human Development* (1981). The classic studies are Whiting and Child, *Child Training and Personality: A Cross-Cultural Study* (1953); Whiting and Whiting, *Children of Six Cultures: A Psychocultural Analysis* (1975); and more recently, Whiting and Edwards, *Children of Different Worlds: The Formation of Social Behavior* (1988).

The Fels Institute longitudinal study is described in Kagan and Moss, *Birth to Maturity* (1962). The best sources on the longitudinal archives housed at the Institute of Human Development (IHD) in Berkeley are Eichorn, Clausen, Haan, Honzik, and Mussen (eds.), *Present and Past in Middle Life* (1981); and Block, *Lives Through Time* (1971).

FURTHER READING

Chapter 14

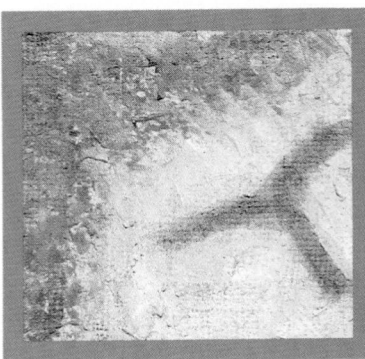

Detail, Little Hope.

Personality Theory and Assessment

In Chapter 13, we defined personality as the characteristic patterns of thought, emotion, and behavior that define an individual's personal style and influence his or her interactions with the environment. Accordingly, personality psychology seeks a) to describe and to explain individual differences—the diverse ways in which individuals differ from one another, and b) to synthesize the many processes that can influence an individual's interactions with the environment—biology, development, learning, thinking, emotion, motivation, and social interaction—into an integrated account of the total person. The study of personality is the most ambitious subfield of psychology.

In this chapter, we shall look at the four major approaches to personality and the empirical methods they employ to measure or assess personality. We shall also return to a theme touched on briefly in Chapter 1 by comparing the portraits of the human personality that emerge from their different philosophies of human nature. In what ways are we free and in what ways are our actions determined by causes beyond our control? Are we basically good, neutral, or evil? Fixed or modifiable? Active or passive? What constitutes psychological health and unhealth? These are not empirical questions, and theories of personality do not explicitly attempt to answer them. But each approach does have implicit answers—underlying presumptions about the nature of human personality that give the approach a distinctive flavor. Historically, these more philosophical factors have been as important as the empirical data in provoking controversies and in winning converts for the competing accounts of personality.

In reading about each of the approaches to personality, it is important to keep in mind that many, if not most, contemporary psychologists are eclectic: they pick and choose among the diverse approaches to arrive at their own integrated view of personality; some would even claim that they subscribe to no theory at all, but simply do neutral empirical research on problems that interest them. In psychology's earlier days, competing schools of thought were much more in evidence, the battle lines more firmly drawn. Nevertheless, we shall see that contemporary controversies are still quite lively.

TRAIT APPROACH

Personality Types

The study of personality is not only the most ambitious subfield of psychology, it is also the oldest. In 400 B.C., Hippocrates suggested that there were four basic personality types, associated with the four bodily humors. According to his theory, an excess of black bile produces the melancholic (depressed) type; an excess of yellow bile produces the choleric (irritable) type; blood produces the sanguine (optimistic) type; and phlegm produces the phlegmatic (calm, stolid) type.

A more differentiated typology was published by Theophrastus (372–287 B.C.), Aristotle's successor as head of the Lyceum in Athens. He proposed a set of 30 personality types, which he presented in a series of character vignettes. Each sketch began with a brief definition of the dominant characteristic of the type and then described several behaviors typical of the type.

Among his characters were the Liar, the Tasteless Man, the Flatterer, and the Penurious Man. For example,

> Penuriousness is economy carried beyond all measure. A Penurious Man is one who goes to a debtor to ask for his half-obol interest before the end of the month. At a dinner where expenses are shared, he counts the number of cups each person drinks and he makes a smaller libation to Artemis than anyone. . . . If his wife drops a copper, he moves furniture, beds, chests and hunts in the curtains. . . . The coffers of the penurious men are moldy and the keys rust. . . . They have hair cut short and do not put on their shoes until midday; and when they take their cloak to the fuller they urge him to use plenty of earth so that it will not be spotted so soon. (Quoted in Allport, 1937, p. 57)

Body physique has also been a popular basis for personality typologies. The idea that body build and personality characteristics are related is reflected in such popular stereotypes as "fat people are jolly," or "skinny people are intellectuals." Shakespeare's Julius Caesar remarked, "Let me have men about me that are fat; sleek-headed men, and such as sleep o' nights. Yond Cassius has a lean and hungry look; he thinks too much: such men are dangerous. . . . Would he were fatter" (*Julius Caesar*, Act 1, Scene 2).

In the 1940s, the American physician William Sheldon reported correlations between three bodily physiques, called *somatotypes*, and temperament: the endomorphic (soft and round) somatotype has a relaxed, sociable temperament; the mesomorphic (muscular and athletic) somatotype has an energetic, assertive, courageous temperament; and the ectomorphic (tall and thin) somatotype has a restrained, fearful, introverted, artistic temperament (Sheldon, 1954). Sheldon's evidence, however, was not very strong, and his methods left open the possibility that his temperament ratings simply reflected popular stereotypes. When individuals are rated on specific behaviors rather than on global traits, there are no strong associations between body types and personality (Mischel, 1968). Although most contemporary psychologists do not consider somatotyping useful, some have continued to refine the system and to present confirming data (Carter & Heath, 1971).

The theories discussed above are called *type theories* because they propose that individuals can be categorized into discrete types that are qualitatively different from one another. Typologies have been useful in many sciences. In chemistry, the periodic chart of the elements is a refinement of earlier typologies of physical substances. In biology, the concepts of a species and of sex (male and female) are both type concepts. Nevertheless, type theories of personality are currently not very popular. The very simplicity that makes them appealing also makes them less capable of capturing the complexity and variability of human personality. Even so, some psychologists have called for a revival of typological thinking in personality, arguing that typologies have been rejected for the wrong reasons and that their virtues have been overlooked (Bem, 1983; Gangestad & Snyder, 1985; Kagan, 1989).

Personality Traits

Whereas typologies comprise discontinuous categories (like male and female), traits are conceived of as continuous dimensions. For example, rather than categorizing body physiques into one of three pure types, Sheldon rated them on three dimensions, using 7-point rating scales. Thus, a 2–7–4 would be low on endomorphy, high on mesomorphy, and moderate

A trait theorist might describe the individual on the left as bold and adventurous and the individual on the right as quiet and reflective.

on ectomorphy. More generally, trait theories of personality assume that persons vary simultaneously on a number of personality dimensions or scales. We might rate an individual on scales of intelligence, emotional stability, aggressiveness, and so on. To arrive at a global description of personality, we would need to know the individual's rating on a number of scales, and how much of each trait he or she possessed. Actually, we are all trait theorists. When we informally describe ourselves and others with such adjectives as "aggressive," "cautious," "excitable," "intelligent," or "anxious," we are using a layperson's version of trait theory. Our informal theories serve the same purposes as those of the formal trait theorists: they enable us to characterize consistencies in an individual's behavior and thereby to anticipate how he or she will respond to particular situations.

Trait psychologists attempt to go beyond our everyday trait conceptions of personality, however. Specifically, they seek a) to arrive at a manageably small set of trait descriptors that can encompass the diversity of human personality, b) to craft ways of measuring personality traits reliably and validly, and c) to discover the relationships among traits and between traits and specific behaviors. Different trait theorists have approached these tasks in different ways.

Trait Theories

GORDON ALLPORT   One of the most influential trait theorists was Harvard psychologist Gordon Allport, who died in 1967. His major works on personality were *Personality: A Psychological Interpretation* (1937) and *Pattern and Growth in Personality* (1961). Allport regarded traits as the basic building blocks of psychological organization, serving to integrate what would otherwise be dissimilar stimuli and responses. For example, consider a woman for whom the trait of friendliness is central. For her, sitting next to a stranger on an airplane, visiting the family, and working with others at the office are all equivalent situations in that they all evoke what is for her an interrelated set of responses: being interested, personable, helpful, pleasant, outgoing, warm, and attentive. In other words, her trait of friendliness serves as a unifying element, creating an equivalence class of stimuli, an equivalence class of responses, and providing the link between them.

Mother Theresa's cardinal disposition is altruism.

Allport distinguished between *common traits* and *personal dispositions*. Common traits are trait dimensions on which individuals can be compared with one another. Personal dispositions refer to the unique patterning or configuration of traits within the individual. Two people may both be honest but may differ in the way that honesty relates to their other traits. One, sensitive to the feelings of others, may tell a "white lie" on occasion; for him, sensitivity ranks higher than honesty. The other, ranking honesty higher, is scrupulously honest no matter whom he offends. People may also possess the same trait but for different motives. For example, two people may both be conscientious—one because he is concerned about how he appears to other people; the other because he wants to keep his life neat and orderly, and being conscientious serves this purpose.

Traits also differ in the extent to which they influence the person's behavior. Allport viewed personal dispositions as being organized in a kind of hierarchy, some having a more pervasive influence on an individual's behavior than others; he distinguished among cardinal, central, and secondary dispositions. A few people may have one dominant disposition that influences virtually all aspects of their behavior. Allport called these *cardinal dispositions*. A saintly, religious figure such as Mother Theresa might be said to have the cardinal disposition of altruism. Less pervasive but still quite general tendencies to respond are called *central dispositions*. Most of us have 5 to 10 central dispositions that serve to organize and direct many aspects of our lives. For the woman described earlier, friendliness would be a central disposition. Finally, we all have numerous more specific and narrow interests or tendencies to respond that Allport called *secondary dispositions*; a preference for certain kinds of clothes or a tendency to keep a neat desk but a sloppy personal appearance would be examples. Some of these are perhaps more appropriately characterized as attitudes.

Most trait psychologists focus on what Allport called the common traits, because these lend themselves better to quantitative analysis and the systematic comparison of individuals with one another. In contrast, Allport's notion of personal dispositions lends itself primarily to the in-depth study of individual lives and experiences. While acknowledging the usefulness of quantitative methods and the study of common traits, Allport himself remained convinced that they failed to capture what he considered the essence of personality—individuality. The systematic study of individuality is relatively neglected in contemporary personality psychology, and some psychologists have even questioned whether it is science rather than biography. Later in this chapter, however, we shall see how Allport's more individualized approach offers one solution to a recurring paradox in the study of personality: How can one reconcile the concept of traits with the observation that most people are inconsistent in their behavior from one situation to another?

FACTOR-ANALYTIC THEORIES The English language contains approximately 18,000 words that refer to characteristics of behavior. As we noted above, one task of trait psychology is to reduce these to a manageable number of traits that can encompass the diversity of human personality. Gordon Allport and a colleague addressed this problem by actually going through the unabridged dictionary and reducing the 18,000 trait-like words to a list of about 4,500 terms by eliminating obscure words and close synonyms. They then organized the list into psychologically meaningful subsets (Allport & Odbert, 1936).

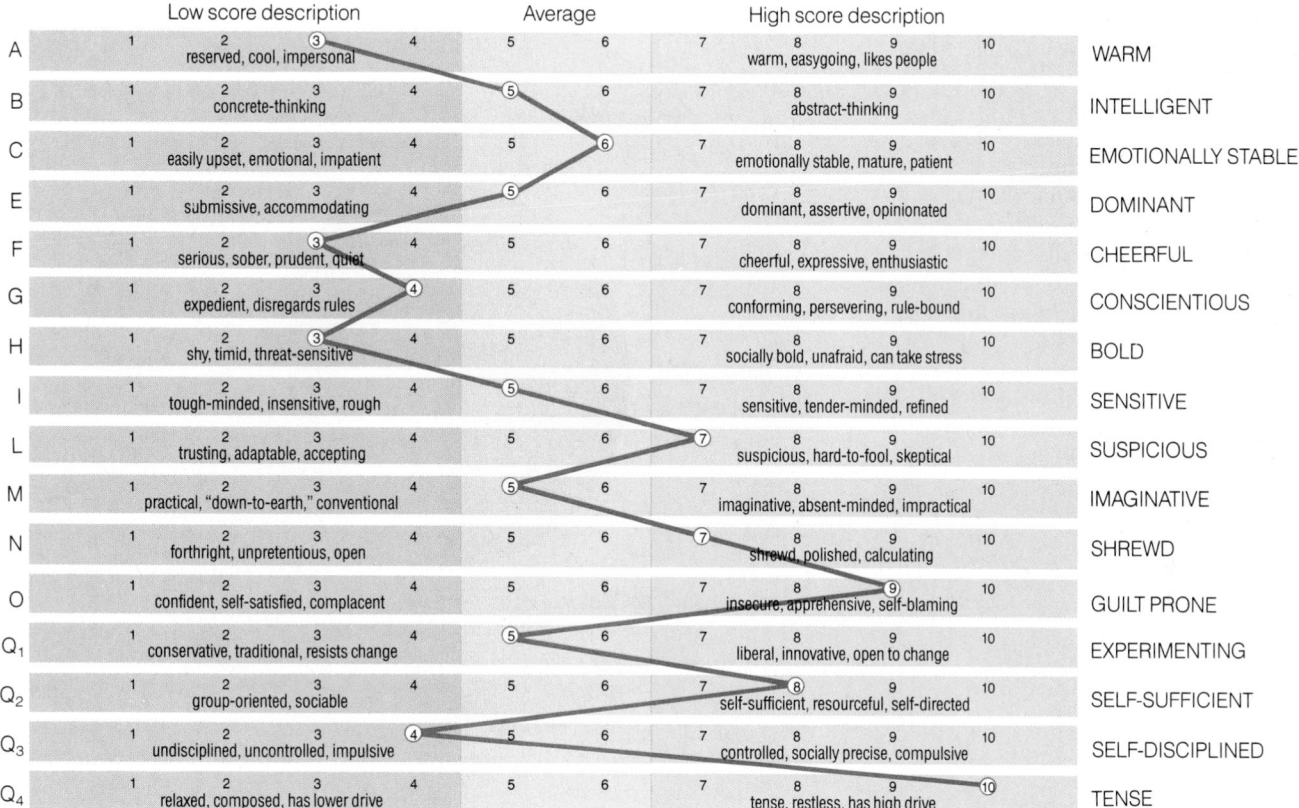

	Low score description	Average	High score description	
A	1 2 ③ 4 reserved, cool, impersonal	5 6	7 8 9 10 warm, easygoing, likes people	WARM
B	1 2 3 4 concrete-thinking	⑤ 6	7 8 9 10 abstract-thinking	INTELLIGENT
C	1 2 3 4 easily upset, emotional, impatient	5 ⑥	7 8 9 10 emotionally stable, mature, patient	EMOTIONALLY STABLE
E	1 2 3 4 submissive, accommodating	⑤ 6	7 8 9 10 dominant, assertive, opinionated	DOMINANT
F	1 2 ③ 4 serious, sober, prudent, quiet	5 6	7 8 9 10 cheerful, expressive, enthusiastic	CHEERFUL
G	1 2 3 ④ expedient, disregards rules	5 6	7 8 9 10 conforming, persevering, rule-bound	CONSCIENTIOUS
H	1 2 ③ 4 shy, timid, threat-sensitive	5 6	7 8 9 10 socially bold, unafraid, can take stress	BOLD
I	1 2 3 4 tough-minded, insensitive, rough	⑤ 6	7 8 9 10 sensitive, tender-minded, refined	SENSITIVE
L	1 2 3 4 trusting, adaptable, accepting	5 6	⑦ 8 9 10 suspicious, hard-to-fool, skeptical	SUSPICIOUS
M	1 2 3 4 practical, "down-to-earth," conventional	⑤ 6	7 8 9 10 imaginative, absent-minded, impractical	IMAGINATIVE
N	1 2 3 4 forthright, unpretentious, open	5 6	⑦ 8 9 10 shrewd, polished, calculating	SHREWD
O	1 2 3 4 confident, self-satisfied, complacent	5 6	7 8 ⑨ 10 insecure, apprehensive, self-blaming	GUILT PRONE
Q₁	1 2 3 4 conservative, traditional, resists change	⑤ 6	7 8 9 10 liberal, innovative, open to change	EXPERIMENTING
Q₂	1 2 3 4 group-oriented, sociable	5 6	7 ⑧ 9 10 self-sufficient, resourceful, self-directed	SELF-SUFFICIENT
Q₃	1 2 3 ④ undisciplined, uncontrolled, impulsive	5 6	7 8 9 10 controlled, socially precise, compulsive	SELF-DISCIPLINED
Q₄	1 2 3 4 relaxed, composed, has lower drive	5 6	7 8 9 ⑩ tense, restless, has high drive	TENSE

The idea of consulting the dictionary to construct a vocabulary for scientific purposes is not as wrongheaded as it may first appear. The motivating assumption is that through linguistic evolution, the lexicon of a natural language will encode most, if not all, of the important distinctions between persons that make a difference in everyday life. The natural language embodies the accumulated wisdom of the ages, and the unabridged dictionary is the written record of that wisdom.

Several subsequent researchers began with the Allport-Odbert list and carried the work further by using the method of *factor analysis*. As we noted in Chapter 12, factor analysis is a statistical technique that examines the intercorrelations among a number of measures and, by grouping those that are most highly correlated, reduces them to a smaller number of independent dimensions, called *factors*.

The most extensive factor-analytic studies of personality have been conducted by Raymond Cattell (1957; 1966). He first condensed the Allport-Odbert list to under 200 terms by further eliminating rare words and near synonyms. He then had people rate their friends on these personality traits and factor analyzed the results. This analysis yielded 12 personality factors, to which he added 4 more obtained by factor analyzing self-ratings. Although Cattell gives his factors strange-sounding technical names (for example, *affectia* versus *sizia*), he also supplies more familiar labels (*outgoing* versus *reserved*). Some of his other factors are *stable–emotional, dominant–submissive,* and *imaginative–practical*.

Cattell has devised a questionnaire to measure his 16 basic traits: the Sixteen Personality Factor Questionnaire (16 PF, for short). The yes or no

Personality Profiles *The trait names represent the 16 personality factors obtained by factor analysis of a large number of ratings. Factors A–O were obtained from factor analyses of ratings of one person by another; the 4 Q factors were found only in data from self-ratings. A personality test based on the 16 factors measures the level of each factor, and the scores can be graphed as a profile. (From R. B. Cattell, 1986, The Administrator's Manual for the 16 Personality Factor Questionnaire, copyright © 1972, 1979, 1986 by the Institute for Personality and Ability Testing, Inc. All rights reserved. Reproduced by permission.)*

FIGURE 14-1
Eysenck's Personality Factors *The figure shows the two major factors that emerge from factor-analytic studies of the intercorrelations between traits by Eysenck and others. The Stable–Unstable axis defines the* neuroticism *factor; the Introverted–Extraverted axis defines the* extraversion *factor. The other terms in the outer ring indicate where other traits are placed with respect to these two factors. The inner ring shows how the "four temperaments" of Hippocrates might correspond to the more contemporary system. (After Eysenck & Rachman 1965)*

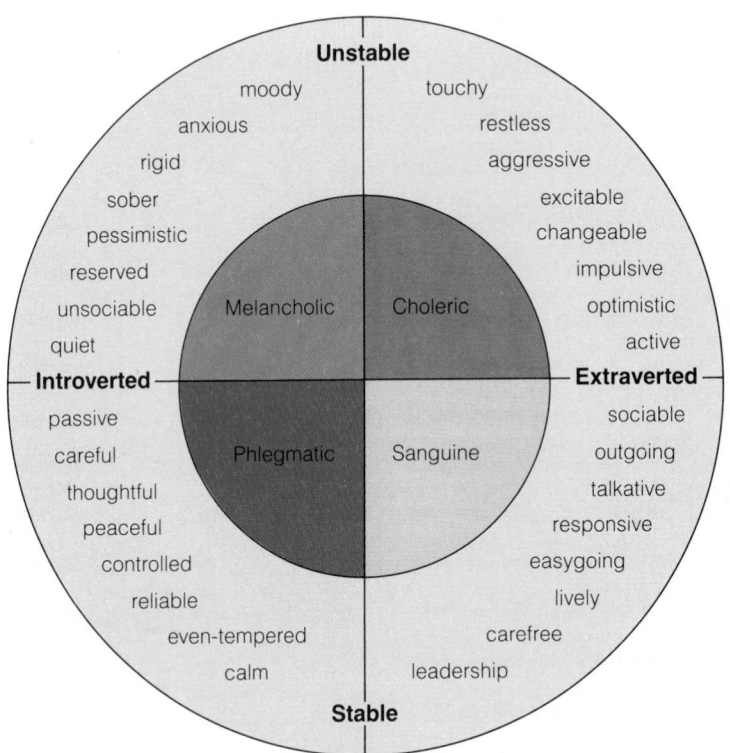

answers that a subject gives to more than 100 questions are compiled to yield a score for each factor. For example, answering "no" to the question "Do you tend to keep in the background on social occasions?" will earn a point toward the dominant side of the dominant–submissive scale. By plotting an individual's test score for each factor on a single graph, the tester arrives at a personality profile that is a kind of shorthand description of the individual's personality.

A second major theorist using factor analysis is the British psychologist Hans Eysenck. He agrees with Cattell's overall approach, but believes that a better and more stable set of factors can be obtained by using a more restrictive kind of factor analysis (Eysenck, 1953). His major factors are introversion–extraversion—a dimension first identified by the psychoanalyst Carl Jung—and emotional instability–stability, which he calls *neuroticism.* (Recently, Eysenck has added *Psychoticism* as a third dimension, but it is not as well established or researched as the other two.)

Introversion–extraversion refers to the degree to which a person's basic orientation is turned inward toward the self or outward toward the external world. At the introversion end of the scale are individuals who are shy and prefer to work alone; they tend to withdraw into themselves, particularly in times of emotional stress or conflict. At the extraversion end are individuals who are sociable and prefer occupations that permit them to work directly with other people; in times of stress, they seek company. Neuroticism or instability–stability is a dimension of emotionality, with moody, anxious, temperamental, and maladjusted individuals at the neurotic or unstable end, and calm, well-adjusted individuals at the other. Figure 14-1 shows how these two dimensions combine to organize a number of subtraits that are correlated with the factors. For historical purposes, Eysenck has included in this figure the four ancient temperaments of Hippocrates' typology to illustrate how they might relate to his more contemporary system.

TRAIT FACTOR	REPRESENTATIVE TRAIT SCALES
Neuroticism	Calm–Worrying Hardy–Vulnerable Secure–Insecure
Extraversion	Retiring–Sociable Quiet–Talkative Inhibited–Spontaneous
Openness	Conventional–Original Unadventurous–Daring Conservative–Liberal
Agreeableness	Irritable–Good-natured Ruthless–Soft-hearted Selfish–Selfless
Conscientiousness	Careless–Careful Undependable–Reliable Negligent–Conscientious

TABLE 14-1
Five Trait Factors *The table presents five trait factors that reliably emerge when a wide variety of assessment instruments are factor analyzed. The adjective pairs are examples of trait scales that characterize each of the factors. (After McCrae & Costa, 1987)*

How many basic personality factors are there? Even with a rigorous analytic procedure like factor analysis, there is no definitive answer. As we have seen, Cattell arrives at the number 16; Eysenck at 2 (or 3). Other investigators arrive at still different numbers. We encountered a similar situation in Chapter 12, where we saw that the number of factors defining the concept of intelligence could be 1 (Spearman's general intelligence factor, *g*), 7 (Thurstone's *primary mental abilities*), or as many as 150 (Guilford, 1982).

Some of the discrepancy occurs because different trait scales are put into the analysis initially; some occurs because different types of data are being analyzed (for example, peer-ratings versus self-ratings); and some occurs because different factor analytic methods are employed—it is not as cut and dried a technique as it may first seem. But much of the disagreement is a matter of taste. A researcher who prefers a more differentiated or fine-grained description of personality will stop the factor analysis earlier and accept more factors, arguing that important distinctions would be lost if the factors were further merged. Another researcher, like Eysenck, will prefer to merge several lower-level factors into more general ones, arguing that the resulting factors will be more stable (more likely to reemerge in other analyses). For example, when Cattell's 16 factors are themselves factor analyzed, Eysenck's 2 factors emerge as superfactors.

Despite these disagreements, however, a consensus is emerging among many trait researchers that five trait dimensions may provide the best compromise. Although the five factors were originally identified through a factor analysis of the Allport-Odbert trait list (Norman, 1963), the same five have now emerged from a wide variety of measuring techniques (Digman & Inouye, 1986; McCrae & Costa, 1987). There is still disagreement about how best to name and interpret the factors, but one reasonable way to summarize them is with the acronym NEOAC: Neuroticism, Extraversion, Openness to Experience, Agreeableness, and Conscientiousness. Table 14-1 displays some representative examples of the trait scales that characterize each of the five factors.

An individual may be withdrawn in some situations and outgoing in others.

Evaluation of Trait Approach

The trait approach is not in itself a theory of personality but a general orientation and set of methods for assessing stable characteristics of persons. It is the approach typically adopted by researchers who claim no allegiance to a particular theory but who claim to be merely "gathering the facts." For example, our discussion of personality through the life course in Chapter 13 implicitly adopted a trait approach. The approach becomes a theory only when an investigator asserts that a particular trait or set of traits is the most important and attempts to build the structure of personality on it.

At the beginning of this chapter, we noted that personality psychology has two separate tasks. The first involves specifying the variables on which individuals differ from one another. The second involves synthesizing the general processes of human functioning into an integrated account of the total person. Trait approaches have been most successful at specifying the variables of personality, having much to say about the *content* of individual differences and virtually nothing to say about the dynamic *processes* of personality functioning. By themselves, traits are static creatures that just sit there. Trait psychologists who have sought more complete theories of personality have had to look elsewhere for the dynamic aspects of their accounts. For example, when attempting to understand how personality is shaped and modified, Allport adopted a humanistic approach and Eysenck employs a learning theory. We will examine these approaches later in the chapter.

The major criticism of the trait approach is that its basic underlying assumption may be untrue: perhaps traits do not even exist. Perhaps individuals are so variable in their behavior across time and situations that it is not valid to think of them as possessing trait-like characteristics. This is a startling charge. The assumption that persons display cross-situational consistencies in their behavior—that they possess traits—seems so obviously true that it is practically synonymous with our definition of personality. Yet, we are all aware that our own behavior may vary widely from one situation to another. We may assume a dominant role with our friends but not with parents and teachers; even with friends, we may be dominant on some occasions and docile on others. For this reason trait measures of personality have not been as successful in predicting behavior across situations as psychologists had hoped or expected. How can we reconcile the observation that persons are *not* consistent across situations with our intuitions that they *are* consistent across situations? This has been a major topic in contemporary personality psychology and we will devote an entire section to it at the end of the chapter.

PSYCHOANALYTIC APPROACH

Sigmund Freud, the creator of psychoanalytic theory, is one of the towering intellectual figures of the twentieth century. Whatever its shortcomings as a scientific theory, the psychoanalytic account of personality remains the most comprehensive, far-reaching, and influential theory of personality ever created. Its impact extends well beyond psychology, influencing the social sciences, the humanities, the arts, and society generally. Even though psychoanalytic theory plays a less central role in psychology today than it did 40 or 50 years ago, many of its ideas have been absorbed into the mainstream of psychological thinking. Even parents who have done nothing more than raise their children with the occasional guidance of psychiatrist Benjamin Spock's bestselling *Baby and Child Care* are more like Freudian psychologists than they realize.

Freud began his scientific career as a neurologist, treating patients suffering from various "nervous" disorders by using conventional medical procedures. Because these often failed, he tried and then abandoned the technique of hypnosis. Eventually, he discovered the method of *free association*, in which a patient is instructed to say everything that comes to mind, regardless of how trivial or embarrassing it may seem. By listening carefully to these verbal associations, Freud detected consistent themes that were manifestations of unconscious wishes and fears. He found similar themes in the recall of dreams and early childhood memories.

Freud compared the human mind to an iceberg. The small part that shows above the surface of the water represents conscious experience; the much larger mass below water level represents the unconscious, a storehouse of impulses, passions, and inaccessible memories that affect our thoughts and behavior. Freud was not the first to discover unconscious mental influences—even Shakespeare includes them in his plays—but Freud was the first to give them primary importance in the everyday functioning of the normal personality.

Closely allied with Freud's focus on unconscious processes was his determinism about human behavior. *Psychological determinism* is the doctrine that all thoughts, emotions, and actions have causes. Freud maintained not only that all psychological events are caused, but that most of them are caused by unsatisfied drives and unconscious wishes. In one of his earliest publications, *The Psychopathology of Everyday Life* (1901), Freud argued that dreams, humor, forgetting, and slips of the tongue ("Freudian slips") all serve to relieve psychological tension by gratifying forbidden impulses or unfulfilled wishes.

Freud's writings fill 24 volumes. His first major contribution, *The Interpretation of Dreams*, was published in 1900, and his final treatise, *An Outline of Psychoanalysis*, was published in 1940, a year after his death. We can present only the barest outline of Freud's theory of personality here.

Personality Structure

Freud believed that personality is composed of three major systems: the *id*, the *ego*, and the *superego*. Each system has its own functions, but the three interact to govern behavior.

THE ID   The id is the most primitive part of the personality, from which the ego and the superego later develop. It is present in the newborn infant and consists of the basic biological impulses (or drives): the need to eat, to drink, to eliminate wastes, to avoid pain, and to gain sexual (sensual) pleasure. Freud believed that aggression is also a basic biological drive (see Chapter 11). In fact, he believed that the sexual and aggressive drives were the most important instinctual determinants of personality throughout life. The id seeks immediate gratification of these impulses. Like a young child, the id operates on the *pleasure principle*: it endeavors to obtain pleasure and to avoid pain, regardless of the external circumstances.

THE EGO   Children soon learn that their impulses cannot always be gratified immediately. Hunger must wait until someone provides food. The satisfaction of relieving bladder or bowel pressure must be delayed until the bathroom is reached. Certain impulses—hitting someone or playing with the genitals—may elicit punishment from a parent. A new part of the personality, the ego, develops as the young child learns to consider the demands of reality. The ego obeys the *reality principle*: the gratification of impulses must be delayed until the appropriate environmental conditions are found. For example, taking the real world into consideration, the ego delays satisfaction of sexual impulses until conditions are appropriate. It is essentially the executive of the personality: it decides what actions are appropriate and which id impulses will be satisfied and in what manner. The ego mediates among the demands of the id, the realities of the world, and the demands of the superego.

THE SUPEREGO   The third part of the personality, the superego, is the internalized representation of the values and morals of society as taught to the child by the parents and others. It is essentially the individual's conscience. The superego judges whether an action is right or wrong. The id seeks pleasure, the ego tests reality, and the superego strives for perfection. The superego develops in response to parental rewards and punishments. It incorporates all the actions for which the child is punished or reprimanded, as well as all the actions for which the child is rewarded.

Initially, parents control children's behavior directly by reward and punishment. Through the incorporation of parental standards into the superego, a child brings behavior under his or her own control. Children no longer need anyone to tell them it is wrong to steal; their superego tells them. Violating the superego's standards, or even the impulse to do so, produces anxiety—which was originally the anxiety over the loss of parental love. According to Freud, this anxiety is largely unconscious but may be felt as guilt. If parental standards are overly rigid, the individual may be guilt-

"Very well, I'll introduce you. Ego, meet Id. Now get back to work."

Toilet training is one of a child's first experiences with imposed control.

ridden and inhibit all aggressive or sexual impulses. In contrast, an individual who fails to incorporate any standards for acceptable social behavior will have few behavioral constraints and may engage in excessively self-indulgent or criminal behavior. Such a person is considered to have a weak superego.

The three components of personality are often in opposition: the ego postpones the gratification that the id wants immediately, and the superego battles with both the id and the ego because behavior often falls short of the moral code it represents. In the well-integrated personality, the ego remains in firm but flexible control; the reality principle governs.

Personality Dynamics

CONSERVATION OF ENERGY   The science of physics was remarkably successful in the nineteenth century, and Freud was greatly influenced by the German physicist Hermann von Helmholtz, who argued that physiological events could also be explained by the same principles that had been so successful in physics. Freud was particularly impressed by the principle of the conservation of energy—which states that energy may be changed into different forms but is neither created nor destroyed—and he postulated that humans are also closed energy systems. There is a constant amount of psychic energy for any given individual, which Freud called *libido* (Latin for lust), reflecting his view that the sexual drive was primary.

One corollary of the conservation of energy principle is that if a forbidden act or impulse is suppressed, its energy will seek an outlet somewhere else in the system, possibly appearing in disguised form. The desires of the id contain psychic energy that must be expressed in some way, and prohibiting their expression does not abolish them. Aggressive impulses, for example, may be displaced to racing sports cars, playing chess, or to a sarcastic sense of humor. Dreams and neurotic symptoms are also manifestations of psychic energy that has been prevented from direct expression.

ANXIETY AND DEFENSE   Individuals with an urge to do something forbidden become anxious; expressing the impulse in disguised form can avoid punishment by society or condemnation by the superego, and thereby reduce the anxiety. Freud described several additional strategies the individual can use to prevent or reduce anxiety. These strategies are called the ego's *mechanisms of defense*. The most basic defense mechanism is *repression*, in which the ego pushes a threatening thought or forbidden impulse out of awareness into the unconscious; from the outside it appears that the individual has simply forgotten the aversive thought or impulse.

Defense mechanisms form the basis of Freud's theory of maladaptive behavior and will be examined more fully in Chapter 15. At this point, we will note only that people differ in the balance among their id, ego, and superego systems and in the defenses they use to deal with anxiety. The individual's approach to a problem situation reflects his or her manner of coping with the conflicting demands of the id, the ego, and the superego.

Personality Development

Freud believed that during the first 5 years of life, the individual progresses through several developmental stages that affect personality. Applying a broad definition of sexuality, he called these periods *psychosexual stages*. During each stage, the pleasure-seeking impulses of the id focus on a particular area of the body and on activities connected with that area.

Freud called the first year of life the *oral stage* of psychosexual development. During this period, infants derive pleasure from nursing and sucking. Indeed, they will put their thumb or anything else they can reach into their mouths. During the second year of life, the *anal stage*, children have their first experience with imposed control in the form of toilet training. Gratification presumably is derived from withholding or expelling feces. In the *phallic stage*, from about age 3 to age 6, children begin to derive pleasure from fondling their genitals. They observe the differences between males and females and begin to direct their awakening sexual impulses toward the parent of the opposite sex.

It is during the phallic stage that children must resolve the *Oedipal conflict*. This conflict is clearest in the case of a boy. Around the age of 5 or 6, the boy's sexual impulses are directed toward the mother. This leads him to perceive his father as a rival for his mother's affection. Freud called this situation the Oedipal conflict, after Sophocles' play in which Oedipus Rex unwittingly kills his father and marries his mother. According to Freud, the boy also fears that his father will retaliate against these sexual impulses by castrating him. Freud labeled this fear *castration anxiety* and considered it to be the prototype of all later anxieties provoked by forbidden internal desires. In a normal case of development, the boy simultaneously reduces this anxiety and settles for vicarious gratification of his feelings toward his mother by *identifying* with his father—internalizing an idealized perception of his father's attitudes and values. This successful resolution of the Oedipal conflict also marks the successful formation of the superego—the acquisition of conscience and moral ideas.

The same process in a girl is analogous but more complicated—and even more controversial. The cross-cultural taboo against incest is often cited as evidence for the universality of the Oedipal conflict; the taboo is seen as society's attempt to control the Oedipal situation.

Resolution of the Oedipal conflict also terminates the phallic stage and is succeeded by the *latency period*, which lasts from about age 7 to age 12. During this sexually quiescent time, children become less concerned with their bodies and turn their attention to the skills needed for coping with the environment. Finally, adolescence and puberty usher in the *genital stage*, the mature phase of adult sexual concerns and pleasures.

Freud felt that special problems at any stage could arrest (or *fixate*) development and have a lasting effect on the individual's personality. Libido would remain attached to the activities appropriate for that stage. Thus, a person who was weaned very early and who did not have enough sucking pleasure might become fixated at the oral stage. As an adult, this person may be excessively dependent on others and overly fond of such oral pleasures as eating, drinking, and smoking. Such a person is called an *oral personality*. A person fixated at the anal stage of psychosexual development may be abnormally concerned with cleanliness, orderliness, and saving and may tend to resist external pressure—the *anal personality*. Inadequate resolution of the oedipal conflict can lead to a weak sense of morality, difficulties with authority figures, and many other problems. Note that Freud's theory thus contains a type theory within it—the psychosexual typology.

Modifications of Freud's Theory

Freud modified his theories throughout his life. As a good scientist, he remained open to new data, revising earlier positions as new observations accumulated that could not be accommodated by the theory. For example, one of Freud's major insights was his realization that his patients' reports of childhood seductions were not literally true, but reflected their own early sexual fantasies. (Ironically, the increased sensitivity to child sexual abuse in recent years has led some to argue that Freud's original assumption about the reality of the seductions was probably more correct (Masson, 1984).) Similarly, he revised his theory of anxiety quite late in his career. Freud's theory has been further extended by his daughter Anna, who has played a particularly important role in clarifying the mechanisms of defense (1937) and in applying psychoanalytic theory to the practice of child psychiatry (1958).

But if Freud was open to new data, he was emphatically *not* open to dissenting opinions. He was particularly adamant that his colleagues and followers not question the libido theory and the centrality of sexual motivation in the functioning of personality. This dogmatism forced a break between Freud and many of his most brilliant associates—some of whom went on to develop rival theories that placed more emphasis on motivational processes other than sexuality. These former associates included Carl Jung and Alfred Adler, as well as later theorists such as Karen Horney, Harry Stack Sullivan, and Erich Fromm.

These dissidents and other, more recent psychoanalytic theorists all place more stress on the role of the ego. They believe that the ego is present at birth, develops independently of the id, and performs functions other than finding realistic ways of satisfying id impulses. These ego functions are learning how to cope with the environment and making sense of experience. Ego satisfactions include exploration, manipulation, and competency in performance. This approach ties the concept of the ego more closely to cognitive processes.

One important part of this new direction is called *object relations theory*, which deals with the child's attachments to people over the course of development. Object relations theorists have not rejected the concept of the id or the importance of biological drives in motivating behavior, but they have an equal interest in such questions as the degree of psychological separateness

A boy identifying with his father.

from parents, the degree of attachment to and involvement with other people versus self-preoccupation, and the strength of the individual's feelings of self-esteem and competency.

Although we did not identify it as such, Erik Erikson's stage theory of development—which we discussed in Chapter 3—is an example of a revised psychoanalytic theory. Erikson himself was trained as a psychoanalyst by Anna Freud, and he perceives his own views as expanding rather than altering Freudian theory. Instead of viewing developmental stages in terms of their psychosexual functions, Erikson sees them as *psychosocial* stages involving primarily ego processes. For Erikson, the important feature of the first year of life is not that it focuses on oral gratification, but that the child is learning to trust (or mistrust) the environment as a satisfier of needs. The important feature of the second year of life is not that it focuses on anal concerns such as toilet training, but that the child is learning autonomy. Toilet training just happens to be a frequent arena of conflict in which the child's striving for autonomy clashes with new obedience demands by parents. Erikson's theory also adds more stages in order to encompass the entire life span.

Psychoanalytic Portrait of Human Personality

At the beginning of this chapter, we noted that each approach to personality carries with it an intrinsic philosophy of human nature. To what extent are we free or determined? Good, neutral, or evil? Fixed or modifiable? Active or passive? What constitutes psychological health?

From our description of Freud's theory, you have probably already formed an impression of his views on these matters—especially the question of psychological freedom versus determinism. Freud is often compared with Copernicus and Darwin. Like these two other intellectual pioneers, Freud was accused of undermining the stature and dignity of humanity. The astronomer Copernicus demoted the earth from its position as center of the universe to one of several planets moving around a minor star; Darwin demoted the human species to a descendent of apes. Freud took the next step by emphasizing that human behavior is determined by forces beyond our control, thereby depriving us of our free will and psychological freedom. By emphasizing the unconscious status of our motivations, he deprived us of our rationality; and, by stressing the sexual and aggressive nature of those motivations, he dealt the final blow to our dignity.

Psychoanalytic theory also draws a dark portrait of human personality as basically evil. Without the restraining forces of society and its internalized representative, the superego, humans would destroy themselves. Freud was a deeply pessimistic man. He was forced to flee from Vienna when the Nazis invaded in 1938 and died in September of 1939, the very month that World War II began. He saw these events as the natural consequence of the human aggressive drive when it is not held in check.

Human personality is also relatively fixed. According to psychoanalytic theory, our personalities are basically determined by fixed inborn drives and by environmental events in the first five years of life. Only extensive psychoanalysis can undo some of the negative consequences of early experiences, and it can do so in only limited ways. We also emerge from psychoanalytic theory as relatively passive creatures. It is true that the ego is in an active struggle with the id and superego, but we seem mainly to be impotent, passive pawns of this drama being played out in our unconscious. And finally, for Freud, psychological health consisted of firm but flexible ego control over the impulses of the id. As Freud noted, the goal of psychoanalysis was to ensure that "Where the id was, there shall ego be" (1933).

Evaluation of Psychoanalytic Approach

Psychoanalytic theory is so broad in scope that it cannot simply be pronounced true or false. But whether it is correct or incorrect in its particulars is virtually irrelevant to its overall impact on our culture and to the value of some of its scientific contributions. For example, Freud's method of free association opened up an entirely new database of observations that had never before been explored systematically. Second, the notion that our behavior is frequently a compromise between our wishes and our fears accounts for many of the apparent contradictions in human behavior better than any other theory of personality. As a theory of *ambivalence*, psychoanalytic theory has no peer. Third, Freud's recognition that unconscious processes play an important role in much of our behavior is almost universally accepted—although these processes are often reinterpreted in learning-theory or information-processing terms.

Nevertheless, as a scientific theory, the psychoanalytic account has been persistently criticized for its inadequacy (for example, Grünbaum, 1984). One of the main criticisms is that many of its concepts are ambiguous and difficult to define or measure objectively. For example, it would be difficult to test the conservation of energy principle very precisely, because there is no way of measuring libido. Also, psychoanalytic theory assumes that very different behaviors may be signs of the same underlying motive. For example, a mother who feels resentful of her child may be abusive, or she may deny her hostile impulses by becoming overly concerned and protective toward the child—what Freud would call a *reaction formation* (see Chapter 15). When opposing behaviors are said to result from the same underlying motive, it is difficult to confirm the presence or absence of the motive or to make predictions that can be empirically verified.

When researchers *have* managed to put the theory to empirical test, it has achieved a mixed record. For example, efforts to link adult personality characteristics to psychosexually relevant events in childhood have generally met with negative outcomes (Sears, Maccoby, & Levin, 1957; Sewell & Mussen, 1952). When relevant character traits *are* identified, they appear to be related to similar character traits in the parents (Beloff, 1957; Hetherington & Brackbill, 1963). Thus, even if a relationship were to be found between toilet-training practices and adult personality traits, it could have arisen because both are linked with a parental emphasis on cleanliness and order. In such a case, a simple learning-theory explanation—parental reinforcement and the child's modeling of the parents—would be a more economical explanation of the adult traits than the psychoanalytic hypothesis.

A particularly instructive test of psychoanalytic theory was conducted by the anthropologist Malinowski (1927). He had read Freud's account of the oedipal conflict and how boys often reveal their hostility toward their fathers in nightmares in which the father is maimed or killed. According to Freud, such dreams symbolically fulfill the boy's wish to get rid of the rival for his mother's affection. Malinowski collected dream reports from boys in the Trobriand Islands, where uncles rather than fathers are responsible for disciplining boys. He found *no* instances of nightmares in which fathers suffered but several in which uncles met with disaster. Because Freud had based his theory on observations in a culture in which the father was both the mother's lover *and* the son's disciplinarian, he had no way of determining which function created the son's hostility. The Trobriand Island culture provided Malinowski with a natural laboratory in which the two functions were separated, thereby permitting him to demonstrate that it is the discipline, not oedipal rivalry, that creates the hostility.

This outcome should also remind us that Freud based his theory on observations of a very narrow range of people—primarily upper-middle-class neurotics in Victorian Vienna. In hindsight, many of Freud's cultural biases are now obvious, particularly in his theories about women. For example, his theory that female psychosexual development is shaped by "penis envy," and by the accompanying feelings of unworthiness due to the lack of such equipment, is certainly inadequate in view of our current awareness of the role that social factors play in gender identification (Chodorow, 1978). It was probably not her brother's penis that a little girl during the Victorian era envied but his greater independence, power, and social status.

Despite these criticisms, however, the remarkable feature of Freud's theory is how well it did manage to transcend its narrow observational base. For example, many experimental studies of the defense mechanisms and reactions to conflict have supported the theory in contexts quite different from those in which Freud developed the theory (for example, Blum, 1953; Erdelyi, 1985; Holmes, 1974; Sears, 1943; 1944; Silverman, 1976). In general, the structural theory (ego, id, and superego), the psychosexual theory, and the energy concept have not fared well over the years. Even some psychoanalytic writers are prepared to abandon or to modify them substantially (for example, Kline, 1972; Schafer, 1976). On the other hand, Freud's dynamic theory—especially his theory of anxiety and the mechanisms of defense—has withstood the test of time, research, and observation. There is a continuing interest in reformulating psychoanalytic theory in more testable terms and subjecting it to further experimental evaluation (Silverman & Weinberger, 1985).

SOCIAL-LEARNING APPROACH

In contrast to both trait and psychodynamic approaches to personality, social-learning approaches emphasize the importance of *environmental*, or *situational*, determinants of behavior. For social-learning theorists, behavior is the result of a continuous interaction between personal and environmental variables. Environmental conditions shape behavior through learning; a person's behavior, in turn, shapes the environment. Persons and situations influence each other reciprocally. To predict behavior, we need to know how the characteristics of the individual interact with the characteristics of the situation. The social-learning approach is the contemporary descendent of *behaviorism* and its outgrowth, *stimulus-response psychology*, which were dominant in the first half of this century (see Chapter 1 and Appendix II).

Social Learning and Conditioning

OPERANT CONDITIONING The effect of other people—the rewards and punishments they provide—is an important influence on an individual's behavior. Accordingly, social learning is considered to be a special case of *operant conditioning* and the processes related to it that we discussed in Chapter 7. According to social-learning theory, individual differences in behavior result in large part from differences in the kinds of learning experiences a person encounters in the course of growing up. Some behavior patterns are learned through direct experience: the individual is rewarded or punished for behaving in a certain manner. But a person acquires many responses without direct reinforcement, through *observational*, or *vicarious*, learning (see Chapter 11). People can learn by observing the actions of others and by noting the consequences of those actions. It would be a slow and inefficient process indeed if all of our behavior had to be learned through the direct reinforcement of our responses. According to social-learning theorists, reinforcement is not *necessary* for learning, although it may *facilitate* learning by focusing the individual's attention in the appropriate direction.

Although reinforcement is not necessary for learning, it is crucial to the performance of learned behavior. A main assumption of social-learning theory is that people behave in ways that are likely to produce reinforcement. A person's repertoire of learned behaviors is extensive; the particular action chosen in a specific situation depends on the expected outcome. Most adolescent girls know how to fight, having watched male classmates or television characters aggress by hitting with the fist, kicking, and so on. But since this kind of behavior is seldom reinforced in girls, it is unlikely to occur except under unusual circumstances.

The reinforcement that controls the expression of learned behavior may be *direct* (tangible rewards, social approval or disapproval, or alleviation of aversive conditions), *vicarious* (observation of someone receiving reward or punishment for behavior similar to one's own), or *self-administered* (evaluation of one's own performance with self-praise or self-reproach).

According to social-learning theorists, a person's actions in a given situation depend on the specific characteristics of the situation, the individual's appraisal of the situation, and past reinforcement for behavior in similar situations (or observations of others in similar situations). People behave consistently insofar as the situations they encounter and the roles they are expected to play remain relatively stable.

Most social behaviors, however, are not uniformly rewarded in all settings. The individual learns to discriminate the contexts in which certain behavior is appropriate and those in which it is not. To the extent that a person is rewarded for the same response in many different situations, *generalization* takes place, ensuring that the same behavior will occur in a variety of settings. Thus, a boy who is reinforced for physical aggression at home, as well as at school and at play, will probably develop a personality that is pervasively aggressive. But, more often, aggressive responses are differentially rewarded, and learned *discriminations* determine the situations in which the individual will display aggression (for example, aggression is acceptable on the football field but not in the classroom). For this reason, social-learning theorists challenge the usefulness of characterizing persons with trait terms like "aggressive," arguing that such terms obscure the cross-situational variability of behavior.

CLASSICAL CONDITIONING   Operant conditioning and its related processes apply to *behavior*, the major focus of social-learning approaches. In order to account for *emotion* or *affect*, social-learning theorists add *classical conditioning* to their account of personality (see Chapter 7). For example, when a child is punished by a parent for engaging in some forbidden activity,

Children may learn drinking habits by observing their parents.

the punishment elicits the physiological responses that we associate with guilt or anxiety. Subsequently, the child's behavior may itself elicit those same responses; he or she will feel guilty when engaging in the forbidden behavior. In the terminology of classical conditioning, we would say that the behavior becomes a *conditioned stimulus* by being paired with the *unconditioned stimulus* of punishment; the anxiety becomes the *conditioned response*. For the social-learning theorist, it is classical conditioning that produces the internalized source of anxiety that Freud labeled the superego. Like operant conditioning, classical conditioning can also operate vicariously and can generalize to stimuli that have not been directly conditioned.

Person Variables

We noted earlier that personality psychology seeks to specify both the variables on which individuals differ from one another and the general processes of personality functioning. Trait approaches have been most successful at the first task, having much to say about the *content* of individual differences and virtually nothing to say about the dynamic *processes* of personality functioning. Psychoanalytic theory has attempted to do both.

In contrast, the social-learning approach has typically been all process and no content. Because the approach sees every individual's personality as the unique product of an idiosyncratic reinforcement history and emphasizes the degree to which behavior varies across situations, it has not attempted to classify individuals into types or to rate them on traits. Recently, however, a few social-learning theorists have begun to consider individual differences in a systematic way, focusing on *person variables* that seem likely to interact with particular situations to affect behavior. One prominent social-learning theorist, Walter Mischel, has proposed the following variables:

1. *Competencies: What can you do?* Competencies include intellectual abilities, social and physical skills, and other special abilities.

2. *Encoding strategies: How do you see it?* People differ in the way they selectively attend to information, encode (represent) events, and group the information into meaningful categories. An event perceived by one person as threatening may be seen by another as challenging.

3. *Expectancies: What will happen?* Expectations about the consequences of different behaviors will guide the individual's choice of behavior. If you cheat on an examination and are caught, what do you expect the consequences to be? If you tell your friend what you really think of him or her, what will happen to your relationship? Expectations about our own abilities will also influence behavior: we may anticipate the consequences of a certain behavior but fail to act because we are uncertain of our ability to execute the behavior.

4. *Subjective values: What is it worth?* Individuals who have similar expectancies may choose to behave differently because they assign different values to the outcomes. Two students may expect a certain behavior to please their professor; however, this outcome is important to one student but is not important to the other.

5. *Self-regulatory systems and plans: How can you achieve it?* People differ in the standards and rules they adopt for regulating their behavior (including self-imposed rewards for success or punishments for failure), as well as in their ability to make realistic plans for reaching a goal. (After Mischel, 1973; 1986)

All of these person variables (sometimes referred to as cognitive social-learning person variables) interact with the conditions of a particular situation to determine what an individual will do in that situation.

Social-Learning Portrait of Human Personality

Like the psychoanalytic approach, the social-learning approach to personality is very deterministic. In contrast to the psychoanalytic approach, however, it pays very little attention to biological determinants of behavior and focuses exclusively on environmental determinants. Like its parent, behaviorism, the social-learning approach has been strongly influenced by the ideas of Darwin. Just as evolution works through natural selection to shape the species to be adaptive to its ecology, so the processes of learning—especially operant conditioning—shape the individual's behavioral repertoire to be adaptive to his or her environment. Inherently, we are neither good nor evil, but extraordinarily modifiable. John Watson, founder of the behaviorist movement in the United States, argued that a human being is a blank slate (*tabula rasa*) at birth. As he stated the case:

> Give me a dozen healthy infants, well-formed, and my own specified world to bring them up in and I'll guarantee to take any one at random and to train him to become any type of specialist I might select—doctor, lawyer, artist, merchant-chief and, yes, even beggar-man and thief, regardless of his talents, penchants, tendencies, abilities, vocations, and race of his ancestors. (1930, p. 104)

Few social-learning theorists would take such an extreme view today. Nevertheless, social-learning theory shares with its predecessor a cheery optimism about our ability to change human behavior by changing the environment. Such a view is nicely congruent with American pragmatism and American ideology about equality, so it is not surprising that behaviorism was popular in the United States. Interestingly, the other society with a similar view concerning the modifiability of human personality is the Soviet Union, birthplace of Pavlov and classical conditioning. It is not accidental that both these societies have embraced a conditioning-based view of human behavior, whereas more traditional class-based societies like England and Germany have produced Charles Darwin, ethologists, trait theorists, and Sigmund Freud.

Even though the human personality that emerges from the social-learning approach is modifiable, it still has a passive quality to it. We still seem to be shaped primarily by forces beyond our control. This portrait is changing, however, as social-learning approaches increasingly emphasize the individual's active role in selecting and modifying the environment, thereby permitting the person to become a causal force in his or her own life. As we shall see, however, this is still not sufficiently active for the humanistic or phenomenological theorists. In particular, they do not believe that it is sufficient to define psychological health merely as optimal adaptation to the environment.

Evaluation of Social-Learning Approach

Through its emphasis on specifying the environmental variables that evoke specific behaviors, social-learning theory has made a major contribution to both clinical psychology and personality theory. It has led us to see

Charles Darwin.

human actions as reactions to specific environments, and it has helped us to focus on the way in which environments control our behavior and how they can be changed to modify behavior. As we will see in Chapter 17, the careful application of learning principles has proved successful in changing maladaptive behavior. Social-learning theorists have also challenged the notion that individuals are cross-situationally consistent, forcing other personality theorists to reexamine the fundamental assumptions of their approaches.

Social-learning theorists have been criticized for overemphasizing the importance of situational influences on behavior and thus losing the person in personality psychology (Carlson, 1971). And, as we shall see later, many personality theorists are unwilling to concede that personality has as little cross-situational consistency as social-learning theory implies.

PHENOMENOLOGICAL APPROACH

The phenomenological approach to the study of personality focuses on the individual's *subjective experience*—his or her personal view of the world. Phenomenological theories differ from the theories we have discussed so far in that they generally are not concerned with the person's motivational or reinforcement history or with predicting behavior. They focus instead on how the individual perceives and interprets events in his or her current environment; that is, the focus is on the individual's *phenomenology*. Among the subvarieties of the phenomenological approach, the most central is *humanistic psychology*.

Humanistic Psychology

During the first half of this century, the psychoanalytic and behavioristic approaches were dominant in psychology. In 1962, a group of psychologists founded the Association of Humanistic Psychology. They offered humanistic psychology as a "third force," an explicit set of alternative assumptions and concerns to those that characterized the other two approaches. To define its mission, the Association adopted a set of four principles:

1. *The experiencing person is of primary interest.* Humans are not simply objects of study. They must be described and understood in terms of their own subjective views of the world, their perceptions of self, and their feelings of self-worth. The central question each person must face is "Who am I?" In order to learn how the individual attempts to answer this question, the psychologist must become a partner with the individual in the quest for existential meaning.

2. *Human choice, creativity, and self-actualization are the preferred topics of investigation.* Humanistic psychologists reject the psychoanalytic approach, believing that a psychology based on crippled personalities could only produce a crippled psychology. They also reject behaviorism, a psychology devoid of consciousness derived primarily from the study of lower organisms. People are not simply motivated by basic drives like sex or aggression or physiological needs like hunger and thirst. They have a need to develop their potentials and capabilities. Growth and self-actualization should be the criteria of psychological health, not merely ego control or adjustment to the environment.

3. *Meaningfulness must precede objectivity in the selection of research problems.* The humanistic psychologists believe that too often psychological research is guided by the methods available rather than by the importance of the problems to be investigated. They argue that we should study important human and social problems, even if that sometimes means adopting less rigorous methods. And while psychologists should strive to be objective in collecting and interpreting observations, their choice of research topics can and should be guided by values. In this sense, research is not value-free; values are not something psychologists should pretend not to have or feel they have to apologize for.

4. *Ultimate value is placed on the dignity of the person.* Persons are basically good. The objective of psychology is to understand, not to predict or control people. Even referring to them as "subjects" is considered by many humanistic psychologists to degrade their dignity as full partners in the quest for understanding human personality.

Psychologists who share the values of the Association come from diverse theoretical backgrounds. For example, the trait theorist Gordon Allport was clearly a humanistic psychologist, and we have already pointed out that several psychoanalysts held humanistic views of motivation that diverged from Freud's views—such as Carl Jung, Alfred Adler, and Erik Erikson. But it is Carl Rogers and Abraham Maslow whose theoretical views lie at the center of the humanistic movement.

CARL ROGERS   Like Freud, Carl Rogers (1902–1987) developed his theory from his work with emotionally troubled people (Rogers, 1951; 1959; 1963; 1970). Rogers was impressed with what he saw as the individual's innate tendency to move in the direction of growth, maturity, and positive change. He came to believe that the basic force motivating the human organism is the actualizing tendency—a tendency toward fulfillment or actualization of all the capacities of the organism. A growing organism seeks to fulfill its potential within the limits of its heredity. A person may not always clearly perceive which actions lead to growth and which actions are regressive. But once the course is clear, the individual chooses to grow rather than to regress. Rogers did not deny that there are other needs, some of them biological, but he saw them as subservient to the organism's motivation to enhance itself.

Rogers' belief in the primacy of actualization forms the basis of his nondirective or *person-centered therapy*. This method of psychotherapy assumes that every individual (given the proper circumstances) has the motivation and ability to change and that the individual is the person best qualified to decide on the direction that such change should take. The therapist's role is to act as a sounding board while the individual explores and analyzes his or her problems. This approach differs from psychoanalytic therapy, during which the therapist analyzes the patient's history to determine the problem and devise a course of remedial action. (See Chapter 17 for a discussion of various approaches to psychotherapy.)

The central concept in Rogers' theory of personality is the *self*. The self, or self-concept (Rogers uses the terms interchangeably), became the cornerstone of his theory. The self consists of all the ideas, perceptions, and values that characterize "I" or "me"; it includes the awareness of "what I am" and "what I can do." This perceived self, in turn, influences both the person's perception of the world and his or her behavior. For example, a woman who perceives herself as strong and competent views the world quite differently and therefore acts differently from a woman who considers herself weak and

Carl Rogers Writing on the Phenomenological Approach *"The best vantage point for understanding behavior is from the internal frame of reference of the individual himself."*

"The organism has one basic tendency and striving—to actualize, maintain, and enhance the experiencing organism."

"When the individual perceives and accepts into one consistent and integrated system all his sensory and visceral experiences, then he is necessarily more understanding of others and is more accepting of others as separate individuals." (Rogers, 1951)

ineffectual. The self-concept does not necessarily reflect reality: a person may be highly successful and respected but still view himself or herself as a failure.

According to Rogers, the individual evaluates every experience in relation to this self-concept. People want to behave in ways that are consistent with their self-image; experiences and feelings that are not consistent are threatening and may be denied admittance to consciousness. This is essentially Freud's concept of repression, although Rogers felt that such repression is neither necessary nor permanent. (Freud would say that repression is inevitable and that some aspects of the individual's experiences always remain unconscious.)

The more areas of experience that a person denies because they are inconsistent with his or her self-concept, the wider the gulf between the self and reality and the greater the potential for maladjustment. An individual whose self-concept is incongruent with personal feelings and experiences must defend himself or herself against the truth because the truth will result in anxiety. If the incongruence becomes too great, the defenses may break down, resulting in severe anxiety or other forms of emotional disturbance. The well-adjusted person, in contrast, has a self-concept that is consistent with thought, experience, and behavior; the self is not rigid, but flexible, and can change as it assimilates new experiences and ideas.

The other self in Rogers' theory is the *ideal* self. We all have a conception of the kind of person we would like to be. The closer the ideal self is to the real self, the more fulfilled and happy the individual becomes. A large discrepancy between the ideal self and the real self results in an unhappy, dissatisfied person.

Thus, two kinds of incongruence can develop: one, between the self and the experiences of reality; the other, between the self and the ideal self. Rogers had some hypotheses about how these incongruences may develop.

Martin Luther King fulfilled Maslow's criteria for a self-actualizer.

DEVELOPMENT OF THE SELF   Rogers believed that people are likely to become more fully functioning if they are brought up with *unconditional positive regard*. This means that they feel themselves valued by parents and others even when their feelings, attitudes, and behaviors are less than ideal. If parents offer only *conditional positive regard*—valuing the child only when he or she behaves, thinks, or feels correctly—the child is likely to distort his or her self-concept. For example, feelings of competition and hostility toward a younger sibling are natural, but parents disapprove of hitting a baby brother or sister and usually punish such actions. Children must somehow integrate this experience into their self-concept. They may decide that they are bad and so may feel ashamed. They may decide that their parents do not like them and so may feel rejected. Or they may deny their feelings and decide they do not want to hit the baby. Each of these attitudes contains a distortion of the truth. The third alternative is the easiest for children to accept, but in so doing, they deny their real feelings, which then become unconscious. The more people are forced to deny their own feelings and to accept the values of others, the more uncomfortable they will feel about themselves. Rogers suggested that the best approach is for the parents to recognize the child's feelings as valid while explaining the reasons why hitting is not acceptable.

ABRAHAM MASLOW   The psychology of Abraham Maslow (1908–1970) overlaps with that of Carl Rogers in many ways. Maslow was first attracted to behaviorism and carried out studies in primate sexuality and

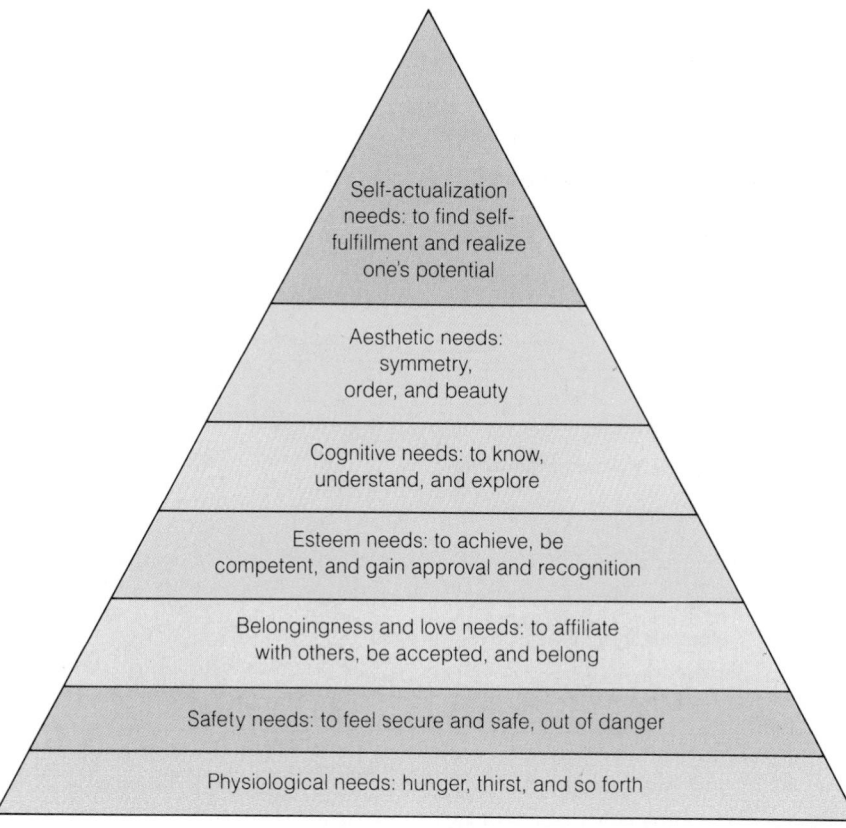

FIGURE 14-2
Maslow's Hierarchy of Needs *Needs that are low in the hierarchy must be at least partially satisfied before needs that are higher in the hierarchy become important sources of motivation.* (After Maslow, 1954)

dominance. He was already moving away from behaviorism when his first child was born, after which he remarked that anyone who observes a baby cannot be a behaviorist. He was influenced by psychoanalysis, but eventually became critical of its theory of motivation and developed his own. Specifically, he proposed that there is a *hierarchy of needs*, ascending from the basic biological needs to the more complex psychological motivations that become important only after the basic needs have been satisfied (see Figure 14-2). The needs at one level must be at least partially satisfied before those at the next level become important determiners of action. When food and safety are difficult to obtain, the satisfaction of those needs will dominate a person's actions and higher motives are of little significance. Only when basic needs can be satisfied easily will the individual have the time and energy to devote to aesthetic and intellectual interests. Artistic and scientific endeavors do not flourish in societies in which people must struggle for food, shelter, and safety. The highest motive—*self-actualization*—can only be fulfilled after all other needs are fulfilled.

Maslow decided to study *self-actualizers*—men and women who had made extraordinary use of their potential. He began by studying the lives of eminent historical figures such as Spinoza, Thomas Jefferson, Abraham Lincoln, Jane Addams, Albert Einstein, and Eleanor Roosevelt. In this way, he arrived at a composite picture of a self-actualizer. The distinguishing characteristics of such persons are listed in Table 14-2, along with some of the behaviors that Maslow believed could lead to self-actualization.

Maslow extended his study to a population of college students. Selecting students who fit his definition of self-actualizers, Maslow found this group to

Eleanor Roosevelt was one of Maslow's examples of a self-actualizer.

TABLE 14-2
Self-Actualization *Listed are the personal qualities that Maslow found to be characteristic of self-actualizers and the behaviors he considered important to the development of self-actualization.* (After Maslow, 1967)

CHARACTERISTICS OF SELF-ACTUALIZERS

Perceive reality efficiently and are able to tolerate uncertainty

Accept themselves and others for what they are

Spontaneous in thought and behavior

Problem-centered rather than self-centered

Have a good sense of humor

Highly creative

Resistant to enculturation, although not purposely unconventional

Concerned for the welfare of humanity

Capable of deep appreciation of the basic experiences of life

Establish deep, satisfying interpersonal relationships with a few, rather than many, people

Able to look at life from an objective viewpoint

BEHAVIORS LEADING TO SELF-ACTUALIZATION

Experience life as a child does, with full absorption and concentration

Try something new rather than sticking to secure and safe ways

Listen to your own feelings in evaluating experiences rather than to the voice of tradition or authority or the majority

Be honest; avoid pretenses or "game playing"

Be prepared to be unpopular if your views do not coincide with those of most people

Assume responsibility

Work hard at whatever you decide to do

Try to identify your defenses and have the courage to give them up

---

be in the healthiest 1 percent of the population; these students showed no signs of maladjustment and were making effective use of their talents and capabilities (Maslow, 1970).

Many people experience transient moments of self-actualization, which Maslow called *peak experiences.* A peak experience is an experience of being characterized by happiness and fulfillment—a temporary, nonstriving, non-self-centered state of perfection and goal attainment. Peak experiences may occur in different intensities and in various contexts: creative activities, appreciation of nature, intimate relationships with others, parental experiences, aesthetic perceptions, or athletic participation. After asking a large number of college students to describe any experience that came close to being a peak experience, Maslow attempted to summarize their responses. They spoke of wholeness, perfection, aliveness, uniqueness, effortlessness, self-sufficiency, and the values of beauty, goodness, and truth.

Personal Construct Theory

Humanistic psychologists are concerned with how individuals feel about and perceive themselves in terms of personal value or worth. *Personal construct theory* takes a more cognitive approach to the individual's phenomenology. According to George Kelly (1905–1966), the originator of personal construct theory, trait psychologists try to characterize a person on personality dimensions that the psychologists themselves have constructed. In contrast, Kelly believed that the psychologist's goal should be to discover the dimensions that individuals themselves use to interpret or to *construe* themselves and their social worlds. These dimensions are the individual's own *personal constructs*, and they constitute the basic units of analysis in Kelly's theory (1955).

More generally, Kelly believed that individuals should be viewed as intuitive scientists. Like formal scientists, they observe the world, formulate and test hypotheses about it, and make up theories about it. Like the psychologists who study them, human subjects also construe or abstract behavior—categorizing, interpreting, labeling, and judging themselves and their world. And, like scientists, individuals can entertain bad theories, beliefs that hinder them in daily life and lead them to bias their interpretations of events and persons, including themselves. (In Chapter 18, we discuss in depth the person-as-scientist view of social information processing.)

In Kelly's view, the purpose of therapy or counseling is to help the person construct more effective interpretations, construals, or theories of the world. If a client claims that he is unable to stand up to authority, the therapist's job is not to determine the truth or falsity of the assertion but to encourage the individual to explore what the implications of viewing himself that way are for his daily life and to consider alternative hypotheses about his behaviors. In order to get clients to construe themselves and their social worlds from different perspectives, Kelly used the technique of role playing. For example, the client who claimed he cannot stand up to authority might be asked to role-play his boss, construing the situation as he thinks his boss might. This often helped clients to interpret their own behaviors very differently.

Kelly also devised an ingenious measuring instrument for eliciting a person's personal constructs, the *Role Construct Repertory Test* or "Rep Test." (We will discuss this instrument in the section on personality assessment.)

Phenomenological Portrait of Human Personality

As a matter of principle, phenomenological psychologists—especially humanistic psychologists—have been quite explicit about the values and philosophical presuppositions that underlie their approach to human personality. The four principles set forth by the Association of Humanistic Psychology, which we summarized earlier, draw sharp contrasts between the humanistic portrait of human personality and the portraits drawn by the psychoanalytic and behavioristic approaches.

The phenomenological approach does not dispute that biological and environmental variables can determine behavior, but it emphasizes the individual's own role in defining and creating his or her destiny. Individuals are basically good, striving for growth and self-actualization. They are also modifiable and active. Phenomenological psychologists set a particularly high criterion for psychological health. Mere ego control or adaptation to the environment is not sufficient. Only an individual who is growing toward self-actualization can be said to be psychologically healthy. In other words, psychological health is a process not an end state.

Philosophical positions also have political implications. We pointed out earlier that the philosophical assumptions of behaviorism are quite compatible with American ideology. Its assumption that all humans are created equal—as blank slates—and are infinitely modifiable by the environment provides a psychological rationale for politically liberal programs that seek to improve the environments of those who are disadvantaged.

In contrast, the humanistic approach provides support for a much more radical politics. Anything that retards the fulfillment of one's potential—that prevents any human being from becoming all he or she can be—is evil and should be challenged. If women in the 1950s were happy and well-adjusted to traditional sex roles, the criterion of psychological health defined by behaviorism was satisfied. Nothing was amiss. But from the humanistic perspective, consigning all women to the same role is evil—no matter how appropriate that role might be for some women—because it prevents many women from reaching their maximum potential. It is not accidental that the rhetoric of liberation movements—such as women's liberation and gay liberation—echoes the rhetoric of humanistic psychology. Betty Friedan's 1963 book, *The Feminine Mystique*, is often credited with initiating the contemporary feminist movement. Friedan criticizes the sexism of Freud and has little good to say about the bland liberalism of behaviorism, but she does have one major hero from the world of psychology: Abraham Maslow.

Evaluation of Phenomenological Approach

By focusing on the individual's unique perception and interpretation of events, the phenomenological approach brings back the role of private experience to the study of personality. More than any other theory we have discussed, the theories of Rogers and Maslow concentrate on the whole, healthy person and emphasize a positive, optimistic view of human personality. However, a phenomenological theory of personality is incomplete; it does not provide a sufficient analysis of the causes of behavior. A person's self-concept may be an important determinant of behavior, but what determines the particular self-concept he or she holds? Just how does the self-concept affect behavior? These theories do not say.

Phenomenological psychologists emphasize that they study important problems even if they do not always have rigorous methods for investigating them. They have a point; investigating trivial problems just because one has a convenient method for doing so does little to advance the science of psychology. Moreover, the phenomenological psychologists have been increasingly ingenious over the years at devising new methods for assessing self-concepts, personal constructs, and conducting studies that genuinely treat the individual as an equal partner in the research enterprise. Nevertheless, critics can and do question the quality of the evidence in support of the humanistic claims. For example, to what extent are the characteristics of self-actualizers a consequence of a psychological process called self-actualization, and to what extent are they merely reflections of the particular value systems held by Rogers and Maslow? Where, they ask, is the evidence for Maslow's hierarchy of needs?

Phenomenological psychologists are also vulnerable to a criticism that is the mirror image of a criticism they have leveled at Freud. They have

Humanistic psychology has provided the psychological rationale for questioning traditional sex roles.

criticized Freud for attempting to build a complete theory of personality on observations of neurotic individuals. But critics point out that Rogers and Kelly both built their theories on observations of relatively healthy college students. Accordingly, their theories are best suited to young, well-functioning people who have the luxury of worrying about needs at the top of Maslow's hierarchy. The application of these theories to seriously malfunctioning individuals or to socially, culturally, or economically disadvantaged individuals is less apparent.

And finally, some have even criticized the values espoused by the phenomenological theorists. Many observers believe that America already has too obsessive a concern with the individual and too little concern for the welfare of the larger society. A psychology that raises individual self-fulfillment and actualization to the top of the value hierarchy is *too* compatible with American ideology; it provides a psychological "sanction for selfishness" (Wallach & Wallach, 1983). Where in the humanistic hierarchy is the need to care for others or to contribute to the welfare of the larger society?

PERSONALITY ASSESSMENT

The objective assessment of personality serves a number of practical needs in our society. In selecting individuals for high-level positions, employers need to know something about their honesty, their ability to handle stress, and so on. In helping students to make career choices, counselors can offer wiser advice if they know something about a student's personality, in addition to his or her school performance. Decisions about the kind of treatment that will be most beneficial to an emotionally disturbed person or that will help to rehabilitate a convicted felon require an objective assessment of the individual's personality.

Beyond these practical concerns, methods of assessing personality are essential to the study of personality itself—no matter what theoretical approach one prefers. Although each of the four approaches to personality we have discussed in this chapter can use any of several assessment methods, each tends to favor an assessment strategy tailored to its theoretical concerns. For this reason, we have grouped the assessment methods in this section according to the theoretical approaches.

General Considerations

In Chapter 12, we introduced some of the requirements of a good test of mental abilities. With some additional complexities, the same criteria apply to tests of personality. Specifically, a good test must have *reliability* and *validity*.

RELIABILITY   If a test or method of assessment is *reliable*, it will give reproducible and consistent results. Reliability is typically assessed by correlating two sets of scores. For example, when the same test is given to the same group of people on two occasions, their scores on the first occasion should correlate highly with their scores on the second. If they do, then the test is said to have *temporal stability* or *test-retest reliability*. A similar measure of *alternate form reliability* assesses the degree to which two forms of the same test yield equivalent scores. Another common measure of reliability is *internal consistency*, the degree to which the separate questions or items on a test are all measuring the same thing. This can be assessed by correlating the score obtained by a group of individuals on each item with their total scores. Any item that is not correlated with the total score is an unreliable item; it is failing to contribute to what the test is measuring. Discarding unreliable items "purifies" a test by increasing its internal consistency. As the number of reliable items on a test increases, the reliability of the test's total score also increases.

A special kind of reliability check is required when subjective judgments are involved in an assessment. For example, if two observers independently rate a group of nursery-school children for aggression, we can correlate the ratings of the two observers. This will yield an index of *interscorer agreement* or *interjudge reliability*. This measure of reliability would also be calculated if two or more judges were asked to read presidential inaugural addresses and to rate them for optimism or to count the number of negative references to the Soviet Union.

VALIDITY   Reliability assesses the degree to which a test is measuring *something*, but good reliability does not guarantee that the test is measuring what it is intended to measure; it does not guarantee that the test has *validity*. As we noted in Chapter 12, a humor test containing jokes that are hard to understand might well be reliable, but the test might be measuring verbal intelligence or educational achievement rather than sense of humor. In some instances the validity of a test can be assessed by correlating the test score with some external criterion. This correlation is called a *validity coefficient*. For example, the positive correlation between scores on the Scholastic Aptitude Test (SAT) and freshman grades in college indicates that the test has reasonable validity. This kind of validity is called *criterion* or *empirical validity*. Because of sensitivity to race and sex discrimination, the courts are increasingly requiring agencies or companies that use tests for personnel selection to

provide evidence that those tests correlate with on-the-job performance—that they have criterion or empirical validity.

If a researcher is designing a test to measure some concept or construct that is part of a theory, it is not always possible to compute a validity coefficient, because it is not clear what the external criterion should be. How, for example, should a researcher assess the validity of a test for achievement motivation? One can think of a number of possibilities. The test could be given to business executives to see if the test correlates with their salaries. Perhaps the test will correlate with teachers' ratings of the ambitiousness of their students. The problem is that there is no single criterion the researcher is willing to accept as the ultimate "true" answer. It would be nice if the test correlated with executive salaries, but if it did not, the researcher would not be willing to judge the test to be invalid. This is known as the *criterion problem* in personality psychology, and the validity the researcher is seeking to establish is called *construct validity*.

The construct validity of a new assessment instrument is established through the process of research itself. The researcher uses his or her theory both to construct the instrument and to generate predictions from the theory. Studies using the new instrument are then conducted to test those predictions. To the extent that the results of several converging studies are positive, both the theory and the instrument are validated simultaneously. Most often, mixed results suggest ways in which both the theory and the instrument need to be modified.

Trait Assessment

PERSONALITY RATINGS The most direct way of assessing how much of a particular trait an individual possesses is to ask those who know the person well to rate him or her on a scale of that trait. For example, a rater might be asked to rate the person on the trait of friendliness using a 7-point scale that ranges from "not at all friendly" to "very friendly." Often such scales label the two ends of the scale with opposite traits—for example, "domineering–submissive" or "conscientious–unreliable." Individuals can also rate themselves.

As we saw earlier, a number of trait theorists adopted this method as a starting point for their systems by selecting trait terms culled from the unabridged dictionary. For example, Cattell applied factor analysis to trait rating scales of this kind to identify the 16 basic personality factors that form the basis of his system. Twelve of his factors came from peer ratings and four came from self-ratings.

Q SORT One kind of rating method that deserves special mention is the *Q sort*, which we described in detail in Chapter 13. In the Q-sort technique, the rater (sorter) is given a set of cards, each containing a personality statement (for example, "Is cheerful"), and is asked to describe an individual's personality by sorting them into piles. The rater places statements that are least descriptive of the individual in pile 1 on the left and those that are most descriptive in pile 9 on the right. The other statements are distributed in the intermediate piles, thereby assigning each Q item a score ranging from 1 to 9. (Some Q sorts use fewer or more than 9 piles.)

At first glance, this would seem no different from asking raters to rate the individual on a set of traits, using a 9-point rating scale. And, in fact, the

CRITICAL DISCUSSION

Testimonial Validity and Other Nonsense

If you own a microcomputer, you can buy an inexpensive program that analyzes handwriting. When it was first introduced, the computer magazines gave it glowing reviews. Sometimes it was so embarrassingly accurate at describing a reviewer's personality that he or she was reluctant to print the full description in the review. Testimonials attesting to its accuracy have also appeared in advertisements for the program. Many are similar to the following:

> For the first time things that I have been vaguely aware of have been put into concise and constructive statements which I would like to use as a plan for improving myself.

> It appears to me that the results . . . are unbelievably close to the truth.

This method of evaluating an assessment instrument by gathering opinions on its accuracy from those who have been assessed establishes what we suggest should be called its *testimonial validity*. It is a frequently used method—especially by astrologers, fortune-tellers, medical quacks, and other hucksters. In short, it is bunk.

Studies have shown that people tend to view generalized descriptions as accurate summaries of their own personality. In several experiments, college students were given a personality inventory. A few days later, they were handed typed reports in sealed envelopes and asked to rate the accuracy of the evaluations. Unknown to the subjects, all the personality descriptions were identical. Most students in such

item scores *can* be used in this way if the researcher wishes. But there is an important difference. When filling out rating scales, a rater is implicitly comparing the individual with other individuals (for example, a rating of "very friendly" implies that the individual is very friendly compared with other individuals). When performing a Q sort, however, a rater is explicitly comparing each trait with other traits *within* the same individual (for example, placing the item "friendly" in pile 9 implies that, compared with other traits, friendliness stands out as uniquely descriptive of the individual).

The difference between the two kinds of ratings parallels Allport's distinction between *common traits* and *personal dispositions*. Common traits are those on which individuals can be compared with one another; personal dispositions refer to the unique *patterning* or *configuration* of traits within the individual. It is this unique patterning that is captured by the Q-sort method. The technique thus offers a quantitative way of partially capturing what Allport considered to be the most important feature of personality: individuality.

As we described in Chapter 13, two Q sorts can be compared with each other quantitatively by computing a correlation between them, thereby assessing the degree to which two individuals are similar to one another in their overall personality configurations. If two Q sorts are descriptions of the same individual at two different times, then the correlation assesses the test-retest reliability of the technique or the continuity of that individual's overall personality over time. If two Q sorts are descriptions of a single individual made by two raters, then the correlation assesses interjudge reliability or the degree to which two persons perceive the same individual similarly. (For example, in marital counseling, it could be helpful to assess the degree to which two spouses agree or disagree in their perceptions of each other.) If one of the Q sorts is a description of some hypothetical ideal type (for example, the optimally adjusted personality), then the correlation between an individual's Q sort and the ideal sort assesses the degree to which the person approximates the ideal. A complete description of the Q-sort technique has been written by Block (1961/1978).

studies say that the description fits them fairly well (Forer, 1949). The two testimonials quoted above actually came from two subjects in a study of this type (Ulrich, Stachnik & Stainton, 1963). This phenomenon has been dubbed the *Barnum effect*, in reference to the frequently quoted statement by the circus entrepreneur P. T. Barnum, "There's a sucker born every minute."

Check it out for yourself. Here is your personal report:

- You have a tendency to be critical of yourself. At times, you are extraverted, affable, sociable, while at other times you are introverted, wary, reserved.

- You pride yourself on being an independent thinker and do not accept others' opinions without satisfactory proof.

- Some of your aspirations tend to be pretty unrealistic.

- Under stressful circumstances, you occasionally experience some feelings of self-doubt.

- Although you have considerable affection for your parents, there have been times when you disagreed with them.

- Your sexual adjustment has presented problems for you.

In addition to using such general statements, some fortune-tellers and entertainers who claim to "read minds" are quite skilled in picking up cues from the individual's appearance and reactions and then elaborating the statements and tailoring them even more closely to the particular person.

Let the consumer beware. Testimonial validity isn't valid.

PERSONALITY INVENTORIES   A personality inventory is essentially a questionnaire in which the person reports his or her reactions or feelings in certain situations. The personality inventory resembles a structured interview in that it asks the same questions of each person, and the answers are usually given in a form that can be easily scored, often by computer. A personality inventory may be designed to measure a single dimension of personality (such as anxiety level) or several personality traits simultaneously. Again, Cattell provides an example. After he had derived his factors from trait rating scales, he composed questions that best represented each factor and assembled them into a test that yielded a score for each factor—his Sixteen Personality Factor Questionnaire (16 PF). For example, an individual who answers no to the question "Do you tend to keep in the background on social occasions?" earns a point toward the dominant side of the dominant–submissive factor.

In composing his questions, Cattell was using his theory of the 16 factors as a guide. This is called the *rational* method of construction. A different method of test construction—the *empirical* or *criterion* method—was used in the development of the Minnesota Multiphasic Personality Inventory (MMPI).

MINNESOTA MULTIPHASIC PERSONALITY INVENTORY   The MMPI is composed of approximately 550 statements about attitudes, emotional reactions, physical and psychological symptoms, and past experiences. The subject responds to each statement by answering "true," "false," or "cannot say." Some sample test items follow:

- I have never done anything dangerous for the thrill of it.

- I daydream very little.

- My mother or father often made me obey, even when I thought it was unreasonable.

- At times my thoughts have raced ahead faster than I could speak them.

TABLE 14-3

MMPI Scales *The first three scales are "validity" scales, which help to determine whether the person has answered the test items carefully and honestly. For example, the F (Frequency) scale measures the degree to which infrequent or atypical answers are given. A high score on this scale usually indicates that the individual was careless or confused in responding. (However, high F scores often accompany high scores on the Schizophrenia scale, which measures bizarre thinking.) The remaining "clinical" scales were originally named for categories of psychiatric disorders, but interpretation now emphasizes personality attributes rather than diagnostic categories.*

SCALE NAME	SCALE ABBREVIATION	INTERPRETATION OF HIGH SCORES
Lie	L	Denial of common frailties
Frequency	F	Invalidity of profile
Correction	K	Defensive, evasive
Hypochondriasis	Hs	Emphasis on physical complaints
Depression	D	Unhappy, depressed
Hysteria	Hy	Reacts to stress by denying problems
Psychopathic deviancy	Pd	Lack of social conformity; often in trouble with the law
Masculinity–femininity	Mf	Feminine orientation (males); masculine orientation (females)
Paranoia	Pa	Suspicious
Psychasthenia	Pt	Worried, anxious
Schizophrenia	Sc	Withdrawn, bizarre thinking
Hypomania	Ma	Impulsive, excitable
Social introversion–extraversion	Si	Introverted, shy

The responses are scored according to their correspondence to answers given by people with different kinds of psychological problems (see Table 14-3).

The MMPI was developed to aid clinicians in diagnosing personality disturbances. But instead of assuming specific personality traits and formulating questions to measure them, the test designers gave hundreds of test questions to groups of individuals. Each group was known to differ from the norm on a particular criterion. Only the questions that discriminated between groups were retained to form the inventory. For example, to develop a scale of items that distinguish between paranoid and normal individuals, the same questions were given to two groups. The criterion group consisted of individuals who were hospitalized with the diagnosis of paranoid disorder; the control group comprised people who had never been diagnosed as having psychiatric problems but who were similar to the criterion group in age, sex, socioeconomic status, and other important variables. Questions that at face value might seem to distinguish normal from paranoid individuals (for instance, "I think that most people would lie to get ahead") may or may not do so when put to an empirical test. In fact, patients diagnosed as paranoid were significantly *less* apt to respond "true" to this statement than were normal individuals.

Since the MMPI is derived from differences between criterion and control groups, it does not really matter whether what the person says is true. What is important is the fact that he or she says it. If schizophrenics answer "true" and normal subjects answer "false" to the statement "My mother never loved me," their answers distinguish the two groups regardless of how their

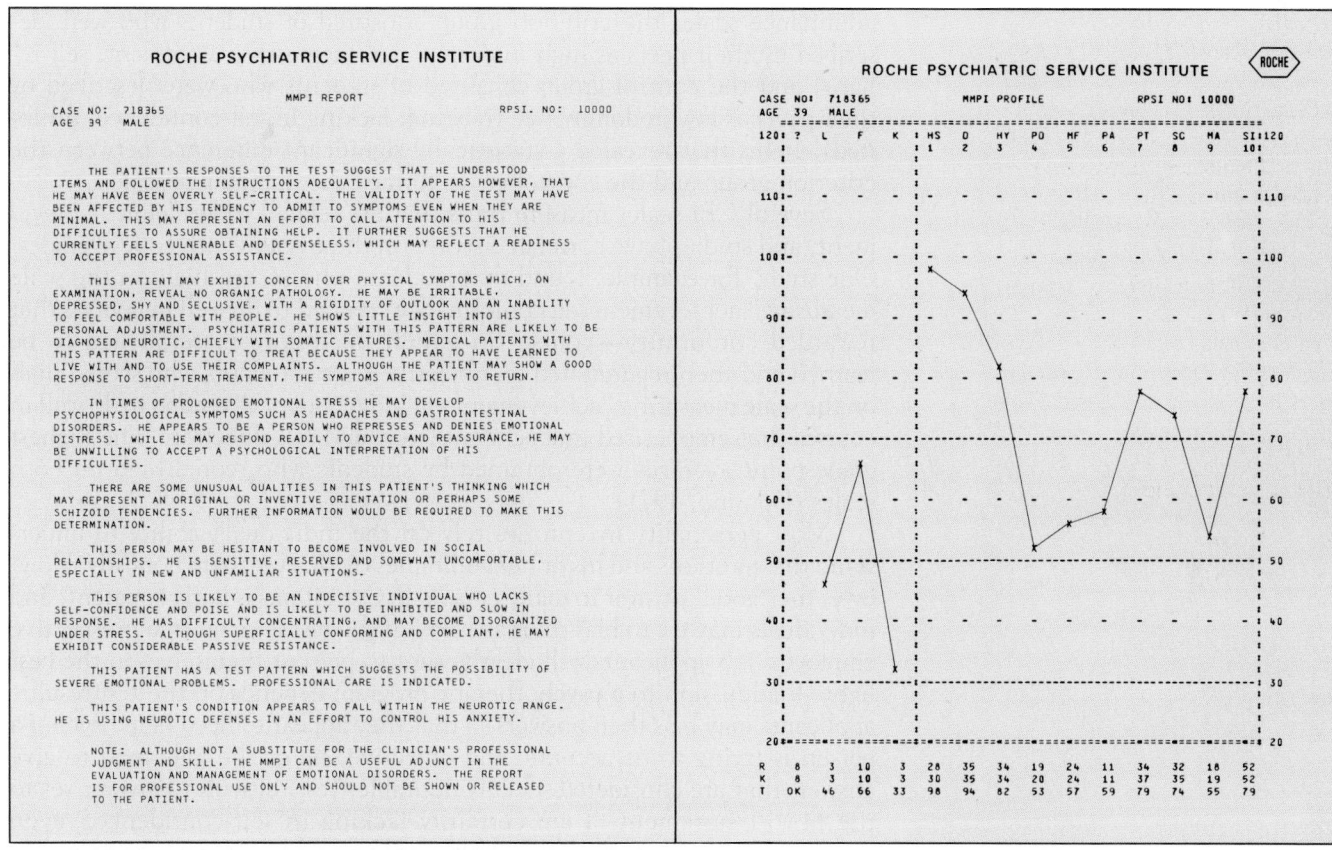

FIGURE 14-3
Computer Printout of an MMPI Profile with Interpretation

mothers actually behaved. This is an advantage of a test based on the method of empirical construction over one based on a test constructor's assumption that certain answers indicate specific personality traits. The disadvantage is that one does not really have a theoretical understanding of the connection between the test responses and the personality characteristics they identify.

Although the MMPI scales were originally designed to identify people with serious personality disorders, they have been widely used in studying normal populations. Sufficient data have been collected to provide personality descriptions of people with different patterns of high and low scores on the various scales. A recent development is the use of a computer to score and interpret the test results (see Figure 14-3). Because the MMPI does not adequately sample some of the traits useful in describing the normal personality (such as conscientiousness or cooperativeness), psychologists recommend that it be supplemented with tests that measure a broader range of normal personality characteristics (Costa, Zonderman, McCrae, & Williams, 1985).

CALIFORNIA PSYCHOLOGICAL INVENTORY Another personality test based on the method of empirical construction is the California Psychological Inventory (CPI). The CPI uses some of the same questions as the MMPI but is designed to measure more "normal" personality traits. The CPI scales measure such traits as dominance, sociability, self-acceptance, responsibility, and socialization. The comparison groups for some of the scales were obtained by asking high-school and college students to designate the classmates they would rate high or low on the trait in question. Thus, for the dominance scale, the criterion group consisted of students who were described by their peers as high in dominance (aggressive, confident, self-reliant) and the control group consisted of students who were described by their peers as low in dominance (retiring, lacking in self-confidence, inhibited). Items that revealed a statistically significant difference between the criterion group and the control group formed the dominance scale.

Several CPI scales measure traits that are related to academic achievement, and studies have correlated scores on these scales with college grades. One study, for example, found that students who scored high on the scale measuring "achievement via conformance" tended to do well in courses that rewarded conformity—courses in which fixed core material had to be learned and then regurgitated on objective tests. Students who scored high on the scale measuring "achievement via independence" tended to do well in courses that emphasized independent study and self-direction. The highest grade point averages were obtained by students who scored high on both scales (Domino, 1971).

Most personality inventories rely on the individual's ability to understand the questions and his or her willingness to answer them honestly. However, the "good" answer to many personality test items is fairly apparent, and individuals may try to bias their answers. If the test is given by a prospective employer, job applicants will clearly want to present themselves in the best light. If admission to a psychotherapy program depends on the test results, applicants may bias their answers so that they appear to need help. Even if a person is trying to be accurate and objective, he or she may tend to give answers that are considered socially desirable. It is difficult to answer yes to the MMPI statement "I am certainly lacking in self-confidence," even though you may feel that way. Self-confidence is a desirable trait in our society; to be lacking in self-confidence is socially undesirable.

Another personality variable that influences test responses is the tendency of some people to acquiesce—to agree with the questions. For example, a person might answer yes to "I am a happy and carefree person" and later to "I frequently have periods when I am extremely depressed." The test results would reflect something about the person's behavior—a tendency to agree with questions—but would tell us little about the individual's general mood. To counteract agreement tendencies, test constructors try (whenever possible) to reverse the wording of questions to provide yes and no versions of each item. Various other methods have been used to counteract deliberate falsifying, tendencies toward social desirability, and acquiescence on personality inventories, but they have been only partially successful.

Psychoanalytic Assessment

As you might expect, psychologists who take a psychoanalytic approach to personality are particularly interested in assessing unconscious wishes, motivations, and conflicts. They need assessment methods that reproduce as closely as possible the method of free association, in which the individual is free to say whatever comes to mind. Clearly the fixed structure of personality inventories—specific questions to which the individual must respond by selecting one of the answers presented—is not well-suited to this purpose. Accordingly, they have developed *projective tests*. A projective test presents an ambiguous stimulus to which the person may respond as he or she wishes. Theoretically, because the stimulus is ambiguous and does not demand a specific response, the individual *projects* his or her personality onto the stimulus. Projective tests tap the individual's imagination and are based on the assumption that the person reveals something about himself or herself through imaginative productions. Two of the most widely used projective techniques are the Rorschach Test and the Thematic Apperception Test.

RORSCHACH TEST   The Rorschach Test, developed by the Swiss psychiatrist Hermann Rorschach in the 1920s, consists of a series of 10 cards, each displaying a rather complex inkblot like the one shown in Figure 14-4. Some of the blots are color; some are black and white. The subject is instructed to look at one card at a time and report everything the inkblot resembles. After the subject has finished the 10 cards, the examiner usually goes over each response, asking the subject to clarify some responses and to tell what features of the blot gave a particular impression.

The subject's responses may be scored in various ways. Three main categories are location (whether the response involves the entire inkblot or a part of it), determinants (whether the subject responds to the shape of the blot, its color, or differences in texture and shading), and content (what the response represents). Most testers also score responses according to frequency of occurrence; for example, a response is "popular" if many people assign it to the same inkblot.

Several elaborate scoring systems have been devised based on these categories. But most of these systems proved to have limited predictive value. Consequently, many psychologists base their interpretations on an impressionistic evaluation of the response record, as well as on the subject's general reaction to the test situation (for example, whether the individual is defensive, open, competitive, cooperative, and so on).

In 1974, a new system was introduced that attempted to extract and combine the validated portions of all the scoring systems into one complete system. It has undergone extensive revision and is now supplemented by a computer scoring service and software for microcomputers (Exner, 1986). Although this system looks more promising than previous efforts, not enough studies have accumulated to evaluate its validity with any confidence.

FIGURE 14-4
Rorschach Inkblot *The subject is asked to tell what is seen in the blot; it may be viewed from any angle.*

Some of the Rorschach inkblots are in color, similar to this example.

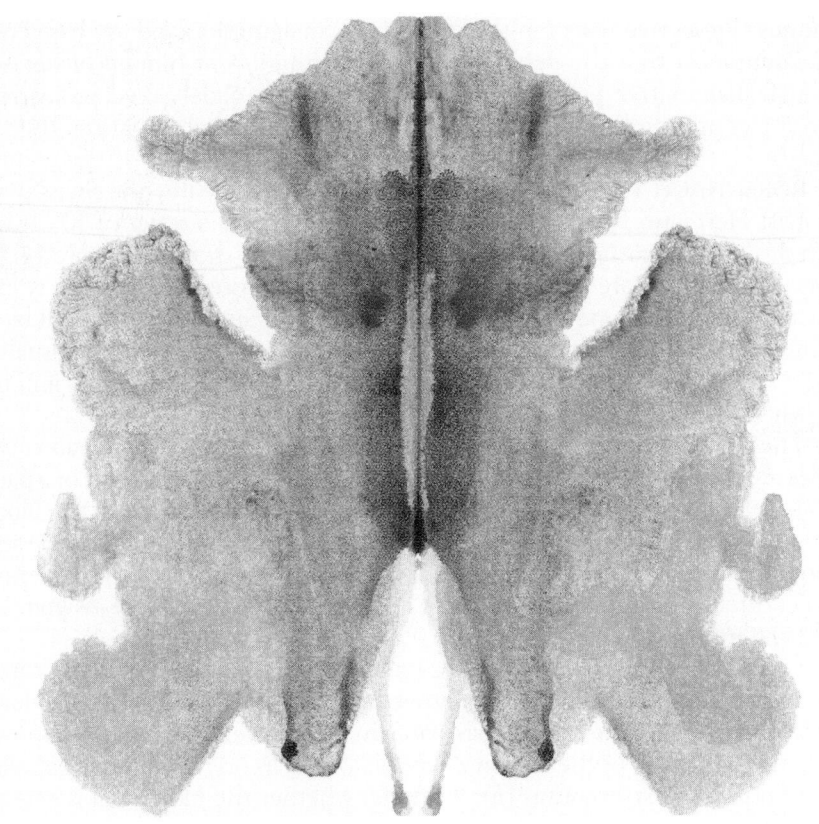

THEMATIC APPERCEPTION TEST   Another popular projective test, the Thematic Apperception Test (TAT), was developed at Harvard University by Henry Murray in the 1930s. The subject is shown as many as 20 ambiguous pictures of persons and scenes, similar to the one in Figure 14-5, and is asked to make up a story about each. The subject is encouraged to give free rein to his or her imagination and to tell whatever story comes to mind. The test is intended to reveal basic themes that recur in a person's imaginative productions. Apperception is a readiness to perceive in certain ways based on prior experiences. People interpret ambiguous pictures according to their apperceptions and elaborate stories in terms of preferred plots or themes that reflect personal fantasies. If particular problems are bothering the subject, they may become evident in a number of the stories or in striking deviations from the usual theme in one or two stories. When shown a picture similar to the one in Figure 14-5, a 21-year-old male told the following story:

> She has prepared this room for someone's arrival and is opening the door for a last general look over the room. She is probably expecting her son home. She tries to place everything as it was when he left. She seems like a very tyrannical character. She led her son's life for him and is going to take over again as soon as he gets back. This is merely the beginning of her rule, and the son is definitely cowed by this overbearing attitude of hers and will slip back into her well-ordered way of life. He will go through life plodding down the tracks she has laid down for him. All this represents her complete domination of his life until she dies. (Arnold, 1949, p. 100)

Although the original picture shows only a woman standing in an open doorway looking into a room, the subject's readiness to talk about his

FIGURE 14-5
Thematic Apperception Test *This picture is similar to the pictures used on the Thematic Apperception Test. The pictures usually have elements of ambiguity so that the subject can "read into" them something from personal experience or fantasy.*

relationship with his mother led to this story of a woman's domination of her son. Facts obtained later confirmed the clinician's interpretation that the story reflected the subject's own problems.

In analyzing responses to the TAT cards, the psychologist looks for recurrent themes that may reveal the individual's needs, motives, or characteristic way of handling interpersonal relationships.

PROBLEMS WITH PROJECTIVE TESTS   Many other projective tests have been devised. Some ask the subject to draw pictures of people, houses, trees, and so on. Others involve completing sentences that start with "I often wish . . . ," "My mother . . . ," or "I feel like quitting when they. . . ." In fact, any stimulus to which a person can respond in an individualistic way could be considered the basis for a projective test. But most projective tests have not been subjected to enough research to establish their usefulness in assessing personality.

The Rorschach Test and the TAT, in contrast, have been intensively researched. The results, however, have not always been encouraging. Reliability of the Rorschach Test has been generally poor because the interpretation of responses is too dependent on the clinician's judgment; the same test protocol may be evaluated quite differently by two trained examiners. And attempts to demonstrate the Rorschach's ability to predict behavior or discriminate between groups have met with limited success. The new comprehensive system, mentioned above, may prove more successful.

The TAT has fared somewhat better. When specific scoring systems are used (for example, to measure achievement motives or aggressive themes), the interscorer reliability is fairly good. But the relationship of TAT scores to overt behavior is complex. Preoccupations are not necessarily acted on. A person who produces a number of stories with aggressive themes may not actually behave aggressively. The individual may be compensating for a need to inhibit aggressive tendencies by expressing such impulses in fantasy. When inhibitions about expressing aggression and strength of aggressive tendencies are estimated from the TAT stories, the relationship to behavior becomes more predictable. Among boys whose tests indicated that they were not very inhibited, the correlation between amount of aggression in the TAT stories and overt aggression was .55. Among boys showing a high degree of inhibition, the correlation between the number of aggressive themes and overt aggression was −.50 (Olweus, 1969).

Defenders of the Rorschach Test and the TAT point out that it is not fair to expect accurate predictions based on test responses alone; story themes or responses to inkblots are meaningful only when considered in light of additional information, such as the person's life history, other test data, and observations of behavior. The skilled clinician uses the results of projective tests to make tentative interpretations about the individual's personality and then verifies or discards them, depending on further information. The tests are helpful in suggesting possible areas of conflict to be explored.

Social-Learning Assessment

Because of their primary focus on behavior and its situational determinants, psychologists who take a social-learning approach to personality have developed several methods for recording behavior in naturalistic settings. One group of researchers has constructed an elaborate electronic system for recording the behavior of children in free-play settings. By holding down buttons on a console, a single observer is able to record up to 12 different categories of ongoing behavior simultaneously (for example, "talking," "sitting alone"). The continuous record of behavior is sufficiently precise to enable researchers to relate even small changes in a child's behavior to events and to other children's behavior in the situation (Lovaas, Freitag, Gold, & Kassorla, 1965). Another research program has developed ingenious methods for recording the detailed interactions between highly aggressive children and their family members in everyday settings like the dinner table (Patterson, 1976).

Many behavioral assessments are conducted in conjunction with therapeutic techniques based on social-learning principles (see Chapter 17). In one study of height phobia, fear of heights was assessed by measuring the distance that individuals would climb on a fire escape. After receiving therapy, they were assessed again by having them take an elevator to a roof garden and attempt to count passing cars below for 2 minutes (Lazarus, 1961).

Individuals are often assessed by training them to be self-observers. For example, individuals in behavioral therapy are often asked to keep daily diaries of their activities in order to help the therapist pinpoint sources of anxiety. One study of adolescents provided each subject with an electronic paging device. Whenever they were beeped by the experimenter during the day, they stopped whatever they were doing and filled out a form, recording their current activity and their current level of self-esteem (Savin-Williams & Jaquish, 1981).

As psychologists who take a social-learning approach have become more cognitive in recent years, they have also begun to measure cognitions relevant to behavior, such as expectancies. In one study, patients who had suffered heart attacks were given a list of daily situations that might cause emotional strain (such as complaining to an unsympathetic sales person about poor service) and were asked to indicate whether they thought they could manage the situation and, if so, to rate how confident they felt about doing

"Leave us alone! I am a behavior therapist! I am helping my patient overcome a fear of heights!"

so (Bandura, et al., 1985). And finally, social-learning researchers have occasionally recorded physiological variables in order to assess ongoing emotional reactions to situations.

Phenomenological Assessment

For phenomenologically oriented psychologists, there is only one valid source for the information they find crucial: the individual himself or herself. Their most common tool is the interview. In early research, investigators would select excerpts from interviews taken during therapy sessions and attempt to discern how the clients' verbalizations reflected changes in their self-concepts during the course of therapy. More recently, they have developed reliable scoring systems for categorizing self-references into theoretically relevant categories, such as approving self-references (Mardsen, 1971; Truax & Mitchell, 1971).

Q SORT   The Q sort technique has already been described in the section on trait assessment. We mention it again here because Carl Rogers pioneered its use as a phenomenological assessment instrument for examining the self-concept. Rogers' Q set contains statements like "I am satisfied with myself"; "I have a warm emotional relationship with others"; and "I don't trust my emotions." In Rogers' procedure, individuals first sort themselves as they actually are—their *real self*—and then sort themselves as they would like to be—their *ideal self*. The correlation between the two sorts indexes the *self–ideal discrepancy*. A low or negative correlation corresponds to a large self–ideal discrepancy, implying feelings of low self-esteem and lack of personal worth—one index of maladjustment.

By repeating this procedure several times during the course of therapy, Rogers could assess the effectiveness of therapy. In one study, correlations between self and ideal Q sorts of individuals seeking therapy averaged − .01 prior to therapy, but increased to + .58 following therapy. The same correlation for a matched control group not receiving therapy did not change (Butler & Haigh, 1954). In other words, the therapy had significantly reduced these individuals' perception of the discrepancy between their real selves and their ideal selves. Note that this could also occur if an individual did not change his or her perception of the real self but instead lowered unrealistic aspirations for the ideal self.

THE ROLE CONSTRUCT REPERTORY TEST   The personal construct theory of George Kelly has its own unique assessment device, the *Role Construct Repertory Test*, or "Rep Test." Kelly designed it as a way of eliciting the personal constructs an individual uses to interpret or construe his or her interpersonal world. On this test, subjects or clients fill in a matrix or *grid* like the one shown in Figure 14-6.

Along the top of the grid is a list of people who are important to the individual. These might be supplied by the assessor or the subject, but they usually include "myself," and sometimes include "my ideal self." On each line of the grid, the assessor has circled three of the cells. For example, in the first row of the figure, the assessor has circled the cells in the columns labeled "myself," "my mother," and "my best friend." The subject is asked to consider these three people and to place an "X" in the cells of the two people who are most similar to each other but different from the third. As shown in the first

FIGURE 14-6
Role Construct Repertory Test *In each row, the subject compares three of the persons listed at the top of the grid, placing an "X" under the two who are most alike. He or she then describes how they are alike by writing in the* construct. *Finally, the subject describes how the third person is different from the other two by writing in the* contrast. *This subject indicates that he sees himself and his mother as both being* witty *and different from his best friend, who is seen as* humorless. *The procedure is repeated for each row in the matrix.*

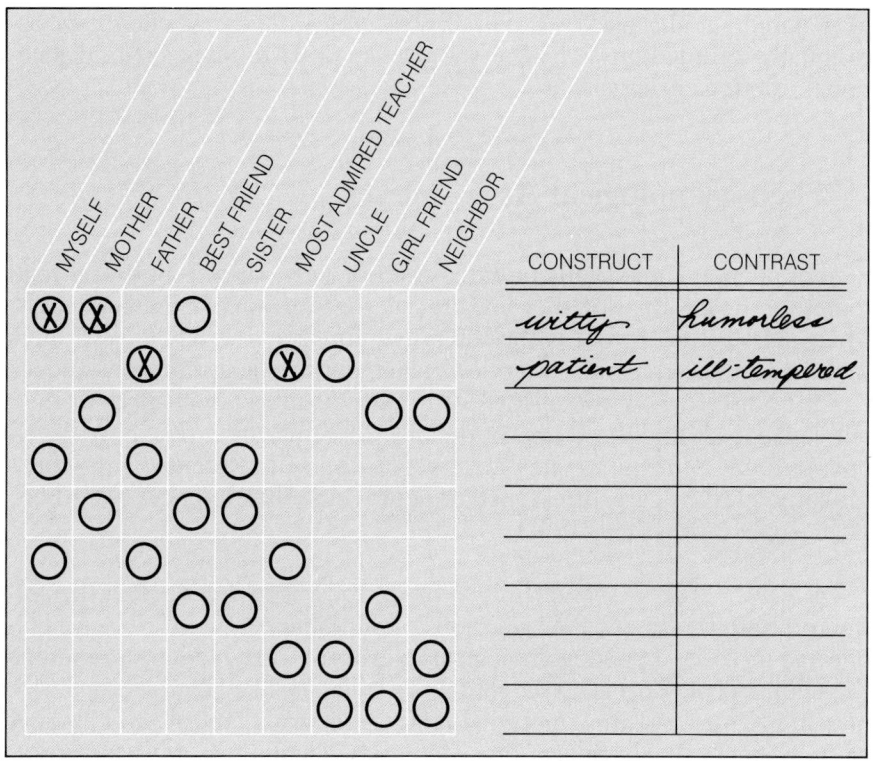

row, this (male) subject considers himself and his mother to be the most similar pair. He is then asked, "In what way are you and your mother alike but different from your best friend?" In this case, the subject has indicated that he and his mother are both *witty*. This description is called his *construct*. Next, he is asked "In what way is your friend different from you and your mother?" He has responded with the answer that his friend is *humorless*. This description is called his *contrast*. For this subject, then, the dimension *witty–humorless* is one of the personal constructs he uses to interpret or construe his interpersonal world.

Note that a construct–contrast pair need not constitute logical opposites. For example, this subject might have labeled himself and his mother as *witty*, but then labeled his best friend as *serious* or *introverted* or *prefers-to-listen-to-humor-rather-than-to-initiate-it*. If that is how he construes the two poles of the dimension, then that is what Kelly wants to know. The Rep Test is designed to assess the *individual's* constructs, not the psychologist's.

This procedure is repeated with several other triads in the set. By looking at the entire set, the investigator or therapist can explore a number of themes that seem to characterize the individual's construal of the world. For example, some clients will reveal through this procedure that they see the entire world in authoritarian terms; dimensions like *strong–weak, powerful–powerless*, and so forth might appear repeatedly. Or an individual might reveal that she always pairs herself with males on the construct end of dimensions while placing other women on the contrast end.

The Rep Test is a very general procedure and is not restricted to construing persons. For example, an individual may be asked to consider triads of situations or events. (Which two are alike but different from the third? Taking an examination; going out on a blind date; encountering a spider.) The technique has proved valuable both for research on people's constructs and for counseling. There are even specialized mathematical techniques for analyzing the grid and abstracting structural features of the individual's construct system (such as the degree of cognitive complexity it reveals).

CONSISTENCY PARADOX

As we noted earlier, the assumption that persons display cross-situational consistencies in their behavior seems so obviously true that it is practically synonymous with our definition of personality. This was certainly the view of Theophrastus when he informed us that penurious men go to collect interest from their debtors before it is due, move the furniture looking for a lost coin, count the number of cups each person drinks at dinner parties where expenses are shared, and postpone putting on their shoes until midday so they will not be worn out so soon.

Although the assumption of cross-situational consistency is most explicit in type and trait theories of personality, it is also present in psychoanalytic and phenomenological theories. For example, even when overt behaviors appear inconsistent—as when a mother who resents her child shows hostility on one day and exaggerated love and concern the next—psychoanalytic theory assumes that a consistent unconscious motivation produces both behaviors. Phenomenological theories assume that the self-concept integrates our behavior and thus provides consistency.

But dissenting voices were heard as long ago as the sixteenth century, when the French essayist Michel de Montaigne wrote an essay entitled "Of the Inconsistency of Our Actions." In it, he sounded very much like a contemporary behaviorist in his insistence that the situation (neighboring circumstances) determines behavior:

> In view of the natural instability of our conduct, it has often seemed to me that even good authors are wrong to insist on weaving a consistent and solid fabric out of us. . . . He who would judge [us] in detail and distinctly, bit by bit would more often hit upon the truth. . . . The surest thing, in my opinion, would be to trace [our actions] to the neighboring circumstances without getting into any further research and without drawing from them any other conclusions. (1580/1943, pp. 118, 120)

The consistency issue was first addressed empirically 60 years ago, when a series of studies explicitly set out to assess consistency across situations. The best known of these studies was the classic investigation of character by Hartshorne and May in the late 1920s. They gave some 11,000 elementary- and high-school students a large number of behavioral tests designed to measure the traits of altruism, self-control, and honesty in a number of different situations—at home, in the classroom, during athletic competition, and in church. To test honesty, for instance, the children were placed in situations where they had a chance to be dishonest while believing they would not be detected—to keep some of the money they were given to play with, to cheat on a test, to report falsely about the number of push-ups they could do, or the amount of work done at home. The correlations among behaviors in the different situations turned out to be quite low. For example, correlating scores on any two tests used to measure honesty yielded an average correlation of .23. These low correlations led Hartshorne and May to conclude that

CRITICAL DISCUSSION

Are Our Intuitions about Consistency Wrong?

Research by social psychologists on the processes of social inference has revealed a number of biases and shortcomings in our abilities to draw valid judgments from the data of everyday experience. (We discuss these in detail in Chapter 18.) This research suggests that there are a number of plausible reasons why our intuitions might be in error about consistency. Here are six:

1. Our preconceived notions of how people behave may lead us to generalize beyond our actual observations. We may fill in the missing data according to our implicit personality theories of which traits and behaviors go together. Moreover, research shows that when we expect two behaviors to be correlated, we tend to see them as correlated even when they are not. Stereotypes of how a "homosexual," a "career woman," or an "athlete" behaves may cause us to attribute greater consistency to a person's actions than actual observations warrant.

2. Many features of an individual remain fairly constant—physical appearance, manner of speaking, expressive gestures, and so on. These constancies help to create an impression that the personality is consistent as well.

3. Our presence can cause people to behave in certain ways. Thus, our acquaintances may appear to behave consistently because we are present as a stimulus during every observation we make. They may behave quite differently when we are not there.

4. Because the actions of another person are such a salient feature of any scene, we tend to overestimate the extent to which behavior is caused by personality characteristics and underestimate the importance of situational forces that may cause the person to act as he or she does. If we observe someone behaving aggressively, we assume that the person has an aggressive disposition and will behave similarly in other settings, even though the situational factors may be quite different. This tendency to underestimate situational influences on behavior has been called the *fundamental attribution error* (see Chapter 18).

5. The set of situations in which we observe most individuals is usually more limited than we realize. For example, we are so familiar with the warm, sincere personalities of the network news anchors on the national nightly newscasts that we would be shocked if we learned that one of them cheated on a spouse or kicked the family poodle. Because we see them so often, we mistakenly assume that we also see them in a variety of situations. As a

---

neither honesty nor dishonesty is a unified character trait; behavior is specific to the situation (Hartshorne & May, 1929).

The debate was reactivated some 40 years later by Walter Mischel (1968). After reviewing additional studies that had accumulated since the Hartshorne-May inquiry, Mischel also concluded that people are quite variable in their behavior across situations. He found that the correlations between trait measures on personality tests and actual behavioral observations of the same traits in real situations were quite low for most studies—typically less than .30. Correlations between measures of the same trait in two different situations were equally low (Mischel, 1968).

The paradox that sustains the debate and accounts for its historical durability is this: our intuitions tell us that individuals are consistent; the research tells us that they are not. Intuitions or research? Which one is wrong?

Recent research in social psychology lends some support to those who believe that our intuitions about consistency might be wrong (see the Critical Discussion, "Are Our Intuitions about Consistency Wrong?"). Despite these findings, however, some psychologists continue to maintain that our intuitions capture the reality of personality more faithfully than does the research (Bem & Allen, 1974; Bem, 1983). Their argument is an extension of Gordon Allport's view of personality and provides the first of several proposed solutions to the consistency paradox, the *person-centered solution*.

result we feel we know them well and readily generalize about their behavior—assuming a consistency that is unwarranted.

This example is particularly telling, because the behavior of news anchors is so severely constrained and so situationally determined

that it could not possibly convey very much about their personalities. If they deviated even slightly from their prescribed role—if they slouched in their chairs or stood up to stretch, for example—they would be fired.

6. Our language entices us to think about human behavior in trait terms. As we noted earlier, there are about 18,000 trait terms in our language, nearly five percent of the entire lexicon. In contrast, we have an impoverished and awkward vocabulary for labeling situations. But language is not only a *cause* of how we think, it is also the *result* of how we think. The fact that our language is so unbalanced in this way probably indicates that we have always found it more important to classify persons rather than situations.

This discussion has presented only the case for the prosecution. The case for the defense appears in the remainder of this section.

Tom Brokaw fits the stereotype of a network news anchor.

Person-Centered Solution

We saw earlier that Gordon Allport believed that personality psychology should be less concerned with comparing individuals across common traits and more concerned with the unique pattern or configuration of personal dispositions within the individual. We shall refer to the first strategy as the *trait-centered approach* and Allport's suggested strategy as the *person-centered approach*. The important difference between the two approaches is illustrated by Allport's response to the findings of Hartshorne and May that the children they observed in their study were not consistently honest or dishonest across situations. He noted that the low correlations "prove only that children are not consistent *in the same way*, not that they are inconsistent with *themselves*" (1937, p. 250). What did he mean by this?

Consider the two behaviors of lying and stealing, which were relatively uncorrelated in the study. One child may lie in order to avoid hurting the feelings of the teacher, whereas another may steal pennies in order to buy social acceptance from his or her peers. The first child might be consistently empathic and sensitive across situations, the second child consistently insecure about acceptance across situations. But for neither of these two children do the behaviors of lying and stealing belong together in a common equivalence class representing an honesty–dishonesty dimension. Honesty and dishonesty are categories in the head of the investigator—a personal construct or way of construing behavior. They are not categories that capture the coherence of either of these children's behaviors. If Hartshorne and May had measured empathy and sensitivity across situations, the first child would have shown up as consistent; if they had measured insecurity across situations, the second child would have shown up as consistent. As Allport said, the children are not inconsistent with themselves; they are only inconsistent with the investigator's theory that lying and stealing represent "the same thing." This, according to Allport, is the fallacy of the trait-centered approach to personality.

In contrast, our intuitions appear to follow the person-centered strategy. Consider how we approach the task of describing a friend. We do not invoke a fixed set of trait terms that we apply to everyone. Instead, we first review our friend's behavior and then select a small set of traits that strike us as pertinent *precisely because* they seem to conform to the patterning of our friend's behavior.

If John always does his schoolwork early, is meticulous about his personal appearance, and is always punctual, it may well occur to us to describe him as conscientious. On the other hand, if he is always conscientious about his schoolwork but negligent in these other areas, we may well describe him as a totally dedicated student who has time for little else. The important point is that we are not likely to characterize him as someone who is inconsistently conscientious. That is, we do not first impose a trait term—"conscientious"—on him and then judge him to be inconsistent. Instead, we first attempt to discern a recognizable pattern to his behaviors and only then to put a label on that pattern.

This, then, is the essence of our intuitive approach to personality, and it is the argument of Bem and Allen that in terms of the underlying logic and fidelity to reality, our intuitions about consistency are right; the research is wrong (Bem & Allen, 1974; Bem, 1983).

Aggregation Solution

In our discussion of reliability, we noted that as the number of items on a test increases, the reliability of the entire test increases. For example, the correlation between any two items on the Wechsler Adult Intelligence Scales (WAIS) (see Chapter 12) is only about .16. Clearly it would be absurd to expect an individual's answer to a single item to correlate with his or her intelligence in nontest situations; in other words, a one-item test would have virtually no validity. But because many such items are aggregated on the WAIS, the reliability of the total test score is .96, and its validity—its correlation with many nontest behaviors—is quite impressive.

With this in mind, it is instructive to look at the studies that find little cross-situational consistency in behavior. Most are based on only one or two measures of behavior. For example, a typical study may try to relate helpfulness in one situation (giving money to charity) with helpfulness in another (coming to the aid of a person in distress). This is analogous to trying to correlate one item on the WAIS with one of the other items. Low correlations should be expected. Other studies may correlate an individual's score on a scale measuring aggression with an aggressive behavior in a laboratory experiment. Because the aggression scale is an aggregate of many items, it is probably reliable, but the likely *unreliability* of the single laboratory measure of aggression is rarely considered and almost never actually assessed.

A history of childhood temper tantrums may lead to marital strife in adulthood.

In other words, a more accurate estimate of cross-situational consistency would be obtained if investigators combined several behavioral measures of the same trait to arrive at an aggregated score, just as they have always done with their tests. For example, much higher correlations are found in the Hartshorne and May study when aggregated scores are used. When the children's aggregated scores on half of the honesty tests are correlated with those on the other half of the tests, the correlation is .72. This is much higher than the average correlation of a .23 between any two tests for honesty and indicates considerable consistency (Rushton, Jackson, & Paunonen, 1981).

The method of aggregation can also be used to demonstrate the stability of traits over time. In one study, observers followed people for 4 weeks and rated them on variables related to their sociability or their tendency to be impulsive. Although the correlations for any 2 days were quite low, the ratings averaged over the first 14 days correlated .81 with the ratings averaged over the second 14 days (Epstein, 1977). Thus, it appears that we can find considerable consistency in traits, given a large enough sample of behavior.

The aggregation solution also resolves another paradox. In Chapter 13, we reported impressive continuities between childhood personality characteristics (like ill-temperedness and dependency) and adult outcomes thirty years later (like occupational status and marital stability). But how can this be so if simple behaviors are not consistent across situations even when measured within days of each other? The answer, of course, is that the childhood personality characteristics comprised aggregated observations over 3 years and the adult outcomes similarly reflected the consequences of many aggregated behaviors. We cannot predict whether a boy who has a temper tantrum one day when he is ten will have a fight with his wife one day when he is 40. But we *can* predict from the sum of his temper tantrums over three years in late childhood to a divorce precipitated by several adult years of marital strife.

Interactional Solution

The interactional solution to the consistency debate represents the emerging consensus among personality psychologists that an adequate theory of personality must attend to the characteristics of both the person and the situation. Moreover, most personality psychologists now recognize the diverse ways in which the person and the situation interact to produce behavior.

We anticipated this resolution in Chapter 13, where we described in detail how the interactions between our genotypes (inherited characteristics) and our environments interact to shape our personalities. The person-situation interactions that produce behavior are directly analogous to the genotype-environment interactions that shape personality in the first place.

First, an individual's personality and the situation contribute jointly to behavior just as a child's genotype and the environment contribute jointly to the shaping of personality. In addition, situations become a function of our personalities through the same three forms of dynamic interaction that cause the environment to become a function of the child's personality: *reactive*, *evocative*, and *proactive*.

REACTIVE INTERACTION   Different individuals exposed to the same situation experience it, interpret it, and react to it differently. The person who interprets a hurtful act as the product of hostility will react differently from the person who interprets it as the product of insensitivity. It is here that the phenomenological psychologists have a major contribution to make through their concern with each individual's interpretation of situations.

EVOCATIVE INTERACTION   Every individual's personality evokes distinctive responses from others. A person who acts in an abrasive manner is apt to evoke more hostile responses from the social environment than one who is tactful and sensitive to the feelings of others. Here the social-learning theorists have taken the lead by providing the necessary conceptual and methodological tools for analyzing reciprocal behavioral interactions.

PROACTIVE INTERACTION   Each individual's personality leads him or her to seek out some situations and to avoid others. A person who feels the need to dominate others might seek confrontation, whereas a more submissive individual would try to avoid such situations. The sociable student will choose to take an informal seminar rather than a large class. And once an individual is in a situation, he or she can shape it further: it will be the sociable student who suggests moving the evening seminar to the local tavern.

The existence of dynamic person–situation interactions complicates the study of personality and challenges researchers to be more creative in the strategies they pursue for studying personality. For example, the hallmark of the experimental laboratory is the control of conditions; subjects assigned to the same conditions must experience the same treatment if valid inferences are to be drawn. Moreover, subjects should be randomly assigned to conditions. But if individuals differ from one another primarily in their interpretations of situations, in the characteristic responses they evoke from others in situations, in their selection of which situations to enter in the first place, and in their tendencies to reshape the situations they enter, then psychologists who use only the laboratory to study personality will never see its major manifestations.

Clearly, personality psychology needs the contribution of all the approaches discussed in this chapter more than ever. In attempting to provide a complete, integrated account of the total person, the study of personality remains the most ambitious subfield of psychology.

1. *Personality* refers to the characteristic patterns of thought, emotion, and behavior that define an individual's personal style and influence his or her interactions with the environment. Personality psychology seeks a) to describe and to explain individual differences, and b) to synthesize the processes that can influence an individual's interactions with the environment into an integrated account of the total person.

2. *Type theories* propose that individuals can be categorized into discrete types that are qualitatively different from one another. Currently, *typologies* are not very popular in psychology. *Trait theories* assume that an individual's personality can be described by its position on a number of continuous dimensions, or scales, each of which represents a trait. A major task of trait theorists is to derive a manageably small set of trait descriptors that can encompass the diversity of human personality. The method of factor analysis has often been used for this purpose. Five factors that are found fairly consistently in factor-analytic studies of personality are *Neuroticism* (maladjustment), *Extraversion, Openness to Experience, Agreeableness*, and *Conscientiousness*. Gordon Allport, Raymond Cattell, and Hans Eysenck are three of the most prominent trait theorists.

3. Freud's *psychoanalytic theory* holds that many behaviors, including dreams and slips of the tongue, are caused by unconscious motivations. Personality is primarily determined by the biological drives of sex and aggression and by experiences that occur during the first 5 years of life. Freud's theory of *personality structure* views personality as composed of the *id*, the *ego*, and the *superego*, which are often in conflict. The id operates on the *pleasure principle*, seeking immediate gratification of biological impulses. The ego obeys the *reality principle*, postponing gratification until it can be achieved in socially acceptable ways. The *superego* (conscience) imposes *moral standards* on the individual. In a well-integrated personality, the ego remains in firm but flexible control over the id and superego; the reality principle governs.

4. Freud's theory of *personality dynamics* proposes that there is a constant amount of psychic energy (*libido*) for each individual. If a forbidden act or impulse is suppressed, its energy will seek an outlet in some other form, such as dreams or neurotic symptoms. The theory assumes that repressed id impulses cause anxiety, which can be reduced by *defense mechanisms*.

5. Freud's theory of *personality development* proposes that individuals pass through *psychosexual stages* (such as oral, anal, phallic) and must resolve the *oedipal conflict*, in which the young child sees the same-sex parent as a rival for the affection of the opposite-sex parent. Freud's theory of anxiety and defense mechanisms has fared better over the years than his structural and developmental theories. Psychoanalytic theory has been modified by others like Jung, Adler, Horney, Sullivan, Fromm, and Erikson—all of whom place more emphasis on functions of the ego and on motives other than sex and aggression.

6. *Social-learning theory* assumes that personality differences result from variations in learning experiences. Responses may be learned through observation, without reinforcement, but reinforcement is important in determining whether the learned responses will be *performed*. A person's behavior depends on the specific characteristics of the situation in interaction with the individual's appraisal of the situation and reinforcement history. People behave consistently only insofar as the situations they encounter and the roles they are expected to play remain relatively stable.

7. *Phenomenological theories* are concerned with the individual's subjective experience. *Humanistic psychology* was founded as the "third force," an explicit alternative to psychoanalytic and behavioristic approaches. Humanistic psychologists like Carl Rogers and Abraham Maslow emphasize a person's self-concept and striving for growth, or self-actualization. George Kelly's *personal construct theory* focuses on the concepts or constructs individuals use to interpret or *construe* their world.

8. Tests for assessing personality must demonstrate that they yield reproducible and consistent results (*reliability*) and that they measure what they are intended to measure (*validity*). Tests designed to measure a construct that is part of a theory (for example, motivation to affiliate) achieve *construct validity* when predictions from the theory are confirmed in studies using the test.

9. Ratings made on trait dimensions (such as "friendly–unfriendly") can be made by individuals describing themselves or by people who know them well. The *Q-sort* technique requires the rater to sort statements typed on cards into piles ranging from statements that are least characteristic to statements that are most characteristic of the individual. Whereas rating scales implicitly compare an individual with other individuals across traits, the Q sort explicitly compares each trait with other traits *within* a single individual, thereby describing the *patterning* or *configuration* of traits that compose his or her personality.

10. *Personality inventories* are questionnaires on which individuals report their reactions or feelings in certain situations. Responses to subsets of items are summed to yield scores on separate scales or factors within the inventory. Items on some inventories are composed or selected on the basis of a theory; this is called the *rational* method of test construction. Alternatively, items can be selected because they correlate with some criterion; for example, an item to which schizophrenics answer "true" significantly more often than do nonschizophrenics would be retained as an item for a schizophrenia scale. This is called the *empirical* or *criterion* method of test construction. The Minnesota Multiphasic Personality Inventory (MMPI) and the California Psychological Inventory (CPI) are examples of empirically constructed tests.

11. Psychologists who take the psychoanalytic approach prefer less structured assessment instruments called *projective tests*, such as the Rorschach Test and the Thematic Apperception Test (TAT). Because the test stimuli are ambiguous, it is assumed that the individual projects his or her personality onto the stimulus, thereby revealing unconscious wishes and motives. Psychologists who take the social-learning approach prefer to observe behavior directly in natural settings. Psychologists who take the phenomenological approach focus on the individual's own perceptions and interpretations. These can be assessed by analyzing interviews. The *Role Construct Repertory Test* is specifically designed within the framework of Kelly's *personal construct theory* to elicit the concepts or constructs individuals use to interpret or *construe* their world.

12. There is a long-standing discrepancy between our intuitive assumption—embodied in most theories of personality—that individuals are consistent across situations and studies that seem to demonstrate that they are not. Studies that find low correlations between measures of the same trait in two different situations or between personality test scores and situational measures of the trait support the contention of social-learning theorists that behavior is more dependent on the situation than on enduring traits. In reply, Allport and others have argued that the low correlations only demonstrate that individuals are not consistent in the same way, not that they are inconsistent across situations in their personal dispositions. Others have demonstrated that consistency increases if measures are *aggregated* across situations or over time.

13. *Interactionism* resolves the debate by recognizing that behavior results from an ongoing reciprocal interaction between personal dispositions and situational variables. In particular, individuals a) differentially react to situations, b) evoke

different responses from others in situations, and c) differentially select and shape situations. As a result, situations themselves become a function of the individual's personality through the processes of *reactive*, *evocative*, and *proactive* interaction.

FURTHER READING

General books on personality include Hall, Lindzey, Loehlin, and Manosevitz, *Introduction to Theories of Personality* (1985); Mischel, *Introduction to Personality* (4th ed., 1986); Feshbach and Weiner, *Personality* (2nd ed., 1986); Singer, *The Human Personality: An Introductory Textbook* (1984); and Phares, *Introduction to Personality* (1984).

For a social-learning approach to personality, see Bandura, *Social Learning Theory* (1977); and Mischel, *Introduction to Personality* (4th ed., 1986).

Freud's theories are presented in their most readable form in his *New Introductory Lectures on Psychoanalysis* (1933; reprint ed., 1965). Other references for psychoanalytic theories of personality include Holzman, *Psychoanalysis and Psychopathology* (1970); and Eagle, *Recent Developments in Psychoanalysis: A Critical Evaluation* (1984).

The phenomenological viewpoint is represented in Maddi and Costa, *Humanism in Personology: Allport, Maslow, and Murray* (1972); and Keen, *A Primer in Phenomenological Psychology* (1982). For Carl Rogers' views, see Rogers and Stevens, *Person to Person: The Problem of Being Human* (1967); and Rogers, *Carl Rogers on Personal Power* (1977). *Personality and Personal Growth* (2nd ed., 1984) by Frager and Fadiman focuses on the personality theories that are most concerned with understanding human nature and includes a section on such Eastern theories of personality as Yoga, Zen Buddhism, and Sufism.

Aiken, *Assessment of Personality* (1989) is a general text on methods of assessing personality. Cronbach, *Essentials of Psychological Testing* (4th ed., 1984), also contains chapters on personality measurement.

Paul Klee. The Artist at the Window, *1909.*
Watercolor and colored chalk, 11¾″ x 9¼″, Collection Felix Klee, Bern. (70)

PART VII

Stress, Psychopathology, and Therapy

Chapter 15

Detail, The Artist at the Window.

Stress and Coping

Regardless of how resourceful we may be in coping with problems, the circumstances of life inevitably involve stress. Our motives are not always easily satisfied: obstacles must be overcome, choices need to be made, and delays have to be tolerated. Today's rapidly paced society creates pressures for each of us. We are constantly faced with a sense of urgency, the pressure to accomplish more and more in less and less time. Stress from the environment and our jobs—air and noise pollution, traffic congestion, job deadlines, and work overload—are increasingly present in our everyday lives. Each of us develops characteristic ways of responding to such pressures. To a large extent, our responses to stressful situations determine how adequately we adjust to life. In the next three chapters, we will look at the ways in which people respond to stress and what happens when inadequate coping techniques pose a threat to adjustment. We will also discuss a variety of abnormal behaviors and the methods used to treat them.

CONCEPT OF STRESS

Stress has become a popular topic. We are flooded with information about its harmful effects and how it can be managed or prevented. But what is stress? There is little agreement on how the term should be defined. Different researchers define it differently, depending on their orientations. In general terms, stress is a state that occurs when people a) are faced with events they perceive as endangering their physical or psychological well-being, and b) are unsure of their ability to deal with these events. Stress includes the environmental events that are perceived as threatening (*stressors*) and the person's reactions to them (*stress responses*).

Some researchers have focused on stressors. They have studied catastrophic events, such as fires, earthquakes, and nuclear disasters, as well as more chronic stressful situations such as imprisonment and overcrowding. They have also studied the relationship between the accumulation of stressful life events (such as job loss, divorce, or the death of a loved one) and the risk of subsequent illness. And they have tried to identify the characteristics of a situation that make it stressful.

Other researchers have focused on stress responses. They have tried to identify the cognitive, emotional, physiological, and behavioral responses that occur when an individual is faced with demanding or threatening situations.

One of the most striking features about the experience of stress is the powerful influence of psychological factors. People show marked individual differences in their reaction to stressors. Even physiological responses to painful stimuli can be influenced by the way we think about them. While some situations are stressful for everyone (life-threatening illness or the loss of a loved one), many less dramatic experiences (taking an examination, arguing with a friend, getting stuck in traffic) are very stressful for some people, but not for others. To understand stress, we need to know how the individual appraises a situation in terms of his or her particular motives and resources for coping with the situation.

In Chapter 11 we discussed how the cognitive appraisal of a situation influences the quality and intensity of the emotion experienced. When we talk specifically about stress, cognitive appraisal is the process of evaluating

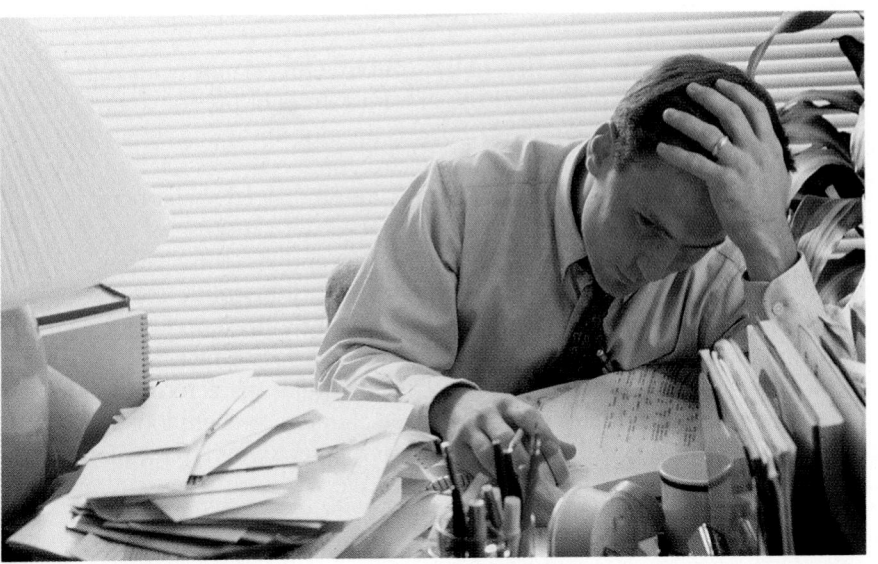

an event with respect to its significance for a person's well-being. This appraisal is twofold. The *primary appraisal* asks, What does this mean to me? Am I okay or am I in trouble? The *secondary appraisal* asks, What can I do about the situation? The primary appraisal may judge the situation as a) irrelevant to the person's well-being, b) benign-positive, or c) stressful. A situation appraised as stressful involves three types of judgments. The person may judge that he or she has already sustained some damage (for example, the loss of a loved one, an incapacitating injury, or damage to esteem). Or the judgment may involve the *threat* of such damage or loss. A third judgment is that the situation is a *challenge*: there are potential benefits to the individual, but these also contain risks (Lazarus & Folkman, 1984).

A job promotion may be viewed as both a threat and a challenge. Either way, the situation is stressful because an individual must mobilize coping efforts to meet new demands. The main difference is that challenge appraisals are characterized by pleasurable emotions such as eagerness and excitement, whereas threat is characterized by negative emotions such as fear and anxiety. In a study of stress related to taking examinations, most students reported feelings of both threat and challenge two days before a midterm exam (Folkman & Lazarus, 1985).

If the primary appraisal evaluates the situation as stressful (I'm in trouble), then the secondary appraisal answers the question, What, if anything, can I do about it? The answer to a given stressful event depends on the person's past experiences in similar situations and his or her resources—problem-solving skills, morale, social supports, and material resources.

PHYSIOLOGICAL REACTIONS TO STRESS

The body reacts by initiating a complex sequence of innate responses to a perceived threat. If the threat is dealt with quickly, these emergency responses subside, and our physiological state returns to normal. If the stressful situation continues, a different set of internal responses occurs as we attempt to adapt to a chronic stressor.

Stress Response

Whether you fall into an icy river, encounter a knife-wielding assailant, or are terrified by your first parachute jump, your body responds in similar ways. Regardless of the stressor, your body automatically prepares to handle the emergency. Quick energy is needed, so the liver releases extra sugar (glucose) to fuel the muscles, and hormones are released that stimulate the conversion of fats and proteins to sugar. The body's metabolism increases in preparation for expending energy on physical action. Heart rate, blood pressure, and breathing rate increase, and the muscles tense. At the same time, certain unessential activities, such as digestion, are curtailed. Saliva and mucus dry up, thereby increasing the size of the air passages to the lungs. Thus, an early sign of stress is a dry mouth. Endorphins, the body's natural painkillers, are secreted, and the surface blood vessels constrict to reduce bleeding in case of injury. The spleen releases more red blood cells to help carry oxygen, and the bone marrow produces more white corpuscles to fight infection.

Most of these physiological changes result from activation of two neuro-endocrine systems controlled by the hypothalamus: the *sympathetic system* and the *adrenal-cortical system*. The hypothalamus has been called the brain's stress center because of its dual function in emergencies. Its first function is to activate the sympathetic division of the autonomic nervous system (see Chapter 2). Nerve impulses from the hypothalamus are transmitted to nuclei in the brain stem that control the functioning of the autonomic nervous system. The sympathetic division of the autonomic system acts directly on the smooth muscles and internal organs to produce some of the bodily changes described above—for example, increased heart rate, elevated blood pressure, dilated pupils. The sympathetic system also stimulates the inner core of the adrenal glands (the adrenal medulla) to release the hormones *epinephrine* (adrenaline) and *norepinephrine* into the blood stream. Epinephrine has the same effect on the muscles and organs as the sympathetic nervous system does (for example, it increases heart rate and blood pressure) and thus serves to perpetuate a state of arousal. Norepinephrine, through its action on the pituitary gland, is indirectly responsible for the release of extra sugar from the liver (see Figure 15-1).

The above events describe only the first function of the hypothalamus: activation of the sympathetic system. The hypothalamus carries out its second function (activation of the adrenal-cortical system) by signaling the *pituitary gland*, which lies just below it (refer back to Figure 2-7), to secrete two important hormones. One of these stimulates the thyroid gland which, in turn, makes more energy available to the body. The other, *adrenocorticotrophic hormone* (ACTH), is the body's "major stress hormone" (see Chapter 2). ACTH stimulates the outer layer of the adrenal glands (the adrenal cortex) resulting in the release of a group of hormones (the major one is cortisol) that regulate the blood levels of glucose and of certain minerals. The amount of cortisol in blood or urine samples is often used as a measure of stress. ACTH also signals other endocrine glands to release about 30 hormones, each of which plays a role in the body's adjustment to emergency situations.

This innate pattern of responses has been called the "fight-or-flight" response because it prepares the organism to attack or flee (Cannon, 1929). The response pattern is triggered by a wide variety of physical and psychological stressors. While the physiological components of the fight-or-flight response are valuable in helping an individual deal with a physical threat

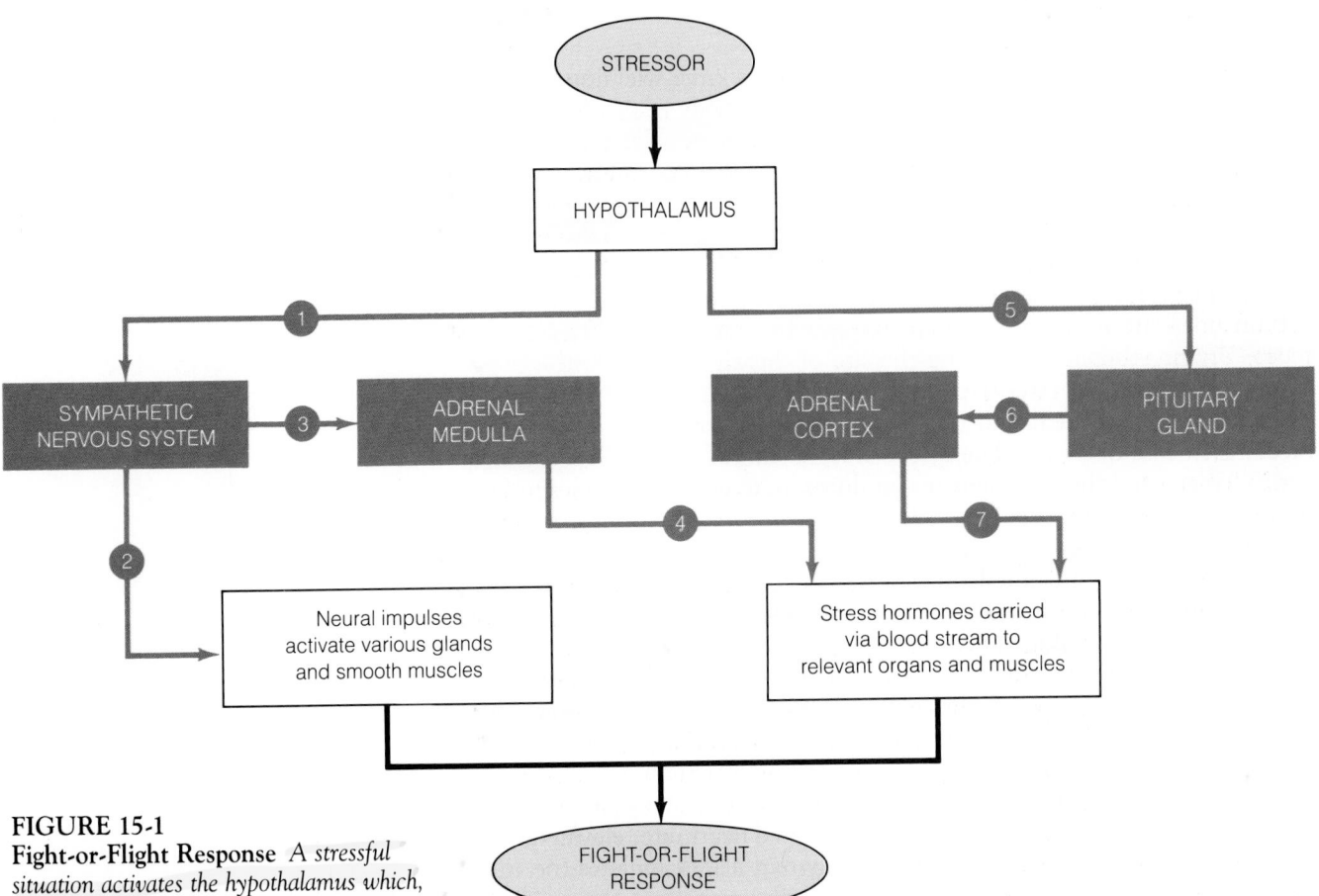

FIGURE 15-1
Fight-or-Flight Response *A stressful situation activates the hypothalamus which, in turn, controls two neuroendocrine systems: the sympathetic system (shown in red) and the adrenal-cortical system (shown in green). The sympathetic nervous system, responding to neural impulses from the hypothalamus (1), activates various organs and smooth muscles under its control (2). For example, it increases heart rate and dilates the pupils. The sympathetic nervous system also signals the adrenal medulla (3) to release epinephrine and norepinephrine into the bloodstream (4). The adrenal-cortical system is activated when the hypothalamus secretes CRF, a chemical that acts on the pituitary gland lying just below the hypothalamus (5). The pituitary gland, in turn, secretes the hormone ACTH, which is carried via the bloodstream to the adrenal cortex (6) where it stimulates the release of a group of hormones, including cortisol, that regulate blood glucose levels (7). ACTH also signals the other endocrine glands to release some 30 hormones. The combined effect of the various stress hormones carried via the bloodstream plus the neural activity of the sympathetic division of the autonomic nervous system constitute the fight-or-flight response.*

requiring immediate action, they are not very adaptive for dealing with many modern-day sources of stress. In situations in which action is impossible or in which the threat continues and must be dealt with over an extended period of time, such intense physiological arousal can be harmful.

Laboratory studies with animals have shown that prolonged exposure to a stressor produces a number of bodily changes: enlarged adrenal glands, shrunken lymph nodes, and stomach ulcers (Selye, 1979). These changes decrease the organism's ability to resist other stressors, including infectious and disease-producing agents. As we will see later, chronic arousal can make a person susceptible to illness.

Variations of the Stress Response

Initially, researchers believed that the stress response pattern we have described was *nonspecific*—that is, it occurred automatically and in roughly the same form to a wide range of noxious events or stressors. But contemporary theorists emphasize the importance of cognitive and emotional factors in determining physiological reactions to stressful events. Thus, whether or not a particular stressor elicits a stress reaction and the pattern of that reaction depends on the meaning of the situation for the individual.

Physiological arousal in response to a stressor may represent a mixture of *distress* (anxiety, fear) and *effort* (active attempts to cope with the situation).

Evidence indicates that the pattern of physiological responses varies depending on the relative amounts of distress and effort (Frankenhaeuser, 1983). In a situation that involves effort with a minimum of distress (the individual is coping effectively and does not feel threatened), the sympathetic system is more active than the adrenal-cortical system. This type of stress response is indicated by elevated levels of epinephrine and norepinephrine in the blood. In a situation that involves distress without effort (either the individual feels helpless to act or no coping response is possible), the adrenal-cortical system is more active than the sympathetic system. This type of stress response is indicated by elevated blood levels of cortisol. Most stressful situations involve both distress and effort and, consequently, both systems are activated to varying degrees.

We have focused on the negative aspects of the physiological arousal elicited by stressors. Studies have shown, however, that exposure to intermittent stressors can have later benefits in the form of "physiological toughness." In essence, intermittent stress (occasional exposure but with recovery periods) leads to stress tolerance later on (Dienstbier, 1989). For example, young rats who are removed from their cages and handled daily (a stressor for them) are less fearful when exposed to other stressors as adults and show a quicker return to their normal levels of the stress hormones (Levine, 1960; Meaney et al., 1987). Rats who were "toughened" by having to swim in cold water for a period of 14 consecutive days performed better on a later swim test and showed less depletion of epinephrine and norepinephrine than rats who had received no prior exposure to cold water (Weiss et al., 1975).

The physiological responses that appear to be beneficial are those associated with effort and arousal of the sympathetic system. Increases in epinephrine and norepinephrine have been found to correlate positively with performance on a variety of tasks (from students taking tests to paratroopers engaged in training jumps): high levels of these hormones in blood and urine were related to better performance (Johansson & Frankenhaeuser, 1973; Ursin, 1978). The physiological responses related to poor performance are the ones associated with distress and arousal of the adrenal-cortical system.

Research on the positive aspects of stress arousal is still in an exploratory stage. The interaction between the sympathetic system and the adrenal-cortical system is exceedingly complex, and it is difficult to determine their separate effects using current research methods (primarily, measures of the chemistry of the blood and/or urine). However, the idea that stressors can have beneficial effects under certain circumstances has generated increased interest among researchers.

PSYCHOLOGICAL REACTIONS TO STRESS

Some negative emotions acompany the physiological responses that occur with stress, as well as an impairment of cognitive functioning.

Cognitive Impairment

Performance on a task, particularly a complex task, tends to deteriorate at high levels of emotional arousal (refer back to Figure 11-5). Stress impairs our ability to concentrate and to organize our thoughts logically. Instead of concentrating on the task at hand, our thinking tends to be dominated by

worries about the consequences of our actions and by self-deprecatory thoughts. For instance, students who are especially prone to worry about examinations—a condition called *test anxiety*—tend to worry about possible failures and about their inadequacies. They can become so distracted by these negative thoughts that they fail to follow instructions and neglect or misinterpret obvious information cues provided by the questions. As anxiety mounts, they have difficulty retrieving facts they had learned well.

In times of stress, people tend to resort to behavior patterns that have worked in the past. The cautious person may become even more cautious and withdraw entirely, whereas the aggressive person may lose control and strike out heedlessly in all directions. If the initial attempts at coping are unsuccessful, anxiety often intensifies and the individual becomes more rigid in his or her efforts, unable to perceive alternative solutions to the problem. People have been trapped in flaming buildings because they persisted in pushing against exit doors that opened inward; in their panic, they failed to consider the possibility of an alternative action.

Emotional Responses

Stressful situations produce emotional reactions ranging from exhilaration (when the event is appraised as a demanding but manageable challenge) to the more common emotions of anxiety, anger, discouragement, and depression. If the stressful situation continues, our emotions may switch back and forth among any of these, depending on the success of our coping efforts.

ANXIETY The primary response to a situation appraised as threatening is anxiety. By anxiety, we mean the unpleasant emotion characterized by such terms as "worry," "apprehension," "tension," and "fear" that we all experience at times in varying degrees. Different theorists conceptualize anxiety differently, depending on what they view as threatening for people. Consequently, we will not attempt to provide a more precise definition.

Anxiety is generally characterized as either normal or neurotic, depending on whether or not an individual's reaction seems appropriate to the situation that caused it. Normal anxiety, or *objective anxiety*, is adaptive; it motivates the person to deal with the harmful situation. *Neurotic anxiety*, which is out of proportion to the actual danger posed (such as stage fright), often reduces the person's ability to cope. We will discuss neurotic anxiety reactions in Chapter 16 when we consider phobias and other anxiety disorders.

Freud viewed objective anxiety as a realistic response to external danger, synonymous with fear. He believed that neurotic anxiety stems from unacceptable internal impulses that the individual is trying to control. Since these impulses are largely unconscious, the person is not aware of the reason for his or her anxiety. Many psychologists still find it meaningful to distinguish between fear and anxiety. However, since it is not clear that the two emotions can be differentiated—either on the basis of physiological responses or on the basis of the individual's descriptions of feelings—we will use the terms "anxiety" and "fear" interchangeably. Just as there are varying degrees of anxiety, ranging from mild apprehension to panic, there are probably varying degrees of awareness of the cause of an individual's discomfort. People who suffer from internal conflicts often have some idea of why they are anxious, even though they cannot specify all the factors involved clearly.

Freud believed that neurotic anxiety is the result of an unconscious conflict between *id impulses* (mainly sexual and aggressive) and the constraints imposed by the *ego* and *superego* (see Chapter 14). Many id impulses pose a threat to the individual because they are contradictory to personal or social values. A young girl may not consciously acknowledge that she has strong hostile feelings toward her mother because these feelings conflict with her belief that a child should love her parents. If she acknowledged her true feelings, she would destroy her self-concept as a loving daughter and would risk the loss of her mother's love and support. When she begins to feel angry toward her mother, the aroused anxiety serves as a *signal* of potential danger. The girl then engages in *defensive maneuvers* to exclude anxiety-producing impulses from her conscious awareness. These maneuvers, or defense mechanisms, form an important part of Freud's theory of maladaptive behavior and will be discussed later.

When a person reacts with intense anxiety to a situation that others view as only mildly stressful, then we assume that the source of danger is associated more with internal feelings than with the external stressor. While Freud saw unconscious conflicts as the internal source of anxiety, behaviorists have focused on ways in which anxiety becomes associated with certain situations via learning. For instance, a little girl who is punished by her parents whenever she rebels against their wishes and attempts to assert herself eventually learns to associate the pain of punishment with assertive behavior. When she thinks about asserting her own wishes and defying her parents, she becomes anxious.

Sometimes fears learned in childhood are difficult to extinguish. If a child's first reaction is to avoid or escape the anxiety-producing situation, he or she may not be able to determine when the situation is no longer dangerous. The little girl who has been punished for assertive behavior may never learn that it is appropriate for her to express her wishes in certain situations.

Another approach suggests that people experience anxiety whenever they encounter a situation that seems beyond their control. It might be a new situation that we must organize and integrate into our view of the world and

While aggression is not an inevitable response to frustration, it is one of them.

of ourselves. It might be an ambiguous situation—as many of our experiences are—that we must fit into our concept of how the world operates. A feeling of being helpless and not in control of what is happening seems central to the experience of anxiety. As we will see later, the degree of anxiety we feel in stressful situations is largely dependent on how much control we believe we have over the situation.

ANGER AND AGGRESSION   Another common reaction to a stressful situation is anger, which may lead to aggression. Laboratory studies have shown that some animals behave aggressively in response to a variety of stressors, including overcrowding, electric shock, and the failure to receive an expected food reward. If a pair of animals is shocked in a cage from which they cannot escape, they begin fighting when the shock starts and stop fighting when it ends.

Children often become angry and exhibit aggressive behavior when they experience *frustration*. As we noted in Chapter 11, the *frustration-aggression hypothesis* assumes that whenever a person's effort to reach a goal is blocked, an aggressive drive is induced that motivates behavior to injure the object—or person—causing the frustration. While research has shown that aggression is not an inevitable response to frustration, it is certainly one of them. When one child takes a toy from another, the second is likely to attack the first in an attempt to regain the toy. Adults usually express their aggression verbally rather than physically; they are more apt to exchange insults than they are blows.

Direct aggression toward the source of frustration is not always possible or wise. Sometimes the source is vague and intangible. The person does not know what to attack but feels angry and seeks an object on which to vent these feelings. Sometimes the individual responsible for the frustration is so powerful that an attack would be dangerous. When circumstances block direct attack on the cause of frustration, aggression may be *displaced*: the aggressive action may be directed toward an innocent person or object rather than toward the actual cause of the frustration. A man who is reprimanded at work may take out unexpressed resentment on his family. A student, angry at her professor for an unfair grade, may blow up at her roommate. A child frustrated by experiences at school may resort to vandalism of school property.

APATHY AND DEPRESSION Complicating the study of human behavior is the tendency of different individuals to respond to similar situations in different ways. Although a common response to frustration is active aggression, the opposite response of withdrawal and apathy is also common. If the stressful conditions continue and the individual is not successful in coping with them, apathy may deepen into depression.

We do not know why one person reacts with aggression and another reacts with apathy to the same situation, but it seems likely that learning is an important factor. Reactions to frustration can be learned in much the same manner as other behaviors. Children who strike out angrily when frustrated and find that their needs are then satisfied (either through their own efforts or because a parent rushes to placate them) will probably resort to the same behavior the next time their motives are thwarted. Children whose aggressive outbursts are never successful (they find they have no power to satisfy their needs by means of their own actions) may give up and withdraw when confronted with subsequent frustrating situations.

Studies have shown that animals and people can learn to be helpless when faced with stressful situations. The theory of *learned helplessness* originated with a series of laboratory experiments discussed in some detail in Chapter 7. A dog placed in a shuttle box (an apparatus with two compartments separated by a barrier) quickly learns to jump to the opposite compartment to escape a mild electric shock delivered to its feet through a grid on the floor. If a light is turned on a few seconds before the grid is electrified, the dog can learn to avoid the shock entirely by jumping to the safe compartment when signaled by the light. However, if the dog has had a previous history of being in another enclosure in which shocks are unavoidable and

Prisoners in a Nazi concentration camp at the moment of liberation (Buchenwald, Germany, 1945).

CRITICAL DISCUSSION

Coping with Captivity

Imagine yourself locked in a small, windowless cell with no one to talk to, no books or newspapers to read, and no paper or pencil with which to write. Months go by with no chance for you to breathe fresh air or to see the sun, moon, grass, or trees. The sparse food your captors provide is of little nutritional value; you are constantly hungry. Injuries and illnesses go untreated; there is no medical or dental care. Your hands are often bound, and you may be chained to your bed for days on end.

It is difficult to conceive of many situations that would engender greater feelings of frustration, helplessness, and hopelessness. Yet many United States servicemen captured during the Korean and Vietnam wars endured this type of solitary confinement for months or, in some cases, for years. One factor that helped the Vietnam prisoners cope with captivity was their previous training in prison-survival techniques.

Studies of people who are confined as hostages, as prisoners of war, or as inmates of concentration camps indicate that apathy and depression are common reactions to frustrating and traumatic conditions from which there is no hope of escape. Faced with continual deprivation, torture, and threats of death, many prisoners become detached, emotionless, and indifferent to events taking place around them. Some may abandon any attempt to cope with the situation or to continue living. Interviews with American servicemen released from prison camps after the Korean War showed that almost all experienced feelings of withdrawal and apathy at some time during their imprisonment. Some men gave up altogether; they curled up on their bunks and waited to die, making no effort to eat or to take care of themselves. Two remedies seemed helpful in saving a man close to death: getting him on his feet and doing something, no matter how trivial, and getting him interested in some current or future project. In a sense both remedies provided the individual with a goal toward which he could direct his efforts (Strassman, Thaler, & Schein, 1956).

Concern about the reactions of American prisoners during the Korean War led military officials to develop programs that would prepare servicemen to cope with the frustrations of imprisonment. Reports from men imprisoned during the Vietnam War indicate that their survival training had been helpful. Knowing how to keep physically and mentally active, to provide support for each other, and to focus on ways to solve daily problems did much to combat depression and

inescapable—where nothing the animal does terminates the shock—then it is very difficult for the dog to learn the avoidance response in a new situation when it is appropriate. The animal simply sits and endures the shock in the shuttle box, even though an easy jump to the opposite compartment would eliminate discomfort. Some dogs never learn, even if the experimenter demonstrates the proper procedure by carrying them over the barrier.

The experimenters concluded that the animals had learned through prior experience that they were helpless to avoid the shock and so gave up trying to do so, even in a new situation. This learned helplessness was difficult to overcome (Overmeier & Seligman, 1967).

Numerous experiments have attempted to demonstrate learned helplessness with human subjects, but the results have been difficult to interpret. Uncontrollable events do not always produce helplessness and passivity; sometimes they generate invigorated effort (Wortman & Brehm, 1975). Clearly, the animal model of learned helplessness is too simple to provide a comprehensive account of human behavior. As we will see when we discuss depression in the next chapter, the theory of learned helplessness has been elaborated to take into account the attributions a person makes about negative events. It is not uncontrollable events per se but how the individual interprets them that creates feelings of helplessness and depression. Nevertheless, the feeling that we have control over our lives and over what happens to us is an extremely important factor in our ability to cope with stress.

feelings of helplessness. Returned POWs reported that the most helpful behaviors included communication, thinking about the future, and physical exercise. The least useful behaviors were thinking about suicide, talking to oneself, and worrying about the family (Richlin, 1977).

In many North Vietnamese prison camps, the prisoners were placed in solitary cells, and rules forbidding communication were strictly enforced by the guards. To be caught talking to a fellow prisoner meant severe torture. However, some POWs developed ingenious methods of communication, which they taught to each other. The sounds of finger tapping, coughing, spitting, and clearing the throat were used to convey messages. A prisoner could also communicate by dragging his sandals according to a code as he walked past another prisoner's cell. And a POW sweeping the prison compound could send a message to every prisoner in the area by the way he moved his broom (Stockdale, 1984).

Having strategies for coping with the stress of imprisonment appears to have aided survival. Although American POWs were held captive in Vietnam more than twice as long (8 years in some cases) as American POWs in Korea, the servicemen who had been imprisoned in Vietnam returned in better physical and emotional condition than did the Korean War POWs. The prisoner mortality rate in Vietnam during captivity was much lower as well: roughly 38 percent of all American servicemen imprisoned during the Korean War did not survive captivity, whereas only about 15 percent of the American POWs in Vietnam died while imprisoned.

However, before concluding that survival training produced the differences in mortality rates, we should realize that the Korean and Vietnam POWs differed in other respects. Most of the men captured during the Korean War were in the infantry. Some were officers, but the majority were enlisted men. Most of the men imprisoned in

North Vietnam were pilots. On the average, they were more mature at the time of capture (average age 31 years) and more highly educated than the Korean POWs. Due to the nature of pilot selection procedures, the Vietnam POWs were also probably more emotionally stable and highly motivated than the average serviceman. Their maturity, emotional stability, and intellectual resources undoubtedly played vital roles in their ability to survive. Another factor that contributed to the lower survival rate in Korea was the extreme cold to which POWs were subjected, which depleted their physical strength.

Thus, survival training was not the only variable affecting the ability of Vietnam POWs to endure imprisonment. However, such preparation does appear to help people cope with the stress of captivity. As a result, the United States government now provides survival training for military and diplomatic personnel who have a high risk of capture.

SOURCES OF STRESS

Countless events create stress. Some are major changes affecting large numbers of people—events such as war, nuclear accidents, and earthquakes. Others are major changes in the life of an individual—for instance, moving to a new area, changing jobs, getting married, losing a friend, suffering a serious illness. In addition to the big changes that require major adjustments are life's little hassles, such as losing your wallet, getting stuck in traffic, arguing with your boss, and so on.

Although it has become popular to focus on external stressors, the source of stress can be within the individual in the form of a *conflict* between opposing motives.

Traumatic Events

The most obvious sources of stress are traumatic events—situations of extreme danger that are outside the range of usual human experience. These include natural disasters, such as earthquakes and floods; man-made disasters, such as wars and nuclear accidents; catastrophic accidents, such as car or plane crashes; and physical assaults, such as rape or attempted murder.

Victims of the 1988 earthquake in Armenia.

These traumatic events produce severe stress responses in everyone and require extensive and prolonged coping efforts.

While the immediate reactions to traumatic events vary widely (depending on the nature and severity of the catastrophe and its degree of unexpectedness), a common behavior pattern—the *disaster syndrome*—has been observed. At first the victims are stunned, dazed, and appear to be unaware of their injuries or of danger. They may wander around in a disoriented state. In the next stage they are still passive and unable to initiate even simple tasks, but will follow orders readily. In the third stage they become anxious and apprehensive, have difficulty concentrating, and may repeat the story of the catastrophe over and over again.

Experiencing a traumatic event that is beyond the normal range of human suffering can have a profound and prolonged effect on the individual. Some survivors of catastrophes develop a syndrome that is called *post-traumatic stress disorder*. The major symptoms include: a) feeling *numb* to the world, with a lack of interest in former activities and a sense of estrangement from others; b) reliving the trauma repeatedly in memories and in dreams; and c) anxiety, which may manifest itself in sleep disturbances, difficulty concentrating, and over-alertness. Some individuals feel guilty about surviving when others have not.

Post-traumatic stress disorder may develop immediately after the disaster, or it may be brought on by some minor stress weeks or even months later. And it may last a long time. A study of survivors of the Nazi concentration camps found that 97 percent were still troubled with anxiety 20 years after they were freed from the camps. Many still relived the traumas of persecution in their dreams and were fearful that something terrible would happen to their spouses or their children whenever they were out of sight (Krystal, 1968).

Post-traumatic stress disorder became widely accepted as a diagnostic category because of difficulties experienced by Vietnam veterans. Although stress reactions to the horrors of battle had been noted in earlier wars (in World War I it was called "shell shock"; in World War II, "combat fatigue"), veterans of Vietnam seemed especially prone to develop the long-term symptoms we have described. A recent survey estimated that 15 percent of

Vietnam veterans have suffered from post-traumatic stress disorder since their discharge (Centers for Disease Control, 1988).

The soldiers who fought in Vietnam were young (average age 19) and the conditions of warfare were unusual: absence of clear front lines, unpredictable attacks in dense jungle conditions, difficulty in distinguishing between Vietnamese allies and enemies, and the lack of support for the war on the home front. To this day, some Vietnam veterans still reexperience in memories or in dreams the traumatic events that happened to them. As one veteran wrote: "The war is over in history. But it never ended for me" (Marbly, 1987, p. 193).

The awareness that extraordinary traumas can have long-lasting effects on the victims has led to attempts to prevent post-traumatic stress disorders. Many community and national organizations are now prepared to send in teams of mental health professionals immediately following a major disaster to talk with the survivors about their experiences and to help them deal with their emotions. It is too early to evaluate the effectiveness of these types of interventions, but most observers believe that they will help reduce the likelihood of post-traumatic stress disorders.

Life Changes

Any change in life that requires a person to adapt to new circumstances can cause stress, regardless of whether or not the change is beneficial. The arrival of a new baby, for example—an event usually anticipated with joy—causes numerous readjustments in the lives of both parents. Studies of personal histories suggest that physical and emotional disorders tend to cluster around periods of major change.

In an attempt to measure the impact of life changes, two researchers developed the *Life Events Scale*, shown in Table 15-1 (Holmes & Rahe, 1967). The life events are ranked in order from the most stressful (death of a spouse) to the least stressful (minor violations of the law). To arrive at this scale, the investigators examined thousands of interviews and medical histories to identify the kinds of events that people found stressful. Because marriage (a positive event, but one that requires a considerable amount of adjustment) appeared to be a critical event for most people, it was placed in the middle of the scale and was assigned an arbitrary value of 50. The investigators then asked approximately 400 men and women (of varying ages, backgrounds, and marital status) to compare marriage with a number of other life events. They were asked such questions as, "Does the event call for more or less readjustment than marriage?" and "Would the readjustment take shorter or longer to accomplish?" Those interviewed were then asked to assign a point value to each event on the basis of their evaluation of its severity and the time required for adjustment. These ratings were used to construct the scale in Table 15-1.

You may not agree with the exact ordering of these events. Studies have shown some cultural and age differences. For example, older adults rank sex difficulties thirteenth from the top in terms of stressfulness, while adolescents put them fifth (Ruch & Holmes, 1971). European subjects rank death of a close family member as less stressful than do American subjects. Nevertheless, consensus tends to be high (Holmes, 1979).

To determine the amount of life change an individual has experienced, the person is asked to indicate which of the events listed on the scale happened to them over a fixed period of time (for example, the past 6 months or

TABLE 15-1
Life Events Scale *This scale, also known as the Holmes and Rahe Social Readjustment Rating Scale, measures stress in terms of life changes.* (After Holmes & Rahe, 1967)

LIFE EVENT	VALUE
Death of spouse	100
Divorce	73
Marital separation	65
Jail term	63
Death of close family member	63
Personal injury or illness	53
Marriage	50
Fired from job	47
Marital reconciliation	45
Retirement	45
Change in health of family member	44
Pregnancy	40
Sex difficulties	39
Gain of new family member	39
Business readjustment	39
Change in financial state	38
Death of close friend	37
Change to different line of work	36
Foreclosure of mortgage	30
Change in responsibilities at work	29
Son or daughter leaving home	29
Trouble with in-laws	29
Outstanding personal achievement	28
Wife begins or stops work	26
Begin or end school	26
Change in living conditions	25
Revision of personal habits	24
Trouble with boss	23
Change in residence	20
Change in school	20
Change in recreation	19
Change in church activities	19
Change in social activities	18
Change in sleeping habits	16
Change in eating habits	15
Vacation	13
Christmas	12
Minor legal violations	11

the past 2 years). The values of the events are summed to give a total life-change score. The investigator then looks at the relationship between life-change scores and the individual's physical and emotional health.

Studies using this method have found that high life-change scores (total-ing 300 or higher) are associated with an increased frequency of various illnesses, psychological disorders, athletic injuries, and even traffic accidents (Holmes & Masuda, 1974; Rahe & Arthur, 1977).

To account for the findings relating life changes to illness, the developers of the Life Events Scale hypothesized that the more major changes an individual experiences, the greater effort the individual must expend to adapt. This effort presumably lowers the body's natural resistance to disease. However, other researchers have questioned these conclusions for the following reasons:

1. It is difficult to separate the effects of stress from such factors as diet, smoking, drinking, and other general health habits. Individuals who are trying to cope with major life changes (a new job, the loss of a spouse) may increase their alcohol intake, may eat more snack foods, may get less sleep, and may fail to exercise. An increased susceptibility to illness in such cases is more likely to stem from changes in health habits than from the direct action of stress on resistance to disease.

2. The health data for life-change studies are derived from self-reports and/or medical reports. People differ in their tendencies to focus on physical symptoms and to seek medical help; a stomachache that one person ignores may send another person to the doctor. Moreover, people are more apt to focus on symptoms and go to a doctor if they are discontented with their lives than if they are happily involved in activities they enjoy. Thus, stress may be more important in triggering help-seeking behavior than in triggering actual illness.

3. Some of the items on the Life Events Scale may be the *result* of illness rather than the cause. An individual's poor emotional or physical health may contribute to marital, job, and financial difficulties or to changes in social activities and sleeping habits.

4. The Life Events Scale assumes that change, per se, is stressful. However, subsequent research has not found *positive* life changes to be related to poor health, and sometimes the absence of change (boredom) is stressful. Whether or not change (or its absence) is stressful depends on the individual's personal history and present life circumstances.

More recently developed scales deal with this last objection by asking individuals to indicate the desirability and impact of each event—to judge it as good or bad and to estimate its effect on their lives. Thus, whether a new job or a change of residence is good or bad is left up to the person answering the survey. Studies using these ratings have found that people with a large number of events they regard as bad are more likely to report physical and emotional problems 6 months later (Sarason, Johnson, & Siegel, 1978; Dohrenwend et al., 1978). Uncontrollable negative life events (death of a loved one, job loss, sudden illness) are especially associated with depression (Dohrenwend & Dohrenwend, 1974).

Despite the criticisms of life-events studies, there does appear to be a relationship between life changes and health; the cumulative effects of adapting to environmental demands may lower the body's resistance to disease. However, the correlations are low (typically .30 or less). The majority of individuals manage to cope with life changes without becoming ill. Clearly, other factors are involved. We will discuss some of these in a later section.

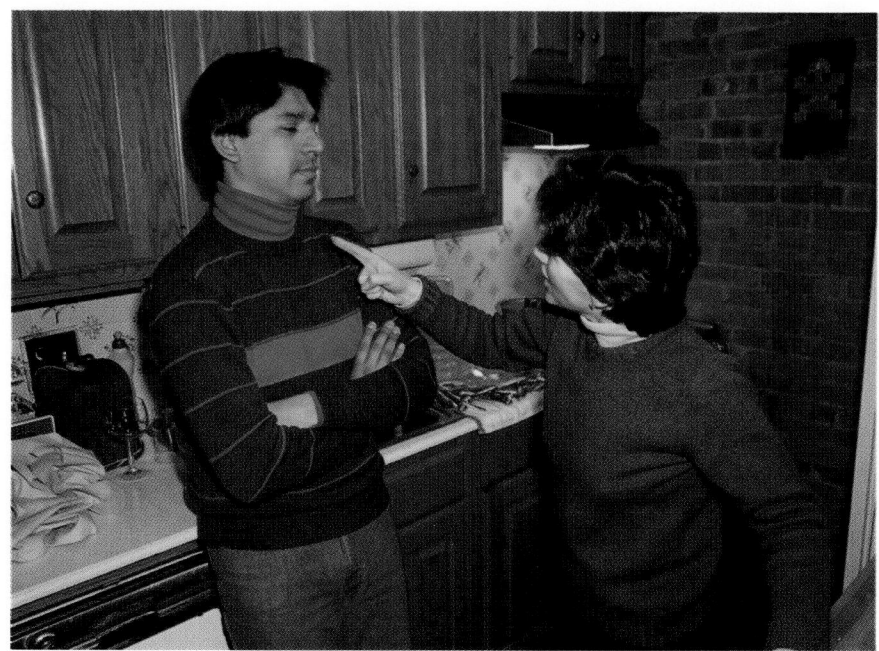

Daily Hassles

Perhaps it is not the major life events but the minor frustrations and annoyances in our daily lives that produce the greatest stress. To investigate this possibility, a group of investigators conducted a year-long study of the effects of life's daily hassles on middle-aged men and women. They gave their subjects life-events questionnaires and checklists on which to record the "hassles," or irritating things that happened every day, as well as the "uplifts," or pleasant things. Examples of hassles include misplacing items, concerns about owing money, too many interruptions, too many responsibilities, not enough time for family, and arguments. The researchers found that the accumulation of daily hassles was an even better predictor of emotional and physical health than were the major events in people's lives (DeLongis et al., 1982).

It appears, too, that the stressfulness of major life changes is partly a function of the daily hassles they create. For example, a widow's grief over the loss of her husband may be compounded when she has to cope with such unfamiliar responsibilities as auto repairs, handling the changed finances, and preparing tax returns. To the extent that life changes (job loss, divorce, death of a loved one) disrupt an individual's patterns of daily living, they are apt to create hassles.

Again, there are large individual differences in the way people react to daily hassles. While the majority of subjects report depressed or anxious moods and an increase in physical symptoms on days that are full of hassles, about a third report the opposite: increases in daily stress were accompanied by somewhat improved health and mood (DeLongis, Folkman, & Lazarus, 1988). Those who seem to thrive when stress levels increase tend to have greater self-esteem and more friends and relatives they can count on for emotional support. We will discuss the ways in which social supports can help to buffer stress in the next section.

People with high self-esteem see themselves as able to cope with a broad array of problems and are less likely to feel overwhelmed when confronted

Self-esteem helps an individual cope with stressful demands.

with stressful demands than people who do not have positive views of themselves. Indeed, what a person considers a hassle depends a lot on his or her coping skills. For example, an individual who is well organized and realistic in scheduling time and work will have fewer deadline hassles than one who procrastinates. A person who is skillful in interpersonal relationships will have fewer hassles with fellow workers than one who is not.

Conflict

Unresolved conflicts are another source of stress. Conflict occurs when a person must choose between incompatible, or mutually exclusive, goals or courses of action. Many of the things people desire prove to be incompatible. You want to play on your college volleyball team but cannot devote the time required and still earn the grades necessary to apply to graduate school. You want to join your friends for a pizza party but are afraid you will fail tomorrow's exam if you don't stay home and study. You *don't* want to go to your uncle's for dinner but you *don't* want to listen to your mother's complaints if you reject the invitation. The goals in these instances are incompatible because the action needed to achieve one automatically prevents you from reaching the other.

Even if two goals are equally attractive—for example, you receive two good job offers—you may agonize over the decision and experience regrets after making a choice. This stress would not have occurred if you had been offered only one job.

Conflict may also arise when two inner needs or motives are in opposition. In our society, the conflicts that are the most pervasive and difficult to resolve generally occur between the following motives:

■ *Independence versus dependence* In times of stress, we may want to resort to the dependence characteristics of childhood, to have someone take care of us and solve our problems. But we are taught that the ability to stand on our own and to assume responsibilities is a mark of maturity.

- *Intimacy versus isolation*   The desire to be close to another person and to share our innermost thoughts and emotions may conflict with the fear of being hurt or rejected if we expose too much of ourselves.

- *Cooperation versus competition*   In our society much emphasis is placed on competition and success. Competition begins in early childhood among siblings, continues through school, and culminates in business and professional rivalry. At the same time, we are urged to cooperate and to help others.

- *Impulse expression versus moral standards*   Impulses must be regulated to some degree in all societies. We noted in Chapter 3 that much of childhood learning involves internalizing the cultural restrictions placed on innate impulses. Sex and aggression are two areas in which our impulses frequently conflict with moral standards, and violation of these standards can generate feelings of guilt.

These four areas present the greatest potential for serious conflict. Trying to find a workable compromise between opposing motives can create considerable stress.

Situational Factors that Influence Stress

Cognitive appraisal, self-esteem, and coping skills are personal variables that influence the severity of stress. People respond differently to the same stressful situation, depending on its meaning for them and the amount of confidence they have in their ability to cope with it. But certain characteristics of the stressor have been found to influence the severity of stress— namely, its predictability and controllability. Another situational factor that exerts a powerful influence on the experience of stress is the availability of social supports.

PREDICTABILITY   Being able to predict the occurrence of a stressful event—even if the individual cannot control it—usually reduces the severity of the stress. Laboratory experiments show that both human beings and animals prefer predictable aversive events to unpredictable ones. In one study, rats were given a choice between a signaled shock and an unsignaled shock. If the rat pressed a bar at the start of a series of shock trials, each shock was preceded by a warning tone. If the rat failed to press the bar, no warning tones sounded during that series of trials. All of the rats quickly learned to press the bar, showing a marked preference for predictable shock (Abbott, Schoen, & Badia, 1984).

Human subjects generally choose predictable over unpredictable shocks, too. They also show less emotional arousal and report less distress while waiting for predictable shocks to occur, and they perceive predictable shocks as less aversive than unpredictable ones of the same intensity (Katz & Wykes, 1985). How do we explain these results? With unpredictable shock, there is no safe period; with predictable shock, the subject (human or animal) can relax to some extent until the signal warns that shock is about to occur. Another possibility is that a warning signal before an aversive event allows the subject to initiate some sort of preparatory process that acts to lessen the effects of a noxious stimulus on the nervous system.

In real-life situations, lack of predictability—or *uncertainty*—can make it very difficult for an individual to deal with stressful events. For example, one of the major problems faced by cancer patients who receive treatment is that they cannot be sure whether or not they have been cured until many years have passed. Every day they must confront the uncertainty of a potentially disastrous future.

A similar gnawing uncertainty has created chronic stress for people who lived near Three Mile Island (Middletown, Pennsylvania) when an accident at the nuclear power plant released radioactive gases. Many of the residents believe that they were exposed to radiation and are apprehensive about the future effects of that exposure. Compared to a control group, these residents reported more emotional and physical problems and showed poorer task performance 2 years after the accident (Baum, Gatchel, Fleming, & Lake, 1981).

Another example is women whose husbands were reported missing in action in Vietnam. Not knowing whether their husbands were alive or dead made it difficult for them to resolve their grief and proceed with their lives. Compared with wives of men who were killed in action and with wives of men who were prisoners, women married to MIAs showed the poorest physical and emotional health (Hunter, 1979).

CONTROLLABILITY Having some control over a stressful event also reduces the severity of the stress. In one study, subjects were shown color photographs of victims of violent deaths. The experimental group could terminate the viewing by pressing a button. The control subjects saw the same photographs for the time duration determined by the experimental group, but they could not terminate exposure. The experimental group showed much less anxiety (measured by the galvanic skin response, GSR) in response to the photographs than did the group that had no control over the duration of viewing (Geer & Maisel, 1972).

In another study, two groups of subjects were exposed to a loud, extremely unpleasant noise. Subjects in one group were told that they could terminate the noise by pressing a button, but they were urged not to do so unless it was absolutely necessary. Subjects in the other group had no control over the noise. None of the subjects who had a control button actually pressed it, so the noise exposure was the same for both groups. Nevertheless, performance on subsequent problem-solving tasks was significantly worse for the group that had no control, indicating that they were more disturbed by the noise than was the group that had the potential for control. The belief that we can control the duration of an aversive event appears to lessen anxiety, even if the control is never exercised or if the belief is erroneous (Glass & Singer, 1972).

SOCIAL SUPPORTS The emotional support and concern of other people can make stress more bearable. Divorce, the death of a loved one, or a serious illness is usually more devastating if an individual must face it alone. A study of Israeli parents who had lost a son (either through accidents or in the Yom Kippur War) found that bereavement exacted a heavier toll for those who were widowed or divorced. Their mortality rate in the 10-year period following their loss was higher than the mortality rate for parents who could share their grief with each other (Levav et al., 1988).

Numerous studies indicate that people who have many social ties (spouse, friends, relatives, and group memberships) live longer and are less apt to succumb to stress-related illnesses than are people who have few supportive social contacts (Cohen & Wills, 1985). Friends and family can provide support in many ways. They can bolster self-esteem by loving us despite our problems. They can provide information and advice, companionship to distract us from our worries, and financial or material aid. All of these tend to reduce

Disasters tend to rally individuals to work toward a common goal.

feelings of helplessness and to increase our confidence in our ability to cope.

Sometimes, however, family and friends can increase the stress. Minimizing the seriousness of the problem or giving blind assurance that everything will be all right may produce more anxiety than failing to offer support at all. A study of graduate students facing crucial examinations suggests that spouses who are realistically supportive ("I'm worried, but I know you'll do the best you can") are more helpful than spouses who deny any possibility of failure ("I'm not worried; I'm sure you'll pass"). In the latter case, the student has to worry not only about failing the exam but also about losing respect in the eyes of the spouse (Mechanic, 1962).

Stress is easier to tolerate when the cause of the stress is shared by others. Community disasters (floods, earthquakes, tornadoes, wars) often seem to bring out the best in people (Nilson et al., 1981). Individual anxieties and conflicts tend to be forgotten when people are working together against a common enemy or toward a common goal. For example, during the intensive bombing of London in World War II there was a marked decline in the number of people seeking help for emotional problems.

COPING WITH STRESS

Because the anxiety and physiological arousal created by stressful situations are highly uncomfortable, the individual is motivated to do something to alleviate the discomfort. The process by which a person attempts to manage stressful demands is called *coping*, and it takes two major forms. One focuses on the problem: the individual evaluates the stressful situation and does something to change or avoid it. The other focuses on the emotional response to the problem: the individual tries to reduce anxiety without dealing directly with the anxiety-producing situation. The former is referred to as *problem-focused coping* and the latter as *emotion-focused coping* (Lazarus & Folkman, 1984).

Suppose that you receive a warning that you are about to fail a course required for graduation. You might confer with the professor, devise a work schedule to fulfill the requirements, and then follow it; or you might decide that you cannot fulfill the requirements in the time remaining and so sign up to retake the course in summer school. Both of these actions are problem-focused methods of coping. On the other hand, you might try to reduce your anxiety about the failure warning by refusing to acknowledge the possibility of failing or by convincing yourself that a college degree is worthless—or you might deaden your anxiety with alcohol. These are emotion-focused coping strategies.

Each individual deals with stressful situations in his or her unique way, often using a combination of problem-focused and emotion-focused strategies. In most instances, problem solving is the healthier approach. But not all problems can be solved. In such instances as an incapacitating illness or the loss of a loved one, individuals may need to reduce emotional distress until they can face the situation in its entirety. We often use emotion-focused coping to maintain hope, to keep up our morale so that we can continue to function. In general, emotion-focused forms of coping are more likely to occur when a person is experiencing a high level of stress and has decided that nothing can be done to modify the threatening conditions. Problem-focused forms of coping, on the other hand, are more probable at moderate

© 1980 United Features Syndicate

levels of stress, where the situation is appraised as changeable (Lazarus & Folkman, 1984).

Some emotion-focused strategies are behavioral—for example, engaging in physical exercise to get one's mind off a problem, taking a drink, venting anger, seeking emotional support from friends. Others are cognitive: examples are temporarily setting aside thoughts about the problem—"I decided it wasn't worth worrying about"—and reducing the threat by changing the meaning of the situation—"I decided her friendship wasn't that important to me." These two statements indicate that the person is reappraising a stressful situation to make it less of a threat.

Our reappraisal of a problem may be realistic: perhaps, on second thought, the problem is not worth serious concern. Sometimes, however, in seeking to reduce anxiety we deceive ourselves and distort the reality of the situation.

Defense Mechanisms as Emotion-Focused Coping

Freud used the term *defense mechanisms* to refer to unconscious processes that defend a person against anxiety by distorting reality in some way. These emotion-focused strategies do not alter the stressful situation; they simply change the way the person perceives or thinks about it. Thus, all defense mechanisms involve an element of *self-deception*.

The word "mechanism" is not the most appropriate term, because it implies that a form of mechanical device is involved. Freud was influenced by the nineteenth-century tendency to think of the human being as a complicated machine. Actually, we will be talking about some emotion-focused strategies that people employ to minimize anxiety in situations they cannot handle effectively. But since "defense mechanism" is still the most commonly applied term, we will continue to use it.

We all use defense mechanisms at times. They help us over the rough spots until we can deal more directly with the stressful situation. Defense mechanisms indicate personality maladjustment only when they become the dominant mode of responding to problems.

REPRESSION   Freud considered *repression* to be the basic, and most important, defense mechanism. In repression, impulses or memories that are too frightening or painful are excluded from conscious awareness. Memories that evoke shame, guilt, or self-deprecation are often repressed. Freud believed that repression of certain childhood impulses is universal. He maintained that all young boys have feelings of sexual attraction toward the mother and feelings of rivalry and hostility toward the father (the *Oedipus conflict*); these impulses are repressed to avoid the painful consequences of acting on them. In later life, an individual may repress feelings and memories that could cause anxiety because they are inconsistent with his or her self-concept. Feelings of hostility toward a loved one and experiences of failure may be banished from conscious memory.

Repression must be distinguished from *suppression*. Suppression is the process of deliberate self-control, keeping impulses and desires in check (perhaps holding them privately while denying them publicly) or temporarily pushing aside painful memories in order to concentrate on a task. Individuals are aware of suppressed thoughts but are largely unaware of impulses or memories that are repressed.

Freud believed that repression is seldom completely successful. The repressed impulses threaten to break through into consciousness; the individual becomes anxious (although unaware of the reason) and employs one of the following defense mechanisms to keep the partially repressed impulses from awareness. Thus, these other defense mechanisms are said to aid repression.

RATIONALIZATION   When the fox in Aesop's fable rejected the grapes he could not reach "because they were sour," he illustrated a defense mechanism known as *rationalization*. Rationalization does not mean "to act rationally," as one might assume; it is the assignment of logical or socially desirable motives to what we do so that we seem to have acted rationally. Rationalization serves two purposes: it eases our disappointment when we fail to reach a goal ("I didn't want it anyway"), and it provides us with acceptable motives for our behavior. If we act impulsively or on the basis of motives we do not wish to acknowledge even to ourselves, we rationalize what we have done to place our behavior in a more favorable light.

In the search for the "good" reason rather than the "true" reason, individuals make a number of excuses. These excuses are usually plausible; they simply do not tell the whole story. For example, "My roommate failed to wake me" or "I had too many other things to do." Both statements may be true, but they are perhaps not the real reasons for the individual's failure to perform the behavior in question. Individuals who are really concerned set an alarm clock or find the time.

An experiment involving posthypnotic suggestion (see Chapter 6) demonstrates the process of rationalization. A subject under hypnosis is told that when he wakes from the trance he will watch the hypnotist. When the hypnotist takes off her glasses, the subject will raise the window, but he will not remember that the hypnotist told him to do this. Aroused from the trance, the subject feels a little drowsy but presently circulates among the people in the room and carries on a normal conversation, furtively watching the hypnotist. When the hypnotist casually removes her glasses, the subject feels an impulse to open the window. He takes a step in that direction but hesitates. Unconsciously, he mobilizes his wishes to be a reasonable person; seeking a reason for his impulse to open the window, he says "Isn't it a little stuffy in here?" Having found the needed excuse, he opens the window and feels more comfortable (Hilgard, 1965).

REACTION FORMATION   Sometimes individuals can conceal a motive from themselves by giving strong expression to the opposite motive. Such a tendency is called *reaction formation*. A mother who feels guilty about not wanting her child may become overindulgent and overprotective to assure the child of her love and to assure herself that she is a good mother. In one case, a mother who wished to do everything for her daughter could not

© 1975 United Features Syndicate

understand why the child was so unappreciative. At great sacrifice, she had the daughter take expensive piano lessons and assisted her in the daily practice sessions. Although the mother thought she was being extremely kind, she was actually being very demanding—in fact, hostile. She was unaware of her own hostility, but when confronted with it, the mother admitted that she had hated piano lessons as a child. Under the conscious guise of being kind, she was unconsciously being cruel to her daughter. The daughter vaguely sensed what was going on and developed symptoms that required psychological treatment.

Some people who crusade with fanatical zeal against loose morals, alcohol, and gambling may be manifesting reaction formation. Often such individuals have a background of earlier difficulties with these problems, and their zealous crusading may be a means of defending themselves against the possibility of backsliding.

PROJECTION   All of us have undesirable traits that we do not acknowledge, even to ourselves. One unconscious mechanism, *projection*, protects us from recognizing our own undesirable qualities by assigning them in exaggerated amounts to other people. Suppose you have a tendency to be critical of or unkind to other people, but you would dislike yourself if you admitted this tendency. If you are convinced that the people around you are cruel or unkind, your harsh treatment of them is not based on *your* bad qualities—you are simply "giving them what they deserve." If you can assure yourself that everybody else cheats on college examinations, your unacknowledged tendency to take some academic shortcuts is not so bad. Projection is really a form of rationalization, but it is so pervasive in our culture that it merits discussion in its own right.

INTELLECTUALIZATION   *Intellectualization* is an attempt to gain detachment from a stressful situation by dealing with it in abstract, intellectual terms. This kind of defense is frequently a necessity for people who must deal with life-and-death matters in their daily job. The doctor who is continually confronted with human suffering cannot afford to become emotionally involved with each patient. In fact, a certain amount of detachment may be essential for the doctor to function competently. This kind of intellectualization is a problem only when it becomes such a pervasive life-style that individuals cut themselves off from all emotional experiences.

DENIAL   When an external reality is too unpleasant to face, an individual may deny that it exists. The parents of a fatally ill child may refuse to admit that anything is seriously wrong, even though they are fully informed of the diagnosis and the expected outcome. Because they cannot tolerate the pain that acknowledging reality would produce, they resort to the defense mechanism of *denial*. Less extreme forms of denial may be seen in individuals who consistently ignore criticism, fail to perceive that others are angry with them, or disregard all kinds of clues suggesting that a marriage partner is having an affair.

Sometimes, denying facts may be better than facing them. In a severe crisis, denial may give the person time to face the grim facts at a more gradual pace. For example, victims of a stroke or a spinal cord injury might give up altogether if they were fully aware of the seriousness of their conditions. Hope gives the individual the incentive to keep trying. Servicemen who have faced combat or imprisonment report that denying the possibility of death helped them to function. In these situations, denial clearly has an adaptive value. On the other hand, the negative aspects of denial are evident when people postpone seeking medical help: for example, a woman may deny that a lump in the breast may be cancerous and so delay going to a physician.

DISPLACEMENT The last defense mechanism we consider fulfills its function (reduces anxiety) while partially gratifying the unacceptable motive. Through the mechanism of *displacement*, a motive that cannot be gratified in one form is directed into a new channel. An example of displacement was provided in our discussion of anger that could not be expressed toward the source of frustration and was redirected toward a less threatening object.

Freud felt that displacement was the most satisfactory way of handling aggressive and sexual impulses. The basic drives cannot be changed, but the object toward which a drive is directed can be changed. For example, sexual impulses toward the parents cannot be safely gratified, but such impulses can be displaced toward a more suitable love object. Erotic impulses that cannot be expressed directly may be expressed indirectly in creative activities such as art, poetry, and music. Hostile impulses may find socially acceptable expression through participation in contact sports.

It seems unlikely that displacement actually eliminates the frustrated impulses, but substitute activities do help to reduce tension when a basic drive is thwarted. For example, the activities of mothering, being mothered, or seeking companionship may help to reduce the tension associated with unsatisfied sexual needs.

Problem-Focused Coping

In coping with the stressful situation itself, rather than with the emotions it generates, we can flee from the problem or we can try to find some way of altering or solving it. Strategies for solving problems include defining the problem, generating alternative solutions, weighing the alternatives in terms of costs and benefits, choosing among them, and implementing the selected alternative. How skillfully the individual employs these strategies depends on his or her range of experiences, intellectual ability, and capacity for self-control.

Problem-focused strategies can also be directed inward: the person changes something about himself or herself instead of changing the environment. Changing one's level of aspiration, finding alternative sources of gratification, and learning new skills are examples. When a person's job is a chronic source of stress, for instance, inwardly directed strategies might be the best solution.

It should be emphasized that most people use *both* emotion-focused and problem-focused coping in dealing with the stresses of daily life. Several studies asked people to record the stressful events they experienced over the course of a year. The subjects reported on a checklist the thoughts and behaviors they used to handle the demands of each event. The results indicate that almost everyone used both emotion-focused and problem-focused strategies to deal with virtually every stressful encounter (Folkman & Lazarus, 1980; Folkman et al., 1986).

Sometimes the two forms of coping can facilitate each other. For example, a student feels extremely anxious at the beginning of a major exam. But as she turns her attention to taking the exam, her anxiety diminishes. In this instance, problem-focused coping (turning to the task) reduces emotional distress. Sometimes emotion-focused and problem-focused coping can impede each other. A person suffering over having to make a difficult decision finds the distress unbearable and, in order to reduce distress, makes a premature decision. Here, the strategy used to reduce distress interferes with effective problem solving.

STRESS AND ILLNESS

Attempts to adapt to the continued presence of a stressor may deplete the body's resources and make it vulnerable to illness. Chronic stress can lead to such physical disorders as ulcers, high blood pressure, and heart disease. It can also impair the immune system, decreasing the body's ability to fight invading bacteria and viruses. Indeed, doctors estimate that emotional stress plays an important role in more than half of all medical problems.

Psychosomatic disorders are physical disorders in which emotions are believed to play a central role. The term "psychosomatic" is derived from the Greek words *psyche* ("mind") and *soma* ("body"). A common misconception is that people with psychosomatic disorders are not really sick and do not need medical attention. On the contrary, the symptoms of psychosomatic illness reflect physiological disturbances associated with tissue damage and pain; a peptic ulcer caused by stress is indistinguishable from an ulcer that results from long-term heavy usage of aspirin.

Traditionally, research in psychosomatic medicine focused on such illnesses as asthma, hypertension (high blood pressure), ulcers, colitis, and rheumatoid arthritis. Researchers looked for relationships between specific illnesses and characteristic attitudes toward, or ways of coping with, stressful life events. For example, individuals with hypertension were said to feel that life was threatening and, consequently, they must be on guard at all times. Those suffering from colitis were believed to be angry but unable to express their anger. However, most studies that reported characteristic attitudes to be related to specific illnesses have not been replicated. Thus, the hypothesis that people who share the same ways of reacting to stress will be vulnerable to the same illnesses has generally not been confirmed. An important exception is the research on coronary heart disease and Type A behavior patterns, as we will see shortly.

Today the focus of psychosomatic research is much broader, and the term "psychosomatic medicine" is being replaced by *behavioral medicine*. Behavioral medicine is an interdisciplinary field that attracts specialists from psychology and medicine. It seeks to learn how social, psychological, and biological variables combine to cause illness, and how behavior and environments can be changed to promote health.

Heart Disease

Coronary heart disease is a leading cause of death and chronic illness in the United States. It occurs when the coronary blood vessels that supply the heart muscle are narrowed or closed (by the gradual build-up of a hard, fatty substance called placque), blocking the flow of oxygen and nutrients to the heart. Three factors that have long been known to increase the risk of coronary heart disease are high blood pressure, smoking, and high levels of cholesterol in the blood. More recently a behavior pattern, called *Type A*, has been identified that is believed to be another risk factor.

TYPE A BEHAVIOR PATTERN   Physicians had noted over the years that heart attack victims tended to be hostile, aggressive, impatient persons who were overinvolved in their work. In the 1950s two cardiologists defined a constellation of behaviors (the Type A behavior pattern) that seemed to characterize patients with coronary heart disease (Friedman & Rosenman, 1974). People who exhibit this Type A behavior pattern are described as extremely competitive and achievement oriented; they have a sense of time urgency, find it difficult to relax, and become impatient and angry when confronted with delays or with people they view as incompetent. Although outwardly self-confident, they are presumably prey to constant feelings of self-doubt; they push themselves to accomplish more and more in less and less time. Some common Type A behaviors are listed in Table 15-2. Type B people are those who do not exhibit the characteristics listed for Type A. Type B individuals are able to relax without feeling guilty and to work without becoming agitated; they lack a sense of urgency, with its accompanying impatience, and are not easily roused to anger.

To examine the relationship between Type A behavior and coronary heart disease, more than 3,000 healthy, middle-age men were evaluated by means of a structured interview. The interview was designed to be irritating. The interviewer kept the subject waiting without explanation and then asked a series of questions about being competitive, hostile, and pressed for time. Examples are: "Do you ever feel rushed or under pressure?"; "Do you

TABLE 15-2
Type A Behaviors *Some behaviors that characterize people prone to coronary heart disease.* (After Friedman & Rosenman, 1974)

Thinking of or doing two things at once

Scheduling more and more activities into less and less time

Failing to notice or be interested in the environment or things of beauty

Hurrying the speech of others

Becoming unduly irritated when forced to wait in line or when driving behind a car you think is moving too slowly

Believing that if you want something done well, you have to do it yourself

Gesticulating when you talk

Frequent knee jiggling or rapid tapping of your fingers

Explosive speech patterns or frequent use of obscenities

Making a fetish of always being on time

Having difficulty sitting and doing nothing

Playing nearly every game to win, even when playing with children

Measuring your own and others' success in terms of numbers (number of patients seen, articles written, etc.)

Lip clicking, head nodding, fist clenching, table pounding, or sucking in of air when speaking

Becoming impatient while watching others do things you think you can do better or faster

Rapid eye blinking or ticlike eyebrow lifting

---

eat quickly?"; "Would you describe yourself as ambitious and hard driving, or relaxed and easy going?"; "Do you resent it if someone is late?" The interviewer interrupted, asked questions in a challenging manner, and threw in nonsequiturs. The interview was scored more on the way the person behaved in answering the questions than on the answers themselves. For example, extreme Type A people spoke loudly in an explosive manner, talked over the interviewer so as not to be interrupted, appeared tense and tight-lipped, and described hostile incidents with great emotional intensity. Classic Type B people sat in a relaxed manner, spoke slowly and softly, were easily interrupted, and smiled often.

After the subjects were classified as Type A or Type B, they were followed for 8½ years. During that period, Type A men had twice as many heart attacks or other forms of coronary heart disease than did Type B men. These results held up even after diet, age, smoking, and other variables were taken into account (Rosenman et al., 1975). Other studies confirmed this two-fold risk and linked Type A behavior to heart disease in both men and women (Haynes, Feinleib, & Kannel, 1980; Kornitzer et al., 1982). In addition, Type A behavior has been correlated with severity of coronary artery blockage as determined at autopsy or in X-ray studies of the inside of coronary blood vessels (Friedman et al., 1968; Williams et al., 1988).

After reviewing the evidence, in 1981 the American Heart Association decided that Type A behavior should be classified as a risk factor for coronary heart disease. However, two more recent studies failed to find any link between Type A behavior and heart disease (Case et al., 1985; Shekelle et al., 1983). While some researchers attribute this failure to the way Type A individuals were assessed in these studies, others believe that the definition of Type A behavior, as originally formulated, is too diffuse. They argue that time urgency and competitiveness are *not* the most important components; the crucial variable may be hostility.

HOSTILITY AND TYPE A BEHAVIOR   Several studies have found that a person's level of hostility is a better predictor of heart disease than is his or her overall level of Type A behavior (Thoresen, Telch, & Eagleston, 1981; Dembroski et al., 1985). In an attempt to examine further the anger component of Type A behavior, a number of studies have used personality tests rather than interviews to measure hostility. For example, a 25-year study of 118 lawyers found that those who scored high on hostility traits on a personality inventory taken in law school were five times as likely to die before age 50 as classmates who were not hostile (Barefoot et al., 1989). In a similar follow-up study of physicians, hostility scores obtained in medical school predicted the incidence of coronary heart disease as well as mortality from all causes (Barefoot, Williams, & Dahlstrom, 1983). In both studies, this relationship was independent of the effects of smoking, age, and high blood pressure. There is some evidence that anger that is repressed, or held in, may be more destructive to one's heart than anger that is overtly expressed (Spielberger et al., 1985; Wright, 1988).

Hostility is a good predictor of heart disease.

How does Type A behavior or its component trait of hostility lead to coronary heart disease? One plausible biological mechanism is the way the individual's sympathetic nervous system responds to stress. When exposed to stressful experimental situations (for example, when faced with threat of failure, harassment, or competitive task demands), most subjects report feeling angry, irritated, and tense. However, subjects who score high on hostility as a trait show much larger increases in blood pressure, heart rate, and the secretion of stress-related hormones than subjects with low hostility scores (Suarez & Williams, 1989). The same results have been found when Type A subjects are compared with Type B subjects (Manuck & Kranz, 1986). The sympathetic nervous systems of hostile and/or Type A individuals appear to be hyperresponsive to stressful situations. All of these physiological changes can damage the heart and blood vessels.

It has been suggested that hostile and non-hostile people may have fundamentally different nervous systems. When non-hostile individuals are aroused and upset, their parasympathetic nervous systems act like a stop switch to calm them down. Hostile individuals may have a weak parasympathetic nervous system. When they are angered, their adrenalin fires off and they stay unpleasantly aroused. As a consequence, they interact with the world differently (Williams, 1989).

MODIFYING TYPE A BEHAVIOR   A project aimed at modifying Type A behavior and involving more than 1,000 individuals who have experienced at least one heart attack reports considerable success. The subjects in the experimental group were helped to change their Type A behavior. For example, to reduce their sense of time urgency, individuals were asked to practice standing in line (a situation Type A individuals find extremely irritating) and to use the opportunity to reflect on things that they do not normally have time to think about, or to watch people, or to strike up a conversation with a stranger. Treatment also included learning to express themselves without exploding at people and to alter certain specific behaviors (such as interrupting the speech of others or talking or eating hurriedly), reevaluating basic beliefs (such as the notion that success depends on the quantity of work produced), and finding ways to make the home and work environment less stressful (such as reducing the number of unnecessary social engagements).

The critical dependent variable in this study is the occurrence of another heart attack. By the end of the study, 4½ years later, the experimental group had a cardiac recurrence rate almost half that of control subjects who were not taught how to alter their life-style pattern. Clearly, learning to modify Type A behavior is beneficial to one's health (Friedman et al., 1985).

This study also found hostility to be the most significant predictor of heart disease. Individuals who suffered a subsequent heart attack, many of whom died, did not differ from individuals who remained healthy in terms of total Type A scores, family background, and overall measures of chronic stress. But they scored two or three times higher on measures of hostile behavior.

OCCUPATIONAL AND SOCIAL STRESS   Personality traits, such as hostility and Type A behavior, are not the only psychological variables that are related to the development of cardiovascular disease. Researchers have also examined the role of occupational stress and social stress. For example, two factors that determine the stressfulness of a job are its *demands* (in terms of workload, responsibilities, and role conflicts) and its *controllability* (the ability of the worker to control the speed, nature, and conditions of work). Highly demanding jobs and jobs in which the worker has little control are both associated with feelings of distress and with an increased death rate from coronary heart disease (Karasek et al., 1981; Karasek et al., 1982). The most stressful occupations are those that combine high demand and low control. An example might be an assembly line job in which rapid, high-quality production is expected and the work is machine-paced rather than self-paced.

In one study, some 900 middle-aged men and women were followed over a 10-year period and examined for the development of heart disease. Two independent methods—occupational titles and the subjects' self-reports of their own feelings about the job—were used to classify workers along the dimensions of job demand and job control. The results showed that both men and women in occupations classified as "high strain" (high demand combined with low control) had a risk of coronary heart disease 1½ times greater than those in other occupations. The risk was even higher when self-report measures were used, demonstrating the influence of individual cognitive appraisal on the experience of stress.

High family demands in addition to a stressful job can adversely affect a woman's cardiovascular health. Employed women in general are not at a higher risk of coronary heart disease than housewives. However, employed mothers are more likely to develop heart disease. The likelihood of the disease increases with the number of children for working women but not for housewives (Hayne & Feinleib, 1980).

Experimental studies with animals have shown that disruption of the social environment can induce pathology that resembles coronary artery disease (Manuck, Kaplan, & Matthews, 1986). Some of the key experiments have been conducted with a type of macaque monkey whose social organization involves the establishment of stable hierarchies of social dominance; dominant and submissive animals can be identified within a given group based on the animals' social behavior. The introduction of unfamiliar

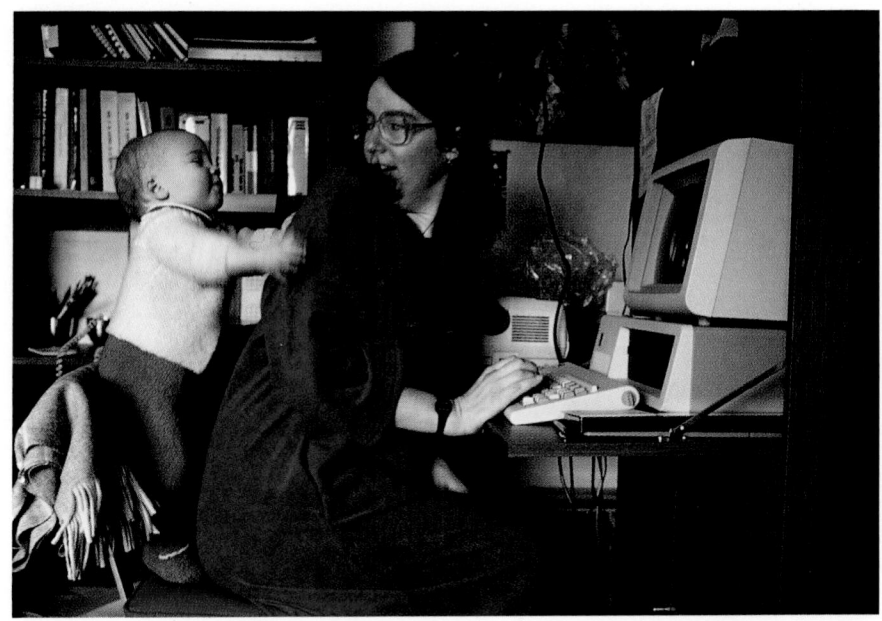

Coping with the demands of job and motherhood can be stressful.

monkeys into an established social group is a stressor that leads to increased aggressive behavior as group members attempt to reestablish a social dominance hierarchy (Manuck, Kaplan, & Matthews, 1986).

In these studies, some monkey groups remained stable with fixed memberships; other groups were stressed by the repeated introduction of new members. After about 2 years under these conditions, the high ranking or dominant males in the unstable social condition showed more extensive atherosclerosis (the build-up of placque on the artery walls) than the subordinate males. No differences in coronary disease were evident between dominants and subordinates in the stable social condition (Kaplan et al., 1982).

The dominant males in the unstable group showed higher rates of aggressive contact and more disruption of "friendly" social behavior (mutual grooming, passive body contact). In essence, the aggressive behaviors observed in male monkeys who developed the most coronary disease resemble characteristics of hostility and Type A behavior that predict heart disease in humans.

The results of these experiments reinforce the point that the effects of a stressor depend more on characteristics of the individual than on the objective situation. In this case, the animal's level of dominance determined how the stressor (introduction of unfamiliar animals) influenced its behavior and physiology.

The Immune System

One relatively new area of research in behavioral medicine is *psychoimmunology*, the study of how the body's immune system is affected by psychological variables. The immune system is a surveillance mechanism that protects the body from disease-causing microorganisms. It regulates our susceptibility to cancers, infectious diseases, allergies, and autoimmune disorders (that is, diseases such as rheumatoid arthritis, in which the immune cells attack the normal tissue of the body). Evidence is mounting that stress affects the ability of the immune system to defend the body.

CRITICAL DISCUSSION

Controlling Physiological Responses to Stress

Among the techniques that have been used to help people control their physiological responses to stressful situations are *biofeedback, relaxation training, cognitive behavior therapy,* and *aerobic exercise.*

In biofeedback training, individuals receive information (feedback) about an aspect of their physiological state and then attempt to alter that state. For example, in a procedure for learning to control tension headaches, electrodes are attached to the forehead so that any movement in the forehead muscle can be electronically detected, amplified, and fed back to the person as an auditory signal. The signal, or tone, increases in pitch when the muscle contracts and decreases when it relaxes. By learning to control the pitch of the tone, the individual learns to keep the muscle relaxed. (Relaxation of the forehead muscle usually ensures relaxation of scalp and neck muscles also.) After 4 to 8 weeks of biofeedback training, the subject learns to recognize the onset of tension and to reduce it without feedback from the machine (Tarler-Benlolo, 1978).

Physiological processes that are controlled by the autonomic nervous system, such as heart rate and blood pressure, have traditionally been assumed to be automatic and not under voluntary control. However, experiments in the 1960s showed that rats could be operantly conditioned (see Chapter 7) to raise or lower their heart rates (DiCara & Miller, 1968). Subsequent laboratory studies have demonstrated that human subjects can also learn to modify heart rate and blood pressure (see the figure). The results of these studies have led to new procedures for treating patients with high blood pressure (hypertension). One procedure is to show patients a graph of their blood pressure while it is being monitored and to teach them techniques for relaxing different muscle groups. The patients are instructed to tense their muscles (for example, to clench a fist or to tighten the abdomen), release the tension, and notice the difference in sensation. By starting with the feet and ankle muscles and progressing through the body to the muscles that control the neck and face, the patients learn to modify muscular tension. This combination of biofeedback with relaxation training has proved effective in lowering blood pressure for some individuals (Tarler-Benlolo, 1978).

Reviews of numerous studies using biofeedback and relaxation training to control headaches and hypertension conclude that the most important variable is *learning how to relax* (Runck, 1980). Some people may learn to relax faster when they receive biofeedback. Others may learn to relax equally well when they receive training in muscle

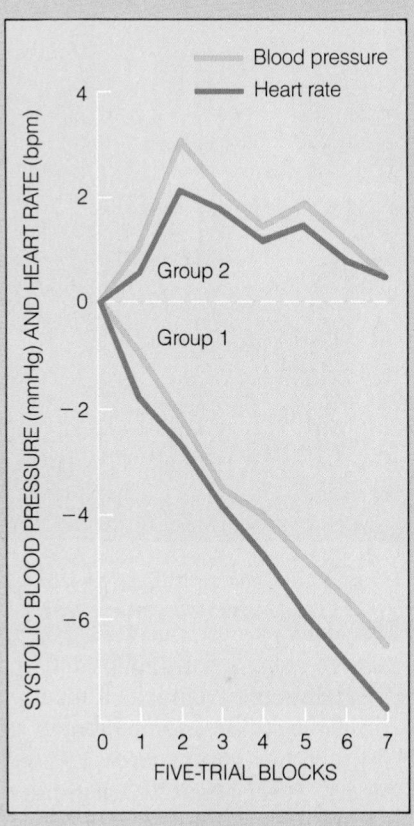

Operant Conditioning of Blood Pressure and Heart Rate *One group of subjects received biofeedback (a light and a tone) whenever their blood pressure and heart rate decreased simultaneously (Group 1); the other group received the same feedback whenever their blood pressure and heart rate increased simultaneously (Group 2). The subjects achieved significant simultaneous control of blood pressure and heart rate during a single conditioning session. The group reinforced for lowering both functions achieved increasingly more control over trials; the group reinforced for raising both functions was less consistent. (After Schwartz, 1975)*

Academic pressures, bereavement, and marital disruption are some of the stressful events that have been associated with impaired immune responses. For example, during examination periods college students have lower levels of an antibody in their blood that defends against respiratory infections (Jemmott et al., 1985), and medical students show lowered immune functioning on a number of blood-sample measures (Glaser et al., 1985; Glaser et al., 1986). A study of men whose wives had died from breast cancer demonstrated that the responsiveness of the men's lymphocytes (a

relaxation without any specific biofeedback. The usefulness of relaxation training seems to depend on the individual. Some people who are not conscientious about taking drugs to relieve high blood pressure are more responsive to relaxation training, whereas others who have learned to control their blood pressure through relaxation may eventually drop the procedure because they find it too time-consuming.

People who are able to control their physiological responses through biofeedback and relaxation training in the laboratory will have more difficulty doing so in actual stressful situations, particularly if they continue to interact in ways that make them tense. Consequently, an additional approach to stress management focuses on changing the individual's cognitive and behavioral responses to stressful situations. *Cognitive behavior therapy* attempts to help people identify the kinds of stressful situations that produce their physiological symptoms and to alter the way they cope with these situations. For example, a man who suffers from tension headaches would be asked to begin by keeping a record of their occurrence and rating the severity of each headache and the circumstances in which it occurred. Next he is taught how to monitor his responses to these stressful events and is asked to record his feelings, thoughts, and behavior prior to, during, and following the event. After a period of self-monitoring, certain relationships often become evident among situational variables (for example, criticism by a supervisor or coworker); thoughts ("I can't do anything right"); and emotional, behavioral, and physiological responses (depression, withdrawal, and headache).

The next step is trying to identify the expectations or beliefs that might explain the headache reactions (for example, "I expect to do everything perfectly, so the slightest criticism upsets me" or "I judge myself harshly, become depressed, and end up with a headache"). The final and most difficult step is trying to change something about the stressful situation, the individual's way of thinking about it, or the individual's behavior. The options might include finding a less stressful job, recognizing that the need to perform perfectly leads to unnecessary anguish over errors, or learning to behave more assertively in interactions instead of withdrawing.

This capsule summary of cognitive behavior therapy for coping with stressful situations does not do justice to the procedures involved. A more detailed description is found in Chapter 17. Biofeedback, relaxation training, and cognitive behavior therapy have all proved useful in helping people control their physiological responses to stress. Some research suggests that the improvement gained with cognitive behavior therapy is more likely to be maintained over time (Holroyd, Appel, & Andrasik, 1983). This is not surprising, since the complex demands of everyday life often require flexible coping skills; being able to relax may not be an effective method of coping with some of life's stresses. Programs for stress management frequently employ a combination of biofeedback, relaxation training, and cognitive behavior modification techniques.

Another factor important in controlling stress is physical fitness. Individuals who regularly engage in aerobic exercise (any sustained activity that increases heart rate and oxygen consumption, such as jogging, swimming, or cycling) show significantly lower heart rates and blood pressure in response to stressful situations than individuals who do not exercise regularly (Holmes & McGilley, 1987; Holmes & Roth, 1985). In addition, aerobic exercise has proven more helpful than relaxation training for people who are depressed (McCann & Holmes, 1984; Roth & Holmes, 1987). In view of these findings, many stress management programs also emphasize aerobic fitness.

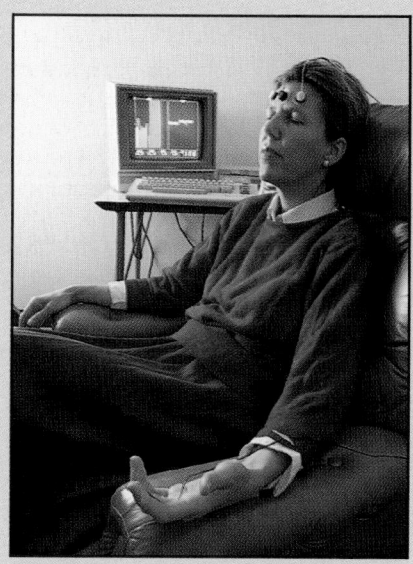

In this biofeedback procedure for treating headaches, the sensors measure forehead muscle contractions and finger temperature. Cold fingers are often a sign of tension.

class of white blood cells that is an essential part of the immune system) declined significantly within the month following their wives' deaths, and in some cases remained low for a year thereafter (Schleifer et al., 1979). Individuals of both sexes who have recently been separated or divorced show poorer immune functioning than matched control subjects who are still married, even though no significant differences were found between the two groups in health-related behaviors such as smoking and diet (Kiecolt-Glaser et al., 1987; Kiecolt-Glaser et al., 1988).

FIGURE 15-2
Yoked Controls in a Stress
Experiment *A series of electrical shocks*
are preprogrammed to be delivered
simultaneously to the tails of the two
animals. The rat on the left can terminate
a shock when it occurs by pressing the lever
in front of him. The rat on the right has
no control in the situation (his lever is
inoperative) but he is yoked to the first rat.
That is, the yoked rat is electrically wired
in series to the first rat; when the first
rat receives a shock, the yoked rat
simultaneously receives the same shock
and it remains on until the first rat presses
his lever. The lever presses of the yoked rat
have no effect on the shock sequence for
either animal.

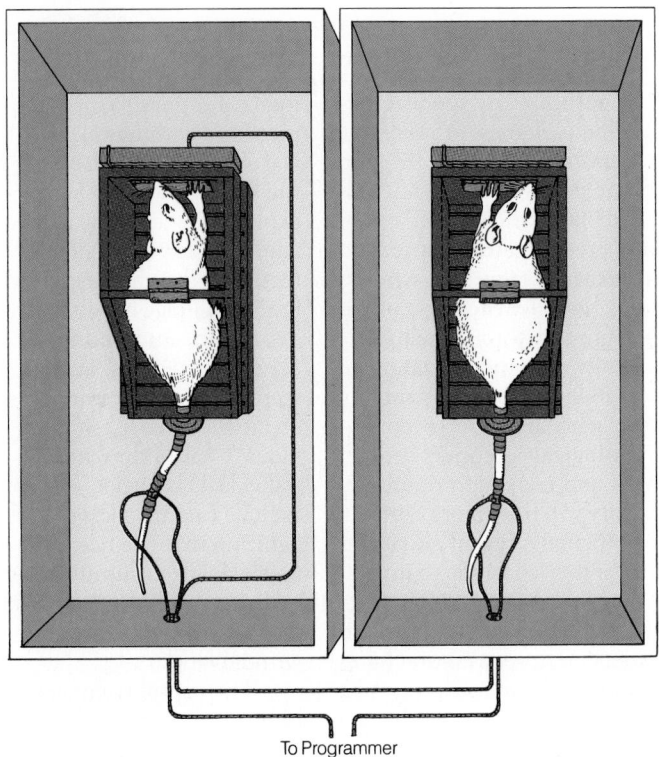

To Programmer

These and similar studies indicate that a decline in immune functioning frequently accompanies stressful life events. However, factors such as prior health and recent exposure to pathogens are important in determining actual illness.

There is evidence too that psychological factors that reduce stress can attenuate these adverse immunological changes. One factor that appears to be important is the extent to which an individual can control the stress. Controllability, as noted earlier, is one of the variables that reduces the severity of stress. A series of animal studies demonstrates that uncontrollable shock has a much greater effect on the immune system than controllable shock. In these experiments, rats are subjected to electric shock. One group can press a lever to turn off the shock. The other animals, the yoked controls, receive an identical sequence of shocks but their levers are ineffective (see Figure 15-2).

In one study using this procedure, the investigator looked at how readily the rats' *T-cells* (a type of lymphocyte that kills invading viruses) multiplied when "challenged" by an invader. They found that the T-cells from rats who could control the shock multiplied as readily as did those from rats who were not stressed at all. T-cells from rats exposed to uncontrollable shock, on the other hand, multiplied only weakly. Thus, shock (stress) interfered with the immune response only in rats who could not control them (Laudenslager et al., 1983).

In another study, the investigators implanted tumor cells into rats, gave them shocks, and recorded whether the rats' natural defenses rejected the cells or whether they developed into tumors. Only 27 percent of the rats given uncontrollable shocks rejected tumors, whereas 63 percent of the rats who could turn the shocks off rejected tumors—even though the rats received identical amounts of shock (Visintainer, Volpicelli, & Seligman, 1982).

Perhaps when stressful life events result in suppressed immune responses, they do so because the individuals feel that they have no control over the negative event. In one study on the effects of marital separation or divorce on immune functioning, the partner who had initiated the separation (the one more in control of the situation) was less distressed, reported better health, and showed better immune system functioning than the non-initiator (Kiecolt-Glaser et al., 1988).

We noted earlier that social supports can reduce the effects of stress. In the study of medical students mentioned above, those students who scored high on a scale measuring loneliness (who had few friends) showed the poorest immune functioning when faced with the stress of examinations. And a similar relationship between loneliness scores and lowered immune functioning has been found among psychiatric patients (Kiecolt-Glaser et al., 1984). Certainly loneliness is a major component of the stress caused by bereavement or marital disruption. Individuals who have the companionship and support of friends and relatives are healthier mentally and physically than those with few social supports.

The immune system is incredibly complicated, employing a number of different weapons that interact to defend the body. Much remains unknown about how it does the job, and even less is known about its relationship to the nervous system. Scientists once believed that the immune system operated quite independently, isolated from other physiological systems. But current studies are making it increasingly evident that the immune system and the nervous system have numerous anatomical and physiological connections. To mention one example, researchers are discovering that lymphocytes have receptors for a number of different neurotransmitters. Thus, these immune system cells are equipped to receive messages from the nervous system that may alter the way they behave.

As research in psychoimmunology yields additional information about the links between the nervous and immune systems, we will gain a clearer understanding of how mental attitudes affect health.

Loneliness can be a major source of stress.

Stress-Resistant Individuals

Some people experience one stressful event after another and do not break down. Others are seriously upset by even low-level stressors. As noted throughout the chapter, two variables that mediate the effects of stressors are the individual's cognitive appraisal of the situation and his or her resources for coping with it. Several investigators have attempted to determine more precisely the personality characteristics that make people resistant to stress. In one study, more than 600 men who were executives or managers in the same company were given checklists and were asked to describe all of the stressful events and illnesses they had experienced over the previous 3 years. Two groups were selected for comparison: the first group scored above average on both stressful events and illness; the second group scored equally high on stress but *below average* on illness. Members of both groups then filled out detailed personality questionnaires. Analysis of the results indicated that the high-stress/low-illness men differed from the men who became ill under stress on three major dimensions: they were more actively involved in their work and social lives, they were more oriented toward challenge and change, and they felt more in control of events in their lives (Kobasa, 1979).

Of course, it could be argued that these personality differences were the *result* rather than the *cause* of illness. For example, it is hard for people to be involved in work or social activity when they are ill. The investigators therefore conducted a longitudinal study that considered the personality characteristics of business executives before they became ill, then monitored their life stress scores and the extent of their illnesses for a period of 2 years. The results showed that the executives whose attitudes toward life could be rated high on involvement, feelings of control, and positive responses to change remained healthier than the men who scored low on these dimensions (Kobasa, Maddi, & Kahn, 1982). The most important factor appears to be attitude toward change. People who view change as a challenge—for example, regarding the loss of a job as an opportunity to pursue a new career rather than as a setback—are apt to experience less stress and to turn the situation to their advantage.

The personality characteristics of stress-resistant or hardy individuals have been summarized by the terms "commitment," "control," and "challenge." These characteristics are interrelated with the factors we have discussed as influencing the severity of stress. For example, commitment to relationships with other people provides social support in times of stress. The sense of being in control of life events reflects feelings of competency and also influences the way in which stressful events are appraised. People who feel they are able to exert control over stressful situations (instead of feeling helpless) are more likely to take action to remedy the situation. Challenge also involves cognitive evaluation, the belief that change is normal in life and should be viewed as an opportunity for growth rather than as a threat to security.

⚡ CHAPTER SUMMARY

1. Stress is a state that occurs when people a) are faced with events they perceive as endangering their physical or psychological well-being, and b) are uncertain of their ability to deal with these events. Stress includes the environmental events that are perceived as threatening (*stressors*) and the person's reactions to them (*stress responses*).

2. The person's cognitive appraisal determines the degree of stress. The *primary appraisal* evaluates a situation as either irrelevant, benign-positive, or stressful (that is, constituting loss, threat of loss, or challenge). The *secondary appraisal* evaluates the individual's resources for coping with the threat.

3. The pattern of physiological reactions that prepares the organism to deal with a perceived threat (the *fight-or-flight response*) is controlled by the hypothalamus (the brain's stress center). The hypothalamus has a dual function in emergencies: it activates the *sympathetic system* and also the *adrenal-cortical system*. Depending on the relative amounts of distress and effort in a given stressful situation, one of these systems may be more active than the other.

4. Psychological reactions to stress include *cognitive impairment* (difficulty in concentrating and rigidity of behavior) and such diverse emotional responses as *anxiety* (both objective and neurotic), *anger* and *aggression* (both direct and displaced), and *apathy* and *depression* (which may reflect *learned helplessness*).

5. Sources of stress include *traumatic events*, major *life changes*, *daily hassles*, and *conflict* between opposing motives. The ability to *predict* the occurrence of a stressful event and to exert some *control* over its duration reduces the severity of stress, as does the *social support* provided by other people.

6. In coping with stressful situations, people use a combination of *problem-focused strategies*, aimed at changing the situation in some way, and *emotion-focused strategies*, aimed at reducing anxiety without dealing directly with the problem. Some emotion-focused strategies that distort reality are called *defense mechanisms*. They include *repression*, *rationalization*, *reaction formation*, *projection*, *intellectualization*, *denial*, and *displacement*.

7. *Psychosomatic disorders* are physical disorders in which emotions are believed to play a central role. *Behavioral medicine*, an interdisciplinary field, seeks to discover how social, psychological, and biological variables combine to cause illness, and how behavior and environment can be changed to promote health.

8. Chronic stress can contribute to physical disorders, such as coronary heart disease, and can increase our vulnerability to infectious diseases by impairing the functioning of the body's immune system. *Type A personality* characteristics (hostile, impatient, time-pressured, and ambitious) predispose a person to heart disease. An inability to control stressful events appears to play a role in decreased immune functioning.

9. The personality characteristics of stress-resistant individuals (those who remain healthy despite many stressful life events) can be summarized by the terms *commitment*, *control*, and *challenge*.

 FURTHER READING

Stress and Stress Management: Research and Applications (1984) by Hamberger and Lohr discusses the different models of stress, some relevant research findings, and various methods for controlling stress. *Stress, Appraisal, and Coping* (1984) by Lazarus and Folkman emphasizes the role of cognitive appraisal in determining stress. For a cognitive behavior approach to stress prevention and management, see Meichenbaum and Jaremko (eds.), *Stress Reduction and Prevention* (1983); and a paperback, *Stress Inoculation Training* (1985), by Meichenbaum.

The *Handbook of Clinical Health Psychology* (1982), edited by Millon, Green, and Meagher, includes articles on most of the topics discussed in this chapter and also covers issues in the developing field of health psychology—for example, coping with the problems of life-threatening illness, chronic illness and disability, aging, and patient compliance with medical procedures. See also *Behavioral Medicine: The Biopsychological Approach* (1985), edited by Schneiderman and Tapp, and *Mechanisms of Psychological Influence on Physical Health* (1989), edited by Carstensen and Neale. For a review of research on stress and heart disease see *Handbook of Stress, Reactivity, and Cardiovascular Disease* (1986), edited by Matthews.

A classic account of defense mechanisms is given by Anna Freud in *The Ego and the Mechanisms of Defense* (rev. ed., 1967). An introductory treatment may be found in Coleman, Butcher, and Carson, *Abnormal Psychology and Modern Life* (7th ed., 1984).

Chapter 16

Detail, The Artist at the Window.

Abnormal Psychology

ost of us have periods when we feel anxious, depressed, unreasonably angry, or inadequate in dealing with life's complexities. Trying to lead a satisfying and meaningful life is not easy in an era of rapid social and technological change. Many of our traditional assumptions about work, religion, sex, marriage, and family are being questioned, and the social values that gave our grandparents a sense of security no longer provide clear guidelines for behavior. It is an unusual person who manages to get through life without periods of loneliness, self-doubt, and despair. In fact, about a third of Americans will experience a severe enough mental or emotional problem at least once during their lifetime that, if diagnosed, would be classified as a mental disorder (Regier et al., 1988).

In this chapter, we will look at some individuals who have serious mental disorders and some who have developed self-destructive life-styles. The behaviors we discuss are classified as "abnormal," but as we will see, the dividing line between "normal" and "abnormal" behavior is far from clear.

ABNORMAL BEHAVIOR

Defining Abnormality

What do we mean by "abnormal" behavior? By what criteria do we distinguish it from "normal" behavior? There is no general agreement, but most attempts to describe abnormality are based on one or more of the following definitions.

DEVIATION FROM STATISTICAL NORMS   The word *abnormal* means "away from the norm." Many characteristics, such as height, weight, and intelligence, cover a range of values when measured over a population. Most people fall within the middle range of height, while a few individuals are abnormally tall or abnormally short. One definition of abnormality is based on *statistical frequency*: abnormal behavior is statistically infrequent or deviant from the norm. But according to this definition, the person who is extremely intelligent or extremely happy would be classified as abnormal. Thus, in defining abnormal behavior, we must consider more than statistical frequency.

DEVIATION FROM SOCIAL NORMS   Every society has certain standards, or norms, for acceptable behavior; behavior that deviates markedly from these norms is considered abnormal. Usually, but not always, such behavior is also statistically infrequent in that society. However, several problems arise when deviation from social norms is used as a criterion for defining abnormality.

Behavior that is considered normal by one society may be considered abnormal by another. For example, members of some African tribes do not consider it unusual to hear voices when no one is actually talking or to see visions when nothing is actually there, but such behaviors are considered abnormal in most societies. Another problem is that the concept of abnormality changes over time within the same society. Most Americans would have considered smoking marijuana or appearing nearly nude at the beach abnormal behaviors 30 years ago. Today, such behaviors tend to be viewed as differences in life-style rather than as signs of abnormality.

Thus, ideas of normality and abnormality differ from one society to another and over time within the same society. Any definition of abnormality must include more than social compliance.

MALADAPTIVENESS OF BEHAVIOR   Rather than defining abnormal behavior in terms of deviance from either statistical or societal norms, many social scientists believe that the most important criterion is how the behavior affects the well-being of the individual or of the social group. According to this criterion, behavior is abnormal if it is *maladaptive*, if it has adverse effects on the individual or on society. Some kinds of deviant behavior interfere with the welfare of the individual (a man who is so fearful of crowds that he cannot ride the bus to work; an alcoholic who drinks so heavily that he or she cannot keep a job; a woman who attempts suicide). Other forms of deviant behavior are harmful to society (an adolescent who has violent aggressive outbursts; a paranoid individual who plots to assassinate national leaders). If we use the criterion of maladaptiveness, all of these behaviors would be considered abnormal.

PERSONAL DISTRESS   A fourth criterion considers abnormality in terms of the individual's subjective feelings of distress rather than the individual's behavior. Most people diagnosed as mentally ill feel acutely miserable. They are anxious, depressed, or agitated and may suffer from insomnia, loss of appetite, or numerous aches and pains. Sometimes personal distress may be the only symptom of abnormality; the individual's behavior may appear normal to the casual observer.

None of these definitions provides a completely satisfactory description of abnormal behavior. In most instances, all four criteria—statistical frequency, social deviation, maladaptive behavior, and personal distress—are considered in diagnosing abnormality.

What Is Normality?

Normality is even more difficult to define than abnormality, but most psychologists would agree that the following qualities indicate emotional well-being. These characteristics do not make sharp distinctions between the mentally healthy and the mentally ill; rather, they represent traits that the normal person possesses to a *greater degree* than the individual who is diagnosed as abnormal.

1. *Efficient perception of reality*   Normal individuals are fairly realistic in appraising their reactions and capabilities and in interpreting what is going on in the world around them. They do not consistently misperceive what others say and do, and they do not consistently overevaluate their abilities and tackle more than they can accomplish, nor do they underestimate their abilities and shy away from difficult tasks.
2. *Self-knowledge*   Well-adjusted people have some awareness of their own motives and feelings. Although none of us can fully understand our feelings or behavior, normal people have more self-awareness than individuals who are diagnosed as mentally ill.
3. *An ability to exercise voluntary control over behavior*   Normal individuals feel fairly confident about their ability to control their behavior. Occasionally,

Self-Portrait with Bandaged Ear *by Vincent van Gogh (1887).*

they may act impulsively, but they are able to restrain sexual and aggressive urges when necessary. They may fail to conform to social norms, but their decision to act as such is voluntary rather than the result of uncontrollable impulses.

4. *Self-esteem and acceptance* Well-adjusted people have some appreciation of their own self-worth and feel accepted by those around them. They are comfortable with other people and are able to react spontaneously in social situations. At the same time, they do not feel obligated to subjugate their opinions to those of the group. Feelings of worthlessness, alienation, and lack of acceptance are prevalent among individuals who are diagnosed as abnormal.

5. An *ability to form affectionate relationships* Normal individuals are able to form close and satisfying relationships with other people. They are sensitive to the feelings of others and do not make excessive demands on others to gratify their own needs. Often, mentally disturbed people are so concerned with protecting their own security that they become extremely self-centered. Preoccupied with their own feelings and strivings, they seek affection but are unable to reciprocate. Sometimes they fear intimacy because their past relationships have been destructive.

6. *Productivity* Well-adjusted people are able to channel their abilities into productive activity. They are enthusiastic about life and do not need to drive themselves to meet the demands of the day. A chronic lack of energy and excessive susceptibility to fatigue are often symptoms of psychological tension resulting from unresolved problems.

The Scream *by Edvard Munch (1893).*

Some people turn to creative work as an outlet for their unresolved conflicts. The artists van Gogh and Munch were probably seriously disturbed (judging from descriptions of their behavior), and one wonders if their creative powers would have been as great if they had been better adjusted emotionally. The question is debatable, but it is clear from accounts of the lives of these artists that their works were produced at great expense in the form of pain to themselves and to those close to them. Although a few disturbed people manage to turn their troubles to their advantage, most mentally ill individuals are unable to use their full creative abilities because their emotional problems inhibit productivity.

Classifying Abnormal Behavior

A broad range of behaviors has been classified as abnormal. Some abnormal behaviors are acute and transitory, resulting from particularly stressful events, whereas others are chronic and lifelong. Some abnormal behaviors result from disease or damage to the nervous system. Others are the products of undesirable social environments or faulty learning experiences. Often these factors overlap and interact. Each person's behavior and emotional problems are unique; no two individuals behave in exactly the same manner or share the same life experiences. However, enough similarities exist for mental health professionals to classify cases into categories.

A classification system has advantages and disadvantages. If the various types of abnormal behavior have different causes, we can hope to uncover them by grouping individuals according to similarities in behavior and then looking for other ways in which the persons may be similar. A diagnostic label also enables those who work with disturbed individuals to communicate information more quickly and concisely. The diagnosis of *schizophrenia* indicates quite a bit about a person's behavior. Knowing that an individual's symptoms are similar to those of other patients (whose progress followed a

TABLE 16-1
Categories of Mental Disorders *Listed are the main diagnostic categories of DSM-III-R. Each category includes numerous subclassifications. Personality disorders and developmental disorders (such as mental retardation and delayed language) are coded on Axis II. (After American Psychiatric Association, 1987)*

1. **Disorders usually first evident in infancy, childhood, or adolescence**
   Includes mental retardation, hyperactivity, childhood anxieties, eating disorders (for example, anorexia and bulimia), speech disorders, and other deviations from normal development.

2. **Organic mental disorders**
   Disorders in which the functioning of the brain is known to be impaired, either permanently or transiently; may be the result of aging, degenerative diseases of the nervous system (for example, syphilis or Alzheimer's disease), or the ingestion of toxic substances (for example, lead poisoning or drugs).

3. **Psychoactive substance use disorders**
   Includes excessive use of alcohol, barbiturates, amphetamines, cocaine, and other drugs that alter behavior. Marijuana and tobacco are also included in this category, which is controversial.

4. **Schizophrenia**
   A group of disorders characterized by loss of contact with reality, marked disturbances of thought and perception, and bizarre behavior. At some phase of the illness delusions or hallucinations almost always occur.

5. **Delusional (paranoid) disorders**
   Disorders characterized by excessive suspicions and hostility accompanied by feelings of being persecuted; reality contact in other areas is satisfactory.

6. **Mood disorders**
   Disturbances of normal mood; the person may be extremely depressed, abnormally elated, or may alternate between periods of elation and depression.

7. **Anxiety disorders**
   Includes disorders in which anxiety is the main symptom (generalized anxiety or panic disorders) or anxiety is experienced unless the individual avoids certain feared situations (phobic disorders) or tries to resist performing certain rituals or thinking persistent thoughts (obsessive-compulsive disorders). Also includes post-traumatic stress disorder.

8. **Somatoform disorders**
   The symptoms are physical, but no organic basis can be found and psychological factors appear to play the major role. Included are conversion disorders (for example, a woman who resents having to care for her invalid mother suddenly develops a paralyzed arm) and hypochondriasis (excessive preoccupation with health and fear of disease when there is no basis for concern).

particular course or who benefited from a certain kind of treatment) is also helpful in deciding how to treat the patient.

Disadvantages arise, however, if we allow a diagnostic label to carry too much weight. Labeling induces us to overlook the unique features of each case and to expect the person to conform to the classification. We may also forget that a label for maladaptive behavior is not an explanation of that behavior; the classification does not tell us how the behavior originated or what maintains the behavior.

The classification of mental disorders used by most mental health professionals in this country is the *Diagnostic and Statistical Manual of Mental Disorders*, 3rd edition, revised (DSM-III-R, for short), which corresponds generally to the international system formulated by the World Health

9. **Dissociative disorders**
   Temporary alterations in the functions of consciousness, memory, or identity
   due to emotional problems. Included are amnesia (the individual cannot recall
   anything about his or her history following a traumatic experience) and multiple
   personality (two or more independent personality systems existing within the
   same individual).

10. **Sexual disorders**
    Includes problems of sexual identity (for example, transsexualism), sexual
    performance (for example, impotence, premature ejaculation, and frigidity),
    and sexual aim (for example, sexual interest in children). Homosexuality is
    considered a disorder only when the individual is unhappy with his or her sexual
    orientation and wishes to change it.

11. **Sleep disorders**
    Includes chronic insomnia, excessive sleepiness, sleep apnea, sleepwalking, and
    narcolepsy.

12. **Factitious disorders**
    Physical or psychological symptoms that are intentionally produced or feigned.
    Differs from malingering in that there is no obvious goal, such as disability
    payments or the avoidance of military service. The best-studied form of this
    disorder is called Münchausen syndrome: the individual's plausible presentation
    of factitious physical symptoms results in frequent hospitalizations.

13. **Impulse control disorders**
    Includes kleptomania (compulsive stealing of objects not needed for personal
    use or their monetary value), pathological gambling and pyromania (setting fires
    for the pleasure or relief of tension derived thereby).

14. **Personality disorders**
    Long-standing patterns of maladaptive behavior that constitute immature and
    inappropriate ways of coping with stress or solving problems. Antisocial
    personality disorder and narcissistic personality disorder are two examples.

15. **Conditions not attributable to a mental disorder**
    This category includes many of the problems for which people seek help, such
    as marital problems, parent-child difficulties, and academic or occupational
    problems.

Organization. The major categories of mental disorders classified by
DSM-III-R are listed in Table 16-1. Some of these disorders will be discussed
in more detail later in the chapter.

DSM-III-R provides an extensive list of subcategories under each of
these headings, as well as a description of the symptoms that must be present
for the diagnosis to be applicable. The complete diagnosis for an individual is
fairly comprehensive. Each person is evaluated on five separate dimensions
or axes. Axis I includes the categories listed in Table 16-1, except for personality disorders and developmental disorders (such as mental retardation or
language problems) that make up Axis II. Axes I and II were separated to
ensure that the presence of long-term disturbances would be considered
when attending to the present one. For example, a person who is now a

heroin addict would be diagnosed on Axis I as having a psychoactive substance use disorder; he might also have a long-standing antisocial personality disorder, which would be listed on Axis II.

The remaining three axes are not needed to make the actual diagnosis but are included to ensure that factors other than a person's symptoms are considered in the overall assessment. The five axes are listed below.

I: The diagnostic category listed in Table 16-1 with the appropriate subclassification. For example, "schizophrenia, paranoid type."

II: A description of the individual's prominent personality characteristics and ways of coping with stress.

III: A list of any current physical disorders that may be relevant to understanding and treating the person.

IV: Documentation of stressful events that may have precipitated the disorder (such as divorce, death of a loved one).

V: An evaluation of how well the individual has functioned socially and occupationally during the previous year.

All of these variables are helpful in determining treatment and prognosis.

You have probably heard the terms "neurosis" and "psychosis" and may be wondering where they fit into the categories of mental disorders listed in Table 16-1. Traditionally, these terms denoted major diagnostic categories. *Neuroses* (plural of *neurosis*) included a group of disorders characterized by anxiety, personal unhappiness, and maladaptive behavior that were seldom serious enough to require hospitalization. The individual could usually function in society, although not at full capacity. *Psychoses* (plural of *psychosis*) included more serious mental disorders. The individual's behavior and thought processes were so disturbed that he or she was out of touch with reality, could not cope with the demands of daily life, and usually had to be hospitalized.

Neither neuroses nor psychoses appear as major categories in DSM-III-R. There are several reasons for this departure from earlier classification systems, but the main one concerns precision of diagnosis. Both categories were fairly broad and included a number of mental disorders with quite dissimilar symptoms. Consequently, mental health professionals did not always agree on the diagnosis for a particular case. DSM-III-R attempts to achieve greater consensus by grouping disorders according to very specific behavioral symptoms, without implying anything about their origins or treatment. The intention is to describe what clinical workers *observe* about individuals who have psychological problems in a way that ensures accurate communication among mental health professionals. Consequently, DSM-III-R includes many more categories than previous editions of the manual. Disorders that were formerly categorized as neuroses (because they were assumed to be ways of coping with internal conflicts) are listed in DSM-III-R under three separate categories: anxiety disorders, somatoform disorders, and dissociative disorders.

Although psychosis is no longer a major category, DSM-III-R recognizes that people diagnosed as having schizophrenia, delusional disorders, some mood disorders, and certain organic mental disorders exhibit *psychotic behavior* at some point during their illness. The individual inaccurately evaluates his or her perceptions and thoughts and makes incorrect inferences about external reality. The person may have *hallucinations* (false sensory experiences, such as hearing voices or seeing strange visions) and/or *delusions* (false

TABLE 16-2
Lifetime Prevalence Rates of Selected Disorders *Listed are the percentage of individuals in the United States population who have experienced one of these mental disorders during their lifetime. These percentages are based on interviews with a sample of 18,571 individuals, age 18 and over, in five major United States cities. (After Regier et al., 1988)*

DISORDER	RATE
Anxiety disorders	14.6%
Mood disorders	8.3%
Schizophrenia	1.3%
Antisocial personality	2.5%
Substance use disorders	16.4%

beliefs, such as the conviction that all thoughts are controlled by a powerful being from another planet).

These issues will become clearer as we look more closely at some of the mental disorders listed in Table 16-1. In the remainder of this chapter, we will examine anxiety disorders, mood disorders, schizophrenia, and one type of personality disorder. Alcoholism and drug dependence (both classified as psychoactive substance use disorders) are covered in Chapter 6. Multiple personality, a dissociative disorder, is also discussed in Chapter 6.

Table 16-2 gives the likelihood of the major mental disorders during one's lifetime. The study on which this table is based found that mental disorders are more common among people under age 45 and more common in women than in men. However, men were twice as likely as women to abuse drugs and five times as likely to abuse alcohol. Antisocial personality disorders affected four times as many men as women, but more women suffered from mood and anxiety disorders.

ANXIETY DISORDERS

Most of us feel anxious and tense in the face of threatening or stressful situations. Such feelings are normal reactions to stress. Anxiety is considered abnormal only when it occurs in situations that most people can handle with little difficulty. *Anxiety disorders* include a group of disorders in which anxiety either is the main symptom (*generalized anxiety* and *panic disorders*) or is experienced when the individual attempts to control certain maladaptive behaviors (*phobic* and *obsessive-compulsive disorders*). (Post-traumatic stress disorder, which involves anxiety following a traumatic event, was discussed in Chapter 15.)

TABLE 16-3
Generalized Anxiety *The statements listed in the table are self-descriptions by individuals who have chronically high levels of anxiety.* (After Sarason & Sarason, 1984)

I am often bothered by the thumping of my heart.

Little annoyances get on my nerves and irritate me.

I often become suddenly scared for no good reason.

I worry continuously and that gets me down.

I frequently get spells of complete exhaustion and fatigue.

It is always hard for me to make up my mind.

I always seem to be dreading something.

I feel nervous and high-strung all the time.

I often feel I cannot overcome my difficulties.

I feel constantly under strain.

Generalized Anxiety and Panic Disorders

A person who suffers from a *generalized anxiety disorder* lives each day in a state of high tension. She or he feels vaguely uneasy or apprehensive much of the time and tends to overreact even to mild stresses. An inability to relax, disturbed sleep, fatigue, headaches, dizziness, and rapid heart rate are the most common physical complaints. In addition, the individual continually worries about potential problems and has difficulty concentrating or making decisions. When the individual finally makes a decision, it becomes the source of further worry ("Did I foresee all possible consequences?" or "Will disaster result?"). Some self-descriptions provided by people with chronically high levels of anxiety appear in Table 16-3.

People who suffer generalized anxiety may also experience panic attacks—episodes of acute and overwhelming apprehension or terror. During panic attacks, the individual feels certain that something dreadful is about to happen. This feeling is usually accompanied by such symptoms as heart palpitations, shortness of breath, perspiration, muscle tremors, faintness, and nausea. The symptoms result from excitation of the sympathetic division of the autonomic nervous system (see Chapter 2) and are the same reactions an individual experiences when extremely frightened. During severe panic attacks, the person fears that he or she will die. The following personal account describes how terrifying such experiences can be:

> I remember walking up the street, the moon was shining and suddenly everything around me seemed unfamiliar, as it would be in a dream. I felt panic rising inside me, but managed to push it away and carry on. I walked a quarter of a mile or so, with the panic getting worse every minute. . . . By now, I was sweating, yet trembling; my heart was pounding and my legs felt like jelly. . . . Terrified, I stood, not knowing what to do. The only bit of sanity left in me told me to get home. Somehow this I did very slowly, holding onto the fence in the road. I cannot remember the actual journey back, until I was going into the house, then I broke down and cried helplessly. . . . I did not go out again for a few days. When I did, it was with my mother and baby to my grandmother's a few miles away. I felt panicky there and couldn't cope with the baby. My cousin suggested we go to my Aunt's house, but I had another attack there. I was sure I was going to die. Following this, I was totally unable to go out alone, and even with someone else I had great difficulty. Not only did I get the panicky fainting spells, but I lived in constant fear of getting them. (Melville, 1977, pp. 1, 14)

People who experience generalized anxiety and panic disorders may have no clear idea of why they are frightened. This kind of anxiety is sometimes called "free-floating" because it is not triggered by a particular event; rather, it occurs in a variety of situations.

Phobias

In contrast to the vague apprehension of generalized anxiety disorders, the fears in phobic disorders are more specific. Someone who responds with intense fear to a stimulus or situation that most people do not consider particularly dangerous is said to have a *phobia*. The individual usually realizes that his or her fear is irrational but still feels anxiety (ranging from strong uneasiness to panic) that can be alleviated only by avoiding the feared object or situation.

Most of us are afraid of something. Snakes, high places, storms, doctors, sickness, injury, and death are the seven fears most commonly reported by adults (Agras, 1975). As you can see from Figure 16-1, the prevalence of specific fears changes with age. There appears to be a continuum between these common fears and phobias, making their distinctions somewhat arbitrary. However, a fear is usually not diagnosed as a phobic disorder unless it interferes considerably with the person's daily life. Examples of phobic disorders would be a woman whose fear of enclosed places prevents her from entering elevators or a man whose fear of crowds prevents him from attending the theater or walking along congested sidewalks.

DSM-III-R divides phobic disorders into three broad categories: simple phobias, social phobias, and agoraphobia. A *simple phobia* is a fear of a specific object, animal, or situation. Irrational fears of snakes, heights, enclosed places, and darkness are examples. Some people may develop a simple phobia but be normal in other respects. In more serious cases, the individual has a number of phobias that interfere with many aspects of life and may be intertwined with obsessive or compulsive behavior (see Box 1).

People with *social phobias* feel extremely insecure in social situations and have an exaggerated fear of embarrassing themselves. Often they are fearful that they will betray their anxiety by such signs as hand tremors, blushing, or a quavering voice. These fears are usually unrealistic: individuals who fear they might shake do not do so; those who fear they will stutter or quaver actually speak quite normally. Fear of public speaking or of eating in public are the most common complaints of socially phobic individuals.

Agoraphobia is the most common phobia among people seeking professional help. It is also the most disabling. The word is Greek for "fear of the marketplace." Individuals suffering from agoraphobia are afraid of entering unfamiliar settings. They avoid open spaces, crowds, and traveling. In extreme cases, the individual may be afraid to leave the familiar setting of home. The following incident in the life of a woman suffering from agoraphobia shows how distressing such fears can be.

> The woman who lives next door is a very nice person and I like her. One day she asked me if I would drive over to a big shopping center that had recently opened about five miles from where we live. I didn't know how to tell her that there isn't a chance in the world that I'd go to that shopping center or any other place outside our neighborhood. She must have seen how upset I got, but I was shaking like a leaf even more inside. I imagined myself in the crowd, getting lost, or passing out. I was terrified by the openness of the shopping center and the crowds. I made an excuse this time, but I don't know what I'll say next time. Maybe I'll just have to let her in on my little bit of craziness. (Sarason & Sarason, 1984, p. 140)

Agoraphobics usually have a history of panic attacks. They become fearful of being incapacitated by an attack away from the security of home and where no one may be available to help them. Crowded enclosed places where escape to safety would be difficult (such as a bus or a theater) are especially terrifying. But agoraphobics also fear open spaces (large bodies of water, bare landscapes, an empty street) and feel more comfortable when the space is circumscribed by trees, or when an enclosed space (perhaps symbolic of home) is easily reached. Agoraphobics are usually very dependent. A large percentage of them exhibited separation anxiety (fear of being away from mother) in childhood, long before developing agoraphobia (Gittelman & Klein, 1985). While simple phobias and social phobias are fairly easy to treat, agoraphobia is much more difficult.

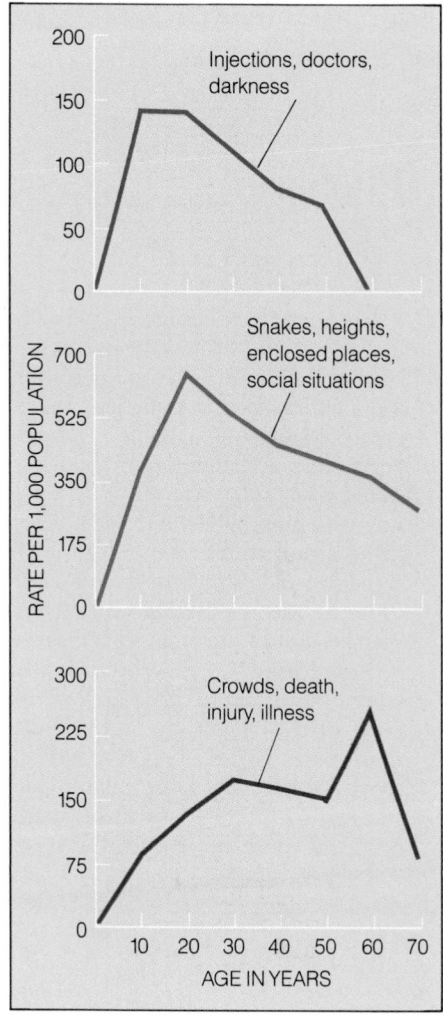

FIGURE 16-1
Fears Change with Age *The graphs show the prevalence of specific fears reported by people of different ages. Fears that follow the same general age pattern are represented together. For example, fears of injections, doctors, and darkness peak at about age 10 and decline thereafter. Fears of snakes, heights, enclosed places, and social situations reach a peak at age 20. Fears of crowds, death, injury, or illness become more prevalent later in life. (After Agras, Sylvester, & Oliveau, 1969)*

Box 1
Phobias

An 18-year-old college freshman came for help at the student health center because each time he left his dormitory room and headed toward class, he experienced a feeling of panic. "It would get so bad at times that I thought I would collapse on the way to class. It was a frightening feeling, and I began to be afraid to leave the dorm." He could not understand these feelings because he was reasonably well pleased with his classes and professors. Even after he returned to the dormitory, he would be unable to face anyone for hours or to concentrate on his homework. But if he remained in or near his room, he felt reasonably comfortable.

During interviews with his therapist, the youth reported other fears, including becoming contaminated by syphilis and growing prematurely bald. Occasionally, these fears were sufficiently intense and persistent to cause him to scrub his hands, genitals, and head compulsively until these parts became red and sometimes even bled. In addition, he touched doorknobs only reluctantly, never drank water from a public fountain, and only used the toilet in his home or dormitory. He realized that his fears were unfounded and exaggerated but also felt that many of his precautions and constant worrying were necessary to avoid even greater "mental anguish."

The student's past history revealed that he had serious concerns about his sexual identity and his adequacy as a male. When he was young, he had avoided playing with the other boys because he could not run as fast or hit a ball as far. His mother had strongly rewarded his tendency not to join others because she was convinced that he would get hurt if he participated in their "roughhousing." He was a late maturer and had spent a traumatic summer at camp about the time that most of his peers were reaching puberty. Discovering that he was sexually underdeveloped in comparison to the other boys, he worried about his deficiency; he wondered whether he was destined to become a girl, and he feared that the other boys might attack him sexually.

Although his puberty made a belated appearance, he continued to worry about his masculine identity and even fantasized on occasion that he was a girl. At these times, he became extremely anxious and seriously considered suicide as a solution.

The therapist's immediate goal in treatment was to remove the student's irrational fear of leaving the dormitory, which was accomplished with the method of systematic desensitization [see Chapter 17]. However, the phobias in this case were clearly part of a deep-rooted problem of sexual identity that would require extensive psychotherapy (Kleinmuntz, 1974, pp. 168–169).

Obsessive-Compulsive Disorders

Individuals with an *obsessive-compulsive disorder* feel compelled to think about things they would rather not think about or perform acts they do not wish to carry out. *Obsessions* are persistent intrusions of unwelcome thoughts or images. *Compulsions* are irresistible urges to carry out certain acts or rituals. Obsessive thoughts may be linked with compulsive acts (for example, thoughts of lurking germs combined with the compulsion to wash eating utensils many times before using them). While people with phobias fear what will happen if they *do* something (enter a crowded elevator or speak in public), people with compulsions fear what will happen if they *don't* do something (wash their hands repeatedly or check the door locks every hour).

At times, all of us have persistently recurring thoughts ("Did I lock the door?") and urges to perform ritualistic behavior (knocking on wood after boasting of good fortune). But when a person has an obsessive-compulsive disorder, such thoughts occupy so much time that they seriously interfere with daily life. The individual recognizes that these thoughts are irrational but is unable to control them. Obsessive thoughts cover a variety of topics, but most often they are concerned with committing aggressive or sexual acts. A mother may have persistent thoughts of drowning her infant in the bathtub. A young man may have recurrent thoughts of exposing his genitals in public or shouting obscenities in church. The likelihood that these thoughts

Box 2
Obsessive Thoughts

A 32-year-old mother of two small children sought help because she was distressed over obsessively intrusive and repugnant thoughts related to injuring or murdering her children. On infrequent occasions, her husband was also a victim. These thoughts were so repugnant, made so little sense, and were so foreign to her conscious feelings that she had been afraid and embarrassed to seek help. She had kept this problem to herself for nearly 2 years, despite considerable psychological pain, tension, and turmoil. Finally, the steadily increasing difficulty had reached an intolerable level.

The thoughts that were so terribly disturbing to this patient really did not differ greatly in quality from what every normal young woman may occasionally feel toward her children. Many less inhibited and more spontaneous young parents than this one might occasionally say, "Oh, I feel just like throwing Johnny out of the window today! He makes me so mad!" Most mothers would not feel threatened by such a thought or guilty about having had it and would probably forget it rather quickly. But this patient greatly feared and condemned such thoughts. To her, the thought was nearly as threatening and as guilt-provoking as the act.

Early in life, this woman had developed a defensive need to deny the presence of all negative feelings. To defend herself against the guilt occasioned by having such terrible thoughts, she endeavored to dissociate herself from them—to deny that they were her thoughts. "It's just awful words that pop into my head. . . . They have nothing at all to do with the way I feel. They couldn't be my thoughts at all. . . ."

The patient had been raised by an anxious and insecure mother who was unable to permit herself or her children the slightest expression of negative feelings. The daughter soon realized that any feelings other than loving ones must be repressed or denied. The patient was the eldest of three siblings and had been assigned undue responsibility for their care. She felt deprived of her share of her parents' affection, was greatly resentful of her younger sister and brother, and fantasized about what it would be like if they were not around. Her occasional murderous fantasies about them were accompanied by tremendous guilt and anxiety. As a result, the fantasies and associated emotional feelings had been completely repressed from conscious awareness. These early conflicts were reactivated during her marriage when the needs of her husband and children seemed to take precedence over her own needs (Laughlin, 1967, pp. 324–325).

---

will be transformed into actions is slim. Nevertheless, individuals who experience such obsessive thoughts are horrified by them, cannot understand why they persist, and live in fear that they will perform these dreadful acts. Box 2 reports the history of a young mother who was distressed by recurrent thoughts of murdering her two small children. The kind of prohibition her parents placed on any expression of negative feelings is fairly characteristic of the background of persons who develop obsessive-compulsive disorders. When normal feelings of anger are suppressed or denied, it is hypothesized that they become an alien part of the personality and find expression only in indirect ways.

Compulsive acts range from mild kinds of superstitious behavior (such as not stepping on the cracks in sidewalks or arranging the material on a desk in a precise order before starting an assignment) to elaborate rituals like those described in Box 3.

Most of us find comfort in certain familiar routines or rituals, particularly in times of stress. But people with obsessive-compulsive disorders become intensely anxious when they try to resist their compulsions, and they feel a release of tension once their acts are carried out.

We sometimes label a person who is exceedingly neat, meticulous, and exasperatingly attentive to details a compulsive personality—or sometimes an obsessive-compulsive personality. Such people also tend to be rigid in their thinking and behavior and highly moralistic. It is tempting to suppose

Box 3
Compulsive Rituals

A 30-year-old woman had developed such an elaborate sequence of ritual acts that their consummation occupied most of her waking hours. She could not go to bed at night before she had checked each door and window three times to ensure that it was locked. The gas range and the pilot lights to the furnace and hot water heater also had to be checked to make certain that no gas was escaping. Bathing and dressing took up much of her time; she often took three or four showers in succession—scrubbing her body thoroughly with a special antibacterial cleanser each time—before she was convinced that she was clean enough to put on her clothes. She wore only clothing that could be washed at home, because she did not trust the dry cleaner to remove all possible germs. And each article had to be washed and rinsed three times before she would wear it. Similar hygienic procedures were involved whenever she prepared food: she scalded each dish and utensil with boiling water before and after using it and would not eat a meal unless she had prepared it herself.

This woman had always been unusually neat and clean, but her security operations had intensified over the years until they reached pathological proportions. At times, she realized the foolishness of her precautions, but she experienced intense anxiety whenever she attempted to cut short any of her procedures or omit a step in one of her rituals (R. L. Atkinson, unpublished case report).

that when an obsessive-compulsive personality is under stress, he or she reacts by developing an obsessive-compulsive disorder. However, this hypothesis is not supported by evidence. The results of personality tests indicate that people with *obsessive-compulsive disorders* do not have the characteristics of an *obsessive-compulsive personality* (Rachman & Hodgson, 1980). We should note, in addition, that people with obsessive-compulsive personalities tend to be proud of their meticulousness and attention to detail. Individuals with obsessive-compulsive disorders, in contrast, abhor their symptoms and wish to be rid of them.

Understanding Anxiety Disorders

We do not know why some people become chronically anxious, but their reactions seem to reflect feelings of inadequacy in situations that they perceive as threatening. Theories of anxiety disorders have focused on internal conflicts, learned responses to external events, maladaptive cognitions, and biological factors.

PSYCHOANALYTIC PERSPECTIVE   Psychoanalytic theory assumes that the sources of anxiety are internal and unconscious. The person has repressed certain unacceptable or dangerous impulses that would jeopardize self-esteem or relationships with other people if they were expressed. In situations in which these impulses (usually sexual or aggressive in nature) are likely to be aroused, the individual experiences intense anxiety. Because the source of anxiety is unconscious, the person does not know why he or she feels apprehensive.

From a psychoanalytic viewpoint, phobias are ways of coping with anxiety by displacing it onto an object or situation that can be avoided. For example, the student whose case is reported in Box 1 could avoid the arousal of homosexual impulses by staying in his room away from other men and by not using public restrooms. Obsessions and compulsions also serve to protect the individual from recognizing the true source of his or her anxiety. Obsessive thoughts are unacceptable impulses (hostility, destructiveness, inappropriate sexual urges) that have been repressed and somehow reappear in a disguised form. The individual feels that they are not a part of herself or himself and may commit compulsive acts to undo or atone for forbidden impulses. A mother who is obsessed with thoughts of murdering her infant may feel compelled to check many times during the night to assure herself that the child is well. Compulsive rituals also serve to keep threatening impulses out of the individual's conscious awareness: a person who is continually busy has little opportunity to think improper thoughts or commit improper actions.

BEHAVIORAL PERSPECTIVE   Psychologists who work within the framework of learning theory view anxiety as triggered more by specific external events than by internal conflicts. Generalized anxiety occurs when a person feels unable to cope with many everyday situations and consequently feels apprehensive much of the time. Phobias are viewed as avoidance responses that may be learned either directly from frightening experiences (developing a fear of dogs after being attacked by one) or vicariously by observing fearful responses in others.

The classical conditioning paradigm (see Chapter 7) provides an explanation of how innocuous objects or situations can become the focus of a phobia: a neutral object (the conditioned stimulus) paired with a traumatic event (the unconditioned stimulus) produces fear of the neutral object (the conditioned response). For example, a child who is stung by a bee while picking a yellow flower develops a phobia for yellow flowers. The precipitating trauma, when it can be identified in phobic cases, is well described by classical conditioning. There is considerable evidence from laboratory experiments with animals and humans that pairing a neutral object with a frightening situation produces strong fear of the neutral object. However, there are problems with this explanation of phobias. Simple phobias almost always are restricted to a certain set of objects, rather than to any object that happens to be present at the same time as the traumatic event. Why, for example, are phobias of the dark common, but phobias of pajamas nonexistent, although both are paired with nighttime trauma? Why do we have phobias of snakes and insects but not phobias of kittens or lambs? And why are phobias of knives and guns rare, even though both objects are often paired with injury?

The notion of *prepared conditioning* has been proposed as an explanation. Humans are biologically predisposed, or prepared, to react with fear only to certain classes of dangerous objects or situations. When these objects or situations are paired with trauma, fear conditioning occurs rapidly and is very resistant to extinction (Seligman, 1971; Seligman & Rosenhan, 1984). The majority of common phobias were once actually dangerous to our early ancestors. Natural selection may have favored those ancestors who learned quickly (with only minimal exposure to trauma) that strangers, heights, snakes, large animals, and the dark were dangerous. Evolution may have selected certain objects, all dangerous in an earlier time, that are readily conditionable to trauma. We are less likely to become conditioned to fear other objects (such as lambs, guns, and electric outlets) either because they were never dangerous or because their origin is too recent to have been subject to natural selection. Thus, phobias are instances not of ordinary classical conditioning but of prepared classical conditioning.

A series of laboratory experiments lends support to the idea that people are more prepared to learn to be afraid of certain objects than they are of others. Fear was conditioned in student volunteers using a variety of prepared

conditioned stimuli (pictures of snakes or spiders) and unprepared stimuli (pictures of houses, faces, or flowers). The pictures were followed by a brief, painful electric shock. Fear conditioning, as measured by galvanic skin response (see Chapter 7), occurred much more rapidly to prepared stimuli than to unprepared ones. In fact, conditioning occurred in one pairing of electric shock with pictures of snakes and spiders, but it took four or five pairings for subjects' fear to be conditioned to faces, houses, or flowers. A subsequent experiment found the conditioning properties of guns to be similar to those for flowers, not snakes and spiders (Ohman, Fredrikson, Hugdahl, & Rimmo, 1976).

Viewing phobias as a form of prepared learning helps explain their irrationality and their resistance to extinction. With normal fear conditioning, once the unconditioned stimulus (for instance, the electric shock) is no longer paired with the conditioned stimulus, fear extinguishes rapidly. This does not appear to be the case for prepared fear conditioning. In one study, students were conditioned to fear either snakes and spiders or houses and faces by pairing each with shock. At the end of the conditioning (when the electrodes were removed), fear extinguished immediately to houses and faces but remained intense to snakes and spiders (Hugdahl & Ohman, 1977).

While some phobias appear to result from actual frightening experiences, others may be learned vicariously, through observation. Fearful parents tend to produce children who share their fears. A child who observes his or her parents react with fear to a variety of situations may accept such reactions as normal. Indeed, studies find a high correlation between the fears of a mother and those of her child.

As we will see in the next chapter, the treatment of phobias within the framework of learning theory uses various techniques to extinguish fear responses to the phobic object or situation.

COGNITIVE PERSPECTIVE   A cognitive analysis of anxiety disorders focuses on the way that anxious people think about situations and potential dangers. Individuals who suffer from generalized anxiety tend to make unrealistic appraisals of certain situations, primarily those in which the possibility of danger is remote. They consistently overestimate both the *degree* of harm and the *likelihood* of harm. This kind of mental set makes a person hypervigilant, always on the lookout for signs of danger. For example, a sudden noise in the house is interpreted as burglars; the screech of brakes in the street means one's child is in danger. This hypervigilance and expectation of harm result in continual bodily mobilization for danger. Thus, the physiological responses characteristic of the fight-or-flight reaction (tremors, rapid heart rate, clammy hands, muscle tension) are present much of the time.

The cognitive theory of obsessions assumes that we all have unwanted and repetitive thoughts on occasion. For example, song lyrics or advertising jingles often intrude unbidden into consciousness. But we are able to dismiss them, as well as the more abhorrent thoughts that occasionally run through our heads. The more anxiety-provoking the content of the obsession, the more difficult it is for anyone—obsessive or nonobsessive—to dismiss the thought. And the more stressed we are, the more frequent and intense are these thoughts. If a person is anxious to begin with, obsessive thoughts will be more disturbing and more difficult to dismiss.

If an event triggers a disturbing thought in a nonobsessive person, he or she may find the thought unacceptable but will not become anxious and will easily dismiss it. In contrast, the obsessive person will be made anxious by the thought, and the anxiety will reduce his or her ability to dismiss it. The thought will persist, and the obsessive's inability to disregard it will lead to further anxiety, which will increase his or her susceptibility to the intrusive thought.

Compulsive rituals, according to the cognitive view, are attempts to neutralize the bad thought by an action that ensures safety. Thus, the person obsessed with thoughts of disease and germs washes his hands and food dozens of times. The one obsessed with thoughts that the doors are unlocked checks them many times a night. These rituals are reinforced by the relief from anxiety. But the relief is temporary. The obsessive thoughts return with increased frequency and intensity, and the ritual must be performed each time the thought recurs.

As we will see in the next chapter, the cognitive approach to treating obsessive disorders uses the technique of thought stopping to help the individual terminate obsessive thoughts. The treatment for generalized anxiety and phobias focuses on helping individuals develop more realistic and rational appraisals of themselves and the situations they encounter.

BIOLOGICAL PERSPECTIVE   Anxiety disorders tend to run in families. About 15 percent of parents and siblings of people who have anxiety disorders are similarly affected (Carey & Gottesman, 1981). This finding does not, of course, prove a hereditary basis for such disorders, since these individuals usually live together and thus experience similar environments. However, the results of twin studies provide firmer evidence for an inherited predisposition for panic attacks. Identical twins, as you recall, develop from the same egg and share the same heredity; fraternal twins develop from different eggs and are no more alike genetically than ordinary siblings. An identical twin is three times more likely to suffer from panic attacks if the other twin does than are fraternal twins (Torgersen, 1983).

Scientists have identified a brain chemical (cholecystokinin) that produces panic attacks when injected into individuals who suffer from spontaneous panic attacks (Bradwejn, 1989). Drugs that are capable of preventing panic attacks appear to block the effect of this chemical on neurons. Researchers can also trigger panic attacks in patients by exposing them to carbon dioxide or other substances not found in the brain. These same substances usually have no effect on normal individuals or on phobics who experience anxiety in response to an external stimulus (Lader, 1985).

However, even if panic disorders have a biochemical basis, environmental experiences undoubtedly play an important role. Such disorders may develop through an interaction between biological predispositions and childhood experiences. Some children may be born with a lowered threshold for the arousal of anxiety. These children would be more prone than others to develop separation anxiety if deprived of the mother's care. And, as noted earlier, separation anxiety is often the forerunner of panic disorder in adulthood.

Recent research has also identified a biological basis for obsessive-compulsive disorders: a biochemical abnormality in certain brain areas that may make a person vulnerable to repetitive thoughts and behaviors. PET scan studies (see Chapter 2) of obsessive-compulsive individuals have shown that the metabolic activity in a specific region of their brains (a circuit that runs between the frontal lobes and the basal ganglia) differs from that of normal individuals (Baxter et al., 1988). This region is believed to be involved in the brain's strategy for coping with repeated stimuli and in the control of repetitive movements. In essence, this part of the brain may play a

"Ronald is *extremely* compulsive."

PET scans reveal metabolic differences between the brain of an obsessive-compulsive patient and that of a normal subject. In the photos (three different cross-sections) red corresponds to the highest level of metabolic activity and blue to the lowest level. The obsessive-compulsive individual has elevated levels in several areas, including the basal ganglia.

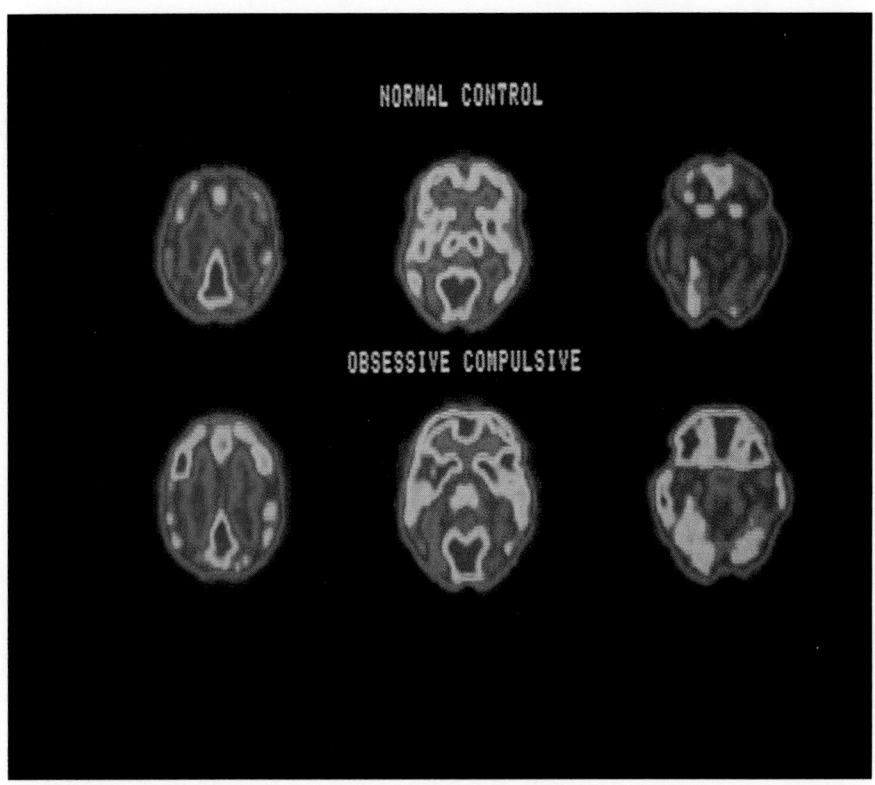

role in telling the rest of the brain to stop worrying about contamination once the hands have been washed or about fire once the stove has been turned off. The exact nature of the brain chemistry abnormality is unknown, and such abnormalities may not be found in all cases of obsessive-compulsive disorders. Nevertheless, treatment with drugs that block the uptake of a neurotransmitter for which the basal ganglia have particularly dense receptors relieves obsessive-compulsive symptoms in about 60 percent of cases (Rapoport, 1989).

The chemical systems in the brain that regulate feelings of anxiety and the symptoms of specific anxiety disorders (such as panic and obsessive-compulsive disorders) undoubtedly involve the complex interaction of a number of neurotransmitters acting on different brain areas. In 1960, a group of drugs called *benzodiazepines* were developed and marketed under such trade names as Valium and Librium. These drugs proved effective in reducing anxiety (see Chapter 17 for a discussion of their merits and disadvantages). Researchers subsequently discovered that the drugs were effective because they bind to specific receptor molecules in certain neurons of the brain, thereby influencing neural transmission (see Chapter 2). The discovery of receptor sites for antianxiety drugs set off a search for a natural body substance that might act in the same way to keep anxiety in proper balance. So far, a natural Valium has not been found, but investigators have learned a great deal about the benzodiazepine receptors and how certain chemicals operate to increase or decrease anxiety (Costa, 1985).

There appear to be three specific docking areas on the benzodiazepine receptor site: one for the benzodiazepine molecule with its antianxiety effects, another for compounds that cause anxiety (the effects of which are blocked by administration of the benzodiazepines), and the third for a group of substances that block the effects of both the benzodiazepines and the anxiety-provoking compounds. The identification of these three receptor sites suggests that some substances secreted in the brain produce the subjective experience of fear and anxiety and other substances block this effect. The ratio of these substances may lead either to an emotionally stable or to an anxious individual (Agras, 1985).

MOOD DISORDERS

In *mood disorders* the person may be severely depressed or manic (wildly elated), or may experience periods of depression as well as periods of mania. Mood disorders are divided into *depressive disorders*, in which the individual has one or more periods of depression without a history of manic episodes, and *bipolar disorders*, in which the individual alternates between periods of depression and periods of elation, usually with a return to normal mood in between the two extremes. Manic episodes without some history of depression are very uncommon.

Depression

Almost everyone gets depressed at times. Most of us have periods when we feel sad, lethargic, and not interested in any activities—even pleasurable ones. Depression is a normal response to many of life's stresses. Among the situations that most often precipitate depression are failure at school or at work, the loss of a loved one, and the realization that illness or aging is depleting one's resources. Depression is considered abnormal only when it is out of proportion to the event and continues past the point at which most people begin to recover.

Although depression is characterized as a disorder of mood, there are actually four sets of symptoms. In addition to emotional (mood) symptoms, there are cognitive, motivational, and physical symptoms. An individual need not have all of these to be diagnosed as depressed, but the more symptoms he or she has, and the more intense they are, the more certain we can be that the individual is suffering from depression.

Sadness and dejection are the most salient emotional symptoms in depression. The individual feels hopeless and unhappy, often has crying spells, and may contemplate suicide. Equally pervasive in depression is the loss of gratification or pleasure in life. Activities that used to bring satisfaction seem dull and joyless. The depressed person gradually loses interest in hobbies, recreation, and family activities. Most depressed patients report that they no longer derive gratification from what had been major interests in life, and many report losing interest in and affection for other people.

The cognitive symptoms consist primarily of negative thoughts. Depressed individuals tend to have low self-esteem, feel inadequate, and blame themselves for their failures. They feel hopeless about the future and are pessimistic that they can do anything to improve their life.

Motivation is at a low ebb in depression. The depressed person tends to be passive and has difficulty initiating activities. The following conversation between a patient and his therapist illustrates this passivity. The man, who

had been hospitalized after a suicide attempt, spent his days sitting motionless in the lounge. His therapist decided to try to engage him in some activities:

Anne

THERAPIST: I understand that you spend most of your day in the lounge. Is that true?
PATIENT: Yes, being quiet gives me the peace of mind I need.
THERAPIST: When you sit here, how's your mood?
PATIENT: I feel awful all the time. I just wish I could fall in a hole somewhere and die.
THERAPIST: Do you feel better after sitting for 2 or 3 hours?
PATIENT: No, the same.
THERAPIST: So you're sitting in the hope that you'll find peace of mind, but it doesn't sound like your depression improves.
PATIENT: I get so bored.
THERAPIST: Would you consider being more active? There are a number of reasons why I think increasing your activity level might help.
PATIENT: There's nothing to do around here.
THERAPIST: Would you consider trying some activities if I could come up with a list?
PATIENT: If you think it will help, but I think you're wasting your time. I don't have any interests.

(Beck, Rush, Shaw & Emery, 1979, p. 200)

The physical symptoms of depression include loss of appetite, sleep disturbances, fatigue, and loss of energy. Since a depressed person's thoughts are focused inward, rather than toward external events, he or she may magnify aches and pains and worry about health.

As we see from this description of its many symptoms, depression can be a debilitating disorder. Fortunately, most depressive episodes are of relatively short duration. Depressed people gradually recover, with or without treatment. About one-quarter of depressive episodes last less than a month, half last less than 3 months, and one-quarter last a year or longer. Only about 10 percent of the latter group do not recover and remain chronically depressed (Lewinsohn, Fenn, & Franklin, 1982). Unfortunately, depressive episodes tend to recur. About half the individuals who have a depressive episode will experience another one. Generally, the more stable a person is before the first episode, the less likely that depression will recur.

Bipolar Disorders

The majority of depressions occur without episodes of mania. But between 5 and 10 percent of mood disorders involve both poles of the mood continuum and are classified as *bipolar disorders*, also known as *manic-depression*. The individual alternates between depression and normal mood and between extreme elation and normal mood. In some cases the cycle between depressive episodes and manic episodes is swift with only a brief return to normality in between.

People experiencing manic episodes behave in a way that appears, on the surface, to be the opposite of depression. During mild manic episodes, the individual is energetic, enthusiastic, and full of self-confidence. He or she talks continually, rushes from one activity to another with little need of sleep, and makes grandiose plans, paying little attention to their practicality. Unlike the kind of joyful exuberance that characterizes normal elation, manic behavior has a driven quality and often expresses hostility more than it does elation.

People experiencing severe manic episodes behave somewhat like the popular concept of a "raving maniac." They are extremely excited and constantly active. They may pace about, sing, shout, or pound the walls for hours. They are angered by attempts to interfere with their activities and may become abusive. Impulses (including sexual ones) are immediately expressed in actions or words. These individuals are confused and disoriented and may experience delusions of great wealth, accomplishment, or power.

Manic episodes can occur without depression, but this is very rare. Usually a depressive episode will occur eventually, once a person has experienced a manic episode. The depression is similar to what we have already described.

Bipolar disorders are relatively rare. Whereas about 6 percent of adult females and 3 percent of adult males in the United States have experienced a major depression at some time, less than 1 percent of the adult population has had a bipolar disorder, which appears to be equally common in men and women. Manic-depression differs from other mood disorders in that it tends to occur at an earlier age, is more likely to run in families, responds to different therapeutic medications, and is apt to recur unless treated. These facts suggest that biological variables play a more important role than psychological variables in bipolar disorders.

Understanding Mood Disorders

Depression is one of the most prevalent emotional disorders. Because depression is so common and can be so debilitating, much effort has been devoted to determining its causes. We will look briefly at several approaches to understanding affective disorders.

PSYCHOANALYTIC PERSPECTIVE   Psychoanalytic theories interpret depression as a *reaction to loss*. Whatever the nature of the loss (loss of a loved one, loss of status, loss of moral support provided by a group of friends), the depressed person reacts to it intensely because the current situation brings back all the fears of an earlier loss that occurred in childhood—that being the loss of parental affection. For some reason, the individual's needs for affection and care were not satisfied in childhood. A loss in later life causes the individual to regress to his or her helpless, dependent state when the original loss occurred. Part of the depressed person's behavior, therefore, represents a cry for love—a display of helplessness and an appeal for affection and security (White & Watt, 1981).

Reaction to loss is complicated by angry feelings toward the deserting person. An underlying assumption of psychoanalytic theories is that people who are prone to depression have learned to repress their hostile feelings because they are afraid of alienating those on whom they depend for support. When things go wrong, they turn their anger inward and blame themselves. For example, a woman may feel extremely hostile toward the employer who fired her. But because her anger arouses anxiety, she uses the defense mechanism of projection to internalize her feelings: she is not angry; rather, others are angry at her. She assumes the employer had a good reason for rejecting her: she is incompetent and worthless.

Psychoanalytic theories suggest that the depressed person's low self-esteem and feelings of worthlessness stem from a childlike need for parental approval. A small child's self-esteem depends on the approval and affection

CRITICAL DISCUSSION

Depression and Suicide

The most disastrous consequence of depression is suicide. Of the reported 25,000 people who end their lives by suicide in the United States every year, the majority are suffering from depression. However, suicide deaths are underreported for a variety of reasons. Because of the stigma attached to suicide, physicians and coroners may be persuaded by the family to list a death as accidental when the circumstances are questionable. In addition, many single-car accidents are probably suicides. And some people who engage in dangerous sports and occupations, who adopt lethal habits (such as heavy use of drugs), or who are physically ill and terminate their medication may be seeking death. Consequently, the number of actual suicides per year may well be closer to 50,000. The number of people who attempt suicide but fail has been estimated at anywhere from two to eight times the number of suicides (Shneidman, 1985).

Women attempt to commit suicide about three times more often than men do, but men succeed in killing themselves more often than women. The greater number of suicide attempts by women is probably related to the greater incidence of depression among women. The fact that men are more successful in their attempts is related to the choice of method. Until recently, women have tended to use less lethal means, such as cutting their wrists or overdosing on sleeping pills; men are more apt to use firearms or carbon monoxide fumes or to hang themselves. However, with the marked increase in the number of women owning guns, suicide by firearms has now become the woman's method of first choice (Wintemute, Teret, Krause, & Wright, 1988). Consequently, the fatality rate for women will change. (Attempted suicides are successful 80 percent of the time when firearms are involved, while only 10 percent of drug or poison ingestions are fatal—a powerful argument for not keeping firearms in the home.)

Among the reasons most frequently cited by those who have attempted suicide are depression, loneliness, ill health, marital problems, and financial or job difficulties (Farberow & Shneidman, 1965; Shneidman, 1985).

The greatest number of suicides occurs among people in their 50s, and the rate continues to be high through age 60 and over. Recently, however, suicide has increased among adolescents and young adults. In fact, the incidence of suicide among 15- to 24-year-olds in the United States has almost tripled over the last two decades (Centers for Disease Control, 1985). Every year some 250,000 young people in this age group attempt suicide, and more than 5,000 of them succeed (Davis, 1983). College students are twice as likely to kill themselves as are nonstudents of the same age (Murphy & Wetzel, 1980).

The increased suicide rate among college students is found not only in the United States but in European countries, India, and Japan, as well. There are a number of possible reasons for the greater despair among college students: living away from home for the first time and having to cope with new problems; trying to stay at the top academically when the competition is much fiercer than it had been in high school; indecision about a career choice; loneliness caused by the absence of long-time friends and anxiety about new ones.

A study of the lives and academic records of college students who committed suicide found that they were moodier, drove themselves harder, and were depressed more frequently than their nonsuicidal classmates. They had also given recurrent warnings of their suicidal intent to others. The major precipitating events appear to have been worry about academic work and physical health and difficulties in their relationships with others (Seiden, 1966). However, we cannot be sure whether these factors caused the suicides or whether academic difficulties and interpersonal problems were secondary to a severe depression. Worry about health is frequently a symptom of depression.

Suicidal college students, on the average, have higher records of academic achievement than their nonsuicidal classmates, whereas most

of the parents. But as a person matures, feelings of worth also should be derived from the individual's sense of his or her own accomplishments and effectiveness. The self-esteem of a person prone to depression depends primarily on external sources: the approval and support of others. When these supports fail, the individual may be thrown into a state of depression.

Psychoanalytic theories of depression, therefore, focus on loss, overdependence on external approval, and internalization of anger. They seem to provide a reasonable explanation for some of the behaviors exhibited by depressed individuals, but they are difficult to prove or to refute. Some studies indicate that people who are prone to depression are more likely than

adolescents who commit suicide have exceptionally poor high-school records. The adolescents tend to be dropouts or to have behavior problems in school. The outstanding characteristic of adolescents who attempt suicide is social isolation: they describe themselves as loners, most have parents who were divorced or separated, a large number have alcoholic parents, and one-fourth were not living at home at the time of their suicide attempt (Rohn et al., 1977).

A major factor contributing to suicide, in addition to depression, is drug abuse. For example, one study of 283 suicides found that nearly 60 percent were drug abusers and 84 percent abused both alcohol and other drugs (Rich, Fowler, Fogarty, & Young, 1988). It is not clear if the drug abuse caused these people to become depressed and kill themselves or if they turned to drugs as a way of coping with depression and killed themselves when the drugs did not help. But in many of the cases drug abuse appears to have preceded the psychological problems.

Young drug abusers (under age 30) who committed suicide had a greater than expected frequency of intense interpersonal conflict or the loss of a spouse or romantic partner in the weeks prior to killing themselves. They may have felt that they had lost their only source of support. And they might have been able to handle the stress without resorting to suicide had their personal resources not been depleted by drug use.

Some individuals commit suicide because they find their emotional distress intolerable and see no solution to their problems other than death. Their sole motivation is to end their life. In other cases, the person does not really wish to die but seeks to impress others with the seriousness of his or her dilemma. The suicide attempt is motivated by a desire to communicate feelings of despair and to change the behavior of other people. Examples would be a woman who takes an overdose of sleeping pills when her lover threatens to leave or a student who does the same when pressured by his parents to achieve beyond his abilities. The suicide attempt is a cry for help.

Some experts use the term *parasuicide* for nonfatal acts in which a person deliberately causes self-injury or ingests a substance in excess of any prescribed or generally recognized therapeutic dosage (Kreitman, 1977). The term "parasuicide" is preferred to "suicide attempt" because it does not necessarily imply a wish to die. As noted earlier, there are many more parasuicides than suicides. However, most people who commit suicidal acts are experiencing such turmoil and stress that their thinking is far from clear. They are not sure whether they want to live or die; they want to do both at the same time, usually one more than the other. Since the best predictor of a future suicide is a prior attempt, all parasuicides should be taken seriously. Few people commit suicide without signaling their intentions to someone. Thus, a person who talks about suicide may actually attempt it. Many communities have established suicide-prevention centers where troubled individuals can seek help, either through telephone contact or in person.

Dramatic instances of suicide, such as jumping from a bridge, are sometimes given sensational coverage by newspapers and television. There is some evidence that such publicity encourages suicidal individuals to act on their impulses. A 7-year California study showed that in the week following a suicide that was highly publicized by the press, the suicide rate rose about 9 percent above the normal rate. Fatal automobile accidents and fatal crashes of private planes (which could be a disguised form of suicide) also increased (Phillips, 1978).

Publicity may also make famous landmarks attractive for would-be suicides. The Golden Gate Bridge in San Francisco is currently the world's favorite suicide spot, with close to 700 officially reported suicide deaths and perhaps an additional 200 deaths that have escaped notice. The Bay Bridge, which is 6 miles away and the same height, is the scene of very few suicides, and those that occur receive little publicity. One researcher found that half the people from the East Bay Area who had committed bridge suicides had traveled across the Bay Bridge in order to leap from the Golden Gate Bridge. Apparently, no one had reversed this process (Seiden, 1981, as cited in Markham, 1981). Thus, media publicity does appear to play a role, perhaps by providing a model for suicide-prone individuals to copy.

the average person to have lost a parent in early life (Roy, 1981; Barnes & Prosen, 1985). But parental loss (through death or separation) is also found in the case histories of people who suffer from other types of mental disorders, and most people who suffer such a loss do not develop emotional problems in adulthood (Tennant, Smith, Bebbington, & Hurry, 1981).

BEHAVIORAL PERSPECTIVE   Learning theorists assume that lack of reinforcement plays a major role in depression. The inactivity of the depressed person and the feelings of sadness are due to a low rate of positive reinforcement and/or a high rate of unpleasant experiences (Lewinsohn, Mischel,

Chaplin, & Barton, 1980; Lewinsohn, Hoberman, Teri, & Hautziner, 1985). Many of the events that precipitate depression (such as the death of a loved one, loss of a job, or impaired health) reduce accustomed reinforcement. In addition, people prone to depression may lack the social skills either to attract positive reinforcement or to cope effectively with aversive events.

Once people become depressed and inactive, their main source of reinforcement is the sympathy and attention they receive from relatives and friends. This attention may initially reinforce the very behaviors that are maladaptive (weeping, complaining, criticizing themselves, talking about suicide). But because it is tiresome to be around someone who refuses to cheer up, the depressed person's behavior eventually alienates even close associates, producing a further reduction in reinforcement and increasing the individual's social isolation and unhappiness. A low rate of positive reinforcement further reduces the individual's activities and the expression of behavior that might be rewarded. Both activities and rewards decrease in a vicious cycle.

COGNITIVE PERSPECTIVE Cognitive theories of depression focus not on what people *do* but on how they view themselves and the world. One of the more influential cognitive theories, developed by Aaron Beck, is derived from extensive therapeutic experience with depressed patients (Beck, 1976; Beck, Rush, Shaw, & Emery, 1979). Beck's theory suggests that individuals prone to depression have developed a general attitude of appraising events from a negative and self-critical viewpoint. They expect to fail rather than to succeed, and they tend to magnify failures and minimize successes in evaluating their performance. (For example, a student who receives a poor grade on only one examination out of many considers himself an academic misfit; a lawyer views herself as inadequate, despite a succession of praiseworthy achievements.) They also tend to blame themselves rather than the circumstances when things go wrong. (When rain dampens spirits at an outdoor buffet, the host blames himself rather than the weather.) According to this view, encouraging depressed people to become more socially active so they can receive more positive reinforcement will not, in itself, be helpful. They will simply find new opportunities to criticize themselves. Instead, cognitive therapy for depression attempts to identify and correct the distorted thinking underlying depression (see Chapter 17). In addition, depressed individuals are taught to master situations they thought were insurmountable.

Another cognitive approach to depression, developed by Martin Seligman, derives from experiments on *learned helplessness* discussed in Chapter 15. According to this theory, people become depressed when they *believe* that their actions make no difference in bringing about either pleasure or pain. Depression is caused by the expectation of future helplessness. A depressed person expects bad events to occur and believes that there is nothing he or she can do to prevent them from happening.

According to Seligman, three dimensions contribute to this feeling of helplessness. The first has to do with whether the person sees the problem as *internal* or *external*. The helplessness theory assumes that a person is more likely to become depressed if he or she believes the problem is internal, the result of his or her personal inability to control the outcome. Thus, a student who fails a course required for graduation and who attributes this failure to inadequate effort (she did not study enough) is more likely to feel depressed than one who attributes his failure to external factors (the teacher did an inferior job of presenting the material, and the final exam was unfair).

The second dimension has to do with whether the person views the situation as *stable* or *unstable*. For example, another student may attribute his course failure to a lack of ability—he worked hard, and his past performance in similar courses also has been poor. According to the theory, this student should be more severely depressed than the two students mentioned above, because he attributes his failure to something internal that is stable (not likely to change in the future).

The third dimension of helplessness has to do with the *global-specific* continuum. A person who interprets what happens as proof that he is totally helpless is more likely to be depressed than someone who sees himself as helpless only in a specific situation. Thus, a student who fails a variety of courses and decides he is stupid is more likely to become depressed than one who fails only language courses and decides he lacks this specific ability.

To summarize, Seligman's theory predicts that individuals who explain negative events in terms of internal, stable, and global causes—"It's me, it's going to last forever, and it's going to affect everything I do"—tend to become depressed when bad events occur (Peterson & Seligman, 1984).

The theories of Beck and Seligman have stimulated a great deal of research on the cognitive processes of depressed individuals, and the results have demonstrated that self-critical attitudes and attributions of helplessness are important components of depression. However, the extent to which such thoughts *precede* rather than *accompany* a depressed episode is far from clear. Both Beck's and Seligman's theories assume that individuals who become depressed possess a stable, traitlike depressive cognitive style that predisposes them to periods of depression. A number of studies using mildly depressed individuals as subjects (mostly college students) have found a relationship between a self-critical and helpless cognitive style and the degree of depression experienced when faced with bad events (Peterson & Seligman, 1984). However, most studies of severely depressed, hospitalized patients find that patterns of depressive cognitions accompany depression but are *not* apparent after a depressive episode. Once the patients' depression had lifted, they did not differ from control subjects (who had never been depressed) in the way they interpreted bad events (Hamilton & Abramson, 1983; Fennell &

Campbell, 1984). Thus a depressive explanatory style may be a *symptom* rather than a *cause* of depression. It is an important symptom, however, because the intensity of a patient's negative beliefs does predict the speed of recovery from a period of depression (Brewin, 1985).

The way a person interprets bad events may be less important for the development of depression than is the belief that one has control over one's life. We noted in Chapter 15 that stressful situations are less disturbing if the individual believes that he or she can exert some control over them. Confidence in one's ability to cope with bad events may increase resistance to depression (Abramson, Metalsky, & Alloy, 1989).

BIOLOGICAL PERSPECTIVE   A tendency to develop mood disorders, particularly bipolar disorders, appears to be inherited. Evidence from twin studies shows that if one identical twin is diagnosed as manic-depressive, there is a 72 percent chance that the other twin will suffer from the same disorder. The corresponding figure for fraternal twins is only 14 percent. These figures, called *concordance rates*, represent the likelihood that both twins will have a specific characteristic, given that one of the twins has the characteristic. The concordance rate for identical twins suffering from depression (40 percent) also exceeds the rate for fraternal twins (11 percent), but the difference between these two rates is much less than is the difference between the rates for manic-depressive twins (Allen, 1976). This comparison indicates that bipolar disorders are more closely related to genetic factors than are depressive disorders.

The specific role that genetic factors play in mood disorders is far from clear. However, it seems likely that a biochemical abnormality is involved. Mounting evidence indicates that our moods are regulated by the *neurotransmitters* that transmit nerve impulses from one neuron to another (see Chapter 2). A number of chemicals serve as neurotransmitters in different parts of the nervous system, and normal behavior requires a careful balance among them. Two neurotransmitters believed to play an important role in mood disorders are *norepinephrine* and *serotonin*. Both of these neurotransmitters, which belong to a class of compounds called *biogenic amines*, are localized in areas of the brain that regulate emotional behavior (the limbic system and the hypothalamus). A widely accepted hypothesis is that depression is associated with a deficiency of one or both of these neurotransmitters and that mania is associated with an excess of one or both of them. However, the evidence is indirect, based largely on the effects that certain drugs have on behavior and on neurotransmitter activity. For example, the drug reserpine, which is used to treat high blood pressure, sometimes produces severe depression as a side effect. Animal research has shown that the drug causes a decrease in the brain levels of serotonin and norepinephrine. In contrast, amphetamines (or "speed"), which produce an emotional high, facilitate the release of both of these neurotransmitters. (However, amphetamines are *not* useful in treating depression, for several reasons.)

Drugs that are effective in relieving depression increase the availability of both norepinephrine and serotonin in the nervous system. Two major classes of antidepressant drugs act in different ways to increase neurotransmitter levels. The *monoamine oxidase* (MAO) *inhibitors* block the activity of an enzyme that can destroy both norepinephrine and serotonin, thereby increasing the concentration of these two neurotransmitters in the brain. The *tricyclic antidepressants* prevent *reuptake* (the process by which neurotransmitters are taken back by the nerve terminals from which they were released) of serotonin and norepinephrine, thereby prolonging the duration of their activity. Since these drugs affect both serotonin and norepinephrine, it is difficult to distinguish between the roles of these two neurotransmitters in depressive disorders. Some studies indicate that serotonin plays the major role; others imply that norepinephrine does. It is possible that each neurotransmitter may be involved but in different subtypes of depression.

Research using new techniques is studying the long-term effects of antidepressants on the neuron's postsynaptic receptors. Antidepressant drugs require time to be effective: both tricyclics and MAO inhibitors take from 1 to 3 weeks before they begin to relieve the symptoms of depression. These observations do not fit with the discovery that the drugs, when they are first taken, increase norepinephrine and serotonin levels only temporarily; after several days, the neurotransmitters return to their previous levels. Thus, an increase in norepinephrine or serotonin per se cannot be the mechanism that relieves depression. Preliminary evidence indicates that these antidepressants increase the sensitivity of both norepinephrine and serotonin postsynaptic receptors. The time frame within which this occurs corresponds well with the course of drug action on symptoms (Charney & Heninger, 1983; Charney, Heninger, & Sternberg, 1984). Thus, even though the patient's levels of norepinephrine or serotonin are low once again, they may be able to use these neurotransmitters more effectively because the receptors receiving them have become more sensitive.

The neurotransmitter systems that regulate mood and emotion are incredibly complex, and we are only beginning to understand them. The fact that some of the newest drugs that have proved successful in relieving depression do not appear to influence serotonin and norepinephrine levels suggests that other neurotransmitter systems are also involved. Several neurotransmitter systems, acting alone or in combination, may be responsible for depressive symptoms (McNeal & Cimbolic, 1986). And bipolar disorders may involve the malfunctioning of yet a different neurotransmitter system (Depue & Iacono, 1989).

There is no doubt that mood disorders involve biochemical changes in the nervous system. The unresolved question is whether the physiological changes are the cause or the result of the psychological changes. For example, people who deliberately behave as if they were experiencing a manic episode exhibit changes in neurotransmitter levels similar to those found among actual manic patients (Post, Kotin, Goodwin, & Gordon, 1973). The depletion of norepinephrine may cause certain kinds of depression, but an earlier link in the causal chain leading to depression may be feelings of helpessness or loss of emotional support.

VULNERABILITY AND STRESS   All of the theories we have discussed make important points about the nature of depression. Inherited physiological characteristics may predispose an individual to extreme mood changes. Early experiences (the loss of parental affection or the inability to gain gratification through one's own efforts) may also make a person *vulnerable* to depression in later life. The kinds of stressful events that depressed patients report precipitated their disorder are usually within the range of normal life experiences; they are experiences most people can handle without becoming abnormally depressed. Thus, the concept of vulnerability is helpful in understanding why some people develop depression but others do not when confronted with a particular stressful experience.

Some additional factors that have been found to increase vulnerability to depression include having few social skills, being poor, being very dependent

Being poor and having young children increases one's vulnerability to depression.

CRITICAL DISCUSSION

Illusion and Well-Being

In discussing cognitive theories of depression, we noted that depressed individuals appraise themselves and the world from a negative viewpoint. They are self-critical; expect to fail rather than succeed; magnify failures and minimize successes in evaluating their performance; and are pessimistic about the future. An ironic possibility is that their appraisals may be closer to reality than those of nondepressed individuals. Those of us who are not depressed may suffer from illusions: we may look at ourselves and the world through rose-colored glasses.

Numerous studies indicate that most people have a) unrealistically positive views of themselves, b) exaggerated perceptions of how much control they have over events, and c) unrealistic optimism about the future (Taylor & Brown, 1988). For example, when asked to indicate how accurately positive and negative personality adjectives describe themselves, normal subjects judged positive traits to be overwhelmingly more characteristic of themselves than negative attributes (Brown, 1986). In addition, most people recall positive information about themselves more readily than negative information (Kuiper et al., 1985); recall successes more often than failures (Silverman, 1964); tend to recall their performance on a task as better than it actually was (Crary, 1966); and attribute positive outcomes to their own ability and negative outcomes to chance factors (Zuckerman, 1979b). When college students, who were interacting on a group task, rated themselves along a number of personality dimensions (for example, friendly, assertive), their ratings were significantly more positive than the ratings of observers who had watched the group interaction (Lewinsohn, Mischel, Chaplin, & Barton, 1980).

Moreover, there seems to be a pervasive tendency to see oneself as better than others. Individuals judge positive personality traits to be *more* descriptive of themselves than of the average person, but see negative personality attributes as *less* descriptive of themselves than of the average person (Brown, 1986). This effect has been documented for a wide range of traits; individuals even believe that their driving ability is superior to others (Svenson, 1981). Because it is logically impossible for most people to be better than the average, these positive views of the self are unrealistic and illusory.

In contrast, people who are depressed are more balanced in their self-perceptions (Watson & Clark, 1984). For example, they a) recall positive and negative information about themselves with equal frequency (Kuiper & MacDonald, 1982); b) offer self appraisals that coincide more closely with the appraisals of objective observers (Lewinsohn et al., 1980); and c) show greater

---

on others, having children under the age of 7, and not having a close and intimate confidant. The last of these appears to be the most important, at least for women, since it has been the most consistently identified over various studies (Brown & Harris, 1978; Campbell, Cope, & Teasdale, 1983; Bebbington, Sturt, Tennant, & Hurry, 1984). Having an intimate, confiding relationship with a husband or friend decreased the risk of a woman's becoming depressed when confronted with a stressful life situation. This is consistent with the research (discussed in Chapter 15) indicating that social supports reduce the severity of stressful events.

Depression has many causes, which may range from being determined almost entirely by an inherited biochemical abnormality to being exclusively the result of psychological or environmental factors. Most cases fall in between the two extremes and involve a mixture of genetic, early developmental, and environmental factors.

SCHIZOPHRENIA

Schizophrenia is the label applied to a group of disorders characterized by severe personality disorganization, distortion of reality, and an inability to function in daily life. It occurs in all cultures, even those that are remote

evenhandedness in their attributions for negative and positive outcomes (Campbell & Fairey, 1985).

Similarly, studies have shown that most people believe they have more control over situations than they actually do. For example, people believe that they have greater control if they personally throw the dice than if someone else does it for them (Fleming & Darley, 1986). People overestimate their degree of control over events that are largely determined by chance: when an expected outcome occurs, they often overestimate the degree to which they were instrumental in bringing it about (Miller & Ross, 1975). Depressed individuals appear less vulnerable to the illusion of control: when outcomes occur as predicted, they provide more accurate estimates of their degree of personal control than do nondepressed people (Greenberg & Alloy, 1989).

Most people are more optimistic about the future than reality warrants. When college students were asked what was possible for them in the future,

they reported four times as many positive as negative possibilities (Markus & Nurius, 1986). People estimated the likelihood that they would experience a variety of pleasant events (such as getting a high-salaried job or having a gifted child) as higher than those of their peers (Weinstein, 1980). Conversely, when asked about their chances of experiencing negative events (a car accident, becoming ill), most people believed they are *less* likely than their peers to do so (Kuiper, MacDonald, & Deery, 1983). In contrast, depressed individuals have a more balanced estimate of their future circumstances (Ruehlman, West, & Pasahow, 1985).

To summarize, most of us have unrealistically positive views of ourselves, an exaggerated belief in our ability to control our environment, and a belief that our future will be better than that of the average person. These positive illusions enable us to cope with an uncertain, and sometimes frightening, world. They provide the motivation to persist in the face of obstacles, and they help us avoid depression.

Traditional views of mental health assert that well-adjusted individuals possess accurate perceptions of themselves and of their ability to control events in their lives. Indeed, the description of normality presented earlier in this chapter includes *efficient perception of reality* as one of the criteria that distinguishes between a normal person and one who is diagnosed as abnormal. The evidence presented here indicates that this criterion should be modified.

Clearly, we need to perceive what is going on in the world and what other people say and do with some degree of accuracy. Nevertheless, positive illusions about our personal qualities and about our ability to control events appear to make us happier, more optimistic, and more willing to undertake challenges. Such illusions may be especially adaptive under circumstances that tend to produce depression. The belief in oneself as a competent, effective person whose future is generally positive helps in overcoming setbacks and blows to our self-esteem (Taylor & Brown, 1988).

---

from the stresses of industrialized civilization, and appears to have plagued humanity throughout history. In the United States, about 6 out of every 1,000 people are treated for schizophrenia in any given year. The disorder usually appears in late adolescence or early adulthood. Sometimes schizophrenia develops slowly as a gradual process of increasing seclusiveness and inappropriate behavior. Sometimes the onset of schizophrenia is sudden, marked by intense confusion and emotional turmoil; such acute cases are usually precipitated by a period of stress in individuals whose lives have tended toward isolation, self-preoccupation, and feelings of insecurity. The case described in Box 4 seems to fall into the latter category, although it lacks the intensity of onset that sometimes occurs.

Characteristics of Schizophrenia

Whether schizophrenia develops slowly or suddenly, the symptoms are many and varied. The primary characteristics of schizophrenia can be summarized under the following headings, although not every person diagnosed as suffering from the disorder will exhibit all of these symptoms.

DISTURBANCES OF THOUGHT AND ATTENTION   Whereas affective disorders are characterized by disturbances of mood, schizophrenia is characterized by disturbances of *thought*. The following excerpt from a

Schizophrenia

WG, a handsome, athletic-looking youth of 19, was admitted to the psychiatric service on the referral of his family physician. The boy's parents said, on his admission, that their son's behavior during the previous several months had changed drastically. He had been an adequate student in high school, but he had had to leave college recently because he was failing all his subjects. He had excelled in a variety of nonteam sports—swimming, weightlifting, track—winning several letters, but now he did not exercise at all. Although he had always been careful about his health and had hardly ever mentioned any physical problems, within the past several weeks he had repeatedly expressed vague complaints about his head and chest, which, he said, indicated that he was "in very bad shape." During the past several days, the patient had spent most of his time sitting in his room, staring vacantly out of his window. He had become (quite uncharacteristically) careless about his personal appearance and habits.

Although there was no doubt that the patient had exhibited serious recent changes in behavior, further conversation with the parents indicated that the patient's childhood and adolescent adjustment had not been healthy. He had always been painfully shy, except in highly structured situations, and had spent much of his free time alone (often working out with weights). He had no really close friends. . . .

The personnel of the psychiatric service found it difficult to converse with the patient; an ordinary diagnostic interview was impossible. For the most part, the boy volunteered no information. He would usually answer direct questions, but often in a flat, toneless way devoid of emotional coloring. Frequently, his answers were not logically connected to the questions. Observers often found it taxing to record their conversations with the patient. After speaking to him for a while, they would find themselves wondering just what the conversation had been about.

At times, the disharmony between the content of the patient's words and his emotional expression was striking. For example, while speaking sympathetically of an acute illness that had rendered his mother bedridden during a portion of the previous fall, the boy giggled constantly.

At times, WG became agitated and spoke with a curious intensity. On one occasion, he spoke of "electrical sensations" and "an electrical current" in his brain. On another, he revealed that when lying awake at night, he often heard a voice repeating the command, "You'll have to do it." The patient felt that he was somehow being influenced by a force outside himself to commit an act of violence—as yet undefined—toward his parents (Hofling, 1975, pp. 372–373).

patient's writings illustrates how difficult it is to understand schizophrenic thinking.

> If things turn by rotation of agriculture or levels in regards and timed to everything; I am referring to a previous document when I made some remarks that were facts also tested and there is another that concerns my daughter she has a lobed bottom right ear, her name being Mary Lou. Much of abstraction has been left unsaid and undone in these productmilk syrup, and others, due to economics, differentials, subsidies, bankruptcy, tools, buildings, bonds, national stocks, foundation craps, weather, trades, government in levels of breakages and fuses in electronics too all formerly states not necessarily factuated. (Maher, 1966, p. 395)

By themselves, the words and phrases make sense, but they are meaningless in relation to each other. The juxtaposition of unrelated words and phrases and the idiosyncratic word associations (sometimes called a "word salad") are characteristic of schizophrenic writing and speech.

The thought disorder in schizophrenia appears to be a general difficulty in filtering out irrelevant stimuli. Most of us are able to focus our attention selectively. From a mass of incoming sensory information, we are able to select the stimuli that are relevant to the task at hand and to ignore the rest. A person who suffers from schizophrenia appears to be unable to screen out irrelevant stimuli. The individual is perceptually receptive to many stimuli at the same time and has trouble making sense of the profusion of inputs, as the following statement by a schizophrenic patient illustrates.

> I can't concentrate. It's diversions of attention that trouble me. I am picking up different conversations. It's like being a transmitter. The sounds are coming through to me, but I feel my mind cannot cope with everything. It's difficult to concentrate on any one sound. (McGhie & Chapman, 1961, p. 104)

The inability to filter out irrelevant stimuli is evident in many aspects of the schizophrenic person's thinking. The disjointed nature of schizophrenic speech reflects the intrusion of irrelevant associations. Often one word will set off a string of associations, as illustrated by the following sentence written by a schizophrenic patient.

> I may be a "Blue Baby" but "Social Baby" not, but yet a blue heart baby could be in the Blue Book published before the war.

> This patient had suffered from heart trouble and may have started out to say "I was a blue baby." The association of "blue baby" with "blue blood" in the sense of social status prompted the interruption of "'Social Baby' not." The last phrase shows the interplay between the two meanings: the intention was to say "yet a blue baby could have been in the Society Blue Book" (Maher, 1966, p. 413).

The disorganized thought processes and irrelevant or idiosyncratic associations that make it difficult to understand what a schizophrenic patient is trying to say are disturbances in the *form* of thought. Equally fundamental to the disorder are disturbances in the *content* of thought. Most schizophrenics show *lack of insight*. When asked what is wrong or why they are hospitalized, they seem to have no appreciation of their condition and little realization that their behavior is unusual. They are also subject to *delusions*, holding beliefs that the rest of society would disagree with or view as misinterpretations of reality. The most common delusions are beliefs that external forces are trying to control the individual's thoughts and actions. These *delusions of influence* include the belief that one's thoughts are being broadcast to the world so that others can hear them, that strange thoughts (not one's own) are being inserted into the individual's mind, or that feelings and actions are being imposed on the person by some external force. Also frequent are beliefs that certain people or certain groups are threatening or plotting against the individual (*delusions of persecution*). Less common are beliefs that the person is powerful and important (*delusions of grandeur*).

A person who has persecutory delusions is called *paranoid*. He or she may become suspicious of friends and relatives, may fear being poisoned, or may complain of being watched, followed, and talked about. So-called motiveless crimes, when an individual attacks or kills someone for no apparent cause, are sometimes committed by people who are later diagnosed as suffering from paranoid schizophrenia.

DISTURBANCES OF PERCEPTION During acute schizophrenic episodes, people often report that the world appears *different* to them (noises seem louder; colors, more intense). Their own bodies may no longer appear the same (their hands may seem to be too large or too small; their legs, overly extended; their eyes, dislocated in the face). Some patients fail to recognize themselves in a mirror or see their reflection as a triple image. The most

German psychiatrist Hans Prinzhorn is responsible for the most extensive collection of artwork by mental patients available. This painting from the collection, by August Neter, illustrates the hallucinations and paranoid fantasies from which many schizophrenic patients suffer.

dramatic disturbances of perception are called *hallucinations*, sensory experiences in the absence of any stimulation from the environment. Hallucinations may occur independently or as part of a delusional belief. Auditory hallucinations (usually voices telling the person what to do or commenting on his or her actions) are the most common. Visual hallucinations (such as seeing strange creatures or heavenly beings) are somewhat less frequent. Other sensory hallucinations (a bad odor emanating from the individual's body, the taste of poison in food, the feeling of being pricked by needles) occur infrequently. Mark Vonnegut, in writing about his own schizophrenic experience, describes his first visual hallucination.

And then one night, as I was trying to get to sleep, I started listening to and feeling my heart beat. Suddenly I became terribly frightened that it would stop. And from out of nowhere came an incredibly wrinkled, iridescent face. Starting as a small point infinitely distant, it rushed forward, becoming infinitely huge. I could see nothing else. My heart had stopped. The moment stretched forever. I tried to make the face go away, but it mocked me. I had somehow gained control over my heartbeat, but I didn't know how to use it. I was holding my life in my hands and was powerless to stop it from dripping through my fingers. I tried to look the face in the eyes and realized I had left all familiar ground.

He, or she, or whatever seemed not to like me much. But the worst of it was it didn't stop coming. It had no respect for my personal space, no inclination to maintain a conversational distance. When I could easily make out all its features, when it and I were more or less on the same scale, when I thought there was maybe a foot or two between us, it had actually been hundreds of miles away, and it kept coming and coming till I was lost somewhere in some pore in its nose and it still kept coming.

There was nothing at all unreal about that face. Its concreteness made the Rock of Gibraltar look like so much cotton candy. I hoped I could get enough rest simply by lying motionless. In any event, the prospect of not sleeping frightened me far less than the possibility of losing contact with the world. (Vonnegut, 1975, pp. 96–98)

DISTURBANCES OF AFFECT   Schizophrenic individuals usually fail to exhibit normal emotional responses. They often are withdrawn and unresponsive in situations that should make them sad or happy. For example, a man may show no emotional response when informed that his daughter has cancer. However, this blunting of emotional expression can conceal inner turmoil, and the person may erupt with angry outbursts.

Sometimes the schizophrenic individual expresses emotions that are inappropriately linked to the situation or to the thought being expressed. For instance, a patient may smile while speaking of tragic events. Since our emotions are influenced by cognitive processes, it is not surprising that disorganized thoughts and perceptions are accompanied by changes in emotional responses. This point is illustrated by the following comment of a schizophrenic patient.

> Half the time I am talking about one thing and thinking about half a dozen other things at the same time. It must look queer to people when I laugh about something that has got nothing to do with what I am talking about, but they don't know what's going on inside and how much of it is running around in my head. You see I might be talking about something quite serious to you and other things come into my head at the same time that are funny and this makes me laugh. If I could only concentrate on one thing at the one time I wouldn't look half so silly. (McGhie & Chapman, 1961, p. 104)

WITHDRAWAL FROM REALITY   During schizophrenic episodes, the individual tends to withdraw from others and to become absorbed in his or her inner thoughts and fantasies. This state of self-absorption is known as *autism* (from the Greek word *autos*, meaning "self"). As the preceding quotation suggests, a person displaying inappropriate emotional behavior may be reacting to what is going on in his or her private world rather than to external events. Self-absorption can be so intense that the person may not know the day or month or where he or she is.

In acute cases of schizophrenia, withdrawal from reality is temporary. In chronic cases, withdrawal may progress to the point where the individual is completely unresponsive to external events, remains silent and immobile for days, and must be cared for like an infant.

DECREASED ABILITY TO FUNCTION   Besides the specific symptoms we have described, schizophrenics have many impairments in their ability to carry out the daily routines of living. If the disorder occurs in adolescence, the individual shows a decreasing ability to cope with school, has limited social skills, and few friends. The adult schizophrenic is usually unsuccessful in obtaining or holding a job. Personal hygiene and grooming deteriorate. The individual becomes more and more seclusive and avoids the company of other people. The signs of schizophrenia are many and varied. Trying to make sense of the variety of symptoms is complicated by the fact that some may result directly from the disorder, while others may be a reaction to life in a mental hospital or to the effects of medication.

Understanding Schizophrenia

More research has been devoted to trying to understand the nature of schizophrenia than to any other mental disorder. In an attempt to explain the disturbances in communication and perception that often characterize

FIGURE 16-2
Genetic Relationships and
Schizophrenia *The lifetime risk of*
developing schizophrenia is largely a function
of how closely an individual is genetically
related to a schizophrenic and not a function
of how much their environment is shared.
In the case of an individual with two
schizophrenic parents, genetic relatedness
cannot be expressed in terms of percentage,
but the regression of the individual's
"genetic value" on that of the parents is 1,
the same as it is for identical twins. (After
Gottesman & Shields, 1982)

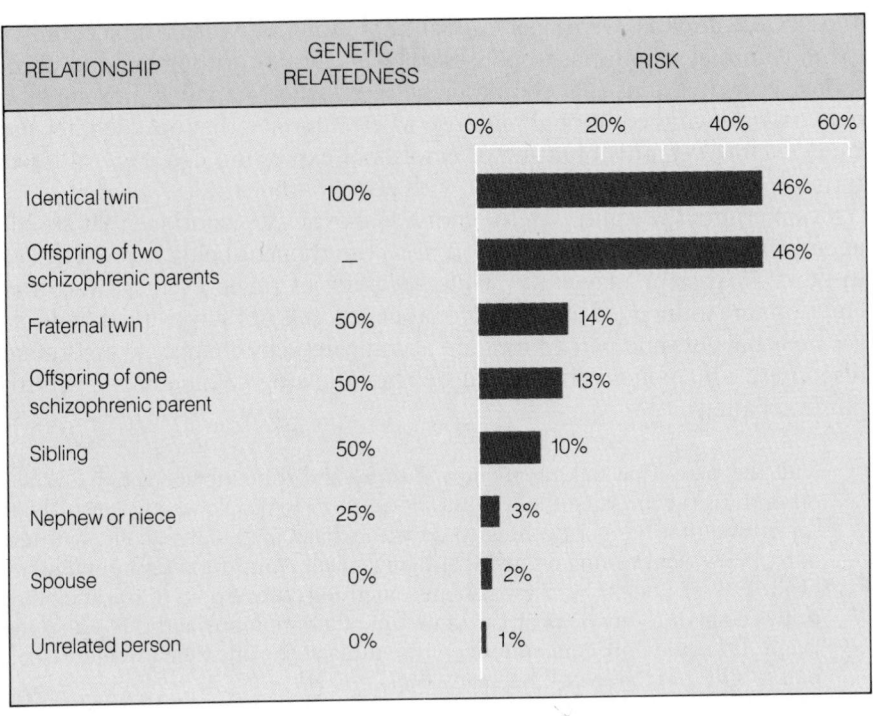

the schizophrenic state, some investigators have studied the cognitive functioning of people diagnosed as schizophrenic—the way they selectively attend to stimuli, store information in memory, and use language. Others have looked at the ways in which schizophrenic individuals differ biologically from other people in terms of genetic inheritance, the functioning of the nervous system, and brain biochemistry. Still others have examined the effects on schizophrenia of such environmental factors as social class, family interaction, and stressful life events.

Despite a voluminous body of research, the causes of schizophrenia are still not understood. Nevertheless, some areas of research are promising, and we will consider three of them here.

BIOLOGICAL PERSPECTIVE   It has become increasingly evident that there is a hereditary predisposition toward developing schizophrenia. Family studies show that relatives of schizophrenics are more likely to develop the disorder than are people from families free of schizophrenia. Figure 16-2 gives the lifetime risk of developing schizophrenia as a function of how closely an individual is genetically related to a person diagnosed as schizophrenic. Note than an identical twin of a schizophrenic is more than 3 times as likely as a fraternal twin to develop schizophrenia and 46 times as likely as an unrelated person to develop the disorder. However, fewer than half of the identical twins of schizophrenics have developed schizophrenia themselves, even though they share the same genes. This fact demonstrates the importance of environmental variables.

The first evidence concerning the means of genetic transmission has come from a study of seven families in England and Iceland that had an unusually high incidence of schizophrenia; 39 out of 104 family members were diagnosed as schizophrenic. Using advanced techniques of molecular biology to study the DNA of afflicted and nonafflicted family members, the

The odds of all four identical quadruplets being diagnosed as schizophrenic are 1 in 2 billion—yet these quadruplets were. They have been in and out of hospitals since high school.

researchers were able to locate a specific region on Chromosome 5 that contained the defective gene or cluster of genes (Sherrington et al., 1988). The gene itself is still unidentified.

A similar study of several generations of a large Swedish family with a high incidence of schizophrenia found that the same region of Chromosome 5 was *not* related to the occurrence of schizophrenia among these individuals (Kennedy et al., 1988), although the researchers expect to find a genetic marker on another chromosome. These findings indicate that schizophrenia has a genetic basis, but that different genes may be involved for different variants of the disorder. This idea reinforces the view that schizophrenia is a group of disorders that produce similar symptoms but have different biological causes. The genetic findings do not, however, rule out the possibility of nongenetic forms of schizophrenia. Some schizophrenics have no history of the disorder in their families.

Assuming that the genetic abnormality produces a defect or imbalance in body chemistry, researchers over the years have sought to find biochemical differences between schizophrenic and normal individuals. A number of differences between the chemistry of blood or urine samples from normals and that of hospitalized schizophrenics have been reported, often heralded as breakthroughs in understanding the cause of schizophrenia. Unfortunately, most of these discoveries either have not been replicable or have been found to be related to a condition of the individual other than his or her schizophrenic disorder. The latter constitutes one of the major problems in the search for a causal explanation of schizophrenia: an abnormality found in schizophrenic patients but not in control subjects may be the *cause* of the disorder or the *result* of the disorder, or it may stem from some aspect of *treatment*. For example, a schizophrenic's first admission to a hospital is often preceded by weeks of intense panic and agitation that undoubtedly produce bodily changes. These changes—related to lack of sleep, inadequate diet, and general stress—cannot be considered the cause of the disorder. Other biochemical abnormalities may be related to treatment. Most schizophrenic patients receive medication, traces of which may remain in the blood for some time.

All of these factors compound the problem of finding differences between schizophrenic and control subjects that tell us something about the origin of schizophrenia. Despite such obstacles, current research, based on increased knowledge of neurotransmitters and the use of new techniques for measuring brain activity, provides promising leads.

Biochemical theories of mood disorders have focused on norepinephrine and serotonin, but research on schizophrenia has centered on *dopamine*, a neurotransmitter active in an area of the brain believed to be involved in the regulation of emotion (the limbic system). The *dopamine hypothesis* proposes that schizophrenia is caused by too much dopamine at certain synapses in the brain. This excess may be due to overproduction of the neurotransmitter or to faulty regulation of the reuptake mechanism by which dopamine returns to and is stored by vesicles in the presynaptic neurons. It might also be due to oversensitive dopamine receptors or to too many dopamine receptors. Evidence for the importance of dopamine comes from two sources. First, drugs that are effective in relieving the symptoms of schizophrenia, called *antipsychotic drugs*, reduce the amount of usable dopamine in the brain. Researchers believe that they do so by blocking the dopamine receptors. These drugs do not cure schizophrenia, but they do reduce hallucinations and delusions, improve concentration, and make schizophrenic symptoms less bizarre. Moreover, the therapeutic effectiveness of a particular drug has been found to parallel its potency in blocking dopamine receptors (Creese, Burt, & Snyder, 1978).

Further evidence that an abnormality in dopamine metabolism may be the underlying cause of schizophrenia comes from observations of the effects of amphetamines, which increase the release of dopamine. Drug users who overdose on amphetamines exhibit psychotic behavior that closely resembles schizophrenia, and their symptoms can be relieved by the same antipsychotic drugs used to treat schizophrenia. When low doses of amphetamines are given to schizophrenic patients, their symptoms become much worse. In these cases, the drug does not produce a psychosis of its own; rather, it exacerbates whatever symptoms the patient may be experiencing (Snyder, 1980).

Thus, enhancing the action of dopamine aggravates schizophrenic symptoms, and blocking dopamine receptors alleviates them. The exact way in which the dopamine metabolisms of schizophrenic and normal individuals differ is not known.

While the dopamine hypothesis seems promising, it still has problems. For example, some schizophrenics do *not* improve when given antipsychotic drugs. Undoubtedly, schizophrenia is not a single disease but a group of disorders; some cases may be due to an excess of dopamine, while others may result from causes as yet unidentified. Investigators are currently using new techniques to obtain detailed pictures of the living human brain. These techniques—positron emission tomography (PET) and computerized axial tomography (CT), discussed in Chapter 2—permit us to study brain activity and look for functional or structural abnormalities. Some of the results with schizophrenics indicate abnormal functioning in a neural circuit connecting the limbic system with the prefrontal cortex. This brain system, which uses dopamine as a neurotransmitter, appears to play an important role in an individual's response to stress. It is also the last brain area to develop and become fully mature. Taken together, these facts have led to the speculation that schizophrenia may result from a brain defect, present at birth, that does

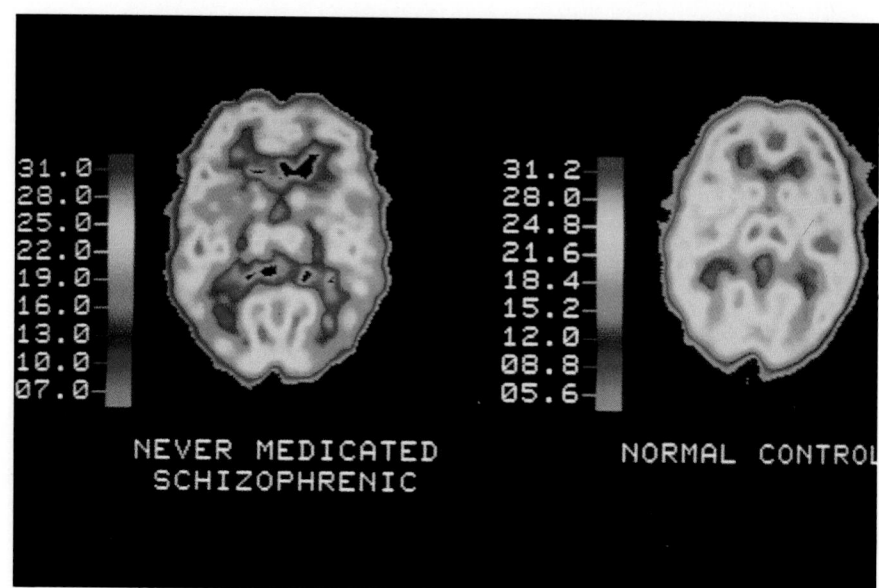

This PET scan shows the metabolic differences between areas of the brain of a schizophrenic patient and that of a normal patient.

not manifest itself until late adolescence or early adulthood when the brain system involved reaches physiological maturity (Weinberger, 1987).

SOCIAL AND PSYCHOLOGICAL PERSPECTIVE Numerous studies in the United States and other countries have revealed that the incidence of schizophrenia is significantly higher among the lower classes than among the middle and upper classes (Dohrenwend, 1973; Strauss, 1982). No one knows why social class is related to schizophrenia, but several explanations have been suggested.

1. *Differential diagnosis* Therapists are reluctant to apply the label "schizophrenia" to higher-income patients because it could have a damaging effect on their clients' careers.
2. *Downward drift* Because their coping skills are poor, individuals who suffer from schizophrenia have difficulty completing their education and getting a decent job. They gradually drift downward in society and become part of the lower classes.
3. *Increased stress* Living under conditions of poverty in areas with high crime rates, run-down housing, and inadequate schools creates enough additional stress to precipitate schizophrenic disorders, particularly in individuals who are genetically predisposed to schizophrenia.

Evidence shows that all of these explanations, especially the last two, may be true (Kosa & Zola, 1975; Brenner, 1982; Fried, 1982).

Research on the role of psychological factors in the development of schizophrenia has focused on relationships within the family. During the 1950s and 1960s numerous investigators recorded detailed observations of families in which one member was diagnosed as schizophrenic in an attempt to determine the kinds of parental attitudes and behaviors that contributed to the disorder. They came to various conclusions, most of which proved difficult to replicate. A major problem was that the families were studied *after* a mental disorder in one family member had affected the entire family. While some of the atypical family interactions may have preceded the onset of the disorder, others may represent reactions to the stresses of living with a

A stressful childhood may contribute to the severity of schizophrenia.

mentally ill person. For example, unclear or conflicting communication between parent and offspring has been identified as a factor that distinguishes between schizophrenic and normal families. The parents are described as communicating in ways that create confusion and uncertainty (Wynn et al., 1977). However, the results of a related study suggest that the parents' communication problems may be a response to unclear communication from their schizophrenic children. In this study the experimenter asked parents and sons, independently, to describe specific objects so that someone listening to their descriptions could identify the objects without seeing them. The descriptions were tape-recorded and played for others in the experiment, including normal and schizophrenic sons and their parents. The investigator found that the parents of schizophrenic sons did not differ from parents of normal sons in their ability to communicate ideas. The poorest communicators were the schizophrenic sons. To quote the investigator, "The communication disorder of the schizophrenic sons had an immediate negative effect not only on the parents of schizophrenic sons but on all parents who heard and attempted to respond to them" (Liem, 1974, p. 445).

A longitudinal study attempted to eliminate the problem inherent in earlier studies by observing family relationships *before* a family member was diagnosed as schizophrenic. The study began with 64 families that contained at least one teenager referred to a psychology clinic for help with mild to moderately severe emotional problems. The adolescents and their families were studied intensively and then followed up for the next 15 years with periodic assessments. The highest incidence of schizophrenia occurred among families in which the parents a) dealt with the adolescent in a critical and hostile manner, and b) were confusing in their communications. The combination of negative parental attitudes and confused communication was more predictive of future schizophrenia than either variable alone (Goldstein, 1987). However, the causal relationship is still not clear. It is possible that communication problems and critical parental attitudes were a consequence of the parents' attempts to cope with a child whose behavior was disturbed or unusual even before he or she was diagnosed as schizophrenic. In other words, is the parents' deviance a cause of the child's maladaptive behavior, or are the child's atypical characteristics a cause of the parents' behavior? This question remains unanswered. But whatever their role in causing the initial schizophrenic behavior, family disorganization and parental rejection are important in determining the severity of the illness and the prognosis for recovery (Roff & Knight, 1981; Anderson, Reiss, & Hogarty, 1986).

In addition to disturbed family relationships, other traumatic events (such as the early death of one or both parents) are found with greater than average frequency in the backgrounds of people who develop schizophrenia. Stressful childhoods of various kinds may contribute to the disorder. In general, the more stressful the childhood, the more severe the schizophrenic disorder.

VULNERABILITY AND STRESS   Most individuals who live in poverty or who experience a disturbing and stressful childhood do *not* develop schizophrenia. While earlier theories of schizophrenia emphasized environmental factors, the explanation that currently has the greatest support views schizophrenia as an inherited brain abnormality that makes the individual vulnerable to the stresses of life. It remains to be seen whether the same brain abnormality is characteristic of all persons diagnosed as schizophrenic, whether there are different brain defects for different types of schizophrenia, or whether some cases of schizophrenia are due solely to environmental causes.

Currently, some 50 longitudinal studies are being conducted with children who have been identified as having a high risk of developing schizophrenia. The studies follow the children from their early years to adulthood in an attempt to pinpoint some of the factors that determine whether or not the disorder will develop. In most of these studies, the children are considered to have a high risk because they have at least one schizophrenic parent (John, Mednick, & Schulsinger, 1982; Steffy et al., 1984; Marcus et al., 1987; Tienari et al., 1987). Other investigators have selected their high-risk group on the basis of psychophysiological measures or behavioral characteristics that they believe to be precursors of schizophrenia (Garmezy, 1974; Mednick et al., 1984).

The high-risk subjects are usually matched with a control group of children who have no family background of mental illness and who show no early signs of psychopathology. The development of both groups is carefully monitored through periodic testing and interviews with parents, teachers, and peers. Once a high-risk subject has a schizophrenic breakdown, he or she is matched both with a subject from the high-risk group who has remained well and with a well member of the control group. Thus, the background of the individual who develops schizophrenia can be compared with that of a high-risk subject and a normal, low-risk subject.

Most of these studies, started in the 1960s and 1970s, are still in progress, and the subjects are now young adults. Some have already become schizophrenic, and many more are expected to do so within the next decade. Consequently, the data available at present consist mainly of comparisons between high-risk and low-risk groups. These data indicate that the high-risk child is similar to an adult schizophrenic in many ways. For example, high-risk children are rated low in social competence and tend to perform poorly on tasks that require sustained attention or abstract thinking.

Preliminary data on high-risk subjects who later developed schizophrenia indicate that they differ from the high-risk subjects who have remained well in the following ways. The subjects who developed the disorder

1. Were more apt to have experienced birth complications that may have affected the functioning of their nervous system.
2. Were more likely to have been separated from their mothers at an early age.
3. Had fathers who were more likely to have been hospitalized, with diagnoses ranging from alcoholism to schizophrenia.
4. Were more likely to show inappropriate behavior in school. The boys were described by their teachers as anxious, lonely, and causing disciplinary problems; the girls, as withdrawn, isolated, and poorly controlled.

When more data from these ongoing high-risk studies become available, we should have a better understanding of how innate and environmental factors interact to produce schizophrenia.

PERSONALITY DISORDERS

Personality disorders are long-standing patterns of maladaptive behavior. In Chapter 14, we described *personality traits* as enduring ways of perceiving or relating to the environment and thinking about oneself. When personality traits become so inflexible and maladaptive that they significantly impair the individual's ability to function, they are called personality disorders. Personality disorders constitute immature and inappropriate ways of coping with stress or solving problems. They are usually evident by early adolescence and may continue throughout adult life.

Unlike people with mood or anxiety disorders, which also involve maladaptive behavior, people who have personality disorders usually do not feel upset or anxious and are not motivated to change their behavior. They do not lose contact with reality or display marked disorganization of behavior, unlike individuals suffering from schizophrenia.

DSM-III-R lists 11 personality disorders. For example, someone who has a *narcissistic personality disorder* is described as having an inflated sense of self-importance, being preoccupied with fantasies of success, constantly seeking admiration and attention, and being insensitive to the needs of others and often exploiting them. *Dependent personality disorders* are characterized by a passive orientation to life, an inability to make decisions or accept responsibility, a tendency to be self-deprecating, and a need for continual support from others.

Most of the personality disorders listed in DSM-III-R have not been the subject of much research. Moreover, the characteristics of the various personality disorders overlap, so that agreement in classifying individuals is poor. The personality disorder that has been studied the most and is the most reliably diagnosed is the antisocial personality (formerly called psychopathic personality).

Antisocial Personality

People who have *antisocial personalities* seem to have little sense of responsibility, morality, or concern for others. Their behavior is determined almost entirely by their own needs. In other words, they lack a *conscience*. Whereas the average person realizes at an early age that some restrictions are placed on behavior and that pleasures must sometimes be postponed in consideration of the needs of others, individuals who have antisocial personalities seldom consider any desires except their own. They behave impulsively, seek immediate gratification of their needs, and cannot tolerate frustration.

The term "antisocial personality" is somewhat misleading, because these characteristics do not describe most people who commit antisocial acts. Antisocial *behavior* results from a number of causes, including membership in a delinquent gang or a criminal subculture, the need for attention and status, loss of contact with reality, and an inability to control impulses. Most juvenile delinquents and adult criminals do have some concern for others (for family or gang members) and some code of moral conduct (you don't betray a friend). In contrast, antisocial *personalities* have little feeling for anyone except themselves and seem to experience little guilt or remorse, regardless of how much suffering their behavior may cause others. Other characteristics of the antisocial personality (sociopath, for short) include a great facility for lying, a need for thrills and excitement with little concern for possible injury, and an inability to alter behavior as a consequence of punishment. Such individuals are often attractive, intelligent, charming people who are quite facile in manipulating others—in other words, good con artists. Their façade of competence and sincerity wins them promising jobs, but they have little staying power. Their restlessness and impulsiveness soon lead them into an escapade that reveals their true nature; they accumulate debts, desert their families, squander company money, or commit crimes. When caught, their declarations of repentance are so convincing that they often escape punishment and are given another chance. But antisocial personalities seldom live up to these declarations; what they say has little relation to what they feel or do (see Box 5).

The two characteristics considered most indicative of an antisocial personality disorder are: a) lack of empathy and concern for others, and b) lack of shame or guilt—the inability to feel remorse for one's actions, regardless of how reprehensible they may be (Hare, 1980).

Understanding Antisocial Personalities

What factors contribute to the development of the antisocial personality? We might expect individuals with such personalities to have been raised by parents who provided no discipline or moral training, but the answer is not that simple. Although some sociopaths come from environments in which antisocial behavior is reinforced and adult criminals serve as models for personality development, many come from good homes and were raised by parents who are prominent and respected members of the community.

As yet, there is no well-supported theory to explain why antisocial personalities develop. Many factors are probably involved and vary from case to case. Current research focuses on biological determinants and on the quality of the parent-child relationship.

Box 5
Antisocial Personality

A 40-year-old man was convicted of check forgery and embezzlement. He was arrested with a young woman, age 18, whom he had married bigamously some months before. She was unaware of the existence of any previous marriage. The subject in this case had already been convicted for two previous bigamous marriages and for 40 other cases of passing fraudulent checks.

The circumstances of his arrest illustrate the impulsivity and lack of insight characteristic of many antisocial personalities. He had gotten a job managing a small restaurant; the absentee owner, who lived in a neighboring town, had arranged to stop by at the end of each week to check on progress and to collect the income. The subject was provided with living quarters over the restaurant, a small salary, and a percentage of the cash register receipts. At the end of the first week, the subject took all the money (he had failed to bank it nightly as he had been instructed) and departed shortly before the employer arrived; he left a series of

vulgar messages scribbled on the walls saying he had taken the money because the salary was "too low." He found lodgings with his wife a few blocks from the restaurant and made no effort to escape detection. He was arrested a few days later.

During the inquiry, it emerged that the subject had spent the past few months cashing checks in department stores in various cities. He would make out the check and send his wife in to cash it; he commented that her genuine innocence of the fact that he had no bank account made her very effective in not arousing suspicion. He had not bothered to use a false name when he signed the checks or the bigamous marriage contract, but he seemed surprised that the police discovered him so quickly.

Inquiry into the subject's past history revealed that he had been educated mostly in private schools and that his parents were financially well-to-do. They had planned for him to go to college, but his academic record was not good enough (although on examination he proved to have superior intelligence). Failing to get into college, he started work as an insurance salesman trainee and did very well. He was a distinguished-looking young man and an exceptionally fluent speaker.

Just as it appeared that he could anticipate a successful career in the insurance business, he ran into trouble because he failed to turn in the checks that customers had given him to pay

their initial premiums. He admitted to having cashed these checks and to spending the money (mostly on clothes and liquor). It apparently did not occur to him that the company's accounting system would quickly discern this type of embezzlement. In fact, he expressed amused indignation at the company's failure to realize that he intended to pay back the money from his salary. No legal action was taken, but he was requested to resign. His parents reimbursed the company for the missing money.

At this point, the subject enlisted in the army and was sent to Officer Candidate School, from which he graduated as a second lieutenant. He was assigned to an infantry unit, where he soon got into trouble that progressed from minor infractions (drunk on duty, smuggling women into his quarters) to cashing fraudulent checks. He was court-martialed and given a dishonorable discharge. From then on, his life followed a pattern of finding a woman to support him (with or without marriage) and then running off with her money to the next woman when life became too tedious.

At his trial, where he was sentenced to five years in prison, he gave a long and articulate speech, pleading clemency for the young woman who was being tried with him, expressing repentance for having ruined her life, and stating that he was glad to have the opportunity to repay society for his crimes (Maher, 1966, pp. 214–215).

BIOLOGICAL FACTORS   The clinical impression that sociopaths experience little anxiety about future discomforts or punishments has been supported by experimental studies. One study compared two groups of adolescent male delinquents selected from the detention unit of a juvenile court. One group had been diagnosed as having antisocial personality disorders; the other, adjustment reactions of adolescence. The experimenters tested galvanic skin response (GSR, see Chapter 11) under stress. Dummy electrodes were attached to each subject's leg, and he was told that in 10 minutes he would be given a very strong but not harmful shock. (A large clock was visible so that the subject knew precisely when the shock was supposed to occur—no shock was actually administered.) The two groups showed no difference in GSR measures during periods of rest or in response to auditory or visual stimulation. However, during the 10 minutes of shock anticipation, the maladjusted group showed significantly more tension than the antisocial group. At the moment when the clock indicated the shock was due, most of the maladjusted subjects exhibited an abrupt drop in skin resistance (indicating a sharp increase in anxiety). *None* of the sociopathic subjects showed this reaction (Lippert & Senter, 1966).

Studies in prisons have shown that, compared to other prisoners, antisocial personalities do not learn to avoid shocks as quickly and do not exhibit as much autonomic nervous system activity under a variety of conditions (Lykken, 1957; Hare, 1970). These findings have led to the hypothesis that sociopaths may have been born with an *underreactive autonomic nervous system*, which would explain why they fail to respond normally to threats of danger that deter most people from antisocial acts. Interpretations must be made with caution, however. It is possible that antisocial personalities may view an experimental situation as a game and may try to play it extra cool by attempting to control their responses.

Subsequent studies using measures of arousal other than the GSR have concluded that sociopaths' arousal levels are low because they are able to ignore or tune out aversive stimuli (Jutai & Hare, 1983; Hare, 1988). In addition, tests of mental functioning indicate that antisocial personalities are deficient in the ability to plan, to change strategies, and to inhibit impulsive actions (Gorenstein, 1982). The above findings provide an explanation for sociopathic behavior. Because his arousal level is low, the sociopath seeks thrills and excitement. Since he has almost no anxiety, it provides little deterrence. Because the sociopath is deficient in planning and in inhibition, he behaves impulsively. These are possible reasons for the sociopath's misconduct without remorse and for his thrill-seeking without regard for society's rules.

PARENTAL INFLUENCES   According to psychoanalytic theory, the development of a conscience, or superego, depends on an affectionate relationship with an adult during early childhood. Normal children internalize their parents' values (which generally reflect the values of society) because they want to be like their parents and fear the loss of their parents' love if they do not behave in accordance with these values. A child who receives no love from either parent does not fear its loss; he or she does not identify with the rejecting parents and does not internalize their rules. Reasonable as this theory seems, it does not conform to all of the data. Many rejected children do not develop antisocial personalities, and some people who do were indulged in childhood.

According to learning theory, antisocial behavior is influenced by the kind of models the parents provide and the kind of behavior they reward. A child may develop an antisocial personality if he or she learns that punishment can be avoided by being charming, lovable, and repentant. A child who is consistently able to avoid punishment by claiming to be sorry and promising never to do it again may learn that it is not the deed that counts but charm and ability to act repentant. If the same child is indulged in other respects and never has to wait or work for a reward, he or she does not learn to tolerate frustration. Two characteristics of sociopaths are a lack of frustration tolerance and the conviction that being charming and appearing contrite excuses wrongdoing. In addition, a child who is always protected from frustration or distress may have no ability to empathize with the distress of others

CRITICAL DISCUSSION

Insanity as a Legal Defense

How should the law treat a mentally disturbed person who commits a criminal offense? Should individuals whose mental faculties are impaired be held responsible for their actions? These questions are of concern to behavioral and social scientists, to members of the legal profession, and to individuals who work with criminal offenders.

Over the centuries, an important part of Western law has been the concept that a civilized society should not punish a person who is mentally incapable of controlling his or her conduct. In 1724, an English court maintained that a man was not responsible for an act if "he doth not know what he is doing, no more than . . . a wild beast." Modern standards of legal responsibility, however, have been based on the M'Naghten decision of 1843.

M'Naghten, a Scotsman, suffered the paranoid delusion that he was being persecuted by the English prime minister, Sir Robert Peel. In an attempt to kill Peel, he mistakenly shot Peel's secretary. Everyone involved in the trial was convinced by M'Naghten's senseless ramblings that he was insane. He was judged not responsible by reason of insanity and sent to a mental hospital, where he remained until his death. But Queen Victoria was not pleased with the verdict—apparently she felt that political assassinations should not be taken lightly—and called on the House of Lords to review the decision. The decision was upheld, and rules for the legal definition of insanity were put into writing. The M'Naghten Rule states that a defendant may be found not guilty by reason of insanity only if he were so severely disturbed at the time of his act that he did not know what he was doing, or if he did know what he was doing, did not know that it was wrong.

The M'Naghten Rule was adopted in the United States, and the distinction of knowing right from wrong remained the basis of most decisions of legal insanity for over a century. Some states added to their statutes the doctrine of "irresistible impulse," which recognizes that some mentally ill individuals may respond correctly when asked if a particular act is morally right or wrong but may be unable to control their behavior.

During the 1970s, a number of state and federal courts adopted a broader legal definition of insanity proposed by the American Law Institute, which states: "A person is not responsible for criminal conduct if at the time of such conduct, as a result of mental disease or defect, he lacks substantial capacity either to appreciate the wrongfulness of his conduct or to conform his conduct to the requirements of the law." The word *substantial* suggests that any incapacity is not enough to avoid criminal responsibility but that total incapacity is not required either. The use of the word *appreciate* rather than *know* implies that intellectual awareness of right or wrong is not enough; individuals must have some understanding of the moral or legal consequences of their behavior before they can be held criminally responsible.

The problem of legal responsibility in the case of mentally disordered individuals became a topic of increased debate in the wake of John Hinckley, Jr.'s, acquittal, by reason of insanity, for the attempted assassination of President Reagan in 1981. Many Americans seem to feel that the insanity defense is a legal loophole that allows too many guilty people to go free. Some legal and mental health professionals argue that the current courtroom procedures—in which psychiatrists and psychologists for the prosecution and the defense present contradictory evidence as to the defendant's mental state—is confusing to the jury and does little to help the cause of justice.

One suggestion is to restrict expert testimony to evidence of abnormality that bears on the defendant's conscious awareness and perception at the time of the crime—that is, the defendant's intent to commit the crime. Other testimony concerning more subtle impairments of judgment and ability to control behavior would no longer be relevant when deciding on a verdict but could be introduced at the time of sentencing. Another proposal calls for a pool of expert witnesses to be selected by the court. These experts would not testify for the prosecution or the

---

(Maher, 1966). Undoubtedly, a number of family interaction patterns foster the development of an antisocial personality.

A longitudinal study that followed up in adulthood a group of individuals who were seen at a child guidance clinic provides evidence of some factors that predict antisocial personality disorders. Ninety percent of an initial sample of 584 cases were located 30 years after their referral to the clinic. An additional 100 control subjects, who lived in the same area but who had not been referred to the clinic, were also followed up in adulthood. The adult subjects were interviewed intensively, and any current maladjustments were

defense but would attempt to arrive at an impartial conclusion regarding the defendant's mental state at the time the crime was committed.

At present, in the United States the laws concerning the insanity defense are in a state of flux. In 1984, Congress passed a bill limiting the insanity test to a determination of whether the defendant knew that he was acting wrongfully. Federal courts are expected to follow this law, and a number of states have passed similar laws.

Twelve states have adopted the verdict "guilty but mentally ill." (In some of these states this verdict replaces the not guilty by reason of insanity verdict; in other states it is an additional option.) Generally, the laws permit a finding of guilty but mentally ill when a defendant is found to have a substantial disorder of thought or mood that afflicted him at the time of the crime and that significantly impaired his judgment, behavior, capacity to recognize reality, or ability to cope with the ordinary demands of life. The effect of this mental illness, however, falls short of legal insanity. The person subject to this verdict would be given psychotherapeutic treatment in jail or would be treated in a mental hospital and returned to jail when he or she was deemed fit to complete the sentence. The problem remains as to whether treatment in either place would be sufficient to rehabilitate the individual.

Despite public concern that the insanity defense may be a loophole in the criminal law, actual cases of acquittal by reason of insanity are quite rare.

Jurors seem reluctant to believe that people are not morally responsible for their acts, and lawyers, knowing that an insanity plea is apt to fail, tend to use it only as a last resort. Fewer than 1 percent of defendants charged with serious crimes are found not guilty by reason of insanity.

It is too early to tell how the addition of a guilty but mentally ill alternative will affect this percentage. Preliminary studies suggest that jurors prefer this verdict and that providing it as an option may have two results: a) the tendency to judge defendants who are clearly psychotic and would formerly have been declared not guilty by reason of insanity to be guilty but mentally ill; and b) the tendency to judge defendants with personality disorders (primarily antisocial personalities), who are not mentally ill in the sense intended by law and who would formerly have been found guilty, to be guilty but mentally ill (Roberts, Golding, & Fincham, 1987).

The question of mental disorder exerts its greatest impact earlier in the legal process. Many accused people who are mentally ill never come to trial. In the United States, the law requires that the defendant be *competent to stand trial*. An individual is judged competent to stand trial if he or she is able a) to understand the charges, and b) to cooperate with a lawyer in preparing a defense. The competency issue is basic to the American ideal of a fair trial and is quite separate from the question of whether the person was "insane" at the time the crime was committed. In a preliminary hearing, the judge receives evidence about the accused's mental competency. The judge may drop the charges and commit the individual to a psychiatric facility (if the crime is not serious) or commit the accused and file the charges until he or she is deemed competent to stand trial. Because court calendars are congested and trials are expensive, judges often prefer to deal with mentally disturbed defendants in this way, particularly if they believe that the psychiatric hospital will provide adequate treatment and secure confinement.

Many more persons are confined to mental institutions because they are found incompetent to stand trial than because they are found not guilty by reason of insanity. These people, many of whom are not dangerous, often are confined longer than they would have been if they had been convicted of the crime in question. Indeed, before the widespread use of antipsychotic drugs, individuals deemed incompetent to stand trial were often committed to mental institutions for life. However, in 1972, the Supreme Court ruled that defendants found incompetent to stand trial due to mental illness could not be held indefinitely. Judges now attempt to bring such individuals to trial or to release them within 18 months. In deciding on release, the seriousness of the crime and the potential for future dangerous behavior are important considerations. Unfortunately, at present our data for predicting whether an individual is likely to commit a dangerous act are not very reliable.

diagnosed. The most likely candidate for a later diagnosis of antisocial personality disorder was described as a boy who was referred to the guidance clinic for theft or aggression, who had shown a variety of antisocial behaviors, who had a history of truancy, and who showed little guilt over behavior. His childhood involved either inconsistent discipline or no discipline at all. And his father showed antisocial behavior (Robins, 1966). The last two findings support the learning theory emphasis on the kinds of models parents provide and the way they handle rewards and punishments in the development of sociopathic behavior.

CHAPTER SUMMARY

1. The diagnosis of abnormal behavior is based on *statistical frequency*, *social norms*, *adaptiveness of behavior*, and *personal distress*. Characteristics indicative of good mental health include an *efficient perception of reality*, *self-knowledge*, *control of behavior*, *self-esteem*, an *ability to form affectionate relationships*, and *productivity*.

2. DSM-III-R classifies mental disorders according to specific behavioral symptoms. Such a classification system helps to communicate information and provides a basis for research. However, each case is unique, and diagnostic labels should not be used to pigeonhole individuals.

3. Anxiety disorders include *generalized anxiety* (constant worry and tension), *panic disorders* (sudden attacks of overwhelming apprehension), *phobias* (irrational fears of specific objects or situations), and *obsessive-compulsive disorders* (persistent unwanted thoughts, or *obsessions*, combined with urges, or *compulsions*, to perform certain acts).

4. Psychoanalytic theories attribute anxiety disorders to unresolved, unconscious conflicts. Learning theories focus on anxiety as a learned response to external events and invoke the concept of *prepared conditioning* to explain phobias. Cognitive theories emphasize the way anxious people think about potential dangers: their overestimation of the likelihood and degree of harm makes them tense and physiologically prepared for danger; they are unable to dismiss obsessive thoughts and so attempt to neutralize bad thoughts by compulsive acts. Biological theories focus on the interaction of a number of neurotransmitters that regulate feelings of anxiety. Biochemical abnormalities have been identified for panic attacks and obsessive-compulsive disorders.

5. Mood disorders are divided into *depressive disorders* (the individual has one or more periods of depression) and *bipolar disorders* (the individual alternates between periods of depression and periods of elation, or mania). Sadness, loss of gratification in life, negative thoughts, and lack of motivation are the main symptoms of depression. Psychoanalytic theories view depression as a *reactivation of the loss of parental affection* in a person who is *dependent on external approval* and tends *to turn anger inward*. Learning theories focus on *reduced positive reinforcement*.

6. Beck's cognitive theory of depression proposes that individuals prone to depression consistently appraise events from a negative and self-critical viewpoint. Seligman's *learned helplessness* theory attributes depression to an explanatory style that invokes *internal*, *stable*, and *global causes for bad events*. Depressive cognitions accompany depression but may not be a primary cause.

7. Some mood disorders may be influenced by inherited abnormalities in the metabolism of certain *neurotransmitters* (such as *norepinephrine* and *serotonin*). Inherited predispositions and early experiences may make people *vulnerable* to depression when under stress.

8. *Schizophrenia* is characterized by disturbances in the *form of thought* (disorganized thought processses that stem from difficulty in filtering out irrelevant stimuli) and in the *content of thought* (*delusions* and *lack of insight*). Other symptoms include perceptual disturbances (such as *hallucinations*), inappropriate affect, withdrawal, and impaired functioning. Research on the causes of schizophrenia has focused on evidence for a hereditary disposition to the disorder, possible defects in the metabolism of neurotransmitters (the *dopamine hypothesis*), social factors, and deviant family relationships. Studies of high-risk children point to some predictors of schizophrenia.

9. *Personality disorders* are long-standing patterns of maladaptive behavior that constitute immature and inappropriate ways of coping with stress or solving problems. Individuals classified as having *antisocial personalities* are impulsive, show little guilt, are concerned only with their own needs, and are frequently in trouble with the law. An underreactive nervous system, parental modeling of antisocial behavior, and lack of (or inconsistent) discipline are possible explanations for this disorder.

General textbooks on abnormal psychology include Davison and Neale, *Abnormal Psychology: An Experimental Clinical Approach* (4th ed., 1986); Sarason and Sarason, *Abnormal Psychology: The Problem of Maladaptive Behavior* (6th ed., 1989); Seligman and Rosenhan, *Abnormal Psychology* (1984); Coleman, Butcher, and Carson, *Abnormal Psychology and Modern Life* (8th ed., 1988); Goldstein, Baker, and Jamison, *Abnormal Psychology: Experiences, Origins, and Interventions* (2nd ed., 1986).

The hereditary aspects of mental illness are reviewed in Plomin, DeFries, and McClearn, *Behavioral Genetics: A Primer* (2nd ed., 1989); and in Gottesman and Shields, *Schizophrenia: The Epigenetic Puzzle* (1982).

Panic: Facing Fears, Phobias, and Anxiety (1985) by Agras provides an interesting discussion of the way fears develop into phobias. *Schizophrenia* (1981) by Strauss and Carpenter provides a readable account of the disorder, its possible causes, and treatment. The world of psychosis from the patient's viewpoint is graphically described in Green, *I Never Promised You a Rose Garden* (1971); and Vonnegut, *The Eden Express* (1975). In *Holiday of Darkness* (1982) by Endler, a well-known psychologist provides an account of his personal battle with depression and discusses the effects of various treatments.

FURTHER READING

Chapter 17

Detail, The Artist at the Window.

Methods of Therapy

In this chapter, we will look at methods for treating abnormal behavior. Some of these methods focus on helping individuals gain an understanding of the causes of their problems, some attempt to modify thoughts and behavior directly, some involve biological interventions, and some specify ways in which the community can help. The treatment of mental disorders is closely linked to theories about the causes of such disorders. A brief history of the treatment of the mentally ill will illustrate how methods change as theories about human nature and the causes of its disorders change.

HISTORICAL BACKGROUND

According to one of the earliest beliefs (espoused by the ancient Chinese, Egyptians, and Hebrews), a person with a mental disorder was possessed by evil spirits. These demons were exorcised by such techniques as prayer, incantation, magic, and the use of purgatives concocted from herbs. If these treatments were unsuccessful, more extreme measures were taken to ensure that the body would be an unpleasant dwelling place for the evil spirit. Flogging, starving, burning, and even stoning to death were not infrequent forms of treatment.

The first progress in understanding mental disorders was made by the Greek physician Hippocrates (circa 460–377 B.C.), who rejected demonology and maintained that mental disorders were the result of a disturbance in the balance of body fluids. Hippocrates, and the Greek and Roman physicians who followed him, argued for a more humane treatment of the mentally ill. They stressed the importance of pleasant surroundings, exercise, proper diet, massage, and soothing baths, as well as some less desirable treatments, such as bleeding, purging, and mechanical restraints. Although there were no institutions for the mentally ill during this period, many individuals were cared for with great kindness by physicians in temples dedicated to the Greek and Roman gods.

This progressive view of mental illness did not continue, however. Primitive superstitions and a belief in demonology were revived during the Middle Ages. The mentally ill were considered to be in league with Satan and to possess supernatural powers with which they could cause floods, pestilence, and injuries to others. Seriously disturbed individuals were treated cruelly: people believed that by beating, starving, and torturing the mentally ill, they were punishing the devil. This type of cruelty culminated in the witchcraft trials that sentenced to death thousands of people (many of them mentally ill) during the fifteenth, sixteenth, and seventeenth centuries.

Early Asylums

In the latter part of the Middle Ages, cities created asylums to cope with the mentally ill. These asylums were simply prisons; the inmates were chained in dark, filthy cells and were treated more as animals than as human beings. It was not until 1792, when Philippe Pinel was placed in charge of an asylum in Paris, that some improvements were made. As an experiment, Pinel was allowed to remove the chains that restrained the inmates. Much to

Phillippe Pinel in the courtyard of the hospital of Salpêtrière.

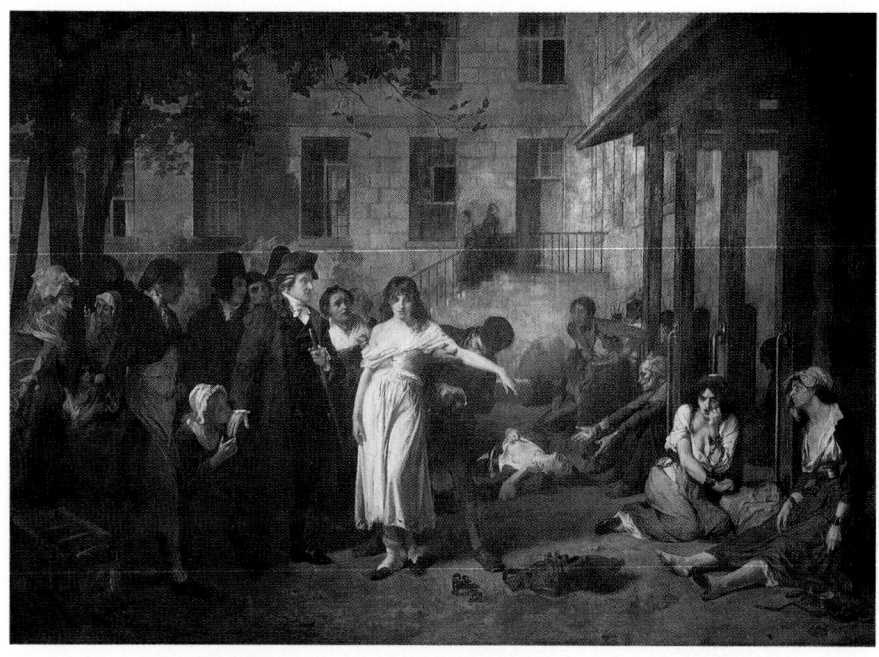

As late as the early nineteenth century, English asylums used rotating devices in which patients were whirled around at high speeds.

the amazement of skeptics who thought Pinel was mad to unchain such "animals," the experiment was a success. When released from their restraints, placed in clean, sunny rooms, and treated kindly, many people who for years had been considered hopelessly insane improved enough to leave the asylum.

By the beginning of the twentieth century, the fields of medicine and psychology were making great advances. In 1905, a mental disorder known as *general paresis* was shown to have a physical cause: a syphilis infection acquired many years before the symptoms of the disorder appeared. General paresis is characterized by a gradual decline in mental and physical functions, marked personality changes, and delusions and hallucinations. Without treatment, death occurs within a few years. The syphilis spirochete remains in the body after the initial genital infection disappears, and it gradually destroys the nervous system. At one time, general paresis accounted for more than 10 percent of all admissions to mental hospitals, but today few cases are reported, due to the effectiveness of penicillin in treating syphilis (Dale, 1975).

The discovery that general paresis was the result of a disease encouraged those who believed that mental illness was biological in origin. At about the same time, Sigmund Freud and his followers laid the groundwork for understanding mental illness in terms of psychological factors; likewise Pavlov's laboratory experiments demonstrated that animals could become emotionally disturbed if forced to make decisions beyond their capacities.

Despite these scientific advances, in the early 1900s the public still did not understand mental illness and viewed mental hospitals and their inmates with fear and horror. Clifford Beers undertook the task of educating the public about mental health. As a young man, Beers developed a bipolar disorder and was confined for 3 years in several private and state hospitals. Although chains and other methods of torture had been abandoned long before, the straitjacket was still widely used to restrain excited patients. Lack of funds made the average state mental hospital—with its overcrowded wards, poor food, and unsympathetic attendants—a far from pleasant place to live. After his recovery, Beers wrote about his experiences in the now-famous book *A Mind That Found Itself* (1908), which aroused considerable

The "crib"—a restraining device used in a New York mental institution in 1882.

public interest. Beers worked ceaselessly to educate the public about mental illness and helped to organize the National Committee for Mental Hygiene. In 1950, this organization joined with two related groups to form the National Association for Mental Health. The mental hygiene movement played an invaluable role in stimulating the organization of child-guidance clinics and community mental health centers to aid in the prevention and treatment of mental disorders.

Modern Treatment Facilities

Mental hospitals have been upgraded markedly since the time of Beers, but there is still much room for improvement. Most people who require hospitalization for mental disorders are first admitted to the psychiatric ward of a general hospital, where their condition is evaluated. If more than a brief period of hospitalization is indicated, they may be transferred to a public or private mental hospital. The best of these hospitals are comfortable and well-kept places that provide a number of therapeutic activities: individual and group psychotherapy, recreation, occupational therapy (designed to teach skills, as well as to provide relaxation), and educational courses to help patients prepare for a job upon release from the hospital. The worst are primarily custodial institutions where inmates lead a boring existence in run-down, overcrowded wards and receive little treatment except for medication. Most mental hospitals fall somewhere in between these two extremes.

Beginning in the early 1960s emphasis shifted from treating mentally disturbed individuals in hospitals to treating them in their own communities. This movement toward *deinstitutionalization* was motivated partly by the recognition that hospitalization has some inherent disadvantages, regardless of how good the facilities may be. Hospitals remove people from the social support of family and friends and from their patterns of daily life; they tend to make people feel "sick" and unable to cope with the world; and they encourage dependency. They are also very expensive.

During the 1950s psychotherapeutic drugs (discussed later in this chapter) were discovered that could relieve depression and anxiety and reduce psychotic behavior. When these drugs became widely available in the 1960s, it was possible for many hospitalized patients to be discharged and returned home to be treated as outpatients. The Community Mental Health Centers Act of 1963 made federal funds available for the establishment of community treatment centers. These community mental health centers were designed to provide outpatient treatment and a number of other services, including short-term hospitalization and partial hospitalization. Partial hospitalization

FIGURE 17-1
Patients in Mental Hospitals *The*
number of patients cared for in United
States state and county mental hospitals has
decreased dramatically over the past 35
years.

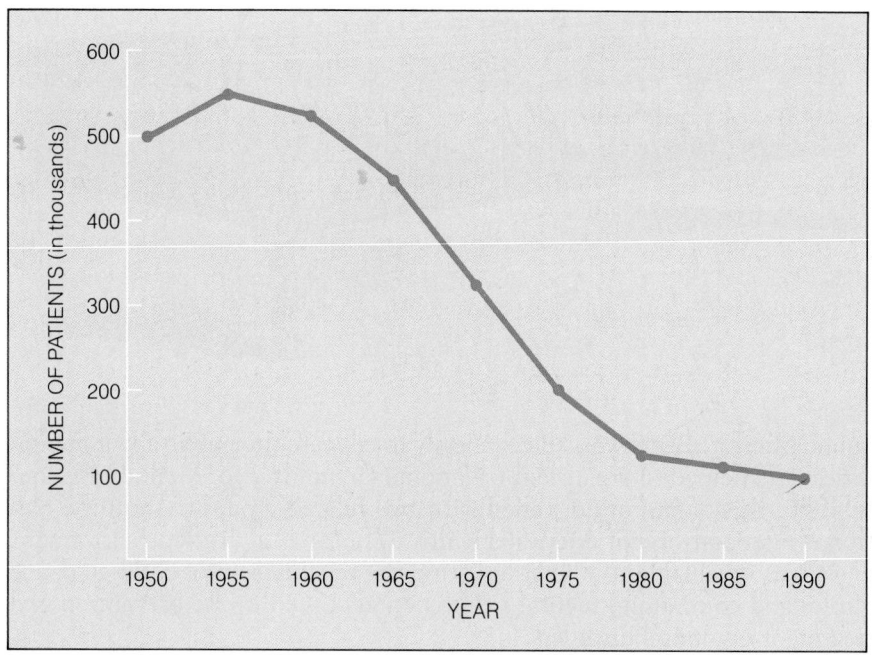

is more flexible than traditional hospitalization: individuals may receive treatment at the center during the day and return home in the evening or may work during the day and spend nights at the center. Unfortunately, most centers are currently so overcrowded that they cannot begin to provide beds and services for the many mentally ill people who need them.

As Figure 17-1 shows, the number of patients treated in state and county mental hospitals has decreased dramatically over the past 35 years. For some patients the policy of deinstitutionalization has worked. The services of the mental health centers, along with help from their families and the use of psychotherapeutic drugs, have enabled them to resume a satisfactory life. For others, however, deinstitutionalization has had unfortunate consequences, largely because the facilities in most communities are far from adequate.

Many individuals who improve with hospitalization and could manage on their own with assistance do not receive adequate follow-up care in terms of outpatient therapy or help in finding friends, housing, and jobs. As a consequence, they lead a revolving door existence, going in and out of institutions between unsuccessful attempts to cope on their own. About half of all patients discharged from state hospitals are readmitted within a year.

Some discharged patients are too incapacitated to even attempt to support themselves or to function without custodial care; they may live in dirty, overcrowded housing or roam the streets. The disheveled man standing on the corner talking to himself and shouting gibberish may be one victim of deinstitutionalization. The woman with all of her worldly possessions in a shopping bag who spends one night in the doorway of an office building and the next in a subway station, may be another. A large proportion of street people suffer from some sort of mental disorder.

The increasing visibility of homeless mentally-ill individuals, particularly in large cities, has aroused public concern and prompted a move toward reinstitutionalization. However, an important ethical issue is involved. If such people are not readjusting to society, should they be involuntarily committed to a mental hospital? One of the most cherished civil rights in a democratic society is the right to liberty. It is essential that any commitment proceedings safeguard this right.

Some experts believe that legal action is warranted only if a person is potentially dangerous to others. But dangerousness is difficult to predict. Studies have shown that mental health professionals are poor at predicting whether a person will commit a dangerous act (Monahan, 1976). Moreover, our legal system is designed to protect people from preventative detention. A person is assumed innocent until proven guilty by the courts, and prisoners are released from penitentiaries even though statistics show that most will commit additional crimes. Should mentally ill individuals not have the same rights? And what about the person who appears self-destructive, more dangerous to himself than to others? Should he be committed? These complex issues have yet to be resolved.

Aside from the legal issues, the problem of providing care for the mentally ill remains. Funds need to be directed toward two areas. One is the improvement of outpatient services to help those who can make it on their own with adequate assistance. The other is the development of alternative residential facilities (such as small-group homes) for patients who are unable to function outside of a sheltered environment, as well as for those who need help in the transition from hospital to independent living. Evidence indicates that residential treatment centers cost less to operate and are more effective for many patients than are traditional hospitals (Kiesler, 1982).

Professions Involved in Psychotherapy

Whether a person receives therapy in a hospital, a community mental health center, a private clinic, or an office, several different types of professionals may be involved. A psychiatrist, a clinical psychologist, and a psychiatric social worker may work together or independently on a given case.

A *psychiatrist* has an M.D. degree and has taken postgraduate training, called a residency, during which he or she received supervision in the diagnosis of abnormal behavior, drug therapy, and psychotherapy. Subsequently,

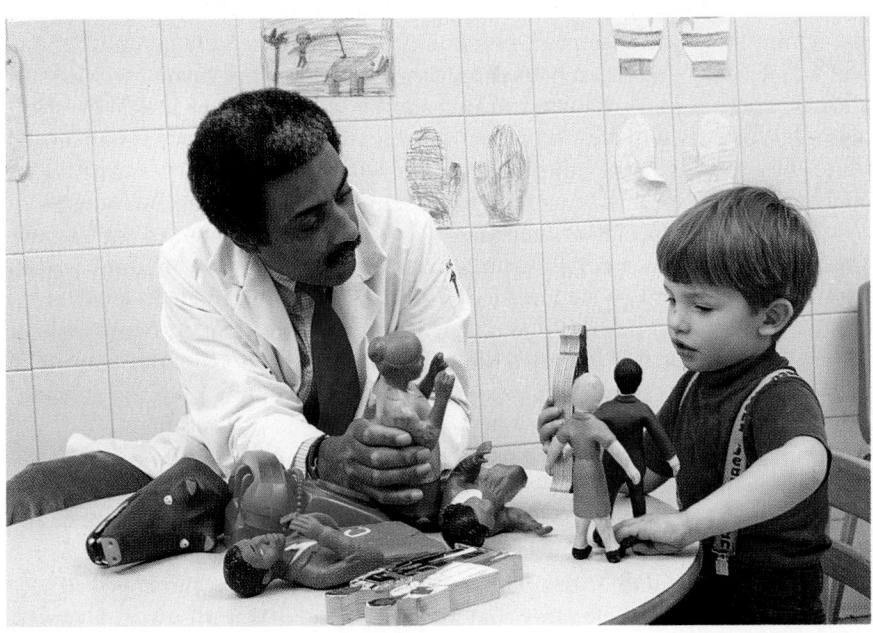

A child psychiatrist works with a young patient.

A clinical psychologist talking with a client.

many but not all psychiatrists take an examination in psychiatry and become board-certified. As a physician, the psychiatrist is the only mental health professional who can prescribe medication and, in most states, hospitalization.

The term *psychoanalyst* is reserved for individuals who have received specialized training at a psychoanalytic institute learning the methods and theories derived from Freud. The program usually takes several years, during which the trainees must undergo their own personal psychoanalysis as well as treat several clients psychoanalytically while under supervision. Until recently, most psychoanalytic institutes required their graduates to have an M.D. degree. Thus, most psychoanalysts are psychiatrists. However, the vast majority of psychiatrists are not psychoanalysts.

A *clinical psychologist* has a Ph.D. in psychology, which entails 4 to 5 years of graduate study, and has served special internships in the fields of testing and diagnosis, psychotherapy, and research. The clinical psychologist administers and interprets psychological tests, conducts psychotherapy, and is also active in research. A *counseling psychologist* has earned an M.A. or a Ph.D. and has had graduate training similar to that of the clinical psychologist, but usually with less emphasis on research. The training is concerned more with problems of adjustment than with mental disorders and often concentrates on specific areas such as student, marriage, or family counseling.

A psychiatric social worker usually has a master's degree in social work (M.S.W.) as well as special training in interviewing, psychotherapy, and in extending treatment procedures to the home and community. In addition to conducting psychotherapy, the social worker is often called on to collect information about the patient's home situation and to assist the patient in getting help from community resources (such as hospitals, schools, and social agencies).

Sometimes, these professionals work as a team. The psychiatrist prescribes psychotherapeutic medications and monitors their effectiveness; the psychologist sees the same client in individual or group psychotherapy; the social worker monitors the home environment. In mental hospitals a fourth professional is available: the *psychiatric nurse*. Psychiatric nursing is a field within the nursing profession that requires special training in the understanding and treatment of mental disorders. In our discussion of psychotherapeutic techniques, we will not specify the profession of the psychotherapists; we will assume that they are trained and competent members of any one of these professions.

TECHNIQUES OF PSYCHOTHERAPY

Psychotherapy refers to the treatment of mental disorders by psychological (rather than physical or biological) means. The term embraces a variety of techniques, all of which are intended to help emotionally disturbed individuals modify their behavior, thoughts, and emotions so that they can develop more useful ways of dealing with stress and with other people. Some psychotherapists believe that modification of behavior is dependent on the individual's understanding of his or her unconscious motives and conflicts (psychoanalysts, for example). Others feel that people can learn to cope with their problems without necessarily exploring the factors that have led to their development (behavior therapists and cognitive behavior therapists, for example). Despite differences in techniques, most methods of psychotherapy have certain basic features in common. They involve a helping relationship between two people: the client (patient) and the therapist. The client is encouraged to discuss intimate concerns, emotions, and experiences freely without fear of being judged by the therapist or having confidences betrayed. The therapist, in turn, offers sympathy and understanding, engenders trust, and tries to help the client develop more effective ways of handling his or her

Psychoanalysis

Psychoanalytic theories of personality (see Chapter 14) assume that within each individual are opposing forces (the *id*, the *ego*, and the *superego*) that make internal conflicts inevitable. These conflicts, of which the person may or may not be aware, have a powerful influence on personality development and on the ability to handle life stresses. Freud believed that psychological disorders are the result of conflicts, usually originating in early childhood, of which the individual is *not* aware; the impulses and emotions involved have been repressed to the unconscious.

Unconscious conflicts between the aggressive and sexual impulses of the id and the constraints imposed by the ego and superego were considered by Freud to be the most crucial for later maladjustment. For example, a young boy may naturally feel hostile toward the new baby brother who usurps some of the parental love that was once exclusively his. If the parents refuse to acknowledge the boy's feelings and severely punish any expression of anger toward the baby, the boy must deny these impulses in order to retain his parents' love. The unwanted impulse to hurt the baby (and any emotions or memories associated with this impulse) may be pushed out of consciousness. These unconscious feelings of sibling rivalry may influence relationships in later life, perhaps taking the form of intense jealousy of and competition with friends and co-workers. Because the original conflict was repressed, the individual will have no awareness of the source of these emotions.

A key assumption of psychoanalysis is that a person's current problems cannot be successfully resolved without a thorough understanding of their

Freud's office in Vienna offered the comfort of his famous couch, as well as a collection of Egyptian, Greek, and Roman antiquities.

unconscious basis in the early relationships with parents and siblings. The goal of psychoanalysis is to bring conflicts (repressed emotions and motives) into awareness so that they can be dealt with in a more rational and realistic way.

FREE ASSOCIATION AND DREAM ANALYSIS   One of the main techniques psychoanalysts use to facilitate the recovery of unconscious conflicts is *free association*. The client is encouraged to give free rein to thoughts and feelings and to say whatever comes to mind without editing or censoring. This is not easy to do, however. In conversation, we usually try to keep a connecting thread running through our remarks and to exclude irrelevant ideas. In addition, most of us have spent a lifetime learning to be cautious and to think before speaking; thoughts that strike us as inappropriate, stupid, or shameful usually remain unspoken.

With practice, however, and with encouragement from the analyst, free association becomes easier. But even individuals who conscientiously try to give free rein to their thoughts will occasionally find themselves blocked. When a patient remains silent, abruptly changes the subject, or is unable to recall the details of an event, the analyst assumes that the person is resisting the recall of certain thoughts or feelings. Freud believed that blocking, or *resistance*, results from the individual's unconscious control over sensitive areas and that these are precisely the areas that should be explored.

Another technique often used with free association is *dream analysis*. Freud believed that dreams were "the royal road to the unconscious"; they represented an unconscious wish or fear in disguised form. He distinguished between the *manifest* (obvious, conscious) *content* and the *latent* (hidden, unconscious) *content* of dreams (see Chapter 6). By talking about the manifest content of a dream and then free associating to that content, the analyst and client attempt to discern the unconscious meaning.

TRANSFERENCE   In psychoanalysis, the patient's attitudes toward the analyst are considered to be an important part of treatment. Sooner or later, the client develops strong emotional responses to the psychoanalyst.

Sometimes the responses are positive and friendly; sometimes, negative and hostile. Often these reactions are inappropriate to what is taking place in the therapy sessions. The tendency for the client to make the therapist the object of emotional responses is known as *transference*: the client expresses attitudes toward the analyst that the client actually feels toward other people who are, or were, important in his or her life. Freud assumed that transference represents relics of childhood reactions to parents, and he utilized this transference of attitudes as a means of explaining to patients the childhood origin of many of their concerns and fears. By pointing out how their clients are reacting to them, analysts help their patients achieve a better understanding of how they react to others. The following excerpt shows an analyst's use of transference, followed by the use of free association.

PATIENT: I don't understand why you're holding back on telling me if this step is the right one for me at this time in my life.

ANALYST: This has come up before. You want my approval before taking some action. What seems to be happening here is that one of the conflicts you have with your wife is trying to get her approval of what you have decided you want to do, and that conflict is occurring now between us.

PATIENT: I suppose so. Other people's approval has always been very important to me.

ANALYST: Let's stay with that for a few minutes. Would you free associate to that idea of getting approval from others. Just let the associations come spontaneously—don't force them.

(Woody & Robertson, 1988, p. 129)

INTERPRETATION   The analyst helps the client gain *insight* into the nature of the unconscious conflicts that are the source of his or her difficulties through *interpretation*. An interpretation is a hypothesis that summarizes a segment of the client's behavior and offers an explanation of its motivation. In the previous excerpt, the analyst offers an interpretation by comparing the patient's behavior in the therapy situation (seeking approval for a proposed action) to the kind of approval-seeking behavior that causes conflict with his wife. The client appears to tentatively accept the interpretation.

Interpretation may also take the form of calling attention to the patient's resistances—a sudden blocking of free association, changing the subject, or forgetting an appointment. All of these behaviors may indicate that the client is trying to avoid uncomfortable topics. Interpretations must be skillfully timed; that is, made at a point when unconscious material is close to awareness and the patient is ready to accept painful insights. An interpretation offered before a client is ready to accept it may only arouse anxiety and defensiveness.

WORKING THROUGH   As an analysis progresses, the patient goes through a lengthy process of reeducation known as *working through*. By examining the same conflicts over and over as they have appeared in a variety of situations, the client comes to understand them and to see how pervasive certain of his attitudes and behaviors are. By working through painful childhood emotions during therapy, the person becomes strong enough to face these emotions with less anxiety and to deal with them in a more realistic manner.

Psychoanalysis is a lengthy, intensive, and expensive process. Client and analyst usually meet for 50-minute sessions several times a week for at least a year, and often several years. Psychoanalysis is most successful with individuals who are highly motivated to solve their problems, who can verbalize their feelings with some ease, and who can afford it.

Psychoanalytic Psychotherapies

Since Freud's time, numerous forms of psychotherapy based on Freudian concepts have developed. They share in common the premise that mental disorders stem from unconscious conflicts and fears, but they differ from classical psychoanalysis in a number of ways and are usually called *psychoanalytic psychotherapies*. (The term *psychodynamic therapies* is also used.) As noted in Chapter 14, the ego analysts (such as Karen Horney and Heinz Hartman) placed greater emphasis on the role of the rational, problem-solving ego in directing behavior and correspondingly less emphasis on the role of unconscious sexual and aggressive drives. They sought to strengthen the functions of the ego, in particular self-esteem and feelings of competency, so that the individual could deal more constructively with current anxieties and interpersonal relationships. Their general strategy was a) to give the client insight into how the past continues to influence the present, and b) to develop the client's awareness of what can be done in the present to correct the harmful effects of the past.

The techniques of psychoanalysis have been modified too. Contemporary psychoanalytic psychotherapy is usually briefer, more flexible, and less intense. Sessions are scheduled less frequently, usually once a week. There is less emphasis on a complete reconstruction of childhood experiences and more attention to problems arising from the way the individual is currently interacting with others. Free association is often replaced with a direct discussion of critical issues, and the psychoanalytic psychotherapist may be more direct, raising pertinent topics when it seems appropriate rather than waiting for the client to bring them up. While transference is still considered an important part of the therapeutic process, the therapist may try to limit the intensity of the transference feelings.

Still central, however, is the psychoanalytic therapist's conviction that unconscious motives and fears are at the core of most emotional problems and that insight and the working-through process are essential to a cure. As we will see in the next section, behavior therapists do not agree with these views.

Behavior Therapies

The term *behavior therapy* includes a number of different therapeutic methods based on the principles of learning and conditioning discussed in Chapter 7. Behavior therapists assume that maladaptive behaviors are learned ways of coping with stress and that some of the techniques developed in experimental work on learning can be used to substitute more appropriate responses for maladaptive ones. Whereas psychoanalysis is concerned with understanding how the individual's past conflicts influence behavior, behavior therapy focuses more directly on the behavior itself.

Behavior therapists point out that, although the achievement of insight is a worthwhile goal, it does not ensure behavior change. Often we understand why we behave the way we do in a certain situation but are not able to change our behavior. If you are unusually timid about speaking in class, you

Individuals in an agoraphobia workshop discuss their fear of appearing in public places.

may be able to trace this fear to past events (your father criticized your opinions whenever you expressed them, your mother made a point of correcting your grammar, you had little experience in public speaking during high school because you were afraid to compete with your older brother who was captain of the debate team). Understanding the reasons behind your fear probably will not make it easier for you to contribute to class discussions.

In contrast to psychoanalysis, which attempts to change certain aspects of the individual's personality, behavior therapies tend to focus on fairly circumscribed goals: the modification of maladaptive behaviors in specific situations. Behavior therapists are also more concerned than psychoanalysts with obtaining experimental evaluations of their techniques.

In the initial therapy session a behavior therapist listens carefully to the client's statement of the problem. What exactly does the client want to change? Is it a fear of flying or of speaking in public? A problem with uncontrolled eating or drinking? Feelings of inadequacy and helplessness? An inability to concentrate and get work done? The first step is to define the problem clearly and to break it down into a set of specific therapeutic goals. If, for example, the client complains of general feelings of inadequacy, the therapist will try to get the client to describe these feelings more specifically: to pinpoint the kinds of situations in which they occur and the kinds of behaviors associated with them. Inadequate to do what? To speak up in class or in social situations? To get assignments completed on time? To control eating? Once the behaviors that need changing are specified, the therapist and client work out a treatment program employing some of the procedures we will describe. The therapist chooses the treatment method that is appropriate for the particular problem.

SYSTEMATIC DESENSITIZATION   Systematic desensitization can be viewed as a *deconditioning* or *counterconditioning* process. This procedure is highly effective in eliminating fears or phobias. The principle of the treatment is to substitute a response that is incompatible with anxiety—namely, relaxation. It is difficult to be both relaxed and anxious at the same time. The client is first trained to relax deeply. One way is to progressively relax various muscles, starting, for example, with the feet and ankles and proceeding up the body to neck and facial muscles. The person learns what muscles feel like when they are truly relaxed and how to discriminate various degrees of tension. Sometimes drugs and hypnosis are used to help people who cannot relax otherwise.

The next step is to make up a hierarchy of the anxiety-producing situations. The situations are ranked in order from the one that produces the least anxiety to the one that is most fearful. The client is then asked to relax and experience or imagine each situation in the hierarchy, starting with the one that is least anxiety-producing. (Experiencing the actual situation works best, but an alternative method is to visualize or imagine it.)

An example will make the procedure clearer. Suppose the client is a woman who suffers from agoraphobia (see Chapter 16) and experiences intense anxiety whenever she leaves the security of her home. The anxiety hierarchy might begin with a walk to the corner mailbox. Somewhere around the middle of the list might be a drive to the supermarket, and at the top, a plane trip alone to a distant city. After the woman has learned to relax and has constructed the hierarchy, desensitization begins. She sits with her eyes closed in a comfortable chair while the therapist describes the least anxiety-producing situation to her. If she can imagine herself in the situation without any increase in muscle tension, the therapist proceeds to the next item on the list. If the woman reports any anxiety while visualizing a scene, she concentrates on relaxing; the same scene is visualized until all anxiety is neutralized. This process continues through a series of sessions until the situation that originally provoked the most anxiety now elicits only relaxation. At this point, the woman has been systematically desensitized to anxiety-provoking situations through the strengthening of an incompatible response—relaxation.

Although desensitization through visually imagined scenes has been effective in reducing fears or phobias, it is less effective than desensitization through actual encounters with the feared stimuli. The woman in our hypothetical case would probably lose her fears more readily if she actually exposed herself to the anxiety-producing situations in a sequence of graduated steps and managed to tolerate each situation until her anxiety subsided (Sherman, 1972). Whenever possible, a behavior therapist tries to combine real-life and symbolic desensitization.

POSITIVE REINFORCEMENT AND EXTINCTION   Systematic desensitization is based on principles of classical conditioning: the individual learns to make a new response (relaxation) to stimuli that previously elicited anxiety. *Systematic reinforcement*, based on the principles of operant conditioning (see Chapter 7), has also proved to be an effective method of modifying behavior, especially with children.

The procedure can be illustrated by the case of a third-grade student who was inattentive in school, refused to complete assignments or to participate in class, and spent most of her time daydreaming. In addition, her social skills were poor and she had few friends. The behavior to be reinforced was defined as "on task" behavior, which included paying attention to schoolwork or instructions from the teacher, completing reading assignments, and taking part in class discussions. The reinforcement consisted of beans that were used as tokens to be exchanged for special privileges that the girl valued, such as standing first in line (three beans) or being allowed to stay after school to help the teacher with special projects (nine beans). Anytime the teacher observed the student performing on-task behaviors, she placed one bean in a jar.

During the first 3 months of treatment, the girl completed 12 units of work, compared to 0 units during the 3 months before the reinforcement regime started. In the final 3 months, she completed 36 units and was performing at the same level as the rest of the class. A follow-up the next year showed that the girl was maintaining her academic performance. She also showed a marked improvement in social skills and was accepted more by the other children (Walker, Hedberg, Clement, & Wright, 1981). This is a common finding: improving behavior in one area of life often produces added benefits (Kazdin, 1982).

Reinforcement of desirable responses can be accompanied by extinction of undesirable ones. For example, a young boy who habitually shouts to get his mother's attention could be ignored whenever he does so and reinforced by her attention only when he comes to where she is and speaks in a conversational tone.

Sometimes the behavior that the therapist wants to reinforce occurs infrequently or is totally absent, such as talking in a mute child. In this case, a technique similar to Skinner's *shaping* of behavior (see Chapter 7) is used: responses that approximate the desired behavior are reinforced, and the therapist gradually requires closer and closer approximations until the desired behavior occurs. A procedure of this sort was used to develop language in a seriously disturbed 6-year-old boy whose speech consisted almost entirely of two-word phrases. The boy was trained to respond to pictures showing people in various activities. At first, he was reinforced (with food and praise) for any verbal response to the pictures. Next he was taught to use simple sentences to describe the pictures and was reinforced only when he responded with a sentence. Finally, he learned to use the connective "and" between two sentences and was rewarded only when he produced two correct sentences relevant to a picture (for example, "The boy is reading and the teacher is putting away the book"). Once the boy reached the point where he consistently produced correct compound sentences to the training pictures, trials with new pictures were interspersed among trials with the training stimuli. The boy had to produce complete, grammatically correct, and relevant sentences to the new pictures in order to be rewarded. After 30 half-hour training sessions, the child responded correctly to the novel stimuli on 70 percent of the trials. Moreover, he began describing objects and events in classroom and playground conversations (Stevens-Long, Schwarz, & Bliss, 1976).

Similar procedures have been effective in teaching seriously disturbed (autistic) children to interact with other children, to sit quietly at a desk, and to respond appropriately to questions (see Figure 17-2). Instead of receiving regular breakfasts or lunches, these children were provided with bits of food when their responses approximated the desired behaviors. Although such procedures may seem cruel, they are an effective means of establishing more normal behavior when all other attempts have failed. Once the child begins to respond to primary forms of reward (such as food), social rewards (praise, attention, and special privileges) become effective reinforcers.

A number of mental hospitals have instituted "token economies" on wards with very regressed, chronic patients to induce socially appropriate behavior. Tokens (which can later be exchanged for food and privileges such as watching television) are given for dressing properly, interacting with other patients, eliminating "psychotic talk," helping on the wards, and so on. Such

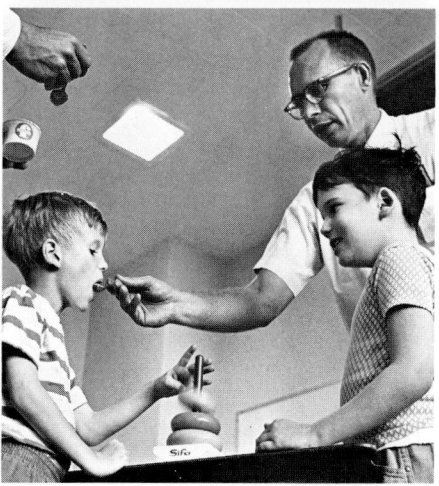

FIGURE 17-2
Behavior Reinforcement *These two autistic children were enrolled in an intensive behavior therapy program at the UCLA Neuropsychiatric Institute. Here they are shown receiving immediate reinforcement in the form of food for interacting with each other. Other techniques included modeling of the appropriate behavior and punishment (electric shock) for self-destructive behavior. The boy on the right, mute and self-destructive when he entered the program, was able to return home in less than a year, and 2 years later he was doing first-grade work in a special school.*

programs have proved successful in improving both the patients' behavior and the general functioning of the ward.

MODELING   Another effective means of changing behavior is *modeling*, which makes use of observational learning. Since observing other models is a principle way in which humans learn, watching people who are displaying adaptive behavior should teach people with maladaptive responses better coping strategies. Observing the behavior of a model (either live or videotaped) has proved effective in reducing fears and teaching new skills.

Many studies using modeling in the treatment of phobias have been carried out by Albert Bandura and his colleagues (Bandura, 1969; 1986). One of their early studies of the treatment of snake phobias illustrates this approach (Bandura, Blanchard, & Ritter, 1969). The subjects were young adults whose fear of snakes was severe enough to restrict their activities in various ways (for example, some could not participate in gardening or hiking for fear of encountering snakes). After an initial test to determine how closely they would approach a live but harmless king snake in a glass tank, the subjects were rated according to their degree of fearfulness and were divided into four matched groups. One group underwent the systematic desensitization procedure described earlier: they learned to relax while imagining increasingly anxiety-provoking situations involving snakes. A second group, after learning muscle relaxation procedures, watched a film in which child and adult models enjoyed progressively more intimate interactions with a large king snake. The subjects were instructed to stop the film if a particular scene provoked anxiety, reverse the film to the beginning of that sequence, and reinduce relaxation. (This procedure is called *symbolic modeling*.) A third group imitated the behavior of a live model as the model performed progressively more fearful activities with the snake (see Figure 17-3). Gradually, the subjects were guided in such activities as touching the snake with a gloved hand, touching the snake with their bare hands, holding the snake, letting it coil around their arms, and finally letting the snake loose in the room, retrieving it, and letting it crawl over their bodies. (This procedure is termed *live modeling with participation*.) The fourth group served as a control group and received no training.

Figure 17-4 indicates the number of snake-approach responses by the subjects before and after the different treatments. All three treatment groups showed improvement in comparison with the control group, but the group that combined live modeling with guided participation achieved the best results. Almost all the subjects in this group completely overcame their fear of snakes.

FIGURE 17-3
Modeling as a Treatment for Snake Phobia *The photos show an individual modeling interactions with a live king snake.*

 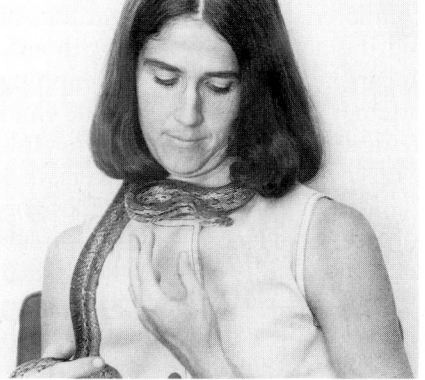 

Children overcoming their fear of snakes.

Subsequent studies have shown that the most effective method of eliminating snake phobias is to start with participant modeling, during which the individual is guided in handling the snake, and then to let the person proceed through various degrees of snake intimacy on his or her own (Bandura, Adams, & Beyer, 1976). In this way, the individual gains a sense of mastery over the situation—a feeling that effective performance is the result of his or her own actions (Bandura, Adams, Hardy, & Howells, 1980).

Modeling is effective in overcoming fears and anxieties because it gives the person a chance to observe someone else go through the anxiety-provoking situation without getting hurt. Watching videotapes of models enjoying a visit to the dentist or going through various hospital procedures has proved successful in helping both children and adults overcome their fears of such experiences (Shaw & Thoresen, 1974; Melamed & Siegel, 1975).

BEHAVIOR REHEARSAL In a therapy session modeling is often combined with role-playing, or *behavioral rehearsal*. The therapist helps the individual rehearse or practice more adaptive behaviors. In the following excerpt, a therapist helps a young man overcome his anxieties about asking girls for dates. The young man has been pretending to talk to a girl over the phone and finishes by asking for a date.

CLIENT: By the way (pause), I don't suppose you want to go out Saturday night?

THERAPIST: Up to actually asking for the date, you were very good. However, if I were the girl, I think I might have been a bit offended when you said, "By the way." It's like your asking her out is pretty casual. Also, the way you phrased the question, you are kind of suggesting to her that she doesn't want to go out with you. Pretend for the moment I'm you. Now, how does this sound: "There is a movie at the Varsity Theater this Saturday that I want to see. If you don't have other plans, I'd like very much to take you."

CLIENT: That sounded good. Like you were sure of yourself and liked the girl, too.

THERAPIST: Why don't you try it.

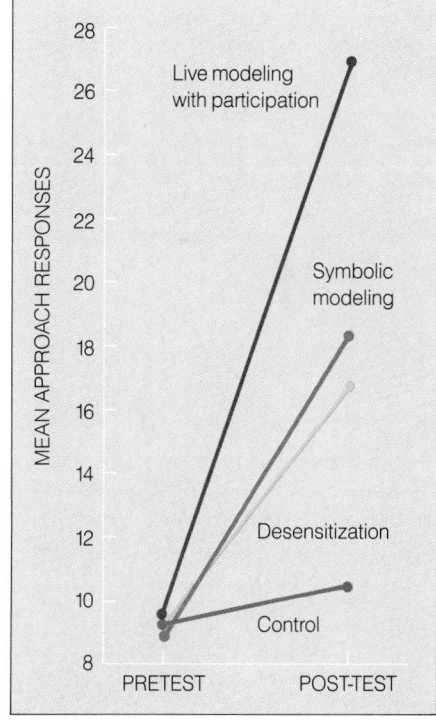

FIGURE 17-4
Treatment of Snake Phobia *The mean number of snake-approach responses by subjects before and after they received different behavior therapy treatments.* (After Bandura, Blanchard, & Ritter, 1969)

CLIENT: You know that movie at the Varsity? Well, I'd like to go, and I'd like to take you Saturday, if you don't have anything better to do.

THERAPIST: Well, that certainly was better. Your tone of voice was especially good. But the last line "if you don't have anything better to do" sounds like you don't think you have too much to offer. Why not run through it one more time.

CLIENT: I'd like to see the show at the Varsity Saturday, and if you haven't made other plans, I'd like to take you.

THERAPIST: Much better. Excellent, in fact. You were confident, forceful, and sincere. (Rimm & Masters, 1979, p. 74)

Another area in which behavioral rehearsal has been used to develop social skills is *assertiveness training*. Some people feel anxious in social situations because they do not know how to speak up for what they feel is right or to say no when others take advantage of them. By practicing *assertive responses* (first in role-playing with the therapist and then in real-life situations), the individual not only reduces anxiety but also develops more effective coping techniques. The therapist determines the kinds of situations in which the person is passive and then helps him or her to think of and to practice some assertive responses that might be effective. The following situations might be worked through during a sequence of therapy sessions:

- Someone steps in front of you in line.
- A friend asks you to do something you do not want to do.
- Your boss criticizes you unjustly.
- You return defective merchandise to a store.
- You are annoyed by the conversation of people behind you in the movies.
- The mechanic did an unsatisfactory job of repairing your car.

Most people do not enjoy dealing with such situations, but some individuals are so fearful of asserting themselves that they say nothing and instead build up feelings of resentment and inadequacy. In assertiveness training, the client rehearses with the therapist effective responses that could be made in such situations and gradually tries them in real life. The therapist tries to teach the client to express his needs in a way that is straightforward and forceful, but not seen by others as hostile or threatening.

SELF-REGULATION Because client and therapist seldom meet more than once per week, the client must learn to control or regulate his or her own behavior so that progress can be made outside the therapy hour. Moreover, if people feel they are responsible for their own improvement, they are more likely to maintain such gains. Self-regulation involves monitoring, or observing, one's own behavior and using various techniques—*self-reinforcement, self-punishment, control of stimulus conditions, development of incompatible responses*—to change the maladaptive behavior. An individual monitors his or her behavior by keeping a careful record of the kinds of situations that elicit the maladaptive behavior and the kinds of responses that are incompatible with it. A person concerned with alcohol dependency would note the kinds of situations in which he or she is most tempted to drink and would try to control such situations or to devise a response that is incompatible with drinking. A man who finds it hard not to join his coworkers in a noontime cocktail might plan to eat lunch at his desk, thereby avoiding the situation. If he is tempted to relax with a drink on arriving home from work,

SELF-MONITORING

Daily Log   Keep a detailed record of everything you eat. Note amount eaten, type of food and caloric value, time of day, and the circumstances of eating. This record will establish the caloric intake that is maintaining your present weight. It will also help to identify the stimuli that elicit and reinforce your eating behavior.

Weight Chart   Decide how much you want to lose and set a weekly goal for weight loss. Your weekly goal should be realistic (between 1 and 2 pounds). Record your weight each day on graph paper. In addition to showing how your weight varies with food intake, this visual record will reinforce your dieting efforts as you observe progress toward your goal.

CONTROLLING STIMULUS CONDITIONS

Use these procedures to narrow the range of stimuli associated with eating:
1. Eat only at predetermined times, at a specific table, using a special place mat, napkin, dishes, and so forth. Do *not* eat at other times or in other places (for example, while standing in the kitchen).
2. Do *not* combine eating with other activities, such as reading or watching television.
3. Keep in the house only those foods that are permitted on your diet.
4. Shop for food only after having had a full meal; buy only those items that are on a previously prepared list.

MODIFYING ACTUAL EATING BEHAVIOR

Use these procedures to break the chain of responses that make eating automatic:
1. Eat very slowly, paying close attention to the food.
2. Finish chewing and swallowing before putting more food on the fork.
3. Put your utensils down for periodic short breaks before continuing to eat.

DEVELOPING INCOMPATIBLE RESPONSES

When tempted to eat at times other than those specified, find a substitute activity that is incompatible with eating. For example, exercise to music, go for a walk, talk with a friend (preferably one who knows you are dieting), study your diet plan and weight graph, noting how much weight you have lost.

SELF-REINFORCEMENT

Arrange to reward yourself with an activity you enjoy (watching television, reading, planning a new wardrobe, visiting a friend) when you have maintained appropriate eating behavior for a day. Plan larger rewards (for example, buying something you want) for a specified amount of weight loss. Self-punishment (other than forgoing a reward) is probably less effective because dieting is a fairly depressing business anyway. But you might decrease the frequency of binge eating by immediately reciting to yourself the aversive consequences or by looking at an unattractive picture of yourself in a bathing suit.

TABLE 17-1
Self-Regulation of Eating *The program illustrates the use of learning principles to help control food intake.* (After Stuart & Davis, 1972; O'Leary & Wilson, 1975)

he might substitute a game of tennis or a jog around the block as a means of relieving tension. Both of these activities would be incompatible with drinking.

Self-reinforcement is rewarding yourself immediately for achieving a specific goal; the reward could be praising yourself, watching a favorite television program, telephoning a friend, eating a favorite food. Self-punishment is arranging some aversive consequence for failing to achieve a goal, such as depriving yourself of something you enjoy (*not* watching a favorite television program, for instance) or making yourself do an unpleasant task (such as cleaning your room). Depending on the kind of behavior the individual wants to change, various combinations of self-reinforcement, self-punishment, or control of stimuli and responses may be used. Table 17-1 outlines a program for self-regulation of eating.

Cognitive Behavior Therapies

The behavior therapy procedures we have discussed thus far have focused on modifying behavior directly with little attention paid to the individual's thinking and reasoning processes. Initially, behavior therapists discounted the importance of cognition, preferring a strict stimulus-response approach. They regarded any consideration of beliefs and attitudes as a return to the kind of unscientific introspection that Watson objected to at the beginning of this century (see Chapter 1). However, in recent years behavior therapists have paid increased attention to the role of cognitive factors—the individual's thoughts, expectations, and interpretation of events—in determining behavior and in mediating behavior change.

Cognitive behavior therapy is a general term for treatment methods that use behavior modification techniques but also incorporate procedures designed to change maladaptive beliefs. The therapist attempts to help people control disturbing emotional reactions, such as anxiety and depression, by teaching them more effective ways of interpreting and thinking about their experiences. For example, as we noted in discussing Beck's cognitive theory of depression (see Chapter 16), depressed individuals tend to appraise events from a negative and self-critical viewpoint. They expect to fail rather than to succeed, and they tend to magnify failures and to minimize successes in evaluating their performance. In treating depression, cognitive behavior therapists try to help their clients recognize the distortions in their thinking and make changes that are more in line with reality. The following dialogue illustrates how a therapist, by carefully directed questioning, makes a client aware of the unrealistic nature of her beliefs.

THERAPIST: Why do you want to end your life?
CLIENT: Without Raymond, I am nothing. . . . I can't be happy without Raymond. . . . But I can't save our marriage.
THERAPIST: What has your marriage been like?
CLIENT: It has been miserable from the very beginning. . . . Raymond has always been unfaithful. . . . I have hardly seen him in the past five years.
THERAPIST: You say that you can't be happy without Raymond. . . . Have you found yourself happy when you are with Raymond?
CLIENT: No, we fight all the time and I feel worse.
THERAPIST: You say you are nothing without Raymond. Before you met Raymond, did you feel you were nothing?
CLIENT: No, I felt I was somebody.

THERAPIST: If you were somebody before you knew Raymond, why do you need him [in order] to be somebody now?

CLIENT: (puzzled) Hmmm. . . .

THERAPIST: If you were free of the marriage, do you think that men might be interested in you—knowing that you were available?

CLIENT: I guess that maybe they would be.

THERAPIST: Is it possible that you might find a man who would be more constant than Raymond?

CLIENT: I don't know. . . . I guess it's possible. . . .

THERAPIST: Then what have you actually lost if you break up the marriage?

CLIENT: I don't know.

THERAPIST: Is it possible that you'll get along better if you end the marriage?

CLIENT: There is no guarantee of that.

THERAPIST: Do you have a *real* marriage?

CLIENT: I guess not.

THERAPIST: If you don't have a real marriage, what do you actually lose if you decide to end the marriage?

CLIENT: (long pause) Nothing, I guess.   (Beck, 1976, pp. 280–291)

The behavioral component of the treatment comes into play when the therapist encourages the client to formulate alternative ways of viewing her situation and then test the implications. For example, the woman in this dialogue might be asked to record her moods at regular intervals and then to note how her depression and feelings of self-esteem fluctuate as a function of what she is doing. If she finds she feels worse after interacting with her husband than when she is alone or is interacting with someone else, this information could serve to challenge her belief that she "can't be happy without Raymond."

Cognitive behavior therapists often combine behavior modification techniques with specific instructions for handling negative thoughts. A program to help someone overcome agoraphobia might include systematic desensitization (at first with imagery and later with actual excursions going progressively farther from home), along with training in positive thinking. The therapist teaches the client to replace self-defeating internal dialogues ("I'm so nervous, I know I'll faint as soon as I leave the house") with positive self-instructions ("Be calm; I'm not alone; even if I have a panic attack there is someone to help me"). Table 17-2 describes a program for the treatment of depression that includes techniques for modifying behavior and for changing attitudes.

Cognitive behavior therapists agree that it is important to alter a person's beliefs in order to bring about an enduring change in behavior. Nevertheless, most maintain that behavioral procedures are more powerful than strictly verbal ones in affecting cognitive processes. For example, to overcome anxiety about giving a speech in class, it is helpful to think positively: "I know the material well, and I'm sure I can present my ideas effectively"; "The topic is interesting, and the other students will enjoy what I have to say." But successfully presenting the speech to a roommate and again before a group of friends will probably do more to reduce anxiety. Successful performance increases our feeling of mastery. In fact, Bandura suggests that all therapeutic procedures that are effective give the person a sense of mastery or *self-efficacy*. Observing others cope and succeed, being verbally persuaded that we can handle a difficult situation, and judging from internal cues that we are relaxed and in control contribute to our feelings of self-efficacy. But the greatest sense of efficacy comes from actual performance, from personal mastery experiences. In essence, nothing succeeds like success (Bandura, 1984).

TABLE 17-2
Coping With Depression *A program for the treatment of depression that combines behavioral and cognitive techniques. This is a condensed description of a 12-session course used successfully to treat depressed individuals in small groups.* (After Lewinsohn, Antonuccio, Steinmetz, & Teri, 1984)

INSTRUCTION IN SELF-CHANGE SKILLS

Pinpointing the target behavior and recording its baseline rate of occurrence; discovering the events or situations that precede the target behavior and the consequences (either positive or negative) that follow it; setting goals for change and choosing reinforcers

RELAXATION TRAINING

Learning progressive muscle relaxation to handle the anxiety that often accompanies depression; monitoring tension in daily situations and applying relaxation techniques

INCREASING PLEASANT EVENTS

Monitoring the frequency of enjoyable activities and planning weekly schedules so that each day contains a balance between negative/neutral activities and pleasant ones

COGNITIVE STRATEGIES

Learning methods for increasing positive thoughts and decreasing negative thoughts; for identifying irrational thoughts and challenging them; and for using self-instructions to help handle problem situations

ASSERTIVENESS TRAINING

Identifying situations in which being nonassertive adds to feelings of depression; learning to handle social interactions more assertively via modeling and role-playing

INCREASING SOCIAL INTERACTION

Identifying the factors that are contributing to low social interaction (such as getting in the habit of doing things alone, feeling uncomfortable due to few social skills); deciding on activities that need to be increased (such as calling friends to suggest getting together) or decreased (such as watching television) in order to improve the level of pleasant social interaction

Humanistic Therapies

Humanistic therapies are based on the phenomenological approach to personality discussed in Chapter 14. While there are different varieties of humanistic therapies, they all emphasize the individual's natural tendency toward growth and self-actualization. Psychological disorders are assumed to arise when the process of reaching one's potential is blocked by circumstances or by other people (parents, teachers, spouses) who try to channel the person's development along lines they find acceptable. When this occurs, the person begins to deny his true feelings. The person's awareness of his uniqueness becomes narrowed and the potential for growth is reduced. Humanistic therapies seek to help people get in touch with their real selves and to make deliberate choices regarding their lives and behavior, rather

Carl Rogers (top right) facilitating discussion in a therapy group.

than letting external events determine their behavior. The goal of humanistic therapy is to help the client to become more fully the person he or she is capable of becoming.

Like the psychoanalyst, the humanistic therapist attempts to increase the person's awareness of underlying emotions and motives. But the emphasis is on what the individual is experiencing in the here and now, rather than in the past. The humanistic therapist does not interpret the person's behavior (as a psychoanalyst might) or try to modify it (as a behavior therapist would) because such actions would impose the therapist's own views on the patient.

The goal of the humanistic therapist is to facilitate exploration of the individual's own thoughts and feelings and to assist the individual in arriving at his or her own solutions. This approach will become clearer as we look at *person-centered therapy* (formerly called *client-centered therapy*), one of the first humanistic therapies.

Person-centered therapy, developed by the late Carl Rogers, is based on the assumption that the client is the best expert on himself or herself and that people are capable of working out the solutions to their own problems. The task of the therapist is to facilitate this progress—not to ask probing questions, to make interpretations, or to suggest courses of action. In fact, Rogers preferred the term "facilitator" to "therapist."

Person-centered therapy can be described rather simply, but in practice it requires great skill and is much more subtle than it first appears. The therapist begins by explaining the nature of the interviews. The responsibility for working out problems is the client's. He or she is free to leave at any time and to choose whether to return. The relationship is private and confidential; the person is free to speak of intimate matters without fear of reproof or of the information being revealed to others. Once the situation is structured, the client does most of the talking. Usually, the client has much to say. The therapist is an interested and alert listener. When the client stops, as though expecting the therapist to say something, the therapist usually acknowledges and accepts the feelings the person has expressed. For example, if a man has

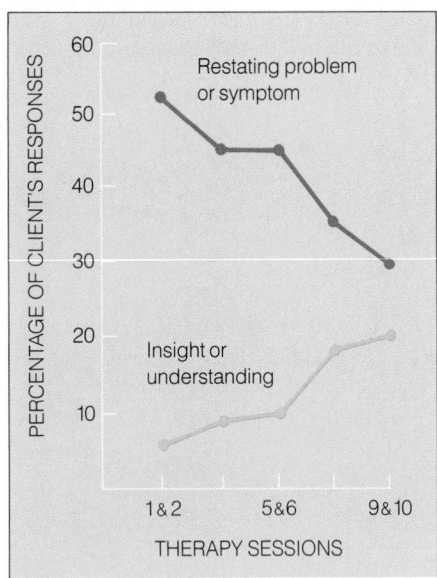

FIGURE 17-5
Changes During Person-Centered Therapy *Description and restatement of the problem on the part of the client gradually gives way during the course of therapy to increased frequency of statements that indicate understanding.* (After Seeman, 1949)

been talking about his nagging mother, the therapist may say, "You feel that your mother tries to control you." The object is to *clarify* the feelings that the person has been expressing, not to judge them or to elaborate on them.

Generally, individuals begin therapy with rather low evaluations of themselves, but in the course of facing their problems and of trying to arrive at solutions, they begin to view themselves more positively. For instance, one client began the initial session with the following statements:

Everything is wrong with me. I feel abnormal. I don't do even the ordinary things of life. I'm sure I will fail on anything I undertake. I'm inferior. When I try to imitate successful people, I'm only acting. I can't go on like this.

By the final interview, the client expressed attitudes that contrasted strikingly with the statements in the first interview:

I am taking a new course of my own choosing. I am really changing. I have always tried to live up to others' standards that were beyond my abilities. I've come to realize that I'm not so bright, but I can get along anyway. I no longer think so much about myself. I'm much more comfortable with people. I'm getting a feeling of success out of my job. I don't feel quite steady yet and would like to feel that I can come for more help if I need it. (Snyder et al., 1947)

To determine whether this kind of progress is typical, researchers have analyzed recorded interviews. When clients' statements are classified and plotted, the course of therapy turns out to be fairly predictable. In the early interviews, people spend a good deal of time talking about their problems and describing symptoms. During the course of therapy, they make more and more statements that indicate they are achieving an *understanding* of their particular problems. By classifying all clients' remarks as either "problem restatements" or "statements of understanding and insight," the progressive increase in insight as therapy proceeds becomes evident (see Figure 17-5).

What do person-centered therapists do to bring about these changes? Rogers believed that the most important qualities for a therapist are empathy, warmth, and genuineness. *Empathy* refers to the ability to understand the feelings the client is trying to express *and* the ability to communicate this understanding to the client. The therapist must adopt the client's frame of reference and must strive to see the problems as the client sees them. By *warmth*, Rogers meant a deep acceptance of the individual as he or she is, including the conviction that this person has the capacity to deal constructively with his or her problems. A therapist who is *genuine* is open and honest and does not play a role or operate behind a professional façade. People are reluctant to reveal themselves to those they perceive as phony. Rogers believed that a therapist who possesses these attributes will facilitate the client's growth and self-exploration (Rogers, 1970; Truax & Mitchell, 1971).

Rogers and his colleagues, by their insistence on an empirical analysis of the therapy process, have contributed much to the field of psychotherapy research. For example, they initiated the practice of tape-recording therapy sessions for subsequent analysis by researchers. Person-centered therapy has some limitations, however. Like psychoanalysis, it appears to be successful only with individuals who are fairly verbal and who are motivated to discuss their problems. For people who do not voluntarily seek help or who are seriously disturbed and are unable to discuss their feelings, more directive methods are usually necessary. In addition, by using the client's self-reports as the only measure of psychotherapeutic effectiveness, the person-centered

TABLE 17-3
Some Approaches to Psychotherapy

NAME	FOCUS	METHODS
Gestalt therapy	To become aware of the whole personality by working through unresolved conflicts and discovering those aspects of the individual's being that are blocked from awareness. Emphasis is on becoming intensely aware of how one is feeling and behaving at the moment.	Therapy in a group setting, but therapist works with one individual at a time. Acting out fantasies, dreams, or the two sides to a conflict are methods used to increase awareness. Combines psychoanalytic emphasis on resolving internal conflicts with behaviorist emphasis on awareness of one's behavior and humanistic concern for self-actualization.
Reality therapy	To clarify the individual's values and to evaluate current behavior and future plans in relation to these values. To force the individual to accept responsibility.	Therapist helps the individual perceive the consequences of possible courses of action and decide on a realistic solution or goal. Once a plan of action is chosen, a contract may be signed in which the client agrees to follow through.
Rational-Emotive therapy	To replace certain irrational ideas (It is essential to be loved and admired by everyone all the time; I should be competent in all respects; People have little control over their sorrow and unhappiness) with more realistic ones. Assumes that cognitive change will produce emotional changes.	Therapist attacks and contradicts the individual's ideas (sometimes subtly, sometimes directly) in an attempt to persuade her or him to take a more rational view of the situation. Similar to Beck's cognitive therapy, but therapist is more direct and confrontive.
Transactional analysis	To become aware of the intent behind the individual's communications; to eliminate subterfuge and deceit so that the individual can interpret his or her behavior accurately.	Therapy in a group setting. Communications between married couples or group members are analyzed in terms of the part of the personality that is speaking—"parent," "child," or "adult" (similar to Freud's superego, id, and ego)—and the intent of the message. Destructive social interactions or games are exposed for what they are.
Hypnotherapy	To relieve the symptoms and strengthen ego processes by helping the individual set reality aside and make constructive use of imagery.	Therapist uses various hypnotic procedures in an attempt to reduce conflict and doubt by focusing the individual's attention, to modify symptoms through direct suggestion or displacement, and to strengthen the individual's ability to cope.

therapist ignores behavior outside of the therapy session. Individuals who feel insecure and ineffective in their interpersonal relationships often need help in modifying their behavior.

An Eclectic Approach

There are many variations of psychotherapy in addition to the ones we have discussed here. Several other approaches to psychotherapy are listed in Table 17-3. Most psychotherapists do not adhere strictly to any *single* method. Instead, they take an *eclectic approach*, selecting from the different techniques the ones they feel are most appropriate for the individual client. Although their theoretical orientation may be toward a particular method or school (for example, more psychoanalytic than behaviorist), eclectic psychotherapists feel free to discard the concepts they view as not especially helpful and to select techniques from other schools. In short, they are flexible in their approach to therapy.*

In dealing with a highly anxious individual, for instance, an eclectic psychotherapist might first prescribe tranquilizers or relaxation training to help reduce the person's level of anxiety. (Most psychoanalysts would not take this approach, however, because they believe that anxiety is necessary to motivate the client to explore his or her conflicts.) To help the client understand the origins of his or her problems, the eclectic therapist might discuss certain aspects of the patient's history but might feel it unnecessary to explore childhood experiences to the extent that a psychoanalyst would. The therapist might use educational techniques, such as providing information about sex and reproduction to help relieve the anxieties of an adolescent boy who feels guilty about his sexual impulses or explaining the functioning of the autonomic nervous system to reassure an anxious woman that some of her symptoms, such as heart palpitations and hand tremors, are not indications of a disease.

Recognizing that often no single therapeutic approach deals successfully with all aspects of a problem, more and more therapists are specializing in specific problems. For example, some clinicians specialize in problems of sexual dysfunction. They learn all they can about the physiological processes that lead to orgasm; the effect of drugs (such as alcohol, tranquilizers, and other medications) on sexual performance; and the way in which such factors as anxiety, sexual traumas, and poor communication between partners contribute to sexual dysfunction. Once sex therapists have learned all there is to know about the variables involved in normal and abnormal sexual functioning, they examine the various therapeutic systems to see what techniques can be applied to specific problems. Although sex therapists may draw on all of the approaches we have discussed, biological and cognitive behavioral methods are most often used in treating sexual dysfunctions.

Other therapists specialize in anxiety, depression, alcoholism, and marital problems. Some concentrate on certain age groups, seeking to learn all they can about the problems of children, adolescents, or the aged. Within their special areas, therapists generally use an eclectic, or integrative, approach.

Group and Family Therapy

Many emotional problems involve an individual's difficulties in relating to others, including feelings of isolation, rejection, and loneliness and the inability to form meaningful relationships. Although the therapist can help the individual to work out some of these problems, the final test lies in how well the person can apply the attitudes and responses learned in therapy to relationships in everyday life. *Group therapy* permits clients to work out their problems in the presence of others, to observe how other people react to their behavior, and to try out new methods of responding when old ones prove unsatisfactory. It is often used as a supplement to individual psychotherapy.

Therapists of various orientations (psychoanalytic, humanistic, and cognitive behaviorist) have modified their techniques to be applicable to therapy groups. Group therapy has been used in a variety of settings: in hospital wards and outpatient psychiatric clinics, with parents of disturbed children, and with teenagers in correctional institutions, to name a few. Typically, the

---

*The term *integrative psychotherapy* is sometimes used instead of eclectic psychotherapy.

Alcoholics Anonymous is an example of a self-help group.

groups consist of a small number of individuals (6 to 12 is considered optimal) who have similar problems. The therapist usually remains in the background, allowing the members to exchange experiences, to comment on one another's behavior, and to discuss their own problems as well as those of the other members. However, in some groups the therapist is quite active. For example, in a group desensitization session, people who share the same phobias (such as fear of flying or anxieties about tests) may be led together through a systematic desensitization hierarchy. Or in a session for training social skills, a group of shy and unassertive individuals may be coached by the therapist in a series of role-playing scenes.

Group therapy has several advantages over individual therapy. It saves therapist time because one therapist can help several people at once. An individual can derive comfort and support from observing that others have similar, perhaps more severe problems. A person can learn vicariously by watching how others behave and can explore attitudes and reactions by interacting with a variety of people, not just with the therapist. Groups are particularly effective when they provide the participants with opportunities to acquire new social skills through modeling and to practice these skills in the group.

Most groups are led by a trained therapist. However, the number and variety of self-help groups—groups that are conducted without a professional therapist—are increasing. Self-help groups are voluntary organizations of people who meet regularly to exchange information and to support each other's efforts to overcome a common problem. *Alcoholics Anonymous* is the best known of the self-help groups. Another is *Recovery, Inc.*, an organization open to former mental patients. Other groups help people cope with specific stressful situations such as bereavement, divorce, and single parenthood. Table 17-4 lists a variety of self-help groups.

MARITAL AND FAMILY THERAPY   Problems in communicating feelings, satisfying one's needs, and responding appropriately to the needs and demands of others become intensified in the intimate context of marriage and family life. To the extent that they involve more than one client and focus on

TABLE 17-4
Examples of Self-Help Groups *Listed are some of the self-help groups available in one large community.* (After San Diego Mental Health Association, 1989)

AIDS Counseling Program
AIRS (teenage chemical dependency)
Adult Children of Alcoholics
Adults Molested as Children
Affective Disorders Group (mood disorders)
Al-Anon (families of alcoholics)
Ala-Teen (teenage alcohol abuse)

Alcoholics Anonymous
Alzheimer's Disease Family Support Group
Arthritis Support Group
Battered Women's Support Group
Bi-Polar Support Group (manic-depression)
CREATE (college students recovering from mental illness)
Emotional Health Anonymous
Epilepsy Support Group
Gay Men's Coming Out Group
Grandmother's Support Group (mothers of teenage mothers)
Lesbian Support Group

Loss Support (grief recovery)
Make Today Count (breast cancer support)
Narcotics Anonymous
PMS Association (Pre-Menstrual Syndrome)
Parent Aid (parents at risk for child abuse)
Parents United (sexual abuse)
Parkinson's Disease Support Group
Pre Ala-Teen (child alcohol dependency)
Project Return (recovering mental patients)
Recovery Inc.
Phobia Foundation
Single Parent Support Group
Sudden Infant Death Syndrome
Survivors of Suicide
Teen Mothers Support Group
Victims of Homicide (family and loved ones)
Voices (schizophrenic support group)

interpersonal relationships, *marital therapy* and *family therapy* can be considered specialized forms of group therapy.

The high divorce rate and the number of couples seeking help for difficulties centering around their relationship have made marital, or couple, therapy a growing field. Studies show that joint therapy for both partners is more effective in solving marital problems than is individual therapy for only one partner (Gurman & Kniskern, 1981).

There are many approaches to marital therapy, but most focus on helping the partners communicate their feelings, develop greater understanding and sensitivity to each other's needs, and work on more effective ways of handling their conflicts. Some couples enter marriage with very different, and often unrealistic, expectations about the roles of husband and wife, which can wreak havoc with their relationship. The therapist can help them clarify their expectations and work out a mutually agreeable compromise. Sometimes the couple negotiates *behavioral contracts*, agreeing on the behavior changes each person is willing to make in order to create a more satisfying relationship and specifying the rewards and penalties they can use with each other to ensure the changes.

Marriage counseling (left) and family therapy (right).

Family therapy overlaps with marital therapy but has a somewhat different origin. It developed in response to the discovery that many people who improved in individual therapy while away from their family—often in institutional settings—relapsed when they returned home. It became apparent that many of these people came from a disturbed family setting that required modification itself if the individual's gains were to be maintained. The basic premise of family therapy is that the problem shown by the identified patient is a sign that something is wrong with the entire family; the *family system* is not operating properly. The difficulty may lie in poor communication among family members or in an alliance between some family members that excludes others. For example, a mother whose relationship with her husband is unsatisfactory may focus all her attention on her son. As a result, the husband and daughter feel neglected and the son, upset by his mother's smothering and the resentment directed toward him by his father and sister, develops problems in school. While the boy's school difficulties may be the reason for seeking treatment, it is clear that they are only a symptom of a more basic family problem.

In family therapy, the family meets regularly with one or two therapists (usually a male and a female). The therapist, while observing the interactions among family members, tries to help each member become aware of the way he or she relates to the others and how his or her actions may be contributing to the family's problems. Sometimes videotape recordings are played back to make the family members aware of how they interact with each other. Other times, the therapist may visit the family in the home to observe conflicts and verbal exchanges as they occur in their natural setting. It often becomes apparent that problem behaviors are being reinforced by the responses of family members. For example, a young child's temper tantrums or a teenager's eating problems may be inadvertently reinforced by the attention they elicit from the parents. The therapist can teach the parents to monitor their own and their children's behavior, to determine how their reactions may be reinforcing the problem behavior, and then to alter the reinforcement contingencies.

EFFECTIVENESS OF PSYCHOTHERAPY

How effective is psychotherapy? Which methods work best? These questions are not easy to answer. Research into the effectiveness of psychotherapy is hampered by several major difficulties. How do we decide whether an individual has improved? What measures of improvement are valid? How do we know what caused the change?

Evaluating Psychotherapy

Evaluating the effectiveness of psychotherapy is a very difficult task because so many variables must be considered. For instance, a large percentage of people with psychological problems get better without any professional treatment. This phenomenon is called *spontaneous remission*, a term borrowed from medicine. Many physical illnesses run a certain course, and barring complications, the individual will recover without specific treatment. However, the word "spontaneous" is not really appropriate in describing recovery from psychological disorders without professional help. Some mental disorders do improve by themselves, simply with the passage of time—much like the common cold. This is particularly true of depression. But more often, improvement that occurs in the absence of treatment is not spontaneous; rather, it is the result of external events—usually changes in the individual's life situation or the help of another person.

Many emotionally disturbed people who do not seek professional assistance are able to improve with the help of a nonprofessional, such as a friend, teacher, or religious adviser. We cannot consider these recoveries to be spontaneous; but since they are not due to psychotherapy, they are included in the rate of spontaneous remission, which ranges from about 30 to 60 percent, depending on the particular disorder being studied (Bergin & Lambert, 1978). To allow for those who would have improved without treatment, any evaluation of psychotherapy must compare a treated group with an untreated control group. Psychotherapy is judged to be effective if the client's improvement after therapy is greater than any improvement that occurs without therapy over the same period. The ethical problem of allowing someone to go without treatment is usually resolved by composing the control group of individuals on a waiting list. Members of the waiting-list control group are interviewed at the start of the study to gather baseline information but receive no treatment until the study has ended. Unfortunately, the longer the study (and time is needed to measure improvement, especially with insight therapies), the harder it is to maintain people on a waiting list.

A second major problem in evaluating psychotherapy is measuring the outcome. How do we decide whether a person has been helped by therapy? We cannot always rely on the individual's own assessment. Some people report that they are feeling better simply to please the therapist or to convince themselves that their money was well spent. The *hello–goodbye effect* has long been recognized by therapists. At the beginning of therapy (the "hello"), people tend to exaggerate their unhappiness and their problems to convince the therapist that they really need help. At the end of therapy (the "goodbye"), they tend to exaggerate their well-being to express appreciation to the therapist for his or her efforts or to convince themselves that their time and money were not wasted. These phenomena must be considered when evaluating the client's view of his or her progress.

The therapist's evaluation of the treatment as successful cannot always be considered an objective criterion, either. The therapist has a vested interest in proclaiming that the client is better. But sometimes the changes that the therapist observes during the therapy session do not carry over into real-life situations. Assessment of improvement, therefore, should include at least three independent measures: the client's evaluation of progress; the therapist's evaluation; and the judgment of a third party, such as family members and friends or a clinician not involved in the treatment.

Other outcome measures that may be used in evaluating the effectiveness of psychotherapy include scores on tests (such as the Minnesota Multiphasic Personality Inventory or the Beck Depression Inventory) and, in the case of behavior therapy, changes in the target behavior (such as a decrease in compulsive acts). Measures of improvement in a person's life outside of the therapy situation—performing more effectively at work or school, drinking less, a decrease in antisocial activities—are more meaningful but are often difficult to obtain in long-term studies of psychotherapeutic effectiveness.

Despite these problems, researchers have been able to conduct many psychotherapy evaluation studies. Rather than discuss individual studies, we will look at a major evaluation that attempted to answer the question of whether psychotherapy works. The investigators located 475 published studies that compared at least one therapy group with an untreated control group. Using a complicated statistical procedure called meta-analysis (see Chapter 6), they determined the magnitude of effect for each study by comparing the average change produced in treatment (on measures such as self-esteem, anxiety, and achievement in work and school) with that of the control group. They concluded that individuals receiving therapy were better off than those who had received no treatment. The average psychotherapy patient showed greater improvement than 80 percent of the untreated control-group patients (Smith, Glass, & Miller, 1980).

A subsequent review that analyzed a new sample of studies yielded comparable results (Shapiro & Shapiro, 1982). When we look at improvement rates as a function of the number of therapy sessions (see Figure 17-6), it is clear that treated groups show a rate of change that is above and beyond spontaneous remission estimates. By the eighth therapy session approximately 50 percent of patients are measurably improved, and 75 percent have shown improvement by the end of 6 months of weekly psychotherapy.

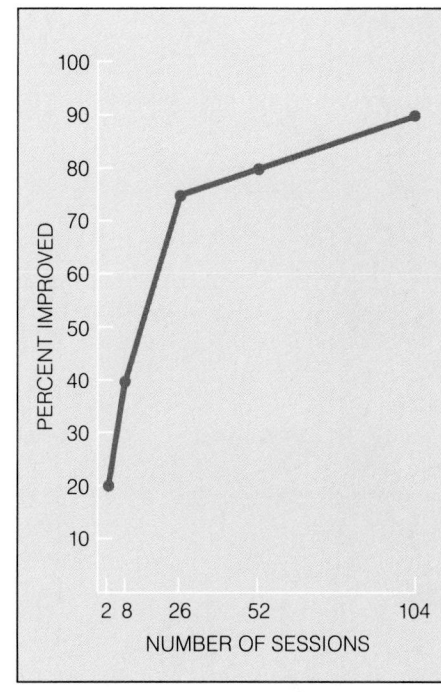

FIGURE 17-6
Improvement with Psychotherapy
The figure shows the relationship between the number of sessions of individual psychotherapy and the percentage of patients improved. Improvement was rated by independent researchers following the termination of treatment. (After Howard, Kopta, Krause, & Orlinsky, 1986)

Comparing Psychotherapies

Psychotherapy produces greater improvement than no treatment, but are the different therapeutic approaches equally effective? A number of reviews have analyzed studies in which the results of different psychotherapies were compared (for example, Bergin & Lambert, 1978; Smith, Glass, & Miller, 1980; Rachman & Wilson, 1980). The conclusion of most of these reviews is that there is little difference in effectiveness between therapies. This conclusion, disturbing to some therapists, has been called the "Dodo bird verdict," in reference to the Dodo bird in *Alice in Wonderland* who said "Everyone has won and all must have prizes." How can therapies that espouse such different methods produce such similar results? Numerous possible explanations have been suggested (see Stiles, Shapiro, & Elliott, 1986). We will mention only two.

Perhaps certain therapies are effective for certain problems or disorders but are relatively ineffective for others. When specific therapies are used to treat a wide range of disorders, they may help some cases but not others. Thus, averaging results over cases may conceal the special strengths of a particular therapy. We need to know which treatment is effective for which problem.

There are some clues. We know, for example, that systematic desensitization and modeling are effective for eliminating specific fears or phobias, whereas psychoanalytic and person-centered therapies are not. When we want to change specific behaviors, cognitive behavior therapies generally work better than insight therapies. But if the goal is self-understanding, then more global therapies such as psychoanalytic and person-centered therapy are appropriate.

We know, too, that none of the psychotherapies are very successful in treating schizophrenia or bipolar disorders. However, psychotherapy can be beneficial (when used in combination with some of the biological therapies described in the next section) in helping the patient deal with the problems of daily living. The task for future evaluators is to determine the disorder for which each therapy is particularly effective. Matching the right therapy and therapist with the right patient will improve the overall effectiveness of treatment.

Another reason why different psychotherapies may be equally effective in helping clients is because they all share certain factors. It may be these common factors, rather than the specific therapeutic techniques employed, that promote positive change.

Common Factors in Psychotherapies

One school of therapy emphasizes insight; another, modeling and reinforcement; and yet another, empathy and warmth. But perhaps these variables are not the crucial ones. Other factors that are common to most psychotherapies, but which receive little emphasis when therapists write about what they do, may be more important (Garfield, 1980; Orlinsky & Howard, 1987).

AN INTERPERSONAL RELATIONSHIP OF WARMTH AND TRUST   Regardless of the type of therapy provided, in a good therapeutic relationship, client and therapist have mutual respect and regard for one another. The client must believe that the therapist understands and is concerned with his or her problems. Although behavior therapy may sound like a rather impersonal procedure when it is described in a textbook, studies indicate that experienced behavior therapists show as much empathy and depth of interpersonal involvement as experienced psychoanalytically oriented therapists (Sloane et al., 1975). A therapist who understands our problems and believes we can solve them earns our trust, which increases our sense of competence and our confidence that we can succeed.

REASSURANCE AND SUPPORT   Our problems often seem insurmountable and unique to us. Discussing them with an expert who accepts our difficulties as not unusual and indicates that they can be resolved is reassuring. Having someone help us with problems we have not been able to solve alone also provides a sense of support and a feeling of hope. In fact, the most successful therapists, regardless of their method of psychotherapy, are those

A relationship of mutual respect and trust is important to successful psychotherapy.

who form a helpful, supportive relationship with their clients (Luborsky et al., 1985).

DESENSITIZATION   We have already talked about systematic desensitization, the specific techniques of behavior therapy aimed at helping individuals to lose their fear of certain objects or situations. But many types of psychotherapy can encourage a broader kind of desensitization. When we discuss events and emotions that have been troubling us in the accepting atmosphere of a therapy session, they gradually lose their threatening quality. Problems that we brood about alone can become magnified beyond proportion; sharing problems with someone else often makes them seem less serious. Several other hypotheses can also explain how desensitization occurs in psychotherapy. For example, putting events that are disturbing into words may help us reappraise the situation in a more realistic manner. From the viewpoint of learning theory, repeatedly discussing distressing experiences in the security of a therapeutic setting (where punishment is not forthcoming) may gradually extinguish the anxiety associated with them. Whatever the process, desensitization does appear to be a factor common to many kinds of psychotherapy.

REINFORCEMENT OF ADAPTIVE RESPONSES   Behavior therapists use reinforcement as a technique to increase positive attitudes and actions. But any therapist in whom a client places trust and confidence functions as a reinforcing agent; that is, the therapist tends to express approval of the behaviors or attitudes deemed conducive to better adjustment and to ignore or express disapproval of maladaptive attitudes or responses. Which responses are reinforced depends on the therapist's orientation and therapeutic goals. The use of reinforcement may be intentional or unintentional; in some instances, the therapist may be unaware that he or she is reinforcing or failing

CRITICAL DISCUSSION

The Placebo Response

Placebos are commonly used in research on the effectiveness of drugs. A placebo is an inert substance (known to have no pharmacological effect) that is made to look like an active drug—in essence, a sugar pill. Placebos are used in drug research as controls a) for the patients' expectations that the medicine will make them feel better, b) for the researcher's belief that the medicine is effective, and c) for the beneficial effects of extra attention from nurses and other personnel that stem from being a research subject. A *double-blind* procedure is usually employed: one group of patients is given the drug and a comparable group is given the placebo, but neither the patients nor the researchers (or whoever judges the results) knows until the end of the study which pills contain the active medication and which are the placebos. Since both the patients and the researchers are blind to the nature of the pills, the method is termed double-blind. If the rate of improvement is greater in those who received the drug, then the drug is considered to be therapeutically effective. If both groups of patients show similar improvement, then whatever positive response occurs with the drug is considered to be a placebo effect and the drug is judged to be ineffective.

All responses that cannot be explained on the basis of actual drug effects are considered to be placebo responses—that is, due to unknown and nonpharmacological causes. Such unknown causes are generally assumed to be psychological in nature.

Placebo responses can be very powerful. For example, 40 percent of patients who were suffering from a painful heart disease (angina pectoris) reported marked relief from their symptoms after undergoing a diagnostic procedure that they believed was an operation to cure the problem (Beecher, 1961). In treating psychological disorders, placebos are often as effective as medication. A review of studies in which patients were given either an antianxiety drug or a placebo found that improvement rates for patients receiving placebos were usually as good as, and often better than, the rates for those receiving drugs (Lowinger & Dobie, 1969).

Until the beginning of modern scientific medicine, almost all medications were placebos. Patients were given every conceivable substance—crocodile dung, lozenges of dried vipers, spermatic fluid of frogs, spiders, worms, and human excrement—prepared in every possible manner to treat their symptoms. Throughout medical history, patients have been purged, poisoned, leached, bled, heated, frozen, sweated, and shocked (Shapiro & Morris, 1978). Since physicians and healers traditionally have held positions of honor and respect, their "treatments" must have helped at least some of their patients. We assume their effectiveness was due to the placebo response. Scientists also attribute documented cases of faith healing and various forms of miraculous cures to placebo effects.

Some clinicians have suggested that the placebo response may be one of the reasons why psychotherapy works (Lieberman & Dunlap, 1979; Wilkins, 1984). According to this view, almost any method of psychotherapy should show positive results if the client believes it will be effective. If this is true, it becomes important for the therapist to convey to the client his or her conviction that the method of treatment will be successful.

---

to reinforce a particular client behavior. For example, person-centered therapists believe in letting the client determine what is discussed during the therapy sessions and do not wish to influence the trend of the client's conversation. However, reinforcement can be subtle; a smile, a nod of the head, or a simple "um hmm" following certain client statements may increase the likelihood of their recurrence.

Since the goal of all psychotherapies is to bring about a change in the client's attitudes and behaviors, some type of learning must take place in therapy. The therapist needs to be aware of his or her role in influencing the client by means of reinforcement and should use this knowledge consciously to facilitate desired changes.

UNDERSTANDING OR INSIGHT   All of the psychotherapies we have been discussing provide the client with an *explanation* of his or her difficulties—how they arose, why they persist, and how they can be changed. For the individual in psychoanalysis, this explanation may take the form of a

The idea that placebo responses play a central role in psychotherapy is disturbing to some clinicians. They feel that it links psychotherapy with quackery or charlatanism and implies that the process is one of self-deception. This is not the case. Physicians and psychotherapists have known for a long time that a patient's attitudes and beliefs are very important in determining the effectiveness of treatment. Any treatment will be more effective if the patient believes in it and is motivated to use it in the proper manner. Rather than deny the importance of the placebo effect, it would be better to continue investigating the variables that contribute to it.

In addition, researchers who wish to demonstrate the effectiveness of a specific therapeutic technique should control for the placebo response. Sophisticated studies do this by including a placebo control group, as well as an untreated control group. For example, an experiment designed to test the efficacy of systematic desensitization in reducing anxiety about public speaking included the following groups: systematic desensitization, insight therapy, attention-placebo, and untreated control. The subjects in the attention-placebo group met with a sympathetic therapist who led them to believe that a pill would reduce their overall sensitivity to stress. To convince them, the therapist had them listen to a "stress tape" (presumably one used in training astronauts to function under stress) for several sessions after ingesting the "tranquilizer." In reality, the pill was a placebo and the tape contained nonverbal sounds that had been found in other research to be boring rather than stressful. In this way, the researcher raised the subjects' expectations that their speech anxiety would be lessened by taking a pill. The results of this study revealed that the systematic desensitization group improved (they reduced their speech anxiety) much more than the no-treatment group and more than the attention-placebo and insight therapy groups, who reacted about the same to their forms of therapy. The latter two groups, however, did show significant improvement (Paul, 1967). By including the attention-placebo group, the experimenter was able to conclude that the success of the systematic desensitization procedure was not due solely to the placebo effect.

The mechanism that causes placebo responses is unknown. Numerous hypotheses have been proposed, but so far there is little empirical verification for any of them. One group of explanations focuses on social influence (see Chapter 19). Because patients tend to view physicians and therapists as socially powerful individuals, they may be very suggestible to the influence of such authorities and may be easily persuaded that beneficial results will occur. In addition, the role of patient entails certain prescribed behaviors. A good patient is one who gets better; getting better justifies the therapists' initial concern and subsequent interest.

Other explanations focus on the individual's expectations. The person who administers the treatment may communicate, by intended or unintended means, expectations about the effects of the treatment. The patients also arrive with certain expectations, based on their previous experiences. Expectations that one will get better and a strong desire that it happen are the essential ingredients of hope. And hope can have a powerful influence on our emotions and bodily processes. Some researchers speculate that this influence may be mediated by the endorphin group of neurotransmitters. We noted in Chapter 2 how endorphins, the "brain's natural opiates," affect mood and the subjective experience of pain. Endorphins may turn out to play an important role in the placebo response.

gradual understanding of repressed childhood fears and the ways in which these unconscious feelings have contributed to current problems. A behavior therapist might inform the client that current fears are the result of previous conditioning and can be conquered by learning responses that are incompatible with the current ones. A client seeing a cognitive behavior therapist might be told that his or her difficulties stem from the irrational belief that one must be perfect or must be loved by everyone.

How can such different explanations all produce positive results? Perhaps the precise nature of the insights and understanding provided by the therapist is relatively unimportant. It may be more important to provide the client with an explanation for the behavior or feelings that he or she finds so distressing and to present a set of activities (such as free association or relaxation training) that both therapist and client believe will alleviate the distress. When a person is experiencing disturbing symptoms and is unsure of their cause or how serious they might be, he or she will feel reassured contacting a professional who seems to know what the problem is and offers ways of relieving it. The knowledge that change is possible gives the individual hope, and hope is an important variable in facilitating change. (See the Critical Discussion, "The Placebo Response.")

Our discussion of common factors among psychotherapies is not intended to deny the value of some specific treatment methods. Perhaps the most effective therapist is one who recognizes the importance of the common factors and utilizes them in a planned manner for all patients, but who also selects the specific procedures most appropriate for each individual case. This suggests that the training of future therapists should be more eclectic, less committed to a particular school of psychotherapy, and more open to a variety of procedures. It should encourage a systematic search for the procedures that are most effective and efficient for specific problems.

BIOLOGICAL THERAPIES

The biological approach to abnormal behavior assumes that mental disorders, like physical illnesses, are caused by biochemical or physiological dysfunctions of the brain. Several biological theories were mentioned in discussing the etiology of schizophrenia and the mood disorders in Chapter 16. Biological therapies include the use of drugs, electroconvulsive shock, and surgical procedures.

Psychotherapeutic Drugs

By far the most successful biological therapy is the use of drugs to modify mood and behavior. The discovery in the early 1950s of drugs that relieved some of the symptoms of schizophrenia represented a major breakthrough in the treatment of severely disturbed individuals. Intensely agitated patients no longer had to be physically restrained by straitjackets, and patients who had been spending most of their time hallucinating and exhibiting bizarre behavior became more responsive and functional. As a result, psychiatric wards became more manageable, and patients could be discharged more quickly. A few years later, the discovery of drugs that could relieve severe depression had a similar beneficial effect on hospital management and population. We saw in Figure 17-1 the reduction in the number of mental-hospital residents that occurred following the introduction of antipsychotic and antidepressant drugs. About the same time, a group of drugs were being developed to relieve anxiety.

ANTIANXIETY DRUGS Drugs that reduce anxiety belong to the family called *benzodiazepines*. They are commonly known as *tranquilizers* and are marketed under such trade names as Valium (diazepam), Librium (chlordiazepoxide), and Xanax (alprazolam). These drugs reduce tension and cause drowsiness. Like alcohol and the barbiturates, they depress the action of the central nervous system. Family physicians often prescribe tranquilizers to help people cope during difficult periods in their lives. The drugs are also used to treat anxiety disorders, withdrawal from alcohol, and physical disorders related to stress. For example, antianxiety drugs may be combined with systematic desensitization in the treatment of a phobia to help the individual relax when confronting the feared situation.

Although tranquilizers may be useful on a short-term basis, the overall benefits are debatable, and such drugs clearly are overprescribed and misused. Until quite recently (before some of the dangers became apparent), Valium and Librium were the two most widely prescribed drugs in this country (Julien, 1988). The dangers of tranquilizer overuse are several. Depending on a pill to relieve anxiety may prevent a person from exploring the *cause* of the anxiety and from learning more effective ways of coping with tension. More importantly, long-term use of tranquilizers can lead to physical dependency, or addiction (see Chapter 6). Although tranquilizers are not as addictive as barbiturates, tolerance does develop with repeated use and the individual experiences severe withdrawal symptoms if the drug is discontinued. In addition, tranquilizers impair concentration, including driving performance, and can cause death if combined with alcohol.

ANTIPSYCHOTIC DRUGS   Most of the *antipsychotic drugs* that relieve the symptoms of schizophrenia belong to the family called *phenothiazines*. Examples are Thorazine (chlorpromazine) and Prolixin (fluphenazine). These drugs have been called "major tranquilizers," but the term is not really appropriate, because they do not act on the nervous system in the same way as barbiturates or antianxiety drugs. They may cause some drowsiness and lethargy, but they do not induce deep sleep even in massive doses (the person can be easily aroused). They also seldom create the pleasant, slightly euphoric feeling associated with low doses of antianxiety drugs. In fact, the psychological effects of the antipsychotic drugs when administered to normal individuals are usually unpleasant. Hence, these drugs are seldom abused.

In Chapter 16, we discussed the theory that schizophrenia is caused by excessive activity of the neurotransmitter dopamine. Antipsychotic drugs block dopamine receptors. Because the drug's molecules are structurally similar to dopamine molecules, they bind to the postsynaptic receptors of dopamine neurons, thereby blocking the access of dopamine to its receptors. (The drug itself does not activate the receptors.) A single synapse has many receptor molecules. If all of them are blocked, transmission across the synapse will fail. If only some of them are blocked, transmission will be weakened. The clinical potency of an antipsychotic drug is directly related to its ability to compete for dopamine receptors.

Neurons that have receptors for dopamine are concentrated in the reticular system, the limbic system, and the hypothalamus. The reticular system selectively filters the flow of messages from the sense organs to the cerebral cortex and controls the individual's state of arousal. The limbic system and the hypothalamus are important in the regulation of emotion. Alteration of neural activity in these areas may account for the calming effects of antipsychotic drugs, although we have no idea as yet of the processes involved.

Whatever their method of action, antipsychotic drugs are effective in alleviating the hallucinations and confusion of an acute schizophrenic episode and in restoring rational thought processes. These drugs do not cure schizophrenia; most patients must continue to receive a maintenance dosage in order to function outside of a hospital. Many of the characteristic symptoms of schizophrenia—emotional blunting, seclusiveness, difficulties in sustaining attention—remain. Nevertheless, antipsychotic drugs shorten the length of time patients must be hospitalized, and they prevent relapse. Studies of schizophrenics living in the community find that the relapse rate for those taking one of the phenothiazines is typically half the relapse rate of those receiving a placebo (Hogarty et al., 1979).

Unfortunately, antipsychotic drugs do not help all schizophrenic patients. In addition, the drugs have unpleasant side effects—dryness of the mouth, blurred vision, difficulty concentrating—that prompt many patients to discontinue their medication. With long-term usage, more serious side effects may also occur (for example, low blood pressure and a muscular disorder in which there are involuntary movements of the mouth and chin). Researchers continue to search for drugs that will relieve the symptoms of schizophrenia with fewer side effects.

ANTIDEPRESSANT DRUGS   *Antidepressant drugs* help to elevate the mood of depressed individuals. These drugs energize rather than tranquilize, apparently by increasing the availability of two neurotransmitters (norepinephrine and serotonin) that are deficient in some cases of depression (see Chapter 16). The two major classes of antidepressant drugs act in different ways to increase neurotransmitter levels. The *monoamine oxidase* (MAO) *inhibitors* (examples are Nardil and Parnate) block the activity of an enzyme that can destroy both norepinephrine and serotonin, thereby increasing the concentration of these two neurotransmitters in the brain. The *tricyclic antidepressants* (examples are Tofranil and Elavil) prevent the *reuptake* of serotonin and norepinephrine, thereby prolonging the duration of the neurotransmitters' actions. (Recall that *reuptake* is the process by which neurotransmitters are drawn back into the nerve terminals that released them.) Both classes of drugs have proved effective in relieving certain types of depression, presumably those caused more by biological factors than environmental ones. However, like the antipsychotic drugs, the antidepressants can produce some undesirable side effects.

Antidepressants are not stimulants, as amphetamines are (see Chapter 6); they do not produce feelings of euphoria and increased energy. In fact, a patient may undergo several weeks of medication before a change in mood is observed. This is one reason why electroconvulsive therapy, which acts more quickly, is sometimes the preferred treatment for severely depressed, suicidal individuals. We will discuss electroconvulsive therapy in the next section.

Antidepressants are not effective in treating the depression that occurs with bipolar disorders. However, another drug, lithium, has proved very successful. Lithium reduces extreme mood swings and returns the individual to a more normal state of emotional equilibrium. Although the effectiveness of this drug has been known for more than 40 years, researchers have only recently discovered how its complex action on certain neurotransmitters achieves this normalizing effect (Worley, Heller, Snyder, & Baraban, 1988).

Drug therapy has successfully reduced the severity of some types of mental disorders. Many individuals who would require hospitalization otherwise can function within the community with the help of these drugs. On the other hand, there are limitations to the application of drug therapy. All therapeutic drugs can produce undesirable side effects. In addition, many psychologists feel that these drugs alleviate symptoms without requiring the individual to face the personal problems that may be contributing to the disorder. Biochemical abnormalities undoubtedly play a role in schizophrenia and in the more severe mood disorders, but psychological factors are also important. Attitudes and methods of coping with problems that have developed gradually over a lifetime cannot be changed by the administration of a drug. When therapeutic drugs are prescribed, psychotherapeutic help is usually also required.

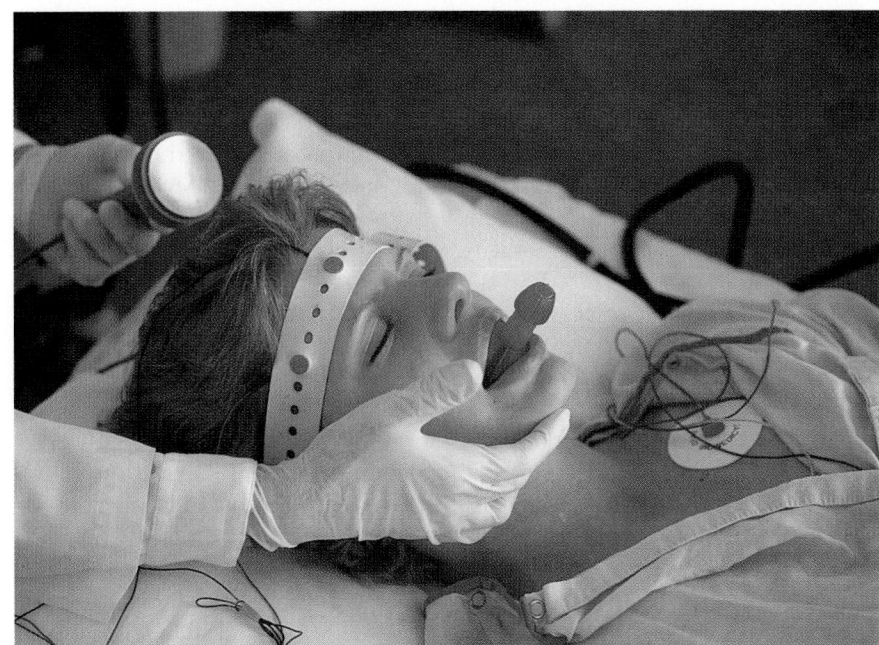

A patient being prepared for electroconvulsive therapy.

Electroconvulsive Therapy and Psychosurgery

In *electroconvulsive therapy* (ECT), also known as *electroshock therapy*, a mild electric current is applied to the brain to produce a seizure similar to an epileptic convulsion. ECT was a popular treatment from about 1940 to 1960, before antipsychotic and antidepressant drugs became readily available. Today, ECT is used only in cases of severe depression when patients fail to respond to drug therapy.

ECT has been the subject of much controversy and public apprehension for several reasons. At one time, it was used indiscriminately in mental hospitals to treat such disorders as alcoholism and schizophrenia, for which it produced no beneficial results. Before more refined procedures were developed, ECT was a frightening experience for the patient, who was often awake until the electric current triggered the seizure and produced momentary unconsciousness. The patient frequently suffered confusion and memory loss afterward. Occasionally, the intensity of the muscle spasms accompanying the brain seizure resulted in physical injuries.

Today, ECT involves little discomfort. The patient is given a short-acting anesthesia and then is injected with a muscle relaxant. A brief, very weak electric current is delivered to the brain either across both temples or to the temple on the side of the nondominant cerebral hemisphere. The minimum current required to produce a brain seizure is administered, since the seizure itself—*not* the electricity—is therapeutic. The muscle relaxant prevents the convulsive spasm of body muscles and possible injury. The individual awakens within a few minutes and remembers nothing about the treatment. Four to six treatments are usually administered over a period of several weeks.

The most troublesome side effect of ECT is memory loss. Some patients report a gap in memory for events that occurred up to 6 months before ECT, as well as an impaired ability to retain new information for a month or two following treatment. However, if very low dosages of electricity are used (the amount is carefully calibrated for each patient to be just sufficient to produce a seizure), memory problems are minimal (Sackeim & Malitz, 1985).

No one knows how the electrically induced seizures relieve depression. Brain seizures do cause the massive release of a number of neurotransmitters, including norepinephrine and serotonin; deficiencies of these two neurotransmitters may be an important factor in some cases of depression (see Chapter 16). Currently researchers are trying to determine the similarities and dissimilarities between ECT and antidepressant drugs in terms of the way each affects neurotransmitters. However it works, ECT is effective in bringing people out of severe, immobilizing depression and does so faster than drug therapy (Janicak et al., 1985).

In *psychosurgery*, selected areas of the brain are destroyed by cutting nerve fibers or by ultrasonic irradiation. Most often, the fibers that connect the frontal lobes with the limbic system or with certain regions of the hypothalamus are destroyed. (Both the limbic system and the hypothalamus are believed to play important roles in emotion.) Psychosurgery is a highly controversial procedure, and congressional committees have investigated the issue of whether it should be legally banned. Some early surgical methods produced individuals who were relaxed and cheerful (no longer violent or suicidal) but whose brains were so impaired that they could not function efficiently. Newer techniques appear to cause minimal intellectual impairment, and the procedure may help severely depressed and suicidal patients, or those who suffer from intractable pain, when all other forms of treatment have failed (Valenstein, 1980).

ENHANCING MENTAL HEALTH

The prevention and treatment of mental disorders is a problem of tremendous concern for both the community and the nation. Early in this chapter, we noted that the Community Mental Health Centers Act, passed by Congress in 1963, provided funds for the establishment of community mental health centers so that people could be treated close to family and friends rather than in large state psychiatric hospitals. These community centers provide short-term hospitalization, outpatient treatment, and a 24-hour emergency service. They are also concerned with preventing emotional problems and so consult with schools, juvenile courts, and other community agencies.

Federal funding for community mental health centers has been cut drastically in recent years, greatly diminishing services for the poor. Increased efforts by states, communities, and volunteer organizations are essential to help fill the void.

Community Resources and Paraprofessionals

A variety of community resources have been developed in response to the psychological needs of different groups. One such resource is the *halfway house*, where patients who have been hospitalized can live while making the transition back to an independent life in the community. Residential centers are also available to people recovering from alcohol and drug problems, to delinquent or runaway youths, and to battered wives. *Rap centers*, where troubled teenagers can discuss their problems with each other and with sympathetic counselors, play an important role in many communities; *youth centers* provide job counseling, remedial education, and help with family and personal problems.

A telephone hotline for suicide prevention.

CRISIS INTERVENTION *Crisis intervention* provides immediate help for individuals and families undergoing intense stress. During periods of acute emotional turmoil, people often feel overwhelmed and incapable of dealing with the situation. They may not be able to wait for a therapy appointment, or they may not know where to turn. One form of crisis intervention is provided by 24-hour, walk-in services, often in a community mental health center, where the individual receives immediate attention. There, a therapist helps to clarify the problem, provides reassurance, suggests a plan of action, and mobilizes the support of other agencies or family members. This kind of therapy is usually short-term (five or six sessions) and provides the support the person requires to handle the crisis at hand. Such short-term intervention often prevents the need for hospitalization.

Another form of crisis intervention is the *telephone hot line*. Telephone crisis centers are usually staffed by volunteers under the direction of mental health professionals. Some focus specifically on suicide prevention; others are more general and help distressed callers find the particular kind of assistance they need. The volunteers usually receive training that emphasizes listening with care, evaluating the potential for suicide, conveying empathy and understanding, providing information about community resources, giving hope and reassurance, and recording the caller's name and phone number before he or she hangs up so that a professional can follow up on the problem. Most major cities in the United States have developed some form of telephone hot line to help people who are undergoing periods of severe stress, as well as specialized hot lines to deal with child abuse, rape victims, battered wives, and runaways. The phone numbers are widely publicized in the hope of reaching those who need help.

PARAPROFESSIONALS AS THERAPISTS Most of the community programs we have discussed could not function without the help of paraprofessionals. Because the need for psychological services outstrips the supply of available therapists, concerned citizens can play a valuable role. People of all ages and backgrounds have been trained to work in the area of community mental health. College students have served as companions for hospitalized patients. Older individuals who have successfully raised families have been trained as mental health counselors to work with adolescents in community clinics, to counsel parents of youngsters who have behavior problems, and to work with schizophrenic children. Former mental patients, recovered drug

FIGURE 17-7
Residential Program for Delinquent Youths *A family conference at Achievement Place—a group home for youngsters with behavior problems who are referred by the courts. The youngsters and their professional teacher-parents meet daily to discuss rules of conduct, decide on consequences for violations of the rules, criticize aspects of the program, and evaluate a peer manager who oversees many of the activities.*

addicts, and exconvicts have been trained to help those faced with problems similar to the ones they have experienced.

Many residential mental health programs are run by nonprofessionals in consultation with trained therapists. An outstanding example is Achievement Place, which is a home-style facility in Kansas where couples act as surrogate parents for a group of youngsters referred by the courts because of their delinquent behavior (see Figure 17-7). Behavior therapy methods are used to extinguish aggressive behavior and to reward social skills. Follow-up data show that youths who graduate from Achievement Place have fewer contacts with courts and police and achieve slightly higher grades than do individuals who are placed on probation or in a traditional institution for delinquents (Fixsen, Phillips, Phillips, & Wolf, 1976). At present, there are 80 Achievement Places throughout the United States modeled after the original Kansas facility.

Promoting Your Own Emotional Well-Being

Aside from seeking professional help, there are many ways that each of us can positively influence our own psychological well-being. By monitoring our feelings and behavior we can determine the kinds of actions and situations that cause us pain or get us into difficulty, and, conversely, the kinds that benefit us the most. By trying to analyze our motives and abilities, we can enhance our capacity to make active choices in our lives, instead of passively accepting what comes.

The problems that people face vary greatly, and there are no universal guidelines for staying psychologically healthy. However, a few general suggestions have emerged from the experiences of therapists.

ACCEPT YOUR FEELINGS Strong emotions can produce anxiety. Anger, sorrow, fear, and a feeling of having fallen short of ideals or goals are all unpleasant emotions, and we may try to escape anxiety by denying these feelings. Sometimes we try to avoid anxiety by facing situations unemotionally, which leads to a false kind of detachment or cool that may be destructive. We may try to suppress all emotions, thereby losing the ability to accept as normal the joys and sorrows that are a part of our involvement with other people.

Unpleasant emotions are a normal reaction to many situations. There is no reason to be ashamed of feeling homesick, of being afraid when learning to ski, or of becoming angry at someone who has disappointed us. These emotions are natural, and it is better to recognize them than to deny them. When emotions cannot be expressed directly (for example, it may not be wise to tell off your boss), it helps to find another outlet for releasing tension. Taking a long walk, pounding a tennis ball, or discussing the situation with a friend can help to dissipate anger. As long as you accept your right to feel emotion, you can express it in indirect or substitute ways when direct channels of expression are blocked.

KNOW YOUR VULNERABILITIES   Discovering the kinds of situations that upset you or cause you to overreact may help to guard against stress. Perhaps certain people annoy you. You could avoid them, or you could try to understand just what it is about them that disturbs you. Maybe they seem so poised and confident that they make you feel insecure. Trying to pinpoint the cause of your discomfort may help you to see the situation in a new light. Perhaps you become very anxious when you have to speak in class or present a paper. Again, you could try to avoid such situations, or you could gain confidence by taking a course in public speaking. (Many colleges offer courses specifically aimed at learning to control speech anxiety.) You could also reinterpret the situation. Instead of thinking "Everyone is waiting to criticize me as soon as I open my mouth," you could tell yourself "The class will be interested in what I have to say, and I'm not going to let it worry me if I make a few mistakes."

Many people feel especially anxious when they are under pressure. Careful planning and spacing of work can help you avoid feeling overwhelmed at the last minute. The strategy of purposely allowing more time than you think you need to get to classes or to appointments can eliminate one source of stress.

DEVELOP YOUR TALENTS AND INTERESTS   People who are bored and unhappy seldom have many interests. Today's college and community programs offer almost unlimited opportunities for people of all ages to explore their talents in many areas, including sports, academic interests, music, art, drama, and crafts. Often, the more you know about a subject, the more interesting it (and life) becomes. In addition, the feeling of competency gained from developing skills can do a great deal to bolster self-esteem.

BECOME INVOLVED WITH OTHER PEOPLE   Feelings of isolation and loneliness form the core of most emotional disorders. We are social beings, and we need the support, comfort, and reassurance provided by other people. Focusing all of your attention on your own problems can lead to an unhealthy preoccupation with yourself. Sharing your concerns with others often helps you to view your troubles in a clearer perspective. Also, being concerned for the welfare of other people can reinforce your feelings of self-worth.

KNOW WHEN TO SEEK HELP   Although these suggestions can help to promote emotional well-being, there are limits to self-understanding and self-help. Some problems are difficult to solve alone. Our tendency toward self-deception makes it hard to view problems objectively, and we may not know all of the possible solutions. When you feel that you are making little headway in gaining control over a problem, it is time to seek professional help from a counseling or clinical psychologist, a psychiatrist, or some other trained therapist. The willingness to seek help is a sign of emotional maturity, not a sign of weakness; do not wait until you feel overwhelmed. Obtaining psychological help when it is needed should be as accepted a practice as going to a physician for medical problems.

▣ CHAPTER SUMMARY

1. Treatment of the mentally ill has progressed from the ancient notion that abnormal behavior resulted from the possession of evil spirits that needed to be punished, to custodial care in ill-kept and isolated asylums, to modern mental hospitals and community mental health centers. The policy of *deinstitutionalization* (despite its good intentions) has created the problem of homeless mentally-ill, causing concern about civil rights and adequate care.

2. *Psychotherapy* is the treatment of mental disorders by psychological means. One type of psychotherapy is *psychoanalysis*, which was developed by Freud. He believed that unconscious conflicts between the aggressive and sexual impulses of the id and the constraints imposed by the ego and superego were the cause of most mental disorders. Through the methods of *free association* and *dream analysis*, repressed thoughts and feelings are brought to the patient's awareness. By *interpreting* these dreams and associations, the analyst helps the individual gain *insight* into his or her problems. *Transference*, the tendency to express feelings toward the analyst that the client has for important people in his or her life, provides another source of interpretation. Through the processes of *working through*, the individual becomes able to cope with problems more realistically.

3. *Psychoanalytic psychotherapies*, based on Freudian concepts, are briefer than psychoanalysis and place more emphasis on the problem-solving functions of the ego (as opposed to the id's sexual and aggressive impulses) and the individual's current interpersonal problems (as opposed to a complete reconstruction of childhood experiences).

4. *Behavior therapies* apply methods based on learning principles to *modify* the individual's behavior. These methods include *systematic desensitization* (the individual learns to relax in situations that previously produced anxiety), *reinforcement* of adaptive behaviors and *extinction* of maladaptive ones, *modeling* and *rehearsal* of appropriate behavior, and techniques for *self-regulation* of behavior.

5. *Cognitive behavior therapies* use behavior modification techniques but also incorporate procedures for changing maladaptive beliefs. The therapist helps the individual to replace irrational interpretations of events with more realistic ones.

6. *Humanistic therapies* help individuals to become aware of their real selves and to solve their problems with a minimum of therapist intervention. Carl Rogers, who developed *person-centered psychotherapy*, believed that the therapist's characteristics necessary for the client's growth and self-exploration are *empathy*, *warmth*, and *genuineness*.

7. Rather than adhering strictly to any single method, most therapists take an *eclectic* approach, selecting from the different techniques the ones most appropriate for a given client. Some therapists specialize in treating specific problems, such as alcoholism, sexual dysfunction, or depression.

8. *Group therapy* provides an opportunity for the individual to explore his or her attitudes and behavior in interaction with others who have similar problems. *Marital therapy* and *family therapy* are specialized forms of group therapy that help couples, or parents and children, to learn more effective ways of relating to one another and of handling their problems.

9. The effectiveness of psychotherapy is hard to evaluate because of the difficulty of defining a *successful outcome* and of controlling for *spontaneous remission*. Research indicates that psychotherapy does help but that different approaches

do not differ greatly in effectiveness. Factors common to the various psychotherapies—a *warm and trustful interpersonal relationship, reassurance and support, desensitization, insight,* and *reinforcement of adaptive responses*—may be more important in producing positive change than are specific therapeutic methods.

10. *Biological therapies* include *electroconvulsive therapy* (ECT), *psychosurgery,* and the use of *psychotherapeutic drugs.* Of these three treatments, drug therapy has proved by far to be the most successful. *Antianxiety drugs* are used to reduce severe anxiety and to help individuals cope with life crises. *Antipsychotic drugs* have proved effective in the treatment of schizophrenia, *antidepressants* help to elevate the mood of depressed patients, and *lithium* has been successful in treating bipolar disorders.

11. The prevention and treatment of mental disorders is of great concern in our society. Community resources that offer help include *halfway houses, residential centers* for people who have special problems, and various forms of *crisis intervention.* We can promote our own emotional health by accepting our feelings as natural, discovering our vulnerabilities, developing talents and interests, becoming involved with others, and recognizing when to seek professional help.

◢ FURTHER READING

Interesting material on the historical treatment of the mentally ill can be found in Veith, *Hysteria: The History of a Disease* (1970); and Bell, *Treating the Mentally Ill: From Colonial Times to the Present* (1980).

A review of the various methods of psychotherapy is provided by Woody and Robertson, *Becoming a Clinical Psychologist* (1988); and Corsini, *Current Psychotherapies* (1984). *Psychotherapy: An Eclectic Approach* (1980) by Garfield describes the process of psychotherapy, the features common to most psychotherapies, and psychotherapy research. *The Handbook of Psychotherapy and Behavior Change* (3rd ed., 1986) by Garfield and Bergin includes a historical overview and comprehensive coverage of research in almost all areas of application.

For an introduction to psychoanalytic methods, see Menninger and Holzman, *Theory of Psychoanalytic Technique* (2nd ed., 1973). For person-centered therapy, see *On Becoming a Person: A Therapist's View of Psychotherapy* (1970) and *Carl Rogers on Personal Power* (1977), both by Rogers. The principles of behavior therapy are presented in Craighead, Kazdin, and Mahoney, *Behavior Modification: Principles, Issues, and Applications* (2nd ed., 1981). The application of cognitive-behavior therapy to a variety of mental disorders is described in *Cognitive Psychotherapy: Theory and Practice* (1988), edited by Perris, Blackburn, and Perris. *Panic: Facing Fears, Phobias, and Anxiety* (1985) by Agras describes behavior therapy methods for overcoming fears.

An overview of group therapy is presented in Yalom, *The Theory and Practice of Group Psychotherapy* (3rd ed., 1985). For a cognitive-behavioral approach to marital and couple therapy see Beck, *Love is Never Enough* (1988).

Drugs for Mental Illness: A Revolution in Psychiatry (1983), a paperback by Lickey and Gordon, presents a very readable summary of biological research on the major mental disorders. It includes case histories and describes diagnostic procedures, evidence of drug effectiveness, and how psychotherapeutic drugs affect the brain.

For ways to modify your own behavior, see Karoly and Kanfer, *Self-Management and Behavior Change* (1982); and Watson and Tharp, *Self-Directed Behavior: Self-Modification for Personal Adjustment* (4th ed., 1985). *Necessary Losses* (1986) by Viorst, written from a psychoanalytic viewpoint, is a sensitive and wise analysis of how we grow and change through the losses that are an inevitable part of life.

Paul Klee. Strange Garden, 1923.
Watercolor on gesso on fabric bordered with gouache and ink, mounted on light
cardboard, 15¾" x 11⅜", The Metropolitan Museum of Art, The Berggruen Klee
Collection, 1984. (1984.531) (160)

PART VIII Social Behavior

Chapter 18

Detail, Strange Garden.

Social Information Processing

Social psychology is the study of social interaction, of how we think, feel, and act in the presence of other people, and how, in turn, our thoughts, feelings, and actions are influenced by others. How do we perceive and interpret the behaviors and motives of others? How consistent are our social beliefs, attitudes, and behaviors? What determines whom we like and dislike? What are the processes of social influence?

Social psychologists base their approach to such topics on two fundamental observations. Both of these have been mentioned earlier (see Chapters 13 and 14), but they are especially relevant to the study of social interaction. The first is that human behavior is a function of both the person and the situation. Each person brings a unique set of personal attributes to a situation, leading different persons to act in different ways in the same situation. But each situation also brings a unique set of forces to bear on the person, leading him or her to act in different ways in different situations.

The second observation is that if persons define situations as real, they are real in their consequences (Thomas & Thomas, 1928). That is, people do not react simply to the objective features of a situation but to their own subjective interpretations, or cognitive appraisals, of it. This is one reason why different persons behave in different ways in the same objective situation. The person who interprets a hurtful act as the product of hostility reacts differently from the person who interprets that same act as the product of insensitivity. Thus, an understanding of social interaction requires a particularly detailed understanding of social information processing—the ways in which we perceive and interpret the behaviors and motives of others. Accordingly, this chapter deals entirely with social information processing. Chapter 19 will discuss social influence.

INTUITIVE SCIENCE OF SOCIAL JUDGMENTS

We are all psychologists. In attempting to understand other people and ourselves, we are informal scientists who construct our own intuitive theories of human behavior. In doing so, we face the same basic tasks as the formal scientist (Nisbett & Ross, 1985). First, we *observe* or *collect data* ("My friend Chris asserts that women should have the right to obtain abortions"; "Lee Yamuri achieved the highest score on the math test"; "My heart is pounding"). Second, we try to *detect covariation,* to discern what goes with what ("Most people who oppose the death penalty appear to support the right to abortion"; "On the average, Asians seem to do better in math and science than non-Asians"; "My heart seems to pound when Robin is near"). And third, we attempt to *infer cause and effect,* to evaluate what causes what ("Does Chris support the right to abortion out of genuine conviction or because of peer pressure to express liberal attitudes?" "Do Asian students excel in math and science because they are inherently smarter or because their families stress the value of education?" "Am I in love with Robin or is it just sexual passion?").

Our intuitive attempts to apply scientific reasoning to everyday life work surprisingly well. Social interaction would be chaos if our informal theories

Exit polling helps the media predict elections.

of human behavior did not possess substantial validity. But we also make a number of systematic errors in arriving at social judgments, and, ironically, our theories themselves often interfere with accurate information processing. As we shall see, our theories can actually shape our perceptions of the data, distort our estimates of what goes with what, and bias our evaluations of cause and effect.

Collecting Data

The first difficulty we face as informal scientists is collecting our data in a systematic and unbiased way. When a survey researcher wants to estimate how many Americans support a woman's right to abortion, he or she takes great care to ensure that a random or representative sample of people are contacted so that the numbers of Catholics, Protestants, men, women, and so forth are interviewed in proportion to their percentage of the total population. But when we, as informal survey researchers, try to make this estimate intuitively, our major source of data is likely to be the people we know personally. Obviously this is not a representative sample of the population.

Another major source of data for us is the mass media, which also provide a nonrandom and nonrepresentative sample of data. For example, the media necessarily give more attention to a small number of antiabortion protestors publicly demonstrating at a medical clinic than they do to a larger number of people who silently support the clinic's abortion service. The media are not being biased here in the usual sense; they are simply reporting the news. But the data they give us are still not a reliable sample from which to estimate public opinion.

A survey researcher also keeps accurate records of the data. But in everyday life, we constantly accumulate information in our heads, and then later, when we are called on to make some judgment, we must attempt to recall the pertinent data from memory. Thus, not only are the data we collect a biased sample in the first place, but the data we actually bring to bear on our social judgments are further biased by problems of selective recall.

VIVIDNESS One of the factors that influences the information we attend to is its *vividness*. Research has shown that our estimates and judgments are often more influenced by vivid information than by pallid information of equal or greater reliability (Nisbett & Ross, 1985).

In one study, introductory psychology students who planned to major in psychology were given information about upper-level psychology courses and then asked to indicate which courses they planned to take. The subjects either heard two or three students make some informal remarks about each course in a face-to-face session or they saw a statistical summary of course evaluations made by students who had already taken the courses (made on five-point scales from Poor to Excellent). The subjects were more influenced in their choices by the face-to-face remarks than by the statistical summary—even if the summary was accompanied by written quotations of those same remarks. The vivid face-to-face information was more influential than the pallid written information even though it was based on less complete and representative data (Borgida & Nisbett, 1977).

In a study showing the effects of vividness on judgments based on recalled information, subjects read testimony allegedly from a trial in which a person of otherwise good character was accused of drunk driving. Half the subjects read pallid prosecution testimony and vivid defense testimony,

The vividness of an event influences our judgment of it.

while the other half read vivid prosecution testimony and pallid defense testimony. For example, in describing the man's behavior at a party before he left to drive home, the pallid prosecution testimony stated that he had staggered against a table, knocking a bowl to the floor. The vivid version stated that he had knocked a bowl of guacamole dip to the floor, splattering the dip all over the white shag carpet. Pallid defense testimony argued that the man was not drunk because he was alert enough to avoid an oncoming car, whereas the vivid version had him avoiding a bright orange Volkswagen. Note that the vivid descriptions should not logically affect the nature of the evidence, and in fact, the vividness of testimony did not affect subjects' judgments of the defendant's guilt immediately after they had read the testimony. But when subjects were asked to judge the defendant's guilt again the next day, subjects who had read the vivid prosecution testimony shifted toward guilty verdicts and those who read the vivid defense testimony shifted toward nonguilty verdicts (Reyes, Thompson, & Bower, 1980).

A review of several studies reveals that the vividness effect appears to occur only when both a vivid and a nonvivid presentation compete for our attention simultaneously. Apparently, the vivid information is more salient and, hence, is stored in memory more effectively than the nonvivid information at the time of presentation (Taylor & Thompson, 1982).

The vividness effect is a particular problem with information from the mass media. Even if reporters scrupulously gave equal coverage to both the vivid and nonvivid sides of an issue, our own information processing tendencies would supply the bias. The studies described here suggest, for example, that even if a television newscast reports the results of a survey, showing that a national majority supports abortion rights, we are still more likely to store and later recall the vivid pictures of the antiabortion protest as the relevant data about public opinion.

SCHEMATA   Even if we could collect data in a systematic and unbiased way, our perceptions of the data can still be biased by our existing expectations and preconceptions (our theories) of what the data *should* look like.

Whenever we perceive any object or event, we compare the incoming information with our memories of previous encounters with similar objects and events. In earlier chapters, we saw that often our memories of objects and events are not photograph-like reproductions of the original stimuli, but simplified reconstructions of our original perceptions. As noted in Chapter 8, such representations or memory structures are called *schemata* and are the result of perceiving and thinking in terms of mental representations of classes of people, objects, events, or situations. The process of searching for the schema in memory that is most consistent with the incoming data is called *schematic processing*. Schemata and schematic processing permit us to organize and process an enormous amount of information with great efficiency. Instead of having to perceive and remember all the details of each new object or event, we can simply note that it is like one of our preexisting schemata and encode or remember only its most prominent features. Schematic processing typically occurs rapidly and automatically; usually we are not even aware that any processing of information is taking place at all.

For example, we have schemata for different kinds of people. When someone tells you that you are about to meet an extravert, you retrieve your extravert schema in anticipation of the coming encounter. The extravert schema consists of a set of interrelated traits such as sociability, warmth, and possibly loudness and impulsiveness. General person-schemata like these are sometimes called *stereotypes*. We also have schemata of particular persons, such as the president of the United States, our best friend, and even ourselves, as we shall see later.

Research confirms that schemata help us to process information. For example, if people are explicitly instructed to remember as much information as they can about a stimulus person, they actually remember less than if they are simply told to try to form an impression of the person (Hamilton, 1979). The instruction to form an impression induces the subjects to search for various person-relevant schemata that help them organize and recall material better. Without schemata and schematic processing, we would simply be overwhelmed by the information that inundates us. We would be very poor information processors.

But the price we pay for such efficiency is a bias in our perception of the data. Consider, for example, the impression you form of Jim from the following observations of his behavior.

> Jim left the house to get some stationery. He walked out into the sun-filled street with two of his friends, basking in the sun as he walked. Jim entered the stationery store, which was full of people. Jim talked with an acquaintance while he waited to catch the clerk's eye. On his way out, he stopped to chat with a school friend who was just coming into the store. Leaving the store, he walked toward the school. On his way he met the girl to whom he had been introduced the night before. They talked for a short while, and then Jim left for school. After school Jim left the classroom alone. Leaving the school, he started on his long walk home. The street was brilliantly filled with sunshine. Jim walked down the street on the shady side. Coming down the street toward him, he saw the pretty girl whom he had met on the previous evening. Jim crossed the street and entered a candy store. The store was crowded with students, and he noticed a few familiar faces. Jim waited quietly until he caught the counterman's eye and then gave his order. Taking his drink, he sat down at a side table. When he had finished his drink he went home. (Luchins, 1957, pp. 34–35)

What impression do you have of Jim? Do you think of him as friendly and outgoing or shy and introverted? If you think Jim is better described as

CONDITIONS	PERCENTAGE RATING JIM AS FRIENDLY
Friendly description only	95
Friendly first—unfriendly last	78
Unfriendly first—friendly last	18
Unfriendly description only	3

TABLE 18-1
Schematic Processing and the Primacy Effect *Once a schema of Jim has been established, later information is assimilated to it.* (After Luchins, 1957)

friendly, you agree with 78 percent of people who read this description. But examine the description closely; it is actually composed of two very different portraits. Up to the sentence that begins "After school, Jim left . . . ," Jim is portrayed in several situations as fairly friendly. After that point, however, a nearly identical set of situations shows him to be much more of a loner. In fact, 95 percent of the people who are shown only the first half of the description rate Jim as friendly, whereas only 3 percent of the people who are shown only the second half rate him as friendly. Thus, in the combined description that you read, Jim's friendliness seems to win out over his unfriendliness. But when individuals read the same description with the unfriendly half of the paragraph appearing first, only 18 percent rate Jim as friendly; Jim's unfriendly behavior leaves the major impression (see Table 18-1). In general, the first information we receive has the greater impact on our overall impressions. This is known as the *primacy effect.*

The primacy effect has been found repeatedly in several different kinds of impression formation studies, including studies using real rather than hypothetical persons. For example, subjects who watched a male student attempt to solve a series of difficult multiple-choice problems were asked to assess his general ability (Jones et al., 1968). Although the student always solved exactly 15 of the 30 problems correctly, he was judged more capable if the successes came mostly at the beginning of the series than if they came near the end. Moreover, when asked to recall how many problems the student had solved, subjects who had seen the 15 successes bunched at the beginning estimated an average of 20.6, whereas subjects who had seen the successes at the end estimated an average of 12.5.

Although several factors contribute to the primacy effect, it appears to be primarily a consequence of schematic processing. When we are first attempting to form our impressions of a person, we actively search in memory for the person schema or schemata that best match the incoming data. At some point we make a preliminary decision: this person is friendly (or some such judgment). We then assimilate any further information to that schema and dismiss any discrepant information as not representative of the real person we have come to know. For example, when explicitly asked to reconcile the apparent contradictions in Jim's behavior, subjects sometimes say that Jim is really friendly but was probably tired by the end of the day (Luchins, 1957). Our perceptions become schema-driven and therefore relatively impervious to new data. Our theory of Jim, which has already been established, shapes our perception of all subsequent data about him.

Such theories can also affect the retrieval of data from memory. For example, in Chapter 8 we described a study in which subjects read statements about a woman's early life (for example, "Although she never had a

CRITICAL DISCUSSION

The Gender Schema

Most of the schemata discussed in this section apply to limited domains of objects or events, helping us to organize and interpret small and specific areas of everyday life (such as particular persons or particular events). But some schemata have a much wider scope, organizing broad areas of experience and becoming, in effect, a set of lenses through which we view vast aspects of our world. Gender is often such a schema because in most cultures the distinction between male and female tends to organize many features of daily life. Not only are young boys and girls expected to acquire sex-specific skills and behaviors, they are also expected to have or to acquire sex-specific self-concepts and personality attributes—in other words, to be masculine or feminine as defined by that particular culture. You will recall from Chapter 3 that the process by which a society teaches children to conform to such expectations is called *sex typing*.

Psychologist Sandra Bem (1981) has suggested that in addition to learning the specific concepts and behaviors that the culture associates with being male or female, the child also learns to perceive and organize diverse kinds of information in terms of a *gender schema*. According to her theory, individuals who are sex-typed use the gender schema more than individuals who are not sex-typed.

In her research, Bem identifies sex-typed persons by asking individuals to rate themselves on a list of sex-typed personality traits. Individuals who rate themselves high on stereotypically masculine traits (such as "assertive," "independent") but low on stereotypically feminine traits (such as "compassionate," "tender") are defined as masculine; individuals with the reverse pattern are defined as feminine; and individuals who describe themselves as having both masculine and feminine traits are defined as *androgynous* ("andro" means male; "gyn" means female).

In a series of studies validating this classification procedure, androgynous individuals displayed both masculine independence and feminine nurturance, whereas sex-typed individuals (masculine men and feminine women) tended to display only the behavior stereotypically considered appropriate

---

steady boyfriend in high school, she did go out on dates"). At a subsequent session, subjects were further told either that she had adopted a lesbian lifestyle as an adult or that she had gotten married. When asked to recall what they remembered about her earlier history, subjects selectively recalled facts and events that were consistent with their new schema about her. For example, subjects who were told she became a lesbian were more likely to remember that she never had a steady boyfriend, whereas subjects who were told she married were more likely to remember that she went out on dates (Snyder & Uranowitz, 1978). This study illustrates how a new schema can affect the recall of *old* data. The primacy effect demonstrates how a preexisting schema can affect the interpretation of *new* data.

SCRIPTS   In addition to schemata of people, we also have schemata for events and social interactions. Such schemata are called *scripts* (Abelson, 1976). One of the most familiar is the greeting script. When we greet an acquaintance with the phrase "How are you," the script calls for the response "Fine. How are you?" A person who responds instead with a long list of woes fails to understand this common social script. Some scripts are more complex and abstract. When we are invited to a birthday party, we invoke a general birthday party script, an abstract picture or cognitive structure in our minds that informs us of what would be appropriate to wear, reminds us to take a gift, and generally helps us to anticipate what will take place. Like other schemata, scripts permit us to process information quickly and automatically—even mindlessly—by permitting us to gloss over the particular details of each new interaction.

This aspect of scripts was amusingly demonstrated in an experiment in which a person about to use a copy machine was approached by an experi-

for their sex (Bem, 1975; Bem, Martyna, & Watson, 1976).

In one study designed to test whether or not sex-typed individuals use the gender schema to organize information, subjects were shown a list of words and were later asked to recall as many of the words as they could in any order. The list included proper names, animal names, verbs, and articles of clothing. Half of the proper names were male and half were female, and one third of the words within each of the other categories had been rated by judges as masculine (for instance "gorilla," "hurling," "trousers"), one third as feminine (for instance "butterfly," "blushing," "bikini"), and one third as neutral (for instance "ant," "stepping," "sweater"). Research in memory has shown that if an individual has encoded a number of words in terms of an underlying schema or network of associations, then think-

ing of one schema-related word enhances the probability of thinking of another. Accordingly, an individual's sequence of recall should reveal runs or clusters of words that are linked in memory by the schema. If a subject thinks of an animal word, he or she is likely to think next of another animal word. Note that subjects in this experiment could cluster words either according to semantic category (proper names, animals, verbs, clothing) or according to gender.

The individuals who were sex-typed showed significantly more gender clustering than did individuals who were not sex-typed. For example, if a sex-typed person happened to recall the feminine animal, "butterfly," he or she was more likely to follow that with another feminine word such as "bikini," whereas an individual who was not sex-typed was more likely to follow "butter-

fly" with another animal name. Thus, sex-typed subjects were more likely to link words together in memory on the basis of gender; as the theory predicts, they were more likely to use the gender schema to organize information.

Bem believes that the lesson to be learned from gender schema theory is *not* that every individual ought to be androgynous, to be both masculine and feminine. That prescription would constrain the person from being a unique individual just as much as the traditional prescription would that men must be masculine and women must be feminine. Rather, she argues that human behaviors and personality attributes should cease to have gender and that society should stop projecting gender into situations in which it is irrelevant. The individual, in short, should not have to be androgynous, but the society should be less gender schematic.

menter who asked for permission to use the machine first (Langer, Blank, & Chanowitz, 1978). The experimenter stated that she had either a small or a large number of copies to make and made the request in one of three ways:

1. Request only: "Excuse me. I have 5 [20] pages. May I use the Xerox machine?"

2. Request plus genuine reason: "Excuse me, I have 5 [20] pages. May I use the Xerox machine because I'm in a rush?"

3. Request plus nonreason: "Excuse me, I have 5 [20] pages. May I use the Xerox machine because I have to make copies?"

The amount of compliance obtained by each of these requests is shown in Table 18-2 (p. 690); it displays the percentage of subjects who complied with the request in each condition. Not surprisingly, the smaller 5-page request always obtains more compliance than the larger 20-page request. Moreover, the request plus reason (request 2) obtains more compliance than the request only (request 1). As we have all learned, accompanying a request with a reason is not only the polite request script but the most effective one as well.

The critical results are those for request 3—request plus nonreason. It appears to follow the polite script, but the reason given—"I have to make copies"—conveys no information. Why else would someone want to use a copy machine if not to make copies? Thus, despite its appearance, request 3 conveys no more information than request 1. As we see in Table 18-2 (p. 690), when the request plus a nonreason embedded in the proper script is small, it obtains the same result as a genuine reason. Apparently the person responds to the form of the request without thinking about its meaning. But when the request is large, it apparently triggers the person to think more

TABLE 18-2
Automatic Processing of the Request Script *When the request was small, a nonreason couched in the appropriate script format was as effective as a genuine reason. When the request was large, a nonreason was no more effective than no reason at all.* (After Langer, Blank, & Chanowitz, 1978)

CONDITION	PERCENTAGE OF SUBJECTS COMPLYING WITH REQUEST TO USE THE COPY MACHINE	
	SMALL REQUEST	LARGE REQUEST
Request only	60	24
Request plus genuine reason	94	42
Request plus nonreason	93	24

carefully about its meaning, and hence the nonreason becomes no more effective than no reason at all.

THEORIES   Schemata and scripts are actually minitheories of everyday objects and events. But more elaborate theories also affect our perception of data. In one particularly elegant demonstration of this, students who held strongly divergent beliefs about whether or not capital punishment (the death penalty) acts as a deterrent for potential murderers read a summary of two purportedly authentic studies. One of the studies appeared to show that capital punishment was a deterrent, and the other appeared to show that it was not (Lord, Ross, & Lepper, 1979). The students also read a critique of each study that criticized its methodology. The results showed that students on both sides of the issue found the study supporting their own position to be significantly more convincing and better conducted than the other study. Moreover, they were more convinced about the correctness of their initial position than they were before reading about *any* evidence! One disturbing implication of these results is that evidence introduced into public debate in the hope of resolving an issue—or at least moderating extreme views—will tend instead to polarize public opinion even further. Proponents of each side will pick and choose from the evidence so as to bolster their initial opinions (Nisbett & Ross, 1985, p. 171).

Both the pro-Israeli and pro-Arab groups believed media coverage of the 1982 Lebanon massacre was biased against their side.

In 1982, a tragic series of events in the Middle East permitted researchers to examine how strongly held beliefs affect the perception of information in a real-life situation. Israeli-supported elements in Lebanon massacred a number of civilians in Lebanese refugee camps. Television coverage of the event was extensive, and Israel's role was quite controversial. The researchers questioned both pro-Israeli and pro-Arab individuals about the television news coverage. They found that each group believed that media coverage had been biased against its side. For example, pro-Israeli subjects estimated that only 17 percent of the references to Israel in the news programs were favorable, whereas pro-Arab subjects estimated that 42 percent of the references to Israel were favorable. Pro-Israeli subjects estimated that 57 percent of the references to Israel were unfavorable, whereas pro-Arab subjects estimated that only 26 percent were unfavorable. Both groups predicted that neutral viewers had been swayed in the direction hostile to their own beliefs (Vallone, Ross, & Lepper, 1985). This is an example of how our theories shape our perceptions of data.

Detecting Covariation

When two things vary in relation to each other (for instance, height and weight or education and income), they are said to *covary* or *correlate*. The detection of such covariation or correlation is a fundamental task in every science, and as intuitive scientists of human behavior, we perceive—or think we perceive—such correlations all the time ("People who are against capital punishment seem more likely to hold a pro-choice position on abortion"; "Asians seem to do better in math and science than non-Asians"; "My heart seems to pound when Robin is near").

Research shows, however, that we are not very good at this task. Once again, it is our theories that mislead us. In particular, when our schemata or theories lead us to expect two things to covary, we overestimate the correlation between them, even seeing illusory correlations that do not exist. But when we do not have a theory, we underestimate the correlation, even failing to spot a correlation that is strongly present in the data.

This was convincingly demonstrated in a series of studies initiated by two researchers who were puzzled by the fact that clinical psychologists routinely report associations between patients' responses to projective tests (see Chapter 14) and their personality characteristics or symptoms, even though research studies repeatedly fail to find such correlations. First the researchers obtained reports from 32 clinicians who, in the course of their practices, had analyzed the Rorschach inkblot responses of many homosexual men. These clinicians reported that homosexual men are more likely than heterosexual men to see anal images, feminine clothing, and three other kinds of images in the inkblots—despite the fact that carefully controlled research studies have failed to confirm the validity of these images as indicators of male homosexuality. Moreover, only 2 of the 32 clinicians listed either of two Rorschach signs (a monster image in one of the inkblots and an animal-human image in another) that some research studies *have* shown to be valid indicators of male homosexuality (Chapman & Chapman, 1969).

The researchers suggest that the invalid images are erroneously seen to correlate with homosexuality because they are part of a popular stereotype—a schema—of male homosexuality, whereas the two valid images are not detected because they are not part of the stereotype. Several experiments have now confirmed their hypothesis.

Student subjects in one of these experiments were asked to study a set of Rorschach cards. Each card contained the inkblot, a description of the image the patient reported seeing in it, and a statement of two characteristics that the patient displayed. The reported images included five stereotyped but invalid signs of homosexuality, the two unstereotyped but valid signs, and unrelated control signs (for example, food images). The characteristics were either homosexuality ("has sexual feelings toward other men") or unrelated characteristics ("feels sad and depressed much of the time"). The cards were carefully constructed so that no sign was systematically associated with homosexuality.

After studying all of the cards, subjects were presented with four characteristics and asked to report if they had noticed "any general kind of thing that was seen most often by men" with this characteristic. Like the practicing clinical psychologists, subjects erroneously reported the invalid signs—but not the valid signs or the control signs—to be associated with homosexuality. Even when the cards were reconstructed so that the valid signs were associated with homosexuality 100 percent of the time, subjects still reported seeing the nonexistent correlation with the invalid signs more than twice as often as the perfect correlation with the valid signs.

As intuitive scientists, we are theory-driven. We see covariations our theories have prepared us to see and fail to see covariations our theories have not prepared us to see.

SELF-FULFILLING STEREOTYPES   As the studies just described indicate, our schemata of classes of persons—stereotypes—are actually miniature theories of covariation. The stereotype of an extravert or a homosexual is a theory of what particular traits or behaviors go with certain other traits or behaviors. For this reason stereotypes have also been called *implicit personality theories* (Schneider, 1973).

Stereotypes have a bad reputation because they are associated with prejudice and discrimination. But it is important to recognize that the thinking process behind stereotypes—schematic processing—is not itself evil or pathological. Because it is simply not possible to deal with every new person as a unique individual, our use of schemata or working stereotypes is inevitable until further experiences either refine or discredit the schemata. For example, some students from rural areas of the country who attend college in New York City spend their first few weeks of college thinking that all New Yorkers are Jews and all Jews are New Yorkers. There is not necessarily any malice or ill will behind such a stereotype; the new student has simply not yet seen enough Catholic New Yorkers or Texas Jews to sort the social environment into more accurate and finely differentiated categories or schemata. Many of our stereotypes are of this benign variety and are discarded as our experiences multiply.

As we have seen, however, schemata are resistant to change, because they lead us to misperceive the very data that could potentially disconfirm them. For this reason alone, stereotypes are not so easily discarded, even as experiences multiply. But there is an even more insidious process at work: our schemata influence not only perceptions but also our behaviors and social interactions. Our stereotypes can lead us to interact with those we stereotype in ways that cause them to fulfill our expectations. Thus, our stereotypes can become both self-perpetuating and self-fulfilling.

This was illustrated in a study in which white college students played the role of job interviewers. They were assigned to interview both black and white job applicants, who were actually confederates of the experimenters.

The experimenters found that the subjects (the interviewers) were less friendly when interviewing black applicants than when interviewing white applicants. The subjects also maintained greater interpersonal distance, made more speech errors, and terminated the interview sooner when interviewing the black applicants.

But that was only the first part of the study. The experimenters then trained white interviewers to reproduce both the friendly and the less friendly interviewing styles shown by the original subjects. New subjects—all white—were then recruited, this time to play the role of the job applicants. Some received the friendly interview treatment; others, the less friendly treatment. Viewing videotapes of the interviews, judges later rated the subjects' performance and composure. The results showed that those being interviewed (the subjects) who received the less friendly pattern of behavior from the interviewer (as had the black applicants in the first experiment) were rated significantly lower on their own performance and demeanor than were those who had received the more friendly pattern (Word, Zanna, & Cooper, 1974). This study indicates that prejudiced individuals may interact in ways that actually evoke the stereotyped behaviors and thus sustain the prejudice.

Stereotypes may be self-fulfilling in more profound ways, actually shaping the long-term personalities of those stereotyped. Evidence for this comes from research on physical attractiveness. First, a commonly held stereotype is that physically attractive persons have many other desirable characteristics. In one study, male and female subjects were shown photographs of men and women from a college yearbook and were asked to rate the pictured individuals on a number of traits. The photographs had been previously rated as very attractive, average, or unattractive. Compared to the unattractive individuals, the more attractive individuals were rated as being more sensitive, kind, interesting, strong, poised, sociable, outgoing, exciting, and sexually responsive. They were also rated as having higher status, more likely to get married, likely to have a more successful marriage, and likely to be happier (Dion, Berscheid, & Walster, 1972).

Second, evidence shows that such a stereotype can be self-fulfilling, even in a brief interaction. In one study, male students engaged in a 10-minute telephone conversation with a female student they had never seen but whom they believed to be either physically attractive or unattractive. The experimenters established this belief by showing the man a photograph allegedly taken of his phone partner—a photograph whose attractiveness was, in fact, unrelated to the actual attractiveness of the woman on the telephone. Analyses of the conversations showed that men who believed they were talking to an attractive woman were friendlier, more outgoing, and more sociable than were men who believed they were talking to a less attractive woman. This is interesting in itself, but there is more. The telephone conversations were recorded on two-track tapes, and judges listened to the woman's half of each conversation without hearing the male partner and without knowing the partner's belief about the woman's attractiveness. These judges rated women whose partners believed they were attractive as more sociable, poised, and humorous than women whose partners believed they were unattractive. So, the men's stereotype of physically attractive women became self-fulfilling in a 10-minute telephone conversation (Snyder, Tanke, & Berscheid, 1977).

Finally, indirect evidence suggests that this self-fulfilling process has long-term effects in the real world; the common stereotype of the physically attractive person appears to have a grain of truth. In one study, male students

The attractiveness stereotype attributes many desirable characteristics to good-looking individuals.

spoke on the telephone for about 5 minutes with female students they had never seen and then rated the women's social skills. Independent observers rated the physical attractiveness of the women. The researchers found that the more attractive women were, in fact, rated higher in social skills by their telephone partners than were the less attractive women (Goldman & Lewis, 1977). Other studies have shown that physical attractiveness is correlated with a positive self-concept (Lerner & Karabenick, 1974), good mental health (Adams, 1981), assertiveness and self-confidence (Dion & Stein, 1978; Goldman & Lewis, 1977; Jackson & Huston, 1975), and a variety of other positive characteristics.

The suggestion, then, is that more attractive individuals have higher self-esteem, better mental health, and greater social skills than do unattractive individuals because the former are treated better in everyday life. They develop these desirable traits because they are hired first, paid more, promoted faster, and so forth. And, as we shall see later in this chapter, they also have the edge in dating and mating.

Inferring Causality

The heart of most sciences is the discovery of causes and effects. Similarly, as intuitive scientists, we feel we truly understand some instance of human behavior when we know why it occurred or what caused it. Suppose, for example, a famous athlete endorses a breakfast cereal on television. Why does she do it? Does she really like the cereal, or is she doing it for the money? A man kisses his female companion at the end of an evening out. Is this just a social norm, or is he really fond of her? Perhaps this particular man kisses everyone. Or perhaps everyone would kiss this particular woman. You give a five-dollar donation to Planned Parenthood. Why? Are you altruistic? Were you being pressured? Do you need a tax writeoff? Do you believe in the work of the organization?

Each of these cases creates an attribution problem. We see some behavior—perhaps our own—and must decide to which of many possible causes the action should be attributed. In social psychology the task of attempting to infer the causes of behavior is known as the *attribution problem*, and the study of the attribution process has become a central concern in social psychology (Heider, 1958; Kelley, 1967).

Inferring cause and effect is a special case of detecting covariations. Suppose that you wake up one morning with a runny nose. You see that the azaleas in your yard have just bloomed and hypothesize that they are causing your sniffles. Note how you test this hypothesis. You look to see if your symptoms come and go as you enter and leave areas containing azaleas. That is, you run an experiment to see if your symptoms and azaleas covary. Does the effect come and go with the suspected cause? If it does, azaleas are convicted. But if your sniffles remain constant—there is no covariation—then there is nothing distinctive about azaleas, and you conclude that they are not the cause. Thus you use the *distinctiveness* of your reactions to the suspected stimulus as a criterion for deciding if it caused the problem.

Another criterion is *consistency*. If you had the same symptoms the last 3 years when the azaleas bloomed, you are fairly certain that they are the culprit. But if this is the first time the symptoms have occurred—this is not a consistent event—you might not be so certain.

Finally, you call your doctor, who says that yours is the sixteenth such complaint of the day and that "this always happens when the azaleas bloom." In other words, you are not unique. Others share the same reaction to the same stimulus. This is the criterion of *consensus*.

Thus you attempt to detect a covariation that satisfies three criteria: the effect must vary only with the suspected cause (distinctiveness); it must do so every time the experiment is conducted (consistency); and other people must get the same result (consensus).

We use these same criteria when we attempt to understand the behavior of our friends and acquaintances (Kelley, 1973). Suppose that Julia raves about a recent meal at a Chinese restaurant. In very general terms, there are three potential causes of her praise. The first is the stimulus itself: maybe the food really *was* terrific. The second possible source of the praise is something about the person: Julia is a real Chinese-food nut. The third possibility is the particular situation: it was her birthday and anything would have seemed great to her. To choose among these three classes of causes, we again invoke the three criteria of distinctiveness, consistency, and consensus. If she praises no restaurants but this one (distinctiveness), does so every time she eats there (consistency), as does everyone else (consensus), then the restaurant must be terrific. But if Julia praises all Chinese restaurants all the time, we are probably learning more about Julia than about the restaurant. Finally, if she has never praised any restaurant before—including this one—and nobody else in Julia's party liked it much, then we can probably conclude that something about this particular situation (such as her birthday) is coloring her perceptions of the meal.

Research confirms that people do, in fact, utilize these criteria in this way (McArthur, 1972), but research also reveals that we frequently fail to apply the criteria correctly or sufficiently (Nisbett & Ross, 1985). The main problem—as you must be able to guess by now—is that we have theories of causality that bias our inferences.

FUNDAMENTAL ATTRIBUTION ERROR   As several of the above examples illustrate, one of the major attribution tasks we face daily is deciding whether an observed behavior reflects something unique about the person (his or her attitudes, personality characteristics, and so forth) or something about the situation in which we observe the person. If we infer that

"Folks, I endorse Scrunchies because I *eat* Scrunchies. As God is my witness, I don't just *say* I eat them, I really and truly *do* eat them. In fact, folks, I never eat anything but. And if you don't believe me, I can supply documentation from my personal physician."

Drawing by Ross; © 1976 *The New Yorker Magazine*, Inc.

something about the person is primarily responsible for the behavior (for instance, the athlete really loves the cereal), then our inference is called an *internal* or *dispositional attribution* ("disposition" here refers to a person's beliefs, attitudes, and personality characteristics). If, however, we conclude that some external cause is primarily responsible for the behavior (for instance, money, social norms, threats), it is called an *external* or *situational attribution*.

The founder of modern attribution theory Fritz Heider noted that an individual's behavior is so compelling to observers that they take it at face value and give insufficient weight to the circumstances surrounding it (1958). Recent research has confirmed Heider's speculation. We underestimate the situational causes of behavior, too easily jumping to conclusions about the dispositions of the person. Another way of stating it is that we (in Western society, at any rate) have a schema of cause and effect in human behavior that gives too much weight to the person and too little to the situation. One psychologist has termed this bias toward dispositional attributions rather than situational attributions the fundamental attribution error (Ross, 1977).

In one of the first studies to reveal this bias, subjects read a debater's speech that either supported or attacked Cuba's leader Fidel Castro. The subjects were explicitly told that the debater had been assigned which side of the issue to argue by the debate coach; the debater had no choice. Despite this knowledge, when asked to estimate the individual's actual attitude toward Castro, subjects inferred that the individual held a position close to the one argued in the debate. In other words, the subjects made a dispositional attribution even though situational forces were fully sufficient to account for the behavior (Jones & Harris, 1967). This effect is quite powerful. Even when the subjects themselves dictate the opinion that someone is to express, they still tend to see the person as actually holding that opinion (Gilbert & Jones, 1986). The effect occurs even if the presentations are deliberately designed to be drab and unenthusiastic and the speaker simply reads a transcribed version of the speech in a monotone and uses no gestures (Schneider & Miller, 1975).

Intuitive Science of Self-Judgments

As informal scientists of human behavior, one of our major tasks is understanding ourselves. As we shall see, the judgments we make about our own thoughts, emotions, behaviors, motives, and personalities are governed by many of the same processes that govern our judgments of others.

SELF-SCHEMA   Just as we have schemata about extraverts, the president of the United States, and our best friend, so too, we have a schema about ourselves—a set of organized self-concepts stored in memory (Markus, 1977). When you see a job advertisement for a peer counselor, you can evaluate the match between your counselor schema and your self-schema to decide whether you should apply. Like other schemata, the self-schema permits us to organize and process information with great efficiency. For example, people can recall a list of words better if they are told to decide whether each word describes themselves as they go through the list (Ganellen & Carver, 1985; Rogers, Kuiper, & Kirker, 1977). The self-schema also influences the way we attend to and recall information about ourselves. We spend more time attending to information that confirms our self-concepts than to information that is discrepant with them (Swann & Read, 1981); we remember such information better; and, we regulate our behaviors so that they are consistent with our self-schema (Markus & Sentis, 1982).

The self-schema also interacts with other schemata. For example, we saw earlier that individuals who are sex-typed organize information about the world in terms of a gender schema. Research shows that they also organize information about themselves—their self-schema—in terms of the gender schema. In one study, they were much faster at rating themselves on sex-typed traits than on other traits. For instance, masculine males rated themselves more quickly on the masculine trait "assertive" than on a sex-neutral trait like "honest." They had encoded both their self-concepts and the terms for sex-typed personality traits according to the gender schema; instead of reviewing their personality in detail, all they had to do was look up the trait in the schema to see if it was there. In contrast, individuals who were not sex-typed—who organize neither their self-concepts nor personality trait terms according to the gender schema—were no faster on sex-typed traits than they were on sex-neutral traits (Girvin, 1978, as cited in Bem, 1981; Markus, Crane, Bernstein, & Siladi, 1982).

SELF-PERCEPTION   We saw in Chapter 11 that we often judge what emotion we are experiencing through a process of cognitive appraisal. Although the physiological arousal of our autonomic nervous system provides us with the information that we are experiencing an emotion, the more subtle judgment of *which* emotion we are experiencing often depends on our perceptions—our cognitive appraisals—of the surrounding circumstances. This suggests the more general possibility that we may rely on cues external to ourselves in order to make judgments about many of our inner states.

This possibility is the basis for *self-perception theory* by Daryl Bem (1972), who proposes that we make judgments about ourselves using the same inferential processes—and making the same kinds of errors—that we use for making judgments about others. Specifically, the theory proposes that individuals come to know their own attitudes, emotions, and other internal states partially by inferring them from observations of their own behavior and the circumstances in which this behavior occurs. Thus to the extent that internal cues are weak, ambiguous, or uninterpretable, the individual is like any outside observer who must rely on external cues to infer the individual's inner states.

These propositions may seem strange, because we generally assume that we have direct knowledge of our own feelings and beliefs. But this is not always true. Consider the common remark, "This is my second sandwich; I guess I was hungrier than I thought." Clearly the speaker originally misjudged an internal state and has now decided on the basis of behavioral self-observation that he or she was wrong. Similarly, the self-observation "I've been biting my nails all day; something must be bugging me" is based on the same external evidence that might lead a friend to remark, "You've been biting your nails all day; something must be bugging you."

Self-perception theory is nicely illustrated by an *induced-compliance* experiment originally conducted in order to test Festinger's theory of *cognitive dissonance* (1957), which is discussed later in the chapter. Male college students were taken one at a time to a small room to work for an hour on dull, repetitive tasks (stacking spools and turning pegs). After completing the tasks, some subjects were offered $1 to tell the next subject that the tasks had been fun and interesting. Others were offered $20 to do this. All subjects complied with the request. Later they were asked how much they had enjoyed the tasks. As shown in Figure 18-1, subjects who had been paid only $1

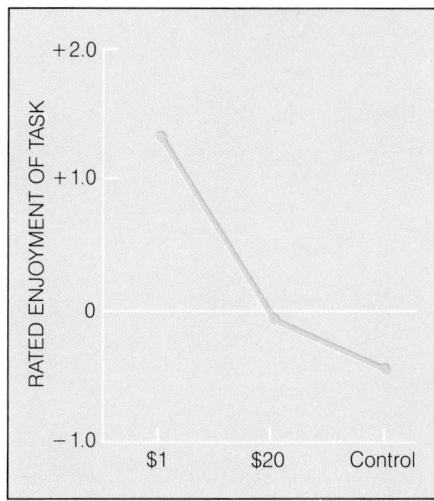

FIGURE 18-1
Induced-Compliance Experiment *The smaller incentive for agreeing to say the tasks were interesting led subjects to infer that they had actually enjoyed the tasks. The larger incentive did not.* (After Festinger & Carlsmith, 1959)

stated that they had, in fact, enjoyed the tasks. But subjects who had been paid $20 did not find them significantly more enjoyable than control subjects who were not asked to speak to another subject (Festinger & Carlsmith, 1959). The small incentive for complying with the experimenter's request—but not the large incentive—led individuals to *believe* what they had heard themselves say. Why should this be so?

Self-perception theory proposes that, just as we try to decide whether an athlete on television really loves the cereal she endorses or whether she is just saying so for the money, so too, the subjects in this experiment looked at their own behavior (saying that the tasks were interesting) and had to solve the attribution problem, "Why did I say this?" It further proposes that they solved the problem the same way an outside observer would. Such a hypothetical observer, hearing the individual say the tasks were enjoyable, must decide whether to make a dispositional attribution (he did it because he believes it) or a situational attribution (he did it for the money). When the individual is paid only $1, the observer is more likely to make a dispositional attribution: "He wouldn't be willing to say it for only $1 and so must have actually enjoyed the tasks." But if the individual is paid $20, the observer is more likely to make a situational attribution: "Anyone would have done it for $20, so I can't judge his attitude toward the tasks on the basis of his statement." If we assume that the individual follows the same inferential process as this outside observer, then subjects paid $1 make a dispositional attribution about their own behavior: "I must think the tasks were enjoyable; otherwise, I would not have said so." But subjects paid $20 attribute their behavior to this situational factor and thus express attitudes toward the tasks that do not differ from those expressed by control group subjects who made no statements to another subject.

FUNDAMENTAL ATTRIBUTION ERROR   There is a subtle point about the findings in this experiment. We know that all the subjects were willing to comply with the experimenter's request to tell the next subject that the tasks were enjoyable—even subjects who were offered only $1 to do so. But the subjects themselves do not know this. Thus, when subjects paid $1 implicitly conclude that they must think the tasks are enjoyable because otherwise they would not have complied with the request, they are wrong. They should be concluding that they complied with the request because they were paid $1. In other words, the subjects are making a dispositional attribution about their own behavior when they should be making a situational attribution. They are committing the fundamental attribution error.

An amusing demonstration of the fundamental attribution error was illustrated in a study in which pairs of male or female subjects were recruited to participate in a question-and-answer game of general knowledge. One member of the pair was randomly assigned to be the questioner and to make up 10 difficult questions to which he or she knew the answers (for example, "What is the world's largest glacier?"). The other subject served as the contestant and attempted to answer the questions. When the contestant failed a question, the questioner would give the answer. In a reenactment of the study, observers also watched the contest. After the game was completed, both participants and observers were asked to rate the level of general knowledge possessed by the questioner and the contestant, relative to the "average student." It is important to note that participants and observers all knew that the roles of questioner and contestant had been assigned randomly.

As Figure 18-2 shows, questioners judged both themselves and the contestant to be about average in level of general knowledge. But contestants

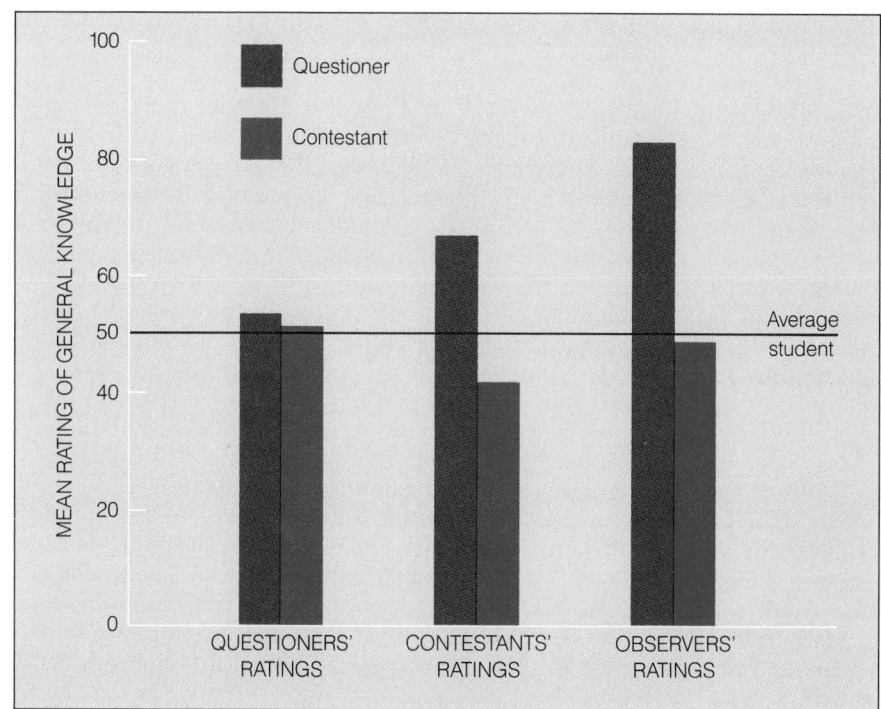

FIGURE 18-2
Fundamental Attribution Error *Ratings of questioners and contestants after they had participated in a quiz game. The questioner is rated as superior by both the contestant and observers even though the questioner had an overwhelming situational advantage. Both contestants and observers gave too much weight to dispositional causes and too little to situational causes. (After Ross, Amabile, & Steinmetz, 1977)*

rated the questioner as superior and themselves as inferior to the average student. They attributed the outcome of the game to their (and the questioner's) level of knowledge rather than taking into account the overwhelming situational advantage enjoyed by the questioner—who gets to omit any questions to which he or she does not know the answer. Observers, aware that the questioner could ask questions which neither they nor the contestant could answer, rated the questioner's level of knowledge even higher. In other words, both contestants and observers gave too much weight to dispositional causes and too little to situational causes—the fundamental attribution error (Ross, Amabile, & Steinmetz, 1977).

One implication of this study is that people who select the topics discussed in a conversation will be seen as more knowledgeable than those who passively let others set the agenda—even if everyone is aware of the differential roles being played. This, in turn, has implications for contemporary sex roles. Research has shown that men talk more than women in mixed-sex interactions (Henley, Hamilton, & Thorne, 1985); they interrupt more (West & Zimmerman, 1983); and they are more likely to raise the topics discussed (Fishman, 1983). The questioner-contestant study implies that one consequence of these sex-role patterns is that women leave most mixed-sex interactions thinking themselves less knowledgeable than the men, with bystanders of both sexes sharing this illusion. The moral is clear: the fundamental attribution error can work for or against you. If you want to appear knowledgeable both to yourself and to others, learn how to structure the situation so that you control the choice of topics discussed. Be the questioner, not the contestant.

THEORIZING ABOUT ONESELF   Self-perception theory draws a portrait of two selves in one, a subject-self and a psychologist-self. The subject-self behaves and the psychologist-self attempts to interpret or explain the behavior—displaying the same biases and making the same kinds of errors as

CRITICAL DISCUSSION

Information Processing Biases: Cognitive or Motivational?

So far, we have implied that information processing biases are rooted in cognitive or perceptual factors. But when dealing with an individual's interpretation of his or her own behavior, we must also consider the possibility that the biases are motivational—that the individual distorts self-judgments in order to enhance or defend his or her self-image. The Freudian defense mechanisms, discussed in Chapter 15, are examples of such motivational processes. A question currently under debate within social psychology is whether the biases of the kind we have been discussing in this chapter can all be ex-

plained by cognitive factors or whether some of them require motivational explanations. For example, we have interpreted the findings of the $1–$20 experiment (in which the smaller incentive led subjects to believe their own statement that they had enjoyed the tasks) as a purely cognitive phenomenon of self-perception, a set of self-attributions biased by the fundamental attribution error. But as we shall see later, these same results can also be interpreted motivationally.

Even judgments that appear to be obviously self-serving can stem from purely cognitive factors. When college students are asked to explain examination grades they have received, they tend to attribute A and B grades to personal internal factors such as ability and effort and C, D, and F grades to external factors such as test difficulty and bad luck (Bernstein, Stephan, & Davis, 1979). In one study, subjects played a competitive game that was rigged so that winners and losers were randomly determined. Winners attributed their wins to skill and effort, whereas losers blamed their losses on

luck (Snyder, Stephan, & Rosenfeld, 1976). Similarly, gamblers tend to attribute wins to their gambling skills or strategies, whereas they interpret their losses as near misses due to flukes (Gilovich, 1983). But even though these judgments are self-serving, they are not necessarily the product of motivational processes. Because we usually try to succeed and rarely try to fail, it makes some sense to attribute our successes to internal factors and failures to external factors. We fail *despite* our abilities and efforts, not because of them. And if we have a history of success, then it is certainly rational to attribute an unexpected failure to external rather than to enduring internal causes. Thus, these apparently self-serving attributions may not only derive from purely cognitive factors, but may well be correct! On the other hand, one well-designed study controlled for the subjects' expectancies of success and failure and still found self-serving bias (Ross & Sicoly, 1979).

The same interpretive problem arises in another pervasive self-enhancement phenomenon—which

any intuitive scientist. We saw a similar idea in Chapter 6, in which we discussed Hilgard's *neodissociation theory* of hypnosis. According to this theory, there is a "hidden observer," a mental structure that monitors everything that happens during hypnosis, including events that the subject is not consciously aware of perceiving.

Recent research in neuropsychology suggests that the concept of an observing self and an observed self may be more than a simple metaphor. In Chapter 2, we reported research on patients who had the two hemispheres of their brain surgically separated for medical reasons. Because the language area of the brain is located in the left hemisphere, such patients cannot verbally describe visual stimuli presented to the right cerebral hemisphere. Subsequent experiments have suggested to one neuropsychologist that there is a *left-brain interpreter* that attempts to understand feelings and behaviors originating in other parts of the brain (Gazzaniga, 1985).

In one of Gazzaniga's experiments, a picture of a chicken claw was presented to the left hemisphere of a split-brain patient while a picture of a snow scene was presented to the right hemisphere. Under these conditions, the left hemisphere does not register the snow scene. The patient was then shown an array of pictures and asked to choose those associated with the pictures presented. The obviously correct associations were a picture of a chicken for the chicken claw and a shovel for the snow scene. The patient

we might call the Lake Wobegon effect, after the fictional community in which "all the women are strong, all the men are handsome, and all the children are above average." In 1976–1977, the College Entrance Examination Board surveyed the nearly one million high-school seniors who took the Scholastic Aptitude Test, asking them to compare themselves with their peers. Seventy percent of the seniors described themselves as above average in leadership ability; only 2 percent rated themselves as below average. When asked about their ability to get along with others, *all* the seniors rated themselves as at least average, 60 percent rated themselves in the top 10 percent, and 25 percent rated themselves in the top 1 percent (Myers, 1987, p. 92). Most business people see themselves as more ethical than the average business person (Brenner & Molander, 1977); most drivers—including drivers who have been hospitalized for accidents—describe themselves as safer and more skillful than the average driver (Svenson, 1981); and 94 percent of all college professors say they do above-average work (Cross, 1977).

Research suggests that both cognitive and motivational factors might play a role in the Lake Wobegon effect. One cognitive factor derives from the ambiguity of the rating task itself: does leadership ability mean the ability to get the task done or to resolve conflicts within the group? Does the above-average professor excel at giving lectures, conducting small seminars, doing research, serving on committees, designing curricula, or advising students? Because the criteria are usually left unspecified when we make such judgments, we are free to select the criterion on which we do best and then to employ that criterion to judge how well we do. When asked how she compares with other professors, the superb lecturer is likely to think primarily of her lecturing ability as the central criterion and rate herself as above average. She is not likely to think of her indifferent committee work as relevant to the judgment. Through this selective cognitive process, virtually all professors can claim—honestly and correctly—that they do above-average work. Research supports this explanation, showing, for example, that the more criteria that can be used to define "doing well," the stronger the Lake Wobegon effect becomes (Dunning, Meyerowitz, & Holzberg, 1989). On the other hand, motivational factors also appear to play a role. When students from a business school were led to believe that specific social skills were more important than specific business skills for being a successful executive, they raised their self-evaluations of these social skills and lowered their self-evaluations of the specific business skills. The reverse occurred when they were led to believe that the business skills were the more important (Dunning, Story, & Tan, 1989).

These examples illustrate how difficult it is to resolve the debate over cognitive versus motivational explanations of self-enhancing biases in self-judgments. Some authors have argued that the opposing positions are formulated in ways that do not even permit the debate to be resolved on empirical grounds (Tetlock & Levi, 1982).

chose both of the correct pictures, pointing to the shovel with the left hand (which is controlled by the right hemisphere) and the chicken with the right hand. When asked why he chose these items, he replied, "Oh, that's simple. The chicken claw goes with the chicken, and you need a shovel to clean out the chicken shed." The left-brain interpreter—ignorant of the snow scene but seeing his hand choose the picture of the shovel—made up a plausible theory to explain the behavior.

In another experiment, the written command "laugh" was presented to a patient's right hemisphere. The patient laughed, and when asked why, said "You guys come up and test us every month. What a way to make a living!" When the command "walk" was flashed to the right hemisphere of another patient, he stood up and began to leave, explaining that he had decided to get a Coke.

Understanding our emotions also appears to require the left-brain interpreter. In one experiment, a film depicting one person throwing another into a fire was shown to the right hemisphere of a split-brain patient. As expected, she could not describe what she saw, but she described herself as feeling kind of scared and jumpy. As an aside to a colleague, she then said, "I know I like Dr. Gazzaniga, but right now I'm scared of him for some reason." Denied a knowledge of the source of the emotion, the left-brain interpreter came up with a plausible theory to explain the felt emotional state.

In general, when people are asked to account for their preferences, behaviors, and emotional states, they tend to identify causes that seem plausible—even when those causes are not operative—and to overlook actual causes that seem less plausible (Nisbett & Wilson, 1977). For example, several studies have asked individuals to keep daily records of their moods and the factors that might affect them (the day of the week, the weather, the amount they slept, and so forth). At the end of each study, the individuals were asked to judge how much each of the factors had affected their moods. There was little relationship between their perceptions of how important a factor was and how well it actually correlated with their moods. In fact, individuals were no better at predicting how well the day of the week or the weather had predicted their moods than strangers who were simply asked to make plausible intuitive estimates (Wilson, Laser, & Stone, 1982).

People who suffer bouts of insomnia often arrive at a number of plausible but incorrect reasons for their sleeplessness (Storms & Nisbett, 1970). They rarely identify known factors like exercising or eating before bedtime, an overheated room, or an irregular sleeping schedule. Later in this chapter, we shall discuss the possibility that sexual attraction can also be based on misattribution.

INTUITIVE LOGIC OF SOCIAL ATTITUDES

Except for the consideration of possible motivational biases in self-attributions, our discussion of social information processing has focused exclusively on cognitive functioning, the processes of perceiving and thinking. With the concept of *attitude*, social psychology's most central concept, we can begin to incorporate affective functioning—emotions and feelings—into our portrait of the person as a processor of social information.

Attitudes are likes and dislikes—affinities for and aversions to objects, persons, groups, situations, or any other identifiable aspects of the environment, including abstract ideas and social policies. We often express our attitudes in opinion statements: "I love oranges"; "I can't abide Republicans." But even though they express feelings, attitudes are often linked to cognitions, specifically to beliefs about the attitude objects ("Oranges contain lots of vitamins"; "Republicans have no compassion for the poor"). Moreover, attitudes are sometimes linked to actions we take with respect to the attitude objects ("I eat an orange every morning"; "I never vote for Republicans"). Accordingly, social psychologists have typically studied attitudes as one component of a three-part system. The beliefs constitute the *cognitive* component; the attitude is the *affective* component; and the actions constitute the *behavioral* component.

Prior sections of this chapter have focused on how well we do as intuitive empirical scientists in making social judgments. It was appropriate to ask whether our judgments were true or false, correct or incorrect, accurate or inaccurate. But attitudes cannot be objectively judged to be right or wrong, hence the more appropriate question to ask is whether or not they are logically consistent with one another, with their associated beliefs, and with their associated actions. In this section, then, we assess not our adequacy as intuitive empirical scientists but our adequacy as intuitive logicians.

start here

Cognitive Consistency

Certain opinions seem to go together. For example, people who support affirmative action often seem to be the same people who advocate stronger gun control, oppose book censorship, and are most concerned about nuclear disarmament. On the surface these diverse attitudes do not seem to follow one another logically. Yet knowing that a person holds one of the attitudes often permits us to guess the others with fair accuracy, and there does seem to be a kind of logic involved. The attitudes all appear to follow more or less from a common set of underlying values that we might label as "liberal."

The same kind of logic can be discerned among "conservative" attitudes. Many people who oppose affirmative action and gun control laws cite their belief in the value of individual freedom as the basis for their opinions. Even those who disagree with such opinions can appreciate the logic involved. But many such freedom-loving individuals also feel that women belong in the home, that marijuana use should be more heavily penalized, and that homosexual behavior should be illegal. Here the logic is less than clear, yet these opinions, too, seem strangely predictable.

In short, people's attitudes often appear to have a kind of internal logic to them, but it is not usually a strict kind of formal logic. Instead, it is a kind of psycho-logic, and it is this psycho-logic that social psychologists have studied under the label of *cognitive consistency*. The basic premise of cognitive consistency theories is that we all strive to be consistent in our beliefs, attitudes, and behaviors, and that inconsistency acts as an irritant or a stimulus that motivates us to modify or change them until they form a coherent, if not logical, package.

CONSISTENCY AMONG BELIEFS   One of the earliest studies of cognitive consistency assessed the degree to which sets of beliefs did, in fact, follow the rules of formal logic. Subjects in the study were given a questionnaire containing 48 propositions that had been taken from 16 logical syllogisms. A *logical syllogism* contains three propositions—two premises and a conclusion drawn from those premises. For example, three of the propositions were drawn from the following syllogism:

> Any form of recreation that constitutes a serious health menace will be outlawed by the City Health Authority.

> The increasing water pollution in this area will make swimming a serious health menace.

> Swimming at the local beaches will be outlawed by the City Health Authority.

The propositions did not appear in syllogistic form on the questionnaire; rather, they were dispersed among propositions from other syllogisms and filler items.

High-school students filled out the questionnaire by indicating their belief in the truth of each proposition on a numerical scale. About a week later, these students received persuasive messages that argued for the truth of the first premise in each syllogism but did not mention the second premises or the conclusions. After receiving the messages, the students again indicated how much they believed each of the 48 propositions.

After the persuasion the results showed a significant change toward stronger belief in the propositions explicitly mentioned in the persuasive messages, as might be expected. Of greater interest, however, was a

Nuclear disarmament and liberal values seem to go together.

TABLE 18-3
Freedom and Equality Rankings as a Function of Civil Rights Attitudes
Three groups of individuals with different attitudes toward civil rights demonstrations ranked "freedom" and "equality" among a list of 12 values. Although all subjects ranked the value of "freedom" high, only those most favorable toward civil rights demonstrations ranked "equality" high. (After Rokeach, 1968)

	PARTICIPATED	SYMPATHETIC	UNSYMPATHETIC
Freedom	1	1	2
Equality	3	6	11

significant, though smaller, change toward a stronger belief in the unmentioned conclusions—as a cognitive consistency hypothesis would predict (McGuire, 1960).

CONSISTENCY AMONG ATTITUDES   We implied earlier that a person's attitudes might cohere because they all derive from a core set of underlying values. A *value* can be defined as a basic attitude toward certain broad modes of conduct (for example, "courage," "honesty," "friendship") or certain end states of existence (for example, "equality," "salvation," "freedom," "self-fulfillment") (Rokeach, 1968; Rokeach, 1973). Values are thus a kind of attitude, but they refer to ends, not means. A woman who has a positive attitude toward money, for instance, might explain it by saying that money would allow her to retire, retirement would permit her to take music lessons, and music lessons would help her attain self-fulfillment. Money, retirement, and music lessons do not qualify as values because they are all seen as means not ends—means toward the value of self-fulfillment. Such labels as "liberal" and "conservative" enable us to predict many of an individual's attitudes because these two terms refer to broad underlying values that are shared by large segments of the population. In fact, Americans—liberals and conservatives alike—share many values, and our differences of opinion stem from the relative importance we assign to them.

This was nicely illustrated in a study in which individuals were asked to rank 12 values in the order of the values' importance to them. The investigator was particularly interested in the values "freedom" and "equality," and he tallied the rankings of these two values separately for individuals who had participated in civil rights demonstrations during the 1960s; for individuals who had not participated in the demonstrations but who were sympathetic to them; and for individuals who were unsympathetic to them. Table 18-3 shows how each of these groups ranked "freedom" and "equality" in the list of 12. As the table shows, freedom ranked high for all groups, but equality was considered relatively unimportant (next to last among the 12 values) for those unsympathetic to civil rights demonstrations.

The investigator then conducted a study similar to the one for syllogisms described earlier to see if inconsistency could induce attitude or value change. After obtaining students' value rankings and their attitudes toward civil rights demonstrations, he discussed with them the low ranking given to equality by those unsympathetic to civil rights demonstrations and speculated aloud that maybe such individuals cared a great deal about their own freedom but were indifferent to other people's freedom. Students were invited to ponder their own values and attitudes in this light. Three weeks later and then again 3 to 5 months later, they were asked to rank their values and state their attitudes once more.

This study, like the syllogism study, found that inconsistency produced attitude change. In particular, students who had ranked equality high but who were initially against civil rights demonstrations became more pro-civil rights while retaining the importance of equality in their value rankings. Interestingly, the change in civil rights attitudes was greater after 3 to 5 months than it was only 3 weeks after the experiment—as if the changes needed time to filter down through the belief system. Finally, students who had initially ranked equality low but were pro-civil rights raised the importance of equality in their value rankings and retained their pro-civil rights attitudes (Rokeach, 1968).

CONSISTENCY BETWEEN BELIEFS AND ATTITUDES   Consistency between our beliefs and our attitudes is a common occurrence in daily life. If we come to believe that a certain automobile is highly reliable, gives a comfortable ride, and has good gas mileage, then we are likely to have a favorable attitude toward it. In such cases our attitude seems to arise naturally and inevitably from the supporting beliefs. A number of researchers over the years have shown that it is even possible to make quantitative predictions of people's attitudes by using numerical scales and algebraic formulas to combine the relevant underlying beliefs and values (see Rosenberg, 1956; Fishbein, 1963). This kind of consistency closely follows the rules of formal logic demonstrated in the syllogism study.

But even the syllogism study revealed a kind of consistency between beliefs and attitudes that formal logic does not anticipate: there was a high correlation between the degree to which subjects believed the 48 propositions from the syllogisms to be true and their attitudes toward those propositions. The more they believed a proposition to be true, on the average, the more they thought it to be desirable. Furthermore, when subjects changed their degree of belief in a proposition, they also changed their attitude toward it. This kind of consistency is often called *rationalization*. If we come to believe that something is true, then we persuade ourselves that it is desirable as well. The reverse sequence of reasoning may also take place: because we believe something to be desirable, we persuade ourselves that it is true. This is called *wishful thinking*. Both rationalization and wishful thinking could account for the correlation between the belief ratings and the attitude ratings. Both produce a consistency not of logic, but of psycho-logic.

A kind of wishful thinking was explored more directly in a clever study that changed individuals' attitudes through hypnosis and then sought to determine whether any associated beliefs also changed. In one variation, subjects were hypnotized and told that when they awoke they would be very much in favor of black families moving into white neighborhoods. "The mere idea . . . will give you a happy, exhilarated feeling. Although you will not remember this suggestion having been made, it will strongly influence your feelings after you have awakened" (Rosenberg, 1960, pp. 26–27). Note that nothing was said about any beliefs that might underlie attitudes toward integrated neighborhoods. Nevertheless, such beliefs changed as a result of the hypnotic suggestion. For example, after being awakened, subjects were less likely than before the experiment to see integrated neighborhoods as lowering property values. Some also rated the maintenance of property values as less important than they had earlier. Even after the posthypnotic suggestion was removed, some of the belief changes persisted. As we noted in our earlier discussion of theorizing about oneself, when the actual causes of our thoughts, emotions, or behavior are obscure, we (or our left-brain interpreters) will make up plausible explanations for them. In this study, the new beliefs provide a rationale for the altered attitudes.

"And don't waste your time canvassing the whole building, young man. We all think alike."

Drawing by Stevenson; © 1980 *The New Yorker Magazine,* Inc.

CONSISTENCY BETWEEN ATTITUDES AND BEHAVIOR   A major reason for studying attitudes is the expectation that they enable us to predict behavior. A political candidate is interested in a survey of voter attitudes only if the attitudes expressed relate to voting behavior. The assumption that a person's attitudes determine his or her behavior is deeply ingrained in Western thinking, and in many instances the assumption holds. For example, a survey of presidential campaigns from 1952 to 1964 reveals that 85 percent of the voters surveyed showed a correspondence between their attitudes 2 months before the election and their actual vote in the election (Kelley & Mirer, 1974).

But in other cases, the assumption of attitude-behavior consistency appears to be violated. The classic study usually cited in this connection was conducted during the 1930s. A white professor traveled across the United States with a young Chinese couple. At that time, there was quite strong prejudice against Asians and there were no laws against racial discrimination in public accommodations. The three travelers stopped at over 200 hotels, motels, and restaurants and were served at all the restaurants and all but one of the hotels and motels without problem. Later, a letter was sent to all of the establishments visited asking them whether or not they would accept a Chinese couple as guests. Of the 128 replies received, 92 percent said they would not. In other words, these proprietors expressed attitudes that were much more prejudiced than their behavior (LaPiere, 1934).

This study illustrates that behavior is determined by many factors other than attitudes, and these other factors affect attitude-behavior consistency. One obvious factor is the degree of constraint in the situation: we must often act in ways that are not consistent with what we feel or believe. As children, we ate asparagus that we detested, and as adults we attend lectures and dinner parties that we would compare unfavorably to our experience with asparagus. In the racial discrimination study, the prejudiced proprietors may have found it difficult to act on their prejudices when actually faced with an Asian couple seeking service. Public accommodation laws against discrimination now make it even more difficult to display such prejudices than it was in 1934. Peer pressure can exert similar influences on behavior. For example, a teenager's attitude toward marijuana is moderately correlated with his or her actual use of marijuana, but the number of marijuana-using friends the teenager has is an even better predictor (Andrews & Kandel, 1979).

In general, attitudes tend to predict behavior best when they are a) strong and consistent; b) based on the person's direct experience; and c) specifically related to the behavior being predicted. We shall look briefly at each of these.

Strong and consistent attitudes predict behavior better than weak or ambivalent attitudes. This is illustrated by the surveys of presidential voting, mentioned earlier. Most of the attitude-vote inconsistencies came from voters with weak or ambivalent attitudes. Many such voters experience ambivalence because they are cross-pressured by friends and associates who do not agree with one another. For example, a Jewish businessperson belongs to an ethnic group that generally holds liberal political positions, but she also belongs to a business community that frequently holds conservative political positions, particularly on economic issues. When it comes time to vote, such a person is subjected to conflicting pressures. Ambivalence and conflict can arise from within the person as well. When the cognitive and affective components (the beliefs and the attitudes, respectively) are not consistent with one another, then attitudes are usually not reliable predictors of behavior (Norman, 1975).

Behavior is more predictable for individuals whose attitudes toward AIDS stem from direct experience.

Attitudes based on direct experience predict behavior better than do attitudes formed from just reading or hearing about an issue. For example, during a housing shortage at a university, many freshmen had to spend the first few weeks of the term in crowded temporary housing. Researchers measured attitudes of students toward the housing crisis and their willingness to sign and distribute petitions or to join committees to study it. For students who actually had to live in the temporary housing, there was a high correlation between their attitude toward the crisis and their willingness to take action to solve it. But for students who had not directly experienced the temporary housing, no such correlation existed (Regan & Fazio, 1977). There are many more examples of a strong relationship between behaviors and attitudes based on direct experiences, and these can be interpreted as evidence for the importance of the self-perception process described earlier (Fazio & Zanna, 1981).

And finally, attitudes specifically related to the behavior being assessed tend to predict better than attitudes only generally related. For example, general environmental attitudes in one study were not related to a willingness to take action on behalf of the Sierra Club, but attitudes specifically toward the Sierra Club were strongly related (Weigel, Vernon, & Tognacci, 1974). Similarly, attitudes toward birth control correlated only .08 with a woman's use of oral contraceptives over a 2-year span, but attitudes toward the pill in particular correlated .7 with that behavior (Davidson & Jaccard, 1979).

COGNITIVE DISSONANCE THEORY   Our discussion of attitude-behavior consistency has covered only half the topic so far. We have examined how attitudes might lead to behavior, but it is also possible for behavior to lead to attitudes. The most influential theory of this sequence of events has been Leon Festinger's theory of cognitive dissonance. Like cognitive consistency theories in general, cognitive dissonance theory assumes that there is a drive toward cognitive consistency; two cognitions that are inconsistent with one another will produce discomfort that motivates the person to remove the inconsistency and bring the cognitions into harmony. This inconsistency-produced discomfort is called *cognitive dissonance* (Festinger, 1957).

Although cognitive dissonance theory speaks generally about many kinds of inconsistency, it has been the most provocative in predicting that engaging in behavior that is counter to one's attitudes creates dissonance pressure to change the attitudes so they are consistent with the behavior. The theory further states that engaging in counterattitudinal behavior produces the most dissonance, and hence the most attitude change, when there are no other consonant reasons for engaging in the behavior. This was illustrated in an experiment that we have already discussed in the context of self-perception theory, the $1–$20 induced-compliance experiment by Festinger and Carlsmith (1959).

Recall that subjects in this study were induced to tell a waiting subject that a series of dull tasks had been fun and interesting. Subjects who had been paid $20 to do this did not change their attitudes, but subjects who had been paid only $1 came to believe that the tasks had, in fact, been enjoyable. According to cognitive dissonance theory, being paid $20 provides a very consonant reason for complying with the experimenter's request to lie to the waiting subject, and hence the person experiences little or no dissonance. The inconsistency between the person's compliance and his or her attitude toward the tasks is swamped by the far greater consistency between the compliance and the incentive for complying. Accordingly, the subjects who were paid $20 did not change their attitudes; the subjects who were paid $1, however, had no consonant reason for complying. Accordingly, they experienced dissonance, which they reduced by coming to believe that they really did enjoy the tasks. The general conclusion is that dissonance-causing behavior will lead to attitude change in induced-compliance situations when the behavior can be induced with a *minimum* amount of pressure, whether in the form of reward or punishment.

Experiments with children have confirmed the prediction about minimal punishment. If children obey a very mild request not to play with an attractive toy, they come to believe that the toy is not as attractive as they first thought—a belief that is consistent with their observation that they are not playing with it. But if the children refrain from playing with the toy under a strong threat of punishment, they do not change their liking for the toy (Aronson & Carlsmith, 1963; Freedman, 1965).

Cognitive dissonance theory successfully predicts a number of other attitude change phenomena as well, and it has inspired extensive research and intensive debate.

COMPETING THEORIES OF INDUCED COMPLIANCE   As we have now seen, both cognitive dissonance theory and self-perception theory claim to explain the results of induced-compliance studies. Dissonance theory is a motivational theory because it proposes that the inconsistency between the behavior and the person's initial attitude motivates him or her to change that attitude. In contrast, self-perception theory implies that the person's initial attitude is irrelevant and there is no discomfort produced by the behavior. People are seen not as *changing* their attitudes but as *inferring* what their own attitudes must be by observing their behavior. There is no drive or motivational process involved.

A third theory, *impression management theory*, proposes that subjects in such studies are motivated to make a good impression on the experimenter. In low incentive conditions (such as the $1 payment), their behavior appears to be an expression of their true attitudes, and hence expressing a contrary attitude at the end of the session would make them look inconsistent. Accordingly, they express an attitude consistent with their behavior. The attitude changes, then, are not seen as a result of internal cognitive dynamics but of a motivated attempt to avoid looking bad in a situation contrived by the experimenter (Tedeschi & Rosenfeld, 1981).

Each of these theories has been supported by several studies, and each of the theories has also generated data that the other theories cannot explain. Several investigators have now concluded that all the theories may be partially correct, and the focus of research should be on specifying when and where each theory applies (Baumeister & Tice, 1984; Fazio, Zanna, & Cooper, 1977; Paulhus, 1982).

This is a common outcome in the history of science. Scientists rarely adopt a new theory and discard another because a crucial experiment decides between them. Most often they switch theories because they are more interested in the problems that can be explored with the new theory and simply abandon for a time the problems dealt with by the original paradigm (Kuhn, 1970). For example, during the 1960s, when social psychologists were more interested in attitude change phenomena, cognitive dissonance theory was very popular. But when attention shifted to problems of attribution in the 1970s, self-perception theory seemed to provide a more congenial set of concepts.

Outside the Laboratory

Although the evidence for consistency among beliefs, attitudes, and behaviors seems impressive, psychologists and political scientists who have analyzed the public mind outside the social psychology laboratory are quite divided in their views about the ideological coherence of public opinion on important social and political issues (Kinder & Sears, 1985). One of those who believes the public to be ideologically innocent has said:

> As intellectuals and students of politics we are disposed by training and sensibility to take political ideas seriously. . . . We are therefore prone to forget that most people take them less seriously than we do, that they pay little attention to issues, rarely worry about the consistency of their opinions, and spend little or no time thinking about the values, presuppositions and implications that distinguish one political orientation from another (McClosky, quoted by Abelson, 1968).

An example of such nonconsistency was revealed in a national survey taken by the *New York Times* and CBS News in the late 1970s. The survey showed that a majority of Americans said they disapprove of "most government-sponsored welfare programs." Yet 81 percent said they approve of the government's "program providing financial assistance for children raised in low-income homes where one parent is missing" (Aid to Families with Dependent Children, a major welfare program). Similarly, 81 percent endorsed the government's "helping poor people buy food for their families at cheaper prices" (the essence of the federal food-stamp program) and 82 percent approved of paying for health care for poor people (the Medicaid program). This pattern of support was similar among almost all types of people—rich and poor, liberal and conservative, Democrat and Republican.

An earlier national survey, designed specifically to probe this kind of inconsistency, found a similar contradiction between an *ideological* conservatism and an *operational* liberalism in attitudes toward welfare. One out of four

Americans was classified as conservative on questions concerning the general concept of welfare but simultaneously classified as liberal on questions concerning specific welfare programs (Free & Cantril, 1967).

It is important to be cautious about accusing someone of being inconsistent, however, because his or her opinions may simply be inconsistent with the ideological framework of the investigator. Inconsistency may be in the eye of the beholder. Thus, opposition to capital punishment is usually characterized as a liberal position, whereas opposition to legalized abortion is usually thought of as a conservative position. And yet there is a quite logical coherence to the views of a person who, being against all taking of life, opposes both capital punishment and legalized abortion. Another example is provided by libertarians, who are opposed to any government interference in our lives. They are conservative on economic issues (the free market should govern the economic system) and in their opposition to government-enforced civil rights laws. But they are liberal on personal social issues, believing, for example, that the government should not criminalize the use of marijuana or concern itself with our private sexual behavior. To libertarians, both conservatives and liberals are inconsistent.

Nevertheless, the evidence suggests that most citizens do not organize their beliefs and attitudes according to any kind of overall ideology; nonconsistency, if not inconsistency, seems more prevalent than consistency. This has led one investigator to propose that many of our opinions exist as isolated *opinion molecules*. Each molecule is made up of a) a belief, b) an attitude, and c) a perception of social support for the opinion. In other words, each opinion molecule contains a fact, a feeling, and a following (Abelson, 1968): "It's a fact that when my Uncle Charlie had back trouble, he was cured by a chiropractor [*fact*]"; "You know, I feel that chiropractors have been sneered at too much [*feeling*], and I'm not ashamed to say so because I know a lot of people who feel the same way [*following*]." Or, "Americans don't really want the Equal Rights Amendment [*following*], and neither do I [*feeling*]. It would lead to unisex bathrooms [*fact*]."

Opinion molecules serve important social functions. First, they act as conversational units, giving us something coherent to say when a particular topic comes up in conversation. They also give a rational appearance to our unexamined agreement with friends and neighbors on social issues. But most important, they serve as badges of identification with our important social groups. They reinforce our group identifications. Thus, the fact and the feeling are less important ingredients of an opinion molecule than the following.

In general, this chapter has treated beliefs, attitudes, and values as products of cognitive processes. In Chapter 19, we shall examine them as products of social processes.

SOCIAL PSYCHOLOGY OF INTERPERSONAL ATTRACTION

Of all our attitudes, the most important are undoubtedly our attitudes toward other people. The questions that often concern us most whenever we meet new people are whether or not they like us and we like them. Beyond the initial encounter, our concerns often center on how to nurture and guide the relationship from an initial liking or attraction to a deeper friendship or possibly even to intimacy and love. It is probably not an exaggeration to say that fostering personal relationships is a top priority for most people much of the time. Accordingly, social psychologists have long been interested in the factors that promote liking or interpersonal attraction, and they have recently shown a willingness to study love and intimacy as well. Some of the findings have confirmed commonly held notions about liking and loving, but others have produced surprises. We begin with liking—namely, friendship and the early stages of more intimate love relationships.

Determinants of Liking

When Great Britain's Prince Charles married a few years ago, social psychologists were not surprised that he married "the girl next door," a very attractive woman whom he had known for years and who shared many of his social background characteristics and attitudes. As we shall see, these are precisely the determinants of interpersonal attraction: physical attractiveness, proximity, familiarity, and similarity.

PHYSICAL ATTRACTIVENESS   To most of us there is something mildly undemocratic about the possibility that a person's physical appearance is a determinant of how well others like him or her. Unlike character, niceness, and other personal attributes, physical appearance is a factor over which we have little control, and hence it seems unfair to use it as a criterion for liking someone. In fact, surveys taken over a span of several decades have shown that people do not rank physical attractiveness as very important in their liking of other people (Perrin, 1921; Tesser & Brodie, 1971).

But research on actual behavior shows otherwise. A group of psychologists set up a "computer dance" in which each person was randomly paired with a partner. At intermission each person filled out an anonymous questionnaire evaluating his or her date. In addition, the experimenters obtained several personality test scores for each person, as well as an independent estimate of his or her physical attractiveness. The results showed that only physical attractiveness played a role in how much each person was liked by his or her partner. None of the measures of intelligence, social skills, or personality were related to the partners' liking for one another (Walster, Aronson, Abrahams, & Rottmann, 1966). Moreover, the importance of physical attractiveness continues to operate not only on first dates but on subsequent ones as well (Mathes, 1975).

The importance of physical attractiveness is not confined just to dating and mating patterns. For example, physically attractive boys and girls (5 and 6 years of age) are more popular with their peers than are less attractive children (Dion & Berscheid, 1972). Even adults are affected by a child's physical attractiveness. One investigator had women read a description of an aggressive act committed by a 7-year-old child. The description was accompanied by a photograph of either an attractive or an unattractive child. The women believed that the attractive child was less likely than the unattractive child to commit a similar aggressive act in the future (Dion, 1972).

Why is physical attractiveness so important? Part of the reason is the popular stereotype of physically attractive people that was discussed earlier. Beautiful people are not only thought to have more beautiful personalities, but there is some evidence that they actually do—in part because we treat them more beautifully and they react accordingly.

Research also suggests that our own social standing and self-esteem are enhanced when we are seen with physically attractive companions. Both men and women are rated more favorably when they are with an attractive romantic partner or friend than when they are with an unattractive companion (Sheposh, Deming, & Young, 1977; Sigall & Landy, 1973). But there is an interesting twist to this: both men and women are rated *less* favorably when they are seen with a *stranger* who is physically more attractive than they (Kernis & Wheeler, 1981). Apparently they suffer by comparison when compared with the other person. This effect has been found in other studies. For example, male college students who had just watched a television show starring beautiful young women gave lower attractiveness ratings to a photograph of a more typical-looking woman—as did both men and women who were first shown a photograph of a highly attractive woman (Kenrick & Gutierres, 1980).

Fortunately, there is hope for the unbeautiful among us. First of all, physical attractiveness appears to decline in importance when a marriage partner is being chosen (Stroebe, Insko, Thompson, & Layton, 1971). And, as we shall see, several more democratic factors can work in our favor.

PROXIMITY   An examination of 5,000 marriage license applications in Philadelphia in the 1930s found that one-third of the couples lived within five blocks of each other (Rubin, 1973). Research shows that the best single predictor of whether two people are friends is how far apart they live. In a study of friendship patterns in apartment houses, residents were asked to name the three people they saw socially most often. Residents mentioned 41 percent of neighbors who lived in the apartment next door, 22 percent of those who lived two doors away (about 30 feet) and only 10 percent of those who lived at the other end of the hall (Festinger, Schachter, & Back, 1950).

Studies of college dormitories show the same effect. After a full academic year, roommates were twice as likely as floormates to be friends, and floormates were more than twice as likely as dormitory residents in general to be friends (Priest & Sawyer, 1967). A study of male trainees at the Training Academy of the Maryland State Police is even more striking. The Academy assigns trainees to dormitory rooms and classroom seats by name in alphabetical order. Thus the closer two trainees' last names are alphabetically, the more likely they are to spend time in close proximity to one another. The researchers asked trainees who had been at the Academy for 6 months to name their three closest friends there. Despite an intensive training course in which all trainees get to know one another quite well, there was a strong alphabetical proximity effect. On the average, each person chosen as a best friend was only 4.5 letters away from the person who chose him—an alphabetical proximity significantly closer than the 15.3 letters expected by chance (Segal, 1974).

There are cases, of course, in which neighbors and roommates hate one another, and the major exception to the friendship-promoting effect of proximity seems to occur when there are initial antagonisms. In a test of this, a subject waited in a laboratory with a female confederate who acted in either a pleasant or an unpleasant way toward the subject. When she acted pleasantly, the closer she sat to the subject the better she was liked; when she acted unpleasantly, the closer she sat to the subject, the less she was liked. Proximity simply increased the intensity of the initial reaction (Schiffenbauer & Schiavo, 1976). But because most initial encounters probably range from neutral to pleasant, the most frequent result of sustained proximity is friendship.

Certainly, unbeknownst to William Evans, the perfect woman for him is a waitress in Caracas named Ramona. Good luck, Bill.

Those who believe in miracles when it comes to matters of the heart may believe that there is a perfect mate chosen for each of us waiting to be discovered somewhere in the world. But if this is true, the far greater miracle is the frequency with which Fate conspires to place this person within walking distance.

FAMILIARITY   One of the major reasons that proximity creates liking is that it increases *familiarity,* and there is now abundant research that familiarity all by itself—sheer exposure—increases liking (Zajonc, 1968). This *familiarity breeds liking* effect is a quite general phenomenon. For example, rats repeatedly exposed to either the music of Mozart or Schoenberg come to prefer the composer they have heard, and humans repeatedly exposed to selected nonsense syllables or Chinese characters come to prefer those they have seen most often. The effect even occurs when individuals are unaware that they have been previously exposed to the stimuli (Moreland & Zajonc, 1979; Wilson, 1979). More germane to the present discussion is a study in which subjects were exposed to pictures of faces and then asked how much they thought they would like the person shown. The more frequently they had seen a particular face, the more they said they liked it and thought they would like the person (see Figure 18-3). Similar results are obtained when individuals are exposed to one another in actual interaction.

In one clever demonstration of the *familiarity breeds liking* effect, the investigators took photographs of college women and then prepared prints of both the original face and its mirror image. These prints were then shown to the women themselves, their women friends, and their lovers. The women themselves preferred the mirror-image prints by a margin of 68 percent to 32 percent, but the friends and lovers preferred the nonreversed prints by a margin of 61 percent to 39 percent (Mita, Dermer, & Knight, 1977). Can you guess why?

The moral is clear. If you are not beautiful or you find your admiration of someone unreciprocated, be persistent and hang around. Proximity and familiarity are your most powerful weapons.

SIMILARITY   There is an old saying that "opposites attract," and lovers are fond of recounting how different they are from each other: "I love boating, but she prefers mountain climbing." "I'm in engineering, but he's a history major." What such lovers overlook is that they both like outdoor activities; they are both preprofessionals; they are both Democrats; they are both the same nationality; the same religion; the same social class; the same educational level; and they are probably within 3 years of each other in age and within 5 IQ points of each other in intelligence. In short, the old saying is mostly false.

Research all the way back to 1870 supports this conclusion. Over 99 percent of the married couples in the United States are of the same race; 94 percent are of the same religion. Moreover, statistical surveys show that husbands and wives are significantly similar to each other not only in sociological characteristics—such as age, race, religion, education, and socioeconomic class—but also with respect to psychological characteristics like intelligence and physical characteristics such as height and eye color (Rubin, 1973). A study of dating couples finds the same patterns, in addition to finding that couples were also similar in their attitudes about sexual behavior and sex roles. Moreover, couples who were most similar in background at the beginning of the study were most likely to be together 1 year later (Hill, Rubin, & Peplau, 1976). Of particular pertinence to our earlier discussion of

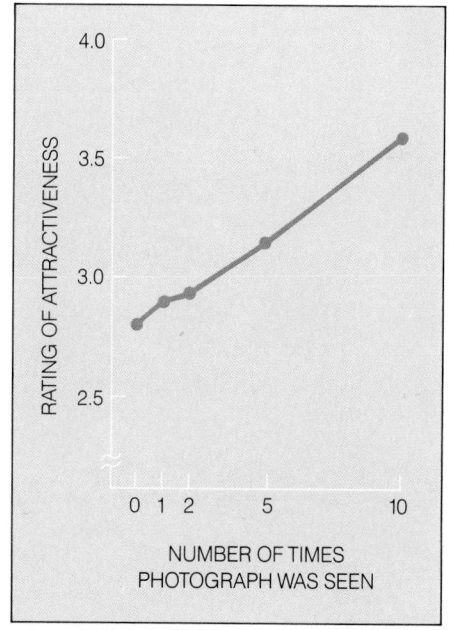

FIGURE 18-3
Familiarity Breeds Liking *Subjects were asked to rate photographs of unknown faces according to how much they thought they would like the person. The lowest ratings of attractiveness were made by subjects who had never seen the photograph before; the highest ratings of attractiveness were made by subjects who had seen the photograph most often. (After Zajonc, 1968)*

The saying "opposites attract" is a myth: couples tend to have many common attributes.

physical attractiveness is the finding that couples are closely matched on this dimension as well, a finding that has shown up in several studies (Berscheid & Walster, 1978).

For example, in one study, judges rated photographs of each partner of 99 couples for physical attractiveness without knowing who was paired with whom. The physical attractiveness ratings of the couples matched each other significantly more closely than did the ratings of photographs that were randomly paired into couples (Murstein, 1972). Similar results were obtained in a real-life field study in which separate observers rated the physical attractiveness of members of couples in bars and theater lobbies and at social events (Silverman, 1971).

This matching of couples on physical attractiveness is usually explained in terms of the *expectancy-value theory* of decision making. This theory states that we consider not only the reward value of the particular choice—the potential partner's attractiveness—but also the expectancy of success—the probability the person is willing to pair up with us. Put bluntly, less attractive people seek less attractive people because they expect to be rejected by someone more attractive than themselves. A study of a video dating service found that both men and women were most likely to pursue a relationship with someone who matched them in physical attractiveness. Only the most attractive people sought dates with the most attractive partners (Folkes, 1982). The overall result of this chilling marketplace process is attractiveness similarity: most of us end up with partners who are about as attractive as we are.

But similarities on dimensions other than physical attractiveness are probably even more important over the long-term course of a relationship. A longitudinal study of 135 married couples, discussed in Chapter 13, found that spouses who were more similar to each other in personality also resembled each other more in terms of how much they enjoyed similar daily activities like visiting friends, going out for dinner, and participating in community activities and professional meetings. These couples also reported less marital conflict and greater closeness, friendliness, and marital satisfaction than less similar spouses (Caspi & Herbener, 1989).

In an ambitious study of similarity and friendship, male students received free room for the year in a large house at the University of Michigan in exchange for their participation. On the basis of information from tests and questionnaires, some men were assigned roommates who were quite similar to them and others were assigned roommates who were quite dissimilar. The investigator observed the friendship patterns that developed over the course of the year, obtaining more questionnaire and attitude data from the participants at regular intervals. In all other respects the men lived as they would in any dormitory.

Roommates who were initially similar generally liked each other and ended up as better friends than those who were dissimilar. When the study was repeated with a new group of men the next year, however, the familiarity breeds liking effect turned out to be even more powerful than similarity. Regardless of whether low or high similarity had been the basis for room assignments, roommates came to like each other (Newcomb, 1961).

One reason that similarity produces liking is probably that people value their own opinions and preferences and enjoy being with others who validate their choices, possibly boosting their self-esteem in the process. But perhaps the major reason that similarity produces liking is just a repeat of factors we have seen before—proximity and familiarity. Both social norms and situational circumstances throw us together with people who are like us. Most religious groups prefer (or insist) that their members date and mate within the religion, and cultural norms regulate what is considered acceptable in terms of race and age matches—a couple comprising an older woman and a younger man is still viewed as inappropriate. Situational circumstances also play an important role. Many couples meet in college or graduate school, thus assuring that they will be similar in educational level, general intelligence, professional aspirations, and probably in age and socioeconomic status. Moreover, tennis players will have met on the tennis courts, political liberals at an antiapartheid rally, and gay people at a meeting of the Gay People's Union.

Despite all this, the saying that opposites attract may still apply to certain complementary personality traits (Winch, Ktsanes, & Ktsanes, 1954). To take the most obvious example, one partner may be quite dominant and thus require someone who is relatively more submissive. A person with strong preferences may do best with someone who is very flexible or even wishy-washy. This has been called the *need-complementarity hypothesis*. But even in the case of complementary traits an underlying similarity of attitudes can often be discerned. For example, the marital relationship in which the husband is dominant and the wife is submissive will be smooth only if both agree on the desirability of these traditional sex roles. Even successful complementarity requires a basic similarity of attitudes favoring the dissimilarity.

The major problem with the need-complementarity hypothesis, however, is that there is not much evidence for it (Levinger, Senn, & Jorgensen, 1970). In one study, marital adjustment among couples married for up to 5 years was found to depend more on similarity than on complementarity (Meyer & Pepper, 1977). Attempts to identify the pairs of personality traits that bring about complementarity have not been very successful. When all is said and done, it is similarity that wins the day.

Love

Love is more than just intense liking. Most of us know people we like very much but do not love, and some of us have experienced even passionate love for someone we do not particularly like. Research confirms these everyday observations. One of the first researchers to study romantic love compiled a number of statements that people thought reflected liking and loving and constructed separate scales to measure each (Rubin, 1973). Items on the liking scale tap the degree to which the other person is regarded as likable, respected, admired, and having maturity and good judgment. Items on the love scale tap three main themes: a sense of attachment ("It would be hard for me to get along without _____"), a sense of caring for the other person ("I would do almost anything for _____"), and a sense of trust ("I feel that I can confide in _____ about virtually everything"). The two scales are only moderately correlated with each other: .56 for men and .36 for women. When members of dating couples are asked the straightforward question "Would you say that you and _____ are in love," their answers are correlated .63 and .53 with the man's and the woman's love scale scores, respectively. The correlations with the liking scale scores are significantly lower (.36 for men and .29 for women).

SOCIAL PENETRATION   Both liking and early infatuation can move toward greater closeness and intimacy through a process of *social penetration* (Altman & Taylor, 1973). Social penetration has both breadth and depth. Breadth refers to the number of different areas of the partners' lives and personalities that are involved in the relationship, and depth refers to the degree to which the pair know and share things that are close to the cores of their personalities—fears, anxieties, uncertainties, hopes, and so forth.

The key to social penetration is *reciprocal self-disclosure*; the partners must reveal themselves to each other, and this can be a very delicate process. At the beginning of a relationship, there is a *strong norm of reciprocity*; as one person begins to disclose things about himself or herself, the other person must also be willing to do so. In this way, trust builds up and intimacy increases. Research shows that the pace of self-disclosure is very important. If one of the partners discloses too much too soon, it can cause the other person to pull back (Rubin, 1975).

In romantic relationships these days, self-disclosure takes place rather early. In one recent study, most of the couples who had been going together an average of 8 months had engaged in full and equal disclosure about very personal and private areas of their lives (Rubin, Hill, Peplau, & Dunkel-Schetter, 1980). About three-fourths of the women and men said they had fully revealed their feelings about their sexual relationship, almost half had fully disclosed their thoughts about the future of the relationship, and over half had provided full information about their previous sexual experiences. One-third of each sex had revealed fully those things about themselves that they were most ashamed of.

Such rapid and full self-disclosure has not always been the norm. In one study, both college students and senior citizens were asked to describe relationships characteristic of 22-year-olds of their own generations. The results showed that today's young people expect couples to disclose both positive and negative feelings more openly and freely than had previous generations (Rands & Levinger, 1979). Up through the 1950s, the middle-class norm emphasized much more self-restraint and self-protectiveness. The sexual revolution of the 1960s changed not only sexual behavior but also social norms

Reciprocal self-disclosure is important in a relationship.

concerning self-disclosure (Altman & Taylor, 1973). This was the era of the encounter group and instant intimacy. Although much of the popularity of encounter groups has declined, the new norms of self-disclosure in romantic relationships have been sustained.

LOVE AND MARRIAGE   The concept of romantic love is an old one, but the belief that it has much to do with marriage is more recent and far from universal. In some non-Western cultures, marriage is still considered to be a contractual or financial arrangement that has nothing whatever to do with love. In our own society, the link between love and marriage has actually become stronger over the past 25 years. Over the years, college students have been asked "if a man (woman) had all the other qualities you desired, would you marry this person if you were not in love with him (her)?" In 1967, about 65 percent of the men but only 24 percent of college women said that they would refuse to marry such a person (the majority of women were undecided; only 4 percent actually said yes) (Kephart, 1967). The recent feminist movement had just begun at that time, and it may be that women were then more likely than now to consider marriage a necessary condition for their own financial security. When the survey was repeated in 1984, 85 percent of both men and women said that they would refuse to marry without being in love. In fact, many young men and women believe that if romantic love disappears from the marriage relationship, that is sufficient reason to end it (Simpson, Campbell, & Berscheid, 1986).

Some of these young people may equate romantic love with its *passionate* component, an intensely emotional state in which "tender and sexual feelings, elation and pain, anxiety and relief, altruism and jealousy coexist in a confusion of feelings" (Berscheid & Walster, 1978, p. 171). In contrast, couples who have been happily married for many years are more likely to emphasize the *companionate* component of romantic love, the "affection we feel for those with whom our lives are deeply intertwined." The characteristics of

The passionate component of romantic love becomes less important than the companionate component in later life.

CRITICAL DISCUSSION

Passion by Misattribution

In his first-century Roman handbook *The Art of Love*, Ovid offered advice on romantic conquest to both men and women. Among his more intriguing suggestions to a man was that he take any woman in whom he is interested to the gladiator contests, where she could be easily aroused to passion. He did not say why this should be so, however. It was not until 1887 that a psychological explanation for this bit of wisdom was offered:

Love can only be excited by strong and vivid emotion, and it is almost immaterial whether these emotions are agreeable or disagreeable. The Cid wooed the proud heart of Donna Ximene, whose father he had slain, by shooting one after another of her pet pigeons (Adolf Horwicz, quoted in Finck, 1887, p. 240)

These romantic tactics should strike a familiar chord. As discussed earlier, we often judge what emotion we are experiencing through a process of cognitive appraisal. Although the physiological arousal of our autonomic nervous system provides us with the information that we are experiencing an emotion, the more subtle judgment of *which* emotion we are experiencing often depends on our cognitive appraisals of the surrounding circumstances. Ovid and Horwicz are suggesting that a person who is physiologically aroused—by whatever means—might attribute that arousal to love or sexual passion—to the advantage of any would-be lover who happens to be at hand.

There is now experimental evidence for this supposition. In a study conducted in a natural setting, an attractive female experimenter approached men who were alone and were crossing a rickety, swaying bridge suspended 230 feet above rocks and shallow rapids. The assumption was that being on this bridge produced high physiological arousal due to fear. She asked them to help her with a psychological study by filling out a questionnaire right then and there. Among other things, the questionnaire asked the man to write an imaginative story to a picture (see the discussion of the Thematic Apperception Test—TAT—

companionate love are trust, caring, tolerance of the partner's flaws and idiosyncrasies, and an emotional tone of warmth and affection rather than high-pitched emotional passion. One investigator suggests that as a relationship continues over time, interdependence grows and the potential for strong emotion actually increases (Berscheid, 1983). This can be seen when longtime partners experience intense feelings of loneliness and desire when temporarily separated from each other or in the emotional devastation typically experienced by someone who loses a longtime partner. But, paradoxically, because companionate couples become so compatible and coordinated in their daily routines, the actual frequency of strong emotions is usually fairly low.

The importance of the companionate component of love is illustrated in a study that compared long-term marriages in the United States—where couples claim to marry for love—with marriages in Japan that had been arranged by the couples' parents. As expected, the American marriages started out with a higher level of expressed love and sexual interest than did the Japanese arranged marriages. But the amount of love expressed decreased in both groups until there were no differences between the two groups after 10 years (Blood, 1967). As the sixteenth Century writer Giraldi put it: "The history of a love affair is in some sense the drama of its fight against time."

This decline of expressed love did not necessarily spell marital failure, however. Many couples in this study reported quite gratifying marriages, marriages that had evolved into a deep companionate love characterized by communication between the partners, an equitable division of labor, and equality of decision-making power. The moral would appear to be that passionate love might be terrific for starters, but the sustaining forces of a good

in Chapter 14). After he had completed the questionnaire, the woman offered him her telephone number in case he was interested in knowing more about the study. In control conditions, a male experimenter was used or the experimenter approached men who were crossing a non-arousing, low, stable bridge. The stories were scored for sexual imagery and a record was kept of which men later telephoned the experimenter. The investigators found more sexual imagery in stories by men who encountered the female experimenter in the high arousal condition than in stories by men in the low arousal condition. There was very little sexual imagery in the stories by men who had encountered the male experimenter in either condition. Men who encountered the female experimenter in the high arousal condition were also the most likely to telephone later (Dutton & Aron, 1974).

Perhaps you can detect flaws in this study. Maybe only macho men cross the high bridge and only wimps cross the low bridge, and it is this difference in subject populations that produces the differential results. Or perhaps the woman herself acted differently or appeared more attractive on the high bridge than on the low bridge. To control for these and other difficulties, several additional studies have now been conducted. In one series of studies, male subjects were physiologically aroused in one of three ways: by running in place, by watching a videotape of a comedy routine, or by watching a videotape of a grisly killing. They then watched a tape of a woman who was dressed and made up to look either attractive or unattractive. Finally, all subjects rated the woman on several scales, including her general attractiveness and the degree to which they would be interested in dating her and kissing her. No matter how the arousal had been obtained, these subjects liked the attractive woman *more* and the unattractive woman *less* than did control subjects who had not been aroused (White, Fishbein, & Rutstein, 1981). The high arousal intensified both positive and negative reactions to the woman. Other research demonstrates that aroused subjects are especially likely to be attracted to an attractive woman when they are distracted from the true source of their arousal (White & Kight, 1984).

Perhaps you should keep these studies in mind when considering whether to buy tickets for next season's hockey games.

long-term relationship are less exciting, undoubtedly require more work, and have more to do with equality than with passion. A disappointment for romantics, perhaps, but heartening news for advocates of sexual equality.

CHAPTER SUMMARY

1. *Social psychology* is the study of social interaction, of how we think, feel, and act in the presence of other people, and of how, in turn, our thoughts, feelings, and actions are influenced by others. Social psychology emphasizes that human behavior is a function of both the person and the situation.

2. In attempting to understand others and ourselves, we construct intuitive theories of human behavior by performing the same tasks as a formal scientist: *collecting data, detecting covariation*, and *inferring causality*. Our theories themselves, however, can shape our perceptions of the data, distort our estimates of covariation, and bias our evaluations of cause and effect. For example, we tend to notice and recall information that is vivid rather than pallid, and this biases our social judgments.

3. *Schematic processing* is the perceiving and interpreting of incoming information in terms of simplified memory structures called *schemata*. Schemata of classes of persons are called *stereotypes*; schemata of events and social interactions are called *scripts*. Schemata constitute miniature theories of everyday objects and events. They allow us to process social information efficiently by permitting us to encode and to remember only the unique or most prominent features of a new object or event.

4. Because schemata constitute simplifications of reality, schematic processing produces biases and errors in our processing of social information. In forming impressions of other people, for example, we are prone to the *primacy effect*; the

first information we receive evokes an initial schema and, hence, becomes more powerful in determining our impression than does later information. In general, schematic processing produces perceptions that are resistant to change and relatively impervious to new data.

5. We are not very accurate at detecting covariations or correlations between variables. When our schemata or theories lead us to expect two things to covary, we overestimate their actual correlation; but when we do not have a theory, we underestimate their correlation.

6. Stereotypes, like other schemata, are resistant to change. Moreover, they can be self-perpetuating and self-fulfilling, because they influence those who hold them to behave in ways that actually evoke the stereotyped behavior.

7. *Attribution* is the process by which we attempt to interpret and to explain the behavior of other people—that is, to discern the causes of their actions. We tend to attribute an action or event to a potential cause with which it covaries—provided that it varies only with that potential cause (*distinctiveness*), and does so over several occasions (*consistency*), and for several observers (*consensus*).

8. One major attribution task is to decide whether someone's action should be attributed to *dispositional* causes (the person's personality or attitudes) or to *situational* causes (social forces or other external circumstances). We tend to give too much weight to dispositional factors and too little to situational factors. This bias has been called the *fundamental attribution error*.

9. The judgments we make about ourselves are governed by many of the same processes that govern our judgments of others. *Self-perception theory* proposes that we are two selves in one. The subject-self behaves and the psychologist-self attempts to interpret or explain the behavior—displaying the same biases and making the same kinds of errors as any intuitive scientist. For example, we often commit the fundamental attributions error when interpreting our own behavior, erroneously attributing our actions to our dispositions when situational factors are responsible. Research on split-brain patients suggests that the two-selves theory is not just a metaphor. The left side of the brain appears to house the portion of the brain that interprets perceptions and emotions registered in other parts of the brain.

10. *Attitudes* are likes and dislikes for identifiable aspects of the environment—objects, persons, events, or ideas. Attitudes are the *affective* component of a three-part system that also includes beliefs (the *cognitive* component) and actions (the *behavioral* component). A major question in attitude research is the degree of consistency among these components, particularly between attitudes and behavior. In general, attitudes predict behavior best when they are a) strong and consistent, b) based on the person's direct experience, and c) specifically related to the behavior being predicted.

11. *Cognitive dissonance theory* proposes that when a person's actions are inconsistent with his or her attitudes, the discomfort produced by this dissonance leads the person to bring the attitudes into line with the actions. *Self-perception theory* and *impression management theory* offer alternative explanations for the same phenomenon. All three theories may be partially correct under different circumstances.

12. Social scientists are divided in their views about the degree to which citizens hold coherent opinions about social and political issues. Many opinions appear to serve social rather than intellectual functions for the person such as reinforcing his or her group identifications.

13. Many factors influence whether we will be attracted to someone. The most important are *physical attractiveness*, *proximity*, *familiarity*, and *similarity*. Both liking and early infatuation can move toward greater intimacy through a process of *social penetration*. The key to social penetration is reciprocal self-disclosure.

14. The link between love and marriage is historically recent and far from universal. In our own society the link has become closer over the past 25 years, with more

women and men today refusing to marry someone they do not love. Romantic love has both *passionate* and *companionate* components. The former is characterized by intense emotion, whereas the latter is characterized by trust, caring, tolerance of the partner's flaws, and an emotional tone of warmth and affection. Cross-cultural studies suggest that the sustaining forces of a good long-term relationship have less to do with the passionate component of romantic love and more to do with the companionate component. These marriages are characterized by communication between the partners, an equitable division of labor, and equality of decision making.

FURTHER READING

The major theme of this chapter—that persons act as informal scientists in arriving at social judgments—is treated in detail in Nisbett and Ross, *Human Inference: Strategies and Shortcomings of Social Judgment* (1985). A number of books deal in more depth with the other topics discussed. Recommended are Bem, *Beliefs, Attitudes, and Human Affairs* (1970); Gazzaniga, *The Social Brain* (1985); Kelley et al. (eds.), *Close Relationships* (1983); and Aronson, *The Social Animal* (5th ed., 1988).

Three comprehensive textbooks in this area are Brown, *Social Psychology: The Second Edition* (1986); Myers, *Social Psychology* (2nd ed., 1987); Sears, Peplau, Freedman, and Taylor, *Social Psychology* (6th ed., 1988). More advanced treatments are available in Lindzey and Aronson (eds.), *The Handbook of Social Psychology* (3rd ed., 1985).

Chapter 19

Social Influence

Detail, Strange Garden.

In Chapter 18, we defined social psychology, in part, as the study of *social influence*—the ways in which an individual's thoughts, feelings, and behaviors are influenced by others. For most of us, social influence is exemplified by the direct and deliberate attempts of persons or groups to change our beliefs, attitudes, or behaviors. For example, a parent attempts to make a child eat spinach; a television commercial tries to induce us to buy a particular product; a religious cult attempts to persuade a young person to abandon school and family and devote full loyalty to a higher mission.

But many forms of social influence are indirect or unintentional. For example, we shall see that the mere physical presence of other persons can affect us in a number of subtle ways. We are also influenced by *social norms*—implicit rules and expectations that dictate what we ought to think and how we ought to behave; these range from the trivial to the profound. Social norms tell us to face forward when riding in an elevator and govern how long we can gaze at a stranger before being considered rude. More profoundly, they can create and maintain an ideology of racism or sexism in a society. As we shall see, the success of direct and deliberate social influence itself often depends on our unwitting and automatic allegiance to social norms.

Because social norms can influence us even when others are not actually present, the definition of social influence usually includes how an individual's thoughts, feelings, and behaviors are influenced by the actual, imagined, or implied presence of others (G. Allport, 1985). It is social influence in this broader sense that concerns us in this chapter.

After discussing our diverse responses to the mere presence of others, we will examine three kinds of responses to more direct social influence attempts (Kelman, 1961):

1. *Compliance*   The person at whom the influence is directed (the "target") publicly conforms to the wishes of the influencing source but does not change his or her private beliefs or attitudes. (The child eats the spinach but continues to dislike it.)

2. *Internalization*   The target changes his or her beliefs, attitudes, or behaviors because of a genuine belief in the validity of the position advocated by the influencing source. (A middle-aged man gives up smoking after reading the Surgeon General's warnings that smoking causes cancer.)

3. *Identification*   The target changes his or her beliefs, attitudes, or behaviors in order to *identify with* or to be like an influencing source that is respected or admired. (A high-school girl takes up smoking in order to be like a group of older girls she admires.)

Social influence is central to human interaction and communal life. Cooperation, community, altruism, and love all involve social influence. But we tend to take these phenomena for granted and to focus our concern on influences that cause us grief. Accordingly, just as the chapter on abnormal psychology focuses on the dark side of individual behavior, this chapter also dwells on the dark side of social behavior. Some of the findings are disturbing, even depressing. But just as the study of abnormal psychology has led to effective therapies, the study of problematic social influences has led us to more effective ways of dealing with them. As we shall see, the principles of social influence that can produce evil are the same principles that can produce the antidote to evil.

PRESENCE OF OTHERS

Social Facilitation

In 1897, the psychologist Norman Triplett was examining the speed records of bicycle racers and he noticed that many cyclists achieved higher speeds when they raced against each other than when they raced against the clock. This led him to perform one of social psychology's earliest laboratory experiments. He instructed children to turn a fishing reel as fast as possible for a fixed period of time. Sometimes two children worked at the same time in the same room, each with his or her own reel. Other times they worked alone. Although his published data are difficult to interpret, Triplett reported that many children worked faster in *coaction*—that is, when another child doing the same task was present—than when they worked alone.

Since this experiment, many studies have demonstrated the facilitating effects of coaction with both human and animal subjects. For example, college students will complete more multiplication problems in coaction than when alone (F. H. Allport, 1920; 1924), worker ants in groups will dig more than three times as much sand per ant than when alone (Chen, 1937), and many animals will eat more food if other members of their species are present (Platt, Yaksh, & Darby, 1967). Soon after Triplett's experiment on coaction, psychologists discovered that the presence of a passive spectator—an audience rather than a coactor—also facilitates performance. For example, the presence of an audience had the same facilitating effect on students' multiplication performance as did that of the coactors in the earlier study (Dashiell, 1930). These coaction and audience effects have been called *social facilitation*.

But even this simplest case of social influence turns out to be more complicated than social psychologists first thought. For example, researchers found that subjects made more errors on the multiplication problems when in coaction or in the presence of an audience than when they performed alone (Dashiell, 1930). In other words, the quality of performance declined even though quantity increased. In other studies, however, the quality of performance improved when coactors or audiences were present (for example, Dashiell, 1935; Cottrell, 1972). How can these contradictions be reconciled?

A close examination has revealed that behaviors showing improved performance in the presence of coactors or audiences usually involve either highly practiced responses or instinctive responses, such as eating. When performing such behaviors, the most likely or most dominant response is the correct one. Behaviors showing impaired performance are those in which the most likely or most dominant response is likely to be wrong. On a multiplication problem, for example, there are many wrong responses but only one correct one. A well-known principle of motivation explains this pattern of findings: a high level of drive or arousal tends to energize the dominant responses of an organism. If the mere presence of another member of the species raises the general arousal or drive level of an organism, then simple or well-learned behaviors should show social facilitation, because these behaviors would be the dominant response. More complex behavior or behavior just being learned—in which the dominant or most likely response is more apt to be incorrect—would be impaired (Zajonc, 1965; 1980).

A number of experiments with both human and animal subjects tested this theory of social facilitation. In one particularly clever study, cockroaches

COACTION BOXES

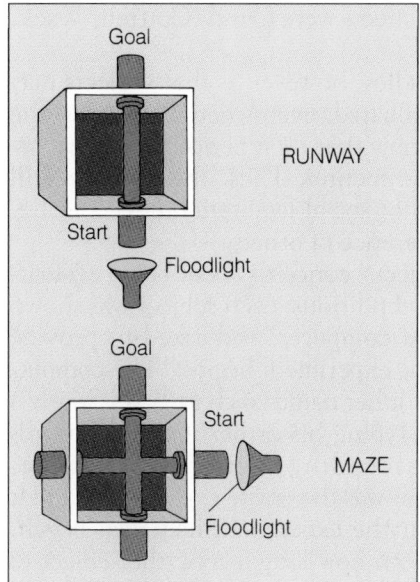

AUDIENCE BOXES

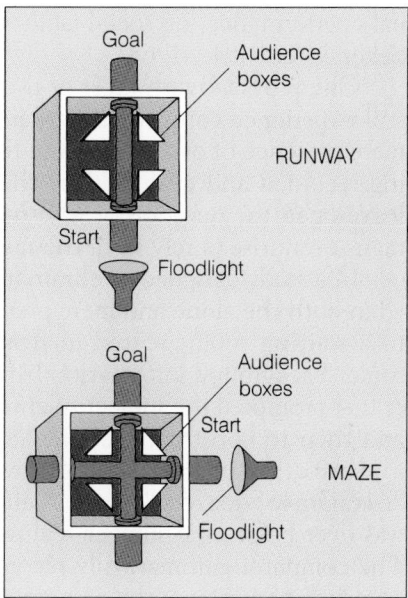

FIGURE 19-1
Social Facilitation Experiment *Diagrams of runways and mazes used in Zajonc's social facilitation experiment with cockroaches.* (After Zajonc, 1965)

were able to run down a straight runway into a darkened goal box to escape a bright floodlight (see Figure 19-1). Researchers found that the roaches reached the goal box faster if they ran in pairs than if they ran alone. But when the escape response was made more complicated by requiring the roaches to make a right-angle turn to find the goal box, pairs of roaches took longer to reach the box than did single roaches. In other words, the presence of coactors facilitated performance in the simple runway but impaired performance in the complex runway (Zajonc, Heingartner, & Herman, 1969). This experiment was repeated by having all of the roaches run alone, but with an audience of four roaches that watched from small plexiglass boxes set alongside the runways. Again, the presence of other roaches—even if they were just spectators—facilitated performance when the dominant response (running down the straight runway) was correct and impaired performance when the dominant response was incorrect.

Studies with human subjects have also confirmed this theory of social facilitation. One such study was a direct analogue of the cockroach study, showing that human subjects learn a simple maze faster, but a complex maze more slowly, when an audience is present than when it is not (Hunt & Hillery, 1973). People also memorize easy word lists faster, but difficult word lists more slowly, in the presence of an audience than when alone (Cottrell, Rittle, & Wack, 1967).

Because social facilitation effects occur in lower organisms, they would not seem to be due to complex cognitive processes. But one theory suggests that social facilitation in humans is due not to the mere presence of others but to feelings of competition or to concerns about being evaluated, and it is these cognitive concerns that raise the drive level. Even the early studies of coaction found that, if all elements of rivalry and competition were removed, social facilitation effects were reduced or eliminated (Dashiell, 1930). Other studies show that audience effects vary, depending on how much the person feels that he or she is being evaluated. For example, social facilitation effects are enhanced if an expert watches but diminished if the audience consists only of "undergraduates who want to watch a psychology experiment" (Henchy & Glass, 1968; Paulus & Murdock, 1971). In one study, when the

TABLE 19-1
Social Facilitation in the Presence of Another Individual *When subjects either are being evaluated or are merely in the presence of another individual, they perform an easy task more quickly but a difficult task more slowly than they would if alone. The dependent variable is the mean time (in seconds) required to complete a typing task.* (After Schmitt, Gilovich, Goore, & Joseph, 1986)

	TIME TO COMPLETE TASK	
CONDITION	EASY TASK	DIFFICULT TASK
Alone (Baseline)	15	52
Evaluation	7	63
Mere Presence	10	73

audience wore blindfolds and hence could not watch or evaluate the individual's performance, no social facilitation effects were found (Cottrell, Wack, Sekerak, & Rittle, 1968).

One problem with most of these studies, however, is that subjects may still experience concern about being evaluated, even when alone or in the mere presence of others, because they know that their performances are being recorded and evaluated by the experimenter. Thus, these studies still leave open the question of whether or not social facilitation effects in humans ever arise purely from the mere presence of others.

In a study designed to eliminate subjects' concerns about being evaluated in both the alone and mere presence conditions, each subject was shown to a waiting room, seated in front of a computer, and asked to provide some "background information before the experiment begins." The computer first prompted the subject to enter his or her name (such as "Joan Smith") and then to construct a code name by typing his or her name backwards and alternating each letter with ascending digits (for example, "h1t2i3m4S5n6a7o8J"). In actuality, that was the entire experiment, and it was over before the subject realized that the experiment had even begun. The computer automatically recorded both how long it took the subject to type his or her name (the easy task) and to type the code name (the difficult task). One group of subjects typed while alone in the room (alone condition). Another group of subjects typed while the experimenter looked over their shoulders (evaluation condition). A third group typed in the presence of a blindfolded person who wore headphones, faced away from the subject, and was said to be waiting to be in a sensory deprivation experiment (mere presence condition).

The results revealed that social facilitation effects *can* be produced by the mere presence of another individual (see Table 19-1). Compared with subjects in the alone condition, subjects in both the evaluation and mere presence conditions performed the easy task more quickly but the difficult task more slowly—the characteristic pattern of social facilitation (Schmitt, Gilovich, Goore, & Joseph, 1986).

Two additional theories have been proposed to account for social facilitation effects. *Distraction-conflict theory* suggests that the presence of others distracts the person, causing a conflict over how to allocate attention between the others and the task to be performed. It is this attentional conflict—rather than the mere presence of another person or a concern over being evaluated—that raises the drive level and causes social facilitation effects (Sanders & Baron, 1975; Baron, 1986). *Self-presentation theory* proposes that the presence of others enhances the individual's desire to present a favorable image. On easy tasks this leads to more effort and concentration and thus to improved performance. On difficult tasks, however, this desire magnifies the frustrations imposed by the tasks and leads to embarrassment, withdrawal, or excessive anxiety, all of which lead to poorer performance (Bond, 1982). There are research results that support each of these theories, and it seems likely that all of the proposed processes—mere presence, concern over evaluation, distraction-conflict, and desire to present a favorable image—contribute to social facilitation effects (Sanders, 1984).

Deindividuation

At about the same time that Triplett was performing his laboratory experiment on social facilitation, another observer of human behavior,

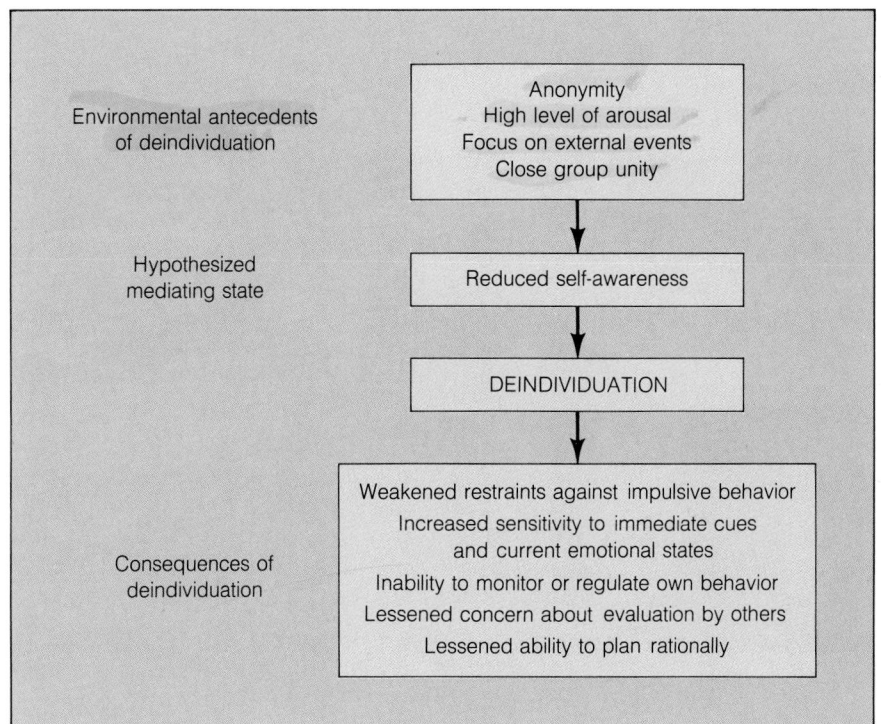

FIGURE 19-2
Antecedents and Consequences of Deindividuation *One explanation of crowd behavior traces it to a loss of personal identity in certain group situations.* (After Diener, 1979)

Gustave LeBon, was taking a less dispassionate view of group coaction. In his book *The Crowd* (1895), he complained that "the crowd is always intellectually inferior to the isolated individual. . . . The mob man is fickle, credulous, and intolerant, showing the violence and ferocity of primitive beings . . . women, children, savages, and lower classes . . . operating under the influence of the spinal cord." LeBon believed that the aggressive and immoral behaviors shown by lynch mobs (and, in his view, by the underclasses during the French Revolution) spread by contagion through a mob or crowd, breaking down the moral sense and self-control of men—if not also of women, children, or savages. This caused crowds to commit destructive acts that no lone individual would commit.

Despite his obvious prejudices, LeBon's observations have some validity. The modern counterpart to his theory is built on the concept of *deindividuation*, a concept first proposed by Festinger, Pepitone, and Newcomb (1952) and extended by Zimbardo (1970) and Diener (1979; 1980). Their theories propose that certain conditions that are often present in groups can lead individuals to experience a psychological state of *deindividuation*, a feeling that they have lost their personal identities and merged anonymously into the group. This produces diminished restraints against impulsive behavior and the other cognitive and emotional conditions associated with unruly mob behavior. The several antecedents and consequents of deindividuation proposed by Diener are illustrated in Figure 19-2. Note that antecedent conditions lead to deindividuation by producing a state of reduced self-awareness in the individual.

Most studies on deindividuation have explored the effects of the antecedent variable of anonymity. In one study, college women, participating in groups of four, were required to deliver electric shocks to another woman who was supposedly in a learning experiment. Half of the women were deindividuated by making them feel anonymous. They were dressed in bulky

More than 900 followers of religious-cult leader Jim Jones obeyed his orders and committed suicide by poison. Shared beliefs and identification with a charismatic leader can exert a powerful influence on people's actions.

laboratory coats and hoods that hid their faces, and the experimenter only spoke to them as a group, never referring to any of them by name. The remaining women were individuated by having them remain in their own clothes and wear large identification tags. In addition, the women in the second group were introduced to each other by name. During the experiment, each woman had a shock button in front of her that she was to push when the learner made an error. Pushing the button appeared to deliver a shock to the learner. The results showed that the deindividuated women delivered twice as much shock to the learner as did the individuated groups (Zimbardo, 1970).

A clever demonstration of deindividuation took advantage of the Halloween custom of trick-or-treating in identity-hiding costumes. Children out trick-or-treating were greeted at the door by an adult who asked that each child take only one piece of candy. The adult then disappeared into the house briefly, giving the children the opportunity to take more candy. Some of the children had been asked their names while others remained anonymous. The children who came in groups or who remained anonymous stole more candy than did children who came alone or who had given their names to the adult (Diener, Fraser, Beaman, & Kelem, 1976).

These experiments are not definitive, however. For instance, the laboratory coats and hoods in the first study carried negative connotations (they resembled Ku Klux Klan outfits), and it may be that the roles suggested by the costumes, rather than anonymity provided by the costumes, produced the behavior. To test this possibility, the shock experiment was repeated, but this time each subject wore one of three outfits: a Ku Klux Klan-type costume, a nurse's uniform, or her own clothes. The results of the revised experiment did not replicate those of the original study; wearing a Ku Klux Klan-type costume had only a small effect on the level of shock the subjects administered. More significantly, those wearing nurses' uniforms actually gave fewer shocks than did the control group who wore their own clothes, suggesting that a uniform encourages the person to play the kind of role it connotes. Anonymity may increase aggression, but this study shows that such results are not inevitable (Johnson & Downing, 1979).

Deindividuation is a complex process, and the experiments have often confounded a number of different variables (for example, the effects of anonymity with the effects of being part of a group—anonymity seems to be the critical variable, not group membership). Nevertheless, several studies show that the factors hypothesized to produce deindividuation do reduce self-awareness and increase disinhibited behavior as outlined in Figure 19-2 (Diener, 1979; Prentice-Dunn & Rogers, 1980). The theory of deindividuation appears to have some validity for explaining the phenomena that so distressed LeBon. However, other factors are also clearly at work. Some collective behaviors such as revolutions or the mass suicide that occurred within a religious cult at Jonestown, Guyana in 1978 stem from shared and strongly held beliefs among group members or the charisma of a group leader. It is also undoubtedly true that people in a mob may behave irresponsibly because they know they are less likely to be caught and punished than if they committed the same acts alone.

Bystander Intervention

In earlier chapters, we noted that people do not react simply to the objective features of a situation but to their own subjective interpretations of it. In this chapter we have seen that even social facilitation, a primitive kind of social influence, depends in part on the individual's interpretation of what others are doing or thinking. But the process of defining or interpreting the situation is often the very mechanism through which individuals influence one another.

In 1964, Kitty Genovese was murdered outside her home in New York City late at night. She fought back, and the murder took over half an hour. At least 38 neighbors heard her screams for help, but nobody came to her aid. No one even called the police.

The American public was horrified by this incident, and social psychologists began to investigate the causes of what at first was termed "bystander apathy." Their work showed that "apathy" was not a very accurate term, however. It is not simple indifference that prevents bystanders from intervening in emergencies. First, there are realistic deterrents such as physical danger. Second, getting involved may mean lengthy court appearances or other entanglements. Third, emergencies are unpredictable and require quick, unplanned action; few of us are prepared for such situations. Finally, one risks making a fool of oneself by misinterpreting a situation as an emergency when it is not. Researchers concluded that "the bystander to an emergency situation is in an unenviable position. It is perhaps surprising that anyone should intervene at all" (Latané & Darley, 1970, p. 247).

Although we might suppose that the presence of other bystanders would embolden an individual to act despite the risks, research demonstrates the reverse. Often it is the presence of other people that prevents us from intervening. Specifically, the presence of others serves a) to define the situation as a *non*emergency, and b) to diffuse the responsibility for acting.

DEFINING THE SITUATION   Most emergencies begin ambiguously. Is the man who is staggering about ill or simply drunk? Is the woman's life really being threatened, or is it just a family quarrel? Is that smoke or steam pouring

Although many passers-by have noticed the man lying on the sidewalk, no one has stopped to help—to find out if he is asleep, sick, drunk, or dead. If others were not present, someone would be more likely to come to his aid.

out the window? One common way to deal with such dilemmas is to postpone action, to act as if nothing is wrong, and to look around to see how others are reacting. What you are likely to see, of course, are other people who, for the same reasons, are also acting as if nothing is wrong. A state of *pluralistic ignorance* develops—that is, everybody in the group misleads everybody else by defining the situation as a nonemergency. We have all heard about crowds panicking because each person leads everybody else to overreact. The reverse, in which a crowd lulls its members into inaction, may be even more common. Several experiments demonstrate this effect.

In one, male college students were invited to an interview. As they sat in a small waiting room, a stream of smoke began to pour through a wall vent. Some subjects were alone in the waiting room when this occurred, whereas others were in groups of three. The experimenters observed them through a one-way window and waited 6 minutes. Of the subjects tested alone, 75 percent reported the smoke within about 2 minutes. In contrast, fewer than 13 percent of the people tested in groups reported the smoke within the entire 6-minute period, even though the room was filled with smoke. Those who did not report the smoke had decided that it must have been steam, air conditioning vapors, smog, or practically anything but a real fire or emergency. This experiment thus showed that bystanders can define situations as nonemergencies for one another (Latané & Darley, 1968).

But perhaps these subjects were simply afraid to appear cowardly. In a similar study, the "emergency" did not involve personal danger. Subjects in the testing room heard a female experimenter in the next office climb up on a chair to reach a bookcase, fall to the floor, and yell "Oh my god—my foot. . . . I can't move it. Oh . . . my ankle. . . . I can't get this thing off me." She continued to moan for about a minute longer. The entire incident lasted about 2 minutes. Only a curtain separated the woman's office from the testing room in which subjects waited, alone or in pairs. The results confirmed the findings of the smoke study. Of the subjects who were alone, 70 percent came to the woman's aid, whereas only 40 percent of those in two-person groups offered help. Again, those who had not intervened claimed later that they were unsure of what had happened but had decided that it was not serious (Latané & Rodin, 1969). The presence of others in these experiments produced pluralistic ignorance; each person, observing the calmness of the others, resolved the ambiguity of the situation by deciding no emergency existed.

DIFFUSION OF RESPONSIBILITY Pluralistic ignorance can lead individuals to define a situation as a nonemergency, but this process does not explain such incidents as the Genovese murder, in which the emergency is abundantly clear. Moreover, Kitty Genovese's neighbors could not observe one another behind their curtained windows and hence could not tell whether others were calm or panicked. The crucial process here was *diffusion of responsibility*. When each individual knows that many others are present, the burden of responsibility does not fall solely on him or her. Each can think, "Certainly someone else must have done something by now; someone else will intervene."

To test this hypothesis, experimenters placed subjects individually in a booth and told them that they would participate in a group discussion about personal problems faced by college students. To avoid embarrassment, the discussion would be held through an intercom. Each person would speak for 2 minutes. The microphone would be turned on only in the booth of the person speaking, and the experimenter would not be listening. Actually, the voices of all participants except the subject's were tape recordings. On the first round, one of the taped participants mentioned that he had problems with seizures. On the second round, this individual sounded as if he were actually starting to have a seizure and begged for help. The experimenters waited to see if the subject would leave the booth to report the emergency and how long it would take. Note that a) the emergency is not at all ambiguous, b) the subject could not tell how the bystanders in the other booths were reacting, and c) the subject knew the experimenter could not hear the emergency. Some subjects were led to believe that the discussion group consisted only of themselves and the seizure victim. Others were told it was a three-person group; and still others, a six-person group.

Of the subjects who thought that they alone knew of the victim's seizure, 85 percent reported it; of those who thought they were in a three-person group, 62 percent reported the seizure; and only 31 percent of those who thought four other bystanders were present did so (see Figure 19.3). Interviews showed that all the subjects perceived the situation to be a real emergency. Most were very emotional about the conflict between letting the victim suffer and rushing, perhaps foolishly and unnecessarily, for help. In fact, subjects who did not report the seizure seemed more upset than those who did. Clearly we cannot interpret their nonintervention as apathy or indifference. Instead, the presence of others diffused the responsibility for acting (Latané & Darley, 1968).

If pluralistic ignorance and diffusion of responsibility are minimized, will people help one another? Three psychologists used the New York City subway system as their laboratory (Piliavin, Rodin, & Piliavin, 1969). Two male and two female experimenters boarded a subway train separately. The female experimenters took seats and recorded the results, while the two men remained standing. As the train moved along, one of the men staggered forward and collapsed, remaining prone and staring at the ceiling until he received help. If no help came, the other man finally helped him to his feet. Several variations of the study were tried: the victim either carried a cane (so he would appear ill) or smelled of alcohol (so he would appear drunk). Sometimes the victim was white; other times, black. There was no ambiguity;

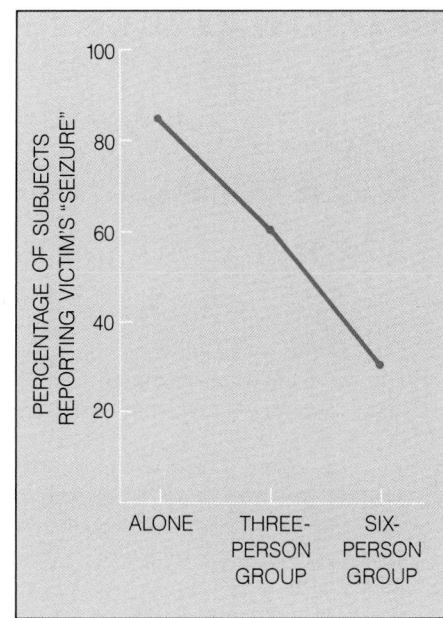

FIGURE 19-3
Diffusion of Responsibility *The percentage of subjects who reported a victim's apparent seizure declined as the number of other people the subject believed were in his or her discussion group increased.* (After Darley & Latané, 1968)

CRITICAL DISCUSSION

Social Impact Theory

Each of the social influence phenomena discussed in this chapter has one or more theories that attempt to explain it. One of the investigators who initiated the research on bystander intervention has attempted to construct a more abstract theory that would summarize, if not exactly explain, all of these phenomena. He has called this a theory of *social impact* (Latané, 1981). The purpose of such a theory is not to replace the individual theories, but to incorporate them into a more general framework as special cases.

Two propositions of the theory are of interest here. The first proposition is illustrated in Figure 1 and states that the social impact of any source of influence on a target individual increases with the number, immediacy, and strength or importance of the sources. For example, this proposition predicts that social facilitation effects will increase with the number of coactors or audience members present, with their immediacy or salience to the individual, and with their importance to the individual. Thus we have seen that social facilitation effects are weaker if an audience is blindfolded (less immediacy), and they are stronger if the audience consists of an expert rather than of undergraduates (greater importance).

A number of studies outside the arena of social facilitation are also consistent with this proposition. For example, when reciting a poem before an audience, individuals rate themselves as increasingly nervous as the number and the status of audience members increase (Latané & Harkins, 1976). Stutterers reading aloud in front of an audience stutter more as the audience increases in size (Porter, 1939). We will see additional illustrations of this proposition later when we discuss conformity and obedience.

The second proposition is illustrated in Figure 2 and states that the social impact of a source *decreases* as the number, immediacy, and importance of *targets* increases. Thus, the first proposition deals with the multiplication of impact due to multiple sources of influence; the second, with the diffusion of impact over multiple targets. For example, the second proposition describes the diffusion of responsibility in emergency situations: the more bystanders present in an emergency situation, the less pressure there is on any particular bystander to intervene.

A number of other studies also support this diffusion-of-impact proposition. For example, we illustrated the multiplication-of-impact proposition by noting that performers become increasingly nervous as the size of the audience increases—as the number of sources impinging on a single target increases. The diffusion-of-impact

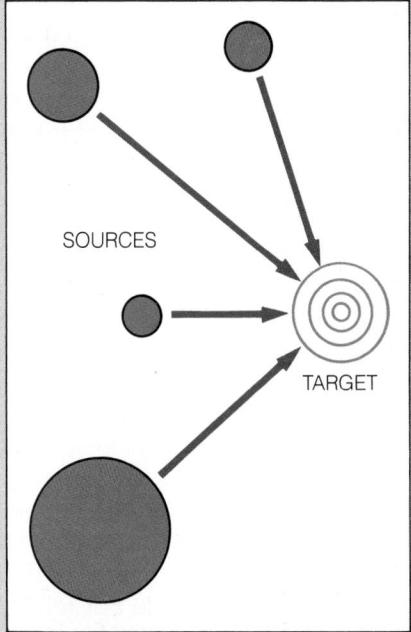

FIGURE 1
Multiplication of Social Impact *The social impact of a source of influence on a target individual increases with the number of sources (the number of circles), the immediacy of the sources (the nearness of the circles), and the strength or importance of the sources (the size of the circles). (After Latané, 1981)*

clearly the victim needed help. Diffusion of responsibility was minimized because each bystander could not continue to assume that someone else was intervening. Therefore, people should help.

The results supported this optimistic expectation. The victim with the cane received spontaneous help on over 95 percent of the trials, within an average of 5 seconds. The drunk victim received help in half of the trials, on the average within 2 minutes. Both black and white cane victims were aided by black and white bystanders. There was no relationship between the number of bystanders and the speed of help, suggesting that diffusion of responsibility had indeed been minimized. And all of this occurred on the New York City subway system! This not only tends to support the proposed explanations of bystander nonintervention but should help us revise our stereotypes about New York City subway riders.

proposition is illustrated by a study of performers in a talent show. Solo performers were about six times more nervous than those who performed in a 10-person act (Jackson & Latané, 1981). The impact of the source (the audience) was diffused over several targets (the performers).

In another study of impact diffusion, records were kept of how much diners in a restaurant tipped the waiter or waitress. The researchers reasoned that one motive for leaving a tip is a feeling of obligation and that this feeling of obligation should be diffused or divided when several diners share the check. In the restaurant they studied, the average tip was about 15 percent. An individual dining alone tipped an average of nearly 19 percent, whereas parties of five to six people tipped less than 13 percent (Freeman, Walker, Borden, & Latané, 1975). A study of Billy Graham's evangelical rallies varying in size from 2,000 to 143,000 persons revealed that the percentage of people present who were willing to come forward and inquire into Christianity declined as the size of the rally increased (Latané, 1981).

One of the major phenomena predicted by the diffusion-of-impact proposition is *social loafing*. In the 1920s, a German researcher named Ringelmann conducted an unpublished study on how collective action influenced individual effort. Workers were asked to pull as hard as they could on a rope working alone, in a group of three, or in a group of six people. Even though total group effort increased with group size, the effort of each member decreased, with six-person groups performing at only 36 percent of potential capacity (calculated as the sum of individual-based efforts) (Moede, 1927, as reported by Latané, 1981). More recent studies have replicated this finding using different kinds of tasks (Petty, Harkins, Williams, & Latané, 1977; Latané, Williams, & Harkins, 1979).

Perhaps you have noticed an apparent contradiction here. The presence of coactors is supposed to produce social facilitation—increased drive and effort—not social loafing. According to social impact theory, the critical difference lies in the role played by the "others" in the situation. When each person performs a task independently, the others put competitive or evaluative pressure on each other. There are many sources acting on each individual target; thus, multiplication of impact occurs (Figure 1). When a group of individuals work on a shared task, the experimenter serves as a single source and his or her influence is diffused over many targets; hence, Figure 2 applies. Cognitive processes may also contribute to social loafing. Each person may believe that others in the group are not contributing their fair share and thus be less motivated to work to capacity. Or each individual may feel that his or her own contribution will be less recognizable when working in a group, leading to a diffusion of responsibility. A more recent study found that social loafing decreases when the task is made more challenging and when individuals believe they can make a unique contribution to the group effort (Harkins & Petty, 1982).

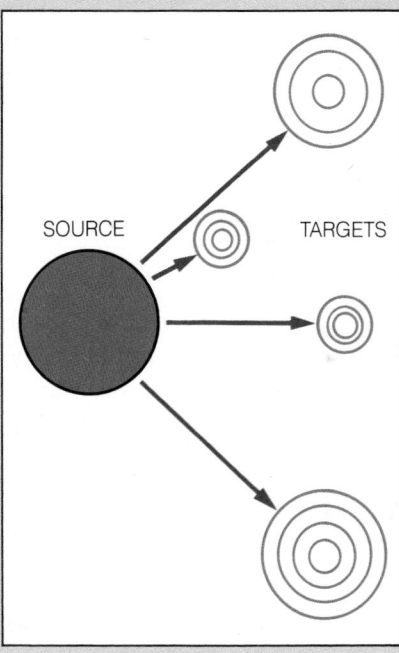

FIGURE 2
Diffusion of Social Impact *The impact of a source decreases as the number, immediacy, and importance of targets increase.* (After Latané, 1981)

ROLE OF HELPING MODELS In the subway study, as soon as one person moved to help, many others followed. This suggests that just as individuals use other people as models to define a situation as a nonemergency (pluralistic ignorance), they also use other people as models to indicate when to be helpful. This possibility was tested in a study by counting the number of drivers who stopped to help a woman whose car had a flat tire (the test car). During some test periods, another car with a flat tire (the model car) was parked alongside the highway, one-quarter mile before the test car. The model car was raised on a jack and a woman was watching a man change the flat tire. Of 4,000 passing cars, 93 people stopped to help the woman alone in the test car: 35 stopped when there was no model car before the test car and 58 when there was—a statistically significant difference. This experiment indicates that others not only help us decide when *not* to act in an emergency but also serve as models to show us how and when to be good Samaritans (Bryan & Test, 1967).

ROLE OF INFORMATION Would you be more likely to intervene in an emergency now that you have read this section? An experiment at the University of Montana suggests that you would. Undergraduates were either given a lecture or shown a film based on the material discussed in this section. Two weeks later, each undergraduate was confronted with a simulated emergency while walking with one other person (a confederate of the experimenters). A male victim was sprawled on the floor of a hallway. The confederate did not react as if the situation were an emergency. Of those who had heard the lecture or seen the film, 43 percent offered help, compared with only 25 percent of those who had not—a statistically significant difference (Beaman, Barnes, Klentz, & McQuirk, 1978). For society's sake, perhaps you should reread this section!

COMPLIANCE

As we noted at the beginning of the chapter, social influence produces *compliance* when a target individual publicly conforms to the wishes of an influencing source but does not change his or her private beliefs or attitudes. When a source obtains compliance by setting an example, we call that compliance *conformity*; when a source obtains compliance by wielding authority, we call it *obedience*. In both cases, an individual complies because the source has the power to administer rewards and punishments. Most often these are social rewards and punishments, such as approval and disapproval or acceptance and rejection. In this section we examine both conformity to peer pressure and obedience to authority.

Conformity to a Majority

When we are in a group, we may find ourselves in the minority on some issue. This is a fact of life to which most of us have become accustomed. If we decide that the majority is a more valid source of information than our own experience, we may change our minds and conform to the majority opinion. But imagine yourself in a situation in which you are sure that your own opinion is correct and that the group is wrong. Would you yield to social pressure under those circumstances? This is the kind of conformity that social psychologist Solomon Asch decided to investigate in a series of classic studies (1952; 1955; 1958).

In Asch's standard procedure, a single subject was seated at a table with a group of seven to nine others (actually confederates of the experimenter). The group was shown a display of three vertical lines of different lengths, and members of the group were asked to judge which line was the same length as a standard drawn in another display (see Figure 19-4). Each individual announced his or her decision in turn, and the subject sat in the next to the last seat. The correct judgments were obvious, and on most trials everyone gave the same response. But on several predetermined critical trials, the confederates had been instructed to give the wrong answer. Asch then observed the amount of conformity this procedure would elicit from his subjects.

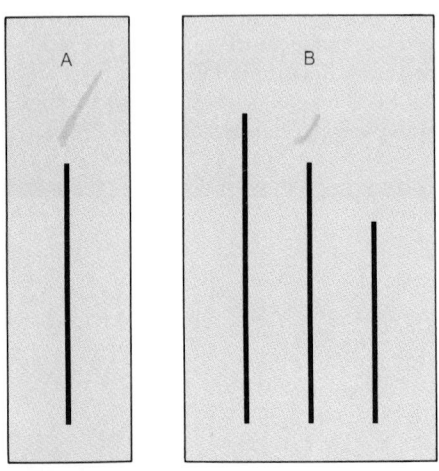

FIGURE 19-4
Representative Stimulus in Asch's Study *After viewing display A, the subjects were told to pick the matching line from display B. The displays shown here are typical in that the correct decision is obvious.* (After Asch, 1958)

Resistance of Majority Opinion *(top)* All of the group members except the man sixth from the left are confederates previously instructed to give uniformly wrong answers on 12 of the 18 trials. Number 6, who has been told he is participating in an experiment in visual judgment, therefore finds himself a lone dissenter when he gives the correct answers. *(bottom left)* The subject, showing the strain of repeated disagreement with the majority, leans forward anxiously to look at the exhibit in question. *(bottom right)* This particular subject persists in his opinion, saying that "he has to call them as he sees them."

The results were striking. Even though the correct answer was always obvious, the average subject conformed to the group consensus on 32 percent of the critical trials, and 74 percent of the subjects conformed at least once. Moreover, the group did not have to be large to obtain such conformity. When Asch varied the size of the group from 2 to 16, he found that a group of 3 or 4 confederates was just as effective at producing conformity as were larger groups (Asch, 1958).

Why didn't the obviousness of the correct answer provide support for the individual's independence from the majority? Why isn't a person's confidence in his or her ability to make simple sensory judgments a strong force against conformity?

According to one line of argument, it is precisely the obviousness of the correct answer in the Asch experiment that produces the strong forces *toward* conformity (Ross, Bierbrauer, & Hoffman, 1976). Disagreements in real life typically involve difficult or subjective judgments such as which economic policy will best reduce inflation or which of two paintings is more aesthetically pleasing. In these cases, we expect to disagree with others occasionally; we even know that being a minority of one in an otherwise unanimous group is a plausible, if uncomfortable, possibility.

The Asch situation is much more extreme. Here the individual is confronted with unanimous disagreement about a simple physical fact, a bizarre and unprecedented occurrence that appears to have no rational explanation. Subjects are clearly puzzled and tense. They rub their eyes in disbelief and jump up to look more closely at the lines. They squirm, mumble, giggle in embarrassment, and look searchingly at others in the group for some clue to the mystery. After the experiment, they offer halfhearted hypotheses about optical illusions or suggest—quite aptly—that perhaps the first person occasionally made mistakes and each successive person followed suit because of conformity pressures (Asch, 1952).

Consider what it means to dissent from the majority under these circumstances. Just as the judgments of the group seem incomprehensible to the subject, so the subject believes that his or her dissent will be incomprehensible to the group. Group members will surely judge him or her to be incompetent, even out of touch with reality. Similarly, if the subject dissents repeatedly, this will seem to constitute a direct challenge to the group's competence, a challenge that requires enormous courage when one's own perceptual abilities are suddenly and inexplicably called into question. Such a challenge violates a strong social norm against insulting others. This fear of "What will they think of me?" and "What will they think I think of them?" inhibits dissent and generates the strong pressures to conform in the Asch situation.

Conformity pressures are far less strong when the group is not unanimous. If even one confederate breaks with the majority, the amount of conformity drops from 32 percent of the trials to about 6 percent. In fact, a group of eight containing only one dissenter produces less conformity than a unanimous majority of three (Asch, 1958). Surprisingly, the dissenter does not even have to give the correct answer. Even when the dissenter's answers are *more* incorrect than the majority's, the spell is broken and subjects are more inclined to give their own correct judgments (Asch, 1955; Allen & Levine, 1969). Nor does it matter who the dissenter is. A black dissenter reduces the conformity rate among racially prejudiced white subjects just as effectively as a white dissenter (Malof & Lott, 1962). [In a variation that approaches the absurd, conformity was significantly reduced even though the subjects thought the dissenter was so visually handicapped that he could not see the stimuli (Allen & Levine, 1971).] It seems clear that the presence of but one other deviant to share the potential disapproval or ridicule of the group permits the subject to dissent without feeling totally isolated. Social impact theory (see the previous Critical Discussion) would describe this as a result of diffusing the social forces over a large number of targets.

If Asch's conformity situation is unlike most situations in real life, why did Asch use a task in which the correct answer was obvious? The reason is that he wanted to study pure public conformity, uncontaminated by the possibility that subjects were actually changing their minds about the correct answers. In other words, he was investigating compliance, not internalization. Several variations of Asch's study have utilized more difficult or subjective judgments, and although they may reflect life more faithfully, they do not permit us to assess the effects of pure pressure to conform to a majority when we are certain that our own minority judgment is correct. (Ross, Bierbrauer, & Hoffman, 1976).

Obedience to Authority

In Nazi Germany from 1933 to 1945, millions of innocent people were systematically put to death in concentration camps. The mastermind of this horror, Adolph Hitler, may well have been a psychopathic monster. But he could not have done it alone. What about all those who ran the day-to-day operations, who built the ovens and gas chambers, filled them with human beings, counted bodies, and did the necessary paperwork? Were they all monsters, too?

Not according to social philosopher Hannah Arendt (1963), who covered the trial of Adolph Eichmann, a Nazi war criminal who was found guilty and was executed for causing the murder of millions of Jews. She described him as a dull, ordinary, unaggressive bureaucrat who saw himself as a little cog in a big machine. The recent publication of a partial transcript of Eichmann's pretrial interrogation supports Arendt's view. Several psychiatrists found Eichmann to be quite sane, and his personal relationships were quite normal. He sincerely believed that the Jews should have been allowed to emigrate to a separate territory and had argued that position within Hitler's security service. Moreover, he had a Jewish mistress in secret—a crime for an SS officer—and a Jewish half cousin whom he arranged to have protected during the war (Von Lang & Sibyll, 1983).

Arendt subtitled her book about Eichmann *A Report on the Banality of Evil* and concluded that most of the "evil men" of the Third Reich were just ordinary people following orders from superiors. This suggests that all of us might be capable of such evil and that Nazi Germany was an event less wildly alien from the normal human condition than we might like to think. As Arendt put it, "in certain circumstances the most ordinary decent person can become a criminal." This is not an easy conclusion to accept because it is more comforting to believe that monstrous evil is done only by monstrous persons. In fact, our emotional attachment to this explanation of evil was vividly shown by the intensity of the attacks on Arendt and her conclusions.

The problem of obedience to authority arose again in 1969, when a group of American soldiers serving in Vietnam killed a number of civilians in the community of My Lai, claiming that they were simply following orders. Again the public was forced to ponder the possibility that ordinary citizens are willing to obey authority in violation of their own moral consciences.

This issue was explored empirically in a series of important and controversial studies conducted by Stanley Milgram (1963; 1974) at Yale University. Ordinary men and women were recruited through a newspaper ad that offered four dollars for one hour's participation in a "study of memory." On

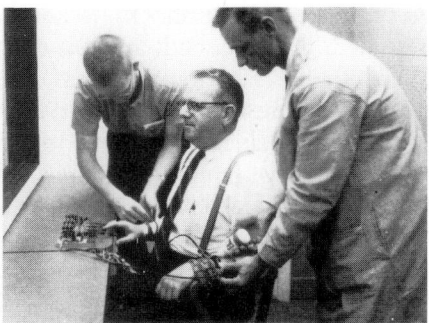

Milgram Experiment *(top left) The "shock generator" used in Milgram's experiment on obedience. (top right) The victim is strapped into the "electric chair." (bottom left) A subject receives the sample shock before starting the "teaching session." (bottom right) A subject refuses to go on with the experiment. Most subjects became deeply disturbed by the role they were asked to play, whether they continued in the experiment to the end or refused at some point to go on.* (From the film *Obedience*, distributed by New York University Film Library; copyright © 1965 by Stanley Milgram)

FIGURE 19-5
Milgram Obedience Experiment *The subject was told to give the learner a more intense shock after each error. If the subject objected, the experimenter insisted it was necessary to go on.* (After Milgram, 1974)

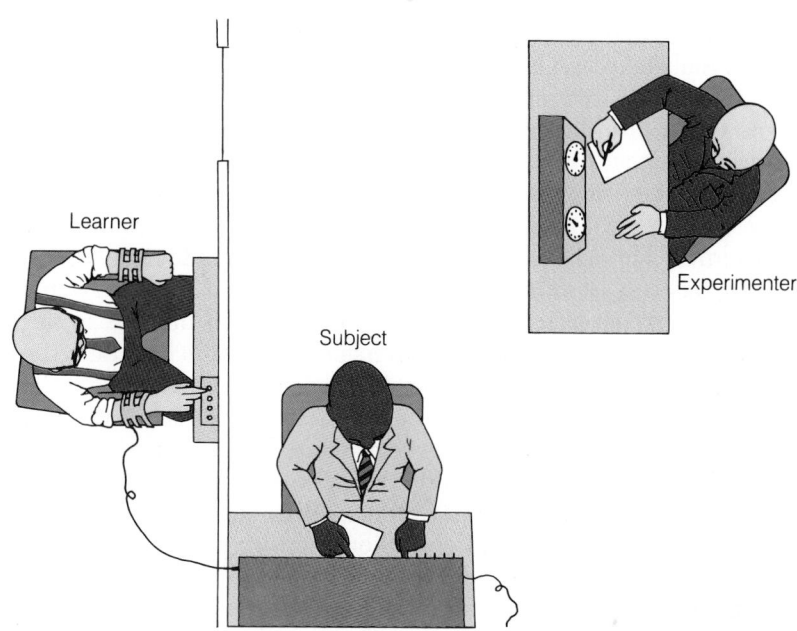

Learner

Subject

Experimenter

arriving at the laboratory, the subject was told that he or she would be playing the role of teacher in the study. The subject was to read a series of word pairs to another subject and then test that learner's memory by reading the first word of each pair and asking him to select the correct second word from four alternatives. Each time the learner made an error, the subject was to press a lever that delivered an electric shock to him.

The subject watched while the learner was strapped into an electrically wired chair and an electrode was attached to his wrist. The subject was then seated in an adjoining room in front of a shock generator whose front panel contained 30 lever switches set in a horizontal line. Each switch was labeled with a voltage rating, ranging in sequence from 15 to 450 volts, and groups of adjacent switches were labeled descriptively, ranging from "Slight Shock" up to "Danger: Severe Shock." When a switch was depressed, an electric buzz sounded, lights flashed, and the needle on a voltage meter deflected to the right. To illustrate how it worked, the subject was given a sample shock of 45 volts from the generator. As the procedure began, the experimenter instructed the subject to move one level higher on the shock generator after each successive error (see Figure 19-5).

The learner did not, of course, actually receive any shocks. He was a 47-year-old, mild-mannered accountant who had been specially trained for his role. As he began to make errors and the shock levels escalated, he could be heard protesting through the adjoining wall. As the shocks became stronger, he began to shout and curse. At 300 volts he began to kick the wall, and at the next shock level (marked "Extreme Intensity Shock"), he no longer answered the questions or made any noise. As you might expect, many subjects began to object to this excruciating procedure, pleading with the experimenter to call a halt. But the experimenter responded with a sequence of prods, using as many as necessary to get the subject to go on: "Please continue"; "The experiment requires that you continue"; "It is absolutely essential that you continue"; and "You have no other choice—you *must* go on." Obedience to authority was measured by the maximum amount of shock the subject would administer before refusing to continue.

Milgram found that 65 percent of the subjects continued to obey throughout, going all the way to the end of the shock series (450 volts). Not one subject stopped prior to administering 300 volts—the point at which the learner began to kick the wall (see Figure 19-6). What produces such obedience?

Milgram suggests that the potential for obedience to authority is such a necessary requirement for communal life that it has probably been built into our species by evolution. The division of labor in a society requires that individuals have the capacity to subordinate and coordinate their own independent actions to serve the goals and purposes of the larger social organization. Parents, school systems, and businesses all nurture this capacity further by reminding the individual about the importance of following the directives of others who "know the larger picture." To understand obedience in a particular situation, then, we need to understand the factors that persuade individuals to relinquish their autonomy and become voluntary agents of the system. Four such factors—social norms, surveillance, buffers, and ideological justification—are well illustrated in the Milgram experiments.

SOCIAL NORMS   By replying to the advertisement and agreeing to be in the study, subjects in Milgram's experiments had voluntarily assented to an implicit contract to cooperate with the experimenter, to follow the directions of the person in charge, and to see the job through to completion. This is a very strong social norm, and we tend to underestimate how difficult it is to break such an agreement and to go back on our implied word to cooperate.

The experiment was also designed to reinforce this norm by making it particularly difficult to stop once it had begun. The procedure starts rather innocently as an experiment in memory and then gradually escalates. Once subjects begin to give shocks and to raise the shock levels, there is no longer a natural stopping point. By the time they want to quit, they are trapped. The experimenter makes no new demands, only that they continue to do what they are already doing. In order to break off, they must suffer the guilt and embarrassment of acknowledging that they were wrong to begin at all. And the longer they put off quitting, the harder it is to admit their misjudgment in going as far as they have. It is easier to continue. Imagine how much less obedience there would be if subjects had to begin by giving the strongest shock first.

Finally, the potential quitter faces a dilemma over violating a social norm of etiquette (being polite) similar to the one confronting a subject in the Asch situation. Dissenting in that case implied that the subject thought the group was incompetent. Dissenting in the Milgram situation is equivalent to accusing the experimenter of being immoral—an even more compelling force that pushes the subject to stay in line and go along with the experiment.

If social norms like these can produce so much obedience in Milgram's studies, then it is easy to imagine how much more powerful the penalties for quitting would be in Nazi Germany or in military service once one has already "signed on."

SURVEILLANCE   An obvious factor in the Milgram experiment is the constant presence or surveillance of the experimenter. When the experimenter left the room and issued his orders by telephone, obedience dropped from 65 percent to 21 percent (Milgram, 1974). Moreover, several of the subjects who continued under these conditions cheated by administering

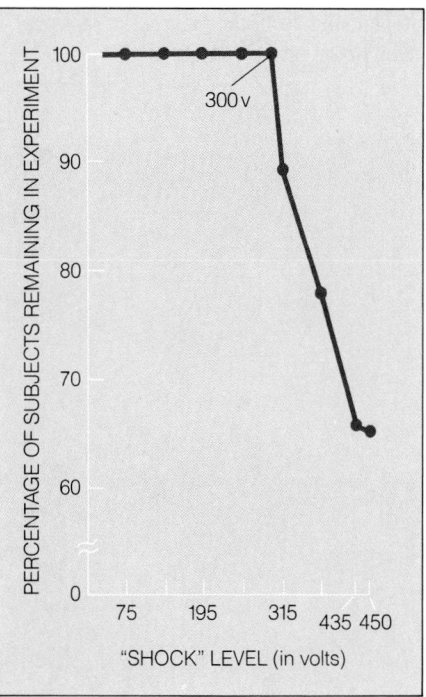

FIGURE 19-6
Obedience to Authority *The percentage of subjects willing to administer a punishing shock did not begin to decline until the intensity level of the shock reached 300 volts (the danger level). (After Milgram, 1963)*

Remoteness from the final act of violence: War Room of the Pentagon.

shocks of lower intensity than they were supposed to without telling the experimenter. In general, continued compliance rests on continuing surveillance, because the influencing agent is obtaining only public conformity from the target individual, not private acceptance. As we shall see in later sections, social influence based on processes of internalization or identification does not require surveillance for its maintenance.

BUFFERS   Milgram's subjects believed that they were committing acts of violence, but there were several buffers that obscured this fact or diluted the immediacy of the experience. For example, the learner was in the next room, out of sight and unable to communicate. Milgram reports that obedience drops from 65 percent to 40 percent if the learner is in the same room as the subject. If the subject must personally ensure that the learner holds his hand on the shock plate, obedience declines to 30 percent. The more direct the person's experience with the victim—the fewer buffers between the person and the consequences of his or her act, in other words—the less the person will obey.

The most common buffer found in warlike situations is the remoteness of the person from the final act of violence. Thus, Adolph Eichmann argued that he was not directly responsible for killing Jews; he merely arranged for their deaths indirectly. Milgram conducted an analogue to this "link-in-the-chain" situation by requiring a subject only to pull a switch that enabled another teacher (a confederate) to deliver the shocks to the learner. Under these conditions, obedience soared: a full 93 percent of the subjects continued to the end of the shock series. In this situation, the subject can shift the blame to the person who actually delivers the shock.

The shock generator itself served as a buffer—an impersonal mechanical agent that actually delivered the shock. Imagine how obedience would have declined if subjects were required to hit the learner with their fists. In real life, we have analogous technologies that permit us to destroy distant fellow humans by remote control, thereby removing us from the sight of their suffering. Although we probably all agree that it is worse to kill thousands of people by pushing a button that releases a guided missile than it is to beat one individual to death with a rock, it is still psychologically easier to push the button. Such are the effects of buffers.

IDEOLOGICAL JUSTIFICATION   The fourth and most important factor producing voluntary obedience is the individual's acceptance of an *ideology*—a set of beliefs and attitudes—that legitimates the authority of the person in charge and justifies following his or her directives. Nazi officers such as Eichmann believed in the primacy of the German state and hence in the legitimacy of orders issued in the name of its ideology. Similarly, the American soldiers who followed orders to shoot enemy civilians in Vietnam had already committed themselves to the premise that national security requires strict obedience to military commands.

In the Milgram experiments, the "importance of science" is the ideology that legitimates even quite extraordinary demands. Some critics of the Milgram experiments have argued that they were artificial, that the prestige of a scientific experiment led people to obey without questioning the dubious procedures in which they participated, and that people in real life would never do such a thing. Indeed, when Milgram repeated his experiment in a rundown set of offices and removed any association with Yale University from the setting, obedience dropped from 65 percent to 48 percent (Milgram, 1974).

But this criticism misses the major point. The prestige of science is not an irrelevant artificiality but an integral part of Milgram's demonstration. Science serves precisely the same legitimating role in the experiment that the German state served in Nazi Germany and that national security serves in wartime killing. A belief in the primacy of scientific research is the ideology that prompts individuals to relinquish their personal moral autonomy and to voluntarily subordinate their own independence to goals and purposes of a larger social organization.

Obedience to Authority in Everyday Life

Because the Milgram experiments have been criticized for being artificial (see Orne & Holland, 1968), it is instructive to look at an example of obedience to authority under more ordinary conditions. Researchers investigated whether nurses in public and private hospitals would obey an order that violated hospital rules and professional practice (Hofling et al., 1966). While on regular duty, the subject (a nurse) received a phone call from a doctor she knew to be on the staff but had not met: "This is Dr. Smith from Psychiatry calling. I was asked to see Mr. Jones this morning, and I'm going to have to see him again tonight. I'd like him to have had some medication by the time I get to the ward. Will you please check your medicine cabinet and see if you have some Astroten? That's ASTROTEN." When the nurse checked the medicine cabinet, she saw a pillbox labeled:

ASTROTEN

5 mg. capsules

Usual dose: 5 mg.

Maximum daily dose: 10 mg.

CRITICAL DISCUSSION

Power of Situational Influences

In Chapter 18, we saw that people typically overestimate the role of personal dispositional factors and underestimate the role of situational factors in controlling behavior—the *fundamental attribution error*. Studies on conformity and obedience illustrate this point—not through their results, but through our *surprise* at their results. We simply do not expect the situational forces to be as effective as they are. When college students are told about Milgram's procedures (but not given the results) and are asked whether they would continue to administer the shocks in the Milgram situation after the learner begins to pound on the wall, about 99 percent of the students say they would not (Aronson, 1988). Milgram himself surveyed psychiatrists at a leading medical school; they predicted that most subjects would refuse to go on after reaching 150 volts, that only about 4 percent would go beyond 300 volts, and that fewer than 1 percent would go all the way to 450 volts. In one study, subjects were asked to estimate obedience rates after they had reenacted the entire Milgram procedure, complete with shock apparatus and a tape recording of the protesting learner. Whether they played the role of the actual subject or the role of an observer, all subjects continued to vastly underestimate the compliance rates actually obtained by Milgram, as shown in the figure (Bierbrauer, 1973).

The nursing study on administering medication yields comparable results. When nurses who had not been subjects were given a complete description of the situation and asked how they themselves would respond, 83 percent reported that they would not have given the medication, and most of them thought a majority of nurses would also refuse. Of 21 nursing students asked the same question, all of them reported that they would not have given the medication as ordered.

There is an amusing footnote to the nursing study. The study was conducted and reported by psychiatrists, and they offer a psychoanalytic explanation for the nurses' compliance—complete with references to Oedipal feelings that female nurses are likely to have for male doctors. Most contemporary social psychologists are likely to regard such dispositional talk as superfluous—even silly—and to believe that the situational forces in this study are quite sufficient to account for the 95 percent compliance rate observed. In short, they are likely to believe that the authors of the nursing study are themselves committing the fundamental attribution error.

In sum, our *reactions* to conformity and obedience experiments dramatically illustrate a major lesson of social psychology: we seriously underestimate the extent and power of social and situational forces on human behavior.

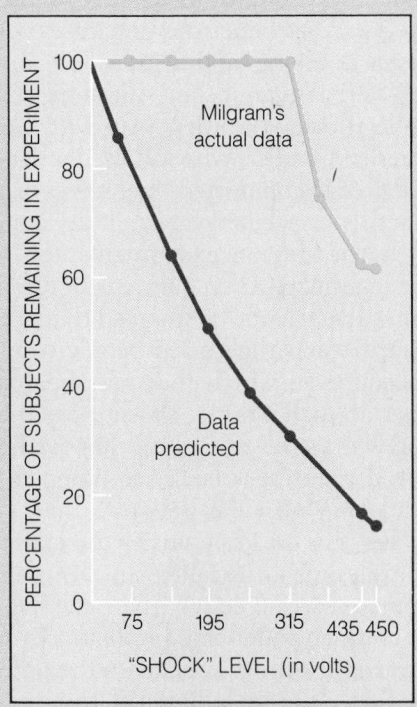

Predicted and Actual Compliance *The upper curve presents the Milgram data and shows the percentage of subjects who remained obedient in the situation, continuing to administer shocks as the voltage increased. The lower curve is from a study in which role-playing subjects participated in a reenactment of the Milgram experiment and attempted to predict what percentage of the actual subjects would continue to be obedient as shock increased. The role-playing subjects vastly underestimated the magnitude of the situational forces and the likelihood of obedience in the Milgram situation. (After Bierbrauer, 1973)*

After she reported that she had found it, the doctor continued, "Now will you please give Mr. Jones a dose of 20 milligrams of Astroten. I'll be up within 10 minutes; I'll sign the order then, but I'd like the drug to have started taking effect." A staff psychiatrist, posted unobtrusively nearby, terminated each trial by disclosing its true nature when the nurse either poured the medication (actually a harmless placebo), refused to accept the order, or tried to contact another professional.

This order violated several rules. The dose was clearly excessive. Medication orders are not permitted to be given by telephone. The medication was unauthorized—that is, it was not on the ward stock list clearing it for use. Finally, the order was given by an unfamiliar person. Despite all this, 95 percent of the nurses started to give the medication. Moreover, the telephone calls were all brief, and the nurses put up little or no resistance. None of them insisted on a written order, although several sought reassurance that the doctor would arrive promptly. In interviews after the experiment, all the nurses stated that such orders had been received in the past and that doctors became annoyed if the nurses balked.

Rebellion

One reason compliance experiments generate so much conformity and obedience may be that the social pressures in these studies are directed toward a lone individual. According to social impact theory, social influence will be less powerful if it is diffused over many target individuals, suggesting that a group of individuals might be less susceptible to it—perhaps even showing a bit of rebellion. We have already seen some data to support this suggestion: a subject in the Asch conformity situation is less likely to go along with the group's incorrect judgments if there is at least one other dissenter.

A similar phenomenon occurs in the Milgram obedience situation. In one variation of the procedure, two additional confederates were employed. They were introduced as subjects who would also play teacher roles. Teacher 1 would read the list of word pairs; Teacher 2 would tell the learner if he was right or wrong; and Teacher 3 (the subject) would deliver the shocks. The confederates complied with the instructions through the 150-volt shock, at which point Teacher 1 informed the experimenter that he was quitting. Despite the experimenter's insistence that he continue, Teacher 1 got up from his chair and sat in another part of the room. After the 210-volt shock, Teacher 2 also quit. The experimenter then turned to the subject and ordered him to continue alone. Only 10 percent of the subjects were willing to complete the series in this situation. In a second variation, there were two experimenters rather than two additional teachers. After a few shocks, they began to argue—one of them saying that they should stop the experiment; the other saying they should continue. Under these circumstances, not a single subject would continue despite the orders to do so by the second experimenter (Milgram, 1974).

In these variations, the instigation to nonconformity or disobedience came from planted confederates. A more recent experiment explored the possibility that groups of subjects with no confederates present would be moved to rebel against unjust authority. Citizens from a nonuniversity community were recruited by phone for 10 dollars to spend 2 hours at a local Holiday Inn assisting in research on "group standards" sponsored by a fictitious company, the Manufacturer's Human Relations Consultants, or MHRC (Gamson, Fireman, & Rytina, 1982). Nine subjects, both male and female, were recruited for each group session. When they arrived, they were given a letter explaining that legal cases sometimes hinge on the notion of community standards and that MHRC collects evidence on such standards by bringing together concerned citizens for group discussion. The subjects were then seated in front of video cameras and microphones at a U-shaped table, where they filled out a background questionnaire and signed a "participation agreement" giving MHRC permission to videotape them as they engaged in group discussion. The man in charge, who introduced himself as the coordinator, then read the background of a pending court case. The basic facts were as follows:

> A service station manager was suing an oil company because it had canceled the franchise on his service station. The oil company had conducted an investigation of the man and discovered that he was living with a woman to whom he was not married. The company claimed that his life-style violated the moral standards of the local community and that he would therefore not be able to maintain good relations with customers; accordingly, they decided to revoke his franchise license. The man sued for breach of contract and invasion of privacy, arguing that the company was out to get him because he had publicly criticized the company's gas pricing policies in a local television interview.

After presenting the case, the coordinator asked the group to discuss it while being videotaped. After a general discussion, the cameras were turned off and the group was given a short break. Before resuming the videotaping, the coordinator requested three of the group members to argue as if they were personally offended by the station manager's life-style. This second discussion was taped, there was another break, and three additional individuals were designated to argue in the same way in the next discussion. Finally, the coordinator asked each individual to go on camera alone and voice objections to the station manager's affair, stating an intention to boycott the station, and arguing that the manager should lose his franchise. Group members were also told that they would be asked to sign notarized affidavits giving MHRC the right to introduce the tapes as evidence in court after editing them as it saw fit.

As MHRC's motives began to dawn on them, all but one of the 33 groups in this experiment began to dissent: "Can you assure us that the court is going to know these aren't our real opinions?"; "Would you mind leaving the tape on while you give us these instructions, so that it doesn't appear . . ."; "Do these professional people know what you're doing in fact is suborning perjury?" (Gamson, Fireman, & Rytina, 1982, pp. 62, 65). One group even decided to take direct action by gathering up materials from the table and taking them to the local newspaper.

Overall, 16 of the 33 groups rebelled completely—all members refused to sign the final affidavit—and a majority refused to do so in 9 additional groups. Only a minority refused in the remaining 8 groups, although a number of dissenting comments were voiced. Compared to the Milgram situation, then, obedience to authority had clearly been undermined in this study. But why?

The two studies differ in several respects, so we cannot be certain that the important difference was having a group rather than a lone individual as the target. Nevertheless, this seems to be the most likely factor. In fact, the circumstances producing rebellion in the MHRC study appear to be the same ones we have seen operating in other group contexts: defining the situation and conformity.

In the bystander intervention studies, we noted that individuals in a group define an ambiguous situation for one another. Subjects in the MHRC study were given ample opportunity during the breaks to define and clarify the situation for one another by sharing their suspicions of MHRC's motives. Some of the comments were "How are people going to know that these aren't our opinions?"; "We don't want to be faced with the situation where you read in the *New York Times* one day that thanks to a new method of litigation [group laughter] that this poor schnook [group laughter] lost his license" (Gamson, Fireman, & Rytina, 1982, pp. 101, 102).

The preliminary questionnaires also indicated that 80 to 90 percent of the subjects initially disagreed with the position they were asked to take: they were quite tolerant of an unmarried man and woman living together; they were critical of large oil companies; and they believed that an employee's private life was none of a company's business. The group members could also share these opinions with one another. The researchers compared the 23 groups in which a majority of subjects initially held dissenting opinions with the 10 groups that initially held fewer dissenting opinions. They found that 65 percent of the former groups produced complete rebellion—nobody signed the affidavits—whereas only 10 percent of the latter groups rebelled completely. A majority of the groups also contained some individuals who had been active in past protests and strikes, and these groups were also more likely to rebel than groups without such role models. Lone subjects in the Milgram obedience studies obviously had none of these opportunities for sharing information, receiving social support for dissent, or seeing role models for disobedience.

But before we congratulate the human species for heroic independence and autonomy in the face of social pressure, we should consider the implication of these findings more closely. They suggest that many of the individuals in the groups were not choosing between obedience and autonomy but between obedience and conformity: obey the coordinator or conform to the developing group norm to disobey. As the researchers observed, "Many were uncertain at this point, waiting to see what others would do, delaying decision as long as possible. Ultimately, they were faced with an unavoidable choice—to sign or not to sign—and loyalty to the group became one major factor in their decision." They also report that some who had already signed the affidavit crossed out their names or tore up the form. As one subject told the coordinator, "I didn't personally say anything I didn't believe, but I'm not going to sign this either, if the rest of the group isn't signing" (Gamson, Fireman, & Rytina, 1982, p. 99).

Obeying or conforming may not strike you as a very heroic choice. But these are among the processes that provide the social glue for the human species. Several years before this study was conducted, a social historian noted that "disobedience when it is not criminally but morally, religiously or politically motivated is always a collective act and it is justified by the values of the collectivity and the mutual engagements of its members" (Walzer, 1970, p. 4).

INTERNALIZATION

Individuals are said to comply when they change their behavior in accordance with the wishes of a source of influence who exercises power and maintains continued surveillance over the individual. But in everyday life, most sources of influence strive to obtain change that the individual "believes in" and that will therefore sustain itself after the source has departed. Such change is called *internalization*. Certainly the major goal of parents, educators, clergy, politicians, and advertisers is internalization, not just compliance. In general, internalization is obtained by an influence source who

Billy Graham is one of the clergy's most persuasive spokesmen.

either a) presents a persuasive message that is itself compelling, or b) is perceived by the individual as credible, possessing both expertise and trustworthiness. In this section, we examine processes of influence designed to persuade rather than coerce.

Minority Influence

A number of European scholars have been critical of social psychological research in North America because of its preoccupation with conformity and the influence of the majority on the minority. As they correctly point out, intellectual innovation, social change, and political revolution often occur because an informed and articulate minority—sometimes a minority of one—begins to convert others to its point of view (Moscovici, 1976). Why not study innovation and the influence that minorities can have on the majority?

To make their point, these European investigators deliberately began their experimental work by setting up a laboratory situation virtually identical to Asch's conformity situation. Subjects were asked to make a series of simple perceptual judgments in the face of confederates who consistently gave the incorrect answer. But instead of placing a single subject in the midst of several confederates, these investigators planted two confederates, who consistently gave incorrect responses, in the midst of four real subjects. The experimenters found that the minority was able to influence about 32 percent of the subjects to make at least one incorrect judgment. For this to occur, however, the minority had to remain consistent throughout the experiment. If they wavered or showed any inconsistency in their judgments, they were unable to influence the majority (Moscovici, Lage, & Naffrechoux, 1969).

Since this initial demonstration of minority influence, many additional studies have been conducted in both Europe and North America, including several that required groups to debate social and political issues rather than to make simple perceptual judgments. The general finding is that minorities can move majorities toward their point of view if they present a consistent position without appearing rigid, dogmatic, or arrogant. Such minorities are perceived to be more confident and, occasionally, more competent than the majority (Maass & Clark, 1984). Minorities are also more effective if they argue a position that is consistent with the developing social norms of the larger society. For example, in two experiments in which feminist issues were discussed, subjects were moved significantly more by a minority position that was in line with recent social norms (feminist) than by one opposed to these new norms (antifeminist) (Paicheler, 1976, 1977).

But the most interesting finding from this research is that the majority members in these studies show internalization—a change of private attitudes—not just compliance or public conformity. In fact, minorities sometimes obtain internalization from majority members even when they fail to obtain public conformity. In one study, groups of subjects read a purported summary of a group discussion of gay rights held by five undergraduates like themselves. In all cases four discussants had favored one position and a minority of one had consistently favored the opposite position. In some discussions, the majority had been for gay rights and the minority against; in other discussions, the majority and minority positions were reversed. After reading the summary, subjects voiced considerable public agreement with the majority view—regardless of whether it had been for or against gay rights—but

Action by a minority can change the attitude of the majority.

written ratings revealed that opinions had shifted toward the minority position (Maass & Clark, 1983).

These findings serve to remind us that the majorities of the world typically have the social power to approve and disapprove, to accept or reject, and it is this power that can obtain compliance. In contrast, minorities rarely have such social power. But if they have credibility, then they have the power to produce internalization and, hence, innovation, social change, and revolution.

Processes of Persuasion

Just as the practices of Nazi Germany under Hitler prompted social psychologists to be interested in obedience to authority, so propaganda efforts on both sides in World War II prompted them to study persuasion. Intensive research began in the late 1940s at Yale University, where investigators sought to determine the characteristics of successful persuasive communicators, successful communications, and the kinds of persons who are most easily persuaded (Hovland, Janis, & Kelley, 1953). As research on these topics continued over the years, a number of interesting phenomena were discovered but few general principles emerged. The results became increasingly complex and difficult to summarize, and every conclusion seemed to require several "it-depends" qualifications. Recently, however, the situation has improved markedly. Social psychology's contemporary interest in information processing (see Chapter 18) has stimulated new thinking about persuasion and has given rise to theories that provide a more unified framework for understanding its many complexities.

COGNITIVE RESPONSE THEORY   Among the new approaches to persuasion are several variations of *cognitive response theory*. This theory proposes that persuasion induced by a communication is actually self-persuasion produced by the thoughts that the person generates while reading, listening to, or even just anticipating the communication. These thoughts can be about the content of the communication itself or about other aspects of the situation, such as the credibility of the communicator. If the communication evokes thoughts supportive of the position being advocated, the individual will move toward that position; if the communication evokes unsupportive thoughts (such as counterarguments or disparaging thoughts about the communicator), the individual will remain unconvinced or even *boomerang*—shift away from the position being advocated (Greenwald, 1968; Petty, Ostrom, & Brock, 1981).

A number of studies support this theory. In one, each subject read a communication containing arguments on a controversial issue and wrote a one-sentence reaction (cognitive response) to each argument. One week later the subjects were unexpectedly given a memory test asking them to recall both the arguments in the communication and their written reactions to those arguments. Subjects' opinions on the issue were assessed both before receiving the communication and then, again, at the time of the memory test 1 week later. The results showed that the amount of opinion change produced by the communication was significantly correlated with both the supportiveness of subjects' reactions to the communication and to subjects' later recall of those reactions, but it was *not* significantly correlated with subjects' recall of the arguments themselves (Love & Greenwald, 1978). This experiment not only supports the theory, but also explains what had previously been a puzzling observation—that the persistence of opinion change is often unrelated to an individual's memory for the arguments that produced that change.

Cognitive response theory also proposes that a persuasive communication will be *unsuccessful* to the extent that the target individual is both motivated to generate counterarguments against the position being advocated and has the ability and opportunity to do so. As we shall now see, this proposal provides a unified explanation for several long-standing phenomena of persuasion.

ONE-SIDED VERSUS TWO-SIDED COMMUNICATION   A tactical decision facing any persuasive communicator is whether to present only the side of the issue favorable to his or her conclusions or to present both sides of the issue and to argue explicitly against the opposing side. This was explored empirically as early as 1945 by psychologists in the United States Army's Information and Education Division. After the Allies had defeated Germany in World War II, the Army did not want soldiers to be overconfident about the ease of defeating the Japanese, with whom the United States was still at war. The psychologists designed two radio broadcasts that argued that the war would last at least 2 more years. One broadcast presented only arguments in favor of that conclusion. The other broadcast presented arguments on both sides; for example, it raised and responded to the counterargument that the United States now had the advantage of fighting the war on only one front.

The researchers found that for soldiers who already agreed that the war would last a long time, the one-sided broadcast was *more* effective than the two-sided broadcast. The two-sided broadcast apparently alerted them to counterarguments they would not have thought of otherwise and thus weakened the effect of the broadcast. But for soldiers who initially disagreed with the communication's conclusion, the one-sided broadcast was *less* effective (Hovland, Lumsdaine, & Sheffield, 1949). These soldiers already possessed a set of counterarguments that they could generate while hearing the broadcast. Moreover, they were more likely to perceive the one-sided broadcast as biased and hence to generate unfavorable thoughts about its credibility. Later research has shown that just being aware that opposing arguments exist renders a one-sided communication less persuasive than a two-sided one (Jones & Brehm, 1970).

There is an additional advantage to two-sided communications. Regardless of whether they agree or disagree with the position advocated, individuals exposed to two-sided communications are more resistant to later counterpropaganda than are individuals exposed to one-sided communications (Lumsdaine & Janis, 1953). Two-sided communications not only expose individuals to counterarguments but to the refutations of those counterarguments as well, giving those individuals a new set of contrary cognitive responses to generate when later exposed to communications from the opposing side.

Learning how to generate counterarguments can inoculate young people against peer pressure to use drugs.

INOCULATION AGAINST PERSUASION   As we have just seen, two-sided communications can serve to immunize an individual's newly acquired opinions against counterattack. Psychologist William McGuire decided to pursue this biological analogy by asking whether it was possible to inoculate people against persuasion as we inoculate them against a virus. Would a weak attack on an individual's beliefs stimulate him or her to marshal counterarguments against a full blown attack the same way a vaccination containing a weakened form of a virus stimulates the body to produce antibodies against it?

To perform this feat, McGuire needed "germ free" beliefs—beliefs that had not previously been exposed to attack. For this purpose, he selected *cultural truisms*, beliefs that are so widely believed that nobody thinks of questioning them (for example, "It's a good idea to brush your teeth after every meal if at all possible"). First, he confirmed that attacking such beliefs with strong arguments could markedly diminish an individual's belief in them. (Did you know that the American Dental Association has warned that too much toothbrushing can damage your gums?) He then showed that subjects who first received a mild attack on their belief in a truism and then read or wrote an essay refuting this attack were better able to resist a subsequent strong attack. Moreover, this inoculation defense was more effective than a supportive defense in which subjects simply read paragraphs presenting arguments in favor of the truism. This was seen as analogous to giving a person vitamins to bolster the body's general resistance (Papageorgis & McGuire, 1961; McGuire & Papageorgis, 1961; McGuire, 1964).

FOREWARNING   Mildly attacking individuals' beliefs is not the only way to stimulate them to marshal counterarguments against persuasion. A simple *forewarning* that they are about to receive a communication with which they will disagree is also sufficient. Even a warning issued only 2 minutes before receiving the communication is sufficient to produce resistance to it (Freedman & Sears, 1965; Hass & Grady, 1975), and research shows that forewarned subjects do, in fact, utilize this time to construct counterarguments (Petty & Cacioppo, 1977). Unwarned subjects will also show resistance to a communication if they are simply instructed to list their thoughts on the topic beforehand. This demonstrates that it is not forewarning per se that induces resistance to a communication but the anticipatory thinking about the topic.

PRACTICAL APPLICATIONS   As we noted earlier, social psychologists initiated research on persuasion in response to practical problems involved in the prosecution of World War II. Although much of the subsequent research has been conducted in laboratories, exposing college students to communications on relatively unimportant issues, there has always been an interest in the practical applications of the findings. Cognitive response theory is no exception.

For example, one education program has been designed to inoculate junior high-school students against peer pressure to smoke. High-school students conducted sessions in which they taught seventh-graders how to generate counterarguments. For example, in role-playing sessions they were taught to respond to being called "chicken" for not taking a cigarette by saying things like "I'd be a real chicken if I smoked just to impress you." They were also taught to respond to advertisements implying that liberated women smoke by saying, "She's not really liberated if she is hooked on tobacco." Several inoculation sessions were held during seventh and eighth grades, and records were kept of how many of the students smoked from the beginning of the study through the ninth grade. The results show that inoculated students were half as likely to smoke as students at a matched junior high school that used a more typical smoking education program (McAlister, Perry, Killen, Slinkard, & Maccoby, 1980). Similar programs have been designed to inoculate elementary-school children against being taken in by deceptive television commercials (Cohen, 1980; Feshbach, 1980).

CENTRAL VERSUS PERIPHERAL ROUTES OF PERSUASION Although research on cognitive response theory has focused primarily on the individual's thoughts about the substantive arguments in a communication, the individual may also respond to other features of the situation—such as cues about the communicator's credibility. Richard Petty and John Cacioppo, two major contributors to cognitive response theory, have recently clarified the persuasion domain even further by demonstrating the importance of distinguishing between two routes that persuasion can take in producing belief and attitude change (Petty & Cacioppo, 1981; 1986).

Persuasion is said to follow the *central route* when the individual responds to substantive information about the issue under consideration. This can be information contained in the persuasive communication itself or information that is part of the individual's preexisting knowledge. Most of the research on cognitive response theory explores this route. Persuasion is said to follow the *peripheral route* when the individual responds instead to noncontent cues in a communication (such as the sheer number of arguments it contains) or to cues in the communication context (such as the credibility of the communicator or the pleasantness of the surroundings).

As we have seen, the central route to persuasion is available only when the individual is both motivated to generate thoughts in response to the substantive contents of a communication and has the ability and opportunity to do so. The peripheral route is available when the individual is unable or unwilling to put in the cognitive work required to process the content of the communication. Several factors can influence which route will be available. One such factor is personal involvement. If a communication addresses an issue in which the individual has a personal stake, he or she is more likely to attend carefully to the arguments. In such a case, the individual is also likely to have a rich store of prior information and opinion on the issue—which can provide many cognitive responses to the communication. On the other hand, if an issue has no personal relevance for the individual, he or she is not likely to make much of an effort either to support or to refute arguments about it. What happens then?

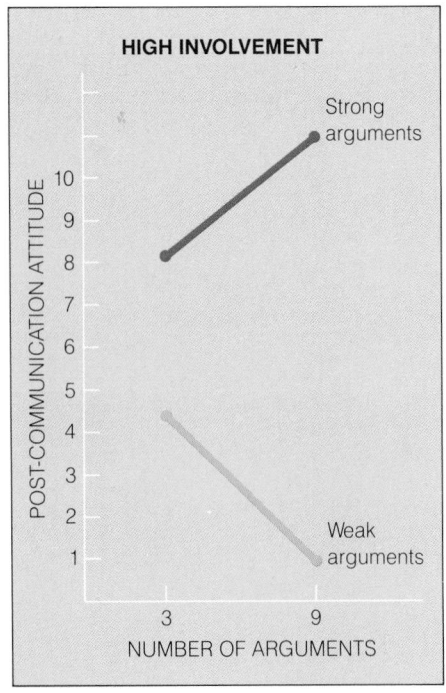

FIGURE 19-7
Post-Communication Attitudes *When subjects have high involvement in the issue, nine strong arguments produce* more *agreement with the essay than three strong arguments but nine weak arguments produce* less *agreement than three weak arguments.* (After Petty & Cacioppo, 1984)

According to one recent theory, when we are unwilling or unable to process the content of a communication, we may utilize simple rules of thumb—called *heuristics*—to infer the validity of its arguments. Examples of such rules might include "Messages with many arguments are more likely to be valid than messages with few arguments"; "Politicians always lie"; or "College professors know what they are talking about." This is called a *heuristic theory* of persuasion (Chaiken, 1980; Eagly & Chaiken, 1984). (In Chapter 18, we called such heuristics *scripts* and demonstrated that they permit us to process information efficiently but mindlessly—that is, without really paying attention to its content.)

This entire line of reasoning has been tested in several studies. In one rather complex study, college undergraduates read an essay allegedly written by the chairperson of a university committee charged with advising the chancellor on changes in academic policy. The essay advocated that the university institute a comprehensive examination that every undergraduate would have to pass in his or her major field before being permitted to graduate. In order to manipulate the personal involvement of the students in the issue, half of them were told that any policy changes adopted by the chancellor would be instituted the following year (high involvement), whereas the other half were told that any changes would take effect in 10 years (low involvement). Different forms of the essay were also used. Some contained strong arguments; others contained weak arguments. Some contained only three arguments; others contained nine.

The post-communication attitudes of students in the high-involvement conditions are shown in Figure 19-7. It can be seen that strong arguments produced more favorable attitudes overall than did weak arguments. But more importantly, nine strong arguments produced *greater* agreement with the essay than did three strong arguments, whereas nine weak arguments produced *less* agreement with the essay than did three weak arguments. How do the theories account for these patterns?

The theory about routes of persuasion predicts that students in the high-involvement conditions will be motivated to process the essay's substantive arguments and thus generate topic-relevant cognitive responses. This is the central route of persuasion, the route that cognitive response theory is designed to handle. Specifically, the theory predicts that strong arguments will evoke more supportive cognitive responses and fewer counterarguments than will weak arguments and will thus produce more agreement with the essay—as, indeed, they did. Moreover, nine strong arguments should be more persuasive than three strong arguments because the more strong arguments the individual encounters, the more supportive cognitive responses he or she will generate. In contrast, nine weak arguments should be *less* persuasive than three weak arguments because the more weak arguments the individual encounters, the more counterarguments he or she will generate. These predictions accord with the findings displayed in Figure 19-7.

As shown in Figure 19-8, a very different pattern emerges for students in the low-involvement conditions. Here the theory about routes of persuasion predicts that students in the low-involvement conditions will not be motivated to scrutinize the essay's arguments closely and will instead rely on simple heuristics to evaluate its merits and form their attitudes. This is the peripheral route, the route that the heuristic theory of persuasion is designed to handle. Specifically, the theory suggests that an individual in this setting will not even bother to determine whether the arguments are strong or weak but will simply invoke the heuristic rule: "Messages with many arguments are more likely to be valid than messages with few arguments." Thus, strong

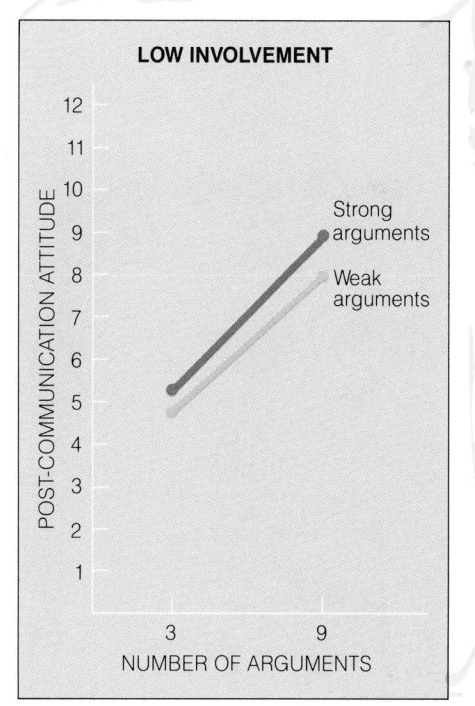

FIGURE 19-8
Post-Communication Attitudes *When subjects have low involvement in the issue, nine arguments produce more agreement than three arguments, regardless of whether the arguments are strong or weak.*

arguments will be no more effective than weak arguments, and nine arguments will be more persuasive than three arguments—regardless of whether they are strong or weak. This is precisely the pattern shown in Figure 19-8: overall, there were no significant differences between strong and weak arguments, but nine arguments were more effective than three arguments in both conditions (Petty & Cacioppo, 1984).

An experiment that varied the expertise of the communicator rather than the number of arguments found similar results: whereas subjects in the high-involvement conditions were more influenced by the strength of the arguments, subjects in the low-involvement conditions relied more on the heuristic "Arguments made by an expert are more valid than arguments made by a nonexpert" (Petty, Cacioppo, & Goldman, 1981).

The complexity of the results in these studies should give you some idea of how chaotic the findings from persuasion research must have appeared before the recent theories imposed some order on them. The findings remain complex, but at least they now fall into some sensible patterns.

Mass Media Persuasion

The mass media have had an enormous effect on our society. Television, in particular, has become a potent social presence in our lives. By age 16, the average child has spent more time in front of the television set than in the classroom (Waters & Malamud, 1975), and it is estimated that one-third of all American adults watch an average of 4 or more hours of television per day (Gerbner & Gross, 1976). Understandably, many people have been concerned about the influences of the mass media on our beliefs, attitudes, and behaviors. In Chapter 11 we discussed the effects of television violence on behavior. Here we look at the success of media persuasion.

Given the amount of money that companies and candidates spend on television advertising, one would conclude that persuasion via the mass media must be very effective. But it depends on how you look at it. In a highly competitive market or in a close political campaign, a competitive edge of a few percentage points makes an enormous difference. Media advertising can sometimes provide that extra edge. It can also create knowledge of and demand for a new product or create name recognition for a political unknown. Finally, intense long-term media promotion can help a group of manufacturers dominate a particular market, even though they are in close competition.

An example of this is provided by pharmaceutical advertising. Despite repeated medical findings that all nonprescription pain relievers provide the same amount of relief, equally fast and with equal safety, the market is totally dominated by three or four heavily advertised national brands (Consumers Union, 1980). Such advertising costs money, and these national brands cost consumers up to seven times more than the unadvertised brands available in virtually every drug store and supermarket. If you use one of these well-known brands, your headache dollar is spent primarily for the privilege of being persuaded to spend it, and you have first-hand knowledge that media persuasion is effective (Bem, 1970). But before concluding that you are simply gullible, you should note that the issue of which pain reliever to use is a very low-involvement issue. There is no compelling reason to expend considerable cognitive effort in order to evaluate the claims made in the commercials. Even expensive brands require a relatively small financial outlay, and it is efficient to rely on some simple heuristic like "Nationally advertised brands are probably safe and effective. Why take chances on an unknown

John F. Kennedy and Richard M. Nixon meet just prior to the first television debate of the 1960 presidential campaign.

brand?" If we really cared about the issue, we would be willing to invest more cognitive effort—by reading *Consumer Reports*, for example—in order to be better informed.

In general, when one examines how small a proportion of its intended audience mass media persuasion affects or how little it affects a single individual's beliefs or attitudes on important issues, the effectiveness of media persuasion looks unimpressive. For example, after an intensive image-building campaign for the oil industry, 13 percent of the sample surveyed had become more favorable, but 9 percent had become less favorable (Watson, 1966). During the 1960 presidential campaign, 55 percent of the adult population watched the first presidential campaign debates (between John F. Kennedy and Richard M. Nixon); 80 percent watched at least one of the debates. Moreover, there was a clear perception among journalists that Kennedy won the debates. But research surveys showed that there were no substantial changes in votes as a result of the debates (Katz & Feldman, 1962). The 1980 debate between Jimmy Carter and Ronald Reagan was held 1 week before the presidential election and is often cited as a major influence in Reagan's last minute victorious surge. But a CBS News poll taken immediately after the debate showed that only 7 percent of viewers changed their preference from Carter to Reagan and 1 percent of Reagan's supporters moved to Carter. Again, in a close race such tiny percentages can be important, but they do not reveal a significant influence on the part of the mass media. Why aren't the mass media more influential?

NOBODY IS WATCHING   Perhaps the most mundane, but most critical, reason that media influence is so limited is that only a small proportion of the target audience is watching or paying attention. For example, even though the Nielsen ratings show that the average household has a television set on almost 7 hours per day, one study found that 19 percent of the time the television set was on, nobody was in the room, and an additional 21 percent of the time people were in the room but no one was watching. Even when

This scene, from a television commercial sponsored by the Stanford Heart Disease Prevention Program, features a local man who reports that he can now run marathon races after having lost 60 pounds.

people were watching, they were often doing other things, including ironing, playing games, talking on the telephone, and dancing (Comstock et al., 1978).

Moreover, with the exception of events such as the presidential debates, most political news and advertising reach only a tiny proportion of the population. A majority of adult Americans do not see any national news broadcast in an average 2-week period (Robinson, 1971). Even those who do watch fail to retain much of what they see. One telephone survey found that viewers could recall fewer than 2 of the 20 news stories covered on the national news earlier in the evening. Even when reminded of the stories, viewers still could not remember having heard half of them (Neuman, 1976).

SELECTIVE EXPOSURE   A second reason the media fail to change our beliefs and attitudes is that we are more likely to be exposed to opinions we already agree with. Democrats listen mainly to speeches by Democrats; Republicans, to speeches by Republicans. Liberals read *The New Republic* but are unlikely to read *The National Review*. Research shows that most selective exposure is unintentional; we simply tend to be around sources of information that support our views. The conservative business person probably reads the *Wall Street Journal* because he or she is interested in business news; the fact that it also supports his or her political views is incidental. Again, the major obstacle facing a would-be persuader is to get the message to us in the first place.

SELECTIVE ATTENTION   Even the persuader who does get the message to us cannot control very well how we attend to it. This was shown in two clever experiments in which subjects listened to persuasive communications that were difficult to hear because of static in the sound channel. In order to hear the message more clearly the subject could push a button that removed the static (Brock & Balloun, 1967; Kleinhesselink & Edwards, 1975). The subjects were more likely to remove the static from messages that supported their views than from messages that did not. For example, students who were strongly in favor of legalizing marijuana removed the static from neutral messages, from messages supporting legalization, and even from messages opposing legalization with arguments that were easy to refute; but they let the static interfere when the messages opposed legalization with arguments that were difficult to refute (Kleinhesselink & Edwards, 1975).

SELECTIVE INTERPRETATION   Even when we listen carefully to a message, we are likely to interpret it in the context of our own beliefs and attitudes. Political figures learn to state their positions—or nonpositions—with enough ambiguity so that the maximum number of people can interpret the message as agreeing with their own position. Moreover, messages from sources we already agree with will be perceived as more supportive of our own positions than they might actually be. For example, in presidential elections, voters tend to see the positions taken by the presidential candidates they prefer as being more consistent with their own views than they actually are (Granberg & Brent, 1974).

A SUCCESSFUL COUNTEREXAMPLE   It is clear that the mass media are not going to brainwash us. When we consider the many obstacles a would-be persuader faces in trying to reach us, it is a wonder that mass media persuasion works at all. But in some cases these obstacles have been overcome, as the following study demonstrates.

In 1972, the Stanford Heart Disease Prevention Program launched a three-community field study to see if people could be persuaded to alter their exercise, smoking, and dietary habits in the interest of reducing their risk of heart disease (Maccoby, Farquhar, Wood, & Alexander, 1977). This was a collaborative effort involving social psychologists, communication experts, media production people, and cardiovascular disease specialists. Note that such an effort not only faces the usual obstacles of media persuasion already discussed, but it also requires people to change deeply embedded habits, such as smoking and overeating. Accordingly, the research team put everything they knew about persuasion, communication, and behavior modification into the program.

Two northern California communities (each with a population of about 13,000) were selected to be the experimental communities; and a third community, similar to the others, served as the control. A randomly selected sample of about 400 people in each of the three communities was surveyed before, during, and after the 2-year study in order to assess the effects of the campaign. Over the 2 years, the entire population of the experimental communities was exposed to about 3 hours of television programs, over 50 television spot announcements, 100 radio spots, several hours of radio programming, weekly newspaper columns, and newspaper advertisements and stories that dealt with heart disease and its prevention. Posters were put up in buses, stores and worksites, and printed material was sent via direct mail to the participants. The campaign was presented in both English and Spanish.

The research team found that the level of knowledge about risk factors associated with heart disease increased dramatically in the two experimental communities, showing about a 30 percent increase, compared with about a 6 percent increase for the control community (Maccoby, Farquhar, Wood, & Alexander, 1977). Figure 19-9 shows that participants in the experimental communities demonstrated significantly greater decreases than the control community participants in saturated fat intake, cigarette smoking, plasma-cholesterol levels, systolic blood pressure, and overall probability of contracting heart disease (Farquhar et al., 1977).

These results are even more impressive when compared with results obtained from a specially selected group of participants who were enrolled in an

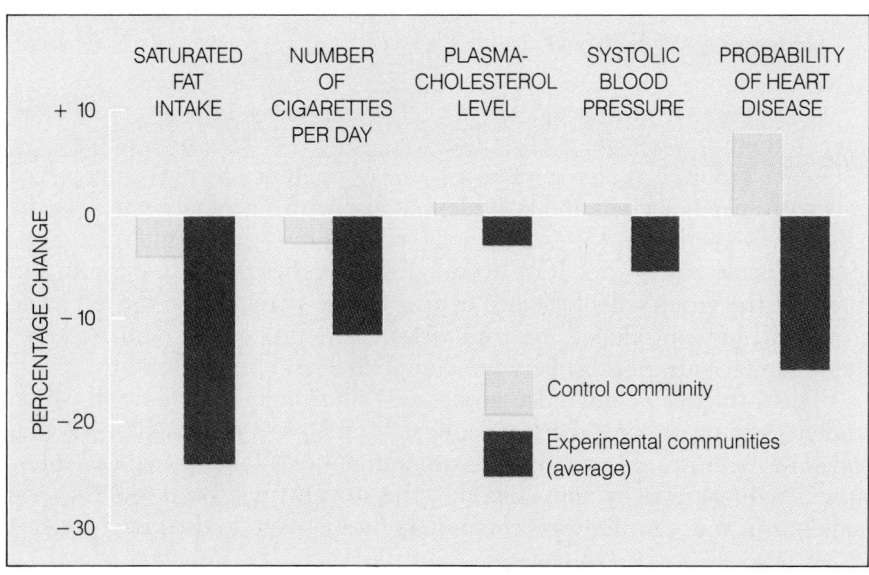

FIGURE 19-9
Mass Media Persuasion Campaign *An intensive 2-year mass media campaign successfully persuaded citizens from the experimental communities to alter their daily habits in order to reduce their risk of developing heart disease. (After Farquhar et al., 1977)*

intensive 10-week program involving weekly face-to-face sessions of counseling and instruction on how to reduce the risk of heart disease. These were all people identified as being at high risk for contracting such disease. During the second year of the program, the individuals again received counseling and were encouraged to maintain any previous changes. The participants were also exposed to the overall media campaign. The results showed that this group significantly reduced their risk-related behaviors during the first year of the program, doing better than media-only participants. But by the end of the second year the media-only campaign had almost caught up, producing nearly as much change as the intensive counseling (Farquhar et al., 1977). This highly successful study has led to several others, both in North America and other countries. The original Stanford group now conducts workshops for communities that wish to implement such programs on their own (Farquhar, Maccoby, & Solomon, 1984).

This study shows that persuasion via the mass media *can* be effective if carefully and intensively carried out. It is also important to note that the sources of influence in this study had very high credibility. They were experts on the topic of heart disease, and their motives in trying to obtain behavior change from the target audience could not be seen as self-serving—as a product commercial or political speech would be. Credibility is the key to internalization.

IDENTIFICATION

Nearly every group to which we belong, from our family to the society as a whole, has an implicit or explicit set of beliefs, attitudes, and behaviors that it considers correct. Any member of the group who strays from these social norms risks isolation and social disapproval. Thus, through social rewards and punishments, the groups to which we belong obtain compliance from us. In addition, if we respect or admire other individuals or groups, we may obey their norms and adopt their beliefs, attitudes, and behaviors in order to be like them, to identify with them. This is the process of *identification*.

Reference Groups

Groups with whom we identify are called our *reference groups*, because we refer to them in order to evaluate and to regulate our opinions and actions. Reference groups can also serve as a frame of reference by providing us not only with specific beliefs and attitudes but also with a general perspective by which we view the world—an ideology or set of ready-made interpretations of social issues and events. If we eventually adopt these views as our own and integrate the group's ideology into our own value system, then the reference group will have produced internalization. The process of identification, then, can provide a bridge between compliance and internalization.

The influence of reference groups was illustrated by a study in which students at a progressive teachers' college listened to a recorded speech that called for a return to traditional classroom methods. The speech was interrupted several times by applause. Half the students had been told that the audience in the recording was composed of students from their own college;

Many children identify with professional athletes.

the other half, that it was composed of local townspeople. Those who believed the applause came from fellow students changed their opinions about progressive education in the direction advocated in the speech more than did those who believed the applause came from outsiders (Kelley & Woodruff, 1956).

An individual does not necessarily have to be a member of a reference group in order to be influenced by its values. For example, lower-class individuals often use the middle class as a reference group. A young, aspiring athlete may use professional athletes as a reference group, adopting their views and otherwise trying to model himself or herself after them.

Life would be simple if each of us identified with only one reference group. But most of us identify with several reference groups, which often leads to conflicting pressures. We noted in Chapter 18, for example, that the Jewish businessperson might experience cross-pressures because his or her ethnic reference group usually holds more liberal political positions than does his or her business reference group. But perhaps the most enduring example of competing reference groups is the conflict that many young people experience between their family reference group and their college or peer reference group. The most extensive study of this conflict is Theodore Newcomb's classic Bennington Study—an examination of the political attitudes of the entire population of Bennington College, a small, politically liberal college in Vermont. The dates of the study (1935–1939) are a useful reminder that this is not a new phenomenon.

Today, Bennington College tends to attract liberal students, but in 1935 most students came from wealthy, conservative families. (It is coed today, but in 1935 it was a women's college.) Over two-thirds of the parents of Bennington students were affiliated with the Republican party. The Bennington College community was liberal during the 1930s, but this was not why most of the women selected the college.

Newcomb's main finding was that with each year at Bennington, students moved further away from their parents' attitudes and closer to the attitudes of the college community. For example, in the 1936 presidential campaign about 66 percent of parents favored the Republican candidate,

Landon, over the Democratic candidate, Roosevelt. Landon was supported by 62 percent of the Bennington freshmen, 43 percent of the sophomores, but only 15 percent of the juniors and seniors.

For most of the women, increasing liberalism reflected a deliberate choice between the two competing reference groups. Two women discuss how they made this choice:

> All my life I've resented the protection of governesses and parents. At college I got away from that, or rather, I guess I should say, I changed it to wanting the intellectual approval of teachers and more advanced students. Then I found that you can't be reactionary and be intellectually respectable.

> Becoming radical meant thinking for myself and, figuratively, thumbing my nose at my family. It also meant intellectual identification with the faculty and students that I most wanted to be like. (Newcomb, 1943, pp. 134, 131)

Note that the second woman uses the term "identification" in the sense that we have been using it. Note, too, how the women describe a mixture of change produced by social rewards and punishments (compliance) and change produced by an attraction to an admired group whom they strive to emulate (identification).

From Identification to Internalization

As mentioned earlier, reference groups also serve as frames of reference by providing their members with new perspectives on the world. The Bennington community, particularly the faculty, gave students a perspective on the depression of the 1930s and the threat of World War II that their wealthy and conservative home environments had not, and this began to move them from identification to internalization:

> It didn't take me long to see that liberal attitudes had prestige value. . . . I became liberal at first because of its prestige value; I remain so because the problems around which my liberalism centers are important. What I want now is to be effective in solving problems.

> Prestige and recognition have always meant everything to me. . . . But I've sweat blood in trying to be honest with myself, and the result is that I really know what I want my attitudes to be, and I see what their consequences will be in my own life. (Newcomb, 1943, pp. 136–137)

Many of our most important beliefs and attitudes are probably based initially on identification. Whenever we start to identify with a new reference group, we engage in a process of trying on the new set of beliefs and attitudes they prescribe. What we really believe is in flux, capable of changing from day to day. The first year of college often has this effect on students; many of the views students bring from the family reference group are challenged by students and faculty from very different backgrounds, with different beliefs. Students often try on the new beliefs with great intensity and strong conviction, only to discard them for still newer beliefs when the first set does not quite fit. This is a natural process of growth. Although the process never really ends for people who remain open to new experiences, it is greatly accelerated during the college years, before the person has formed a nucleus of permanent beliefs on which to build more slowly and less radically. The

Reference groups provide their members with a ready-made viewpoint on social issues.

real work of college is to evolve an ideological identity from the several beliefs and attitudes that are tested in order to move from identification to internalization.

As noted earlier, the advantage of internalization over compliance is that the changes are self-sustaining. The original source of influence does not have to monitor the individual to maintain the induced changes. The test of internalization, then, is the long-term stability of the induced beliefs, attitudes, and behaviors. Was the identification-induced liberalism of Bennington women maintained when the students returned to the real world? The answer is yes. A follow-up study of the Bennington women 25 years later found they had remained liberal. For example, in the 1960 presidential election, 60 percent of Bennington alumni preferred the Democrat Kennedy over the Republican Nixon, compared with fewer than 30 percent of women from a similar socioeconomic class and geographical location and with a similar educational level. Moreover, about 60 percent of Bennington alumni were politically active, most (66 percent) within the Democratic party (Newcomb, Koening, Flacks, & Warwick, 1967).

But we never outgrow our need for identification with supporting reference groups. The political attitudes of Bennington women remained stable, in part, because they selected new reference groups—friends and husbands—after college who supported the attitudes they developed in college. Those who married more conservative men were more likely to be politically conservative in 1960. As Newcomb noted, we often select our reference groups because they share our attitudes, and then our reference groups, in turn, help to develop and to sustain our attitudes. The relationship is circular. The distinction between identification and internalization is a useful one for understanding social influence, but in practice it is not always possible to disentangle them.

College freshmen "try on" new beliefs.

CHAPTER SUMMARY

1. Social psychology is, in part, the study of how an individual's thoughts, feelings, and behaviors are influenced by others. Three processes of social influence have been identified: a) *compliance*, in which the person publicly conforms outwardly to the wishes of the influencing source but does not change his or her private beliefs or attitudes; b) *internalization*, in which the person changes his or her beliefs, attitudes, or behaviors because he or she genuinely believes in the validity of the position advocated by the influencing source; and c) *identification*, in which the person changes his beliefs, attitudes, or behaviors in order to identify with or be like an influencing source that is respected or admired.

2. We are also influenced by *social norms*, implicit rules and expectations that tell us what we ought to think and how we ought to behave. Because norms influence us even when others are not actually present, the definition of social psychology includes the study of how an individual's thoughts, feelings, and behaviors are influenced by the *actual, imagined,* or *implied presence* of others.

3. Both humans and animals respond more quickly when in the presence of other members of their species. This *social facilitation* occurs whether the others are performing the same task (coactors) or are simply watching (an audience). The presence of others appears to raise the organism's drive level. For humans, cognitive factors, such as a concern with evaluation, also play a role.

4. The uninhibited aggressive behavior sometimes shown by mobs and crowds may be the result of a state of *deindividuation*, in which individuals feel that they have lost their personal identities and have merged into the group. Anonymity and close group unity seem to reduce self-awareness and contribute to deindividuation. Some of the consequences of deindividuation are weakened restraints

against impulsive behavior, increased sensitivity to immediate cues and current emotional states, and a lessened concern about the evaluation by others.

5. A bystander to an emergency is less likely to intervene or help if in a group than if alone. Two major factors that deter intervention are *defining the situation* and *diffusion of responsibility*. By attempting to appear calm, bystanders may define the situation for each other as a nonemergency, thereby producing a state of *pluralistic ignorance*. The presence of other people also diffuses responsibility so that no one person feels the necessity to act. Bystanders are more likely to intervene when these factors are minimized, particularly if at least one person displays helping behavior.

6. *Social impact theory* summarizes many phenomena of social influence by proposing that a) the social impact or effectiveness of influence on a target individual *increases* with the number, immediacy, and importance of the sources of influence; and b) the social impact of a source of influence *decreases* as the number, immediacy, and importance of targets increase.

7. When a source of influence obtains compliance by setting an example, it is called *conformity*. When the source obtains compliance by wielding authority, it is called *obedience*. Asch found that a unanimous group exerts strong pressure on an individual to conform to the group's judgments—even when those judgments are clearly wrong. Much less conformity is observed if the group is not unanimous.

8. Milgram's studies demonstrated that people would obey an experimenter's order to deliver strong electric shocks to an innocent victim. Factors conspiring to produce the high obedience rates include *social norms* (for example, the implied contract to continue the experiment until completed); the *surveillance* of the experimenter; *buffers* that distance the person from the consequences of his or her acts; and the *legitimating role of science*, which leads people to abandon their autonomy to the experimenter.

9. Obedience to authority can be undermined—and rebellion provoked—if the individual is with a group whose members have the opportunity to share their opinions, can give each other social support for dissenting, and can provide role models for disobedience. But the individual may then have to choose between obedience to the authority and conformity to the group that has decided to rebel.

10. Studies of conformity and obedience reveal that situational factors exert more influence over behavior than most of us realize. We tend to underestimate situational forces on behavior.

11. Obtaining internalization—actual belief and attitude change—usually requires a source of influence who either a) presents a persuasive communication that is itself compelling, or b) is perceived by the individual to be credible, possessing both expertise and trustworthiness. A minority of persons within a larger group can move the majority toward its point of view if it presents and maintains a consistent dissenting position without appearing rigid, dogmatic, or arrogant.

12. *Cognitive response theory* proposes that persuasion induced by a communication is actually self-persuasion produced by the thoughts that the person generates while reading or hearing the communication. If the communication evokes thoughts supportive of the position being advocated, the individual will move toward that position; if the communication evokes unsupportive thoughts—such as counterarguments or disparaging thoughts about the communicator—the individual will remain unpersuaded. The theory provides a unified explanation for several previously discovered phenomena of persuasion.

13. Persuasion can take two routes in producing belief and attitude change: the *central route*, in which the individual responds to the substantive arguments of a communication, and the *peripheral route*, in which the individual responds to noncontent cues in a communication (such as the number of arguments) or to context cues (such as the credibility of the communicator or the pleasantness of the surroundings). A communication about an issue of personal relevance is

more likely to generate thoughts in response to the communication's substantive arguments. When an issue is of little personal relevance or when people are unwilling or unable to respond to the substantive content of a communication, they tend to use simple *heuristics*—rules of thumb—to judge the merits of the communication.

14. Despite the amount of money spent on persuasion in the mass media, the effects are not great. People tend not to attend to the persuasive message; they expose themselves primarily to opinions they already agree with; they tune out messages they disagree with; and they tend to interpret the message as more similar to their original beliefs than it actually is. However, a large-scale, 2-year campaign aimed at changing people's habits in order to reduce the risk of heart disease showed that the mass media can be very effective when correctly used.

15. In the process of *identification* we obey the norms and adopt the beliefs, attitudes, and behaviors of groups that we respect and admire. We use such *reference groups* to evaluate and regulate our opinions and actions. A reference group can regulate our attitudes and behavior by administering social rewards and punishments or by providing us with a frame of reference, a ready-made interpretation of events and social issues.

16. Most of us identify with more than one reference group, and this can lead to conflicting pressures on our beliefs, attitudes, and behaviors. College students frequently move away from the views of their family reference group toward the college reference group. These new views are usually sustained because a) they become internalized, and b) we tend to select new reference groups after college—spouses and friends—that share our views.

FURTHER READING

Many of the topics in this chapter are covered in paperback books written for general audiences, often by the original investigators. Aronson, *The Social Animal* (5th ed., 1988), covers several topics in social influence. Milgram, *Obedience to Authority* (1974) is well worth reading, especially before forming an opinion about this controversial series of studies. Latané and Darley, *The Unresponsive Bystander: Why Doesn't He Help?* (1970) is a report by two of the original researchers in that area. Petty and Cacioppo, *Attitudes and Persuasion: Classic and Contemporary Approaches* (1981) is an excellent summary of both earlier and current work on persuasion written by two active researchers and theorists in the area. LeBon's classic book, *The Crowd* (1895), is available in several editions.

The Bennington Study and its followup of both the original women and Bennington College itself are reported in Newcomb, *Personality and Social Change* (1943); and in Newcomb, Koening, Flacks, and Warwick, *Persistence and Change: Bennington College and Its Students after Twenty-Five Years* (1967).

Three comprehensive textbooks in this area are Roger Brown, *Social Psychology: The Second Edition* (1986); Myers, *Social Psychology* (2nd ed., 1987); Sears, Peplau, Freedman, and Taylor, *Social Psychology* (6th ed., 1988). More technical, in-depth treatments are available in Lindzey and Aronson (eds.), *The Handbook of Social Psychology* (3rd ed., 1985).

Appendix I

How to Read a Textbook: The PQRST Method

A central topic in psychology is the analysis of learning and memory. Almost every chapter of this book refers to these phenomena; Chapter 7 ("Learning and Conditioning") and Chapter 8 ("Memory") are devoted exclusively to learning and memory. In this appendix we review a method for reading and studying information presented in textbook form. The theoretical ideas underlying this method are discussed in Chapter 8; the method is described here in greater detail for readers who wish to apply it in studying this textbook.

This approach for reading textbook chapters, called the PQRST method, has been shown to be very effective in improving a reader's understanding of and memory for key ideas and information. The method takes its name from the first letter of the five steps one follows in reading a chapter— *Preview, Question, Read, Self-recitation, Test.* The steps or stages are diagramed in the figure below. The first and last stages (Preview and Test) apply to the chapter as a whole; the middle three stages (Question, Read, Self-recitation) apply to each major section of the chapter as it is encountered.*

STAGE P (PREVIEW)   In the first step, you preview the entire chapter by skimming through it to get an idea of major topics. This is done by reading the chapter outline and then skimming the chapter, paying special attention to the headings of main sections and subsections and glancing at pictures and illustrations. The most important aspect of the preview stage is to read carefully the summary at the end of the chapter once you have skimmed through the chapter. Take time to consider each point in the summary; questions will come to mind that should be answered later as you read the full text. The

---

*The PQRST method as described here is based on the work of Thomas and H. A. Robinson (1982) and Spache and Berg (1978); their work, in turn, is based on the earlier contributions of R. P. Robinson (1970). In some sources, the name SQ3R is used instead of PQRST. The S, the Q, and the three Rs stand for the same five steps, but are relabeled as Survey, Question, Read, Recite, and Review. We find PQRST to be easier to remember than SQ3R.

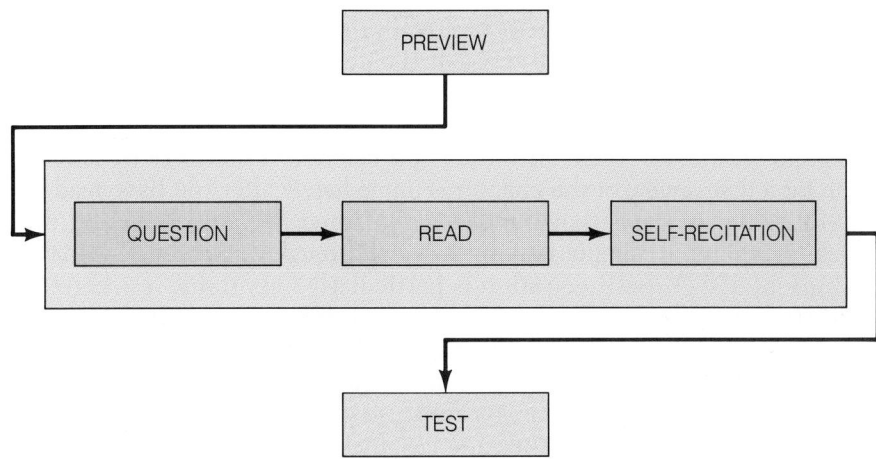

PQRST Method *The first and last stages apply to the chapter as a whole, whereas the middle three stages apply to each section of the chapter as it is encountered.*

preview stage will give you an overview of the topics covered in the chapter and how they are organized.

STAGE Q (QUESTION)   As noted earlier, you should apply Stages Q, R, and S to each major section of the chapter as it is encountered. The typical chapter in this textbook has about five to eight major sections, each section beginning with a heading set in large, capital blue letters. Work through the chapter one section at a time, applying Stages Q, R, and S to each section before going on to the next section. Before reading a section, read the heading of the section and the headings of the subsections. Then turn the topic headings into one or more questions that you should expect to answer while reading the section. Ask yourself: "What are the main ideas the author is trying to convey in this section?" This is the Question Stage.

STAGE R (READ)   Next, read the section carefully for meaning. As you read, try to answer the questions you asked in Stage Q. Reflect on what you are reading, and try to make connections to other things you know. You may choose to mark or underline key words or phrases in the text. Try, however, not to mark more than 10 to 15 percent of the text. Too much underlining defeats the intended purpose, which is to make key words and ideas stand out for later review. It is probably best to delay taking notes until you have read the entire section and encountered all the key ideas, so you can judge their relative importance.

STAGE S (SELF-RECITATION)   After you have finished reading the section, try to recall the main ideas and recite the information. Self-recitation is a powerful means of fixing the material in your memory. Put the ideas into your own words and recite the information (preferably aloud or, if you are not alone, to yourself). Check against the text to be sure that you have recited the material correctly and completely. Self-recitation will reveal blanks in your knowledge and help you organize the information in your mind. After you have completed one section of the chapter in this way, turn to the next section and again apply Stages Q, R, and S. Continue in this manner until you have finished all sections of the chapter.

STAGE T (TEST)   When you have finished reading the chapter, you should test and review all of the material. Look over your notes and test your recall for the main ideas. Try to understand how the various facts relate to each other and how they were organized in the chapter. The test stage may require that you thumb back through the chapter to check key facts and ideas. You should also reread the chapter summary at this time; as you are doing so, you should be able to add details to each entry in the summary. Don't put off the test stage until the night before an examination. The best time for a first review of the chapter is immediately after you have read it.

Research indicates that the PQRST method is very helpful and definitely preferable to simply reading straight through a chapter (Thomas & Robinson, 1982). Self-recitation is particularly important; it is better to spend a significant percentage of study time in an active attempt to recite than it is to devote the entire time to reading and rereading the material (Gates, 1917). Studies also show that a careful reading of the summary of the chapter *before* reading the chapter itself is especially productive (Reder & Anderson, 1980). Reading the summary first provides an overview of the chapter that helps organize the material as you read through the chapter. Even if you choose not to follow every step of the PQRST method, special attention should be directed to the value of self-recitation and reading the chapter summary as an introduction to the material.

The PQRST method and various other study skills, including taking lecture notes and preparing for and taking examinations, are discussed in an excellent book entitled *Building Better Study Skills: Practical Methods for Succeeding in College*, published by the American College Testing Program, Iowa City, Iowa. As its subtitle indicates, this book focuses on practical methods for achieving personal and academic success in college.

Appendix II

Brief History of Psychology

Although psychology is a young science, people throughout history have been concerned with psychological issues. Books on the history of psychology discuss the views of early Greek philosophers, especially those of Plato and Aristotle. After the Greeks, Saint Augustine (A.D. 354–430) is considered the next great precursor of modern psychology because of his interest in introspection and his curiosity about psychological phenomena, including the behavior of infants and of crowds at chariot races. Descartes (1596–1650) left his mark on psychology by theorizing that animals are machines that can be studied much as other machines are studied. He also introduced the concept of reflex action, which has occupied a significant place in psychology. Many prominent philosophers of the seventeenth and eighteenth centuries—Leibnitz, Hobbes, Locke, Kant, and Hume, to name five—grappled with psychological questions.

ROOTS OF CONTEMPORARY PSYCHOLOGY

Two Early Approaches

In the nineteenth century, two theories of the mind competed for support. One, known as *faculty psychology*, was a doctrine of inherited mental powers. According to this theory, the mind has a few distinct and independent "faculties" or mental agencies—such as thinking, feeling, and willing—that account for its activities. These faculties were further broken into subfaculties: we remember through the subfaculty of memory, imagine through the subfaculty of imagination, and so on. Faculty psychology encouraged early nineteenth-century *phrenologists*, such as Gall, to try to localize special faculties in different parts of the brain.

The *association psychologists* held an opposing view. They denied inborn faculties of the mind; instead, they limited the mind's content to ideas that

Wilhelm Wundt.

enter by way of the senses and then become associated through such principles as similarity, contrast, and contiguity. They explained all mental activity through the *association of ideas*—a concept principally developed by British philosophers.

Both faculty psychology and association psychology have present-day counterparts. The search for mental abilities as factors in psychological tests is related to faculty psychology. Current research on memory and learning is related to earlier association theory. Faculty psychology took note of the inherited aspects of behavior, whereas associationism emphasized the environment as the determiner of behavior. The environment versus heredity issue runs throughout the history of psychology.

Wundt's Laboratory

Wilhelm Wundt is given credit for founding psychology as an academic discipline. The founding date is usually cited as 1879, the year that Wundt established the first formal psychological laboratory at the University of Leipzig in Germany. Wundt's research was primarily concerned with the senses, especially vision; but he and his coworkers also studied attention, emotion, and memory.

Wundt's psychology relied on *introspection* as a method of studying mental processes. The introspective method was inherited from philosophy, but Wundt added a new dimension to the concept. Pure self-observation was not sufficient; it had to be supplemented by experiments. His experiments systematically varied some physical dimension of a stimulus, and the introspective method was used to determine how these physical changes modified consciousness.

Wundt's approach to research can be illustrated by one of his experiments on *reaction time*. In this experiment, the subject was required to press a key as quickly as possible after the onset of a light, and the subject's reaction time was carefully measured. Wundt found that the response time was longer when a subject paid careful attention to detecting the onset of light than it was when the subject's attention was directed to making a quick finger movement to press the key. The subject reacted very quickly in both cases, but there was a difference in reaction time of about .1 second. To explain this strange finding, Wundt distinguished between *perception* and *apperception*. When attention was focused on the finger movement, simple perception occurred and the light triggered the response promptly. But when attention was focused on the stimulus, an additional activity of apperception occurred, which involved a "richer" perception of the light. Wundt decided that this apperception required about .1 second. His interpretation is no longer accepted, for we now know that the processes intervening between stimulus and response are organized in more complex ways; but such studies helped to launch psychology as an experimental science.

Until his death in 1920, Wundt's personal influence on psychology was singularly important. Many pioneers in American psychology were trained in Wundt's laboratory. The first formal psychology laboratory in the United States was established in 1883 at Johns Hopkins University by G. Stanley Hall (who had studied with Wundt), although William James had set up a small demonstration laboratory at Harvard by 1875. The first person to be called "professor of psychology" in the United States was J. McKeen Cattell, another Wundt student, who acquired that title at the University of

Pennsylvania in 1888. Before the end of the 1890s, Wundt's students were to be found in many American universities.

Other Roots of Contemporary Psychology

Although the impetus for establishing psychological laboratories came largely from Germany, there were other influences. In England, Sir Francis Galton was a pioneer in the study of individual differences and exerted an important influence on the development of intelligence tests. Galton invented the statistical technique of correlation and developed the index that later became known as the *coefficient of correlation*.

The influence of the theory of evolution through natural selection, propounded by Charles Darwin, also came from England. Darwin's theory established the continuity between animals and human beings and thus led to comparative studies in psychology.

Another area of influence on psychology came from medicine, especially from the treatment of the mentally ill. Hypnotism, for example, has a long history as a form of therapy, dating from the work of Anton Mesmer in the late 1700s. Another Viennese physician, Sigmund Freud, founded psychoanalysis early in the present century.

Sir Francis Galton.

SCHOOLS OF PSYCHOLOGY

Structuralism and Functionalism

When scientific psychology emerged in the latter part of the nineteenth century, researchers were making great advances in chemistry and physics by analyzing complex compounds (molecules) into their elements (atoms). These successes encouraged psychologists to look for the mental elements of which more complex experiences were composed. If the chemist made headway by analyzing water into hydrogen and oxygen, perhaps the psychologist could make progress by considering the taste of lemonade (perception) as a molecule of conscious experience to be analyzed into elements (sensations)—such as sweet, bitter, cold, and whatever—that could be identified by introspection. This was the approach taken by Wundt and his students; its major proponent in the United States was E. B. Titchener, a Wundt-trained psychologist at Cornell University. Since the goal was to specify mental structures, Titchener introduced the term *structuralism* to describe this brand of psychology.

But there was vigorous opposition to the purely analytical character of structuralism. William James—a distinguished psychologist at Harvard University—was impatient with the restrictions on psychology as it was developing under the structuralists. James felt that less emphasis should be placed on analyzing the elements of consciousness and more emphasis should be placed on understanding its fluid, streaming, personal character. His principal interest was in studying how the mind worked so that an organism could adapt to its environment. Because James asked how consciousness functions (particularly in the adaptive process), his approach to psychology was named *functionalism*. James' writing on *habits* as a mode of adaptation helped set the

William James.

Important Dates in the History of Psychology

B.C. 400	Hippocrates relates personality characteristics to body types and proposes a physiological (as opposed to demonological) theory of mental illness.
B.C. 350	Aristotle stresses the objective observation of man's behavior and proposes three principles to account for the association of ideas.
A.D. 400	Saint Augustine, influenced by Platonic ideas, makes careful introspections in his *Confessions*.
1650	René Descartes characterizes the mind–body relationship as one of interaction.
1651	Thomas Hobbes foreshadows associationism by declaring that all ideas come from sensory experience.
1690	John Locke carries Hobbes' notion a step further by declaring that at birth the mind is a blank slate (*tabula rasa*).
1749	David Hartley formalizes a doctrine of associationism and suggests a neurological basis for memory.
1781	Immanuel Kant's *Critique of Pure Reason* attacks associationism and the nativistic approach; it strongly influences later philosophers and psychologists.
1809	Franz Gall and Johann Spurzheim give prominence through phrenology to the study of mental faculties and brain function.
1821	Pierre Flourens performs the first significant experiments in localization of brain functions.
1822	Friedrich Bessel measures individual differences in reaction time for astronomical observations.
1838	Johannes Müller formulates the doctrine of specific nerve energies.
1846	Ernst Weber derives the first quantitative law in psychology.
1850	Hermann von Helmholtz measures the rates of conduction of nerve impulses.
1859	Charles Darwin publishes *The Origin of Species*, propounding the theory of evolution through natural selection.
1860	Gustav Fechner publishes *Elements of Psychophysics*, in which he presents various methods for measuring the relationship between physical stimuli and sensations.
1869	Sir Francis Galton studies individual differences and applies Darwin's concept of selective adaptation to the evolution of races.
1879	Wilhelm Wundt opens the first formal psychological laboratory at the University of Leipzig.
1883	G. Stanley Hall establishes the first psychological laboratory in America at Johns Hopkins University.
1885	Hermann Ebbinghaus publishes the first experimental studies of memory.

1890   William James' *Principles of Psychology* is published in the United States.

1892   Edward Titchener at Cornell University establishes "structuralism" as a major influence in American psychology.

1898   Edward Thorndike performs some of the first controlled experiments on animal learning.

1900   Sigmund Freud publishes *The Interpretation of Dreams*, which presents many of his ideas on psychoanalysis.

1905   Alfred Binet and Theodore Simon devise the first intelligence test.

1906   Ivan Pavlov publishes the results of his studies on classical conditioning.

1908   William McDougall's publication of *An Introduction to Social Psychology* marks the formal inauguration of the field of social psychology.

1912   Max Wertheimer publishes the first formulation of Gestalt psychology.

1913   John B. Watson exerts a major impact on the course of psychology with his behaviorist manifesto.

1917   Wolfgang Köhler publishes the results of his studies on problem solving in primates.

1922   Edward Tolman presents his initial ideas on purposive behaviorism.

1929   Karl Lashley publishes *Brain Mechanisms and Intelligence*.

1935   Louis Thurstone develops factor analysis.

1938   B. F. Skinner publishes *The Behavior of Organisms*, which summarizes early research on operant conditioning.

1949   Donald Hebb, in *Organization of Behavior*, presents a theory that bridges the gap between neurophysiology and psychology.

1950   William Estes lays the foundation for a mathematical approach to theories of learning.

1954   The Swiss psychologist Jean Piaget publishes *The Construction of Reality in the Child*, which focuses attention on cognitive development.

1957   Noam Chomsky publishes *Syntactic Structures*, a book that presents a cognitive approach to language behavior.

1958   Herbert Simon and colleagues publish *Elements of a Theory of Human Problem Solving*, which reformulates classical psychological problems in terms of information-processing models.

1962   David Hubel and Torsten Weisel discover the relationship between the activity of individual neurons in the visual cortex to specific features of a visual stimulus.

1979   The journal *Cognitive Science* and a society by the same name was founded, serving to catalyze research on the representational and computational capacities of the mind.

Events since 1980 are not listed because not enough time has elapsed to judge their long-term impact on the field.

stage for a psychology that included the learning process as a central topic of study.

Interest in adaptation was influenced by Darwin's theory of natural selection. Consciousness evolved, so the argument ran, only because it served some purpose in guiding the activities of the individual. With this emphasis on the functional role of consciousness came a recognition that the introspective method of structuralism was too restrictive. To find out how the organism adapts to its environment, the functionalists argued that data derived from introspection had to be supplemented by observations of actual behavior, including the study of animal behavior and the development of behavior (developmental psychology). Thus, functionalism broadened the scope of psychology to include behavior as a dependent variable. But along with the structuralists, functionalists still regarded psychology as the science of conscious experience and the principal investigative method as introspection.

Structuralism and functionalism played important roles in the early development of psychology. Because each viewpoint provided a systematic approach to the field, the two were considered competing *schools of psychology*. As psychology developed, other schools evolved and vied for leadership. By 1920, structuralism and functionalism were being displaced by three newer schools: behaviorism, Gestalt psychology, and psychoanalysis.

Behaviorism

Of the three new schools, behaviorism had the greatest influence on scientific psychology. Its founder, John B. Watson, reacted against the tradition of his time—that conscious experience was the province of psychology—and boldly proclaimed a psychology *without* introspection. Watson made no assertions about consciousness when he studied the behavior of animals and infants. He decided not only that the results of animal psychology and child psychology could stand on their own as a science, but also that they set a pattern that adult psychology might well follow.

In order to make psychology a science, Watson said, psychological data must be open to public inspection like the data of any other science. Behavior is public; consciousness is private. Science should deal with public facts. Because psychologists were growing impatient with introspection, the new behaviorism caught on rapidly, particularly in the 1920s; for a time, most of the younger psychologists in the United States called themselves "behaviorists." In Russia, the work of Ivan Pavlov on the conditioned response was regarded as an important area of research by the behaviorists. The conditioned response was being investigated in the United States in a limited way before the advent of behaviorism, but Watson was responsible for its subsequent widespread influence on psychology.

Watson argued that nearly all behavior is the result of conditioning, and that the environment shapes our behavior by reinforcing specific habits. The conditioned response was viewed as the smallest indivisible unit of behavior, an "atom of behavior" from which more complicated behaviors could be built. All types of complex behavioral repertoires arising from special training or education were regarded as nothing more than an interlinked fabric of conditioned responses.

Behaviorists found it congenial to discuss psychological phenomena as beginning with a stimulus and ending with a response—giving rise to the term *stimulus-response (S-R) psychology*. S-R psychologists went beyond the

John B. Watson.

earlier behaviorists in their willingness to infer hypothetical processes between the stimulus input and the response output, processes that were called *intervening variables.*

If broad definitions are used, so that "stimulus" refers to a whole class of antecedent conditions and "response" refers to a whole class of outcomes (actual behavior and products of behavior), S-R psychology becomes merely a psychology of independent and dependent variables. Viewed in this way, S-R psychology is not a particular theory but a *language* that can be used to make psychological information explicit and communicable. As such, the S-R outlook is widely prevalent in psychology today.

Gestalt Psychology

At about the same time that Watson announced behaviorism in America, Gestalt psychology was appearing in Germany. The word *Gestalt* translates from the German as "form" or "configuration," and the psychology announced by Max Wertheimer in 1912 was a psychology concerned with the organization of mental processes. The position came to be identified most closely with Wertheimer and his colleagues Kurt Koffka and Wolfgang Köhler, all of whom migrated to the United States.

The earliest Gestalt experiments dealt with perceived motion, particularly the *phi phenomenon.* When two separated lights are flashed in succession (provided the timing and spatial locations are proper), the subject sees a single light moving from the position of the first light to that of the second. The phenomenon of apparent motion was familiar, but the Gestalt psychologists sensed the theoretical importance of the patterning of stimuli in producing the effect. Our experiences depend on the *patterns* formed by stimuli and on the *organization* of experience, they decided. What we see is relative to background, to other aspects of the whole. The whole is different from the sum of its parts; the whole consists of parts in relationship.

Although the Gestalt psychologists did not subscribe to the introspective psychology of their day any more than Watson did, they were vigorous opponents of behaviorism. They did not want to give up a kind of free introspection that goes by the name of *phenomenology.* They wanted to be able to ask a person what something looked like, what it meant. They were interested in the perception of motion, in how people judged sizes, and in the appearance of colors under changes in illumination.

The importance of perception in all psychological events has led those influenced by Gestalt psychology to a number of perception-centered interpretations of learning, memory, and problem solving. These interpretations, spoken of as forms of cognitive theory, were instrumental in laying the groundwork for current developments in cognitive psychology.

Psychoanalysis

Sigmund Freud introduced psychoanalytic psychology to the United States in a series of lectures given at Clark University in 1909 on the invitation of psychologist G. Stanley Hall. Thus, the first scholarly recognition of Freud's work in the United States came from psychologists. Freud's influence became so pervasive that those who know nothing else about psychology have at least a nodding acquaintance with psychoanalysis.

Wolfgang Köhler.

Sigmund Freud.

If one of Freud's theories is to be singled out for consideration along with behaviorism and Gestalt psychology, it is his interpretation of the *unconscious*. Basic to Freud's theory of the unconscious is the conception that the unacceptable (forbidden, punished) wishes of childhood are driven out of awareness and become part of the unconscious, where they remain influential. The unconscious presses to find expression, which it does in numerous ways, including dreams, slips of speech, and unconscious mannerisms. The method of psychoanalysis—free association under the guidance of the analyst—is itself a way of helping unconscious wishes find verbal expression. In classical Freudian theory, these unconscious wishes were almost exclusively sexual. This emphasis on childhood sexuality was one of the barriers to the acceptance of Freud's theories when they were first announced.

RECENT DEVELOPMENTS

Despite the important contribution of Gestalt psychology and psychoanalysis, psychology was dominated by behaviorism until World War II, particularly in the United States. With the end of the war, interest in psychology increased and many people were attracted to careers in the field. Sophisticated instruments and electronic equipment became available, and a wider range of problems could be examined. This expanded program of research made it evident that earlier theoretical approaches were too restrictive.

This viewpoint was strengthened by the development of computers in the 1950s. Computers, properly programmed, were able to perform tasks—such as playing chess and proving mathematical theorems—that previously could only be done by human beings. It became apparent that the computer offered psychologists a powerful tool with which to theorize about psychological processes. A series of brilliant papers, published in the late 1950s by Herbert Simon (who was later awarded the Nobel prize) and his colleagues, indicated how psychological phenomena could be *simulated* using the computer. Many old psychological issues were recast in terms of *information-processing systems*. The human being could now be viewed as a processor of information. The senses provide an input channel for information; mental operations are applied to the input; the transformed input creates a mental structure that is stored in memory; that structure interacts with others in memory to generate a response. The power of the computer permitted psychologists to theorize about complex mental processes and investigate the implications of the theory by simulating it on a computer. If the response (output) stage of the computer simulation agreed with the observed behavior of actual people, the psychologist could have some confidence in the theory.

The information-processing approach provided a richer and more dynamic approach to psychology than S-R theory with its intervening variables. Similarly, the information-processing approach permitted some of the speculations of Gestalt psychology and psychoanalysis to be formulated in a precise fashion as programs in a computer; in this way, earlier ideas about the nature of the mind could be made concrete and checked against actual data.

Another factor that led to a changing viewpoint in psychology in the 1950s was the development of modern linguistics. Prior to that time, linguists were primarily concerned with a description of a language; now they began to theorize about the mental structures required to comprehend and to speak a language. Work in this area was pioneered by Noam Chomsky, whose

Herbert Simon.

book *Syntactic Structures*, published in 1957, provided the basis for an active collaboration between psychologists and linguists. A rapid development of the field of *psycholinguistics* followed, providing the first significant psychological analyses of language.

At the same time, important advances were occurring in neuropsychology. A number of discoveries about the brain and the nervous system established clear relationships between neurobiological events and mental processes. It became increasingly difficult to assert, as some of the early behaviorists had, that a science of psychology could be established without links to neurophysiology.

The development of information-processing models, psycholinguistics, and neuropsychology has produced a psychology that is highly cognitive in orientation. There is no agreed-on definition of *cognitive psychology*, but its principal concern is the scientific analysis of mental processes and mental structures. Cognitive psychology is not exclusively concerned with thought and knowledge. Its early concerns with the representation of knowledge and human thought led to the label "cognitive psychology," but the approach has been expanded to all areas of psychology, including motivation, perception, psychopathology, and social psychology.

During this century, the focus of psychology has come full circle. After rejecting conscious experience as ill-suited to scientific investigation and turning to the study of behavior, psychologists are once again theorizing about the mind, but this time with new and more powerful tools. The gain from behaviorism has been an emphasis on the objectivity and reproducibility of findings—an emphasis that has found a place in cognitive psychology.

From a historical perspective, it is too early to judge the long-term significance of recent developments in psychology. What is evident, however, is that there is great excitement in the field today, and many psychologists believe that it is in a period of revolutionary change and progress. Understanding how the mind works is a challenge that deserves the best intellectual effort we can put forth.

FURTHER READING

For a general survey of the history of psychology, see Hilgard, *Psychology in America: A Historical Survey* (1987); Watson, *The Great Psychologists: From Aristotle to Freud* (4th ed., 1978); Wertheimer, *A Brief History of Psychology* (rev. ed., 1979); and Schultz, *A History of Modern Psychology* (4th ed., 1987). See also Boring, *A History of Experimental Psychology* (2nd ed., 1950); and Herrnstein and Boring, *A Source Book in the History of Psychology* (1965).

Appendix III

Statistical Methods and Measurement

Much of the work of psychologists calls for making measurements—either in the laboratory or under field conditions. This work may involve measuring the eye movements of infants when first exposed to a novel stimulus, recording the galvanic skin response of people under stress, counting the number of trials required to condition a monkey that has a prefrontal lobotomy, determining achievement test scores for students using computer-assisted learning, or counting the number of patients who show improvement following a particular type of psychotherapy. In all these examples, the *measurement operation* yields numbers; the psychologist's problem is to interpret them and to arrive at some general conclusions. Basic to this task is *statistics*—the discipline that deals with collecting numerical data and with making inferences from such data. The purpose of this appendix is to review certain statistical methods that play an important role in psychology.

This appendix is written on the assumption that the problems students have with statistics are essentially problems of clear thinking about data. An introductory acquaintance with statistics is *not* beyond the scope of anyone who understands enough algebra to use plus and minus signs and to substitute numbers for letters in equations.

DESCRIPTIVE STATISTICS

Statistics serves, first of all, to provide a shorthand description of large amounts of data. Suppose that we want to study the college entrance examination scores of 5,000 students recorded on cards in the registrar's office. These scores are the raw data. Thumbing through the cards will give us some impressions of the students' scores, but it will be impossible for us to keep all of them in mind. So we make some kind of summary of the data, possibly averaging all the scores or finding the highest and lowest scores. These statistical summaries make it easier to remember and to think about the data. Such summarizing statements are called *descriptive statistics*.

TABLE 1

Raw Scores *College entrance examination scores for 15 students, listed in the order in which they were tested.*

84	75	91
61	75	67
72	87	79
75	79	83
77	51	69

TABLE 2

Frequency Distribution *Scores from Table 1 accumulated with class intervals of 10.*

CLASS INTERVAL	NUMBER OF PERSONS IN CLASS
50–59	1
60–69	3
70–79	7
80–89	3
90–99	1

Frequency Distributions

Items of raw data become comprehensible when they are grouped in a *frequency distribution*. To group data, we must first divide the scale along which they are measured into intervals and then count the number of items that fall into each interval. An interval in which scores are grouped is called a *class interval*. The decision of how many class intervals the data are to be grouped into is not fixed by any rules but is based on the judgment of the investigator.

Table 1 provides a sample of raw data representing college entrance examination scores for 15 students. The scores are listed in the order in which the students were tested (the first student tested had a score of 84; the second, 61; and so on). Table 2 shows these data arranged in a frequency distribution for which the class interval has been set at 10. One score falls in the interval from 50 to 59, three scores fall in the interval from 60 to 69, and so on. Note that most scores fall in the interval from 70 to 79 and that no scores fall below the 50 to 59 interval or above the 90 to 99 interval.

A frequency distribution is often easier to understand if it is presented graphically. The most widely used graph form is the *frequency histogram*; an example is shown in the top panel of Figure 1. Histograms are constructed by drawing bars, the bases of which are given by the class intervals and the heights of which are determined by the corresponding class frequencies. An alternative way of presenting frequency distributions in graph form is to use a *frequency polygon*, an example of which is shown in the bottom panel of Figure 1. Frequency polygons are constructed by plotting the class frequencies at the center of the class interval and connecting the points obtained by straight lines. To complete the picture, one extra class is added at each end of the distribution; since these classes have zero frequencies, both ends of the figure will touch the horizontal axis. The frequency polygon gives the same information as the frequency histogram but by means of a set of connected lines rather than bars.

In practice, we would obtain a much greater number of items than those plotted in Figure 1, but a minimum amount of data is shown in all of the illustrations in this appendix so that you can easily check the steps in tabulating and plotting.

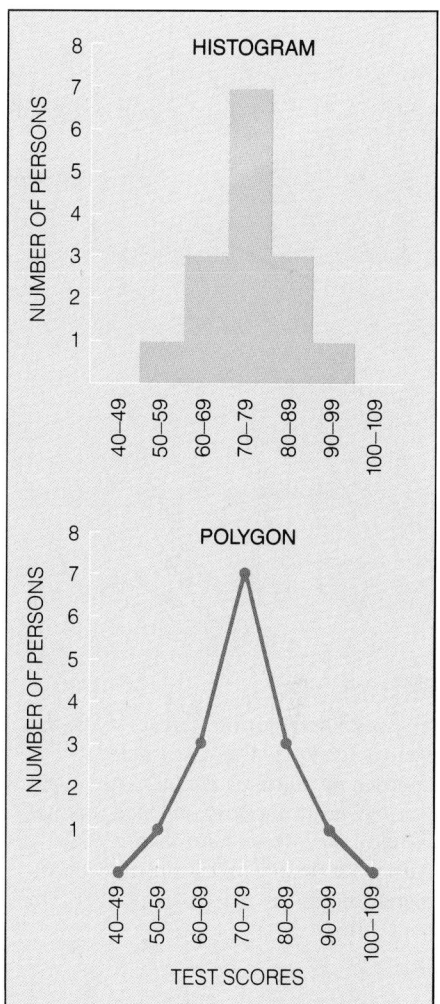

FIGURE 1
Frequency Diagrams *The data from Table 2 are plotted here. A frequency histogram is on the top; a frequency polygon, on the bottom.*

Measures of Central Tendency

A *measure of central tendency* is simply a representative point on our scale—a central point with scores scattered on either side. Three such measures are commonly used: the *mean*, the *median*, and the *mode*.

The *mean* is the familiar arithmetic average obtained by adding the scores and dividing by the number of scores. The sum of the raw scores in Table 1 is 1125. If we divide this by 15 (the number of students' scores), the mean turns out to be 75.

The *median* is the score of the middle item, which is obtained by arranging the scores in order and then counting into the middle from either end. When the 15 scores in Table 1 are placed in order from highest to lowest, the eighth score from either end turns out to be 75. If the number of cases is even, we simply average the two cases on either side of the middle. For instance, the median of 10 items is the arithmetic average of the fifth and sixth cases.

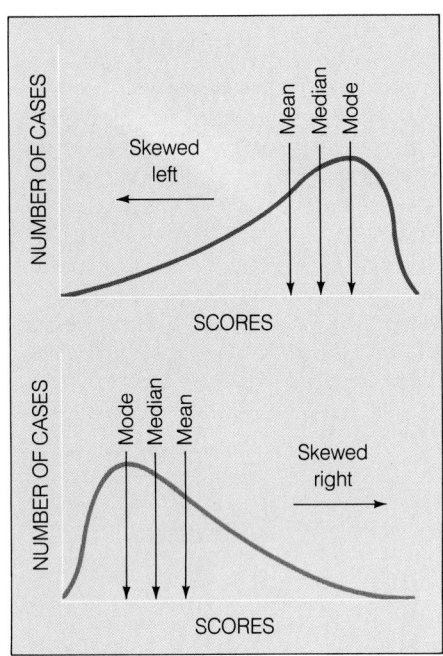

FIGURE 2
Skewed Distribution Curves *Note that skewed distributions are designated by the direction in which the tail falls. Also note that the mean, median, and mode are not identical for a skewed distribution; the median commonly falls between the mode and the mean.*

The *mode* is the most frequent score in a given distribution. In Table 1, the most frequent score is 75; hence, the mode of the distribution is 75.

In a *symmetrical distribution*, in which the scores are distributed evenly on either side of the middle (as in Figure 1), the mean, median, and mode all fall together. This is not true for distributions that are *skewed*, or unbalanced. Suppose we want to analyze the departure times of a morning train. The train usually leaves on time; occasionally it leaves late, but it never leaves early. For a train with a scheduled departure time of 8:00 A.M., one week's record might be as follows:

M	8:00	Mean = 8:07
Tu	8:04	Median = 8:02
W	8:02	Mode = 8:00
Th	8:19	
F	8:22	
Sat	8:00	
Sun	8:00	

The distribution of departure times in this example is skewed because of the two late departures; they raise the mean departure time but do not have much effect on the median or the mode.

Skewness is important because, unless it is understood, the differences between the median and the mean may sometimes be misleading (see Figure 2). If, for example, two political parties are arguing about the prosperity of the country, it is possible for the mean and median incomes to move in opposite directions. Suppose that a round of wage increases has been combined with a reduction in extremely high incomes. The median income might have gone up while the mean went down. The party wanting to show that incomes were getting higher would choose the median, whereas the party wishing to show that incomes were getting lower would choose the mean.

The mean is the most widely used measure of central tendency, but there are times when the mode or the median is a more meaningful measure.

Measures of Variation

Usually more information is needed about a distribution than can be obtained from a measure of central tendency. For example, we need a measure to tell us whether scores cluster closely around their average or whether they scatter widely. A measure of the spread of scores around the average is called a *measure of variation*.

Measures of variation are useful in at least two ways. First, they tell us how representative the average is. If the variation is small, we know that individual scores are close to it. If the variation is large, we cannot use the mean as a representative value with as much assurance. Suppose that clothing is being designed for a group of people without the benefit of precise measurements. Knowing their average size would be helpful, but it also would be important to know the spread of sizes. The second measure provides a yardstick that we can use to measure the amount of variability among the sizes.

To illustrate, consider the data in Figure 3, which show frequency distributions of entrance examination scores for two classes of 30 students. Both classes have the same mean of 75, but they exhibit clearly different degrees of variation. The scores of all the students in Class I are clustered close to the mean, whereas the scores of the students in Class II are spread over a wide

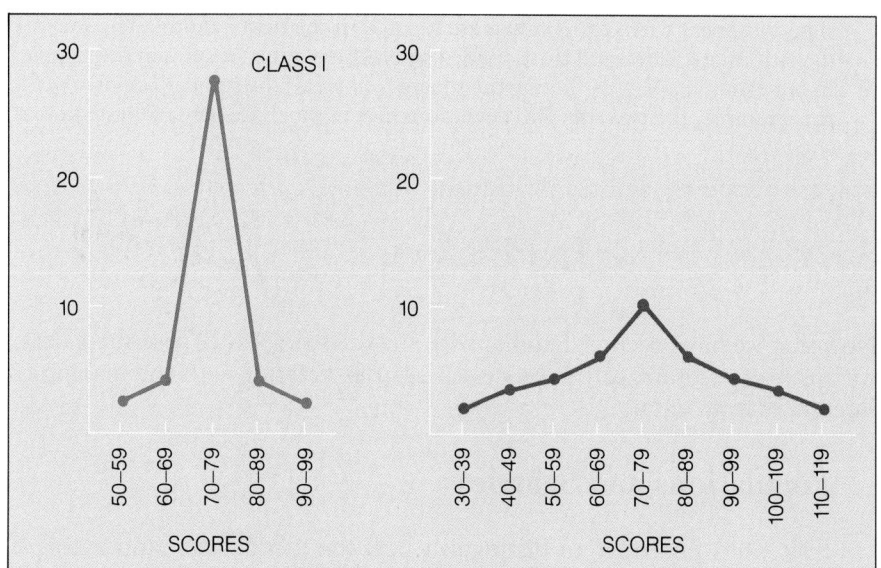

FIGURE 3
Distributions Differing in Variation *It is easy to see that the scores for Class I cluster closer to the mean than the scores for Class II, even though the means of the two classes are identical (75). For Class I, all the scores fall between 60 and 89, with most of the scores falling in the interval from 70 through 79. For Class II, the scores are distributed fairly uniformly over a wide range from 40 through 109. This difference in variability between the two distributions can be measured using the standard deviation, which is smaller for Class I than for Class II.*

range. Some measure is required to specify more exactly how these two distributions differ. Two measures of variation frequently used by psychologists are the *range* and the *standard deviation*.

To simplify arithmetic computation, we will suppose that five students from each class seek entrance to college and that their entrance examination scores are as follows:

Student scores from Class I:
73, 74, 75, 76, 77 (mean = 75)

Student scores from Class II:
60, 65, 75, 85, 90 (mean = 75)

We will now compute the measures of variation for these two samples.

The *range* is the spread between the highest score and the lowest score. The range of scores for the five students from Class I is 4 (from 73 to 77); the range of scores from Class II is 30 (from 60 to 90).

The range is easy to compute, but the *standard deviation* is more frequently used because it has certain properties that make it the preferred measure. One such property is that it is an extremely sensitive measure of variation because it accounts for every score, not just extreme values as the range does. The standard deviation, denoted by the lowercase Greek letter *sigma* (σ), measures how far the scores making up a distribution depart from that distribution's mean. The deviation *d* of each score from the mean is computed and squared; then the average of these squared values is obtained. The standard deviation is the square root of this average. Written as a formula,

$$\sigma = \sqrt{\frac{\text{sum of } d^2}{N}}$$

Specimen Computation of the Standard Deviation The scores for the samples from the two classes are arranged in Table 3 (p. 778) for computation of the standard deviation. The first step involves subtracting the mean from each score (the mean is 75 for both classes). This operation yields positive *d* values for scores above the mean and negative *d* values for scores below the mean. The minus

TABLE 3
Computation of the Standard Deviation

CLASS I SCORES (MEAN = 75)		
	d	d^2
77 − 75 =	2	4
76 − 75 =	1	1
75 − 75 =	0	0
74 − 75 =	−1	1
73 − 75 =	−2	4
		10

Sum of d^2 = 10
Mean of d^2 = $\frac{10}{5}$ = 2.0
Standard deviation (σ) = $\sqrt{2.0}$ = 1.4

CLASS II SCORES (MEAN = 75)		
	d	d^2
90 − 75 =	15	225
85 − 75 =	10	100
75 − 75 =	0	0
65 − 75 =	−10	100
60 − 75 =	−15	225
		650

Sum of d^2 = 650
Mean of d^2 = $\frac{650}{5}$ = 130
Standard deviation (σ) = $\sqrt{130}$ = 11.4

signs disappear when the d values are squared in the next column. The squared deviations are added and then divided by N, the number of cases in the sample; in our example, $N = 5$. Taking the square root yields the standard deviation. In this example, the two standard deviations give us much the same information as the ranges. *

STATISTICAL INFERENCE

Now that we have become familiar with statistics as a way of describing data, we are ready to turn to the processes of interpretation—to the making of inferences from data.

Populations and Samples

First, it is necessary to distinguish between a *population* and a *sample* drawn from that population. The United States Census Bureau attempts to describe the whole population by obtaining descriptive material on age, marital status, and so on from everyone in the country. The word *population* is appropriate to the census because it represents *all* the people living in the United States.

In statistics, the word "population" is not limited to people or animals or things. The population may be all of the temperatures registered on a thermometer during the last decade, all of the words in the English language, or all of any other specified supply of data. Often we do not have access to the total popluation, and so we try to represent it by a sample drawn in a *random* (unbiased) fashion. We may ask some questions of a random fraction of the people, as the United States Census Bureau has done as part of recent censuses; we may derive average temperatures by reading the thermometer at specified times, without taking a continuous record; we may estimate the number of words in the encyclopedia by counting the words on a random number of pages. These illustrations all involve the selection of a *sample* from the popluation. If any of these processes are repeated, we will obtain slightly different results due to the fact that a sample does not fully represent the whole population and therefore contains *errors of sampling*. This is where statistical inference enters.

A sample of data is collected from a population in order to make inferences about that population. A sample of census data may be examined to see whether the population is getting older, for example, or whether there is a trend of migration to the suburbs. Similarly, experimental results are studied to determine what effects experimental manipulations have had on behavior—whether the threshold for pitch is affected by loudness, whether child-rearing practices have detectable effects later in life. To make *statistical inferences*, we have to evaluate the relationships revealed by the sample data. These inferences are always made under some degree of uncertainty due to

---

*For this introductory treatment, we will use *sigma* (σ) throughout. However, in the scientific literature, the lowercase letter s is used to denote the standard deviation of a *sample* and σ is used to denote the standard deviation of the *population*. Moreover, in computing the standard deviation of a sample s, the sum of d^2 is divided by $N-1$ rather than by N. For reasonably large samples, however, the actual value of the standard deviation is only slightly affected whether we divide by $N-1$ or N. To simplify this presentation, we will not distinguish between the standard deviation of a sample and that of a population; instead, we will use the same formula to compute both. For a discussion of this point, see Phillips (1988).

sampling errors. If the statistical tests indicate that the magnitude of the effect found in the sample is fairly large (relative to the estimate of the sampling error), then we can be confident that the effect observed in the sample holds for the population at large.

Thus, statistical inference deals with the problem of making an inference or judgment about a feature of a population based solely on information obtained from a sample of that population. As an introduction to statistical inference, we will consider the normal distribution and its use in interpreting standard deviations.

Normal Distribution

When large amounts of data are collected, tabulated, and plotted as a histogram or polygon, they often fall into a roughly bell-shaped symmetrical distribution known as the *normal distribution*. Most items fall near the mean (the high point of the bell), and the bell tapers off sharply at very high and very low scores. This form of curve is of special interest because it also arises when the outcome of a process is based on a large number of *chance* events all occurring independently. The demonstration device displayed in Figure 4 illustrates how a sequence of chance events gives rise to a normal distribution. The chance factor of whether a steel ball will fall to the left or right each time it encounters a point where the channel branches results in a symmetrical distribution: more balls fall straight down the middle, but occasionally one reaches one of the end compartments. This is a useful way of visualizing what is meant by a chance distribution closely approximating the normal distribution.

The normal distribution (Figure 5) is the mathematical representation of the idealized distribution approximated by the device shown in Figure 4. The normal distribution represents the likelihood that items within a normally distributed population will depart from the mean by any stated amount. The percentages shown in Figure 5 represent the *percentage of the area* lying under the curve between the indicated scale values; the total area under the curve represents the whole population. Roughly two-thirds of the cases (68 percent) will fall between plus and minus one standard deviation from the mean ($\pm1\sigma$); 95 percent of the cases within $\pm2\sigma$; and virtually all cases (99.7 percent) within $\pm3\sigma$. A more detailed listing of areas under portions of the normal curve is given in Table 4 (p. 780).

Using Table 4, let us trace how the 68 percent and 95 percent values in Figure 5 are derived. We find from Column 3 of Table 4 that between -1σ and the mean lies .341 of the total area and between $+1\sigma$ and the mean also lies .341 of the area. Adding these values gives us .682, which is expressed in Figure 5 as 68 percent. Similarly, the area between -2σ and $+2\sigma$ is $2 \times .477 = .954$, which is expressed as 95 percent.

These percentages have several uses. One is in connection with the interpretation of standard scores, to which we turn next. Another is in connection with tests of significance.

Scaling of Data

In order to interpret a score, we often need to know whether it is high or low in relation to other scores. If a person taking a driver's test requires .500 seconds to brake after a danger signal, how can we tell whether the performance is fast or slow? Does a student who scores 60 on a physics examination

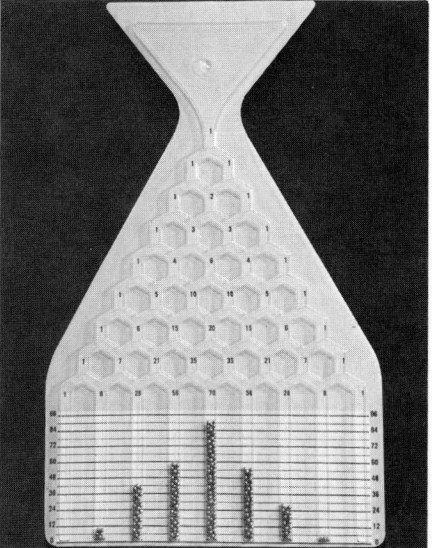

FIGURE 4
Device to Demonstrate a Chance Distribution *The board is held upside down until all the steel balls fall into the reservoir. Then the board is turned over and held vertically until the balls fall into the nine columns. The precise number of balls falling into each column will vary from one demonstration to the next. On the average, however, the heights of the columns of balls will approximate a normal distribution, with the greatest height in the center column and gradually decreasing heights in the outer columns.*

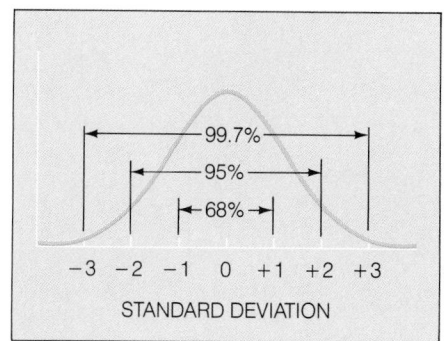

FIGURE 5
Normal Distribution *The normal distribution curve can be constructed using the mean and the standard deviation. The area under the curve below -3σ and above $+3\sigma$ is negligible.*

TABLE 4
Area of the Normal Distribution as
Proportion of Total Area

STANDARD DEVIATION	(1) AREA TO THE LEFT OF THIS VALUE	(2) AREA TO THE RIGHT OF THIS VALUE	(3) AREA BETWEEN THIS VALUE AND MEAN
-3.0σ	.001	.999	.499
-2.5σ	.006	.994	.494
-2.0σ	.023	.977	.477
-1.5σ	.067	.933	.433
-1.0σ	.159	.841	.341
-0.5σ	.309	.691	.191
0.0σ	.500	.500	.000
$+0.5\sigma$	.691	.309	.191
$+1.0\sigma$	.841	.159	.341
$+1.5\sigma$	.933	.067	.433
$+2.0\sigma$	.977	.023	.477
$+2.5\sigma$	.994	.006	.494
$+3.0\sigma$	.999	.001	.499

pass the course? To answer questions of this kind, we have to derive a *scale* against which the scores can be compared.

RANKED DATA   By placing scores in rank order from high to low, we derive one kind of scale. An individual score is interpreted on the basis of where it ranks among the group of scores. For example, the graduates of West Point know where they stand in their class—perhaps 35th or 125th in a class of 400.

STANDARD SCORES   The standard deviation is a convenient unit to use in scaling because we can interpret how far away 1σ or 2σ is from the mean (see Table 4). A score based on a multiple of the standard deviation is known as a *standard score*. Many scales used in psychological measurement are based on the principle of standard scores.

Specimen Computations of Standard Scores   Table 1 presented college entrance scores for 15 students. Without more information, we do not know whether these scores are representative of the population of all college applicants. On this examination, however, we will assume that the population mean is 75 and the standard deviation is 10.

What, then, is the *standard score* for a student who had 90 on the examination? We must express how far this score lies above the mean in multiples of the standard deviation.

Standard score for grade of 90:

$$\frac{90 - 75}{10} = \frac{15}{10} = 1.5\sigma$$

As a second example, consider a student with a score of 53.

Standard score for grade of 53:

$$\frac{53 - 75}{10} = \frac{-22}{10} = -2.2\sigma$$

In this case, the minus sign tells us that the student's score is below the mean by 2.2 standard deviations. Thus, the sign of the standard score (+ or −) indicates whether the score is above or below the mean, and its value indicates how far from the mean the score lies in standard deviations.

How Representative Is a Mean?

How useful is the mean of a sample in estimating the population mean? If we measure the height of a random sample of 100 college students, how well does the sample mean predict the true population mean (that is, the mean height of *all* college students)? These questions raise the issue of making an *inference* about a population based on information from a sample.

The accuracy of such inferences depends on *errors of sampling*. Suppose we were to select two random samples from the same population and compute the mean for each sample. What differences between the first and the second mean could be expected to occur by chance?

Successive random samples drawn from the same population will have different means, forming a distribution of *sample means* around the *true mean* of the population. These sample means are themselves numbers for which the standard deviation can be computed. We call this standard deviation the *standard error of the mean*, or σ_M, and can estimate it on the basis of the following formula:

$$\sigma_M = \frac{\sigma}{\sqrt{N}}$$

where σ is the standard deviation of the sample and N is the number of cases from which each sample mean is computed.

According to the formula, the size of the standard error of the mean decreases as the sample size increases; thus, a mean based on a large sample is more trustworthy (more likely to be close to the actual population mean) than a mean based on a smaller sample. Common sense would lead us to expect this. Computations of the standard error of the mean permit us to make clear assertions about the degree of uncertainty in our computed mean. The more cases in the sample, the more uncertainty has been reduced.

Significance of a Difference

In many psychological experiments, data are collected on two groups of subjects; one group is exposed to certain specified experimental conditions, and the other serves as a control group. The question is whether there is a difference in the mean performance of the two groups, and if such a difference is observed, whether it holds for the population from which these groups of subjects have been sampled. Basically, we are asking whether a difference between two sample means reflects a true difference or whether this difference is simply the result of sampling error.

As an example, we will compare the scores on a reading test for a sample of first-grade boys with the scores for a sample of first-grade girls. The boys score lower than the girls as far as mean performances are concerned, but there is a great deal of overlap; some boys do extremely well, and some girls do very poorly. Thus, we cannot accept the obtained difference in means without making a test of its *statistical significance*. Only then can we decide

TABLE 5
Significance of a Difference *Two examples that compare the difference between means are shown above. The difference between means is the same (8 kilograms) in both the top and the bottom panel. However, the data in the bottom panel indicate a more reliable difference between means than do the data in the top panel.*

STRENGTH OF GRIP IN KILOGRAMS, RIGHT-HANDED MEN	STRENGTH OF GRIP IN KILOGRAMS, LEFT-HANDED MEN
40	40
45	45
50	50
55	55
100	60
Sum 290	Sum 250
Mean 58	Mean 50

STRENGTH OF GRIP IN KILOGRAMS, RIGHT-HANDED MEN	STRENGTH OF GRIP IN KILOGRAMS, LEFT-HANDED MEN
56	48
57	49
58	50
59	51
60	52
Sum 290	Sum 250
Mean 58	Mean 50

whether the observed differences in sample means reflect true differences in the population or are due to sampling error. If some of the brighter girls and some of the duller boys are sampled by sheer luck, the difference could be due to sampling error.

As another example, suppose that we have set up an experiment to compare the grip strength of right-handed and left-handed men. The top panel of Table 5 presents hypothetical data from such an experiment. A sample of five right-handed men averaged 8 kilograms stronger than a sample of five left-handed men. In general, what can we infer from these data about left-handed and right-handed men? Can we argue that right-handed men are stronger than left-handed men? Obviously not, because the averages derived from most of the right-handed men would not differ from those from the left-handed men; the one markedly deviant score of 100 tells us we are dealing with an uncertain situation.

Now suppose that the results of the experiment were those shown in the bottom panel of Table 5. Again, we find the same mean difference of 8 kilograms, but we are now inclined to have greater confidence in the results, because the left-handed men scored consistently lower than the right-handed men. Statistics provides a precise way of taking into account the reliability of the mean differences so that we do not have to depend solely on intuition to determine that one difference is more reliable than another.

These examples suggest that the significance of a difference will depend on both the size of the obtained difference and the variability of the means being compared. From the standard error of the means, we can compute the *standard error of the difference between two means* σ_{D_M}. We can then evaluate the obtained difference by using a *critical ratio*—the ratio of the obtained difference between the means D_M to the standard error of the difference between the means:

$$\text{Critical ratio} = \frac{D_M}{\sigma_{D_M}}$$

This ratio helps us to evaluate the significance of the difference between the two means. As a rule of thumb, a critical ratio should be 2.0 or larger for the difference between means to be accepted as significant. Throughout this book, statements that the difference between means is "statistically significant" indicate that the critical ratio is at least that large.

Why is a critical ratio of 2.0 selected as statistically significant? Simply because a value this large or larger can occur by chance only 5 out of 100 times. Where do we get the 5 out of 100? We can treat the critical ratio as a standard score because it is merely the difference between two means, expressed as a multiple of its standard error. Referring to Column 2 in Table 4, we note that the likelihood is .023 that a standard deviation as high as or higher than +2.0 will occur by chance. Because the chance of deviating in the opposite direction is also .023, the total probability is .046. This means that 46 times out of 1,000, or about 5 times out of 100, a critical ratio as large as 2.0 would be found by chance if the population means were identical.

The rule of thumb that says a critical ratio should be at least 2.0 is just that—an arbitrary but convenient rule that defines the "5 percent level of significance." Following this rule, we will make fewer than 5 errors in 100 decisions by concluding on the basis of sample data that a difference in means exists when in fact there is none. The 5 percent level need not always be used; a higher level of significance may be appropriate in certain experiments, depending on how willing we are to make an occasional error in inference.

Specimen Computation of the Critical Ratio   The computation of the critical ratio calls for finding the *standard error of the difference between two means*, which is given by the following formula:

$$\sigma_{D_M} = \sqrt{(\sigma_{M_1})^2 + (\sigma_{M_2})^2}$$

In this formula, σ_{M_1} and σ_{M_2} are the standard errors of the two means being compared.

As an illustration, suppose we wanted to compare reading achievement test scores for first-grade boys and girls in the United States. A random sample of boys and girls would be identified and given the test. We will assume that the mean score for the boys was 70 with a standard error of .40 and that the mean score for the girls was 72 with a standard error of .30. On the basis of these samples, we want to decide whether there is a real difference between the reading achievement of boys and girls in the population as a whole. The sample data suggest that girls do achieve better reading scores than boys, but can we infer that this would have been the case if we had tested all the girls and all the boys in the United States? The critical ratio helps us make this decision.

$$\sigma_{D_M} = \sqrt{(\sigma_{M_1})^2 + (\sigma_{M_2})^2}$$
$$= \sqrt{.16 + .09} = \sqrt{.25}$$
$$= .5$$

$$\text{Critical ratio} = \frac{D_M}{\sigma_{D_M}} = \frac{72 - 70}{.5} = \frac{2.0}{.5} = 4.0$$

Because the critical ratio is well above 2.0, we may assert that the observed mean difference is statistically significant at the 5 percent level. Thus, we can conclude that there is a reliable difference in performance on the reading test between boys and girls. Note that the sign of the critical ratio could be positive or negative, depending on which mean is subtracted from which; when the critical ratio is interpreted, only its magnitude (not its sign) is considered.

COEFFICIENT OF CORRELATION

Correlation refers to the concomitant variation of paired measures. Suppose that a test is designed to predict success in college. If it is a good test, high scores on it will be related to high performance in college and low scores will be related to poor performance. The *coefficient of correlation* gives us a way of stating the degree of relationship more precisely. (This topic was discussed on pp. 19–21. You may find it helpful to review that material.)

Product-Moment Correlation

The most frequently used method of determining the coefficient of correlation is the *product-moment method*, which yields the index conventionally designated r. The product-moment coefficient r varies between perfect positive correlation ($r = +1.00$) and perfect negative correlation ($r = -1.00$). Lack of any relationship yields $r = .00$.

TABLE 6
Computation of a Product-Moment Correlation

STUDENT	ENTRANCE TEST (x-score)	FRESHMAN GRADES (y-score)	(dx)	(dy)	(dx)(dy)
Adam	71	39	6	9	+ 54
Bill	67	27	2	− 3	− 6
Charles	65	33	0	3	0
David	63	30	− 2	0	0
Edward	59	21	− 6	− 9	+ 54
Sum	325	150	0	0	+ 102
Mean	65	30			

$$\sigma_x = 4 \qquad \sigma_y = 6 \qquad r = \frac{\text{Sum }(dx)(dy)}{N\sigma_x\sigma_y} = \frac{+102}{5 \times 4 \times 6} = +.85$$

The formula for computing the product-moment correlation is

$$r = \frac{\text{Sum }(dx)(dy)}{N\sigma_x\sigma_y}$$

Here, one of the paired measures has been labeled the x-score; the other, the y-score. The dx and dy refer to the deviations of each score from its mean, N is the number of paired measures, and σ_x and σ_y are the standard deviations of the x-scores and the y-scores.

The computation of the coefficient of correlation requires the determination of the sum of the (dx)(dy) products. This sum, in addition to the computed standard deviations for the x-scores and y-scores, can then be entered into the formula.

Specimen Computation of Product-Moment Correlation Suppose that we have collected the data shown in Table 6. For each subject, we have obtained two scores—the first being a score on a college entrance test (to be labeled arbitrarily the x-score) and the second being freshman grades (the y-score).

Figure 6 is a *scatter diagram* of these data. Each point represents the x-score and y-score for a given subject; for example, the uppermost right-hand point is for Adam (labeled A). Looking at these data, we can easily detect that there is some positive correlation between the x-scores and the y-scores. Adam attained the highest score on the entrance test and also earned the highest freshman grades; Edward received the lowest scores on both. The other students' test scores and grades are a little irregular, so we know that the correlation is not perfect; hence, r is less than 1.00.

We will compute the correlation to illustrate the method, although no researcher would consent, in practice, to determining a correlation for so few cases. The details are given in Table 6. Following the procedure outlined in Table 3, we compute the standard deviation of the x-scores and then the standard deviation of the y-scores. Next, we compute the (dx)(dy) products for each subject and total the five cases. Entering these results in our equation yields an r of +.85.

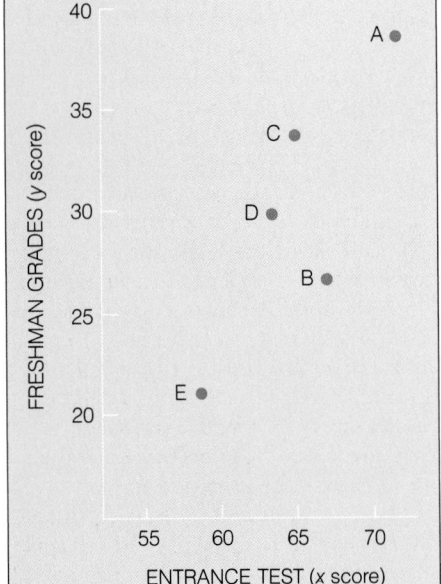

FIGURE 6
Scatter Diagram *Each point represents the x- and y-scores for a particular student. The letters next to the points identify the students in the data table (A = Adam, B = Bill, and so on).*

Interpreting a Correlation Coefficient

We can use correlations in making predictions. For example, if we know from past experience that a certain entrance test correlates with freshman grades, we can predict the freshman grades for beginning college students who have taken the test. If the correlation were perfect, we could predict their grades without error. But r is usually less than 1.00, and some errors in prediction will be made; the closer r is to 0, the greater the sizes of the errors in prediction.

Although we cannot go into the technical problems of predicting freshman grades from entrance examinations or of making other similar predictions, we can consider the meanings of correlation coefficients of different sizes. It is evident that with a correlation of 0 between x and y, knowledge of x will not help to predict y. If weight is unrelated to intelligence, it does us no good to know a subject's weight when we are trying to predict his or her intelligence. At the other extreme, a perfect correlation would mean 100 percent predictive efficiency—knowing x, we can predict y perfectly. What about intermediate values of r? Some appreciation of the meaning of correlations of intermediate sizes can be gained by examining the scatter diagrams in Figure 7.

In the preceding discussion, we did not emphasize the sign of the correlation coefficient, since this has no bearing on the strength of a relationship. The only distinction between a correlation of $r = +.70$ and $r = -.70$ is that increases in x are accompanied by increases in y for the former, and increases in x are accompanied by decreases in y for the latter.

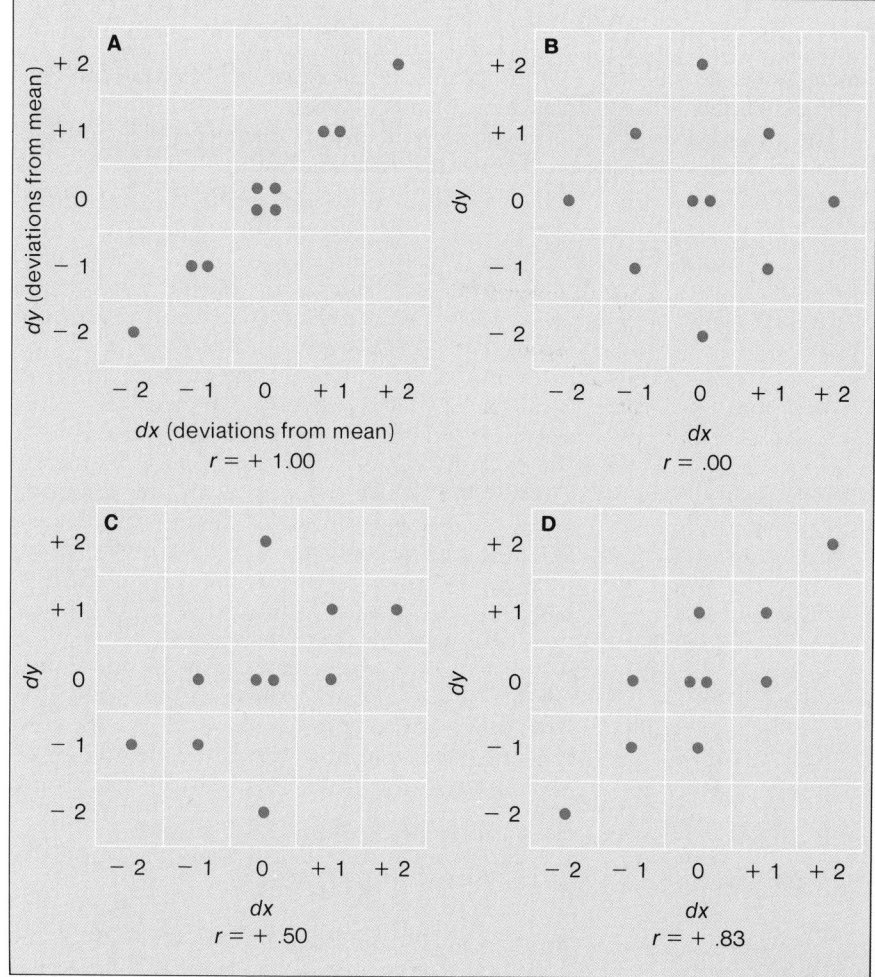

FIGURE 7
Scatter Diagrams Illustrating Correlations of Various Sizes *Each dot represents one individual's score on two tests, x and y. In A, all cases fall on the diagonal and the correlation is perfect (r= +1.00); if we know a subject's score on x, we know that it will be the same on y. In B, the correlation is 0; knowing a subject's score on x, we cannot predict whether it will be at, above, or below the mean on y. For example, of the four subjects who score at the mean of x (dx=0), one makes a very high score on y (dy=+2), one a very low score (dy=−2), and two remain average. In both C and D, there is a diagonal trend to the scores, so that a high score on x is associated with a high score on y and a low score on x with a low score on y, but the relationship is imperfect. It is possible to check the value of the correlations by using the formulas given in the text for the coefficient of correlation. The computation has been greatly simplified by presenting the scores in the deviation form that permits entering them directly into the formulas. The fact that the axes do not have conventional scales does not change the interpretation. For example, if we assigned the values 1 through 5 to the x and y coordinates and then computed r for these new values, the correlation coefficients would be the same.*

Although the correlation coefficient is one of the most widely used statistics in psychology, it is also one of the most widely misused procedures. Those who use it sometimes overlook the fact that r does not imply a cause-and-effect relationship between x and y. When two sets of scores are correlated, we may suspect that they have some causal factors in common, but we cannot conclude that one of them causes the other (see p. 21).

Correlations sometimes appear paradoxical. For example, the correlation between study time and college grades has been found to be slightly negative (about $-.10$). If a causal interpretation were assumed, we might conclude that the best way to raise grades would be to stop studying. The negative correlation arises because some students have advantages over others in grade making (possibly due to better college preparation), so that often those who study the hardest are those who have difficulty earning the best grades.

This example provides sufficient warning against assigning a causal interpretation to a coefficient of correlation. It is possible, however, that when two variables are correlated, one may be the cause of the other. The search for causes is a logical one, and correlations can help us by providing leads to experiments that can verify cause-and-effect relationships.

FURTHER READING

There are a number of textbooks on statistics written from the viewpoint of psychological research. Examples are McCall, *Fundamental Statistics for Behavioral Sciences* (4th ed., 1986); Welkowitz, Ewen, and Cohen, *Introductory Statistics for the Behavioral Sciences* (3rd ed., 1982); Loftus and Loftus, *Essence of Statistics* (1982); Hinkle, Wiersma, and Jurs, *Applied Statistics for the Behavioral Sciences* (2nd ed., 1988); and Phillips, *How to Think About Statistics* (1988).

The role of statistics in the design of psychological experiments is discussed in Keppel and Saufley, *Introduction to Design and Analysis* (1980).

Appendix IV

Psychology Journals

Listed alphabetically are some of the major American psychology journals and a description of the types of articles they publish. These journals are available in most college and university libraries; current issues of the journals usually can be found on racks in an open area of the library. An excellent introduction to psychology can be gained by spending some time perusing recent issues of these journals.

- *American Psychologist:* Official papers of the American Psychological Association; articles on psychology; comments, announcements, and lists of regional, national, and international conventions.

- *Animal Learning and Behavior:* Studies of animal learning, motivation, emotion, and comparative animal behavior.

- *Behavioral Neuroscience:* Original research papers concerned with the biological bases of psychological phenomena; studies cover the entire range of relevant biological and neural sciences.

- *Cognitive Psychology:* Theory and research in the area of cognitive processes and related fields of psychology.

- *Contemporary Psychology:* Critical reviews of recent books, films, and other media; brief notes on new texts; previews of textbooks in psychology.

- *Developmental Psychology:* Studies of the variables influencing growth, development, and aging.

- *Journal of Abnormal Psychology:* Basic research and theory in the field of abnormal behavior, its determinants, and its correlates.

- *Journal of Applied Psychology:* Theoretical and research contributions in applied fields such as business and industry; government, urban, and consumer affairs; legal, health, transportation, defense, and educational systems; and space and other new environments.

- *Journal of Comparative Psychology:* Research reports in comparative psychology; laboratory and field studies of the behavioral patterns of various species as they relate to such factors as evolution, development, ecology, and functional significance.

- *Journal of Consulting and Clinical Psychology:* Research and theory concerning clinical psychology, including psychological diagnoses, psychotherapy, personality, and psychopathology.

- *Journal of Counseling Psychology:* Theory, research, and practice concerning counseling and related activities of counselors and personnel workers.
- *Journal of Educational Psychology:* Studies of learning and teaching, including measurement of psychological development, methods of instruction, and school adjustment.
- *Journal of Experimental Psychology–Animal Behavior Processes:* Studies of the basic mechanisms of perception, learning, motivation, and performance, especially with infrahuman animals.
- *Journal of Experimental Psychology–General:* Long, integrative reports leading to an advance in knowledge of interest to all experimental psychologists.
- *Journal of Experimental Psychology–Human Learning and Memory:* Studies of human acquisition, retention, and transfer processes.
- *Journal of Experimental Psychology–Human Perception and Performance:* Studies of information-processing operations as they relate to experience and performance.
- *Journal of Mathematical Psychology:* Theoretical contributions in all fields of psychology in which the work involves theories or models employing mathematical methods, formal logic, or computer simulation.
- *Journal of Personality and Social Psychology:* Research on personality dynamics, group processes, and the psychological aspects of social structure.
- *Journal of Phenomenological Psychology:* Theoretical and empirical contributions to psychology that emphasize a humanistic-phenomenological approach.
- *Memory and Cognition:* Studies of human memory and learning, conceptual processes, psycholinguistics, problem solving, thinking, decision making, and skilled performance.
- *Perception and Psychophysics:* Studies that deal with sensory processes, perception, and psychophysics.
- *Physiological Psychology:* Basic studies in structural, chemical, and electrical aspects of brain organization and functions that have implications for behavior.
- *Psychological Abstracts:* Noncritical abstracts of the world's literature in psychology and related subjects.
- *Psychological Bulletin:* Evaluative reviews of research literature and discussions of research methodology in psychology.
- *Psychological Review:* Theoretical contributions attempting to integrate and discuss a broad range of psychological phenomena.
- *Psychology and Aging:* Focuses on adult development and aging. The journal's two major aims are to disseminate new research findings and to highlight the importance of the physiological and behavioral aspects of aging.
- *Psychometrika:* Articles on the development of quantitative models for psychological phenomena, including new mathematical and statistical techniques for the evaluation of psychological data.

Glossary

The glossary defines the technical words that appear in the text and some common words that have special meanings when used in psychology. No attempt is made to give the range of meanings beyond those used in the text. For fuller definitions and other shades of meaning, consult any standard dictionary of psychology.

A

ability. Demonstrable knowledge or skill. Ability includes aptitude and achievement. See also *achievement, aptitude.*

abreaction. In psychoanalysis, the process of reducing emotional tension by reliving (in speech or action or both) the experience that caused the tension.

absolute threshold. The intensity or frequency at which a stimulus becomes effective or ceases to become effective, as measured under experimental conditions. See also *difference threshold, threshold.*

accommodation. The process by which the lens of the eye varies its focus.

acetylcholine. The most common of the neurotransmitters. It is found in many synapses in the brain and spinal cord, and is particularly prevalent in an area of the brain called the hippocampus, which plays a key role in the formation of new memories. See also *neurotransmitter.*

achievement. Acquired ability, such as school attainment in spelling. See also *aptitude.*

achromatic colors. Black, white, and gray. See also *chromatic colors.*

acquisition. The stage during which a new response is learned and gradually strengthened. See also *classical conditioning.*

ACTH. See *adrenocorticotropic hormone.*

action potential. Synonymous with *nerve impulse.* The wave of electrical activity that is transmitted down the axon of the neuron when the cell membrane becomes depolarized. See also *depolarization, graded potentials, resting potential.*

acupuncture. A healing procedure developed in China in which needles are inserted in the skin at critical points and twirled, eliminating pain. See also *gate control theory of pain.*

addiction. See *physical dependence.*

additive mixture. The mixture of colored lights; two spotlights of different colors focused on the same spot yield an additive color mixture. See also *subtractive mixture.*

ADH. See *antidiuretic hormone.*

adipocytes. Special fat cells in the body. Obese individuals have many more of them and thus, perhaps, a higher body fat base line.

adolescence. The period of transition from childhood to adulthood during which the individual develops to sexual maturity. See also *puberty.*

adolescent growth spurt. A period of rapid physical growth that accompanies the onset of puberty.

adrenal gland. One of a pair of endocrine glands located above the kidneys. The medulla of the gland secretes the hormones epinephrine and norepinephrine. The cortex of the gland secretes a number of hormones, collectively called the *adrenocortical hormones,* which include cortisol. See also *endocrine gland.*

adrenalin. See *epinephrine.*

adreno-cortical system. A neuro-endocrine system activated in response to stress. On a signal from the hypothalamus, the pituitary gland secretes a number of hormones. One stimulates the thyroid gland to make more energy available; the other (adrenocorticotropic hormone, ACTH) triggers the outer layer of the adrenal gland (the adrenal cortex) to release some 30 hormones (including cortisol) which play a role in the body's adjustment to emergencies. See also *adrenocorticotropic hormone, cortisol.*

adrenocorticotropic hormone (ACTH). A hormone released by the pituitary gland in response to stress; known as the body's major "stress" hormone. It is carried by the bloodstream to the adrenal glands and various other organs of the body, causing the release of some 30 hormones, each of which plays a role in the body's adjustment to emergency situations. See also *corticotropin-release factor.*

affective experience. An emotional experience, whether pleasant or unpleasant, mild or intense. See also *emotion.*

afferent neuron. See *sensory neuron.*

afterimage. The sensory experience that remains when a stimulus is withdrawn. Usually refers to visual experience—for example, the negative afterimage of a picture or the train of colored images that results after staring at the sun.

age regression. In hypnosis, the reliving through fantasy of experiences that are based on early memories or that are appropriate to a younger age. See also *hypnosis.*

aggregated score. A combination of several measures of the same behavior or characteristic.

aggression. Behavior intended to harm another person. See also *hostile aggression, instrumental aggression.*

agoraphobia. Fear of being alone or being in a public place where escape might be difficult or help unavailable should the individual be incapacitated by a panic attack. See also *panic disorder, phobia.*

AI. See *artificial intelligence.*

all-or-none principle. The rule that the nerve impulse in a single neuron is independent of the strength of stimulation; the neuron either responds completely (fires its action potential) or not at all.

alpha waves. See *electroencephalogram.*

alternative form reliability. The consistency between two or more versions of the same test when given to the same person. See also *reliability.*

ambivalence. Simultaneous liking and disliking of an object or person; the conflict caused by an incentive that is at once positive and negative. See also *conflict.*

Ames room. A perceptual illusion; specifically, a room that when viewed through a peephole leads to distortions in size judgments. See also *size constancy.*

amnesia. A partial or complete loss of memory. May be due to psychological factors (for example, emotional trauma) or physiological factors (some form of brain damage) and may involve loss of memory for events occurring prior to or subsequent to the amnesia-causing trauma. See also *anterograde amnesia, retrograde amnesia.*

amphetamines. Central nervous system stimulants that produce restlessness, irritability, anxiety, and rapid heart rate. Dexedrine sulfate ("speed") and methamphetamine ("meth") are two types of amphetamines. See also *depressants, stimulants.*

amygdala. A brain structure located below the cerebral cortex that is involved in consolidation of new memories. See also *diencephalon, hippocampus.*

anal stage. The second stage in Freud's psychoanalytic theory of psychosexual development, following the oral stage. The sources of gratification and conflict have to do with the expulsion and retention of feces. See also *psychosexual development.*

androgens. The collective name for male sex hormones, of which testosterone, secreted by the testes, is best known. See also *gonads.*

androgyny. The condition in which some male and some female characteristics are present in the same individual. An *androgynous* individual has both so-called masculine and feminine personality traits.

angiotensin. A hormone critical in the regulation of thirst. When produced, it induces a feeling of thirst as well as an appetite for salt.

anorexia nervosa. An eating disorder, which mainly afflicts young women, and which is characterized by an extreme, self-imposed weight loss. See also *bulimia.*

anterograde amnesia. Loss of memory for events and experiences occurring subsequent to an amnesia-causing trauma; the patient is unable to acquire new informaton, although recall of information learned prior to the onset may be largely unaffected. See also *amnesia, retrograde amnesia.*

anthropology. The science that studies chiefly preliterate ("primitive") societies. Its main divisions are archaeology (the study of the physical monuments and remains from earlier civilizations), physical anthropology (concerned with the anatomical differences among men and their evolutionary origins), linguistic anthropology, and social anthropology (concerned with social institutions and behavior). See also *behavioral sciences.*

antianxiety drug. Central nervous system depressant that reduces tension. Causes some drowsiness but less than barbiturates. Examples are Valium and Librium (syn. *tranquilizer*).

antidepressant. Drug used to elevate the mood of depressed individuals, presumably by increasing the availability of the neurotransmitters norepinephrine and/or serotonin. Examples are imipramine (Tofranil), isocarboxazid (Marplan), and tranylcypromine (Parnate).

antidiuretic hormone (ADH). Hormone secreted by the pituitary gland that signals the kidney to reabsorb water into the bloodstream instead of excreting it as urine.

antipsychotic drug. A drug that reduces psychotic symptoms, used most frequently in the treatment of schizophrenia. Chlorpromazine and reserpine are examples (syn. *neuroleptic drug*). See also *psychotic behavior.*

antisocial personality. A type of personality disorder marked by impulsivity, inability to abide by the customs and laws of society, and lack of anxiety or guilt regarding behavior (syn. *sociopathic personality, psychopathic personality*).

anxiety. A state of apprehension, tension, and worry. Synonymous with fear for some theorists, although others view the object of anxiety (such as a vague danger or foreboding) as less specific than the object of a fear (such as a vicious animal). See also *neurotic anxiety, objective anxiety.*

anxiety disorders. A group of mental disorders characterized by intense anxiety or by maladaptive behavior designed to relieve anxiety. Includes generalized anxiety and panic disorders, phobic and obsessive-compulsive disorders. Major category of DSM-III-R covering most of the disorders formerly called neuroses. See also *generalized anxiety disorder, neurosis, obsessive-compulsive disorder, panic disorder, phobic disorder, post-traumatic stress disorder.*

anxiety hierarchy. A list of situations or stimuli to which a person responds with anxiety ranked in order from the least anxiety-producing to the most fearful. Used by behavior therapists in systematically desensitizing patients to feared stimuli by associating deep relaxation with the situations rather than anxiety. See also *behavior therapy, systematic desensitization.*

apathy. Listlessness, indifference; one of the consequences of frustration. See also *frustration.*

aphagia. Inability to eat. See also *hyperphagia.*

aphasia. Impairment or loss of ability to articulate words or comprehend speech.

apnea. A sleep disturbance characterized by inhibited breathing during sleep.

apparent motion. See *phi phenomenon, stroboscopic motion.*

appetitive behavior. Seeking behavior. See also *aversive behavior.*

aptitude. The capacity to learn—for instance, a person's typing aptitude prior to practice on a typewriter. Aptitude tests are designed to predict the outcome of training, hence to predict future ability on the basis of present ability. See also *achievement.*

arousal level. The principle according to which people seek an optimal level of drive or arousal.

artificial intelligence (AI). A field of research combining computer science and cognitive psychology; it is concerned with a) using computers to simulate human thought processes and b) devising computer programs that act "intelligently" and can adapt to changing circumstances. In essence, it is the science of making machines (computers) do things that are normally done by the human mind. See also *cognitive psychology, cognitive science, computer simulation.*

assertiveness training. The use of behavioral rehearsal to help an individual learn to express his or her needs in an effective, nonhostile manner.

association areas. Areas of the cerebral cortex that are not directly concerned with sensory or motor processes; they integrate inputs from various sensory channels and presumably function in learning, memory, and thinking.

associative learning. Learning that certain contingencies (or relations) exist between events; learning that one event is associated with another.

astigmatism. In vision, an optical defect that prevents horizontal and vertical contours from being in focus simultaneously. See also *strabismus.*

attachment. The tendency of the young organism to seek closeness to particular individuals and to feel more secure in their presence.

attention. The focusing of perception leading to heightened awareness of a limited range of stimuli. It has both overt behavioral components and internal components. See also *orienting reflex*.

attitude. A like or dislike; an affinity for or aversion to objects, persons, groups, situations or other aspects of the environment including abstract ideas and social policies. Treated by social psychologists as one component in a three-part system. Beliefs constitute the cognitive component; the attitude is the affective component; actions constitute the behavioral component.

attribution. The process by which we attempt to explain the behavior of other people. Attribution theory deals with the rules people use to infer the causes of observed behavior. See also *dispositional attribution, situational attribution*.

authoritarian parents. Parents who exercise a high level of control over their children's behavior without warmth, nurturance, or two-way communication. See also *authoritative parents, child-centered parents, indulgent parents, neglecting parents, parent-centered parents*.

authoritative parents. Parents who combine a high level of control over their children's behavior with warmth, nurturance, and two-way communication. See also *authoritarian parents, child-centered parents, indulgent parents, neglecting parents, parent-centered parents*.

autism. Absorption in fantasy to the exclusion of interest in reality; a symptom of schizophrenia. See also *schizophrenia*.

autistic thinking. A form of associative thinking, controlled more by the thinker's needs or desires than by reality; wishful thinking. See also *rationalization*.

automatic writing. Writing that the writer is unaware of (does not know that he or she is producing); familiar in hypnosis. See also *hypnosis*.

autonomic nervous system. The division of the peripheral nervous system that regulates smooth muscle (organ and glandular) activities. It is divided into the sympathetic and parasympathetic divisions. See also *parasympathetic division, peripheral nervous system, sympathetic division*.

autoshaping. A shaping procedure that involves aspects of both operant and classical conditioning and does not require the presence of an experimenter. See also *shaping of behavior*.

average. See *measure of central tendency*.

aversive behavior. Avoidance behavior. See also *appetitive behavior*.

aversive conditioning. A form of conditioning in which an undesirable response is extinguished through association with punishment; has been used in behavior therapy to treat alcoholism, smoking, and sexual problems. See also *behavior therapy, counterconditioning*.

avoidance learning. A form of conditioned behavior in which an organism learns to avoid a punishing event by responding to a warning signal. See also *conditioning*.

awareness. See *consciousness*.

axon. That portion of a neuron that transmits impulses to other neurons. See also *dendrite, neuron*.

B

BAC. See *blood alcohol concentration*.

Barnum effect. Refers to the readiness of people to believe that general descriptions, as given in astrological characterizations, refer to them personally.

basal mental age. In individual tests of the Binet type, the highest age level at which, and below which, all tests are passed. See also *mental age*.

basic level. In a hierarchy of concepts, the level at which one first categorizes an object.

basilar membrane. A membrane of the ear within the coils of the cochlea supporting the organ of Corti. Movements of the basilar membrane stimulate the hair cells of the organ of Corti, producing the neural effects of auditory stimulation. See also *cochlea, organ of Corti*.

behavior. Those activities of an organism that can be observed by another organism or by an experimenter's instruments. Included within behavior are verbal reports made about subjective, conscious experiences. See also *conscious processes*.

behavior genetics. The study of the inheritance of behavioral characteristics.

behavior modification. See *behavior therapy*.

behavior therapy. A method of psychotherapy based on learning principles. It uses such techniques as counter-conditioning, reinforcement, and shaping to modify behavior (syn. *behavior modification*). See also *cognitive behavior therapy*.

behavioral assessment. Personality appraisal through direct observations of behavior, often in controlled or contrived social situations. See also *personality assessment*.

behavioral medicine. An interdisciplinary field that focuses on how social, psychological, and biological variables contribute to illness and how behavior and environments can be changed to promote health. An outgrowth of earlier research on psychosomatic aspects of illness. See also *psychosomatic disorder*.

behavioral perspective. An approach to psychology that focuses only on observable behavior, and tries to explain it in terms of its relation to environmental events. See also *behaviorism*.

behavioral sciences. The sciences concerned in one way or another with the behavior of humans and lower organisms (especially social anthropology, psychology, and sociology but including some aspects of biology, economics, political science, history, philosophy, and other fields of study.)

behaviorism. A school or system of psychology associated with the name of John B. Watson; it defined psychology as the study of behavior and limited the data of psychology to observable activities. In its classical form it was more restrictive than the contemporary behavioral viewpoint in psychology.

belief-driven learning. A kind of associative learning in which people have prior beliefs about the relation that has to be learned; learning is driven by the beliefs as well as by the input. See also *data-driven learning*.

binocular cues. See *distance cues*.

binocular disparity. The fact that an object projects slightly different images on the two retinas due to the different positions of the right and left eyes.

binocular parallax. A cue for depth perception that arises because any visible point will differ slightly in its direction to the two eyes. See also *binocular disparity*.

biofeedback. A procedure that permits individuals to monitor their own physiological processes (such as heart rate, blood pressure) which they are normally unaware of, to learn to control them.

biological perspective. An approach to psychology that tries to explain behavior in terms of electrical and chemical events taking place inside the body, particularly within the brain and nervous system.

biological therapy. Treatment of personality maladjustment or mental illness by drugs, electric shock, or other methods directly affecting bodily processes. See also *psychotherapy*.

bipolar cells. Cells in the retina that transmit electrical impulses from photoreceptors to ganglion cells. See also *ganglia, photoreceptors, retina*.

bipolar disorder. A mood disorder in which people experience episodes of depression and mania (exaggerated excitement) or of mania alone. Typically the individual alternates between the two extremes, often with periods of normal mood in between (syn. *manic-depression*). See also *depression, mood disorder*.

blind spot. An insensitive area of the retina where the nerve fibers from the ganglion cells join to form the optic nerve.

blocking. A phenomenon in classical conditioning: if one conditioned stimulus

blocking (*continued*)
reliably predicts an unconditioned stimulus, and another conditioned stimulus is added, the relation between the added conditioned stimulus and the unconditioned stimulus will not be learned.

blood alcohol concentration (BAC). The concentration, in milligrams, of alcohol per 100 milliliters of blood. The legal definition of intoxication in most states is a blood alcohol concentration of .10 percent (100 milligrams of alcohol per 100 milliliters of blood).

blood pressure. The pressure of the blood against the walls of the blood vessels. Changes in blood pressure following stimulation serve as one indicator of emotion.

brain stem. The structures lying near the core of the brain; essentially all of the brain with the exception of the cerebrum and the cerebellum and their dependent parts.

brightness. The dimension of color that describes its nearness in brilliance to white (as contrasted to black). A bright color reflects more light than a dark one. See also *hue, saturation.*

Broca's area. A portion of the left cerebral hemisphere involved in the control of speech. Individuals with damage in this area have difficulty enunciating words correctly and speak in a slow and labored way; their speech often makes sense, but it includes only key words.

bulimia. An eating disorder, which mainly afflicts young women, and which is characterized by episodes of binge eating, followed by attempts to purge the excess by means of vomiting and laxatives. See also *anorexia nervosa.*

C

Cannon-Bard theory. A classical theory of emotion proposed by Cannon and Bard. The theory states that an emotion-producing stimulus activates the cortex and bodily responses at the same time; bodily changes and the experience of emotion occur simultaneously. See also *cognitive-appraisal theory, James-Lange theory.*

cardiac muscle. A special kind of muscle found only in the heart. See also *smooth muscle, striate muscle.*

cardinal disposition. In Gordon Allport's personality theory, a personality trait that influences virtually all aspects of an individual's behavior. Only a few people have a cardinal disposition; most have a small number of *central dispositions* and a large number of *secondary dispositions*. See also *central disposition, common disposition, personal disposition, secondary disposition.*

case history. A biography obtained for scientific purposes; the material is sometimes supplied by interview, sometimes collected over the years. See also *longitudinal study.*

castration. Surgical removal of the gonads; in the male, removal of testes; in the female, removal of the ovaries.

catharsis. Reduction of an impulse or emotion through direct or indirect expression, particularly verbal and fantasy expression.

central core. The most central and the evolutionally oldest portion of the brain. It includes structures that regulate basic life processes, including most of the brain stem. See also *brain stem, cerebellum, hypothalamus, reticular system.*

central disposition. In Gordon Allport's personality theory, a personality trait that influences many aspects of an individual's behavior. Most people have a small number of *central dispositions* and a much larger number of *secondary dispositions*. See also *cardinal disposition, common disposition, personal disposition, secondary disposition.*

central fissure. A fissure of each cerebral hemisphere that separates the frontal and parietal lobes (syn. *fissure of Rolando*).

central nervous system. In vertebrates, the brain and spinal cord, as distinct from the nerve trunks and their peripheral connections. See also *autonomic nervous system, peripheral nervous system.*

cerebellum. Lobed structure attached to the rear of the brain stem that regulates muscle tone and coordination of intricate movements.

cerebral cortex. The surface layer of the cerebral hemispheres in higher animals, including humans. It is commonly called gray matter because its many cell bodies give it a gray appearance in cross section, in contrast with the myelinated nerve fibers that make up the white matter in the center.

cerebral hemispheres. Two large masses of nerve cells and fibers constituting the bulk of the brain in humans and other higher animals. The hemispheres are separated by a deep fissure, but connected by a broad band of fibers, the corpus callosum (syn. cerebrum). See also *cerebral cortex, left hemisphere, right hemisphere, split-brain subject.*

cerebrum. See *cerebral hemispheres.*

child-centered parents. Parents who are highly involved in their children's lives, contrasted with parent-centered parents, who are more occupied with their own interests and activities than those of their children. See also *authoritarian parents, authoritative parents, indulgent parents, neglecting parents, parent-centered parents.*

childhood amnesia. The inability to recall events from the first years of one's life.

chlorpromazine. See *antipsychotic drug.*

chromatic colors. All colors other than black, white, and gray; for instance, red, yellow, blue. See also *achromatic colors.*

chromosome. Rodlike structures found in pairs in all the cells of the body, carrying the genetic determiners (genes) that are transmitted from parent to offspring. A human cell has 46 chromosomes, arranged in 23 pairs, one member of each pair deriving from the mother, one from the father. See also *gene.*

chronological age (CA). Age from birth; calendar age. See also *mental age.*

chunk. The largest meaningful unit of information that can be stored in short-term memory; short-term memory holds 7 ± 2 chunks. See also *short-term memory.*

cilia. Hairlike structures that are sometimes parts of receptors.

circadian rhythm. A cycle or rhythm that is roughly 24 hours long. Sleep-wakefulness, body temperature, and water excretion follow a circadian rhythm, as do a number of behavioral and psychological variables.

clairvoyance. Perception of objects or events that do not provide a stimulus to the known senses (for example, identifying a concealed playing card, the identity of which is unknown). See also *extrasensory perception, parapsychology, precognition, psi, psychokinesis, telepathy.*

classical concept. A concept where every instance must have every property mentioned in the concept. An example is the concept of *bachelor*; every instance must have the properties of being adult, male, and unmarried. See also *fuzzy concept.*

classical conditioning. Conditioned-response experiments conforming to the pattern of Pavlov's experiment. The main feature is that the originally neutral conditioned stimulus, through repeated pairing with the unconditioned one, acquires the response originally given to the unconditioned stimulus. See also *operant conditioning.*

claustrophobia. Fear of closed places. See also *phobia.*

client-centered therapy. See *person-centered therapy.*

clinical psychologist. A psychologist, usually with a Ph.D. degree, trained in the diagnosis and treatment of emotional or behavioral problems and mental disorders. See also *counseling psychologist, psychiatrist.*

closure. A Gestalt principle of grouping, wherein elements are grouped together so as to complete figures with gaps. See also *good continuation.*

cocaine. A central nervous system stimulant derived from leaves of the coca plant. Increases energy, produces euphoria, and in large doses causes paranoia.

cochlea. The portion of the inner ear containing the receptors for hearing. See also *basilar membrane, organ of Corti.*

coding. See *encoding.*

coding by pattern. Coding the quality of a sensation in terms of the pattern of neural firing. See also *coding by specificity.*

coding by specificity. Coding the quality of a sensation in terms of the specific neurons involved. See also *coding by pattern, doctrine of specific nerve energies.*

coefficient of correlation. A numerical index used to indicate the degree of correspondence between two sets of paired measurements. The most common kind is the product-moment coefficient designated by *r.*

cognition. An individual's thoughts, knowledge, interpretations, understandings, or ideas. See also *cognitive processes.*

cognitive appraisal. The interpretation of an event or situation with respect to one's goals and well-being. The cognitive appraisal of an event influences both the quality and intensity of the emotion experienced and the degree of perceived threat.

cognitive behavior therapy. A psychotherapy approach that emphasizes the influence of a person's beliefs, thoughts, and self-statements on behavior. Combines behavior therapy methods with techniques designed to change the way the individual thinks about self and events. See also *behavior therapy.*

cognitive dissonance. The condition in which one has beliefs or attitudes that disagree with each other or with behavioral tendencies; when such cognitive dissonance arises, the subject is motivated to reduce the dissonance through changes in behavior or cognition.

cognitive map. A hypothetical structure in memory that preserves and organizes information about the various events that occur in a learning situation; a mental picture of the learning situation. See also *schema.*

cognitive perspective. An approach to psychology that focuses on mental processes such as perceiving, remembering, reasoning, deciding, and problem solving, and tries to explain behavior in terms of these mental processes. See also *cognitive psychology, cognitive science.*

cognitive processes. Mental processes of perception, memory, and information processing by which the individual acquires information, makes plans, and solves problems.

cognitive psychology. A general approach to psychology that stresses the role of mental processes in understanding behavior. The cognitive psychologist explains behavior at the level of mental representations and the mental processes that operate on these representations to produce products (including responses). The approach is not re-

stricted to the study of thought and knowledge; its early concerns with these topics led to the label "cognitive psychology," but in recent years the approach has been generalized to all areas of psychology. See also *artificial intelligence, cognitive science, information-processing model.*

cognitive response theory. A theory that proposes that persuasion induced by a communication is actually self-persuasion produced by the thoughts that the individual generates while receiving or even just anticipating the communication.

cognitive science. A term introduced in the 1970s to focus attention on how humans acquire and organize knowledge; a "new" science dedicated to understanding cognition. In addition to psychology, the disciplines relevant to cognitive science are neuroscience, linguistics, philosophy, mathematics, and computer science (particularly that branch of computer science known as artificial intelligence). See also *artificial intelligence, cognitive psychology.*

cognitive-appraisal theory. A theory of emotion that proposes that the subjective emotional state is a function of the individual's appraisal, or analysis, of the emotion-arousing situation. A state of physiological arousal can produce different emotions (even antithetical ones) depending on how the person appraises the situation. See also *Cannon-Bard theory, James-Lange theory.*

color blindness. Defective discrimination of chromatic colors. See also *dichromatism, monochromatism, red-green color blindness, trichromatism.*

color circle. An arrangement of chromatic colors on the circumference of a circle in the order in which they appear in the spectrum but with the addition of nonspectral reds and purples. The colors are so arranged that those opposite each other are complementaries in additive mixture. See also *color solid.*

color constancy. The tendency to see a familiar object as of the same color, regardless of changes in illumination on it that alter its stimulus properties. See also *perceptual constancy.*

color solid. A three-dimensional representation of the psychological dimensions of color, with hue around the circumference, saturation along each radius, and brightness from top to bottom. See also *color circle.*

color-opponent cells. In color vision, cells that respond only to their two opponent colors. See also *opponent-color theory.*

common disposition. In Gordon Allport's personality theory, a trait on which different individuals can be compared with one another. Contrasted with *personal disposi-*

tion, which refers to the unique patterning or configuration of traits within the individual. See also *cardinal disposition, central disposition, personal disposition, secondary disposition.*

complementary colors. Two colors that in additive mixture yield either a gray or an unsaturated color of the hue of the stronger component.

complex cell. A cell in the visual cortex that responds to a bar of light or straight edge of a particular orientation located anywhere in the visual field. See also *simple cell.*

compliance. A response to social influence in which the person at whom the influence is directed publicly conforms to the wishes of the influencing sources but does not change his or her private beliefs or attitudes. When a source obtains compliance by setting an example, it is called *conformity;* when a source obtains compliance by wielding authority, it is called *obedience.* See also *identification, internalization.*

compulsion. A repetitive action that a person feels driven to make and is unable to resist; ritualistic behavior. See also *obsession, obsessive-compulsive disorder.*

computer program. See *program.*

computer simulation. The use of a computer to simulate a phenomenon or system in order to study its properties. In psychology, the simulation usually involves an attempt to program a computer to mimic how the mind processes information and solves problems. In this sense, the computer program is literally a theory of how the mind functions. See also *artificial intelligence, cognitive psychology, information-processing model.*

computerized axial tomography (CT). A computer-based procedure that analyzes data obtained by a scanning beam of X rays to provide a picture of a cross-sectional slice through the body or brain.

concept. The properties or relationships common to a class of objects or ideas. Concepts may be of concrete things (such as the concept *poodle* referring to a given variety of dog) or of abstract ideas (such as *equality, justice, number*), implying relationships common to many different kinds of objects or ideas. See also *classical concept, fuzzy concept.*

concrete operational stage. Piaget's third stage of cognitive development (ages 7 to 12 years) during which a child becomes capable of logical thought and achieves conservation concepts. See also *conservation.*

conditioned emotion. An emotional response acquired by conditioning: one aroused by a stimulus that did not originally evoke it. See also *conditioning.*

conditioned reinforcer. A stimulus that has become reinforcing through prior association with a reinforcing stimulus (syn.

conditioned reinforcer (*continued*) *secondary reinforcer*). See also *reinforcing stimulus*.

conditioned response (CR). In classical conditioning, the learned or acquired response to a conditioned stimulus; in other words, to a stimulus that did not evoke the response originally. See also *conditioned stimulus, unconditioned response, unconditioned stimulus*.

conditioned stimulus (CS). In classical conditioning, a stimulus previously neutral that comes to elicit a conditioned response through association with an unconditioned stimulus. See also *conditioned response, unconditioned response, unconditioned stimulus*.

conditioning. The process by which conditioned responses are learned. See also *classical conditioning, operant conditioning*.

conduction loss. A hearing deficit in which threshold elevation (loss of sensitivity) occurs equally at all frequencies as the result of poor conduction in the middle ear. See also *sensory-neural loss*.

cone. In the eye, a specialized cell of the retina found predominantly in the fovea and more sparsely throughout the retina. The cones mediate both chromatic and achromatic sensations. See also *fovea, retina, rod*.

conflict. The simultaneous presence of opposing or mutually exclusive impulses, desires, or tendencies. See also *ambivalence*.

connectionist models. Models of cognitive processes (like perception) that incorporate a network of nodes, with excitatory and inhibitory connections between them.

connotative meaning. The suggestive and emotional meanings of a word or symbol, beyond its denotative meaning. Thus, *naked* and *nude* both refer to an unclothed body (denotative meaning), but they have somewhat different connotations. See also *denotative meaning*.

conscience. An internal recognition of standards of right and wrong by which the individual judges his or her conduct. See also *superego*.

conscious processes. Events such as perceptions, private thoughts, and dreams, of which only the person is aware. They are accessible to others through verbal report or by way of inference from other behavior (syn. *experience, awareness*).

consciousness. We are conscious when we are aware of external events, reflect on past experiences, engage in problem solving, are selective in attending to some stimuli rather than others, and deliberately choose an action in response to environmental conditions and personal goals. In short, consciousness has to do with a) *monitoring* ourselves and our environment so that percepts, memories, and thoughts are accurately represented in awareness; and b) *controlling* ourselves and our environment so that we are able to initiate and terminate behavioral and cognitive activities. In some contexts, the term is used as a synonym for *awareness*.

conservation. Piaget's term for the ability of the child to recognize that certain properties of objects (such as mass, volume, number) do not change despite transformations in the appearance of the objects. See also *preoperational stage*.

construct validity. The ability of a test or assessment instrument to confirm predictions of the theory underlying some theoretical concept or construct. Confirming results validate both the concept and the assessment instrument simultaneously. See also *criterion problem, validity*.

constructive memory. Using general knowledge stored in memory to construct and elaborate a more complete and detailed account of some events.

contemporary consequences. Outcomes in an individual's life that result from a childhood personality disposition that he or she has carried into adulthood from childhood. See also *cumulative consequences, path analysis*.

contrast sensitivity. In visual perception, the ability to discriminate between dark and light stripes under various conditions.

control group. In an experimental design contrasting two groups, that group not given the treatment whose effect is under study. See also *experimental group*.

control processes. Regulatory processes that serve to establish equilibrium or monitor goal-directed activities. See also *homeostasis*.

conventional morality. Level II of Kohlberg's stages of moral reasoning, in which actions are evaluated in terms of external sanctions; in other words, whether the actions gain approval from others and adhere to laws and social norms. See also *postconventional morality, preconventional morality*.

core. The part of a concept that contains the properties that are more essential for determining membership in the concept. See also *prototype*.

cornea. The transparent surface of the eye through which light enters and rays are bent inward to begin image formation. See also *lens, pupil, retina*.

corpus callosum. A large band of nerve fibers connecting the two cerebral hemispheres.

correlation. See *coefficient of correlation*.

correlational method. A research method used to determine whether some difference that is not under the researcher's control is associated, or correlated, with another difference of interest. See also *coefficient of correlation*.

corticotropin-release factor (CRF). A substance secreted by neurons in the hypothalamus in response to stress. It, in turn, is carried through a channel-like structure to the pituitary gland, causing ACTH (the body's major "stress" hormone) to be released. See also *adrenocorticotropic hormone*.

cortisol. One of the steroid hormones produced by the adrenal glands. It has many effects on the body, including the formation of glucose, the reduction of inflammation, and the retention of water. Its level in the blood is used as a measure of stress. See also *adrenal glands, adreno-cortical system*.

counseling psychologist. A trained psychologist usually with a Ph.D. or Ed.D. degree, who deals with personal problems not classified as illness, such as academic, social, or vocational problems of students. He or she has skills similar to those of the clinical psychologist but usually works in a nonmedical setting. See also *clinical psychologist, psychiatrist*.

counterconditioning. In behavior therapy, the replacement of a particular response to a stimulus by the establishment of another (usually incompatible) response.

CRF. See *corticotropin-release factor*.

criterion. a) A set of scores or other records against which the success of a predictive test is verified. b) A standard selected as the goal to be achieved in a learning task; for example, the number of runs through a maze to be made without error as an indication that the maze has been mastered.

criterion method of test construction. See *empirical method of test construction*.

criterion problem. The difficulty that arises in validating a test or assessment instrument when there is no criterion behavior the investigator is willing to accept as the "true" measure of the concept being evaluated. See also *construct validity, validity*.

criterion validity. The ability of a test or assessment instrument to predict the behavior it is designed to predict (syn. *empirical validity*). See also *criterion, validity*.

critical period. A stage in development during which the organism is optimally ready to learn certain response patterns. There is some evidence for a critical period in language learning; a child not exposed to language prior to adolescence has great difficulty acquiring language thereafter.

cross-pressure. Conflicting social influences on an individual's beliefs, attitudes, or behaviors. Usually arises when a person identifies with more than one reference group.

cues to distance. See *distance cues*.

culture-fair test. A type of intelligence test that has been constructed to minimize bias due to the differing experiences of children raised in a rural rather than an urban culture or in a lower-class rather than in a middle-class or upper-class culture (syn. *culture-free test*).

cumulative consequences. Outcomes in an individual's life that result from the cumulative effects of some childhood personality disposition. The childhood disposition initiates a chain of events that culminates in the later outcomes—even if the individual no longer carries the disposition as an adult. See also *contemporary consequences, path analysis*.

cumulative curve. A graphic record of the responses emitted during an operant conditioning session. The slope of the cumulative curve indicates the rate of response.

D

dark adaptation. The increased sensitivity to light when the subject has been continuously in the dark or under conditions of reduced illumination. See also *light adaptation*.

data-driven learning. A kind of associative learning in which people have no prior beliefs about the relation that has to be learned; learning is driven only by the input or data. See also *belief-driven learning*.

db. See *decibel*.

decibel (db). A measure of sound intensity. A change of 10 decibels corresponds to a change in sound power of 10 times; 20 decibels, a change of 100 times; and so forth.

deductive reasoning. Reasoning about arguments in which the conclusion cannot be false if the premises are true. See also *inductive reasoning*.

defense mechanisms. In Freud's psychoanalytic theory, the strategies used by the ego to ward off or to reduce anxiety. These consist of adjustments made unconsciously, either through action or the avoidance of action, to keep from recognizing personal motives that might threaten self-esteem or heighten anxiety. Repression, denial, and projection are examples.

degradation. The process in which enzymes in the membrane of a receiving neuron react with a neurotransmitter to break it up chemically and make it inactive; one method (in addition to reuptake) of terminating a neurotransmitter's action. See also *neurotransmitter, reuptake*.

deindividuation. A psychological state in which persons feel that they have lost their personal identities and have merged anonymously into a group. Hypothesized to be the basis for the impulsive, aggressive behaviors sometimes shown by mobs and crowds.

delayed conditioning. A classical conditioning procedure in which the CS begins several seconds or more before the onset of the UCS and continues with it until the response occurs. See also *simultaneous conditioning, trace conditioning*.

delta waves. See *electroencephalogram*.

delusion. False beliefs characteristic of some forms of psychotic disorder. They often take the form of delusions of grandeur or delusions of persecution. See also *hallucination, illusion, paranoid schizophrenia*.

dendrite. The specialized portion of the neuron that (together with the cell body) receives impulses from other neurons. See also *axon, neuron*.

denial. A defense mechanism by which unacceptable impulses or ideas are not perceived or allowed into full awareness. See also *defense mechanisms*.

denotative meaning. The primary meaning of a symbol, something specific to which the symbol refers or points (for example, my street address is denotative; whether I live in a desirable neighborhood is a connotative meaning secondary to the address itself). See also *connotative meaning*.

deoxyribonucleic acid (DNA). The basic hereditary material of all organisms; a nucleic acid polymer incorporating the sugar deoxyribose. In higher organisms, the great bulk of DNA is located within the chromosomes.

dependent variable. The variable whose measured changes are attributed to (or correspond to) changes in the independent variable. In psychological experiments, the dependent variable is often a response to a measured stimulus. See also *independent variable*.

depolarization. Change in the resting potential of the nerve cell membrane in the direction of the action potential; the inside of the membrane becomes more positive. See also *action potential, resting potential*.

depressants. Psychoactive drugs that tend to reduce arousal. Alcohol, barbiturates, and opiates are examples.

depression. A mood disorder characterized by sadness and dejection, decreased motivation and interest in life, negative thoughts (for example, feelings of helplessness, inadequacy, and low self-esteem) and such physical symptoms as sleep disturbances, loss of appetite, and fatigue. See also *mood disorder*.

depth perception. The perception of the distance of an object from the observer or the distance from front to back of a solid object. See also *distance cues*.

determinism. See *psychological determinism*.

developmental psychologist. A psychologist whose research interest lies in studying the changes that occur as a function of the growth and development of the organism, in particular the relationship between early and later behavior.

deviation IQ. An intelligence quotient (IQ) computed as a standard score with a mean of 100 and a standard deviation of 15 (Wechsler) or 16 (Stanford–Binet), to correspond approximately to traditional intelligence quotient. See also *intelligence quotient*.

dichromatism. Color blindness in which either the red-green or the blue-yellow system is lacking. The red-green form is relatively common; the blue-yellow form is the rarest of all forms of color blindness. See also *monochromatism, red-green color blindness, trichromatism*.

diencephalon. A cluster of nuclei, located below the cerebral cortex, that is involved in the consolidation of new memories. See also *amygdala, hippocampus*.

difference reduction. A problem-solving strategy in which one sets up subgoals that, when obtained, put one in a state closer to the goal. See also *means-ends analysis, working backwards*.

difference threshold. The minimum difference between a pair of stimuli that can be perceived under experimental conditions. See also *absolute threshold, just noticeable difference, threshold, Weber's law*.

diffusion of responsibility. The tendency for persons in a group situation to fail to take action (as in an emergency) because others are present, thus diffusing the responsibility for acting. A major factor in inhibiting bystanders from intervening in emergencies.

discrimination. a) In perception, the detection of differences between two stimuli. b) In conditioning, the differential response to the positive (reinforced) stimulus and to the negative (nonreinforced) stimulus. See also *generalization*. c) In social psychology, prejudicial treatment, as in racial discrimination.

discriminative stimulus. A stimulus that becomes an occasion for an operant response; for example, a knock that leads one to open the door. The stimulus does not elicit the operant response in the same sense that a stimulus elicits respondent behavior. See also *operant behavior*.

displaced aggression. Aggression against a person or object other than that which was (or is) the source of frustration. See also *scapegoat*.

displacement. a) A defense mechanism whereby a motive that may not be directly expressed (such as sex or aggression) appears in a more acceptable form. See also *defense mechanism.* b) The principle of loss of items from short-term memory as too many new items are added. See also *chunk, short-term memory.*

dispositional attribution. Attributing a person's actions to internal dispositions (attitudes, traits, motives), as opposed to situational factors. See also *situational attribution.*

dissociation. The process whereby some ideas, feelings, or activities lose relationship to other aspects of consciousness and personality and operate automatically or independently.

dissonance. a) In music, an inharmonious combination of sounds; contrasted with consonance. b) In social psychology, Festinger's term for discomfort arising from a perceived inconsistency between one's attitudes and one's behavior. See also *cognitive dissonance.*

distance cues. a) In vision, the monocular cues according to which the distance of objects is perceived—such as superposition of objects, perspective, light and shadow, and relative movement—and the binocular cues used in stereoscopic vision. See also *stereoscopic vision.* b) In audition, the corresponding cues governing perception of distance and direction, such as intensity and time differences of sound reaching the two ears.

dizygotic (DZ) twins. Twins developed from separate eggs. They are no more alike genetically than ordinary brothers and sisters and can be of the same or different sexes (syn. *fraternal twins*). See also *monozygotic twins.*

DNA. See *deoxyribonucleic acid.*

doctrine of specific nerve energies. The proposal that the brain codes qualitative differences between sensory modalities by the specific neural pathways involved.

dominance. The higher status position when social rank is organized according to a dominance–submission hierarchy; commonly found in human societies and in certain animal groups.

dominant gene. A member of a gene pair, which, if present, determines that the individual will show the trait controlled by the gene, regardless of whether the other member of the pair is the same or different (that is, recessive). See also *recessive gene.*

dopamine. A neurotransmitter of the central nervous system believed to play a role in schizophrenia. It is synthesized from an amino acid by the action of certain body enzymes and, in turn, is converted into norepinephrine. See also *neurotransmitter, norepinephrine.*

dopamine hypothesis. The hypothesis that schizophrenia is related to an excess of the neurotransmitter dopamine; either schizophrenics produce too much dopamine or are deficient in the enzyme that converts dopamine to norepinephrine. See also *dopamine, norepinephrine, schizophrenia.*

double blind. An experimental design, often used in drug research, in which neither the investigator nor the patients know which subjects are in the treatment and which in the nontreatment condition until the experiment has been completed.

Down's syndrome. A form of mental deficiency produced by a genetic abnormality (an extra chromosome on pair 21). Characteristics include a thick tongue, extra eyelid folds, and short, stubby fingers (syn. *mongolism*).

drive. a) An aroused condition of the organism based on deprivation or noxious stimulation, including tissue needs, drug or hormonal conditions, and specified internal or external stimuli, as in pain. b) Loosely, any motive. See also *motive, need.*

drive-reduction theory. The theory that a motivated sequence of behavior can be best explained as moving from an aversive state of heightened tension (or drive) to a goal state in which the drive is reduced. The goal of the sequence, in other words, is drive reduction. See also *drive, incentive theory, motive, need.*

DSM-III-R. The third edition of the *Diagnostic and Statistical Manual of the American Psychiatric Association,* revised.

dual-memory theory. A theory that distinguishes between a short-term memory of limited capacity and a virtually unlimited long-term memory. Information can only be encoded into long-term memory via short-term memory. See also *long-term memory, short-term memory.*

DZ twins. See *dizygotic twins.*

E

eardrum. The membrane at the inner end of the auditory canal, leading to the middle ear. See also *middle ear.*

ectomorphic type. A tall, thin physique postulated by Sheldon's type theory to be associated with an introverted, artistic temperament. See also *endomorphic type, mesomorphic type, somatotypes, type theory.*

educational psychologist. A psychologist whose research interest lies in the application of psychological principles to the education of children and adults in schools. See also *school psychologist.*

EEG. See *electroencephalogram.*

efferent neuron. See *motor neuron.*

ego. In Freud's tripartite division of the personality, the rational part or controlling self. Operates on the *reality principle,* holding back the impulses of the id until they can be satisfied in socially approved ways. See also *id, superego.*

ego analyst. A psychoanalyst who focuses on the integrative, positive functions of the ego (for example, coping with the environment) rather than the functions of the id (for example, gratifying sexual impulses). Heinz Hartman and David Rapaport are considered ego analysts. See also *ego, id, psychoanalyst.*

eidetic imagery. The ability to retain visual images of pictures that are almost photographic in clarity. Such images can be described in far greater detail than would be possible from memory alone. See also *mental imagery.*

elaboration. A memory process wherein one expands verbal material so as to increase the number of ways to retrieve the material.

electroconvulsive therapy (ECT). A treatment for severe depression in which a mild electric current is applied to the brain, producing a seizure similar to an epileptic convulsion. Also known as *electroshock therapy.*

electroencephalogram (EEG). A record obtained by attaching electrodes to the scalp (or occasionally to the exposed brain) and amplifying the spontaneous electrical activity of the brain. Familiar aspects of the EEG are alpha waves (8–13 Hz) and delta waves of slower frequency.

electroshock therapy. See *electroconvulsive therapy.*

emotion. The condition of the organism during affectively toned experience, whether mild or intense. See also *affective experience.*

emotion-focused coping. Ways of reducing anxiety or stress that do not deal directly with the anxiety-producing situation; defense mechanisms are a form of emotion-focused coping. See also *problem-focused coping.*

empirical method of test construction. Selecting items for a test or assessment instrument by comparing the responses of some criterion group (for example, paranoid individuals) with a control group and retaining only those that discriminate between the two groups. Also called the criterion method of test construction. See also *rational method of test construction.*

empirical validity. See *criterion validity.*

empiricism. The view that behavior is learned as a result of experience. See also *nativism.*

encoding. Transforming a sensory input into a form (code) that can be processed by the memory system.

endocrine gland. A ductless gland, or gland of internal secretion, that discharges its products directly into the bloodstream. The hormones secreted by the endocrine glands are important chemical integrators of bodily activity. See also *hormone.*

endomorphic type. A soft, round physique postulated by Sheldon's type theory to be associated with a relaxed, sociable temperament. See also *ectomorphic type, mesomorphic type, somatotypes, type theory.*

endorphins. A group of neurotransmitters in the brain released in response to stress that have the effect of blocking pain. Opiates, a class of drugs that includes heroin and morphine, are similar in molecular shape to endorphins and mimic this naturally occurring substance.

engineering psychologist. A psychologist who specializes in the relationship between people and machines, seeking, for example, to design machines that minimize human error.

epinephrine. The principal hormone secreted by the adrenal medulla in response to stressful situations. Its effects are similar to those brought about by stimulation of the sympathetic division of the autonomic nervous system (for example, arousal, increased heart rate and blood pressure). It is also an excitatory neurotransmitter in the central nervous system (syn. *adrenalin*). See also *adrenal gland, norepinephrine.*

equilibratory senses. The senses that give discrimination of the position of the body in space and of the movement of the body as a whole. See also *kinesthesis, semicircular canals, vestibular sacs.*

ESP. See *extrasensory perception.*

estrogens. A group of female sex hormones produced principally by the ovaries. They are responsible for the development of female body characteristics and hair distribution, and for preparing the reproductive system for pregnancy. See also *androgens.*

estrous cycle. Recurring episodes of sexual receptivity that precede ovulation in most female mammals. They are characterized by rising and falling levels of estrogens and progesterone in the bloodstream. See also *estrogens, progesterone.*

ethology. An interdisciplinary science combining zoology, biology, and psychology to study animal behavior, primarily in the natural environment of the species being observed. Most of the work has been on insects, birds, and fish, but in recent years the approach has been applied to human behavior. Naturalistic observation characterizes the approach, and the theoretical ideas tend to focus on the interplay of genetic and environmental factors in understanding behavior. See also *imprinting, instinct.*

evocative interaction. The interaction between individuals and their environments that arises because the behavior of different individuals evokes different responses from others. See also *proactive interaction, reactive interaction.*

evoked potential. An electrical discharge in some part of the nervous system produced by stimulation elsewhere. The measured potential is commonly based on response averaging by a computer.

exemplar strategy. A categorization strategy in which a) old instances of a concept are memorized and b) a new item is declared a member of that concept if it is sufficiently similar to the memorized instances.

excitatory synapse. A synapse at which the neurotransmitter changes the membrane permeability of the receiving cell in the direction of depolarization. See also *depolarization, inhibitory synapse, synapse.*

expectation. An anticipation or prediction of future events based on past experience and present stimuli.

experimental design. A plan for collecting and treating the data of a proposed experiment. The design is evolved after preliminary exploration, with the aims of economy, precision, and control, so that appropriate inferences and decisions can be made from the data.

experimental group. In an experimental design contrasting two groups, that group of subjects given the treatment whose effect is under investigation. See also *control group.*

experimental method. The method of investigation of natural events that seeks to control the variables involved so as to more precisely define cause-and-effect relationships. Most frequently done in a laboratory, but need not be. See also *observational method, variable.*

experimental psychologist. A psychologist whose research interest is in the laboratory study of general psychological principles as revealed in the behavior of lower organisms and human beings.

explicit memory. The kind of memory that underlies a conscious recollecton of something in the past. See also *implicit memory.*

extinction. a) The experimental procedure, following classical or operant conditioning, of presenting the conditioned stimulus without the usual reinforcement. b) The reduction in response that results from this procedure. See also *reinforcement.*

extracellular fluid. Fluid, including the blood, outside the cells; one of the critical variables monitored in the control of thirst.

extrasensory perception (ESP). Response to external stimuli without any known sensory contact. See also *clairvoyance,* *parapsychology, precognition, psi, psychokinesis, telepathy.*

extraversion. See *introversion–extraversion.*

F

fact memory. The kind of memory that presumably stores factual information. See also *skill memory.*

factor analysis. A statistical method used in test construction and in interpreting scores from batteries of tests. The method enables the investigator to compute the minimum number of determiners (factors) required to account for the intercorrelations among the scores on the tests making up the battery. See also *general factor, special factor.*

family therapy. Psychotherapy with the family members as a group rather than treatment of the patient alone. See also *group therapy.*

feature detector. A general term for any perceptual mechanism that detects distinctive features in a complex display. An example is a line (or edge) detector in vision. Since anything we see can be approximated by a series of line segments at angles to each other, feature detectors have been postulated to be the building blocks for recognizing more complex forms.

Fechner's law. The assertion that the perceived magnitude of a stimulus increases in proportion to the logarithm of its physical intensity.

fetal alcohol syndrome. Abnormal development of the fetus and infant caused by maternal alcohol consumption during pregnancy. Features of the syndrome include retarded growth, small head circumference, a flat nasal bridge, a small midface, shortened eyelids, and mental retardation.

figure-ground perception. Perceiving a pattern as foreground against a background. Patterns are commonly perceived this way even when the stimuli are ambiguous and the foreground–background relationships are reversible.

file-drawer problem. A problem that arises because studies that fail to obtain positive results are less likely to be published than studies that do obtain positive results. (Failed studies are thus said to "go into the file drawer" rather than being published.) The file-drawer effect causes the database of known studies to be biased toward confirming studies.

filter. Any device that allows some things to pass through it and not others; for example, an electronic device that allows only particular sound frequencies to pass or an optical lens that transmits only certain wavelengths of light. Various types of

filter (*continued*)
filters are embedded in the sensory system (optical, mechanical, chemical, neural) that pass some signals and not others. A neuron in the sensory system that is preceded by a filter will respond only to signals that pass through the filter; such a neuron is said to be "tuned" to those signals. See also *specific neuron code hypothesis*.

fixation. In Freud's psychoanalytic theory, arrested development through failure to pass beyond one of the earlier stages of psychosexual development or to change the objects of attachment (such as fixated at the oral stage or fixated on the mother).

flashbulb memory. A vivid and relatively permanent record of the circumstances in which one learned of an emotionally charged, significant event.

flow chart. A diagramatic representation of the sequence of choices and actions in an activity.

formal operational stage. Piaget's fourth stage of cognitive development (age 12 and up) in which the child becomes able to use abstract rules.

fovea. In the eye, a small area in the central part of the retina, packed with cones; in daylight, the most sensitive part of the retina for detail vision and color vision. See also *cone, retina*.

fraternal twins. See *dizygotic twins*.

free association. a) The form of word-association experiment in which the subject gives any word he or she thinks of in response to the stimulus word. b) In psychoanalysis, the effort to report without modification everything that comes into awareness.

free recall. A memory task in which a subject is given a list of items (usually one at a time) and is later asked to recall them in any order.

Freudian slip. In psychoanalytic theory, a mistake or substitution of words in speaking or writing that is contrary to the speaker's conscious intention and presumably expresses wishes or thoughts repressed to the unconscious.

frontal lobe. A portion of each cerebral hemisphere, in front of the central fissure. See also *occipital lobe, parietal lobe, temporal lobe*.

frustration. a) As an event, the thwarting circumstances that block or interfere with goal-directed activity. b) As a state, the annoyance, confusion, or anger engendered by being thwarted, disappointed, defeated.

frustration-aggression hypothesis. The hypothesis that frustration (thwarting a person's goal-directed efforts) induces an aggressive drive, which, in turn, motivates aggressive behavior.

fundamental. The frequency being played in a musical note.

fundamental attribution error. The tendency to underestimate situational influences on behavior and assume that some personal characteristic of the individual is responsible; the bias toward dispositional rather than situational attributions. See also *attribution, dispositional attribution, situational attribution*.

fuzzy concept. A concept in which one primarily relies on prototype properties in determining membership, and hence cannot always be sure of one's decisions. See also *prototype*.

G

GABA. See *gamma-aminobutyric acid*.

galvanic skin response (GSR). Changes in electrical conductivity of, or activity in, the skin, detected by a sensitive galvanometer. The reactions are commonly used as an emotional indicator.

gamma-aminobutyric acid (GABA). An important inhibitory neurotransmitter.

ganglia (sing. *ganglion*). A collection of nerve cell bodies and synapses, constituting a center lying outside the brain and spinal cord, as in the sympathetic ganglia. See also *nuclei*.

gate control theory of pain. According to this theory, the sensation of pain requires not only that pain receptors be activated, but also that a neural gate in the spinal cord allow these signals to continue to the brain. Pressure stimulation tends to close the gate; this is why rubbing a hurt area can relieve pain. Attitudes, suggestions, and drugs may act to close the gate.

gender identity. The degree to which one regards oneself as male or female. See also *sex role, sex typing*.

gender schema. An abstract cognitive structure that organizes a diverse array of information in terms of its male–female connotations. According to gender schema theory, sex-typed individuals are more likely to use a gender schema than non-sex-typed individuals. See also *schema, sex typing*.

gene. The basic unit of hereditary transmission, localized within the chromosomes. Each chromosome contains many genes. Genes are typically in pairs, one member of the pair being found in the chromosome from the father, the other in the corresponding chromosome from the mother. See also *chromosome, dominant gene, recessive gene*.

general factor (g). a) A general ability underlying test scores, especially in tests of intelligence, as distinct from special abilities unique to each test. b) A general ability with which each of the primary factors correlates. See also *factor analysis, special factor*.

General Problem Solver (GPS). A computer program to simulate human problem solving by setting up subgoals and reducing the discrepancies to each subsequent subgoal. See also *simulation*.

generalization. a) In concept formation, problem solving, and transfer of learning, the detection by the learner of a characteristic or principle common to a class of objects, events, or problems. b) In conditioning, the principle that once a conditioned response has been established to a given stimulus, similar stimuli will also evoke that response. See also *discrimination*.

generalized anxiety disorder. An anxiety disorder characterized by persistent tension and apprehension. May be accompanied by such physical symptoms as rapid heart rate, fatigue, disturbed sleep, and dizziness. See also *anxiety disorders*.

genetics. That branch of biology concerned with heredity and the means by which hereditary characteristics are transmitted.

genital stage. In Freud's psychoanalytic theory, the final stage of psychosexual development, culminating in sexual union with a member of the opposite sex. See also *psychosexual development*.

genotype. In genetics, the characteristics that an individual has inherited and will transmit to his or her descendants, whether or not the individual manifests these characteristics. See also *phenotype*.

Gestalt psychology. A system of psychological theory concerned primarily with perception that emphasizes pattern, organization, wholes, and field properties.

glia cells. Supporting cells (not neurons) composing a substantial portion of brain tissue; recent speculation suggests that they may play a role in neural conduction.

gonads. Testes in the male, ovaries in the female. As duct glands, the sex glands are active in mating behavior, but as endocrine glands their hormones affect secondary sex characteristics as well as maintaining functional sexual activity. The male hormones are known as androgens, the female hormones as estrogen and progesterone (syn. *sex glands*). See also *androgens, endocrine gland, estrogens, progesterone*.

good continuation. A Gestalt principle of grouping, wherein elements are grouped together in order to form an unbroken contour. See also *closure*.

graded potentials. Potential changes of varying size induced in a neuron's dendrites or cell body by stimulation from synapses from other neurons. When the graded potentials reach a threshold of depolarization, an action potential occurs. See also *action potential, depolarization.*

gradient of texture. If a surface is perceived visually as having substantial texture (hard, soft, smooth, rough, and so on) and if the texture has a noticeable grain, it becomes fine as the surface recedes from the viewing person, producing a gradient of texture that is important in judgments of slant and of distance. See also *distance cues.*

group test. A test administered to several people at once by a single tester. A college exam is usually a group test.

group therapy. A group discussion or other group activity with a therapeutic purpose participated in by more than one client or patient at a time. See also *psychotherapy.*

GSR. See *galvanic skin response.*

gustation. The sense of taste.

H

habit. A learned stimulus-response sequence. See also *conditioned response.*

habituation. The reduction in the strength of a response to a repeated stimulus. In general, almost any stimulus will produce habituation; for example, a pure tone sounded for a half-hour may decrease as much as 20 db in perceived loudness.

hair cells. In audition, hairlike receptors in the cochlea that bend due to vibration of the basilar membrane and then send electrical impulses to the brain. See also *basilar membrane, cochlea.*

hallucination. A sense experience in the absence of appropriate external stimuli; a misinterpretation of imaginary experiences as actual perceptions. See also *delusion, illusion, schizophrenia.*

hallucinogens. Drugs whose main effect is to change perceptual experience and "expand consciousness." LSD and marijuana are examples (syn. *psychedelic drugs*).

halo effect. The tendency to bias our perception of another person in the direction of one particular characteristic that we like or dislike.

heritability. The proportion of the total variability of a trait in a given population that is attributable to genetic differences among individuals within that population.

hermaphrodite. An individual born with genitals that are ambiguous in appearance or that are in conflict with the internal sex glands. See also *transsexual.*

heroin. An extremely addictive central nervous system depressant derived from opium. See also *opiates.*

hertz (Hz). The wave frequency of a sound source, or other cyclical phenomena, measured in cycles per second.

heterosexual. A person who is attracted to and seeks sexual relations with members of the opposite sex.

heuristic. In problem solving, a strategy that can be applied to a variety of problems and that usually, but not always, yields a correct solution.

heuristic theory of persuasion. A theory that proposes that when we are unwilling or unable to process the content of a persuasive communication, we evaluate its validity by utilizing simple rules of thumb (*heuristics*). One such rule might be "messages with many arguments are more likely to be valid than messages with few arguments."

hidden observer. A metaphor to describe the concealed consciousness in hypnosis, inferred to have experiences differing from, but parallel to, the hypnotic consciousness.

hierarchies of concepts. The relationships among individual concepts. See also *concept.*

hierarchy of needs. Maslow's way of classifying needs and motives, ascending from basic biological needs to a peak of self-actualization, supposedly the highest human motive.

hippocampus. A brain structure located below the cerebral cortex, that is involved in the consolidation of new memories; its role seems to be that of a cross-referencing system, linking together aspects of a particular memory that are stored in separate parts of the brain. See also *amygdala.*

home sign. A system of gestures used by deaf children that initially functions as a kind of simple pantomime but eventually takes on the properties of a language.

homeostasis. An optimal level of organic function, maintained by regulatory mechanisms known as homeostatic mechanisms; for example, the mechanisms maintaining a uniform body temperature.

homosexual. A person who prefers to have sexual relations with others of the same sex. Can be male or female, but female homosexuals are often termed *lesbians.* Not to be confused with transsexual. See also *transsexual.*

hormone. A chemical messenger produced by an organ in one part of the body and transported through the bloodstream to other parts of the body where it has a specific effect on cells that recognize its message. See also *endocrine gland.*

hostile aggression. Aggression whose primary aim is to inflict injury. See also *instrumental aggression.*

hue. The dimension of color from which the major color names are derived (red, yellow, green, and so on), corresponding to wavelength of light. See also *brightness, saturation.*

humanistic psychology. A psychological approach that emphasizes the uniqueness of human beings; it is concerned with subjective experience and human values. Often referred to as a third force in psychology in contrast to behaviorism and psychoanalysis. See also *phenomenology.*

hunger drive. A drive based on food deprivation. See also *drive, specific hunger.*

hypercomplex cell. A cell in the visual cortex that responds to a particular kind of stimulus in a particular orientation and length. See also *complex cell, feature detector, simple cell.*

hyperphagia. Pathological overeating. See also *aphagia.*

hypnosis. The responsive state achieved following a hypnotic induction or its equivalent. In this state, one person (the subject) responds to suggestions offered by another person (the hypnotist) and experiences alterations in perception, memory, and voluntary action.

hypnotic induction. The procedure used in establishing hypnosis in a responsive person. It usually involves relaxation and stimulated imagination. See also *hypnosis.*

hypnotic trance. The dreamlike state of heightened suggestibility induced in a subject by a hypnotist. See also *posthypnotic suggestion.*

hypothalamus. A small but very important structure located just above the brain stem and just below the thalamus. Considered a part of the central core of the brain, it includes centers that govern motivated behavior such as eating, drinking, sex, and emotions; it also regulates endocrine activity and maintains body homeostasis. See also *lateral hypothalamus, ventromedial hypothalamus.*

hypothesis testing. Gathering information and testing alternative explanations of some phenomenon.

hypothetical construct. One form of inferred intermediate mechanism. The construct is conceived of as having properties of its own, other than those specifically required for the explanation; for example, drive that is inferred from the behavior of a deprived organism and is used in the explanation of later behavior.

Hz. See *hertz.*

I

id. In Freud's tripartite division of the personality, the most primitive part, consisting of the basic biological impulses (or drives). The source of psychic energy or *libido.* Operates on the *pleasure principle*, endeavor-

id (*continued*)
ing to obtain pleasure and to avoid pain, regardless of external circumstances. See also *ego, libido, superego.*

ideal self. In Carl Roger's theory, the conception of the kind of person one would like to be. A large discrepancy between the ideal self and the real self creates unhappiness and dissatisfaction. See also *self-concept.*

identical twins. See *monozygotic twins.*

identification. a) The normal process of acquiring appropriate social roles in childhood through copying, in part unconsciously, the behavior of significant adults; for example, the child's identification with his or her like-sexed parent. See also *imitation.* b) Close affiliation with others of like interest, such as identifying with a group. c) A response to social influence in which the person changes his or her beliefs, attitudes, or behaviors in order to be like an influencing source that is respected or admired. See also *compliance, internalization, reference group.*

identification figures. Adult models (especially parents) copied, partly unconsciously, by the child. See also *identification.*

identity confusion. A stage of development characteristic of some adolescents (and others) in which various identifications have not been harmonized and integrated into a sense of personal identity. See also *identification, identity formation.*

identity formation. The process of achieving adult personality integration, as an outgrowth of earlier identifications and other influences. See also *identification.*

illusion. In perception, a misinterpretation of the relationships among presented stimuli so that what is perceived does not correspond to physical reality, especially, but not exclusively, an optical or visual illusion. See also *delusion, hallucination.*

illusory conjunctions. In perception, an incorrect pairing of features from two different objects.

imitation. Behavior that is modeled on or copies that of another. See also *identification.*

implicit memory. The kind of memory that underlies perceptual and cognitive skills. It is often expressed as an improvement on some perceptual or cognitive task without any conscious recollection of the experiences that led to the improvement. See also *explicit memory.*

impossible figures. A figure in which recognition is normal when attending to each part, but the parts do not fuse into a single coherent picture.

imprinting. A term used by ethologists for a species-specific type of learning that occurs within a limited period early in the life of the organism and is relatively unmodifiable thereafter, such as young ducklings learning to follow one adult female (usually the mother) within 11–18 hours after birth. But whatever object they are given to follow at this time, they will thereafter continue to follow. See also *ethology.*

incentive. a) A tangible goal object that provides the stimuli that lead to goal activity. b) Loosely, any goal. See also *negative incentive, positive incentive.*

incentive theory. A theory of motivation that emphasizes the importance of negative and positive incentives in determining behavior; internal drives are not the sole instigators of activity. See also *drive-reduction theory.*

independent variable. The variable under experimental control with which the changes studied in the experiment are correlated. In psychological experiments, the independent variable is often a stimulus, responses to which are the dependent variables under investigation. See also *dependent variable.*

individual differences. Relatively persistent dissimilarities in structure or behavior among persons or members of the same species.

induced motion. The perception of motion caused when a larger object surrounding a smaller object moves; the smaller object may appear to be the one that is moving even if it is stationary. See also *stroboscopic motion.*

inductive reasoning. Reasoning about arguments in which it is improbable that the conclusion is false if the premises are true. See also *deductive reasoning.*

indulgent parents. Responsive, child-centered parents who exercise low levels of control over their children's behavior and place few demands on them. See also *authoritarian parents, authoritative parents, child-centered parents, neglecting parents, parent-centered parents.*

infancy. The period of helplessness and dependency in humans and other organisms; in humans, roughly the first 2 years.

information-processing model. In general, a model based on assumptions regarding the flow of information through a system; usually best realized in the form of a computer program. In cognitive psychology, theories of how the mind functions are often represented in the form of an information-processing model. By simulating the model on a computer, one can study the properties and implications of the theory. See also *cognitive psychology, computer simulation, model.*

inhibitory synapse. A synapse at which the neurotransmitter changes the membrane permeability of the receiving cell in the direction of the resting potential; in other words, keeps it from firing. See also *excitatory synapse, synapse.*

inner ear. The internal portion of the ear containing, in addition to the cochlea, the vestibular sacs and the semicircular canals. See also *cochlea, semicircular canals, vestibular sacs.*

insight. a) In problem-solving experiments, the perception of relationships leading to solution. Such a solution can be repeated promptly when the problem is again confronted. b) In psychotherapy, the discovery by the individuals of dynamic connections between earlier and later events so that they come to recognize the roots of their conflicts.

insomnia. Dissatisfaction with the amount or quality of one's sleep. The diagnosis is subjective because many people who complain of insomnia are found to have normal sleep when studied in the laboratory, whereas others who do not complain of insomnia are found to have detectable sleep disturbances. See also *apnea.*

instinct. The name given to unlearned, patterned, goal-directed behavior, which is species-specific, as illustrated by nest-building in birds or by the migration of salmon (syn. *species-specific behavior*). See also *ethology.*

instrumental aggression. Aggression aimed at obtaining rewards other than the victim's suffering. See also *hostile aggression.*

insulin. The hormone secreted by the pancreas. See also *hormone.*

intellectualization. A defense mechanism whereby a person tries to gain detachment from an emotionally threatening situation by dealing with it in abstract, intellectual terms. See also *defense mechanisms.*

intelligence. a) That which a properly standardized intelligence test measures. b) The ability to learn from experience, think in abstract terms, and deal effectively with one's environment. See also *intelligence quotient, mental age.*

intelligence quotient (IQ). A scale unit used in reporting intelligence test scores, based on the ratio between mental age and chronological age. The decimal point is omitted so that the average IQ for children of any one chronological age is set at 100. See also *chronological age, deviation IQ, mental age.*

interactionism. In personality-developmental theory, a framework in which personality is seen as resulting from the interaction between the child's genotype (inherited characteristics) and the environment in which he or she is raised. In personality theory, a framework in which behavior is seen as resulting from the interaction between consistent personality dispositions or traits and the situations in which people find themselves. See also *evocative interaction, proactive interaction, reactive interaction.*

interaural intensity. The difference in intensity of sounds reaching the two ears; it aids in the localization of sounds at high frequencies. See also *interaural time difference.*

interaural time difference. The difference in time between the arrival of sound waves at the two ears; it aids in the localization of sounds at low frequencies. See also *interaural intensity.*

interjudge reliability. The consistency achieved by two or more observers when assessing or rating some behavior (for example, in rating the aggressiveness of nursery-school children). Also called interscorer agreement. See also *reliability.*

intermittent reinforcement. See *partial reinforcement.*

internal consistency. A form of test reliability. Specifically, the homogeneity of a set of items on a test, the degree to which they are all measuring the same variable. See also *reliability.*

internalization. A response to social influence in which the person changes his or her beliefs, attitudes, or behaviors because he or she genuinely believes in the validity of the position advocated by the influencing source. The incorporation of someone else's opinions or behaviors into one's own value system. See also *compliance, identification.*

interneurons. Neurons in the central nervous system that receive messages from sensory neurons and send them to other interneurons or to motor neurons. See also *motor neuron, sensory neuron.*

interpretation. In psychoanalysis, the analyst's calling attention to the patient's resistances in order to facilitate the flow of associations; also the explanation of symbols, as in dream interpretation. See also *resistance.*

interscorer agreement. See *interjudge reliability.*

intervening variable. A process inferred to occur between stimulus and response, thus accounting for one response rather than another to the same stimulus. The intervening variable may be inferred without further specification, or it may be given concrete properties and become an object of investigation.

interview. A conversation between an investigator (the interviewer) and a subject (the respondent) used for gathering pertinent data for the subject's benefit (as in the psy-

chotherapeutic interview) or for information-gathering (as in a sample survey).

intracellular fluid. Water contained within the body's cells; one of the critical variables monitored in the control of thirst.

introspection. a) A form of trained self-observation, in which individuals describe the content of their consciousness without the intrusion of meanings or interpretations. b) Any form of reporting on subjective (conscious) events or experiences. See also *phenomenology.*

introversion–extraversion. The personality dimension first identified by Carl Jung that refers to the degree to which a person's basic orientation is turned inward toward the self or outward toward the external world. At the introversion end are shy individuals who tend to withdraw into themselves; at the extraversion end are sociable individuals who prefer to be with others.

ion channel. A specialized protein molecule that permits specific ions to enter or leave cells. Some ion channels open or close in response to appropriate neurotransmitter molecules; others open or close in response to voltage changes across the cell membrane. This process regulates depolarization and the firing of nerve impulses.

J

James–Lange theory. A classical theory of emotion, named for the two men who independently proposed it. The theory states that the stimulus first leads to bodily responses, and then the awareness of these responses constitutes the experience of emotion. See also *Cannon–Bard theory, cognitive-appraisal theory.*

jnd. See *just noticeable difference.*

just noticeable difference (jnd). A barely perceptible physical change in a stimulus; a measure of the difference threshold. The term is used also as a unit for scaling the steps of sensation corresponding to increase in the magnitude of stimulation. See also *difference threshold, Weber's law.*

K

key-word method. A technique for learning vocabulary of a foreign language via an intermediate key word related to the sound of the foreign word and the meaning of the English equivalent. See also *mnemonics.*

kinesthesis. The muscle, tendon, and joint senses, yielding discrimination of position and movement of parts of the body. See also *equilibratory senses.*

Klinefelter's syndrome. An abnormal condition of the sex chromosomes (XXY instead

of XX or XY); the individual is physically a male with penis and testicles but has marked feminine characteristics.

L

latency. a) A temporal measure of response, referring to the time delay between the occurrence of the stimulus and the onset of the response. b) In Freud's psychoanalytic theory, a period in middle childhood, roughly the years 6–12, when both sexual and aggressive impulses are said to be in a somewhat subdued state, so that the child's attention is directed outward, and curiosity about the environment makes him or her ready to learn. See also *psychosexual development.*

latent content. The underlying significance of a dream (such as the motives or wishes being expressed by it) as interpreted from the manifest content. See also *interpretation, manifest content.*

latent learning. Learning that is not demonstrated by behavior at the time of learning but can be shown to have occurred by increasing the reinforcement for such behavior.

lateral fissure. A deep fissure at the side of each cerebral hemisphere, below which lies the temporal lobe (syn. *fissure of Sylvius*).

lateral hypothalamus (LH). An area of the hypothalamus important to the regulation of food intake. Electrical stimulation of this area will make an experimental animal start to eat; destruction of brain tissue here causes an animal to stop eating. See also *hypothalamus, ventromedial hypothalamus.*

law of effect. The phenomenon that any behavior that is followed by reinforcement is strengthened; from the infinite pool of possible responses, those that lead to reinforcement are repeated, whereas those that do not are extinguished. Some argue that the law of effect is comparable to the principle of natural selection: adaptive responses are selected from the pool of possible responses and their occurrence is made more likely by reinforcement, whereas nonadaptive responses are allowed to become extinct. See also *reinforcement.*

learned helplessness. A condition of apathy or helplessness created experimentally by subjecting an organism to unavoidable trauma (such as shock, heat, or cold). Being unable to avoid or escape an aversive situation produces a feeling of helplessness that generalizes to subsequent situations.

learning. A relatively permanent change in behavior that occurs as the result of practice. Behavior changes due to maturation

learning (*continued*)
or temporary conditions of the organism (such as fatigue, the influence of drugs, adaptation) are not included.

learning curve. A graph plotting the course of learning, in which the vertical axis (ordinate) plots a measure of proficiency (amount per unit time, time per unit amount, errors made, and so on), while the horizontal axis (abscissa) represents some measure of practice (trials, time, and so on.)

left hemisphere. The left cerebral hemisphere. Controls the right side of the body and, for most people, speech and other logical, sequential activities (syn. *major hemisphere*). See also *cerebral hemispheres, corpus callosum, right hemisphere, split-brain subject.*

left-brain interpreter. A portion of the brain that attempts to interpret or to explain feelings and behaviors originating in other parts of the brain. See also *cerebral hemisphere, corpus callosum, split-brain subject.*

lens. The part of the eye that helps focus light rays on a single point of the retina. See also *cornea, pupil, retina.*

lesbian. See *homosexual.*

LH. See *lateral hypothalamus.*

libido (Latin for lust). In Freud's psychoanalytic theory, the psychic energy of the id. See also *id.*

lie detector. See *polygraph, voice stress analyzer.*

light adaptation. The decreased sensitivity of the eye to light when the subject has been continuously exposed to high levels of illumination. See also *dark adaptation.*

lightness constancy. The tendency to see a familiar object as of the same brightness, regardless of light and shadow that change its stimulus properties. See also *perceptual constancy.*

limbic system. A set of structures in and around the midbrain, forming a functional unit regulating motivational-emotional types of behavior, such as waking and sleeping, excitement and quiescence, feeding, and mating.

linguistic relativity hypothesis. The proposition that one's thought processes, the way one perceives the world, are related to one's language.

lithium carbonate. A compound based on lithium, an element related to sodium. Has been successful in treating bipolar disorders.

localized functions. Behavior controlled by known areas of the brain; for example, vision is localized in the occipital lobes.

location constancy. The tendency to perceive the place at which a resting object is located as remaining the same even though

the relationship to the observer has changed. See also *perceptual constancy.*

long-term memory (LTM). The relatively permanent component of the memory system, as opposed to short-term memory. See also *short-term memory.*

longitudinal study. A research method that studies an individual through time, taking measurements at periodic intervals. See also *case history.*

loudness. An intensity dimension of hearing correlated with the amplitude of the sound waves that constitute the stimulus. Greater amplitudes yield greater loudnesses. See also *pitch, timbre.*

LSD. See *lysergic acid diethylamide.*

lysergic acid diethylamide. A powerful psychoactive drug capable of producing extreme alterations in consciousness, hallucinations, distortions in perception, and unpredictable mood swings.

M

magnetic resonance imaging (MRI). A computer-based scanning procedure that uses strong magnetic fields and radio-frequency pulses to generate a picture of a cross section of the brain or body. Provides greater precision than the CT scanner.

major hemisphere. See *left hemisphere.*

manic-depression. See *bipolar disorder.*

manifest content. The remembered content of a dream, the characters, and their actions, as distinguished from the inferred latent content. See also *latent content.*

mantra. See *transcendental meditation.*

MAO. See *monoamine oxidase.*

MAOI. See *monoamine oxidase inhibitor.*

marijuana. The dried leaves of the hemp plant; also known as hashish, "pot," or "grass." Hashish is actually an extract of the plant material and, hence, is usually stronger than marijuana. Intake may enhance sensory experiences and produce a state of euphoria.

marital therapy. Psychotherapy with both members of a couple aimed at resolving problems in their relationship (syn. *couples therapy*). See also *psychotherapy.*

masochism. A pathological desire to inflict pain on oneself or to suffer pain at the hands of others. See also *sadism.*

maternal drive. The drive, particularly in animals, induced in the female through bearing and nursing young, leading to nest-building, retrieving, and other forms of care. See also *drive.*

maturation. Growth processes in the individual that result in orderly changes in behavior, whose timing and patterning are relatively independent of exercise or expe-

rience though they may require a normal environment.

maze. A device used in the study of animal and human learning, consisting of a correct path and blind alleys.

mean. The arithmetical average; the sum of all scores divided by their number. See also *measure of central tendency.*

means-ends analysis. A problem-solving strategy in which one compares one's current state to the goal state in order to find the most important difference between them; eliminating this difference then becomes the main subgoal. See also *difference reduction, working backwards.*

measure of central tendency. A value representative of a frequency distribution, around which other values are dispersed; for example, the mean, median, or mode of a distribution of scores. See also *mean, median, mode.*

measure of variation. A measure of the dispersion or spread of scores in a frequency distribution, such as the range or the standard deviation. See also *standard deviation.*

mechanisms of defense. See *defense mechanisms.*

median. The score of the middle case when cases are arranged in order of size of score. See also *measure of central tendency.*

meditation. An altered state of consciousness in which the individual is extremely relaxed and feels divorced from the outside world; the individual loses self-awareness and gains a sense of being involved in a wider consciousness. This meditative state is achieved by performing certain rituals, including regulating breathing, sharply restricting one's field of attention, and assuming yogic body positions. A commercialized form of meditation has been widely promoted under the name of *transcendental meditation* or *TM.*

memory decay. A major cause of forgetting in short-term memory in which information simply fades with time.

memory span. The number of items (digits, letters, words) that can be reproduced in order after a single presentation; usually 7 ± 2. See also *chunk, short-term memory.*

memory trace. The inferred change in the nervous system that persists between the time something is learned and the time it is recalled.

menarche. The first menstrual period, indicative of sexual maturation in a girl. See also *menstruation.*

menstruation. The approximately monthly discharge from the uterus. See also *menarche.*

mental age (MA). A scale unit proposed by Binet for use in intelligence testing. If an intelligence test is properly standardized, a representative group of children of age 6 should earn an average mental age of 6, those of age 7, a mental age of 7, and so on. A child whose MA is above his or her chronological age (CA) is advanced; one whose MA lags behind is retarded. See also *chronological age, intelligence quotient.*

mental imagery. Mental pictures used as an aid to memory. *Not* the same as eidetic imagery. See also *eidetic imagery.*

mental retardation. Subnormal intellectual functioning with impairment in social adjustment.

mental rotation. The notion that a mental image of an object can be rotated in the mind in a fashion analogous to rotating the real object.

mesomorphic type. A muscular, athletic physique postulated by Sheldon's type theory to be associated with an assertive, energetic temperament. See also *ectomorphic type, endomorphic type, somatotypes, type theory.*

meta-analysis. A statistical technique that treats the accumulated studies of a particular phenomenon as a single grand experiment and each study as a single observation.

method of constant stimuli. A psychophysical method for determining sensory thresholds. Stimuli with magnitudes varying around the threshold are presented to a subject many times to see what percentage of the time the subject detects them. See also *psychophysical methods.*

method of loci. An aid to serial memory. Verbal material is transformed into mental images, which are then located at successive positions along a visualized route, such as an imaged walk through the house or down a familiar street.

middle ear. The part of the ear that transmits sound waves from the outer ear to the oval window through an air-filled cavity. See also *inner ear, outer ear.*

minor hemisphere. See *right hemisphere.*

mnemonics. A system for improving memory often involving a set of symbols that can substitute for the material to be remembered; for example, in attempting to remember a number sequence, one may translate the sequence into letters of the alphabet that in turn approximate words that are easily remembered.

mode. The most frequent score in a distribution, or the class interval in which the greatest number of cases fall. See also *measure of central tendency.*

model. a) Miniature systems are often constructed according to a logical, mathematical, or physical model. That is, the principles according to which data are organized and made understandable parallel those of the model; for instance, the piano keyboard is a model for understanding the basilar membrane; the thermostat is a model for the feedback principle of homeostasis. b) In behavior therapy, one who *models* or performs behaviors that the therapist wishes the patient to imitate.

modeling. In social learning theory, the process by which a person learns social and cognitive behaviors by observing and imitating others.

modularity thesis. The proposal that the mind consists of a number of innate mental structures (modules), controlling such activities as language and visual perception, that are associated with specific neural structures and operate outside of conscious awareness and voluntary control.

mongolism. See *Down's syndrome.*

monoamine oxidase (MAO). One of the enzymes responsible for the breakdown of a group of neurotransmitters called biogenic amines (norepinephrine, dopamine, and serotonin are examples); believed to be important in the regulation of emotion. Drugs that inhibit the action of this enzyme (MAO inhibitors) are used in treating depression. See also *antidepressant, monamine oxidase inhibitor, neurotransmitter.*

monoamine oxidase inhibitor (MAOI). A class of drugs used to treat depression; the drug inhibits the action of an enzyme (monoamine oxidase) that breaks down certain neurotransmitters (such as dopamine, norepinephrine, and serotonin), thereby prolonging the action of these neurotransmitters. See also *antidepressant, monoamine oxidase, neurotransmitter.*

monochromatism. Total color blindness, the visual system being achromatic. A rare disorder. See also *dichromatism, trichromatism.*

monocular cues. See *distance cues.*

monozygotic (MZ) twins. Twins developed from a single egg. They are always of the same sex and commonly much alike in appearance, although some characteristics may be in mirror image; for example one right-handed, the other left-handed (syn. *identical twins*). See also *dizygotic twins.*

mood disorder. A mental disorder characterized by disturbances of mood. Depression, mania (exaggerated excitement), and bipolar disorders in which the individual experiences both extremes of mood are examples. See also *bipolar disorder, depression.*

moon illusion. A perceptual illusion that makes the moon appear as much as 50 percent larger when it is near the horizon than when it is at its zenith, even though at both locations the moon produces the same retinal image.

morpheme. The smallest meaningful unit in the structure of a language, whether a word, base, or affix; such as *man, strange, ing, pro.* See also *phoneme.*

motion aftereffect. The illusion of movement in a static object that occurs after viewing motion for an extended period of time; the aftereffect occurs in the opposite direction of the viewed motion.

motivation. A general term referring to the regulation of need-satisfying and goal-seeking behavior. See also *motive.*

motive. Any condition of the organism that affects its readiness to start on or continue in a sequence of behavior.

motor area. A projection area in the brain lying in front of the central fissure. Electrical stimulation commonly results in movement, or motor, responses. See also *somatosensory area.*

motor neuron. A neuron, or nerve cell, that conveys messages from the brain or spinal cord to the muscles and glands (syn. *efferent neuron*). See also *sensory neuron.*

MRI. See *magnetic resonance imaging.*

multiple personality. The existence of two or more integrated and well-developed personalities within the same individual. Each personality has its own set of memories and characteristic behaviors. Typically, the attitudes and behavior of the alternating personalities are markedly different.

myelin sheath. The fatty sheath surrounding certain nerve fibers known as myelinated fibers. Impulses travel faster and with less energy expenditure in myelinated fibers than in unmyelinated fibers.

MZ twins. See *monozygotic twins.*

N

nanometer (nm). A billionth of a meter. Wavelength of light is measured in nanometers.

narcissism. Self-love; in Freud's psychoanalytic theory, the normal expression of pregenital development.

narcolepsy. A sleep disturbance characterized by an uncontrollable tendency to fall asleep for brief periods at inopportune times.

narcotics. See *opiates.*

nativism. The view that behavior is innately determined. See also *empiricism.*

nature-nurture issue. The problem of determining the relative importance of heredity (nature) and the result of upbringing in the particular environment (nurture) on mature ability.

need. A physical state involving any lack or deficit within the organism. See also *drive, motive.*

negative incentive. An object or circumstance away from which behavior is directed when the object or circumstance is perceived or anticipated. See also *positive incentive.*

negative reinforcement. Reinforcing a response by the removal of an aversive stimulus. See also *negative reinforcer.*

negative reinforcer. Any stimulus that, when removed following a response, increases the probability of the response. Loud noise, electric shock, and extreme heat or cold classify as negative reinforcers. See also *punishment.*

neglecting parents. Parents who exercise low levels of control over their children's behavior and are more occupied with their own interests and activities than those of their children. Extreme neglecting parents are emotionally unavailable to their children, being detached, emotionally uninvolved and uninterested in them. See also *authoritarian parents, authoritative parents, child-centered parents, indulgent parents, parent-centered parents.*

nerve. A bundle of elongated axons belonging to hundreds or thousands of neurons, possibly both afferent and efferent neurons. Connects portions of the nervous system to other portions and to receptors and effectors. See also *axon, neuron.*

nerve cell. See *neuron.*

neuron. The nerve cell; the basic unit of a synaptic nervous system.

neurosis (pl. *neuroses*). A mental disorder in which the individual is unable to cope with anxieties and conflicts and develops symptoms that he or she finds distressing, such as obsessions, compulsions, phobias, or anxiety attacks. In Freud's psychoanalytic theory, neurosis results from the use of defense mechanisms to ward off anxiety caused by unconscious conflicts. No longer a diagnostic category of DSM-III-R. See also *anxiety disorders, obsessive-compulsive disorder, phobia.*

neurotic anxiety. Fear that is out of proportion to the actual danger posed (such as stage fright). See also *anxiety, objective anxiety.*

neuroticism. The name of the emotional instability–stability dimension in Eysenck's factor-analytic theory of personality. Moody, anxious, and maladjusted individuals are at the neurotic or unstable end; calm, well-adjusted individuals are at the other. See also *introversion–extraversion.*

neurotransmitter. A chemical involved in the transmission of nerve impulses across the synapse from one neuron to another. Usually released from small vesicles in the synaptic terminals of the axon in response to the action potential; diffuses across synapse to influence electrical activity in another neuron. See also *dopamine, epinephrine, norepinephrine, serotonin.*

NMDA. See *N-methyl D-aspartate receptor.*

N-methyl D-aspartate receptor (NMDA receptor). A receptor molecule that requires two successive chemical signals to activate it; the first signal makes the receptor more responsive (a phenomenon known as long-term potentiation) so that when a second chemical signal occurs (the neurotransmitter glutanate), the receptor is activated. NMDA receptors are particularly dense in the hippocampus and may explain how memories are stored by linking neurons to form new neural circuits. See also *hippocampus, neurotransmitter, receptor molecule.*

noncontingent reinforcement. Reinforcement not contingent on a specific response.

noradrenalin. See *norepinephrine.*

norepinephrine. One of the hormones secreted by the adrenal medulla; its action in emotional excitement is similar in some, but not all, respects to that of epinephrine. It is also a neurotransmitter of the central nervous system. Norepinephrine synapses can be either excitatory or inhibitory. Believed to play a role in depression and bipolar disorders (syn. *noradrenaline*). See also *adrenal gland, epinephrine.*

norm. An average, common, or standard performance under specified conditions; for example, the average achievement test score of 9-year-old children or the average birth weight of male children. See also *social norms, test standardization.*

normal curve. The plotted form of the normal distribution.

normal distribution. The standard symmetrical bell-shaped frequency distribution, whose properties are commonly used in making statistical inferences from measures derived from samples. See also *normal curve.*

nuclei (sing. *nucleus*). A collection of nerve cell bodies grouped in the brain or spinal cord. See also *ganglia.*

null hypothesis. A statistical hypothesis that any difference observed among treatment conditions occurs by chance and does not reflect a true difference. Rejection of the null hypothesis means that we believe the treatment conditions are actually having an effect.

O

object constancy. See *perceptual constancy.*

object permanence. Piaget's term for the child's realization that an object continues to exist even though it is hidden from view. See also *sensorimotor stage.*

object relations theory. An outgrowth of psychoanalytic theory that deals with the person's attachments to others over the course of development. Emphasizes ego functioning more than did classical psychoanalytic theory.

object size. The size of an object as determined from measurement at its surface. When size constancy holds, the observer perceives a distant object as being near its object size. See also *retinal size.*

objective anxiety. Fear that is proportionate to the danger posed.

observational method. Studying events as they occur in nature, without experimental control of variables; for instance, studying the nest-building of birds or observing children's behavior in a play situation. See also *experimental method.*

obsession. A persistent, unwelcome, intrusive thought, often suggesting an aggressive or sexual act. See also *compulsion, obsessive-compulsive disorder.*

obsessive-compulsive disorder. An anxiety disorder taking one of three forms: a) recurrent thoughts, often disturbing and unwelcome (obsessions); b) irresistible urges to repeat stereotyped or ritualistic acts (compulsions); c) both of these in combination. See also *anxiety disorders.*

occipital lobe. A portion of the cerebral hemisphere, behind the parietal and temporal lobes. See also *frontal lobe, parietal lobe, temporal lobe.*

Oedipal conflict. In Freud's psychoanalytic theory, the conflict that arises during the phallic stage of psychosexual development in which the individual is sexually attracted to the parent of the opposite sex and perceives the same-sex parent as a rival. See also *phallic stage, psychosexual development.*

olfaction. The sense of smell.

olfactory epithelium. The specialized skin within the nasal cavity that contains the receptors for the sense of smell.

operant behavior. Behavior defined by the stimulus to which it leads rather than by the stimulus that elicits it; such as behavior leading to reward (syn. *instrumental behavior*). See also *respondent behavior.*

operant conditioning. The strengthening of an operant response by presenting a reinforcing stimulus if, and only if, the response occurs (syn. *instrumental conditioning, reward learning*). See also *classical conditioning.*

opiates. Opium or one of its chemical derivatives: codeine, morphine, or heroin. Central nervous system depressants that relieve pain and produce euphoria, all highly addictive (syn. *narcotics*). See also *heroin.*

opinion molecule. A cognitive unit comprising a belief, an attitude, and a perception of social support for the individual's view on the matter. For example, "I believe that Democrats are compassionate toward the poor" (*belief*); "I prefer having Democrats in office" (*attitude*); "And I think the American people agree with me" (*perception of social support*).

opponent-color theory. A theory of color perception that postulates two types of color-sensitive units that respond in opposite ways to the two colors of an opponent pair. One type of unit responds to red or green, the other to blue or yellow. Since a unit cannot respond in two ways at once, reddish-greens and yellowish-blues cannot occur. See also *trichromatic theory, two-stage color theory.*

opponent-process theory. In emotion, the theory that assumes the brain is organized to oppose or suppress emotional responses, whether they are pleasurable or aversive.

optic nerve. In vision, a nerve formed out of axons of the ganglion cells, which leads to the brain. See also *bipolar cells, ganglion cells, photoreceptors, retina.*

oral behavior. Behavior deriving from the infant's need to suck or, more generally, to be fed through the mouth.

oral stage. In Freud's psychoanalytic theory, the first stage of psychosexual development; pleasure derives from the lips and mouth, as in sucking at the mother's breast. See also *psychosexual development.*

organ of Corti. In the ear, the actual receptor for hearing, lying on the basilar membrane in the cochlea and containing the hair cells where the fibers of the auditory nerve originate (syn. *Tunnel of Corti*). See also *basilar membrane, cochlea.*

orienting reflex. a) A nonspecific response to change in stimulation involving depression of cortical alpha rhythm, galvanic skin response, pupillary dilation, and complex vasomotor responses (a term introduced by Russian psychologists). b) Head or body movements that orient the organism's receptors to those parts of the environment in which stimulus changes are occurring.

osmoreceptors. Hypothesized cells in the hypothalamus that respond to dehydration by stimulating the release of ADH by the pituitary gland, which, in turn, signals the kidneys to reabsorb water into the bloodstream. See also *antidiuretic hormone, volumetric receptors.*

otoliths. "Ear stones." See also *vestibular sacs.*

outer ear. The external ear and auditory canal, whose purpose is to funnel sound waves towards the inner ear. See also *inner ear, middle ear.*

ovarian hormones. See *estrogen, progesterone.*

overextension. The tendency of a child, in learning a language, to apply a new word too widely; for example, to call all animals "doggie."

overtone. A higher frequency tone, a multiple of the fundamental frequency, that occurs when a tone is sounded by a musical instrument. See also *timbre.*

P

paired-associate learning. The learning of stimulus-response pairs, as in the acquisition of a foreign language vocabulary. When the first member of a pair (the stimulus) is presented, the subject's task is to give the second member (the response).

pancreas. A bodily organ situated near the stomach. As a duct gland, it secretes pancreatic juice into the intestines, but some specialized cells function as an endocrine gland, secreting the hormone insulin into the bloodstream. See also *endocrine gland.*

pandemonium theory. An early effort in the field of artificial intelligence to build a computer-based machine that could simulate the process of pattern recognition. The system was designed for the recognition of hand-printed letters, and many psychologists argue that it has important resemblances to human recognition. See also *artificial intelligence, simulation.*

panic disorder. An anxiety disorder in which the individual has sudden and inexplicable episodes of terror and feelings of impending doom accompanied by physiological symptoms of fear (such as heart palpitations, shortness of breath, muscle tremors, faintness). See also *anxiety, anxiety disorders.*

parallel processing. A theoretical interpretation of information processing in which several sources of information are all processed simultaneously. See also *serial processing.*

paranoid schizophrenia. A schizophrenic reaction in which the patient has delusions of persecution. See also *schizophrenia.*

parapsychology ("beside psychology"). A subfield of psychology that studies psi phenomena (extrasensory perception and psychokinesis). See also *clairvoyance, extrasensory perception, precognition, psi, psychokinesis, telepathy.*

parasympathetic division. A division of the autonomic nervous system, the nerve fibers of which originate in the cranial and sacral portions of the spinal cord. Active in relaxed or quiescent states of the body and to some extent antagonistic to the sympathetic division. See also *sympathetic division.*

parathyroid glands. Endocrine glands adjacent to the thyroid gland in the neck, whose hormones regulate calcium metabolism, thus maintaining the normal excitability of the nervous system. Parathyroid inadequacy leads to tetany. See also *endocrine gland.*

parent-centered parents. Parents who are more occupied with their own interests and activities than those of their children; contrasted with child-centered parents who are highly involved in their children's lives. See also *authoritarian parents, authoritative parents, child-centered parents, indulgent parents, neglecting parents.*

parietal lobe. A portion of the cerebral hemisphere, behind the central fissure and between the frontal and occipital lobes. See also *frontal lobe, occipital lobe, temporal lobe.*

partial reinforcement. Reinforcing a given response only some proportion of the times it occurs (syn. *intermittent reinforcement*). See also *reinforcement, reinforcement schedule.*

path analysis. A correlational procedure that divides an overall correlation between two variables into separate components or paths. For example, path analysis can help to determine whether a link between childhood temper tantrums and later occupational problems is direct or is due to some intervening link like dropping out of school. See also *contemporary consequences, cumulative consequences.*

pattern recognition. The perceptual process of determining what an object is.

percept. The result of the perceptual process; that which the individual perceives.

perception. A general term to describe the whole process of how we come to know what is going on around us; the entire sequence of events from the presentation of a physical stimulus to the phenomenological experiencing of it. Perception is viewed as a set of subprocesses that occur in a multilevel, interactive system. The lower levels in this system, the parts closely associated with the sense organs, are called sensory processes. See also *sensory processes.*

perceptual constancy. The tendency to see objects as relatively unchanged under widely altered conditions of illumination, distance, and position. See also *color constancy, lightness constancy, location constancy, shape constancy, size constancy.*

perceptual defense. The supposed prevention of an individual's conscious perceptual system from recognizing an anxiety-producing situation perceived by the individual's unconscious perceptual system.

perceptual patterning. The tendency to perceive stimuli according to principles such as proximity, similarity, continuity, and closure. Emphasized by Gestalt psychologists. See also *figure-ground perception, Gestalt psychology.*

performance. Overt behavior, as distinguished from knowledge or information not translated into action. The distinction is important in theories of learning.

peripheral nervous system. That part of the nervous system outside the brain and spinal cord; it includes the autonomic nervous system and the somatic nervous system. See also *autonomic nervous system, somatic nervous system.*

personal construct. In George Kelly's theory of personality, a dimension used by an individual to interpret or "construe" his or her environment. Considered by Kelly to be the basic unit of personality organization.

personal disposition. In Gordon Allport's personality theory, the unique patterning or configuration of traits within an individual. See also *cardinal disposition, central disposition, common trait, secondary disposition.*

personality. The characteristic patterns of thought, emotion, and behavior that define an individual's personal style and influence his or her interactions with the environment.

personality assessment. The measurement or appraisal of personality. See also *behavioral assessment.*

personality disorders. Ingrained, habitual, and rigid patterns of behavior or character that severely limit the individual's adaptive potential; often society sees the behavior as maladaptive whereas the individual does not.

personality dynamics. Theories of personality that stress personality dynamics are concerned with the interactive aspects of behavior (as in conflict resolution), with value hierarchies, with the permeability of boundaries between differentiated aspects of personality, and so on. Contrasted with developmental theories, though not incompatible with them.

personality inventory. An inventory for self-appraisal, consisting of many statements or questions about personal characteristics and behavior that the person judges to apply or not to apply to him or her. See also *projective test.*

personality profile. A chart plotting the ratings of a number of traits of the same individual on a common scale in parallel rows so that the pattern of traits can be visually perceived. See also *trait.*

personality psychologist. A psychologist whose area of interest focuses on classifying individuals and studying the differences between them. This specialty overlaps both developmental and social psychologists to some extent. See also *developmental psychologist, social psychologist.*

person-centered therapy. A method of psychotherapy developed by Carl Rogers in which the therapist is nondirective and reflective and does not interpret or advise. The operating assumption is that the client is the best expert on his or her problems and can work them out in a nonjudgmental, accepting atmosphere. Formerly called client-centered therapy (syn. *nondirective counseling*).

PET scan. See *positron emission tomography.*

phallic stage. In Freud's psychoanalytic theory, the stage of psychosexual development in which gratification is associated with stimulation of the sex organs and sexual attachment is to the parent of the opposite sex. See also *Oedipal stage, psychosexual development.*

phenomenological perspective. An approach to psychology that focuses on subjective experience and tries to describe it from each individual's unique perspective. See also *humanistic psychology.*

phenomenology. The study of an individual's subjective experience or unique perception of the world. Emphasis is on understanding events from the subject's point of view rather than focusing on behavior. See also *humanistic psychology, introspection.*

phenotype. In genetics, the characteristics that are displayed by the individual organism—such as eye color or intelligence—as distinct from those traits that one may carry genetically but not display. See also *genotype.*

pheromones. Special chemicals secreted by many animals that float through the air to attract other members of the same species. They represent a primitive form of communication.

phi phenomenon. Stroboscopic motion is its simpler form. Commonly produced by successively turning on and off two separated stationary light sources; as the first is turned off and the second turned on, the subject perceives a spot of light moving from the position of the first to that of the second. See also *stroboscopic motion.*

phobia. Excessive fear in the absence of real danger. See also *agoraphobia, claustrophobia.*

phobic disorder. An anxiety disorder in which phobias are severe or pervasive enough to interfere seriously with the individual's daily life. See also *anxiety disorders, phobia.*

phoneme. The smallest unit in the sound system of a language; it serves to distinguish utterances from one another. See also *morpheme.*

photoreceptors. The chemicals in rods and cones responsible for transducing light into electrical impulses. See also *cones, rods, transduction.*

physical dependence. With repeated use of a drug, an individual can become dependent on that drug. Physical dependence is characterized by tolerance (with continued use, the individual must take more and more of the drug to achieve the same effect) and withdrawal (if use is discontinued, the person experiences unpleasant physical symptoms) (syn. *addiction*).

physiological motive. A motive based on an evident bodily need, such as the need for food or water.

physiological psychologist. A psychologist concerned with the relationship between physiological functions and behavior.

physiology. That branch of biology concerned primarily with the functioning of organ systems within the body.

pitch. A qualitative dimension of hearing correlated with the frequency of the sound waves that constitute the stimulus. Higher frequencies yield higher pitches. See also *loudness, timbre.*

pituitary gland. An endocrine gland joined to the brain just below the hypothalamus. It consists of two parts, the anterior pituitary and the posterior pituitary. The anterior pituitary is the more important part because of its regulation of growth and of other endocrine glands (syn. *hypophysis*). See also *endocrine gland.*

place theory of pitch. A theory of hearing that associates pitch with the place on the basilar membrane where activation occurs. See also *temporal theory of pitch.*

placebo. An inert substance used in place of an active drug; given to the control group in an experimental test.

pleasure principle. In Freud's psychoanalytic theory, the strategy followed by the *id*, seeking to obtain pleasure and to avoid pain, regardless of external circumstances. See also *id, reality principle.*

pluralistic ignorance. The tendency for persons in a group to mislead each other about a situation; for example, to define an emergency as a nonemergency because others are remaining calm and are not taking action.

polygenic traits. Characteristics—intelligence, height, emotional stability—determined by many sets of genes.

polygraph. A device that measures simultaneously several physiological responses that accompany emotion; for instance, heart and respiration rate, blood pressure, and GSR. Commonly known as a "lie detector" because of its use in determining the guilt of a subject through responses while he or she answers questions. See also *voice stress analyzer.*

pop-out effect. A phenomenon in perception, wherein when searching for a primitive feature in a large array, the target feature seems to "pop out."

population. The total universe of all possible

cases from which a sample is selected. The usual statistical formulas for making inferences from samples apply when the population is appreciably larger than the sample—for instance, 5 to 10 times larger than the sample. See also *sample*.

positive incentive. An object or circumstance toward which behavior is directed when the object or circumstance is perceived or anticipated. See also *negative incentive*.

positive reinforcement. Reinforcing a response by the presentation of a positive stimulus. See also *positive reinforcer*.

positive reinforcer. Any stimulus that, when applied following a response, increases the probability of the response (syn. *reward*). See also *negative reinforcer*.

positron emission tomography (PET). A computer-based scanning procedure that measures the radioactivity of glucose molecules to map the metabolic activities of the living brain.

postconventional morality. Level III of Kohlberg's stages of moral reasoning in which actions are evaluated in terms of their adherence to principles essential to the community welfare and/or personal ethics. See also *conventional morality, preconventional morality*.

posthypnotic amnesia. A particular form of posthypnotic suggestion in which the hypnotized person forgets what has happened during the hypnosis until signaled to remember. See also *posthypnotic suggestion*.

posthypnotic suggestion. A suggestion made to a hypnotized person that he or she will perform in a prescribed way (commonly to a prearranged signal) when no longer hypnotized. The activity is usually carried out without the subject's awareness of its origin. See also *hypnosis*.

post-traumatic stress disorder. An anxiety disorder in which a stressful event that is outside the range of usual human experience, such as military combat or a natural disaster, brings in its aftermath such symptoms as a re-experiencing of the trauma and avoidance of stimuli associated with it, a feeling of estrangement, a tendency to be easily startled, nightmares, recurrent dreams, and disturbed sleep. See also *anxiety disorder*.

PQRST method. A technique for reading and studying information presented in textbook form. The method takes its name from the first letter of the five steps one follows in reading a textbook chapter: *Preview, Question, Read, Self-recitation, Test*.

pragmatic rules. Rules used in deductive reasoning that are less abstract than logical rules, but still applicable to many different domains of life. An example is the *permission rule*.

precognition. Perception of a future event that could not be anticipated through any known inferential process (for example, predicting that a particular number will come up on the next throw of dice). See also *clairvoyance, extrasensory perception, parapsychology, psi, psychokinesis, telepathy*.

preconscious memories. Memories and thoughts that are not part of your consciousness at this moment, but that can be brought to consciousness when needed. They include specific memories of personal events as well as information accumulated over a lifetime. See also *consciousness*.

preconventional morality. Level I of Kohlberg's stages of moral reasoning in which actions are evaluated in terms of outcome (whether the actions avoid punishment or lead to reward) without any concept of right or wrong. See also *conventional morality, postconventional morality*.

preferential looking method. A method of examining infants' perceptual preferences by presenting them two stimuli simultaneously and noting the amount of time the infants gaze at each object.

prejudice. A prejudgment that something or someone is good or bad on the basis of little or no evidence; an attitude that is firmly fixed, not open to free and rational discussion, and resistant to change.

preoperational stage. Piaget's second stage of cognitive development (ages 2–7 years). The child can think in terms of symbols but does not yet comprehend certain rules or operations, such as the principle of conservation. See also *conservation*.

prepared conditioning. The proposal that humans are biologically predisposed, or prepared, by evolutionary selection to associate fear with objects or situations that were dangerous in earlier times. Explains why people develop phobias (conditioned fears) of snakes and heights but not of lambs or guns. See also *classical conditioning*.

primacy effect. a) In memory experiments, the tendency for initial words in a list to be recalled more readily than later words. b) In studies of impression formation, the tendency for initial information to carry more weight than information received later.

primary abilities. The abilities, discovered by factor analysis, that underlie intelligence test performance. See also *factor analysis*.

primary sex characteristics. The structural or physiological characteristics that make possible sexual union and reproduction. See also *secondary sex characteristics*.

proactive interaction. The interaction between individuals and their environments that arises because different individuals

choose to enter different situations and to shape those situations differently after entering them. See also *evocative interaction, reactive interaction*.

proactive interference. The interference of earlier learning with the learning and recall of new material. See also *retroactive interference*.

probe. In studies of memory, a digit or other item from a list to be remembered that is presented as a cue to the subject; for example, the subject could be asked to give the next digit in the list.

problem-focused coping. Reducing anxiety or stress by dealing in some way with the anxiety-producing situation. Escaping the situation or finding a way to alter it are examples. See also *emotion-focused coping*.

problem-solving strategies. The various strategies that can be employed in solving a problem. Of special interest are a class of strategies that involve breaking the solution to a problem into a series of subgoals. The subgoals are to be accomplished as intermediate steps toward ultimately reaching the final goal.

product-moment correlation. See *coefficient of correlation*.

progesterone. A female sex hormone produced by the ovaries; it helps prepare the uterus for pregnancy and the breasts for lactation.

program. a) A plan for the solution of a problem; often used interchangeably with "routine" to specify the precise sequence of instructions enabling a computer to solve a problem. b) In teaching, a set of materials arranged so as to maximize the learning process.

projection. A defense mechanism by which people protect themselves from awareness of their own undesirable traits by attributing those traits excessively to others. See also *defense mechanisms*.

projective test. A personality test in which subjects reveal ("project") themselves through imaginative productions. The projective test gives much freer possibilities of response than the fixed-alternative personality inventory. Examples of projective tests are the Rorschach Test (ink blots to be interpreted) and the Thematic Apperception Test (pictures that elicit stories). See also *personality inventory*.

prolactin. Pituitary hormone prompting the secretion of milk. See also *hormones*.

proposition. A sentence or component of a sentence that asserts something, the predicate, about somebody (or something), the subject. All sentences can be broken into propositions.

prosopagnosia. The inability to recognize familiar faces; in severe cases, the person

prosopagnosia (continued) may be unable to recognize his or her own face.

prototype. The part of a concept that contains the properties that describe the best examples of the concept. See also *core*.

psi. Processes of information and/or energy exchange not currently explicable in terms of known physical mechanisms. See also *clairvoyance, extrasensory perception, parapsychology, precognition, psychokinesis, telepathy*.

psychedelic drugs. See *hallucinogens*.

psychiatric nurse. A nurse specially trained to deal with patients suffering from mental disorders. See also *psychiatrist*.

psychiatric social worker. A social worker trained to work with patients and their families on problems of mental health and illness, usually in close relationship with psychiatrists and clinical psychologists. See also *clinical psychologist, psychiatrist*.

psychiatrist. A medical doctor specializing in the treatment and prevention of mental disorders both mild and severe. See also *clinical psychologist, psychoanalyst*.

psychiatry. A branch of medicine concerned with mental health and mental illness. See also *psychiatrist, psychoanalyst*.

psychoactive drugs. Drugs that affect one's behavior and thought processes. See also *depressants, hallucinogens, stimulants*.

psychonalysis. a) The method developed by Freud and extended by his followers for treating neuroses. b) The system of psychological theory growing out of experiences with the psychoanalytic method.

psychoanalyst. A psychotherapist, usually trained as a psychiatrist, who uses methods related to those originally proposed by Freud for treating neuroses and other mental disorders. See also *clinical psychologist, psychiatrist*.

psychoanalytic perspective. An approach to psychology that tries to explain certain kinds of behaviors in terms of unconscious beliefs, fears, and desires. See also *psychoanalysis*.

psychoanalytic psychotherapy. A method of treating mental disorders based on the theories of Freud but briefer and less intense than psychoanalysis. Less emphasis on exploration of childhood experiences and more attention to the client's current interpersonal problems. See also *psychoanalysis*.

psychodrama. A form of spontaneous play acting used in psychotherapy.

psychogenic. Caused by psychological factors (such as emotional conflict or faulty habits) rather than by disease, injury, or other somatic cause; functional rather than organic.

psychoimmunology. An area of research in behavioral medicine that studies how the body's immune system is affected by psychological variables. See also *behavioral medicine*.

psychokinesis (PK). Mental influence over physical events without the intervention of any known physical force (for example, willing that a particular number will come up on the throw of dice). See also *clairvoyance, extrasensory perception, parapsychology, precognition, psi, telepathy*.

psycholinguistics. The study of the psychological aspects of language and its acquisition.

psychological determinism. The doctrine that all thoughts, emotions, and actions have causes.

psychological motive. A motive that is primarily learned rather than based on biological needs.

psychology. The science that studies behavior and mental processes.

psychometric function. A curve plotting the percentage of times the subject reports detecting a stimulus against a measure of the physical energy of the stimulus.

psychopathic personality. See *antisocial personality*.

psychopharmacology. The study of the effects of drugs on behavior.

psychophysical methods. Procedures used to determine thresholds of sensory modalities.

psychophysics. A name used by Fechner for the science of the relationship between mental processes and the physical world. Now usually restricted to the study of the sensory consequences of controlled physical stimulation.

psychosexual development. In Freud's psychoanalytic theory, the idea that development takes place through stages (oral, anal, phallic, latent, genital), each stage characterized by a zone of pleasurable stimulation and appropriate objects of sexual attachment, culminating in normal heterosexual mating. See also *anal stage, genital stage, latency, oral stage, phallic stage, psychosocial stages*.

psychosis (pl. *psychoses*). A severe mental disorder in which thinking and emotion are so impaired that the individual is seriously out of contact with reality. No longer a major diagnostic category in DSM-III-R. See also *psychotic behavior*.

psychosocial stages. A modification by Erikson of the psychoanalytic theory of psychosexual development, giving more attention to the social and environmental problems associated with the various stages of development and adding some adult stages beyond genital maturing. See also *psychosexual development*.

psychosomatic disorder. Physical illness that has psychological causes (syn. *psychophysiological disorder*).

psychosurgery. A form of biological therapy for abnormal behavior. Involves destroying selected areas of the brain, most often the nerve fibers connecting the frontal lobes to the limbic system and/or the hypothalamus.

psychotherapy. Treatment of personality maladjustment or mental illness by psychological means, usually, but not exclusively, through personal consultation. See also *biological therapy*.

psychotic behavior. Behavior indicating gross impairment in reality contact as evidence by delusions and/or hallucinations. May result from damage to the brain or from a mental disorder such as schizophrenia or a bipolar disorder. See also *psychosis*.

puberty. The period during which the reproductive organs become functionally mature. The development of the secondary sex characteristics (particularly the growth and pigmentation of underarm and pubic hair) marks the onset of puberty and the capacity for reproduction, the culmination. See also *adolescent growth spurt, secondary sex characteristics*.

punishment. A procedure used to decrease the strength of a response by presenting an aversive stimulus whenever the response occurs. Note that such a stimulus when applied would be a punisher; when removed, it would act as a negative reinforcer, reinforcing whatever led to its removal. See also *negative reinforcer*.

pupil. In the eye, a circular opening in the iris (the colored part of the eye) that expands and contracts, varying according to the intensity of light present. See also *cornea, lens, retina*.

Q

Q-sort technique. An assessment technique by which a rater provides a systematic description of an individual's personality by sorting a set of personality statements (for example, "Has a wide range of interests") into groups, ranging from those that are least descriptive to those that are most descriptive of the individual.

R

rapid eye movements (REMs). Eye movements that usually occur during dreaming and that can be measured by attaching small electrodes laterally to and above the subject's eye. These register changes in electrical activity associated with movements of the eyeball in its socket.

rapport. a) A comfortable relationship between the subject and the tester, ensuring cooperation in replying to test questions.

b) A similar relationship between therapist and patient. c) A special relationship of hypnotic subject to hypnotist.

rating scale. A device by which raters can record their judgments of others (or of themselves) on the traits defined by the scale.

rational method of test construction. The procedure of generating or selecting items for a test or assessment instrument by using an underlying theory. See also *empirical method of test construction.*

rationalization. A defense mechanism in which self-esteem is maintained by assigning plausible and acceptable reasons for conduct entered on impulsively or for less acceptable reasons. See also *defense mechanisms.*

reaction formation. A defense mechanism in which a person denies a disapproved motive through giving strong expression to its opposite. See also *defense mechanisms.*

reaction time. The time between the presentation of a stimulus and the occurrence of a response. See also *latency.*

reactive interaction. The interaction between individuals and their environments that arises because different individuals interpret, experience, and react to situations in different ways. See also *evocative interaction, proactive interaction.*

reality principle. In Freud's psychoanalytic theory, the strategy followed by the *ego,* holding back the impulses of the id until they can be satisfied in socially approved ways. See also *ego, pleasure principle.*

receiver-operating-characteristic curve (ROC curve). The function relating the probability of hits and false alarms for a fixed signal level in a detection task. Factors influencing response bias may cause hits and false alarms to vary, but their variation is constrained to the ROC curve. See also *signal detection task.*

recency effect. In memory experiments, the tendency for the last words in a list to be recalled more readily than other list words.

receptive field. In vision, a region of the retina that is associated with a specific cortical neuron; when a stimulus appears anywhere in the field, the associated neuron fires. See also *feature detector.*

receptor. A specialized portion of the body sensitive to particular kinds of stimuli and connected to nerves composed of afferent neurons (such as the retina of the eye). Used more loosely, the organ containing these sensitive portions (such as the eye or the ear).

receptor molecule. A protein molecule situation in a cell membrane that is sensitive to a particular chemical, such as a neurotransmitter. When the appropriate chemical stimulates a receptor molecule, changes occur in the cell membrane either

increasing or decreasing its permeability. Some neurotransmitters have an excitatory effect when locked to their receptors; others have an inhibitory effect. See also *neurotransmitter.*

recessive gene. A member of a gene pair that determines the characteristic trait or appearance of the individual only if the other member of the pair is recessive. If the other member of the pair is dominant, the effect of the recessive gene is masked. See also *dominant gene.*

recoding. A process for improving short-term memory by grouping items into a familiar unit or chunk.

recognition. To recognize something is to associate it correctly with a category, such as "chair," or with a specific name, such as "John Jones." It is a high-level process that requires learning and remembering.

recurrent inhibition. A process whereby some receptors in the visual system when stimulated by nerve impulses inhibit the firing of other visual receptors, thus making the visual system responsive to changes in illumination.

red-green color blindness. The commonest form of color blindness, a variety of dichromatism. In the two subvarieties, red-blindness and green-blindness, both red and green vision are lacking, but achromatic bands are seen at different parts of the spectrum. See also *color blindness, dichromatism.*

reduced stimulation study. An experimental situation in which sensory stimulation is markedly reduced (syn. *sensory deprivation study*).

reductionism. In psychology, a kind of explanation that tries to explain (or reduce) psychological notions to biological ones.

reference group. Any group to which an individual refers for comparing, judging, and deciding on his or her opinions, and behaviors. We are said to "identify" with such groups. See also *identification.*

refractory phase. The period of temporary inactivity in a neuron after it has fired once.

registration. A term to describe receptive processing in which information is processed but not perceived. See also *perception.*

regression. A return to more primitive or infantile modes of response.

rehearsal. The conscious repetition of information in short-term memory, usually involving speech. The process facilitates the short-term recall of information and its transfer to long-term memory. See also *dual-memory theory.*

reincarnation. The belief in rebirth; in other words, that a person has lived before.

reinforcement. a) In classical conditioning, the experimental procedure of following

the conditioned stimulus by the unconditioned stimulus. b) In operant conditioning, the analogous procedure of following the occurrence of the operant response by the reinforcing stimulus. c) The process that increases the strength of conditioning as a result of these arrangements. See also *negative reinforcement, partial reinforcement, positive reinforcement.*

reinforcement schedule. A well-defined procedure for reinforcing a given response only some proportion of the time it occurs. See also *partial reinforcement.*

reinforcing stimulus. a) In classical conditioning, the unconditioned stimulus. b) In operant conditioning, the stimulus that reinforces the operant (typically, a reward) (syn. *reinforcer*). See also *negative reinforcer, positive reinforcer.*

relative height. In perception, a monocular cue for depth. Among identical objects, those that are higher in an image are perceived as being further away. See also *distance cues, relative size, superposition.*

relative size. In perception, a monocular cue for depth. If an image contains an array of objects of similar shape, the smaller objects are perceived as being further away. See also *distance cues, relative height, superposition.*

relaxation training. Training in various techniques for relaxing muscle tension. The procedure is based on Jacobson's progressive relaxation method, in which the person learns how to relax muscle groups one at a time, the assumption being that muscular relaxation is effective in bringing about emotional relaxation.

releaser. A term used by ethologists for a stimulus that sets off a cycle of instinctive behavior. See also *ethology, instinct.*

reliability. The self-consistency of a test as a measuring instrument. Reliability is measured by a coefficient of correlation between scores on two halves of a test, alternate forms of the test, or retests with the same test; a high correlation signifies high consistency of scores for the population tested. See also *validity.*

REMs. See *rapid eye movements.*

repression. a) A defense mechanism in which an impulse or memory that is distressing or might provoke feelings of guilt is excluded from conscious awareness. See also *defense mechanisms, suppression.* b) A theory of forgetting.

Rescorla–Wagner model. A model of classical conditioning. It assumes that the amount of conditioning between a conditioned stimulus and an unconditioned stimulus on any trial depends on the predictability of the unconditioned stimulus; the less predictable the unconditioned stimulus, the greater the amount of conditioning.

reserpine. See *antipsychotic drugs.*

resistance. In psychoanalysis, a blocking of free association; a psychological barrier against bringing unconscious impulses to the level of awareness. Resistance is part of the process of maintaining repression. See also *interpretation, repression.*

respondent behavior. A type of behavior corresponding to reflex action, in that it is largely under the control of and predictable from the stimulus (syn. *elicited behavior*). See also *operant behavior.*

response. a) The behavioral result of stimulation in the form of a movement or glandular secretion. b) Sometimes, any activity of the organism, including central responses (such as an image or fantasy) regardless of whether the stimulus is identified and whether identifiable movements occur. c) Products of the organism's activity, such as words typed per minute.

resting potential. The electrical potential across the nerve cell membrane when it is in its resting state (in other words, not responding to other neurons); the inside of the cell membrane is slightly more negative than the outside. See also *action potential.*

reticular system. A system of ill-defined nerve paths and connections within the brain stem, lying outside the well-defined nerve pathways, and important as an arousal mechanism.

retina. The portion of the eye sensitive to light, containing the rods and the cones. See also *cone, rod.*

retinal image. The image projected onto the retina by an object in the visual field.

retinal size. The size of the retinal image of an object; retinal size decreases in direct proportion to the object's distance. See also *object size.*

retrieval. Locating information in memory.

retroactive interference. The interference in recall of something earlier learned by something subsequently learned. See also *proactive interference.*

retrograde amnesia. Loss of memory for events and experiences occurring in a period of time prior to the amnesia-causing trauma; usually considered to be a failure of the ability to retrieve the information rather than a true loss of that information. See also *amnesia, anterograde amnesia.*

reuptake. The process by which a neurotransmitter is "taken up" again (reabsorbed) by the synaptic terminals from which it had been released. See also *neurotransmitter, synaptic terminals.*

reward. A synonym for *positive reinforcement.* See also *positive reinforcement.*

right hemisphere. The right cerebral hemisphere. Controls the left side of the body and, for most people, spatial and patterned activities (syn. *minor hemisphere*). See also *cerebral hemispheres, corpus callosum, left hemisphere, split-brain subject.*

ROC curve. See *receiver-operating-characteristic curve.*

rod. In the eye, an element of the retina mediating achromatic sensation only; particularly important in peripheral vision and night vision. See also *cone, retina.*

role playing. A method for teaching attitudes and behaviors important to interpersonal relations by having the subject assume a part in a spontaneous play, whether in psychotherapy or in leadership training.

S

saccade. The quick, almost instantaneous movement of the eyes between eye fixations.

sadism. A pathological motive that leads to inflicting pain on another person. See also *masochism.*

sample. A selection of scores from a total set of scores known as the "population." If selection is random, an unbiased sample results; if selection is nonrandom, the sample is biased and unrepresentative. See also *population.*

satiety sensors. Detectors located in different parts of the digestive or thirst systems that signal that the needed nutrients or fluids are on their way and that feeding or drinking can stop.

saturation. The dimension of color that describes its purity; if highly saturated, it appears to be pure hue and free of gray, but if of low saturation, it appears to have a great deal of gray mixed with it. See also *brightness, hue.*

scaling. Converting raw data into types of scores more readily interpreted, such as ranks, centiles, standard scores.

scapegoat. A form of displaced aggression in which an innocent but helpless victim is blamed or punished as the source of the scapegoater's frustration. See also *displaced aggression.*

schema (pl. *schemata*). Some psychologists use the term to designate specific theoretical ideas about mental events; others use it in a very broad and vaguely defined sense. However used, the term refers to cognitive structures stored in memory that are abstract representations of events, objects, and relationships in the real world. It is a key ingredient of cognitive theories of psychological phenomena. See also *cognitive map, schematic processing.*

schematic processing. The cognitive process of searching for the schema in memory that is most consistent with the incoming information. See also *schema.*

schizoid. Having some characteristics that resemble schizophrenia but are less severe. Occurs with higher frequency in families of schizophrenics and thus tends to support a genetic basis for schizophrenia. See also *schizophrenia.*

schizophrenia. A group of mental disorders characterized by major disturbances in thought, perception, emotion, and behavior. Thinking is illogical and usually includes delusional beliefs; distorted perceptions may take the form of hallucinations; emotions are flat or inappropriate; bizarre behavior includes unusual postures, stereotyped movements, and "crazy talk." The individual withdraws from other people and from reality. Inherited brain or biochemical abnormalities are implicated.

school psychologist. A professional psychologist employed by a school or school system, with responsibility for testing, guidance, research, and so on. See also *educational psychologist.*

script. A schema or abstract cognitive representation of events and social interactions (for example, a birthday party). See also *schema.*

secondary disposition. In Gordon Allport's personality theory, one of an individual's many narrow and specific personality traits. Contrasted with a *cardinal* or a *central disposition.* See also *cardinal disposition, central disposition, common trait, personal disposition.*

secondary sex characteristics. The physical features distinguishing the mature male from the mature female, apart from the reproductive organs. In humans, the deeper voice of the male and the growth of the beard are illustrative. See also *primary sex characteristics.*

selective breeding. A method of studying genetic influences by mating animals that display certain traits and selecting for breeding from among their offspring those that express the trait. If the trait is primarily determined by heredity, continued selection for a number of generations will produce a strain that breeds true for that trait.

self-actualization. A person's fundamental tendency toward maximal realization of his or her potentials; a basic concept in humanistic theories of personality such as those developed by Maslow and Rogers.

self-concept. The composite of ideas, feelings, and attitudes people have about themselves. For some theorists, self-concept is synonymous with the *self.*

self-consciousness. A state of heightened self-awareness; the disposition to be self-attentive.

self-perception. The individual's awareness of himself or herself; differs from self-consciousness because it may take the form of objective self-appraisal. See also *self-consciousness.*

self-perception theory. The theory that attitudes and beliefs are influenced by observations of one's own behavior; sometimes we judge how we feel by observing how we act.

self-regulation. In behavior therapy, monitoring one's own behavior and using techniques such as self-reinforcement or controlling stimulus conditions to modify maladaptive behavior. See also *behavior therapy.*

self-schema (pl. *self-schemata*). A generalization or theory about oneself derived from past experience. Self-schemata are assumed to influence the way we selectively attend to, process, and recall personally relevant information (syn. *self-concept*). See also *schema.*

semantic conditioning. A form of classical conditioning in which semantic concepts are used as the conditioned stimuli and generalization occurs through semantic similarities.

semicircular canals. Three curved tubular canals, in three planes, which form part of the labyrinth of the inner ear and are concerned with equilibrium and motion. See also *equilibratory senses.*

sensation. The conscious experience associated with a very simple stimulus like the onset of a tone or light. At one time, the distinction between sensation and perception had great theoretical importance with perception viewed as a combination of sensations. Today, the dividing line between sensation and perception is much less clear, and it seems best to view such experiences as lying along a continuum.

sensorimotor stage. Piaget's first stage of cognitive development (birth–2 years) during which the infant discovers relationships between sensations and motor behavior. See also *object permanence.*

sensory adaptation. The reduction in sensitivity that occurs with prolonged stimulation and the increase in sensitivity that occurs with lack of stimulation; most noted in vision, smell, taste, and temperature sensitivity. See also *dark adaptation, light adaptation.*

sensory modalities. The individual senses.

sensory-neural loss. A hearing deficit in which threshold elevation (loss of sensitivity) is greater at high rather than low frequencies. See also *conduction loss.*

sensory neuron. A neuron, or nerve cell, that conveys messages to the brain or spinal cord from the sense receptors informing the organism about events in the environment or within the body (syn. *afferent neuron*). See also *motor neuron, receptor.*

sensory processes. The subprocesses of the perceptual system that are closely associated with the sense organs. Sensory processes provide selectively filtered information about the stimuli that impinge on us; higher-level processes use this information to form a mental representation of the scene. See also *filter, perception.*

septal area. A portion of the brain deep in the central part, between the lateral ventricles, that appears to yield a state akin to pleasure when stimulated electrically (in a rat, at least).

serial memory search. Comparing a test stimulus in sequence to each item in short-term memory. See also *short-term memory.*

serial processing. A theoretical interpretation of information processing in which several sources of information are processed in a serial order; only one source being attended to at a time. See also *parallel processing.*

serotonin. A neurotransmitter in both the peripheral and central nervous systems. It is an inhibitory transmitter whose actions have been implicated in various processes including sleep, the perception of pain, and mood disorders (depression and manic-depression). See also *neurotransmitter.*

set point. In an analysis of feeding and hunger, the weight at which an individual body functions best.

sex role. The full complement of attitudes and behaviors that a society considers appropriate for the individual because of his or her sex. See also *sex typing.*

sex typing. The acquisition of attitudes and behaviors that a society considers appropriate for the individual because of his or her sex. Distinguished from *gender identity,* which is the degree to which one regards oneself as male or female. See also *sex role.*

sex-linked trait. A trait determined by a gene transmitted on the same chromosomes that determine sex, such as red-green color blindness. See also *X, Y chromosome.*

shape constancy. The tendency to see a familiar object as of the same shape regardless of the viewing angle. See also *perceptual constancy.*

shaping of behavior. Modifying operant behavior by reinforcing only those variations in response that deviate in the direction desired by the experimenter.

shock therapy. See *electroconvulsive therapy.*

short-term memory (STM). The assumption that certain components of the memory system have limited capacity and will maintain information for only a brief time. The definition varies somewhat from theory to theory. See also *long-term memory.*

sibling. A brother or a sister.

sibling rivalry. Jealousy between siblings, often based on their competition for parental affection.

signal detectability theory. A theory of the sensory and decision processes involved in psychophysical judgments, with special reference to the problem of detecting weak signals in noise. See also *signal detection task.*

signal detection task. A procedure whereby the subject must judge on each trial whether a weak signal was embedded in a noise background. Saying "yes" when the signal was presented is called a *hit* and saying "yes" when the signal was not presented is called a *false alarm.* See also *receiver-operating-characteristic curve.*

simple cell. A cell in the visual cortex that responds to a bar of light or straight edge of a particular orientation and location in the visual field. See also *complex cell.*

simple phobia. Excessive fear of a specific object, animal, or situation in the absence of real danger. See also *phobia, phobic disorder.*

simulation. See *computer simulation.*

simultaneous conditioning. A classical conditioning procedure in which the CS begins a fraction of a second before the onset of the UCS and continues with it until the response occurs. See also *delayed conditioning, trace conditioning.*

sine wave. A cyclical wave that when plotted corresponds to the plot of the trigonometric sine function. The sound waves of pure tones yield this function when plotted.

situational attribution. Attributing a person's actions to factors in the situation or environment, as opposed to internal attitudes and motives. See also *dispositional attribution.*

size constancy. The tendency to see a familiar object as of its actual size regardless of its distance. See also *perceptual constancy.*

size-distance invariance principle. The proposal that the perceived size of an object is equal to the product of the retinal size of the object and the perceived distance of the object.

skill memory. The kind of memory that presumably stores perceptual and motor skills, such as the ability to ride a bicycle. See also *fact memory.*

smooth muscle. The type of muscle found in the digestive organs, blood vessels, and other internal organs. Controlled via the autonomic nervous system. See also *cardiac muscle, striate muscle.*

social facilitation. The phenomenon in which an organism performs responses more rapidly when other members of its species are present.

social impact theory. A general theory of social influence that proposes that the impact of any source of influence on a target individual increases as the number, immediacy, and importance of sources increases, but decreases as the number, immediacy, and importance of targets decreases.

social learning theory. The application of

social learning theory (*continued*) learning theory to the problems of personal and social behavior (syn. *social behavior theory*).

social loafing. The phenomenon in which individuals put in less effort when working in concert with others than when working alone.

social norms. A group or community's unwritten rules that govern its members' behavior, attitudes, and beliefs.

social penetration. A process through which individuals move from liking or early infatuation toward greater closeness and intimacy by getting to know one another better through reciprocal self-disclosure.

social phobia. Extreme insecurity in social situations accompanied by an exaggerated fear of embarrassing oneself. See also *phobia, phobic disorder.*

social psychologist. A psychologist who studies social interaction and the ways in which individuals influence one another.

socialization. The shaping of individual characteristics and behavior through the training that the social environment provides.

sociology. The science dealing with group life and social organization in literate societies. See also *behavioral sciences.*

sociopathic personality. See *antisocial personality.*

somatic nervous system. A division of the peripheral nervous system consisting of nerves that connect the brain and spinal cord with the sense receptors, muscles, and body surface. See also *autonomic nervous system, peripheral nervous system.*

somatosensory area. Area in the parietal lobe of the brain that registers sensory experiences, such as heat, cold, touch, and pain (syn. *body-sense area*). See also *motor area.*

somatotypes. Types of bodily physiques postulated by Sheldon's type theory to be associated with personality temperaments. See also *ectomorphic type, endomorphic type, mesomorphic type, type theory.*

spatial frequency. In perception, the distance between successive dark bars in a grating consisting of alternating dark and light bars. Spatial frequency is a determinant of visual resolution. See also *contrast sensitivity.*

spatial localization. The perceptual process of determining where in the visual field an object is. See also *pattern recognition.*

spatial resolution. The ability to see spatial patterns. Visual actuity and the contrast threshold are measures of spatial resolution.

speaker's intention. The speaker's goal in uttering a particular sentence, which is distinct from the actual content of the sentence.

special factor(s). A specialized ability underlying test scores, especially in tests of intelligence; for example, a special ability in mathematics, as distinct from general intelligence. See also *factor analysis, general factor.*

species-specific behavior. See *instinct.*

specific hunger. Hunger for a specific food incentive, such as a craving for sweets. See also *hunger drive.*

specific neuron code hypothesis. According to this hypothesis, the sensory system contains different types of neurons, each tuned to (responsive to) specific features of a stimulus and each evoking a particular sensation. The fact that specific neurons are tuned to particular sensory features occurs because filters are appropriately located at lower levels in the sensory system. From this theoretical perspective, a scene is represented in our mind not by a picture, but by a coded message composed of sensations that correspond to specific features of the stimulus. See also *feature detector, filter.*

spindle. An EEG characteristic of Stage 2 sleep, consisting of short bursts of rhythmical responses of 13–16 Hz; slightly higher than alpha. See also *electroencephalogram.*

split-brain subject. A person who has had an operation that severed the corpus callosum, thus separating the functions of the two cerebral hemispheres. See also *cerebral hemispheres, corpus callosum.*

spontaneous remission. Recovery from an illness or improvement without treatment.

sports psychology. The study of human behavior in sport. The goal of much of the work is to help athletes develop psychological skills that maximize performance and enhance the sport experience. For example, hypnosis and biofeedback have been used to control an athlete's anxiety level during competition and mental imagery has been employed to help perfect the synchrony and flow of certain body movements.

spreading activation. A proposed model of retrieval from long-term memory in which activation subdivides among paths emanating from an activated mental representation.

spurious association. A plausible but nonexistent relation between two stimuli. Human learners frequently report such relations when trying to learn less-than-perfect relations.

S-R psychology. See *stimulus-response psychology.*

stabilized retinal image. The image of an object on the retina when special techniques are used to counteract the minute movements of the eyeball that occur in normal vision. When an image is thus stabilized it quickly disappears, suggesting that the changes in stimulation of retinal cells pro-

vided by the eye movements are necessary for vision.

stages of development. Developmental periods, usually following a progressive sequence, that appear to represent qualitative changes in either the structure or the function of the organism (such as Freud's psychosexual stages, Piaget's cognitive stages).

standard deviation. The square root of the mean of the squares of the amount by which each case departs from the mean of all the cases (syn. *root mean square deviation*).

state-dependent learning. Learning that occurs during a particular biological state—such as when drugged—so that it can only be demonstrated or is most effective when the person is put in the same state again.

statistical significance. The trustworthiness of an obtained statistical measure as a statement about reality; for example, the probability that the population mean falls within the limits determined from a sample. The expression refers to the reliability of the statistical finding and not to its importance.

statistics. The discipline that deals with sampling data from a population of individuals, and then drawing inferences about the population from the sample. See also *statistical significance.*

stereoscopic vision. a) The binocular perception of depth and distance of an object owing to the overlapping fields of the two eyes. b) The equivalent effect when slightly unlike pictures are presented individually to each eye in a stereoscope. See also *distance cues.*

stereotype. A schema, or abstract cognitive representation, of the personality traits or physical attributes of a class or group of people. The schema is usually an overgeneralization, leading us to assume that every member of the group possesses the particular characteristic; for instance the false stereotype that all male homosexuals are effeminate. See also *schema.*

steroids. Complex chemical substances, some of which are prominent in the secretions of the adrenal cortex and may be related to some forms of mental illness. See also *adrenal gland.*

stimulants. Psychoactive drugs that increase arousal. Amphetamines, cocaine, and caffeine are examples.

stimulation-produced analgesia. An analgesic effect produced by the stimulation of a region of the midbrain. See also *gate control theory of pain.*

stimulus (pl. *stimuli*). a) Some specific physical energy impinging on a receptor sensitive to that kind of energy. b) Any objectively describable situation or event (whether outside or inside the organism) that is the occasion for an organism's response. See also *response*.

stimulus-response (S-R) psychology. A psychological view that all behavior is in response to stimuli and that the appropriate tasks of psychological science are those identifying stimuli, the responses correlated with them, and the processes intervening between stimulus and response.

STM. See *short-term memory*.

strabismus. In vision, a lack of binocular depth perception caused by a person's eyes not pointing in the same direction early in life. See also *astigmatism*.

stress. Defined variously as a) a response, the pattern of psychological and physiological responses that occur in difficult situations; b) a stimulus, an event or set of circumstances that requires an unusual response; c) a transaction, a relationship between the person and the environment that is appraised by the person as taxing his or her resources and endangering his or her well-being.

striate muscle. Striped muscle; the characteristic muscles controlling the skeleton, as in the arms and legs. Activated by the somatic, as opposed to the autonomic, nervous system. See also *cardiac muscle, smooth muscle*.

stroboscopic motion. An illusion of motion resulting from the successive presentation of discrete stimulus patterns arranged in a progression corresponding to movement, such as motion pictures. See also *phi phenomenon*.

subconscious processes. A considerable body of research indicates that we register and evaluate stimuli that we are not consciously aware of. The stimuli are said to influence us subconsciously or to operate at a subconscious level of awareness. See also *consciousness*.

subtractive mixture. Color mixture in which absorption occurs so that results differ from additive mixture obtained by mixing projected lights. Subtractive mixture occurs when transparent colored filters are placed one in front of the other and when pigments are mixed. See also *additive mixture*.

superego. In Freud's tripartite division of the personality, the part that represents the internalization of the values and morals of society; the conscience that controls the expression of the id's impulses through moral scruples. See also *conscience, ego, id*.

superposition. In perception, a monocular cue for depth. If an object has contours that cut through those of another, obstructing the other object's view, the overlapping object is perceived as being nearer. See also *distance cues, relative height, relative size*.

suppression. A process of self-control in which impulses, tendencies to action, and wishes to perform disapproved acts are in awareness but not overtly revealed. See also *repression*.

survey method. A method of obtaining information by questioning a large sample of people.

symbol. Anything that stands for or refers to something other than itself.

sympathetic division. A division of the autonomic nervous system, characterized by a chain of ganglia on either side of the spinal cord, with nerve fibers originating in the thoracic and lumbar portions of the spinal cord. Active in emotional excitement and to some extent antagonistic to the parasympathetic division (syn. *sympathetic system*). See also *parasympathetic division*.

synapse. The close functional connection between the axon of one neuron and the dendrites or cell body of another neuron. See also *excitatory synapse, inhibitory synapse*.

synaptic terminals. Small swellings at the end of axon branches that enclose synaptic vesicles containing neurotransmitters. See also *neurotransmitter, synapse, synaptic vesicles*.

synaptic vesicles. Small spherical or irregularly shaped structures within a synaptic terminal that contain neurotransmitters; when stimulated, they discharge the neurotransmitters. See also *neurotransmitter, synapse, synaptic terminals*.

syntactic analysis. In language, an analysis that divides a sentence into noun phrases and verb phrases, and then divides these phrases into smaller units like nouns, adjectives, and verbs.

systematic desensitization. A behavior therapy technique in which hierarchies of anxiety-producing situations are imagined (or sometimes confronted in reality) while the person is in a state of deep relaxation. Gradually the situations become dissociated from the anxiety response. See also *anxiety hierarchy, behavior therapy, counterconditioning*.

T

tabula rasa. Latin, meaning *blank slate*. The term refers to the view that human beings are born without any innate knowledge or ideas; all knowledge is acquired through learning and experience. Proposed by the 17th- and 18th-century British empiricists (Locke, Hume, Berkeley, Hartley).

tachistoscope. An instrument for the brief exposure of words, symbols, pictures, or other visually presented material; sometimes called a T-scope.

taste buds. Receptors for taste located in clusters on the tongue and around the mouth.

T-cell (thymus-dependent cell). A type of lymphocyte that recognizes and destroys foreign antigens (enzymes, toxins, or other substances) and thus plays an important role in the body's immune response.

telegraphic speech. A stage in the development of speech in which the child preserves only the most meaningful and perceptually salient elements of adult speech. The child tends to omit prepositions, articles, prefixes, suffixes, and auxiliary words.

telepathy. Thought transference from one person to another without the mediation of any known channel of sensory communication (for example, identifying a playing card merely being thought of by another person). See also *clairvoyance, extrasensory perception, parapsychology, precognition, psi, psychokinesis*.

temperament. An individual's characteristic mood, sensitivity to stimulation, and energy level. Temperament is usually conceptualized as a genetic predisposition because striking differences in reactivity to stimulation, general mood, and activity level can be observed in newborns.

temperature regulation. The process by which an organism keeps its body temperature relatively constant.

temporal lobe. A portion of the cerebral hemisphere, at the side below the lateral fissure and in front of the occipital lobe. See also *frontal lobe, occipital lobe, parietal lobe*.

temporal theory of pitch. A theory of pitch perception which assumes that the neural impulses traveling up the auditory nerve correspond to a tone's vibrations. If the neural response follows the waveform of the sound, then the auditory system could pick out and respond to this overall frequency. See also *place theory of pitch*.

temporal stability. See *test-retest reliability*.

test battery. A collection of tests whose composite scores are used to appraise individual differences.

test method. A method of psychological investigation. Its advantages are that it allows the psychologist to collect large quantities of useful data from many people, with a minimum of disturbance of their routines of existence and with a minimum of laboratory equipment.

test profile. A chart plotting scores from a number of tests given to the same individual (or group of individuals) in parallel rows on a common scale, with the scores connected by lines, so that high and low scores can be readily perceived. See also *trait profile*.

test standardization. The establishment of norms for interpreting scores by giving a

test standardization (*continued*) test to a representative population and by making appropriate studies of its reliability and validity. See also *norm, reliability, validity.*

test-retest reliability. The consistency of a test when given over successive occasions to the same person (syn. *temporal stability*). See also *reliability.*

testosterone. The primary male sex hormone produced by the testes; it is important for the growth of the male sex organs and the development of the secondary male sex characteristics. It influences the sex drive. See also *androgens, secondary sex characteristics.*

texture gradient. A cue for perceiving depth directly. When viewing a surface in perspective, the elements that make up the featured surface appear to be packed closer and closer together, giving an impression of depth. See also *distance cues.*

thalamus. Two groups of nerve cell nuclei located just above the brain stem and inside the cerebral hemispheres. Considered a part of the central core of the brain. One area acts as a sensory relay station, the other plays a role in sleep and waking; this portion is considered part of the limbic system. See also *hypothalamus.*

theory. A set of assumptions (axioms) advanced to explain existing data and predict new events; usually applicable to a wide array of phenomena.

thinking. The ability to imagine or represent objects or events in memory and to operate on these representations. Ideational problem solving as distinguished from solution through overt manipulation.

threshold. The transitional point at which an increasing stimulus or an increasing difference not previously perceived becomes perceptible (or at which a decreasing stimulus or previously perceived difference becomes imperceptible). The value obtained depends in part on the methods used in determining it. See also *absolute threshold, difference threshold.*

thyroid gland. An endocrine gland located in the neck, whose hormone thyroxin is important in determining metabolic rate. See also *endocrine gland.*

timbre. The quality distinguishing a tone of a given pitch sounded by one instrument from that sounded by another. The differences are due to overtones and other impurities. See also *overtone.*

tip-of-the-tongue phenomenon. The experience of failing to recall a word or name when we are quite certain we know it.

TM. See *meditation.*

T-maze. An apparatus in which an animal is presented with two alternative paths, one of which leads to a goal box. It is usually used with rats and lower organisms. See also *maze.*

tolerance. The need to take more and more of a drug to achieve the same effect. An important factor in physical dependency on drugs.

trace conditioning. A classical conditioning procedure in which the CS terminates before the onset of the UCS. See also *delayed conditioning, simultaneous conditioning.*

trait. A persisting characteristic or dimension of personality according to which individuals can be rated or measured. See also *personality profile.*

trait profile. A chart plotting the ratings of a number of traits of the same individual on a common scale in parallel rows so that the pattern of traits can be visually perceived (syn. *psychograph*). See also *test profile, trait.*

trait theory. The theory that human personality is most profitably characterized by the scores that an individual makes on a number of scales, each of which represents a trait or dimension of his or her personality.

tranquilizer. A drug that reduces anxiety and agitation, such as *Valium.*

transcendental meditation (TM). See *meditation.*

transducer. A device such as an electrode or gauge that, in psychophysiology, converts physiological indicators into other forms of energy that can be recorded and measured.

transduction. The translation of a physical energy into electrical signals by specialized receptor cells. See also *receptor cells.*

transference. In psychoanalysis, the patient's unconsciously making the therapist the object of emotional response, transferring to the therapist responses appropriate to other persons important in the patient's life history.

transsexual. An individual who is physically one sex but psychologically the other. Transsexuals sometimes resort to surgery and hormonal treatment to change their physical appearance. They do not, however, consider themselves to be homosexual. See also *homosexual.*

trichromatic theory. A theory of color perception that postulates three basic color receptors (cones), a ''red'' receptor, a ''green'' receptor, and a ''blue'' receptor. The theory explains color blindness by the absence of one or more receptor types (syn. *Young–Helmholtz theory*). See also *opponent-color theory, two-stage color theory.*

trichromatism. Normal color vision, based on the classification of color vision according to three color systems: black-white, blue-yellow, and red-green. The normal eye sees all three; the colorblind eye is defective in one or two of the three systems. See also *dichromatism, monochromatism.*

tricyclic antidepressant. A class of antidepressants that relieve the symptoms of depression by preventing the reuptake of the neurotransmitters serotonin and norepinephrine, thereby prolonging their action. Imipramine (brand names, Tofranil and Elavil) is the drug most commonly prescribed. See also *antidepressant.*

Turner's syndrome. An abnormal condition of the sex chromosomes in which a female is born with one X chromosome instead of the usual XX. See also *X chromosome.*

two-point threshold. A kind of pressure threshold; it is the minimum distance by which two thin rods touching the skin must be separated before they are felt as two points rather than one.

two-stage color theory. A theory of color vision that postulates three types of cones (in agreement with trichromatic theory) followed by red-green and yellow-blue opponent processes (in agreement with opponent-color theory). This theory accounts for much of what is known about color vision, and serves as a prototype for the analysis of other sensory systems. See also *opponent-color theory, trichromatic theory.*

type A and type B. Two contrasting behavior patterns found in studies of coronary heart disease. Type A people are rushed, competitive, aggressive, and overcommitted to achieving; type Bs are more relaxed and feel less pressure. Type As are at risk for heart disease.

type theory. The theory that human subjects can profitably be classified into a small number of classes or types, each class or type having characteristics in common that set its members apart from other classes or types. See also *trait theory.*

U

unconditioned response (UCR). In classical conditioning, the response given originally to the unconditioned stimulus used as the basis for establishing a conditioned response to a previously neutral stimulus. See also *conditioned response, conditioned stimulus, unconditioned stimulus.*

unconditioned stimulus (UCS). In classical conditioning, a stimulus that automatically elicits a response, typically via a reflex, without prior conditioning. See also *conditioned response, conditioned stimulus, unconditioned response.*

unconscious inference. A term used by the German scientist Hermann von Helmholtz to describe the process by which the perceiver progresses from experiencing sensations evoked by an object to recognizing the properties of the object. We make this inference automatically and unconsciously, and eventually we do not even notice the sensations on which it is based. Helmholtz argued that unconscious inference is the basis of many perceptual phenomena, including distance and object perception.

unconscious motive. A motive of which the subject is unaware or aware of in distorted form. Because there is no sharp dividing line between conscious and unconscious, many motives have both conscious and unconscious aspects.

unconscious processes. Memories, impulses, and desires that are not available to consciousness. According to the psychoanalytic theories of Sigmund Freud, painful memories and wishes are sometimes repressed—that is, diverted to the unconscious where they continue to influence our actions even though we are not aware of them. See also *consciousness.*

V

validity. The predictive significance of a test for its intended purposes. Validity can be measured by a coefficient of correlation between scores on the test and the scores that the test seeks to predict; in other words, scores on some criterion. See also *criterion, reliability.*

validity coefficient. The correlation between a test score and some criterion to which the test is supposed to predict. See also *criterion, validity.*

value. A basic attitude toward broad modes of conduct (for example, courage, honesty) or end-states of existence (for example, equality, salvation). See also *attitude.*

variable. One of the conditions measured or controlled in an experiment. See also *dependent variable, independent variable.*

variance. The square of a standard deviation.

ventromedial hypothalamus (VMH). Area of the hypothalamus important to the regulation of food intake. Electrical stimulation of this area will make an experimental animal stop eating; destruction of brain tissue here produces voracious eating, eventually leading to obesity. See also *hypothalamus, lateral hypothalamus.*

vestibular apparatus. An organ in the inner ear that contains receptors for body movement and kinesthesis.

vestibular sacs. Two sacs in the labyrinth of the inner ear, called the *saccule* and *utricle,* which contain the otoliths ("ear stones"). Pressure of the otoliths on the hair cells in the gelatinous material of the utricle and saccule gives us the sense of body tilt or linear acceleration. See also *equilibratory senses.*

vicarious learning. Learning by observing the behavior of others and noting the consequences of that behavior (syn. *observational learning*).

visual acuity. The threshold for the minimum size of detail that a person can visually detect.

visual area. A projection area lying in the occipital lobe. In humans, damage to this area produces blindness in portions of the visual field corresponding to the amount and location of the damage.

visual cliff. An experimental apparatus with glass over a patterned surface, one half of which is just below the glass and the other half, several feet below. Used to test the depth perception of animals and human infants.

visual field. The total visual array acting on the eye when it is directed toward a fixation point.

visual-evoked potentials. A method of studying perception using electrodes placed on the back of the head over the visual cortex. The electrodes record electrical responses related to how well the observer can discriminate a presented stimulus.

VMH. See *ventromedial hypothalamus.*

voice stress analyzer. A device that graphically represents changes in a person's voice associated with emotion. Used in lie detection. See also *polygraph.*

volumetric receptors. Hypothesized receptors that regulate water intake by responding to the volume of blood and body fluids. Renin, a substance secreted by the kidneys into the bloodstream, may be one volumetric receptor; it constricts the blood vessels and stimulates the release of the hormone, angiotensin, which acts on cells in the hypothalamus to produce thirst. See also *osmoreceptors.*

voluntary processes. Activities selected by choice and controlled or monitored according to intention or plan. See also *control processes.*

W

Weber's law. A law stating that the difference threshold is proportional to the stimulus magnitude at which it is measured. The law is not accurate over the full stimulus range. See also *difference threshold.*

Wernicke's area. A portion of the left cerebral hemisphere involved in language understanding. Individuals with damage in this area are not able to comprehend words; they can hear words, but they do not know their meanings.

working backwards. A problem-solving strategy in which one works backwards from the goal towards the current state. See also *difference reduction, means-ends analysis.*

working through. In psychoanalytic therapy, the process of reeducation by having patients face the same conflicts over and over in the consultation room, until they can independently face and master the conflicts in ordinary life.

X

X chromosome. A chromosome that, if paired with another X chromosome, determines that the individual will be a female. If it is combined with a Y chromosome, the individual will be a male. The X chromosome transmits sex-linked traits. See also *chromosome, sex-linked trait, Y chromosome.*

XYY syndrome. An abnormal condition in which a male has an extra Y sex chromosome; reputedly associated with unusual aggressiveness, although the evidence is not conclusive. See also *Y chromosome.*

Y

Y chromosome. The chromosome that, combined with an X chromosome, determines maleness. See also *chromosome, sex-linked trait, X chromosome.*

Young–Helmholtz theory. See *trichromatic theory.*

Z

zygote. A fertilized ovum or egg. See also *dizygotic twins, monozygotic twins.*

Copyrights and Acknowledgments and Illustration Credits

Chapter 4 (*continued*)
Wadsworth, Inc. Reprinted by permission of the publisher. **4-24** Adapted from *Human Anatomy* by Anthony J. Gaudin and Kenneth C. Jones, copyright © 1988 by Harcourt Brace Jovanovich, Inc., reproduced by permission of the publisher. **4-25** Adapted from *Sensation and Perception*, Third Edition by Stanley Coren and Laurence Ward, copyright © 1989 by Harcourt Brace Jovanovich, Inc., reproduced by permission of the publisher. **4-27** Moore, B. C. J. (1978) "Psychophysical tuning curves measured in simultaneous and forward masking," *Journal of the Acoustical Society of America*, 63:524–32. Adapted with permission of the American Institute of Physics. **4-29, 4-30** Adapted from *Human Anatomy* by Anthony J. Gaudin and Kenneth C. Jones, copyright © 1988 by Harcourt Brace Jovanovich, Inc., reproduced by permission of the publisher. **4-31** Reprinted with permission from Erickson (1963) "Sensory neural patterns and gustation," in Zotterman (ed.), *Olfaction and Taste*, Vol. I, pp. 205–13, copyright © 1963 by Pergamon Press, Inc. **4-32** From Weinstein, S. (1968) "Intensive and extensive aspects of tactile sensitivity as a function of body part, sex and laterality," in Kenshalo, D. R. (ed.), *The Skin Senses*, 1968. Courtesy of Charles C. Thomas, Publisher, Springfield, Illinois. **4-33** Kosambi, D. D. (1967) "Living prehistory in India," *Scientific American*, 216:105. Copyright © D. D. Kosambi; reprinted by permission of Dr. Meera Kosambi and Mr. Bijoy B. Sarkar. **4-34** Adapted from *Sensation and Perception*, Third Edition by Stanley Coren and Laurence Ward, copyright © 1989 by Harcourt Brace Jovanovich, Inc., reproduced by permission of the publisher. **pg. 136** Adapted from *Visual Perception* by T. N. Cornsweet, copyright © 1970 by Harcourt Brace Jovanovich, Inc., reproduced by permission of the publisher. **pg. 137 (top)** Adapted from *Sensation and Perception*, Third Edition, by Stanley Coren and Laurence Ward, copyright © 1989 by Harcourt Brace Jovanovich, Inc., reproduced by permission of the publisher. **pg. 137 (bottom)** Campbell, F. W. and Robson, J. G. (1968) "Application of Fourier analysis to the visibility of gratings," *Journal of Physiology*, 197:551–66. Adapted by permission of The Physiological Society. **pg. 145** Nick Fasciano/ © 1983 Discover Publications.

Chapter 5
5-1 Kaiser Porcelain, Ltd., London, England. **5-2** Salvador Dali, *Slave Market with Disappearing Bust of Voltaire*, 1940. The Salvador Dali Museum, St. Petersburg, Florida. **5-4** From Banks, W. P. and Prinzmetal, W. (1976) "Configurational effects in visual information processing," *Perception and Psychophysics*, 19:361–67. Reprinted by permission of the Psychonomic Society, Inc. **5-5** From Prinzmetal, W. and Banks, W. P. (1977) "Good continuation affects visual detection, " *Perception and Psychophysics*, 21:389–95. Reprinted by permission of the Psychonomic Society, Inc. **5-8 (left)** © B. Hrynewych/Stock, Boston. **5-8 (right)** © M. Winter/Stock, Boston. **5-12** Triesman, A. and Gormican, S. (1988) "Feature analysis in early vision: Evidence from search asymmetries," *Psychological Review*, 95:15–48. Copyright © 1988 by the APA. Adapted by permission of the publisher and the author. **5-16** Reicher, G. M. (1969) "Perceptual recognition as a function of the meaningfulness of the material," *Journal of Experimental Psychology*, 81:275–80. Copyright © 1969 by the APA. Adapted by permission of the publisher and the author. **5-18** Morr, D. and Nishihara, H. K. (1978) "Representation and recognition of three-dimensional shapes," *Proceedings of the Royal Society of London*, 200 (Series B), 269–94. Adapted by permission of the Royal Society. **5-20** Biederman, I. (1987) "Recognition of components: A theory of human image understanding," *Psychological Review*, 94:115–47. Copyright © 1987 by the APA. Adapted with permission of the publisher and the author. **5-22** From Fisher, G. H. (1967) "Perception of ambiguous stimulus materials," *Perception and Psychophysics*, 2:421–22. Reprinted by permission of the Psychonomic Society, Inc. **5-24** Yarbus, D. L. (1967) *Eye Movements and Vision*, Plenum Publishing Corporation. Reproduced by permission of the publisher. **5-26** Triesman, A. and Gelade, G. (1980) "A feature integration theory of attention," *Cognitive Psychology*, 12:97–136. Adapted by permission of Academic Press. **5-30** © Norm Snyder, New York. **5-31** From *Sensation and Perception*, 2/E by E. Bruce Goldstein, copyright © 1984 by Wadsworth, Inc. Reprinted by permission of the publisher. **5-32** Photo by David Linton; © 1989 Ann Linton. **5-33** Ginsberg, A. (1983) "Contrast perception in the human infant," unpub. manuscript, reproduced in *Sensation and Perception*, 2/E by E. Bruce Goldstein, copyright © 1984 by Wadsworth, Inc. Reprinted by permission of the publisher. Photo courtesy Wadsworth, Inc. **5-34** © William Vandivert, *Scientific American*, April 1960, cover photo. **5-35** Blakemore, C. and Cooper, G. F. (1970) "Development of the brain depends on the visual environment," Reprinted by permission from *Nature*, 228:478. Copyright © 1970 Macmillan Magazines, Ltd. **5-36**

Hein, A. and Held, R. (1967) "Dissociation of the visual placing response into elicited and guided components," *Science*, 158:390–92 (Oct. 20, 1967), copyright © 1967 by the AAAS. **5-37** Held, R. and Hein, A. (1963) "Movement-produced stimulation in the development of visually guided behavior," *Journal of Comparative and Physiological Psychology*, 56:872-76. Copyright © 1963 by the APA. Reprinted by permission of the publisher and the author. **pg. 178** Just, M. A. and Carpenter, P. A. (1980) "A theory of reading: From eye fixations to comprehension," *Psychological Review*, 87:329–54. Copyright © 1980 by the APA. Adapted by permission of the publisher and the author.

Chapter 6
6-1 Ludwig, A. M., et al. (1972) "The objective study of a multiple personality," *Archives of General Psychiatry*, 26:298–310. Copyright © 1972 American Medical Association. **6-2** Adapted from McGuinness, J. for W. C. Dement (1978) *Some Must Watch While Some Must Sleep*, copyright © 1972, 1974, by W. C. Dement, a Portable Stanford Book, published by permission of Stanford Alumni Association, Stanford University. **6-6** Data from the National Highway and Traffic Safety Administration. **6-8** Adapted from *Hypnotic Susceptibility* by Ernest Hilgard, copyright © 1965 by Harcourt Brace Jovanovich, Inc., reproduced by permission of the publisher. **6-9** Cooper, L. M. (1979) "Hypnotic amnesia," reprinted with permission from Erika Fromm and Ronald E. Shor, HYPNOSIS: DEVELOPMENTS IN RESEARCH AND NEW PERSPECTIVES (New and revised 2nd ed.) (New York: Aldine de Gruyter) Copyright © 1979 by Erika Fromm and Ronald E. Shor.

Chapter 7
7-2 Pavlov, E. P. (1927) *Conditioned Reflexes*, Oxford: Oxford University Press. Adapted by permission of the publisher. **7-3** Hovland, C. I. (1937) "The sensory generalization of conditioned responses with varying frequencies of tone," *Journal of General Psychology*, 17:125–48. Reprinted with permission of the Helen Dwight Reid Educational Foundation. Published by Heldref Publications, 4000 Albemarle St., N.W., Washington D.C. 20016. Copyright © 1937. **7-4** Fuhrer, M. J. and Baer, P. E. (1965) "Differential classical conditioning: Verbalization of stimulus contingencies," *Science*, 150:1479–81 (Dec. 10, 1965), copyright © 1965 by the AAAS. **7-6** © Richard Wood/The Picture Cube. **7-7** From "Learning in the autonomic nervous system," by L. V. DiCara, *Scientific Ameri-*

References

The numbers in boldface following each reference give the text pages on which the article or book is cited. Citations in the text are made by author and date of publication.

A

ABBOTT, B. B., SCHOEN, L. S., & BADIA, P. (1984). Predictable and unpredictable shock: Behavioral measures of aversion and physiological measures of stress. PSYCHOLOGICAL BULLETIN, 96, 45–71. **571**

ABELSON, R. P. (1968). Computers, polls, and public opinion—Some puzzles and paradoxes. TRANSACTION, 5, 20–27. **709, 710**

ABELSON, R. P. (1968). Psychological implication. In R. P. Abelson, E. Aronson, W. J. McGuire, T. M. Newcomb, M. J. Rosenberg, & P. H. Tannenbaum (Eds.), THEORIES OF COGNITIVE CONSISTENCY: A SOURCEBOOK. Chicago: Rand McNally. **710**

ABELSON, R. P. (1976). Script processing in attitude formation and decision making. In J. S. Carroll & J. W. Payne (Eds.), COGNITION AND SOCIAL BEHAVIOR. Hillsdale, NJ: Erlbaum. **688**

ABERNATHY, E. M. (1940). The effect of changed environmental conditions upon the results of college examinations. JOURNAL OF PSYCHOLOGY, 10, 293–301. **309**

ABRAMSON, L. Y., METALSKY, G. I., & ALLOY, L. B. (1989). Hopelessness depression: A theory-based subtype of depression. PSYCHOLOGICAL REVIEW, 969, 358–372. **614**

ADAMS, G. R. (1981). The effects of physical attractiveness on the socialization process. In G. W. Lucher, K. A. Ribbens, & J. A. McNamara, Jr. (Eds.), PSYCHOLOGICAL ASPECTS OF FACIAL FORM. Craniofacial Growth Series. Ann Arbor: University of Michigan. **694**

ADAMS, J. L. (1974). CONCEPTUAL BLOCK-BUSTING. Stanford, CA: Stanford Alumni Association. **351**

ADAMS, M., & COLLINS, A. (1979). A schema-theoretic view of reading. In R. O. Freedle (Ed.), NEW DIRECTIONS DISCOURSE PROCESSING (Vol. 12). Norwood, NJ: Ablex. **336**

ADELSON, E. (1982). Saturation and adaptation in the rod system. VISION RESEARCH, 22, 1299–1312. **128**

AGRAS, W. S. (1975). Fears and phobias. STANFORD MAGAZINE, 3, 59–62. **599**

AGRAS, W. S. (1985). PANIC: FACING FEARS, PHOBIAS, AND ANXIETY. New York: Freeman. **607, 635, 679**

AGRAS, W. S., SYLVESTER, D., & OLIVEAU, D. (1969). The epidemiology of common fears and phobias. COMPREHENSIVE PSYCHIATRY, 10, 151–156. **599**

AIKEN, L. R. (1989). ASSESSMENT OF PERSONALITY. Boston: Allyn & Bacon. **551**

AINSWORTH, M. D. S. (1979). Infant–mother attachment. AMERICAN PSYCHOLOGIST, 34, 932–937. **89, 90**

AINSWORTH, M. D. S., BLEHAR, M. C., WALTERS, E., & WALL, S. (1978). PATTERNS OF ATTACHMENT: A PSYCHOLOGICAL STUDY OF THE STRANGE SITUATION. Hillsdale, NJ: Erlbaum. **89**

AKERS, C. (1984). Methodological criticisms of parapsychology. In S. Krippner (Ed.), ADVANCES IN PARAPSYCHOLOGICAL RESEARCH (Vol. 4). Jefferson, NC: McFarland. **238**

ALBERTS, B., BRAY, D., LEWIS, J., RAFF, M., ROBERTS, K., & WATSON, J. D. (1983). MOLECULAR BIOLOGY OF THE CELL. New York: Garland. **36, 67**

ALLEN, M. G. (1976). Twin studies of affective illness. ARCHIVES OF GENERAL PSYCHIATRY, 35, 1476–1478. **614**

ALLEN, V. L., & LEVINE, J. M. (1969). Consensus and conformity. JOURNAL OF EXPERIMENTAL AND SOCIAL PSYCHOLOGY, 5 (4), 389. **736**

ALLEN, V. L., & LEVINE, J. M. (1971). Social support and conformity: The role of independent assessment of reality. JOURNAL OF EXPERIMENTAL SOCIAL PSYCHOLOGY, 7, 48–58. **736**

ALLPORT, F. H. (1920). The influence of the group upon association and thought. JOURNAL OF EXPERIMENTAL PSYCHOLOGY, 3, 159–182. **724**

ALLPORT, F. H. (1924). SOCIAL PSYCHOLOGY. Boston: Houghton Mifflin. **724**

ALLPORT, G. W. (1937). PERSONALITY: A PSYCHOLOGICAL INTERPRETATION. New York: HENRY HOLT. **504, 505, 545**

ALLPORT, G. W. (1961). PATTERNS AND GROWTH IN PERSONALITY. New York: Holt, Rinehart & Winston. **505**

ALLPORT, G. W. (1985). The historical background of social psychology. In G. Lindzey & E. Aronson (Eds.), THE HANDBOOK OF SOCIAL PSYCHOLOGY (3rd ed.). New York: Random House. (Article originally published 1954) **723**

ALLPORT, G. W., & ODBERT, H. S. (1936). Trait-names: A psycholexical study. PSYCHOLOGICAL MONOGRAPHS, 47 (1, No. 211). **506**

ALTMAN, I., & TAYLOR, D. A. (1973). SOCIAL PENETRATION: THE DEVELOPMENT OF INTERPERSONAL RELATIONSHIPS. New York: Holt, Rinehart & Winston. **716, 717**

AMERICAN PSYCHIATRIC ASSOCIATION. (1987). DIAGNOSTIC AND STATISTICAL MANUAL OF MENTAL DISORDERS (3rd ed., rev.). Washington, DC: American Psychiatric Association. **594**

AMOORE, J. E. (1970). THE MOLECULAR BASIS OF ODOR. Springfield, IL: Thomas. 147

ANASTASI, A. (1982). PSYCHOLOGICAL TESTING (5th ed.). New York: Macmillan. 473

ANCOLI-ISRAEL, S., KRIPKE, D. F. & MASON, W. (1987). Characteristics of obstructive and central sleep apnea in the elderly: An interim report. BIOLOGICAL PSYCHIATRY, 22, 741–750. 207

ANDERSON, C. M., REISS, D. J., & HOGARTY, G. E. (1986). SCHIZO-PHRENIA AND THE FAMILY. New York: Guilford Press. 627

ANDERSON, J. R. (1983). THE ARCHITEC-TURE OF COGNITION. Cambridge, MA: Harvard University Press. 286, 295, 296, 319

ANDERSON, J. R. (1985). COGNITIVE PSY-CHOLOGY AND ITS IMPLICATIONS (2nd ed.). New York: Freeman. 29, 293, 319, 349, 350

ANDERSON, J. R. (1989). COGNITIVE PSY-CHOLOGY AND ITS IMPLICATIONS (3rd ed.). New York: Freeman. 29, 293, 319

ANDREASEN, N. C. (1988). Brain imaging: Applications in psychiatry. SCIENCE, 239, 1381–1388. 45

ANDREWS, K. H., & KANDEL, D. B. (1979). Attitude and behavior. AMERICAN SOCIOLOGICAL REVIEW, 44, 298–310. 706

ARDREY, R. (1966). THE TERRITORIAL IM-PERATIVE. New York: Dell. 426

ARENDT, H. (1963). EICHMANN IN JERUSA-LEM: A REPORT ON THE BANALITY OF EVIL. New York: Viking Press. 737

ARMSTRONG, S. L., GLEITMAN, L. R., & GLEITMAN, H. (1983). What some concepts might not be. COGNITION, 13, 263–308. 323

ARNOLD, M. (1949). A demonstrational analysis of the TAT in a clinical setting. JOURNAL OF ABNORMAL AND SOCIAL PSY-CHOLOGY, 44, 97–111. 538

ARONSON, E. (1988). THE SOCIAL ANIMAL (5th ed.). San Francisco: Freeman. 719, 721, 742, 761

ARONSON, E., & CARLSMITH, J. M. (1963). The effect of the severity of threat on the devaluation of forbidden behavior. JOURNAL OF ABNORMAL AND SOCIAL PSY-CHOLOGY, 66, 584–588. 708

ASCH, S. E. (1952). SOCIAL PSYCHOLOGY. Englewood Cliffs, NJ: Prentice-Hall. 734, 736

ASCH, S. E. (1955). Opinions and social pressures. SCIENTIFIC AMERICAN, 193, 31–35. 734, 736

ASCH, S. E. (1958). Effects of group pressure upon modification and distortion of judgments. In E. E. Maccoby, T. M. New-comb, & E. L. Hartley (Eds.), READINGS IN SOCIAL PSYCHOLOGY (3rd ed.). New York: Holt, Rinehart & Winston. 734, 735, 736

ASLIN, R. N. (1987). Visual and auditory development in infancy. In J. D. Osofsky (Ed.), HANDBOOK OF INFANT DEVELOP-MENT (2nd ed.). New York: Wiley. 76

ASLIN, R. N., & BANKS, M. S. (1978). Early visual experience in humans: Evidence for a critical period in the development of binocular vision. In S. Schneider, H. Liebowitz, H. Pick, & H. Stevenson (Eds.), PSYCHOLOGY, FROM BASIC RE-SEARCH TO PRACTICE. New York: Plenum. 189

ATKINSON, R. C. (1975). Mnemotechnics in second-language learning. AMERICAN PSYCHOLOGIST, 30, 821–828. 308

ATKINSON, R. C. (1976). Teaching children to read using a computer. AMERICAN PSYCHOLOGIST, 29, 169–178. 18

ATKINSON, R. C., HERRNSTEIN, R. J., LINDZEY, G., & LUCE, R. D. (Eds.). (1988). STEVENS' HANDBOOK OF EXPERI-MENTAL PSYCHOLOGY (Vols. 1 and 2). New York: Wiley. 155, 319

ATKINSON, R. C., & SHIFFRIN, R. M. (1971). The control of short-term memory. SCIENTIFIC AMERICAN, 224, 82–90. 289

ATKINSON, R. C., & SHIFFRIN, R. M. (1977). Human memory: A proposed system and its control processes. In G. H. Bower (Ed.), HUMAN MEMORY: BASIC PROCESSES. New York: Academic Press. 289

AVERILL, J. R. (1983). Studies on anger and aggression: Implications for theories of emotion. AMERICAN PSYCHOLOGIST, 38, 1145–1160. 431

AWAYA, S., MIYAKE, Y., IMAYUMI, Y., SHIOSE, Y., KNADA, T., & KOMURO, K. (1973). Amblyopia. JAPANESE JOURNAL OF OPHTHAMOLOGY, 17, 69–82. 189

AX, A. (1953). The physiological differentiation between fear and anger in humans. PSYCHOSOMATIC MEDICINE, 15, 433–442. 405

B

BAARS, B. J. (1988). COGNITIVE THEORY OF CONSCIOUSNESS. New York: Cambridge University Press. 243

BADDELEY, A. D. (1982). YOUR MEMORY: A USER'S GUIDE. New York: Macmillan. 319

BADDELEY, A. D. (1986). WORKING MEM-ORY. New York: Oxford University Press. 288, 291, 319

BADDELEY, A. D., & HITCH, G. J. (1974). Working memory. In G. H. Bower (Ed.), THE PSYCHOLOGY OF LEARNING AND MOTIVATION (Vol. 8). New York: Academic Press. 288

BADDELEY, A. D., & HITCH, G. J. (1977). Recency re-examined. In S. Dornic (Ed.), ATTENTION AND PERFORMANCE (Vol. 6). Hillsdale, NJ: Erlbaum. 291

BADDELEY, A. D., THOMPSON, N., & BUCHANAN, M. (1975). Word length and the structure of short-term memory. JOURNAL OF VERBAL LEARNING AND VER-BAL BEHAVIOR, 14, 575–589. 286

BAER, D. J., & CORRADO, J. J. (1974). Heroin addict relationships with parents during childhood and early adolescent years. JOURNAL OF GENETIC PSYCHOLOGY, 124, 99–103. 225

BAER, P. E., & FUHRER, M. J. (1968). Cognitive processes during differential trace and delayed conditioning of the G.S.R. JOURNAL OF EXPERIMENTAL PSY-CHOLOGY, 78, 81–88. 251

BAHRICK, L. E., & WATSON, J. S. (1985). Detection of intermodel pro-prioceptive-visual contingency as a potential basis of self-perception in infancy. DE-VELOPMENTAL PSYCHOLOGY, 21, 693–973. 84, 85

BANDUCCI, R. (1967). The effect of mother's employment on the achievement, aspirations, and expectations of the child. PERSONNEL AND GUIDANCE JOUR-NAL, 46, 263–267.

BANDURA, A. (1969). PRINCIPLES OF BE-HAVIOR MODIFICATION. New York: Holt, Rinehart & Winston. 650

BANDURA, A. (1973). AGGRESSION: A SO-CIAL LEARNING ANALYSIS. Englewood Cliffs, NJ: Prentice-Hall. 425, 429, 433

BANDURA, A. (1977). SOCIAL LEARNING THEORY. Englewood Cliffs, NJ: Prentice-Hall. 425, 433, 551

BANDURA, A. (1984). Recycling misconceptions of perceived self-efficacy. COGNI-TIVE THERAPY AND RESEARCH, 8, 231–255. 655

BANDURA, A. (1986). SOCIAL FOUNDA-TIONS OF THOUGHT AND ACTION: A SO-CIAL COGNITIVE THEORY. Englewood Cliffs, NJ: Prentice-Hall. 425, 650

BANDURA, A., ADAMS, N. E., & BEY-ER, J. (1976). Cognitive processes mediating behavioral change. JOURNAL OF PER-SONALITY AND SOCIAL PSYCHOLOGY, 35, 125–139. 651

BANDURA, A., ADAMS, N. E., HARDY, A. B., & HOWELLS, G. N. (1980). Tests of the generality of self-efficacy theory. COGNITIVE THERAPY AND RESEARCH, 4, 39–66. 651

BANDURA, A., BLANCHARD, E. B., & RITTER, B. (1969). The relative efficacy of desensitization and modeling approaches for inducing behavioral, affective, and attitudinal changes. JOURNAL OF PERSONALITY AND SOCIAL PSYCHOLOGY, 13, 173–199. 650, 651

BANDURA, A., & MCDONALD, F. J. (1963). Influence of social reinforcement and the behavior of models in shaping children's moral judgments. JOURNAL OF ABNORMAL AND SOCIAL PSYCHOLOGY, 67, 274–281. **99**

BANDURA, A., TAYLOR, C. B., EWART, C. K., MILLER, N. M., & DE-BUSK, R. F. (1985). Exercise testing to enhance wives' confidence in their husbands' cardiac capability soon after clinically uncomplicated acute myocardial infarction. AMERICAN JOURNAL OF CARDIOLOGY, 55, 635–638. **541**

BANKS, M. S. (1982). The development of spatial and temporal contrast sensitivity. CURRENT EYE RESEARCH, 2, 191–198. **186**

BANKS, W. P., & PRINZMETAL, W. (1976). Configurational effects in visual information processing. PERCEPTION AND PSYCHOPHYSICS, 19, 361–367. **159**

BANKS, W. P., & SALAPATEK, P. (1983). Infant visual perception. In P. H. Mussen (Ed.), HANDBOOK OF CHILD PSYCHOLOGY: VOL. 2. INFANCY AND DEVELOPMENTAL PSYCHOBIOLOGY. New York: Wiley. **76**

BANYAI, E. I., & HILGARD, E. R. (1976). A comparison of active-alert hypnotic induction with traditional relaxation induction. JOURNAL OF ABNORMAL PSYCHOLOGY, 85, 218–224. **229**

BARBOUR, H. G. (1912). Die wirkung unmittelbarer erwarmung und abkuhlung der warmenzentrum auf die korpertemperatur. ACHIV FUR EXPERIMENTALLE PATHALOGIE UND PHARMAKOLOGIE, 70, 1–26. **363**

BAREFOOT, J. C., DODGE, K. A., PETERSON, B. L., DAHLSTROM, W. G., & WILLIAMS, R. B., JR. (1989). The Cook-Medley hostility scale: Item content and ability to predict survival. PSYCHOSOMATIC MEDICINE, 51, 46–57. **581**

BAREFOOT, J. C., WILLIAMS, R. B., & DAHLSTROM, W. G. (1983). Hostility, CHD incidence, and total mortality: A 25-year follow-up study of 255 physicians. PSYCHOSOMATIC MEDICINE, 45, 59–63. **581**

BARLOW, H. B., BLAKEMORE, C., & PETTIGREW, J. D. (1967). The neural mechanism of binocular depth discrimination. JOURNAL OF PHYSIOLOGY, 193, 327–342. **161**

BARLOW, H. B., & MOLLON, J. D. (1982). THE SENSES. Cambridge: Cambridge University Press. **155**

BARNES, G. E., & PROSEN, H. (1985). Parental death and depression. JOURNAL OF ABNORMAL PSYCHOLOGY, 94, 64–69. **611**

BARON, J. (1988). THINKING AND DECIDING. Cambridge: Cambridge University Press. **356**

BARON, R. S. (1986). Distraction-conflict theory: Progress and problems. In L. Berk-owitz (Ed.), ADVANCES IN EXPERIMENTAL SOCIAL PSYCHOLOGY (Vol. 19). New York: Academic Press. **726**

BARRERA, M. E., & MAURER, D. (1981). Recognition of mother's photographed face by the three-month-old infant. CHILD DEVELOPMENT, 52, 714–716. **187**

BARRY, H., CHILD, I., & BACON, M. (1959). Relation of child training to subsistence economy. AMERICAN ANTHROPOLOGIST, 61, 51–63. **485, 486**

BARSALOU, L. W. (1987). The content and organization of autobiographical memories. In U. Neisser & E. Winograd (Eds.), REMEMBERING RECONSIDERED: ECOLOGICAL AND TRADITIONAL APPROACHES TO THE STUDY OF MEMORY. New York: Cambridge University Press. **317**

BARTLETT, F. C. (1932). REMEMBERING: A STUDY IN EXPERIMENTAL AND SOCIAL PSYCHOLOGY. Cambridge: Cambridge University Press. **315**

BARTOSHUK, L. M. (1979). Bitter taste of saccharin: Related to the genetic ability to taste the bitter substance propylthiourial (PROP). SCIENCE, 205, 934–935. **148**

BATTERSBY, W., & WAGMAN, I. (1962). Neural limits of visual excitability: Pt. 4. Spatial determinants of retrochiasmal interaction. AMERICAN JOURNAL OF PHYSIOLOGY, 203, 359–365. **128**

BAUM, A., GATCHEL, R. J., FLEMING, R., & LAKE, C. R. (1981). CHRONIC AND ACUTE STRESS ASSOCIATED WITH THE THREE MILE ISLAND ACCIDENT AND DECONTAMINATION: PRELIMINARY FINDINGS OF A LONGITUDINAL STUDY. Technical report submitted to the U.S. Nuclear Regulatory Commission. **572**

BAUMEISTER, R. F., & TICE, D. M. (1984). Role of self-presentation and choice in cognitive dissonance under forced compliance: Necessary or sufficient causes? JOURNAL OF PERSONALITY AND SOCIAL PSYCHOLOGY, 43, 838–852. **709**

BAUMRIND, D. (1967). Childcare practices anteceding three patterns of preschool behavior. GENETIC PSYCHOLOGY MONOGRAPHS, 75, 43–88. **478**

BAUMRIND, D. (1971). Current patterns of parental authority. DEVELOPMENTAL PSYCHOLOGY MONOGRAPHS, 1, 1–103. **478**

BAXTER, L. R., JR., SCHWARTZ, J. M., MAZZIOTTA, J. C., PHELPS, M. E., PAHL, J. J., GUZE, M. D., & FAIRBANKS, L. (1988). Cerebral glucose metabolic rates in nondepressed patients with obsessive-compulsive disorder. AMERICAN JOURNAL OF PSYCHIATRY, 145, 1560–1563. **605**

BAYLEY, N. (1970). Development of mental abilities. In P. Mussen (Ed.), CARMICHAEL'S MANUAL OF CHILD PSYCHOLOGY (Vol. 1). New York: Wiley. **467**

BEAMAN, A. L., BARNES, P. J., KLENTZ, B., & MCQUIRK, B. (1978). Increasing helping rates through information dissemination: Teaching pays. PERSONALITY AND SOCIAL PSYCHOLOGY BULLETIN, 4, 406–411. **734**

BEATON, A. (1986). LEFT SIDE/RIGHT SIDE: A REVIEW OF LATERALITY RESEARCH. New Haven: Yale University Press. **67**

BEBBINGTON, P., STURT, E., TENNANT, C., & HURRY, J. (1984). Misfortune and resilience: A community study of women. PSYCHOLOGICAL MEDICINE, 14, 347–363. **616**

BECK, A. T. (1976). COGNITIVE THERAPY AND THE EMOTIONAL DISORDERS. New York: International Universities Press. **512, 655**

BECK, A. T. (1988). LOVE IS NEVER ENOUGH. New York: Harper & Row. **679**

BECK, A. T., RUSH, A. J., SHAW, B. F., & EMERY, G. (1979). COGNITIVE THERAPY OF DEPRESSION. New York: Guilford Press. **608, 612**

BEE, H. (1985). THE DEVELOPING CHILD (4th ed.). New York: Harper & Row. **113**

BEECHER, H. K. (1961). Surgery as placebo. JOURNAL OF AMERICAN MEDICAL ASSOCIATION, 176, 1102–1107. **668**

BEERS, C. W. (1908). A MIND THAT FOUND ITSELF. New York: Doubleday. **638**

BÉKÉSY, G. VON. (1960). EXPERIMENTS IN HEARING (E. G. Weaver, Trans.). New York: McGraw-Hill. **142**

BELL, A. P., & WEINBERG, M. S. (1978). HOMOSEXUALITIES: A STUDY OF DIVERSITY AMONG MEN AND WOMEN. New York: Simon & Schuster. **385, 388**

BELL, A. P., WEINBERG, M. S., & HAMMERSMITH, S. K. (1981). SEXUAL PREFERENCE: ITS DEVELOPMENT IN MEN AND WOMEN. Bloomington: Indiana University Press. **385, 386**

BELL, L. V. (1980). TREATING THE MENTALLY ILL: FROM COLONIAL TIMES TO THE PRESENT. New York: Praeger. **679**

BELL, R. Q. (1968). A reinterpretation of the direction of effects in studies of socialization. PSYCHOLOGICAL REVIEW, 75, 81–95. **478**

BELLEZZA, F. S., & BOWER, G. H. (1981). Person stereotypes and memory for people. JOURNAL OF PERSONALITY AND SOCIAL PSYCHOLOGY, 41, 856–865. **315**

BELOFF, H. (1957). The structure and origin of the anal character. GENETIC PSYCHOLOGY MONOGRAPHS, 55, 141–172. **517**

BELSKY, J., & ROVINE, M. (1988). Nonmaternal care in the first year of life and security of infant–parent attachment. CHILD DEVELOPMENT, 59, 157–167. **94**

BELSKY, J., ROVINE, M., & TAYLOR, D. (1984). The Pennsylvania infant and

BELSKY, J. (continued) family development project III: The origins of individual differences in infant–mother attachment: Maternal and infant contributions. CHILD DEVELOPMENT, 55, 718–728. 90

BEM, D. J. (1970). BELIEFS, ATTITUDES AND HUMAN AFFAIRS. Belmont, CA: Brooks/Cole. 719, 721, 752

BEM, D. J. (1972). Self-perception theory. In L. Berkowitz (Ed.), ADVANCES IN EXPERIMENTAL SOCIAL PSYCHOLOGY (Vol. 6). New York: Academic Press. 697

BEM, D. J. (1983). Toward a response style theory of persons in situations. In R. A. Dienstbier & M. M. Page (Eds.), NEBRASKA SYMPOSIUM ON MOTIVATION 1982: PERSONALITY CURRENT THEORY AND RESEARCH (Vol. 30, pp. 201–231). Lincoln: University of Nebraska Press. 504, 544, 546

BEM, D. J., & ALLEN, A. (1974). On predicting some of the people some of the time: The search for cross-situational consistencies in behavior. PSYCHOLOGICAL REVIEW, 81, 506–520. 544, 546

BEM, S. L. (1975). Sex-role adaptability: One consequence of psychological androgyny. JOURNAL OF PERSONALITY AND SOCIAL PSYCHOLOGY, 31, 634–643. 689

BEM, S. L. (1981). Gender schema theory: A cognitive account of sex-typing. PSYCHOLOGICAL REVIEW, 88, 354–364. 688, 697

BEM, S. L., MARTYNA, W., & WATSON, C. (1976). Sex-typing and androgyny: Further explorations of the expressive domain. JOURNAL OF PERSONALITY AND SOCIAL PSYCHOLOGY, 34, 1016–1023. 689

BENBOW, C. P. (1988). Sex differences in mathematical reasoning ability in intellectually talented preadolescents: Their nature, effects, and possible causes. BEHAVIORAL AND BRAIN SCIENCES, 11, 169–232. 456

BENBOW, C. P., & STANLEY, J. C. (1980). Sex differences in mathematical ability: Fact or artifact? SCIENCE, 210, 1262–1264.

BENSON, H. (1975). THE RELAXATION RESPONSE. New York: Morrow. 243

BENSON, H., & FRIEDMAN, R. (1985). A rebuttal to the conclusions of David S. Holmes' article: "Meditation and somatic arousal reduction." AMERICAN PSYCHOLOGIST, 40, 725–728. 227

BENSON, H., KOTCH, J. B., CRASSWELLER, K. D., & GREENWOOD, M. M. (1977). Historical and clinical considerations of the relaxation response. AMERICAN SCIENTIST, 65, 441–443. 227

BERGIN, A. E., & LAMBERT, M. J. (1978). The evaluation of therapeutic outcomes. In S. L. Garfield & A. E. Bergin (Eds.), HANDBOOK OF PSYCHOTHERAPY AND BEHAVIOR CHANGE (2nd ed.). New York: Wiley. 664, 665

BERGSON, H. (1911). MATTER AND MEMORY. New York: Macmillan. 306

BERKOWITZ, L. (1965). The concept of aggressive drive. In L. Berkowitz (Ed.), ADVANCES IN EXPERIMENTAL SOCIAL PSYCHOLOGY (Vol. 2). New York: Academic Press. 430

BERLIN, B., & KAY, P. (1969). BASIC COLOR TERMS: THEIR UNIVERSALITY AND EVOLUTION. Los Angeles: University of California Press. 326

BERNSTEIN, W. M., STEPHAN, W. G., & DAVIS, M. H. (1979). Explaining attributions for achievement: A path analytic approach. JOURNAL OF PERSONALITY AND SOCIAL PSYCHOLOGY, 37, 1810–1821. 700

BERRY, J. W. (1967). Independence and conformity in subsistence-level societies. JOURNAL OF PERSONALITY AND SOCIAL PSYCHOLOGY, 7, 415–418. 486

BERSCHEID, E. (1983). Emotion. In H. H. Kelley, E. Berscheid, A. Christensen, J. H. Harvey, T. L. Huston, G. Levinger, E. McClintock, L. A. Peplau, & D. R. Peterson (Eds.), CLOSE RELATIONSHIPS. New York: Freeman. 718

BERSCHEID, E., & WALSTER, E. H. (1978). INTERPERSONAL ATTRACTION (2nd ed.). Menlo Park, CA: Addison-Wesley. 714, 717

BIEDERMAN, I. (1981). On the semantics of a glance at a scene. In M. Kubovy & J. Pomerantz (Eds.), PERCEPTUAL ORGANIZATION. Hillsdale, NJ: Erlbaum. 172

BIEDERMAN, I. (1987). Recognition by components: A theory of human image understanding. PSYCHOLOGICAL REVIEW, 94, 115–147. 171, 172

BIEDERMAN, I., & JU, G. (1988). Surface versus edge-based determinants of visual recognition. COGNITIVE PSYCHOLOGY, 20, 38–64. 165

BIERBRAUER, G. (1973). ATTRIBUTION AND PERSPECTIVE: EFFECTS OF TIME, SET, AND ROLE ON INTERPERSONAL INFERENCE. Unpublished doctoral dissertation, Stanford University. 742

BINET, A., & SIMON, T. (1905). New methods for the diagnosis of the intellectual level of subnormals. ANNALS OF PSYCHOLOGY, 11, 191. 444, 459

BISIACH, E., & LUZZATI, C. (1978). Unilateral neglect of representational space. CORTEX, 14, 129–133. 347

BLAKEMORE, C., & COOPER, G. F. (1970). Development of the brain depends on the visual environment. NATURE, 228, 477–478. 189

BLASI, A. (1980). Bridging moral cognition and moral action: A critical review of the literature. PSYCHOLOGICAL BULLETIN, 88, 1–45. 100

BLASS, E. M., & EPSTEIN, A. N. (1971). A lateral preoptic osmosensitive zone for thirst in the rat. JOURNAL OF COMPARATIVE AND PHYSIOLOGICAL PSYCHOLOGY, 76, 378–394. 384

BLISS, E. L. (1980). Multiple personalities: Report of fourteen cases with implications for schizophrenia and hysteria. ARCHIVES OF GENERAL PSYCHIATRY, 37, 1388–1397. 201

BLOCK, J. (1961/1978). THE Q-SORT METHOD IN PERSONALITY ASSESSMENT AND PSYCHIATRIC RESEARCH. Palo Alto: Consulting Psychologists Press. 490, 532

BLOCK, J. (1971). LIVES THROUGH TIME. Berkeley: Bancroft. 488, 490, 501

BLOCK, J. H. (1980). Another look at sex differentiation in the socialization behavior of mothers and fathers. In F. Denmark & J. Sherman (Eds.), PSYCHOLOGY OF WOMEN: FUTURE DIRECTIONS OF RESEARCH. New York: Psychological Dimensions. 96

BLOCK, J. H. (1982). Psychological development of female children and adolescents. In P. W. Berman & E. R. Ramey (Eds.), WOMEN: A DEVELOPMENTAL PERSPECTIVE. Washington, DC: Department of Health and Human Services. 93

BLOOD, R. O. (1967). LOVE MATCH AND ARRANGED MARRIAGE. New York: Free Press. 718

BLUM, G. S. (1953). PSYCHOANALYTIC THEORIES OF PERSONALITY. New York: McGraw-Hill. 518

BLUM, R., & ASSOCIATES. (1972). HORATIO ALGER'S CHILDREN. San Francisco: Jossey-Bass. 225

BOFF, K. R., KAUFMAN, L., & THOMAS, J. P. (Eds.). (1986). HANDBOOK OF PERCEPTION AND HUMAN PERFORMANCE: Vol. 1. SENSORY PROCESSES AND PERCEPTION. New York: Wiley. 155

BOLLES, R. C. (1970). Species-specific defense reactions and avoidance learning. PSYCHOLOGICAL REVIEW, 77, 32–48. 270

BOND, C. F. (1982). Social facilitation: A self-presentational view. JOURNAL OF PERSONALITY AND SOCIAL PSYCHOLOGY, 42, 1042–1050. 726

BOND, L. A., & JOFFE, J. M. (Eds.). (1982). FACILITATING INFANT AND EARLY CHILDHOOD DEVELOPMENT. Hanover, NH: University Press of New England. 473

BOONE, J. A., & ADESSO, V. J. (1974). Racial differences on a black intelligence test. JOURNAL OF NEGRO EDUCATION, 43, 429–536. 452

BORGIDA, E., & NISBETT, R. E. (1977). The differential impact of abstract versus concrete information on decisions. JOUR-

NAL OF APPLIED SOCIAL PSYCHOLOGY, 7, 258–271. **684**

BORING, E. G. (1930). A new ambiguous figure. AMERICAN JOURNAL OF PSYCHOLOGY, 42, 444–445. **172**

BORING, E. G. (1942). SENSATION AND PERCEPTION IN THE HISTORY OF EXPERIMENTAL PSYCHOLOGY. New York: Appleton-Century-Crofts. **117**

BORING, E. G. (1950). A HISTORY OF EXPERIMENTAL PSYCHOLOGY (2nd ed.). New York: Appleton-Century-Crofts. **773**

BOUCHARD, T. J. (1976). Genetic factors in intelligence. In A. R. Kaplan (Ed.), HUMAN BEHAVIOR GENETICS. Springfield, IL: Charles Thomas. **467**

BOUCHARD, T. J. (1984). Twins reared apart and together: What they tell us about human diversity. In S. Fox (Ed.), THE CHEMICAL AND BIOLOGICAL BASES OF INDIVIDUALITY. New York: Plenum. **476**

BOUCHARD, T. J., & MCGUE, M. (1981). Familial studies of intelligence: A review. SCIENCE, 212, 1055–1059. **466**

BOWER, G. H. (1981). Mood and memory. AMERICAN PSYCHOLOGIST, 6, 129–148. **301, 421**

BOWER, G. H., BLACK, J. B., & TURNER, T. R. (1979). Scripts in memory for text. COGNITIVE PSYCHOLOGY, 11, 177–220. **315**

BOWER, G. H., & CLARK, M. C. (1969). Narrative stories as mediators for serial learning. PSYCHONOMIC SCIENCE, 14, 181–182. **310**

BOWER, G. H., CLARK, M. C., WINZENZ, D., & LESGOLD, A. (1969). Hierarchical retrieval schemes in recall of categorized word lists. JOURNAL OF VERBAL LEARNING AND VERBAL BEHAVIOR, 8, 323–343. **297**

BOWER, G. H., & HILGARD, E. R. (1981). THEORIES OF LEARNING (5th ed.). Englewood Cliffs, NJ: Prentice-Hall. **29, 279**

BOWER, G. H., & SPRINGSTON, F. (1970). Pauses as recoding points in letter series. JOURNAL OF EXPERIMENTAL PSYCHOLOGY, 83, 421–430. **289**

BOWER, S. A., & BOWER, G. H. (1976). ASSERTING YOURSELF. Reading, MA: Addison-Wesley. **679**

BOWER, T. G. R. (1982). DEVELOPMENT IN INFANCY (2nd ed.). San Francisco: Freeman. **188, 193**

BOWERS, K. S., & MEICHENBAUM, D. H. (Eds.). (1984). THE UNCONSCIOUS RECONSIDERED. New York: Wiley. **243**

BOWLBY, J. (1973). ATTACHMENT AND LOSS: VOL. 2. SEPARATION: ANXIETY & ANGER. New York: Basic Books. **86**

BOYNTON, R. (1979). HUMAN COLOR VISION. New York: Holt, Rinehart & Winston. **155**

BRADSHAW, G. L., & ANDERSON, J. R. (1982). Elaborative encoding as an explanation of levels of processing. JOURNAL OF VERBAL LEARNING AND VERBAL BEHAVIOR, 21, 165–174. **293**

BRADWEJN, J., KOSZYCKI, D., & METERISSIAN, G. (1989). Cholescystokinin tetrapeptide induces panic attacks identical to spontaneous panic attacks in patients suffering from panic disorder. CANADIAN JOURNAL OF PSYCHIATRY (in press). **605**

BRANSFORD, J. D., BARCLAY, J. R., & FRANKS, J. J. (1972). Sentence memory: A constructive versus interpretive approach. COGNITIVE PSYCHOLOGY, 3, 193–209.

BRANSFORD, J. D., & JOHNSON, M. K. (1973). Considerations of some problems of comprehension. In W. G. Chase (Ed.), VISUAL INFORMATION PROCESSING. New York: Academic Press. **316**

BRAUN, B. G. (1986). TREATMENT OF MULTIPLE PERSONALITY DISORDER. Washington, DC: American Psychiatric Press. **201, 243**

BREGMAN, A. S., & REIDNICKY, A. I. (1975). Auditory segregation: Stream of streams? JOURNAL OF EXPERIMENTAL PSYCHOLOGY: HUMAN PERCEPTION AND PERFORMANCE, 1, 263–267. **160**

BRELAND, K., & BRELAND, M. (1961). The misbehavior of organisms. AMERICAN PSYCHOLOGIST, 16, 681–684. **269**

BRELAND, K., & BRELAND, M. (1966). ANIMAL BEHAVIOR. New York: Macmillan. **259**

BRENNER, C. (1980). A psychoanalytic theory of affects. In R. Plutchik & H. Kellerman (Eds.), EMOTION: THEORY, RESEARCH, AND EXPERIENCE (Vol. 1). New York: Academic Press. **411**

BRENNER, M. H. (1982). Mental illness and the economy. In D. L. Parron, F. Solomon, & C. D. Jenkins (Eds.), BEHAVIOR, HEALTH RISKS, AND SOCIAL DISADVANTAGE. Washington, DC: National Academy Press. **625**

BRENNER, S. N., & MOLANDER, E. A. (1977, January–February). Is the ethics of business changing? HARVARD BUSINESS REVIEW, pp. 57–71. **701**

BREWER, W. F., & NAKAMURA, G. V. (1984). The nature and functions of schemas. In R. S. Wyer & T. K. Srull (Eds.), HANDBOOK OF SOCIAL COGNITION (Vol. 1). Hillsdale, NJ: Erlbaum. **317**

BREWIN, C. R. (1985). Depression and causal attributions: What is their relation? PSYCHOLOGICAL BULLETIN, 98, 297–300. **614**

BRIDGER, W. H. (1961). Sensory habituation and discrimination in the human neo-

nate. AMERICAN JOURNAL OF PSYCHIATRY, 117, 991–996. **74**

BROADBENT, D. E. (1958). PERCEPTION AND COMMUNICATION. London: Pergamon Press. **176**

BROCK, T. C., & BALLOUN, J. L. (1967). Behavior receptivity to dissonant information. JOURNAL OF PERSONALITY AND SOCIAL PSYCHOLOGY, 6, 413–428. **754**

BROOKS-GUNN, J., & FURSTENBERG, F. F., JR. (1989). Adolescent sexual behavior. AMERICAN PSYCHOLOGIST, 44, 249–257. **102**

BROOKS-GUNN, J., & RUBLE, D. N. (1983). The experience of menarche from a developmental perspective. In J. Brooks-Gunn & A. C. Petersen (Eds.), GIRLS AT PUBERTY: BIOLOGICAL AND PSYCHOLOGICAL PERSPECTIVES. New York: Plenum. **102**

BROWN, A. E. (1936). Dreams in which the dreamer knows he is asleep. JOURNAL OF ABNORMAL PSYCHOLOGY, 31, 59–66. **209**

BROWN, A. L., BRANSFORD, J. D., FERRARA, R. A., & CHAMPIONE, J. C. (1983). Learning, remembering, and understanding. In J. H. Flavell & E. M. Markman (Eds.), HANDBOOK OF CHILD PSYCHOLOGY: VOL. 3. COGNITIVE DEVELOPMENT. New York: Wiley. **85**

BROWN, D. P. (1977). A model for the levels of concentrative meditation. INTERNATIONAL JOURNAL OF CLINICAL AND EXPERIMENTAL HYPNOSIS, 25, 236–273. **226**

BROWN, E. L., & DEFFENBACHER, K. (1979). PERCEPTION AND THE SENSES. Oxford: Oxford University Press. **151**

BROWN, G. W., & HARRIS, T. (1978). SOCIAL ORIGINS OF DEPRESSION: A STUDY OF PSYCHIATRIC DISORDER IN WOMEN. London: Tavistock. **616**

BROWN, J. D. (1986). Evaluations of self and others: Self-enhancement biases in social judgments. SOCIAL COGNITION, 4, 353–376. **146, 385, 387, 616**

BROWN, P. L., & JENKINS, H. M. (1968). Autoshaping of the pigeon's keypeck. JOURNAL OF THE EXPERIMENTAL ANALYSIS OF BEHAVIOR, 11, 1–8. **260**

BROWN, R. (1973). A FIRST LANGUAGE: THE EARLY STAGES. Cambridge, MA: Harvard University Press. **357**

BROWN, R. (1986). SOCIAL PSYCHOLOGY: THE SECOND EDITION. New York: Free Press. **326, 346, 719, 721, 761**

BROWN, R., CAZDEN, C. B., & BELLUGI, U. (1969). The child's grammar from 1 to 3. In J. P. Hill (Ed.), MINNESOTA SYMPOSIUM ON CHILD PSYCHOLOGY (Vol. 2). Minneapolis: University of Minnesota Press. **340**

BROWN, R., & KULIK, J. (1977). Flash-bulb memories. COGNITION, 5, 73–99. **299**

BROWN, R., & MCNEILL, D. (1966). The "tip-of-the-tongue" phenomenon. JOURNAL OF VERBAL LEARNING AND VERBAL BEHAVIOR, 5, 325–337. **294**

BROWN, T. H., CHAPMAN, P. F., KAIRISS, E. W., & KEENAN, C. L. (1988). Long-term synaptic potentiation. SCIENCE, 242, 724–727. **40**

BROWNELL, K. (1988). Yo-yo dieting. PSYCHOLOGY TODAY, 22, 20–23. **373**

BROZAN, N. (1985, March 13). U.S. leads industrialized nations in teenage births and abortions. NEW YORK TIMES, p. 1. **105**

BRUCH, H. (1973). EATING DISORDERS: OBESITY, ANOREXIA NERVOSA, AND THE PERSON WITHIN. New York: Basic Books. **376, 377**

BRUNER, J. S., OLVER, R. R., GREENFIELD, P.M., & collaborators. (1966). STUDIES IN COGNITIVE GROWTH. New York: Wiley. **321**

BRUYER, R., LATERRE, C., SERON, X., & collaborators. (1983). A case of prosopagnosia with some preserved covert remembrance of familiar faces. BRAIN AND COGNITION, 2, 257–284. **415**

BRYAN, J. H., & TEST, M. A. (1967). Models and helping: Naturalistic studies in aiding behavior. JOURNAL OF PERSONALITY AND SOCIAL PSYCHOLOGY, 6, 400–707. **734**

BURNETT, S. A. (1986). Sex-related differences in spatial ability: Are they trivial? AMERICAN PSYCHOLOGIST, 41, 1012–1014. **456**

BUSS, A. H., & PLOMIN, R. (1984). TEMPERAMENT: EARLY DEVELOPING PERSONALITY TRAITS. Hillsdale, NJ: Erlbaum. **475**

BUTLER, J. M., & HAIGH, G. V. (1954). Changes in the relation between self-concepts and ideal concepts consequent upon client-centered counseling. In C. R. Rogers & R. F. Dymond (Eds.), PSYCHOTHERAPY AND PERSONALITY CHANGE: COORDINATED STUDIES IN THE CLIENT-CENTERED APPROACH. Chicago: University of Chicago Press. **541**

BUTT, D. S. (1987). THE PSYCHOLOGY OF SPORT: THE BEHAVIOR, MOTIVATION, PERSONALITY AND PERFORMANCE OF ATHLETES (2nd ed.). New York: Van Nostrand Reinhold. **243**

BUTTERFIELD, E. L., & SIPERSTEIN, G. N. (1972). Influence of contingent auditory stimulation on nonnutritional sucking. In J. Bosma (Ed.), ORAL SENSATION AND PERCEPTION: THE MOUTH OF THE INFANT. Springfield, IL: Charles B. Thomas. **75**

C

CAGGIULA, A. R., & HOEBEL, B. G. (1966). A "copulation-reward site" in the posterior hypothalamus. SCIENCE, 153, 1284–1285. **380**

CAMPBELL, E. A., COPE, S. J., & TEASDALE, J. D. (1983). Social factors and affective disorder: An investigation of Brown and Harris's model. BRITISH JOURNAL OF PSYCHIATRY, 143, 548–553. **616**

CAMPBELL, F. W., & ROBSON, J. G. (1968). Application of Fourier analysis to the visibility of gratings. JOURNAL OF PHYSIOLOGY, 197, 551–566. **137**

CAMPBELL, H. J. (1973). THE PLEASURE AREAS. London: Eyre Methuen. **265**

CAMPBELL, J. D., & FAIREY, P. J. (1985). Effects of self-esteem, hypothetical explanations, and verbalization of expectancies on future performance. JOURNAL OF PERSONALITY AND SOCIAL PSYCHOLOGY, 48, 1097–1111. **617**

CANNON, W. B. (1927). The James-Lange theory of emotions: A critical examination and an alternative theory. AMERICAN JOURNAL OF PSYCHOLOGY, 39, 106–124. **405**

CANNON, W. B. (1929). BODILY CHANGES IN PAIN, HUNGER, FEAR, AND RAGE. New York: Appleton. **557**

CARAMAZZA, A., & ZURIF, E. B. (1976). Dissociation of algorithmic and heuristic processes in language comprehension: Evidence from aphasia. BRAIN AND LANGUAGE, 3, 572–582. **345**

CAREY, G., & GOTTESMAN, I. I. (1981). Twin and family studies of anxiety, phobic, and obsessive disorders. In D. F. Klein & J. Rabkin (Eds.), ANXIETY: NEW RESEARCH AND CHANGING CONCEPTS. New York: Haven Press. **605**

CARLSON, N. R. (1985). PHYSIOLOGY OF BEHAVIOR (3rd ed.). Boston: Allyn & Bacon. **399**

CARLSON, N. R. (1988). FOUNDATIONS OF PHYSIOLOGICAL PSYCHOLOGY. Boston: Allyn & Bacon. **67**

CARLSON, R. (1971). Where is the person in personality research? PSYCHOLOGICAL BULLETIN, 75, 203–219. **522**

CARR, K. D., & COONS, E. E. (1982). Rats' self-administered nonrewarding brain stimulation to ameliorate aversion. SCIENCE, 215, 1516–1517. **265**

CARROL, E. N., ZUCKERMAN, M., & VOGEL, W. H. (1982). A test of the optimal level of arousal theory of sensation-seeking. JOURNAL OF PERSONALITY AND SOCIAL PSYCHOLOGY, 42, 572–575. **397**

CARROLL, D. W. (1985). PSYCHOLOGY OF LANGUAGE. Monterey, CA: Brooks/Cole. **357**

CARROLL, J. B. (1988). Individual differences in cognitive functioning. In R. C. Atkinson, R. J. Herrnstein, G. Lindzey, & R. D. Luce (Eds.), STEVENS' HANDBOOK OF EXPERIMENTAL PSYCHOLOGY (Vol. 2). New York: Wiley. **461**

CARSKADON, M. A., MITLER, M. M., & DEMENT, W. C. (1974). A comparison of insomniacs and normals: Total sleep time and sleep latency. SLEEP RESEARCH, 3, 130. **206**

CARSTENSEN, L. L., & NEALE, J. M. (1989). MECHANISMS OF PSYCHOLOGICAL INFLUENCE ON PHYSICAL HEALTH. New York: Plenum. **589**

CARTER, J. E., & HEATH, B. (1971). Somatotype methodology and kinesiology research. KINESIOLOGY REVIEW, 2, 10. **504**

CARTERETTE, E. C., & FRIEDMAN, M. P. (Eds.). (1974–1978). HANDBOOK OF PERCEPTION (Vols. 1–11). New York: Academic Press. **155**

CARTWRIGHT, R. D. (1974). The influence of a conscious wish on dreams: A methodological study of dream meaning and function. JOURNAL OF ABNORMAL PSYCHOLOGY, 83, 387–393. **209**

CARTWRIGHT, R. D. (1978). A PRIMER ON SLEEP AND DREAMING. Reading, MA: Addison-Wesley. **243**

CARVER, R. P. (1981). READING COMPREHENSION AND READING THEORY. Springfield, IL: Thomas. **179**

CASE, R. B., HELLER, S. S., CASE, N. B., & MOSS, A. J. (1985). Type A behavior and survival after acute myocardial infarction. NEW ENGLAND JOURNAL OF MEDICINE, 312, 737. **581**

CASPI, A., BEM, D. J., & ELDER, G. H., JR. (1989). Continuities and consequences of interactional styles across the life course. JOURNAL OF PERSONALITY, 56, 375–406. **494, 496**

CASPI, A., ELDER, G. H., JR., & BEM, D. J. (1987). Moving against the world: Life-course patterns of explosive children. DEVELOPMENTAL PSYCHOLOGY, 22, 303–308. **494, 495, 496**

CASPI, A., ELDER, G. H., JR., & BEM, D. J. (1989). MOVING TOWARD THE WORLD: LIFE-COURSE PATTERNS OF DEPENDENT CHILDREN. Unpublished manuscript, Harvard University. **496**

CASPI, A., & HERBENER, E. S. (1989). CONTINUITY AND CHANGE: ASSORTIVE MARRIAGE AND THE CONSISTENCY OF PERSONALITY IN ADULTHOOD. Unpublished manuscript, Harvard University. **493, 715**

CASTELLUCI, V., & KANDEL, E. R. (1976). Presynaptic facilitation as a mechanism for behavioral sensitization in Aplysia. SCIENCE, 194, 1176–1178. **255**

CATTELL, R. B. (1957). PERSONALITY AND MOTIVATION STRUCTURE AND MEASUREMENT. New York: Harcourt Brace Jovanovich. **507**

CATTELL, R. B. (1966). THE SCIENTIFIC ANALYSIS OF PERSONALITY. Chicago: Aldine. **507**

CATTELL, R. B. (1986). THE HANDBOOK FOR THE 16 PERSONALITY FACTOR QUESTIONNAIRE. Champaign, IL: Institute for Personality and Ability Testing. **507**

CENTERS FOR DISEASE CONTROL (1985). SUICIDE SURVEILLANCE 1970–1980. U.S. Department of Health and Human Services, Public Health Service, Violent Epidemiology Branch, Center for Health Promotion and Education. **610**

CERELLA, J. (1985). Information processing rates in the elderly. PSYCHOLOGICAL BULLETIN, 98, 67–83. **111**

CHAIKEN, S. (1980). Heuristic versus systematic information processing and the use of source versus message cues in persuasion. JOURNAL OF PERSONALITY AND SOCIAL PSYCHOLOGY, 39, 752–766. **751**

CHAPMAN, L. J., & CHAPMAN, J. P. (1967). Genesis of popular but erroneous diagnostic observations. JOURNAL OF ABNORMAL PSYCHOLOGY, 72, 193–204. **276**

CHAPMAN, L. J., & CHAPMAN, J. P. (1969). Illusory correlation as an obstacle to the use of valid psychodiagnostic signs. JOURNAL OF ABNORMAL PSYCHOLOGY, 74, 271–280. **691**

CHARNEY, D. S., & HENINGER, G. R. (1983). Monoamine receptor sensitivity and depression: Clinical studies of antidepressant effects on serotonin and noradrenergic function. PSYCHOPHARMACOLOGY BULLETIN, 20, 213–223. **615**

CHARNEY, D. S., HENINGER, G. R., & STERNBERG, D. E. (1984). Serotonin function and mechanism of action of antidepressant treatment: Effects of amitriptyline and desipramine. ARCHIVES OF GENERAL PSYCHIATRY, 41, 359–365. **615**

CHASE, W. G., & SIMON, H. A. (1973). The mind's eye in chess. In W. G. Chase (Ed.), VISUAL INFORMATION PROCESSING. New York: Academic Press. **352**

CHAUDURI, H. (1965). PHILOSOPHY OF MEDITATION. New York: Philosophical Library. **225**

CHEN, S. C. (1937). Social modification of the activity of ants in nest-building. PHYSIOLOGICAL ZOOLOGY, 10, 420–436. **724**

CHENG, P. W., HOLYOAK, K. J., NISBETT, R. E., & OLIVER, L. (1986). Pragmatic versus syntactic approaches to training deductive reasoning. COGNITIVE PSYCHOLOGY, 18, 293–328. **330**

CHESS, S., & THOMAS, A. (1982). Infant bonding: Mystique and reality. AMERICAN JOURNAL OF ORTHO-PSYCHIATRY, 52, 213–222. **91**

CHI, M., GLASER, R., & REES, E. (1982). Expertise in problem solving. In R. Sternberg (Ed.), ADVANCES IN THE PSYCHOLOGY OF HUMAN INTELLIGENCE (Vol. 1). Hillsdale, NJ: Erlbaum. **352**

CHIPEUR, H. M., ROVINE, M. J., & PLOMIN, R. (1989, June). LISREL MODELING: GENETIC AND ENVIRONMENTAL INFLUENCES ON IQ REVISITED. Presented at the Annual Meeting of the Behavior Genetics Association, Charlottesville, VA. **466**

CHODOROW, N. (1978). THE REPRODUCTION OF MOTHERING. Los Angeles: University of California Press. **518**

CHOMSKY, N. (1965). ASPECTS OF THE THEORY OF SYNTAX. Cambridge, MA: MIT Press. **333**

CHOMSKY, N. (1972). LANGUAGE AND MIND (2nd ed.). New York: Harcourt Brace Jovanovich. **343**

CHOMSKY, N. (1980a). On cognitive structures and their development: A reply to Piaget. In M. Piatelli-Palmarini (Ed.), LANGUAGE AND LEARNING: THE DEBATE BETWEEN JEAN PIAGET AND NOAM CHOMSKY. Cambridge, MA: Harvard University Press. **342**

CHOMSKY, N. (1980b). RULES AND REPRESENTATIONS. New York: Columbia University Press. **357**

CHURCHLAND, P. M. (1988). MATTER AND CONSCIOUSNESS. Cambridge: MIT Press. **243**

CHURCHLAND, P. S., & SEJNOWSKI, T. J. (1988). Perspectives on cognitive neuroscience. SCIENCE, 242, 741–745. **15**

CLARK, E. V. (1983). Meanings and concepts. In P. H. Mussen (Ed.), HANDBOOK OF CHILD PSYCHOLOGY. New York: Wiley. **338**

CLARK, H. H. (1984). Language use and language users. In G. Lindzey & E. Aronson (Eds.), THE HANDBOOK OF SOCIAL PSYCHOLOGY (Vol. 2, 3rd ed.). New York: Harper & Row. **337**

CLARK, H. H., & CLARK, E. V. (1977). PSYCHOLOGY AND LANGUAGE: AN INTRODUCTION TO PSYCHOLINGUISTICS. New York: Harcourt Brace Jovanovich. **328, 357**

CLARKE-STEWART, K. A. (1973). Interactions between mothers and their young children: Characteristics and consequences. MONOGRAPHS OF THE SOCIETY FOR RESEARCH IN CHILD DEVELOPMENT, 38(6 & 7, Serial No. 153). **90, 478**

CLARKE-STEWART, K. A. (1978). Popular primers for parents. AMERICAN PSYCHOLOGIST, 35, 359–369. **92**

CLARKE-STEWART, K. A. (1982). DAYCARE. Cambridge, MA: Harvard University Press. **94, 95**

CLARKE-STEWART, K. A. (1989). Infant day care: Maligned or malignant? AMERICAN PSYCHOLOGIST, 44, 266–273. **94**

CLARKE-STEWART, K. A., & FEIN, G. G. (1983). Early childhood programs. In P. H. Mussen (Ed.), HANDBOOK OF CHILD PSYCHOLOGY: VOL. 2. INFANCY AND DEVELOPMENTAL PSYCHOBIOLOGY. New York: Wiley. **95**

COE, W. C., & SARBIN, T. R. (1977). Hypnosis from the standpoint of a contextualist. ANNALS OF THE NEW YORK ACADEMY OF SCIENCES, 296, 2–13. **234**

COHEN, N. J., & SQUIRE, L. R. (1980). Preserved learning and retention of pattern-analyzing skill in amnesia: Dissociation of knowing how and knowing that. SCIENCE, 210, 207–209. **303**

COHEN, S. (1980, September). TRAINING TO UNDERSTAND TELEVISION ADVERTISING: EFFECTS AND SOME POLICY IMPLICATIONS. Paper presented at the annual meeting of the American Psychological Association, Montreal. **750**

COHEN, S., & WILLS, T. A. (1985). Stress, social support, and the buffering hypothesis. PSYCHOLOGICAL BULLETIN, 98, 310–357. **572**

COLBY, A., KOHLBERG, L., & collaborators. (1987). THE MEASUREMENT OF MORAL JUDGMENT: VOL. 1. THEORETICAL FOUNDATIONS AND RESEARCH VALIDATION. New York: Cambridge University Press. **97**

COLBY, A., KOHLBERG, L., GIBBS, J., & LIEBERMAN, M. A. (1983). A longitudinal study of moral judgment. MONOGRAPHS OF THE SOCIETY FOR RESEARCH IN CHILD DEVELOPMENT, 48(No. 200), 1–2. **99**

COLE, M. (1981). Mind as a cultural achievement: Implications for IQ testing. Annual Report, 1979–1980. Research and Clinical Center for Child Development. Faculty of Education, Hokkaido University, Sapporo, Japan. **453**

COLE, M., & COLE, S. R. (1989). THE DEVELOPMENT OF CHILDREN. New York: Scientific American Books. **74, 95, 113**

COLEMAN, J. C., BUTCHER, J. N., & CARSON, R. C. (1984). ABNORMAL PSYCHOLOGY AND MODERN LIFE (7th ed.). Glenview, IL: Scott, Foresman. **589, 635**

COLES, R. (1986). THE MORAL LIFE OF CHILDREN. Boston: Atlantic Monthly Press. **113**

COLLINS, A. M., & LOFTUS, E. G. (1975). A spreading-activation theory of semantic processing. PSYCHOLOGICAL REVIEW, 82, 407–428. **324**

COLLINS, H. M. (1974). The TEA set: Tacit knowledge and scientific networks. SCIENCE STUDIES, 4, 165–186. 237

COMSTOCK, G., CHAFFEE, S., KATZMAN, N., MCCOMBS, M., & ROBERTS, D. (1978). TELEVISION AND HUMAN BEHAVIOR. New York: Columbia University Press. 754

CONDRY, J., & CONDRY, S. (1976). Sex differences: A study in the eye of the beholder. CHILD DEVELOPMENT, 47, 812–819. 93

CONGER, J. J., & PETERSON, A. C. (1983). ADOLESCENCE AND YOUTH: PSYCHOLOGICAL DEVELOPMENT IN A CHANGING WORLD (3rd ed.). New York: Harper & Row. 113

CONLEY, J. J. (1984). The hierarchy of consistency: A review and model of longitudinal findings on adult individual differences in intelligence, personality, and self-opinion. PERSONALITY AND INDIVIDUAL DIFFERENCES, 5, 11–25. 488

CONLEY, J. J. (1985). Longitudinal stability of personality traits: A multitrait-multimethod-multioccasion analysis. JOURNAL OF PERSONALITY AND SOCIAL PSYCHOLOGY, 49, 1266–1282. 488

CONRAD, R. (1964). Acoustic confusions in immediate memory. BRITISH JOURNAL OF PSYCHOLOGY, 55, 75–84. 283

CONSUMERS UNION (1980). THE MEDICINE SHOW (5th ed.). Mount Vernon, NY: Consumers Union of U.S. 572

COOPER, L. A., & SHEPARD, R. N. (1973). Chronometric studies of the rotation of mental images. In W. G. Chase (Ed.), VISUAL INFORMATION PROCESSING. New York: Academic Press. 348

COOPER, L. M. (1979). Hypnotic amnesia. In E. Fromm, & R. E. Shor (Eds.), HYPNOSIS: DEVELOPMENTS IN RESEARCH AND NEW PERSPECTIVES (rev. ed.). New York: Aldine. 231

COOPERSMITH, S. (1967). THE ANTECEDENTS OF SELF-ESTEEM. San Francisco: Freeman. 480

CORDUA, G. D., MCGRAW, K. O., & DRABMAN, R. S. (1979). Doctor or nurse: Children's perception of sex-typed occupations. CHILD DEVELOPMENT, 50, 590–593. 97

COREN, S., PORAC, C., & WARD, L. M. (1984). SENSATION AND PERCEPTION (2nd ed.). Orlando: Academic Press. 137, 155

COREN, S., & WARD, L. M. (1989). SENSATION AND PERCEPTION. San Diego: Harcourt Brace Jovanovich. 155, 193

CORKIN, S., COHEN, N. J., SULLIVAN, E. V., CLEGG, R. A., ROSEN, T. J., & ACKERMAN, R. H. (1985). Analyses of global memory impairments of different etiologies. In D. S. Olton, E. Gamzu, & S. Corkin (Eds.), MEMORY DYSFUNCTION. New York: New York Academy of Sciences. 302

CORNELL, E. H., & MCDONNELL, P. M. (1986). Infants' acuity at twenty feet. INVESTIGATIVE OPHTHALMOLOGY AND VISUAL SCIENCE, 27, 1417–1420. 76

CORSINI, R. J. (1984). CURRENT PSYCHOTHERAPIES (3rd ed.). Itasca, IL: Peacock. 679

COSCINA, D. V., & DIXON, L. M. (1983). Body weight regulation in anorexia nervosa: Insights from an animal model. In F. L. Darby, P. E. Garfinkel, D. M. Garner, & D. V. Coscina (Eds.), ANOREXIA NERVOSA: RECENT DEVELOPMENTS. New York: Allan R. Liss. 372

COSTA, E. (1985). Benzodiazepine/GABA interactions: A model to investigate the neurobiology of anxiety. In A. H. Tuma & J. D. Maser (Eds.), ANXIETY AND THE ANXIETY DISORDERS. Hillsdale, NJ: Erlbaum. 606

COSTA, P. T., & MCCRAE, R. R. (1980). Still stable after all these years: Personality as a key to some issues in aging. In P. B. Bolles & O. G. Brim (Eds.), LIFE-SPAN DEVELOPMENT AND BEHAVIOR (Vol. 3). New York: Academic Press. 110

COSTA, P. T., JR., ZONDERMAN, A. B., MCCRAE, R. R., & WILLIAMS, R. B., JR. (1985). Content and comprehensiveness in the MMPI: An item factor analysis in a normal adult sample. JOURNAL OF PERSONALITY AND SOCIAL PSYCHOLOGY, 48, 925–933. 535

COTMAN, C. W., MONAGHAN, D. T., OTTERSON, O. P., & STORM-MATHISEN, J. (1987). Excitatory amino acids in the brain-focus on NMDA. TRENDS IN NEUROSCIENCE, 10(7), 263–265. 40

COTTRELL, N. B. (1972). Social facilitation. In C. G. McClintock (Ed.), EXPERIMENTAL SOCIAL PSYCHOLOGY. New York: Holt, Rinehart & Winston. 724

COTTRELL, N. B., RITTLE, R. H., & WACK, D. L. (1967). Presence of an audience and list type (competitional or non-competitional) as joint determinants of performance in paired-associates learning. JOURNAL OF PERSONALITY, 35, 425–434. 725

COTTRELL, N. B., WACK, D. L., SEKERAK, G. J., & RITTLE, R. H. (1968). Social facilitation of dominant responses by the presence of an audience and the mere presence of others. JOURNAL OF PERSONALITY AND SOCIAL PSYCHOLOGY, 9, 245–250. 726

CRAIGHEAD, L. W., STUNKARD, A. J., & O'BRIEN, R. M. (1981). Behavior therapy and pharmacotherapy for obesity. ARCHIVES OF GENERAL PSYCHIATRY, 38, 763–768. 375

CRAIGHEAD, W. E., KAZDIN, A. E., & MAHONEY, M. J. (1981). BEHAVIOR MODIFICATION: PRINCIPLES, ISSUES, AND APPLICATIONS (2nd ed.). Boston: Houghton Mifflin. 679

CRAIK, F. I. M., & LOCKHART, R. S. (1972). Levels of processing: A framework for memory research. JOURNAL OF VERBAL LEARNING AND VERBAL BEHAVIOR, 11, 671–684. 290

CRAIK, F. I. M., & WATKINS, M. J. (1973). The role of rehearsal in short-term memory. JOURNAL OF VERBAL LEARNING AND VERBAL BEHAVIOR, 12, 599–607. 290

CRARY, W. G. (1966). Reactions to incongruent self-experiences. JOURNAL OF CONSULTING PSYCHOLOGY, 30, 246–252. 616

CREESE, I., BURT, D. R., & SNYDER, S. H. (1978). Biochemical actions of neuroleptic drugs. In L. L. Iversen, S. D. Iversen, & S. H. Snyder (Eds.), HANDBOOK OF PSYCHOPHARMACOLOGY (Vol. 10). New York: Plenum. 624

CRICK, F., & MITCHISON, G. (1983). The function of dream sleep. NATURE, 304, 111–114. 210

CRICK, F., & MITCHISON, G. (1986). REM sleep and neural nets. JOURNAL OF MIND AND BEHAVIOR, 7, 229–250. 210

CRONBACH, L. J. (1984). ESSENTIALS OF PSYCHOLOGICAL TESTING (4th ed.). New York: Harper & Row. 473, 551

CROSS, P. (1977). Not can but will college teaching be improved? NEW DIRECTIONS FOR HIGHER EDUCATION, 17, 1–15. 701

CROWDER, R. G. (1976). PRINCIPLES OF LEARNING AND MEMORY. Hillsdale, NJ: Erlbaum. 319

CURTISS, S. (1977). GENIE: A PSYCHOLINGUISTIC STUDY OF A MODERN DAY 'WILD CHILD.' New York: Academic Press. 343

D

D'ANDRADE, R. G. (1967). REPORT ON SOME TESTING AND TRAINING PROCEDURES AT BASSAWA PRIMARY SCHOOL, ZARIA, NIGERIA. Unpublished manuscript. 453

DALE, A. J. D. (1975). Organic brain syndromes associated with infections. In A. M. Freedman, H. I. Kaplan, & B. J. Sadock (Eds.), COMPREHENSIVE TEXTBOOK OF PSYCHIATRY (Vol. 2), 1, 1121–1130. Baltimore, MD: Williams & Wilkins. 638

DAMON, W. (1977). THE SOCIAL WORLD OF THE CHILD. San Francisco: Jossey-Bass. 100

DAMON, W. (1983). SOCIAL AND PERSONALITY DEVELOPMENT. New York: Norton & Company. 501

DANEMAN, M., & CARPENTER, P. A. (1981). Individual differences in working memory and reading. JOURNAL OF VERBAL

LEARNING AND VERBAL BEHAVIOR, *19*, 450–466. **288**

DARIAN-SMITH, I. (Ed.). (1984). HANDBOOK OF PHYSIOLOGY: THE NERVOUS SYSTEM: SECTION 1, VOL. 3. SENSORY PROCESSES. Bethesda, MD: American Physiological Society. **155**

DARLEY, C. F., TINKLENBERG, J. R., ROTH, W. T., HOLLISTER, L. E., & ATKINSON, R. C. (1973). Influence of marijuana on storage and retrieval processes in memory. MEMORY AND COGNITION, *1*, 196–200. **17**

DARLEY, J. M., & LATANÉ, B. (1968). Bystander intervention in emergencies: Diffusion of responsibility. JOURNAL OF PERSONALITY AND SOCIAL PSYCHOLOGY, *8*, 377–383. **731**

DARLINGTON, R. B. (1986). Long-term effects of preschool programs. In U. Neisser (Ed.), THE SCHOOL ACHIEVEMENT OF MINORITY CHILDREN. Hillsdale, NJ: Erlbaum. **469**

DARWIN, C. (1859). ON THE ORIGIN OF THE SPECIES. London: Murray. **70**

DARWIN, C. (1872). THE EXPRESSION OF EMOTION IN MAN AND ANIMALS. New York: Philosophical Library. **413**

DASHIELL, J. F. (1930). An experimental analysis of some group effects. JOURNAL OF ABNORMAL AND SOCIAL PSYCHOLOGY, *25*, 190–199. **724, 725**

DASHIELL, J. F. (1935). Experimental studies of the influence of social situations on the behavior of individual human adults. In C. Murchison (Ed.), HANDBOOK OF SOCIAL PSYCHOLOGY. Worcester, MA: Clark University. **724**

DAVIDSON, A. R., & JACCARD, J. J. (1979). Variables that moderate the attitude-behavior relations: Results of a longitudinal survey. JOURNAL OF PERSONALITY AND SOCIAL PSYCHOLOGY, *37*, 1364–1376. **707**

DAVIDSON, E. S., YASUNA, A., & TOWER, A. (1979). The effects of television cartoons on sex-role stereotyping in young girls. CHILD DEVELOPMENT, *50*, 597–600. **96**

DAVIDSON, J. (1988). PATTERNS OF SEXUAL AROUSAL. New York: Guilford Press. **379**

DAVISON, G. C., & NEALE, J. M. (1986). ABNORMAL PSYCHOLOGY: AN EXPERIMENTAL CLINICAL APPROACH (4th ed.). New York: Wiley. **635**

DE CASPER, A. J., & FIFER, W. P. (1980). Of human bonding: Newborns prefer their mother's voices. SCIENCE, *208*, 1174–1176. **75**

DEIKMAN, A. J. (1963). Experimental meditation. JOURNAL OF NERVOUS AND MENTAL DISEASE, *136*, 329–373. **225**

DELK, J. L., & FILLENBAUM, S. (1965). Differences in perceived color as a function of characteristic color. AMERICAN JOURNAL OF PSYCHOLOGY, *78*, 290–293. **133**

DELONGIS, A., COYNE, J. C., DAKOF, G., FOLKMAN, S., & LAZARUS, R. S. (1982). Relationship of daily hassles, uplifts, and major life events to health status. HEALTH PSYCHOLOGY, *1*, 119–136. **569**

DELONGIS, A., FOLKMAN, S., & LAZARUS, R. S. (1988). The impact of daily stress on health and mood: Psychological and social resources as mediators. JOURNAL OF PERSONALITY AND SOCIAL PSYCHOLOGY, *54*, 486–495. **569**

DEMBROSKI, T. M., MACDOUGALL, J. M., WILLIAMS, B., & HANEY, T. L. (1985). Components of Type A hostility and anger: Relationship to angiographic findings. PSYCHOSOMATIC MEDICINE, *47*, 219–233. **581**

DEMENT, W. C. (1960). The effect of dream deprivation. SCIENCE, *131*, 1705–1707. **208**

DEMENT, W. C., & KLEITMAN, N. (1957). The relation of eye movements during sleep to dream activity: An objective method for the study of dreaming. JOURNAL OF EXPERIMENTAL PSYCHOLOGY, *53*, 339–346. **202**

DEMENT, W. C., & WOLPERT, E. (1958). The relation of eye movements, bodily motility, and external stimuli to dream content. JOURNAL OF EXPERIMENTAL PSYCHOLOGY, *55*, 543–553. **209**

DENNIS, W. (1960). Causes of retardation among institutional children: Iran. JOURNAL OF GENETIC PSYCHOLOGY, *96*, 47–59. **79**

DENNIS, W. (1973). CHILDREN OF THE CRECHE. Englewood Cliffs, NJ: Prentice-Hall. **79**

DENNY, N. W. (1980). Task demands and problem-solving strategies in middle-age and older adults. JOURNAL OF GERONTOLOGY, *35*, 559–564. **111**

DEPUE, R. A., & IACONO, W. G. (1989). Neurobehavioral aspects of affective disorders. In M. R. Rosenzweig & L. W. Porter (Eds.), ANNUAL REVIEW OF PSYCHOLOGY (Vol. 40). Palo Alto, CA: Annual Reviews, Inc. **615**

DER SIMONIAN, R., & LAIRD, N. M. (1983). Evaluating the effect of coaching on SAT scores: A meta-analysis. HARVARD EDUCATIONAL REVIEW, *53*, 1–15. **457**

DEVALOIS, R. L., & DEVALOIS, K. K. (1980). Spatial vision. ANNUAL REVIEW OF PSYCHOLOGY, *31*, 309–341. **167**

DEVALOIS, R. L., & JACOBS, G. H. (1984). Neural mechanisms of color vision. In I. Darian-Smith (Ed.), HANDBOOK OF PHYSIOLOGY (Vol. 3). Bethesda, MD: American Physiological Society. **135**

DICARA, L. V. (1970). Learning in the autonomous nervous system. SCIENTIFIC AMERICAN, *222*, 30–39. **258**

DICARA, L. V., & MILLER, W. E. (1968). Instrumental learning of systolic blood-pressure responses by curarized rats. PSYCHOSOMATIC MEDICINE, *30*, 489–494. **584**

DIENER, E. (1979). Deindividuation, self-awareness, and disinhibition. JOURNAL OF PERSONALITY AND SOCIAL PSYCHOLOGY, *37*, 1160–1171. **727, 729**

DIENER, E. (1980). Deindividuation: The absence of self-awareness and self-regulation in group members. In P. B. Paulus (Ed.), THE PSYCHOLOGY OF GROUP INFLUENCE. Hillsdale, NJ: Erlbaum. **727**

DIENER, E., FRASER, S. C., BEAMAN, A. L., & KELEM, R. T. (1976). Effects of deindividuation variables on stealing among Halloween trick-or-treaters. JOURNAL OF PERSONALITY AND SOCIAL PSYCHOLOGY, *33*, 178–183. **728**

DIENSTBIER, R. A. (1989). Arousal and physiological toughness: Implications for mental and physical health. PSYCHOLOGICAL REVIEW, *96*, 84–100. **559**

DIGMAN, J. M., & INOUYE, J. (1986). Further specification of the five robust factors of personality. JOURNAL OF PERSONALITY AND SOCIAL PSYCHOLOGY, *50*, 116–123. **509**

DION, K. K. (1972). Physical attractiveness and evaluations of children's transgressions. JOURNAL OF PERSONALITY AND SOCIAL PSYCHOLOGY, *24*, 207–213. **711**

DION, K. K., & BERSCHEID, E. (1972). PHYSICAL ATTRACTIVENESS AND SOCIAL PERCEPTION OF PEERS IN PRESCHOOL CHILDREN. Unpublished manuscript, University of Minnesota, Minneapolis. **711**

DION, K. K., BERSCHEID, E., & WALSTER, E. (1972). What is beautiful is good. JOURNAL OF PERSONALITY AND SOCIAL PSYCHOLOGY, *24*, 285–290. **693**

DION, K. K., & STEIN, S. (1978). Physical attractiveness and interpersonal influence. JOURNAL OF EXPERIMENTAL SOCIAL PSYCHOLOGY, *14*, 97–108. **694**

DOBELLE, W. H., MEADEJOVSKY, M. G., & GIRVIN, J. P. (1974). Artificial vision for the blind: Electrical stimulation of visual cortex offers hope for a functional prosthesis. SCIENCE, *183*, 440–444. **145**

DOHRENWEND, B. S. (1973). Social status and stressful life events. JOURNAL OF PERSONALITY AND SOCIAL PSYCHOLOGY, *28*, 225–235. **625**

DOHRENWEND, B. S., & DOHRENWEND, B. P. (Eds.). (1974). STRESSFUL LIFE EVENTS: THEIR NATURE AND EFFECTS. New York: Wiley. **568**

DOHRENWEND, B. S., KRASSNOFF, L., ASKENASY, A. R., & DOHRENWEND,

DOHRENWEND, B. S., (*continued*) B. P. (1978). Exemplification of a method for scaling life events: The PERI events scale. JOURNAL OF HEALTH AND SOCIAL BEHAVIOR, *19*, 205–229. **568**

DOLLARD, J., DOOB, L. W., MILLER, N. E., MOWRER, O. H., & SEARS, R. R. (1939). FRUSTRATION AND AGGRESSION. New Haven: Yale University Press. **423**

DOMINO, G. (1971). Interactive effects of achievement orientation and teaching style of academic achievement. JOURNAL OF EDUCATIONAL PSYCHOLOGY, *62*, 427–431. **536**

DOMJAN, M. (1983). Biological constraints on instrumental and classical conditioning: Implications for general process theory. THE PSYCHOLOGY OF LEARNING AND MOTIVATION, *17*, 215–277. **271**

DOMJAN, M., & BURKHARD, B. (1986). THE PRINCIPLES OF LEARNING AND BEHAVIOR. Monterey, CA: Brooks/Cole. **279**

DOWLING, J. E., & BOYCOTT, B. B. (1966). Organization of the primate retina. PROCEEDINGS OF THE ROYAL SOCIETY OF LONDON (Series B), *166*, 80–111. **126**

DUCLAUZ, R., & KENSHALO, D. R. (1980). Response characteristics of cutaneous warm fibers in the monkey. JOURNAL OF NEUROPHYSIOLOGY, *43*, 1–15. **151**

DUNCKER, D. K. (1929). Uber induzierte bewegung (ein Beitrag zur Theorie optisch wahrgenomener Bewegung). PSYCHOLOGISCH FORSCHUNG, *12*, 129–180. [Summary in W. D. Ellis (1938), A SOURCEBOOK OF GESTALT PSYCHOLOGY. London: Kegan Paul, Trench, Trubner.] **163**

DUNNING, D., MEYEROWITZ, J. A., & HOLZBERG, A. (1989). AMBIGUITY AND SELF-EVALUATION: DISTORTED SELF-ASSESSMENTS ARE PROMPTED BY IDIOSYNCRATIC DEFINITIONS OF TRAITS AND ABILITIES. Unpublished manuscript, Cornell University. **701**

DUNNING, D., STORY, A. L., & TAN, P. L. (1989). THE SELF AS MODEL OF EXCELLENCE IN SOCIAL EVALUATION. Unpublished manuscript, Cornell University. **701**

DURLACH, N. I., & COLBURN, H. S. (1978). Binaural phenomena. In E. C. Carterette & M. J. Friedman (Eds.), HANDBOOK OF PERCEPTION (Vol. 4). New York: Academic Press. **143**

DUTTON, D. G., & ARON, A. P. (1974). Some evidence for heightened sexual attraction under conditions of high anxiety. JOURNAL OF PERSONALITY AND SOCIAL PSYCHOLOGY, *30*, 510–517. **719**

E

EAGLE, M. N. (1984). RECENT DEVELOPMENTS IN PSYCHOANALYSIS: A CRITICAL EVALUATION. New York: McGraw-Hill. **551**

EAGLY, A. H., & CHAIKEN, S. (1984). Cognitive theories of persuasion. In L. Berkowitz (Ed.), ADVANCES IN EXPERIMENTAL SOCIAL PSYCHOLOGY (Vol. 17). New York: Academic Press. **751**

EBBESEN, E., DUNCAN, B., & KONEČNI, V. (1975). Effects of content of verbal aggression on future verbal aggression: A field experiment. JOURNAL OF EXPERIMENTAL PSYCHOLOGY, *11*, 192–204. **430**

ECCLES, J. S., & JACOBS, J. E. (1986). Social forces shape math attitudes and performance. SIGNS, *11*, 367–380. **455**

EDWARDS, C. P., & WHITING, B. B. (1980). Differential socialization of girls and boys in light of cross-cultural research. In C. Super & S. Harkness (Eds.), ANTHROPOLOGICAL PERSPECTIVES ON CHILD DEVELOPMENT. San Francisco: Jossey-Bass. **485**

EELLS, K., DAVIS, A., HAVIGHURST, R. J., HERRICK, V. E., & TYLER, R. W. (1951). INTELLIGENCE AND CULTURAL DIFFERENCES. Chicago: University of Chicago Press. **452**

EGAN, J. P. (1975). SIGNAL DETECTION THEORY AND ROC ANALYSIS. New York: Academic Press. **123**

EGELAND, B., & SROUFE, L. A. (1981a). Attachment and early maltreatment. CHILD DEVELOPMENT, *52*, 44–52. **480**

EGELAND, B., & SROUFE, L. A. (1981b). Developmental sequelae of maltreatment in infancy. NEW DIRECTIONS FOR CHILD DEVELOPMENT, *11*, 77–92. **480**

EIBL-EIBESFELDT, I. (1970). ETHOLOGY: THE BIOLOGY OF BEHAVIOR (E. Klinghammer, Trans.). New York: Holt, Rinehart & Winston. **86, 426**

EICH, J., WEINGARTNER, H., STILLMAN, R. C., & GILLIAN, J. C. (1975). State-dependent accessibility of retrieval cues in the retention of a categorized list. JOURNAL OF VERBAL LEARNING AND VERBAL BEHAVIOR, *14*, 408–417. **298**

EICHORN, D. H., CLAUSEN, J. A., HAAN, N., HONZIK, M. P., & MUSSEN, P. H. (Eds.). (1981). PRESENT AND PAST IN MIDDLE LIFE. New York: Academic Press. **501**

EIMAS, P. D. (1975). Speech perception in early infancy. In L. B. Cohen & P. Salapatek (Eds.), INFANT PERCEPTION: FROM SENSATION TO COGNITION (Vol. 2). New York: Academic Press. **75**

EIMAS, P. D. (1985). The perception of speech in early infancy. SCIENTIFIC AMERICAN, *252*, 46–52. **338**

EKMAN, P. (1982). EMOTIONS IN THE HUMAN FACE (2nd ed.). New York: Cambridge University Press. **413, 433**

EKMAN, P. (1985). TELLING LIES: CLUES TO DECEIT IN THE MARKETPLACE, POLITICS, AND MARRIAGE. New York: Norton. **433**

EKMAN, P., LEVENSON, R. W., & FRIESON, W. V. (1983). Autonomic nervous system activity distinguishes among emotions. SCIENCE, *221*, 1208–1210. **405**

EKSTROM, R. B., FRENCH, J. W., HARMAN, H. H., & DERMAN, D. (1976). MANUAL FOR KIT OF FACTOR-REFERENCED COGNITIVE TESTS, 1976. Princeton, NJ: Educational Testing Service. **461**

EKSTROM, R. B., FRENCH, J. W., & HARMAN, H. H. (1979). Cognitive factors: Their identification and replication. MULTIVARIATE BEHAVIORAL RESEARCH MONOGRAPHS. Ft. Worth, TX: Society for Multivariate Experimental Psychology. **461**

EMMERT, E. (1881). Grössenverhaltnisse der nachbilder. KLIN. MONATSBL. D. AUGENHEILK., *19*, 443–450. **181**

ENDLER, N. S. (1982). HOLIDAY OF DARKNESS. New York: Wiley. **635**

ENGEN, T. (1982). THE PERCEPTION OF ODORS. New York: Academic Press. **155**

EPSTEIN, S. (1967). Toward a unified theory of anxiety. In B. A. Maher (Ed.), PROGRESS IN EXPERIMENTAL PERSONALITY RESEARCH (Vol. 4). New York: Academic Press. **418**

EPSTEIN, S. (1977). Traits are alive and well. In D. Magnusson & N. S. Endler (Eds.), PERSONALITY AT THE CROSSROADS: CURRENT ISSUES IN INTERACTIONAL PSYCHOLOGY. Hillsdale, NJ: Erlbaum. **547**

ERDELYI, M. H. (1985). PSYCHOANALYSIS: FREUD'S COGNITIVE PSYCHOLOGY. New York: Freeman. **175, 301, 518**

ERDELYI, M. H., & APPLEBAUM, G. A. (1973). Cognitive masking: The disruptive effect of an emotional stimulus upon the perception of contiguous neutral items. BULLETIN OF THE PSYCHONOMIC SOCIETY, *1*, 59–61. **175**

ERICSSON, K. A., CHASE, W. G., & FALOON, S. (1980). Acquisition of a memory skill. SCIENCE, *208*, 1181–1182. **307**

ERIKSON, E. H. (1963). CHILDHOOD AND SOCIETY (2nd ed.). New York: Norton. **86, 108**

ERIKSON, R. R. (1963). Sensory neural patterns and gustation. In Y. Zoterman (Ed.), OLFACTION AND TASTE (Vol. 1). Oxford: Pergamon Press. **86, 149, 150**

ERON, L. D. (1987). The development of aggressive behavior from the perspective of a developing behaviorism. AMERICAN PSYCHOLOGIST, *42*, 435–442. **424, 429**

ERON, L. D., HUESMANN, L. R., LEFKOWITZ, M. M., & WALDER, L. O. (1972). Does television violence cause ag-

REFERENCES **A-45**

gression? AMERICAN PSYCHOLOGIST, 27, 253–263. **7, 431**

ERVIN-TRIPP, S. (1964). Imitation and structural change in children's language. In H. Lenneberg (Ed.), NEW DIRECTIONS IN THE STUDY OF LANGUAGE. Cambridge, MA: MIT Press. **340**

ESTES, W. K. (1972). An associative basis for coding and organization in memory. In A. W. Melton & E. Martin (Eds.), CODING PROCESSES IN HUMAN MEMORY. Washington, DC: Winston. **298**

ESTES, W. K. (Ed.). (1975–1979). HANDBOOK OF LEARNING AND COGNITIVE PROCESSES (Vols. 1–6). Hillsdale, NJ: Erlbaum. **279**

ETCOFF, N. L. (1985). The neuropsychology of emotional expression. In G. Goldstein & R. E. Tarter (Eds.), ADVANCES IN CLINICAL NEUROPSYCHOLOGY (Vol. 3). New York: Plenum. **415**

EVANS, C. (1984). LANDSCAPES OF THE NIGHT: HOW AND WHY WE DREAM. New York: Viking. **210**

EXNER, J. (1986). THE RORSCHACH: A COMPREHENSIVE SYSTEM (2nd ed.) (Vol. 1). New York: Wiley. **537**

EYFERTH, K., BRANDT, U., & WOLFGANG, H. (1960). FARBIGE KINDER IN DEUTSCHLAND. Munich: Juventa. **469**

EYSENCK, H. J. (1953). THE STRUCTURE OF HUMAN PERSONALITY. New York: Wiley. **508**

EYSENCK, H. J., & RACHMAN, S. (1965). THE CAUSES AND CURES OF NEUROSIS: AN INTRODUCTION TO MODERN BEHAVIOR THERAPY BASED ON LEARNING THEORY AND THE PRINCIPLES OF CONDITIONING. San Diego: Knapp. **50**

F

FANCHER, R. E. (1985). THE INTELLIGENCE MEN: MAKERS OF THE IQ CONTROVERSY. New York: Norton. **473**

FANTZ, R. L. (1961). The origin of form perception. SCIENCE, 204, 66–72. **76, 185, 187**

FANTZ, R. L. (1970). Visual perception and experience in infancy: Issues and approaches. In National Academy of Science, EARLY EXPERIENCE AND VISUAL INFORMATION PROCESSING IN PERCEPTUAL AND READING DISORDERS (pp. 351–381). New York: National Academy of Science. **187**

FANTZ, R. L., ORDY, J. M., & UDELF, M. S. (1962). Maturation of pattern vision in infants during the first six months. JOURNAL OF COMPARATIVE AND PHYSIOLOGICAL PSYCHOLOGY, 55, 907–917. **185**

FARAH, M. J. (1988). Is visual imagery really visual? Overlooked evidence from neuropsychology. PSYCHOLOGICAL REVIEW, 95, 307–317. **348**

FARBEROW, N. L., & SHNEIDMAN, E. S. (1965). THE CRY FOR HELP. New York: McGraw-Hill. **610**

FARQUHAR, J. W., MACCOBY, N., WOOD, P. D., & collaborators. (1977). Community education for cardiovascular health. THE LANCET, 1(8023), 1192–1195. **755, 756**

FARQUHAR, J. W., MACCOBY, N., & SOLOMON, D. S. (1984). Community applications of behavioral medicine. In W. D. Gentry (Ed.), HANDBOOK OF BEHAVIORAL MEDICINE. New York: Guilford Press. **756**

FAUST, I. M. (1984). Role of the fat cell in energy balance physiology. In A. T. Stunkard & E. Stellar (Eds.), EATING AND ITS DISORDERS. New York: Raven Press. **375**

FAZIO, R., & ZANNA, M. P. (1981). Direct experience and attitude-behavior consistency. In L. Berkowitz (Ed.), ADVANCES IN AN EXPERIMENTAL SOCIAL PSYCHOLOGY (Vol. 14). New York: Academic Press. **707**

FAZIO, R., ZANNA, M. P., & COOPER, J. (1977). Dissonance and self-perception: An integrative view of each theory's proper domain of application. JOURNAL OF EXPERIMENTAL SOCIAL PSYCHOLOGY, 13, 464–479. **709**

FECHNER, G. T. (1860/1966). ELEMENTS OF PSYCHOPHYSICS (H. E. Adler, Trans.). New York: Holt, Rinehart & Winston. **120**

FEINGOLD, A. (1988). Cognitive gender differences are disappearing. AMERICAN PSYCHOLOGIST, 43, 95–103. **455**

FELDMAN, H., GOLDIN-MEADOW, S., & GLEITMAN, L. R. (1978). Beyond Herodotus: The creation of language by linguistically deprived children. In A. Lock (Ed.), ACTION, GESTURE, AND SYMBOL: THE EMERGENCE OF LANGUAGE. London: Academic Press. **343**

FENNELL, M. J. V., & CAMPBELL, E. H. (1984). The cognitions questionnaire: Specific thinking errors in depression. BRITISH JOURNAL OF CLINICAL PSYCHOLOGY, 23, 81–92. **614**

FESHBACH, N. D. (1980, September). THE CHILD AS PSYCHOLOGIST AND ECONOMIST: TWO CURRICULA. Paper presented at the annual meeting of the American Psychological Association, Montreal. **750**

FESTINGER, L. (1957). A THEORY OF COGNITIVE DISSONANCE. Stanford University Press. **697, 707**

FESTINGER, L., & CARLSMITH, J. M. (1959). Cognitive consequences of forced compliance. JOURNAL OF ABNORMAL AND SOCIAL PSYCHOLOGY, 58, 203–210. **697, 698, 708**

FESTINGER, L., PEPITONE, A., & NEWCOMB, T. M. (1952). Some conse-

quences of deindividuation in a group. JOURNAL OF ABNORMAL AND SOCIAL PSYCHOLOGY, 47, 383–389. **727**

FESTINGER, L., SCHACHTER, S., & BACK, K. (1950). SOCIAL PRESSURES IN INFORMAL GROUPS: A STUDY OF HUMAN FACTORS IN HOUSING. New York: Harper & Row. **712**

FIELD, J. (1987). The development of auditory-visual localization in infancy. In B. E. McKenzie & R. H. Day (Eds.), PERCEPTUAL DEVELOPMENT IN EARLY INFANCY. Hillsdale, NJ: Erlbaum. **75**

FINCK, H. T. (1887). ROMANTIC LOVE AND PERSONAL BEAUTY: THEIR DEVELOPMENT, CAUSAL RELATIONS, HISTORIC AND NATIONAL PECULIARITIES. London: Macmillan. **718**

FINKE, R. A. (1985). Theories relating mental imagery to perception. PSYCHOLOGICAL BULLETIN, 98, 236–259. **347**

FISHBEIN, M. (1963). An investigation of the relationships between beliefs about an object and the attitude toward that object. HUMAN RELATIONS, 16, 233–240. **705**

FISHER, G. H. (1967). Preparation of ambiguous stimulus materials. PERCEPTION AND PSYCHOPHYSICS, 2, 421–422. **173**

FISHMAN, P. (1983). Interaction: The work women do. In B. Thorne, C. Kramarae, & N. Henley (Eds.), LANGUAGE, GENDER, AND SOCIETY. Rowley, MA: Newbury House. **699**

FIXSEN, D. L., PHILLIPS, E. L., PHILLIPS, E. A., & WOLF, M. M. (1976). The teaching-family model of group home treatment. In W. E. Craighead, A. E. Kazdin, & M. J. Mahoney (Eds.), BEHAVIOR MODIFICATION: PRINCIPLES, ISSUES, AND APPLICATIONS. Boston: Houghton Mifflin. **676**

FLAVELL, J. H. (1970). Development studies of mediated behavior. In H. W. Reese & L. P. Lipsett (Eds.), ADVANCES IN CHILD DEVELOPMENT AND BEHAVIOR (Vol. 5). New York: Academic Press. **85**

FLAVELL, J. H. (1985). COGNITIVE DEVELOPMENT (2nd ed.). Englewood Cliffs, NJ: Prentice-Hall, **113**

FLEMING, J., & DARLEY, J. M. (1986). PERCEIVING INTENTION IN CONSTRAINED BEHAVIOR: THE ROLE OF PURPOSEFUL AND CONSTRAINED ACTION CUES IN CORRESPONDENCE BIAS EFFECTS. Unpublished manuscript, Princeton University, Princeton, NJ. **617**

FLODERUS-MYRED, B., PETERSEN, N., & RASMUSON, I. (1980). Assessment of heritability for personality based on a short form of the Eysenck Personality Inventory. BEHAVIOR GENETICS, 10, 153–161. **476**

FODOR, J. A. (1981). REPRESENTATIONS: PHILOSOPHICAL ESSAYS ON THE FOUNDA-

FODOR, J. A. (continued) TIONS OF COGNITIVE SCIENCE. Cambridge, MA: MIT Press. **15, 198**

FODOR, J. A. (1983). THE MODULARITY OF MIND. Cambridge, MA: MIT Press. **198**

FODOR, J. A., BEVER, T. G., & GARRETT, M. F. (1974). THE PSYCHOLOGY OF LANGUAGE: AN INTRODUCTION TO PSYCHOLINGUISTICS AND GENERATIVE GRAMMAR. New York: McGraw-Hill. **357**

FODOR, J. A., & PYLYSHYN, Z. W. (1981). How direct is visual perception? Some reflections of Gibson's "ecological approach." COGNITION, 9, 139–196. **162**

FOLKES, V. S. (1982). Forming relationships and the matching hypothesis. PERSONALITY AND SOCIAL PSYCHOLOGY BULLETIN, 8, 631–636. **714**

FOLKMAN, S., & LAZARUS, R. S. (1980). An analysis of coping in a middle-aged community sample. JOURNAL OF HEALTH AND SOCIAL BEHAVIOR, 21, 219–239. **578**

FOLKMAN, S., & LAZARUS, R. S. (1985). If it changes it must be a process: A study of emotion and coping during three stages of a college examination. JOURNAL OF PERSONALITY AND SOCIAL PSYCHOLOGY, 48, 150–170. **556**

FOLKMAN, S., LAZARUS, R. S., DUNKELSCHETTER, C., DELONGIS, A., & GRUEN, R. (1986). The dynamics of a stressful encounter: Cognitive appraisal, coping, and encounter outcomes. JOURNAL OF PERSONALITY AND SOCIAL PSYCHOLOGY, 50, 992–1003. **578**

FORDHAM, S., & OGBU, J. U. (1986). Black students' school success: Coping with the "burden of 'acting white.'" THE URBAN REVIEW, 18, 176–206. **469**

FOREM, J. (1973). TRANSCENDENTAL MEDITATION: MAHARISHI MAHESH YOGI AND THE SCIENCE OF CREATIVE INTELLIGENCE. New York: Dutton. **226**

FORER, B. R. (1949). The fallacy of personal validation: A classroom demonstration of gullibility. JOURNAL OF ABNORMAL AND SOCIAL PSYCHOLOGY, 44, 118–123. **533**

FOSS, D. J., & HAKES, D. T. (1978). PSYCHOLINGUISTICS: AN INTRODUCTION TO THE PSYCHOLOGY OF LANGUAGE. Englewood Cliffs, NJ: Prentice-Hall. **357**

FOX, R., ASLIN, R. N., SHEA, S. L., & DUMAIS, S. T. (1980). Stereopsis in human infants. SCIENCE, 207, 323–324. **187**

FRAGER, R., & FADIMAN. J. (1984). PERSONALITY AND PERSONAL GROWTH (2nd ed.). New York: Harper & Row. **551**

FRANKENBURG, W. K., & DODDS, J. B. (1967). The Denver developmental screening test. JOURNAL OF PEDIATRICS, 71, 181–191. **72**

FRANKENHAEUSER, M. (1983). The sympathetic-adrenal and pituitary-adrenal response to challenge: Comparison between the sexes. In T. M. Dembroski, T. H. Schmidt, & G. Blumchen (Eds.), BIOBEHAVIORAL BASES OF CORONARY HEART DISEASE. Basel: Karger. **559**

FRANKLIN, J. (1987). MOLECULES OF THE MIND. New York: Atheneum. **39**

FRANZOI, S. L., DAVIS, M. H., & YOUNG, R. D. (1985). The effects of private self-consciousness and perspective taking on satisfaction in close relationships. JOURNAL OF PERSONALITY AND SOCIAL PSYCHOLOGY, 48, 1584–1594.

FRASE, L. T. (1975). Prose processing. In G. H. Bower (Ed.), THE PSYCHOLOGY OF LEARNING AND MOTIVATION (Vol. 9). New York: Academic Press. **293**

FRAZIER, K. (Ed.). (1986). SCIENCE CONFRONTS THE PARANORMAL. Buffalo: Prometheus Books. **243**

FRAZIER, K. (1987). Psychic's imagined year fizzles (again). SKEPTICAL INQUIRER, 11, 335–336. **240**

FREE, L. A., & CANTRIL, H. (1967). THE POLITICAL BELIEFS OF AMERICANS. New Brunswick, NJ: Rutgers University Press. **710**

FREEDMAN, J. L. (1965). Long-term behavioral effects of cognitive dissonance. JOURNAL OF EXPERIMENTAL SOCIAL PSYCHOLOGY, 1, 145–155. **708**

FREEDMAN, J. L., & SEARS, D. O. (1965). Warning, distraction, and resistance to influence. JOURNAL OF PERSONALITY AND SOCIAL PSYCHOLOGY, 1, 262–266. **749**

FREEDMAN, S., WALKER, M. R., BORDEN, R., & LATANÉ, B. (1975). Diffusion of responsibility and restaurant tipping: Cheaper by the bunch. PERSONALITY AND SOCIAL PSYCHOLOGY BULLETIN, 1, 584–587. **733**

FRENCH, G. M., & HARLOW, H. F. (1962). Variability of delayed-reaction performance in normal and brain-damaged rhesus monkeys. JOURNAL OF NEUROPHYSIOLOGY, 25, 585–599. **50**

FREUD, A. (1958). Adolescence. THE PSYCHOANALYTIC STUDY OF THE CHILD, 13, 255–278. **515**

FREUD, A. (1946/1967). THE EGO AND THE MECHANISMS OF DEFENSE (rev. ed.). New York: International Universities Press. **515, 589**

FREUD, S. (1885/1974). COCAINE PAPERS (edited and introduction by R. Byck; notes by A. Freud). New York: Stonehill. **220**

FREUD, S. (1900/1953). THE INTERPRETATION OF DREAMS (Reprint ed.) (Vol. 4, 5). London: Hogarth Press. **211, 512**

FREUD, S. (1901/1960). PSYCHOPATHOLOGY OF EVERYDAY LIFE (Standard ed.) (Vol. 6). London: Hogarth Press. **511**

FREUD, S. (1905/1948). THREE CONTRIBUTIONS TO THEORY OF SEX (4th ed.; A. A. Brill, Trans.). New York: Nervous and Mental Disease Monograph. **13, 304, 305**

FREUD, S. (1915/1976). Repression. In J. Strachey (Ed. and Trans.), THE COMPLETE PSYCHOLOGICAL WORKS: STANDARD EDITION (Vol. 14). London: Hogarth Press. **411**

FREUD, S. (1920/1975). BEYOND THE PLEASURE PRINCIPLE. New York: Norton. **433**

FREUD, S. (1932/1963). Why war? In P. Reiff (Ed.), FREUD: CHARACTER AND CULTURE. New York: Collier. **426**

FREUD, S. (1933/1965). Revision of the theory of dreams. In J. Strachey (Ed. and Trans.), NEW INTRODUCTORY LECTURES ON PSYCHOANALYSIS (Vol. 22, Lect. 29). New York: Norton. **211, 433, 517, 551**

FREUD, S. (1940). An outline of psychoanalysis. INTERNATIONAL JOURNAL OF PSYCHOANALYSIS, 21, 27–84. **512**

FRICKE, B. G. (1975). REPORT TO THE FACULTY. Ann Arbor: Evaluation and Examinations Office, University of Michigan. **454**

FRIED, I., MATEER, C., OJEMANN, G., WOHNS, R., & FEDIO, P. (1982). Organization of visuospatial functions in human cortex. BRAIN, 105, 349–371. **415**

FRIED, M. (1982). Disadvantage, vulnerability, and mental illness. In D. L. Parron, F. Solomon, & C. D. Jenkins (Eds.), BEHAVIOR, HEALTH RISKS, AND SOCIAL DISADVANTAGE. Washington, DC: National Academy Press. **625**

FRIEDAN, B. (1963). THE FEMININE MYSTIQUE. New York: Dell Publishing. **528**

FRIEDMAN, M., & ROSENMAN, R. H. (1974). TYPE A BEHAVIOR AND YOUR HEART. New York: Knopf. **579, 580**

FRIEDMAN, M., ROSENMAN, R. H., STRAUS, R., WURM, M., & KOSITCHECK, R. (1968). The relationship of behavior pattern A to the state of coronary vasculature. AMERICAN JOURNAL OF MEDICINE, 44, 525–537. **580**

FRIEDMAN, M., THORESEN, C. E., GILL, J. J., & collaborators. (1985, March). ALTERATION OF TYPE A BEHAVIOR AND ITS EFFECT UPON CARDIAC RECURRENCES IN POST-MYOCARDIAL INFARCTION SUBJECTS: SUMMARY RESULTS OF THE RECURRENT CORONARY PREVENTION PROJECT. Paper presented at meetings of the Society of Behavioral Medicine, New Orleans. **582**

FRIEDMAN, M. I., & STRICKER, E. M. (1976). The physiological psychology of hunger: A physiological perspective. PSYCHOLOGICAL REVIEW, 83, 401–431. **370**

FRISCHHOLZ, E. J. (1985). The relationship among dissociation, hypnosis, and child abuse in the development of multiple personality disorder. In R. P. Kluft (Ed.), CHILDHOOD ANTECEDENTS OF MULTIPLE PERSONALITY. Washington, DC: American Psychiatric Press. **201**

FROMM, E. (1970). Age regression with unexpected reappearance of a repressed childhood language. INTERNATIONAL JOURNAL OF CLINICAL AND EXPERIMENTAL HYPNOSIS, 18, 79–88. **231**

FROMM, E., & SHOR, R. E. (Eds.). (1979). HYPNOSIS: DEVELOPMENTS IN RESEARCH AND NEW PERSPECTIVES (2nd ed.). Chicago: Aldine. **243**

FUNKENSTEIN, D. (1955). The physiology of fear and anger. SCIENTIFIC AMERICAN, 192, 74–80. **405**

FURSTENBERG, F. F., JR., BROOKS-GUNN, J., & MORGAN, S. P. (1987). ADOLESCENT MOTHERS IN LATER LIFE. New York: Cambridge Press. **104**

G

GALANTER, E. (1962). Contemporary psychophysics. In R. Brown & collaborators (Eds.), NEW DIRECTIONS IN PSYCHOLOGY (Vol. 1). New York: Holt, Rinehart & Winston. **119**

GALLISTEL, C. R. (1973). Self-stimulation: The neurophysiology of reward and motivation. In J. A. Deutsch (Ed.), THE PHYSIOLOGICAL BASIS OF MEMORY. New York: Academic Press. **267**

GALOTTI, K. M. (1989). Approaches to studying formal and everyday reasoning. PSYCHOLOGICAL BULLETIN, 105, 331–351. **463**

GAMSON, W. B., FIREMAN, B., & RYTINA, S. (1982). ENCOUNTERS WITH UNJUST AUTHORITY. Homewood, IL: Dorsey Press. **743, 744, 745**

GANELLEN, R. J., & CARVER, C. S. (1985). Why does self-reference promote incidental encoding? JOURNAL OF PERSONALITY AND SOCIAL PSYCHOLOGY, 21, 284–300. **696**

GANGESTAD, S., & SNYDER, M. (1985). To carve nature at its joints: On the existence of discrete classes in personality. PSYCHOLOGICAL REVIEW, 92, 317–349. **504**

GARCIA, J., & KOELLING, R. A. (1966). A relation of cue to consequence in avoidance learning. PSYCHONOMIC SOCIETY, 4, 123–124. **269, 271**

GARDNER, B. T., & GARDNER, R. A. (1972). Two-way communication with an infant chimpanzee. In A. M. Schrier & F. Stollnitz (Eds.), BEHAVIOR OF NONHUMAN PRIMATES (Vol. 4). New York: Academic Press. **345, 346**

GARDNER, H. (1975). THE SHATTERED MIND. New York: Knopf. **344, 345**

GARDNER, H. (1983). FRAMES OF MIND: THE THEORY OF MULTIPLE INTELLIGENCES. New York: Basic Books. **464, 465**

GARDNER, H. (1985). THE MIND'S NEW SCIENCE: A HISTORY OF THE COGNITIVE REVOLUTION. New York: Basic Books. **26, 29**

GARDNER, M. (1981). SCIENCE: GOOD, BAD, AND BOGUS. New York: Prometheus. **243**

GARFIELD, S. L. (1980). PSYCHOTHERAPY: AN ECLECTIC APPROACH. New York: Wiley-Interscience. **666, 679**

GARFIELD, S. L., & BERGIN, A. E. (Eds.). (1986). HANDBOOK OF PSYCHOTHERAPY AND BEHAVIOR CHANGE (3rd ed.). New York: Wiley. **679**

GARFINKEL, P. E., & GARDNER, D. M. (1982). ANOREXIA NERVOSA: A MULTIDISCIPLINARY PERSPECTIVE. New York: Brunner/Mazel. **376**

GARMEZY, N. (1974). Children at risk: The search for the antecedents of schizophrenia: Pt. 2. Ongoing research programs, issues and intervention. SCHIZOPHRENIA BULLETIN, 1(9), 55–125. **627**

GARRETT, M. F. (1975). The analysis of sentence production. In G. H. Bower (Ed.), THE PSYCHOLOGY OF LEARNING AND MOTIVATION (Vol. 9). New York: Academic Press. **334**

GARROW, J. (1978). The regulation of energy expenditure. In G. A. Bray (Ed.), RECENT ADVANCES IN OBESITY RESEARCH (Vol. 2). London: Newman. **373**

GATES, A. I. (1917). Recitation as a factor in memorizing. ARCHIVES OF PSYCHOLOGY, No. 40. **311, 764**

GAZZANIGA, M. S. (1985). THE SOCIAL BRAIN: DISCOVERING THE NETWORKS OF MIND. New York: Basic Books. **700, 719, 721**

GEEN, R. G., BEATTY, W. W., & ARKIN, R. M. (1984). HUMAN MOTIVATION: PHYSIOLOGICAL, BEHAVIORAL, AND SOCIAL APPROACHES. Boston: Allyn & Bacon. **397, 399**

GEEN, R. G., & QUANTY, M. B. (1977). The catharsis of aggression. In L. Berkowitz (Ed.), ADVANCES IN EXPERIMENTAL SOCIAL PSYCHOLOGY (Vol. 10). New York: Academic Press. **430**

GEER, J., & MAISEL, E. (1972). Evaluating the effects of the prediction-control confound. JOURNAL OF PERSONALITY AND SOCIAL PSYCHOLOGY, 23, 314–319. **572**

GEISLER, W. S. (1978). Adaptation, afterimages and cone saturation. VISION RESEARCH, 18, 279–289. **119**

GELMAN, R., & GALLISTEL, C. R. (1978). THE YOUNG CHILD'S UNDERSTANDING OF NUMBER: A WINDOW ON EARLY COGNITIVE DEVELOPMENT. Cambridge, MA: Harvard University Press. **84**

GERBNER, G., & GROSS, L. (1976). The scary world of television's heavy viewer. PSYCHOLOGY TODAY, 9, 41–45. **752**

GESCHWIND, N. (1972). Language and the brain. SCIENTIFIC AMERICAN, 226, 10, 76–83. **345**

GESCHWIND, N. (1979). Specializations of the human brain. SCIENTIFIC AMERICAN, 241, 180–199. **54**

GESCHWIND, N. (1984). The biology of cerebral dominance: Implications for cognition. COGNITION, 17, 193–208. **389**

GESCHWIND, N., & GALABURDA, A. M. (1987). CEREBRAL LATERALIZATION. Cambridge, MA: MIT Press. **50, 55**

GESELL, A., & THOMPSON, H. (1929). Learning and growth in identical twins: An experimental study by the method of co-twin control. GENETIC PSYCHOLOGY MONOGRAPHS, 6, 1–123. **79**

GIBBS, J., YOUNG, R. C., & SMITH, G. P. (1973). Cholecystokinin decreases food intake in rats. JOURNAL OF COMPARATIVE AND PHYSIOLOGICAL PSYCHOLOGY, 84, 484–495. **367**

GIBSON, E. J., & WALK, R. D. (1960). The "visual cliff." SCIENTIFIC AMERICAN, 202, 64–71. **187**

GIBSON, J. J. (1950). THE PERCEPTION OF THE VISUAL WORLD. Boston: Houghton Mifflin. **162**

GIBSON, J. J. (1966). THE SENSES CONSIDERED AS PERCEPTUAL SYSTEMS. Boston: Houghton Mifflin. **162, 193**

GIBSON, J. J. (1979). THE ECOLOGICAL APPROACH TO VISUAL PERCEPTION. Boston: Houghton Mifflin. **162, 163, 165, 193**

GILBERT, D. T., & JONES, E. E. (1986). Perceiver-induced constraint: Interpretations of self-generated reality. JOURNAL OF PERSONALITY AND SOCIAL PSYCHOLOGY, 50, 269–280. **696**

GILL, M. M. (1972). Hypnosis as an altered and regressed state. INTERNATIONAL JOURNAL OF CLINICAL AND EXPERIMENTAL HYPNOSIS, 20, 224–337. **234**

GILLIN, J. C. (1985). Sleep and dreams. In G. L. Klerman, M. M. Weissman, P. S. Applebaum, & L. H. Roth (Eds.), PSYCHIATRY (Vol. 3). Philadelphia: Lippincott. **204**

GILLUND, G., & SHIFFRIN, R. M. (1984). A retrieval model for both recognition and recall. PSYCHOLOGICAL REVIEW, 91(1), 1–61. **298**

GILOVICH, T. (1983). Biased evaluation and persistence in gambling. JOURNAL OF PERSONALITY AND SOCIAL PSYCHOLOGY, 40, 797–808. **700**

GINSBERG, A. (1983). CONTRAST PERCEPTION IN THE HUMAN INFANT. Unpublished manuscript. **186**

GIRVIN, B. (1978). THE NATURE OF BEING SCHEMATIC: SEX-ROLE, SELF-SCHEMAS AND DIFFERENTIAL PROCESSING OF MASCULINE AND FEMININE INFORMATION. Unpublished doctoral dissertation, Stanford University. **697**

GITTELMAN, R., & KLEIN, D. F. (1985). Childhood separation anxiety and adult agoraphobia. In A. H. Tuma & J. D. Maser (Eds.), ANXIETY AND THE ANXIETY DISORDERS. Hillsdale, NJ: Erlbaum. **599**

GLASER, R., KIECOLT-GLASER, J. K., STOUT, J. C., TARR, K. L., SPEICHER, C. E., & HOLLIDAY, J. E. (1985). Stress-related impairments in cellular immunity. PSYCHIATRY RESEARCH, 16, 233–239. **584**

GLASER, R., RICE, J., SPEICHER, C. E., STOUT, J. C., & KIECOLT-GLASER, J. K. (1986). Stress depresses interferon production by leukocytes concomitant with a decrease in natural killer-cell activity. BEHAVIORAL NEUROSCIENCE, 100, 675–678. **584**

GLASS, A. L., & HOLYOAK, K. J. (1986). COGNITION (2nd ed.). New York: Random House. **319**

GLASS, D. C., & SINGER, J. E. (1972). URBAN STRESS: EXPERIMENTS ON NOISE AND SOCIAL STRESSORS. New York: Academic Press. **572**

GLASS, G. V., MCGAW, B., & SMITH, M. L. (1981). META-ANALYSIS IN SOCIAL RESEARCH. Beverly Hills, CA: Sage. **236**

GLUCK, M. A., & THOMPSON, R. F. (1987). Modeling the neural substrates of associative learning and memory: A computational approach. PSYCHOLOGICAL REVIEW, 94, 176–191. **255**

GOLDBERG, R. J. (1978). DEVELOPMENT IN THE FAMILY AND SCHOOL CONTEXT: WHO IS RESPONSIBLE FOR THE EDUCATION OF YOUNG CHILDREN IN AMERICA? Paper presented at the National Association for the Education of Young Children Annual Conference, New York City. **94**

GOLDBERG, S., PERLMUTTER, M., & MYERS, N. (1974). Recall of related and unrelated lists by two-year-olds. JOURNAL OF EXPERIMENTAL CHILD PSYCHOLOGY, 18, 1–8. **85**

GOLDHABER, D. (1986). LIFE-SPAN HUMAN DEVELOPMENT. San Diego: Harcourt Brace Jovanovich. **501**

GOLDIN-MEADOW, S. (1982). The resilience of recursion: A structure within a conventional model. In E. Wanner & L. R. Gleitman (Eds.), LANGUAGE ACQUISITION: THE STATE OF THE ART. Cambridge, MA: Cambridge University Press. **73**

GOLDMAN, W., & LEWIS, P. (1977). Beautiful is good: Evidence that the physically attractive are more socially skillful. JOURNAL OF EXPERIMENTAL SOCIAL PSYCHOLOGY, 13, 125–130. **694**

GOLDSTEIN, E. B. (1984). SENSATION AND PERCEPTION (2nd ed.). Belmont, CA: Wadsworth. **124, 129, 135, 149, 162, 165, 183, 186**

GOLDSTEIN, E. B. (1989). SENSATION AND PERCEPTION (3rd ed.). Belmont, CA: Wadsworth. **153**

GOLDSTEIN, M. J. (1987). The UCLA High Risk Project. SCHIZOPHRENIA BULLETIN, 13, 505–514. **627**

GOLDSTEIN, M. J., BAKER, B. L., & JAMISON, K. R. (1986). ABNORMAL PSYCHOLOGY: EXPERIENCES, ORIGINS, AND INTERVENTIONS (2nd ed.). Boston: Little, Brown. **635**

GOLEMAN, D. (1988, October 18). Chemistry of sexual desire yields its elusive secret. NEW YORK TIMES. **379**

GOLEMAN, D. J. (1977). THE VARIETIES OF MEDITATIVE EXPERIENCE. New York: Dutton. **243**

GOODALL, J. (1978). Chimp killings: Is it the man in them? SCIENCE NEWS, 113, 276. **427**

GOODGLASS, H., & BUTTERS, N. (1988). Psychobiology of cognitive processes. In R. C. Atkinson, R. J. Herrnstein, G. Lindzey, & R. D. Luce (Eds.), STEVENS' HANDBOOK OF EXPERIMENTAL PSYCHOLOGY (Vol. 2). New York: Wiley. **50**

GOOSSENS, F. A. (1987). Maternal employment and day care: Effects on attachment. In L. W. C. Tavecchio & M. H. Van Ijzendoorn (Eds.), ATTACHMENT IN SOCIAL NETWORKS. Amsterdam: North-Holland. **94**

GORDON, E. (1967). A three-year longitudinal predictive validity study of the musical aptitude profile. STUDIES IN THE PSYCHOLOGY OF MUSIC (Vol. 5). Iowa City: University of Iowa Press. **438**

GORENSTEIN, E. E. (1982). Frontal lobe functions in psychopaths. JOURNAL OF ABNORMAL PSYCHOLOGY, 91, 368–379. **631**

GORRELL, P. (1987). SOME PERCEPTUAL CONSEQUENCES OF AMBIGUITY. Unpublished doctoral dissertation, University of Connecticut. **336**

GOTTESMAN, I. I., & SHIELDS, J. (1982). SCHIZOPHRENIA: THE EPIGENETIC PUZZLE. New York: Cambridge University Press. **622, 635**

GOULD, J. L., & MARLER, P. (1987). Learning by instinct. SCIENTIFIC AMERICAN, 256, 74–85. **271**

GOY, R. W. (1968). Organizing effect of androgen on the behavior of rhesus monkeys. In R. F. Michael (Ed.), ENDOCRINOLOGY OF HUMAN BEHAVIOR. London: Oxford University Press. **389**

GRAF, P., & MANDLER, G. (1984). Activation makes words more accessible, but not necessarily more retrievable. JOURNAL OF VERBAL LEARNING AND VERBAL BEHAVIOR, 23, 553–568. **306**

GRANBERG, D., & BRENT, E. E. (1974). Dove–hawk placements in the 1968 election: Application of social judgment and balance theories. JOURNAL OF PERSONALITY AND SOCIAL PSYCHOLOGY, 29, 687–695. **754**

GREEN, D. M., & SWETS, J. A. (1966). SIGNAL DETECTION THEORY AND PSYCHOPHYSICS. New York: Wiley. **123**

GREEN, D. M., & WIER, C. C. (1984). Auditory perception. In I. Darian-Smith (Ed.), HANDBOOK OF PHYSIOLOGY (Vol. 3). Bethesda, MD: American Physiological Society. **142**

GREEN, H. (1971). I NEVER PROMISED YOU A ROSE GARDEN. New York: New American Library. **635**

GREENBERG, J. S., & ALLOY, L. B. (1989). Depression versus anxiety: Differences in self and other schemata. In L. B. Alloy (Ed.), COGNITIVE PROCESSES IN DEPRESSION. New York: Guilford Press. **617**

GREENWALD, A. G. (1968). Cognitive learning, cognitive response to persuasion, and attitude change. In A. G. Greenwald, T. C. Brock, & T. M. Ostrom (Eds.), PSYCHOLOGICAL FOUNDATIONS OF ATTITUDES. New York: Academic Press. **748**

GREGG, V. H. (1986). INTRODUCTION TO HUMAN MEMORY. Boston: Routledge and Kegan Paul. **319**

GRICE, H. P. (1975). Logic and conversation. In G. Harman & D. Davidson (Eds.), THE LOGIC OF GRAMMAR. Encino, CA: Dickinson. **337**

GRIGGS, R. A., & COX, J. R. (1982). The elusive thematic-materials effect in Watson's selection task. BRITISH JOURNAL OF PSYCHOLOGY, 73, 407–420. **329**

GRODZINSKI, Y. (1984). The syntactic characterization of agrammatism. COGNITION, 16, 99–120. **345**

GROVES, P. M., & REBEC, G. V. (1988). INTRODUCTION TO BIOLOGICAL PSYCHOLOGY (3rd ed.). Dubuque, IA: Brown. **35, 39, 67**

GRÜNBAUM, A. (1984). THE FOUNDATIONS OF PSYCHOANALYSIS. Berkeley, CA: University of California Press. **517**

GUILFORD, J. P. (1982). Cognitive psychology's ambiguities: Some suggested remedies. PSYCHOLOGICAL REVIEW, 89, 48–49. **461, 509**

GULEVICH, G., DEMENT, W. C., & JOHNSON, L. (1966). Psychiatric and EEG observations on a case of prolonged wakefulness. ARCHIVES OF GENERAL PSYCHIATRY, 15, 29–35. **206, 208**

GURMAN, A. S., & KNISKERN, D. P. (1981). HANDBOOK OF FAMILY THERAPY. New York: Brunner/Mazel. **662**

H

HABER, R. N. (1969). Eidetic images. SCIENTIFIC AMERICAN, 220, 36–55. **284**

HAITH, M. M., BERGMAN, T., & MOORE, M. J. (1977). Eye contact and face scanning in early infancy. SCIENCE, 198, 853–855. **76**

HALIKAS, J. A., GOODWIN, D. W., & GUZE, S. B. (1971). Marijuana effects: A survey of regular users. JOURNAL OF AMERICAN MEDICAL ASSOCIATION, 217, 692–694. **223**

HALL, C. S., LINDZEY, G., LOEHLIN, J. C., & MANOSEVITZ, M. (1985). INTRODUCTION TO THEORIES OF PERSONALITY. New York: Wiley. **551**

HAMBERGER, L. K., & LOHR, J. M. (1984). STRESS AND STRESS MANAGEMENT: RESEARCH AND APPLICATIONS. New York: Springer. **589**

HAMBURG, D., & TRUDEAU, M. B. (Eds.). (1981). BIOBEHAVIORAL ASPECTS OF AGGRESSION. New York: Alan Liss. **379, 433**

HAMILTON, D. L. (1979). A cognitive-attributional analysis of stereotyping. In L. Berkowitz (Ed.), ADVANCES IN EXPERIMENTAL SOCIAL PSYCHOLOGY (Vol. 12). New York: Academic Press. **686**

HAMILTON, E. W., & ABRAMSON, L. Y. (1983). Cognitive patterns and major depressive disorder: A longitudinal study in a hospital setting. JOURNAL OF ABNORMAL PSYCHOLOGY, 92, 173–184. **613**

HARE, R. D. (1970). PSYCHOPATHY: THEORY AND RESEARCH. New York: Wiley. **631**

HARE, R. D. (1978). Psychopathy and physiological activity during anticipation of an aversive stimulus in a distraction paradigm. PSYCHOPHYSIOLOGY, 15, 165–172. **631**

HARE, R. D. (1980). A research scale for the assessment of psychopathy in criminal populations. PERSONALITY AND INDIVIDUAL DIFFERENCES, 1, 111–119. **629**

HARKINS, S. G., & PETTY, R. E. (1982). Effects of task difficulty and task uniqueness on social loafing. JOURNAL OF PERSONALITY AND SOCIAL PSYCHOLOGY, 43, 1214–1229. **733**

HARLOW, H. F. (1971). LEARNING TO LOVE. San Francisco: Albion. **382**

HARLOW, H. F., HARLOW, M. K., & MEYER, D. R. (1950). Learning moti-vated by a manipulation drive. JOURNAL OF EXPERIMENTAL PSYCHOLOGY, 40, 228–234. **395**

HARLOW, H. F., & SUOMI, S. J. (1979). Nature of love—simplified. AMERICAN PSYCHOLOGIST, 25, 161–168. **88**

HARRE, R., & LAMB, R. (Eds.). (1983). THE ENCYCLOPEDIC DICTIONARY OF PSYCHOLOGY. Cambridge, MA: MIT Press. **228**

HARRIS, M. J., & ROSENTHAL, R. (1988). INTERPERSONAL EXPECTANCY EFFECTS AND HUMAN PERFORMANCE RESEARCH. Washington, DC: National Academy Press. **238**

HARTIGAN, J. A., & WIGDOR, A. K. (Eds.). (1989). FAIRNESS IN EMPLOYMENT TESTING. Washington, DC: National Academy Press. **472**

HARTMANN, E. (1984). THE NIGHTMARE. New York: Basic Books. **204, 205**

HARTSHORNE, H., & MAY, M. A. (1929). STUDIES IN THE NATURE OF CHARACTER: *Vol. 2.* STUDIES IN SERVICE AND SELF CONTROL. New York: Macmillan. **544**

HARTUP, W. W., & COATES, B. (1967). Imitation of a peer as a function of reinforcement from the peer group and rewardingness of the model. CHILD DEVELOPMENT, 38, 1003–1016. **92**

HARTUP, W. W., & MOORE, S. G. (1963). Avoidance of inappropriate sex-typing by young children. JOURNAL OF CONSULTING PSYCHOLOGY, 27, 467–473. **95**

HASS, R. G., & GRADY, K. (1975). Temporal delay, type of forewarning, and resistance to influence. JOURNAL OF EXPERIMENTAL SOCIAL PSYCHOLOGY, 11, 459–469. **749**

HAURI, P. (1982). SLEEP DISORDERS. Kalamazoo, MI: Upjohn. **243**

HAWKINS, R. D., & KANDEL, E. R. (1984). Is there a cell-biological alphabet for simple forms of learning? PSYCHOLOGICAL REVIEW, 91, 375–391. **255**

HAYES, C. E. (Ed.). (1987). RISKING THE FUTURE: ADOLESCENT SEXUALITY, PREGNANCY, AND CHILDBEARING. Washington, DC: National Academy Press. **104**

HAYNES, S. G., & FEINLEIB, M. (1980). Women, work, and coronary heart disease: Prospective findings from the Framingham heart study. AMERICAN JOURNAL OF PUBLIC HEALTH, 70, 133–141. **582**

HAYNES, S. G., FEINLEIB, M., & KANNEL, W. B. (1980). The relationship of psychosocial factors to coronary heart disease in the Framingham Study: Pt. 3. Eight-year incidence of coronary heart disease. AMERICAN JOURNAL OF EPIDEMIOLOGY, 111(1), 37–58. **508**

HEBB, D. O. (1972). TEXTBOOK OF PSYCHOLOGY (3rd ed.). Philadelphia: Saunders. **232, 420**

HEBB, D. O. (1982). Understanding psychological man: A state-of-the-science report. PSYCHOLOGY TODAY, 16, 52–53. **232**

HECHT, S., & HSIA, Y. (1945). Dark adaptation following light adaptation to red and white lights. JOURNAL OF THE OPTICAL SOCIETY OF AMERICA, 35, 261–267. **127**

HECHT, S., SHLAER, S., & PIRENNE, M. H. (1942). Energy, quanta, and vision. JOURNAL OF GENERAL PHYSIOLOGY, 25, 819–840. **119**

HEIDER, F. (1958). THE PSYCHOLOGY OF INTERPERSONAL RELATIONS. New York: Wiley. **695, 696**

HEIN, A., & HELD, R. (1967). Dissociation of the visual placing response into elicited and guided components. SCIENCE, 158, 390–392. **190**

HELD, R. (1965). Plasticity in sensory motor systems. SCIENTIFIC AMERICAN, 21(5), 84–94. **191**

HELD, R., & HEIN, A. (1963). Movement produced stimulation in the development of visually guided behavior. JOURNAL OF COMPARATIVE AND PHYSIOLOGICAL PSYCHOLOGY, 56, 872–876. **191**

HELMHOLTZ, H. (1909). WISSENSCHAFTLICHE ABHANDLONGEN (II, pp. 764–843). **161, 182**

HEMMI, T. (1969). How we have handled the problem of drug abuse in Japan. In F. Sjoqvist & M. Tottie (Eds.), ABUSE OF CENTRAL STIMULANTS. New York: Raven Press. **219**

HENCHY, T., & GLASS, D. C. (1968). Evaluation apprehension and social facilitation of dominant and subordinate responses. JOURNAL OF PERSONALITY AND SOCIAL PSYCHOLOGY, 10, 446–454. **725**

HENLEY, N., HAMILTON, M., & THORNE, B. (1985). Womanspeak and manspeak: Sex differences and sexism in communication, verbal and nonverbal. In A. G. Sargent (Ed.), BEYOND SEX ROLES. St. Paul, MN: West. **699**

HENSEL, H. (1973). Cutaneous thermoreceptors. In A. Iggo (Ed.), HANDBOOK OF SENSORY PHYSIOLOGY (Vol. 2). Berlin: Springer-Verlag. **151**

HERBERT, N. (1987). QUANTUM REALITY: BEYOND THE NEW PHYSICS. Garden City, NY: Anchor. **241**

HERDT, G. H. (Ed.). (1984). RITUALIZED HOMOSEXUALITY IN MELANESIA. Berkeley: University of California Press. **382**

HERMAN, C. P., & POLIVY, J. (1980). Restrained eating. In A. J. Stunkard (Ed.), OBESITY. Philadelphia: Saunders. **371**

HERRNSTEIN, R. J., & BORING, E. G. (1965). SOURCE BOOK IN THE HISTORY OF

HERRNSTEIN, R. J. (*continued*) PSYCHOLOGY. Cambridge, MA: Harvard University Press. **773**

HESS, E. H. (1958). "Imprinting" in animals. SCIENTIFIC AMERICAN, *198*, 81–90. **392**

HESS, E. H. (1972). "Imprinting" in a natural laboratory. SCIENTIFIC AMERICAN, *227*, 24–31. **393**

HETHERINGTON, E. M., & BRACKBILL, Y. (1963). Etiology and covariation of obstinacy, orderliness, and parsimony in young children. CHILD DEVELOPMENT, *34*, 919–943. **517**

HEWITT, P., & MASSEY, J. O. (1969). CLINICAL CLUES FROM THE WISC. Palo Alto, CA: Consulting Psychologists Press. **452**

HILGARD, E. R. (1961). Hypnosis and experimental psychodynamics. In H. Brosin (Ed.), LECTURES ON EXPERIMENTAL PSYCHIATRY. Pittsburgh: Pittsburgh University Press. **20, 230**

HILGARD, E. R. (1965). HYPNOTIC SUSCEPTIBILITY. New York: Harcourt Brace Jovanovich. **230, 575**

HILGARD, E. R. (1968). THE EXPERIENCE OF HYPNOSIS. New York: Harcourt Brace Jovanovich. **243**

HILGARD, E. R. (1977). DIVIDED CONSCIOUSNESS: MULTIPLE CONTROLS IN HUMAN THOUGHT AND ACTION. New York: Wiley-Interscience. **232, 233, 243**

HILGARD, E. R. (1987). PSYCHOLOGY IN AMERICA: A HISTORICAL SURVEY. San Diego: Harcourt Brace Jovanovich. **29, 773**

HILGARD, E. R., & HILGARD, J. R. (1975). HYPNOSIS IN THE RELIEF OF PAIN. Los Altos, CA: Kaufmann. **233**

HILGARD, E. R., HILGARD, J. R., MACDONALD, H., MORGAN, A. H., & JOHNSON, L. S. (1978). Covert pain in hypnotic analgesia: Its reality as tested by the real-simulator design. JOURNAL OF ABNORMAL PSYCHOLOGY, *87*, 655–663. **233**

HILGARD, J. R. (1979). PERSONALITY AND HYPNOSIS: A STUDY OF IMAGINATIVE INVOLVEMENT (2nd ed.). Chicago: University of Chicago Press. **230, 243**

HILL, C., RUBIN, Z., & PEPLAU, L. A. (1976). Breakups before marriage: The end of 103 affairs. JOURNAL OF SOCIAL ISSUES, *32*, 147–168. **713**

HILL, J. P. (1988). Adapting to menarche: Familial control and conflict. In M. R. Gunnar & W. A. Collins (Eds.), THE MINNESOTA SYMPOSIA ON CHILD PSYCHOLOGY (Vol. 21). Hillsdale, NJ: Erlbaum. **102**

HIRSCH, J., & BATCHELOR, B. R. (1976). Adipose tissue cellularity and human obesity. CLINICAL ENDOCRINOLOGY AND METABOLISM, *5*, 299–311. **375**

HIRSCH, H. V. B., & SPINELLI, D. N. (1970). Visual experience modifies distribution of horizontally and vertically oriented receptive fields in cats. SCIENCE, *168*, 869–871. **189**

HIRSH, S. R., & NATELSON, B. J. (1981). Electrical brain stimulation and food reinforcement dissociated by demand elasticity. PHYSIOLOGY AND BEHAVIOR, *18*, 141–150. **267**

HIRST, W. (1982). The amnesic syndrome: Descriptions and explanations. PSYCHOLOGICAL BULLETIN, *91*(3), 435–460. **302**

HOBSON, J. A. (1988). THE DREAMING BRAIN. New York: Basic Books. **206, 209, 243**

HOBSON, J. A. (1989). SLEEP. New York: Freeman. **202, 205**

HOCHBERG, J. (1978). PERCEPTION (2nd ed.). Englewood Cliffs, NJ: Prentice-Hall. **175**

HOCK, E. (1980). Working and nonworking mothers and their infants: A comparative study of maternal caregiving characteristics and infant social behavior. MERRILL PALMER QUARTERLY, *26*, 79–102. **94**

HOEBEL, B. G., & TEITELBAUM, P. (1966). Effects of force-feeding and starvation on food intake and body weight on a rat with ventromedial hypothalamic lesions. JOURNAL OF COMPARATIVE AND PHYSIOLOGICAL PSYCHOLOGY, *61*, 189–193. **368**

HOFLING, C. K. (1975). TEXTBOOK OF PSYCHIATRY FOR MEDICAL PRACTICE (3rd ed.). Philadelphia: Lippincott. **618**

HOFLING, C. K., BROTZMAN, E., DALRYMPLE, S., GRAVES, N., & PIERCE, C. M. (1966). An experimental study in nurse–physician relationships. JOURNAL OF NERVOUS AND MENTAL DISEASE, *143*, 171–180. **741**

HOGARTY, G. E., SCHOOLER, N. R., ULRICH, R., MUSSARE, F., FERRO, P., & HERRON, E. (1979). Fluphenazine and social therapy in the after care of schizophrenic patients. ARCHIVES OF GENERAL PSYCHIATRY, *36*, 1283–1294. **672**

HOHMANN, G. W. (1962). Some effects of spinal cord lesions on experienced emotional feelings. PSYCHOPHYSIOLOGY, *3*, 143–156. **404**

HOHMANN, M., BANET, B., & WEIKART, D. (1979). YOUNG CHILDREN IN ACTION. Ypsilanti, MI: High Scope Press. **404, 469**

HOLDEN, C. (1975). Lie detectors: PSE gains audience despite critic's doubt. SCIENCE, *190*, 359–362. **407**

HOLLAND, J. H., HOLYOAK, K. J., NISBETT, R. E., & THAGARD, P. R. (1986). INDUCTION: PROCESSES OF INFERENCE, LEARNING, AND DISCOVERY. Cambridge, MA: MIT Press. **356**

HOLMES, D. S. (1974). Investigations of repression: Differential recall of material experimentally or naturally associated with ego threat. PSYCHOLOGICAL BULLETIN, *81*, 632–653. **301, 518**

HOLMES, D. S. (1984). Meditation and somatic arousal reduction: A review of the evidence. AMERICAN PSYCHOLOGIST, *39*, 1–10. **227**

HOLMES, D. S. (1987). The influence of meditation versus rest on physiological arousal: A second examination. In M. A. West (Ed.), THE PSYCHOLOGY OF MEDITATION. New York: Oxford University Press. **227**

HOLMES, D. S., & MCGILLEY, B. M. (1987). Influence of a brief aerobic training program on heart rate and subjective response to stress. PSYCHOSOMATIC MEDICINE, *49*, 366–374. **585**

HOLMES, D. S., & ROTH, D. L. (1985). Association of aerobic fitness with pulse rate and subjective responses to psychological stress. PSYCHOPHYSIOLOGY, *22*, 525–529. **585**

HOLMES, T. H., & MASUDA, M. (1974). Life change and stress susceptibility. In B. S. Dohrenwend & B. P. Dohrenwend (Eds.), STRESSFUL LIFE EVENTS: THEIR NATURE AND EFFECTS. New York: Wiley. **567, 568**

HOLMES, T. H., & RAHE, R. H. (1967). The social readjustment rating scale. JOURNAL OF PSYCHOSOMATIC RESEARCH, *11*, 213–218. **567, 568**

HOLROYD, K. A., APPEL, M. A., & ANDRASIK, F. (1983). A cognitive-behavioral approach to psychophysiological disorders. In D. Meichenbaum & M. E. Jaremko (Eds.), STRESS REDUCTION AND PREVENTION. New York: Plenum. **585**

HOLWAY, A. H., & BORING, E. G. (1941). Determinants of apparent visual size with distance variant. AMERICAN JOURNAL OF PSYCHOLOGY, *54*, 21–37. **182**

HOLYOAK, K., KOH, K., & NISBETT, R. E. (1989). A theory of conditioning: Inductive learning within rule-based default hierarchies. PSYCHOLOGICAL REVIEW, *96*, 315–340. **253**

HOLZMAN, P. S. (1970). PSYCHOANALYSIS AND PSYCHOPATHOLOGY. New York: McGraw-Hill. **551**

HOMME, L. E., DE BACA, P. C., DEVINE, J. V., STEINHORST, R., & RICKERT, E. J. (1963). Use of the Premack principle in controlling the behavior of nursery-school children. JOURNAL OF THE EXPERIMENTAL ANALYSIS OF BEHAVIOR, *6*, 544. **263**

HONIG, W. K., & STADDON, J. E. R. (Eds.). (1977). HANDBOOK OF OPERANT BEHAVIOR. Englewood Cliffs, NJ: Prentice-Hall. **279**

HONORTON, C. (1985). Meta-analysis of psi Ganzfeld research: A response to Hyman. JOURNAL OF PARAPSYCHOLOGY, 49, 51–91. **235, 236, 239**

HOOD, D. C., & FINKELSTEIN, M. A. (1983). A case for the revision of textbook models of color vision: The detection and appearance of small, brief lights. In J. D. Mollon & L. T. Sharpe (Eds.), COLOUR VISION: PHYSIOLOGY AND PSYCHOPHYSICS. London: Academic Press. **135**

HOOK, E. B. (1973). Behavioral implications of the human XYY genotype. SCIENCE, 179, 139–150. **63**

HOPKINS, J. R. (1977). Sexual behavior in adolescence. JOURNAL OF SOCIAL ISSUES, 33, 67–85. **383**

HORNE, J. (1988). WHY WE SLEEP. New York: Oxford University Press. **204, 205, 208, 243**

HOVLAND, C., JANIS, I., & KELLEY, H. H. (1953). COMMUNICATION AND PERSUASION. New Haven: Yale University Press. **747, 748**

HOVLAND, C. I., LUMSDAINE, A. A., & SHEFFIELD, F. D. (1949). Experiments on mass communication. STUDIES IN SOCIAL PSYCHOLOGY IN WORLD WAR II (Vol. III). Princeton, NJ: Princeton University Press. **748**

HOWARD, K. I., KOPTA, S. M., KRAUSE, M. S., & ORLINSKY, D. E. (1986). The dose-effect relationship in psychotherapy. AMERICAN PSYCHOLOGIST, 41, 159–164. **665**

HUBEL, D. H., & WIESEL, T. N. (1963). Receptive fields of cells in striate cortex of very young, visually inexperienced kittens. JOURNAL OF NEUROPHYSIOLOGY, 26, 994–1002. **188**

HUBEL, D. H., & WIESEL, T. N. (1968). Receptive fields and functional architecture of monkey striate cortex. JOURNAL OF PHYSIOLOGY, 195, 215–243. **166**

HUESMANN, L. R., ERON, L. D., LEFKOWITZ, M. M., & WALDER, L. O. (1984). Stability of aggression over time and generations. DEVELOPMENTAL PSYCHOLOGY, 20, 1120–1134. **424**

HUGDAHL, K., & OHMAN, A. (1977). Effects of instruction on acquisition and extinction of electrodermal response to fear-relevant stimuli. JOURNAL OF EXPERIMENTAL PSYCHOLOGY: HUMAN LEARNING AND MEMORY, 3(5), 608–618. **604**

HUNT, D. D., & HAMPSON, J. L. (1980). Follow-up of 17 biologic male transsexuals after sex reassignment surgery. AMERICAN JOURNAL OF PSYCHIATRY, 137, 432–438. **391**

HUNT, E. (1985). Verbal ability. In R. J. Sternberg (Ed.), HUMAN ABILITIES: AN INFORMATION-PROCESSING APPROACH. New York: Freeman. **461**

HUNT, M. (1974). SEXUAL BEHAVIOR IN THE 1970S. Chicago: Playboy Press. **383, 384**

HUNT, P. J., & HILLERY, J. M. (1973). SOCIAL FACILITATION AT DIFFERENT STAGES IN LEARNING. Paper presented at the Midwestern Psychological Association Meetings, Cleveland. **725**

HUNTER, E. J. (1979, May). COMBAT CASUALTIES WHO REMAIN AT HOME. Paper presented at Western Regional Conference of the Interuniversity Seminar, "Technology in Combat." Navy Postgraduate School, Monterey, CA. **572**

HUNTER, I. M. L. (1974). MEMORY. Baltimore: Penguin. **314**

HURVICH, L., & JAMESON, D. (1957). An opponent-process theory of color vision. PSYCHOLOGICAL REVIEW, 64, 384–404. **135**

HURVICH, L. M. (1981). COLOR VISION. Sunderland, MA: Sinauer Associates. **135, 155**

HUSTON, A. C. (1983). Sex-typing. In P. H. Mussen (Ed.), HANDBOOK OF CHILD PSYCHOLOGY: VOL. 4. SOCIALIZATION, PERSONALITY, AND SOCIAL DEVELOPMENT. New York: Wiley. **95**

HUSTON-STEIN, A., & HIGGINS-TRENK, A. (1978). Development of females from childhood through adulthood: Career and feminine role orientations. In P. B. Baltes (Ed.), LIFE-SPAN DEVELOPMENT AND BEHAVIOR (Vol. 1). New York: Academic Press. **94**

HYDE, J. S., & LINN, M. C. (1988). Gender differences in verbal ability: A meta-analysis. PSYCHOLOGICAL BULLETIN, 104, 53–69. **455**

HYMAN, R. (1985). The Ganzfeld psi experiment: A critical appraisal. JOURNAL OF PARAPSYCHOLOGY, 49, 3–49. **236**

HYMAN, R., & HONORTON, C. (1986). A joint communique: The psi Ganzfeld controversy. JOURNAL OF PARAPSYCHOLOGY, 50, 351–364. **236, 239**

I

IMPERATO-MCGINLEY, J., PETERSON, R. E., GAUTIER, T., & STURLA, E. (1979). Androgens and the evolution of male gender identity among male pseudohermaphrodites with 5 alpha reductase deficiency. NEW ENGLAND JOURNAL OF MEDICINE, 300, 1233–1237. **390**

INSTITUTE OF MEDICINE. (1982). MARIJUANA AND HEALTH. Washington, DC: National Academy Press. **223**

ISEN, P. M. (1985). The asymmetry of happiness and sadness in effects on memory in normal college students. JOURNAL OF EXPERIMENTAL PSYCHOLOGY: GENERAL, 114, 388–391. **421**

ISEN, P. M., SHALKER, T. E., CLARK, M., & KARP, L. (1978). Affect, accessibility of material in memory, and behavior: A cognitive loop? JOURNAL OF PERSONALITY AND SOCIAL PSYCHOLOGY, 36, 1–12. **422**

J

JACKENDOFF, R. (1987). CONSCIOUSNESS AND THE COMPUTATIONAL MIND. Cambridge, MA: MIT Press. **243**

JACKSON, D. J., & HUSTON, T. L. (1975). Physical attractiveness and assertiveness. JOURNAL OF SOCIAL PSYCHOLOGY, 96, 79–84. **694**

JACKSON, J. M., & LATANÉ, B. (1981). All alone in front of all those people: Stage fright as a function of number and type of coperformers and audience. JOURNAL OF PERSONALITY AND SOCIAL PSYCHOLOGY, 40, 73–85. **733**

JACOBS, W. J., & NADEL, W. (1985). Stress-induced recovery of fears and phobias. PSYCHOLOGICAL REVIEW, 92, 512–531. **250**

JACOBSON, A., & KALES, A. (1967). Somnambulism: All-night EEG and related studies. In S. S. Kety, E. V. Evarts, & H. L. Williams (Eds.), SLEEP AND ALTERED STATES OF CONSCIOUSNESS. Baltimore: Williams & Wilkins. **210**

JACOBSON, A. L., FRIED, C., & HOROWITZ, S. D. (1967). Classical conditioning, pseudoconditioning, or sensitization in the planarian. JOURNAL OF COMPARATIVE AND PHYSIOLOGICAL PSYCHOLOGY, 64, 73–79. **250**

JACOBY, L. L., & DALLAS, M. (1981). On the relationship between biographical memory and perceptual learning. JOURNAL OF EXPERIMENTAL PSYCHOLOGY: GENERAL, 110, 306–340. **306**

JAHN, R. G., & DUNNE, B. J. (1987). MARGINS OF REALITY. San Diego: Harcourt Brace Jovanovich. **241**

JAMES, W. (1884). What is an emotion? MIND, 9, 188–205. **404**

JANET, P. (1889). L'AUTOMISMEPSYCHOLOGIQUE. Paris: Felix Alcan. **199**

JANICAK, P. C., DAVIS, J. M., GIBBONS, R. D., ERICKSEN, S., CHANG, S., & GALLAGHER, P. (1985). Efficacy of ECT: A meta-analysis. AMERICAN JOURNAL OF PSYCHIATRY, 142(3), 297–302. **674**

JANOWITZ, H. D., & GROSSMAN, M. I. (1949). Some factors affecting the food intake of normal dogs and dogs' esophagostomy and gastric fistula. AMERICAN JOURNAL OF PHYSIOLOGY, 159, 143–148. **367**

JASMOS, T. M., & HAKMILLER, K. L. (1975). Some effects of lesion level, and emotional cues on affective expression in

JASMOS, T. M. (*continued*)
spinal cord patients. PSYCHOLOGICAL RE-PORTS, 37, 859–870. **404**

JEMMOTT, J. B., III, BORYSENKO, M., MCCLELLAND, D. C., CHAPMAN, R., MEYER, D., & BENSON, H. (1985). Academic stress, power motivation, and decrease in salivary secretory immunoglobulin: A secretion rate. LANCET, 1, 1400–1402. **584**

JENKINS, H. M., & MOORE, B. R. (1973). The form of the autoshaped response with food or water reinforcers. JOURNAL OF THE EXPERIMENTAL ANALYSIS OF BEHAVIOR, 20, 163–181. **261**

JENNINGS, D., AMABILE, T. M., & ROSS, L. (1982). Informal covariation assessment: Data-based versus theory-based judgments. In A. Tversky, D. Kahneman, & P. Slovic (Eds.), JUDGMENT UNDER UNCERTAINTY: HEURISTICS AND BIASES. New York: Cambridge University Press. **277**

JENSEN, A. R. (1980). BIAS IN MENTAL TESTING. New York: Free Press. **467, 468**

JENSEN, A. R. (1985). The nature of the black–white difference on various psychometric tests: Spearman's hypothesis. THE BEHAVIORAL AND BRAIN SCIENCES, 8, 193–263. **468**

JOHN, R. S., MEDNICK, S. A., & SCHULSINGER, F. (1982). Teacher reports as a predictor of schizophrenia and borderline schizophrenia: A Bayesian decision analysis. JOURNAL OF ABNORMAL PSYCHOLOGY, 91, 399–413. **627**

JOHNSON, E. J., & TVERSKY, A. (1983). Affect, generalization, and the perception of risk. JOURNAL OF PERSONALITY AND SOCIAL PSYCHOLOGY, 45, 20–31. **422**

JOHNSON, R. D., & DOWNING, L. L. (1979). Deindividuation and valence of cues: Effects on prosocial and antisocial behavior. JOURNAL OF PERSONALITY AND SOCIAL PSYCHOLOGY, 37, 1532–1538. **729**

JOHNSON, R. N. (1972). AGGRESSION IN MAN AND ANIMALS. Philadelphia: Saunders. **433**

JOHNSON-LAIRD, P. N. (1983). MENTAL MODELS: TOWARD A COGNITIVE SCIENCE OF LANGUAGE, INFERENCE, AND CONSCIOUSNESS. Cambridge, MA: Harvard University Press. **330**

JOHNSON-LAIRD, P. N. (1985). The deductive reasoning ability. In R. J. Sternberg (Ed.), HUMAN ABILITIES: AN INFORMATION-PROCESSING APPROACH. New York: Freeman. **351**

JOHNSON-LAIRD, P. N. (1988). THE COMPUTER AND THE MIND: AN INTRODUCTION TO COGNITIVE SCIENCE. Cambridge, MA: Harvard University Press. **193**

JOHNSTON, L. D., O'MALLEY, P. M., & BACHMAN, J. G. (1989). ILLICIT DRUG USE, SMOKING, AND DRINKING BY AMERICA'S HIGH SCHOOL STUDENTS, COLLEGE STUDENTS, AND YOUNG ADULTS, 1975–1987. Rockville, MD: National Institute on Drug Abuse. **212, 213, 215, 221**

JONES, E. E., & HARRIS, V. A. (1967). The attribution of attitudes. JOURNAL OF EXPERIMENTAL SOCIAL PSYCHOLOGY, 3, 1–24. **696**

JONES, E. E., ROCK, L., SHAVER, K. G., GOETHALS, G. R., & WARD, L. M. (1968). Pattern of performance and ability attribution: An unexpected primacy effect. JOURNAL OF PERSONALITY AND SOCIAL PSYCHOLOGY, 9, 317–340. **687**

JONES, H. C., & LOVINGER, P. W. (1985). THE MARIJUANA QUESTION AND SCIENCE'S SEARCH FOR AN ANSWER. New York: Dodd, Mead. **223**

JONES, L. V. (1984). White–black achievement differences: The narrowing gap. AMERICAN PSYCHOLOGIST, 39, 1207–1213. **454, 457, 469**

JONES, R. A., & BREHM, J. W. (1970). Persuasiveness of one- and two-sided communications as a function of awareness that there are two sides. JOURNAL OF EXPERIMENTAL SOCIAL PSYCHOLOGY, 6, 47–56. **749**

JUDD, D. B., & KELLY, K. L. (1965). The ISCC-NBS method of designating colors and a dictionary of color names. U.S. NATIONAL BUREAU OF STANDARDS CIRCULAR, 553(2nd ed.). **129**

JULESZ, B. (1971). FOUNDATIONS OF CYCLOPEAN PERCEPTION. Chicago: University of Chicago Press. **161**

JULIEN, R. M. (1988). DRUGS AND THE BODY. New York: Freeman. **67, 243**

JULIEN, R. M. (1988). A PRIMER OF DRUG ACTION (5th ed.). New York: Freeman. **243, 671**

JUNG, R. (1984). Sensory research in historical perspective: Some philosophical foundations of perception. In I. Darian-Smith (Ed.), HANDBOOK OF PHYSIOLOGY (Vol. 3). Bethesda, MD: American Physiological Society. **117**

JUST, M. A., & CARPENTER, P. A. (1980). A theory of reading: From eye fixations to comprehension. PSYCHOLOGICAL REVIEW, 87, 329–354. **178**

JUST, M. A., & CARPENTER, P. A. (1987). THE PSYCHOLOGY OF READING AND LANGUAGE COMPREHENSION. Boston: Allyn & Bacon, Inc. **288**

JUTAI, J. W., & HARE, R. D. (1983). Psychopathy and selective attention during performance of a complex perceptual-motor task. PSYCHOPHYSIOLOGY, 20, 140–151. **631**

K

KAGAN, J. (1979). Overview: Perspectives on human infancy. In J. D. Osofsky (Ed.), HANDBOOK OF INFANT DEVELOPMENT. New York: Wiley-Interscience. **71, 87**

KAGAN, J. (1989). Temperamental contributions to social behavior. AMERICAN PSYCHOLOGIST, 44, 668–674. **504**

KAGAN, J., KEARSLEY, R., & ZELAZO, P. R. (1978). INFANCY: ITS PLACE IN HUMAN DEVELOPMENT. Cambridge, MA: Harvard University Press. **94**

KAGAN, J., & KLEIN, R. E. (1973). Cross-cultural perspectives on early development. AMERICAN PSYCHOLOGIST, 28, 947–961. **80**

KAGAN, N., & MOSS, H. A. (1962). BIRTH TO MATURITY. New York: Wiley. **491, 501**

KAHNEMAN, D., SLOVIC, P., & TVERSKY, A. (Eds.). (1982). JUDGMENT UNDER UNCERTAINTY: HEURISTICS AND BIASES. New York: Cambridge University Press. **356**

KAIL, R. (1984). THE DEVELOPMENT OF MEMORY IN CHILDREN (2nd ed.). New York: Freeman. **113**

KAIL, R., & PELLEGRINO, J. W. (1985). HUMAN INTELLIGENCE: PERSPECTIVES AND PROSPECTS. New York: Freeman. **473**

KAMIN, L. J. (1969). Predictability, surprise, attention, and conditioning. In B. A. Campbell & R. M. Church (Eds.), PUNISHMENT AND AVERSIVE BEHAVIOR. New York: Appleton-Century-Crofts. **252**

KAMIN, L. J. (1976). Heredity, intelligence, politics, and psychology. In N. J. Block & G. Dworkin (Eds.), THE IQ CONTROVERSY. New York: Pantheon. **467, 468**

KANDEL, D. B. (1975). Stages in adolescent involvement in drug use. SCIENCE, 190, 912–914. **224**

KANDEL, D. B., DAVIES, M., KARUS, D. K., & YAMAGUCHI, K. (1986). The consequences in young adulthood of adolescent drug involvement. ARCHIVES GENERAL PSYCHIATRY, 43, 746–754. **224**

KANDEL, E. R. (1979). Small systems of neurons. In R. Thompson (Ed.), THE BRAIN. San Francisco: Freeman. **254, 255**

KAPLAN, J. (1983). THE HARDEST DRUG: HEROIN AND PUBLIC POLICY. Chicago: University of Chicago Press. **243**

KAPLAN, J. R., MANUCK, S. B., CLARKSON, T. B., LUSSO, F. M., & TAUB, D. B. (1982). Social status, environment, and atherosclerosis in cynomolgus monkeys. ARTERIOSCLEROSIS, 2, 359–368. **583**

KAPLAN, R. M., & SACCUZZO, D. P. (1989). PSYCHOLOGICAL TESTING: PRINCIPLES AND ISSUES. Pacific Grove, CA: Brooks/Cole. **473**

KARASEK, R., BAKER, D., MARXER, F., AHLBOM, A., & THEORELL, T. (1981). Job decision latitude, job demands, and cardiovascular disease: A prospective study of Swedish men. AMERICAN

JOURNAL OF PUBLIC HEALTH, 71, 694–705. **582**

KARASEK, R. A., THEORELL, T. G., SCHWARTZ, J., PIEPER, C., & ALFREDSSON, L. (1982). Job, psychological factors and coronary heart disease: Swedish prospective findings and U.S. prevalence findings using a new occupational inference method. ADVANCES IN CARDIOLOGY, 29, 62–67. **582**

KATZ, E., & FELDMAN, J. J. (1962). The debates in the light of research: A survey of surveys. In S. Kraus (Ed.), THE GREAT DEBATES. Bloomington: Indiana University Press. **753**

KATZ, R., & WYKES, T. (1985). The psychological difference between temporally predictable and unpredictable stressful events: Evidence for information control theories. JOURNAL OF PERSONALITY AND SOCIAL PSYCHOLOGY, 48, 781–790. **571**

KAZDIN, A. E. (1982). Symptom substitution, generalization, and response covariation: Implications for psychotherapy outcome. PSYCHOLOGICAL BULLETIN, 91, 349–365. **649**

KEEN, E. (1982). A PRIMER IN PHENOMENOLOGICAL PSYCHOLOGY. New York: Holt, Rinehart & Winston. **551**

KEESEY, R. E., & POWLEY, T. L. (1975). Hypothalamic regulation of body weight. AMERICAN SCIENTIST, 63, 558–565. **369**

KEIL, F. C., & BATTERMAN, N. A. (1984). Characteristic-to-defining shift in the development of word meaning. JOURNAL OF VERBAL LEARNING AND VERBAL BEHAVIOR, 23, 221–236. **325**

KELLEY, H. H. (1967). Attribution theory in social psychology. In D. Levine (Ed.), NEBRASKA SYMPOSIUM ON MOTIVATION (Vol. 15). Lincoln: University of Nebraska Press. **695**

KELLEY, H. H. (1973). The processes of causal attribution. AMERICAN PSYCHOLOGIST, 28, 107–128. **695**

KELLEY, H. H., BERSCHEID, E., & collaborators (Eds.). (1983). CLOSE RELATIONSHIPS. New York: Freeman. **719, 721**

KELLEY, H. H., & WOODRUFF, C. L. (1956). Members' reactions to apparent group approval of a counternorm communication. JOURNAL OF ABNORMAL AND SOCIAL PSYCHOLOGY, 52, 67–74. **757**

KELLEY, S., JR., & MIRER, T. W. (1974). The simple act of voting. AMERICAN POLITICAL SCIENCE REVIEW, 68, 572–591. **706**

KELLY, G. A. (1955). THE PSYCHOLOGY OF PERSONAL CONSTRUCTS. New York: Norton. **527**

KELMAN, M. C. (1961). Processes of opinion change. PUBLIC OPINION QUARTERLY, 25, 57–78. **723**

KEMLER-NELSON, D. G. (1984). The effect of intention on what concepts are acquired. JOURNAL OF VERBAL LEARNING AND VERBAL BEHAVIOR, 23, 734–759. **325**

KENNEDY, J. L., GIUFFRA, L. A., & collaborators (1988). Evidence against linkage of schizophrenia to markers on chromosome 5 in northern Swedish pedigree. NATURE, 336, 167–170. **623**

KENRICK, D. T., & GUTIERRES, S. E. (1980). Contrast effects and judgments of physical attractiveness: When beauty becomes a social problem. JOURNAL OF PERSONALITY AND SOCIAL PSYCHOLOGY, 38, 131–140. **712**

KENSHALO, D. R., NAFE, J. P., & BROOKS, B. (1961). Variations in thermal sensitivity. SCIENCE, 134, 104–105. **151**

KEPHART, W. M. (1967). Some correlates of romantic love. JOURNAL OF MARRIAGE AND THE FAMILY, 29, 470–474. **717**

KEPPEL, G., & SAUFLEY, W. H., JR. (1980). INTRODUCTION TO DESIGN AND ANALYSIS. San Francisco: Freeman. **786**

KERNIS, M. H., & WHEELER, L. (1981). Beautiful friends and ugly strangers: Radiation and contrast effects in perception of same-sex pairs. JOURNAL OF PERSONALITY AND SOCIAL PSYCHOLOGY, 7, 617–620. **712**

KIECOLT-GLASER, J. K., FISHER, B. S., OGROCKI, P., STOUT, J. C., SPEICHER, C. E., & GLASER, R. (1987). Marital quality, marital disruption, and immune function. PSYCHOSOMATIC MEDICINE, 49, 13–33. **585**

KIECOLT-GLASER, J. K., KENNEDY, S., MALKOFF, S., FISHER, L., SPEICHER, C. E., & GLASER, R. (1988). Marital discord and immunity in males. PSYCHOSOMATIC MEDICINE, 50, 213–229. **585, 587**

KIECOLT-GLASER, J. K., RICKER, D., GEORGE, J., MESSICK, G., SPEICHER, C. E., GARNER, W., & GLASER, R. (1984). Urinary cortisol levels, cellular immunocompetence, and loneliness in psychiatric inpatients. PSYCHOSOMATIC MEDICINE, 46, 15–23. **587**

KIESLER, C. A. (1982). Mental hospitals and alternative care: Noninstitutionalization as potential policy for mental patients. AMERICAN PSYCHOLOGIST, 34, 349–360. **641**

KIHLSTROM, J. F. (1984). Conscious, subconscious, unconscious: A cognitive view. In K. S. Bowers & D. Meichenbaum (Eds.), THE UNCONSCIOUS: RECONSIDERED. New York: Wiley. **196**

KIHLSTROM, J. F. (1985). Hypnosis. ANNUAL REVIEW OF PSYCHOLOGY, 36, 385–418. **228, 229, 232**

KIHLSTROM, J. F. (1987). The cognitive unconscious. SCIENCE, 237, 1445–1452. **197, 198, 231, 234**

KIMBLE, G. A., & PERLMUTER, L. C. (1970). The problem of volition. PSYCHOLOGICAL REVIEW, 77, 361–384. **257**

KIMMEL, D. C., & WEINER, I. B. (1985). ADOLESCENCE: A DEVELOPMENTAL TRANSITION. Hillsdale, NJ: Erlbaum. **113**

KINDER, D. R., & SEARS, D. O. (1985). Public opinion and political action. In G. Lindzey & E. Aronson (Eds.), THE HANDBOOK OF SOCIAL PSYCHOLOGY (3rd ed.). New York: Random House. **709**

KINSEY, A. C., POMEROY, W. B., & MARTIN, C. E. (1948). SEXUAL BEHAVIOR IN THE HUMAN MALE. Philadelphia: Saunders. **22, 383**

KINSEY, A. C., POMEROY, W. B., MARTIN, C. E., & GEBHARD, P. H. (1953). SEXUAL BEHAVIOR IN THE HUMAN FEMALE. Philadelphia: Saunders. **22, 383**

KINTSCH, W., & BUSCHKE, H. (1969). Homophones and synonyms in short-term memory. JOURNAL OF EXPERIMENTAL PSYCHOLOGY, 80, 403–407. **291**

KLATZKY, R. L. (1980). HUMAN MEMORY: STRUCTURES AND PROCESSES (2nd ed.). San Francisco: Freeman. **319**

KLATZKY, R. L., LEDERMAN, S. J., & METZGER, V. A. (1985). Identifying objects by touch: An expert system. PERCEPTION AND PSYCHOPHYSICS, 37, 299–302. **150**

KLEINHESSELINK, R. R., & EDWARDS, R. W. (1975). Seeking and avoiding belief-discrepant information as a function of its perceived refutability. JOURNAL OF PERSONALITY AND SOCIAL PSYCHOLOGY, 31, 787–790. **754**

KLEINMUNTZ, B. (1974). ESSENTIALS OF ABNORMAL PSYCHOLOGY. New York: Harper & Row. **600**

KLINE, P. (1972). FACT AND FANCY IN FREUDIAN THEORY. London: Methuen. **518**

KLINEBERG, O. (1938). Emotional expression in Chinese literature. JOURNAL OF ABNORMAL AND SOCIAL PSYCHOLOGY, 33, 517–520. **414**

KLUFT, R. P. (Ed.). (1985). CHILDHOOD ANTECEDENTS OF MULTIPLE PERSONALITY. Washington, DC: American Psychiatric Press. **243**

KNITTLE, J. L., & HIRSCH, J. (1968). Effect of early nutrition on the development of rat epididymal fat pads: Cellularity and metabolism. JOURNAL OF CLINICAL INVESTIGATION, 47, 2091. **375**

KNOX, V. J., CRUTCHHELD, L., & HILGARD, E. R. (1975). The nature of task interference in hypnotic dissociation: An investigation of hypnotic behavior. INTERNATIONAL JOURNAL OF CLINICAL AND EXPERIMENTAL HYPNOSIS, 23, 305–323. **232, 233**

KOBASA, S. C. (1979). Stressful life events, personality, and health: An in-

KOBASA, S. C. (*continued*)
quiry into hardiness. JOURNAL OF PERSON-ALITY AND SOCIAL PSYCHOLOGY, 37, 1–11. **587**

KOBASA, S. C., MADDI, S. R., & KAHN, S. (1982). Hardiness and health: A prospective study. JOURNAL OF PERSONALITY AND SOCIAL PSYCHOLOGY, 42, 168–177. **588**

KOBASIGAWA, A., ARAKAKI, K., & AWIGUNI, A. (1966). Avoidance of feminine toys by kindergarten boys: The effects of adult presence or absence, and an adult's attitudes toward sex-typing. JAPA-NESE JOURNAL OF PSYCHOLOGY, 37, 96–103. **96**

KOHLBERG, L. (1969). Stage and sequence: The cognitive-developmental approach to socialization. In D. A. Goslin (Ed.), HANDBOOK OF SOCIALIZATION THE-ORY AND RESEARCH. Chicago: Rand McNally. **97, 98, 99**

KOHLBERG, L. (1973). Implications of developmental psychology for education: Examples from moral development. EDUCA-TIONAL PSYCHOLOGIST, 10, 2–14. **99**

KOHLBERG, L. (1984). THE PSYCHOLOGY OF MORAL DEVELOPMENT: THE NATURE AND VALIDITY OF MORAL STAGES. New York: Harper & Row. **113**

KOHLBERG, L. (1984). THE PSYCHOLOGY OF MORAL DEVELOPMENT: *Vol. 1.* MORAL STAGES AND THE LIFE CYCLE; *Vol. 2.* ESSAYS ON MORAL DEVELOPMENT. New York: Harper & Row. **97**

KOHLER, W. (1925). THE MENTALITY OF APES. New York: Harcourt Brace. (Reprint ed., 1976. New York: Liveright.) **273, 279**

KOLB, B., & WHISHAW, I. Q. (1985). FUNDAMENTALS OF HUMAN NEUROPSY-CHOLOGY (2nd ed.). San Francisco: Freeman. **67**

KOLODNER, J. L. (1983). Maintaining organization in a dynamic long-term memory. COGNITIVE SCIENCE, 7, 243–280. **317**

KOOB, G. F., & BLOOM, F. E. (1988). Cellular and molecular mechanisms of drug dependence. SCIENCE, 242, 715–723. **218**

KORNER, A. F. (1973). Individual differences at birth: Implications for early experience and later development. In J. C. Westman (Ed.), INDIVIDUAL DIFFERENCES IN CHILDREN. New York: Wiley. **77**

KORNITZER, M., MAGOTTEAU, V., & collaborators. (1982). Angiographic findings and the Type A pattern assessed by means of the Bortner scale. JOURNAL OF BEHAVIORAL MEDICINE, 5, 313–320. **580**

KOSA, J., & ZOLA, I. K. (Eds.). (1975). POVERTY AND HEALTH: A SOCIOLOGICAL ANALYSIS. Cambridge, MA: Harvard University Press. **625**

KOSAMBI, D. D. (1967). Living prehistory in India. SCIENTIFIC AMERICAN, 215, 105. **152**

KOSSLYN, S. M. (1980). IMAGE AND MIND. Cambridge, MA: Harvard University Press. **348, 349, 356**

KOSSLYN, S. M. (1983). GHOSTS IN THE MIND'S MACHINE. New York: Norton. **347, 356**

KOSSLYN, S. M. (1988). Aspects of a cognitive neuroscience of mental imagery. SCIENCE, 240, 1621–1626. **56**

KOSSLYN, S. M., BALL, T. M., & REISER, B. J. (1978). Visual images preserve metric spatial information: Evidence from studies of image scanning. JOURNAL OF EXPERIMENTAL PSYCHOLOGY: HUMAN PERCEPTION AND PERFORMANCE, 4, 47–60. **349**

KOTELCHUCK, M. (1976). The infant's relationship to the father: Experimental evidence. In M. Lamb (Ed.), THE ROLE OF THE FATHER IN CHILD DEVELOPMENT. New York: Wiley. **92**

KOULACK, D., & GOODENOUGH, D. R. (1976). Dream recall and dream recall failure: An arousal-retrieval model. PSYCHOLOGICAL BULLETIN, 83, 975–984. **209**

KREITMAN, N. (1977). PARASUICIDE. London: Wiley. **611**

KRIPKE, D. F. (1985). Biological rhythms. In G. L. Klerman, M. M. Weissman, P. S. Applebaum, & L. H. Roth (Eds.), PSYCHI-ATRY (Vol. 3). Philadelphia: Lippincott. **202**

KRIPKE, D. F., & GILLIN, J. C. (1985). Sleep disorders. In G. L. Klerman, M. M. Weissman, P. S. Applebaum, & L. N. Roth (Eds.), PSYCHIATRY (Vol. 3). Philadelphia: Lippincott. **206**

KUBIS, J. F. (1962). Cited in B. M. Smith, The polygraph. In R. C. Allainson (Ed.), CONTEMPORARY PSYCHOLOGY. San Francisco: Freeman. **406**

KUHN, D., NASH, S. C., & BRUCKEN, L. (1978). Sex role concepts of two- and three-year-olds. CHILD DEVELOPMENT, 49, 445–451. **96**

KUHN, T. S. (1970). THE STRUCTURE OF SCIENTIFIC REVOLUTIONS (2nd ed.). Chicago: University of Chicago Press. **709**

KUIPER, N. A., & MACDONALD, M. R. (1982). Self- and other perception in mild depressives. SOCIAL COGNITION, 1, 233–239. **616**

KUIPER, N. A., MACDONALD, M. R., & DERRY, P. A. (1983). Parameters of a depressive self-schema. In J. Suls & A. G. Greenwald (Eds.), PSYCHOLOGICAL PER-SPECTIVES ON THE SELF (Vol. 2). Hillsdale, NJ: Erlbaum. **617**

KUIPER, N. A., OLINGER, L. J., MAC-DONALD, M. R., & SHAW, B. F. (1985). Self-schema processing of depressed and nondepressed content: The ef-fects of vulnerability on depression. SO-CIAL COGNITION, 3, 77–93. **616**

KUMAN, I. G., FEDROV, C. N., & NO-VIKOVA, L. A. (1983). Investigation of the sensitive period in the development of the human visual system. ZH. VYSHP. NERV. DEYAT (JOURNAL OF HIGHER NERVOUS AC-TIVITY), 33, 434–441. **73**

KUNST-WILSON, W. R., & ZAJONC, R. B. (1980). Affective discrimination of stimuli that cannot be recognized. SCI-ENCE, 207, 557–558. **175, 412**

KURTZ, P. (Ed.). (1985). A SKEPTIC'S HANDBOOK OF PARAPSYCHOLOGY. Buffalo: Prometheus Books. **243**

L

LADER, M. (1985). Benzodiasepines, anxiety, and catecholamines: A commentary. In A. H. Tuma & J. D. Maser (Eds.), ANX-IETY AND THE ANXIETY DISORDERS. Hillsdale, NJ: Erlbaum. **605**

LAGERSPETZ, K., VIEMERO, V., & AKADEMI, A. (1986). Television and aggressive behavior among Finnish children. In L. R. Huesmann & L. D. Eron (Eds.), TELEVISION AND THE AGGRESSIVE CHILD. New York: Erlbaum. **431**

LAIRLI, J. D. (1974). Self-attribution of emotion: The effects of expressive behavior on the quality of emotional experience. JOURNAL OF PERSONALITY AND SOCIAL PSYCHOLOGY, 29, 475–486. **416**

LAMB, M. E., & BORNSTEIN, M. H. (1987). DEVELOPMENT IN INFANCY: AN IN-TRODUCTION (2nd ed.). New York: Random House. **113**

LAMB, M. E., THOMPSON, R. A., GARDNER, W. P., CHARNOV, E. L., & ESTES, D. (1984). Security of infantile attachment as assessed in the "Strange Situation": Its study and biological interpretation. BEHAVIORAL AND BRAIN SCIENCES, 7, 127–154. **91**

LAND, E. H. (1977). The retinex theory of color vision. SCIENTIFIC AMERICAN, 237(6), 108–128. **180**

LANGER, E. J., BLANK, A., & CHANOWITZ, B. (1978). The mindlessness of ostensibly thoughtful action. JOUR-NAL OF PERSONALITY AND SOCIAL PSY-CHOLOGY, 36, 635–642. **689, 690**

LANGLOIS, J. H., & DOWNS, A. C. (1980). Mothers, fathers, and peers as socialization agents of sex-typed play behaviors in young children. CHILD DEVELOP-MENT, 51, 1237–1247. **96**

LAPIERE, R. (1934). Attitudes versus actions. SOCIAL FORCES, 13, 230–237. **706**

LARKIN, J. H., MCDERMOTT, J., SI-MON, D. P., & SIMON, H. A. (1980). Expert and novice performance in solving physics problems. SCIENCE, *208*, 1335–1342. **353**

LATANÉ, B. (1981). The psychology of social impact. AMERICAN PSYCHOLOGIST, *36*, 343–356. **732, 733**

LATANÉ, B., & DARLEY, J. M. (1968). Group inhibition of bystander intervention in emergencies. JOURNAL OF PERSONALITY AND SOCIAL PSYCHOLOGY, *10*, 215–221. **730, 731**

LATANÉ, B., & DARLEY, J. M. (1970). THE UNRESPONSIVE BYSTANDER: WHY DOESN'T HE HELP? New York: Appleton-Century-Crofts. **729, 761**

LATANÉ, B., & HARKINS, S. G. (1976). Crossmodality matches suggest anticipated stage fright, a multiplicative power function of audience size and status. PERCEPTION AND PSYCHOPHYSICS, *20*, 482–488. **732**

LATANÉ, B., & RODIN, J. (1969). A lady in distress: Inhibiting effects of friends and strangers on bystander intervention. JOURNAL OF EXPERIMENTAL AND SOCIAL PSYCHOLOGY, *5*, 189–202. **731**

LATANÉ, B., WILLIAMS, K. D., & HARKINS, S. G. (1979). Many hands make light work: The causes and consequences of social loafing. JOURNAL OF PERSONALITY AND SOCIAL PSYCHOLOGY, *37*, 822–832. **733**

LAUDENSLAGER, M. L., RYAN, S. M., DRUGAN, R. C., HYSON, R. L., & MAIER, S. F. (1983). Coping and immunosuppression: Inescapable but not escapable shock suppresses lymphocyte proliferation. SCIENCE, *221*, 568–570. **586**

LAUER, J., & LAUER, R. (1985). Marriages made to last. PSYCHOLOGY TODAY, *19*(6), 22–26. **110**

LAUGHLIN, H. P. (1967). THE NEUROSES. Washington, DC: Butterworths. **601**

LAURENCE, J. R. (1980). DUALITY AND DISSOCIATION IN HYPNOSIS. Unpublished masters thesis, Concordia University, Montreal. **233**

LAZAR, I., & DARLINGTON, R. (1982). Lasting effects of early education: A report from the Consortium for Longitudinal Studies. MONOGRAPHS OF THE SOCIETY FOR RESEARCH IN CHILD DEVELOPMENT, *47*, 2–3. **469**

LAZARUS, R. S. (1961). Group therapy of phobic disorders by systematic desensitization. JOURNAL OF ABNORMAL AND SOCIAL PSYCHOLOGY, *63*, 504–510. **540**

LAZARUS, R. S., & FOLKMAN, S. (1984). STRESS, APPRAISAL, AND COPING. New York: Springer. **556, 573, 574, 589**

LAZARUS, R. S., KANNER, A. D., & FOLKMAN, S. (1980). Emotions: A cognitive-phenomenological analysis. In R. Plutchik & H. Kellerman (Eds.), EMOTION: THEORY, RESEARCH, AND EXPERI-

ENCE (Vol. 1). New York: Academic Press. **408**

LE BON, G. (1895). THE CROWD. London: Ernest Benn. **727, 761**

LEE, V. E., BROOKS-GUNN, J., & SCHNUR, E. (1988). Does Head Start work? A 1-year follow-up comparison of disadvantaged children attending Head Start, no preschool, and other preschool programs. DEVELOPMENTAL PSYCHOLOGY, *24*, 210–222. **469**

LENNEBERG, E. H. (1967). BIOLOGICAL FOUNDATIONS OF LANGUAGE. New York: Wiley. **343**

LERNER, R., KARSON, M., MEISELS, M., & KNAPP, J. R. (1975b). Actual and perceived attitudes of late adolescents: The phenomenon of the generation gaps. JOURNAL OF GENETIC PSYCHOLOGY, *126*, 197–207. **103**

LERNER, R. M., & KARABENICK, S. A. (1974). Physical attractiveness, body attitudes, and self-concept in late adolescents. JOURNAL OF YOUTH AND ADOLESCENCE, *3*, 307–316. **694**

LEVAV, I., FRIEDLANDER, Y., KARK, J. D., & PERITZ, E. (1988). An epidemiologic study of mortality among bereaved parents. THE NEW ENGLAND JOURNAL OF MEDICINE, *319*, 457–461. **572**

LEVINE, R. A. (1980). Anthropology and child development. NEW DIRECTIONS FOR CHILD DEVELOPMENT, *8*, 71–86. **485**

LEVINE, S. (1960). Stimulation in infancy. SCIENTIFIC AMERICAN, *202*, 80–86. **559**

LEVINGER, G., SENN, D. J., & JORGENSEN, B. W. (1970). Progress toward permanence in courtship: A test of the Kerckhoff-Davis hypotheses. SOCIOMETRY, *33*, 427–443. **715**

LEVINSON, D. J., DARROW, C., KLEIN, E. B., LEVINSON, M. H., & MCKEE, B. (1978). THE SEASONS OF A MAN'S LIFE. New York: Knopf. **110**

LEVY, J. (1985). Right brain, left brain: Facts and fiction. PSYCHOLOGY TODAY, *19*(5), 38–44. **56**

LEWINSOHN, P. M., ANTONUCCIO, D. O., STEINMETZ, J. L., & TERI, L. (1984). THE COPING WITH DEPRESSION COURSE: PSYCHOEDUCATIONAL INTERVENTION FOR UNIPOLAR DEPRESSION. Eugene, OR: Castalia. **656**

LEWINSOHN, P. M., FENN, D., & FRANKLIN, J. (1982). THE RELATIONSHIP OF AGE OF ONSET TO DURATION OF EPISODE IN UNIPOLAR DEPRESSION. Unpublished manuscript, University of Oregon. **608**

LEWINSOHN, P. M., HOBERMAN, H., TERI, L., HAUTZINER, M. (1985). An integrative theory of depression. In S. Reiss & R. Bootsin (Eds.), THEORETICAL ISSUES IN BEHAVIOR THERAPY. New York: Academic Press. **512, 611, 612**

LEWINSOHN, P. M., MISCHEL, W., CHAPLIN, W., & BARTON, R. (1980). Social competence and depression: The role of illusory self-perceptions. JOURNAL OF ABNORMAL PSYCHOLOGY, *89*, 203–212. **512, 611, 616**

LEWONTIN, R. C., ROSE, S., & KAMIN, L. J. (1984). NOT IN OUR GENES: BIOLOGY, IDEOLOGY, AND HUMAN NATURE. New York: Pantheon. **473**

LEY, R. G., & BRYDEN, M. P. (1982). A dissociation of right and left hemispheric effects for recognizing emotional tone and verbal content. BRAIN AND COGNITION, *1*, 3–9. **416**

LIBERMAN, A. M., COOPER, F., SHANKWEILER, D., & STUDERT-KENNEDY, M. (1967). Perception of the speech code. PSYCHOLOGICAL REVIEW, *74*, 431–459. **333**

LICKEY, M. E., & GORDON, B. (1983). DRUGS FOR MENTAL ILLNESS. New York: Freeman. **679**

LIEBERMAN, L. R., & DUNLAP, J. T. (1979). O'Leary and Borkovec's conceptualization of placebo: The placebo paradox. AMERICAN PSYCHOLOGIST, *34*, 553–554. **668**

LIEM, J. H. (1974). Effects of verbal communications of parents and children: A comparison of normal and schizophrenic families. JOURNAL OF CONSULTING AND CLINICAL PSYCHOLOGY, *42*, 438–450. **626**

LINDZEY, G., & ARONSON, E. (Eds.). (1985). THE HANDBOOK OF SOCIAL PSYCHOLOGY (3rd ed.). Hillsdale, NJ: Erlbaum. **721, 761**

LINN, M. C., & HYDE, J. S. (1989, February). GENDER, MATHEMATICS, AND SCIENCE. Paper presented at the annual meeting of the American Association for the Advancement of Science, San Francisco. **455**

LINN, R. L. (1982). Ability testing: Individual differences, prediction, and differential prediction. In A. Wigdor & W. Gardner (Eds.), ABILITY TESTING: USES, CONSEQUENCES, AND CONTROVERSIES. Washington, DC: National Academy Press. **454, 457**

LIPPERT, W. W., & SENTER, R. J. (1966). Electrodermal responses in the sociopath. PSYCHONOMIC SCIENCE, *4*, 25–26. **631**

LIVINGSTONE, M., & HUBEL, D. (1988). Segregation of form, color, movement, and depth: Anatomy, physiology, and perception. SCIENCE, *240*, 740–750. **157, 158**

LOEB, G. (1985). The functional replacement of the ear. SCIENTIFIC AMERICAN, *252*(2), 104–111. **144, 145**

LOEHLIN, J. C., LINDZEY, G., & SPUHLER, J. N. (1975). RACE DIFFERENCES IN INTELLIGENCE. San Francisco: Freeman. **468**

LOFTUS, E. F., & LOFTUS, G. R. (1980). On the permanence of stored information in the human brain. AMERICAN PSYCHOLOGIST, 35, 409–420. **296**

LOFTUS, E. F., SCHOOLER, J. W., & WAGENAAR, W. A. (1985). The fate of memory: Comment on McCloskey and Zaragoza. JOURNAL OF EXPERIMENTAL PSYCHOLOGY: GENERAL, 114(3), 375–380. **313**

LOFTUS, G. R., & LOFTUS, E. F. (1975). HUMAN MEMOS: THE PROCESSING OF INFORMATION. New York: Halsted Press. **313**

LOFTUS, G. R., & LOFTUS, E. F. (1982). ESSENCE OF STATISTICS. Monterey, CA: Brooks/Cole. **786**

LOGUE, A. W. (1986). THE PSYCHOLOGY OF EATING AND DRINKING. New York: Freeman. **399**

LOOMIS, A. L., HARVEY, E. N., & HOBART, G. A. (1937). Cerebral states during sleep as studied by human potentials. JOURNAL OF EXPERIMENTAL PSYCHOLOGY, 21, 127–144. **202**

LOOMIS, J. M., & LEDERMAN, S. J. (1986). Tactual perception. In K. Boff, L. Kaufman, & J. Thomas (Eds.), HANDBOOK OF PERCEPTION AND HUMAN PERFORMANCE (Vol. 1). New York: Wiley. **150**

LORD, C. G., ROSS, L., & LEPPER, M. R. (1979). Biased assimilation and attitude polarization: The effects of prior theories on subsequently considered evidence. JOURNAL OF PERSONALITY AND SOCIAL PSYCHOLOGY, 37, 2098–2109. **690**

LORENZ, K. (1966). ON AGGRESSION. New York: Harcourt Brace Jovanovich. **426**

LORENZ, K. (1981). THE FOUNDATIONS OF ETHOLOGY. New York: Springer-Verlag. **399, 426**

LOVAAS, O. I., FREITAG, S., GOLD, V. J., & KASSORLA, I. C. (1965). Recording apparatus for observation of behaviors of children in free-play settings. JOURNAL OF EXPERIMENTAL CHILD PSYCHOLOGY, 2, 108–120. **540**

LOVE, R. E., & GREENWALD, A. C. (1978). Cognitive responses to persuasion as mediators of opinion change. JOURNAL OF SOCIAL PSYCHOLOGY, 104, 231–241. **748**

LOWINGER, P., & DOBIE, S. (1969). What makes the placebo work? A study of placebo response rate. ARCHIVES OF GENERAL PSYCHIATRY, 20, 84–88. **668**

LUBORSKY, L. L., MCCLELLAN, A. T., WOODY, G. E., O'BRIEN, E. P., & AUERBACH, A. (1985). Therapist success and its determinants. ARCHIVES OF GENERAL PSYCHIATRY, 42, 602–611. **667**

LUCHINS, A. (1957). Primacy-recency in impression formation. In C. I. Hovland (Ed.), THE ORDER OF PRESENTATION IN PERSUASION. New Haven: Yale University Press. **686, 687**

LUDWIG, A. M., BRANDSMA, J. M., WILBUR, C. B., BENDFELDT, F., & JAMESON, D. H. (1972). The objective study of a multiple personality. ARCHIVES OF GENERAL PSYCHIATRY, 26, 298–310. **200**

LUMSDAINE, A. A., & JANIS, I. L. (1953). Resistance to counter-propaganda produced by one-sided and two-sided propaganda presentations. PUBLIC OPINION QUARTERLY, 17, 311–318. **749**

LUNDIN, R. W. (1985). THEORIES AND SYSTEMS OF PSYCHOLOGY (3rd ed.). Lexington, MA: Heath. **29**

LURIA, Z., & RUBIN, J. Z. (1974). The eye of the beholder: Parents' views on sex of newborns. AMERICAN JOURNAL OF ORTHOPSYCHIATRY, 44, 512–519. **93**

LYCAN, W. G. (1987). CONSCIOUSNESS. Cambridge, MA: MIT Press. **243**

LYKKEN, D. T. (1957). A study of anxiety in the sociopathic personality. JOURNAL OF ABNORMAL AND SOCIAL PSYCHOLOGY, 55, 6–10. **631**

LYKKEN, D. T. (1980). A TREMOR IN THE BLOOD: USES AND ABUSES OF THE LIE DETECTOR. New York: McGraw-Hill. **407, 433**

LYKKEN, D. T. (1982). Research with twins: The concept of emergencies. THE SOCIETY FOR PSYCHOPHYSIOLOGICAL RESEARCH, 19, 361–373. **476**

LYKKEN, D. T. (1984). Polygraphic interrogation. NATURE, 307, 681–684. **406**

LYONS-RUTH, K., CONNELL, D. B., ZOLL, D., & STAHL, J. (1987). Infants at social risk: Relations among infant maltreatment, maternal behavior, and infant attachment behavior. DEVELOPMENTAL PSYCHOLOGY, 23, 223–232. **90**

M

MAASS, A., & CLARK, R. D., III. (1983). Internalization versus compliance: Differential processes underlying minority influence and conformity. EUROPEAN JOURNAL OF SOCIAL PSYCHOLOGY, 13, 45–55. **747**

MAASS, A., & CLARK, R. D., III. (1984). Hidden impact of minorities: Fifteen years of minority influence research. PSYCHOLOGICAL BULLETIN, 95, 428–450. **746**

MACCOBY, E. E., & MARTIN, J. A. (1983). Socialization in the context of the family: Parent–child interaction. In P. H. Mussen (Ed.), HANDBOOK OF CHILD PSYCHOLOGY: VOL. 4. SOCIALIZATION, PERSONALITY, AND SOCIAL DEVELOPMENT. New York: Wiley. **106, 478, 479**

MACCOBY, N., FARQUHAR, J. W., WOOD, P. D., & ALEXANDER, J. (1977). Reducing the risk of cardiovascular disease: Effects of a community-based campaign on knowledge and behavior. JOURNAL OF COMMUNITY HEALTH, 3, 100–114. **755**

MACKENZIE, B. (1984). Explaining race differences in IQ: The logic, the methodology, and the evidence. AMERICAN PSYCHOLOGIST, 39, 1214–1233. **468**

MACKINTOSH, N. J. (1983). CONDITIONING AND ASSOCIATIVE LEARNING. New York: Oxford University Press. **279**

MADDI, S., & COSTA, P. (1972). HUMANISM IN PERSONOLOGY: ALLPORT, MASLOW, AND MURRAY. Chicago: Aldine. **551**

MAHER, B. A. (1966). PRINCIPLES OF PSYCHOTHERAPY: AN EXPERIMENTAL APPROACH. New York: McGraw-Hill. **618, 619, 630, 632**

MAIER, S. F., & SELIGMAN, M. E. P. (1976). Learned helplessness: Theory and evidence. JOURNAL OF EXPERIMENTAL PSYCHOLOGY: GENERAL, 105, 3–46. **261**

MAIN, M., & CASSIDY, J. (1988). Categories of response to reunion with parents at age 6: Predictable from infant attachment classifications and stable over a 1-month period. DEVELOPMENTAL PSYCHOLOGY, 24, 415–426. **91**

MALINOWSKI, B. (1927). SEX AND REPRESSION IN SAVAGE SOCIETY. London: Humanities Press. **517**

MALOF, M., & LOTT, A. J. (1962). Ethnocentrism and the acceptance of Negro support in a group pressure situation. JOURNAL OF ABNORMAL AND SOCIAL PSYCHOLOGY, 65, 254–258. **736**

MALONEY, L. T., & WANDELL, B. A. (1986). Color constancy: A method for recovering surface spectral reflectance. JOURNAL OF THE OPTICAL SOCIETY OF AMERICA, 3, 29–33. **180**

MALT, B. C. (1985). The role of discourse structure in understanding anaphora. JOURNAL OF MEMORY AND LANGUAGE, 24, 271–289. **288**

MANDLER, G. (1982). MIND AND EMOTION. New York: Norton. **433**

MANUCK, S. B., KAPLAN, J. R., & MATTHEWS, K. A. (1986). Behavioral antecedents of coronary heart disease and atherosclerosis. ARTERIOSCLEROSIS, 6, 1–14. **582, 583**

MANUCK, S. B., & KRANTZ, D. S. (1986). Psychophysiologic reactivity in coronary heart disease and essential hypertension. In K. A. Matthews, S. M. Weiss, T. Detre, T. M. Dembroski, B. Falkner, S. B. Manuck, & R. B. Williams, Jr. (Eds.), HANDBOOK OF STRESS, REACTIVITY, AND CARDIOVASCULAR DISEASE. New York: Wiley. **581**

MARBLY, N. (1987). But you weren't there. In T. Williams (Ed.), POST-TRAUMATIC STRESS DISORDERS: A HANDBOOK FOR CLI-

NICIANS. Cincinnati, OH: Disabled American Veterans. **567**

MARCEL, A. J. (1983). Conscious and unconscious perception: An approach to the relations between phenomenal experience and perceptual processes. COGNITIVE PSYCHOLOGY, 15, 238–300. **173**

MARCUS, J., HANS, S. L., NAGLER, S., AUERBACK, J. G., MIRSKY, A. F., & AUBREY, A. (1987). A review of the NIMH Israeli Kibbutz–city study. SCHIZOPHRENIA BULLETIN, 13, 425–438. **627**

MARSDEN, G. (1971). Content analysis studies of psychotherapy: 1954 through 1968. In A. E. Bergin & S. L. Garfield (Eds.), HANDBOOK OF PSYCHOTHERAPY AND BEHAVIOR CHANGE. New York: Wiley. **541**

MARKHAM, M. (1981). Suicide without depression. PSYCHIATRIC NEWS, 8, 24–25. **611**

MARKMAN, E. (1987). How children constrain the possible meanings of words. In U. Neisser (Ed.), CONCEPTS AND CONCEPTUAL DEVELOPMENT: ECOLOGICAL AND INTELLECTUAL FACTORS IN CATEGORIZATION. New York: Cambridge University Press. **338**

MARKS, D., & KAMMANN, R. (1980). THE PSYCHOLOGY OF THE PSYCHIC. Buffalo, NY: Prometheus Books. **242, 243**

MARKUS, H. (1977). Self-schemata and processing information about the self. JOURNAL OF PERSONALITY AND SOCIAL PSYCHOLOGY, 35, 63–78. **696**

MARKUS, H., CRANE, M., BERNSTEIN, S., & SILADI, M. (1982). Self-schemas and gender. JOURNAL OF PERSONALITY AND SOCIAL PSYCHOLOGY, 42, 38–50. **697**

MARKUS, H., & NURIUS, P. (1986). Possible selves. AMERICAN PSYCHOLOGIST, 41, 954–969. **617**

MARKUS, H., & SENTIS, K. (1982). The self in social information processing. In J. Suls (Ed.), PSYCHOLOGICAL PERSPECTIVES ON THE SELF (Vol. 1). Hillsdale, NJ: Erlbaum. **697**

MARKUS, H., & SMITH, J. (1981). The influence of self-schemas on the perception of others. In N. Cantor & J. Kihlstrom (Eds.), PERSONALITY, COGNITION, AND SOCIAL INTERACTION. Hillsdale, NJ: Erlbaum. **697**

MARLATT, G. A., BAER, J. S., DONOVAN, D. M., & KIVLAHAN, D. R. (1988). Addictive behaviors: Etiology and treatment. In M. R. Rosenzweig & L. W. Porter (Eds.), ANNUAL REVIEW OF PSYCHOLOGY (Vol. 39). Palo Alto, CA: Annual Reviews. **225**

MARLER, P. (1970). A comparative approach to vocal learning: Song development in white-crowned sparrows. JOURNAL

OF COMPARATIVE AND PHYSIOLOGICAL PSYCHOLOGY, 7, 1–25. **271**

MARR, D. (1982). VISION. San Francisco: Freeman. **157, 165, 193**

MARR, D., & NISHIHARA, H. K. (1978). Representation and recognition of three-dimensional shapes. PROCEEDINGS OF THE ROYAL SOCIETY, LONDON, 200 (Series B), 269–294. **171**

MARRON, J. E. (1965). SPECIAL TEST PREPARATION: ITS EFFECTS ON COLLEGE BOARD SCORES AND THE RELATIONSHIP OF EFFECTED SCORES TO SUBSEQUENT COLLEGE PERFORMANCE. Office of the Director of Admissions and Registrar. West Point, NY: U.S. Military Academy. **457**

MARSHALL, G., & ZIMBARDO, P. G. (1979). Affective consequences of inadequately explained physiological arousal. JOURNAL OF PERSONALITY AND SOCIAL PSYCHOLOGY, 37, 970–988. **409**

MASLACH, C. (1979). The emotional consequences of arousal without reason. In C. E. Izard (Ed.), EMOTION IN PERSONALITY AND PSYCHOPATHOLOGY. New York: Plenum. **409**

MASLOW, A. H. (1954). MOTIVATION AND PERSONALITY. New York: Harper & Row. **525**

MASLOW, A. H. (1967). Self-actualization and beyond. In J. F. T. Bugenthal (Ed.), CHALLENGES OF HUMANISTIC PSYCHOLOGY. New York: McGraw-Hill. **526**

MASLOW, A. H. (1970). MOTIVATION AND PERSONALITY (2nd ed.). New York: Harper & Row. **526**

MASSON, J. M. (1984). THE ASSAULT ON TRUTH. New York: Farrar, Straus & Giroux. **515**

MASTERS, W. H., & JOHNSON, V. E. (1966). HUMAN SEXUAL RESPONSE. Boston: Little, Brown. **21**

MATARAZZO, J. D., & WIENS, A. W. (1977). Black Intelligence Test of Cultural Homogeneity and Wechsler Adult Intelligence Scale scores of black and white police applicants. JOURNAL OF APPLIED PSYCHOLOGY, 62, 57–63. **452**

MATAS, L., AREND, R. A., & SROUFE, L. A. (1978). Continuity of adaption in the second year: The relationship between quality of attachment and later competence. CHILD DEVELOPMENT, 49, 547–556. **91, 477**

MATHES, E. W. (1975). The effects of physical attractiveness and anxiety on heterosexual attraction over a series of five encounters. JOURNAL OF MARRIAGE AND THE FAMILY, 37, 769–773. **711**

MATTHEWS, D. F. (1972). Response patterns of single neurons in the tortoise olfactory epithelium and olfactory bulb. JOURNAL OF GENERAL PHYSIOLOGY, 60, 166–180. **147**

MATTHEWS, K. A., WEISS, S. M., DETRE, T., DEMBROSKI, T. M., FALKNER, B., MANUCK, S. B., & WILLIAMS, R. B., JR. (Eds.). (1986). HANDBOOK OF STRESS, REACTIVITY, AND CARDIOVASCULAR DISEASE. New York: Wiley. **589**

MAYER, R. E. (1983). THINKING, PROBLEM SOLVING AND COGNITION. New York: Freeman. **356**

MCALISTER, A., PERRY, C., KILLEN, J., SLINKARD, L. A., & MACCOBY, N. (1980). Pilot study of smoking, alcohol and drug abuse prevention. AMERICAN JOURNAL OF PUBLIC HEALTH, 70, 719–721. **750**

MCARTHUR, L. A. (1972). The how and what of why: Some determinants and consequences of causal attribution. JOURNAL OF PERSONALITY AND SOCIAL PSYCHOLOGY, 22, 171–193. **695**

MCBURNEY, D. H. (1978). Psychological dimensions and the perceptual analysis of taste. In E. C. Carterette & M. P. Friedman (Eds.), HANDBOOK OF PERCEPTION (Vol. 6A). New York: Academic Press. **149**

MCCALL, R. B. (1986). FUNDAMENTAL STATISTICS FOR BEHAVIORAL SCIENCES (4th ed.). San Diego: Harcourt Brace Jovanovich. **786**

MCCANN, I. L., & HOLMES, D. S. (1984). Influence of aerobic exercise on depression. JOURNAL OF PERSONALITY AND SOCIAL PSYCHOLOGY, 46, 1142–1147. **585**

MCCARTHY, R. A., & WARRINGTON, E. K. (1987a). The double dissociation of short-term memory for lists and sentences. BRAIN, 10, 1545–1563. **288**

MCCARTHY, R. A., & WARRINGTON, E. K. (1987b). Understanding: A function of short-term memory? BRAIN, 110, 1565–1578. **288**

MCCARTNEY, K., & PHILLIPS, D. (1988). Motherhood and child care. In B. Birns & D. Hay (Eds.), DIFFERENT FACES OF MOTHERHOOD. New York: Plenum. **94**

MCCLEARN, G. E., & FOCH, T. T. (1988). Behavioral genetics. In R. C. Atkinson, R. J. Herrnstein, G. Lindzey, & R. D. Luce (Eds.), STEVENS' HANDBOOK OF EXPERIMENTAL PSYCHOLOGY (Vol. 1). New York: Wiley. **64**

MCCLELLAND, J. L., & RUMELHART, D. E. (1981). An interactive model of context effects in letter perception: Pt. 1. An account of basic findings. PSYCHOLOGICAL REVIEW, 88, 375–407. **170**

MCCLELLAND, J. L., RUMELHART, D. E., & THE PDP RESEARCH GROUP. (1986). PARALLEL DISTRIBUTED PROCESSING: EXPLORATIONS IN THE MICROSTRUCTURE OF COGNITION. VOLUME 2: PSYCHOLOGICAL AND BIOLOGICAL MODELS.

MCCLELLAND, J. L. (*continued*) Cambridge, MA: Bradford Books/MIT Press. **169**

MCCLINTOCK, M. K. (1971). Menstrual synchrony and suppression. NATURE, *229*, 244–245. **146**

MCCLOSKEY, M., WIBLE, C. G., & COHEN, N. J. (1988). Is there a flashbulb-memory system? JOURNAL OF EXPERIMENTAL PSYCHOLOGY, *117*, 171–181. **300**

MCCLOSKEY, M., & ZARAGOZA, M. (1985). Misleading post-event memory impairment hypotheses. JOURNAL OF EXPERIMENTAL PSYCHOLOGY: GENERAL, *114*, 1–16. **313, 314**

MCCRAE, R. R., & COSTA, P. T., JR. (1987). Validation of the five-factor model of personality across instruments and observers. JOURNAL OF PERSONALITY AND SOCIAL PSYCHOLOGY, *52*, 81–90. **509**

MCDOUGALL, W. (1908). SOCIAL PSYCHOLOGY. New York: G. P. Putnam's Sons. **392**

MCFARLAND, D. (1985). ANIMAL BEHAVIOUR: PSYCHOBIOLOGY, ETHOLOGY AND EVOLUTION. Menlo Park, CA: Benjamin-Cummings. **399**

MCGAUGH, J. L., & HERZ, M. J. (1972). MEMORY CONSOLIDATION. San Francisco: Albion. **296**

MCGAUGH, J. L., JENSEN, R. A., & MARTINEZ, J. L., JR. (1979). Sleep, brain state, and memory. In R. Drucker-Colin, M. Shkurovich, & M. B. Sterman (Eds.), THE FUNCTIONS OF SLEEP. New York: Academic Press. **208**

MCGHIE, A., & CHAPMAN, J. (1961). Disorders of attention and perception in early schizophrenia. BRITISH JOURNAL OF MEDICAL PSYCHOLOGY, *34*, 103–116. **619, 621**

MCGINNIES, E. (1949). Emotionality and perceptual defense. PSYCHOLOGICAL REVIEW, *56*, 244–251. **174**

MCGRAW, M. D. (1935). GROWTH: A STUDY OF JOHNNY AND JIMMY. Englewood Cliffs, NJ: Prentice-Hall. **79**

MCGUIRE, W. J. (1960). A syllogistic analysis of cognitive relationships. In C. I. Hovland & M. J. Rosenberg (Eds.), ATTITUDE ORGANIZATION AND CHANGE. New Haven: Yale University Press. **704**

MCGUIRE, W. J. (1964). Inducing resistance to persuasion: Some contemporary approaches. In L. Berkowitz (Ed.), ADVANCES IN EXPERIMENTAL SOCIAL PSYCHOLOGY (Vol. 1). New York: Academic Press. **749**

MCGUIRE, W. J., & PAPAGEORGIS, D. (1961). The relative efficacy of various types of prior belief-defense in producing immunity against persuasion. JOURNAL OF ABNORMAL AND SOCIAL PSYCHOLOGY, *62*, 327–337. **749**

MCKENNA, R. J. (1972). Some effects of anxiety level and food cues on the eating behavior of obese and normal subjects. JOURNAL OF PERSONALITY AND SOCIAL PSYCHOLOGY, *22*, 311–319. **372**

MCNEAL, E. T., & CIMBOLIC, P. (1986). Antidepressants and biochemical theories of depression. PSYCHOLOGICAL BULLETIN, *99*, 361–374. **615**

MEANEY, M. J., AITKENS, D. H., BERKEL, C., BHATNAGAR, S., SARRIEAU, A., & SAPOLSKY, R. M. (1987). POST-NATAL HANDLING ATTENUATES AGE-RELATED CHANGES IN THE ADRENOCORTICAL STRESS RESPONSE AND SPATIAL MEMORY DEFICITS IN THE RAT. Paper presented at the 17th Annual Meeting of the Society of Neuroscience, New Orleans. **559**

MECHANIC, D. (1962). STUDENTS UNDER STRESS. New York: Free Press. **573**

MEDNICK, S. A., CUDECK, R., GRIFFITH, J. J., TALOVIC, S. A., & SCHULSINGER, F. (1984). The Danish High-Risk Project: Recent methods and findings. In H. F. Watt, E. J. Anthony, L. C. Wynne, & J. E. Rolf (Eds.), CHILDREN AT RISK FOR SCHIZOPHRENIA. New York: Cambridge University Press. **627**

MEICHENBAUM, D. H. (1985). STRESS INOCULATION TRAINING. New York: Pergamon. **589**

MEICHENBAUM, D. H., & JAREMKO, M. E. (Eds.). (1983). STRESS REDUCTION AND PREVENTION. New York: Plenum. **589**

MELAMED, B. G., & SIEGEL, L. J. (1975). Reduction of anxiety in children facing hospitalization and surgery by use of filmed modeling. JOURNAL OF CONSULTING AND CLINICAL PSYCHIATRY, *43*, 511–521. **651**

MELVILLE, J. (1977). PHOBIAS AND OBSESSIONS. New York: Coward, McCann, & Geoghegan. **598**

MELZAK, R. (1973). THE PUZZLE OF PAIN. New York: Basic Books. **152**

MENNINGER, K., & HOLZMAN, P. S. (1973). THEORY OF PSYCHOANALYTIC TECHNIQUE (2nd ed.). New York: Basic Books. **679**

MENZIES, R. (1937). Conditioned vasomotor responses in human subjects. JOURNAL OF PSYCHOLOGY, *4*, 75–120. **250**

MERVIS, C. B., & PANI, J. R. (1981). Acquisition of basic object categories. COGNITIVE PSYCHOLOGY, *12*, 496–522. **326**

MERVIS, C. B., & ROSCH, E. (1981). Categorization of natural objects. In M. R. Rosenz & L. W. Porter (Eds.), ANNUAL REVIEW OF PSYCHOLOGY (Vol. 21). Palo Alto, CA: Annual Reviews. **324**

MESSER, S. (1967). Implicit phonology in children. JOURNAL OF VERBAL LEARNING AND VERBAL BEHAVIOR, *6*, 609–613. **338**

MEYER, J. P., & PEPPER, S. (1977). Need compatibility and marital adjustment in young married couples. JOURNAL OF PERSONALITY AND SOCIAL PSYCHOLOGY, *35*, 331–342. **715**

MICHOTTE, A. (1963). THE PERCEPTION OF CAUSALITY. New York: Basic Books. **164**

MILES, L. E., RAYNAL, D. M., & WILSON, M. A. (1977). Blind man living in normal society has circadian rhythm of 24.9 hours. SCIENCE, *198*, 421–423. **202**

MILGRAM, S. (1963). Behavioral study of obedience. JOURNAL OF ABNORMAL AND SOCIAL PSYCHOLOGY, *67*, 371–378. **737, 739**

MILGRAM, S. (1974). OBEDIENCE TO AUTHORITY: AN EXPERIMENTAL VIEW. New York: Harper & Row. **737, 738, 739, 741, 743, 761**

MILLER, D. T., & ROSS, M. (1975). Self-serving biases in attribution of causality: Fact or fiction? PSYCHOLOGICAL BULLETIN, *82*, 213–225. **617**

MILLER, G. A. (1956). The magical number seven plus or minus two: Some limits on our capacity for processing information. PSYCHOLOGICAL REVIEW, *63*, 81–97. **284, 289**

MILLER, G. A. (1965). Some preliminaries to psycholinguistics. AMERICAN PSYCHOLOGIST, *20*, 15–20. **340**

MILLER, G. A., & GILDEA, P. M. (1987). How children learn words. SCIENTIFIC AMERICAN, *257*, 94–99. **338**

MILLER, N. E. (1969). Learning of visceral and glandular responses. SCIENCE, *169*, 434–445. **258**

MILLER, N. E. (1985). The value of behavioral research on animals. AMERICAN PSYCHOLOGIST, *40*, 423–440. **258**

MILLER, P. H. (1989). THEORIES OF DEVELOPMENTAL PSYCHOLOGY (2nd ed.). New York: Freeman. **113**

MILLER-JONES, D. (1989). Culture and testing. AMERICAN PSYCHOLOGIST, *44*, 360–366. **453**

MILLON, T., GREEN, C., & MEAGHER, R. (Eds.). (1982). HANDBOOK OF CLINICAL HEALTH PSYCHOLOGY. New York: Plenum. **589**

MILNER, B. (1964). Some effects of frontal lobectomy in man. In J. M. Warren & K. Akert (Eds.), THE FRONTAL GRANULAR CORTEX AND BEHAVIOR. New York: McGraw-Hill. **50**

MILNER, B., CORKIN, S., & TEUBER, H. L. (1968). Further analysis of the hippocampal amnesic syndrome: 14-year follow-up study of H. M. NEUROPSYCHOLOGIA, *6*, 215–234. **282**

MINIUM, E. W., & CLARK, R. W. (1982).

ELEMENTS OF STATISTICAL REASONING. New York: Wiley. **786**

MISCHEL, W. (1968). PERSONALITY AND ASSESSMENT. New York: Wiley. **504, 544**

MISCHEL, W. (1973). Toward a cognitive social learning reconceptualization of personality. PSYCHOLOGICAL REVIEW, 80, 272–283. **520**

MISCHEL, W. (1986). INTRODUCTION TO PERSONALITY (4th ed.). New York: Holt, Rinehart & Winston. **520, 551**

MISCHEL, W., & MISCHEL, H. (1976). A cognitive social learning approach to morality and self-regulation. In T. Lickona (Ed.), MORAL DEVELOPMENT AND BEHAVIOR. New York: Holt, Rinehart & Winston. **100**

MISHKIN, M., & APPENZELLER, T. (1987). The anatomy of memory. SCIENTIFIC AMERICAN, 256, 80–89. **157, 297**

MISHKIN, M., MALAMUT, B., & BACH-EVALIER, J. (1984). Memories and habits: Two neural systems. In G. T. Lynch, J. L. McGaugh, & N. M. Weinberger (Eds.), NEUROBIOLOGY OF LEARNING AND MEMORY. New York: Guilford Press. **305**

MITA, T. H., DERMER, M., & KNIGHT, J. (1977). Reversed facial images and the mere-exposure hypothesis. JOURNAL OF PERSONALITY AND SOCIAL PSYCHOLOGY, 35, 597–601. **713**

MITCHEL, J. S., & KEESEY, R. E. (1974). The effects of lateral hypothalamic lesions and castration upon the body weight of male rats. BEHAVIORAL BIOLOGY, 11, 69–82. **369**

MITCHELL, D. E., & WILKINSON, F. (1974). The effect of early astigmatism on the visual resolution of gratings. JOURNAL OF PHYSIOLOGY, 243, 739–756. **189**

MOEDE, W. (1927). Die richtlinien der liestungs-psychologie. INDUSTRIELLE PSYCHOTECHNIK, 4, 193–207. **733**

MOERMAN, D. E. (1981). Edible symbols: The effectiveness of placebos. In T. A. Sebok & R. Rosenthal (Eds.), THE CLEVER HANS PHENOMENON (Annals of the New York Academy of Sciences, Vol. 364). New York: New York Academy of Science. **237**

MONAHAN, J. (1976). The prevention of violence. In J. Monahan (Ed.), COMMUNITY MENTAL HEALTH AND THE CRIMINAL JUSTICE SYSTEM. Elmsford, NY: Pergamon Press. **641**

MONEY, J. (1980). Endocrine influences and psychosexual status spanning the life cycle. In H. M. Van Praag (Ed.), HANDBOOK OF BIOLOGICAL PSYCHIATRY (Part 3). New York: Marcel Dekker. **387, 389**

MONEY, J. (1987). Sin, sickness, or status? Homosexual gender identity and psycho-

neuroendocrinology. AMERICAN PSYCHOLOGIST, 42, 384–400. **390**

MONEY, J., SCHWARTZ, M., & LEWIS, V. G. (1984). Adult heterosexual status and fetal hormonal masculinization and demasculinization: 46, XX congenital virilizing adrenal hyperplasia and 46, XY androgen-insensitivity syndrome compared. PSYCHONEUROENDOCRINOLOGY, 9, 405–414. **387**

MONEY, J., WIEDEKING, C., WALKER, P. A., & GAIN, D. (1976). Combined antiandrogenic and counseling programs for treatment of 46 XY and 47 XXY sex offenders. In E. Sacher (Ed.), HORMONES, BEHAVIOR AND PSYCHOPATHOLOGY. New York: Raven Press. **378**

MONSELL, S. (1979). Recency, immediate recognition memory, and reaction time. COGNITIVE PSYCHOLOGY, 10, 465–501. **287**

MONTAGU, A. (Ed.). (1978). LEARNING NONAGGRESSION: THE EXPERIENCE OF NONLITERATE SOCIETIES. New York: Oxford University Press. **433**

MONTAIGNE, M. D. (1580/1943). Of the inconsistency of our actions. In D. M. Frame (Trans.), SELECTED ESSAYS. Roslyn, NY: Walter J. Black. **543**

MOOK, D. C. (1987). MOTIVATION: THE ORGANIZATION OF ACTION. New York: Norton. **392, 399, 433**

MOORE, B. C. J. (1978). Psychophysical tuning curves measured in simultaneous and forward masking. JOURNAL OF THE ACOUSTICAL SOCIETY OF AMERICA, 63, 524–532. **141**

MOORE, B. C. J. (1982). AN INTRODUCTION TO THE PSYCHOLOGY OF HEARING (2nd ed.). New York: Academic Press. **155**

MORAY, N. (1969). ATTENTION: SELECTIVE PROCESSES IN VISION AND HEARING. London: Hutchinson. **176**

MORELAND, R. L., & ZAJONC, R. B. (1979). Exposure effects may not depend on stimulus recognition. JOURNAL OF PERSONALITY AND SOCIAL PSYCHOLOGY, 37, 1085–1089. **713**

MORRISON, D. M. (1985). Adolescent contraceptive behavior: A review. PSYCHOLOGICAL BULLETIN, 98, 538–568. **104, 105**

MOSCOVICI, S. (1976). SOCIAL INFLUENCE AND SOCIAL CHANGE. London: Academic Press. **746**

MOSCOVICI, S., LAGE, E., & NAFFRECHOUX, M. (1969). Influence of a consistent minority on the responses of a majority in a color perception task. SOCIOMETRY, 32, 365–379. **746**

MOSKOWITZ, H. R., KUMRAICH, V., SHARMA, H., JACOBS, L., & SHARMA, S. D. (1975). Cross-cultural

difference in simple taste preference. SCIENCE, 190, 1217–1218. **148**

MOULTON, D. G. (1977). Minimum oderant concentrations detectable by the dog and their implications for olfactory sensitivity. In D. Miller-Schwarze and M. M. Mozell (Eds.), CHEMICAL SIGNALS IN VERTEBRATES. New York: Plenum. **147**

MOVSHON, J. A., & VAN SLUYTERS, R. C. (1981). Visual neural development. ANNUAL REVIEW OF PSYCHOLOGY, 32, 477–522. **189**

MUNROE, R. H., MUNROE, R. L., & WHITING, B. B. (Eds.). (1981). HANDBOOK OF CROSS-CULTURAL HUMAN DEVELOPMENT. New York: Garland STPM Press. **501**

MURDOCK, B. B., JR. (1962). The serial position effect in free recall. JOURNAL OF EXPERIMENTAL PSYCHOLOGY, 64, 482–488. **290**

MURPHY, G., & KOVACH, J. (1972). HISTORICAL INTRODUCTION TO MODERN PSYCHOLOGY (3rd ed.). New York: Harcourt Brace Jovanovich. **29**

MURPHY, G. E., & WETZEL, R. D. (1980). Suicide risk by birth cohort in the United States, 1949 to 1974. ARCHIVES OF GENERAL PSYCHIATRY, 37, 519–523. **610**

MURSTEIN, B. I. (1972). Physical attractiveness and marital choice. JOURNAL OF PERSONALITY AND SOCIAL PSYCHOLOGY, 22, 8–12. **714**

MUSSEN, P. H. (Ed.). (1983). HANDBOOK OF CHILD PSYCHOLOGY (4th ed.). New York: Wiley. **113**

MUSSEN, P. H., CONGER, J. J., KAGAN, J., & HUSTON, A. C. (1984). CHILD DEVELOPMENT AND PERSONALITY (6th ed.). New York: Harper & Row. **113**

MYERS, D. G. (1987). SOCIAL PSYCHOLOGY (2nd ed.). New York: McGraw-Hill. **701, 719, 721, 761**

N

NAKAYAMA, K. (1985). Biological image motion-processing. VISION RESEARCH, 25, 625–660. **164, 165**

NAKAYAMA, K., & TYLER, C. W. (1981). Psychophysical isolation of movement sensitivity by removal of familiar position cues. VISION RESEARCH, 21, 427–433. **163**

NARANJO, C., & ORNSTEIN, R. E. (1977). ON THE PSYCHOLOGY OF MEDITATION. New York: Penguin. **243**

NATHANS, J., THOMAS, D., & HOGNESS, D. S. (1986). Molecular genetics of human color vision: The genes encoding blue, green, and red pigments. SCIENCE, 232, 193–202. **131**

NEALE, M. C., & STEVENSON, J. (1989). Rater bias in the EASI Temperament Scales: A twin study. JOURNAL OF PERSONALITY AND SOCIAL PSYCHOLOGY, 56, 446–455. **475**

NEBES, R. D., & SPERRY, R. W. (1971). Cerebral dominance in perception. NEUROPSYCHOLOGIA, 9, 247. **53**

NEGRETE, J. C., & KWAN, M. W. (1972). Relative value of various etiological factors in short-lasting, adverse psychological reactions to cannabis smoking. INTERNAL PHARMACOPSYCHIATRY, 7, 249–259. **223**

NEISSER, U. (1981). John Dean's memory: A case study. COGNITION, 9, 1–22. **292**

NEISSER, U. (Ed.). (1982). MEMORY OBSERVED: REMEMBERING IN NATURAL CONTEXTS. San Francisco: Freeman. **291, 299, 319**

NEISSER, U. (Ed.). (1986). THE SCHOOL ACHIEVEMENT OF MINORITY CHILDREN. Hillsdale, NJ: Erlbaum. **453, 468**

NELSON, T. O. (1977). Repetition and depth of processing. JOURNAL OF VERBAL LEARNING AND VERBAL BEHAVIOR, 16, 152–171. **290**

NEUGARTEN, B. (1968). Adult personality: Toward a psychology of the life cycle. In B. Neugarten (Ed.), MIDDLE AGE AND AGING. Chicago: University of Chicago Press. **111**

NEUMAN, W. R. (1976). Patterns of recall among television news viewers. PUBLIC OPINION QUARTERLY, 40, 115–123. **754**

NEWCOMB, M. D., & BENTLER, P. M. (1988). CONSEQUENCES OF ADOLESCENT DRUG USE. Newbury Park, CA: Sage. **225**

NEWCOMB, T. M. (1943). PERSONALITY AND SOCIAL CHANGE. New York: Dryden Press. **494, 758, 761**

NEWCOMB, T. M. (1961). THE ACQUAINTANCE PROCESS. New York: Holt, Rinehart & Winston. **715**

NEWCOMB, T. M., KOENING, K. E., FLACKS, R., & WARWICK, D. P. (1967). PERSISTENCE AND CHANGE: BENNINGTON COLLEGE AND ITS STUDENTS AFTER TWENTY-FIVE YEARS. New York: Wiley. **494, 759, 761**

NEWELL, A., & SIMON, H. A. (1972). HUMAN PROBLEM SOLVING. Englewood Cliffs, NJ: Prentice-Hall. **350, 356**

NICKLAUS, J. (1974). GOLF MY WAY. New York: Simon & Schuster. **228**

NILSON, D. C., NILSON, L. B., OLSON, R. S., & MCALLISTER, B. H. (1981). THE PLANNING ENVIRONMENT REPORT FOR THE SOUTHERN CALIFORNIA EARTHQUAKE SAFETY ADVISORY BOARD. Redlands, CA: Social Research Advisory & Policy Research Center. **573**

NININGER, H. H. (1933). OUR STONE-PELTED PLANET. Boston: Houghton Mifflin. **241**

NISAN, M., & KOHLBERG, L. (1982). Universality and variation in moral judgment: A longitudinal and cross-sectional study in Turkey. CHILD DEVELOPMENT, 53, 865–876. **99**

NISBETT, R. E. (1968). Taste, deprivation, and weight determinants of eating behavior. JOURNAL OF PERSONALITY AND SOCIAL PSYCHOLOGY, 10, 107–116. **372**

NISBETT, R. E. (1972). Hunger, obesity, and the ventromedial hypothalamus. PSYCHOLOGICAL REVIEW, 79, 433–453. **376**

NISBETT, R. E., FONG, G. T., LEHMAN, D. R., & CHENG, P. W. (1987). Teaching reasoning. SCIENCE, 238, 625–631. **332**

NISBETT, R. E., & ROSS, L. (1985). HUMAN INFERENCE: STRATEGIES AND SHORTCOMINGS OF SOCIAL JUDGMENT (reprint ed.). Englewood Cliffs, NJ: Prentice-Hall. **683, 684, 690, 695, 719, 721**

NISBETT, R. E., & WILSON, T. D. (1977). Telling more than we can know: Verbal reports on mental processes. PSYCHOLOGICAL REVIEW, 84, 231–259. **702**

NORMAN, D. A. (1976). MEMORY AND ATTENTION: AN INTRODUCTION TO HUMAN INFORMATION PROCESSING (2nd ed.). New York: Wiley. **309**

NORMAN, R. (1975). Affective-cognitive consistency, attitudes, conformity, and behavior. JOURNAL OF PERSONALITY AND SOCIAL PSYCHOLOGY, 32, 83–91. **706**

NORMAN, W. T. (1963). Toward an adequate taxonomy of personality attributes: Replicated factor structure in peer nomination personality ratings. JOURNAL OF ABNORMAL AND SOCIAL PSYCHOLOGY, 66, 574–583. **509**

O

O'BRIEN, M., & HUSTON, A. C. (1985). Development of sex-typed play behavior in toddlers. DEVELOPMENTAL PSYCHOLOGY, 21(5), 866–871. **94**

O'DONNELL, J. A., & CLAYTON, R. R. (1982). The stepping stone hypothesis: Marijuana, heroin, and causality. CHEMICAL DEPENDENCIES, 4(3). **224**

O'LEARY, K. D., & WILSON, G. T. (1975). BEHAVIOR THERAPY: APPLICATION AND OUTCOME. Englewood Cliffs, NJ: Prentice-Hall. **653**

OFFIR, C. (1982). HUMAN SEXUALITY. San Diego: Harcourt Brace Jovanovich. **370, 379, 380, 399**

OGBU, J. U. (1986). The consequences of the American caste system. In U. Neisser (Ed.), THE SCHOOL ACHIEVEMENT OF MINORITY CHILDREN. Hillsdale, NJ: Erlbaum. **469**

OHMAN, A., FREDRIKSON, M., HUGDAHL, K., & RIMMO, P. (1976). The premise of equipotentiality in human classical conditioning: Conditioned electrodermal responses to potentially phobic stimuli. JOURNAL OF EXPERIMENTAL PSYCHOLOGY: GENERAL, 105, 313–337. **604**

OLTON, D. S. (1978). Characteristics of spatial memory. In S. H. Hulse, H. F. Fowler, & W. K. Honig (Eds.), COGNITIVE PROCESSES IN ANIMAL BEHAVIOR. Hillsdale, NJ: Erlbaum. **272**

OLTON, D. S. (1979). Mazes, maps, and memory. AMERICAN PSYCHOLOGIST, 34, 583–596. **272**

OLTON, D. S., & SAMUELSON, R. J. (1976). Remembrance of places passed: Spatial memory in rats. JOURNAL OF EXPERIMENTAL PSYCHOLOGY: ANIMAL BEHAVIOR PROCESS, 2, 96–116. **273**

OLWEUS, D. (1969). PREDICTION OF AGGRESSION. Scandinavian Test Corporation. **540**

ORLINSKY, D. E., & HOWARD, K. I. (1987). A generic model of psychotherapy. JOURNAL OF INTEGRATIVE AND ECLECTIC PSYCHOTHERAPY, 6, 6–27. **666**

ORNE, M. T., & HOLLAND, C. C. (1968). On the ecological validity of laboratory deceptions. INTERNATIONAL JOURNAL OF PSYCHIATRY, 6, 282–293. **741**

ORNSTEIN, P. A., & NAUS, M. J. (1985). Effects of the knowledge base on children's memory strategies. In H. W. Reese (Ed.), ADVANCES IN CHILD DEVELOPMENT AND BEHAVIOR (Vol. 19). New York: Academic Press. **86**

ORTONY, A., CLORE, G. L., & COLLINS, A. (1988). THE COGNITIVE STRUCTURE OF EMOTIONS. Cambridge, MA: Cambridge University Press. **433**

OSHERSON, D. N. (1976). LOGICAL ABILITIES IN CHILDREN: Vol. 4. REASONING AND CONCEPTS. Hillsdale, NJ: Erlbaum. **329**

OSOFSKY, J. D. (Ed.). (1987). HANDBOOK OF INFANT DEVELOPMENT (2nd ed.). New York: Wiley. **113**

OVERMEIER, J. B., & SELIGMAN, M. E. P. (1967). Effects of inescapable shock upon subsequent escape and avoidance responding. JOURNAL OF COMPARATIVE AND PHYSIOLOGICAL PSYCHOLOGY, 63, 28. **564**

OWEN, D. R. (1972). The 47 XYY male: A review. PSYCHOLOGICAL REVIEW, 78, 209–233. **63**

P

PAICHELER, G. (1976). Norms and attitude change: Pt. 1. Polarization and styles of behavior. EUROPEAN JOURNAL OF SOCIAL PSYCHOLOGY, 6, 405–427. **746**

PAICHELER, G. (1977). Norms and attitude change: Pt. 2. The phenomenon of bipolarization. EUROPEAN JOURNAL OF SOCIAL PSYCHOLOGY, 7, 5–14. **746**

PALLONE, N. J. (1961). Effects of short- and long-term developmental reading courses upon SAT verbal scores. PERSONNEL AND GUIDANCE JOURNAL, 39, 654–657. **457**

PALMER, F. H., & ANDERSON, L. W. (1979). Long-term gains from early intervention: Findings from longitudinal studies. In E. Zigler & J. Valentine (Eds.), PROJECT HEAD START: A LEGACY OF THE WAR ON POVERTY. New York: Free Press. **469**

PALMER, J. A., HONORTON, C., & UTTS, J. (1988). REPLY TO THE NATIONAL RESEARCH COUNCIL STUDY ON PARAPSYCHOLOGY. Research Triangle Park, NC: Parapsychological Association, Inc. **237**

PALMER, S. E. (1975). The effects of contextual scenes on the identification of objects. MEMORY AND COGNITION, 3, 519–526. **172**

PAPAGEORGIS, D., & MCGUIRE, W. J. (1961). The generality of immunity to persuasion produced by pre-exposure to weakened counterarguments. JOURNAL OF ABNORMAL AND SOCIAL PSYCHOLOGY, 62, 475–481. **749**

PATEL, V. L., & GROEN, G. J. (1986). Knowledge-based solution strategies in medical reasoning. COGNITIVE SCIENCE, 10, 91. **353**

PATTERSON, F. G. (1978). The gestures of a gorilla: Language acquisition in another pongid. BRAIN AND LANGUAGE, 5, 72–97. **346**

PATTERSON, F. G., & LINDEN, E. (1981). THE EDUCATION OF KOKO. New York: Holt, Rinehart & Winston. **346**

PATTERSON, G. R. (1976). The aggressive child: Victim and architect of a coercive system. In L. A. Hamerlynck, L. C. Handy, & E. J. Mash (Eds.), BEHAVIOR MODIFICATION AND FAMILIES: 1. THEORY AND RESEARCH. New York: Brunner/Mazel. **540**

PATTERSON, G. R., LITTMAN, R. A., & BRICKER, W. A. (1967). Assertive behavior in children: A step toward a theory of aggression. MONOGRAPHS OF THE SOCIETY FOR RESEARCH IN CHILD DEVELOPMENT (Serial No. 113), 5. **429**

PAUL, G. L. (1967). Insight versus desensitization in psychotherapy two years after termination. JOURNAL OF CONSULTING PSYCHOLOGY, 31, 333–348. **669**

PAULHUS, D. (1982). Individual differences, self-presentation and cognitive dissonance: Their concurrent operation in forced compliance. JOURNAL OF PERSONALITY AND SOCIAL PSYCHOLOGY, 43, 838–852. **709**

PAULUS, P. B., & MURDOCK, P. (1971). Anticipated evaluation and audience presence in the enhancement of dominant responses. JOURNAL OF EXPERIMENTAL SOCIAL PSYCHOLOGY, 7, 280–291. **725**

PAVLOV, I. P. (1927). CONDITIONED REFLEXES. New York: Oxford University Press. **249, 279**

PECK, J. W., & NOVIN, D. (1971). Evidence that osmoreceptors mediating drinking in rabbits are in the lateral preoptic area. JOURNAL OF COMPARATIVE AND PHYSIOLOGICAL PSYCHOLOGY, 74, 134–137. **364**

PELLEGRINO, J. W. (1985). Inductive reasoning ability. In R. J. Sternberg (Ed.), HUMAN ABILITIES: AN INFORMATION-PROCESSING APPROACH. New York: Freeman. **463**

PEPLAU, L. A., RUBIN, Z., & HILL, C. T. (1977). Sexual intimacy in dating relationships. JOURNAL OF SOCIAL ISSUES, 33, 86–109. **384**

PERLMUTTER, M., & HALL, E. (1985). ADULT DEVELOPMENT AND AGING. New York: Wiley. **113**

PERRIN, F. A. C. (1921). Physical attractiveness and repulsiveness. JOURNAL OF EXPERIMENTAL PSYCHOLOGY, 4, 203–217. **711**

PERRIS, C., BLACKBURN, I. M., & PERRIS, H. (Eds.). (1988). COGNITIVE PSYCHOTHERAPY: THEORY AND PRACTICE. New York: Springer-Verlag. **679**

PETERSEN, A. C. (1988a). Pubertal change and psychosocial development. In D. L. Baltes, R. M. Featherman, & R. M. Lerner (Eds.), LIFE-SPAN DEVELOPMENT AND BEHAVIOR (Vol. 9). New York: Academic Press. **101**

PETERSEN, A. C. (1988b). Adolescent development. In M. R. Rosenzweig & L. W. Porter (Eds.), ANNUAL REVIEW OF PSYCHOLOGY (Vol. 39). Palo Alto, CA: Annual Reviews. **106**

PETERSON, C. (1988). PERSONALITY. San Diego: Harcourt Brace Jovanovich. **29**

PETERSON, C., & SELIGMAN, M. E. P. (1984). Causal explanations as a risk factor for depression: Theory and evidence. PSYCHOLOGICAL REVIEW, 91, 347–374. **613**

PETTY, R. E., & CACIOPPO, J. T. (1977). Forewarning, cognitive responding, and resistance to persuasion. JOURNAL OF PERSONALITY AND SOCIAL PSYCHOLOGY, 35, 645–655. **749**

PETTY, R. E., & CACIOPPO, J. T. (1981). ATTITUDES AND PERSUASION: CLASSIC AND CONTEMPORARY APPROACHES. Dubuque, IA: Wm. C. Brown. **750, 761**

PETTY, R. E., & CACIOPPO, J. T. (1984). The effects of involvement on responses to argument quantity and quality: Central and peripheral routes to persuasion. JOURNAL OF PERSONALITY AND SOCIAL PSYCHOLOGY, 46, 69–81. **750, 752**

PETTY, R. E., & CACIOPPO, J. T. (1986). Elaboration likelihood model of persuasion. In L. Berkowitz (Ed.), ADVANCES IN EXPERIMENTAL SOCIAL PSYCHOLOGY (Vol. 19). New York: Academic Press. **750**

PETTY, R. E., CACIOPPO, J. T., & GOLDMAN, R. (1981). Personal involvement as a determinant of argument-based persuasion. JOURNAL OF PERSONALITY AND SOCIAL PSYCHOLOGY, 41, 847–855. **752**

PETTY, R. E., HARKINS, S. G., WILLIAMS, K. D., & LATANÉ, B. (1977). The effects of group size on cognitive effort and evaluation. PERSONALITY AND SOCIAL PSYCHOLOGY BULLETIN, 3, 575–578. **733**

PETTY, R. E., OSTROM, T. M., & BROCK, T. C. (1981). Historical foundations of the cognitive response approach to attitudes and persuasion. In R. E. Petty, T. M. Ostrom, & T. C. Brock (Eds.), COGNITIVE RESPONSES IN PERSUASION. Hillsdale, NJ: Erlbaum. **748**

PHARES, E. J. (1984). INTRODUCTION TO PERSONALITY. Columbus, OH: Merrill. **551**

PHILLIPS, D. P. (1978). Airplane accident fatalities increase just after newspaper stories about murder and suicide. SCIENCE, 201, 748–749. **611**

PHILLIPS, J. L., JR. (1981). PIAGET'S THEORY: A PRIMER. San Francisco: Freeman. **113**

PHILLIPS, J. L., JR. (1988). HOW TO THINK ABOUT STATISTICS. San Francisco: Freeman. **29, 778, 786**

PHOENIX, C. H., GOY, R. H., & RESKO, J. A. (1968). Psychosexual differentiation as a function of androgenic stimulation. In M. Diamond (Ed.), REPRODUCTION AND SEXUAL BEHAVIOR. Bloomington: Indiana University Press. **389**

PIAGET, J. (1952). THE ORIGINS OF INTELLIGENCE IN CHILDREN. New York: International Universities Press. **395**

PILIAVAN, I. M., RODIN, J., & PILIAVIN, J. A. (1969). Good Samaritanism: An underground phenomenon? JOURNAL OF PERSONALITY AND SOCIAL PSYCHOLOGY, 13, 289–399. **731**

PILLIMER, D. B. (1984). Flashbulb memories of the assassination attempt on President Reagan. COGNITION, 16, 63–80. **300**

PINKER, S. (1984). LANGUAGE LEARNABILITY AND LANGUAGE DEVELOPMENT. Cambridge, MA: Harvard University Press. **357**

PINKER, S., & PRINCE, A. (1988). On language and connectionism: Analysis of a parallel distributed processing model of

PINKER, S. (*continued*)
language acquisition. COGNITION, 28, 71–193. **341**

PIRCHIO, M., SPINELLI, D., FIORENTINI, A., & MAFFEI, L. (1978). Infant contrast sensitivity evaluated by evoked potentials. BRAIN RESEARCH, *141*, 179–184. **186**

PLATT, J. J., YAKSH, T., & DARBY, C. L. (1967). Social facilitation of eating behavior in armadillos. PSYCHOLOGICAL REPORTS, *20*, 1136. **724**

PLOMIN, R. (1986). DEVELOPMENT, GENETICS, AND PSYCHOLOGY. Hillsdale, NJ: Erlbaum. **64, 67, 473, 501**

PLOMIN, R. (1989). Environment and genes: Determinants of behavior. AMERICAN PSYCHOLOGIST, *44*, 105–111. **467**

PLOMIN, R., & DANIELS, D. (1987). Why are children in the same family so different from one another? BEHAVIORAL AND BRAIN SCIENCES, *10*, 1–60. **484**

PLOMIN, R., DEFRIES, J. C., & LOEHLIN, J. C. (1977). Genotype–environment interaction and correlation in the analysis of human behavior. PSYCHOLOGICAL BULLETIN, *84*, 309–322. **481**

PLOMIN, R., DEFRIES, J. C., & MCCLEARN, G. E. (1989). BEHAVIORAL GENETICS: A PRIMER (2nd ed.). New York: Freeman. **473, 635**

PLOMIN, R., PEDERSEN, N. L., MCCLEARN, G. E., NESSELROADE, J. R., & BERGEMAN, C. S. (1988). EAS temperaments during the last half of the life span: Twins reared apart and twins reared together. PSYCHOLOGY AND AGING, *3*, 43–50. **475**

PLUTCHIK, R. (1980). A general psychoevolutionary theory of emotion. In R. Plutchik & H. Kellerman (Eds.), EMOTION: THEORY, RESEARCH AND EXPERIENCE (Vol. 1). New York: Academic Press. **410, 433**

PLUTCHIK, R., & KELLERMAN, H. (Eds.). (1980). EMOTION: THEORY, RESEARCH, AND EXPERIENCE (Vol. 1). New York: Academic Press. **433**

POLIVY, J., & HERMAN, C. P. (1985). Dieting and binging: A causal analysis. AMERICAN PSYCHOLOGIST, *40*, 193–201. **372**

POPE, K. S., & SINGER, J. L. (Eds.). (1978). THE STREAM OF CONSCIOUSNESS. New York: Plenum. **243**

PORTER, H. (1939). Studies in the psychology of stuttering: Pt. 14. Stuttering phenomena in relation to size and personnel of audience. JOURNAL OF SPEECH DISORDERS, *4*, 323–333. **732**

POSNER, M. I., & KEELE, S. W. (1967). Decay of visual information from a single letter. SCIENCE, *158*, 137–139. **284**

POSNER, M. I., & MARIN, O. S. M. (Eds.). (1985). MECHANISMS OF ATTENTION: VOL. 11. ATTENTION AND PERFORMANCE. Hillsdale, NJ: Erlbaum. **193**

POSNER, M. I., PETERSEN, S. E., FOX, P. T., & RAICHLE, M. E. (1988). Localization of cognitive operations in the human brain. SCIENCE, *240*, 1627–1631. **45**

POST, R. M., KOTIN, J., GOODWIN, F. K., & GORDON, E. (1973). Psychomotor activity and cerebrospinal fluid amine metabolites in affective illness. AMERICAN JOURNAL OF PSYCHIATRY, *130*, 67–72. **615**

POWLEY, T. L., & KEESEY, R. E. (1970). Relationship of body weight to the lateral hypothalamic feeding syndrome. JOURNAL OF COMPARATIVE AND PHYSIOLOGICAL PSYCHOLOGY, *70*, 25–36. **369**

PREMACK, D. (1959). Toward empirical behavior laws: Pt. 1. Positive reinforcement. PSYCHOLOGICAL REVIEW, *66*, 219–233. **262**

PREMACK, D. (1962). Reversibility of the reinforcement relation. SCIENCE, *136*, 255–257. **263**

PREMACK, D. (1971). Language in chimpanzees? SCIENCE, *172*, 808–822. **345**

PREMACK, D. (1985a). "Gavagai!" Or the future history of the animal language controversy. COGNITION, *19*, 207–296. **275**

PREMACK, D. (1985b). GAVAGAI! THE FUTURE OF THE ANIMAL LANGUAGE CONTROVERSY. Cambridge, MA: MIT Press. **279**

PREMACK, D., & PREMACK, A. J. (1983). THE MIND OF AN APE. New York: Norton. **275, 345**

PRENTICE-DUNN, S., & ROGERS, R. W. (1980). Effects of deindividuating situational cues and aggressive models on subjective deindividuation and aggression. JOURNAL OF PERSONALITY AND SOCIAL PSYCHOLOGY, *39*, 104–113. **729**

PRESSLEY, M., LEVIN, J. R., & DELANEY, H. D. (1982). The mnemonic keyword method. REVIEW OF EDUCATIONAL RESEARCH, *52*, 61–91. **308**

PRIEST, R. F., & SAWYER, J. (1967). Proximity and peership: Bases of balance in interpersonal attraction. AMERICAN JOURNAL OF SOCIOLOGY, *72*, 633–649. **712**

PRINZMETAL, W., & BANKS, W. P. (1977). Good continuation affects visual detection. PERCEPTION AND PSYCHOPHYSICS, *21*, 389–395. **160**

PULKKINEN, L. (1982). Self-control and continuity from childhood to adolescence. In P. B. Baltes & O. G. Brim, Jr. (Eds.), LIFE-SPAN DEVELOPMENT AND BEHAVIOR (Vol. 4). New York: Academic Press. **480**

PUTNAM, F. W., JR. (1984). Cited in R. M. Restak, THE BRAIN. New York: Bantam. **200**

R

RAAIJMAKERS, J. G., & SHIFFRIN, R. M. (1981). Search of associative memory. PSYCHOLOGICAL REVIEW, *88*, 93–134. **298**

RABIN, A. I., & BEIT-HALLAHMI, B. (1982). TWENTY YEARS LATER: KIBBUTZ CHILDREN GROWN UP. New York: Springer. **470**

RACHLIN, H. (1980). Economics and behavioral psychology. In J. E. R. Staddon (Ed.), LIMITS TO ACTION. New York: Academic Press. **266**

RACHMAN, S. J., & HODGSON, R. J. (1980). OBSESSIONS AND COMPULSIONS. Englewood Cliffs, NJ: Prentice-Hall. **602**

RACHMAN, S. J., & WILSON, G. T. (1980). THE EFFECTS OF PSYCHOLOGICAL THERAPY (2nd ed.). Elmsford, NY: Pergamon Press. **665**

RAHE, R. H., & ARTHUR, R. J. (1977). Life-change patterns surrounding illness experience. In A. Monat & R. S. Lazarus (Eds.), STRESS AND COPING. New York: Columbia University Press. **568**

RAMEY, C. T. (1981). Consequences of infant day care. In B. Weissbound & J. Musick (Eds.), INFANTS: THEIR SOCIAL ENVIRONMENTS. Washington, DC: National Association for the Education of Young Children. **94**

RANDS, M., & LEVINGER, G. (1979). Implicit theories of relationship: An intergenerational study. JOURNAL OF PERSONALITY AND SOCIAL PSYCHOLOGY, *37*, 645–661. **716**

RAPAPORT, D. (1942). EMOTIONS AND MEMORY. Baltimore: Williams & Wilkins. **299**

RAPOPORT, J. L. (1989, March). The biology of obsessions and compulsions. SCIENTIFIC AMERICAN, *260*, 83–89. **606**

RAVUSSIN, E., & collaborators. (1988). Reduced rate of energy expenditure as a risk factor for body-weight gain. THE NEW ENGLAND JOURNAL OF MEDICINE, *318*, 467–472. **373**

RAY, O. S. (1983). DRUGS, SOCIETY, AND HUMAN BEHAVIOR (3rd ed.). St. Louis: Mosby. **243**

RAY, W. J., & RAVIZZA, R. (1984). METHODS TOWARD A SCIENCE OF BEHAVIOR AND EXPERIENCE (2nd ed.). Belmont, CA: Wadsworth. **29**

RAYNER, K. (1978). Eye movements in reading and information processing. PSYCHOLOGICAL BULLETIN, *85*, 618–660. **178**

RAYNER, K., INHOFF, A. W., MORRISON, R. E., SLOWIACZEK, M. L., & BERTERA, J. H. (1981). Masking of foveal and parafoveal vision during eye fixations in reading. JOURNAL OF EXPERIMEN-

TAL PSYCHOLOGY: HUMAN PERCEPTION AND PERFORMANCE, 7, 167–179. **179**

REED, S. K. (1981). COGNITION: THEORY AND APPLICATIONS. Monterey, CA: Brooks/Cole. **319**

REGAN, D., BEVERLEY, K. I., & CYNADER, M. (1979). The visual perception of motion depth. SCIENTIFIC AMERICAN, 241(1), 136–151. **164**

REGAN, D. T., & FAZIO, R. (1977). On the consistency between attitudes and behavior: Look to the method of attitude formation. JOURNAL OF EXPERIMENTAL SOCIAL PSYCHOLOGY, 13, 28–45. **707**

REGIER, D. A., BOYD, J. H., & collaborators. (1988). One-month prevalence of mental disorders in the United States. ARCHIVES OF GENERAL PSYCHIATRY, 45, 977–986. **591, 596**

REICHER, G. M. (1969). Perceptual recognition as a function of the meaningfulness of the material. JOURNAL OF EXPERIMENTAL PSYCHOLOGY, 81, 275–280. **169**

REISEN, A. H. (1947). The development of visual perception in man and chimpanzee. SCIENCE, 106, 107–108. **188**

REISENZEIN, R. (1983). The Schachter theory of emotion: Two decades later. PSYCHOLOGICAL BULLETIN, 94, 239–264. **409, 417**

REITMAN, J. S. (1974). Without surreptitious rehearsal, information in short-term memory decays. JOURNAL OF VERBAL LEARNING AND VERBAL BEHAVIOR, 13, 365–377. **286**

RESCORLA, R. A. (1967). Pavlovian conditioning and its proper control procedures. PSYCHOLOGICAL REVIEW, 74, 71–80. **251**

RESCORLA, R. A. (1972). Informational variables in Pavlovian conditioning. In G. H. Bower (Ed.), PSYCHOLOGY OF LEARNING AND MOTIVATION (Vol. 6). New York: Academic Press. **252**

RESCORLA, R. A. (1980). Overextension in early language development. JOURNAL OF CHILD LANGUAGE, 7, 321–335. **338**

RESCORLA, R. A. (1987). A Pavlovian analysis of goal-directed behavior. AMERICAN PSYCHOLOGIST, 42(2), 119–129. **255**

RESCORLA, R. A., & WAGNER, A. R. (1972). A theory of Pavlovian conditioning: Variations in the effectiveness of reinforcement and nonreinforcement. In P. H. Black & W. F. Prokasy (Eds.), CLASSICAL CONDITIONING II. New York: Appleton-Century-Crofts. **252**

REST, J. R. (1983). Morality. In P. H. Mussen (Ed.), HANDBOOK OF CHILD PSYCHOLOGY: VOL. 3. COGNITIVE DEVELOPMENT. New York: Wiley. **100**

REYES, R. M., THOMPSON, W. L., & BOWER, G. H. (1980). Judgmental biases resulting from differing availabilities of arguments. JOURNAL OF PERSONALITY AND SOCIAL PSYCHOLOGY, 39, 2–12. **685**

REYNOLDS, D. V. (1969). Surgery in the rat during electrical analgesia induced by focal brain stimulation. SCIENCE, 164, 444–445. **153**

RICE, B. (1978). The new truth machine. PSYCHOLOGY TODAY, 12, 61–78. **407**

RICH, C. L., FOWLER, R. C., FOGARTY, L. A., & YOUNG, D. (1988). San Diego suicide study. ARCHIVES OF GENERAL PSYCHIATRY, 45, 589–592. **611**

RICHLIN, M. (1977, September 3). POSITIVE AND NEGATIVE RESIDUALS OF PROLONGED STRESS. Paper presented at Military Family Research Conference, San Diego. **565**

RIESE, M. L. (1987). Temperament stability between the neonatal period and 24 months. DEVELOPMENTAL PSYCHOLOGY, 23, 216–222. **78**

RIMM, D. C., & MASTERS, J. C. (1979). BEHAVIOR THERAPY: TECHNIQUES AND EMPIRICAL FINDINGS (2nd ed.). New York: Academic Press. **652**

RIPS, L. J. (1983). Cognitive processes in propositional reasoning. PSYCHOLOGICAL REVIEW, 90, 38–71. **329**

RIPS, L. J. (1986). Deduction. In R. J. Sternberg & E. E. Smith (Eds.), THE PSYCHOLOGY OF HUMAN THOUGHT. New York: Cambridge University Press. **330**

ROBERTS, C. F., GOLDING, S. L., & FINCHAM, F. D. (1987). Implicit theories of criminal responsibility: Decision-making and the insanity defense. LAW AND HUMAN BEHAVIOR, 11, 207–232. **633**

ROBINS, L. (1974). THE VIETNAM DRUG ABUSER RETURNS. New York: McGraw-Hill. **217**

ROBINS, L. N. (1966). DEVIANT CHILDREN GROWN UP. Baltimore, MD: Williams & Wilkins. **633**

ROBINSON, D. L., & WURTZ, R. (1976). Use of an extra-retinal signal by monkey superior colliculus neurons to distinguish real from self-induced stimulus movement. JOURNAL OF NEUROPHYSIOLOGY, 39, 852–870. **180**

ROBINSON, J. P. (1971). The audience for national television news programs. PUBLIC OPINION QUARTERLY, 35, 403–405. **754**

ROBINSON, R. P. (1970). EFFECTIVE STUDY. New York: Harper & Row. **762**

ROCK, I. (1983). THE LOGIC OF PERCEPTION. Cambridge, MA: MIT Press. **162, 193**

RODIN, J. (1981). Current status of the internal-external hypothesis of obesity: What went wrong? AMERICAN PSYCHOLOGIST, 36, 361–372. **370, 372**

ROFF, J. D., & KNIGHT, R. (1981). Family characteristics, childhood symptoms, and adult outcome in schizophrenia. JOURNAL OF ABNORMAL PSYCHOLOGY, 90, 510–520. **627**

ROFFWARG, H. P., HERMAN, J. H., BOWER-ANDERS, C., & TAUBER, E. S. (1978). The effects of sustained alterations of waking visual input on dream content. In A. M. Arkin, J. S. Antrobus, & S. J. Ellman (Eds.), THE MIND IN SLEEP. Hillsdale, NJ: Erlbaum. **209**

ROGERS, C. R. (1951). CLIENT-CENTERED THERAPY. Boston: Houghton Mifflin. **523**

ROGERS, C. R. (1959). A theory of therapy, personality, and interpersonal relationships, as developed in the client-centered framework. In S. Koch (Ed.), FORMULATIONS OF THE PERSON AND THE SOCIAL CONTEXT (Vol. 3). New York: McGraw-Hill. **523**

ROGERS, C. R. (1963). The actualizing tendency in relation to motives and to consciousness. In M. Jones (Ed.), NEBRASKA SYMPOSIUM ON MOTIVATION. Lincoln: University of Nebraska Press. **523**

ROGERS, C. R. (1970). ON BECOMING A PERSON: A THERAPIST'S VIEW OF PSYCHOTHERAPY. Boston: Houghton Mifflin. **523, 658, 679**

ROGERS, C. R. (1977). CARL ROGERS ON PERSONAL POWER. New York: Delacorte Press. **551, 679**

ROGERS, C. R., & STEVENS, B. (1967). PERSON TO PERSON: THE PROBLEM OF BEING HUMAN. New York: Pocket Books. **551**

ROGERS, T. B., KUIPER, N. A., & KIRKER, W. S. (1977). Self-reference and the encoding of personal information. JOURNAL OF PERSONALITY AND SOCIAL PSYCHOLOGY, 35, 677–688. **696**

ROHN, R. D., SARTES, R. M., KENNY, T. J., REYNOLDS, B. J., & HEALD, F. P. (1977). Adolescents who attempt suicide. JOURNAL OF PEDIATRICS, 90, 636–638. **611**

ROITBLATT, H. L. (1987). INTRODUCTION TO COMPARATIVE COGNITION. New York: Freeman. **279**

ROKEACH, M. (1968). BELIEFS, ATTITUDES, AND VALUES. San Francisco: Jossey-Bass. **704, 705**

ROKEACH, M. (1973). THE NATURE OF HUMAN VALUES. New York: Free Press. **704**

ROLAND, P. E., & FRIBERG, L. (1985). Localization of cortical areas activated by thinking. JOURNAL OF NEUROPHYSIOLOGY, 53, 1219–1243. **348**

ROSCH, E. (1974). Linguistic relativity. In A. Silverstein (Ed.), HUMAN COMMUNICATION: THEORETICAL PERSPECTIVES. New York: Halsted Press. **327**

ROSCH, E. (1978). Principles of categorization. In E. Rosch & B. L. Lloyd (Eds.),

ROSCH, E. (*continued*)
COGNITION AND CATEGORIZATION. Hillsdale, NJ: Erlbaum. **323**

ROSE, J. E., BRUGGE, J. F., ANDERSON, D. J., & HIND, J. E. (1967). Phase-locked response to lower frequency tones in single auditory nerve fibers of the squirrel monkey. JOURNAL OF NEUROPHYSIOLOGY, 309, 769–793. **142**

ROSEMAN, I. J. (1979, September). COGNITIVE ASPECTS OF EMOTION AND EMOTIONAL BEHAVIOR. Paper read at the 87th Annual Convention of the American Psychological Association, New York City. **410**

ROSEMAN, I. J. (1984). Cognitive determinants of emotions: A structural theory. In P. Shaver (Ed.), REVIEW OF PERSONALITY AND SOCIAL PSYCHOLOGY: VOL. 5. EMOTIONS, RELATIONSHIPS, AND HEALTH. Beverly Hills, CA: Sage. **410**

ROSEN, J. C., & SOLOMON, L. J. (Eds.). (1985). PREVENTION IN HEALTH PSYCHOLOGY. Vermont Conference on the Primary Prevention of Psychopathology (8th:1983: University of Vermont): University Press of New England. **589**

ROSENBERG, M. J. (1956). Cognitive structure and attitudinal affect. JOURNAL OF ABNORMAL AND SOCIAL PSYCHOLOGY, 53, 367–372. **705**

ROSENBERG, M. J. (1960). An analysis of affective-cognitive consistency. In C. I. Hovland & M. J. Rosenberg (Eds.), ATTITUDE ORGANIZATION AND CHANGE. New Haven: Yale University Press. **705**

ROSENBLITH, J. F., & SIMS-KNIGHT, J. (1985). IN THE BEGINNING: DEVELOPMENT IN THE FIRST TWO YEARS. Monterey, CA: Brooks/Cole. **113**

ROSENMAN, R. H., BRAND, R. J., JENKINS, C. D., FRIEDMAN, M., STRAUS, R., & WRUM, M. (1975). Coronary heart disease in the Western Collaborative Group Study: Final follow-up experience of 8½ years. JOURNAL OF THE AMERICAN MEDICAL ASSOCIATION, 233, 872–877. **580**

ROSENTHAL, R. (1966). EXPERIMENTER EFFECTS IN BEHAVIORAL RESEARCH. New York: Appleton-Century-Crofts. **237**

ROSENTHAL, R. (1984). META-ANALYTIC PROCEDURES FOR SOCIAL RESEARCH. Beverly Hills, CA: Sage. **236**

ROSENZWEIG, M. R., & LEIMAN, A. L. (1989). PHYSIOLOGICAL PSYCHOLOGY (2nd ed.). Lexington, MA: Heath. **67, 399**

ROSS, L. (1977). The intuitive psychologist and his shortcomings: Distortions in the attribution process. In L. Berkowitz (Ed.), ADVANCES IN EXPERIMENTAL SOCIAL PSYCHOLOGY (Vol. 10). New York: Academic Press. **696**

ROSS, L., AMABILE, T. M., & STEINMETZ, J. L. (1977). Social roles, social control, and biases in social-perception processes. JOURNAL OF PERSONALITY AND SOCIAL PSYCHOLOGY, 35, 485–494. **699**

ROSS, M., & SICOLY, F. (1979). Egocentric biases in availability and attribution. JOURNAL OF PERSONALITY AND SOCIAL PSYCHOLOGY, 37, 322–336. **700**

ROSS, R., BIERBRAUER, G., & HOFFMAN, S. (1976). The role of attribution processes in conformity and dissent: Revisiting the Asch Situation. AMERICAN PSYCHOLOGIST, 31, 148–157. **735, 736**

ROTH, D. L., & HOLMES, D. S. (1987). Influence of aerobic exercise training and relaxation training on physical and psychological health following stressful life events. PSYCHOSOMATIC MEDICINE, 49, 355–365. **585**

ROTHBART, M., & LEWIS, S. (1988). Inferring category attributes from exemplar attributes: Geometric shapes and social categories. JOURNAL OF PERSONALITY AND SOCIAL PSYCHOLOGY, 55, 861–872. **323**

ROVEE-COLLIER, C., & HAYNE, H. (1987). Reactivation of infant memory: Implications for cognitive development. In H. W. Reese (Ed.), ADVANCES IN CHILD DEVELOPMENT AND BEHAVIOR (Vol. 20). New York: Academic Press. **77**

ROY, A. (1981). Role of past loss in depression. ARCHIVES OF GENERAL PSYCHIATRY, 38(3), 301–302. **611**

ROYCE, J. R., & MOS, L. P. (Eds.). (1981). HUMANISTIC PSYCHOLOGY: CONCEPTS AND CRITICISMS. New York: Plenum. **29**

RUBIN, D. C. (Ed.). (1986). AUTOBIOGRAPHICAL MEMORY. New York: Cambridge University Press. **304**

RUBIN, Z. (1973). LIKING AND LOVING. New York: Holt, Rinehart & Winston. **109, 712, 713, 716**

RUBIN, Z. (1975). Disclosing oneself to a stranger: Reciprocity and its limits. JOURNAL OF EXPERIMENTAL SOCIAL PSYCHOLOGY, 11, 233–260. **716**

RUBIN, Z., HILL, C. T., PEPLAU, L. A., & DUNKEL-SCHETTER, C. (1980). Self-disclosure in dating couples: Sex roles and ethic of openness. JOURNAL OF MARRIAGE AND THE FAMILY, 42, 305–317. **716**

RUCH, J. C. (1975). Self-hypnosis: The result of heterohypnosis or vice versa? INTERNATIONAL JOURNAL OF CLINICAL AND EXPERIMENTAL HYPNOSIS, 23, 282–304. **229**

RUCH, J. C., MORGAN, A. H., & HILGARD, E. R. (1973). Behavioral predictions from hypnotic responsiveness scores when obtained with and without prior induction procedures. JOURNAL OF ABNORMAL PSYCHOLOGY, 82, 543–546. **230**

RUCH, L. O., & HOLMES, T. H. (1971). Scaling of life change: Comparison of direct and indirect methods. JOURNAL OF PSYCHOSOMATIC RESEARCH, 15, 221–227. **567**

RUDERMAN, A. J. (1986). Dietary restraint: A theoretical and empirical review. PSYCHOLOGICAL BULLETIN, 99, 247–262. **371**

RUEHLMAN, L. S., WEST, S. G., & PASAHOW, R. J. (1985). Depression and evaluative schemata. JOURNAL OF PERSONALITY, 53, 46–92. **617**

RUMBAUGH, D. M. (Ed.). (1977). LANGUAGE LEARNING BY A CHIMPANZEE: THE LANA PROJECT. New York: Academic Press. **346**

RUMELHART, D. E., & MCCLELLAND, J. L. (1987). Learning the past tenses of English verbs: Implicit rules or parallel distributed processing? In B. MacWhinney (Ed.), MECHANISMS OF LANGUAGE ACQUISITION. Hillsdale, NJ: Erlbaum. **341**

RUMELHART, D. E., MCCLELLAND, J. L., & THE PDP RESEARCH GROUP. (1986). PARALLEL DISTRIBUTED PROCESSING: EXPLORATIONS IN THE MICROSTRUCTURE OF COGNITION. VOLUME 1: FOUNDATIONS. Cambridge, MA: Bradford Books/MIT Press. **169, 193**

RUNCK, B. (1980). BIOFEEDBACK: ISSUES IN TREATMENT ASSESSMENT. National Institute of Mental Health Science Reports. **584**

RUSHTON, J. P., JACKSON, D. N., & PAUNONEN, S. V. (1981). Personality: Nomothetic or idiographic? A response to Kenrick and Stringfield. PSYCHOLOGICAL REVIEW, 88, 582–589. **547**

RUSSEK, M. (1971). Hepatic receptors and the neurophysiological mechanisms controlling feedback behavior. In S. Ehreupreis (Ed.), NEUROSCIENCES RESEARCH (Vol. 4). New York: Academic Press. **367**

RUSSELL, M. J. (1976). Human olfactory communication. NATURE, 260, 520–522. **76, 146**

RUSSELL, M. J., SWITZ, G. M., & THOMPSON, K. (1980). Olfactory influence on the human menstrual cycle. PHARMACOLOGY, BIOCHEMISTRY AND BEHAVIOR, 13, 737–738. **146**

RUTHERFORD, W. (1886). A new theory of hearing. JOURNAL OF ANATOMY AND PHYSIOLOGY, 21, 166–168. **141**

RUTTER, M. (1979). Maternal deprivation 1972–1978: New findings, new concepts, new approaches. CHILD DEVELOPMENT, 50, 283–305. **477**

RYLE, G. (1949). THE CONCEPT OF MIND. San Francisco: Hutchinson. **303**

S

SACHS, J. D. S. (1967). Recognition memory for syntactic and semantic aspects of connected discourse. PERCEPTION AND PSYCHOPHYSICS, 2, 437–442. **292**

SACKEIM, H. A., PORTNOY, S., NEELEY, P., STEIF, B. L., DECINA, P., & MALITZ, S. (1985). Cognitive consequences of low dosage ECT. In S. Malitz & H. A. Sackeim (Eds.), ELECTROCONVULSIVE THERAPY: CLINICAL AND BASIC RESEARCH ISSUES. Annals of the New York Academy of Science. **673**

SALAMY, J. (1970). Instrumental responding to internal cues associated with REM sleep. PSYCHONOMIC SCIENCE, 18, 342–343. **209**

SALAPATEK, P. (1975). Pattern perception in early infancy. In L. B. Cohen & P. Salapatek (Eds.), INFANT PERCEPTION: FROM SENSATION TO COGNITION (Vol. 1). New York: Academic Press. **187**

SANDERS, G. S. (1984). Self-presentation and drive in social facilitation. JOURNAL OF EXPERIMENTAL SOCIAL PSYCHOLOGY, 20, 312–322. **726**

SANDERS, G. S., & BARON, R. S. (1975). The motivating effects of distraction on task performance. JOURNAL OF PERSONALITY AND SOCIAL PSYCHOLOGY, 32, 956–963. **726**

SARASON, I. G., JOHNSON, J. H., SIEGEL, J. M. (1978). Assessing the impact of life changes: Development of the life experiences survey. JOURNAL OF CONSULTING AND CLINICAL PSYCHOLOGY, 46, 932–946. **568**

SARASON, I. G., & SARASON, B. R. (1984). ABNORMAL PSYCHOLOGY: THE PROBLEM OF MALADAPTIVE BEHAVIOR. Englewood Cliffs, NJ: Prentice-Hall. **598, 599, 635**

SATINOFF, E., & RUTSTEIN, J. (1970). Behavioral thermoregulations in rats with anterior hypothalamic lesions. JOURNAL OF COMPARATIVE AND PHYSIOLOGICAL PSYCHOLOGY, 71, 72–82. **363**

SATINOFF, E., & SHAN, S. Y. (1971). Loss of behavioral thermoregulation after lateral hypothalamic lesions in rats. JOURNAL OF COMPARATIVE AND PHYSIOLOGICAL PSYCHOLOGY, 72, 302–312. **363**

SATTLER, J. M. (1988). ASSESSMENT OF CHILDREN. San Diego: Jerome M. Sattler. **447, 449, 473**

SAUNDERS, D. R. (1985). On Hyman's factor analyses. JOURNAL OF PARAPSYCHOLOGY, 49, 86–88. **238**

SAVIN-WILLIAMS, R. C., & JAQUISH, G. A. (1981). The assessment of adolescent self-esteem: A comparison of methods. JOURNAL OF PERSONALITY, 49, 324–336. **540**

SAXE, L., DOUGHERTY, D., & CROSS, T. (1985). The validity of polygraph testing. AMERICAN PSYCHOLOGIST, 40, 355–366. **406**

SCARR, S. (1981). RACE, SOCIAL CLASS, AND INDIVIDUAL DIFFERENCES IN IQ. Hillsdale, NJ: Erlbaum. **473**

SCARR, S. (1984). MOTHER CARE/OTHER CARE. New York: Basic Books. **95**

SCARR, S. (1988). How genotypes and environments combine: Development and individual differences. In N. Bolger, A. Caspi, G. Downey, & M. Moorehouse (Eds.), PERSONS IN CONTEXT: DEVELOPMENTAL PROCESSES. New York: Cambridge University Press. **481, 482, 483, 484**

SCARR, S., & MCCARTNEY, K. (1983). How people make their own environments: A theory of genotype-environment effects. CHILD DEVELOPMENT, 54, 424–435. **481, 482, 483, 484**

SCARR, S., & WEINBERG, R. A. (1976). IQ test performance of black children adopted by white families. AMERICAN PSYCHOLOGIST, 31, 726–739. **466, 469**

SCARR, S., WEINBERG, R. A., & LEVINE, A. (1986). UNDERSTANDING DEVELOPMENT. San Diego: Harcourt Brace Jovanovich. **501**

SCHACHTER, S. (1971). EMOTION, OBESITY, AND CRIME. New York: Academic Press. **404**

SCHACHTER, S., & SINGER, J. E. (1962). Cognitive, social, and physiological determinants of emotional state. PSYCHOLOGICAL REVIEW, 69, 379–399. **408**

SCHACTEL, E. G. (1947). On memory and child amnesia. PSYCHIATRY, 10, 1–26. **305**

SCHACTER, D. L. (1987). Implicit memory: History and current status. JOURNAL OF EXPERIMENTAL PSYCHOLOGY: LEARNING, MEMORY AND COGNITION, 3, 501–518. **305**

SCHAEFFER, J., ANDRYSIAK, T., & UNGERLEIDER, J. T. (1981). Cognition and long-term use of ganja (cannabis). SCIENCE, 213, 456–466. **223**

SCHAFER, R. (1976). A NEW LANGUAGE FOR PSYCHOANALYSIS. New Haven: Yale University Press. **518**

SCHAIE, K. W., & WILLIS, S. L. (1986a). ADULT DEVELOPMENT AND AGING (2nd ed.). Boston: Little, Brown. **110**

SCHAIE, K. W., & WILLIS, S. L. (1986b). Can decline in intellectual functioning in the elderly be reversed? DEVELOPMENTAL PSYCHOLOGY, 22, 223–232. **111**

SCHANK, R. C. (1982). DYNAMIC MEMORY. New York: Cambridge University Press. **336**

SCHIFF, W., & FOULKE, E. (1982). TACTUAL PERCEPTION: A SOURCEBOOK. Cambridge: Cambridge University Press. **155**

SCHIFFENBAUER, A., & SCHIAVO, R. S. (1976). Physical distance and attraction: An intensification effect. JOURNAL OF EXPERIMENTAL SOCIAL PSYCHOLOGY, 12, 274–282. **712**

SCHIFFMAN, H. R. (1982). SENSATION AND PERCEPTION: AN INTEGRATED APPROACH (2nd ed.). New York: Wiley. **155**

SCHIFFMAN, S. S., & ERICKSON, R. P. (1980). The issue of primary tastes versus a taste continuum. NEUROSCIENCE AND BIOBEHAVIORAL REVIEWS, 4, 109–117. **149**

SCHLEIFER, S. J., KELLER, S. E., MCKEGNEY, F. P., & STEIN, M. (1979, March). THE INFLUENCE OF STRESS AND OTHER PSYCHOSOCIAL FACTORS ON HUMAN IMMUNITY. Paper presented at the 36th Annual Meeting of the Psychosomatic Society, Dallas. **585**

SCHMITT, B. H., GILOVICH, T., GOORE, N., & JOSEPH, L. (1986). Mere presence and social facilitation: One more time. JOURNAL OF EXPERIMENTAL SOCIAL PSYCHOLOGY, 22, 242–248. **726**

SCHNEIDER, A. M., & TARSHIS, B. (1986). AN INTRODUCTION TO PHYSIOLOGICAL PSYCHOLOGY (3rd ed.). New York: Random House. **67**

SCHNEIDER, D. J. (1973). Implicit personality theory: A review. PSYCHOLOGICAL BULLETIN, 79, 294–309. **692**

SCHNEIDER, D. J., & MILLER, R. S. (1975). The effects of enthusiasm and quality of arguments on attitude attribution. JOURNAL OF PERSONALITY, 43, 693–708. **696**

SCHNEIDERMAN, N. S., & TAPP, J. T. (Eds.). (1985). BEHAVIORAL MEDICINE: THE BIOPSYCHOSOCIAL APPROACH. New York: Erlbaum. **589**

SCHRADER, W. B. (1971). The predictive validity of College Board Admissions tests. In W. H. Angoff (Ed.), THE COLLEGE BOARD ADMISSIONS TESTING PROGRAM: A TECHNICAL REPORT ON RESEARCH AND DEVELOPMENT ACTIVITIES RELATING TO THE SCHOLASTIC APTITUDE TEST AND ACHIEVEMENT TESTS. New York: College Entrance Examination Board. **454**

SCHUCKIT, M. A. (1989). DRUG AND ALCOHOL ABUSE: A CLINICAL GUIDE TO DIAGNOSIS AND TREATMENT (3rd ed.). New York: Plenum. **216, 243**

SCHULTZ, D. (1987). A HISTORY OF MODERN PSYCHOLOGY (4th ed.). New York: Academic Press. **29, 773**

SCHVANEVELDT, R. W., & MEYER, D. E. (1973). Retrieval and comparison processes in semantic memory. In S. Kornblum (Ed.), ATTENTION AND

SCHVANEVELTD, R. W. (continued) PERFORMANCE (Vol. 4). New York: Academic Press. 173

SCHWARTZ, B. (1982). Failure to produce response variability with reinforcement. JOURNAL OF THE EXPERIMENTAL ANALYSIS OF BEHAVIOR, 37, 171–181. 267

SCHWARTZ, B. (1989). PSYCHOLOGY OF LEARNING AND BEHAVIOR (3rd ed.). New York: Norton. 256, 279

SCHWARTZ, B., & GAMZU, E. (1977). Pavlovian control of operant behavior. In W. K. Honig & J. E. R. Staddon (Eds.), HANDBOOK OF OPERANT BEHAVIOR. Englewood Cliffs, NJ: Prentice-Hall. 261

SCHWARTZ, G. E. (1975). Biofeedback, self-regulation, and the patterning of physiological processes. AMERICAN SCIENTIST, 63, 314–324. 584

SEAMON, J. G., BRODY, N., & KAUFF, D. M. (1983). Affective discrimination of stimuli that are not recognized: Effects of shadowing, masking, and cerebral laterality. JOURNAL OF EXPERIMENTAL PSYCHOLOGY: LEARNING, MEMORY AND COGNITION, 9, 544–555. 412

SEARS, D. O., PEPLAU, L. A., FREEDMAN, J. L., & TAYLOR, S. E. (1988). SOCIAL PSYCHOLOGY (6th ed.). Englewood Cliffs, NJ: Prentice-Hall. 719, 721, 761

SEARS, R. R. (1943). Survey of objective studies of psychoanalytic concepts. SOCIAL SCIENCE RESEARCH COUNCIL BULLETIN (No. 51). 518

SEARS, R. R. (1944). Experimental analyses of psychoanalytic phenomena. In J. M. Hunt (Ed.), PERSONALITY AND THE BEHAVIOR DISORDERS (Vol. 1). New York: Ronald. 518

SEARS, R. R., MACCOBY, E. E., & LEVIN, H. (1957). PATTERNS OF CHILD REARING. New York: Harper & Row. 517

SEEMAN, J. (1949). A study of the process of nondirective therapy. JOURNAL OF CONSULTING PSYCHOLOGY, 13, 157–168. 658

SEGAL, M. W. (1974). Alphabet and attraction: An unobtrusive measure of the effect of propinquity in a field setting. JOURNAL OF PERSONALITY AND SOCIAL PSYCHOLOGY, 30, 654–657. 712

SEIDEN, R. H. (1966). Campus tragedy: A study of student suicide. JOURNAL OF ABNORMAL PSYCHOLOGY, 71, 388–399. 610

SEIDENBERG, M. S., & PETITTO, L. A. (1979). Signing behavior in apes. COGNITION, 7, 177–215. 346

SEIFERT, C. M., ROBERTSON, S. P., & BLACK, J. B. (1985). Types of inferences generated during reading. JOURNAL OF MEMORY AND LANGUAGE, 24, 405–422. 313

SEKULER, R., & BLAKE, R. (1985). PERCEPTION. New York: Knopf. 155

SEKULER, R., & GANZ, L. (1963). A new aftereffect of seen movement with a stabilized retinal image. SCIENCE, 139, 1146–1148. 164

SEKULER, R., HUTMAN, L. P., & OWSLEY, C. J. (1980). Human aging and spatial vision. SCIENCE, 209, 1255–1256. 137

SELFRIDGE, O., & NEISSER, U. (1959). Pattern recognition by machine. SCIENTIFIC AMERICAN, 203, 60–80. 137, 169

SELIGMAN, M. E. P. (1971). Phobias and preparedness. BEHAVIOR THERAPY, 2, 307–320. 603

SELIGMAN, M. E. P. (1975). HELPLESSNESS. San Francisco: Freeman. 253, 262

SELIGMAN, M. E. P., & ROSENHAN, D. L. (1984). ABNORMAL PSYCHOLOGY. New York: Norton. 603, 635

SEWELL, W. H., & MUSSEN, P. H. (1952). The effects of feeding, weaning, and scheduling procedures on childhood adjustment and the formation of oral symptoms. CHILD DEVELOPMENT, 23, 185–191. 517

SHAFFER, L. F. (1947). Fear and courage in aerial combat. JOURNAL OF CONSULTING PSYCHOLOGY, 11, 137–143. 403

SHAPIRO, A. K., & MORRIS, L. A. (1978). The placebo effect in medical and psychological therapies. In S. L. Garfield & A. E. Bergin (Eds.), HANDBOOK OF PSYCHOTHERAPY AND BEHAVIOR CHANGE (2nd ed.). New York: Wiley. 668

SHAPIRO, D. A., & SHAPIRO, D. (1982). Meta-analysis of comparative therapy outcome studies: A replication and refinement. PSYCHOLOGICAL BULLETIN, 92, 581–604. 665

SHAPIRO, D. H. (1985). Clinical use of meditation as a self-regulation strategy: Comments on Holme's 1984 conclusions and implications. AMERICAN PSYCHOLOGIST, 40, 719–722. 227

SHAPLEY, R., & LENNIE, P. (1985). Spatial frequency analysis in the visual system. ANNUAL REVIEW OF NEUROSCIENCES, 8, 547–583. 167

SHAW, D. W., & THORESEN, C. E. (1974). Effects of modeling and desensitization in reducing dentist phobia. JOURNAL OF COUNSELING PSYCHOLOGY, 21, 415–420. 651

SHEEHY, G. (1976). PASSAGES. New York: Dutton. 110

SHEINGOLD, K., & TENNEY, Y. J. (1982). Memory for a salient childhood event. In U. Neisser (Ed.), MEMORY OBSERVED: REMEMBERING IN NATURAL CONTEXTS. San Francisco: Freeman. 6, 305

SHEKELLE, R., NEATON, J. D., JACOBS, D., HULLEY, S., & BLACKBURN, H. (1983). TYPE A BEHAVIOR PATTERN IN MRFIT. A paper presented to the American Heart Association Council on Epidemiology Meetings, San Diego. 581

SHELDON, W. H. (1954). ATLAS OF MEN: A GUIDE FOR SOMATOTYPING THE ADULT MALE AT ALL AGES. New York: Harper & Row. 504

SHEPARD, R. N., & COOPER, L. A. (1982). MENTAL IMAGES AND THEIR TRANSFORMATIONS. Cambridge, MA: MIT Press, Bradford Books. 347, 349, 356

SHEPOSH, J. P., DEMING, M., & YOUNG, L. E. (1977, April). THE RADIATING EFFECTS OF STATUS AND ATTRACTIVENESS OF A MALE UPON EVALUATING HIS FEMALE PARTNER. Paper presented at the annual meeting of the Western Psychological Association, Seattle. 712

SHERMAN, A. R. (1972). Real-life exposure as a primary therapeutic factor in the desensitization treatment of fear. JOURNAL OF ABNORMAL PSYCHOLOGY, 79, 19–28. 648

SHERRINGTON, R., BRYNJOLFSSON, J., & collaborators. (1988). Localization of a susceptibility locus for schizophrenia on chromosome 5. NATURE, 336, 164–167. 623

SHNEIDMAN, E. A. (1985). DEFINITION OF SUICIDE. New York: Wiley. 610

SIGALL, H., & LANDY, D. (1973). Radiating beauty: The effects of having a physically attractive partner on person perception. JOURNAL OF PERSONALITY AND SOCIAL PSYCHOLOGY, 31, 410–414. 712

SILVERMAN, I. (1964). Self-esteem and differential responsiveness to success and failure. JOURNAL OF ABNORMAL AND SOCIAL PSYCHOLOGY, 69, 115–119. 616

SILVERMAN, I. (1971). Physical attractiveness and courtship. SEXUAL BEHAVIOR, 1, 22–25. 714

SILVERMAN, L. H. (1976). Psychoanalytic theory: The reports of my death are greatly exaggerated. AMERICAN PSYCHOLOGIST, 31, 621–637. 518

SILVERMAN, L. H., & WEINBERGER, J. (1985). Mommy and I are one: Implications for psychotherapy. AMERICAN PSYCHOLOGIST, 40, 1296–1308. 518

SIMMONS, J. V. (1981). PROJECT SEA HUNT: A REPORT ON PROTOTYPE DEVELOPMENT AND TESTS. Technical Report 746, Naval Ocean Systems Center, San Diego. 260

SIMMONS, R. G., & BLYTH, D. A. (1988). MOVING INTO ADOLESCENCE: THE IMPACT OF PUBERTAL CHANGE AND SCHOOL CONTEXT. New York: Aldine. 102

SIMON, H. A. (1985, June). USING COGNITIVE SCIENCE TO SOLVE HUMAN PROBLEMS. Paper presented at Science and Public Policy Seminar, Federation of Behavioral,

Psychological, and Cognitive Sciences. 354

SIMON, H. A., & GILMARTIN, K. (1973). A simulation of memory for chess positions. COGNITIVE PSYCHOLOGY, 5, 29–46. 352

SIMPSON, J. A., CAMPBELL, B., & BERSCHEID, E. (1986). The association between romantic love and marriage: Kephart 1967 twice revisited. PERSONALITY AND SOCIAL PSYCHOLOGY BULLETIN, 12, 363–372. 717

SINGER, J. L. (1984). THE HUMAN PERSONALITY: AN INTRODUCTORY TEXTBOOK. San Diego: Harcourt Brace Jovanovich. 551

SINGER, J. L., & SINGER, D. G. (1981). TELEVISION, IMAGINATION AND AGGRESSION. Hillsdale, NJ: Erlbaum. 431

SIQUELAND, E. R., & LIPSITT, J. P. (1966). Conditioned head-turning in human newborns. JOURNAL OF EXPERIMENTAL CHILD PSYCHOLOGY, 3, 356–376. 77

SIZEMORE, C. C., & PITTILLO, E. S. (1977). I'M EVE. Garden City, NY: Doubleday. 200

SKEELS, H. M. (1966). Adult status of children with contrasting early life experiences: A follow-up study. MONOGRAPHS OF THE SOCIETY FOR RESEARCH IN CHILD DEVELOPMENT, 31(Serial No. 105). 80

SKEELS, H. M., & DYE, H. B. (1939). A study of the effects of differential stimulation on mentally retarded children. PROCEEDINGS OF THE AMERICAN ASSOCIATION FOR MENTAL DEFICIENCY, 44, 114–136. 80

SKINNER, B. F. (1938). THE BEHAVIOR OF ORGANISMS. New York: Appleton-Century-Crofts. 247, 257, 279

SKINNER, B. F. (1948). "Superstition" in the pigeon. JOURNAL OF EXPERIMENTAL PSYCHOLOGY, 38, 168–172. 261

SKINNER, B. F. (1971). BEYOND FREEDOM AND DIGNITY. New York: Knopf. 248

SKINNER, B. F. (1981). Selection by consequences. SCIENCE, 213, 501–504. 11

SKOLNICK, A. S. (1986). THE PSYCHOLOGY OF HUMAN DEVELOPMENT. San Diego: Harcourt Brace Jovanovich. 113

SKYRMS, B. (1986). CHOICE AND CHANCE: AN INTRODUCTION TO INDUCTIVE LOGIC. Belmont, CA: Dickenson. 328, 330

SLOANE, R. B., STAPLES, F. R., CRISTOL, A. H., YORKSTON, N. J., & WHIPPLE, K. (1975). PSYCHOTHERAPY VERSUS BEHAVIOR THERAPY. Cambridge, MA: Harvard University Press. 666

SLOBIN, D. I. (1971). Cognitive prerequisites for the acquisition of grammar. In C. A. Ferguson & D. I. Slobin (Eds.), STUDIES OF CHILD LANGUAGE DEVELOPMENT. New York: Holt, Rinehart & Winston. 339, 341

SLOBIN, D. I. (1979). PSYCHOLINGUISTICS

(2nd ed.). Glenville, IL: Scott, Foresman. 326, 346

SLOBIN, D. I. (Ed.). (1985). THE CROSS-LINGUISTIC STUDY OF LANGUAGE ACQUISITION. Hillsdale, NJ: Erlbaum. 341

SMART, R. G., & FEJER, D. (1972). Drug use among adolescents and their parents: Closing the generation gap in mood modification. JOURNAL OF ABNORMAL PSYCHOLOGY, 79, 153–160. 225

SMETANA, J. G. (1988). Concepts of self and social convention: Adolescents' and parents' reasoning about hypothetical and actual family conflicts. In M. R. Gunnar & W. A. Collins (Eds.), THE MINNESOTA SYMPOSIA (Vol. 21). Hillsdale, NJ: Erlbaum. 104, 105

SMILANSKY, B. (1974). Paper presented at the meeting of the American Educational Research Association, Chicago. 470

SMITH, C. A., & ELLSWORTH, P. C. (1985). Patterns of cognitive appraisal in emotion. JOURNAL OF PERSONALITY AND SOCIAL PSYCHOLOGY, 48, 813–848. 410

SMITH, C. A., & ELLSWORTH, P. C. (1987). Patterns of appraisal and emotion related to taking an exam. JOURNAL OF PERSONALITY AND SOCIAL PSYCHOLOGY, 52, 475–488. 410

SMITH, D., KING, M., & HOEBEL, B. G. (1970). Lateral hypothalamic control of killing: Evidence for a cholinoceptive mechanism. SCIENCE, 167, 900–901. 424

SMITH, E. E., ADAMS, N., & SCHORR, D. (1978). Fact retrieval and the paradox of interference. COGNITIVE PSYCHOLOGY, 10, 438–464. 298

SMITH, E. E., & MEDIN, D. L. (1981). CATEGORIES AND CONCEPTS. Cambridge, MA: Harvard University Press. 323, 356

SMITH, G. M. (1986). Adolescent personality traits that predict adult drug use. COMPREHENSIVE THERAPY, 22, 44–50. 225

SMITH, M. B. (1973). Is psychology relevant to new priorities? AMERICAN PSYCHOLOGIST, 6, 463–471. 14

SMITH, M. L., GLASS, G. V., & MILLER, T. I. (1980). THE BENEFITS OF PSYCHOTHERAPY. Baltimore: Johns Hopkins University Press. 665

SMUTS, B. B. (1986). Gender, aggression, and influence. In B. Smuts, D. Cheney, R. Seyfarth, R. Wrangham, & T. Struhsaker (Eds.), PRIMATE SOCIETIES. Chicago: University of Chicago Press. 427

SNODGRASS, J. G., LEVY-BERGER, G., & HAYDON, M. (1985). HUMAN EXPERIMENTAL PSYCHOLOGY. New York: Oxford University Press. 29

SNOW, C. (1987). Relevance of the notion of a critical period to language acquisition. In M. H. Bornstein (Ed.), SENSITIVE PE-

RIODS IN DEVELOPMENT: INTERDISCIPLINARY PERSPECTIVES. Hillsdale, NJ: Erlbaum. 343

SNYDER, M. L., & URANOWITZ, S. W. (1978). Reconstructing the past: Some cognitive consequences of person perception. JOURNAL OF PERSONALITY AND SOCIAL PSYCHOLOGY, 36, 941–950. 315, 688

SNYDER, M. L., STEPHAN, W. G., & ROSENFELD, D. (1976). Egotism and attribution. JOURNAL OF PERSONALITY AND SOCIAL PSYCHOLOGY, 33, 435–441. 700

SNYDER, M. L., TANKE, E. D., & BERSCHEID, E. (1977). Social perception and interpersonal behavior: On the self-fulfilling nature of social stereotypes. JOURNAL OF PERSONALITY AND SOCIAL PSYCHOLOGY, 35, 656–666. 693

SNYDER, S. H. (1980). BIOLOGICAL ASPECTS OF MENTAL DISORDER. New York: Oxford University Press. 624

SNYDER, W. U., & collaborators. (1947). CASEBOOK OF NONDIRECTIVE COUNSELING. Boston: Houghton Mifflin. 658

SOLOMON, R. L. (1980). The opponent-process theory of acquired motivation. AMERICAN PSYCHOLOGIST, 35, 691–712. 418, 419

SOLOMON, R. L., & CORBIT, J. D. (1974). An opponent-process theory of motivation: Pt. 1. Temporal dynamics of affect. PSYCHOLOGICAL REVIEW, 81, 119–145. 418

SORENSEN, R. C. (1973). ADOLESCENT SEXUALITY IN CONTEMPORARY AMERICA. New York: World. 102

SPACHE, G., & BERG, P. (1978). THE ART OF EFFICIENT READING (3rd ed.). New York: Macmillan. 762

SPANOS, N. P., & HEWITT, E. C. (1980). The hidden observer in hypnotic analgesia: Discovery or experimental creation? JOURNAL OF PERSONALITY AND SOCIAL PSYCHOLOGY, 39, 1201–1214. 233

SPANOS, N. P., WEEKES, J. R., & BERTRAND, L. D. (1985). Multiple personality: A social psychological perspective. JOURNAL OF ABNORMAL PSYCHOLOGY, 94, 362–376. 201

SPEARMAN, C. (1904). "General intelligence" objectively determined and measured. AMERICAN JOURNAL OF PSYCHOLOGY, 15, 201–293. 460

SPEATH, J. L. (1976). Characteristics of the work setting and the job as determinants of income. In W. H. Sewell, R. M. Hauser, & D. L. Featherman (Eds.), SCHOOLING AND ACHIEVEMENT IN AMERICAN SOCIETY. New York: Academic Press. 454

SPENCE, K. W. (1964). Anxiety (drive) level and performance in eyelid conditioning. PSYCHOLOGICAL BULLETIN, 61, 129–139. 237

SPERRY, R. W. (1970). Perception in the absence of neocortical commissures. In PERCEPTION AND ITS DISORDERS (Res. Publ. A.R.N.M.D., Vol. 48). New York: The Association for Research in Nervous and Mental Disease. **50, 53**

SPIELBERGER, C. D., JOHNSON, E. H., RUSSELL, S. F., CRANE, R. S., JACOBS, G. A., & WORDEN, T. J. (1985). The experience and expression of anger: Construction and validation of an anger expression scale. In M. A. Chesney & R. H. Rosenman (Eds.), ANGER AND HOSTILITY IN CARDIOVASCULAR AND BEHAVIORAL DISORDERS. New York: Hemisphere/McGraw-Hill. **581**

SPOEHR, K. T., & LEHMKUHLE, S. W. (1982). VISUAL INFORMATION PROCESSING. San Francisco: Freeman. **193**

SPRINGER, S. P., & DEUTSCH, G. (1989). LEFT BRAIN, RIGHT BRAIN (3rd ed.). San Francisco: Freeman. **56, 67**

SQUIRE, L. R. (1986). Mechanisms of memory. SCIENCE, 232, 1612–1619.

SQUIRE, L. R. (1987). MEMORY AND BRAIN. New York: Oxford University Press. **38, 46, 67, 319**

SQUIRE, L. R., & BUTTERS, N. (Eds.). (1984). THE NEUROPSYCHOLOGY OF MEMORY. New York: Guilford Press. **319**

SQUIRE, L. R., & COHEN, N. J. (1984). Human memory and amnesia. In J. L. McGaugh, G. T. Lynch, & N. M. Weinberger (Eds.), THE NEUROBIOLOGY OF LEARNING AND MEMORY. New York: Guilford Press. **302**

SQUIRE, L. R., & FOX, M. M. (1980). Assessment of remote memory: Validation of the television test by repeated testing during a seven-day period. BEHAVIORAL RESEARCH METHODS AND INSTRUMENTATION, 12, 583–586. **296**

SQUIRE, L. R., COHEN, N. J., & NADEL, L. (1984). The medial temporal region and memory consolidations: A new hypothesis. In H. Weingartner and E. Parker (Eds.), MEMORY CONSOLIDATION. Hillsdale, NJ: Erlbaum. **296**

SROUFE, A., FOX, N., & PANCAKE, V. (1983). Attachment and dependency in developmental perspective. CHILD DEVELOPMENT, 54, 1615–1627. **477**

STAATS, A. W. (1968). LANGUAGE, LEARNING AND COGNITION. New York: Holt, Rinehart & Winston. **247**

STADDON, J. E. R. (1983). ADAPTIVE BEHAVIOR AND LEARNING. New York: Cambridge University Press. **279**

STAPP, J., & FULCHER, R. (1981). The employment of APA members. AMERICAN PSYCHOLOGIST, 36, 1263–1314. **23, 24**

STAYTON, D. J. (1973, March). INFANT RESPONSES TO BRIEF EVERYDAY SEPARATIONS: DISTRESS, FOLLOWING, AND GREETING. Paper presented at the meeting of the Society for Research in Child Development. **90**

STEFFY, R. A., ASARNOW, R. S., ASARNOW, J. R., MACCRIMMON, D. J., & CLEGHORN, J. M. (1984). The McMaster-Waterloo High-Risk Project: Multifaceted strategy for high-risk research. In H. F. Watt, E. J. Anthony, L. C. Wynne, & J. E. Rolf (Eds.), CHILDREN AT RISK FOR SCHIZOPHRENIA. New York: Cambridge University Press. **627**

STEINBERG, L. (1987). Impact of puberty on family relations: Effects of pubertal status and pubertal timing. DEVELOPMENTAL PSYCHOLOGY, 23, 451–460. **104**

STEINBROOK, R. (1987, July 30). AIDS threat changes life style of one in five. LOS ANGELES TIMES, pt. I, p. 1. **103**

STELLAR, J. R., & STELLAR, E. (1985). THE NEUROBIOLOGY OF MOTIVATION AND REWARD. New York: Springer-Verlag. **265, 268, 392, 399**

STERNBACH, R. A. (Ed.). (1986). THE PSYCHOLOGY OF PAIN (2nd ed.). New York: Raven. **155**

STERNBERG, R. J. (1985). BEYOND IQ: A TRIARCHIC THEORY OF HUMAN INTELLIGENCE. New York: Cambridge University Press. **462, 463**

STERNBERG, R. J. (1986). INTELLIGENCE APPLIED: UNDERSTANDING AND INCREASING YOUR INTELLECTUAL SKILLS. San Diego: Harcourt Brace Jovanovich. **473**

STERNBERG, R. J. (Ed.). (1982). HANDBOOK OF HUMAN INTELLIGENCE. New York: Cambridge University Press. **473**

STERNBERG, R. J. (Ed.). (1984). HUMAN ABILITIES: AN INFORMATION-PROCESSING APPROACH. New York: Freeman. **473**

STERNBERG, R. J., & SMITH, E. E. (Eds.). (1988). THE PSYCHOLOGY OF HUMAN THOUGHT. Cambridge, MA: Cambridge University Press. **356**

STERNBERG, R. J., & WAGNER, R. K. (Eds.). (1986). PRACTICAL INTELLIGENCE. New York: Cambridge University Press. **463**

STERNBERG, S. (1966). High-speed scanning in human memory. SCIENCE, 153, 652–654. **287**

STERNGLANZ, S. H., & SERBIN, L. A. (1974). Sex-role stereotyping in children's television programs. DEVELOPMENTAL PSYCHOLOGY, 10, 710–715. **96**

STEUER, F. B., APPLEFIELD, J. M., & SMITH, R. (1971). Televised aggression and the interpersonal aggression of preschool children. JOURNAL OF EXPERIMENTAL CHILD PSYCHOLOGY, 11, 422–447. **431**

STEVENS-LONG, J., SCHWARZ, J. L., & BLISS, D. (1976). The acquisition of compound sentence structure in an autistic child. BEHAVIOR THERAPY, 7, 397–404. **649**

STILES, W. B., SHAPIRO, D. A., & ELLIOTT, R. (1986). Are all psychotherapies equivalent? AMERICAN PSYCHOLOGIST, 41, 165–180. **665**

STOCKDALE, J. B. (1984). A VIETNAM EXPERIENCE. Stanford: Hoover Press. **565**

STOKES, D. M. (1987). Theoretical parapsychology. In S. Krippner (Ed.), ADVANCES IN PARAPSYCHOLOGICAL RESEARCH (Vol. 5). Jefferson, NC: McFarland. **241**

STORMS, M. D. (1981). A theory of erotic orientation development. PSYCHOLOGICAL REVIEW, 88, 340–353. **386**

STORMS, M. D., & NISBETT, R. E. (1970). Insomnia and the attribution process. JOURNAL OF PERSONALITY AND SOCIAL PSYCHOLOGY, 2, 319–328. **702**

STRASSMAN, H. D., THALER, M. B., & SCHEIN, E. H. (1956). A prisoner of war syndrome: Apathy as a reaction to severe stress. AMERICAN JOURNAL OF PSYCHIATRY, 112, 998–1003. **564**

STRAUSS, J. S. (1982). Behavioral aspects of being disadvantaged and risk for schizophrenia. In D. L. Parron, F. Solomon, & C. D. Jenkins (Eds.), BEHAVIOR, HEALTH RISKS, AND SOCIAL DISADVANTAGE. Washington, DC: National Academy Press. **625**

STRAUSS, J. S., & CARPENTER, W. T., JR. (1981). SCHIZOPHRENIA. New York: Plenum. **635**

STREISSGUTH, A. P., CLARREN, S. K., & JONES, K. L. (1985). Natural history of the fetal alcohol syndrome: A 10-year follow-up of eleven patients. THE LANCET, 2(8446), 85–91. **215**

STRICKER, E. M. (1983). Thirst and sodium appetite after colloid treatment in rats: Role of the renin-angiotensin-aldosterone system. BEHAVIORAL NEUROSCIENCE, 97, 725–737. **370**

STRICKER, E. M., ROWLAND, N., SALLER, C. F., & FRIEDMAN, M. I. (1977). Homeostasis during hypoglycemia: Central control of adrenal secretion and peripheral control of feeding. SCIENCE, 196, 79–81. **366**

STRICKER, E. M., & VERBALIS, J. G. (1988). Hormones and behavior: The biology of thirst and sodium appetite. AMERICAN SCIENTIST, 76, 261–268. **365**

STROEBE, W., INSKO, C. A., THOMPSON, V. D., & LAYTON, B. D. (1971). Effects of physical attractiveness, attitude similarity, and sex on various aspects of interpersonal attraction. JOURNAL OF PERSONALITY AND SOCIAL PSYCHOLOGY, 18, 79–91. **712**

STRONGMAN, K. T. (1978). THE PSYCHOLOGY OF EMOTION (2nd ed.). New York: Wiley. **433**

STUART, R. B., & DAVIS, B. (1972). SLIM CHANCE IN A FAT WORLD. Champaign, IL: Research Press. **653**

STUNKARD, A. J. (Ed.). (1980). OBESITY. Philadelphia: Saunders. **399**

STUNKARD, A. J. (1982). Obesity. In M. Hersen, A. Bellack, A. Kazdin (Eds.), INTERNATIONAL HANDBOOK OF BEHAVIOR MODIFICATION AND THERAPY. New York: Plenum. **376**

STUNKARD, A. J., FOCH, T. T., & HRUBEC, Z. (1986). A twin study of human obesity. JOURNAL OF THE AMERICAN MEDICAL ASSOCIATION, 256, 51–54. **375**

SUAREZ, E. C., & WILLIAMS, R. B. (1989). Situational determinants of cardiovascular and emotional reactivity in high- and low-hostile men. PSYCHOSOMATIC MEDICINE, 51, 404–418. **581**

SUEDFELD, P. (1975). The benefits of boredom: Sensory deprivation considered. AMERICAN SCIENTIST, 63, 60–69. **395**

SUEDFELD, P., & BAKER-BROWN, G. (1986). Restricted environmental stimulation therapy and aversive conditioning in smoking cessation: Active and placebo effects. BEHAVIORAL RESPIRATORY THERAPY, 24, 421–428. **395**

SUEDFELD, P., & COREN, S. (1989). Perceptual isolation, sensory deprivation, and rest: Moving introductory psychology texts out of the 1950s. CANADIAN PSYCHOLOGY/PSYCHOLOGIE CANADIENNE, 30, 17–29. **396**

SUOMI, S. J. (1977). Peers, play, and primary prevention in primates. In PROCEEDINGS OF THE THIRD VERMONT CONFERENCE ON THE PRIMARY PREVENTION OF PSYCHOPATHOLOGY: PROMOTING SOCIAL COMPETENCE AND COPING IN CHILDREN. Hanover, NH: University Press of New England. **92**

SUOMI, S. J., HARLOW, H. F., & MCKINNEY, W. T. (1972). Monkey psychiatrist. AMERICAN JOURNAL OF PSYCHIATRY, 28, 41–46. **394**

SVAETICHIN, G. (1956). Spectral response curves from single cones. ACTA PHYSIOLOGICA SCANDINAVICA, 39(Suppl. 134), 17–46. **135**

SVENSON, O. (1981). Are we all less risky and more skillful than our fellow drivers? ACTA PSYCHOLOGICA, 47, 143–148. **616, 701**

SWANN, W. B., JR., & READ, S. J. (1981). Acquiring self-knowledge: The search for feedback that fits. JOURNAL OF PERSONALITY AND SOCIAL PSYCHOLOGY, 41, 1119–1128. **696**

SWINNEY, D. A. (1979). Lexical access during sentence comprehension: Consideration of context effects. JOURNAL OF VERBAL LEARNING AND VERBAL BEHAVIOR, 18, 645–659. **335**

SYER, J., & CONNOLLY, C. (1984). SPORTING BODY, SPORTING MIND: AN ATHLETE'S GUIDE TO MENTAL TRAINING. Cambridge, MA: Cambridge University Press. **228, 243**

T

TAKAHASHI, K. (1986). Examining the Strange Situation procedure with Japanese mothers and 12-month-old infants. DEVELOPMENT PSYCHOLOGY, 22, 265–270. **91**

TANENHAUS, M. G., LEIMAN, J., & SEIDENBERG, M. (1979). Evidence for multiple stages in the processing of ambiguous words in syntactic contexts. JOURNAL OF VERBAL LEARNING AND VERBAL BEHAVIOR, 18, 427–441. **335**

TANNER, J. M. (1970). Physical growth. In P. H. Mussen (Ed.), CARMICHAEL'S MANUAL OF CHILD PSYCHOLOGY (Vol. 1, 3rd ed.). New York: Wiley. **101**

TARLER-BENLOLO, L. (1978). The role of relaxation in biofeedback training. PSYCHOLOGICAL BULLETIN, 85, 727–755. **584**

TART, C. T. (1971). ON BEING STONED: A PSYCHOLOGICAL STUDY OF MARIJUANA INTOXICATION. Palo Alto, CA: Science and Behavior Books. **223**

TART, C. T., & DICK, L. (1970). Conscious control of dreaming: Pt. 1. The post-hypnotic dream. JOURNAL OF ABNORMAL PSYCHOLOGY, 76, 304–315. **210**

TART, C. T. (1979). Measuring the depth of an altered state of consciousness, with particular reference to self-report scales of hypnotic depth. In E. Fromm & R. E. Shor (Eds.), HYPNOSIS: DEVELOPMENTS IN RESEARCH AND NEW PERSPECTIVES (2nd ed.). New York: Aldine. **230**

TARTTER, V. C. (1986). LANGUAGE PROCESSES. New York: Holt, Rinehart & Winston. **357**

TASHKIN, D. P., COULSON, A., CLARK, V., & collaborators. (1985). Respiratory symptoms and lung function in heavy habitual smokers of marijuana alone and with tobacco, smokers of tobacco alone and nonsmokers. AMERICAN REVIEW OF RESPIRATORY DISEASE, 131, A198. **223**

TAVRIS, C. (1984). ANGER: THE MISUNDERSTOOD EMOTION. New York: Simon & Schuster. **433**

TAVRIS, C., & OFFIR, C. (1977). THE LONGEST WAR: SEX DIFFERENCES IN PERSPECTIVE. New York: Harcourt Brace Jovanovich. **384**

TAVRIS, C., & SADD, S. (1977). THE REDBOOK REPORT ON FEMALE SEXUALITY. New York: Dell, **383**

TAYLOR, S. E., & BROWN, J. D. (1988). Illusion and well-being: A social psychological perspective on mental health. PSYCHOLOGICAL BULLETIN, 103, 193–210. **616, 617**

TAYLOR, S. E., & THOMPSON, S. C. (1982). Stalking the elusive vividness effect. PSYCHOLOGICAL REVIEW, 89, 155–181. **685**

TEASDALE, T. W., & OWEN, D. R. (1984). Heredity and familial environment in intelligence and education level: A sibling study. NATURE, 309, 620–622. **467**

TEDESCHI, J. T., & ROSENFELD, P. (1981). Impression management and the forced compliance situation. In J. T. Tedeschi (Ed.), IMPRESSION MANAGEMENT THEORY AND SOCIAL PSYCHOLOGICAL RESEARCH. New York: Academic Press. **709**

TEITELBAUM, P., & EPSTEIN, A. N. (1962). The lateral hypothalamic syndrome: Recovery of feeding and drinking after lateral hypothalamic lesions. PSYCHOLOGICAL REVIEW, 69, 74–90. **368**

TELLEGEN, A., LYKKEN, D. T., BOUCHARD, T. J., JR., WILCOX, K. J., SEGAL, N. L., & RICH, S. (1988). Personality similarity in twins reared apart and together. JOURNAL OF PERSONALITY AND SOCIAL PSYCHOLOGY, 54, 1031–1039. **476**

TELLER, D. Y., MORSE, R., BORTON, R., & REGAL, D. (1974). Visual acuity for vertical and diagonal gratings in human infants. VISION RESEARCH, 14, 1433–1439. **186**

TEMPLIN, M. C. (1957). CERTAIN LANGUAGE SKILLS IN CHILDREN: THEIR DEVELOPMENT AND INTERRELATIONSHIPS. Minneapolis: University of Minnesota Press. **338**

TENNANT, C., SMITH, A., BEBBINGTON, P., & HURRY, J. (1981). Parental loss in childhood: Relationship to adult psychiatric impairment and contact with psychiatric services. ARCHIVES OF GENERAL PSYCHIATRY, 38, 309–314. **611**

TERKEL, J., & ROSENBLATT, J. S. (1972). Humoral factors underlying maternal behavior at parturition: Cross transfusion between freely moving rats. JOURNAL OF COMPARATIVE AND PHYSIOLOGICAL PSYCHOLOGY, 80, 365–371. **391**

TERRACE, H. S., PETITTO, L. A., SANDERS, D. J., & BEVER, T. G. (1979). Can an ape create a sentence? SCIENCE, 206, 891–902. **346**

TESSER, A., & BRODIE, M. (1971). A note on the evaluation of a "computer date." PSYCHONOMIC SCIENCE, 23, 300. **711**

TESTA, T. J. (1975). Effects of similarity of location and temporal intensity pattern of conditioned and unconditioned stimuli on the acquisition of conditioned suppression in rats. JOURNAL OF EXPERIMENTAL

TESTA, T. J. (continued)
PSYCHOLOGY: ANIMAL BEHAVIOR PROCESSES, 1, 114–121. **271**

TETLOCK, P. E., & LEVI, A. (1982). Attribution bias: On the inconclusiveness of the cognition-motivation debate. JOURNAL OF EXPERIMENTAL SOCIAL PSYCHOLOGY, 18, 68–88. **701**

THE STEERING COMMITTEE OF THE PHYSICIANS' HEALTH STUDY RESEARCH GROUP. (1988). Preliminary report: Findings from the aspirin component of the ongoing Physicians' Health Study. NEW ENGLAND JOURNAL OF MEDICINE, 318, 262–264. **237**

THIGPEN, C. H., & CLECKLEY, H. (1957). THE THREE FACES OF EVE. New York: McGraw-Hill. **200**

THOMAS, A., & CHESS, S. (1977). TEMPERAMENT AND DEVELOPMENT. New York: Brunner/Mazel. **78, 475**

THOMAS, E. L., & ROBINSON, H. A. (1982). IMPROVING READING IN EVERY CLASS. Boston: Allyn & Bacon. **311, 762, 764**

THOMAS, W. I., & THOMAS, D. S. (1928). THE CHILD IN AMERICA. New York: Knopf. **683**

THOMPSON, J. K., JARVIE, G. J., LAKEY, B. B., & CURETON, K. J. (1982). Exercise and obesity: Etiology, physiology, and intervention. PSYCHOLOGICAL BULLETIN, 91, 55–79. **374**

THOMPSON, R. A., LAMB, M., & ESTES, D. (1982). Stability of infant–mother attachment and its relationship to changing life circumstances in an unsettled middle-class sample. CHILD DEVELOPMENT, 53, 144–148. **91**

THOMPSON, W. R. (1954). The inheritance and development of intelligence. PROCEEDINGS OF THE ASSOCIATION FOR RESEARCH ON NERVOUS AND MENTAL DISEASE, 33, 209–231. **64**

THORESEN, C. E., TELCH, M. J., & EAGLESTON, J. R. (1981). Altering Type A behavior. PSYCHOSOMATICS, 8, 472–482. **581**

THORNDIKE, R. L., HAGEN, E. P., & SATTLER, J. M. (1986). STANFORD-BINET INTELLIGENCE SCALE: GUIDE FOR ADMINISTERING AND SCORING THE FOURTH EDITION. Chicago: Riverside. **446**

THORNDYIKE, E. L. (1898). Animal intelligence: An experimental study of the associative processes in animals. PSYCHOLOGICAL MONOGRAPHS, 2(8). **255**

THURSTONE, L. L. (1938). Primary mental abilities. PSYCHOMETRIC MONOGRAPHS (No. 1). Chicago: University of Chicago Press. **460**

THURSTONE, L. L., & THURSTONE, T. G. (1963). SRA PRIMARY ABILITIES.

Chicago: Science Research Associates. **461**

TIENARI, P., SORRI, A., LAHTI, I., NAARALA, M., WAHLBERG, K., et al. (1987). Interaction of genetic and psychosocial factors in schizophrenia. The Finnish adoptive family study: A longitudinal combination of the adoptive family strategy and the risk research strategy. SCHIZOPHRENIA BULLETIN, 13, 477–484. **627**

TIMBERLAKE, W., & ALLISON, J. (1974). Response deprivation: An empirical approach to instrumental performance. PSYCHOLOGICAL REVIEW, 81, 146–164. **264**

TOLMAN, E. C. (1932). PURPOSIVE BEHAVIOR IN ANIMALS AND MEN. New York: Appleton-Century-Crofts. (Reprint ed., 1967. New York: Irvington.) **272, 279**

TOMPKINS, S. S. (1980). Affect as amplification: Some modifications in theory. In R. Plutchik & H. Kellerman (Eds.), EMOTION: THEORY, RESEARCH AND EXPERIENCE (Vol. 1). New York: Academic Press. **417**

TORGERSEN, S. (1983). Genetic factors in anxiety disorders. ARCHIVES OF GENERAL PSYCHIATRY, 40, 1085–1089. **605**

TOURANGEAU, R., & ELLSWORTH, P. C. (1979). The role of facial responses in the experience of emotion. JOURNAL OF PERSONALITY AND SOCIAL PSYCHOLOGY, 37, 1519–1531. **416**

TRAUPMANN, J., & HATFIELD, E. (1981). Love and its effects on mental and physical health. In R. W. Fogel, E. Hatfield, S. B. Kiesler, & E. Shanas (Eds.), AGING: STABILITY AND CHANGE IN THE FAMILY. New York: Academic Press. **109**

TREISMAN, A. (1969). Strategies and models of selective attention. PSYCHOLOGICAL REVIEW, 76, 282–299. **176**

TREISMAN, A., & GELADE, G. (1980). A feature-integration theory of attention. COGNITIVE PSYCHOLOGY, 12, 97–136. **176**

TREISMAN, A., & GORMICAN, S. (1988). Feature analysis in early vision: Evidence from search asymmetries. PSYCHOLOGICAL REVIEW, 95, 15–48. **167**

TREISMAN, A., & SCHMIDT, H. (1982). Illusory conjunctions in the perception of objects. COGNITIVE PSYCHOLOGY, 14, 107–141. **177**

TRINDER, J. (1988). Subjective insomnia without objective findings: A pseudodiagnostic classification. PSYCHOLOGICAL BULLETIN, 103, 87–94. **206**

TRUAX, C. B., & MITCHELL, K. M. (1971). Research on certain therapist interpersonal skills in relation to process and outcome. In A. E. Bergin & S. L. Garfield (Eds.), HANDBOOK OF PSYCHOTHERAPY AND BEHAVIOR CHANGE: AN EMPIRICAL ANALYSIS. New York: Wiley. **541, 658**

TULVING, E. (1974). Cue-dependent forgetting. AMERICAN SCIENTIST, 62, 74–82. **294**

TULVING, E. (1983). THE ELEMENTS OF EPISODIC MEMORY. New York: Oxford University Press. **319**

TULVING, E. (1985). How many memory systems are there? AMERICAN PSYCHOLOGIST, 40, 385–398. **303**

TULVING, E., & PEARLSTONE, Z. (1966). Availability versus accessibility of information in memory for words. JOURNAL OF VERBAL LEARNING AND VERBAL BEHAVIOR, 5, 381–391. **294**

TVERSKY, A., & KAHNEMAN, D. (1973). On the psychology of prediction. PSYCHOLOGICAL REVIEW, 80, 237–251. **331**

TVERSKY, A., & KAHNEMAN, D. (1983). Extensional versus intuitive reasoning: The conjunction fallacy in probability judgment. PSYCHOLOGICAL REVIEW, 90, 293–315. **332**

TYHURST, J. S. (1951). Individual reactions to community disaster. AMERICAN JOURNAL OF PSYCHIATRY, 10, 746–769. **420**

TYLER, H. (1977). The unsinkable Jeane Dixon. THE HUMANIST, 37, 6–9. **240**

U

ULLMAN, S. (1979). THE INTERPRETATION OF VISUAL MOTION. Cambridge, MA: MIT Press. **165**

ULRICH, R. E., STACHNIK, T. J., & STAINTON, N. R. (1963). Student acceptance of generalized personality interpretations. PSYCHOLOGICAL REPORTS, 13, 831–834. **533**

URSIN, H. (1978). Activation, coping, and psychosomatics. In H. Ursin, E. Baade, & S. Levine (Eds.), PSYCHOBIOLOGY OF STRESS: A STUDY OF COPING MEN. New York: Academic Press. **559**

UTTS, J. (1986). The Ganzfeld debate: A statistician's perspective. JOURNAL OF PARAPSYCHOLOGY, 50, 393–402. **237**

V

VAILLANT, G. (1977). ADAPTATION TO LIFE. Boston: Little, Brown. **110**

VALENSTEIN, E. S. (1980). A prospective study of cingulatomy. In E. S. Valenstein (Ed.), THE PSYCHOSURGERY DEBATE: SCIENTIFIC, LEGAL, AND ETHICAL PERSPECTIVES. San Francisco: Freeman. **674**

VALLONE, R. P., ROSS, L., & LEPPER, M. R. (1985). The hostile media phenomenon: Biased perception and perceptions of media bias in coverage of the Beirut massacre. JOURNAL OF PERSONALITY AND SOCIAL PSYCHOLOGY, 49, 577–585. **691**

VAN CANTFORT, P. E., & RIMPAU, J. B. (1982). Sign language studies with children and chimpanzees. SIGN LANGUAGE STUDIES, 34, 15–72. **346**

VAN EEDEN, F. (1913). A study of dreams. PROCEEDINGS OF THE SOCIETY FOR PSYCHICAL RESEARCH, 26, 431–461. **209**

VEITH, I. (1970). HYSTERIA: THE HISTORY OF A DISEASE. Chicago: University of Chicago Press. **679**

VIORST, J. (1986). NECESSARY LOSSES. New York: Faucett Gold Medal. **679**

VISINTAINER, M. A., VOLPICELLI, J. R., & SELIGMAN, M. E. P. (1982). Tumor rejection in rats after inescapable or escapable shock. SCIENCE, 216, 437–439. **586**

VON LANG, J., & SIBYLL, C. (Eds.). (1983). EICHMANN INTERROGATED (R. Manheim, Trans.). New York: Farrar, Straus & Giroux. **737**

VONNEGUT, M. (1975). THE EDEN EXPRESS. New York: Bantam. **620, 635**

W

WADDEN, T. A., & ANDERTON, C. H. (1982). The clinical use of hypnosis. PSYCHOLOGICAL BULLETIN, 91, 215–243. **233**

WAGNER, A. R. (1981). SOP: A model of automatic memory processing in animal behavior. In N. E. Spear & R. R. Miller (Eds.), INFORMATION PROCESSING IN ANIMALS: MEMORY MECHANISMS. Hillsdale, NJ: Erlbaum. **253**

WAGNER, M. W., & MONNET, M. (1979). Attitudes of college professors toward extrasensory perception. ZETETIC SCHOLAR, 5, 7–17. **241**

WALD, G., & BROWN, P. K. (1965). Human color vision and color blindness. COLD SPRING HARBOR SYMPOSIA ON QUANTITATIVE BIOLOGY, 30, 345–359. **133**

WALDROP, M. M. (1987). The workings of working memory. SCIENCE, 237, 1564–1567. **307**

WALKER, C. E., HEDBERG, A., CLEMENT, P. W., & WRIGHT, L. (1981). CLINICAL PROCEDURES FOR BEHAVIOR THERAPY. Englewood Cliffs, NJ: Prentice-Hall. **649**

WALKER, E. (1978). EXPLORATIONS IN THE BIOLOGY OF LANGUAGE. Monterey, VT: Bradford Books. **378**

WALLACH, M. A., & WALLACH, L. (1983). PSYCHOLOGY'S SANCTION FOR SELFISHNESS. San Francisco: Freeman. **529**

WALSTER, E., ARONSON, E., ABRAHAMS, D., & ROTTMANN, L. (1966). Importance of physical attractiveness in dating behavior. JOURNAL OF PERSONALITY AND SOCIAL PSYCHOLOGY, 4, 508–516. **711**

WALTERS, J. M., & GARDNER, H. (1986). The theory of multiple intelligences: Some issues and answers. In R. J. Sternberg & R. K. Wagner (Eds.), PRACTICAL INTELLIGENCE. New York: Cambridge University Press. **465**

WALZER, M. (1970). OBLIGATIONS. Cambridge, MA: Harvard University Press. **745**

WARRINGTON, E. K., & SHALLICE, T. (1972). Neuropsychological evidence of visual storage in short-term memory tasks. QUARTERLY JOURNAL OF EXPERIMENTAL PSYCHOLOGY, 24, 30–40. **282**

WARRINGTON, E. K., & WEISKRANTZ, L. (1978). Further analysis of the prior learning effect in amnesic patients. NEUROPSYCHOLOGIA, 16, 169–177. **303**

WASON, P. C., & JOHNSON-LAIRD, P. N. (1972). PSYCHOLOGY OF REASONING: STRUCTURE AND CONTENT. London: Batsford. **329**

WATERS, E., WIPPMAN, J., & SROUFE, L. A. (1979). Attachment, positive affect, and competence in the peer group: Two studies in construct validation. CHILD DEVELOPMENT, 50, 821–829. **91, 477**

WATERS, H. F., & MALAMUD, P. (1975). Drop that gun, Captain Video. NEWSWEEK, 85, 81–82. **752**

WATKINS, M. J., HO, E., & TULVING, E. (1976). Context effects in recognition memory for faces. JOURNAL OF VERBAL LEARNING AND VERBAL BEHAVIOR, 15, 505–518. **299**

WATSON, D., & CLARK, L. A. (1984). Negative affectivity: The disposition to experience aversive emotional states. PSYCHOLOGICAL BULLETIN, 96, 465–490. **616**

WATSON, D. L., & THARP, R. G. (1985). SELF-DIRECTED BEHAVIOR: SELF-MODIFICATION FOR PERSONAL ADJUSTMENT (4th ed.). Belmont, CA: Wadsworth. **679**

WATSON, J. (1930). BEHAVIORISM (rev. ed.). New York: Norton. **521**

WATSON, J. B. (1928). PSYCHOLOGICAL CARE OF INFANT AND CHILD. New York: Norton.

WATSON, J. B. (1950). BEHAVIORISM. New York: Norton. **70**

WATSON, J. S. (1983). CONTINGENCY PERCEPTION IN EARLY SOCIAL DEVELOPMENT. Unpublished paper, University of California, Berkeley. **84**

WATSON, R. I. (1978). THE GREAT PSYCHOLOGISTS: FROM ARISTOTLE TO FREUD (4th ed.). Philadelphia: Lippincott. **773**

WAUGH, N. C., & NORMAN, D. A. (1965). Primary memory. PSYCHOLOGICAL REVIEW, 72, 89–104. **286**

WEBB, W. B. (1975). SLEEP THE GENTLE TYRANT. Englewood Cliffs, NJ: Prentice-Hall. **202, 208**

WEBER, E. H. (1834/1978). CONCERNING TOUCH (H. E. Ross, Trans.). New York: Academic Press. **120**

WECHSLER, D. (1958). THE MEASUREMENT AND APPRAISAL OF ADULT INTELLIGENCE. Baltimore: Williams. **448, 459**

WECHSLER, D. (1974). WECHSLER INTELLIGENCE SCALE FOR CHILDREN, REVISED. New York: Psychological Corporation. **448**

WEIGEL, R. H., VERNON, D. T. A., & TOGNACCI, L. N. (1974). Specificity of the attitude as a determinant of attitude-behavior congruence. JOURNAL OF PERSONALITY AND SOCIAL PSYCHOLOGY, 30, 724–728. **707**

WEINBERGER, D. R. (1987). Implications of normal brain development for the pathogenesis of schizophrenia. ARCHIVES OF GENERAL PSYCHIATRY, 44, 660–669. **625**

WEINGARTNER, H., GRAFMAN, J., BOUTELLE, W., KAYE, W., & MARTIN, P. R. (1983). Forms of memory failure. SCIENCE, 221, 380–382. **304**

WEINSTEIN, N. D. (1980). Unrealistic optimism about future events. JOURNAL OF PERSONALITY AND SOCIAL PSYCHOLOGY, 39, 806–820. **617**

WEINSTEIN, S. (1968). Intensive and extensive aspects of tactile sensitivity as a function of body part, sex, and laterality. In D. R. Kenshalo (Ed.), THE SKIN SENSES. Springfield, IL: Thomas. **151**

WEISS, J. M., GLAZER, H. I., POHORECKY, L. A., BRICK, J., & MILLER, N. E. (1975). Effects of chronic exposure to stressors on avoidance-escape behavior and on brain norepinephrine. PSYCHOSOMATIC MEDICINE, 37, 522–534. **559**

WELKOWITZ, J., EWEN, R. B., & COHEN, J. (1982). INTRODUCTORY STATISTICS FOR THE BEHAVIORAL SCIENCES (3rd ed.). San Diego: Harcourt Brace Jovanovich. **786**

WENGER, E. (1987). ARTIFICIAL INTELLIGENCE AND TUTORING SYSTEMS. Los Angeles: Morgan Kaufmann Publishers, Inc. **463**

WERTHEIMER, M. (1912). Experimentelle Studien uber das Sehen von Beuegung. ZEITSCHRIFT FÜR PSYCHOLOGIE, 61, 161–265. **159, 163**

WERTHEIMER, M. (1979). A BRIEF HISTORY OF PSYCHOLOGY (rev. ed.). New York: Holt, Rinehart & Winston. **29, 773**

WEST, C., & ZIMMERMAN, D. H. (1983). Small insults: A study of interruptions in cross-sex conversations between unacquainted persons. In B. Thorne, C. Kramarae, & N. Henley (Eds.), LANGUAGE, GENDER, AND SOCIETY. Rowley, MA: Newbury House. **699**

WEST, M. A. (Ed.). (1987). THE PSYCHOLOGY OF MEDITATION. New York: Oxford University Press. **224, 243**

WETZLER, S. E., & SWEENEY, J. A. (1986). Childhood amnesia: An empirical demonstration. In D. C. Rubin (Ed.), AUTOBIOGRAPHICAL MEMORY. New York: Cambridge University Press. **304**

WEVER, E. G. (1949). THEORY OF HEARING. New York: Wiley. **141**

WHITE, C. (1977). Unpublished doctoral dissertation, Catholic University, Washington, DC. **372**

WHITE, G. L., & KIGHT, T. D. (1984). Misattribution of arousal and attraction: Effects of salience of explanations for arousal. JOURNAL OF EXPERIMENTAL SOCIAL PSYCHOLOGY, 20, 55–64. **719**

WHITE, G. L., FISHBEIN, S., & RUTSTEIN, J. (1981). Passionate love and the misattribution of arousal. JOURNAL OF PERSONALITY AND SOCIAL PSYCHOLOGY, 41, 56–62. **719**

WHITE, R. W., & WATT, N. F. (1981). THE ABNORMAL PERSONALITY (5th ed.). New York: Wiley. **609**

WHITING, B. B., & EDWARDS, C. P. (1988). CHILDREN OF DIFFERENT WORLDS: THE FORMATION OF SOCIAL BEHAVIOR. Cambridge, MA: Harvard University Press. **485, 501**

WHITING, B. B., & WHITING, J. W. M. (1975). CHILDREN OF SIX CULTURES: A PSYCHOCULTURAL ANALYSIS. Cambridge, MA: Harvard University Press. **485, 501**

WHITING, J. W. M., & CHILD, I. (1953). CHILD TRAINING AND PERSONALITY: A CROSS-CULTURAL STUDY. New Haven: Yale University Press. **485, 501**

WHORF, B. L. (1956). Science and linguistics. In J. B. Carroll (Ed.), LANGUAGE, THOUGHT AND REALITY: SELECTED WRITINGS OF BENJAMIN LEE WHORF. Cambridge, MA: MIT Press. **326**

WIESEL, T. N., & HUBEL, D. H. (1974). Ordered arrangement of orientation columns in monkeys lacking visual experience. JOURNAL OF COMPARATIVE NEUROLOGY, 158, 307–318. **188**

WIGDOR, A. K., & GARNER, W. R. (Eds.). (1982). ABILITY TESTING: USES, CONSEQUENCES, AND CONTROVERSIES. Washington, DC: National Academy Press. **473**

WILKES, A. L., & KENNEDY, R. A. (1969). Relationship between pausing and retrieval latency in sentences of varying grammatical form. JOURNAL OF EXPERIMENTAL PSYCHOLOGY, 79, 241–245. **335**

WILKINS, W. (1984). Psychotherapy: The powerful placebo. JOURNAL OF CONSULTING AND CLINICAL PSYCHOLOGY, 52, 570–573. **668**

WILLIAMS, D. C. (1959). The elimination of tantrum behavior by extinction procedures. JOURNAL OF ABNORMAL AND SOCIAL PSYCHOLOGY, 59, 269. **257**

WILLIAMS, M. D., & HOLLAN, J. D. (1981). The process of retrieval from very long-term memory. COGNITIVE SCIENCE, 5, 87–119. **309**

WILLIAMS, R. B., Jr. (1989). THE TRUSTING HEART: GREAT NEWS ABOUT TYPE A BEHAVIOR. New York: Random House. **581**

WILLIAMS, R. B., JR., BAREFOOT, J. C., HANEY, T. L., HARRELL, F. E., BLUMENTHAL, J. A., PRYOR, D. B., & PETERSON, B. (1988). Type A behavior and angiographically documented coronary atherosclerosis in a sample of 2,289 patients. PSYCHOSOMATIC MEDICINE, 50, 139–152. **580**

WILLIAMS, R. L. (1972). THE BITCH TEST (BLACK INTELLIGENCE TEST OF CULTURAL HOMOGENEITY). St. Louis: Black Studies Program, Washington University. **452**

WILLIS, S. L. (1985). Towards an educational psychology of the older adult learner: Intellectual and cognitive bases. In J. E. Birren & K. W. Schaie (Eds.), HANDBOOK OF THE PSYCHOLOGY OF AGING (2nd ed.). New York: Van Nostrand Reinhold. **111**

WILSON, E. O. (1963). Pheromones. SCIENTIFIC AMERICAN, 208(5), 100–114. **146**

WILSON, E. O. (1983, October). Statement cited in "Mother nature's murderers," DISCOVERY, pp. 79–82. **427**

WILSON, T. D., LASER, P. S., & STONE, J. I. (1982). Judging the predictors of one's mood: Accuracy and the use of shared theories. JOURNAL OF EXPERIMENTAL SOCIAL PSYCHOLOGY, 18, 537–556. **702**

WILSON, W. R. (1979). Feeling more than we can know: Exposure effects without learning. JOURNAL OF PERSONALITY AND SOCIAL PSYCHOLOGY, 37, 811–821. **713**

WINCH, R. F., KTSANES, T., & KTSANES, V. (1954). The theory of complementary needs in mate selection: An analytic and descriptive study. AMERICAN SOCIOLOGICAL REVIEW, 29, 241–249. **714, 715**

WINTEMUTE, G. J., TERET, S. P., KRAUS, J. F., & WRIGHT, M. W. (1988). The choice of weapons in firearm suicides. AMERICAN JOURNAL OF PUBLIC HEALTH, 18, 824–826. **610**

WISE, R. A. (1984). Neuroleptic and operant behavior: The anhedonia hypothesis. BEHAVIOR AND BRAIN SCIENCES, 5, 39–87. **267**

WITKIN, H. A., MEDNICK, S. A., SCHULSINGER, F., & collaborators. (1976). Criminality in XYY and XXY men, SCIENCE, 193, 547–555. **63**

WOLFE, D. A. (1985). Child-abusive parents: An empirical review and analysis. PSYCHOLOGICAL BULLETIN, 97, 462–482. **391**

WOLMAN, B. B., DALE, L. A., SCHMEIDLER, G. R., & ULLMAN, M. (Eds.). (1985). HANDBOOK OF PARAPSYCHOLOGY. New York: Van Nostrand & Reinhold. **243**

WOOD, G. (1986). FUNDAMENTALS OF PSYCHOLOGICAL RESEARCH (3rd ed.). Boston: Little, Brown. **29**

WOODWORTH, R. S. (1938). EXPERIMENTAL PSYCHOLOGY. New York: Henry Holt and Company. **147**

WOODY, R. H., & ROBERTSON, M. (1988). BECOMING A CLINICAL PSYCHOLOGIST. Madison, CT: International Universities Press. **645, 679**

WORD, C. O., ZANNA, M. P., & COOPER, J. (1974). The nonverbal mediation of self-fulfilling prophecies in interracial interaction. JOURNAL OF EXPERIMENTAL SOCIAL PSYCHOLOGY, 10, 109–120. **693**

WORLEY, P. F., HELLER, W. A., SNYDER, S. H., & BARABAN, J. M. (1988). Lithium blocks a phosphoinositide-mediated cholinergic response in hippocampal slices. SCIENCE, 239, 1428–1429. **672**

WORTMAN, C. B., & BREHM, J. W. (1975). Responses to uncontrollable outcomes: An integration of reactance theory and the learned helplessness model. ADVANCES IN EXPERIMENTAL AND SOCIAL PSYCHOLOGY, 8, 277–286. **564**

WRIGHT, L. (1988). The Type A behavior pattern and coronary artery disease: Quest for the active ingredients and the elusive mechanism. AMERICAN PSYCHOLOGIST, 43, 2–14. **581**

WRIGHT, W. D. (1946). RESEARCHES ON NORMAL AND COLOR DEFECTIVE VISION. London: Henry Kimpton. **130**

WYNN, L. C., SINGER, M. T., BARTKO, J., & TOOHEY, M. L. (1977). Schizophrenics and their families: Research on parental communication. In J. Tanner (Ed.), DEVELOPMENTS IN PSYCHIATRIC RESEARCH. London: Hodder & Stoughton. **626**

Y

YALOM, I. D. (1985). THE THEORY AND PRACTICE OF GROUP PSYCHOTHERAPY (3rd ed.). New York: Basic Books. **679**

YARBUS, D. L. (1967). EYE MOVEMENTS AND VISION. New York: Plenum. **174**

YESAVAGE, J. A., LEIER, V. O., DENARI, M., & HOLLISTER, L. E. (1985). Carry-over effect of marijuana intoxication on aircraft pilot performance: A preliminary report. AMERICAN JOURNAL OF PSYCHIATRY, *142*, 1325–1330. **223**

YOST, W. A., & NIELSON, D. W. (1985). FUNDAMENTALS OF HEARING (2nd ed.). New York: Holt, Rinehart & Winston. **140, 155**

YOUNG, T. (1807). A COURSE OF LECTURES ON NATURAL PHILOSOPHY. London: William Savage. **133**

YOUNISS, J., & SMOLLAR, J. (1985). ADOLESCENT RELATIONS WITH MOTHERS, FATHERS, AND FRIENDS. Chicago: University of Chicago Press. **103, 113**

YU, B., ZHANG, W., JING, Q., PENG, R., ZHANG, G., & SIMON, H. A. (1985). STM capacity for Chinese and English language materials. MEMORY AND COGNITION, *13*, 202–207. **285**

YUSSEN, S. R., & BERMAN, L. (1981). Memory predictions for recall and recognition in first-, third-, and fifth-grade children. DEVELOPMENTAL PSYCHOLOGY, *17*, 224–229. **85**

Z

ZAJONC, R. B. (1965). Social facilitation. SCIENCE, *149*, 269–274. **724, 725**

ZAJONC, R. B. (1968). Attitudinal effects of mere exposure. JOURNAL OF PERSONALITY AND SOCIAL PSYCHOLOGY. Monograph Supplement 9(2), 1–29. **713**

ZAJONC, R. B. (1980). Compresence. In P. B. Paulus (Ed.), PSYCHOLOGY OF GROUP INFLUENCE. Hillsdale, NJ: Erlbaum. **412, 724**

ZAJONC, R. B. (1984). On the primacy of affect. AMERICAN PSYCHOLOGIST, *39*, 117–123. **412**

ZAJONC, R. B., HEINGARTNER, A., & HERMAN, E. M. (1969). Social enhancement and impairment of performance in the cockroach. JOURNAL OF PERSONALITY AND SOCIAL PSYCHOLOGY, *13*, 83–92. **725**

ZAJONC, R. B., MURPHY, S. T., & INGLEHART, M. (1989). Feeling and facial efference: Implications of the vascular theory of emotion. PSYCHOLOGICAL REVIEW, *96*, 395–416. **412, 417**

ZAMANSKY, H. S., & BARTIS, S. P. (1985). The dissociation of an experience: The hidden observer observed. JOURNAL OF ABNORMAL PSYCHOLOGY, *94*, 243–248. **232, 233**

ZEIGLER, H. P., & LEIBOWITZ, H. (1957). Apparent visual size as a function of distance for children and adults. AMERICAN JOURNAL OF PSYCHOLOGY, *70*, 106–109. **188**

ZELAZO, P. R., ZELAZO, N. A., & KOLB, S. (1972). Walking: In the newborn. SCIENCE, *176*, 314–315. **79**

ZELNIK, M., & KANTER, J. F. (1977). Sexual and contraceptive experience of young unmarried women in the United States, 1976 and 1971. FAMILY PLANNING PERSPECTIVES, *9*, 55–71. **102**

ZHANG, G., & SIMON, H. A. (1985). STM capacity for Chinese words and idioms: Chunking and acoustical loop hypothesis. MEMORY AND COGNITION, *13*, 193–201. **284**

ZIGLER, E., & BERMAN, W. (1983). Discerning the future of early childhood intervention. AMERICAN PSYCHOLOGIST, *38*, 894–906. **469**

ZIGLER, E. F., & GORDON, E. W. (Eds.). (1981). DAY CARE: SCIENTIFIC AND SOCIAL POLICY ISSUES. Boston: Auburn House. **473**

ZILLMANN, D., & BRYANT, J. (1974). Effect of residual excitation on the emotional response to provocation and delayed aggressive behavior. JOURNAL OF PERSONALITY AND SOCIAL PSYCHOLOGY, *30*, 782–791. **409**

ZIMBARDO, P. G. (1970). The human choice: Individuation, reason and order versus deindividuation, impulse and chaos. In W. J. Arnold & D. Levine (Eds.), NEBRASKA SYMPOSIUM ON MOTIVATION (Vol. 16). Lincoln: University of Nebraska Press. **727, 728**

ZOLA-MORGAN, S., SQUIRE, L. R., & AMARAL, D. G. (1989). Lesions of the hippocampal formation but not lesions of the fornix or the mamalary nuclei produce long-lasting memory impairments in monkeys. JOURNAL OF NEUROSCIENCE, *9*, 898–913. **296**

ZUBEK, J. P. (1969). SENSORY DEPRIVATION: FIFTEEN YEARS OF RESEARCH. New York: Appleton-Century-Crofts. **395**

ZUCKERMAN, M. (1979a). SENSATION-SEEKING: BEYOND THE OPTIMAL LEVEL OF AROUSAL. Hillsdale, NJ: Erlbaum. **397**

ZUCKERMAN, M. (1979b). Attribution of success and failure revisited, or: The motivational bias is alive and well in attribution theory. JOURNAL OF PERSONALITY, *47*, 245–287. **616**

ZUCKERMAN, M., & NEEB, M. (1980). Demographic influences in sensation-seeking and expressions of sensation-seeking in religion, smoking and driving habits. PERSONALITY AND INDIVIDUAL DIFFERENCES, *1*(3), 197–206. **397**

ZURIF, E. B., CARAMAZZA, A., MYERSON, R., & GALVIN, J. (1974). Semantic feature representations for normal and aphasic language. BRAIN AND LANGUAGE, *1*, 167–187. **345**

Index

Page numbers in *italics* refer to figures and tables.